COSIMO DE' MEDICI

AND THE FLORENTINE RENAISSANCE

COSIMO DE' MEDICI
AND THE FLORENTINE
RENAISSANCE

THE PATRON'S OEUVRE

Dale Kent

YALE UNIVERSITY PRESS

New Haven and London

To Gene Brucker,
with gratitude,
for thirty years of constant inspiration,
encouragement, and friendship.

PUBLISHED WITH THE ASSISTANCE OF
THE GETTY GRANT PROGRAM

Designed by Gillian Malpass

Printed in Singapore

Library of Congress Cataloging-in-Publication Data
Kent D. V. (Dale V.)
Cosimo de'Medici and the Florentine Renaissance/Dale Kent.
p. cm.
Includes bibliographical references and index.
ISBN 0-300-08128-6 (alk. paper)
1. Medici, Cosimo de', 1389-1464 – Art patronage. 2. Arts. Italian – Italy – Florence.
3. Arts, Renaissance – Italy – Florence. 4. Florence (Italy) – Social life and customs. I. Title.
NX701.2.M43 K46 2000
945'.5105'092–dc21
00-031038

A catalogue record for this book is available from
The British Library

Frontispiece Benozzo Gozzoli, portrait of Cosimo de' Medici,
Florence, Medici palace, chapel, detail from the east wall

CONTENTS

Preface   ix

PART I   THE PATRON'S OEUVRE   1

Introduction: The Terms of Renaissance Patronage   3
    Defining an oeuvre   3
    Generating a work of art   5
    Articulating identity in images   6
    Artists, patronage networks, and personal letters   7
    Clientelismo *and* mecenatismo: *two sides of the same coin of patronage*   8
    Taste and choice   8

I   Cosimo's Oeuvre   9

II   Cosimo's Letters   15

III   Learning the Lessons of Florentine Culture: Who Cosimo Knew   21
    Cosimo and the humanists   23
    Artists on the Florentine public scene   27

IV   Educating the Patron: What Cosimo Read   33

PART II   THE COMMON CULTURE
OF THE FLORENTINE AUDIENCE:
THE MEDICI SHARE IN THIS   39

V   Venues and Performances   41
    Art and society: political propaganda or a common culture?   41
    Popular poetry and song: performances in the piazza of San Martino   43
    Cosimo at San Martino: patron of charity and popular culture   46
    Civic culture as popular entertainment   50
    Lay confraternities: an education in religious texts and symbols   54
    Sacred plays and civic ceremonies: translating texts into images   59

VI   Compilations and the Corpus of Texts   69
    Vernacular scrapbooks   69
    Populist illustrations for popular texts   75
    *Anthologists: patricians, plebeians, and the "middling sort"; vernacular
      miscellanies in Cosimo's library and Piero de' Medici's* libricciuolo   77

Combining pleasure with profit: the Three Crowns, Dante, Boccaccio, and Petrarch; Brunelleschi's "Fat Carpenter"; Geta and Birria; Lo Za and Burchiello 81
Moral exempla: Aesop's Fables and the classics 82
Devotion: Scripture and quotidian counsel; meditations, confession, penitence, and prayers; the memento mori and the exemplary images of the saints 83
Civic traditions and celebrations: from Brunetto Latini and Villani to the letters of Bruni and Francesco Sforza 88
The fascination of the unknown and the thrill of the exotic: Dati's Globe and the Ethiopian Prester John 90
Storing wisdom in the house of memory 91

VII   Popular Devotion and the Perception of Images 95
Memory and meditation: "with the eyes of the mind more than those of the body"; image and narrative 95
Vision: the power of the image 98
Levels of perception: "The eye is called the first of all the gates / through which the intellect may learn and taste" 101
Poetry, theology, doctrine, and edifying exchange: a scissor-maker's query concerning the Trinity; a goldsmith enquires about the Immaculate Conception 102
Ut pictura poesis (Pictures are like poetry) 104

VIII   Images of Florentine Patronage Refracted through Popular Culture 107
Participants in popular culture as patrons of art 107
Marco Parenti's belt-buckle: a blueprint for a patron's personalized commission 108
The popular appreciation of images expressed in Everyman's commissions 110
Artists sharing and shaping the idiom of popular culture 115
Popular images of Cosimo and his patronage 117
The Florentine popolo as patron of Brunelleschi's cupola: an exemplum for private citizens of patronage in a republic 122

PART III   COSIMO'S RELIGIOUS COMMISSIONS 129

IX   Expiation, Charity, Intercession 131
"The liberal rich man": charity and the patron 131
Images of intercession 136
Death and the patron 138
The Medici patron saints 141
San Marco: the frescoes 149
The San Marco altarpiece: salvation, patronage, and power 155

X   Building "for the Honor of God, and the Honor of the City, and the Memory of Me" 161
Cosimo, "preserver of churches and holy places" 161
Inherited commitments, paternal and papal 162
Ius patronatus and Bosco ai Frati 167
San Marco 171
San Lorenzo, parish church of the Medici neighborhood 179
The old sacristy 186
Cooperating to honor the city, and the orders and cults of the Church 197
The Badia 212

PART IV   THE HOUSE OF THE MEDICI   215

XI   The Palace: Measuring Self on the Urban Map   217
       The palatial debate   217
       Placing the palace and its patron in history: the architectural fusion of
          Florence and Rome   225
       Situating the family in the city   228
       Building for paterfamilias, padrino, *and* pater patriae   230

XII   Accommodating the Patron   239
       "The comfort of his accommodations"   239
       "Per non diviso": family values and the use and decoration of domestic space   241
       Filial piety: the mainly devotional works of art in Cosimo's house 244
       Uccello's Battle of San Romano: *Cosimo, the commune, and warfare: images*
          of fame and defamation, public and private   264
       Heroes classical, Christian, and civic: Donatello's David *and* Judith and
          Holofernes; *The Labors of Hercules*   281
       Decorating and collecting: continuity and change   287
       A cultivated life: gardens and villas   299

XIII   The Chapel in the Heart of the Palace: A Microcosm of
       Medici Patronage   305

PART V   THE PATRON AS "AUCTOR"   329

XIV   Patrons and their Artists: "The Variety of Genius"   331
       The patron's role in the production of art   331
       Artists in the Medici patronage network: the letters   332
       The artist's expertise and the patron's choice   342
       The major partnerships: Donatello and Michelozzo   343

XV   The Patron's Choice: Princes, Patricians, Partisans   347
       Choice and intention   347
       The extent and limitations of Cosimo's political power in Florence:
          was it in fact "princely?"   348
       Cosimo's commissions and those of his princely friends: comparisons, contrasts,
          connections   351
       Florentine precedents for Cosimo's patronage   354
       Emulation, competition, and exchange in the patronage of Cosimo's
          fellow-citizens   356
       A comparable Florentine oeuvre: the patronage of Giovanni Rucellai 357

       Conclusion: An Oeuvre Defines Its Patron: Cosimo's Visible Image   367
       The patron defines himself in relation to his world   367
       The Medici and Florence: continuity and change   370
       Cosimo's visible image   372
       Epilogue: "Returning it all to the Lord": Cosimo's tomb in San Lorenzo 377

       Appendix: A List of What Appear to be Popular Miscellanies
       Compiled from the Pupilli Records   385

Abbreviations   387

Notes   388

List of Works Cited   494

Index   523

Photograph Credits   538

PREFACE

The primary aim of this book is to reexamine the entire body of works of art commissioned by Cosimo de' Medici, or by his sons on behalf of the family, between the early 1420s and his death in 1464, with a view to discerning the interests and themes to which his patronage gave visual expression. Since discovering these depends upon setting Cosimo's commissions in the context of his life, and of the rest of his patronage, personal and political, this book offers a good deal of information about Cosimo (whose last major biographer was C. S. Gutkind, writing in 1938), about Florentine society, and about its governing elite. It does not, however, pretend to be a full or even balanced account of Cosimo's life, still less of his times.

Exchanges between the Medici family and the artists they employed are considered as expressions of their respective roles in the production of works of art, not in any attempt to apportion credit for creativity between patron and artist. As the various themes and arguments of the book are all ultimately related to illuminating the objects Cosimo commissioned, art historians of Florence are likely to be an important part of its audience. Hopefully, however, this book will interest anyone interested in the relation between art and society, and particularly the system of patronage of art by which wealthy and prominent men, in expressing their own identities, enriched the cultures that shaped them. As much as possible of merely academic argument has been relegated to endnotes, which the general reader may ignore.

Nevertheless, this book is unusually long. Many monographs reviewing the oeuvre of a single artist run to several hundred pages; to review the entire opus of the major patron of the Florentine Renaissance, which includes the masterpieces of the age's greatest artists, naturally takes a little longer. Many of the details in parts III–IV of particular commissions and the scholarship concerning them will be eminently familiar to specialists in the field. However, these details appear in a different light when associated and enriched with evidence relating to the concerns of the patron and his audience; moreover, the setting of individual objects in the context of

Cosimo's entire oeuvre results in new insights and perspectives on almost every commission.

For the sake of the general reader, and of Florentine historians who may never really have looked at these objects with a truly critical eye, let alone thought about them as texts to advance their understanding of Cosimo and his patronage, it seemed essential to offer here a relatively full and "self-contained" account of each of Cosimo's commissions, laying out what is collectively known about them without requiring recourse to specialized literature, and presenting the relevant visual and verbal texts in close conjunction. The latter are cited rather than summarized, since apart from the evidence of the objects themselves, what Florentines said is the best clue to what they thought about works of art and the interests these expressed. Only when the reader has before him or her, in all its vivid immediacy, the material necessary to assess at first hand the breadth and richness of Cosimo's patronage oeuvre, and to appreciate its integration with his life and that of his society, can this body of much-discussed works be evaluated afresh.

This study is not offered as a definitive account of Cosimo's patronage. It is animated by the desire to make a beginning in reassembling the Renaissance patron as a whole human being, by looking at his personal, political, and artistic patronage all together, as part of the society and culture in which he lived. In practice that means relating information about patron, artists, commissions, and audience which has previously been considered separately by historians of politics, society, literature, and art. This process involves a certain amount of repetition. The same information must sometimes be considered in more than one context, since one aim of the book is to demonstrate the close connections between the various areas of the patron's activity. This approach also necessitates gathering together as much as possible of the available evidence, rather than mere samples sufficient to support particular points. A good number of pieces of the puzzle are needed before the patterns in Cosimo's patronage begin to emerge. Some scholars see in the same evidence rather different patterns from those I have discerned, and as continuing research uncovers more evidence, future scholars are bound to see still others.

In laying down the design for this book in the early 1980s, I hoped to expand my understanding of Renaissance Florence by exploring a different range of sources and questions than those I had worked on before; I had no clear idea of what I might find. Initially, I envisaged this book as being in some sense a pulling together of the great quantity of recent research relating to the issues that interested me; I hope that it does indeed fulfil something of this function. It turned out, however, to be harder to achieve a harmonious synthesis than I had imagined. Since I had not set out with the intention of revising any particular received views, I found myself differing from other writers much more than I had expected, especially concerning the major themes of Cosimo's oeuvre and the possible motives behind his patronage. Some explanation and justification of these differences is required, and appears in the endnotes.

It seems to me that the richest, most satisfying, and perhaps even the most accurate view of a historical problem, as of life, is one seen from a variety of perspectives. I have made every effort, drawing on a large, varied, and creative literature on Renaissance Florence, to consider Cosimo's patronage from as many different points of view as possible. However, no single study, if it is to be an authentic working out of the author's own insights, and more importantly, intelligible to its readers, can possibly look at any issue from all possible points of view. Some perspectives, moreover, are mutually contradictory. Those which I have found most difficult to integrate into my own are those which claim to offer the sole satisfactory key to the understanding of Cosimo's patronage. Most scholars making this claim, apart from those who focus on the artist and effectively ignore the patron's role, have discerned explicit pretensions to princely authority and status in Cosimo's artistic oeuvre. Their arguments rest on an assumed analogy between this *de facto* leading citizen of a republic and the *de jure* rulers of the principates which were the predominant form of government in this period.

Since my own early work on Cosimo concentrated mainly on his political ambitions, indeed on his calculated exploitation of the obligations of personal patronage to create a group of political partisans, my scepticism concerning the reading of political messages about rulership in Cosimo's oeuvre may strike some readers as ironic, even strange. In fact it is a direct consequence of my interest in the precise mechanisms of Medici power and the awareness of crucial differences, beneath the many surface similarities, between the political arrangements of Renaissance principates and those of the Florentine

republic. The most important of these differences was the persistence in Florence in Cosimo's lifetime of a strong civic republican ideology expressed in art, literature, and performance, as well as politics. This was probably the main political vein tapped by the patronage of the republic's most powerful citizen, although what precisely he intended his audience to read into the civic symbolism of individual commissions is by no means clear.

Cosimo was Florence's leading politician, and therefore anything he said or did was in a sense political. This book presents many examples of the favorable, and probably calculated effect of Cosimo's personal and artistic patronage on his popular image, resulting in the enhancement of his influence and reputation in the city. However, many interpretations of particular works commissioned by Cosimo involve a much narrower conception of what is "political." In effect these readings assume a direct relation between the commission of works of art and the patron's acquisition and maintenance of a greater share of power in the state. The latter must surely be related to constitutional and electoral arrangements rather than works of art. The way in which authority and status are articulated visually in a social setting is another question, which has been imaginatively illuminated by a number of studies of the role of images in social theater. I have tried to pursue this line of enquiry, while keeping in mind that the interpretation of images in their social context is complex, and further complicated by the issue of their form – their relation to the artist's oeuvre and agenda.

The nature and quality of evidence limits what can be known. Law and constitution provide fairly clear evidence of individual or collective political intentions. Although works of art may be considered to be readable texts as much as laws or trials, or political debates, the quest for the recovery of the author's intention – in this case the patron's – is intensely problematic. I have not altogether abandoned this quest, but I have operated on the assumption that it is easier to reconstruct general aims than very specific ones, and that the stated aims of actual protagonists of a situation are a more plausible indication of intention than those which have to be inferred from hypothetical models, or assumptions imported from other periods and places about how things in Florence "must have been."

For example, I took as a provisional guide to Cosimo's oeuvre Giovanni Rucellai's famous declaration that his patronage was undertaken "for the honor of God and the honor of the city and the memory of me." Studies of several other Florentine patrons and their commissions support Rucellai's unusually clear and self-conscious statement of intention, and an examination of Cosimo's oeuvre confirms that he too shared these general impulses. By contrast, the far more specific claims that Cosimo harbored pretensions to princely authority over Florence and used art as a means of "social control" seem to me on closer investigation to be essentially constructions not confirmed by or based upon any concrete contemporary evidence, but rather "cantilevered hypotheses," one assumption building upon another until eventually the whole construct is erroneously assumed to be solid. However, in the end I believe that the question of Cosimo's intentions must remain an open one, which may well be more clearly resolved in the future by the discovery of more conclusive evidence.

The type of evidence on which we focus is the crucial determinant of the picture we obtain. In my early work on the Medici rise to power, I addressed the question of how and why Cosimo came to exercise so much authority in a republic. In search of an answer I drew on transcripts of Cosimo's performances in the political arena of communal councils, and on the private communications in which he directed the activities of his partisans; the Cosimo who emerged from these records, and thus from my studies, was largely a political animal. When I turned, in the preparation of this book, to the evidence of his artistic patronage and the general culture on which he drew in commissioning works of art, I was able to explore more extensively some other dimensions of his experience, leading me to the conclusion that the religious and civic impulses of Cosimo de' Medici and the society he represented may have been more important than political ones in shaping his patronage of art, and its reception. I see this book as representing a progression from an initial investigation of Cosimo's political power in its narrowest and most easily establishable sense of control over political offices (possibly in Florence its most fundamental sense) to a much more challenging and fascinating enterprise, the appreciation of Cosimo's political authority and image in all the richness of its personal and social context, as a product, as well as a determinant, of the nature of Florentine civic life.

The title of this book may raise some expectations that it will not fulfil. Some readers may be frustrated by the limited attention given various important aspects of Florentine social and political life in Cosimo's time, or by the fact that this study is not a biography of Cosimo as traditionally understood. Some may be surprised by the author's avoidance of personal judgment of Cosimo, and interpret this incorrectly as approval of all his works, or the abrogation of the critical faculty. Some clarification of these issues is called for.

A close consideration of Cosimo's politics and patron-age, and his bank, the foundation of all his other achievements, since he was first and foremost a banker, is essential to a balanced view of Cosimo and his role as Florence's leading citizen. However, the present volume, concerned with the artistic products of Cosimo's patronage and their reception, deals only with those areas of Cosimo's life that provide an immediate context for the surviving objects, and that these in turn illuminate. Discussion focuses on elements of social and cultural consensus, rather than on conflict, on the ways in which Medici ascendancy was accepted by various sectors of the Florentine community, rather than on the bitter opposition to the family's increasing power, because it is the body of interests and ideas Cosimo shared with other Florentines, not their differences, that makes sense of his oeuvre and renders it an effective expression of his identity.

I have tried here to show how fundamentally Cosimo's artistic patronage was related to Medici personal and political patronage, but not in order to ennoble Cosimo's political power by associating it with his promotion of a generally admired culture. Cosimo's activities as *paterfamilias*, *padrino*, and *pater patriae*, all governed by traditional patriarchal conceptions of personal relationships, particularly friendship and patronage, that structured and integrated Florentine society and shaped Cosimo's role in it, were examined at length in five chapters which originally constituted the first part of this book. I amputated them to limit its length, and excised in addition a number of subsequent sections dealing with these themes and with the expression in popular literature of a specifically plebeian point of view very different from that of Cosimo and his powerful friends. This material will be published in a second volume entitled *Fathers and Friends: Patronage and Patriarchy in Early Renaissance Florence*.

Insofar as that volume, making much fuller use of the Medici correspondence than is possible in the present one, reveals much more of Cosimo's quotidian life and of his personal relationships with friends, partisans, and family, including his wife, it presents a more three-dimensional picture of the man himself, and of his personal qualities, both positive and negative. However, as I observe in Chapter 2 of this volume, the evidence does not exist for a fully satisfying biography of Cosimo de' Medici, entailing confident explanations and assessments of his actions. Moreover, I am personally disinclined to the sort of moral judgments such an exercise inevitably implies. Were I to judge Cosimo, I would have to do so in terms of my own values and principles and those of my world, and, in that case, I might roundly condemn him as an elitist, sexist, manipulative, and ruthless profiteer who ground the faces of the poor and hypocritically sought to redress this crime with a self-serving "charity." But such anachronistic evaluations of their subjects by historians seem to me unreasonable and pointless. Cosimo's actions were in accordance with the norms, and often the ideals, of his own time; now dead five hundred years, he has passed far beyond my judgment or that of the fleeting present.

It is regrettable that scholars who attempt, as I have done in both volumes, to reconstruct the experience of members of the Florentine elite from their own point of view, are often accused of idealizing, rather than merely describing this. I consider it more useful and creative to try to resurrect the most influential and best-documented figure of the remarkable civilization of early Renaissance Florence than to resolve to bury him beneath the moral censure of another age. But I have no interest in praising him. By the same token, in stressing the role of personal patronage in shaping Florentine political life, I have no wish to neglect, still less to reject the importance of ideas in inspiring human action. My emphasis is dictated by the available evidence rather than by personal choice.

Some historians choose to assert their belief – as yet unsupported by any substantial evidence relating to the fifteenth century – that class conflict must have been a primary and fundamental determinant of effective social and political action in Renaissance Florence, as it has been in the modern world. I have introduced in this volume, and developed much more fully in the next, an argument that conflicting socio-economic interests and the resentments they arouse played out differently in a face-to-face patriarchal pre-modern society committed to the Catholic faith. While there is ample evidence in Florentine sources of the natural resentment of the gross economic inequity that characterized this society, particularly compelling in the popular poems on which my study of Everyman's attitudes so heavily relies, and which are redolent of the rage, pain and shame of the under-privileged and exploited, the modern class consciousness often assumed to exist in this period may well have been inhibited by universally held religious beliefs justifying, and even sanctifying the acceptance of such inequities.

Part I of the book sketches the outline of Cosimo's patronage oeuvre, and what can be recovered of his individual life experience and learning which may have helped to shape it. The point of this exercise is to suggest an approach, profiting from the unique wealth of evidence available to illuminate the life of Florence's leading citizen, to re-creating the patron's point of view. Part II, an exploration of Florentine popular culture as a corpus of texts and performances, and as a complex of attitudes to the visual and its relevance to public and private devo-

tion, which is the main theme of this culture and of Cosimo's oeuvre, describes a vital and comparatively neglected element in the patronage of the powerful. That is the culture common to the artist, the patron, and the audience his oeuvre addresses, constituting the idiom in which they necessarily converse and communicate. This idiom is probably the essential locus of the relation between the art created as a consequence of Cosimo's patronage, and the society of Renaissance Florence, by far the most complex and elusive of the issues this book addresses. The chapters on Florentine popular culture are also vital to understanding just how much information Cosimo brought to his patronage of works of classicizing and devotional art, and how well his audience too was equipped to respond to them.

Parts III and IV confront most explicitly the question of Cosimo's preferences and intentions as a patron. These chapters generally conclude that the celebration of devotional, dynastic, and civic themes predominates in the objects of his patronage, and that these were probably highly effective in enhancing Cosimo's public image and authority, essentially because of the visibly close relation between Cosimo's concerns and those of the Florentine populace at large. Part V seeks to clarify the picture of Cosimo's oeuvre by viewing it from some additional or alternative perspectives; observing the interaction of patron and artist through the letters relating to Medici commissions; comparing Cosimo's commissions with those of his princely friends and his fellow-citizens, particularly Giovanni Rucellai, with a view to establishing the models for Medici patronage, and the degree to which it was distinct from, or similar to, other contemporary oeuvres; finally, after reviewing Cosimo's definition of himself in his patronage of art, attempting to assess how Cosimo's visible image alters or adds to the image which emerges from his more commonly studied activities as banker, statesman, and leading citizen of fifteenth-century Florence.

The endnotes constitute the fullest and most literal acknowledgement of my intellectual debts. Many scholars whose work is cited there have also, over the many years this rather extensive study has consumed, become my friends, assisting me with all the varieties of generosity which friendship comprises. Since for many of these years I had limited access to most of my notes and books, I am particularly grateful for the hospitality of both individuals and institutions, and for the latter's flexibility in allowing me the use of their resources. For this reason, it is difficult in many cases to distinguish between intellectual, institutional, and personal debts. I literally could not name here all the people who have helped me, but I want to thank them all most warmly for the many ways in which they have enriched this book, and hope that they may recognize in it their own contributions.

I would like to mention particularly those who have given my study substantial support and those whose ideas have most profoundly influenced mine. They include: Albert Ascoli, Suzanne Branciforte, Alison Brown, David Brown, Peter Brown, Gene Brucker, Howard Burns, Samuel Cohn, Brian Copenhaver, Gino Corti, Natalie Davis, Kurt Forster, Laurie Fusco, Paul Gehl, Richard Goldthwaite, Margaret Haines, John Hale, John Hand, John Henderson, George Holmes, Rhys Isaac, F. W. Kent, Verlyn Klinkenborg, Irving Lavin, Lauro Martines, Susan McKillop, Henry Millon, John Najemy, Nerida Newbigin, David Peterson, Mark Phillips, Brenda Preyer, William Prizer, Ian Robertson, Diana Robin, Nicolai Rubinstein, Simon Schama, Patricia Simons, John Shearman, Craig Smyth, Lawrence Stone, Randolph Starn, Richard Trexler, Renée Neu Watkins, Ronald Weissman.

I am grateful for institutional and financial support from the Warburg Institute, London; the Institute for Historical Studies, University of London; the Harvard University Center for Italian Renaissance Studies, Villa I Tatti, Florence; the Davis Center for Historical Research, Princeton University; The Newberry Library, Chicago; the National Humanities Center of the United States; the Getty Center for the History of Art and the Humanities; the Center for Advanced Study in the Visual Arts, National Gallery of Art, Washington, D.C.; the Humanities Research Centre, Australian National University; the National Endowment for the Humanities. I am happy to acknowledge the receipt of a Lila Wallace–Reader's Digest Publications Subsidy from Villa I Tatti, and various support from the Senate Research Grants Committee of the University of California, Riverside.

While employed by the National Gallery of Art to work on an interactive multi-media computer display, I enjoyed an unparalleled opportunity to learn from David Brown and John Hand, curators respectively of Italian and northern Renaissance painting, more about artists' formal, as distinct from iconographical techniques for conveying meaning. Patricia Fortini Brown took a major hand in the fate of this book when she recommended it, and me, to Gillian Malpass, every author's dream of an editor by virtue of her imaginative perception of the writer's intentions, and her intelligent role in helping to realize them (she has even allowed me to speak in my own, rather than an academic voice, to the point of permitting, in the title of Chapter 3, the more natural "who" in place of the strictly correct "whom"). Had it not been for her steadfast faith in this enterprise, the book would not have been published in its present form. I want to thank also those who read it in drafts and gave me the benefit of their comments and criticisms, particularly Alison Brown, Gene Brucker, Richard Goldthwaite, Margaret Haines, John Najemy, Brenda Preyer, and John Shearman. Finally, I thank Crispin Robinson for coming to my rescue at the last moment, applying his expertise on the subject to indexing the book just as I would have wanted it done.

Now that it is done, I dedicate this study to all those friends who helped to make it happen. Mostly, however, I worked on the book in solitude, not to say isolation, and I wrote it for my own sustenance and comfort in hard times. To transpose my personal experience into a more appropriately universal key; if an obscure plebeian feminist of the late twentieth century may borrow a few splendid phrases from a famous patrician misogynist of the fifteenth, I would like to cite Machiavelli's description of a historian's day, as being not dissimilar – give or take some very time- and gender-specific details of actions and attitudes – to my own:

> Leaving the wood, I go to a spring . . . I have a book with me, either Dante or Petrarca or one of the lesser poets like Tibullus, Ovid, and the like: I read about their amorous passions and about their loves, I remember my own, and I revel for a moment in this thought. I then move on up the road to the inn, I speak with those who pass . . . I learn many things and note the different and diverse tastes and ways of thinking of men . . . With these men . . . I wipe the mold from my brain and release my feeling of being ill-treated by Fate: I am happy to be driven along this road by her, as I wait to see if she will be ashamed of doing so . . . When evening comes, I return to my home, and I go into my study . . . I enter into the ancient courts of ancient men and am welcomed by them kindly . . . and there I am not ashamed to speak to them, to ask them the reasons for their actions; and they, in their humanity, answer me; and for four hours I feel no boredom, I dismiss every affliction, I no longer fear poverty nor do I tremble at the thought of death: I become completely part of them.

Machiavelli knew the private joy and consolation of escaping from present pains and constraints into the infinite past. His has always seemed to me the most eloquent and compelling argument for the continuing study of history.

I

THE PATRON'S OEUVRE

INTRODUCTION

THE TERMS OF RENAISSANCE PATRONAGE

DEFINING AN OEUVRE

The sophisticated and expensive works of art that survive to embody the Florentine Renaissance of the visual arts as we know it were not just adornments of the environment of fifteenth-century Florentines. They were also a vital medium of self-expression and communication, generated in a dynamic interaction between artists, patrons, and their audience. The relationships between these players in the creative process could take many forms. The interests of artists and patrons might be in harmony, or in conflict. The patron might be the artist's primary, or even exclusive viewer; usually artist and patron together addressed an extensive audience. These two- or three-way relationships between artist, patron, and audience varied in intensity and complexity according to particular personal and social circumstances, and shaped in turn the form of the works of art that were their outcome.[1]

Looking at the art of any period, the object and the artist naturally occupy the center of the picture. Differences in the roles of patrons and audiences in various cultures appear, by contrast, to be great, although much of the difference may lie in the nature or limitations of surviving evidence. Someone has to pay for the production of a costly work of art, and most artists and patrons seek an audience. Comparing the relations of artists, patrons, and audience over a broad spectrum of time and place, artists in Renaissance Florence seemed comparatively dependent upon patrons – although less than in the preceding millennium – and patrons of works of art displayed in public places appeared to be consciously addressing an audience. The Renaissance artist's solution to the expressive problem posed by the patron's commission could never be entirely independent of his patron's interests and the audience's expected response.[2]

A good deal is known about the patrons of Renaissance art, particularly the wealthy and prominent patrons of ambitious and expensive commissions, often much more than is known of the talented but usually less socially elevated artists who realized these commissions. Conversely, while the object itself reveals much of the

expressive problem the artist confronted in representing its formal solution, the patron's expressive problem, although no less real, is less immediately apparent. While form and meaning can hardly be divorced, the patron's main contribution to the act of creation was his desire to express meaning visually. The artist was expected to fulfil his patron's expressive expectations, but these cannot easily be distinguished from his own aspirations, or from the form with which he endowed them.

Unless explicitly stated, the patron's intentions are ultimately unrecoverable. The significant issues and experiences of his life may illuminate otherwise obscure sources of his meaning, but it is difficult to infer direct connections between aspects of the lives of illustrious patrons and particular works they commissioned, even those works the patrons obviously intended to memorialize themselves. Modern patrons tend to articulate such connections. In the fifteenth century the conception of a work of art hardly existed, and there were no common forms of literature, such as the psychological memoir, inviting the patron to record his feelings about the aesthetic qualities of objects, or the meaning they bore for him. Explanations of the Renaissance patron's creative role in individual commissions are thus too often obliged to rest on speculative foundations constructed from scraps of biographical information tenuously relating the patron to ideas and texts randomly chosen from what has aptly been called "the grab-bag of culture."[3]

The concept of an oeuvre is not usually applied by art historians to the patron's production.[4] However, just as the creative issues that preoccupied an artist can be inferred more readily from his entire oeuvre, so the patron's oeuvre – the entire body of work created by his patronage – is the most satisfactory basis on which to reconstruct the meaning he may have invested in particular objects he commissioned. There are some important differences between the implications of an "oeuvre" pertaining to the patron and the customary usage of "oeuvre" to designate the body of an artist's work. The artist's oeuvre as we know it is usually, in the frequent absence of documentation, the contingent construction of a modern connoisseur, arising from often controversial attributions. The artist, on the other hand, is demonstrably the creator of an aesthetic. This may not be true of the patron, but the body of his work is at least a given, consisting by definition of commissions which can be documentably attributed directly or indirectly to his initiative. Overall, as this study of Cosimo's artistic commissions aims to demonstrate, by viewing this body of work as an oeuvre, even in the particular parlance of the student of art, we gain much more in perspective on the role of the patron than we lose in abandoning an arbitrary convention of specialist usage.[5]

Cosimo de' Medici was the leading citizen and the major private patron of the visual arts in Florence in the first half of the fifteenth century. He commissioned objects from most of the distinguished painters, sculptors, architects, and craftsmen of his day, a large and innovative body of work that changed the face of the city and made it then, as now, a magnet for lovers of art. There are distinguishable themes in Cosimo's patronage, regarded as a whole and without excessive concern for the relative quality of the artists who worked for him, or the prestige of the genre in which they worked.[6] The recurrence of these particular themes and interests in Cosimo's patronage gives it a coherence analogous to the oeuvres of artists.

The themes of Cosimo's oeuvre emerge more clearly after connecting information about various areas of his experience previously insufficiently related – the details of Cosimo's many distinguished and complex commissions,[7] of other aspects of his life, culture and patronage,[8] his choices of artists and subjects compared with those of other prominent patrons,[9] and what is known of Florentines' experience and expectations of works of art.[10] Cosimo's patronage oeuvre generally resembles that of other wealthy men of his time; its individuality lies in the unique configuration of the body of works he commissioned, expressing and revealing preoccupations related to his personality, the events of his life, and ideas or images that particularly captured his imagination. As Machiavelli reflected in writing to a friend, "each man governs himself according to his fantasy."[11]

Historians viewing the past through the lens of modern perceptions of self-expression might assume that this last observation relates more to the Renaissance artist than to his patron. Closer attention to the conditions in which works of art were produced reveals that the artist's creativity had in fact to operate within the framework of the patron's fantasy. Although this fantasy contributed to defining the artist's creative problem, it did not preempt the artist's choice of a solution. There is ample evidence, increasing as the fifteenth century progressed, that within the limits set by the patron, many great artists strove

primarily to please themselves, or their professional peers. Cosimo's expectations did not circumscribe Donatello's achievement, although they seem to have been satisfied by it.[12] Michelangelo's creative ambitions conflicted bitterly with his patron's when Pope Julius II changed his mind about commissioning a tomb on the grand scale the artist had imagined. But despite Michelangelo's protests and protestations – he concluded a sonnet to a friend "Defend my painting dead . . . I am no painter,"[13] – the pope's alternative commission to decorate the Sistine chapel ceiling constituted the opportunity for Michelangelo to create a masterpiece.

The enabling fantasy was the patron's, but he too operated within a framework – the expectations of his audience and the culture that shaped them. Modern patronage tends to be driven by personal taste; objects are often purchased for private viewing and pleasure. The Medici collected objects for their personal delectation, but very little of a Renaissance patron's life was private in the modern sense of the word. His sense of self pertained largely to relations nowadays seen as public; its expression envisaged the extensive audience by which most of Cosimo's commissions were made to be seen, and the meaning they were meant to convey was certainly affected by the audience's ability to apprehend it. Cosimo's audience could, and did, bring to the contemplation of his commissions various levels of comprehension, and some sense of these is crucial to uncovering the links between the patron's experience and the works of art he commissioned.

In determining what is relevant to understanding Cosimo's patronage of the visual arts, I have assumed the major importance of his audience. I have also tried to strike a commonsense balance between the extremes that often result from the paucity of explicit testimony from Renaissance patrons about the motives and interests that animated their commissions. It is not enough to show that certain ideas were "in the air":[14] Cosimo's particular choices need to be tied as closely as possible to his own actions, education, and intimate acquaintance.[15] At the same time, he clearly shared many general assumptions current in his time about man's relation to God and society, and the role of the image in expressing it.[16] Since Cosimo is said to have preferred actions to words,[17] it makes sense sometimes to attend to more loquacious contemporaries who articulated these common attitudes.[18]

The tracing of discernible themes through Cosimo's patronage results in a fuller understanding of many individual objects. However, we cannot assume that a wish to articulate these themes entirely accounts for his commissions of complex works of art which pose numerous puzzles of interpretation. Nor is the prevalence of particular themes in the patron's oeuvre a measure of the relative contributions of the patron's ideas and the artist's invention in the objects we behold. Still less could a patron's interests circumscribe a work's significance to each of us, or to its myriad viewers over the centuries.[19] It is important to discover the pattern of Cosimo's patronage, because the objects he commissioned have richer significance when viewed in the context of his life, as they were by his contemporaries. Seen from this perspective, each object tells us in turn something more about its patron, restoring a fundamental layer of the meaning Renaissance works of art bore in their own time.

GENERATING A WORK OF ART

Cosimo de' Medici's costliest and most important commissions were buildings. Filarete spoke of Cosimo in his *Treatise on Architecture*, describing "the delight he says he takes in building."[20] Monastic records enumerated his donations to the convents of San Marco and the Badia, and Medici account books recorded the enormous expenses of construction for the Medici palace and at the church of San Lorenzo.[21] But Cosimo himself left no account of the impulses behind his building program.

However, Giovanni Rucellai, another Florentine banker whose patronage of architecture was almost as notable as Cosimo's, eloquently expressed in his diary his feelings about this most prestigious of a patron's activities: "There are two principal things that men do in this world. The first is to procreate, the second is to build."[22] The many patrician patrons who in the fifteenth-century built palaces to house their progeny in the newly fashionable classicizing style clearly shared Rucellai's view that building was an urgent and primal activity – like making love, as Filarete saw it.[23]

Buildings are among the most remarkable Renaissance "works of art"; objects distinguished in the modern Western cultural tradition by virtue of their aesthetic qualities from the mundane life of the society in which they arose. The Renaissance patron's particular passion for building, however, locates this activity firmly in the realm of the mundane, thus providing a clue to his role in the production of other works of art.[24] At the same time, a growing familiarity with other cultures which make no sharp distinction between art and non-art, seeing the form of the object as inseparable from its function, has begun to put the European aesthetic in historical and cultural perspective.[25]

Rucellai's dictum is important because it presents the patron not just as sponsor, but *auctor*. Giuliano Lapaccini, prior of San Marco, described in detail in his chronicle the activities involved in the convent's rebuilding, and of "its authors, the magnificent Cosimo and Lorenzo de' Medici."[26] Rucellai had Alberti, one of the most distinguished architects of his age, design a splendid marble facade for the church of Santa Maria Novella. He blazoned across it in gleaming letters several feet high, which can be seen from as far away as the steep street of the Costa San Giorgio, on the opposite side of the city, as one descends the hill from the southeastern gate, the words: "I, Giovanni Rucellai, son of Paolo, made this in the year of our Lord 1470."[27]

Nowadays this may seem an extravagant claim, since we are accustomed to regard the artist as the author of his work. However, if we hope to understand the art of the Renaissance, we must understand the patron's point of view. The fifteenth-century patron was not merely the most privileged viewer of the art he commissioned; he was deeply implicated in its authorship.[28] For most of the fifteenth century artists were not considered to be independent creative agents, and could not behave as such. The quattrocento conception of artistic commissions in general derived from Aristotle's classical – and very patriarchal – account of generation: "The female, as female, is passive, and the male, as male, is active, and the principle of the movement comes from him."[29] The patron-progenitor exercised the vital initiative that determined the essential characteristics of artistic progeny; the artist's part was to conceive and give them form. Such a perception prevailed among patrons throughout Cosimo de' Medici's lifetime.

To understand a work of art as "the deposit of a social relationship" between artist, patron, and audience, we need, in Michael Baxandall's words, some "insight into what it was like, intellectually and sensibly, to be a Quattrocento person."[30] There have been many studies of the social conditions in which Renaissance art flourished, and of patrons as initiators or enablers whose agendas established the framework within which artists were obliged to operate. However, neither art historians, preoccupied with the object, and animated by a modern reverence for the artist,[31] nor historians, inclined to see art as an illustration, or even simply a reflection of more fundamental social phenomena, have sufficiently explored the implications of the patron's claims of authorship for the meaning works of art bore in their own time.[32]

This book aims to restore the patron's initiative to its proper place in the picture of quattrocento artistic production. A more general approach to Renaissance art than this book adopts would pay more attention to the balance between the patron's and other perspectives. By the end of the fifteenth century artists had succeeded in shifting the balance of power and credit further in their own favor, and the beginnings of this process are apparent in the chapter of this book dealing with relations between Medici patrons and the artists who worked for them.[33]

In practice there seems to have been no single model for the genesis of art. The respective roles of artists, patrons, humanist advisors, and friends in the conception and realization of any particular commission depended upon its nature and function, and their interests and expertise. There were patterns in quattrocento patronage, but their exploration is largely outside the scope of this study, which examines the process of patronage chiefly with reference to the commissions of Cosimo de' Medici and his family.[34]

Reciprocal obligation to action for mutual advantage is the essence of patronage in all its senses – personal, political, and artistic; cooperation and communication between patrons and groups of artists was crucial to the production of works of art. The most powerful patrons and the most distinguished artists were each *maestri* in their own *botteghe*, the masters of their own workshops, where their authority and fame were the reward of outstanding abilities.[35] At the same time, much earlier than the fifteenth century, the artist's "hoc fecit" (he made this), together with his signature and the incorporation of his self-portrait in his work, had begun to push back strongly against the patron's claims.[36]

ARTICULATING IDENTITY IN IMAGES

Modern students of the fine arts, a discipline based in connoisseurship, have traditionally reversed the Renaissance view to focus on the artist's creativity. Recently, some art historians have paid more attention to the patron's interests and concerns as clues to the ultimate "significance" of the object, but while perceptions of the artist's expressive intentions in individual works have generally been shaped by consideration of his total oeuvre, discussion of the patron's contribution tends to be confined to the specific circumstances leading to a particular commission. Often these are not very illuminating.[37]

Any understanding of works of art is much enhanced by placing them in their total patronage context, and that context properly includes the whole spectrum of the patron's activity – his life's oeuvre, corresponding to that of the artist he employed, and intersecting with it in various and complex ways. This study is animated by a desire to reassemble the patron as the integrated subject of his own activity, rather than the object of academic attention fragmented by disciplines dealing separately with politics, literature, art, and religion, and by scholars excessively preoccupied with anachronistic binary oppositions between public and private, secular and spiritual, individual and corporate.[38]

The commissioning of works of art and the production, consumption, and patronage of diverse genres of writing were among the various means by which the Florentine patron defined and articulated his own and his family's identity, locating them particularly in urban space and historical time.[39] The classical and Christian past, its texts and expressive forms, together with familial and civic traditions, informed the patron's identity and provided the vocabulary, verbal and visual, through which it was articulated and recognized.[40] Viewed as patrician self-definition in a patronage "oeuvre,"[41] the making of Renaissance art appears as an intricate process, neither an expression of the artist's untrameled inspiration as enshrined in the romantic picture of the artist at work,[42] nor some oft-assumed vile compromise between the artist's mysterious creativity and the patron's inscrutable "taste."[43]

The Renaissance patron had at his disposal a vast vocabulary of words, images, and actions. Of the several mutually intelligible languages in which he might express himself – entrepreneurial activity, participation in politics, the cultivation of a dynasty, devotion to God, and charitable works – painting, sculpture, and architecture offered "unusual advantages; unparalleled immediacy, actual presence and permanence."[44] Appreciation of these advantages was not confined to artists or their *cognoscenti*. The power of images was daily apparent to patrons and audience through their role in civic life and in worship; in particular, images helped to create the Christian experience that was the prism through which Renaissance men viewed their world.[45]

The letters and sermons of the Church's most influential mystical thinkers, such as Bernard of Clairvaux and Bridget of Sweden, together with those of outstanding living religious leaders, accustomed Cosimo and his contemporaries to a cultivated response to images, teaching them how to look carefully at the devotional objects that constituted the majority of early Renaissance commissions. Bernard of Clairvaux's sermon on the grief of Mary at Calvary was the original inspiration of countless paintings of the Virgin and Saint John at the foot of the cross, like the one on the wall of Cosimo de' Medici's cell at San Marco.[46]

Sant' Antonino, first as prior of San Marco and later as archbishop of Florence, instructed the laity in his manual on *Living Virtuously* how to meditate before the cross on the Passion of Christ. He described a process of attention to the image "with the eyes of the mind more than those of the body," which is crucial to looking at works of art:

When you have heard mass, or before, or if you want, in your own room, kneel before a crucifix, and . . . consider his face. First, the crown of thorns, ground into his head as far as the brain; then his eyes, full of tears and blood and sweat; then his nose, full of mucous and tears and blood; the mouth, full of bile and spittle and blood; his beard, similarly full of bile and blood and spittle, having been spat upon and raked; then his face, blackened and spat upon, and livid from the blows of the flail and the fist.[47]

The habit of such attention, as the prerequisite for reading an image, could extend to embrace secular objects, of which Giovanni Dominici and Antoninus often disapproved, but which were displayed in Renaissance houses side by side with devotional images.[48] Florentines' favourite reading – the Scriptures, well-known classics and traditional moral literature, like the immensely popular *Fables* of Aesop – similarly encouraged people to regard as a text the visible, natural world,[49] to whose realistic representation Renaissance artists were strongly committed. Quintilian, whose *Institutio Oratoria* was one of the most widely read classical works in the early Renaissance, and one of the manuscripts already in Cosimo's library in 1418, observed that "pictures . . . penetrate into our innermost feelings with such power that at times they seem more eloquent than language itself."[50] For Renaissance men the visual arts were a natural vehicle for the expression of self, and for the realization of their visions of personal and social identity.[51]

ARTISTS, PATRONAGE NETWORKS, AND PERSONAL LETTERS

Identity and power in Florentine society were chiefly constructed and mediated through personal relations. These were formalized in networks of personal patronage. By extending basic familial obligations to "friends," especially of the office-holding class, patronage networks linked the individual or family to the community and its governors, those who had a share in the *stato*.[52] In the language of patronage, younger or less powerful men customarily addressed their older benefactors as "most dear, and like a father to me."[53] Patrons, artists, and their audience were all enmeshed in this web of relationships. Donatello and Michelozzo, artists to whom a large number of Cosimo's commissions have been attributed, were familiars of the Medici household.[54] Most major artists associated with their prominent patrons far beyond the terms of contracts, on which attention has been too exclusively focused in assessing the patron's contribution to shaping works of art. Contracts were

extremely important documents in this legalistic society, serving as records and regulators of all types of agreement and association, but like contracts of marriage or business partnership, contracts between patrons and artists must be read in the context of preexisting social networks; as defining and formalizing at one moment in time ongoing personal relationships out of which specific acts, including the commission of works of art, arose.[55]

The Medici family's personal patronage relationships are brilliantly illluminated by their correspondence. This contains an astonishing variety of incidental information about many otherwise obscure aspects of Florentine life and society. Most letters were generated *faute de mieux*, since important information, as writers constantly observed, was better passed on by word of mouth. Letters paved the way for personal meetings to conduct business *a bocca* (face to face), but they were also the instruments or contracts of patronage. Renaissance networks of patronage and friendship operated much like the Mafia, as associations between men acknowledging their obligation to aid in all his enterprises an *amico degli amici*, a "friend of the friends." Private letters, being the pledges of friendship, were the coin of patronage; their language, precisely calibrated, negotiated, and defined its terms. These terms were not necessarily those of modern friendship, although personal affection was often part of mutual support in political and business enterprises, the sharing of familial and civic interests, and the brotherhood created by common devotional, intellectual, and artistic concerns.[56]

The Medici correspondence was long ago combed for information about important artistic commissions in letters written to or by artists. The resulting small corpus of documents has played an essential role in delineating the picture of relations between artists and patrons.[57] It is often argued that the relatively small number of these letters, and their general concern with practical and pedestrian matters such as payment or delivery date, demonstrate that there was little communication between artists and their patrons, and that the latter were very little involved in the production of the works of art they commissioned. Such arguments *ex silentio*[58] ignore the fact that the evidence of letters is circumscribed by their purpose, which was not to elucidate or communicate a Renaissance aesthetic or to reflect on personal taste. The genre of the functional letter is frequently misunderstood by art historians reading letters out of their social context. Replaced in that context, well-known letters between patrons and artists take on new, and often very different meaning. Forms of speech that strike the modern reader as craven or condescending in fact voiced common social and personal conventions, and may describe a variety of unequal, but often very intimate associations.[59]

The great value of the letters of Cosimo de' Medici, his family, and friends, which are a major source for this study, is in showing how apparently diverse aspects of a patron's life were fundamentally connected, creating a rich context for his patronage of art. This is particularly so since the support and promotion of artists and the acquisition of admired objects were negotiated largely through the same patronage channels as the operations of business and politics, and often by the same familiar group of friends, relatives, and neighbors acting, by their own testimony, in response to the all-encompassing imperatives of personal association and obligation.[60]

CLIENTELISMO AND MECENATISMO: TWO SIDES OF THE SAME COIN OF PATRONAGE

Since the late 1970s there has been a growing awareness that Florence, as a society structured by personal patronage, resembles many others both extinct and extant, especially around the Mediterranean basin. This has led historians to apply to Florence increasingly various models drawn from comparative anthropological and sociological studies, and to modify appropriately a previous tendency to regard Florence as quite unique.[61] However, in the process of comparison and description in theoretical terms, we should not lose sight of the particular qualities of this small city and its sophisticated culture, which first attracted the attention of scholars of art, learning, and society. Fifteenth-century Florence was no more a Mediterranean village than a modern megalopolis.[62]

In response to a new wave of patronage studies, some historians have been keen to sharpen the distinction between *mecenatismo*, the modern Italian term for the support of literature and the arts which has been the traditional meaning of patronage for students of the Renaissance, and the *clientelismo* of personal patronage.[63] This misses the point of the patron's role in a world where patrons and artists were associated in a network of personal bonds, and art and literature were a major means of social and self-definition. Language both prescribes and describes, so it is important to note that in the Italian spoken by Cosimo and his contemporaries there were no such distinctions. Not until much later in the century were these abstract nouns imported from Latin into Italian, and even then they were used relatively infrequently in self-conscious imitation of an admired antique world,[64] where they had signaled a social reality rather different from that which arose from the distinctive Florentine amalgam of classical, Christian, feudal, and mercantile values.[65]

TASTE AND CHOICE

The concept of a patron's oeuvre, on the other hand, stems naturally from fifteenth-century views of patronage. Provided that the term is used with care, it opens up new and broader avenues for approaching a number of important issues, including the vexed question of the role in artistic production of taste, another modern abstraction.[66] Investigating the patron's oeuvre and the taste that shaped it also involves consideration, alongside original commissions, of the patron's collection of ancient and precious objects. Fifteenth-century patrons often valued such objects more highly than the original Renaissance works so prized today. Although not products of the patron's authorship, as evidence of his choice they constitute vital clues to his taste often neglected in scholars' concentration on artistic innovation.[67]

The Medici oeuvre, the most impressive and best-documented of its period, is the essential subject of this book.[68] However, some comparison with the oeuvres of other major patrons is helpful in indicating where Medici patronage choices are particular, and where they embody the interests and values shared by other powerful and cultured men of the age. Recent research on patronage has revealed a more complex picture of cultural debts and exchange within Florence, and between the republic and such other Italian cities as Milan, Naples, Mantua, and Ferrara, all distinct in their constitutional and political arrangements, though in other ways more similar than they may look.[69]

Within Florence, it seems that patronage was often shaped by political affiliation or rivalry. The patronage of Medici friends and followers appears to respond to Medici initiatives, either by emulation or competition.[70] In their own patronage, the Medici may consciously have imitated the example of their Strozzi rivals, who were exiled on account of their wealth and power after the Medici triumph of 1434.[71] Giovanni Rucellai's patronage oeuvre, most comparable to Cosimo's in quantity and quality, richly expressed the particular sense of self that emerges from his diary, or *zibaldone*. This record is invaluable to any study of Florentine patronage because it offers a rarely detailed and self-conscious account of the interests, motives, and mentality of a patron who was unusually reflective, as well as prolific; no other major quattrocento patron articulated so fully the patron's point of view. Rucellai's observation that he had commissioned works of art "for the honor of God and the honor of the city and the memory of me" happily provides at least an entrée into the sensible and intellectual world of the Renaissance patron which this book attempts, as far as it can, to re-create.[72]

I

COSIMO'S OEUVRE

Cosimo de' Medici achieved power in his lifetime and fame beyond it because his outstanding skills in business and politics – civic, Italian, and international – made him a major force in the public life of Renaissance Florence. But he captured the imagination of his contemporaries and has remained an almost legendary figure of history mainly because he used his wealth and power to promote the innovations of the greatest artists of the Florentine Renaissance. The image Cosimo projected as a patron, especially of buildings, is visible in his commissions, more arresting and enduring than the evidence of his political genius. He himself foresaw this. According to his friend and biographer Vespasiano da Bisticci, "he said that one of the greatest mistakes he ever made was not to have begun to spend ten years earlier, since knowing the nature of his city, in less than fifty years' time nothing would be found of him or his family but those few remains of what he had built . . ."[1] Cosimo was a man of deeds rather than words, and his commissions of works of art were among his most eloquent actions.

This book seeks to delineate Cosimo's visible image, to discover what can be seen of Cosimo himself in his patronage of art. To introduce the reader to Cosimo's world, this chapter offers a brief overview of his oeuvre, set in the context of the predominant themes of his life and patronage. In Renaissance Florence celebration of the honor of God, the honor of the city, and the memory of the individual and his family were not alternatives, but a single impulse. This is particularly evident in the extensive patronage of Cosimo and his sons. At the same time, within this framework there was ample room for the expression of personal interests and preoccupations that stamped the Medici oeuvre in Cosimo's lifetime with its highly individual character.[2] His involvement in business and politics, which occupied most of the hours of his days, has been the primary focus of most studies of Cosimo. Less frequently emphasized aspects of his life, which find powerful expression in his patronage, are his loyalty to family, friends, and city, his concern with salvation after death, and his pleasure in the cultivated enjoyment of this life.

Florentines were compelled by that "dear and worthy paternal image" of which Dante spoke in his *Divine Comedy*, and which he personified above all in the figure of Virgil, his guide and protector on his journey down to hell and up the mountain of purgatory.[3] Patriarchal metaphors ordered and integrated the Florentine's world, here and hereafter. They gave coherence to the patronage that imaged that world, as to the patron's life. The primary source of Florentine honor or dishonor was the family, as every articulate patrician attested.[4] For the members of old, wealthy, and powerful families, the honor of the commune was part of the patrimony of the lineage. Cosimo succeeded in identifying the honor of the Medici family with that of the commune more completely than any citizen before him. He did this by extending his patriarchal authority to embrace all of his large lineage – by 1427 he was the acknowledged head of a family of some twenty-seven households – and by making his friends and political supporters honorary extensions of this group, to be seen as dear as fathers, brothers, and sons in affection and obligation.

Cosimo *paterfamilias* of the Medici became *padrino* to a significant proportion of those patricians who held public office, intensifying the patriarchal character of a state which Renaissance Florentines, like the classical Roman forbears with whom they self-consciously identified, conceived as their *patria* – their fatherland. Florentines explicitly acknowledged the fusion of Cosimo's various patriarchal roles when they posthumously awarded him the honorific Roman title *pater patriae*, father of his country. Analogies frequently drawn by Medicean supporters between the protective powers of their earthly father Cosimo and those of their heavenly Father projected his patriarchal image into the realm of eternity.[5]

A major theme of Medici patronage in all its senses is the expression of familial and dynastic solidarity. The descendants of Cosimo's grandfather Averardo, known as "Bicci," became a close-knit group within the lineage that revived the Medici family's failing fourteenth-century fortunes (fig. 1). They did this through the

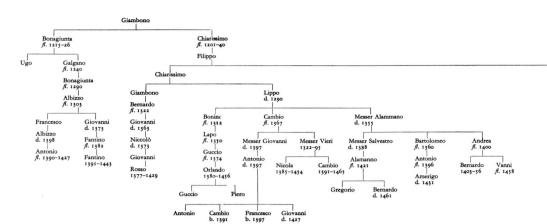

1   Partial genealogy of the Medici family based on those published by De Roover in *The Rise and Decline of the Medici Bank*, and Litta, *Famiglie Celebri Italiani*

commercial success of their bank, which like all their other enterprises flourished in the continuity between generations, and the loyalty and cooperation between members of the line.[6] Well into the fifteenth century a high proportion of the employees of the Medici bank were kinsmen. After the consolidation of the Medici party in the early 1430s factors were regularly drawn from a small pool of close friends and relatives by marriage, including the Bardi, Benci, Martelli, and Portinari families, whose association with their Medici patrons' interests extended the power and influence of the kin-group in business, politics, and society.[7]

Cosimo and Lorenzo, the surviving sons of Giovanni di Bicci, assumed joint control of the bank and other Medici enterprises when Giovanni retired in 1420. The adult brothers, with their wives and children, had continued to live in their father's house; upon Giovanni's death they jointly inherited both house and bank. While primogeniture was not the traditional form of inheritance in Florence, it was customary for the eldest son to move into and maintain the family palace. Enduring three-generation families, including almost adult grandchildren, were comparatively rare, and both a cause and a manifestation of a family's strength.[8] Few quattrocento extended households were longer lived than that of the descendants of Giovanni di Bicci de' Medici, comprising three generations for almost the entire century. After Lorenzo died in 1440, his young son Pierfrancesco remained in Cosimo's household, and the old Medici house became his in the 1450s, when Cosimo and his sons moved with their families into the new palace a few doors down the Via Larga (fig. 92).[9] Piero di Cosimo listed the mourners from "Cosimo's household" at his funeral in 1464, numbering forty-five men and women from both the old house and the new palace on the Via Larga, and from the family villas at Trebbio, Cafaggiolo, and Careggi (figs. 147–9).[10]

Cosimo's earliest artistic commissions were inherited from his father. Giovanni di Bicci built the old sacristy at San Lorenzo to serve as his burial chapel; Cosimo and Lorenzo completed its decoration, which commemorates at once the evangelists, saints, and martyrs of the church and the lineage of their Medici devotees (fig. 77). Before the death of his brother Lorenzo, who was widely admired for his cultivation and learning, all the commissions more commonly associated with Cosimo were in fact, like the bank's contracts, made in their joint names.[11] An early object inscribed to this effect was the reliquary commissioned from Ghiberti in 1426 for the convent church of Santa Maria degli Angeli, where the brothers took part in learned discussions with its humanist prior, their close friend Ambrogio Traversari (fig. 7).[12]

The Medici palace, Cosimo's major secular commission, was the physical embodiment of the Medici house and its honor. Its plan enshrined the continuing solidarity of Bicci's line; it was designed to accommodate all his living descendants into the foreseeable future.[13] Its exterior evoked echoes of the majesty of communal buildings, and its classicizing detail expressed the new enthusiasm for antique forms, as well as some of the dignity and restraint that Cicero, Cosimo's favorite author, thought appropriate to virtuous citizens.[14] Within, it was a luxurious pleasure palace accommodating the highly sophisticated tastes of its residents (fig. 101); a repository of familial objects in the most innovative styles and genres of Florence's rapidly evolving avant-garde art.[15] For example, Mino da Fiesole's busts of Piero, Giovanni, and Piero's wife Lucrezia are the first known examples of portrait busts in the antique manner (figs. 137 and 138).[16]

It is inappropriate to distinguish too sharply between

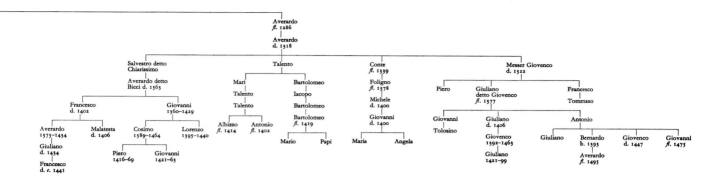

the commissions of Cosimo and his sons. Piero may have done much of the negotiating with artists and craftsmen involved in the palace decoration, as he did with Benozzo Gozzoli, who painted the frescoes of the Journey of the Magi for its chapel, with its portraits of the family and their friends and retainers (fig. 156).[17] No doubt we see there, as in the tabernacles Piero built at San Miniato and the Annunziata (figs. 84 and 85), some expression of his personal preferences and tastes. Cooperation by division of labor between the generations was a strong tradition in the Medici family, reflecting both individual competence and a view of tasks appropriate to youth and age. Probably Cosimo concentrated on building, because this was his major personal interest, and also the prerogative of the patriarch, but since he was the patriarch, nothing else would have been done without his general wish and consent.[18]

Family strength and loyalty were the lifeblood of Florentine society, perhaps its highest ideal. The Medici were typical in the importance they accorded these values, but they were archetypal, as in so many other ways, in the degree to which they succeeded in promoting the honor of their family and in preserving its memory for posterity through their artistic patronage.[19]

"Nothing is more certain than our death, and nothing more uncertain than its hour."[20] This customary preface to charitable bequests in the wills of rich and poor, famous and obscure, voiced the universal belief that a virtuous life was essential to a good death, and that charitable patronage was an important component of this virtue. Cosimo's biographer Vespasiano da Bisticci recorded that Cosimo "wanted God to have mercy on him and to preserve him in the enjoyment of his temporal goods" but "felt some of his money was unjustly acquired." "To lift this weight from his shoulders,"[21] he

began his extensive program of charitable building with the renovation of the Observant Dominican convent of San Marco (fig. 71). Whether Vespasiano's story is literally true or not, Cosimo's desire to expiate his sins is patently a major force driving his patronage.

Cosimo's religious impulses, often reflexively dismissed as conventional piety, or trivialized as guilt about usury,[22] are commonly seen as an incidental element in a primarily self-advertising patronage program expressing his personal power and dynastic ambitions. But it is time that we saw through Burckhardt's myth of the secular Renaissance to the reality of that age's profound and urgent spiritual concerns.[23] Notably, of the commissions for which Cosimo was personally responsible, apart from the family palace, all were for the building and decoration of churches and chapels. Seen together, they represent a powerful strategy for survival in the hereafter.

Giovanni di Bicci, inspired presumably by a play on the Medici name, identified his family with the cult of the early Christian brother physicians, Saints Cosmas and Damian. Twins born to Giovanni's wife Piccarda in 1389 were christened Cosimo and Damiano. Damiano died in 1390, but Cosimo made the doctor saints his own and the Medici family's protectors.[24] They are the central figures of altarpieces he commissioned from Fra Filippo Lippi for Santa Croce, from Alesso Baldovinetti for Cafaggiolo, and from Fra Angelico for San Marco, the Mugello church of Bosco ai Frati rebuilt by the Medici, and another, known as the Annalena altarpiece, for an unknown site, perhaps San Lorenzo (figs. 54–57 and 62).[25]

These representations of the Medici saints were not merely markers to identify the altarpieces as Medici commissions. Their votive functions are most evident in the San Marco altarpiece, where Saint Cosmas turns to the audience, acting as mediator between the viewer and the Virgin, a reminder not only of Cosimo de' Medici's role as patron and power-broker for his friends in Florence, but also of Cosmas's role as Cosimo's "very special friend" interceding for him in heaven.[26] There were many similar works made for the Medici family's domestic contemplation; among them were Filippo Lippi's painted panels of the Annunciation and seven saints, including all the immediate family's onomastic protectors (figs. 121 and 122).[27]

The Medici also adopted the cult of the Magi so popular in Europe in the late Middle Ages. A metaphor for the spiritual progression of the wealthy and powerful toward submission to Christ, it exemplified the compatability in Renaissance Catholicism of devotion with display, the play of imagination, fantasy, and pleasure in religious ceremonies and images.[28] These elements are apparent in the visible influence on Magi images of the visit of Eastern delegates to the church council which met in Florence in 1439 with Cosimo's support. A relatively austere fresco of the Magi, probably by Benozzo Gozzoli, acting as Angelico's assistant, was painted for Cosimo's cell at San Marco (fig. 60), prefiguring the subject of Gozzoli's opulent frescoes for the Medici palace chapel executed in 1459. Many other representations of this theme, by artists including Angelico, Lippi, and Domenico Veneziano, are listed in the inventory of household possessions in the Medici palace compiled after Lorenzo's death in 1492.[29] These pictures were designed to inspire the devotion of their sophisticated patrons, but also to delight their eyes, and to display the artists' powers of invention in the achievement of infinite variety (figs. 117 and 118).

Cassian's *Monastic Institutes* was perhaps the most heavily annotated manuscript in Cosimo's library in 1418, and his major building commissions for the convent of San Marco – his first – and the Badia at Fiesole – his last – also indicate his strong interest in the cloistered life (fig. 91).[30] When in 1444 Cosimo financed the rebuilding of San Marco, he had a special double cell constructed in the lay brothers' corridor for his own use as a spiritual retreat. The fresco of the crucified Christ with saints in Cosimo's cell is similar in form and spirit to the frescoes in the monks' cells and the image in the main cloister of Saint Dominic praying at the foot of the cross; it was personalized for Cosimo's devotion by the inclusion of Saints Cosmas, John, and Peter Martyr (fig. 61). Among the last records for the convent of the Badia compiled in Cosimo's lifetime is a reference to furnishings for "Cosimo's room." In his final years Cosimo obviously found spiritual solace not only in the chapel in his palace, but also at San Marco and the Badia, which he described

as "not an earthly dwelling place, but a heavenly one."[31]

The family's patronage of their parish church of San Lorenzo speaks most clearly of their concern for their immortal souls, although the initiation of the rebuilding and the early patronage of the transept chapels was due to the enterprise, under Medici leadership, of the neighborhood in which their partisans were heavily concentrated. In 1442 Cosimo vastly extended the Medici obligation to San Lorenzo, and the church's obligations to them, by assuming sole responsibility for the rebuilding of the nave and the main chapel (fig. 76). Over the years, the commemorative masses endowed by Cosimo for the souls of his deceased father, mother, brother Lorenzo, and after 1463, his younger son Giovanni, effectively reshaped the liturgy of San Lorenzo, a process crowned by Cosimo's burial before the high altar, at the center of the crossing (fig. 188).[32]

The iconography of the tomb marker refers to Neoplatonic ideas expounded by his humanist friends such as Ficino; the placement of his tomb suggests the influence of early Christian practices promoted by Florentine patristic scholars close to Cosimo, who himself owned and read the writings of the Church Fathers.[33] His patronage oeuvre includes other references to patristic sources, and Lippi's altarpiece for the Medici palace chapel completed just five years before Cosimo's death makes unusual use of one of this tradition's greatest medieval heirs, Saint Bernard of Clairvaux (fig. 163). The appearance with the Virgin of Saint Bernard, patron saint of the Signoria, the governing magistracy of Florence, has important civic connotations as well, like Uccello's fresco of Saint Thomas, symbol of just and virtuous government, for the ancestral Medici church of San Tommaso in the Mercato Vecchio (fig. 82).[34]

Cosimo's epitaph for his father's tomb in the old sacristy (fig. 78) may serve as a reflection on his own patronage, and his quest for immortality through virtuous fame: "If honor in his *patria*, if the glory of his line and of his generosity to all, were free from dark death, he would live happily in that city with his chaste wife, aiding the poor, a haven and enhancement to his friends. But since death conquers all . . .".[35]

"This city is dedicated to commerce, literature, and leisure." Thus Cosimo, speaking in a government debate, once characterized Florence. Within the framework of the wealthy patron's main imperatives, there was ample room for virtuous self-cultivation (the classical conception of leisure), for the rehearsal of learning, and the play of personal pleasure.[36] Cosimo's confidence in himself and in the destiny of his family co-existed with a great admiration for *ingegno* – inventiveness, originality, or genius – in others, enabling him to recognize readily these qualities, which Alberti thought the most important attributes of an artist.[37] Among Florentine patrons Cosimo must surely be considered one of those few "understanding and wise men" to whom even Brunelleschi thought it worth while to explain his inventions.[38] According to Vespasiano, when Cosimo talked with artists, he understood them very well.[39]

The artists Cosimo selected rose superbly to the occasions of his commissions. Paolo Uccello, in love with the possibilities of perspective, may have displayed them for Cosimo's delight in his panels for the Medici house depicting the Battle of San Romano, a representation of the Florentine patron's passionate interest in warfare and admiration for the *condottiere* Niccolò da Tolentino (figs. 125–31).[40] Donatello's prodigious originality generated a wide variety of unique works for the Medici over a period of almost forty years, including the sophisticated marriage of Medici interests in Christian, classical, and civic themes in his bronze *David* (fig. 133),[41] the cycle of saints and church fathers in the old sacristy, representing their collective dynastic and devotional concerns,[42] and the pulpits depicting the Passion and the Resurrection which imaged Cosimo's personal search for salvation (figs. 189–92).[43] After his own death in 1466, the sculptor was buried, at his request, alongside his patron. Michelozzo, on the other hand, performed the esssential function of the Renaissance architect, to serve as his patron's *alter ego* in the creation of a characteristic style.[44]

As in Cosimo's patronage, dynastic, civic, and religious themes were integrated in Petrarch's *Triumphs*; love triumphs over chastity, death over love, fame over death, time over fame, and eternity over all. Cosimo had his own copy of the *Trionfi* by 1418, a splendidly illuminated humanist edition of the text was Piero's first manuscript commission, and Giovanni read Petrarch for diversion at his villa in Fiesole.[45] In 1440 Matteo de' Pasti was gilding an image of the *Triumphs* for Piero,[46] and in 1449 the Triumph of Fame was chosen as the subject of the painted *desco da parto* ordered for the birth of Lorenzo, Cosimo's grandson (fig. 146).[47] These Petrarchan themes appealed to a vast audience in fifteenth-century Florence, animated by the desire, in Dante's words, to know "how man makes himself eternal."[48] In no patronage oeuvre are these themes more consistently and compellingly addressed than in the commissions of Cosimo de' Medici and his sons, who chose as their personal emblem the diamond ring that symbolized eternity, the ultimately triumphant.

2 Cosimo de' Medici, autograph letter to his son Giovanni,
24 June 1442, Florence, ASF, MAP, V, 441

3 Cosimo de' Medici, letter to his son Giovanni, 30 May 1441,
in the hand of Ser Alesso Pelli, Florence, ASF, MAP, V, 399

COSIMO'S LETTERS

Neri di Gino [Capponi] once said to Cosimo: "I wish you would say things clearly so that I could understand you." [Cosimo] replied: "Learn my language."

Angelo Poliziano, *Detti piacevoli*[1]

The Florentine archives are the richest known source of record for any pre-modern European society. Within the limitations of what fifteenth-century men thought it appropriate to record, an enormous amount is known about Cosimo de' Medici and his world. Some thirty thousand personal letters of the Medici family and their correspondents survive for Cosimo's lifetime.[2] Three extensive tax surveys over this period produced lengthy returns detailing Medici assets in business and land, and in the process provided a wealth of information about the family's personal associations and style of life.[3] There are several archives containing accounts of the Medici family's international bank;[4] government records include transcripts of council meetings and debates in which the Medici and their friends participated;[5] diplomatic dispatches illluminate Cosimo's role in Italian politics.[6] There is a large body of literature in Latin and the vernacular, poetry and prose, which throws light on Cosimo's culture and his many and varied intellectual interests.[7]

The public dimension of Cosimo's experience is well documented, but there is very little explicit evidence of what he thought, hoped, or dreamed. He left no direct testimony concerning his feelings about the images he looked at, the literature he read, or the pastimes he enjoyed. The letters written to and by him are the best evidence of his personal allegiances, his daily life, his primary preoccupations, and his ultimate concerns.[8] The correspondence relating to Cosimo falls into five main groups: the family letters, which reveal him as an attentive and loving *paterfamilias*; the letters to friends, chronicling his tireless activity as patron and party boss; his correspondence with the staff of the bank, documenting the shrewd but bold businessman; his letters to his cousin Averardo, displaying the political strategist and patriot; and his statesmanlike correspondence with his friend and ally Francesco Sforza.[9]

The letters Cosimo addressed to his close family and friends are almost the only window on his attitudes to the world. However, even his personal letters fail to answer questions about his cultural preferences – and besides, they are particularly allusive, enigmatic and difficult to decipher. Consequently, some high priests of high culture – of humanism and art – have arbitrarily dismissed as hagiographers biographers who say that Cosimo read Cicero, his collection of classical manuscripts as trophy hunting, and his building as an obvious advertisement of Medici power.[10]

Lack of direct evidence seriously limits what can confidently be said of Cosimo's tastes and "character." This is likely to remain relatively inscrutable, as indeed even contemporaries seem to have found it.[11] Most attempts to write a persuasive life of Cosimo have depended heavily on the testimony of his only contemporary biographer, the bookseller Vespasiano da Bisticci.[12] As Vespasiano was the main provider of books not only for Cosimo's personal library, but also for the libraries of San Marco and the Badia, which involved very large orders, in the course of business he spent a lot of time "in Cosimo's room," and clearly knew him well.[13] Naturally his *Life of Cosimo* emphasizes and approves the literary interests they shared, although, unlike many humanist encomiasts, Vespasiano tempered his admiration with some criticism.[14] He cannot be dismissed as a propagandist; the essential features of his portrait of Cosimo are corroborated by other sources, and in view of this, many of the details of his account may serve to illuminate Cosimo's otherwise shadowy figure.

However, to reach an understanding of Cosimo beyond the arbitrary acceptance or rejection of elements of Vespasiano's "notes toward a biography,"[15] it is necessary "to renounce the illusion of a narrative account" of Cosimo's life or his patronage, "which could claim to be fully authentic, let alone complete: one which offers confident explanations, and deals in the closure of causes and effects."[16] The desire to create a plausible character, even where this conflicts with the historian's "Hippocratic oath" to stick to "what actually happened," has bedeviled biography from its very beginnings, imparting a spurious authority to the authorial voice.[17] Although many recent writers speak about Cosimo with assumed confidence, few have overtly attempted a full-blown biography, and this study is not offered as one. There is insufficient evidence for an entirely convincing personal portrait. The evidence of Cosimo's letters indicates that he himself was very conscious of the operation of the random in human affairs. Constantly calculating, balancing, and maneuvering, his genius lay in his readiness to expect the utterly unforeseen, a lesson as useful to the biographer as to the strategist.

In the absence of self-conscious revelation or even comment from our subject on many of the central concerns of his life, we need to take more critical account of Cosimo's actions, including his patronage of the arts. Although the intentions that animated his commissions are not entirely recoverable, their existence bears witness to many of his interests and achievements. Like Cicero, his favorite classical author, Cosimo knew the value of learning, but he clearly shared something of the orator's view that "to be drawn by study away from the active life is contrary to moral duty. For the whole glory of virtue is in activity . . ."[18] His friend Vespasiano recorded that Cosimo was noted more for deeds than words.[19] The humanist Filelfo, his enemy, agreed.[20] As Aristotle said in his *Poetics*, plot is character.[21]

This study strives not for definitive explanations of Cosimo's patronage, but to make some provisional sense of it in the context of his life, education and activities, and of Florentine society and culture. Some of the fundamental atttitudes and preoccupations that gave coherence to Cosimo's life and to his patronage oeuvre may be reconstructed by posing more modest but more probing questions of his writings and his recorded speech. A brief *ricordo*, a single poem, even apparently unpromising letters, can yield fresh insights, especially if as much attention is paid to their language as to their content. There is a handful of phrases that seem to serve as keys to Cosimo's view of the world, and they will be repeated in different contexts: his insistence in a private letter to his cousin Averardo that sensible men can judge the quality of a soldier or a painting even if they are not experts in warfare or art; his invocation in the poem attributed to him of the classical ideal of art and life, that these should be characterized by "art, ingenuity, order, and measure"; his conception of Florence, more flexible and sophisticated than most historians' conceptions of himself, as a city "of commerce, literature, and leisure."

The main interests underlying Cosimo's patronage in its various senses are revealed in his correspondence with his immediate family. Although no utterance can be assumed to be entirely unselfconscious, the form and function of these domestic letters guarantee a minimum of artifice. Many of his letters are autographs; those written by his household secretary, Ser Alesso Pelli, were obviously dictated and transcribed more or less verbatim, their locution being clearly Cosimo's when compared with Alesso's own letters.[22] The letters scrawled in Cosimo's almost illegible hand were certainly not drafted. They are full of corrections and omissions, often covering a whole large sheet of paper and overflowing onto the reverse, usually reserved for the address (figs. 2–4). Changes in the size and spacing of lines and in the ink suggest that he would begin a letter and keep adding new information or afterthoughts until the paper was full, or as he sometimes noted, he was obliged to stop and consign his letter to a messenger, already mounted on his horse and waiting impatiently at the door to depart. Generally letters were dispatched immediately, the ink scarcely dry on the page.

It is not surprising that Cosimo's letters hardly mention his extensive patronage of art and literature, although he made several references to borrowing, lending, or transporting books, and many letters to and from his sons Piero and Giovanni refer to their interest in collecting antique objects.[23] The purpose of personal letters was to communicate immediately important information – about business, city politics, warfare and diplomacy, the family's movements between their house in Florence and their country villas, and their health, or rather frequent illness. They offer little scope for reflection, although they are full of advice and instruction about action. Since they are also heavily abbreviated, and highly allusive – it is often imposssible to work out who or what Cosimo is talking about – they may seem to reveal very little about Cosimo himself. However, some real sense of Cosimo's otherwise enigmatic personality emerges from his domestic letters, largely because, by contrast with his public appearances and his partisan correspondence, they are not vehicles for self-presentation.

This is not to deny that Cosimo was a master of self-presentation; indeed he carefully crafted and maintained a coherent *persona* to which he owed much of the power and prestige he enjoyed in Florence without formal title. But his image as the ultimate patron probably compelled his fellow citizens precisely because its elements – however honed and polished – were a projection of the self revealed to his family.[24] Cosimo's authority in Florence was unmatched because he *was* – essentially – what Florentines wanted; a man of shrewd and balanced judgment, a spokesman for their values who could overcome republican indecisiveness, at home and abroad, and negotiate strongly on diplomatic and military issues with states whose rulers spoke with a single voice.[25]

4   Ser Alesso di Matteo Pelli (Galluzzi), autograph letter to
Giovanni di Cosimo de' Medici, 28 June 1442, Florence, ASF, MAP, V, 446

Cosimo expressed himself in the genuine idiom of the Florentine populace. In his domestic letters his voice resounds in a few constantly recurring words or phrases that vividly convey his personality and attitudes. They come from the common stock of essential elements of Tuscan vocabulary – itself a clue to Cosimo's effectiveness and appeal – but his usage of them amounts to a distinct and forcefully articulated view of the world. Cosimo was temperamentally inclined to the concrete. He contrasted adversely *indovinare* and *imaginare* – to guess, to imagine, with *vedere il cierto* and *giudicare* – see the facts, judge.[26] He recorded the stream of his thoughts about a shopping list of subjects in long rambling sentences, but his style is essentially plain, direct and vigorous. In this, as in so much else, Cosimo resembles other Florentines of his class and age, but he is also archetypal.

Like the similarly confident and decisive Alberti, Cosimo favored the verb *adoperare* – to put into effect, arrange.[27] It peppers his constant and urgent injunctions to action, reinforced by its opposite, *indugiare*, marking his regular denunciation of slowness or delay.[28] *Spacciare* – to dispatch – was a favorite action verb from the merchant's *bottega*.[29] *Sollecitare*, also involving haste, belongs more to the preacher's repertoire; it implies diligence, but recalls as well the moral dangers of soliciting to sinful acts – like usury and bribery. Cosimo's use of the mercantile verbal metaphor, *fare conto*, was more than just a tic of speech. It signals a whole careful balancing process, "contrapesando l'utile con danno" (weighing the profit against the loss),[30] by which he dealt with any issue, from major financial and diplomatic decisions, to the question of how many horses would be needed to move the family between Florence and Cafaggiolo.[31]

His values are clearly indicated in a phrase from a letter of recommendation: "è valente huomo e buono merchatante," (he is a worthy man and a good merchant),[32] or his assessment of the son of the revered trecento statesman Guido del Palagio as "valente et buono ciptadino" (a worthy and good citizen), the same attributes that other Florentine citizens admired in Cosimo himself.[33] Cosimo's very language identifies him as one of those church-going merchant citizens Michael Baxandall characterized as the chief patrons of Florentine culture. The particular vigor of his speech shows his affinities both with creative artists such as Alberti, and with men of action such as the condottiere duke of Milan.

The substantive issues on which Cosimo wrote most were the state of his business, the welfare of his friends and family, and the business of the state. He recorded at enormous length the details of Florentine military campaigns, foreign diplomacy, and domestic and electoral politics; it seems that Cosimo, like Machiavelli, had been destined by Fortune to talk about politics, or be silent.[34] His remarks on these subjects stress the themes of honor, profit, and glory, which are the end of action, and their obverse, damage and shame.[35] The works of art Cosimo commissioned represented these familial, dynastic, military, and civic interests as he described them in his letters, intertwined.

He told his nephew Pierfrancesco in 1458 that he cared most about the "honor of the house" and the "honor of the city."[36] When in 1429 he saw that the war with Lucca had gone too far for the Florentines to draw back, he wrote to his cousin Averardo, then a commissioner in the field, condemning those who provoked it:

> The commune will incur shame and injury from this, and they are exercising all their ingenuity [ingegnansi] to bring this about, which makes them morally evil men. It seems to me that although we did not favor this undertaking, seeing that the matter has reached the point where the honor of the commune is involved, that everyone must give it every possible support, and I will do so as far as I can, and I advise you to do the same, although I am sure I have no need to say so.[37]

Later he commended Averardo for his patriotism: "You have turned everything to the advantage of the honor of the commune, for which you are to be praised."[38] Toward the end of his life Cosimo was still writing in this vein, stressing to his friend Iacopo Guicciardini the importance of keeping "the affairs of the republic" out of the hands of "those who are known to be moved more by private passions than by the public good."[39]

This is precisely the charge leveled against Cosimo himself, by some of his contemporaries, and by many historians. Perhaps it was justified, but it is clear from his letters that Cosimo did not see himself as having made a choice in favor of private interest at the expense of the good of the commune. Quite the contrary. He spoke much more often in the collective than the singular, and in Cosimo's "we" it is almost impossible to distinguish his interests from those of family, friends, party, and state. He saw all these entities as associated under his protection, the beneficiaries of his careful judgments, his shrewd and decisive actions.[40]

Some historians see blatant contradictions in Cosimo's "character" between the benign patriarch and the ruthless partisan political operator. They argue that the image of Cosimo as pater patriae, "father of his country," is a false one created by courtly sycophants exaggerating Cosimo's paternalistic benevolence, and that the foundation of his power in personal patronage exposes him as rather a padrino, a mafioso "Godfather," than a pater.[41] This reasoning ignores fifteenth-century perceptions expressed in patriarchal metaphors used to describe and connect a whole range of values and behavior pertaining to fatherly figures and ideals.[42] It arises partly from modern perceptions of fathers as necessarily good, and patrons as morally bad. Such prejudices are now appropriately giving way under feminist and populist criticism to post-modern explorations of those various behaviors and social structures, appealing or unappealing, prescribed and governed by the values of patriarchy.[43]

There were frequent conflicts in practice between Cosimo's various obligations. In their fulfilment he contravened dearly held constitutional principles and alienated many leading citizens who wished to see these upheld.[44] But his actions and attitudes were broadly in harmony with the assumption shared by most Florentines that the authority — at once protective, prescriptive, and judgmental — by which a patriarch governed his family, and God his people, was also the appropriate model for the governance of the state.[45] Medici patronage created tangible links of personal relationship between the family and the rulers of the commune, which allowed their various interests to shade together into that special interest — la particolarità or la specialtà — which loyal and virtuous friends, like leaders of their lineage, were committed to defend.[46]

Cosimo wrote to his son Piero in 1463, after the pope appealed to him for assistance with a crusade: "I am obliged to serve the pope in whatever pertains alla mia specialtà."[47] He did not distinguish between political, personal, and religious obligation. The modern assumption that genuine piety must be incompatible with political wheeling and dealing would have astonished most Renaissance citizens, princes and popes. Many other

Medici letters document the profound devotional and charitable concerns so evident in Cosimo's patronage of art. There is no reason to doubt the sincerity of his concluding words to Piero: "I don't care about the other things we discussed, nor on their account would I spend ten ducats. But what I've said I will do, I do first for the honor of God, then for the honor of his Holiness, and ultimately on account of my soul."

Medici friends of the moral stature of Feo Belcari, a leading clerical author of popular devotional poetry and plays, hailed Cosimo as *pater patriae* for his charity long before the commune posthumously allowed him that Ciceronian title of honor. Cosimo's patronage in all its senses expressed that conjunction of concern, along with the commemoration of self, for the honor of God and the honor of the city, so helpfully articulated by Giovanni Rucellai and linked also by Aquinas in a treatise addressed to the king of Cyprus, of which Cosimo possibly owned a copy: charity is the "virtue in which all other virtues are gathered," including love of country, "caritas patriae."[48]

Of course Medici patronage was, in a much subtler sense than is usually understood, highly political.[49] The republic of Florence was not, obviously, a liberal democracy. And "politics" was not just a matter of statesmen making war and law. Cosimo's political power, or rather, in the language of his contemporaries, his *grande autorità*, – his great authority – was not an abstraction, but a function of his relations with others.[50] It was a strategy embracing all of life, an attribute of his identity shaped by all those partisan, patriotic, dynastic, intellectual, and devotional preoccupations expressed in his words and deeds.[51]

The episode of the Medici exile demonstrated the process by which Cosimo's essential attitudes, recorded in intimate letters to members of his immediate family, were eventually and most effectively projected into the public sphere. Exile could have ended a crudely partisan career; Cosimo's sense of himself and his destiny turned it into a triumph. He survived and prospered because by contrast with other Florentine exiles, of whom Dante was the most famous and articulate, Cosimo refused to separate his private interest from the public.[52]

Averardo's grandson Francesco moved into Cosimo's household in Venice while his elders were exiled further afield. In one of many letters to his father describing life with the leaders of the Medici house, the eighteen-year-old Francesco referred to Cosimo's assertion "that he had no wish to return home by any other means than that by which he had left," that is, by order of the Florentine Signoria, and certainly not by means of arms or plots that had been proposed to him.[53] Cosimo's judgment was a shrewd one, made in the same spirit as many others

expressed in his letters. He acted on the precept, noted in his own hand in his copy of Cassian's *Monastic Institutes*, that adversity is the proof of virtue.[54] Having taken this position, he defended it ruthlessly. As we learn from the slightly shocked young Francesco, Cosimo denounced to the Venetian Signoria a distant relative, Mari de' Medici, who approached him with offers of aid from Milan.[55] In all Cosimo's public speech as recorded by his cousin – in Venice, to the emperor, to the pope – Cosimo rigidly maintained his virtuous stance. He was rewarded as early as February 1434 by a letter from a still hostile Signoria praising his conduct as "irreproachable."[56]

In the *ricordi* of his travails in exile – a document that is probably genuine but not at all disingenuous – Cosimo polished the image of the steadfast patriot, and stressed that even after his friends were appointed to power in the Signoria of September 1434 and had urged him to return to Florence he awaited an official command, "not wishing to do anything against the will of the Signoria."[57] When he did return, he received a tumultuous reception, compared by Machiavelli to a Roman triumph, which may have contributed something to the conception of the procession depicted in the Medici chapel frescoes.[58] Cosimo's image could certainly accommodate with ease an association with the symbols of Florentine republicanism, embodied in Donatello's bronze statue of David (fig. 133), which stood in the Medici palace courtyard and bore the inscription: "The victor is whoever defends the fatherland. God crushes the wrath of an enormous foe. Behold! a boy overcame a great tyrant. Conquer, O citizens."[59]

Cosimo's civic virtue was publicly praised in the humanist Lapo da Castiglionchio's dedication to him of a translation of Plutarch's *Life of Themistocles*. He had shown himself "the vigilant and careful steersman [who] fears nothing, but bravely takes on the tempest." He had borne "with the injuries of the *patria* in such a way that during that calamitous exile everyone grieved your ill fortune, approved of your constancy, admired your wisdom. Thus, recalled in great glory to the *patria* by the common consent and desire, richly merited, of every citizen, you bore witness that such misfortunes have not been punishment for crime, but a theme for the illumination of virtue."[60] Praise for Cosimo's circumspection was not confined, however, to humanists and to constitutionalists among the ruling elite. In a popular verse written in 1437 by Anselmo Calderoni, a future herald of the Signoria, Saints Cosmas and Damian appear to the poet in a dream, praising Cosimo for various virtues, including the fact that "at the time Cosimo was in exile/ he could have returned by devious paths./ But like all good Florentines, he never wanted to do that."[61]

Cosimo was a man who believed above all in his own good judgment. In business and politics he was of course an expert. Thinking and writing he saw as requiring a special effort which he referred to as *lavoro*, to which he sometimes declared his *capo* or *cervello* unequal.[62] But Cosimo, like most Renaissance men, recognized a quality common to all great endeavor, from art to the art of war. He was confident that he could judge the quality of artists or soldiers, although he was neither a painter nor a fighter. Giotto's genius, like that of the *condottiere* Francesco Sforza, was plainly apparent to him.[63] It was possible, and indeed necessary to him, to have an opinion on any issue of importance to a Florentine citizen. Reproaching his cousin Averardo once for indecisiveness in his negotiations with the captains of Florence's military forces, he wrote: "I don't say this to rebuke you or to teach you, for this is neither my habit nor my job; but rather optimism confirms me in my opinion, and I see that you hold to yours, and if we continue in this way, they will accept the authority of any clown."[64]

The concept of *ingegno* – *ingegnare, ingegnarsi* – the most resonant of Cosimo's favorite words[65] – was familiar to Florentines from the Tuscan of Dante and Boccaccio. It retained the core of its Ciceronian Latin sense as "the power of the human intellect and spirit by which man discovers himself what he has not learned from others."[66] Giovanni Rucellai described Cosimo as "more endowed with *ingegno* than any one who has ever lived in our city," and as one of the four greatest men of his time, along with Leonardo Bruni and Brunelleschi, who expressed in his design for the cupola of Florence cathedral his divine "ingiengno e fantasia."[67] *Ingegno* embraced and related the sublime and the quotidian. Machines, also designed by Brunelleschi, to move around the actors and the scenery in sacred plays, were known as *ingegni*,[68] and in vulgar parlance *ingegno* was the animating energy of sex.[69]

To Vespasiano, Cosimo was the Godfather of *virtù*, the patron and benefactor of "all those who had any sort of *virtù*," since he so greatly enjoyed observing "the variety of *ingegni*."[70] There is attributed to Cosimo – if he did not write it, it is certainly from the circle of popular poets who frequented his household – a poem in the popular idiom of impossible opposites.[71] It was addressed in 1450 to his friend and ally Francesco Sforza, the *condottiere extraordinaire* recently recognized as duke of Milan. Cosimo's admiration for Sforza was part of his passionate interest in matters military, expressed perhaps in the commission of Uccello's three enormous paintings of the Battle of San Romano and most certainly in his collection of armor,[72] although it remained to his sons and grandsons to assemble really notable collections of arms. Where they were enthusiasts of the joust, he pronounced this surrogate warfare "frivolous" unless the honor of the commune was involved.[73] But clearly he relished the game of war, and was an enthusiast of the related game of chess, which he played with the champion of his age.[74]

Confronted with the republic's problems, Cosimo resolved "operare non meno lo'ngiegno che la forza" – to exercise intellect as much as force.[75] The last line of Cosimo's poem concludes an extended description of a disordered world by affirming the principles which should govern alike politics, life and art:[76] "Sooner shall the sea be plowed and sown/ and fish be seen to swim/ on the mountains and the plain/ than I be separate from that/ to which I am bound:/ to defend your noble stance/ that brings to Lombardy peace or war./ And sooner will nature change its course/ than I should cease to love you/ with art, ingenuity, order and measure."

Arte, ingegno, ordine, and *misura* are key words in the vocabulary of praise of Florentine artists, as of statesmen, scholars, businessmen, and their admirers; as Ghiberti wrote in his *Commentaries* of his second door for the baptistery, it was completed "con ogni arte e misura e ingegno."[77] These commonly admired qualities, recognized in the various achievements of others, signal a complex of shared habits of mind – of values, information, and skills – that helped patrons, politicians, writers, and artists to relate and to communicate their aspirations, to define and to present themselves to each other.[78] This was a major source of the *ingegno*, the energy, that animated the Florentine Renaissance, and brought patrons and artists together in the creative act.

III

LEARNING THE LESSONS OF FLORENTINE CULTURE: WHO COSIMO KNEW

We must look at "living people in concrete situations."

E. H. Gombrich[1]

The subjects of Renaissance art invited elaboration that challenged and extended talented artists and required – and attracted – an informed and visually sophisticated audience to appreciate their work. At the beginning of the fifteenth century, the vast majority of images depicted aspects of the Christian story, for public or private devotion. Simple images of Christ, the Virgin and various saints were of course produced in quantity in workshops at relatively low cost. Works commissioned from distinguished artists by wealthy patrons, and preserved up to the present time in private collections and places of public pride took up the same themes, but these cycles of painted frescoes, sculptured apostles, prophets, and saints, of altarpieces with multiple panels and *predelle*, offered extensive opportunities for more complex and individual representations. Admiration for *istorie* and *invenzione* fueled by precepts from classical literature encouraged distinctive selections from the stories of the Old and New Testaments and the literature extrapolating upon them, which could bear new and more personalized emotional and aesthetic meaning, inspiring new reponses.[2]

As the century progressed, more secular and specifically classical images and objects became popular among patrons to decorate their increasingly sumptuous houses. From the earliest years of the Renaissance revival of the antique, artists had begun to represent both religious and secular subject matter in forms influenced by the principles and practice of art in the ancient world. Architecture was particularly indebted to classical precedents. Nowadays scholars must painstakingly reconstruct the repertoire of symbols and forms, both Christian and classical, which was familiar and immediately recognizable to a fifteenth-century audience; as a consequence, it is easy to exaggerate the inherent complexity of Renaissance representation.

However, classical culture in particular had to be learned and absorbed even then. Artists such as Ghiberti and Brunelleschi strove to master arcane classical forms and récherché subjects the better to express their creativity, and some fresco cycles, for example those Mantegna painted for the Gongaza of Mantua, illustrated complex iconographical programs based on classical texts. Patrons took increasing pride and pleasure in visually displaying their classical, as well as their Christian learning.[3] While works of art may be read in many ways and at various levels, even a fifteenth-century audience would have needed considerable information and viewing experience to appreciate as it did the mastery of form and technique of a Donatello, a Brunelleschi, or a Masaccio, and to interpret easily the images they created.

Traditionally, lovers of art have inclined to see invention and investment with meaning as primarily a consequence of the artist's self-expression. But art, more in the Renaissance than now, was functional – a primary means of communicating common cultural ideas and ideals. The nature of Renaissance art, and the enormous reputation artists began to acquire in their own time, presupposed a large audience of patrons and viewers well versed in Christian and classical culture, and eager to see this repertoire of ideas and forms employed to enhance and particularize the meaning of images that played an important role in their lives. Given that most artists started out as workshop assistants of limited education, the sophistication of so many of their representations presupposes a high degree of interaction and cooperation with cultured men, including their patrons.

To grasp how manifold were the opportunities for interaction in the pool of talented men concentrated in fifteenth-century Florence is crucial to penetrating the meaning of Florentine works of art. Art historians bent on reasserting the artist's creative autonomy are sometimes determined to reduce the meaning of objects to their simplest common denominator, distinguishing sharply – and unrealistically – between image and narrative, object and symbol, arbitrarily dismissing complex iconographical interpretations as figments of the modern scholar's imagination. Part of this campaign is the caricature of imagined mechanistic collaborations between artists, patrons, and scholarly advisors. Patrons and men of learning are represented as visually insensitive, unimaginative, and lacking in the ingenuity to conceive or respond to any but the most obvious visual expressions of ideas or feeling.[4] The artist himself has been reduced on occasion to a simple fellow limited in his inspiration for religious scenes to tales from the *Golden Legend*.[5] Symbolism attributable to the patron is said, somewhat paradoxically, to have "no reference to established set ideas, apart from the whole culture of [the] age."[6] The chapters on the Florentine audience for art and literature will examine more carefully the content of this culture, and the means by which it naturally came to be expressed in visual form.

When we look at "living people in concrete situations," we see that Florence in Cosimo's day was a small and compact city, consisting of some forty thousand people clustered within city walls whose gates at their most distant points were no more than twenty minutes' walking distance from the center (figs. 5 and 6). Modern models of interchange between artists, intellectuals, and their patrons which hover in the shadows of many accounts of Renaissance art are quite inappropriate to the world that produced it. Artists and humanists were neither mere acquaintance, nor simply professional consultants to

patrons, meeting them only at the point of a commission. They were Renaissance men, with an impressively wide variety of interests, and their paths crossed and recrossed, literally as well as metaphorically, in the quotidian pursuit of their common political, financial, charitable, cultural, devotional, and recreational activities. Literature, learning, buildings, and images were part of the environment of educated and intelligent Florentines, and patrons of art mixed constantly in civic, neighborhood, and domestic circles with artists and intellectuals.[7]

However, it is important to be precise about what people read and saw and knew. Arguments that the key to the interpretation of a particular work of art lies in its link to other objects, and especially texts, have been known to rest essentially on the mere fact that the text or the object, however arcane, was known or knowable to someone in roughly the time and place at which the artist and his patron lived.[8] Particularly elaborate iconographical interpretations based on this premise, without the support of any compelling evidence of concrete links, have been in part responsible for a retreat to oversimplification in identifying the likely sources of works of art.

Let us turn to Cosimo, and try to build up a clear and concrete picture of the cultural equipment, apart from a general admiration for creativity, *ingegno*, and *virtù*, that he brought to his extensive patronage. What precisely was the nature of his familiarity with Christian and classical literature that might have furnished him with ideas he wished to express, symbols that had significance to him?

5   View of Florence, called the "chain map," 1490, Florence, Museo di Firenze com'era

6 Map of Florence showing: walls of 1173–5 and 1284–1333; the central squares of (1) the Mercato Vecchio, (2) the grain market (Orsanmichele), and (3) the Mercato Nuovo; and major churches and public buildings

How much might he have absorbed of the genuine spirit of humanist learning or the more profound implications of Christian doctrine? What experience did he have of looking at works of art, and what training in the appreciation of technique and form? What, in sum, would suggest that Cosimo, who made the money he spent on patronage of art from international banking, and owed his eminence to his skills as a wily politician and statesman, was capable of envisaging commissions more sophisticated than simple painted representations of his name-saints, the construction of a serviceable church, or the sculpture of a pleasing figure in the antique style?

COSIMO AND THE HUMANISTS

Accounts of Cosimo's learning and culture have tended to focus on his later, better-documented years, particularly on his interest in Neoplatonic philosophy in the late 1450s and early 1460s. The relation of these ideas to his patronage in the decade before his death is considered below. But to understand the bulk of Cosimo's patronage, which began in earnest after his return from exile in 1434, it is necessary to look back to the culture of the turn of the century that shaped him.[9] Born in 1389, he

was trained as a merchant and banker. He became a cultivated man through long and close association with amateur and professional scholars and artists. This process of self-education began in the first decade of the fifteenth century, and took place under the guidance of men often a generation older than himself. He came to maturity surrounded by the early enthusiasts of the recovery of classical learning; Niccoli, Poggio, Bruni, and Traversari. He was an intimate of this circle and in some ways its focal point.[10] He subsidized and participated in the early discoveries of ancient manuscripts by the humanists Niccoli and Poggio;[11] he witnessed the unveiling of the first exciting classicizing masterpieces of the artists Ghiberti, Brunelleschi, Masaccio, and Donatello. Vespasiano's *Lives* of many of these luminaries depict Cosimo as deeply involved in the intellectual and artistic life of his time, a man who "by long familiarity with learned men had great judgment" and who "when he conversed with painters or sculptors knew what he was talking about."[12]

These claims have often been derided as flattery by modern scholars of humanism and art. Inclined to minimize the patron's role in creativity, they hold Cosimo to professional standards of expertise – past or present – and naturally find him wanting.[13] The breadth and depth of Cosimo's informed lay interest in ideas and images as praised by contemporaries is confirmed by correlating the mass of information from letters, treatises, and wills of the leading literary and artistic figures of his time. Cosimo not only knew them all well; he shared their interests and participated in their activities to a degree that might surprise people with modern businessmen in mind, but was by no means unusual in the fifteenth century. Florentines enjoyed a long tradition of learned amateurs studying under the guidance of professionals. In the late fourteenth century, groups gathered around Luigi Marsili in Santo Spirito, and in the Alberti gardens. In the first decades of the fifteenth century Ambrogio Traversari held discussions at the convent of Santa Maria degli Angeli which included Cosimo and his brother Lorenzo. This tradition continued to the end of the century with the meetings in the Rucellai gardens, the Orti Oricellari, attended by Machiavelli and Savonarola.[14]

According to Vespasiano, Cosimo "was very fond of learned men, and greatly enjoyed conversations with them, and particularly with father Ambruoso of the Angeli, with Messer Lionardo of Arezzo [Bruni], with Nicolaio Nicoli, with Messer Carlo of Arezzo [Marsuppini], and with Messer Poggio [Bracciolini]."[15] This circle of the city's leading humanist scholars was tightly knit, although socially diverse. Some of its members, like Niccoli and Roberto Rossi, were from Florentine families with whom the Medici naturally had much in common. Others,

7   Ghiberti, Reliquary for Saints Protus, Hyacinthus, and Nemesius, Florence, Bargello

including Bruni, Poggio, and Marsuppini, had worked in the papal chancery with which Cosimo was also very familiar, and where perhaps he first encountered them. These three all became chancellors of the Florentine republic. They associated closely with Cosimo in their professional capacity, and soon came by wealth, marriage, and office-holding to share many of the interests of the Florentine patriciate.[16]

Ambrogio Traversari was prior of Santa Maria degli Angeli and later general of the Camaldolensian order. Traversari's extensive correspondence, and the diary he kept during his tour of Camaldolensian houses in 1432/3, are full of affectionate references to the Medici brothers, Cosimo and Lorenzo. Indeed he interrupted his account of his visitations of the houses of the order for Pope Eugenius IV with the news of Cosimo's exile and his response to it. "This event seemed to me a nightmare, because on the eve of my departure I had seen him in very amiable conversation at the palace of the Priors, and Lorenzo had given me not the slightest warning of such a grave act . . . I fell into a profound depression, lamenting not so much the disgrace of these two great friends . . . as the decline of a most noble and flourishing city."[17] Traversari intervened on their behalf with the Venetian government, and even appealed to their arch-rival Rinaldo degli Albizzi, who had led the coup against them, but in vain. Interrupting his journey, he waited in Bologna, hoping to snatch a moment with Lorenzo, "my most dear son," on his way to exile in Venice, and was moved to tears when he visited Cosimo in custody in the palace of the Signoria.

Traversari made his convent of the Angeli the center of patristic scholarship, which greatly interested Cosimo de' Medici; this interest is apparent in the contents of

his library, and in his commissions for San Lorenzo.[18] It seems that Traversari introduced Cosimo to Chrysostom's writings, and according to Vespasiano translated his commentary on the Epistles of Saint Paul while Niccoli transcribed it, and Cosimo looked on.[19] Certainly Cosimo prized his copy of Chrysostom, which he instructed his son Piero to track down as he was leaving Venice after his recall to Florence.[20] At Cosimo's request, Traversari translated Diogenes Laertes from the Greek,[21] and a monk named Michael, his assistant, compiled after Traversari's death an edition of the Camaldolensian's letters which he presented to Cosimo.[22] To house the relics of the early Christian saints Protus, Hyacinthus, and Nemesius in the Angeli's possession, Cosimo and Lorenzo had Ghiberti make a bronze reliquary inscribed with assurances of devotion to their cult (fig. 7).[23] Traversari also made a major contribution to continuing and cultivating Greek studies between the visit of Manuel Chrysoloras in 1399, and the arrival of Giovanni Argyropoulos in the mid-1450s. The Italian encounter with the Greeks at the council designed to reconcile the eastern and western branches of the Church, begun in Ferrara and concluded in Florence, gave great impetus to Florentine interest in Greek culture. Traversari supported Cosimo's proposal to transfer the proceedings to Florence, and was a prominent figure in the negotiations.[24] Indeed he was probably Cosimo de' Medici's main link with the culture of the East, another interest visible in many of Cosimo's artistic commissions.[25]

Vespasiano said Cosimo also studied with Roberto de' Rossi, a leading humanist of the early fifteenth century from a old patrician family.[26] Among Rossi's pupils were other prominent patrician youths of Cosimo's generation, including Luca degli Albizzi, Alessandro Alessandri, and Domenico Buoninsegni, all of whom were supporters of the Medici party in the 1420s and 1430s.[27] Traversari recorded that Lorenzo's teacher was Carlo Marsuppini, and he may have taught Cosimo as well. Marsuppini, another leading humanist, came to Florence in the employ of the papal court, and lectured at the university of Florence in which the Medici, and particularly Lorenzo, took an active interest;[28] Marsuppini later became chancellor of Florence.[29] He was clearly part of the Medici patronage network, which apparently supported his tenure at the Studio against the competing claims of Filelfo.[30] Filelfo, protesting against Medici favoritism toward his enemies Niccoli and Marsuppini, complained to Cosimo about his preferring these intimates: "If I do not frequent your house, as they do daily, that is because I am busy."[31] Marsuppini certainly seems to have known the Medici family well; his letter of consolation to Cosimo and Lorenzo on the death of their mother, Piccarda de' Bueri, expresses much more than conventional sympathy.[32]

Traversari and Bruni both referred in their letters to the Medici brothers' stay in Padua, and their visits to Venice and Verona during the plague of 1430–31, observing that the Medici were accompanied in their retreat, at Cosimo's expense, by Marsuppini and Niccolò Niccoli, as well as by Niccoli's companion Benvenuta, and his nephew Cornelio. Niccoli was an eccentric recluse and scholarly bibliophile who was generally acknowledged in this learned community as the chief arbiter of classical scholarship and taste.[33] He was a leading collector of books and antiquities, and in Poggio Bracciolini's dialogue, *De Nobilitate*, Lorenzo de' Medici speaks admiringly of Niccoli's collection and of what he learned from him of the pleasures of the connoisseur. It is very likely that, as Filelfo claimed, Niccoli paid almost daily visits to the Medici. In 1416 or 1417 Niccoli had left his father's house and stayed for some time in the house of Nerone di Nigi Dietisalvi, a prominent Medicean friend and partisan who lived in Via de' Ginori, which ran along the back of the Medici properties facing onto the Via Larga.[34] In his declaration to the tax officials in 1433 Niccoli acknowledged the Medici family's financial aid; for some years he had owed Cosimo and Lorenzo 355 florins, and "if I had not been supported by their liberality, I would have been forced many years ago to go begging and wandering through the world."[35]

Niccoli's will of 1430, witnessed by Feo Belcari, then a canon of San Lorenzo, entrusted his legendary library to Cosimo and eleven other executors, including such luminaries of the Florentine world of learning as Bruni, Poggio, Marsuppini, and Paolo Toscanelli, together with Franco Sacchetti, Domenico Buoninsegni, and Cosimo's kinsman Nicola di Vieri de' Medici. After 1437 Antonio Manetti, Ambrogio Traversari, Giovanni Becchi, father of Gentile, who was resident priest and tutor in Cosimo's household around the time of Cosimo's death, and Lorenzo della Stufa, one of the Medici family's very closest friends, were added to the number of procurators.[36] It was probably not too difficult for Cosimo to persuade such a group to fulfil Niccoli's wish to put his library at the public disposal by making it the nucleus of the collection he himself bestowed upon San Marco. Niccoli's books were supplemented by gifts from Cosimo's own library, and other manuscripts commissioned from Vespasiano. The document of 6 July 1441, in which the friars of San Marco accepted the terms set by Niccoli's trustees, was witnessed and notarized by Cosimo's secretary Ser Alesso Pelli and Ugolino Martelli, another staunch supporter of the Medici who lived in their near neighborhood.[37] Pending their transfer to San Marco upon the completion of the building, Niccoli's books were apparently kept in the Medici house, and borrowed by the scholarly friends who frequented it; a note to Cosimo's son Giovanni from the same Michael who prepared the edition of Traversari's letters requested permission to borrow a book "which had belonged to our Niccolò Niccoli."[38]

Niccoli's closest friend, apart from the Medici brothers, was Poggio Bracciolini, another former employee of the papal chancery and future chancellor of Florence. It is clear from the many references and greetings to "our Cosmus" sprinkled across the pages of Poggio's correspondence with Niccoli, that Cosimo was a serious participant in the hunt for rare classical manuscripts, and did not merely subsidize the enthusiasms of others when he helped Poggio to acquire them.[39] Poggio and Niccoli were in constant contact with Cosimo, Lorenzo, and also their cousin Nicola di Vieri de' Medici, exchanging books and information concerning them. Poggio wrote of Nicola di Vieri: "As for our Nicolaus . . . I was long ago persuaded that he was my other self, and that everything we had, as is proper in close friendship, we shared with one another; for when I have need of it, I use his property as if it were my own."[40]

In April 1425 Poggio wrote to Niccoli from Rome: "I need Cicero's *Letters to Atticus*, which I copied and which our friend Cosmus now has: for the scribe is writing them pretty inaccurately because of the model. I shall quickly correct them if I have this book of Cosmus', and so send it to me. Ask Cosmus on my behalf to let me have the book for a little while; I shall send it safely back to him. Do the same about the Lactantius and the ten books of Livy."[41] Obviously Cosimo's manuscripts of Cicero and Lactantius, the latter very rare at this time, were an important source for the diffusion in Florence of these works.[42] Poggio, having tracked down the *Ten Decades* of Livy to a monastery in northern Germany, asked Niccoli to talk over this discovery with Cosimo, and make an effort to get the volumes. "See to it that Cosmus writes in detail as soon as possible to Gherardus de Bueris [a relative of Cosimo's mother who represented the Medici bank in Lübeck][43] to go there himself if need be; yes, by all means let him go to the monastery . . . Now you run and urge Cosmus to spend some money to send a letter there safely as soon as possible."[44]

In 1427 Poggio reported to Niccoli on an expedition he had made with Cosimo to search for inscriptions in the ruins of Ostia Antica: "When Cosmus and I went to see the gate we found no inscriptions; for that temple which they are tearing down to get the lime is without inscriptions, but there is an inscription on the Via Ostia near the river bank which I sent you another time; it is on a certain tomb made entirely of marble on which the fasces are carved too."[45] Cosimo may well have applied his observations during this trip to the tomb he and Lorenzo built for their father Giovanni in the old sacristy at San Lorenzo, and he was certainly to make extensive use of inscriptions for many of his artistic commissions.[46] Poggio concluded his account of the destruction of antiquities at Ostia with the regret that "our Cosmus belongs to the Board of Ten [the Florentine war magistracy]. He has a big job and no leisure. I would prefer that it were at another time when he might have put up some opposition to these robbers." He saw little value in Cosimo's contribution to the commune's wars, which helped to make him its leading citizen, by comparison with his ability to advance the cause of knowledge: "I do not see what good he can do [in this job] except to watch the accounts, since other men have charge of running the war."[47]

Although Cosimo believed that Florence's glory lay in its being a city of literature and leisure as well as commerce, lack of leisure obviously limited the time merchant patricians could spend on literature and the pursuit of learning. Poggio wrote to Niccoli of Bartolomeo de' Bardi, manager of the Rome branch of the Medici bank: "You know that Bartholomeus de Bardis, a man very devoted to you and, what I consider important, interested in our work but hemmed in by a host of business responsibilities, can satisfy his desire for study all too little. Sometimes, though, he steals a little time for himself which he spends on reading. He is anxious to have some books which may encourage him to study." Poggio suggested Suetonius, Terence, and Quintus Curtius, all of which Bardi might have borrowed from Cosimo, as they were all in his library by 1418.[48]

Notwithstanding the constraints of humanist epistolary style and philosophy on the expression of personal feeling, it is clear from Poggio's letters that he was fond of the Medici family. He wrote to Niccoli when he heard "that excellent man and lover of his country, Joannes de Medicis, is dead," that

> I was much distressed and still am, not only that our country should lose such a citizen, but also that his sons should lose such a father, and that we should lose such a good and delightful friend, although I ought to say patron.[49] I am sure that both Cosmus and Laurentius are overcome with the greatest grief, as is to be expected from their own nobility of character and their father's. But they must use wisdom, since there is need for it, just as much in adversity as in prosperity. Tell Cosmus not to forget what I once told him, for there is not the same pattern for everything at all times and for all men.[50]

Cosimo's reading and its relation to the main concerns of his life strongly suggests that he shared with professionals like Poggio and Niccoli the humanist valuation of wisdom and virtue derived from learning.[51]

Poggio invoked this wisdom to assuage Lorenzo's grief when they spent some time together in Rome in April, 1429. He wrote to Niccoli: "I am with that delightful man Laurentius every day; and I cannot be separated from him, for I find his character so attractive. I am trying to draw him out of his sadness over his father's death, and to recall to him the pleasures of life. For although the event is very sad, nothing is more foolish than to dwell too long upon something which can neither be avoided nor cured."[52] Among the pleasures of life the two humanists shared with Lorenzo, to whom they were particularly close, was that of laughter, especially if it were slightly risqué, a taste common to learned and popular culture in Renaissance Florence. Poggio wrote to Niccoli once that

> I laughed heartily at the last bit of your letter in which you apologize for what you had written about gluttony and about some other more obscure things which cannot be expressed in Latin unless we are willing to call it "coitus" . . . Laurentius . . . wrote to me that when he told you that . . . I had not been feeling well, you had answered him in these vulgar words: "He would not suffer so much if he took less pleasure in the she-ass," as if that had been the cause of the ailment of all the people who are struck down with this illness, as nearly everybody was. And so when I had heard that you also were suffering from the same kind of disease, I thought your illness had the same cause as you attributed to mine; therefore, I wanted you to be deprived of the cause so that you might recover more quickly, and now that you have done so, I rejoice that you are well.[53]

Poggio's letter of consolation to the Medici brothers when they were exiled appears somewhat stilted by comparison with the warmth of Ambrogio Traversari's. His letter of 17 October to Niccoli shows clearly how much he sympathized and identified with Cosimo's disgrace, but was restrained by caution and a stoic detachment. "I heard of the fall of our Cosmus with misery and with the deepest regret; but such is the state of our times that keeping quiet is safer though less honorable . . . If complaints did any good, I could bewail his private misfortune; but since things once done cannot be altered or reformed, we must be calm in bearing this sudden change of fortune and console ourselves with what the mercy of God has left us."[54] Events proved Poggio wrong, and after the Medici were recalled, the humanist continued to enjoy their friendship and support for the remainder of his life.

Leonardo Bruni, chancellor of the Florentine republic from 1427 to his death in 1444, was also associated with the circle of Niccoli and Poggio, although his relations with the Medici were less intimate than theirs, and his position in the group on the whole more ambiguous. In 1429 Poggio wrote from Terranuova to Niccoli, instructing him to "ask Leonardus for the first part of the Pliny, and the *History of Illustrious Men*, which he translated from Plutarch, and ask Cosmus for his volume, which contains their lives."[55] Bruni had been chancellor of Florence briefly in 1406, before he left to join the court of Pope John XXIII. Since the Medici were the pope's chief bankers, Cosimo and his father Giovanni were part of the papal entourage at the Council of Constance in 1414, where Bruni was acting as John's secretary.[56] Giovanni di Bicci de' Medici was a close friend as well as financial advisor to John XXIII, whose will assigned to his Medici friend the main responsibility for the commission of his tomb, executed by Michelozzo and Donatello under Cosimo's supervision.[57] Another of Cosimo's learned friends from papal circles of this period was Tommaso Parentucelli (da Sarzana), the future Pope Nicholas V. Cosimo extended his friendship and support to this young scholar, who some years later advised Cosimo on the content and organization of the library at San Marco.[58]

After John XXIII's deposition by the council, Cosimo helped Bruni to obtain Florentine citizenship and a tax concession, and when Bruni was elected chancellor of Florence again in 1427, the Medici family's letters suggest they were pleased with this choice.[59] In addition to his official correspondence for the Florentine state, Bruni probably wrote several letters in Latin on Cosimo's behalf.[60] The humanist's presentation to Cosimo of his translation of the pseudo-Aristotelian *Economics* is evidence of their association about the mid-point of Cosimo's life. Cosimo's library contained some of Bruni's translations of important works on moral philosophy, one of the subjects that most interested Cosimo.[61] In view of Cosimo's perception of his own role in Florentine politics and society as perfectly legitimate, it is unlikely that he read Bruni's comments on the Florentine constitution, written in 1439, as a rebuke of the ways in which his own regime had modified it.[62]

The Medici brothers' association with leading humanists was enshrined in their appearance as protagonists in the numerous dialogues these scholars composed. Nicola de' Medici also appeared as a character in several of these.[63] The dialogue was a very particular literary form, a dramatization of the play of ideas and characters, rather than a precise record of opinions ascribable to actual persons.[64] At the same time, the fiction of casting as *dramatis personae* people who might plausibly have had such conversations gave resonance, and perhaps authority to the opinions attributed to them, enabling the author in turn to pay tribute to his "characters." Some of these characterizations were surely meant to flatter; by the same token, since the protagonists were well known in the learned circle in which they moved, it is unlikely that the authors of dialogues would have risked offending the Medici by attributing to them opinions to which they were not sympathetic. Cosimo's brother Lorenzo's expression of pleasure in the acquisition of rare and beautiful objects in Poggio's *On Nobility* is certainly consonant with the ornamentation of the old Medici house, as of the later Medici palace by his brother and nephews. It is equally appropriate that the character of Cosimo in Poggio's *De Infelicitate Principum*, presented as a conversation in Niccoli's library between himself, Cosimo, and Carlo Marsuppini, should dissociate himself from Niccoli's extreme egalitarianism and individualism, by observing that he really had too much to do with popes and princes to talk about them disparagingly.[65] The lineaments of the portraits of Cosimo and his family in humanist dialogues are recognizable in their self-portraits as patrons of art.

ARTISTS ON THE FLORENTINE PUBLIC SCENE

There is much less reliable information concerning artists. Since their primary medium was not the pen, they left comparatively little in the way of first-hand testimony. The only formal writings by artists in the first half of the fifteenth century were Alberti's treatises and Ghiberti's *Commentaries*. Letters and tax reports provide important information concerning artists' practical lives and particular commissions, but they illuminate little of artists' interests and attitudes. Vasari's *Lives of the Artists*, composed in the mid-sixteenth century, have proved far less trustworthy than Vespasiano's *Lives* of quattrocento statesmen, humanists, and religious leaders. Where Vespasiano saw himself as faithfully recording the raw material that would serve some future formal biographer, Vasari explicitly set out to create his own image of the quattrocento artist, largely in his own sixteenth-century likeness. He pressed his sources concerning artists into the service of this aim, often distorting their relations with patrons in the interests of the artists' aggrandizement.[66]

The account of Cosimo's commissions in Parts 3 and 4 of this book reveals much about the Medici family's personal and patronage relations with the artists who worked for them, and these are the specific subject of Chapter 14. Throughout most of Cosimo's lifetime, artists continued to be recruited mainly from among the artisans of the city of Florence, or its surrounding villages and towns.[67] They were therefore less likely than scholars, especially patrician humanists, to come into contact with their patrons in the daily course of business, politics, or government. But an exploration of Florentine popular culture will show that artisans, particularly poets and artists, had much closer connections with patricians and their culture than is often assumed. The architect Brunelleschi, the peer of many of his patrons in birth and office-holding, was an important contributor to the creation of a complex popular culture, and many other artists found in the corpus of popular texts the extensive general knowledge necessary to implement their own and their patrons' visual aspirations.[68]

The remainder of this chapter concerns the highly visible role of artists in the civic environment, and their public relations with the world of learning inhabited by Cosimo and other leading citizens who were also patrons of art.[69] It is appropriate to begin with Leon Battista Alberti who, although scarcely typical, sums up in his person and in his writings the close relations between Florentine innovators in every field. The Alberti were an old and distinguished family closely associated with the Medici. Members of both families were exiled in 1412 for their cooperation in a conspiracy against the current regime, and Leon Battista did not return to Florence until his family was pardoned, probably at the instigation of the Medici, in 1428.[70] A scholar of humanism, but also an enthusiastic supporter of popular culture, in 1441 he organized a contest for the best vernacular poem on friendship. It was modeled on the ancient Roman Certame Coronario after which it was named, and was sponsored by Piero de' Medici.[71] Alberti was a gifted architect, almost certainly responsible for the design of Giovanni Rucellai's palace, his tomb, and his façade for the church of Santa Maria Novella;[72] he also wrote the major early Renaissance treatises on painting, sculpture, and architecture.

On Painting was composed in Latin in Florence in 1435, and later dedicated to Cosimo's friend Giovanfrancesco Gonzaga of Mantua. The author's Italian translation was made in or before July 1436, about the same time that Brunelleschi completed the cupola of the cathedral, and Alberti dedicated it to his friend the architect, since "I recognized in many, but most of all in you, Filippo, and in our great friend the sculptor Donatello, and in the others, Nencio [Ghiberti], Luca [della Robbia] and Masaccio, a genius for every laudable enterprise in no way inferior to any of the ancients who gained fame in these arts."[73] Alberti's recommendations on painting appear to have influenced many artists, including Fra Angelico and Filippo Lippi, both of whom did important work for the Medici. In the 1440s Alberti dedicated

one of his "Dinner Pieces" – *De Uxoria* – to Piero de' Medici, making reference both to their friendship and to his admiration for Cosimo and Piero, "whom I see are so accustomed to give . . . recognition to my writings and literary exercises, that scarcely an hour passes in which you are not reading and committing to memory something that I have written or said."[74] The main ideas of his famous treatise on architecture were almost certainly circulating in Florence by 1450, while the Medici palace was under construction, and when *On Architecture* was published in 1485, Cosimo's grandson Lorenzo was reputed to have literally snatched each new page hot from the press.

Alberti's high-profile and versatile role in Renaissance culture was unique, but most of Florence's leading artists were prominent figures whose work was very much in the public eye. A plethora of major public or corporate commissions in the early years of the fifteenth century led to intensive public viewing and comparison of works of art.[75] In 1401 the Calimala guild held a highly publicized competition for the bronze doors of the baptistery, the talk of the town in its time. The decades that followed saw the unveiling of successive works commissioned by the Opera del Duomo, then at the height of the implementation of its program for the renovation and decoration of the cathedral.[76] The guilds' resolve to express their pride in statues for the niches of the church of Orsanmichele, a project instigated by communal decree in 1406, provided a fresh forum for artists vying with one another for attention. During the first three decades of the quattrocento the completion of a number of high-profile landmark works by private commission, among them Masaccio's decoration of the Brancacci family chapel, and his *Trinity* fresco in the church of Santa Maria Novella, also took place.

Such works attracted the admiration and emulation not only of artists throughout the city and beyond it, but also of other cultural innovators in Florence. While many humanists insisted on the primacy of the written word, Carlo Marsuppini saw the renaissance of the visual arts as a model for the revival of ancient philosophy. In a letter of consolation addressed in 1434 to Cosimo and Lorenzo de' Medici on the recent death of their mother, he appealed to the classical example of stoicism in the face of grief by invoking an analogy with quattrocento artists' imitation of their Greek and Roman predecessors: "If the painters, sculptors and architects of our time can in some part emulate the temples, the gates, the columns, the paintings, the marble figures and bronze statues of the ancients . . . shall we not imitate those ancients whom as Statius says we follow far after, and whose traces we adore?"[77]

Humanists were sometimes consulted concerning important public commissions. This is the context of Bruni's program for the third set of baptistery doors, which has been derided as evidence of humanist insensitivity to art. His proposal shows not that Bruni and other humanists were uninterested in the visual arts − quite the contrary − but rather that humanists, like other observers, were amateurs by comparison with artists in *invenzione* for the media of bronze or stone or paint. Bruni suggested concerning the doors that "whoever has them to design must be well instructed in each episode [*historia*] . . . I would like to be close to the designer to make him grasp every point of significance that the episode carries."[78] Ghiberti did not in fact adhere closely to Bruni's written program, probably because his own design worked better visually, and because he himself was well informed concerning the biblical narrative as well as the classical criteria of design.[79] Whether he entertained the humanist's advice or profited from his historical expertise, is not known.

A good deal is known from Ghiberti's *Commentaries* about the intensity of his interest in learning, as part of the artist's necessary equipment. There is no evidence to confirm or refute Richard Krautheimer's suggestion that when Ghiberti chose to represent the relatively unusual subject of the meeting of Solomon and Sheba on the baptistery doors, he intended to refer to Florence's role in the council of the eastern and western Churches, seeking the advice of the patristic scholar Ambrogio Traversari who had played a major part in the council's negotiations.[80] Given the enormous amount of public interest in the council, and its recurrence as a theme in Cosimo's commissions, the suggestion is eminently plausible. Ghiberti certainly received Traversari's help in obtaining from Aurispa an illustrated Greek manuscript of Athenaeus's work on siege engines, which he later used extensively in his *Commentaries*.[81]

By contrast Bruni, like many non-Florentine humanists,[82] regarded learning as the scholar's prerogative, and spoke patronizingly of artists' intellectual aspirations. In a letter of 1441 he wrote that "an artist who has acquired a certain perfection and standing in his art, such as Apelles in painting or Praxiteles in sculpture, does not need to understand military science or the government of the state, or to have a knowledge of the nature of things. Indeed as Socrates says in the Apology, it is a common vice in artists that one who excels in his own art [craft] deceives himself into thinking that he has other faculties which he has not. An art therefore should be distinguished from other intellectual virtues."[83] Some irritation with this disparaging attitude, which was certainly not shared by Florentine artists or their patrons, may be dis-

cerned in Ambrogio Traversari's reference in a letter to his friend Niccoli to Bruni's proposal for the baptistery doors. This letter implies that Niccoli himself was very interested in the program for these doors, and that Traversari, Poggio, and Niccoli sought an interchange with artists, rather than simply to instruct them.[84]

Vespasiano observed that "Niccoli not only showed great favor to men of letters, but being very well informed about painting, sculpture, and architecture, took great account of all of these, and greatly favored the practitioners of these arts in their work. Pippo di Ser Brunellesco, Donatello, Luca della Robbia, Lorenzo di Bartoluccio; he was close friends with all of them."[85] Niccoli's passionate interest in ancient architecture was sufficiently well known to inspire the ridicule of his literary rival Guarino da Verona. "Who could refrain from bursting into laughter when this man, to demonstrate his understanding of the laws of architecture, stretches out his arms, shows us ancient buildings, pores over the walls, diligently explains the ruins and half-collapsed vaults of the ruined cities . . . telling us how many tiers there were in the ruined theatres, how many columns have fallen . . ."[86] Archaeology naturally caught the imagination of men in love with the remains of the classical past; Poggio rhapsodically described to Niccoli the ruins he had seen at Grottaferrata and Tusculum, and a villa "which must have been Cicero's or have belonged to someone like him."[87]

Michelozzo, the architect of many classicizing buildings for the Medici and their friends, was, significantly, the recipient of Niccoli's only known letter, written at a time when both men frequented the Medici household.[88] Donatello, who was responsible for Cosimo's most brilliant commissions, apparently acted as an arbiter of taste for this circle of learned collectors of classical antiquities. Writing to his friend Niccoli in 1430 from Rome of a number of antique statues he had found, Poggio boasted in particular of one that Donatello had seen "and praised it highly." Donatello's positive judgment on two Roman sarcophagi seen between Lucca and Pisa was sufficient to secure them a place in Matteo Strozzi's collection.[89] Donatello was also said to have advised Cosimo on the repair and display of the statue of Marsyas in his study.[90]

Cosimo's letters show how closely Florence's leading citizens were concerned with any enterprise involving the honor of the commune, and that they also felt themselves perfectly qualified to consider and to judge the relative merits of works of art. These concerns and convictions are embodied in the institution of the *opera*, the lay commission of citizens entrusted by guilds and other communal bodies with responsibility for public buildings and their decoration. Many of the innovations in the art and architecture of the early Renaissance were made in public commissions carried out in this context, and the *opera* was a prime school for the education of private patrons. To be an *operaio* was to hold a position of great prestige, one which could be renounced only in favor of the supreme office of Prior.[91] The outstanding case of wider public involvement in artistic commissions is the project for the cathedral cupola, examined at length in chapter 8, but there are many other similar examples. Most of the commissions by the Opera del Duomo for the decoration of the cathedral called upon the combined skills of a number of artists, craftsmen, and consultants; thus the leading citizens on the committees of *operai* had frequent and immediate contact with artists, and acquired considerable expertise in viewing and judging the visual.[92]

Sometimes they simply put the patron's point of view in the most obvious sense, demanding stained glass for the cathedral windows because they wanted an effect which would be "richer" or "more ornate."[93] But a comment in Antonio Manetti's life of Brunelleschi suggests they were sufficiently informed about these projects to assume practical responsibility for them if necessary. Manetti tells how Brunelleschi left instructions during his absence from the building site of the foundling hospital, sponsored by the silk guild, with the "masons and cutters . . . [and] certain citizens who are heads of the guild, and Operai appointed for this purpose."[94]

A debate of 1433 on the desirable form of the cathedral sacristy cupboards displays the patrician *operaio's* strongly developed personal taste. Maestro Iacopo del Biada favored marble cupboards with bronze doors, the mathematician and astronomer Paolo dal Pozzo Toscanelli thought that the cabinets should be made of fine stone carved by skilled sculptors, and Francesco della Luna and Neri di Gino Capponi preferred intarsia like that of the doors of the first sacristy. Artists participated in this discussion also. Brunelleschi suggested cabinets of colored polished marble with flat bronze decorated doors, and Ghiberti, "not to be outdone, proposed mosaic for the vault and walls, and white marble cupboards with wood intarsia doors."[95]

Much remains to be discovered concerning the ways in which the composition of these committees was determined, and their relation to the political and financial leadership of the commune. Cosimo de' Medici, for example, was one of a committee of four to whom the bankers' guild entrusted the commission of its statue of Saint Matthew for Orsanmichele in 1419. The Orsanmichele figures were among the most notable examples at the time of the monumental bronze statues which had been so popular in the ancient world, and

Cosimo later became one of the few private patrons to commission works in this expensive and technically demanding medium.

Brunelleschi moved in many circles frequented by Cosimo and his family. He held a number of important communal offices, and while these abruptly diminished after the disastrous failure of his plan to divert the Serchio river during Florence's siege of Lucca, his involvement with this engineering project for the war had brought him into direct contact with the Medici and their friends. Averardo, Cosimo's cousin, received letters from his son-in-law Alamanno Salviati, a commissioner in the field, describing the problems associated with the scheme, primarily that the Ten of War had insufficient funds to pay enough men to carry it out. Salviati's notary, Ser Ciaio Ciai, also a Medici partisan, wrote to Averardo on 1 May 1430: "I have looked over his drawing very carefully with Pippo [Brunelleschi] and put to him my doubts, that it will fail to bear the weight of the water. He answers all this with arguments that I don't know enough about it . . . Soon we will see what happens . . ." What happened was that the scheme failed and many Florentines, like the splenetic magnate chronicler Giovanni Cavalcanti, bluntly blamed "some of those madmen of ours, among them Filippo di ser Brunellescho . . ."[96]

Leading citizens and professional artists came together on committees of experts and adjudicators to assess artists and works of art, in order to determine the just price of objects, and when the rejection of commissions, individual or corporate, secular or ecclesiastical, led to arbitration between artists and patrons. That the terms of such judgment might be simply a question of the patrons' taste is suggested in the rejection of Donatello's door for the font of Siena's baptistery because it "did not turn out the way the administrator and advisors liked," or the demand of the Operai del Duomo that Uccello repaint his fresco of Sir John Hawkwood, "because it is not painted appropriately."[97] When the Rucellai family was unsatisfied with a pulpit they commissioned for Santa Maria Novella in 1453, Fra Andrea Rucellai, acting for the family, sought the opinion of several distinguished artists, including Antonio Rossellino and Desiderio da Settignano.[98]

An understanding of the education of the patrician patron, long conceived largely in terms of written sources, should certainly be extended, as Michael Baxandall suggested, to include such skills as dancing and barrel-gauging which might be translated into the appreciation of art.[99] The patron's direct visual experience should also be taken into account in the explication of his oeuvre. Patrons were surrounded by images from birth to death, from *deschi da parto* to burial monuments. Contracts, and the workshop records of a popular artist such as Neri di Bicci, show that patrons often prescribed what they wanted by reference to objects they had seen, which were commissioned or owned by someone else.[100] The chapters on Cosimo's commissions attempt to set them in the context of various public images with which he was obviously familiar.

Cosimo made his only explicit observation about works of art as a comment upon the exercise of judgment as a skill transferable from one field to another. His assurance to his cousin Averardo that although he was not a painter he "would still judge that the figures of Giotto are better than those of Balzanello"[101] may also suggest that he had given some attention, however inexpert, to Giotto's work. This was displayed in various prominent places in Florence, including the Bardi and Peruzzi chapels in Santa Croce, and a small panel of Giotto's was acquired some time in the fifteenth century to hang on the walls of Cosimo's own house.[102] Or perhaps in invoking Giotto as the paradigm of skill, Cosimo was simply repeating conventional wisdom. Nevertheless, his familiarity with contemporary art and artists and the evidence of his own commissions would seem to support Vespasiano's claim that when Cosimo "conversed with painters or sculptors" he "knew what he was talking about."[103]

8   *Nota* sign in Cosimo's hand from his copy of Cassian,
Florence, Biblioteca Medicea Laurenziana, Plut. 16, 31, fol. 78v

EDUCATING THE PATRON: WHAT COSIMO READ

We have children; we don't know how long our own lives will be, but while we live we must advise and educate them, so that when they grow older, or whenever they are abandoned by us, they are equipped with sound principles.

Cosimo de' Medici.[1]

In describing Florence as a city "dedicated to commerce, literature, and leisure,"[2] Cosimo seems to have spoken, as he often did, for many of its leading citizens. A commission moved in 1455 to hire new professors for Florence's university, "since the whole glory and magnificence of the city consists in having wise, well-lettered and worthy citizens."[3] In this intensely intellectual climate, Cosimo could scarcely have enjoyed the unparalleled authority and respect he commanded without something of the "excellent knowledge of letters" Vespasiano attributed to him.[4] And yet some scholars insist that the wisdom his contemporaries admired was "street-wisdom," and that the learning they praised "came from the book of life." The volumes in his library are dismissed as "trophies of his book hunting or, perhaps, relics from his earlier studies,"[5] in the firm if unjustified conviction that "the gouty and astute old banker beneath [the] inapt garlands" bestowed upon him by the humanist Ficino "is clearly very far from being the versatile aristocrat that was becoming the ideal in mid-Quattrocento Florence."[6]

As we have seen, Cosimo was closely associated with most of the leading scholars and creative artists of the generations preceding Ficino's, and often personally involved in their projects. Was he merely an uncomprehending observer of their achievements? Were the subtleties of Brunelleschi and Donatello's use and adaptation of classical forms and themes largely lost upon him? How much precisely did he know and understand of the ideas from classical and Christian literature that were "in the air," and inspired the Florentine Renaissance?

A man's library is a good clue to his learning, and surveys of the inventories of Florentines' libraries suggest that the citizens of this hub of humanism and art were generally extremely well read.[7] And yet Cosimo owned by far the largest and most distinguished collection of books and manuscripts in early fifteenth century Florence, with the exception of Palla Strozzi's.[8] But did he read them? If he did not, it was peculiarly eccentric of him to take his entire library along on a trip for the purpose of establishing a new branch of the bank in Pisa, especially when the clothing and household effects considered indispensable to this relatively extended stay were comparatively few. His *famiglio* noted among the goods transported to Pisa "two trunks in Cosimo's room in which are all the books from his study in Florence, as listed in a notebook contained in the trunks."[9] Cosimo's books had also accompanied him into exile. After his recall, he wrote to Piero, who had remained in Venice to acquire some business experience in the bank's branch there under the guidance of Antonio Martelli, asking him to pack their most valuable volumes with the bed linen so that they would not be damaged on the journey back to Florence.[10] An undated later letter to both his sons in Volterra intructed them to make sure he received some missing "ancient books" in "the small chest decorated with armed men . . . because I need them."[11]

Albinia De La Mare's study of Cosimo's library opens a new and wider window onto his education and tastes. She identified a number of works listed in the inventory of the Medici house made in 1417/18[12] with extant manuscripts, many of them conserved in the Laurenziana library built by the Medici alongside their parish church of San Lorenzo. She redefined the corpus of Cosimo's manuscripts, listing all volumes that bear Cosimo's own *ex libris*, or that can be documented as belonging to Cosimo, copied for him, or presented to him, and she noted that the marginalia in some of these volumes are in the same distinctive hand as the *ex libris* Cosimo himself inscribed in each of his books to identify them as his.[13]

Roberto Sabbadini, who charted the general recovery of classical codices in the fourteenth and fifteenth centuries, described Cosimo as an intelligent collector. De La Mare judged Cosimo's collection of books, as recorded in the inventory of 1417/18, to be "quite an impressive one

for a young man of not quite thirty who was not primarily a scholar."[14] These opinions are in accord with the
judgments of his contemporaries, Poggio, Niccoli, and
Vespasiano, that for a businessman and statesman, Cosimo
was unusually well-read and interested in intellectual
issues.[15]

The nub of the controversy over Cosimo's literacy and
learning is that many modern professional scholars of
humanism have been inclined to judge Cosimo – and
other cultured citizens of Renaissance Florence – by
inappropriate and anachronistic standards. Compared to
professional intellectuals of Cosimo's or our own time, his
knowledge and his philological skills, like those of other
amateurs, were of course limited. Like some historians of
art, some scholars of humanism seem driven by a desire
to enhance the creative achievements of their subjects –
humanists such as Bruni or Ficino – by diminishing the
role of the patrons who supported them. This bizarre
exercise forms part of a larger argument about the relation between ideas and society, framed in terms of such
determinist questions as "Did the manipulative Medici
maintain power by persuading humanists to inject the
citizens of Florence with 'Platonic poison'?"[16] "Were the
humanists 'party intellectuals' or shapers of their patrons'
ideologies?"[17]

All these arguments proceed with equal disregard for
the complex interaction between persons and ideas in the
real world of the past, apparent in the relations between
Cosimo and leading humanists and artists of his time, and
in the popular culture created and shared by a wide range
of citizens of various social positions and occupations.
Renaissance patrons were not above their society, but
part of it; they helped to shape the development of
ideas by which they themselves were shaped. Cosimo de'
Medici and Giovanni Rucellai, major patrons of art and
literature, were not learned in the same sense as Bruni
or Ficino, or creative in the same way as Donatello and
Brunelleschi. They were, however, men of considerable
education and taste. They educated themselves, not to
please their partisans, or to impress their intellectual superiors, but to cultivate virtue, in the hope of living and
dying well, of achieving salvation and a measure of good
fame. Their interest in ideas they shared with others was
part of the pleasure of friendship and sociability in what
they considered "the worthiest and most beautiful *patria*
not only in Christendom, but in the whole world."[18]

Among the aspects of the Renaissance world insufficiently understood by many modern writers is the
importance of oral and shared culture. The numerous colloquia and symposia led by learned clerics and humanists, and the popular fora for the performance of poetry,
songs, and plays, played a major part in citizens' educa-

tion.[19] There is plenty of testimony from scholars close to
the Medici household of Cosimo reading, or having read
to him, Latin works in which he was particularly interested. When it came to reading learned literature, household secretaries and tutors were on hand to help patrons
who were not entirely proficient in Latin. Bartolomeo
Scala read Donato Acciaiuoli's notes of Argyropoulos'
commentary on Aristotle's lectures to the aging Cosimo,
and Panormita much earlier expected that his gift of the
Hermaphrodite – a bravura exercise in the imitation of the
style of classical writers like Martial – might either be
read by Cosimo or read to him.[20] Moreover, many professional scholars, privileging originality, tend to assume
that ideas only matter to original thinkers. They fail to
recognize that familiar, even commonplace ideas and formulations are the necessary aids with which less articulate people in any age define and express their own views
and feelings.[21]

While from a modern ideological perspective, the
studia humanitatis so enthusiastically embraced in the early
Renaissance might appropriately be seen as the culture of
conformism, ensuring the cultural hegemony of the
ruling classes, at the time these studies represented the
rediscovery of the key to wisdom.[22] If Florentine patricians wanted to be learned men as well as patrons of
others' learning, this was because they believed that learning was the path to knowing God, and that along the
way they would find "pleasure and profit."[23] Cosimo's
eighteen-year-old cousin Francesco, who lived in his
uncle's household in Venice where Cosimo and Lorenzo
were exiled, and had received a humanist rather than a
merchant's education, bemoaned his own inability to
master the abacus in the hope of rescuing his family's
business from ruin. But he could at least console himself
with the stoic wisdom of Juvenal: "If you ask my advice,
you will leave it to the gods themselves to provide what
is good for us, and what will be profitable for our affairs;
for in place of what is pleasing, they will give us what is
most appropriate."[24] Cosimo himself thought education
the most precious resource a patriarch could pass on to
his sons, and his son Piero wrote to his own sons Lorenzo
and Giuliano how their grandfather on his deathbed took
comfort "that you had good wits, and bade me educate
you well so that you might be of help to me."[25]

The getting of wisdom was a process best begun at an
early age, when in fact most patricians acquired their
libraries. As early as 1408, when Cosimo was nineteen,
Poggio Braccolini copied a codex of Cicero's *Letters to
Atticus* for him.[26] As Cassian observed in a passage of his
Monastic Institutes marked for attention in Cosimo's copy:
"If we want to reach [the] height of virtue, we must lay
the . . . foundation in youth." All such annotations in

Cosimo's books seem to have been made before about 1420.[27] By the time the 1417/18 inventory was compiled Cosimo, then just short of thirty, had already acquired an impressive collection of books, and the library of the mature Cosimo was to rank with the finest in Italy.[28] His personal library amounted at one point to almost a hundred identifiable volumes, mainly in Latin; later in life he began to pass many of them on to his son Piero, or to the convent of San Marco. There was also a handful of vernacular works, mainly devotional, which will be discussed in the context of the popular culture Cosimo shared with much of the Florentine populace.[29]

The 1417/18 library, some seventy volumes, was according to De La Mare already "in the new mould"; classical texts, especially historians and the works of Cicero, predominated, and a third of the volumes were written in the new humanistic script.[30] Cosimo owned most of the classical works in general currency in the early years of the quattrocento.[31] In addition to these, he possessed "a number of rarities and extreme novelties." Among these were a Tacitus, exceedingly rare in the early fifteenth century, and a prize he may have owed to his friendship with Niccoli.[32] The provenance of many of his books confirms the implication of the letters of Niccoli, Poggio, and Traversari, that their intimacy with Cosimo was based on shared interests in the recovery of accurate classical texts.[33]

By 1418 Cosimo also owned a copy of *On False Religion* by Lactantius, a late classical writer who might be described as an apostle of "civic Christianity."[34] His work was newly and eagerly embraced in the early fifteenth century by Florentine citizens who since their war with the papacy in 1375–8 – dubbed the War of the Eight Saints after the eight Priors of the city's chief magistracy – had been struggling to reconcile religion and patriotism.[35] Cosimo had another copy of Lactantius made about 1435, of an edition of the text based on the sixth-century manuscript discovered at Nonantola in 1426 by Tommaso Parentucelli, later Pope Nicholas V. This ancient manuscript was in the hands of Traversari and Niccoli in Florence in 1431. Cosimo's new Lactantius was particularly fine, and the first of his manuscripts to bear the Medici arms. The Greek passages were added and translated by Cosimo's friend Ambrogio Traversari, in his own hand.[36] Copies of Quintilian, and Asconius's commentaries on five speeches of Cicero, were made for Cosimo from texts that Poggio discovered at the monastery of St. Gall in the summer of 1416, and sent at once to Niccoli and Bruni in Florence.

Cosimo owned a copy of Cato's *De Re Rustica*, an agricultural text still quite rare in the early fifteenth century.[37] When Vespasiano described Cosimo's strong practical interest in the cultivation of vineyards and gardens, he was not simply borrowing a Virgilian topos. His claim is confirmed in the gardens Cosimo had made for both the *casa vecchia* and the new palace, and in the letters of Cosimo's secretary Alesso Pelli, which testify that at times of great stress Cosimo did indeed retire to his estates in the Mugello to work on them.[38] Clearly the collector's items in Cosimo's library also addressed his real personal interests.[39]

The manuscripts themselves are tokens of what he owed to the Florentine tradition of learning, and his continuing cooperation with those who promoted it. Beside the items he obtained with the help of his contemporaries Poggio, Niccoli, and Traversari, Cosimo acquired a number of volumes, including a copy of the sonnets of Petrarch, from the library of Salutati, the early humanist chancellor who presided over the city's intellectual life around the time that Cosimo was born. Cosimo's library reflected his literary sophistication by comparison with his father, whose reading appears to have been mainly devotional; similarly, his own sons Piero and Giovanni were to outstrip him considerably in their knowledge of classical literature.[40]

For another fifteen years after 1418 Cosimo continued to pursue novelties with the advice and help of Niccoli. Poggio's letters testify to the number of precious volumes Cosimo lent to others to be copied; Cosimo's own letters also mention manuscripts lent, or others he borrowed to have copies made.[41] These included an Aulus Gellius obtained from the great humanist teacher Guarino of Verona, then established at the court of Ferrara, and various works of the church fathers Jerome and Augustine, as well as Chrysostom, whose influence is apparent in Medici artistic patronage.[42] After 1435 there is no further evidence that Cosimo commissioned any new manuscripts, and indeed he began as early as the 1440s to give away books; to San Marco to supplement the bequest of Niccoli's library and other items he had specially commissioned for the convent, and to his son Piero, who by then was building an impressive collection of his own. This does not signal a waning of interest in learning, but was the common practice, by which libraries were acquired in youth and passed on, like business enterprises, to men's heirs and the objects of their patronage.[43]

The list of manuscripts which passed to Piero only at his father's death in 1464 could indicate which books Cosimo, even in his last years, was unwilling to relinquish to his sons or others.[44] It included a number of poets, among them Terence, Virgil, Plautus, Martial, and Juvenal, all of whom were already in Cosimo's library in 1418, as well as his schoolbook copy of Ovid's *Epistolae*. This passed eventually to Piero and Giovanfrancesco, the grandsons of Cosimo's brother Lorenzo, who added their *ex libris* to Cosimo's. On the back flyleaf there is an inscription, addressed perhaps to Cosimo's nephew Pierfrancesco, in what appears to be Cosimo's hand, at once a whimsical if somewhat opaque disclaimer of pretensions to erudition, a poignant reference to his sons' ill-health, and a play on the Medici association with doctors: "I am not so much more gifted [than you] that I can afford to talk of my own achievements as an example, for you would blanch so fast that no doctor could diagnose for me the illness from which you are suffering, even worse than that of Piero or Giovanni, which is so acute that it upsets me . . ." (fig. 9).[45]

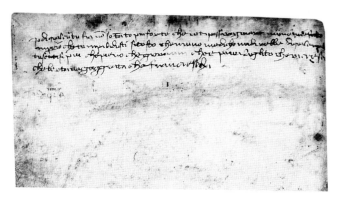

9   Inscription on flyleaf of Cosimo's Ovid, probably in his own hand, Florence, Biblioteca Medicea Laurenziana, Plut. 36, 28, fol. 58v

Cosimo had hung onto a number of prize manuscripts of historical works, whether because he wanted them, or because Piero did not, having already assembled and displayed in his study in the Medici palace a fine collection of new and beautiful humanist manuscripts of classical history, which reflected his own enthusiasm for that subject.[46] Among the volumes which passed to his son only after his death were the *Decades* of Livy, Plutarch's *Lives*, Bruni's *History of Florence*, and the Diogenes Laertius he had commissioned Traversari to translate in the early thirties. Cosimo had also kept the Christian classics he owned already in 1418; Jerome, Augustine, Cassian, Cyprian, Lactantius, and several bibles, psalters, and books of offices. Also in Cosimo's study at the time of his death were volumes of vernacular literature; Dante, Petrarch, and Boccaccio's *Genealogy of the Gods*, and the *Lives* of Saints Cosmas and Damian. These works had equipped Cosimo in his youth with a basic knowledge of much subject matter relevant to his later artistic commissions.

Another perspective on Cosimo's interests and tastes as expressed in his library is offered by those works which were presented to him, and whose dedications he chose to accept.[47] In this group, works of moral philosophy again predominate, constituting two-thirds of the forty-one works or translations dedicated to him, and including six works of Aristotle and twelve of Plato. This list tends to confirm Vespasiano's picture of Cosimo's intellectual interests.[48] However, since some clue to the ideas that may have informed his patronage of the arts is being sought in Cosimo's library, it is worth noting that more than two thirds of the works dedicated to Cosimo were presented to him only in the last seven years of his life, after the last of his major commissions had been made. These late gifts began in 1456–7 with Argyropoulos's translations of Aristotle and continued with the famous editions of Plato that Cosimo ordered from Ficino, which were completed in 1463–4. The dozen or so items that presumably reflect Cosimo's interests in youth and middle age are essentially works on ethics, secular or spiritual.

In the years preceding or during the period of Cosimo's important artistic commissions, he commissioned or accepted Traversari's translations of Diogenes Laertius and the *Sermons* of Saint Ephraem, made in the 1420s, an edition of Traversari's letters prepared by Michael Monachus, two works of Poggio, from the late 1430s and about 1450, respectively, and Bruni's translations of Plato and the pseudo-Aristotelian *Economics*, done between 1420 and 1435. He also accepted in the late fifties and early sixties a copy of Avogadro's remarks *On the Religion and Magnificence of Cosimo*, Lorenzo Pisano's *De Misericordia* (On charity), and Abbot Maffei's treatise *Against the Detractors of Cosimo's Magnificence*, a *pièce d'occasion* relating to Cosimo's rebuilding of the Badia at Fiesole. These three works on charity and magnificence reflect upon Cosimo's later ecclesiastical patronage, and suggest his continuing concern with the moral dilemmas facing the wealthy patrician.[49]

The translations of Plutarch's *Lives*, made around 1434 by Lapo da Castiglionchio and Antonio Pacini, Piero's tutor, are evidence of Cosimo's interest in classical history, which along with his major enthusiasm for the works of Cicero, may well have contributed to his sense of his role as Florence's leading citizen, and to his preference for building, particularly of the Medici palace, in the classical style.[50] The close correspondence between Castiglionchio's dedicatory comparison of Cosimo to classical patriots wronged by their *patria*, and Cosimo's representation of his exile in his own *ricordo* of 1434, might indicate how Cosimo's learning could help shape his life.[51] Iohannes Baldus presented his treatise *De electione medicis* to Cosimo in 1415, and Cosimo and Piero acquired other volumes on medicine which, like the agricultural works in their libraries, suggest that life might also dictate the direction of learning.

If we assume, as seems reasonable from what we have seen of Cosimo's library and its relation to his personal interests, that Cosimo's acceptance of a work dedicated to him by its author is some indication "of the sort of literature Cosimo enjoyed and valued,"[52] then we need to come to terms, as scholars seem reluctant to do, with his acceptance of Panormita's *Hermaphrodite* of 1425. This work, like Poggio's translation of Lucian's *Lucius, vel de Asino*, is often described as "indecent," and its dedication to Cosimo is regarded as an anomaly in view of his reputation for moral virtue.[53] It is indeed notable that among all the ribald jokes circulating in Renaissance Florence, only one of the many pithy sayings attributed to Cosimo in popular collections involves sexual innuendo. However, given the highly conventionalized nature of the genre of Renaissance jokes, that probably reveals more about Cosimo's public image than his personal sense of humor. Ribaldry was a fundamental element of popular literature with which Cosimo was very familiar. The *Hermaphrodite* proved in fact to be one of the most prized of all the manuscripts in the Medici collections. The presentation copy was embellished with a rich initial illumination, but this was restrained by comparison with the illuminated pages added with the *ex libris* of each successive generation; first Piero, and then Lorenzo. The strong strain of homoerotic play and double entendre in both classical and vernacular literature should lead us not to look the other way, but rather to look again at works like Donatello's bronze *David*, with more open and inquiring eyes.[54]

The "Nota" signs which appear in the margins of a dozen of the manuscripts known to have belonged to Cosimo are the most precise and intimate indication of the learning Cosimo might have seen as most applicable to his own life. Albinia De la Mare identified the hand as Cosimo's. The similarity between the hand of the *ex libris* that Cosimo, following Salutati's custom, often cannily placed in the middle of his manuscripts so that it could not be cut out, and the marginal sign *nota*, is indeed striking.[55] An equally compelling indication that these marks are probably Cosimo's is that sometimes they take the form of the distinctive mark of the Medici bank (three dots arranged in a triangle with a tail), a device used by operatives of the bank to authenticate their documents (figs. 8 and 10).[56] Such marks of personal significance were often used in more informal manuscripts to establish ownership and to draw attention to points of particular interest to their owners.

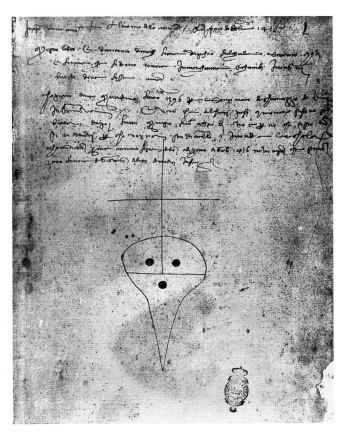

10 Medici bank mark, Florence, Biblioteca Nazionale, Panciatichiano, 71, fol. 1r

The passages indicated seem to relate closely to what is known of Cosimo's general character and interests.[57] The greatest number of marginalia in the sign of the Medici bank occur in Cosimo's copy of Cassian's *Monastic Institutes*. Cosimo's careful reading of this work suggests a concern for the nature and example of monastic life more profound than is usually recognized, and which found expression in his patronage at San Marco, Bosco ai Frati, and the Badia. Passages marked refer to the importance of patience and discretion, a recurring motif of many of Cosimo's letters, and of the diligent pursuit of virtue in youth.[58] One might read in Cassian's noted warning that men whom adversity could not overcome were often undone by prosperity, a reflection on Cosimo's own triumph over exile, and his awareness of the need to remain morally as well as tactically vigilant in his subsequent triumph.[59]

Cosimo marked several passages referring to the temptations of the flesh.[60] He also noted a chapter by Cassian on the evils of envy, which as the opposite of friendship was a prominent theme of classical and popular culture, and the subject of several aphorisms attributed by his contemporaries to Cosimo, as well as a poem addressed to him by Alberti.[61] Passages noted in the other manuscripts are fewer, and many of these, from both classical and Christian authors, are essentially about learning how to acquire wisdom and virtue.[62] From Aristotle's *Ethics*, Cosimo learned that the greatest goods are justice, and the health of mind and body, truths observed perhaps in acute consciousness of his own and his sons' precarious health.[63] In his copy of the *Economics* then attributed to Aristotle, and translated by Bruni for Cosimo when he was still a rather young *paterfamilias*, he noted that neither the city nor the household should be left uncared for, and that the virtuous man should rise before dawn to attend to study and matters domestic. These passages are interesting evidence of Cosimo's familiarity with analogies between the governance of the family and that of the state, a frequent theme of citizen debates on government in the early fifteenth century, and the basic model for his own view of the commune, as it emerges from his private letters and his contributions to those debates.[64]

In his study of Seneca's *Epistles*, Cosimo observed the importance of education to men of various occupations, and the need to progress with age toward the greatest of all virtues, excelling even simplicity, liberality, and constancy – patience.[65] In Caesar's *Commentaries* he took note of the great Roman general's view of the strategic importance in battle of knowing your enemy, an insight he may well have applied in his extremely successful involvement in the commune's warfare. Of course this advice is as generally applicable to everday life as to the military and diplomatic maneuvers with which Cosimo, like Caesar, was so much occupied.[66] Another practical suggestion he observed was a passage from Cicero's *On Oratory*, on how to give counsel in the affairs of the republic. The orator may most successfully sway his audience by appearing to align himself with the majority opinion, a practice which

Cosimo often employed in the councils of leading citizens when he recommended that those present consult the opinions of "cives non mediocres" (not unimportant citizens) before making any decisions.[67] The chapters that follow will look more closely at correlations between the contents of books in Cosimo's library – Quintilian, Propertius, *On Oratory, Orator* – and ideas expressed in particular commissions by Cosimo.

Since Cosimo left no reflective writings in which he was impelled to citations of literature, there is no absolute proof of what he read, nor of what he made of it. But in the light of what is now known of his library, commonsense suggests that the claim that either he did not read the books he owned, or could not understand them, is somewhat perverse.[68] At the same time, in considering what Cosimo read, it is important to recognize the vast gulf between the modern and the Renaissance experience of books and reading. Reading aloud and reading in groups was then a common custom which put technical literacy at less of a premium, and the search for meaning was also a more collective enterprise. Moreover, owning a book meant something very different at a time when the size even of Cosimo's library was so small, by comparison with learned libraries today. The total of written works ultimately available to Cosimo and his contemporaries was minuscule by modern standards; on the other hand, the amount of effort required to procure them was immeasurably greater. Because the number of the revered classics of Greece, Rome, and early Christianity was a finite one, and the sum of knowledge so limited, it was pondered and assimilated in a different fashion.[69]

Nevertheless, most educated Florentines, as the next four chapters show, regarded books in the time-honored way, as repositories of wisdom for the solution of practical problems, and as personal resources to aid in the achievement of a better life. The fact that Cosimo's books seem to have accompanied him wherever he went suggests that he was no exception to this rule.

II

THE COMMON CULTURE OF
THE FLORENTINE AUDIENCE:
THE MEDICI SHARE IN THIS

11   San Martino, Codex Rustici, mid-fifteenth century,
Florence, Seminario Arcivescovile, fol. 25v

V

VENUES AND PERFORMANCES

ART AND SOCIETY: POLITICAL PROPAGANDA OR A COMMON CULTURE?

Since both patrons and artists communicated their ideas and aspirations through objects, their audience played an essential part in the process that created Renaissance works of art. The role in Renaissance art of symbols and figurations as bearers of meaning assumed an audience well versed, not only in the Christian and classical traditions, from which the essential vocabulary of its images was drawn, but familiar as well with cognitive devices, such as metaphor and allegory, that facilitated an association and exchange between words and images. Perhaps on this account most modern discussions of the fifteenth-century artist's expressive intentions have presupposed an informed and appreciative, but often very restricted audience, composed primarily of fellow-artists, discerning patrons, and other *cognoscenti*. More recently, studies focusing on the interests of the patron have envisaged a wider audience for works of art, but one attuned primarily to messages about politics and power encoded in artistic commissions. This model does appear to fit the conditions of much courtly patronage, which supported many leading artists of Renaissance Europe.[1]

However, the plethora of educated patrons living in the small republican city of Florence was an important precondition of the extraordinary intensity of creative innovation by so many talented artists at work there in the early fifteenth century. The sheer number of consumers of art was bound to alter the dynamic between patron, artist, and audience.[2] A handful of members of these groups have left extensive evidence of their related lives and careers; these suggest that particularly remarkable works of art were generated in the fusion of the interests and talents of artists, their patrons, and the Florentine community. As scholars become more interested in the attitudes of Everyman, they have taken more account of the widespread popular enthusiasm for an artist such as Donatello, and major communal projects including the baptistery doors and Brunelleschi's cupola for the cathedral.[3] But as yet, the wealth of available evidence concerning the education and culture of the large mass of literate, but not prominent or highly educated Florentines, who formed a significant part of the city's viewing public, has not been extensively related to the meanings artists and patrons might expect their audience to apprehend in works of art.[4]

The majority of scholars who believe that the "social context" of art contributes to its meaning, many of them reacting against the retrospective application to the Renaissance of the romantic tradition of regarding the artist as the sole creator of his works, have stressed the "political" significance of the commissions of powerful patrons. Naturally the artistic commissions of men involved in government have political significance, as do all their actions, but too often political meaning is simply equated with propaganda.[5] Art has frequently played an important role in promulgating political ideas, not least in the republican communes of the early modern period.[6] However, the relation between ideas espoused by a community and its leaders, and the visual representations of its artists, is a very complex one.

This book asks a simpler question, focusing on people – patrons and artists, individuals or groups of men – and their expressed concerns, rather than trying to relate the abstractions of art and society which are indeed, as Michael Baxandall observed, "unhomologous systematic constructions put upon interpenetrating subject matters."[7] Although immense difficulties beset any attempt, even on the simplest level, to establish and articulate a relation between persons, ideas, and images, to try to do so is nevertheless a necessary step in the recognition that patrons and artists are part of their society and its culture. Artists are generally seen as inevitably expressing in their work something of the values of the society to which they belong, but patrons are more often viewed as puppet-masters, operating above the social scene, pulling the strings.[8]

The next four chapters show how particular elements of a shared culture enabled Florentine patrons and artists to communicate effectively with one another and with their audience. They explore Cosimo de' Medici's involvement in the cultural interests and aspirations of the better part of his Florentine contemporaries, and will serve to suggest the reductive nature of a view of his patronage as essentially "political propaganda." Much of Cosimo's power and popularity as a public figure resided in his ability to stay in the vanguard of civic ideas and action; to be always one of the first to grasp, articulate, and respond to the needs and concerns of his fellow-citizens. This was true in the realm of literary and artistic patronage as of political, diplomatic, and financial intiatives, especially since much of Florentine culture arose from and addressed these practical issues.

A serious obstacle to exploring the more popular culture of any society is the difficulty, sometimes impossibility, of learning very much about people below the threshold of literacy. Luckily in Florence that threshold was unusually low. Florence's educational system probably embraced a higher proportion of the city's inhabitants than that of any other community in Europe. Reading and writing were skills essential to the prosperity of a town primarily engaged in banking, trade, and manufacturing, and commerce fostered a commitment to reading and writing, and to literature, that clearly occupied a good deal of citizens' leisure time. No systematic attempt has yet been made to calculate the number of literate residents of Florence in Cosimo's lifetime, and most estimates so far are based on limited evidence and not entirely convincing. For example, what little we know about the number of schools and schoolmasters in the trecento suggests that the mid-fourteenth-century chronicler Giovanni Villani exaggerated in estimating that well over two-thirds of the male population attended schools where they were taught to read; a figure around one third for the late trecento seems more likely.[9]

Perhaps the most reliable evidence of the literacy of a wide social range of Florentines in the early fifteenth century are the Catasto reports, the declarations of assets and liabilities which were filed first in 1427 by the heads of all households with sufficient income to pay taxes.[10] These citizens' statements, preserved in the government archives in their original form, have been intensively examined for information concerning a variety of issues. Although the rate of literacy they reveal has not yet received much explicit attention, it seems that a high proportion of the 10,000 or so heads of households representing a population of approximately 37,000 wrote their tax reports in their own hands, and the remainder usually managed at least to sign them. These citizens included not only skilled artisans, but men as far down the social scale as cooks and combers of raw wool, including a former wool-carder from the district of the Red Lion, nicknamed "Pennuccia" after the chicken feathers (penne)

from which he also fashioned pens, pillows, and knick-knacks, and a cook who signed his name to a report prepared by a friend, despite shaky orthography and an imperfect grasp of the principle of separating words with spaces (fig. 12).[11]

io pie zo gifuzgrinooze ßato ßa sopza detta iczita

12   Signature to 1427 tax report of a cook, Piero di Fruosino, ASF, Cat., 28, fol. 344r. It reads: "Io Piero di Fruosino o rechato la sopra detta iscritta" ("I, Piero di Fruosino, have rendered what is written above")

There is no reason to believe that the broad configuration of the educational system and the social classes it served had changed much by 1480, when a new survey produced a fresh set of tax returns, rich in information about the details of respondents' lives, which have been systematically examined to illluminate the issue of public literacy. At this time it seems that the families of working poor – artisans, shopkeepers, and workers in the wool industry – made considerable efforts to educate their sons. Those who did so included bakers, beltmakers, butchers, cabinetmakers, cobblers, doubletmakers, petty employees of the commune, flax workers, gold-beaters, small merchants and shopkeepers (merciai), saddlemakers, tailors, and woolworkers.[12]

The traditional culture of the Florentine popolo, shared by both major and minor guildsmen, is recorded in an enormous body of Florentine popular literature, both poetry and prose, which was composed, performed, and enjoyed by a large audience in Cosimo's lifetime. This corpus can be reconstituted from the thousands of informal chapbooks, zibaldoni, or quaderni (notebooks), as their owners called them, compiled by literate Florentines from a wide swathe of the social spectrum.[13] Well known to literary scholars, this material is seldom related by social, political, or art historians to their concerns.[14]

A major component of this literature was the product of Florence's brilliant vernacular culture built upon Dante, Petrarch, and Boccaccio. It also drew heavily on the street traditions of satirical and irreverent plebeian poems (burle e baie), on celebrations of civic events and ideals addressed to the popolo, and above all on the devotional texts articulating religious doctrine and practices.[15] This culture is documented in the writings of thousands of the city's residents, and was available to be read by the thousands more who were literate. It also reached a much larger number orally, through performances in various venues, particularly piazzas and churches. The corpus of Florentine popular literature tells us nothing certainly of the culture of the city's mass of illiterate unskilled workers, but they would have formed part of the audience at such venues as the church of San Martino, located in the heart of one of the city's densest concentrations of wool-working and other industries, where songs and stories were sung or recited almost daily.[16] Transcriptions of these performances in popular compilations give at least a glimpse of the cultural experience of those below the level of literacy, although their individual responses are lost to view.

A customarily loose appplication of the term "popular culture" by many historians and social analysts of both past and present has made its definition, and even discussion, increasingly problematic. In Renaissance Florence the characterization of a distinctively popular culture far less homogeneous than that of the international learned and Latinate elite, in which a number of Florentine patricians also participated, is further complicated by the promotion in the later fifteenth century by intellectuals, including Alberti, Poliziano, and Cristoforo Landino, and their patron Lorenzo de' Medici, of a more sophisticated version of the vernacular tradition, based on the work of Dante, Petrarch, and Boccaccio.[17]

Popular culture in this highly literate urban setting was very different from that of the rural communities which predominated in Europe in this period. The largely undocumented beliefs and customs of the vast majority of the illiterate have been the main focus of most recent studies of "popular" culture in early modern societies. Their authors' imaginative use of innovative methodologies for exploiting forms of evidence other than written records have made these the accepted models for scholars of this burgeoning field. This has led to a current tendency to define popular culture as the belief system of the unlettered.

However, many of these same studies demonstrate the crucial importance, even in predominantly illiterate rural communities, of the culture of partly educated townsmen, some of them artisans. The Friulian miller Menocchio's highly personal view of the world, of man, and of God, and of a universe of cheese permeated by worms, was shown by Carlo Ginzburg to derive from the miller's personal re-framing, in terms of popular beliefs, of extensive reading of the works of men more learned than himself. Popular compilations reveal the existence in Florence of many Menocchios,[18] artisans who, although often disparaged by the wealthy and powerful as part of "the masses" or "the mob,"[19] were also acknowledged by patricians as participants in a common culture widely diffused at all

social levels, and indeed admired as its most gifted creators.[20]

Despite its propensity to generate confusion and contention among scholars, "popular" is the only sensible term (however imprecise) to distinguish (however artificially) the Florentine culture of street performance and personal chapbooks from the learned classicizing culture to which this Renaissance city owes its enduring fame. Overshadowed by scholarly interest in the texts and pedagogical methods of humanism which shaped the elites of Europe up to modern times, this common culture's role in shaping fifteenth-century Florentines, both patricians and plebeians, has been largely ignored.[21] The following characterization of the popular culture of Renaissance Florence and its relevance to Cosimo's artistic commissions attempts to profit from the insights of students of popular culture in various eras without becoming bogged down in competing definitions of this contested area of study. We need to approach the many-faceted culture of fifteenth-century Florence as flexibly as possible in order to appreciate its complex and distinctive nature.

POPULAR POETRY AND SONG: PERFORMANCES IN THE PIAZZA OF SAN MARTINO

Although literary traditions fed and codified Florentine popular culture, the genre was quintessentially oral and performative. Popular poetry in Renaissance Florence, as in the ancient world, was often first sung and then transcribed, and whereas humanists took pride in the esoteric nature of their learning, popular poets and singers measured their success by the size of their audience. This point is underlined by Florence's humanist chancellor Poggio Bracciolini, who first came to the city as a papal secretary, and was one of the group who in 1441 served as judges of the Certame Coronario and scorned the efforts of the *volgare* poets.[22] Among his *Facetiae*, a collection of humorous stories originating from the papal secretaries' informal social gatherings, he tells a tale "Concerning a singer who had promised a recital of the 'Death of Hector'," which derides the audience of popular performances as foolish and credulous: "One of my neighbors, a very simpleminded man, was listening to one of those singers who at the end of his performance, in an attempt to seduce his public, promised for the next day a song on the death of Hector. Our friend gave him some money before he left, begging him not to kill off such a great hero as Hector so quickly. The artist put off this death to another day, and the man continued to pay out money to prolong the hero's life. When he was finally broke," scoffed Poggio, "he had to listen to this song of death a victim of serious misery."[23]

Poggio's fellow humanist Leonardo Bruni, also not a native Florentine, was discomfited that Dante, one of the three literary crowns of Florence, was popular not only with learned men like himself, but also with artisans, to the extent that he could be described as "the poet of wool-workers, bakers, and the like."[24] Readings of Dante were a regular custom not only at the university (Studio) of Florence, frequented by the upper classes, but also at the popular devotional center of Orsanmichele and at the cathedral, the recognized forum for events of interest to the Florentine people at large. Ordinary men rose at dawn to attend these performances.[25] Eventually Bruni, along with other members of the learned elite, found reasons to justify the anomaly of his own admiration for such a popular poet. However, like many distinguished citizens and most humanists, Bruni was unable to embrace that union of the base and exalted which was a major theme of popular culture, as of the practical Christianity that played such a large part in it.

Written texts of significance to the *popolo* were popularized through their incorporation into performances. The recognized venue for the performance of popular culture in Florence was the piazza outside the church of San Martino al Vescovo (fig. 11). A tradition of popular performances in public squares was apparently widespread in northern Italian cities in the age of the communes, but by the fifteenth century it seems to have survived mainly in Florence.[26] From the 1420s a variety of sources from letters to tax reports refer to performances there, and particularly to those "che canta in panca a San Martino" – who sing on the benches at San Martino.[27] The most important days for performances were Sundays and feast-days, which amounted to almost a hundred holidays in each working year. However, transcriptions of recitals also show that they often continued for several days in succession; in effect it would seem that some sort of entertainment was available virtually half the days of each week.[28]

The greatest composers and performers of vernacular poetry and song came to San Martino to entertain an audience of patricians and plebeians gathered together outside the church. Poetry and some prose were recited; very often singers performed their own songs or those of others to the accompaniment of simple melodies like Gregorian chants or melopee, favored at Florentine festivals and performances of sacred dramas; they were played on the viola or chitarra.[29] Improvisation was the essence of this medium. Its most talented practitioners were artisans – shoemakers or barbers, such as Antonio *calzaiuolo*, Burchiello, and Antonio da Baccereto, "who was a barber and now sings on the benches";[30] some of

them became professionals, including the heralds of the Signoria, or Antonio di Guido and Niccolò Cieco, full-time singers who also entertained at the palace of the Signoria or in the homes of such wealthy citizens as the Medici.[31] The most renowned performer of the 1460s, 1470s, and 1480s was Cristoforo, known as "L'Altissimo." The texts of many of his songs were transcribed verbatim by his listeners, and include a number of passages directly addressing and describing his audience. These constitute the fullest account that exists of the performances at San Martino.[32]

As Alberti believed that a painting must involve the spectator, for Cristoforo an artist without an audience was nothing. To make this point he evoked, as had Cosimo de' Medici in his poem to Francesco Sforza, a series of images of the overturning of familiar expectations: "Land without a master, a stone detached from its wall . . . / A twisted statue, a building that collapses,/ a brow without hair, a talent undisplayed,/ a body without a soul, a farmer without grain,/ a lazy artisan, a banker with no money,/ a poor merchant, a valiant defender without a sword,/ a rich man without discipline, a poet without style,/ so I would be, kind listeners, without you/ in making a beginning, a middle and an end./ A silver trumpet with an indecisive sound,/ a tree in full leaf without fruit,/ a noble picture put in a dark place,/ a woman with fine clothes and an ugly face/ . . . a monarch in name, with nothing to rule,/ an angel in name, the epitome of fury,/ I would be, good and wise listeners,/ without the favor of almighty God./ For from him stems originally/ the instinct that makes me speak in verse,/ and secondly from you, who love good work/ and recommend it to others, to make this talent/ blossom, which pleases so many people./ So many men come to listen to me,/ but your coming to fill the benches/ depends on neither me nor you."[33]

L'Altissimo's lines capture the essence of Florentine popular culture, its enthusiastic and socially various audience, and their many shared assumptions and interests. He also underlined the consciously popularizing character of this culture, and the ambiguity of some Florentines' feelings about that: "Sometimes someone says to me:/ 'You humble and abase yourself, poet'." As he explained to his audience: "I do it for pleasure, but it does not drag me down,/ since I have in this street, in this small piazza/ an audience so great and so happy/ that it would make not just me, but a stone proud." He added that if someone should suggest "that I am throwing away my verses at San Martino, I reply,/ 'Oh timid one, behold, this street may be glorified by the worthy picaresque wisdom offered here'./ . . . As a peasant, when he sees the vine and its produce, ready and willing to make wine,/ so I, and my spirit rejoice when I glance over the crowd at San

Martino,/ and see such a noble gathering listening to me."[34]

No doubt the nobility L'Altissimo discerned in his audience was partly that of virtue and intellect, as proclaimed by the poets of the Provençal and Tuscan tradition on which he drew. His "kind and welcome listeners, who are good enough to come here to San Martino," he considered "the ultimate mirror of virtue," but his claim that "I exult that often at San Martino there are so many noble people within my sight," should also be taken literally. Members of many of Florence's leading families, among them Cosimo de' Medici, not only listened to popular poetry at San Martino, but wrote it themselves. Most of their verses have gone largely unnoticed, probably because they are not particularly good poetry, but they are of immeasurable interest to the historian of Florentine society and culture.[35]

Cristoforo's nickname − L'Altissimo, the most exalted − may well have been a verbal play on the reconciliation of social extremes in the nobility of virtue. Conforming to a topos of modesty traditional to both classical and vernacular poetry, he referred to "my base verses," and attributed his success to his noble audience's appreciation of his talents, "which lends me support and aid/ . . . without which I would be little or nothing;/ nor would I have achieved the status of the Highest [*Altezza*, a play on his name] . . . I make myself glorious, though I am an abject man,/ the lowest, base, and with little virtue/ . . . Oh you by whom I raise myself up and am honored/ . . . if I raise myself to heaven with your wings/ this is by your grace, O divine persons."[36]

More literal social mobility was the theme of one of Cristoforo's songs in praise of those of whom it might be asked "of whom was he born?/ Only three days ago he was a peasant/ and seemed to be a worthless louse./ He who is base-born rises all the higher,/ and from a lowly estate reaches a high one . . ." His base-born heroes included the *condottieri* Niccolò Piccinino and Francesco Sforza, the first the most successful leader of the Milanese and Neapolitan forces hostile to Florence in the mid-fifteenth century, the second the Florentine captain who became Cosimo de' Medici's closest friend and political ally, and in 1450 replaced the last of the Visconti as duke of Milan. "Who would ever say of Nicolò Picino, who was the son of a Perugian butcher,/ that he was not sufficiently worthy or noble?/ . . . And Sforza, who was duke of Milan,/ and son of a peasant from Cotignola,/ who was such a worthy and noble captain;/ should these be called vile and miserable?"[37]

Another of Cristoforo's examples of the self-made man was the Florentine citizen Matteo Palmieri, a merchant, historian, and poet: "Matteo Palmieri, whom we see still living among us,/ who was an apothecary at the canto degli Rondini,/ who made himself divine by his virtues,/ and did so much for his *patria*;/ who enriched himself, and was also decorated/ with the laurel crown and the olive branch, and wore a golden cloak,/ and composed poetry which is lofty and esteemed,/ though unjustly it is condemned by some;/[38] who would not call him noble,/ he who acquired so many possessions and so much virtue?" Popularizing the prevalent poetic and humanist view that knowledge and virtue conferred a nobility beyond that of inherited wealth, he declared: "Fathers bequeath money to their sons,/ and the goods which they have acquired,/ but they cannot leave them their virtue,/ nor the nobility of their excellence;/ if there is a virtuous and decorous man/ from whom is descended an ignorant lot,/ should these ignoramuses be called gentlemen?/ You well know they should not, if they do not follow their customs."[39]

The union in virtue of the base and the exalted is of course a major tenet and ideal of Christian faith, the most fundamental and pervasive element of Florentine popular culture.[40] San Martino was only the chief of many churches at which ordinary people performed and listened to devotional texts. Recitals on secular subjects were permeated with references to the religious beliefs the audience shared, and which emphasized the identification of the humble with the sublime in the life of Christ, expressed also in such popular images as Jesus washing the feet of his disciples or the Madonna of Humility, seated not upon a throne as Queen of Heaven, but upon the ground. Performances on feastdays often began with an invocation to the appropriate saint. On 25 March, the feast of the Annunciation, and the first day of the Florentine new year, Cristoforo appealed explicitly to Mary: "O ever Virgin, after the birth and before it,/ mother of your son, O beautiful Virgin,/ more than all other women humble, and more than all others sublime . . . / exalt, I beg you, my verse and my rhyme,/ direct my rhythm, tone and speech,/ by your grace, since this is your day,/ make me please those listening around me . . ."[41]

At the same time, in the well-ordered community that L'Altissimo evoked in his vision of its overturning, each station and occupation had its divinely ordained place and attributes. The roles of the entertainer and his audience are fixed within this scheme; the entertainer's God-given talent flowers through the appreciation of his audience, to whom the Lord allows the good fortune of being present on the benches outside San Martino to hear him. Collectively they represent the virtuous Christian community − of productive farmers, industrious artisans, wealthy bankers, prosperous merchants, and ready protectors. Familiar and desirable in this well-ordered world are – in addition to poets with fine style – harmonious statues, sound buildings, and properly displayed paintings.[42]

L'Altissimo's verses express the prevailing tone of most of the "social comment" in quattrocento popular poetry. For example, patriarchal Christian perceptions of the balance of obligations and responsibilities appropriate to men of various stations had been extrapolated at length half a century earlier in an extremely popular poem by the blind poet Niccolò Cieco. The reciprocal duties of unequals in a patronage society were justified and even sanctified by Christian teaching concerning piety, charity and expiation, shared elements of popular culture that found expression in visual images, including many of Cosimo's commissions.[43]

COSIMO AT SAN MARTINO: PATRON OF CHARITY AND POPULAR CULTURE

The oratory of San Martino stood at the heart of one of the city's four most important wool-processing districts. The manufacture and finishing of woollen cloth was Florence's main industry, and the fine quality fabric produced in this neighborhood was known simply as "San Martino."[44] Many patrician houses had shops here that brought them into personal contact with the artisans and laborers who lived and worked in the district. One of the workers in a woolshop in San Martino established by Cosimo and Lorenzo de' Medici, and managed by Francesco Berlinghieri, wrote to Piero, Cosimo's elder son, asking to be excused from service on the state galleys. In requesting this favor, he appealed to the fact that "I have worked for you and served in your shop, of which Maestro Berlegeri [Berlinghieri] is the *patron*."[45]

The piazza of San Martino lay scarcely more than fifty yards to the east of the church of Orsanmichele. That church and former grain market, situated on the Via Calzaiuoli, had been for most of the fourteenth century the city's major center of popular devotion and the distribution of charity. On the eastern side of the church of San Martino, opposite the entrance to the oratory, was the Torre del Castagna, where in the last years of the thirteenth century the Priors, representing the newly established government of the merchant and artisan guilds, took refuge, in Dino Compagni's evocative phrase, "so that they need not fear the threats of the mighty."[46] The houses of the Alighieri family, where Dante had once lived, lined the street that bordered the church to the north. To the west, the main entrance of the church opened onto the south end of a larger piazza, where the

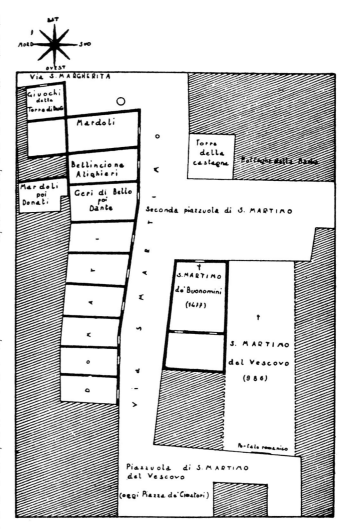

13 Church and oratory of San Martino and adjacent *piazze*, reconstructed by L. Desideri Costa

singers probably performed (fig. 13).[47] San Martino stood in the ancient shadow of the Badia, and fell under its jurisdiction. Its patron saint was the Roman soldier who charitably donated half of his cloak to a beggar; later that night the beggar appeared to Martin in a dream, and revealed that he was Jesus Christ (fig. 14).[48]

In the eleventh century, with the permission of the abbot of the Badia, San Martino was dedicated also to Cosmas and Damian, the Medici saints. This may have attracted Cosimo's attention to the oratory as the site for a charitable confraternity founded in 1442 with the strong support, and almost certainly at the initiative, of the Medici and their friends.[49] The Buonomini of San Martino dedicated themselves to the "shamed" or occasional poor, rather than the destitute; they assisted those families whose circumstances were temporarily reduced by unemployment or altered by the death of a bread-winner, or the birth of an additional child to be fed. The beneficiaries, mostly artisans and their families, came at least weekly to San Martino, bearing name tickets which entitled them to claim their share of the Wednesday distributions of food.[50]

The confraternity of the Buonomini brought together in the same place wealthy patrons performing their traditional duty of Christian charity, beneficiaries largely from the artisan class which produced the major creators of popular culture, and a group from the upper echelons of the artisan ranks and the lower middle class who were prominent in Florence's many pious confraternities. The Buonomini enjoyed the blessing of Archbishop Antoninus and Pope Eugenius IV, both Cosimo's close associates. Among its chief benefactors were many of Cosimo's friends, men influential in the spheres of business, culture, and the Church.[51] The Buonomini themselves included patricians and artisans prominent in the city's charitable "establishment," but minor guildsmen predominated. One of their members was Cosimo's household secretary, Ser Alesso Pelli.[52] The twelve Buonomini personally solicited donations to save the poor from the shame of doing so themselves, and in the 1440s Alesso paid in Cosimo's donations, amounting to some 50 per cent of contributions recorded between 1442 and 1469. Alesso also distributed Cosimo's special Christmas and Easter offerings of ten barrels of vermiglio, one of his favorite wines sent from his own house, and of twenty-five lambs worth five

hundred florins. Thus Medici charity to the Florentine poor via the Buonomini of San Martino was only barely concealed beneath the confraternal veil.[53]

As the center of a popular culture dominated by artisans who were among the chief beneficiaries of the confraternity's charity, San Martino in every symbolic way represented the common interests of Cosimo and Florence's artisan citizens.[54] Feo Belcari, who held the office of canon of San Lorenzo thanks to Medici patronage, and who became the century's most popular author of spiritual songs and sacred plays, was also a member of the Buonomini. He was a particularly close friend of Piero di Cosimo and his wife Lucrezia Tornabuoni, who in her own large corpus of *poemetti sacri* closely emulated Belcari's highly successful style. Belcari perfomed his own works at San Martino, and several of them drew attention to Cosimo's charity to the Florentine people, both as the source of succor for the poor, and as the defender of the Church through the building and decorating of churches. When Cosimo was appointed as one of the *festaiuoli* to organize the Ascension play in 1442, the same year the Buonomini were founded, Feo Belcari praised him in terms that stressed his usefulness to the poor in need of charity, and to the community of the devout intent on preserving and enhancing the shrines of the cult: "Father of your fatherland, gracious and worthy/ conserver of temples and holy places,/ the singular refuge of all those/ who live under the standard of poverty,/ for your good wine slakes our thirst."[55]

Charity was an important theme of popular poetry, just as it was a key component of patrician patronage.[56] The figurative support from his audience to which L'Altissimo referred shaded seamlessly into literal charity and patronage. At least one singer of *laude* at San Martino was a recipient of the charity of the Buonomini.[57] Members of the audience gave money to performers,[58] and the Medici contributed directly to the support of singers with the encouragement of their friends Feo Belcari and the poet-compiler-accountant Michele del Giogante, perhaps the most important figures linking the Medici with the world of popular culture. Michele wrote to Cosimo's son Piero in 1454, beginning his letter with a *quartina* written in red ink: "A pious man, according to Augustine/ has one foot on the ground and the other pointing towards heaven./ Therefore, my dear Signor', with the warm enthusiasm/ of love please relish my instructions." Michele's letter was a recommendation to Piero of the interests of "a young boy, one of us Florentines, about sixteen or seventeen years old," and at that time in the service of a captain of the Venetian army: "And this boy, whom I already put to singing improvisations on the bench at San Martino, of fine intellect and imagination

14   School of Ghirlandaio, *Saint Martin and the Beggar*, c.1490, Florence, Oratory of the Buonomini di San Martino

[*buono ingiengno e fantasia*], really gifted by nature with this skill . . . you already heard sing in Lionardo Bartolini's house, at a splendid dinner he gave for you, where I brought him, and he sang a few stanzas; you must remember it."[59]

He continued:

I think you were also acquainted with his work when he brought with him a very pleasing little book I made for him, and he had sung a good part of the material written in it at San Martino, including a little work maestro Niccolò Cieco performed as a motet at San Martino, which made hundreds of people there weep in sympathy . . . Now this boy, whose father is a very poor old man of about seventy, has an aged mother, and the family has a girl to marry off, and they have been cared for and nourished by a grown son of theirs, the brother of this boy, who has been a bookseller for a long time, and is presently in the employ of Vespasiano, and skilled in his craft, but only with the aid of il Forte's salary [Michele's nickname; he was referring to himself] has this family been kept from extreme necessity. I beg you for the love of God to have this boy brought home when you return, and to give to his old father and mother the joy of seeing him again before they die . . . and so that they may recognize the grace of God in your grace, and always have cause to pray for the living and the dead of all your house.

This letter exposes the intricacy of secular and spiritual responsibility and services owed by the members of various social groups and classes in a patriarchal Christian world. The high visibility of charity and patronage from Medici friends and supporters at San Martino naturally raises the question of how far this center of popular culture served as a forum for the promotion of Medicean political interests. How, and how far Cosimo's patronage of art and popular culture affected the general development of these media is immensely problematic, but the traditions of Florentine popular culture were far too firmly rooted in the Florentine past, as will appear, to permit any easy assumption that this culture was "hegemonized" by the Medici.[60]

Singers compiled their repertoires from a mixture of their own works and those of their friends and contemporaries, with standard traditional selections enumerated in manuals written by and for them. The most famous of these manuals were the *zibaldone* attributed to Antonio Pucci, and the *Cantare dei Cantari,* whose anonymous author, writing some time between 1380 and 1420, specified the works he had found to be most popular. The songs and recitations that moved the audience at San Martino "to tears or admiration" included popular sayings and moral exempla, observations about such subjects of perennial popular appeal as the disposition of women, the education of children, and the character of priests, doctors, and notaries, sacred songs of penance or instruction, songs of love fulfilled, or more often unrequited, medieval romance or historical narrative epics based on the deeds of the ancient Romans, or the origins and history of Florence, and extracts from the Bible and the works of Latin poets and prose writers translated and transposed into rhyme. Antonio Pucci's *zibaldone* also explicitly addressed the rules for composing these works.[61]

Obviously such a repertoire invited, indeed demanded, the rehearsal of a broad range of learning considered indispensable to popular entertainers. This puts the standards of artisan education in a new and interesting light, since, as already observed, the outstanding authors and performers of these works were artisans or entertainment professionals of similar social status. By their attendance at venues for the performance of popular culture such as the church of San Martino, members of the ruling class acknowledged the appeal of popular entertainment and the skills of its artisan practitioners. Although many patricians, including Cosimo de' Medici, took a serious interest at the same time in the culture of the city's intellectual elite, popular culture was an alternative they seem to have found more diverting. It was certainly more accessible. In the popular poetry they themselves wrote and circulated, patricians participated in creating culture far more extensively than they could through exchanges with the literary elite, whom only a few amateurs were erudite enough to match.[62]

Popular entertainers were constantly present in patrician as well as plebeian lives through their service as heralds to the Signoria. The nature of this post is a fascinating indication of the patrician predilection, whether personally or politically inspired, for *popolaresco* culture.[63] In Cosimo's lifetime by far the most important incumbent of the position of singer of *canzoni morali* at the Priors' table, not unlike the minstrel in the hall of a feudal lord, was Antonio di Meglio. Appointed in 1412, by his retirement in 1442 he had transformed his office into that of a spokesman for the city and of its governing regime, with the title of *sindico e referendario* and *miles curialis*, knight of the communal court.[64] Thus, in the period that witnessed the ascendancy of the Medici and their friends in politics and society, the commune's herald wrote and delivered most public speeches on behalf of the Florentine government, with the exception of addresses to the captains of the Florentine military forces, and to extremely distinguished foreign visitors, for example the emperor or the pope. Those speeches, along with the diplomatic letters sent by the Florentine state, were the prerogative of the humanist chancellor. The heralds were in charge of the general ceremonial for all visiting dignitaries;[65] as entertainers to the Signoria at table, they were also the constant companions of the leisure time of the Priors, sequestered in the palace of government for the duration of their office. Gene Brucker has noted the Signoria's particular concern for the financial security of its faithful *familia*. However, the "Canzona of Benuccio the barber, whom our Signoria often sent for, to enjoy his sonnets and ballads, and he could never obtain any payment from them, and so he wrote this *canzona* for them," suggests that they might also be exploited by their patrons.[66]

Prominent patricians including the Medici, and the Albizzi before them, developed close personal relationships with popular entertainers. The singers' poems in praise of individuals prominent in civic life, like the encomia written by Antonio di Meglio and Anselmo Calderoni at the death of Cosimo's brother Lorenzo in 1440, might have been spontaneous tributes to personal friends, commissions from a grateful Signoria to honor its eminent citizens, attempts to ingratiate themselves with the current regime, or a mixture of all of these. The opening lines of Antonio's poem to Lorenzo, emphasizing his civic virtue, suggest that it was commissioned by the Signoria in his honor. However, Calderoni was still in the service of the duke of Urbino when Lorenzo died, and his poem might well have been a tribute from Guido da Montefeltro, a close friend of Cosimo, and an ally and military captain of the forces of the Florentine commune.[67] Commensurate with the scope of their duties, a great number of poems from the pens of the heralds celebrate the commune's battles. A particularly notable example of this genre is Calderoni's salute to the victory of Florence at Anghiari in 1440 over an alliance of Florentine exiles of 1434 with various feudal lords of the Florentine *contado* and the Visconti of Milan. This was acknowledged as a victory of both the Medicean regime – the captains in the field were Neri Capponi and Bernardetto de' Medici – and of the Florentine state.[68] Encomia were written to honor many popes, princes, and *condottieri*, among them Eugenius IV, Francesco Sforza, and Niccolò da Tolentino.

The most popular genre was that of the *canzone morale* – the edifying song – with which the heralds were required to entertain the Priors while they dined. The subjects of such songs ranged from love through politics to devotion, their essential quality being the celebration of some virtuous act. The *canzoni morali* written and performed by Antonio di Meglio included verses "for the instruction of citizens in government," with incipits such as "O excellent fatherland of mine," amorous songs with hidden inscriptions to an admired woman such as Lucrezia de' Medici, a well-known poet and supporter of poets in her own right, and songs in praise "of the three virtues of the Mass and the birth of the Virgin."[69] During Antonio di Meglio's long tenure of the office of herald, there was little difference between the entertainment offered the Signoria in their palace, and that presented to the crowd in the *piazza*. Antonio sang frequently at San Martino, and the star performers there were often brought in to entertain the Priors. In addition to diverting members of a leading families while they resided as public officials in the palace of the Signoria, heralds, like other popular poets, often performed in the homes of these eminent patricians.

The barber-poet Burchiello was one of the few men to criticize the Medici publicly in 1433/34, and he did so in the high savage style of the street singers. At the time he was persecuted and exiled to Siena, but after a period of punishment and ostracism, this very talented poet was praised and sought out as an entertainer by Cosimo's family and their friends. In May 1441 Antonio di Lorenzo della Stufa wrote to Giovanni di Cosimo in Trebbio, full of the news of Maso Pitti's trip to the baths, taking with him "il Burchiello." When in 1445 Giovanni entertained an international group of ambassadors at his house in Rome, Burchiello was the star performer. The Medici and their friends lent him money. Roberto Martelli, head of the Rome branch of the bank, reported to Cosimo from Rome: "I carried your message to Burchiello, and he cannot shake the fever which is making him delirious. These poor men never lack for troubles. First he had no shop, and no money to open one; now that he has a shop he has the quartain fever. He cannot produce sonnets this way." Indeed the barber-poet died shortly thereafter, at the age of forty-four; the Medici family mourned his death, and had his sonnets transcribed in two fine manuscripts for their collection.[70]

When the Medici gave a dinner at Careggi to honor young Galeazzo Maria Sforza, son of the duke of Milan, on the occasion of his visit to Florence in 1459, another popular poet, Antonio di Guido, was chosen to provide the entertainment. The most active and prolific of these versatile Florentine performers in the 1450s, a mere boy when he first sang at San Martino around 1437, he had earned by mid-century an enormous reputation.[71] In a letter to his father, Galeazzo Maria described the impression the singer had made on him:

We heard a maestro Antonio sing, accompanying himself on the chitarra; I think if your Excellency does not know him you must at least have heard him spoken of . . . He sang with such dignity and style that the greatest poet or orator in the world, presented with such a task, would perhaps not have earned such praise for performing it . . . from now on I will be singing his praises, for indeed, his performance was such that everyone showed their wonder and admiration, and especially those who were most learned . . .

Ranking Antonio, the son of an unnamed artisan, with the greatest of Christian and classical poets, Galeazzo Maria continued: "I don't know if Lucan or Dante ever did anything more beautiful, combining so many ancient stories, the names of innumerable ancient Romans, fables, poets, and the names of all the muses . . . I was greatly impressed by him."[72] The apothecary Luca Landucci's equally enthusiastic praise of Antonio as "a singer of improvisations who has surpassed all others in that art" indicates the social breadth of the poet's appeal.[73]

CIVIC CULTURE AS POPULAR ENTERTAINMENT

Popular singers performed their extensive repertoires at various venues, but San Martino was particularly the place where politics became popular entertainment. It was also an important forum for the articulation of civic ideals common to the ruling group, over which Cosimo presided as the city's most influential politician and diplomat, and to the Florentine *popolo,* whose culture incorporated these same ideals. A phenomenally successful businessman and promoter of his family's prosperity and prestige, along with that of their friends and supporters, Cosimo was also a public man, a politician dedicated to the honor and greatness of the Florentine republic, the commune, and its *popolo.* His personal letters show that these commitments were central to Cosimo's identity, and they were appropriately expressed in his commissions of works of art incorporating civic symbols referring to issues of vital importance to the Florentine people.

In addition to being unusually literate, the Florentine populace was particularly politically self-conscious. Popular literature shows that the enthusiasm of the *popolo* for traditional civic ideals, however imperfectly these were realized, was part of the reality of Florentine political and social life. Among the books many Florentines owned, read, or borrowed was Giovanni Villani's *Cronica,* a history of Florence which incorporated the essential elements of the Florentine civic ethos.[74] Fundamental to this ethos was the legend of the Roman foundation of Florence, which was the basis of communal ideology in the thir-

teenth and fourteenth centuries, and became a cornerstone of humanist history in the fifteenth.[75] This legend was a powerful impetus to the incorporation of classical ideas, themes, and personalities into popular vernacular literature and art. Precedents from the Roman republic supported the communal ideal of broad citizen participation in government, and the primacy of public affairs over private loyalties, which led to factionalism, inimical to the common good.[76] These ideas were popularized and transmitted to ordinary Florentines through the use in schools of classical *exempla* of virtue, stressing the strong connection between personal and political virtue.[77] In the course of the fifteenth century public virtue became increasingly linked with the vision of many intensely religious Florentines of the city's divine mission to become an earthly Jerusalem.[78]

Dante's dramatic expression of these central civic themes in his epic poem, a genre that appealed strongly to the Florentine populace, helped to foster throughout Cosimo's lifetime a continuing and lively commitment to them. These ideas were also reinforced by the humanists' infusion of translations of Aristotelian texts into the civic culture of the early fifteenth century. In a much-quoted passage from the *Inferno,* the poet encounters his friend and teacher Brunetto Latini, through whom he voices an impassioned plea, drawing on Aristotelian notions of the *polis* (which had been central to the commune's origins and development in the twelfth and thirteenth centuries) for living Florentines to dedicate themselves to the virtuous civil life, of which Rome had become the epitome.[79] "Il bene del comune," interchangeably "the common good" and "the good of the commune," was the watchword of the *popolo* in the period when its government was paramount, and statesmen of the more restricted regimes of the quattrocento, among them Cosimo de' Medici, continued to invoke this ideal in public and in private.[80] The lines from Latini's *Tesoretto* — that citizens "All in common/ should pull on a rope/ of peace and good deeds,/ because there can be no saving/ a land or city broken by faction" — lived on in the memorable images of Ambrogio Lorenzetti's frescoes *Good and Bad Government* in Siena's civic hall; they were echoed by later poets and compilers of anthologies who continued to celebrate this ethos (fig. 15).[81]

Although the practical political role of the artisan guilds — including the barbers and shoemakers so prominent on the scenes of popular culture — had been marginalized in the electoral processes of the later fourteenth and early fifteenth centuries, the political ideology of the *primo popolo* remained fundamental to Florentine society and culture. Every two months, at the induction of a new group of the Priors who constituted the governing

15   Ambrogio Lorenzetti, *Allegory of Good Government*, detail, *c.*1340, Siena, Palazzo Pubblico, Sala dei Nove, north wall

magistracy, shops were closed and citizens came to listen to an oration on the goals of government, delivered in the vernacular on the platform (*ringhiera*) in front of the palace of the Signoria.[82] This performance, designed to keep the image of civic virtue before the incoming Priors, also served to remind the popular audience of its principles, reiterated in the towering shadow of the civic fortress, with its crenellated battlements displaying the brightly painted shields of the commune's chief corporations and the standard of the commune, the banner of *libertas* (fig. 16). Similar orations were delivered before a general audience of citizens when the commune's military captains received their batons of command, or when foreign ambassadors visited the city. These ceremonies were important opportunities not only for the regime to shape public opinion according to the exigencies of the day, but also for encouraging continuing popular commitment to the whole process of Florentine government, and to pride in the *patria*. Such pride is reflected in many popular poems; these, and the civic and patriotic speeches and protestations made on ceremonial occasions, were among the items most often repeated in recitations at San Martino, just as they continued to be copied and re-copied into personal notebooks.[83]

Particularly popular were poems and speeches that linked Florentine *libertas,* understood primarily as the city's independence from foreign conquest and rule, to her military might. This classical theme was famously

16   Florence, Palazzo Vecchio

elaborated by fifteenth-century humanists from Bruni to Machiavelli, but to the man in the street it translated basically into the vital role of *condottieri*, the leaders of mercenary troops, in preserving Florentine safety and prosperity.[84] Contemporary military captains were the preferred popular heroes. This fact illluminates the Florentine image of David; citizens saw him as the archetypal biblical warrior in the service of God and country, personifying the commune in its battles with foreign powers like the Visconti dukes of Milan. The figure of David appears in countless artistic commissions of the commune or its agencies, including those of the *opera* of the cathedral. Some images depict him more as the sage son of King Solomon or the author of the Psalms than as a warrior. However, it was David the slayer of

17   Andrea del Castagno, *The Youthful David*, painted leather parade shield, *c.*1450, Washington, National Gallery of Art, Widener Collection

Goliath who appeared, for example, on a parade shield painted by Castagno which was borne through the streets of Florence, most likely as part of a procession for the festival of the city's patron saint, John the Baptist (fig. 17).[85]

While Cosimo's intentions in commissioning from Donatello a bronze statue of David, the boy warrior, are endlessly debated, it is clear that this work and the matching bronze of Judith and Holofernes, whose story turns on the same theme, symbolize the winning of freedom from tyranny. This was a key element of Florentine civic ideology in the first half of the fifteenth century, as articulated by the city's humanist chancellors, by its leading citizens in council debates, and in popular verses recited in public places. Cosimo's view that no expense should be spared in a struggle for liberty, expressed in an advisory meeting to the Signoria, obviously represented that of the Florentine populace.[86] This is a vital contemporary context of Cosimo's commission of the bronze *David*, which would have been foremost in the minds of those who glimpsed the statue through the door to the Medici courtyard, as they passed by on the street, or waited on the benches outside for an audience with their patrons within.[87]

Although the Florentine populace valued peace, and the ensuing relief from punishing taxation, it did enjoy the drama and spectacle of war. The exploits of warriors, both past and present, were obviously as interesting to the Florentine in the street as they were to Cosimo de' Medici.[88] L'Altissimo once warned his audience at the beginning of a famous and lengthy performance, comprising ninety-four songs, of his *Reali*, the deeds of the royal houses of France, that "For these cruel horrors, and for the tumult/ you will weep, not only those listeners/ who customarily fill San Martino to the brim with their tears . . ." Nevertheless, so avid was his audience to hear of deeds of arms that they wore him out: "If I am not performing as I am wont,/ O gracious listeners, yes,/ it is because I have sung five whole days in a row,/ and even so, my Muse is not exhausted,/ but my body is worn out with the effort,/ so that my mind is confused./ But worthy listeners gathered here,/ I will make the effort to please you all."[89]

Most eagerly awaited by the audience at San Martino was the current news of war and politics, of military and diplomatic coups.[90] Popular poems particularly celebrated contemporary warriors, including the much-lauded Niccolò da Tolentino, captain of the Florentine forces in the Lucchese war in which Cosimo and his cousin Averardo played a leading part. When Cosimo was exiled by his enemies in 1433, Tolentino wanted to use his troops to rescue him by force; recounting these events a year later in 1434, just before the *condottiere* was assassinated in the Romagna, Cosimo described him as "my very great friend."[91] However, as the defender of Florentine commune against its enemies, Tolentino was also a great popular hero. The commune immortalized the career of its former servant in Castagno's fresco commissioned by the Arte della Lana on its behalf for the cathedral in the 1450s, just as Cosimo may have commissioned from Uccello the three enormous canvases depicting Tolentino's victory at San Romano for his own house. Chapter 12 will consider the relation between Tolentino's role in Florentine history, the artisan poems written in his praise, his depiction in public and private images, and Cosimo's role in civic defence.

After Tolentino's death in 1434, Francesco Sforza took his place in the popular imagination, as he did at the head of the city's troops, and as the most important of the Medici family's network of extra-Florentine friends and allies. Sforza's father, Muzio Attendolo, had perhaps prepared the ground for Francesco's popularity, since he took part in the celebrated conquest of Pisa for the Florentines in 1406, and subsequently captained the city's armies several more times before his death.[92] Leonardo Bruni's oration presenting Francesco Sforza with the captain's baton on behalf of the commune in 1435 became a staple of performances and compilations of popular literature, as did Niccolò Cieco's and Antonio di Meglio's sonnets in praise of Sforza's service to Florence, as he prepared to depart for the battlefield.[93] The man in the street continued to follow Sforza's fortunes over the next two decades as he fought, usually on the Florentine side, in numerous north Italian wars preceding the Peace of Lodi, chiefly negotiated by Cosimo and Sforza, in 1454.[94]

Sforza's military exploits were exciting, and he made a good hero, even in the herald Antonio di Meglio's somewhat stiff diplomatic verse. In a more playful and also very popular verse exchange with Giovanni di Maffeo da Barberino about their common appetites and illnesses, Sforza sprang more naturally to Antonio's mind: "However, I then applied myself so well in bed/ that not even Sforza ever performed better in the saddle than I,/ when I am not constrained by pain."[95] No major Florentine artistic commission, either of the commune or of Cosimo's, ever represented Sforza, probably because he was head of a foreign state after 1450, and it was safer to memorialize and exalt dead heroes than powerful men still living. Sforza survived Cosimo, who died in 1464, by two years. In the last years of Cosimo's life the decoration of the palace of the Medici bank in Milan, under the supervision of his sons Piero and Giovanni, did celebrate in portraits and emblems the close personal association between Cosimo's family and Francesco Sforza.[96]

However, the two men had long been closely associated in the popular mind. If Cosimo was the architect of their alliance, and of Florentine support of Milan, his was a popular choice. A decade before Francesco Sforza's son admired the performance of Antonio di Guido at Careggi, the crowd at San Martino acclaimed the news of his father's acquisition of the lordship of Milan. On 6 March 1450 Sforza sent an envoy with olive branch and trumpet in hand to announce his victory to the Signoria of Florence. This letter appears in several informal collections of popular literature, including one dedicated to praise of Sforza compiled by Michele del Giogante for presentation to the duke and for Piero de' Medici's personal pleasure. Sforza assured the Florentines that "As I have been up to this point a good son and servant of this lofty Signoria, so I intend to be now, and much more in the future, being always ready and willing and prepared to use my state, my troops, my people, my money, and my person for the benefit and preservation and increase of their state, as you may see indeed . . ."[97]

Sforza's victory and the popular response pleased Cosimo, who wrote the following day to his younger son Giovanni in Rome: "You will have heard that the Milanese have recognized the count as their lord and duke, which is excellent news. Here there has been a great celebration and demonstration because . . . everyone is happy about it . . . and because he has sent here letters full of such affection and love."[98] Michele del Giogante thought Sforza's letter so important to every Florentine "that it should be engraved forever on his heart," as in effect it was by its transcription into so many personal anthologies.[99]

The popular poets and their audience rejoiced at a triumph they considered as much Cosimo's as Sforza's, and of almost as much significance to Florence as to Milan. On 8 March 1450 two popular poems in praise of the new duke of Milan were performed at San Martino. One was written by Antonio di Guido,[100] the other by the shoemaker Antonio, "whose renditions are very charming."[101] Antonio's praise was literally in the form of a *lauda*: "O King of Heaven, such is your power,/ so great is your ineffable mercy,/ that the count has assumed by your grace/ such a lordship/ that will be of great benefit to our city./ *Gloria in excelsis Deo* we may sing/ for such a glorious event,/ that the heavens and the earth and the sea should celebrate/ for the health and happiness/ of you, Florence, which will cause you to triumph/ again, since you have the will and the means;/ writing to you he rejoices./ And further we should sing in great praise of Cosimo,/ for his deserved happiness." Cosimo's own poem assuring Sforza that "the world will be turned upside down before/ I should cease continually and always to love you,/ Francesco Sforza, above all else," was almost certainly written in response to Francesco's declaration of undying loyalty to Florence upon his triumph in 1450.[102]

LAY CONFRATERNITIES: AN EDUCATION IN RELIGIOUS TEXTS AND SYMBOLS

Performed in the street or at the table of the Signoria, celebrating love or war or salvation, popular poems and songs were always ultimately framed by moral and spiritual aspirations to which all orders of Florentines subscribed. Artisans were the most active and creative contributors to popular entertainment, but men of every rank enjoyed and supported this culture, and none more than Cosimo de' Medici and his friends. These same individuals and groups cooperated in shaping another vital manifestation of popular civic culture in which citizens of every sort participated – the lay confraternity. The confraternity was the setting in which most Florentines acquired an intimate knowledge of the basic texts and tenets of Christian belief and practice, which naturally determined the forms of devotional art.

Florentine confraternities multiplied in the wake of a wave of intense personal piety that swept Europe in the later fourteenth century, spawning such groups as the Bianchi in Italy, the followers of Wyclif in England and Hus in central Europe, and culminating in the sixteenth century in movements like the Devotio Moderna in the Netherlands, which preceded and presaged the Reformation. While popular religious feeling has been intensively studied in those areas of the north that witnessed epic battles between Catholics and Protestants for the souls of ordinary men, historians have until recently failed to recognize the importance of personal devotion in the centers of what was long seen as the secular civilization of Renaissance Italy.[103] Now numerous studies, particularly of lay confraternities, have shown that lay piety was a major force shaping the lives of ordinary Florentines, and the literary, visual, and performative culture they created.[104]

Confraternities played a vital role in the everyday experience of Renaissance Florentines. By the mid-fifteenth century, there were roughly a hundred such groups meeting in the city, almost twice as many at the end of the century as there had been at its beginning. Although it is impossible to calculate the precise numbers of each company's members, the evidence suggests that most Florentine men, and even some women, belonged to one or another confraternity.[105] These associations provided a form of social security for their members in the

confraternal obligations to assist one another through various charitable activities, including the burial of the dead,[106] but what they offered above all was the opportunity for laymen to participate actively in a corporate religious life. Meeting frequently, once or even several times a week, in small groups in their own chapels or oratories under the supervision of their clerical mentor or *correttore*, *confratelli* had direct and immediate access to the communion of the Mass and to confession.

Whereas at regular church services in Latin, laymen were essentially spectators, at confraternal meetings they said prayers and sang hymns as part of services based on the liturgy, but performed largely in the vernacular. They delivered sermons to their brethren, presented religious plays, and joined in penitential acts, particularly flagellation. In the activities of these brotherhoods, spiritual, social, educational, and expressive elements were blended. At meetings, members broke bread together and contracted obligations to mutual support and charity; they listened to readings of passages from the Scriptures and other sacred and devotional works, including spiritual letters, which were copied and circulated. Confraternal *laude* and sermons, as the main vehicles for lay spiritual self-expression, reveal the breadth and depth of many laypersons' knowledge of Scripture and doctrine, and their ability to relate it to pressing issues of Christian life, including questions of theology.[107]

Confraternities with different spiritual and social emphases attracted different memberships, and some companies catered to particular functional or occupational interests. However, Ronald Weissman's pioneering analysis of the membership lists of some of the major companies shows that in social and geographical terms confraternities generally crossed the boundaries that restricted other Florentine associations. While guilds divided men of different occupations, confraternities brought them together.

Of the 182 men who joined the penitential company of San Paolo in the first decade after its foundation in 1434, fifty were workers in the textile trade. Another eighteen were local tradesmen, many of them vendors of provisions, or engaged in various service occupations. Twelve of San Paolo's new members gave their occupations as masons, sculptors, metalworkers, painters, or as craftsmen otherwise engaged in the decorative arts or construction. Thirty-three described themselves as members of the major guilds; half a dozen were traders in the relatively lucrative commodities of fur and spices, thirteen were judges, notaries, or doctors of law or medicine, and fifteen belonged to the elite merchant guilds of wool and silk manufacturers and bankers.[108] By contrast with associations confined to a particular neighborhood, including the lineage, the *gonfalone*, and the parish, the members of many confraternities came from all over the city.[109] The inclusive character of confraternities, socially and geographically, and their basis in a shared spiritual life that transcended distinctions of wealth and status, made them a vital manifestation of the shared culture of the Florentine *popolo.*

Another essential finding of Weissman's research is that, contrary to a persistent (though unjustified) modern assumption, the merchants and tradesmen of this booming commercial city did not turn to religion as a last resort at the end of lives laid waste by ill-gotten gains.[110] In fact, lay piety was a way of life as much as a preparation for death. Most Florentines joined confraternities in their youth, and their subsequent attendance at meetings was determined less by age than by other social factors affecting them as their lives progressed.[111] Moreover, during the fifteenth century there was a meteoric rise in the popularity of confraternities for *fanciulli,* boys too young to join the adult associations.[112] Thus, Florentines were educated in devotion in spiritual brotherhoods from adolescence to senility.

"Specialist" brotherhoods included the boys' companies, craft associations, and the confraternities of Orsanmichele, the Misericordia, the Bigallo, and the Buonomini di San Martino, who in the tre- and quattrocento successively distributed charity to the needy beyond the ranks of their *confratelli.* Most confraternities were of two main types; either *laudesi* companies, dedicated literally to singing the praises of the Lord, or flagellants, preoccupied with penitence. This distinction has its basis in the Psalms; while disciplinary companies incorporated the penitential psalms into their services, the psalms of praise "resound with 'laudare.'"[113]

The *laudesi* companies were focused on the praise and the cult of the saints, and particularly of the Virgin Mary, which had its origins in the newly personal piety of the twelfth century. This Marian devotion, promoted most successfully by Saint Bernard of Clairvaux, gathered momentum along with the mendicant orders in the thirteenth century, and in Florence flourished in the early decades of Cosimo's lifetime, particularly in the city's dozen or so major *laudesi* confraternities. At confraternal services, members sang *laude* to the glory of God and his saints, and offered prayers for their own and the community's salvation, and for the commemoration of the dead. In the early fifteenth century they performed the first sacred plays, which became an important feature of Florence's distinctive civic and spiritual life, and grew to involve the entire community.[114]

Large numbers of Florentines were encouraged to read, write, and participate in the performance of *laude* in

Italian, not only in churches, but also at various public venues like San Martino, and in civic and sacred ceremonies.[115] Consequently, the *laudesi* confraternities came to play a substantial role in the education of the Florentine community. The major companies of Saint Peter Martyr, Saint Zenobius, Orsanmichele, Saint Agnes and Saint Frediano all conducted schools to teach the *laude* to singers, including young boys.[116] An inventory of the company of San Zanobi included among the devotional objects in its chapel a number of boards bearing lists of indulgences, festivals, and incipits, the opening lines of lauds.[117]

In confraternal worship and performance, music, poetry, and images combined to create a richly textured spiritual experience.[118] Members of the confraternities continued to do their own singing at ordinary services well into the fifteenth century, although there was an increasing tendency, especially with the growing popularity of polyphony, to employ more professional singers. Almost all of these, like the entertainers at secular venues, were artisans.[119] By mid-century ordinary services had given way in most companies to a preoccupation with the fulfilment of bequests for the commemoration of the dead, and above all to the celebration in public processions of the major feasts of the liturgical year, and those of the confraternity's patron saints.[120] Most groups apparently had a formal repertoire of *laude,* corresponding to the days of the liturgical year; these songs were copied into large, often elaborately illuminated books for festal services, and smaller, less ornate ones for everyday use.

Unfortunately, most of these books were lost or destroyed in the suppression of the confraternities in the seventeenth century; very few musical scores survive, and almost never in conjunction with the texts. As a result, little is known of the fundamental musical aspect of *laudesi* experience. It is clear that lyrics were sung to familiar melodies, many of them secular; hence the expression "cantasi come" – sung like – a particular well-known work. Poems on the Passion, and rhymed vernacular paraphrases of the Gospels, in the form of sonnets and *canzoni,* were particularly popular.[121] Some texts were preserved in copies, along with an enormous number of spiritual poems and songs modeled on the confraternal *lauda,* and written by laymen (and women) as well as clerics, for their personal pleasure and for the edification of their friends. They are conserved in the personal compilations surveyed in chapter 6, either as selected items of a more general *zibaldone* of popular literature, or occasionally as separate books; small, compact, easily portable volumes with dog-eared pages that testify to their frequent use, as their owners carried them to church or to other venues for performances.[122] These spiritual songs

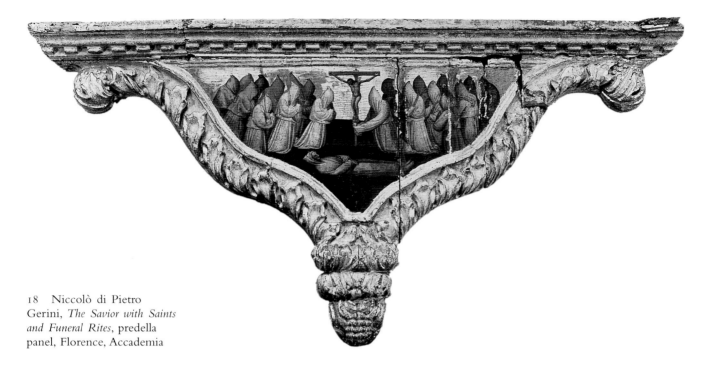

18   Niccolò di Pietro
Gerini, *The Savior with Saints
and Funeral Rites*, predella
panel, Florence, Accademia

and poems are incomparable testimony to how Renaissance Christians felt and thought about God, and about their own relation to Him.

Confraternities also commissioned images to stimulate and give form to prayer and contemplation. In view of their devotion to Marian cults, images of the Madonna of Mercy were among the most popular, and Piero della Francesca's representation of this theme for the confraternity of the Misericordia in his native Borgo Sansepolcro is an unusually sophisticated example of the genre (fig. 49).[123] Only a small proportion of the visual representations made for confraternities have survived, since many took rather ephemeral forms, particularly banners or wax figures made to be carried in processions such as the celebration for the feastday of Saint John the Baptist, patron saint of Florence.[124] An altarpiece by Gerini refers at once to the brothers' sympathetic identification with Christ's Passion, and the confraternal responsibility of burying the dead; in the predella panel, hooded *confratelli* hold up a crucifix before a corpse (fig. 18). Paolo di Stefano, "the Slave," painted a similar scene for the predella of a tabernacle containing an image of the Madonna and Child. The workshop of Neri di Bicci and his father Lorenzo received commissions from the company of Jesus the Pilgrim to depict in the tribuna of its oratory the figures of a pilgrim and flagellants, and a fresco of the Virgin with Saints Anthony and Leonard for the company of San Frediano, which met in the Oltrarno

church of the same name.[125] Occasional evidence survives of lost images made for confraternal chapels or oratories; there is an eighteenth-century copy of the frescoes of Ambrogio Baldesi and Niccolò di Piero Gerini for the facade of the Bigallo, depicting the confraternity's dispensation of charity to the poor.[126]

Confraternities sometimes became the guardians of images believed to have miraculous powers, giving rise to cults that contributed to the popularity and influence of the confraternity. Duccio's great *Madonna*, which hung in the church of Santa Maria Novella, was commissioned by the *laudesi* of Saint Peter Martyr, who met there toward the end of the thirteenth century. A hundred years later, the most important confraternal image was the Madonna of Orsanmichele (fig. 32); her popularity was overtaken in the fifteenth century by that of the Virgin Annunciate, in the church of that name dedicated to her devotion and patronized by Cosimo and Piero de' Medici.[127] Also prominent in the life of the Florentine community was the confraternal fresco in the cathedral, of the Madonna and Child, Our Lady "most full of grace," which was moved to the west wall, south of the main door, around 1397, to accommodate the large crowds who came to adore her.[128]

On the day that he joined the flagellant company of Jesus the Pilgrim, Domenico Pollini wrote in his diary: "I record that this day, the 5th of August 1453, in the name of God, I was accepted into the company of the Pilgrim . . . I thank Omnipotent God who prepares the way for me to do penance for my sins, and so I pray Him to make me persevere in good and fruitful penitence, so that at my end He may by His mercy accept me into eternal life."[129] In the course of the fifteenth century, an age long associated with a worldly sophistication similar to that of classical civilization, the numbers of flagellant companies increased dramatically. In the decades between 1440 and 1460, the period of most of Cosimo de' Medici's commissions of works of art, half of all pious confraternities were pentitential.[130]

While the *laudesi* celebrated their human and humane saints, the purpose of the *disciplinati*, as their statutes announced, was to "commemorate the Passion of our lord Jesus Christ crucified."[131] The *laudesi* occupied themselves with public praise, the disciplinary companies with private contemplation. Both offered their members an opportunity to participate in a corporate religious life, and an education in sacred and devotional texts; in both the veneration of insipiring images played a major part. The figure of Saint Jerome, who became an emblem of fifteenth-century lay piety, fused the images of learning and penitence in the eyes of many patrons of devotional images, including the Medici family.[132] But whereas the *laudesi* sang of penitence and death mainly in the Lament and Passion poems for Holy Week, the *disciplinati* continuously emphasized these themes. Portions of the liturgy, often translated into the vernacular, were transcribed into private compilations to be committed to memory.[133] The officials of the disciplinary company were responsible for instructing its members in the provisions of its statutes and in the commandments, which were frequently read to members.[134]

Disciplinati services were grouped in pairs, taking place either twice a fortnight or twice a month. The first service was occupied with flagellation and penitence, the second with correction and prayer, mirroring the liturgical cycle,[135] which "passed from the days of suffering to the days of joy; the capture, trial, and crucifixion of Christ, to his resurrection and ascension." The penitential psalms were central to these services. As the statutes prescribed,

> the lights are put out, and then they say the Stanza of the Passion. And then a few words are said on the brevity of life, accompanied by an exhortation to the brothers to do well. Then a period of silence follows, after which the brothers whip themselves for the space of time it takes to say five Pater Nosters and Ave Marias. Then they say more prayers followed by the psalm *Miserere Mei Deus* or the *De Profundis Clamavi* [I cried out from the depths] . . . And then they get

dressed again and . . . sing more psalms, lauds, and hymns.[136]

The intensity of this experience is captured in a poem by a member of a prominent Medicean family, Giovanni Ciai. It concludes: "I repent with all my heart that I am filled/ with carnal sin. And so,/ with a whip I often scourge my flanks,/ whence my blood, spilling forth, pools/ around me as I kneel on the ground,/ and mixes with my many tears./ I, who am such a vile worm, have unleashed/ pride against God and my neighbor,/ in which deservedly I am interred."[137]

In their mortifications, members of the penitential confraternities were inspired by the desire to commemorate Christ's Crucifixion, and to imitate his Passion; thus they focused particularly on the Eucharist, the Last Supper, and the veneration of the cross.[138] The Maundy Thursday ceremonies incorporated a literal enactment of the verses from John 13: 1–16, which describe the events of the Last Supper. The passage from the Gospel was read aloud during the ceremony, and guided members as they went through their imitation of Christ's actions.[139] Their feelings as they did so were articulated in a sermon by the layman Poliziano, Lorenzo de' Medici's literary companion and friend, speaking to the members of the confraternity of the Magi: "I invite you to cry with Him in His bitter pain, to become His disconsolate widow: to see His grieving mother, whose heart was pierced with a knife; to cry together with the stones, the sun, with heaven and earth, with all the elements, with the whole world over His incomparable torment . . ."[140] Giovanni Dominici and Archbishop Antoninus exhorted their Florentine flock to practice such devotions with the aid of images;[141] Fra Angelico's frescoes for the cells of the convent of San Marco commissioned by Cosimo de' Medici are among the finest such images of this vein of devotion, and include a Crucifixion for Cosimo's cell in the laybrothers' corridor that is a visual embodiment of the feeling expressed in Poliziano's words.[142]

Cosimo and the confraternities

Florentines feared any large gathering of citizens, even of the members of a single lineage, which might unite to promote a particular cause, thereby transgressing the ideal that each man should vote on the affairs of the republic "according to his individual conscience." The increasing tension between various interest groups within the *reggimento* in the years leading up to the confrontation between members of the Albizzi and Medici factions led to the passing in 1419 and 1426 of laws "contra scandalosos" (against disturbers of the peace), which temporarily suspended the meetings of religious confraternities as potential hotbeds of political intrigue. The *laudesi* company that met in San Lorenzo, the neighborhood church of the Medici family and of many of their partisans, was permanently suppressed in 1432, and its property turned over to the church.[143] After 1434 there is clear evidence that the Medici family did exploit the confraternities as places to promote and consolidate partisan support. Their friends reported to Cosimo and his sons on the secret proceedings of religious companies, particularly concerning elections, which the Medici then took steps to influence.[144]

By the same token, the commitment of members of a confraternity to "assist their brothers in all things," including elections for communal office,[145] naturally led the Medicean regime to fear that its political opponents too might seek a base in the confraternities; also, it seems, with good reason. The Dominican Giovanni Cairoli commented in the 1470s on confraternities of those opposed to the "horrible slavery" of the Medici faction.[146] Whenever the regime experienced or feared a challenge to its authority it passed laws suppressing confraternities or prohibiting citizens eligible to hold major civic offices from attending them. These laws were never uniformly enforced, and were allowed to lapse after some time, but the fear that confraternal obligations to mutual aid could foster conspiracies persisted.[147]

Development and change in religious confraternities was closely related to changes in the Medici regime, and to an increase in the family's authority as the century progressed. By the early 1470s Lorenzo de' Medici was conspicuous as the most influential figure in several of the city's most important companies.[148] His domination of the confraternal scene is often projected back into the lifetime of his grandfather Cosimo, whose relation to these groups was much more ambivalent, as well as simply less clear. Cosimo was a promoter and participant of confraternities in several inseparable capacities; as a Christian, as a citizen, and as the leader of a partisan regime.

The confraternities were the point where Christian charity met intelligent civic provision for the poor, which helped to keep the peace. Such provision was rationalized in the fifteenth century, along with many other areas of government, and the structure and emphases of confraternities changed markedly as a result. Cosimo's initiative in founding the Buonomini di San Martino may have been an attempt to increase his support among artisan families who were its chief beneficiaries; it was also a contribution to the stability of the city, and to the salvation of his own soul. These aims are clearly apparent in the founding document of 1442, which describes the group's dedication to the glory of God and his saints and earthly representatives, to the needs of the shamed poor, and to the salvation of the souls of those responsible for acts of mercy, linking these firmly to "the present famine and the multitude of poor in the city and district of Florence."[149]

The Signoria's amalgamation of the trecento company of the Bigallo with the more affluent Misericordia in 1425, when Cosimo was one of the Bigallo captains, may similarly be adduced as one more example of the assertion of Medici power over the corporate institutions of the commune, or it may be viewed as part of a general trend toward greater efficiency in the provision of charity, in which Florence was admired as an innovator throughout Europe. The abandonment of the oratory of the Bigallo, on the corner of Via Calzaiuoli and Piazza Orsanmichele, may also have been part of the clean-up of the city center in the first decades of the century, along with other communal and guild projects, and the rebuilding of the Parte Guelfa palace. Howard Saalman observed that the interests of the Bigallo came to dominate the merged body in which Cosimo and later his sons were prominent. The cult of Tobias, patron of the Misericordia, was subordinated to that of Saint Peter Martyr, patron saint of the Bigallo and of Cosimo's elder son Piero, born a decade before the merger, in confraternal representations and celebrations. Saalman also noted that less of the organization's income was spent on the care of orphans and the dowering of deserving girls, the traditional concerns of the Misericordia, and more on the building, maintenance, and administration of the various *spedali* or hospitals under the aegis of the Bigallo.

This change of emphasis accorded with a general trend noted by John Henderson, which was due to a new awareness of the problem of indigence, and as Katherine Park has shown, part of a Florentine rationalization of the provision of care for the sick and destitute which was emulated in many other Italian cities.[150] The story of Tobias and the Angel became increasingly popular with both confraternities and merchants in the second half of the fifteenth century, and indeed from 1465 to 1485 more paintings depicting this legend were produced in Florence than all other Italian centers combined.[151] However, the cult of Fra Pietro da Verona, a Dominican who preached in the ancient piazza of Santa Maria Novella from 1243 to 1245, was involved in the foundation of the order of the Servi di Maria, and became Saint Peter Martyr, was of enormous significance to both clergy and laity in quattrocento Florence. The saint's finger was one of the most precious relics conserved in the church of Santa Maria Novella, headquarters of the lay confraternity bearing his name, which was one of the most important devotional companies in the city.[152]

Cosimo's role in the promotion of confraternities was certainly part of a lifetime of participation in the charitable and devotional life of the community, which was the duty of every Christian citizen (not to say the leading citizen of a Christian community with a special spiritual mission), as well as an investment in personal salvation of the sort that underlay most charitable bequests in this period.[153] His patronage of ecclesiastical institutions was larger in scale, but not different in kind from that of other prominent citizens, and if it also served to increase his support as a partisan leader, he had attained that position by virtue of the ready identification of his interests with those of his supporters in every area of their experience, of which the religious, and particularly the confraternal, was of supreme importance.[154]

Cosimo surrounded himself with spiritual advisors in the vanguard of the increasingly demanding devotional spirit that dominated the confraternities. When he undertook the rebuilding of the convent and church of San Marco, he made particular provision for the confraternities that met there; the companies of the Purification, of the Magi, and that of the weavers.[155] He himself was a prominent member of the confraternity of the Magi, which was apparently an influential model for the Platonic Academy, where with Medici support Marsilio Ficino dispensed spiritual as well as philosophical advice.[156] The *laude* of Cosimo's daughter-in-law Lucrezia gave voice to his family's intense personal piety, and Cosimo's commissions of works of art constitute a progressive revelation of the importance of his own devotional life and its effect upon his patronage.

In Cosimo's lifetime, there was a crescendo of religious concern at all social levels. The sermons of such popular preachers as Dominici and San Bernardino were major occasions in the minds of the Florentine public. The wine-merchant Bartolomeo del Corazza took note in his diary of Dominici's sermons delivered in May 1406;[157] San Bernardino's sermons in Florence for Easter 1425 were attended by huge crowds and carefully transcribed for future reference. In the 1430s and 1440s Cosimo's secretary, Ser Alesso Pelli, sought out the most compelling preachers to persuade them to come and address a Florentine audience.[158] Membership in a confraternity reinforced the messages of religious leaders, encouraging and even obliging the laity to master not only the fundamentals of doctrine and worship, but to familiarize themselves with its finer points, and to enquire actively into the nature of their faith. A high proportion of Feo Belcari's output of sacred poems at mid-century consisted of answers in verse to doctrinal questions, on which a large number of patricians and artisans, including the Medici, sought his advice.[159] Popular poets, such as the

shoemaker Giovanni Ciai and the silk merchant Matteo Scambrilla, wrote verses in praise of the Virgin, and in contemplation of the cross.[160] Francesco d'Altobianco degli Alberti's *Moralis Chantilena* was set to music by Antonio Squarcialupi, the greatest composer and musical perfomer of his age.[161]

All this activity gives the lie to suggestions that when Florentines came to look at images of sacred scenes and events, which comprised the bulk of Cosimo's artistic commissions, they brought to them only the most rudimentary religious education, barely enabling them to decipher the attributes of saints or to grasp the symbolic significance of elements of the pictorial narrative.[162] The educated audience of devotional images included not only a ruling group that was far larger than that of any other European polity of comparable size, but an even larger class of artisans able and eager to respond to them.

SACRED PLAYS AND CIVIC CEREMONIES: TRANSLATING TEXTS INTO IMAGES

If the rich and varied content of popular culture equipped ordinary Florentines to appreciate the sophisticated themes of much of the greatest Florentine art, its performative aspects accustomed them to translating ideas into images.[163] San Martino was the customary venue for performances of popular poems and songs, but in many other places, in churches, the chapels of lay religious confraternities, and in the streets of the city, its civic spaces and monuments, through sacred plays and patriotic and devotional processions, Florentines acted out their civic and Christian identity.[164]

The San Giovanni celebrations

An outstanding opportunity for this dramatization was the annual celebration of the feast day of John the Baptist, the city's patron saint. On 24 June, and the days immediately preceding, the city set forth on display everything it stood for. The festivities resembled a live enactment of the themes of literature in praise of cities, like Bonvesin della Riva's description of the wealth of thirteenth-century Milan, or Giovanni Villani's account of the assets of fourteenth-century Florence. The silk merchant Gregorio Dati, writing his *History of Florence* in the early fifteenth century, took a tone very similar to theirs in response to an imaginary interlocutor who asked him to describe the "great festival of San Giovanni Battista, without equal anywhere in the world."[165]

Dati began by explaining that the festival was the culmination of a succession of celebratory feasts in the liturgical calendar, spread across the spring and early summer months of May and June. The feast of San Zanobi, former bishop of Florence and a patron of the city and its cathedral, occurred on 25 May; the movable feasts of these months were the Ascension, Pentecost, Holy Trinity, and Corpus Christi; in 1452 this last also happened to fall on 24 June.[166] To these liturgical feasts the laity added their own joyous celebrations: "whoever had a wedding banquet to give, or another such feast, arranged it at this time, to do honor to the festival." Preparations for the ceremonies, including a horse-race, the *palio*, began two months in advance with the making of banners, costumes, and elaborate wax offerings. Young men and women especially participated, with "hearts full of happiness, dancing, playing and singing, at banquets and jousts and other joyful games, so it seemed that no one had anything else to do at this time up to the eve of San Giovanni."

Simple, rather secular pride and pleasure predominate in the events described by Dati and his immediate contemporaries, who dwelt at length on the rites of spring and youth, and on the lavish display of the products of Florentine trade and manufacture that preceded the procession. "Early in the morning all the guildsmen made a show outside their shops of all their riches, ornaments, and jewels. How many cloths of gold and silk they displayed, enough to clothe ten kingdoms; how many jewels of gold and silver, and hangings and painted panels, and marvellous carvings and goods connected with the business of arms . . ."[167] The display so pleasing to Florentines also characterized Dati's description of "the procession of all the clerics, priests, monks, and friars, from a great number of orders: with so many relics of saints, they amounted to a show of infinite devotion, apart from the marvellous richness of their adornments, for they wore the richest robes that the world offers, garments of gold and silk and embroidered with designs." Following the clergy came members of the lay confraternities, "dressed like angels, playing instruments of every sort and singing marvellously; presenting the most beautiful representations of the saints and their relics to which they did honor."

From this brief description of the confraternities' performances, Dati passed to the afternoon, when richly dressed citizens, assembled under the banners of their districts (*gonfaloni*), walked in procession to the baptistery with their offerings of candles. On the day of the 24th the scene shifted to the seat of government. The piazza outside the palace of the Signoria was curtained off and transformed into a theater accommodating a hundred "towers" made of wood, paper, and wax, painted and elaborately decorated. Each one contained figures of soldiers, horsemen, and dancing girls, made to revolve continually by men stationed inside the towers. When the Priors appeared before the crowd, on the *ringhiera* in front of the palace, they were presented with tributes by representatives of the cities subject to Florentine authority – Pisa, Arezzo, Pistoia, Volterra, Cortona – in a lively demonstration of the commune's imperialist power. Then a great parade of celebrants made offerings at the baptistery, including the wax towers which next day were hung in the church until the following year's feast.[168] After dinner came the climax of the festivities, a horse race from the meadow near Ognissanti, along the Corso to the Porta San Pier Maggiore at the eastern extreme of the city, whence the winner was borne around the city in a triumphal chariot.[169] Dati's final observation concerned the float of the *palio* which was the prize; made of fine velvet, lined with ermine and mink, fringed with silk and fine gold and covered with gold brocade, it "cost six hundred florins or more."

Half a century later Matteo Palmieri's description of the *festa* of San Giovanni in his *Ricordi* noted some major changes in the proceedings, wrought partly in response to Archbishop Antoninus's reforms. Writing in 1454, Palmieri observed that the celebrations were henceforth to occupy four whole days, beginning on the 21st with the *mostra*, the display of the city's wealth in its wares. The 22nd was set aside for "the procession of all the floats [of the confraternities]." These were the focus of his account. Each consisted of a *tableau vivant* of a major event of sacred history, a sort of mobile sacred play; the Battle of the Angels and the Fall of Lucifer, the Creation and Fall of Adam and Eve, Moses and the prophets and sibyls who predicted the birth of Christ, the Annunciation, his Nativity, and the journey of the Magi to adore him, "with a retinue of more than two hundred horses magnificently adorned . . . The Passion and the Entombment are omitted, since they don't seem appropriate to a festival." There followed the representations of limbo and paradise, Christ's Assumption, the quick and the dead, and the Day of Judgment at the end of the world, when. all souls were consigned to heaven or hell. While the companies' tableaux amounted to an even more lavish and ingenious form of display than the traditional towers with their revolving wax figures, they also represented Florentines' growing conviction that the city's wealth consisted not only in the abundance of its worldly produce, but also in its citizens' rich sense of sacred history. They underlined the prominent place of devotion in civic tradition, and fixed in the popular mind the essential elements of the major subjects of sacred art.[170]

Popular comment on public ceremonies

A wealth of ceremony and ritual enriched the quotidian experience of the residents of Florence. From the early fifteenth century, as noted, the heralds of the Signoria and other members of the Priors' *familia* were responsible for orchestrating the festivities accompanying the visits of eminent guests like the pope, the emperor, and various other foreign princes and military leaders. The ceremonial book kept by the herald from the middle of the century documents an increasingly elaborate protocol governing the decoration of the streets through which the guest's entourage might process, and the details of his reception; which dignitaries would go to meet him, and how far within or outside the city they would go.[171] The diaries and poems of merchants and artisans from at least the late trecento show that citizens saw these civic ceremonies as important events in their lives, observing and describing them carefully. This is particularly true of the frequent visits of popes, the celebration of holy days, and the consecration of churches, perhaps because these events were of primary importance to the viewer's own faith and its observance.

The diary of the wine merchant Bartolomeo del Corazza, compiled between 1405 and 1438, is full of descriptions of such ceremonies. The extreme precision of his accounts shows that the man in the street had an excellent eye for visual effects, and was very conscious of the symbolic significance of what he saw.[172] Like most Florentines who recorded the events of this period, Del Corazza saw his city's conquest of Pisa in 1406 as one of the highlights of his age. He recorded how on 9 October, "with the grace of the most high God," representatives of the Florentine war magistracy took possession of the town, and a messenger returned to Florence bearing a large olive branch. "There was great celebration and rejoicing, and one by one the shops were closed. There were so many people in the streets that one could not pass through them on horseback." That night there were fireworks, and on Sunday a solemn mass was celebrated in the baptistery, dedicated to the city's patron. Shops were to remain closed Monday through Wednesday, and all citizens were ordered to attend a "solemn and devout procession." The third morning, "all the clergy gathered around the image of the Madonna of Impruneta, robed and carrying reliquaries, and the companies with their banners . . . It was the richest and most beautiful procession that I have ever seen; mass was said in Santa Liperata [the cathedral], with great solemnity: Fra Giovanni Domenici preached the sermon."[173]

On 14 October there was a joust in the piazza in front of the Church of Santa Croce; Del Corazza described the

19   Donatello, *Saint George*, Florence, Bargello

prizes as "a velvet covered helmet surmounted by an enamelled decoration" and a gold-plated silver lion with a silver olive branch in his hand, mounted on "a very elaborately decorated helmet." There were more than eighteen competitors, mounted on horses covered with cloths bearing beautiful and rich devices, and the horses' caparisons were of velvet embroidered with silver and pearls. "The chief prize," recorded the wine merchant, "went to one of Sforza's soldiers; and truly he carried himself like a St. George."[174]

Del Corazza was writing a decade before Donatello's marble statue for the armorers' niche at Orsanmichele became the archetype of Saint George in Florentine eyes (fig. 19). The grace of this figure captured the imagination of all Florence, particularly of those who admired a virile beauty, like the young man said to have found in Donatello's statue an ideal substitute for a live beloved. However, the figure of Saint George, symbol of the victory of good over evil, had long been a feature of the commune's celebratory procession for the feastday of Saint John the Baptist. It was probably his envisaging of the familiar processional figure that led Del Corazza to recognize in a living man the qualities or attributes of the image of the archetypal warrior saint.[175]

Sacre rappresentazioni

Del Corazza's diary shows how many opportunities there were for the creation in Florentine minds of a subtle relationship, perceived in terms of forms and symbolism, between formal works of art and the visual experience of the ephemeral action of public processions and plays, in which the fifteenth-century Florentine viewer was steeped. This relationship is naturally most complex and most elusive from the point of view of the artist, from which it is usually approached, giving rise to an appropriate stress on the very different representational traditions and problems involved in the production of theater and the production of art.[176]

From the point of view of the audience of these media, their relation may be simpler, and closer. Descriptions of processions and performances such as Del Corazza's, records of workshops such as Neri di Bicci's, and inventories of personal possessions such as Cosimo de' Medici's document the production and collection of banners, edifices, costumes, and ceremonial armor bearing images similar to those created in the more permanent media of painting or sculpture.[177] Often permanent images, like that of the Madonna of Impruneta, or the church paraphernalia and reliquaries displayed at Corpus Christi, were themselves the focus of processions.[178] Sometimes it seems that artists produced works for such occasions with the same characteristics as their more formal commissions for churches and chapels, like the processional shield painted by Castagno around 1450. The image of David that it bore was one of some formal and symbolic sophistication. Based on an ingeniously adapted quotation from classical sculpture, it incorporated an implied narrative in a single perspectival view, an essay in the depiction of movement through an object designed to be seen in motion (fig. 17).[179]

Sacre rappresentazioni relied heavily on images, both visual and verbal. The performances staged in processions, in particular, depended largely on visual effects. In Feo Belcari's plays words and actions, the latter preserved in stage directions, combined to evoke the image.[180] Many performance images appear to be drawn from the general repertoire on which artists also relied; a few mirror particular works of art, confirming that the inventio of major artists so compelled the public imagination that their works came to define the shape of certain sacred scenes, and the appropriate attributes and character of their participants. At the same time the evidence of public response to sacred plays suggests strongly that performance traditions shaped many men's perceptions of the great events of Christian history, and they may also have inspired elements of artists' representations of these events.[181]

The journey of the Magi to Bethlehem to adore the newborn Christ offered splendid opportunities for visual display. Florentines were obviously impressed by the spectacular presentations of the confraternity of the Magi, which met at San Marco. Benozzo Gozzoli probably drew on the effects of these spectacles when he came to represent the Magi in his frescoes for the Medici chapel.[182] Every five years or so, with the blessing and financial support of the commune, the company staged a special celebration on the feast of Epiphany. The story of the Magi unfolded in procession from the palace of the Signoria, signifying Jerusalem and the seat of Herod's secular authority, to Bethlehem, at San Marco.

The Magi were also prominent in the annual Saint John's Day parade. In the entry in his personal chronicle for 1428, Paolo di Matteo Pietrobuoni took particular note of this procession, of the marvelously decorated holy relics borne by the priests, and how "the company of the Magi of San Marco honored the cult with many rich and grand things." Among them was a king "whose dress could not possibly have been more ornate, and behind this king, in the middle of a cloud, there was a little boy about three years old, swaddled, but with his hands kept free, and in one he held a live goldfinch, and with the other he made such natural gestures that a man of forty could not have done better."[183] This is precisely the image of the Christ child in so many devotional paintings; in one hand holding the bird that served as a reminder of his future sacrifice, symbolizing the flight of his soul after death; with the other hand caressing his mother, or greeting or blessing the spectator. Particularly familiar and accessible examples of this image in art were the miracle-working image in the tabernacle in Orsanmichele (fig. 35), and the sculpture of the Madonna and Child for the niche on its south facade, belonging to the guild of physicians and apothecaries. Later in the century, the image of a swaddled Christ was to be reinforced in Florentine visual memory in the form of Andrea della Robbia's terracotta medallions of infants, set in the roundels of the facade of the foundling hospital built by Brunelleschi in the Piazza Santissima Annunziata.[184]

The mid-fifteenth century saw the rise of a new type of sacra rappresentazione with a much stronger textual tradition. The first of these plays, and long the most popular, were written by Feo Belcari, and the earliest documented performance was the representation in 1449, in the church of Santa Maria Maddalena in Cestello, of the Day of Judgment, which Belcari wrote in collaboration with the herald Antonio di Meglio. Although there are no descriptions of the visual impact of their staging to compare with descriptions of the traditional Annunciation, Ascension, and Pentecost plays, the spoken texts of

Belcari's works strongly evoke the visual, in accordance with his view, expressed in the opening lines of his most popular play, *Abraam e Isaac*, that "The eye is called the first of all the gates/ through which the intellect may learn and taste."[185]

Belcari's images of sacred events clearly drew on representations in painting and sculpture with which he was familiar, and which he re-presented in words and actions to his Florentine audience. For example, the passage from the Bible recounting the story of Abraham and Isaac, describes how, just as Abraham drew the knife to slay his son in obedience to God's command, "the angel of the Lord cried out to him from heaven . . . and said: Do not lift your hand against your son."[186] Half a century before Belcari composed his drama the plaques submitted to the Calimala guild in the public competition for the coveted commission for the new bronze doors for the baptistery, in which the two leading contestants were Ghiberti and Brunelleschi, had engraved this scene indelibly upon Florentine minds. After their public viewing, both plaques were preserved, and Brunelleschi's was eventually set in the front of the altar in the old sacristy at San Lorenzo, commissioned by Cosimo's father as his burial chapel. Naturally, both the sculptors translated the angel's command into more compelling visual terms by depicting him hovering near at Abraham's hand. But it was Brunelleschi who with incomparable dramatic immediacy had him seize Abraham's arm at the crucial moment, and it is this gesture that is captured in Belcari's stage directions: "Abraham grasps Isaac's hair with his left hand and raises his right to strike him with the knife and kill him, but an angel appears and seizes Abraham's right hand saying, 'Abraham, Abraham, do not lift your hand/against Isaac so just and pious . . .'" (fig. 20).[187]

Before the rise of this new, more verbal form of *sacra rappresentazione*, the plays staged annually from the 1430s by *laudesi* confraternities, representing key events in the unfolding of the Christian revelation, were renowned for their spectacular visual and technical effects. Among the most famous were the representation of the Annunciation by the company of the Annunciation in the church of San Felice in Piazza, the Ascension performed by the company of Sant' Agnese at the Carmine, and the Pentecost play put on by the company of Santa Maria delle Laude "and of the Holy Spirit" nicknamed Pippione, the "big pigeon," at Santo Spirito.[188]

Most of the delegations to the council of the Eastern and Western churches held in Florence in 1439 arrived in time to take part in the spring liturgical festivities. The fullest and most vivid accounts that exist of the Annunciation and Ascension plays come from the pen of the Russian bishop Abram of Souzdal, on whom they made

20 Brunelleschi, *Abraham and Isaac*, competition plaque for the baptistery doors, Florence, Bargello

as powerful an impression as they did on the Florentine audience he described, as the curtain rose, or rather parted, at San Felice or Santissima Annunziata, the larger church to which the Annunciation play may have been transferred for this occasion. The scene was one made familiar by countless painters, but in the sacred drama the Word was literally made Flesh, incarnating the Christian mysteries only described in Scripture and liturgy:[189]

> When the time came for the spectacle, many people gathered from everywhere for the great and wonderful event, in the hope of seeing the *rappresentazione*, so that a great multitude of people filled the church. For a while they stood in silence, looking up at the scene prepared on the rood screen in the middle of the church. After a while the curtains and hangings are swept open and everybody can see the person acting the part of the pure Virgin Mary, sitting on the magnificent seat beside the bed. It is easy to see, it is a wonderful thing to contemplate, it is full of joy and absolutely ineffable.[190]

Like the figures of philosophy in the trecento plaques depicting the arts on the base of Giotto's bell-tower, or

21   Model of the Ascension play set on the rood screen of Santa Maria del Carmine, reconstructed by Cesare Lisi

22   Model of the machinery for the Annunciation play in San Felice in Piazza, reconstructed by Cesare Lisi

the saints on the bronze doors commissioned by Cosimo and cast by Donatello around this time for the old sacristy at San Lorenzo (figs. 80 and 81), the prophets of the Annunciation play "began to argue with each other, and then each one tore up his scroll and threw it away for being false. But then they leaped up and seized other scrolls and coming forward to the edge of the rood screen they bowed to each other and each one examined the other's scroll and pointed at it, hitting it with his hand and arguing." Then the curtains opened on the tribuna above, transformed into a tableau of heaven with God the Father at its center, surrounded by five hundred lights and by his court of angels, from whence descended, by means of an elaborate system of ropes and pulleys, the angel Gabriel; "his gown was snow white and decorated with gold; just as we see the heavenly angels depicted in paintings." Looking up, the Virgin "saw the Father enthroned in great might and magnificence blessing her from above. When she saw him, she folded her hands on her breast and said to him humbly: 'Behold the handmaiden of the Lord'." Finally, in a burst of light and sound and flame from the fireworks he set off, the angel re-ascended to heaven.

Souzdal praised this spectacle for its high degree of "artifice" or "craft," a quality even more notable in the representation of the Ascension by the company of Sant'Agnese, since the *ingegni*, or stage machinery, was apparently designed by Brunelleschi, who had erected the cathedral cupola without armature, but with the aid of ingenious machines he had devised specially for its construction.[191] The Russian bishop declared that he had never seen anything like the moving parts of the stage setting at the Carmine, also erected on the rood screen of the church, but much more elaborate than at San Felice or Santissima Annunziata (figs. 21 and 22). It consisted of a stone castle with towers and ramparts on the left side of the rood screen, representing Jerusalem, and on the other a hill, representing the Mount of Olives. Above the high altar was a chamber set in the wall, called Heaven, and in front of its opening, God the Father was suspended; around him rotated the planets, and a disc with life-sized painted figures of angels revolved. This image appears in a number of paintings of the period, among them Botticelli's *Mystic Nativity* and Neri di Bicci's *Coronation of the Virgin* (fig. 23).[192]

"When the church is full and silence reigns," Souzdal wrote, "all eyes turn to the rood screen and what is arranged there." The *dramatis personae* make their entrance; Christ, accompanied by angels, the Virgin and Saint Mary Magdalen, and the apostles, barefoot, "and dressed as we see them painted in holy pictures; some have beards, others not, just as they were in reality." Reality and representation merge in the bishop's view as the climax of the spectacle approaches. Proceeding toward the mountain, Jesus ascends the ladder; then with "a peal of thunder, Christ appears on the Mount, and all turn their eyes upwards to see Heaven open, and God the Father floating above, suspended in the air in wondrous fashion, in a great light, which spreads from innumerable lamps; the little boys who represent the heavenly Powers move around him to the sounds of deafening music and sweet singing; the big painted angels on the discs move in the shape of a circle so that they seem to be alive."

> From Heaven . . . there descends on seven ropes an exceedingly beautiful and ingeniously constructed cloud . . . When the cloud is half-way down, Jesus takes two great golden keys and says to Peter: "You are Peter and on this rock I shall build my church and the gates of Hell shall not prevail against it" . . . And when he has blessed him and handed him the keys, he rises up with the aid of seven ropes in the direction of the cloud, blessing Mary and the Apostles with his hand. It is a marvellous sight and without equal; the ropes are set in motion by a very clever and invisible pulley system, so that the person who represents Jesus seems really to rise up by himself, and he reaches a great height without wobbling . . . The cloud is lit up by a multitude of lights which shed their splendour everywhere. But Jesus goes higher and higher, accompanied by the two angels, and soon he steps out next to God the Father, the music ceases, and it grows dark . . . the curtain is drawn back from the place which represents the highest heaven, and there is light again.[193]

Irina Danilova has pointed out that in the original Russian, the word for "spectacle" signified to Bishop Souzdal both representation and vision, at once "marvelous" and "miraculous"; it is the spectator's vision that transforms man-made images into the image of the divine.[194] For artists, painted and sculpted images presented very different possibilities and problems from theatrical performances, in terms of such major quattrocento concerns as the representation of narrative, and of the unity of time and space.[195] The audience of art and theater, accustomed to the imaginative exercises recommended by their spiritual advisors in the contemplation of sacred images, constantly compared painted figures in plays and pictures to living men who seemed to breathe and speak, and living men in plays to the perfection of painted figures; art and theater were similarly the visible manifestations of spiritual forms, elided in their imaginations.

In a more practical and pedestrian sense, these different media were linked in the persons of the many

23 Neri di Bicci, *Coronation of the Virgin*, Baltimore, Walters Art Gallery

artists involved in theatrical representations. Brunelleschi was not the only artist whose *ingegno*, skill or ingenuity, contributed to the effect of the Ascension play, though he was by far the most remarkable and original. Neri di Bicci, in his own workshop the translator and popularizer of images in forms made famous by Lippi and Angelico, was like his father, Bicci di Lorenzo, a captain of the company of Sant'Agnese, and played a leading role in the organization of its festivities.[196] Masolino, Masaccio's partner in painting the frescoes that adorned the chapel of the Brancacci family in the church of the Carmine, painted the clouds for the Ascension play performed there, which the Russian bishop found so remarkable. Piero del Massaio, a painter close to the Medici circle who made the first iconographical maps of mid-century Florence, also contributed to the Carmine decorations. The Magi company enjoyed the services of Michelozzo; in addition to designing decorations for the Medici family's private festivities, he was also one of the *festaiuoli* of the confraternity of the Magi in 1446, along with Cosimo de' Medici.[197]

Indeed Cosimo and his friends were leading participants in the pageants of the company of the Magi. He regularly took part in the company's processions in costume, as we learn from his wife Contessina's note concerning a friend's gift of a fur coat to replace his old cloth of gold cloak, "when we need to do the Magi celebrations again."[198] In 1439 his brother Lorenzo set their household factotum Ser Alesso searching for costumes for the festivities of the working-class *potenza* which met at the Armenian church near the Medici houses; it was the Armenians who put on a representation in the cathedral of the death and resurrection of Christ in honor of the Emperor Frederick's visit in 1452.[199] Cosimo was also a *festaiuolo* for Sant'Agnese's performance of the Ascension play in 1442, and gave alms to help pay for its production.[200] The boys' company of the Purification, which presented the *Prodigal Son* play, written by Piero di Mariano Muzi, a pursemaker, met in San Marco. When Cosimo had the church renovated, they were accommodated in an oratory of their own, for which in 1461 they commissioned with Cosimo's aid an altarpiece by Benozzo Gozzoli.[201] On the completion of the church building in June 1444 Cosimo arranged a solemn procession and a ceremony at which his secretary Ser Alesso Pelli presented the company with the keys to its oratory. According to the confraternal statutes, his reward for this was that "the company should pray to God to grant Cosimo grace for this good deed, to be credited to him in eternal life."[202]

Historians have been generally disinclined to believe that this was all the reward Cosimo expected from his support of confraternities and their performances. As Paola Ventrone has observed, the new more verbal and didactic type of sacred play written by Feo Belcari and others, including the Florentine herald Antonio di Meglio, was generated in a cultural circle dominated by Cosimo and Archbishop Antoninus. These men clearly cooperated to encourage Florentine devotion and its public display in ritual and theater, which obviously pleased the populace; it also contributed to the distinction of the city in the eyes of foreigners such as the emperor or the participants of the church council in 1439, which in turn reflected well on Cosimo de' Medici, Florence's leading citizen. Medici participation in confraternities and their performances also created and reinforced personal relationships, which were the basis of partisanship, and the Medici family's political influence. But to represent all this as a strategy of politico-cultural propaganda is going too far.

Belcari's works were moral and admonitory, concerned with clarifying matters of doctrine; naturally Antoninus supported their performance as part of his program for the religious education of the laity, to stamp out the errors of belief with which his *Summa Theologica* was so preoccupied. Belcari dedicated a number of his works to his Medici patrons, which no doubt helped to promote

the plays, and his own standing in Cosimo's circle, but his preeminence as a spiritual advisor throughout the city made him much more than a Medici "client." Antoninus was a notably strong and steadfast critic and opponent of Medici partisan manipulation; to describe him as "foremost among those who waited on Cosimo's 'court'" distorts the role of both men in Florentine society, as well as their relation to one another. It also misrepresents the role of religion in Florentine culture, and in the personal lives of its citizens, among them the members of the Medici family.[203]

The evolution of Medici power, as of Florentine culture, was a continuing and complex process. Belcari's new style of devotional drama appeared in the very last decade of Cosimo's life. After his death, and particularly after 1470, when the leadership of the Medici family had passed to his grandson Lorenzo, sacred plays, like many other ceremonies and rituals, became more obviously politicized; indeed the plays written by the talented Lorenzo himself helped to transform the genre.[204] No doubt the seeds of this growth of Medici influence over sacred theater were sown many years earlier, but no evidence has yet been offered for the assumption that *sacre rappresentazioni* in Cosimo's day were "a vehicle of Medici propaganda."[205] The *sacre rappresentazioni* of Cosimo's lifetime continued to rest upon a deep-rooted foundation of popular devotion, and an artisan tradition of musical and poetic performance.

Such traditions were not the creation of Cosimo and his friends; they were rather products of, and participants in these traditions. As leaders of Florentine society they influenced the direction of cultural development, but talk of Medici promotion of popular culture as "indoctrination" or "propaganda" raises the same sort of questions as suggestions that the ruling class was "manipulated" by its humanist teachers. How did the content of culture supported by the Medici diverge from what it might otherwise have been, and how could it have increased Medici authority in the very specific arena of political action? Renaissance Florence was a society in which men of every social rank, as an examination of the huge corpus of personal collections of didactic literature reveals, were preoccupied with their own and others' education for various purposes, personal and pious as much as political.

Around the middle of the fifteenth century a growing professionalism in many areas, partly, but by no means entirely the result of Medicean policies in government, began to marginalize traditional corporate groups based on neighborhood, guild, and craft associations.[206] In the course of Cosimo's lifetime amateur participation in various activities, from communal office-holding through warfare and diplomacy to the performance of public ritual, began to give way for a variety of reasons before the rise of professionals. The history of music in Florence in the fourteenth and fifteenth centuries highlights some paradoxes inherent in this development. Blake Wilson observed that polyphony was introduced into Florence by the singers of the *laudesi* companies at the baptistery and the cathedral, who boasted "the oldest written musical tradition in Western sociey to thrive outside the elite circles of aristocracy and clergy." Like so many other manifestations of popular culture, the Florentine experience in music breaks down the assumed equation between elite and written, popular and oral traditions. Musical performances owed their high standards largely to an artisan pride in craft, but the increasing appeal of the polyphonic music they presented eventually put a premium on a level of education to which part-time artisan performers could not aspire.[207] Artistic imperatives, rather than political pressures, were the essential agents of change.

Change in many areas gathered real momentum only after Cosimo's death, perhaps because Cosimo himself had been a product of the late trecento world in which many citizens and corporate groups continued to compete for the pleasure of participating in the city's political, social, and cultural life. In seeking out the forces that shaped Cosimo, his commissions of works of art, the artists who

worked for him, and their audience, it is important to focus on the situation that obtained in his lifetime, however obscure, rather than reading back into that period the conditions of a later age, when the picture is clearer, but substantially altered.

Public processions and plays staged in churches were performed, like the devotional paintings and sculptures made to decorate their chapels, "for the honor and glory of God and the city," as the Signoria explained.[208] Like so much of public and popular culture in the first half of the fifteenth century, these performances were paid for by subsidies from the commune, for the benefit of all its citizens, and by donations from individuals of every rank. They were devised largely by artisans, the members of the *laudesi* confraternities who acted the parts and provided music and song, and by artists who achieved their spectacular decorative and technical effects.[209] Their rapt audience consisted of the entire city, or as much of it as the venues could accommodate. These performances vividly demonstrate the enthusiasm of a Florentine audience for the visual representation of sophisticated and symbolic religious themes like the Incarnation, Ascension, and Transfiguration, represented in Cosimo de' Medici's commissions. They also illustrate the active participation of Cosimo and his friends in the creation and viewing of this common Florentine visual culture.

24   Gregorio Dati, *Sfera*, Florence, Biblioteca Laurenziana, Conv. Soppr. 109, fol. 67r

VI

COMPILATIONS AND THE CORPUS OF POPULAR TEXTS

This city is dedicated to commerce, literature and leisure.

Cosimo de' Medici.[1]

This chapter surveys the wealth of vernacular books and scrapbooks, often copied in their owners' hands, which belonged to men (and even a few women) on every rung of the social ladder of literate citizens, from Cosimo and Piero de' Medici to soapmakers and saddlewrights. Drawing on an extensive repertoire of devotional, antique, and civic literature, these informal personal books preserved the poetry, prose, songs, and snippets of valued information that comprised popular culture. More than many texts well known to historians by mere chance, they reveal what most Florentines were actually reading and hearing in the first half of the fifteenth century. The corpus of texts identified in these manuscripts coincides closely with the repertoire of popular entertainers at San Martino, and with the literary sources of Cosimo's artistic commissions. The works described below shaped the interests and ideas of Florence's major patron of art, and of his audience. They indicate that the vast majority of Christian, classical, political, or literary themes expressed in works of art, particularly those commissioned by the Medici, were not obscure or esoteric, as has often been argued, but eminently familiar to a wide audience of Florentines from their favorite literature.

VERNACULAR SCRAPBOOKS: "OH YOU WHO READ ME, PLEASE DON'T MISLAY ME, FOR I AM THE GUIDE AND COMPANION OF HIM WHO COPIED ME"

The account that follows is based on the study of a few hundred of the thousands of informal books and manuscripts conserved in three major libraries of Florence — the Biblioteca Nazionale, the Riccardiana, and the Laurenziana.[2] Many of these, and perhaps the most interesting, are anthologies of extracts from a variety of texts. These compilations are cognate to the printed chapbooks or commonplace books widely circulated throughout Europe in the early modern centuries. But whereas works later produced *en masse* by printers may well have created popular culture as much as reflecting it, the earlier manuscripts were compiled individually by their owners, or at the owner's request. In seventeenth-century Amsterdam anthologies of the sayings of the apostles, and examples of the wisdom of Solomon from Proverbs, Ecclesiastes, and Ecclesiasticus, were specially published for the instruction of inmates of houses of correction. In fifteenth-century Florence some of the most remarkable and original collections of popular literature were compiled by their owners to pass the time during a stint in prison.[3]

The quintessential compilation is a personal selection from a common cultural repertoire. The importance of these books for understanding popular culture and its relevance to artistic patronage lies in the individual and collective choices they represent.[4] Giovanni Rucellai described his compilation, one of the most sophisticated examples of the genre, as a *zibaldone*, defining it as "a salad of many herbs"; a closer look at his book and his patronage oeuvre in chapter 15 shows how effectively they illuminate one another.[5]

There are certainly "families" of *zibaldoni*. Some leading collectors of popular literature or professional copyists reproduced roughly the same collections several times over, for different friends or clients. A particularly popular set of selections might circulate among a group of friends, each of whom made his own copy. But no two books were precisely the same, because the choices they represented were personal to the owner or compiler. He drew on a living tradition that grew and was modified as new works were written and performed, and as the relevance or significance of traditional texts altered, along with the changing circumstances of individual collectors and the world in which they lived.

In their form and function, compilations were related to the distinctive Florentine genre of the mercantile and familial *ricordo*, with its strong emphasis on counting and accounting. They were inspired by a similar desire to lay down oral traditions in writing before they were lost. Michele del Giogante, compiler of a number of the most interesting collections, was an accountant who kept account of popular culture by transcribing the texts of performances he attended. Benedetto Dei, who described himself as "a good writer, and good on the abacus, and a good accountant," wrote several books filled with lists and numbers – of friends, enemies, places he had been, things he had, and things he lacked, the landmarks of Florence (churches, piazzas, palaces), and the songs and poems he liked best and had memorized.[6] His *Cronica*, the product of a positive obsession with record, documents the interaction of memory, performance, and the written word. Along with his frequent direct address of "my readers and listeners," the structure and rhythm of Dei's prose, and the repetition of key phrases – "somma delle somme," "correvano gli anni" – indicate that his lists of the attributes of his city were meant to be recited and memorized.[7]

This chapter concludes with a discussion of the Florentine concern with the cultivation of memory, as essential to the activation of knowledge. Behind much of the vast Florentine literature of private record, the account books, *prioriste* (lists of those who had held highest civic office), and family genealogies, forms which shaded into one another and eventually into a new conception of the writing of history exemplified in the works of Machiavelli and Guicciardini, was the powerful impulse of the Florentine to transmit the wisdom he had taken pains to acquire to his sons and heirs, as valuable a part of their patrimony as the wealth he had worked to accumulate.[8] This was often the stated aim of copyists and compilers of collections of literature, especially those from the higher social echelons, for whom the maintenance of the traditions of their lineage was of vital social and political, as well as personal importance. As one man wrote on the flyleaf of his book, a classic collection of moral, devotional, civic, and antique works, "This book belongs to Lodovico d'Antonio [notary] of the Signoria, and to his descendants."[9]

The last entry in Lodovico's book was a familiar caution to those who should come after: "Delight and pleasure in the desires of the flesh soon pass away,/ but sin remains for all eternity, and so do our faults and evil deeds."[10] Inscriptions written on the flyleaves of these books, as they passed from one generation to another, testify to the realization of their authors' aim to provide moral instruction to heirs. One of the longer chains of

familial succession can be traced in a volume belonging to the Arrighi, a vulgarization of the fourth *Decade* of Livy. This, along with many similar classical texts, was embraced like a Christian work as a guide to the virtue that was part of the family's spiritual patrimony.[11] The first entry on the flyleaf reads: "This book belongs to me, Simone d'Alessandro di Iacopo Arrighi, and I wrote it in my own hand in the year 1451 and 1452." It passed eventually to

> Simon Girolamo di Giovambatista di Simone di Bartolomeo, who is the heir of the aforesaid Simone di Alessandro di Iacopo Arrighi, who wrote this history in his own hand in the year 1451; and today as I write this we are in the year of our Lord 1584; and the said Simone di Girolamo was born in the year 1583, on the 15th of June, at 19½ hours or thereabouts, a Wednesday. God grant him the grace to be nourished, grow and live in fear of Him and of the most glorious ever Virgin mother Mary.[12]

Indeed the primary purpose of transcribing these vernacular books, apart from the personal pleasure and entertainment they afforded, seems to have been to collect expert information and advice on the lessons of life. One copyist explained in his notebook the uses of literacy: "Those who are literate should concern themselves with good examples; those written here are all truths gained from experience of true and good *exempla*."[13] Mario Guiducci transcribed a number of Iacopo da Voragine's legends of the saints, "thus soothing and minimizing my tribulations."[14] Lionardo di Giovanni Carnesecchi wrote in his *zibaldone*,

> This little book of mine will bring you utility as well as delight, and these two things are necessary to the community of men for diverse ends . . . The delight of speaking and hearing and seeing things that make one glad . . . both soul and body seek these from the world and from God . . . To inspire mercy with the composition and memorization especially of works on hell, on Jesus Christ and all the martyrs who followed him along the path of various torments, so that the fruit may please you more than the flowers . . . Read this book . . . and have regard to the meaning and purpose of speech . . . not only for the consolation and delight of the ears, but with your mind and thought and the labor of your soul . . . so that all things may be perfected and receive the grace of the infinite and powerful God . . . for often the meanest words carry the weight of his majesty . . .[15]

The declaration: "This book belongs to Francesco di Albizzo di Luca di Ser Albizzo," appears no less than eight times on the flyleaf of his book, betraying perhaps an anxiety also suggested in the selection of its contents. His first entry was Boethius's *Consolation*:

> the book dealing with the misery of life . . . This book is called the book of consolation and understanding because it gives comfort to those who feel themselves weighed down by the tribulations of the world, and gives advice to those who have taken the wrong path, to humble themselves and take a new direction, considering their evil state and the sad condition to which they have abandoned themselves in this world, and it gives comfort and strength to the virtuous, to improve themselves through the hope of knowing how to conduct themselves.[16]

Francesco's book also included a number of Feo Belcari's poems of spiritual advice to various correspondents, and his *sacra rappresentazione* of the story of Abraham and Isaac, which turns on paternal love and filial obedience, and was dedicated to Giovanni de' Medici, in a verse expressing the hope that his "glory and honor and fame" would equal that of his father Cosimo. Francesco degli Albizzi's copies of Belcari's works are preceded by a comment apparently addressed to his own son: "I will begin [what follows] in the name of God, for every good and perfect gift proceeds from the father of light. My paternal charity takes such love and delight in your filial subjection to me as I can scarcely convey to you . . . wishing that in time I may inform you, my son, as to the customs you should follow and of the love . . . of God and of the following and other things, and teach you the nature of the virtuous life . . ."[17]

Although Francesco was not among the members of the Albizzi family exiled after the return of the Medici, most of his lineage was damaged by these events. He probably saw in the plight of Boethius, a man whose prospects were also ruined by his political enemies, some parallels with his own life. Compilers tended to select works with obvious relevance to themselves and their own situation; readers related literature to their personal feelings, needs, and experience.[18] Volumes belonging to Rosello Roselli, and to several members of the Benci family, consisting largely of Petrarch's verse, divided the poems into those written before, or after Laura's death. The comments of these copyists suggest they saw the poet not as a long-dead writer, but as a living man with experiences of love and loss similar to their own. Benci concluded his book with a prayer for Petrarch's soul: "Here end the sonnets, songs, madrigals, and other works written by the venerable poet Messer Francesco Petrarca of Florence whose soul may God rest in peace, amen; thanks be to God."[19]

Most anthologists took on the lengthy task of copying their *zibaldoni* themselves.[20] Giovanni Tolosini required over a year to complete his book;[21] others were written rather faster. A vernacular version of Flavius's *Judaic Wars* is inscribed: "This book belongs to Zanobi di Zanobi di Lionardo Bartolini, who copied it in his own hand for himself and his own reading; I began it on 29 August 1465, and finished on 12 October."[22] Zanobi was the grandson of the Lionardo Bartolini at whose house Piero de' Medici first met the great popular performer of San Martino, Antonio di Guido.[23] The shoemaker Giovanni di Zanobi Amadory, "Florentine citizen," did not say how long it took him to finish his selection of works by the church fathers which he began to write in his own hand in 1445,[24] but the manuscript of the soapmaker Antonio di Guido Berti, transcribed with enormous care and enhanced by colored initials, was a labor of love that took more than two years.[25]

Because copying a book represented a large investment of time, many men compiled their collections during a period of enforced leisure, away from the normal demands of home, family, and business. The flyleaf of one which appropriately included several works of Boccaccio, whose *Decameron* supposedly owed its existence to the country sojourn of a group of young Florentines fleeing the plague, reads: "Written in my own hand by Girolamo Morelli during the plague of 1449, for my own pleasure."[26] Several citizens wrote, designed, or had their notaries transcribe compilations while they were serving Florence abroad as Podestà or Captains of the smaller cities of the Florentine dominion.[27] Others, among them Giovanni Cavalcanti, who wrote his famous chronicle to relieve his frustrations during a spell in the Stinche,[28] composed or transcribed edifying literature to sustain their spirits while imprisoned for debt or political crimes. They included a man who signed himself simply "Scharsella in Stinche,"[29] Giuliano de' Ricci,[30] Iacopo di Cocco-Donati,[31] and Andrea de' Medici, who completed his book in prison on 18 June 1468.[32]

Books were viewed as life's moral guides; often they and their authors were seen as literal companions, as Dante saw Virgil. Giuliano di Giovanni de' Bardi wrote on the first page of his book, "O you who read me, please don't mislay me, for I am the guide and companion of him who copied me."[33] Handbooks of liturgical offices and collections of *laude*, used particularly by members of confraternities at their meetings, were compact enough for their owners to carry around with them, and their dog-eared pages testify to constant use. Feo Belcari's notebook, containing a vulgarization of book 1 of Lucan and of the "deeds of Caesar," together with Fazio degli Uberti's poems, was small, slim, and much thumbed, as

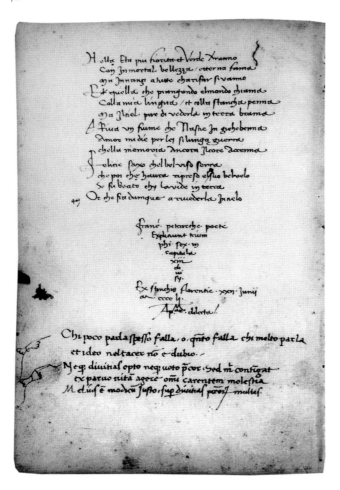

25   Florence, Biblioteca Riccardiana 1133, fol. 36v

pardoned for my sighs./ He who has not love in his heart does not understand it:/ let him be beautiful, lighthearted and in love/ who wants to be my reader."[35]

Books were also communications, a means of sharing wisdom amongst a circle of friends, as well as conveying it to descendants. Using marginal comments and pointing hands to draw attention to particular passages, and directly addressing putative readers, compilers carried on a running commentary on the works they selected. Michele del Giogante, in his collection for Piero de' Medici celebrating Sforza's victory in 1450, sketched elaborate pointing hands in elegant gloves to signal ideas he considered of especial importance "to you, my Piero (fig. 25)."[36] Often selections in *zibaldoni* were introduced by rubrics noting the circumstances in which the work was written or performed, the compiler's judgment on it, and his reasons for including it in his book. These rubrics are enormously valuable, not just as evidence of the provenance of works, but also of how they were chosen, read, and assimilated by their audience.

Some owners advertised the riches of their collections in an index. As one announced: "Written and contained in here is the letter Seneca sent to Lucillus, king of Sicily, on behalf of the Romans, and here are the four cardinal virtues, and here is the Evangel of Saint John, and here are some moral sayings, and here is *Geta and Birria*, and here are the sayings of Aesop painted, along with Birria. Here also is the treatise on nobility by Bonaccorso di Montemagno," described as dealing with "Roman things." The book of Saint John the Evangelist appears in the particularly attractive, accessible, and memorable form

26   Florence, Biblioteca Riccardiana 1591, fol. 84r

might be expected of the *quaderno* of a professional singer.[34] Other scrapbooks, decorated almost as lavishly as volumes for a formal library, were positively seductive. A poem copied in several manuscripts, describing the joy of opening a book by Petrarch, and reminiscent of Filarete's description of Piero de' Medici gloating over his treasure of illuminated manuscripts, is introduced thus: "By Bernardo della Casa, written in front of a work of Petrarch's, the book being richly decorated. First see what I am, you who read me,/ and how beautiful I am; gaze at me bit by bit,/ my letters and pages decorated with gold,/ and look if you have seen my equal in beauty./ And then in my first sonnet read/ what I speak of in . . . rhyme;/ and if you want to understand the art of love by experience,/ choose, my Bernardo, to ask me about it./ Beautiful, as you see, I go in search/ of the beautiful companionship of a servant of love,/ that I may be

of verse, translated by Francesco d'Altobiancho degli Alberti, "a noble and most learned man"; the owner oberved that he had trancribed it "because it is full of grace and truth."[37]

The compiler of this catholic collection inserted himself into the literary landscape of his scrapbook with a large scrawled comment, boldly impressed upon its pages, at the beginning and end of almost every piece (fig. 26). Opposite *Geta and Birria* he added in his rough round hand: "things 144 but well done by a learned and worthy man." The "144" seems to signify "rather risqué," which would be appropriate to this cheerfully ribald work. Writers customarily used code for explicit references to sexual behavior, as they did for political and military secrets.[38] Notably the risqué tone of *Geta and Birria* did not offend its moralizing copyist, who at the end of the last line of "Ave Queen of the heavens, O pious Virgin," a *canzone morale* by Antonio di Meglio which he introduced as "a beautiful poem by an excellent man," concluded: "Here ends this moral song, amen . . . I recommend and devote myself to her, amen, amen." This clearly much-prized compilation is one of the most attractively illustrated, as its owner observed with satisfaction: "the beautiful sayings of Aesop along with his beautiful stories are painted showing Aesop and illustrating the stories of these beautiful tales and sayings."[39]

While many Florentines of varying social status took pleasure and pride in making their own compilations, quite a few patricians left the tiresome task of copying to others. However, the work of these copyists, often notaries and artisans, was not merely servile.[40] Owners might indicate what they wanted included, but in the business of collecting and promulgating useful knowledge, copyists were clearly also bearers of wisdom to their friends or patrons. In the 1430s or 1440s Rosello Roselli, a crony of Giovanni de' Medici, Cosimo's younger son, compiled a book of his own and others' poems for Adovardo di Giovanni Portinari, whose father, uncles, brother, and sons were all factors or managers of the Medici bank. It enshrined the literature that mattered to him so well that he was apparently reluctant to part with it. It was eventually agreed that Rosello would keep the book for a while, and then give it to Giovanni "when he wants it."[41] On the other hand, Giovanni di Tommaso Lapi noted in the front of his book of "chanzoni morali" (edifying poems) that it was written by "a friend . . . and the copying cost nothing because he gave it to me."[42]

Gifts of course served as tributes in Florence, as in many traditional societies.[43] The gift of books is associated also with the didactic social role of many men of middling rank, especially notaries and clergymen, who were both friends of the Medici and members of Florence's charitable and devotional "establishment."[44] Michele del Giogante referred to his anthology in praise of Sforza as the book "I made, that is, more wrote than made, at the behest of my more than superior Piero di Cosimo de' Medici," and prefaced it with this dedicatory poem: "O famed Piero mine, son of Cosimo,/ this little book of mine I call yours,/ because "il Forte" [his own nickname] made it with your advice,/ dreaming, as you know, of serving you in some small way,/ with certain additions which you will see that I make,/ having spent some time gathering them we know where,/ that source from which these things always sprang,/ known to all the crowd, if not to the Count [Sforza]." Putting the best of San Martino's popular culture at his patron's disposal, Michele used this compilation, as he did his letters to Piero, to instruct him in matters of morals and duty.[45]

Ser Baldovino Baldovini honed his notarial skills in the service of such distinguished churchmen as the abbot of San Pancrazio and Antoninus, archbishop of Florence; his protocols are full of acts drawn up on their behalf. He then turned the moral fervor and knowledge of devotional literature fostered by this professional environment to the benefit of the laity. Baldovini made at least two compilations tailored to the special spiritual needs and interests of their Florentine recipients. One of his devotional compilations focusing on Florentine religious traditions contained his own treatise on the Holy Cross; the life of Beata Umiltà of Faenza, "most devoted to the Holy Cross," whose letters to her followers at the hospital of Santa Maria Nuova appear frequently in *zibaldoni*; the life of Santa Margherita, "nun of the monastery of San Giovanni of Faenza," and the life of San Giovanni Gualberto, founder of the Camaldolensians and much revered at San Pancrazio. Piero de' Medici's *tempietto* at San Miniato was built to house his relics.[46]

Another such compilation, comprising the lives of two holy women of Florence, the Beata Umiltà and Santa Umiliana de' Cerchi, and Baldovino's own treatise "Of the Sacrament of the Altar," he presented to the Rucellai family, his eminent neighbors in the district of the Red Lion. The book was offered for their instruction and dedicated to them in affection and admiration. It may have been presented first to Giovanni, the greatest patron of the arts in Florence after Cosimo. Certainly it soon passed to his son Pandolfo, who was to take orders. The dedication reveals that it was written in response to the original owner's request: "You have many times asked me, a man without language and limited in every way, to write something for you about the marvellous works of God manifested in our time, and of the doctrine and *exempla* of those who in our region have been sanctified."[47]

Giovanni Betti presented to "Gismondo d'Agnolo di Lorenzo di Meser Andrea della [Stufa], citizen of Florence," a decorated copy of his poems – "a thousand fantasies [*ghiribizi*]" – which included his own rhymed recommendation of himself to Piero de' Medici. Its last three lines were picked out in bright blue ink: "And I of base intellect/ beg you graciously to accept [this gift], and me your faithful servant, Giovanni Betti." Betti's reuse in a book for Sigismondo della Stufa, whose patronymics refer to the long line of his ancestors devoted to the Medici, of a dedicatory verse originally addressed to Piero, emphasized the Medicean connections of donor and recipient which bound them to one another, and drew particularly flattering attention to the closeness of the Della Stufa to Cosimo and his sons. Betti seems to have done this in somewhat the same spirit as Medici supporters commissioned pictures of the Journey of the Magi containing portraits of the Medici and of themselves.[48]

Many books were compiled progressively, like diaries, over a long period of time. Suddenly a new hand appears, the son's replacing his father's,[49] or a new owner takes up where the previous one left off. Although entries of the early fifteenth century can be broadly distinguished by their handwriting from those made toward its end, there are not many *zibaldoni* for which all the segments subsequently cobbled together can be dated precisely. Of this sample, only nine books were made before 1400, and another sixty-six between 1400 and Cosimo's death in the mid-1460s.[50] In other cases there are signatures and dates referring to particular entries which suggest a *terminus post* or *ante quem* for the collection. A small but significant proportion of the total number of books can be ascribed to a particular owner or copyist.[51] However, the *zibaldone* was by definition a cumulative product. New quires were added and bound in with the old, during the fifteenth century and later.[52] Owners saw themselves as joined by these books to the past, as links in a chain of previous readers, like the one who noted, "This book was written in the year 1416, and now it is the 1677th year, of the seventeenth century."[53]

We can trace the movements of some collections which owners sold to their contemporaries.[54] Bernardo d'Andrea di Lippaccio de' Bardi, a member of the family which supplied the Medici bank with so many partners and general managers, noted that he bought his book, containing a copy of Boccaccio's *Il Filocolo,* from Bernardo del Nero. The original owner had been Nero di Filippo del Nero; the Neri were also close friends and associates of Cosimo de' Medici.[55] Another of Boccaccio's works, *La Teseide,* was copied by Giovanni Tolosini in 1411, and passed first to Matteo di Bartolo, a leather dresser, and then to Giuliano de' Ricci.[56] Some books circulated within a particular community, in one case that of the artisans of the central city. As its first copyist noted: "Here end the Homilies of Saint Gregory written by me Iacopo di Lione, saddlemaker, on the 21st day of February 1445, the second Sunday of Lent. I pray in the name of charity that whoever takes it should give it back for the love of God." He may perhaps have transcribed this work as an act of contrition.

Iacopo sold his book for eight lire "through the mediation of Giovannni di Iacopo da Brucanese, who makes spectacles in Borgo San Lorenzo," to Antonio di Guido di Cristofano, a wool-trimmer, in the Via Porta Rossa, who recorded the transaction on the flyleaf, adding that "whoever borrows this book should return it to me . . . and preserve it from children and oil lamps." This sort of injunction was common, elaborated by one owner with the plea: "Don't let it get mixed up with and ruined by vile things."[57] It evokes a vivid picture of the circumstances in which these books were read; not in formal libraries, like the collections of the classics owned by men such as Cosimo or Palla Strozzi, but in dimly lit rooms amidst the paraphernalia of the quotidian lives of their owners. The volume passed to a third owner who observed: "This book belongs to Donato di Maestro Piero, shoemaker; it cost one lire, four soldi from a woman." Perhaps Antonio had died, and his wife sold off his prized possession for a song.[58]

One man wrote especially forcefully of the perils of lending precious books: "It is always said that one man may injure a hundred,/ although to me it doesn't seem proper;/ but given how I was swindled,/ I intend to follow this precept./ I lent a book to one man, and I must say I regret it,/ for having kept it for a considerable time,/ he swore he had returned it,/ with which I had to be content./ So do not ask me for a loan,/ lest I suffer the usual fate,/ of losing the book and the friendship as well."[59] However, despite these risks, lending books was seen by most men, including Cosimo de' Medici, as one of the duties of friendship.[60] Popular culture was a common culture, not simply in the sense that a wide variety of Florentines read the same texts. The very essence of the compilation was the sharing and dissemination of literature and wisdom in circles where accumulating a large library was not the norm. Owners' admonitions suggest that books were borrowed to be both read and copied, in the manner of classical manuscripts. In an entry proclaiming his ownership of a book "compiled by his own hand," Giuliano di Giovanni de' Bardi added to his injunction not to mislay it, "for I am the guide and companion of him who copied me," that "if there's something you like, copy it for yourself."[61]

Several copyists kept books in common, like the one owned "by Alessandro Cerretani and his friends."[62] A group of scrapbooks belonging to Michele del Giogante, Giovan Matteo Meglio, and Sandro Lotteringhi were written in alternating hands, and included comments and notations addressed by one writer to another. Texts in many books were edited and amended as they circulated; to the common cultural store the individual contributed what he could, and drew from it what he needed.[63]

The transcription of books of religious texts was seen as a contribution to society's shared struggle for salvation, almost a devotional act in itself, as the Flemish painter Jan van Eyck seems to have regarded his meticulous representations of religious subjects.[64] A great-nephew of Giovanni Rucellai inscribed at the end of his copy of the *Vendetta of Christ*: "O you who read this, pray God for me, a sinner."[65] In 1427 Buono di Marcho del Buono di Filippo Marchi, describing himself as one who had "very little luck," put together, perhaps in the hope that God might give him more in the future, a devotional collection including Niccolò Cieco's poem on the Passion, some "Articles of Christian Doctrine," among them the seven acts of mercy, and Giovanni Gherardi's "Tract on an angelic act."[66] A soapmaker finished his *zibaldone* with a fragment from the liturgy in Latin: "Praise be to God whom we acknowledge as our Lord, I finished writing this on Friday the 29th day of December 1396, the day of Saint Thomas the Doubter, by Antonio di Guido di Berto soapmaker, to whom the Lord God give grace at his end, and to all faithful Christians, amen."[67] Goro di Stagio Dati, on the first pages of his book completed in 1380, prayed that its writer would "write and live always with God," and eventually "be gathered into paradise," hoping not only that those who borrowed his book would take good care of it, but that God would bless all those who read it, and that they in turn would pray in all charity for the writer's soul.[68]

POPULIST ILLUSTRATIONS FOR POPULAR TEXTS

Most of these notebooks – *quadernucci*, as their owners often called them – were composed of quires of regular stationer's paper, and written by ordinary men in everyday hands. Even Michele del Giogante's book for Piero was of coarse paper, roughly written and bound. Like letters, notebooks were covered with clarifications and emendations. Sometimes unpretentious volumes were amateurishly embellished for or by their owners, with borders of leaves or lines; initials were colored and filled in with flourishes, or whimsical faces, or simply decorative scribblings expressing the writer's impulse to per-

sonalize his book.[69] A few miscellanies, however, were written in formal hands on fine paper; presentation copies might be beautifully written, bound, and illustrated. Some owners had initials professionally gilded or illuminated; one book signed by its owner, "transcribed by Benedetto Biffoli, a Florentine notary, in 1460," boasted a splendid decorated and gilded first initial, as well as a half-length portrait of Petrarch.[70]

One feature distinguishing books belonging to patricians from those owned by plebeians was the addition of family coats of arms. For example, the only decoration in the notebook of the Milanese ambassador Nicodemo Tranchedini, transcribed in his own hand while he was living in the Medici palace in the 1450s, was the first page, with illuminated initial, frieze, and shield.[71] However, artisans sometimes saw arms as an opportunity for the display of humor or whimsy. When Matteo di Giunto acquired a compilation of Petrarch's *Trionfi* and

27 Florence, Biblioteca Riccardiana 1114, flyleaf

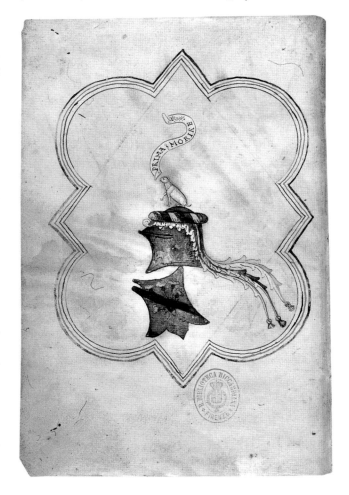

Canzoni richly decorated with a border incorporating a shield with the silver arms on a purple field, the device of its previous, unidentified patrician owner, he added a sketch of his own insignia, a boar's head.[72] One copyist sketched a shield shaped like the quatrefoil panels of the baptistery doors, comprising a bunch of carnations, a helmet with a visor suggesting a smile, surmounted by an ermine, and an inscription, "prima morire," a reference either to a maxim of Pliny or a satirical play upon it in a poem with this incipit, written by Antonio the shoemaker (fig. 27). He also included a rarely copied rhyme by "Andrea che dipigne le sargie" (painter of banners and bedcovers) enquiring of Feo Belcari whether man might be saved by his own merits. His verse and the devotional painting he commissioned from Neri di Bicci are discussed below.[73]

Petrarch's works, particularly the *Triumphs,* which lent themselves perfectly to pictorial elaboration, inspired the overwhelming majority of book illustrations, as they did the decoration of so many household objects, such as chests and birthtrays, commissioned by numerous patrons, including the Medici. Some representations of the *Triumphs* in scrapbooks were richly colored and gilded by professional miniaturists.[74] There are also a number of artists' portraits of Petrarch, and a few of his fellow poet Dante.[75] One book containing Petrarch's *Triumphs* and his treatise on fortune was illustrated perhaps by its owner with a sketch of a bear on a mountain, above him a cloud raining down pellets, and in his left paw a ribbon inscribed with the motto in French, "in a short time the great rain passes" (fig. 28).[76] Several copyists sketched portraits of saints, and a couple drew representations of the Trinity, a favorite theme of the compilers of devotional books, as it was of major artists in the early quattrocento.[77] A later fifteenth-century book belonging to Francesco Teri is interleaved with some of the earliest Italian woodcuts of sacred subjects.[78] Goro Dati's *Sfera,* a rhymed treatise on the regions of the known world, accompanied by maps, appears in many compilations, often with fine watercolor illustrations (fig. 24).[79]

Perhaps the most interesting of the illustrated popular books are a group of three apparently sent to Verrocchio's workshop for decoration. These pen and wash drawings are not in Verrocchio's characteristic "high style," delicate and elegant, but in a simplified, self-consciously popular style, a cruder version of that of Maso Finiguerra; they were presumably executed by one of the lowlier members of the master's workshop. This style matched their texts; the simple moral tales of Aesop, and the humorous verses of *Geta and Birria,* Ghigo (and perhaps also Filippo) Brunelleschi's popular satire based on a Plautus comedy (figs. 29 and 30).[80] The proud but unidentified owner of

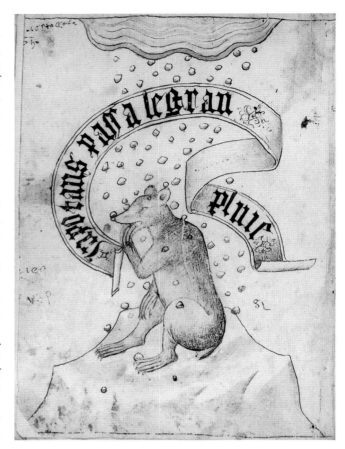

28   Florence, Biblioteca Riccardiana 1103, fol. 10v

the most lavishly illustrated of these books, the man who enumerated its contents in the index with admiring comments repeated in a large rough scrawl on many of its pages, described his possession thus: "This whole book is paid for. It cost ten lire. The painting cost three and a half lire from Andrea del Verrochino whose shop is at the head of the Via Ghibellina. The writing cost seven and a half lire paid to Piero dei Ricci. I paid this money on the 12th of February 1463 [1462 s. f.]. The binding costs more, and I will have to spend more still on this." It is an interesting indication of the value the ordinary man set upon images and artistic talent that the owner of this compilation was willing to give the artist three and a half lire for a dozen sketches, while he paid the scribe only seven and a half lire for four hundred closely copied pages of text.[81]

★   ★   ★

29 Workshop of Verrocchio, illustration of Aesop's *Fables*, Florence, Biblioteca Riccardiana 1591, fol. 85r

30 Workshop of Verrocchio, illustration of *Geta and Birria*, Florence, Biblioteca Riccardiana 1591, fol. 79v

ANTHOLOGISTS: PATRICIANS, PLEBEIANS, AND THE "MIDDLING SORT"; VERNACULAR MISCELLANIES IN COSIMO'S LIBRARY AND PIERO DE' MEDICI'S *LIBRICCIUOLO*

Social status in Renaissance Florence was not easily gauged, being seen by contemporaries as something to be calculated and calibrated with the aid of lists of civic officials, family genealogies, consultation, and careful judgment. However, the owners and transcribers of books and compilations of popular literature clearly comprised an extensive range of patricians, plebeians, and a particularly important third group of Florentines who can only be described as "the middling sort"; not a Marxist middle class, but the *gente mezzana* to whom Florentine social analysts refer.[82] Many were notaries, accountants, apothecaries, or clerics, men who came from, and largely lived in a plebeian social world, but whose professions required

some education, and brought them into contact with members of the political or social elite.[83] It is often assumed that learning, so admired in the Renaissance, trickled down through society from top to bottom, degenerating as it descended. The literary products of the culture of craftsmen bear the same marks of independent creativity as was seen in action on the stage of public performances.

Several of their collections have already been described; the *zibaldone* put together in praise of the Lord by Antonio di Guido, a soapmaker; a book copied by Iacopo di Lione, saddlemaker, which he sold to Antonio di Guido, a wool trimmer, who sold it to Donato di Maestro Piero, shoemaker; the compilations of Giovanfrancesco di Andrea and Giovanni di Zanobi Amadory, both shoemakers, of Francesco di Iacopo di Gianni, an apothecary in the Mercato Vecchio, and the book bought by Matteo di Bartolo, a leather-dresser. There is also the body of works produced by the accountant Michele del

Giogante, sometimes in collaboration with others, including Iacopo di Borgianni, son of a dyer, who adopted the family name Bongianni, and who by the end of his life became quite a prosperous merchant.[84] A large number of books were transcribed for their own or others' use by notaries. "Middling men" like Michele del Giogante, the cleric Feo Belcari, the notary Bernardo Biffoli, and the professional entertainers and heralds of the Signoria, Anselmo Calderoni and Antonio di Meglio, were leading creators and promulgators of popular culture.

Most of these anthologists were also poets whose verses, performed at venues such as San Martino, were staples of popular compilations. Many prominent poets were craftsmen; Niccolò Cieco and Antonio di Guido, the cobblers Giovanni di Cino and Antonio *calzaiuolo*, the barbers Burchiello and Antonio da Bacchereto, and Lo Za. Patricians also wrote poems which they included in their anthologies; often poems appeared first in compilations assembled by their authors. Many personal books were essentially collections of popular poetry, some of it transcribed directly from performances. On the evidence of the most complete modern collection of Florentine popular poetry made to date, of some fifty poets writing in Cosimo's lifetime whose work survives, about half were patricians and the other half artisans, notaries, or ordinary clergymen. The actual proportion of plebeian to patrician poets was undoubtedly much higher, since the work of writers and performers in a mainly oral tradition who lived under infinitely less stable conditions than most patricians is much less likely to have been preserved.[85] Moreover, nearly all the most popular poems, including those most often copied in patrician compilations, were written by artisans, whose rough and satirical style was often imitated by members of the upper class. Many of the most popular poems by major guildsmen, like the *ghiribizzi* (fantasies) of the notary Giovanni Betti, imitated the *burle e baie* (jests and rantings) by Lo Za and Burchiello. The most talented and original patrician poets, such as Francesco di Altobianco degli Alberti and Mariotto Davanzati, were in close personal touch with the cobbler and barber poets, as their verses mourning the passing of Burchiello, the greatest of these, attest.[86]

Surveying the copyists' choices from the canon of the most popular vernacular texts, there seems to be little difference between those of plebeians and patricians. The former were perhaps a little more concerned with devotional texts, which constituted by far the most favored selections of copyists of all social levels. In accordance with the prevailing principle of personal relevance, which appears to have governed most individual selections, poems on the theme of resignation to frustration and pri-

vation appear a little more frequently in artisan compilations. The collection of Antonio di Guido, a soapmaker, included an enormously popular poem by the herald of the Signoria, Antonio di Meglio, beginning: "He who cannot do what he wants, must want what he can." This advice seems particularly appropriate to the less privileged classes, and indeed provides a crucial clue to the quattrocento view of social inequity and injustice as regarded through the lens of resignation to God's will.[87] "He who cannot do what he wants/ must want what he can,/ for it is foolish to wish for what one cannot have./ And I call that man wise who abstains/ from wishing for what he cannot have,/ since our every pleasure and pain/ consists in knowing, wishing, being able – or not . . . And so you who read these observations,/ if you wish to live in peace and serve God,/ wish always to want what you can have."[88]

The main message of this verse is echoed in Antonio di Guido's inscription on the flyleaf of his book: "Let your will be in accordance with that of the Lord,/ and all your desires will be fulfilled." These lines are drawn from the penitential Psalm 37:4, a vital element of the liturgy which was recited at services of flagellant confraternities.[89] The soapmaker's literary selections reflect the moral and devotional tone of the popular culture imbibed by the audience of Cosimo de' Medici's predominantly religious commissions. Antonio began his book with a calendar of saints' days, and much of the rest was taken up with lives of the saints from Iacopo da Voragine's *Golden Legend*. His intention in copying from this work may well have been to provide himself with a selection of everyday moral *exempla*, striving to associate himself, as preachers enjoined, with the holy attributes of each saint on his feastday. Antonio concluded his book with a phrase from the liturgy in praise of God, and a prayer for grace for all faithful Christians.[90]

If the variety and sophistication of the texts in plebeian compilations is surprising, the familiarity of patricians with the corpus of popular vernacular literature might seem equally unexpected in light of a general but rather vague scholarly assumption that the city's ruling class was chiefly steeped in a humanist enthusiasm for the classics. In fact even the most learned and sophisticated of Florentines owned compilations of popular texts. This may largely have escaped the attention of students of literature because more ambitious book collectors such as the Strozzi and the Medici, dedicated to the acquisition of fine manuscripts of classic antique and Christian works, did not include vernacular compilations in their formal inventories, or because their brief references to vernacular books, generally considered a lesser form of literature and listed last, after Latin and Greek texts organized into formal categories of learning, do not indicate their contents.[91]

A number of vernacular works are noted at the end of the inventory of books in Cosimo's study in 1418. Works of the so-called Three Crowns of the Florentine vernacular tradition include Dante's *Canzoni* and several commentaries on *The Divine Comedy* (the epic poem itself is not mentioned), Petrarch's *Sonnets*, and Boccaccio's *Centonovelle, Corbaccio, Teseo, Fiametta*, and various other unnamed works. A life of Dante, perhaps Petrarch's, was due to be returned by Messer Giovanni da Prato at the time the inventory was compiled.[92] These three writers were enormously popular with most compilers of personal scrapbooks. The Medici family interest in Dante is indicated by the efforts of successive generations to repatriate the poet's bones for interment in Santa Maria del Fiore, where he was honored with a memorial by the commune. When the efforts of the Signoria failed, Cosimo himself sent Benedetto Dei "an assiduous observer and researcher of literary treasures both ancient and modern," to negotiate with the lord of Ravenna, where Dante was buried.[93]

Among the devotional texts in Cosimo's library, in addition to the Christian classics, were a Bible, a small catechism (*dottrinale*),[94] and two books of hours, possibly the very popular "Little offices of the Virgin"; a third had been ordered from a bookseller. Cosimo had a translation of Paulus Orosius in Italian, although he owned complete Latin editions of all the classical texts most frequently translated and extracted in popular compilations, including Livy, Caesar, Valerius Maximus, Sallust, Cato, Seneca, Juvenal, Boethius, Quintilian, Ovid's *Epistles*, and above all Cicero – his letters, *On Office-Holding* and *Of Old Age*. The books described in the Medici inventory as "a volume of ecclesiastical writings of Saint Augustine, Saint Bernard and various others" and one of "various works of Saint Jerome and others concerning the lives of the Church Fathers" sound very similar to other Florentines' collections of the writings of these most admired moral authorities, just as many citizens owned copies of the lives and works of their patron saints, like Cosimo's *Life of Saints Cosmas and Damian*. The item described as "I Mappamundi, bello" could well have been a copy of Dati's *Sfera,* commonly known as *il mappamundo*, which contained maps of the three parts of the known world, and was a particular favorite of copyists and anthologists (fig. 24).[95]

The list of Cosimo's vernacular books shows that he chose to read much the same devotional, popular, and patriotic literature as the overwhelming majority of literate Florentines whose choices are reflected in surviving vernacular books and compilations.[96] The contents of

many patrician libraries more modest than his were recorded by the Pupilli officials responsible for administering the estates of wards. Once we come to recognize the format of popular compilations, we realize that most men who owned even half a dozen books had one or more *zibaldoni* among them.[97] The Pupilli inventories, like the repertoire of compilers and copyists, included many works from the vernacular school curriculum which, as Paul Grendler observed in his study of Renaissance education, "developed without any guidance from above."[98] The favorites of adult vernacular culture were used as classroom texts, among them the *Flowers of Virtue* (*Fior di virtù*), the *Letters* of the apostles, and the books of the evangelists. There were also several copies in the inventories of "the book called the story of Troy," and various chivalric romances in verse, as well as volumes of miscellaneous songs. There were numerous devotional, liturgical, catechistic, and meditational works including the penitential psalms, *The Christian Doctrine, The Christian Life*, the offices of the Blessed Virgin, and of the dead, Cavalca's *Lives of the Holy Fathers* and his *Mirror of the Cross, The Golden Legend*, and books of lauds.[99]

Several *zibaldoni* were compiled for or by members of the Medici family in the mid-fifteenth century. Michele del Giogante's book for Piero is the only personalized selection of texts explicitly addressed and presented to a member of Cosimo's immediate family which has been identified to date; notably it is not mentioned in any of the inventories of Piero's books.[100] A number of *zibaldoni* in this relatively small sample bear the Medici arms, although the names of their owners are not inscribed in them, and several were apparently made for Lorenzo.[101] What is known of the culture and function of the scrapbook suggests that more than one was probably made for Cosimo's household; various manuscripts by Michele del Giogante are possible candidates.[102] Andrea de' Medici transcribed a compilation for himself while he was imprisoned in the Stinche between 1461 and 1468; a volume of Dante's works, together with a memory treatise built around the life and illustrated figure of Santa Quaresima, was dedicated to him by its author, Ser Piero di Bonaccorso.[103]

Many of the owners or compilers of collections were closely associated with the Medici as relatives, friends, and business partners. In some cases the similar contents of their *zibaldoni,* featuring civic speeches or poems in praise of the Medici or their *amici*, reinforce the impression that literary anthologies, like pictorial representations, may have served to identify Medici supporters with their patrons' interests. Rosello Roselli, the clerical author of a number of playful love poems, and the companion in leisure and pleasure of the youthful Piero and Giovanni de' Medici, compiled an index of the songs and sonnets of Petrarch, and a collection of witty and amorous verse in the spirit of Boccaccio, for his own and his friends' delectation. Begun "Anno domini 1405, the 15th of October, when I was a boy," it contains a series of figured verses designed around the figure "Oretardi," playing on the consciousness of the passage of time, a prevalent Medicean theme, and perhaps also on the name of the poet's mistress or muse, a possible variant of Oretta. Roselli recorded that he gave this book to Adovardo di Giovanni Portinari, a member of a family closely associated with the Medici in business and friendship, but apparently it continued to circulate among this group of friends.[104]

The trecento artisan poet Antonio Pucci wrote the manual used by most popular entertainers; his family were neighborhood partisans of the Medici as early as 1350.[105] The Bardi were a old Florentine magnate family related to the Medici by Cosimo's marriage to Contessina de' Bardi. Especially in the early decades of the fifteenth century, many of the Medici banking partners came from this clan. One of the earliest signed and dated vernacular scrapbooks belonged to Giuliano di Giovanni di Bardi, and was copied in his own hand in the year 1416.[106] Three brothers of the Benci family, from a branch related to those Benci who were also leading associates of the Medici bank, copied a large number of *zibaldoni*, including their own poetry.[107] Lorenzo, Francesco, and Tommaso di Tommaso di Giovanni di Taddeo Benci recorded in Latin on the flyleaf of their shared book the departure of the Greek members of the church council from Florence on 26 August 1439, a major event for all Florentines, and particularly for the Medici and their friends.[108] Bartolomeo Benci's famous joust of 1473 is commemorated in a *libroncino* charmingly illuminated with the Benci arms and composed by another member of the Medici circle, Filippo Lapaccini, a relative of the Giuliano Lapaccini who oversaw the Medici building at San Marco, and chronicled its progress.[109]

While some copyists came from prosperous and homogenous families of longstanding Medici partisans, others belonged to lineages with members of conditions as diverse as those of Cosimo and Andrea de' Medici. Some suffered serious reversals of fortune in the course of the fifteenth century. The patrician Ricci had been leaders of the ruling class, and allies of the Medici in the conflicts of the late trecento. Giuliano de' Ricci copied a book containing Piero di Crescenzi's *On Agriculture* during a stint in prison; Piero di Giovanni de' Ricci, a poet of some distinction in the style of Burchiello, led a rebellion in 1457 against the Medicean state on behalf of the starving agricultural workers whose plight he lamented in graphic and moving verse.[110]

Iacopo di Niccolò di Cocco Donati, son of the Medici partisan Niccolò di Cocco Donati, who as Gonfalonier of Justice in September 1434 recalled the Medici from exile, and was pilloried for this in a famous poem by Burchiello, ended up destitute in prison only fifteen years after Cosimo's triumphant return. He made at least four compilations, which reveal a great deal about the culture and diverse experience of a man from the inner circle of the Medici friends. His books include his own poetry and almost every classic of the Florentine popular tradition. On the flyleaf of one he wrote: "This little book in which are written many various beautiful and pleasing things in prose and in verse, as you may see by the table of contents, belongs to me, Iacopo di Niccolò di Choccho Donati, a citizen of Florence." Another contained such staples of popular culture as Brunetto Latini's *Tesoretto*, a transcription of the popular vernacular poetry contest, the Certame Coronario, a verse commenting on the widespread custom of singing in the public piazzas of cities, a popular patriotic poem, "Beautiful Florence, O triumphal city," and a memory aid, essential to the mastery of any literary tradition.[111] Iacopo was the copyist who discovered an unknown work by Simone da Siena, "as I the writer, Iacopo di Nicholò, found it written in a copy of Dante's *Commedia* in [Simone's] own hand, which he says he intended to give to Gianni Colonna with a moral song in praise of the house of Colonna." Iacopo completed the book in which he transcribed this verse, which also includes his own sonnet "Laus deo anni," in June 1451, in the Stinche. He referred to this fate by his inclusion in one of his compilations of Antonio di Guido's extremely popular poem, "If I am not first seized by prison, or by death . . ."[112]

Among other books belonging to members of families closely associated with the Medici were Giuliano Quaratesi's version of the legend of Saint John the Baptist, Florence's patron saint, "written by me Giuliano di [Quaratesi]: finished the 10th of December 1458, at 20 hours." On the first folio was a particularly beautiful initial containing the arms of the Quaratesi, whom Cosimo around this time persuaded to take over from him the patronage of San Salvatore al Monte.[113] The widow of Bartolomeo Nasi, Politia de' Pazzi, owned a volume consisting mainly of Dante's and Petrarch's poems. She came from the family of bankers who built the Pazzi chapel, and for most of the fifteenth century were among Cosimo's closest associates; in 1478, fourteen years after his death, they led the conspiracy in which his grandson Giuliano was murdered.[114] A largely devotional anthology containing the *Vendetta of Christ* and Iacopone da Todi's *Laude* was begun in 1469 by Luigi di Donato di Pagholo di Meser Pagholo Rucellai, whose family was linked to the Medici by the marriage of Giovanni

Rucellai's son Bernardo to Cosimo's granddaughter Nannina in 1466.[115]

The hero of the attempted Pazzi conspiracy was Lorenzo de' Medici's intimate crony Sigismondo della Stufa. He protected his friend in the confusion after Giuliano was killed; by this time the Della Stufa had been neighborhood allies of the Medici for more than a century. The several compilations owned by members of the Della Stufa family demonstrate their keen interest in Florentine vernacular literature. Giovanni di Zanobi Betti's presentation copy of his *ghiribizi*, in the spirit of Bocaccio and Burchiello, ended up in Sigismondo della Stufa's hands.[116] His ancestor Giovanni della Stufa had completed part of a book he was compiling for himself "on Palm Sunday 1436"; the volume remained in the family, and the original text was supplemented by several additions; by 1460 it belonged to Giovenco di Lorenzo della Stufa.[117] Another book containing Petrarch's *Trionfi* bears the Della Stufa arms and is illustrated with six large and elaborate illuminations, in the style of Apollonio di Giovanni's *Aeneid*, which was probably made for a member of the Medici circle.[118]

COMBINING PLEASURE WITH PROFIT: THE THREE CROWNS, DANTE, BOCCACCIO, AND PETRARCH; BRUNELLESCHI'S "FAT CARPENTER"; *GETA AND BIRRIA*; LO ZA AND BURCHIELLO

Moral and spiritual perfectibility were the ultimate concerns of popular culture, and in compilations, as in public performances, there is a strong bias in favor of religious and devotional material. Nevertheless, entertainment could be garnered along the road to edification, and the burdens of this earthly pilgrimage lightened by a good laugh. As one copyist observed in his introduction to Antonio Pucci's famous *Beauties of the Mercato Vecchio*, "this work strives to combine pleasure with profit."[119] We turn now to review the texts most popular with anthologists, as with the Medici family, texts that inspired many of Cosimo's commissions and explain their accessibility to his Florentine audience.

By far the most popular of all selections were the works of Dante, Petrarch, and Boccaccio, the "three crowns" of the Florentine vernacular tradition. They appealed alike to the man in the street and to the Latinate humanist, and became in the quattrocento the foundation of a vernacular genre whose tone was not wholly that of either elite or popular culture, but which constituted a bridge between the two. Traces of these writers, of their images and phrases, are everywhere in fifteenth-century verse and prose. The widespread knowledge of these texts is especially interesting since the "three crowns" were apparently not taught in vocational schools. Boccaccio in particular was considered unsuitable for women, and presumably children as well.[120] It seems that the circulation of these texts was as independent as was the curriculum of vernacular schools. There were regular public lectures on Dante, not only at the Studio frequented by the upper classes, but also at Orsanmichele and at the cathedral, attended by the Florentine *popolo*.[121]

The most frequently copied works of Dante were the *Commedia*, his poems, and various apocryphal writings, like the credo and confessions associated with his name.[122] The *Canzoniere*, particularly those addressed to Laura, led the list of Petrarch's preferred works, with the *Triumphs* a close second. These, as already observed, lent themselves especially to illustration; notably they occupy a substantial part of the book belonging to the architect Giuliano da Sangallo. The theme of the *Triumphs* was summarized in more accessible form in a popular poem by Mariotto Davanzati.[123] Also of interest were vulgarizations of Petrarch's *Of the Varieties of Fortune*.[124] Boccaccio's *opus* of course encompassed a wide range of interests and moods, from the Latin *Genealogy of the Gods* to vernacular verses on sacred and profane love, the *Letter to Pino de' Rossi*, and often ribald prose tales, among them the *Centonovelle*. This last work was constantly invoked and emulated by other popular writers, such as Sacchetti, as it was in the letters of Lorenzo di Piero di Cosimo's *brigata* of young friends; Boccaccio set the standard for all those aspiring to write of amatory adventures.[125]

Quattrocento vernacular poetry depended heavily on Dante and Petrarch; compilations included numerous love poems modeled on Petrarch's verses to Laura, written by the copyist or his friends. These were often in the form of a competitive exchange, or *tenzone*; thus compilations of poetry describe the circles in which their collectors moved. Writers were eager to claim their poetic patrimony. Mariotto Davanzati wrote on the death of an unsung poet: "Now what solemn celebrations/ are made for these holy souls,/ but even more for Petrarch and my poet Dante . . ." In his contribution to the Certame Coronario, Davanzati invoked "the arch and support of my life,/ my compatriots Dante and Petrarch,/ without whom I would not dare to speak,/ O lend a hand to my fragile bark."[126] Antonio degli Agli's offering on the same occasion was full of Dantesque imagery: "O Eternal Father, from whom proceeds and falls on us/ every light, every good grace,/ from whence the primal love suffused the world,/ O highest love . . . your worthiness now grasps my heart,/ now inflames the fire of my mind . . ."[127]

In one interesting compilation, Tommaso di Tommaso (?Benci) transcribed several of Boccaccio's works, Dati's *Sfera*, illustrated with beautiful maps, and the *novella* "Il grasso legnaiuolo."[128] This comic tale of the joke played by the architect Brunelleschi on a fat carpenter carries the tradition of Boccaccio and Sacchetti on into the quattrocento. It appears in a number of manuscripts, sometimes alongside *Geta and Birria*, a satirical comic verse written by Ghigo Brunelleschi with additions by Domenico da Prato, and perhaps also by Filippo himself. In the same vein as these two longer works was Brunelleschi's derisive verse exchange with Giovanni da Prato, written in the style of Burchiello.[129] All three of these items associated with Brunelleschi belong to a distinctive genre of popular literature by virtue of their piercing (*aguto*) wit, a rather cruel and subversive humor which Dante saw as characteristic of Florentines, their parody of high culture, and their graphic verbal realism delighting in the vulgar, the ridiculous, and the obscene.

The fat carpenter's tale is a complex comment in this particularly plebeian (*popolaresco*) vein, not simply on Florentine society, but on the nature of knowing, particularly of knowing oneself. *Geta and Birria* is a skit on the grandiose claims of classical scholars, with whom seekers of wisdom and virtue in this society had a markedly love-hate relationship. The distinguishing feature of Birria, the scholar Geta's manservant, is the size not of his intellect, but of his genitals.[130] Lorenzo de' Medici included this work in a selection of Florentine popular literature which he presented to Federigo of Aragon in 1466. Machiavelli read it for diversion under the olive trees in the afternoon, before devoting himself to the serious study of the classics at night, as he observed in his famous letter to Vettori announcing the appearance of *The Prince*.[131]

The objects of satire in popular literature included particularly the clergy, humanists, and homosexuals. The three satirical verse epics of Stefano Finiguerra, known as "Lo Za" or sometimes simply as "the sovereign poet" were very popular, especially the *Buca d'Atene*, which killed all these derided birds with one stone by denouncing in turn each of Florence's most famous learned and clerical homosexuals.[132] The poetic tradition of *burle e baie* (jests and rantings), was elevated to its greatest height by the barber poet Burchiello. Despite his criticisms of the upper classes in general, and of the Medici in particular, he enjoyed the friendship and admiration of most major Florentine writers and artists, as well as a variety of citizens from the literally destitute to Cosimo and his sons. His poetry epitomizes the conjunction in this genre of a huge delight in ridicule with a great respect for the literary repositories of classical and Christian wisdom,

and strong religious feeling. Burchiello was the master of ironic meditations on deprivation, pain, and the transience of life, which touched a chord in serious Christians of every social level. At the same time, his poems were brilliant examples of the acerbic wit that seems in Florentine eyes to have redeemed almost any literary solecism or social blemish.[133]

MORAL *EXEMPLA*: AESOP'S *FABLES* AND THE CLASSICS

Students of humanism have remarked that while the Renaissance brought a new sense of history and cultural relativism to the often uncritical medieval reading of classical texts, most Renaissance men were also impelled to integrate the "pagan" classics with the Christian, and to see the writers, intellectuals, and heroes of the ancient world as moral forerunners of the revelation of Christ. In the pantheon of the literate Florentine, Hercules prefigured David who prefigured Christ, and all three were major images of Medici patronage. The incorporation of antique secular writers into the canon of moralists, in the search for "truths gained from experience of good *exempla*," described by a trecento anthologist, *buffone*, in the introduction to his *zibaldone*, is as marked in these compendia of popular literature as in the curricula of vernacular schools.[134]

Aesop's *Fables*, a Greek text that for centuries had been a classic of popular vernacular literature in western Europe, and was taught in vernacular schools in Florence, continued to be seen in the Renaissance as a rich source of moral *exempla* by citizens from Leon Battista Alberti to Leonardo da Vinci. By comparison with translations made elsewhere in Europe, the fifteenth-century Tuscan versions had a distinctly popularizing tone, like the illustrations that accompanied them in *zibaldoni*, and in the earliest printed books.[135] The variety of texts with which anthologists coupled the fables − from the seven penitential psalms to *Geta and Birria*, suggests that they were valued equally as entertainment and edification.[136] This impression is reinforced by copyists' commentaries and interpolations on the stories they selected from the three hundred or so in circulation at the time. A favorite tale was that of "the cockerel who found a precious stone in the dungheap." One copyist pointed out that "spiritually the cockerel signifies he who pays attention only to earthly and present things and not to their profitable ends, and temporally the cockerel signifies the labors of this world." The precious stone is "the glory of eternal life."[137] A moral message stressed in several fables favoured by Florentine anthologists was that the powerful should not speak disdainfully to the weak; this was also the theme of Niccolò Cieco's extremely popular didactic verse on the different social stations to which God assigns his children in this life.[138]

The works of many well-known writers of antiquity were mined for moral dicta, some spurious, some genuine, described typically in Lodovico della Casa's compilation as "certain authoritative sayings of many worthy men."[139] Particularly popular in compilations, as in school curricula, were Seneca, Cato, Juvenal, and Sallust.[140] Extracts were made of Plutarch's *Lives*, which helped to inspire a number of quattrocento paintings.[141] Sandro Lotteringhi, like several other copyists, noted in his scrapbook this homily: "Plato said that seven sorts of temperance pleased him:/ the first, chastity in youth;/ the second, lightheartedness in age;/ the third, generosity in poverty;/ the fourth, moderation [*misura*] in times of prosperity and in bad times;/ the fifth, humility in greatness;/ the sixth, patience in adversity;/ the seventh, putting up with unfairness or wishes that cannot be fulfilled."[142] Popular comments on classical texts, no less than learned discussions, express an increasing interest in parallels between Renaissance society and that of the classical world. This is particularly apparent in the poems on friendship entered in the vernacular literature competition of the Certame Coronario, which were included in almost every major *zibaldone* of the mid-century. Popular poets saw Cicero's framing of the paradoxical nature of friendship as directly applicable to Renaissance society, saving its transposition into a Christian key.[143]

Cosimo de' Medici stocked his library with Cicero's writings and annotated them in his own hand. Many anthologists also saw Cicero's works as particularly pertinent to their own lives. A book of Bonaccorso di Filippo Adimari copied in 1454 included "the letters of Tullio for the benefit of Marcho Marciello," along with *On Friendship* and *On Old Age*.[144] "The deeds of Caesar" were highly popular, appearing in more than a dozen Riccardiana compilations. A long story in a manuscript also containing Cosimo's poem to Sforza emphasised the relevance of Caesar's founding of cities to the experience of the merchant patrician.[145] Besides numerous single copies, one of them Cosimo's, of the *Consolation of Philosophy* by Boethius, who was an important bridging figure between the classical and Christian traditions, there were long extracts from his work in many compilations. His stoic philosophy harmonized with the increasing austerity of popular religious life in the quattrocento, and his preoccupation with Fortune, a major theme of medieval morality, took on new meaning as the fifteenth-century interest in the classical world advanced.[146]

DEVOTION: SCRIPTURE AND QUOTIDIAN COUNSEL; MEDITATION, CONFESSION, PENITENCE, AND PRAYERS; THE *MEMENTO MORI* AND THE EXEMPLARY IMAGES OF THE SAINTS

Not long ago, when the myth of a secular Renaissance remained relatively unchallenged, it might have seemed surprising that the texts most often copied in informal *quadernucci*, like most books owned by ordinary Florentines, were moral and religious. Now that so much more is known about popular religious practice and devotion, about the role of the sacred in public life and ceremony, and about the importance of confraternal membership in the personal lives of most Florentines, this comes as no surprise.

If the moral component of a popular culture whose chief end was the perfectibility of the individual in this world in preparation for the next was honed by ideals and habits of mind that "trickled down" from the learned elite, much of the energy that thrust works of practical devotion into the forefront of Florentine minds – the offices of the liturgy, *laude*, meditational practice – seems to have surged up from below; from the ranks of the artisan performers and transcribers of this literature who were also the backbone of much of the city's religious life, and particularly of its confraternities. Fundamental Christian texts such as the Scriptures and the works of the church fathers were of course translated from Latin into the vernacular, but there is no reason to associate with any particular social group this harbinger of the Reformation impulse to have the word and the text directly available to the literate individual who did not read Latin. Educated patricians made translations for their own and others' pleasure; Francesco d'Altobianco degli Alberti in particular produced popularizing verse renditions of sacred texts. Most translations, however, were made by "the middling sort"; members of the lesser clergy, originally from the artisan class, and notaries who worked with clergymen and religious organizations.

Of the church fathers, Augustine was popular especially for his sermons. The *City of God*, of which Cosimo owned a fine twelfth-century English copy, was also much transcribed and cited. As one unidentified anthologist observed at the end of his book: "Here ends the 22nd and last book of the *City of God* composed by Saint Augustine, which I the copyist, although most ignorant, judge to be most worthy of praise; and together with its author of blessed memory, I rejoice in such a divine gift, and to the most high God and our Redeemer Jesus Christ I give infinite thanks; who in addition has allowed me, B., to write and finish this work, even if undoubtedly tainted by my flaws, this last day of January 1456 [s. f.]."[147] Augustine was sometimes paired with Jerome; their respective rules for living appear in several books, including one belonging to the Della Stufa, a family very close to the Medici.[148] In 1445 the shoemaker Giovanni di Zanobi Amadori copied into his book Jerome's letter on the death of Eusebius, Augustine's letter to Ciriotto, and Ciriotto's three letters to Jerome.[149] The latter's cult grew in the quattrocento, along with a concern for penance and an interest in the patristic tradition, fostered by such clerical humanists as Ambrogio Traversari. Traversari's friend Cosimo de' Medici, like so many other Florentines, partook in this interest; Cosimo owned a medieval volume of Jerome's works, and there were several images of the saint in the Medici palace.[150] The sayings of Saint Gregory, whose *Moralia* were among Cosimo's favorite reading, were less often cited, although Ser Lamberto di Goccio Lamberteschi included them in a book of devotional material that he completed in 1464.[151] Other Florentines also shared Cosimo's interest in the monastic life as described by Cassian, whose *Collazioni* and "Exhortation to novices" appear in several compilations.[152]

By far the most popular medieval writer, exemplum, and saint was Bernard of Clairvaux. The Marian devotion with which he became identified in the twelfth century was a feature of Florentine *laudesi* companies, and among those works of his most frequently anthologized were his famous *Lauda to the Virgin*, the *Ave Regina Stella* incorporated into confraternal services, and his "Lament of the Virgin beneath the cross." Other popular pieces included his "Commentary on the Song of Solomon," the *Canticle of Canticles*, which one writer copied in 1451 "for the glory and honor of Jesus Christ, bridegroom of the Holy Mother Church," his "Contemplation of the Passion according to the canonical hours," his works on the Mass, its significance, and the "grace that man receives from hearing it," his "Dialogue of the soul with the body," a popular theme of quattrocento *laude*; and various of his sermons and letters on the good government of the family and the state. Also much appreciated were his meditations, particularly his "Meditation on the Passion of Christ" and the "Meditation on the grief of Our Lady," which might have described the scene on the wall of Cosimo's cell at San Marco: "Beside the cross of Jesus stood his mother . . ."[153]

Ironically, most popular of all the writings attributed to him was the Pseudo-Saint Bernard letter to "Messer Count Raimondo," a guide to the virtuous life and to the care of the family addressed to a prominent Florentine feudatory of the territory of Palestine.[154] Saint Bernard's popularity may be explained partly by his

31   Fra Filippo Lippi, *Saint Bernard's Vision of the Virgin*, London, National Gallery

appearance at the climax of Dante's *Divine Comedy*, and by the Signoria's adoption of him as their patron saint some time around the turn of the thirteenth and fourteenth centuries. His inclusion as a figure in the Medici chapel altarpiece by Filippo Lippi probably reflects his prominence in Florentine popular culture.[155] Lippi had painted a panel of Saint Bernard's vision of the Virgin for an earlier patron, who paid an advance to the artist in May 1447 (fig. 31). A central element in the extant painting generally identified with this commission is the association of Bernard not only with his vision, but with books and writing. It shows him seated at his desk hewn out of rock, his books at his side, in the act of reading or transcribing. The saint is deep in contemplation; the Virgin flanked by angels appears before his inner eye.[156]

Selections from the Scriptures in popular compilations often seem to mirror the content of confraternal services. The Psalms appear in a number of compilations, clearly identified with the figure of David, also a symbol of the Florentine republic, who is represented in one of the most important Medici commissions of Cosimo's lifetime.[157] Most frequently copied were the seven penitential psalms, which played a major part in confraternal ritual, especially a verse beginning "Oh Lord God do not admonish me in your fury; in your wrath do not chastise me, but have mercy upon me . . ."[158] Also popular were the Proverbs of Solomon, Ecclesiastes, and the texts describing the lives of the prophets who foretold the coming of Christ. The prophets were often paired in Renaissance images with the evangelists, whose books were perhaps the most popular of all biblical texts. Francesco d'Altobianco degli Alberti's rendition of the Gospel of Saint John in *terze rime* was among the outstanding vernacular translations of the Scriptures. John the Evangelist was of course the subject of many visual representations besides Donatello's stucco decorations for the Medici old sacristy in San Lorenzo. The letters and acts of the apostles were also much copied, along with the Apocalypse of Saint John, the source of images for popular poets and artists in a whole range of works from the baptistery mosaics to Fra Angelico's *Last Judgment* for Traversari's convent of the Angeli.[159]

The many texts of the offices for particular occasions are evidence of the layman's interest in the liturgy; membership of religious confraternities both fostered and required a familiarity with its texts. The transcription of passages from the Divine Offices also indicate the very practical function of these *zibaldoni* as repositories of important information their owners wanted close at hand and readily available for consultation. Also in this category were devotional poems and *laude*, many of them apparently drawn from the repertoire recited by the *confratelli*. The trecento poems of Iacopone da Todi, still performed by *laudesi* confraternities in the quattrocento, and a basic model for the writing of *laude*, appear in a number of compilations.[160]

There were also numerous confessions. The idea of the "good confession" had an enormous hold on the Renaissance imagination, and models for confession were carefully studied. There was great pressure to introspection to account for sin, for men to calculate their moral balance in a Christian application of mercantile habits of mind. Cosimo de' Medici initiated his major ecclesiastical patronage program to even his account with God.[161] Similarly demanding was the process of meditation on the stages, elements and details of the Passion, encouraged particularly by the influential early fifteenth-century Dominican leaders Dominici and Antoninus. The most popular guides to meditation were obviously designed for use with devotional images, encouraging the contemplation of the suffering of Christ and his mother, and the devotee's identification with their pain.[162] Saint Bernard's meditations, as observed, were particularly favored; they turned on the scenes most frequently imaged in devotional art. Also transcribed in several books were guides to meditation written by Antoninus, along with his *Confession*, and his treatises on mortal sins and excommunication.[163]

The scrapbook compiled by Francesco di Nicholò di Teri di Lorenzo Teri was mainly devotional, containing the credo attributed to Dante, a "Reflection on the Holy Mass," the *Legends* of Saint Cecilia, and "Meditations on the Life of Jesus Christ." To these last Teri appended the comment: "This book deals with the life and death of Messer Jesus Christ, praise be to eternal God [*Laud. Deo Senper*]." The text was illustrated with woodcuts depicting the marriage of the Virgin, the Annunciation, the Virgin and Child in glory, the Crucifixion and the Resurrection, this last relating graphic images of corpses to the hope of resurrection through Christ and his saints, and a tree, "symbolizing the fall of worldly states." The treatise on the Resurrection began with a full-page image of Christ rising from the tomb, leaves of blood sprouting from his heart and hands, and an inscription which read: "For the sake of your soul I have suffered this."[164]

Some indication of the reception and internalization of this devotional material appears in the great number of personal prayers copied, and sometimes written, by anthologists. Meditation led naturally to prayer, as in Giovanni Morelli's account of his vision.[165] Sandro Lotteringhi included several prayers in his two compilations. One of these was "a plea to be said when others go to bed: "To bed, to bed, I led my soul and body to God;/I give it to him so he may give it to Saint John,/and assign him to guard it so that the Enemy should not deceive it, should not deceive it;/and then he should give it to Saint Michael, so he may weigh it and/ watch over it well, and then he may give it to Saint Peter so/ he may put it in the kingdom of heaven, amen."/ "But there is another," he added, "to say when you yourself go to bed; I went to my bed Jesus Christ;/ I found there Jesus Christ and Saint Silvester, who made this bed for us,/ and Saint Augustine also set seven lighted candles there,/ with seven angels of God all around my bed, amen."[166]

Cambio da Castello, who described himself as a "student of the authors," collected in his book a number of prayers to be memorized and said on particular occasions, concluding with one that began: "Almighty God, Father and Lord,/ O Supreme wisdom of all eternity . . ."[167] In another book, "a beautiful confession" is followed by a prayer beginning: "Mercy peace and charity we ask of you, O sweet Lord Jesus," and a poem about the folly of taking pleasure in worldly wisdom and friendship by Iacopone da Todi. "Moved by holy madness,/ I want to tell you of my life . . . Listen to this crazy madness/ of the foolishness of my life,/ I who have forty friends;/ I hope to lead a holy life,/ acquiring instead such virtue/ that it will be out of sight./ Moved by holy madness,/ I want to tell you of my life./ Mercy peace and charity/ we beg of you sweet Lord Jesus./ Take up the cross that you may carry it;/ every lover who loves the Lord,/ join the dance singing of love,/ come dancing all impassioned."[168]

A more extreme expression of this same spirit is the *memento mori*, replete with images of fleshly joys mocked by death. This is a predominant theme of selections in compilations, and particularly of *laude* composed by laymen. Clearly recalling the images of the Triumph of Death in the Petrarchan cycle, the *memento mori* is the obverse of a Petrarchan love lyric. The horrific fate that is the end of desire is the fulcrum on which such literature turns.[169] It weighs on the negative side of man's confessional accounting of his ultimate deserts, recounting hard lessons to be learned on the pilgrimage to salvation. The most popular example of this genre was the "Debate between the living man and the dead one," the poetic analogue of the skeleton in the tomb beneath Masaccio's *Trinity* in Santa Maria Novella, which bears the inscription: "As you are now, so once was I. As I am now, so shall you be" (fig. 51).[170] "When an earthly man such as you/ begins to turn his mind to the tomb,/ and you reflect upon it,/ and consider well that you must return/ to the state in which you see/ the man who lies in this dark ditch./ 'Now answer me, you who are buried,/ who recently sojourned in this world,/ where are the garments in which yesterday you were clad?/ Seeing you now adorned with such filth.'/ 'O my brother, do not turn away from me;/ my example may benefit you . . . My head with its hair so blonde/ has disintegrated into carrion encircled by hairs;/ I never thought about this when I lived in the world,/ when I wore a garland perched upon it,/ where there were eyes so enamored,/ now dug out of their hollows,/ I think the worms have eaten them;/ . . . these eyes . . . always sinning against women . . . have now been devoured and my gaze along with them . . .'" The author goes on to describe in excruciating detail how the substance of man's flesh – nose, mouth tongue, hands, arms – is consumed by death. He ends with a call to repentance, before it is too late.[171]

A desire to counterbalance the weight of sin when calculating their fate in the next life led men to seek a remedy in the vast literature of guidance to the virtuous Christian life. Ubiquitous in quattrocento manuscripts were extracts from the thirteenth-century *Fior di virtù*, another text owned by Cosimo, and one whose popularity spread even further with the printing press.[172] The later fourteenth century, following the anxieties of frightful epidemics of plague and acute social upheaval, produced a large quantity of extremely intense, often mystical literature seen as an aid to achieving spiritual perfection. Its continuing relevance to men of the fifteenth century is apparent in the enormous popularity of such authors as Saint Bridget and Fra Giovanni Cavalca. Traces of the influence of their writings appear in the *laude* written by

Cosimo's daughter-in-law Lucrezia Tornabuoni, and in the imagery of the altarpiece for the Medici chapel painted by Filippo Lippi. Saint Bridget was known particularly for her mystical works; among these were her *Revelations*, *Prophecies*, and *Angelic Sermons*.[173] Cavalca's numerous works in personal scrapbooks include his translations of Saint Gregory, the lives of the saints, particularly John the Baptist, a *Meditation on the Life of Christ*, *The Mirror of Christ* and *The Mirror of Sins*, *The Mirror of the Filth of the Heart* and *The Medication of the Heart*. His *Tract on Patience* and his *Treatise on Thirty Forms of Pride*, along with various rhymes and sonnets, stressed above all the need to repudiate the world in favor of penitence and spiritual discipline.[174]

Also valued by Florentine laymen, many of them directly involved in city government, was the counsel of clergymen willing to come to terms with their need to live in the world of politics and business. Many anthologists, among them Michele del Giogante, who put together *zibaldoni* for the Medici, transcribed the correspondence between Guido del Palagio, the city's most eminent statesman of the third quarter of the fourteenth century, and his chief spiritual advisors.[175] Well into the fifteenth century, Florentines saw Guido del Palagio, described by his contemporary Buonaccorso Pitti as "the greatest and most trusted man in Florence," as the ideal of the God-fearing ruler of the city. He might well have served Cosimo as a model for his own life and patronage.[176]

Guido corresponded regularly concerning the conflicts between his civic and spiritual duties with Giovanni dalle Celle, a Vallombrosan hermit, and Luigi Marsili, an Augustinian who from his cell at Santo Spirito presided over a series of legendary colloquies attended by laymen, as well as learned clerics. A friend of Salutati, Marsili amassed one of the more remarkable libraries of his time. Cosimo de' Medici, like Guido del Palagio, was a direct heir of Marsili's wisdom, not only in the form of the letters written to his trecento counterpart, but also of Marsili's books, some of which ended up in Cosimo's library. Guido del Palagio had been one of a group of leading citizens who held office during the War of the Eight Saints, when the governors of Florence opposed the will of the pope, and eventually also the interdict he imposed on the city. Guido sought advice on the spiritual consequences of this defiance from Marsili and Giovanni dalle Celle, who encouraged him to regard patriotism itself as a form of devotion. As Giovanni wrote to him: "Direct your attention first to the honor of God and then to the good state of your city, and it will be easy for you to aid and defend and counsel her, so that she may never come into the hands of her enemies . . . Let your intention be the defence of your *patria*, and in this holy intention you may hold all the offices of the commune without mortal sin . . ."[177] Such literature nourished a civic strain of piety which Savonarola brought to its logical conclusion at the end of the fifteenth century. The vital role of this fusion between the civic and the spiritual in politics and culture in the 1490s has long been acknowledged by historians, and it is important to recognize its expression at mid-century in the praise of Cosimo and his building of churches by Feo Belcari and others.[178]

Guido del Palagio's clerical friends had stressed that even wealthy laymen should practice some measure of renunciation of the flesh, a prominent theme in Cosimo's classical reading and perhaps some explanation of his patronage of monastic institutions.[179] Drawing on one of Cosimo's favorite texts, Saint Gregory's *Moralia*, and representing the world as a "perilous sea," Giovanni dalle Celle advised Guido: "You should see yourself always as a pilgrim in this world, and consider that we are always proceeding, sleeping and waking, toward the harbor of death, as Seneca teaches us in his notebooks, which I sent to your house when I was in Naples." A man should always hold himself a little aloof from the world, "since the world treats us as a man does a pig; wishing to kill it, he fattens it, because he knows it enjoys it, and then he sinks the knife in its heart."[180] In several *zibaldoni*, the correspondence between Guido del Palagio, Luigi Marsili, and Giovanni dalle Celle appears alongside the writings of Saint Bridget. In one it preceded a mid-quattrocento poem by Lodovico d'Antonio [della Casa] which may draw directly on the Vallombrosan's images. "In the desires of the flesh the delight and pleasure soon pass away,/ but the sin remains through all eternity, like all our faults and evil-doing . . ."[181] While prior of the Camaldolensian foundation of Santa Trinita in Florence, before he retired to his cell in the order's convent at Vallombrosa, Giovanni was a powerful advocate of the sort of pentitential exercises practiced by Jerome, whose combination of spiritual discipline and learning so attracted Renaissance Florentines to his cult. Both these attributes of Jerome were represented in paintings, including one by a follower of Angelico depicting him alongside Cosmas and Damian, almost certainly a Medici commission for San Girolamo at Fiesole.[182]

Florentines naturally sought instruction in the writings of contemporary religious leaders.[183] Giovanni Dominici's sermons, especially the "Sermon for Holy Saturday," and his *Book of the Love of Charity*, together with his *Letters* and his *Rule for the Governance of the Family* addressed to the laity, were assiduously copied.[184] Archbishop Antoninus dealt constantly in his office and in his writings with practical spiritual matters. A number of compilations, as

observed, include his recommendations on confessions, excommunications, the sacraments, and a *Treatise on Mortal Sins*. Feo Belcari's edifying verse correspondence, also much copied, is among the most urgent of Florentines' frequent literary expressions of their desire for a better understanding of doctrine.[185] Bernardino of Siena's sermons, especially the famous Easter series preached in Florence in 1425, were collected in the same way as material from performances at San Martino, being transcribed, circulated, and finally preserved for posterity, often in *zibaldoni*. The canonization of the Sienese preacher, and later of Antoninus, so soon after their deaths, reflects the esteem in which their counsel was held, as well perhaps as a wish on the part of many Tuscans, including Cosimo, to add these familiar figures to the ranks of the saints interceding for them in heaven. A laud in honor of San Bernardino appears in at least one book compiled just after his canonization in 1450, and shortly thereafter the Medici had him represented in the altarpiece painted by Baldovinetti for the chapel of their villa at Cafaggiolo.[186]

Self-castigation for sins, and despair of achieving salvation were major themes of the enormous body of *laude* and other spiritual verse written by Florentine laymen and transcribed in their compilations. But whereas fifty years later Luther's sense of his own total depravity, too profound to be redeemed by any virtuous acts he might personally perform, led him to formulate the Protestant doctrine of justification by faith alone, despairing Florentine Catholics put their faith and hope not in their own merits, but in those of the saints, and the power of these saints to intercede on a sinner's behalf with his ultimate judge. Saints were mens' best friends and most perfect patrons, envisaged on the model of earthly friends and patrons such as Cosimo de' Medici; this concept is explicitly imaged in the altarpiece Cosimo commissioned for San Marco.[187] Most anthologies, like mercantile diaries, *ricordi*, and contracts, began with an invocation to the Virgin and other saints to whom the owner or copyist was particularly devoted. Although obviously formulaic, these invocations were far from being a formality. Like declarations of ownership, they might appear on the first or last pages of a book. Sometimes, however, they were hidden, like treasures, in less obvious places. Inscribed on the fourty-fourth folio of one scrapbook is a statement: "Written by me in this parish, that is by me, Sandro di Piero di Lotteringho, on the 10th of July, 1448"; half a dozen folios earlier, after several "lauds in praise of the Virgin Mary," Sandro had inserted the names "Saint Protus, Saint Nemesius, Saint Iacintus," sandwiched between two elaborately drawn Greek crosses. He gave no hint of why these saints' names had suddenly come to his mind; as it happens, they were the three whose relics in the convent of the Angeli had inspired his close friends Cosimo and Lorenzo de' Medici to commission their small bronze reliquary from Ghiberti.[188]

In this review of the devotional literature that appears most often in literary compilations, the saints figure prominently. Fifteenth-century Florentines' understanding of them, the significance of their lives, and the meaning of the attributes associated with them, was drawn from many sources, some of them highly sophisticated. This flatly contradicts the view that artists and their patrons, when they envisaged representations of saints, drew chiefly on the *Golden Legend* of Iacopo da Voragine as a crib. His was the most complete late medieval compilation of saints' lives, and it was indeed very popular. However, extracts from this work usually appear alongside other fundamental devotional literature, coupled with such works as Iacopo Passavanti's *Mirror of True Penitence*, or the sermons and letters of Saint Gregory, Saint Bernard, and Giovanni Dominici. In *The Golden Legend* the lives of the saints, their virtues, miracles and martyrdoms, are presented in the context of the liturgical year, as milestones among the main events of the historical unfolding of the Christian revelation. How that might have affected representations of the saints is a question to which we will return. The care with which fifteenth-century Florentines read *The Golden Legend* and the events it narrated is evident in popular poems and *laude*, as well as in the comments of anthologists. One, for example, concluded his extracts from Iacopo's work with a long comment on the meaning of Advent. Antonio di Guido, the soapmaker, ended his notebook with a prayer: "May the Lord God grant him grace at his end as to all faithful Christians." Of this the deeds and images of the saints gave every sinner a vivid and lively hope.[189]

CIVIC TRADITIONS AND CELEBRATIONS: FROM BRUNETTO LATINI AND VILLANI TO THE LETTERS OF BRUNI AND FRANCESCO SFORZA

Many a literary anthologist, like writers of *ricordi* and returners of tax reports, proudly proclaimed himself "a Florentine." Just as the clerics Giovanni dalle Celle, Dominici, and Savonarola saw patriotism as a part of piety, Dante in his *Divine Comedy* saw the font in the baptistery as the place where Florentines became at once citizens and Christians.[190] Religious preoccupations shaded into the civic and political in many kinds of popular texts. The *ringhiera*, the platform in front of the palace of the

Priors where political speeches were made, was a secular pulpit where speakers similarly equated personal with civic virtue.

Florence's fourteenth-century conflicts of interest with the papacy continued to resurface in the fifteenth century, when not palliated by personal relationships between the pope and leading citizens like Cosimo de' Medici. Indeed after Cosimo's death, tensions eventually reached the point where the Pazzi were named the pope's bankers, and Sixtus IV supported that family's conspiracy against their former Medici friends and patrons. But the many sonnets and civic speeches written in praise of individual popes were repeatedly included in quattrocento *zibaldoni*. The enduring popularity of Giovanni the shoemaker's poem describing Eugenius IV's consecration of Santa Maria del Fiore, like the entries in Bartolomeo del Corazza's diary, shows how much Florentines appreciated the papal presence in their city.[191] Spiritual concerns as well as jurisdictional and territorial ones kept Florentine eyes fixed on the Holy See.

The Florentine populace clearly concurred with Cosimo's view, expressed in the council debates of the 1440s and 1450s, that the city's liberty, her independence from the power of foreign influence, was her greatest treasure. Florentines agreed, albeit often grudgingly, to spend vast sums on their military captains in its defence. Giovanni Gherardi da Prato's "moral song of the *patria* and of liberty" was typical of the patriotic literature to be found in popular compilations,[192] and performances at San Martino show how much *condottieri* were admired as popular heroes. When they accepted the city's baton of authority, military captains were addressed from the platform outside the palace of the Priors by the chancellor on behalf of the Signoria; these speeches, and popular poems written in their honor before and after major battles, appear in a great many compilations. Bruni's orations were particularly admired and often copied, especially those directed to Sigismondo Malatesta and Niccolò da Tolentino. Manetti's oration to Bernardetto de' Medici, after the Florentine troops jointly commanded by him and Neri Capponi defeated the Milanese and the anti-Medicean exiles at Anghiari, was another popular selection. The expensive and largely unsuccessful war against Lucca remained a sore point for Florentines for many years after it ended; Bruni's "Work written in defence of the people of Florence against certain calumniators who condemn the enterprise of the war of Lucca embarked upon by the Florentine people" also enjoyed a wide circulation.[193]

Since the most visible hero of the battlefield for the last thirty years of Cosimo's life was Francesco Sforza, naturally the news of his exploits and the encomia recited in his honor at San Martino were staples of Florentine anthologies.[194] Sforza's image was much enhanced by his victory over the Visconti, the previous ruling dynasty of Milan. The Visconti were the *bêtes noires* of the Florentine republic, which saw itself as having been saved in 1401 from Giangaleazzo Visconti's aggression only by his timely death, interpreted as divine intervention. When a similar situation threatened in 1414, the Florentine herald Antonio di Meglio, in a verse celebrating the Milanese rout at Zagonara, exulted that Giangaleazzo had failed to crush Florence beneath his "tyrant's foot." This attitude may explain the appeal of a tract arguing that: "The Lordship of Milan should be consigned into the hands of the descendants of Sforza/ and never again should the Visconti be its Lords."[195] Other civic occasions marked by speeches featured in compilations were the assumption of office by the republic's leading officials, the Gonfaloniers of Justice, and by foreign Captains and Podestàs, who played a vital role in the function of city government. The government's official letters to cities with which it had important diplomatic relations or which, like Pisa, were part of the Florentine dominion, were also of considerable interest.[196]

Items like these were often grouped together in what might be described as patriotic anthologies.[197] Such collections also included works related to major civic milestones, like Giovanni the shoemaker's poem describing the consecration of the cathedral. In the combination of literary selections can be seen the essential elements of Florentine civic patriotism; classical, feudal, mercantile, Christian. Part of this ethos was the high valuation of heroism and fame, which are major themes of Cosimo's artistic patronage. Contemporary civic heroes were located on a continuum with those of a past that stretched back to the beginnings of ancient civilization. "Marco di Priore di Gino da Prato, notary . . . of the noble and powerful man Iacopo di Niccolò Riccialbani of Florence," when he was Podestà of Montepulciano in 1399, combined in his book a letter attributed to Boccaccio supposedly sent to Frederick Barbarossa, several letters by Bruni including those to Niccolò da Tolentino, works on nobility by Buonaccorso da Montemagno and Guido delle Colonne, and the Trojan stories translated by Mazzeo Bellevuoni, since "naturally men delight in hearing of the deeds of the ancients, and especially of the great and noble things worthy of memory."[198] Compilations preserved the literary sources of a tradition of famous men, imaged so often in paintings like the *uomini illustri* commissioned by Cosimo's father, Giovanni di Bicci de' Medici. Tales of Florentine warriors were copied together with those of the chivalric and classical past, just as in the cycle of *Famous Men* painted in the

Palazzo Vecchio, classical heroes were depicted alongside their medieval and Florentine heirs.[199]

The relations Florence enjoyed with other powerful states similarly reflected on her own reputation. Compilations contained many letters and sonnets in praise of important Italian political figures, not just *condottieri*, but also kings and princes with whom the Florentines had dealings. The Holy Roman Emperor, who sent Cosimo a message of condolence and support when he was exiled in Venice in 1433, visited Florence from time to time on his pilgrimages south to Rome. One of the more celebrated of these occasions occurred in 1451, and is described in great detail in the ceremonial book of the Florentine herald as well as in various *zibaldoni*. Sigismondo Malatesta, lord of Rimini, served from time to time as captain of the Florentine forces, and was a participant on various occasions of significance to the Florentine *popolo*, including the consecration of the cathedral in 1436; his patronage also contributed to the rebuilding of Santissima Annunziata, and his poems were included in Florentine anthologies. The king of Hungary sent an embassy to Florence in 1451, and the Hungarian court's relations with Florence were clearly stimulated by the presence there of a Florentine *condottiere*, Pippo Spano, of the Scolari family, who helped to build the church of the Angeli.[200] The entourage of the king of Naples, a major player on the Florentine diplomatic scene, although not usually on the same side, was entertained and honored in Florence. The Acciaiuoli, among the city's oldest and most distinguished families, had also been feudatories of the king of Naples in the Holy Land, and Nicola Acciaiuoli had served the king as seneschal in the fourteenth century. The rulers of Florence traded on such connections when diplomacy demanded it and the *popolo* took note of them in its *quadernucci*.[201]

An attachment to civic traditions on the part of the *popolo* was reinforced by the recitation and repetition of patriotic texts on state occasions, and again at San Martino. Popular performers also helped to shape this tradition with their original verses on matters of civic interest, often addressed to the Signoria whom they were employed to entertain.[202] Popular interest in civic issues went beyond the glamor of warfare and poems in praise of heroes on the battlefield to the serious business of everyday government. One particularly interesting *quaderno* compiled by Sandro Lotteringhi added to customary selections from the works of Brunetto Latini and Villani's *Chronicle* the edifying tale about the subjugation of private to public welfare recorded by Valerian: "of a man who lamented the death of his enemy because he knew that his life had been devoted to the benefit of the republic, that is, the good of the commune."[203] As we saw in examining the role of the herald in Florentine culture, the *canzona morale* was a specialty of popular entertainers; poets were accepted as authorities on the ethics of politics and government as they were on other matters of morality and religion. Niccolò Cieco commanded a respectful audience for his verses on social harmony, also a basic theme of the *amicizia* poems written for the Certame Coronario. Antonio di Guido, "che canta in san Martino," addressed to his friend and fellow-poet Francesco degli Alberti a discourse "on the government" which began by throwing down a Dantesque gauntlet: "Sleep on, Justinian."[204] The herald Antonio di Meglio entertained Florence's patrician statesmen at table not only with disquisitions on political morality, but also on practical issues of civic organization. Niccolò Cieco lectured the members of the Magi company on the importance of preparing properly, and in an orderly fashion, for the Epiphany celebration. That his views on taxation could also be the stuff of poetry and song might give comfort to those who discern a comment on this theme in Masaccio's frescoes for the Brancacci chapel in the Carmine.[205]

Finally, there was the literature of praise of Florence, transcribed by numerous patriotic anthologists. Many poets directly addressed their native city, personified as a beautiful and gracious lady. Perhaps the best known of these encomia was by Niccolò da Uzzano, a leading anti-Medicean statesmen before his death in 1427, attempting to rouse to action "Lovers of old of the good and beautiful city,/ enhanced by your expenses/ so that all the world tells of her . . ."[206]

THE FASCINATION OF THE UNKNOWN AND THE THRILL OF THE EXOTIC: DATI'S *GLOBE* AND THE ETHIOPIAN PRESTER JOHN

Gregorio Dati's account of the assets of his native city, extracted from his *History of Florence*, sometimes appear in compilations along with his more widely circulated popularization, often beautifully illustrated, of classical geographical studies. Dati's *Globe* (*Sfera* or *Mappamondo*) described the three parts of the then known world; Europe, Asia, and Africa (fig. 24). It was introduced by one copyist as "144 *stanze* called the *Mappamondo*, marvelously beautiful and excellent and delightfully told by Goro di Stagio Dati, our famous citizen." The great popularity of this work, which began to circulate around 1420, bears witness to a lively curiosity in Florence concerning distant worlds. This can be related to the arrival in Florence around 1400 of the Greek text of Ptolemy's

Geography, and the *Geography* of Strabo. Manuscripts of the latter were available in Italy from 1423, but close encounters during the church council of 1439 with Christians from Armenia, Abyssinia and Ethiopia, and Pletho and Toscanelli's related studies of the *Geographia*, perhaps made it seem more immediately relevant to Florentine concerns.[207]

Florentine curiosity concerning the exotic East had long fed on familiar stories of crusading and pilgrimage, like Leonardo Frescobaldi's account of his expedition to the Holy Land in the 1390s, or the letters and dispatches of Florentine merchants in Turkey, sometimes included in personal anthologies. After the Turkish conquest of Constantinople in 1453, the crusading spirit, a concern to defend Christian interests and shrines in the East, was revived in such schemes as Pius II's plan for a new crusade in 1464, which enjoyed the support of Cosimo de' Medici.[208] In the preceding decades, intellectual exchange with the Christian inhabitants of these alien lands, through the visits of eastern scholars and after 1453, their immigration to the West with more Greek manuscripts, had reached a creative high point. At the same time, the government of Florence was in diplomatic contact with countries such as Ethiopia, which sent a delegation to the council. The legendary kingdom of Prester John was marked on contemporary maps of Ethiopia, and his life and chronicles so captured the imagination of Florentines that they thought of him as real. Ser Alesso Pelli, Cosimo's household factotum, referred to the king's communications with the West in a letter to Cosimo's younger son Giovanni, and Michele del Gigante included a substantial selection from this text in a compilation probably made for someone in the Medici circle.[209] After 1440, Eastern costumes, animals, and themes became part of the artist's and performer's as well as the copyist's repertoire; various of Cosimo's commissions of works of art directly express his family's interest in Eastern images and themes.

Most *zibaldoni* were personalized by the addition of snippets of practical information of special interest to their owners. Among these were recipes for favorite dishes and prescriptions of cures for common illnesses. Remedies for sicknesses of body and soul were a specialty of Marsilio Ficino, the young Neoplatonic philosopher and doctor's son whose studies were supported by many Florentine patrons, including the Medici. Although the collections containing his widely circulated *ricette* are beyond the scope of this study, being mostly compiled by members of the ruling elite in the years after Cosimo's death, they continue a long tradition of lay inquiry into such questions as the relation of the soul to God and the nature of Fortune.[210]

The compilations reviewed here are enormously valuable as evidence of the substance and nature of Florentine popular culture, and above all of the sheer variety of its coexistent elements. Florentine minds were enlivened by a miscellany of information from the Bible to Ovid. Whether the anthologists were highly educated or relatively ignorant of formal learning made little difference to the content of these heterogenous collections. Nor did they separate the secular and the spiritual, the solemn, the scary and the side-splitting. They assembled these readings for their relevance to life in all its manifestations.

STORING WISDOM IN THE HOUSE OF MEMORY

Once knowledge was accumulated and conserved in compilations, it had then to be activated in the owner's memory. Transcription was only the first step in this process. Benedetto Dei made long lists of things he had memorized; his enumeration in his *Cronica* of 1473 of the first lines of "Cantari e Sonetti" that he had committed to memory helps to define, only ten years after Cosimo de' Medici's death, the main corpus of popular literature in Cosimo's lifetime. It included a poem which appears in numerous compilations, describing the great snowfall of 1407/8, during which citizens made snowmen in the shape of the Florentine lion (Marzocco) and of Hercules. Other popular items memorized and transcribed by Dei were the poem attributed to Cosimo in praise of Sforza, an elegy on Cosimo's death addressed to Lorenzo di Piero, the *Sfera* of Goro Dati, Lo Za's *Buca di Monte Ferrato*, exposing the associations of Florentine homosexuals, the cobbler Giovanni's poem on the consecration of the cathedral, one of Brunelleschi's poems, Boccaccio's *Ninfale*, the credo attributed to Dante, Burchiello's verses denouncing the return of the Medici in 1434, and a poem in praise of the exploits of the English *condottiere* Sir John Hawkwood, who was memorialized in Uccello's fresco for the cathedral in 1436. Dei committed altogether "ten *novelle* and 139 *storie* and *ternali* to memory," showing just how much information a well-ordered mind could house.[211]

Zanobi di Pagholo d'Agnolo Perini observed in his *quadernuccio* alongside the well-known verse describing the great snowfall of 1408: "In the name of God and his mother Saint Mary and of all the holy court of Paradise amen, amen. Here I record the memory of how on the 17th of January 1407, on the day of Sant'Antonio, the great snow which continued all that month began to fall . . . For I would not consider myself to have even the smallest knowledge if I created no records for the sake of memory of that which I saw in my Florence . . ."[212] As

Machiavelli explained to his friend Vettori, describing how he communed at night with ancient writers in his study, "where I am not ashamed to speak with them and to ask them the reason for their actions, and they in their kindness answer me," he then noted down what he had learned, "because Dante says it does not produce knowledge when we hear but do not remember."[213]

These vivid evocations of the close relation in Renaissance minds between hearing, reading, writing, memorizing, and knowing help to explain the inclusion in many compilations of a treatise on memory. These schema took various forms, some with very individual variations, like the one built by Ser Piero di Ser Bonaccorso around the image of Santa Quaresima.[214] But all basically derived, with more or less explicit acknowledgement, from Cicero's and Quintilian's prescriptions. Among the more personal variants and the most popular in Medici circles were those promulgated by Michele del Giogante.[215] The most interesting of Michele's schemas was devised by the renowned improviser of the 1430s and 1440s, the blind poet Niccolò Cieco, who performed frequently at San Martino and was praised by his fellow poets as "the lodging-house of memories." A native of the Marches, Niccolò Cieco came to Florence in 1432, and in 1435 he moved into Michele's house. Michele was an indefatigable transcriber of Niccolò's performances, translating oral into written culture that could be memorized in turn for future performance. Indeed in one of his *zibaldoni* there is a sonnet of apology that he wrote to his friend Niccolò, referring to a temporary falling out on this account, and prefaced by the following explanation:

> Three stanzas that Michele di Nofri del Giogante wrote for Maestro Niccolò Cieco of Florence on December 30, 1435. Michele . . . wishing to take down in writing the stanzas [Niccolò] sang at San Martino in a correct manner and with the aid of others and having explained this to Niccolò who replied that he was happy about it, Niccolò later became upset and refused to sing any more. For this reason they didn't speak to one another for three days, after which Michele decided to make peace with him by sending him these three stanzas."[216]

The fullest version of Niccolò's treatise is in a compilation Michele made for his own personal use.

> Here I Michele di Nofri di Michele di Maso del Giogante, accountant, will show the principle of learning the art of memory, which was explained to me by Maestro Niccholò Ciecho of Florence in December 1435 when he came here, beginning by allotting places in my house according to the way he told me to, saying

that the first five spaces should be called the first category, and then another five the second, and another five the third category and so on . . . and I began with the first place outside the front door in the alley, and the second around the door, and the third the chest beside the entrance, and the fourth the window, and the fifth the adjacent wall and this was the first category, and then the sixth was the furniture and the seventh the door of the cellar . . . and so on."[217]

This is a Florentine lower middle-class domestication of the schemes described in Quintilian's *Institutions* and Cicero's *De Oratore*, both of which were well known, and were in Cosimo's library by 1418, and in the treatise *Ad Herennium*, a popular text attributed erroneously to Cicero. Its author recommended that to train oneself in the art of memory, one should choose a well-lit, spacious house with a variety of rooms through which the mind can run freely. "Begin by fixing the plan in your imagination; then order the ideas, words, or images that you wish to remember, placing the first thing in the vestibule, the second in the atrium, then more around the impluvium, into side rooms, and even onto statues or paintings. Once you have put everything in its place, whenever you wish to recall something, start again at the entrance and move through the house, where you will find all the images linked one to another as in a chain or a chorus." Once inside his house of memory, a man could start anywhere and move either backward or forward from that point, since it was the spatial order of the storage that allowed for retrieval, as Quintilian pointed out.[218] The precept of the author of *Ad Herennium* that the student of memory must form his own images is followed faithfully in Michele del Giogante's scheme based on his own house, by contrast with the general practice described by Frances Yates of "the regular arrangement of the places in . . . memory rooms (not chosen for their unlikeness to one another and irregularity, as advised in the classical rules)."[219]

The two basic medieval models for memory treatises were the wax tablet, embodying the notion of "engraving" information on the memory, and the "storage room" which could be expanded into a house of memory. There were few, or no post-classical memory treatises earlier than the fifteenth century. So it is particularly significant that the schema used by Florentine artisan poets in the city which gave such impetus to the revival of classical architecture as well as literature is based on the architectural model in preference to the metaphor of the book, which might well have presented itself as a natural choice to men so well versed in the allegorical images of both the Old and New Testaments.[220]

Besides its foundation in the metaphor of architecture, figures and symbols familiar from the arts of painting and sculpture make their appearance in Michele's memory scheme. Alberti, in his treatise *On Painting*, written in 1435, the same year Michele made his transcription, embraced "a view of painting as an art of memory."[221] Michele's scheme illluminates the relation between images and memory in the popular mind. The second part of the treatise deals with the eight "figures" of memory, moving from the known to the unknown, with the aid of imagination.[222] The "actual figure" is for "men, women and other things that you have seen and known and dealt with . . . what you can see and touch," to be associated with places, "or their symbols or devices." The "imaginative figure" is for people or objects "which you have not seen or known or had experience of, except for what you have heard or found in writing . . . You will have heard it said that Hercules was a just and powerful man, and you want to keep his name in your mind, but never having seen or known him . . . you must have faith in your imagining of what he is . . . this is necessary to all the other figures, and none . . . can work without it, because imagination is always open to all forms of language or means of communication."[223]

The "significative figure" takes the first letter of a name and links it to one beginning with the same letter, "which you cannot forget; if you want to remember Sant'Ambrogio and you are called Antonio, use your own name . . . in this chain and group you can retain the other." The "figure of pronunciation," the accidental, is similarly simple; faced with a word without associations, such as "a name in a language you don't understand, divide it into syllables which have meaning in your own language." The "figure of the skill," involves a principle upon which many Florentine lists or descriptions of people were based; "for a man, think of his craft [*arte*] or profession [*uficio*] . . . for a thing, in what profession it is used." The "figure of fame" accords with both classical and Florentine social values, being the recall of the object by its reputation, good or evil. The "figure of the will" depends, like the choice of texts to be preserved in *zibaldoni* and memorized, upon an imaginative conception of the relevance of something to oneself: "Think of this man or woman or thing, of what you would like to do with it . . . or what you would like to see happen to it, whether good or ill . . . like a beautiful palace . . ."[224] The eighth, the "effective figure," required attaching to a man or object the opposite of the truth, "like imagining that you would like to see a good man hanged." Michele assured his readers that "these eight figures of artificial memory constitute every method and manner of being able to remember every name of a man or a woman or other animal or other memorable thing . . . numbers, events, prose, allegories in sermons, the speeches of ambassadors, readings, each and every thing . . ."

Both Quintilian and the author of *Ad Herennium* discussed at length the importance of symbolism and historical allegory, and Cicero equated this with "translation" or "the connection of many metaphors, so that one thing may be said and another understood."[225] As Kristeller observed of the contents of literary anthologies, in these "metaphorical language became a philosophical medium." That is the principle underlying preachers' analyses of images of the Passion of Christ, which specifically relate metaphor and memory to visual images and their viewing.[226] Confraternal devotion and constant listening to sermons, carefully constructed to be memorized, accustomed Florentines to the habit of mind recommended in a Venetian text, *The Garden of Prayer*:

> The better to impress the story of the Passion on your mind, and to memorise each action of it more easily, it is helpful and necessary to fix the places and people in your mind: a city, for example, which will be the city of Jerusalem — taking for this purpose a city that is well known to you. In this city find the principal places in which all the episodes of the Passion would have taken place — for instance, a palace with the supper-room where Christ had the Last Supper with the Disciples, and the house of Anne and that of Caiaphas . . . etc. And then too you must shape in your mind some people, people well-known to you, to rep-

resent for you the people involved in the Passion — the person of Jesus Himself, of the Virgin, Saint Peter, Saint John the Evangelist . . .[227]

Michele's treatise offers a formal method for this imaginative exercise, which extends to the use of familiar visual images and metaphors in popular devotional poetry.[228] As the author of *Ad Herennium* observed, "the artifical memory includes backgrounds and images . . . we first go over a given verse twice or three times to ourselves, and then represent the words by means of images. In this way art will supplement nature."[229]

What Michele del Giogante's memory scheme tells us, apart from what was in his own house, is that the minds of Renaissance men were a mass of associations, a compendium of things that "stood for" other things.[230] This is something we need to understand about their ways of looking at works of art. Artists, as Francis Haskell observed, create memory in works of art by the "self-conscious citation of one work of art by another."[231] This was especially true of Renaissance artists, who tended to build up a framework of customarily connected images that viewers could use to decipher new ones, and which helped to make the practice of viewing an exercise in the rehearsal of learning.[232] The Muses, the goddesses of creative inspiration in poetry, music, and history, were after all the daughters of Jupiter and Mnemosyne, born literally out of memory, which forged the links between past and present, verbal and visual, and the various distinct but ingeniously integrated elements of Florentine popular culture.

POPULAR DEVOTION AND THE PERCEPTION OF IMAGES

There is a large and growing literature exploring how in various times and places men have read the signs of the natural world, their translation of such signs into cultural systems articulating and interpreting religious beliefs, and the symbolic expression of these signs and systems in language, music, and images. In the awareness that the relation between modes of perception and the language of words and images is a complex field of study whose cultivation has barely begun,[1] this chapter attempts only a relatively straightforward reading of the evidence concerning ordinary Florentines' perceptions of sacred images, drawing from the sources on which this book is chiefly based – letters, *ricordi*, popular poetry and literary compilations, and contemporary works of art. It is often suggested that patrons could have very little part in the conception of religious commissions, and that they and their audience perceived devotional images in very simple terms, because their knowledge of Christian doctrine and iconography was very limited. It is clear from the previous chapter that this simply was not so. What follows shows how Florentines could use their comparatively sophisticated understanding of religious doctrine to construct, read, and respond to devotional images, which constituted the bulk of Cosimo's commissions for both private and public viewing.

MEMORY AND MEDITATION: "WITH THE EYES OF THE MIND MORE THAN THOSE OF THE BODY"; IMAGE AND NARRATIVE

Memory systems for the organization of knowledge, particularly those popular in Florence, depended heavily on schemas envisioned "with the eyes of the mind more than those of the body," in Archbishop Antoninus's phrase, instructing the devout on the role of images in spiritual exercises and meditation. Of course his perspective was not precisely that of those who regard images as works of art. But then most fifteenth-century viewers of most quattrocento images saw them as devotional more than decorative. They brought to their viewing a familiar body of texts, devotional and liturgical. Renaissance iconography was therefore not primarily a set of complex and alien signs to be deciphered by learning, but a form of communication natural to most Christian viewers.[2]

Although popular poets in particular were noted for their feats of memory, memorizing essential cultural information, mainly moral and religious, was a universal habit and requirement. Knowledge gleaned from the instruction and entertainment provided in public celebrations and performances, or the devotion practiced in church and confraternity, furnished the equipment needed to create and interpret images. Those who could conserved the memory of this information in writing. Citizens recorded the details of civic ceremonies in their diaries, the *laudesi* companies used boards to propagate their rules and repertoire, the authors of personal anthologies transcribed popular texts, and members of the audience took notes on sermons and performances.[3]

At the heart of popular piety was Everyman's imaginative identification with Christ's pain and his mother's grief. He knew himself to be the direct cause of their sufferings, since Christ died on the cross to redeem his sins, the sins of all the heirs of Adam. The *laude* and devotional poems written or memorized by large numbers of ordinary Florentines show that their identification with the experience of Christ and the Virgin, the archetypes of fleshly mothers and sons, was informed, passionate, and vivid. The role of meditation, recognition, and identification in devotion meant memorizing not only texts but also images, so that verbal and visual memories were naturally fused in these activities. Antoninus's injunction to the contemplation of the crucified Christ in every terrible detail exemplifies the intense attention focused on works of art to achieve the state of mind appropriate to prayer.[4] Antoninus and Dominici, Florence's most compelling religious leaders in Cosimo's lifetime, recognized

32 Orcagna, tabernacle, 1369/70, and Bernardo Daddi, *The Madonna and Child*, 1300–48 Florence, Orsanmichele

and promoted the role of images in evoking, focusing and expressing religious feeling in their congregations from birth to death.

Often cited by historians in this regard is the advice Giovanni Dominici gave to Diamante Salviati on the Christian education of children. "The first regulation is to have pictures of saintly children or young virgins in the home, in which your child, still in swaddling clothes, may take delight and thereby may be gladdened by acts and sights pleasing to childhood. And what I say of pictures applies also to statues. It is well to have the Virgin Mary with the child in arms, with a little bird or apple in his hand . . . So let the child see himself mirrored in the Holy Baptist clothed in camel's skin . . . I should like them to see . . . other such representations as may give them with their milk love of the Virgin, a longing for Christ, a hatred of sin, make them despise vanity, avoid bad company, and begin, through the contemplation of the saints, the contemplation of the supreme Saint of saints . . ." These suggestions made in the first decade of the quattrocento to a mother on the care of her children have been inappropriately adduced as applying to the adult layman's view of art in the full bloom of the Renaissance, particularly in influential accounts by Creighton Gilbert and Charles Hope. On this selective basis Gilbert suggested that the appeal of images to fifteenth-century viewers was "not recondite, nor theological . . . but moral on a very simple level . . . ," alluding only to "what is easily seized . . . working on the genre aspects, so to speak, of our own life."[5]

The evidence of the whole body of lay spiritual activity and literature, from poems and popular compilations to participation in the para-liturgical rituals of confraternities and the performance of *sacre rappresentazioni*, shows precisely the opposite; that the Renaissance audience for images was extremely sophisticated in its knowledge of doctrine, even some theology, and in its envisioning of images to stimulate, refine, and interpret men's perceptions of Christian truths.[6] To focus on just one example from popular didactic literature, from the writing of the other major spiritual guide of Florentines in the early fifteenth century, it is clear that in his pastoral letters and manuals for Christian living Antoninus took for granted his congregation's lifelong cultivation of imaginative resources, including a high level of understanding of the significance of metaphor, analogy, and symbolism.

For example, in an exposition for Holy Thursday of the captivity of the Jews, Antoninus observed how much meaning in the Scriptures "is hidden, for nothing is simply what it seems . . . 'and all things are expressed figuratively,' says the Apostle." The Jews were "figuratively

the Christian people," the Tau was the cross, painted with the blood of the lamb, "which is to say, Jesus Christ." When Jesus spoke of being baptized, he meant "bathed in the flow of his blood onto the column [to which he was tied to be flagellated] . . . The cross . . . and the drunkenness of Noah figures . . . the intoxication of love and desire of human nature for Christ . . . and the pascal lamb figures his Passion, in which the immaculate Lamb of God was roasted "on the spit of the cross by the fire of love and pain . . ."[7] Such an exposition of scripture and other texts and images was rather the norm than the exception in the culture which popular compilers have revealed; a world where Aesop's secular fables and images of them were naturally read by his Christian audience as precedents or analogies of the teachings of Scripture. In this world, the function of art envisaged largely for adults was complex, profound, and fundamental to the devotional experience to create states of mind, revealing the truth of revelation.[8] This was true of images for personal contemplation in private or public, as of images destined to function in a liturgical context in churches or chapels.

For no apparent reason arising from the study of fifteenth-century texts or religious practices, in his study of religious images Charles Hope rejected "iconographical interpretations derived from liturgical practice and devotional texts, as well as suggestions that altarpieces are 'about' aspects of doctrine, such as the Incarnation." He claimed instead to adopt a "commonsensical approach," which essentially means privileging the relatively uninformed assumptions of a twentieth-century secular layman. Reacting against "a tendency to 'theologize' Renaissance religious art" by ascribing "erudite iconographical interpretations to lay patrons," he asserted instead the "normally straightforward devotional concerns of the men and women who ordered altarpieces," meaning mainly their assumed "interest in images of sacred personages rather than narrative representations of historical events." In his elaboration of this argument, Hope confused issues of vital importance to the interpretation of images, not realizing how these "events" were seen as part of the continuous unfolding and manifestation of revelation, uncircumscribed by secular conceptions of the constraints of time and space. He seemed driven, like Gilbert, by a desire to propose more freedom for artists in the working out of religious themes; somewhat paradoxically for his argument he represented artists as "drawing upon the repertory of familiar imagery reiterated in prayers, hymns and other works of art – all known to painter, patron and public."[9]

A study of these works, and of the ambience in which this imagery developed, shows painters, patrons, and their public all closely involved with these elements of popular culture, but perceiving its products as far more complex and profound than Hope's account suggests. His reductive descriptions of imagined contemporary readings of images include such arbitrary and anachronistic propositions as that Christ – the *Salvator mundi* – appears in devotional images of the Madonna and Child not "as a character in his own right, but as an attribute of his mother," or that "most altarpieces are reflections of devotion to the Virgin and the saints, not to Christ," as if the intercessory powers of the Virgin and other saints could have any meaning outside of the framework of Christ's incarnation to redeem man's sins, and his place in heaven at the right hand of God sitting in judgment on sinners.[10]

Much more of Florentines' actual attitudes to images has emerged from our account of popular performances and texts; we turn now to their explicit testimony on this question. Cosimo's friend and fellow-patron of churches and altarpieces, Giuliano Quaratesi, introduced his transcription of the *Legend of Saint John the Baptist*, made so that his readers "are able and know how to meditate and enter into the life of Christ," with a disclaimer. He stressed the simple and diversionary interest of his saint's life, cognate to Dominici's spiritual exercises for children, in relation to the natural progress of Christian meditation toward levels of far higher significance. In describing this he invoked the inherent context of the whole Christian narrative as inevitably recalled by the most casual contemplation of any image of any moment in the lives of Christ, his mother, and their attendant saints.

> I don't intend to enter into such lofty matters, but I want to tell you of his life, meditating and reflecting on him when young and when grown, and whoever reads this should consider his needs. For if his mind is inclined to meditate on the life of Christ, and to consider him as a child and man, and his death and resurrection and the glory of his name, this work is not appropriate for him. But in thinking of him and his ultimate love and that of Messer San Giovanni I have done this for the diversion of feeble minds, and from such a childish work that satisfies the souls of youths, they may gain such spiritual joy as comes from meditating and entering into the life of Christ and of his mother Our Lady, and if they find pleasure in thinking of the life of the saints in such childish ways, how much more will they think on the life of Christ which is perfection, and turning their minds to these small humble meditations they will learn how to enter and contemplate the great things of the saints, and thus will begin to contemplate Messer Gesù Christo in the good deeds of his holy saints. And these are things not demonstrated just by me, but things approved by the

Church. But I delight in considering them, and if it should please you to think of more things or in another way, you may do so, and may wander as you please . . .[11]

Naturally and inevitably, images of saints imply and evoke the well-known narratives of their lives and martyrdoms, drawing behind them a mass of information and lore stored in the mind of the viewer and activated by the appearance of the image. As San Bernardino observed, "to look upon the Cross is to be reminded of Christ's Passion . . . to hear his name is to recollect every aspect of his life: the poverty of the crib, the humility of the carpenter's shop, the penance in the desert, the miracles of the divine charity, the suffering on Calvary, the triumph of the Resurrection and the Ascension."[12]

Much more sophisticated than Quaratesi's *Life of the Baptist*, but still, as already seen, among the simpler and most popular guides to doctrine included in a number of compilations, was Iacopo da Voragine's *The Golden Legend*. This work was not, as Hope suggested, virtually the sole source of the laity's knowledge of the saints; nor was it philosophical or theological. Its author rather proceeded by exposition of passages from the Scripture and authorities woven into narrative accounts of men and women *living* doctrine; these are laden with explanations of elaborate symbolism and "figures of speech." Many apparently straightforward stories are shown to be full of hidden meaning, like the significance in Saint Peter's imagery of the mourning dove representing simplicity, and his sandals, standing for the desires of earthly things, from which man must be unbound. While the chronological arrangement of the work might suggest to the casual reader that it was simply a convenient calendar for the celebration of saints' days, in fact its fundamental purpose was to trace the unfolding of revelation over the course of the liturgical year.[13]

As its author explained in the first lines of his prologue:

> The whole time-span of this present life comprises four distinct periods: the time of deviation or turning from the right way, the time of renewal or of being called back, the time of reconciliation, and the time of pilgrimage. The time of deviation began with Adam, or rather with his turning away from God, and lasted until Moses. The Church represents this period from Septuagesima to Easter, and the Book of Genesis is read, since that book tells of the fall of our first parents. The time of renewal, or being called back, began with Moses and ended with the birth of Christ, during which time mankind was renewed and called back to faith by the prophets. The Church observes it from

the beginning of Advent until the Nativity of the Lord. Isaiah is read then, because he treats clearly of this recall. The time of reconciliation is that during which we were reconciled by Christ, and the Church marks it from Easter to Pentecost: the Book of the Apocalypse, or Revelation, in which the mystery of this reconciliation is fully treated, is read. The time of pilgrimage is that of our present life, for we are on pilgrimage and constantly engaged in warfare . . . [There is] a time of rejoicing, namely, from Christmas to the octave of Epiphany . . . This fourfold division of historic time can be related to the seasons of the year . . . or it may be related to the phases of the day.

This is the framework within which the lives and images of the saints were set and seen.[14]

Familiar devotional literature refers constantly to this personal and historical progression of man from deviation to rejoicing in reconciliation through Christ. Antonio di Guido's devotional sonnets evoke this consciousness so vividly and concisely that it is clear why he was the most admired of all popular poets, and why princes of the sophistication of Sforza's son stood in awe of him. He was able to encapsulate the whole Christian revelation, and the experience of every Christian pilgrim, in one brief *lauda* to the Virgin: "Hail Queen of heaven, O southern star, who wipes away all stain, a crystal fountain./ O living light divine, I come sighing to you, O sweet cure/ by which man is made worthy./ Eve, by her sin, brought a thorn into the world, and you were the one destined to prepare for it the Word incarnate./ Lady, among the joyful, you alone are blessed, a Virgin daughter and mother, handmaid, empress./ In you was circumscribed he who circumscribes heaven,/ and your lovely direct sun/ cleanses my cloudy veil./ By the tears you shed upon the cross of death/ when you looked at Jesus,/ O Virgin give me comfort,/ and cleanse my inveterate filth./ Hail, Queen of heaven, Star of the south.[15]

VISION: THE POWER OF THE IMAGE

The humanist Bartholomeo Fazio, who, as Michael Baxandall observed, is very informative about Renaissance attitudes to images, made an effort to see personally and comment upon as many important new works of art as he could.[16] For Fazio, the key to art was neither narrative nor persons, but rather personality, expressed similarly by artists and poets through metaphor and analogy. Prominent among the literary sources of Fazio's views was Quintilian, the model for Niccolò Cieco and his friend Michele del Giogante in the construction of

their house of memory. Quintilian taught that both words and images could best be fixed in the mind by reference to the particular personal attributes of their subjects. Quintilian also influenced Alberti's *On Painting*, which stressed that the subject of a painting must seem to move, and to move the viewer. This faculty is indeed the fundamental source of the power of the image, apparent in Giovanni Morelli's vision.[17]

33   Spinello Aretino, *Marriage of Saint Catherine*, detail, Florence, Santa Caterina all'Antella

That Florentines were moved by religious images is also demonstrated, if perversely, by occasional acts of iconoclasm. One memorable example is that of the unsuccessful gambler who was tried and executed because in a fit of rage at the Virgin's failure to protect him as he had prayed to her to do, he flung a handful of dung at her image in one of the neighborhood street shrines he passed on his way home.[18] Baxandall's account of humanists'

descriptions of the power of images to move, and his citation of popular exercises in meditation, directed others'
attention to Renaissance responses to images. His own
study of popular attitudes did not, however, proceed far
enough to dispel his impression that conventional phrases
for describing works of art betray a lack of real feeling or
involvement in the process of viewing, or that "religious
observance was institutional to the point of making the
question of individual belief almost irrelevant."[19] Devotional poetry and devotees' responses to religious paintings show the role of individual belief to be in fact crucial
in generating images and responses to them.

Giovanni Morelli, a sometime successful businessman
and statesman, reflected at length in his *Ricordi* on his life's
losses and gains, his hopes and disappointments, his pleasures and pains. His reflections describe a volatile environment shaped by friends, family, and neighbors, a world
in which he enjoyed some success and support, but often
felt betrayed and abandoned. As Richard Trexler pointed
out, this was also Giovanni's perception of his spiritual
life, in crisis after the death of his beloved son.[20] The
climax of his description of this bereavement is the vision
he was vouchsafed as he prayed on his knees at midnight,
before an image of Christ crucified. Morelli, like so many
of the anthologists, emerges from his diary as a man who
studied the writings of such antique moral guides as
Virgil, Boethius, and Seneca, as well as those of Dante,
Boccaccio, and various modern moralists, in addition to
seeking spiritual guidance in various books of the Scriptures by which, as he assured his readers, "you will be
fully instructed in the faith and in the coming of the son
of God, you will have great consolation in your soul,
great joy and great sweetness, you will disdain the world,
you will not be afflicted by your experiences, you will be
bold and knowledgeable in good remedies leading to
salvation."[21]

Morelli's description of his spiritual crisis and vision
shows precisely how pious Florentines accustomed to
seeking wisdom and solace in devotional literature, and
equipped by their reading with a variety of precepts and
beliefs, internalized these messages and effected the transition in their own minds to communion with the figures
and images of these *exempla* through contemplation of
a devotional object. Morelli's experience reveals what
knowledge and expectations the Florentine viewer
brought to an image, and shows how he activated the collective culture on which the artist built in order to move
his viewers. This, not merely an arid set of attributes, is
what the patron invoked when he commissioned a work
"in the usual manner." The viewer, like the patron and
the artist, had a common repertoire of images in his head;
from this, as we may see, Morelli fashioned his vision.

The painted image that inspired it was a scene of the
Crucifixion, such as Cosimo had in his cell at San Marco,
after the Virgin and Child the most popular subject
for devotional paintings made to be contemplated in
the privacy of a domestic, confraternal, or other chapel
(fig. 33).

Tormented by grief and guilt at the death of his young
son Alberto, on the anniversary of his death Morelli rose
from his bed in the middle of the night dressed in a
nightshirt, with the *coreggia* or flail used by the members
of penitential confraternities around his neck. He fell on
his knees before "the figure of the crucified son of God,
to which [Alberto] many times had commended his
bodily health," kissing and embracing the images of
Christ, the Virgin Mary, and Saint John the Evangelist in
the same places as his son had done, contemplating in
turn the sorrow and pain of each of these figures, in
penitence for his own sins for which they had suffered.

> I began first to envisage and contemplate my sins,
> by which I saw that I had severely offended the son
> of God. And then, considering with what hard, bitter
> and gloomy suffering Jesus Christ was crucified, at
> whose figure I gazed, who had redeemed us from
> eternal punishment, my eyes could hardly endure to
> look at him; but by the gift of pity he vouchsafed me,
> I believe, my heart and all my senses moved to the
> greatest tenderness, my eyes bathed my face with tears.
> And remaining thus for quite some time, the weakness
> of my mind was eased, I found comfort, and began to
> pray with devoted psalms and prayers to the crucified
> son of God . . . to pray to him with my eyes, my heart
> and my mind.[22]

Morelli directed his prayers for the salvation of
Alberto's soul to each in turn of the figures in the image
he contemplated. From the Lord he asked forgiveness for
his unworthy self "by the merit of your holy Incarnation"; at this point he recited the scriptural passage which
formed part of the Florentine civic celebration of the
Annunciation. He followed this with the passage from the
Gospel of Saint John concerning the Passion, begging
mercy by virtue in turn of Christ's pity for the disciples
who awaited him in the darkness of the garden, of the
consolation the Virgin received "when you, her son,
appeared to her in glory, of the merit of that great happiness enjoyed by the apostles when you appeared to
them, saying "Peace be with you,'" and finally, "by the
merit of your most glorious Ascension" into paradise.
Meanwhile, his eyes remained fixed on the image and
figure of the crucified Christ.[23]

Then turning his gaze to where on Christ's right, "at
the foot of the cross I saw his pure and holy and blessed

Mother . . . full of the deepest grief and sorrow . . . and considering that my sins were the cause of her great affliction, I did not dare to utter a word . . . but considering in my mind . . . that she had no comfort, but remained alone and abandoned with her son, I felt for this such pain and suffering that I really thought my soul would leave my body . . ." Eventually Morelli asked Mary, "sweet tabernacle of the Son of God," to "make me a participant in your sorrow and in your affliction, so that with full justice, participating in your afflictions, I may merit receiving a pledge of such happiness as your son repurchased for us on the wood of the cross." Adducing the Florentine claim to the Virgin's special protection, he recommended his soul and his son's to

> the living font of mercy . . . the Queen of Heaven . . . our advocate before our Creator . . . and further because we faithful Christians living in the city of Florence consider ourselves, however unworthy, by your special gift to be accepted into your presence . . . as is shown by the many, however undeserved favors, which you have vouchsafed our city by your mercy . . . that, moved by this mercy, you should implore the favor of the Divine Majesty for the salvation of my son's soul . . . that comforted in eternity it should rejoice in the triumphal choir of your beatitude.[24]

Finally he directed his gaze to Saint John,

> the sweet and beloved brother of the transfigured son of the devoted Virgin Mary, at whose feet you kneel in such bitter dejection . . . I lament my sins because my iniquities are borne upon your shoulders . . . you . . . whom the immaculate lamb elected to liberate myself and other sinners from eternal punishment; I, cause of your sorrow, am full of regret, knowing myself inadequate to render the required merits. Incapable of anything else, I beg you, adored saint, that as you undeservedly bear my deserved punishment, that by the grace I beg of you, throughout my life your grief should be the mirror of my sins, so that your splendor should be the constant illumination of the darkness of my mind . . . knowing that reading your Gospel of the holy works of Christ is of more value than the ignorant speech of myself, a sinner . . .[25]

Much comforted, Morelli returned to bed. But tormented by "man's envious Enemy, offended by my prayer,"[26] he tossed and turned, telling over the many grievances and offences he had suffered throughout his life. Finally falling asleep, there appeared to him a vision, granted, he believed, by God and his saints John the Baptist, Anthony of Padua, Benedict, Francis,

and Catherine of Alexandria, to whom Giovanni was especially devoted. Like Petrarch in his quest for self-knowledge, he ascended a mountain, in this case Monte Morello, a landmark of his native countryside, the Mugello. As he looked toward the mountain, he saw a bird, a parrot like those in bestiaries cited in Brunetto Latini's *Trésor* and Boccaccio's *Filocolo*. Figuring, he believed, the soul of his son, it flew down and perched on an olive tree. There it sang a beautiful melody, which turned to jarring notes when it moved to a juniper, then to a fig, a myrtle, and a mountain ash.[27] Morelli then found himself covered in filth by a sow, but as he ascended the mountain, guided by the light of two stars, like Dante on the mount of purgatory he was surrounded by an odor of sweetness, finally encountering not Beatrice, but Saint Catherine. She appeared to him in the form of her traditional iconography, holding in her right hand a palm, and in her left, the wheel on which she was broken, with which she had cut up the sow of lechery. Giovanni interpreted these signs as an injunction to do penance for his sins, taking as his exempla the saints in their purity. Then Catherine touched the bird, and it became an angel, the spirit of Alberto in eternal beatitude, who appeared and undertook to intercede for his living family with the Lord, prophesying his father's long life and extending to him also the promise of salvation. Thus, as Trexler observed, "Giovanni had found a patron, even a father, in his son."[28]

Morelli's account of his vision, although relatively simple, shows how naturally he resorted to the figurative language of his reading from Scriptures and moral literature, weaving stories and symbols and ceremonies he had learned from the liturgy, devotional practice, and visual representations into a complex spiritual narrative with the heuristic aid of an image. This activity seems very distant from the perception of altarpieces as simply "to honor the saints," in the modern sense of the word.[29] It suggests rather that viewers sought complex meanings in images with which they profoundly identified. It appears that even the simplest and most conventional representation of Christ crucified, with the Virgin and Saint John, was laden in the mind of an ordinary merchant and confraternity member such as Morelli with significance sufficient to evoke a narrative vision quite as rich in symbolism as any art historian's interpretation of such a work. A response at least equally as rich could certainly be expected from Cosimo de' Medici, and from the audiences of the considerably more sophisticated images he commissioned.

★   ★   ★

LEVELS OF PERCEPTION: "THE EYE IS CALLED THE FIRST OF ALL THE GATES/THROUGH WHICH THE INTELLECT MAY LEARN AND TASTE"[30]

Feo Belcari introduced his *sacra rappresentazione* of *Abraham and Isaac*, dedicated to Piero de' Medici, with these lines explaining to his audience the means by which his play would entertain and edify them. Their attention would be caught by the images presented in the performance; it would be held, and their understanding engaged, by the words the actors recited. While Belcari's verse may refer in part to the fact that the audience saw the tableau *before* the actors began to speak, the concept of sequential and ascending levels of perception is a fundamental tenet of Christian teaching. Saint Paul's testimony that "now we see through a glass darkly, but then face to face," is just one of the more vivid of scriptural passages justifying this view.[31] Belcari's exposition of these levels of perception is well known. At least three more accounts of the process of progressive epistemological sophistication were written by clerics influential with the laity, and were widely circulated, though in different contexts for different audiences.

The main source of clerical assertions of the superiority of words to images as paths to understanding doctrine was Saint Gregory's justification of the use of images to explain the faith to those who could not read. Images are the books of the unlettered, "for what the Scripture teaches those who read, this same the image shows to those who cannot read, but see."[32] This pronouncement, at the time it was made, was not merely a statement of an accepted truism, but rather part of a heated controversy about attitudes to images. A decree of the Second Nicene Council in 787 prescribed that "the honor shown to the image is transferred to the prototype, and whoever honors an image honors the person represented by it."[33] The Western church, feeling this position to be dangerously close to the adoration of the icon, emphasized in response the function of the image in creating memory, acting as a reminder of the person represented. These various clerical rulings influenced, but did not determine lay attitudes. Some evidence of this is the insertion in Gregory's correspondence of an apocryphal letter describing the power of images to move, and stressing the importance of this quality in images particularly for private devotion, since these were not envisaged in Gregory's time, and hence he had not considered them. As Henk van Os observed, all this was part of "a learning process that lasted for centuries," in which "ordinary believers were trained in spiritual values that had evolved in the claustral world of the monastics," most particularly those relating to the central activities of personal prayer and meditation.[34]

Some eight hundred years later, preaching the faith in perhaps the most literate and aesthetically sophisticated city in Europe, Giovanni Dominici, in the passage cited above, appropriately adapted Gregory's dictum to apply not to the illiterate, but to the pre-literate. Advising a laywoman on the education of her children, in terms very like those adduced by Quaratesi in introducing his transcription of the life of John the Baptist, he advocated the use of images to help children make "a beginning, through considering the saints, of contemplating the supreme Saint of saints." Dominici went on to observe that "painting of the angels and saints is permitted and ordained, for the mental utility of the lowest. For the middling part of humanity, living creatures are the book . . . but the sacred scriptures are mainly for the most perfect." These levels he defines correspond to the development of young children, who can see from birth, but only gradually progress to speaking, and then finally to writing. His suggestions clearly owe something to Saint Gregory's view, but their reference specifically to the limited experience of the children of literate parents is obvious in his mixed metaphor of living creatures as the book.[35]

San Bernardino's exposition of ascending levels of apprehension, which occurs in relation to a comment on Simone Martini's *Annunciation*, was part of his continuing attempt to discourage the faithful from excessive reverence for his famous symbol. He devised this in the form of the letters of the name of Christ (IHS) set in flames, so that churchgoers would have before them constantly, not just the names represented in the arms and devices of the families of chapel patrons, but the name and device of Christ himself. Although he stressed that virtue resided "not [in] the sign, but the thing signified," widespread public adoration of the emblem led to Bernardino being accused of heresy. In the passage cited here, Bernardino described the emblem, in fact an image constructed out of words, as a memory device, like

the pictures which recall to you the Blessed Virgin or other saints, which pictures are made only in memory of the said saints. Note therefore that there are four kinds of letters, each better than the other. The first kind are gross letters for rude folk, as, for example, pictures; the next, for men of the middle sort, are middle letters as, for example, written letters; and these are better than the first. The third are vocal letters, invented for those men who desire actively to busy themselves for charity's sake, pleading and discoursing, in order that they may be learned and may teach others; and these excel the first two. Fourthly and lastly come mental letters, ordained by God for those who desire to persevere always in contemplation; and these are more perfect than the others and exceed them all.[36]

Bernardino invoked the superiority of words over pictures so that he could stress that symbols are merely representations of the sacred, not the "graven images" which God forbids us to worship. The point of progressing from one level of understanding to another was to move from the concrete to the abstract, from action to contemplation.[37]

Iacopo da Voragine's *Golden Legend* was probably written as a manual for the instruction of other clerics. Describing the experience of taking the sacrament, for which the altar of a church is consecrated, he distinguished between clergy and laity, but not primarily between words and images. He represented all the physical senses as working together to move the communicant, considering the eye as the door through which images and words enter together. When we accept the Eucharist offered during the Mass, as Christ commanded, saying:

> Do this in commemoration of me . . . we have a threefold memorial of the Lord's Passion. The first is in writing, i. e., depicted in the images of the Passion of Christ, and this is directed to the eye. Thus the crucifix and the other images in the church are intended to awaken our memories and our devotion, and as a means of instruction; they are the laypeoples' book. The second memorial is the spoken word, namely, the preaching of the Passion of Christ, and this is addressed to the ear. The third is in the sacrament . . . since it really contains and offers to us the body and blood of Christ; and this memorial is directed to the sense of taste. Hence if the depiction of Christ's Passion inflames our love strongly and its preaching more strongly, we should be moved more strongly still by this sacrament, which expresses it so clearly.[38]

Such passages have been wrenched out of context and enlisted by historians anxious to represent Renaissance images as simpler than Renaissance men intended or understood them to be. Replaced in context, these passages are much less prescriptions about the nature of images than descriptions of the paths to greater spiritual sophistication, in which images play a part. Antoninus's brief observations on religious pictures express, like his comments on every other aspect of Florentine life, from law to voting practices, his desire to influence the behavior of the laity in directions prescribed by the Church.[39] They are not accounts of images, or even primarily injunctions about how images should be made or should function. Antoninus's chief concern was to curb misrepresentations of doctrine, whether due to the *inventio* of the artist or the instructions of his patron, and to denounce malpractice by craftsmen as well as their exploitation by employers. When he referred to Nanni di Banco's statues of the four crowned saints in the guild's niche at Orsanmichele, it was as an example relevant to his condemnation of artists who, after the contract is made, prove negligent in the execution of the work in order to finish it faster. Advocating a wage for woodworkers that took into account the labor-intensive nature of intarsia, he added force to his argument by reminding his readers that Mary's husband Joseph was a carpenter, and referred them on this point to Chrysostom's sermon on the Epiphany.[40]

These commentators on art were all clerics who enjoyed considerable prestige as religious leaders, so their comments were well known to the laity. Conversely, they supported specifically clerical agendas, and there is no evidence that the secular patrons who proliferated in the quattrocento were guided primarily by these when contemplating commissions even of devotional images.[41] Notably Alberti, who in his treatise *On Painting* expressed the more general preoccupations of artists and patrons, declared that "a 'historia' you can justifiably praise and admire will be one that reveals itself to be so charming and attractive as to hold the eye of the *learned and unlearned* spectator for a long while and will move his soul."[42]

POETRY, THEOLOGY, DOCTRINE, AND EDIFYING EXCHANGE: A SCISSOR-MAKER'S QUERY CONCERNING THE TRINITY; A GOLDSMITH ENQUIRES ABOUT THE IMMACULATE CONCEPTION

There was in Florence a large and demonstrably influential group of men — poets, painters, members of pious confraternities, both lay and clerical — who clearly grasped the interaction between words and images, and the power of the image to inspire in the viewer a strong personal involvement with the protagonists of the Christian revelation, which would lead eventually to a clearer perception of the doctrines of the faith. A series of verse exchanges between Feo Belcari, master of the sacred play and a leading popular authority on religious issues, and a number of citizens linked by moral and devotional concerns, reveals the existence in Cosimo's lifetime of a circle closely resembling the group known from Marsilio

Ficino's letters to have gathered around him in the era of Lorenzo de' Medici.[43] The Medici were a powerful presence in both circles, but whereas Ficino's friends and followers were nearly all humanist scholars or members of the city's patriciate, Belcari's disciples came from all walks of life, and sought his guidance in mastering even the more abstruse areas of Renaissance dogma and theology. The questions raised in these poetic exchanges between merchants, artisans, and priests concerned the burning theological issues of the day. Their poems focus more sharply what we have learned from the devotional practice of confraternities and the doctrinal themes of sacred plays, of the seriousness and sophistication of popular piety, so often dismissed as "conventional," and of how well equipped Florentines were to decipher even the most complex doctrines relating to images.

Belcari was the supreme example of the fusion in popular culture of entertainment and edification, the virtuous poet who earned fame and glory as a moral educator, the Orphic singer with access to supreme truth. As the shoemaker Antonio put it, "O glorious and blessed singer,/ my salvation depends upon your aid;/ may you enjoy fame and glory in a thousand songs."[44] According to the *canta in panca* Antonio di Guido, Belcari might perhaps surpass Orpheus in sweetness, but he certainly did so in wisdom: "Feo Belcari is infallible in his pronouncements."[45] Confronting this widely accepted characterization more critically, Niccolò Gesuato wrote with heavy irony: "If I did not know, oh my Feo Belcaro,/ that virtue increases when it is praised,/ I would fear to send to you,/not wishing to mar your face with any imperfection . . . What many say is that Orpheus/ has lost his fame, and that you have acquired it . . ./ But I know you are not unaware from what sea/ proceeds this river of living water,/ and that you thank the good Father of Lights,/ for only in him should we glory . . ." Belcari met this challenge briskly in his first line: "I am a publican, but not a Pharisee," a claim that would have brought to any pious mind the passage from Saint Luke, 18:10–14, concerning the two men who went into the temple to pray, one a Pharisee and the other a publican. The Pharisee said to God, "I thank thee that I am not as other men." The publican "would not lift up so much as his eyes to heaven, but smote upon his breast, saying, 'God be merciful to me, a sinner.' I tell you, this man went down to his house justified rather than the other; for every one that exalteth himself shall be abased; and he that humbleth himself shall be exalted."

By his own testimony, Belcari dedicated himself, like Dante, to the exploration and transmission of Christian truths in poetry: "I write to learn,/like an educable man/ . . . for greater hope of achieving blessedness,/ I compose

laude to our invisible God." Belcari represented Cosimo as "the mirror of the true merchant"; Belcari's correspondents, engaged in a similar quest for salvation, recognized the clerical poet as "the mirror of art, a proven talent, lofty and reliable."[46] His "art" embraced the poetic exposition of theology, and the basic themes and points of doctrine that preoccupied Belcari's correspondents included those most frequently presented for general contemplation in images, among them charity, intercession, the Incarnation, the Trinity, and the Last Judgment.

Theologians in Cosimo's day were particularly preoccupied, as can be seen from the discussions which took place during the church council in 1439, with the issue of Incarnation. Italian Catholics, by contrast with members of the Eastern church, were inclined to see God's grace and redemption in the Incarnation of his Son, as much as his sacrifice on the cross. It seems that questions concerning the meaning of the Incarnation occurred as urgently to ordinary men as to leaders of the Church. Antonio di Guido, the star performer at San Martino at mid-century, turned to Belcari to quench "the fire that burns in my mind" as to whether "the eternal Word would have assumed human flesh/ from Mary, if Adam had not sinned." Belcari admitted that, occupied as he was with largely secular cares, he could not claim to penetrate fully the truths of "the sacrosanct, the dear and worthy Scripture/ that makes man more divine than Jove or Mars." Yet it appeared to him that "the immense and holy divine love,/ wishing to make man remarkable/ within and without, did so love him/ that solely to give him glory, and not for a remedy,/ without the sin of Adam would still have assumed/ immortal flesh, and confirmed him in grace."[47]

The mystery of the Incarnation may have been difficult to penetrate, but the doctrine of the Immaculate Conception defeated many believers, including artists who in the course of the Counter-Reformation attempted to depict it in images. Yet the goldsmith Francesco di Matteo, writing to Feo Belcari that his verses engendered "an insatiable thirst that generates/ such lofty thoughts in my base intellect," declared that in pursuing the path to salvation, "I greatly desire to have my doubt resolved,/ as to whether the temple where the son of God was made flesh/ was conceived in original sin." Belcari responded that "the holy church, which includes all truth,/ seeing that her doctors hold diverse opinions in this case,/ has no decree to which we must adhere . . ." However, he declared his own belief that "the blissful being/ was no less perfect than Eve."[48] Not all truths, however, were negotiable; when Banco di Niccolò Bencivenni enquired "if the soul and the spirit are an actual fact," Belcari firmly replied that "every man is obliged to believe/ that the soul is immortal, since the arguments/ are laid down, and without this bridge,/ no one arrives at the blessed Christ."[49]

The author of a verse attributed in some compilations to Maestro Andrea "delle sargie," painter of bedspreads and coverlets, and in others to his son, Francesco, inspired perhaps by Belcari's poems, confided to the poet–priest his doubts concerning the efficacy of the saints, asking him, "if anyone can be saved by the merits of others." Belcari responded that certainly no one attained to eternal glory without benefit of the precious blood shed to extinguish mortal sins, but that Christ also conceded "the heights of heaven to our souls, by virtue of the credit amassed by the great saints."[50] Giovanni Pigli, also the owner of a rich compilation, sought Belcari's opinion on the question of whether "the soul of the damned,/ after being raised with his body incorruptible,/ will stand there at the day of judgment," which the poet answered confidently in the affirmative. Indeed he had written a long and explicit verse on the events of the Last Judgment, climaxing in the scene usually depicted by painters – such as Fra Angelico for Santa Maria degli Angeli – "when all the dead/ shall be raised up and judged by God,/ and divided between hell and paradise" (fig. 45).[51]

When the priest Tomeo de' Pauletti inquired concerning the most direct road to virtue, Belcari replied that there was no higher virtue than charity. Belcari himself had penned a lament in the person of Charity, concerning her unpopularity in Christian Rome, along with humility and piety; the chronicler Giovanni Cavalcanti embellished this idea in a personification of Florence.[52] The poet seems to have practiced what he preached. The scissor-maker Lorenzo di Tommaso, addressing Belcari as his "father and lord" (*padre e duce*) and armed with images drawn from Dante,[53] apologized for his own inadequacy in inquiring about the sources of Belcari's inspiration: "I well understand that I do not shine/ in politic speech, which flows only from a perfect heart;/ but unpolished queries may yet deserve your response." Belcari responded promptly that his secret was to flee "all public affairs, and similarly the great Gold Mountain [*Monte de l'Auro*] of Florence . . . / experience tells me to flee the bustle;/ I submit my soul to the instruction of the heavens." However, when Filippo Lapaccini, a kinsman of the chronicler of San Marco and a patron of Neri di Bicci, enquired whether the stars determine our fates, Belcari replied with a strong assertion of faith in man's liberty, and the superlative power of God's great gift to man, free will.[54]

Notwithstanding some historians' characterizations of lay ignorance, none of these enquiries are those of men disposed to view or commission images alluding only to "what is easily seized." These Florentine merchants, artisans, and clergymen asked the major philosophical questions of the age; the nature of Fortuna preoccupied most of the leading intellectuals of the Renaissance, and the question of free will was to cut to the very heart of the differences between Protestants and Catholics in the era of Reformation.

UT PICTURA POESIS (PICTURES ARE LIKE POETRY)[55]

As Baxandall observed, when Landino wished to comment on the painters of his age, he did not devise an original descriptive vocabulary of his own; he resorted to the authoritative language of Pliny.[56] Other learned writers who, like the humanist Fazio, tried to articulate a response to images that went beyond the accepted, usually classical topoi, often experienced what Baxandall suggested should be read more as a failure of language than of sensibility. Fazio simply resorted to the ancient analogy between painting and poetry: "As you know, there is a great kinship of a sort between painters and poets. A painting indeed is nothing but a silent poem. Both have about an equal concern in the invention and the composition of their works." He stressed the artists' expressive use of metaphor in the same way as the poet's, *ut pictura poesis*; later in the fifteenth century more sophisticated artists took up the same idea in reverse; *ut rhetorica pictura* (the art of oratory is like painting).[57] The analogy between paintings and poems goes beyond subject matter or themes, and their common source in devotional literature and practice, to their reliance on metaphor and symbolism wherein the richest spiritual meaning resided.

The elision of poetry and painting animates much popular devotional verse, which gauges the power of images over ordinary people more accurately than humanists' intellectualizing attempts to describe what they saw. Many poems read like ekphrases of images, as is evident when they are matched against Cosimo's commissions. Associations between ideas, words, and images were also reinforced by inscriptions, of which Cosimo made liberal use. While some art historians may deny that pictures were "about" such doctrines as the Annunciation, many poems clearly were. The doctrinal questions which preoccupied poets like Belcari's verse correspondents were those most frequently implicated in images for devotional meditation, the purpose of which was to penetrate the narrative husk in which the core of the mystery lay concealed.

The power of images to inspire poets had a long and distinguished history in Florence at least from the time of Dante, whose work so strongly influenced quattrocento readers and writers. The specifically visual referents of Dante's images have often been noted. We might, for example, imagine his description of the terraces of purgatory as inspired by the narrative bas-reliefs on ancient obelisks such as Trajan's column, which he had seen in Rome, especially since he explicitly described the cliffs that formed the terraces as lined with marble images like those of the legendary classical sculptor Polyclitus (fig. 34).[58] His quattrocento readers would probably have envisioned from Dante's description something like the scenes in low-relief sculpture of Donatello's pulpits for San Lorenzo; the scene of Christ before Caiaphas and Pilate has just such a column at its center (fig. 189).[59]

Francis Ames-Lewis has suggested that the decorum of representations of the Annunciation probably derived from Dante's description of one of the sculptures in purgatory:

> The angel that came down to earth and brought/ the edict of the age-long wept-for peace/ which broke the long ban and unbarred Heaven's door,/ appeared to us, so life-like was it carved,/ captured in such a gracious gesture/ that it did not seem to be a silent image./ You'd swear it spoke an Ave,/ for she too was pictured there,/ who turned the key/ to unlock the highest love:/ and in her gesture was impressed those words,/ "Ecce ancilla Dei," in the same way/ one stamps a design upon a seal of wax . . .

This passage incorporates the same phrase from the liturgy which artists depicting the Annunciation, among them Simone Martini, were to inscribe on banderoles or on the borders of Mary's garments. A century later San Bernardino demonstrated the reciprocal nature of this continuing exchange between words and images in his evocation of Martini's *Annunciation* to make a point about the modesty of the Virgin (fig. 35).[60]

The association in the patron's perception between poetry and painting, and the view of these as equally acts of devotion, is clearly apparent in the verses of Franco Sacchetti, and the program of frescoes he designed to decorate the oratory of Orsanmichele which housed a miraculous image of the Virgin (fig. 32). In 1398 Sacchetti was one of the captains of the lay confraternity attached to the church, and responsible for the maintenance of its cult. He wrote a group of poems known as the *Capitoli dei Bianchi*, addressed to the Virgin and celebrating the great popular devotional movement which swept Italy in 1399 and led to the foundation of many more confraternities like that at Orsanmichele. In one of these poems,

34   Rome, Trajan's column, detail

a "prayer [to the Virgin] for the author on his own behalf," asking mercy for his soul, Sacchetti cited his poetry, and the frescoes which fostered her cult, as an act of personal devotion contributing to his merits: "for I have spent thirteen years on the tabernacle,/ which surpasses in beauty all others made/ in this century, if I recollect aright./ With the greatest fidelity each story of yours/ is depicted there to demonstrate your glory/ . . . And I have so arranged the whole/ . . . that everyone who will, may grasp its composition,/ . . . with all my ingenuity and astuteness/ I have had it made, having such faith in you . . ."[61]

35   Simone Martini, *Annunciation*, Florence, Uffizi

The verse goes on to describe the subjects of the frescoes, the stained-glass windows, and the marble tabernacle built to showcase the miraculous image. Sacchetti explained how images and words worked together here. "Behind Saint Anne was painted the mystery/ of the Passion, which is the pilgrimage place to which we all come,/ and written the visible prayer,/ so palpable to the Bianchi,/ and many foreigners have made copies of it,/ so that perhaps one of them took it as far as Scotland."[62] Among the saints and prophets by whom the Virgin was surrounded were those most revered by Florentines, the Baptist and John the Evangelist, "Moses there in heaven with the tablets,/and King David, whose writings are not idle tales . . ." The governing theme of the ensemble appears to have been man's progress from allegiance to the law of nature, to written law, and finally to law as illuminated by the light of grace embodied in the Virgin. Light is the ancient metaphor for understanding and grace, employed in poems, *sacre rappresentazioni* and the sacraments of burial and commemorative mass; it was represented with increasing sophistication in Florentine images as a result of the experiments of artists like Lippi in his various *Annunciations*, including at least one for the Medici.[63]

Sacchetti was involved with other projects that married words to images in public places. He was one of the citizens consulted on the proposal, in the first decade of the fifteenth century, to move the Trinity chapel on the south wall of the cathedral the better to accommodate the crowds who flocked to see its altarpiece, depicting the double intercession of Christ and the Virgin joined by inscriptions (fig. 50).[64] He composed some verses to be inscribed in the audience chamber of the Otto di Guardia, while he was a member of this magistracy responsible for public order, praising love of the fatherland, "amar la patria," and the fight for the common good as the virtues which more than any other made it great and powerful. He also wrote the verses concerning the pursuit of truth and justice which were placed alongside a fresco in the Signoria's audience chamber in the Palazzo Vecchio, depicting the doubtful Saint Thomas placing his hand in Christ's wound.[65]

Sacchetti's late trecento description of the frescoes and tabernacle at Orsanmichele is matched and balanced by Antonio di Meglio's sonnet, written half a century later, "in praise of the glorious Virgin Annunciate of Florence, treated in the Gospel of St. Luke," which describes the miraculous image at Santissima Annunziata.[66] Their provision of a tabernacle to house this image caused Feo Belcari to celebrate Cosimo and Piero de' Medici as "conservers and protectors of temples and holy places." Representing the author of the image of the Annunziata as the heir of Saint Luke, who was believed to have painted the original portrait of the Virgin of which all others in a sense partook, Antonio used the words of Scripture and liturgy to describe his response to the painted form of the power of the Virgin herself. "O holy Virgin, glorious mother/ of that eternal and most holy Word,/ of whom you are, besides mother, daughter and spouse,/often already in my bitter torment,/ which like that of so many martyrs afflicts and tears apart/every ounce of my flesh, my bones and nerves,/ I am moved to beg mercy of you . . ." Since, "among your other supreme graces,/ it is given you to do what you will,/ along with the Father, the Son and the Holy Spirit . . . And since on these walls you are so worthily represented /by art and human intellect,/ your figure inspiring him who set his hand to the picture/ with such devotion,/ I pray it should please you that such intense devotion/ should not be in vain in its effect,/ but as if these mercies were asked of your very essence,/ with the greatest fervor,/ there might reside in your figure the power to hear and exhort . . . O blessed Virgin, annunciate by the glorious angel Gabriel . . . hail, full of grace, may God be with you,/ blessed among women,/ who gives light to the blind world!"[67]

As San Bernardino said in a remarkable passage concerning the paradox inherent in the figuration of a theological mystery: "Eternity is present in time, immensity in measure, the Creator in his creature . . . that which cannot be represented in the representation, that which cannot be articulated in the discourse, the inexplicable in speech, the uncircumscribable in place, the invisible in the vision . . ."[68]

VIII

IMAGES OF FLORENTINE PATRONAGE
REFRACTED THROUGH POPULAR CULTURE

PARTICIPANTS IN POPULAR CULTURE AS
PATRONS OF ART

We have observed the close correspondence between Florentines' favorite texts, and the subjects and symbols of their artistic commissions. Unfortunately, for only a handful of patrons, such as Cosimo de' Medici and Giovanni Rucellai, is there enough evidence of both reading habits and oeuvres to permit a precise comparison between texts read and objects acquired. However, there is a strong correlation between the names of those who wrote poetry and made compilations of popular literature, and those who commissioned works of art. Sometimes these are the same individuals; sometimes their kinsmen; such correspondences are obviously more significant in a small cohesive lineage of half a dozen households or less, than in enormous and varied *consorterie* such as the Bardi or the Strozzi. Some of these men have already been mentioned in the preceding chapters concerning written texts; others will appear in the following chapters relating to objects. Their achievements are briefly summarized here to indicate just how many Florentines had a marked and creative interest in both verbal and visual self-expression.[1]

The brothers Lorenzo, Francesco, and Tommaso di Tommaso di Giovanni di Taddeo Benci were prolific poets and copyists of *zibaldoni*; Lorenzo wrote Cosimo a sonnet of consolation when his younger son Giovanni died in 1463, and he was also the author of a *lauda* on the miracle of the Nativity. These Benci were related to the branch of the family who were associates of the Medici bank, including Bartolomeo, the author of a famous and beautifully illustrated account of Giuliano de' Medici's joust of 1473. Giovanni di Amerigo Benci of this line founded the convent of the Murate in 1439, for which he commissioned an Annunciation from Filippo Lippi. Giovanni di Guarnieri Benci had Neri di Bicci set a stained-glass image of Our Lady by Luca della Robbia in a wooden tabernacle for his house.

The Degli Agli, a family prominent in Dante's day, became patrons of the convent of San Domenico at Fiesole in 1419. Antonio degli Agli, much admired as a vernacular poet, was appointed by Giovanni di Bicci as first rector of the canonry of Saints Cosmas and Damian at San Lorenzo, and later became priest at Santa Maria Impruneta, home of the miracle-working black Madonna. He was a patron of Luca della Robbia, and participated in the commissions of the cardinal of Portugal for his chapel in San Miniato. Antonio's household, however, was poor enough to be the objects of the charity of a miller; a largely self-educated scribe and teacher of grammar, Antonio worked originally as an accountant before he became a cleric.[2]

Giuliano Quaratesi composed his own version of the legend of Saint John the Baptist in 1458; his family assumed the patronage of San Salvatore al Monte, adjacent to San Miniato. The ancestral family church of the Quaratesi was San Niccolò Oltrarno, for which they commissioned Gentile da Fabriano's altarpiece of 1424, a sophisticated statement of the nature and use of images. The young sons of Folco Portinari, who lived in Cosimo's house after their father's death, had their family chapel in San Egidio frescoed by Domenicio Veneziano and Castagno around 1439, and Rosello Roselli, a clerical poet who was a close friend of Cosimo's sons, presented them with a personalized compilation he had made for them.

The Bardi were an old and extensive clan; the patronage of their various lines over the centuries included the Santa Croce chapel frescoed by Giotto. One of the earliest signed and dated vernacular scrapbooks of this period belonged to Giuliano di Giovanni di Bardi, and was copied in his own hand in the year 1416; Bernardo d'Andrea di Lippaccio de' Bardi, a member of the family that supplied the Medici bank with so many partners and general managers, owned a compilation of Boccaccio's work. Lorenzo di Larione de' Bardi, of the same line, was the patron of one of the earlier palaces built in the boom which began in the mid-fifteenth century. The Peruzzi, also patrons of a chapel at Santa Croce frescoed by Giotto, were in the fifteenth century collectors of vernacular scrapbooks, and like Giovanni di Bicci de' Medici, employed Dello Delli to decorate one of their houses.

The many compilations owned by members of the Della Stufa family over several generations testify to their keen interest in Florentine popular literature. Giovanni della Stufa had completed part of a book he was compiling for himself "on Palm Sunday 1436"; Sigismondo della Stufa, a close friend of Cosimo's grandson Lorenzo, owned a *zibaldone* with extracts from Augustine and Jerome. Ugo della Stufa, who was one of the original patrons of the San Lorenzo transept chapels, arranged for Lippi to paint a picture for Sigismondo Malatesta. Carlo Martelli wrote several poems on the theme of penitence and was the author of a moving meditation on the Crucifixion. His uncle Bartolomeo was also among the early patrons at San Lorenzo, and may have commissioned the Lippi altarpiece of the Annunciation later found in their chapel. Bartolomeo and his brother Roberto oversaw Medici commissions for Lippi and Benozzo Gozzoli, showing themselves experienced assessors of paintings.

Politia de' Pazzi owned a volume of popular literature consisting mainly of Dante's and Petrarch's poems; she came from the family of bankers who built the Pazzi chapel. Largely devotional compilations were written by or made for members of the Rucellai family, including Giovanni and his sons, in the 1450s and 1460s; Giovanni, the greatest patron in Florence after Cosimo, was himself the author of a sophisticated *zibaldone*. The Carnesecchi were among Fra Angelico's earliest patrons; his image for their family shrine helped to establish his fame. Leonardo Carnesecchi compiled a beautifully illustrated volume of popular literature which later passed to the artist Antonio da San Gallo, who did the intarsia pews for the Medici chapel. Michele del Giogante, one of the more important compilers and poets of the Medici circle, had in his own house images as esoteric as those of Hercules and Abbondanza, the female embodiment of prosperity.

The talented poet Francesco del Benino wrote a sonnet about the phoenix, which seems to have been a family emblem; Neri di Bicci painted a phoenix gazing at the sun for the house of Francesco's brother Piero; for Bernardo del Benino he did a *Transfiguration of Christ*. Francesco was also one of the *operai* of San Felice who assisted Mariano Salvini, general of the Servites, with his commission from Neri di Bicci for an altarpiece for the church. Mariano presided over the patronage at Santissima Annunziata of the Medici and their friends; he was also noted for his work with the confraternities in which young boys received their Christian education. Diamante

Salviati, the beneficiary of Dominici's instruction on the use of images in the education of her children, had Neri di Bicci paint a plaster devotional image of the Madonna and Child within a tabernacle for a bedroom in her house.

Mariotto Davanzati was one of the more eminent and learned vernacular poets; his kinsman Nicolaio di Giovanni commissioned from Neri di Bicci "two nude figures and two dressed in antique armor in plaster" as a gift for Bernardo Baroncelli. Another of the earliest mid-century palaces was built for Tommaso Soderini, whose kinsman Niccolò was also a talented poet. The small artisan family of the Pucci produced the most famous of all popular poets in the fourteenth century; in the fifteenth, they were among the major patrons of Santissima Annunziata. Francesco Inghirami, manager of the Medici woolshop and a poet of the later fifteenth century, was the patron of a chapel at San Lorenzo in 1465.

Iacopo Borgianni, a dyer who became a prosperous businessman in the same period, was both a poet and patron of pictures from artists including Lorenzo di Credi. Niccolò Da Uzzano, known for building the first major palace of the fifteenth century, was also a poet; Luca Pitti, who built perhaps the most pretentious palace of the mid-century series inaugurated by the Medici, was the descendant of the poet and litterateur Bonaccorso Pitti. Branca Brancacci, a mordant poet of the mid-fifteenth century, suffered in the proscriptions after 1434 which also affected the patrons of the famous Brancacci chapel, frescoed by Masaccio and Masolino. The Capponi, patrons at Santa Felicita as well as Santo Spirito, produced military captains who were also writers of *ricordi*, histories, and verse.

More general connections between literary tastes and visual images are apparent in the number of *cassoni* illustrating Petrarch's *Triumphs* or the tales of Troy so popular at San Martino. More constant and profound interaction between an interest in texts and in objects appears in the careers and lives of artists, writers, and citizens, among them Sacchetti, Alberti, Brunelleschi, Leonardo da Vinci, Matteo Palmieri, and Marco Parenti.

MARCO PARENTI'S BELT-BUCKLE: A BLUEPRINT FOR A PATRON'S PERSONALIZED COMMISSION

A study of popular culture shows that modern art historians who attempt to unlock "hidden meanings and allusions in the works of art of the Renaissance, be they theological, philosophical or political," are not, as Gombrich claimed, merely creating their own fantasy worlds of academic erudition. On the contrary, they are imitating the fundamental propensity of Renaissance men to apprehend and order the world through the symbolism of words and images.[3] Sermons and memory devices put this familiarity and fascination with symbols to constant practical use. So did commissions of works of art, although there is very little documentation of this process, which took place chiefly in the minds of patron and artist, and in verbal communications between them.

There are, however, some rare exceptions to this rule. A note from Marco Parenti to his relative and friend Filippo Strozzi, accompanying a silver belt-buckle he was sending as a gift, and explaining the symbolic significance of its design, provides clear evidence of the application of the accumulated knowledge common to literate Florentines, and more importantly, of the habits of mind cultivated in deciphering shared texts, in the creation of a visual image. Parenti described the buckle's design as "a fantasy in my own style," evoking a vivid phrase of Burchiello's much quoted by other popular poets: "my head is full of fantasies."[4] Parenti's head was full of cultural information to be reworked and recombined in his personal fantasy, individual enough to make him feel that his meaning might be indecipherable, even by someone who shared this common knowledge from which his symbolism was drawn. Hence he wrote to Strozzi: "So that you will understand it, I will explain it to you in full."

The buckle incorporated a message in three parts. In the manner of Antoninus's sermons or Michele del Giogante's symbolic inventory of his household possessions,[5] Parenti combined three images to be put on it, "one on the buckle and two on the tongue . . . which I thought of, and which signify three other things." These were "you to whom I am sending it . . . the place where I am sending it to you . . . I, who am sending it to you." In devising his message, Parenti followed the basic rules governing the encoding of meaning in his culture, applying the method of the memory treatise to create his own symbolic associations. "And to signify these things, one needs a figure or representation of some symbol, and knowing of no more notable symbol to signify you, I took your arms, which are moons, and put them in a figure that signifies the moon." Since Strozzi's sign was already a symbol that resonated with classical literary associations, Parenti took the opportunity to rehearse these. "The ancient poets made up certain tales about the moon, which take a long time to tell . . ." He singled out one of "the many ways in which they represented the moon," as Diana, goddess of hunting, and he described her attributes, which he had memorized. Memory failed him in some details, as it often did the authors of literary

scrapbooks: "a bow in her hand, and arrows and dogs, and dressed in fox skins, and a flame on her head with two little wings, which were I forget what . . ."

He improvised, adding other signs, "the better to be understood." To the figure of Diana he joined "a little moon among some clouds under her feet." The image of the moon triggered other popular associations and ideas, namely that "the heavenly signs and their movements delimit time and govern us here below." This led him to the second symbol. "It seemed to me that a device of my own would fit in well, which signifies time, symbolized by a circle." That set off another chain reaction: "to tell you how a circle represents time would be a lenthy task." He noted, however, how mathematicians calculate months and years, and that "by these revolutions and movements of the heavens and of the signs in their orbits time is made, in which, and with which time we associate and organize all our doings and affairs, and so there is a motto that says UTI FERT RES, which means, that's the way things go, to signify that matters and actions are to be accommodated to the times."

Parenti added another layer of meaning to his symbol with the comment that although "the ancient philosophers said that the heavens were moved by separate substances, our theologians say that they are moved by angels." Punning that this "in substance comes to the same thing, I put that angel in the middle, and there you have the second figure." The third figure was, as he noted, well known: "when you want to signify that you are in the Neapolitan kingdom, you see a landscape in which an armed king is reposing, to denote that in a kingdom the power of the king extends everywhere." He concluded his comment in the style of many anthologists of popular compilations: "so you have heard my fantasy, and perhaps it will amuse you."

Parenti also commissioned a pair of *cassoni* for his marriage to Caterina Strozzi, which he ordered from Domenico Veneziano. The notice of the payment he made for these appears in his account book; not surprisingly, there is no reference in this financial log to their subject matter. Giuliano da Maiano's earliest known commission was for Parenti, who ordered from him in 1451 a tabernacle "all'anticha," which was painted by Masaccio's stepbrother, "Lo Scheggia." The tabernacle was to contain a Madonna for Parenti's bedroom.[6] He also assisted his Strozzi in-laws with various other commissions. He was praised for his learning by such distinguished humanist scholars as Alamanno Rinuccini, Donato Acciaiuoli, and Francesco Filelfo, and his friends included Leon Battista Alberti and Vespasiano da Bisticci, who provided him with the books from which he acquired the raw materials for his "fantasy."[7]

However, Parenti's personalized design for a belt-buckle to amuse a friend is barely substantial enough to bear the weight of the scholarly attention it has attracted. This interest is due to the fact that as Creighton Gilbert pointed out, "it is the best single record in this century of a patron's inventing the iconography of any work." Gilbert used Parenti's letter to support his own view of the simple-mindedness of Renaissance patrons, commenting that "the symbolic concept is very elementary . . . the images are commonplace ones . . . their sources unesoteric . . . each such symbol is given just one role, there are no second layers of meaning." This last is patently not true, and in fact Gilbert himself underlined the richness of these symbols' associations in Parenti's mind in observing that "the whole program is the original fancy of the writer, without any specific reference to established set ideas, *apart from the whole culture of his age.*"[8] In this respect Parenti's program represents, however pedestrian its application, the very essence of Renaissance iconography.

The spirit of Parenti's enterprise – the design of the buckle and its accompanying explanation – is precisely that with which the pages of the *zibaldoni* have familiarized us. What separates Parenti's belt-buckle from objects recognized by art historians as masterpieces of "high culture" – the aesthetically remarkable paintings and sculptured figures and buildings fashioned by the skill and imagination of great artists – is the greater solemnity of these genres, the greater skills they demanded, and the greater seriousness of the patron's and artist's intent. The process of invention and recognition is the same. Indeed, what the example of Parenti and his buckle shows is not that Florentine patrons were simpleminded, but how well Florentine popular culture prepared every man to translate his knowledge into visual forms whose meaning is not immediately apparent to the viewer. If modern attempts to decode the resulting images sometimes seem forced and implausible, this is perhaps because nowadays the fifteenth-century repertoire of common ideas and images has become arcane. The cultural games once played by a high proportion of the Florentine populace are now the exclusive province of scholars occupied with an artificial construct of "high culture" divorced from the real world of which it was once part.

THE POPULAR APPRECIATION OF IMAGES
EXPRESSED IN EVERYMAN'S COMMISSIONS

Works of art belonging to patrician patrons had by far the best chance of surviving the centuries. Objects and their documentation were carefully conserved in private palaces and family papers, where many of them may still be found. By contrast, lack of evidence has left scholars largely ignorant of the role of art in ordinary Florentines' lives. Art historians, having studied intensively the most aesthetically distinguished and innovative objects of Renaissance art, most of them arising from the collaboration of prominent patrician families with major artists, have generalized from these about the whole nature of patronage and the impulses behind it. Some have been quick to assume that most ordinary men were probably "philistines."[9]

However, these few well-known objects represented only a portion of a much larger body of works of art, most now lost, commissioned "for the honor of God and the honor of the city and the memory of me," not just by the rich and powerful, but by a whole range of citizens, from little-known major guildsmen through artisans and small businessmen to widows, and even a handful of wage laborers. Their commissions, which consumed a far higher proportion of their meager incomes than those of wealthy patricians, are evidence of the paramount importance of images in the lives of ordinary Florentines.[10] Popular interest in the commissions of great patrons such as Cosimo de' Medici is also implied in the imitation of well-known major works.

Samuel Cohn's study of testaments from six Tuscan cities between the twelfth and fifteenth centuries unearthed a treasure trove of records of plebeian commissions. These commissions were the visual counterparts of chapbooks of popular culture. Cohn's evidence helps to dispel any illusion that art and images were essentially an elite interest.[11] He showed, for the fourteenth century and the very early years of the fifteenth, that the bequest of comparatively inexpensive panel paintings of devotional images had a high priority in the final provisions of butchers, shoemakers, blacksmiths, and even a gardener or a greengrocer.[12]

Some of these plebeian commissions were quite ambitious. In 1343 a Florentine tavern keeper, who also worked as a gravedigger, gave some land to the hospital of Santa Maria della Scala with the stipulation that a statue of the Madonna and Child, to stand at least six feet high, should be erected on the road in front of it.[13] In 1416 a shoemaker from Vinci who worked in Florence left fifty florins to build a chapel in his native village, "furnished and ornamented" with a panel painting of the Virgin Mary and the "blessed saints John the Baptist, Paul the Apostle, Michael the Archangel and Anthony." Like so many patricians, he supplied his chapel with a missal, a chalice, other church furniture, and the salary of a priest to conduct memorial masses.[14] Agostino di Ser Francesco di Ser Giovanni displayed in his 1417 bequest for the chapel of Santa Lucia in the church of Santo Spirito a concern to "conserve and maintain for ever his memory" similar to the spirit that moved his neighbors the Capponi, or the Medici at San Lorenzo. Agostino ordered perpetual masses and divine offices to be celebrated, and his arms to be displayed, "so that they could readily be seen by all," stipulating, like the Medici at San Marco, that "no other banners, plaques, or insignia" be placed next to this chapel or in the space between the chapel and the organ of the church."[15]

Unfortunately, most works of art commissioned by artisans have disappeared. Many were of an ephemeral nature, among them wayside shrines, painted beds for hospitals, and innumerable wax images of sacred figures and family arms that have literally, as Cohn observed, "gone up in smoke." The precarious living conditions of the poor, and the vulnerability to fire of the wooden structures in which they lived, also played a part. A *tavola* of the Madonna made by Neri di Bicci for his neighbor, a barber, which might well have survived in a patrician palace, was destroyed in a blaze that consumed the barber's shop the very afternoon it was delivered.[16]

The workshop book kept from 1452 by Neri di Bicci, third generation of a line of artists that began with Lorenzo di Bicci in the trecento and continued with his son Bicci, father of Neri, into the fifteenth, recorded commissions from patrons of all social levels.[17] Along with numerous artisans, they included Giovanni Rucellai, and other experienced and well-educated patrons such as the Soderini and Davanzati, the cleric Mariano Salviati, general of the Servites and a close friend of the Medici, as well as the syndics of convents and confraternities, and the Florentine Signoria.[18] Neri's detailed accounts of transactions, and the large number of his plebeian customers, allow comparison of their orders and impulses with those of wealthier and more socially distinguished patrons. They also illuminate the place of the artist's *bottegha* in neighborhood and particularly artisan life.[19] Neri di Bicci has not been considered an artist of the first rank, either by his contemporaries or by modern historians, but he worked with sculptors of the caliber of Verrocchio and Giuliano da Maiano, coloring gesso or marble images and gilding tabernacles to house them, often remodeling images and their settings in the newly fashionable classicizing style, with friezes and pilasters.

Most of the workshop's commissions, from patricians or plebeians, were for devotional images, either domestic, or for churches or convents that were the object of the patron's charity. For Giovanni di Guarnieri Benci, Neri provided a wooden tabernacle as a setting for a stained-glass image of Our Lady by Luca della Robbia.[20] Diamante Salviati, in accordance perhaps with Dominici's

earlier advice on the use of images in the education of her children, had Neri paint a plaster devotional image of the Madonna and Child within a tabernacle "in the antique style" for a bedroom in her house.[21] The silk-merchant Leonardo Boni requested the modernization of an old panel depicting "Our Lady" with a newly gilded and carved tabernacle and the addition of a cameo portrait of Saint Jerome, to adorn the main room of his house.[22] In 1461 Diamante Salviati's kinsman Bernardo commissioned a *tavola* of the Coronation of the Virgin with six saints for the high altar of his local church of San Leonardo, on the street of the same name just outside the Porta San Giorgio.[23] Bartolomeo Lenzi also commissioned an altarpiece depicting this subject for the hospital of the Innocenti.[24]

Patrons' specifications for their commissions indicate that they paid close attention to the work being done by artists, and that pictures they had seen on display in the houses of other patrons or in public places influenced their taste and choices. In 1455 the Spini family ordered an altarpiece for their chapel in Santa Trinita, to depict "an Assumption of Our Lady with twelve apostles at her feet and many angels at her side and above her . . . all finely decorated and colored just like the one I did for Carlo Benizzi in Santa Felicità."[25] Jeffrey Ruda described a case brought before the trades' disputes court, the Mercanzia, against Fra Filippo Lippi, in which a patron who had sought out Lippi for his reputation as a "singular and worthy" painter refused to pay for a panel, claiming that the altarpiece he got was not the panel he had ordered, did not contain what he wanted, and was not done by Lippi himself. As Ruda observed, his "agitated testimony shows how a patron of no known cultural pretensions could be intensely concerned with the artistic quality of a painting."[26]

Some patrician commissions stipulated more distinctive features. Pier Francesco Sernigi ordered a tabernacle with gilded columns, decorated with such classicizing details as egg and dart motifs and dentils and a frieze, to be placed in the *camera grande* of his house; within the tabernacle, against an azure and gold ground, Neri was to paint a Christ child alone.[27] Don Mariano Salvini, abbot of the convent of San Felice in Piazza, specified a Christ child depicted in low relief upon a pillow decorated with silk and gold buttons.[28] A more complex commission for the abbot, an altarpiece, was made in November 1459 in personal consultation between the artist and the *operai* of the church, who included Bernardo di Messer Lorenzo Ridolfi, Mariotto Lippi, Goro di Luca di Ghirigoro, Antonio Fantoni, and Francesco del Benino, a well-known popular poet. The *pala* was to depict the Coronation of Our Lady, seated in a cloud with four unnamed saints, with scenes from their lives in the predella. The work with which this commission has been identified is now in the Accademia Gallery in Venice. The predella is missing, and the number of saints is in fact eleven, including Romuald, patron of the Camaldolensian order, Felix, patron of the church, and Bernard, patron of the Signoria; the Medici palace chapel, prominently featuring Saint Bernard, was completed in this same year. If the identification of the altarpiece is correct, it seems that the painter was permitted to embroider considerably upon the original specifications.[29]

A few patrons of "the middling sort" made commissions which were notably up-to-date in subject or form, perhaps in emulation of famous patrician commissions, perhaps because certain subjects and forms appealed to patrons of all sorts. Monna Antonia, a tertiary from Pescia, ordered a tabernacle containing a figure of San Bernardino in 1458, not long after his canonization in 1450, and after his appearance in the Medici altarpiece for Bosco ai Frati painted by Fra Angelico.[30] In 1467 Niccolaio Valentini, a notary of the Mercanzia, furnished Neri with elaborate instructions concerning a tondo of Sant'Antonio, which has been identified with an extant work. The circular picture had only recently come into vogue, following the Medici Magi tondi.[31]

Several of the workshop's patrician customers ordered images of secular subjects, still comparatively rare in this period. Neri rented one of his two botteghe, in Via Porta Rossa, from the Davanzati. In 1464 he was commissioned by Niccolaio di Giovanni Davanzati to make two nude figures in plaster relief, one with a shield in his hand, and two others dressed in antique armor, which cost two large florins, one of the highest prices charged for any object to come out of the workshop. These figures were ordered as a gift for Bernardo Baroncelli.[32] In 1457 Giovanni Speraindio had ordered a head in mezo rilievo colored in oil paint and with a golden crown and armor "in the Roman fashion."[33] While Neri depicted a Transfiguration of Christ for Bernardo del Benino, for the courtyard of the house of his brother Piero he painted a phoenix gazing at the sun. The phoenix, a symbol of resurrection and chastity described by Ovid and Pliny, seems to have been a personal emblem of the Del Benino family, since the poet Francesco del Benino wrote a poem about this bird: "a creature of such amazing vision,/ and so faithful in gazing at the sun,/ that it dies in its rays and then returns to life . . . I have dedicated myself to its way of life,/ in order to be worthy of such a beautiful vision . . ."[34]

At least one of Neri di Bicci's best customers was a dealer. Mariotto Mazzi, a pedlar, dealt in devotional images, ordering paintings in bulk. An entry in the work-shop book for December 1461 refers to payments due for no less than ten pictures of Our Lady, as well as for "two cupids I did for him in a stained-glass window, and one coat of arms I painted a few days ago in a picture belonging to the cardinal of Crana, and for a gilded salt cellar base."[35]

The occupational range of Neri's non-patrician customers was impressively wide. including a stationer, a marriage broker, a factor, a goldbeater, a builder or bricklayer, a blacksmith, a ropemaker, a slippermaker, a fringemaker, and an employee of the Signoria, as well as several leatherworkers, dyers, caskmakers, cobblers and barbers.[36] The range of works of art they commissioned, by comparison with patricians, was rather narrow. Most of them were traditional devotional subjects. Lorenzo, a ropemaker identified as working at the Ponte Rubaconte near the Alberti houses, ordered a tabernacle to be erected on a piece of land he owned outside the city gate at San Minato al Monte in which, Neri di Bicci noted, "I have to paint Our Lady and four saints at her side in the manner he requests, and also to paint the roof and door of the tabernacle." The ropemaker's commission perhaps resembled a still extant image of the Virgin on a throne under a baldachino, in a style favored by Neri di Bicci, on one corner of a house now standing outside the Porta San Miniato.[37]

The only secular image made for a plebeian which was not a familial object, "a large head of a woman with natural coloring and decorated with fine gold," was made for a poet who served as a page to the Signoria.[38] The most common occasions for secular images were the painting of marriage chests and birthtrays which associated Renaissance lineages with the legendary virtues of the protagonists of classical literature. Recent studies have brought forward evidence of an artisan interest in lineage and family traditions cognate to the patrician obsession with these issues, but the surviving visual evidence is very limited.[39] Although men of all classes read Petrarch's Triumphs, which inspired the illustrations of so many painted chests and birthtrays,[40] Neri di Bicci recorded only two or three artisan commissions of cassoni panels or deschi da parto. The workshop of Apollonio di Giovanni and Marco del Buono which specialized in these, so that their bottega book reads like a roll call of Florence's great patrician families, records not a single plebeian commission.[41]

From Neri's workshop, a tailor named Domenicho da Pietrasanta commissioned a birthtray, and paid for it in kind; the garments he made outfitted the artist's entire family.[42] Neri di Bicci painted another desco da parto for the notary Ser Bastiano, for whom he had made a large tabernacle of Our Lady and recolored the face of a plaster

Virgin and Child. On one side of the *desco* was a chess-player, on the other, "certain other things."[43] The only *cassoni* mentioned in Neri's *Ricordanze* were those the artist used to transport a "a little tabernacle for a bed-chamber with Our Lady and two saints by her side" for the blacksmith Antonio dalla Lastra. He was carrying it in a pair of large chests on the back of a horse, when a mule "jumped on top of it," breaking the *cassone* into a dozen pieces which Neri reassembled while Antonio looked on.[44]

Commissioning a work of art was not necessarily a once-in-a-lifetime act, even for artisans. Several of Neri di Bicci's more plebeian customers ordered more than one work from him. While the Medici were unique in possessing a large number of devotional works that filled the rooms of their house as early as 1418, even their friend the accountant Michele del Giogante had decorative images in several rooms of his much smaller dwelling; pictures of Hector, and of a Dacian woman, a bust of Cato and apparently a small statuette of Abbondanza, perhaps a replica of Donatello's *Dovizia*.[45]

Both patricians and plebeians commissioned works not only for domestic display, but also for their local churches or other public places, sometimes as agents for others. A comparatively elaborate Trinity for the church of San Niccolò, Oltrarno, including the saints John the Baptist, Lawrence, Francis, and Leonard, was commissioned by a group of artisans; "Nofri the shoemaker and Piero Dalla Volta blacksmith, and Giovanni fringemaker, executors and agents" of Monna Lionarda, widow of a notary.[46] Like patricians, artisans might be responsible for corporate commissions, particularly for the religious confraternities in which they were so active. Damiano, a leatherworker in the Via Porta Rossa, made an order for the company of San Giorgio who met in the church of that name. The patron's instructions to Neri di Bicci were particularly explicit: "In the middle of the picture I am to do an Annunciation, and on one side San Luca [the apostle who was believed to have made the original image of the Virgin], and on the other whatever saint the patron making the contract wants, and at the bottom in the predella, three little stories of these saints . . ." The work was to be done "in whatever place Damiano wants," and then he and Neri di Bicci were to discuss the price. If they could not agree, they each could call on an arbitrator, "an artisan expert in the art of painting, and they and these said masters should set the price."[47] Neri was also commissioned by a group of dyers to paint a banner with the arms of the company of the Convertite, the reformed prostitutes, whose patron was San Sebastiano, showing the saint at prayer.[48]

Artisans also ordered devotional images for the work-place, as we learn from Neri di Bicci's account of the fire in a barber's shop on the Via Porta Rossa down the street from his own *bottegha*:

Friday, October 14, 1468 . . . Note that on this day I painted and finished for Geri di . . . barber and company, barbers in Porta Rossa, a little tabernacle which they had made to keep in their shop, in which I painted Our Lady on her knees with her Son at her feet, decorated with fine gold and German ultramarine. The very same day the image was burned when their *bottegha* caught fire; both the wood and the painting burned, and in fact no wood remained. I repainted it and sold it to others as recorded in the entry on folio 32. And on the 18th of June 1471, I gave them a little *colmo* like the one I had had of theirs; it was collected by their *compagno* Sìramo, who said he would get someone else to paint it.[49]

Most of the artisan commissions for devotional images were conventional in subject, usually representations of the Madonna and Child, but less wealthy patrons seem to have spared no expense within their means on rich decoration and fashionable form. Neri di Bicci reset many older paintings and plaster sculptures in up-to-date classicizing frames, in addition to making new works with *all'antica* details. "Wednesday, October 31, 1459 . . . I sold to Chimento the barber at the Canto del Giglio a half figure of Our Lady in plaster in low relief with the child at her breast, set in a tabernacle in the antique style with pilasters and architraves, a frieze and cornice, and beneath a framed pendant, the Virgin Mary being decorated in gold and blue."[50] Five years later, Chimento commissioned another devotional image, this time of "Our Lady on her knees on the ground before Our Lord, with a kneeling Saint Lawrence colored and ornamented with gold." Giuliano da Maiano made the tabernacle for this image, which has been associated with a surviving work (fig. 36).[51] For Domenico, the tailor, Neri painted an image for a bedroom with "Our Lady, Saint John and Saint Catherine," which sounds rather like the image before which Giovanni Morelli made his devotions and was vouchsafed his vision.[52] For another tailor, Neri made an image of the Virgin Mary in plaster, set within a gilded wooden ring, as richly decorated as most patrician commissions, and similarly expensive.[53] A dyer and a shoemaker ordered works in plaster and wood in settings *all'antica*, and decorated with costly gold and ultramarine.[54] A blacksmith commissioned a work that was quite elaborate by any standards: "a tabernacle with doors and inside four little stories; the Assumption of Our Lady, the

36   Neri di Bicci, *Virgin and Child with Saint Lawrence*, painted tabernacle panel, Florence, Villa I Tatti, Berenson Collection

37). At least some of the images made in Neri di Bicci's workshop could appeal to buyers of quite dif-ferent social stations; when Francesco da Siena, a marriage broker, failed to collect a relatively large *tavola* with wings that he had ordered from Neri, with the mediation of Iacopo del Piccia, a wool merchant in the Mercato Vecchio, the artist succeeded in selling it to "a slippermaker from San Giovanni."[57]

Apart from the caskmaker who asked simply for "a pair of saints," there is little evidence that even poorer and less educated patrons left the iconography of the commissions they ordered completely to the artist. They do seem in subsequent negotiations to have accepted his advice. Neri di Bicci's *Ricordanze* are particularly valuable for his evocation of the physical circumstances in which commissions were made, carried out, and consigned to their patrons, creating ample opportunity for exchange between the artist and his neighborhood clients. For example, Zanobi di Manno, a caskmaker who lived in the Piazza de' Nerli, ordered an image in the antique style apparently to commemorate the patron of his neighborhood and his own namesaint: "In it he wanted San Zanobi and San Frediano on the occasion of their meeting . . ." In fact there is no tradition of a meeting between these two, and in the extant work identified with this commission, San Frediano appears with Saint Ambrose, as he did in the lives of the saints. Perhaps the

37   Donatello, *Madonna and Child with Four Angels* (Chellini Madonna), London, Victoria and Albert Museum

Annunciation, the Nativity of Christ, and San Giovanni going forth into the desert."[55]

A number of artisan commissions were for brightly painted wood or plaster images. It has been suggested that such works catered to a plebeian taste, corresponding to the lowest of the levels of perception, images for the unlettered, by comparison with more expensive and finely worked marble in low relief which invited a more cerebral response, commensurate with a higher level of understanding with the eyes of the mind. But medieval and Renaissance taste often favored the gaudy painting even of stone capitals, faded now to an austerity more in harmony with modern preferences. It is difficult to establish the original appearance of sculpted images; certainly Neri di Bicci's *bottega* colored some high quality marble reliefs.[56] The surviving products of the workshop of Donatello, the city's most acclaimed sculptor, included alongside the subtlest of marble low reliefs images of painted wood and stucco, and casts for mass production, like the bronze one he gave to his doctor Chellini (fig.

patron had paired in his own mind two saints of personal significance to himself, or perhaps his memory was simply uncertain, like Matteo Palmieri's knowledge of the attributes of the goddess Diana. The artist presumably rectified the mistake, since the lives of the saints were his daily bread, and no doubt he had fresh in his mind Filippo Lippi's depiction of a similar scene of San Frediano and Saint Augustine in the altarpiece for the Barbadori in the local quarter church of Santo Spirito.[58]

While Neri di Bicci catered mainly to a Santo Spirito clientele, with a disproportionately large number of customers from the district of the Green Dragon where he was born, lived, and maintained the workshop he inherited from his father Bicci di Lorenzo, a second workshop across the Arno in Via Porta Rossa gradually became the chief center of his operations and attracted a significant business from that neighborhood as well. Neri's cooperation with other artists such as Giuliano da Maiano and Desiderio da Settignano, whose *botteghe* were located north of the river, also helped to extend his horizons. These frequent exchanges among artists and shops presumably fostered a corporate spirit that helped to balance the fierce competition between artists.

Among those Neri worked with were Maso Finiguerra, who gilded a relief image of the sun with rays radiating from it that may have been San Bernardino's emblem of the name of Christ.[59] For another commission from Neri's workshop Pietro Tazzi "decorated with gold and azure a bedroom tabernacle with the Virgin" that was "carved in marble . . . by the hand of Desiderio [da Settignano.]"[60] A whole group of patrons and artists were involved in a commission for the design of a tapestry for the Signoria. As Neri noted in his *Ricordanze*,

> a few days ago Vetorio the son of Lorenzo di Bartolo who is doing the doors [all the information a Florentine needed to identify Ghiberti!] asked me to help color and design a model of a *spalliera* which has to be redone in tapestry for the platform [*ringhiera*] outside the palace of the Signoria of Florence, and he has also asked Piero del Massaio and Berto the painter and Chimento. So the same day, I Neri took it from the *operai* appointed by the *Signori* of Florence, that is Piero Borsi, Pandolfo Pandolfini, and Recho Capponi, and for our trouble and coloring, we were paid in all 96 lire.[61]

★　　★　　★

ARTISTS SHARING AND SHAPING THE IDIOM OF POPULAR CULTURE

The densely built city of Ambrogio Lorenzetti's fresco depicting Good Government in Siena, packed with shops open to the street where artisans plied their trade in full view of a stream of passers-by, testifies to the very public activities of artisans, among them artists, and their very visible contribution to community life (fig. 38).[62] Neri di Bicci, like his father before him, served as a captain of the confraternity of Sant'Agnese, which met at the church of the Carmine in the district of the Green Dragon, and performed there its famous Ascension play. It is largely thanks to his meticulous records of the expenses of staging the play, and his detailed description of the properties required, that so much is known about the scenery, the costumes, and the activities of the performers.[63]

38 Ambrogio Lorenzetti, *Allegory of Good Government*, c.1340, Siena, Palazzo Pubblico, Sala dei Nove, east wall, detail

Neri di Bicci's *Ricordanze*, the evidence of popular literature, and casual comment in personal *ricordi* all suggest that artists' workshops, easily accessible to an audience of neighbors and patrons, were natural settings for encounters with friends and the exchange of information, places where patrons and their audience could learn about art by seeing artists at work. In the last decade of the century, the popular poet Bongianni heard news of a putative miracle by Savonarola recounted by "two brace of those friars" in the workshop of Lorenzo di Credi, from whom he commissioned an altarpiece.[64] Benedetto Dei, the "poet of Florentine statistics," made a list not of the names of individual artists working in Florence in 1467, but of their workshops, the places where they could be found.[65] Brunelleschi's biographer Manetti first introduced the architect to his audience not as the creator of the cathedral cupola, but as "that Filippo . . . who played the practical joke you admire so much on 'il Grasso.' "[66] As Lauro Martines pointed out, the tale of the trick played by Brunelleschi on the fat carpenter begins with a scene of patricians and artisans socializing and conniving in the workshop, and by the time the story ends, a large and socially varied group of conspirators has joined in the fun. Moreover, the whole ruse of inducing the carpenter to question whether he really knows who he is depends upon the other characters all knowing one another very well. The joke is progressively embroidered by an entire community of artists and writers, revolving around Brunelleschi and his friend Donatello, united in delight in one another's intellect and wit.[67]

Francesco, the son of Andrea delle Sargie, painter of cretonne coverlets, who may himself have written the verse sometimes attributed to his father and addressed to Feo Belcari concerning the saints, was Neri di Bicci's landlord. He inherited his father's *zibaldone* along with the right to collect Neri's rent.[68] The generally close associations between artisan poets and artists is nicely expressed in a sonnet written by Ottavante Barducci, supposedly on behalf of a lady: "written for a friend of his, Michelozzo the sculptor, for a lady who is a neighbor concerning their meeting as he returned to his house." In another poem, which was more of an exercise in social realist portraiture, Barducci compared the apron stained with food that he wore in prison with "the overall of a painter."[69] Cristofano, the son of L'Altissimo, one of San Martino's star performers, became an artist; "Lo Za," "the sovereign poet" of popular satire, was actually Stefano Finiguerra, apparently first cousin to Maso Finiguerra, a leading mid-century artist and engraver in the popular style, whose brother was a goldsmith. A number of notable artists, from Orcagna in the late trecento through Brunelleschi to Michelangelo at the end of the fifteenth century, wrote first-rate popular poetry in the same quintessentially Florentine style as their art.[70]

The artist in his workshop, like the barber or shoemaker poet, the observant apothecary such as Luca Landucci, or the cultivated notary or doctor, was a natural conduit for cultural exchange.[71] While major commissions could take months or even years, most artists' workshops seem to have produced standard items in quantities large enough to attract a regular traffic of such citizen clients as notaries, doctors, barbers, and shoemakers. Neri di Bicci did a brisk trade in colored stucco reliefs, occasionally made in batches of three and four. Even a major artist such as Donatello was interested in making multiple reproductions of his work. His doctor Giovanni Chellini, in a diary he kept from 1425 to 1457, described a gift the artist gave him after an illness, an image of the Virgin and Child with four angels, from which copies might be made. It was, as Chellini explained, "all of bronze, and on the outer side hollowed out so that melted glass could be cast onto it, and it would make the same figures as those on the other side."

Chellini described his famous patient as "the singular and principle master in making figures of bronze and wood and terracotta." He was familiar with some of these commissions, identifying Donatello as the artist "who made the big man which is on top of the chapel above the door of Santa Reparata towards the Servi, and had begun another one 9 braccia high . . ." Chellini's library included Petrarch's treatise *Against Doctors* and a number of books which by their description appear to be *zibaldoni* or *quadernucci* of popular literature, and which he loaned to others. Donatello's doctor seems to have been a good example of the middling sort of man educated by popular culture to an appreciation of art and its patronage. The doctor's diary also records his friendship with Girolamo da Imola, another physician who commissioned an image of the Madonna and Child from Neri di Bicci's workshop. Chellini built a memorial chapel for himself in the convent of San Iacopo in his native San Miniato, dedicated to the doctor saints Cosmas and Damian, and entrusted his tomb to his friend Donatello.[72]

The education and culture of artists was generally that of artisans, although some artists, for example Ghiberti, vied with their better-educated patrons in esoteric knowledge. As artisans, artists were naturally heirs to a rich popular culture which incorporated many of the themes that preoccupied their patrons – fortune, fame, salvation, and the play of metaphor and symbolism. While inventories of the libraries of such later artists as Leonardo survive, with the notable exception of Ghiberti, what is known of the reading of Brunelleschi and his contemporaries must be largely inferred from what they wrote. Leonardo's master, Verrocchio, who was responsible for Cosimo's tomb, kept in his Florentine workshop at the time of his own death a lute, an Italian Bible, the *Trecentonovelle* of Franco Sacchetti, the *Triumphs* of Petrarch, and the *Epistles* (Heroides) of Ovid.[73]

A *zibaldone* owned by Antonio da San Gallo, much of it compiled in the 1450s by Zanobi di Federico Gori, included moral songs by two of the major performers at San Martino, the barber Antonio da Bachereto, writing on desperation, and Maestro Antonio di Guido on government, together with a poem on the seven mortal sins and another on friendship. It also contained the *Triumphs* of Petrarch, and Dati's *Sfera*, beautifully illustrated with maps of the Middle East, Tunisia, Morocco, and the Black Sea.[74] At the death of Benedetto da Maiano, an inventory was made of the books in his and his brother Giuliano's studies. They included copies of Dante's works, Boccaccio's *Centonovelle*, the Bible, the Gospels and the Epistles, the lives of the saints, including particularly the church fathers, an account of the death of Saint Jerome, a dialogue of Saint Gregory, and the miracles of Our Lady. There were also some writings of Saint Bernard, a book of lauds, and one of virtues and vices, the Little Flowers of Saint Francis, a treatise by Saint Antoninus, a history of Florence, a poem of the wars of Charlemagne, the life of Alexander, and extracts from Livy's *Decades*.[75] There is a striking correspondence between the inventories of artists' books, the selections most frequently copied in popular compilations, the titles in Cosimo's library, and the main literary sources of Medicean artistic commissions.

Their reading puts artists right in the mainstream of Florentine popular culture. Patrons, artists, and their audiences drew their understanding of classical and Christian ideas and images from essentially the same texts, and although the patron in the fifteenth century remained the *auctor* of his commissions, there were elements in popular culture that simultaneously encouraged a view of artisans as creators, just as some early medieval accounts of the creation of the world represented God as the supreme artisan.[76] Artisan poets and artists were extravagantly praised for their *ingegno*, an almost divine quality of mind that Florentines discerned in Donatello and Brunelleschi. If as a patron Cosimo governed himself according to his own fantasy, he fulfilled it with the aid of that "variety of *ingegni*" he so admired.

POPULAR IMAGES OF COSIMO AND HIS PATRONAGE

A study of Florentine popular culture is ultimately more valuable to the exploration of Cosimo's patronage for what it reveals about the forces that shaped Cosimo than for what its participants said about him. However, popular images of Cosimo do constitute useful clues to the likely readings and reception of his patronage of art. The chronicler Cavalcanti, himself the scion of an ancient magnate family, wrote that Cosimo's political fortunes flourished

"because the masses had chosen him as their champion and looked on him as a god." His comment was interpreted, particularly by nineteenth-century historians, to mean that the Medici party consisted of men "without political influence, or with very little."[77]

A close analysis of the Medici party, and even of Cavalcanti's protracted account of it, reveals that in fact its leading members were all men of the political class, many of them with long and distinguished records of service to the state. The Medici achieved their ascendancy over Florentine government not by a popular uprising, but with the support of partisans who promoted each other to political office. However, Cavalcanti's testimony to Cosimo's populist public image, together with its elaboration in the verses of popular poets, does illuminate his immense influence as a patron and public figure.

Since the praise of Cosimo in popular literature is so obviously part of the flattery of a powerful patron, what is most interesting is not that he was praised, but how.[78] The image of Cosimo as refracted through the eyes of the popular poets is invaluable evidence of the very positive terms in which his power might be seen. Popular poems praising Cosimo present him above all as the promoter of religious and civic life; the ideal type of the merchant on whom Florentine prosperity depended, the heroic defender of Florentine liberty against foreign aggression,[79] the physician uniquely skilled in the cure of civic ills, the chief patron and *pater* of the Florentine people, the protector of the cult and its shrines.

Anselmo Calderoni, for example, described Cosimo as "the clear mirror of every merchant,/ the true friend of every holy enterprise,/ the honor of famous Florentines,/ the strong shield of the borders of Tuscany,/ the succor of all the needy,/ the helper of wards and widows." These images underline Cosimo's outstanding contribution to the city's commercial and spiritual prosperity, the pride of the Florentine *popolo*, as represented in the procession and performances for the annual civic festival on Saint John the Baptist's feastday.[80] Extravagance on the part of the rich may have been offensive to those who were really poor, but most articulate Florentines delighted in display that could be viewed with collective pride. Unlike humanist encomia which follow classical topoi in praising Cosimo as a ruler (in his middle age as the Aristotelian steersman of the republic, posthumously as the Platonic philosopher-king), most popular poets represented Cosimo as the embodiment of popular ideals. This contributes to the impression that these were the primary terms in which Cosimo framed his patronage of art, and in which it was read by his Florentine audience.

The major and most effective criticism of Cosimo, in his lifetime as after it, was that his manipulation of the

Florentine constitution and its offices had subverted the republic in the manner more of a tyrant than a citizen. His great-grandsons Piero and Giovanni were expelled from the city on this clearly verifiable charge, and only after forty years of domestic struggle, and with the decisive outside support of the Roman church and the Spanish state, were the Medici reinstalled as dukes of their native city. The republican protest was articulated with subtlety and eloquence by Cosimo's fellow patricians, idealists such as Manetti, Acciaiuoli, Palmieri, and Parenti, and with all the coruscating armory of scorn and satire characteristic of the genre by the greatest of popular poets, the barber Burchiello. Burchiello greeted the news of Cosimo's recall from exile in 1434 thus: "O humble people mine, you do not see/how this perfidious tyrant, wicked man,/ harshly with force of veiled deceit/ tramples upon our sovereignty/ . . . He is a dove, but later with full gizzard/ he will be a sea hawk with tawny feathers . . ."[81]

An alternative view was offered by the herald Antonio di Meglio, spokesman for the Florentine commune and for its incumbent officers, in a *canzone* its copyist described as "written in 1434, after the scrutiny for the governing offices of the regime was finished, advising the citizens to recognize what great benefits they had received from God." Antonio represented the recall of Cosimo de' Medici as the result of "happy Fortune and the favor of the heavens." Having first reminded his listeners, in the spirit of Dante, "how many kingdoms, provinces, places, and territories/ were brought to ultimate destruction/ for no other reason than discord," Antonio congratulated them that "by the grace and mercy/ of you yourselves, the example of Rome,/ that rising to such greatness is remembered and followed,/ while you hold dear,/ O free fine sons, the good of the commune . . . By God you are united/ in pulling all together on a single rope." He evoked here the image popularized by Brunetto Latini and preserved, as has been seen, in the compilations of Florentine culture, and in the vivid representations of Ambrogio Lorenzetti's frescoes of Good Government in the town hall at Siena – by mid-fifteenth century part of the Florentine dominion. Declaring his own love and faith in "my fatherland Florence," Antonio concluded with the hope "of further inspiring the citizens of this *patria*/ to flee from vice and follow virtue,/ which after death/ keeps men alive in the world through their fame."[82]

Cosimo was also seen as the ultimate father figure here on earth, the *pater/padrino* interceding with the pope for more indulgences for his people,[83] dispensing his charity in the interests of their salvation, recommending them to his patron saints, depicted in his altarpieces

for public churches, and ultimately to their Heavenly Father.[84] In a series of sonnets addressed to Cosimo and his sons, Feo Belcari praised them not for their political skills or influence in either the public or private spheres, but as fathers of their devoted sons – their friends and the people of Florence. In a prefatory verse to his most famous play, *Abraham and Isaac*, which turned on that issue so close to Florentine hearts, the bond between fathers and sons, Belcari honored Cosimo's younger son Giovanni by associating him in his father's virtues: "Such great gifts and graces you sow,/ O my Giovanni, that with legitimate reason,/ over land and sea,/ your honor and fame is the twin of Cosimo's."

Cosimo he praised as the charitable parent of his people: "Father of your country [*padre della patria*], gracious and worthy/ conserver of temples and holy places,/ the singular refuge of all those/ who live under the standard of poverty,/ for your good wine slakes our thirst . . . When Christ appears in paradise, we all will pray to Him with the greatest love,/ saying, "Bestow upon him this final grace,/ that Cosimo may achieve immortality rejoicing, in happy celebration . . ." Describing himself as "the familiar [*famelico*] of Our Lady," Belcari expressed his gratitude to Cosimo's elder son, Piero, for building the *tempietto* dedicated to her cult in the church of Santissima Annunziata, rejoicing "that it pleased you to spend such a great treasure/ on the chapel of angelic salvation/ which is our path to eternal life." He extolled the patronage of Cosimo and Piero for preserving the city's sacred spaces, "who more than any others have set your hands to this task,/ you and your father with perfection in your hearts/ merit praise from the world, and the great love of God,/ much more than did the great Romans."[85]

The identification of the Medici family with the early Christian doctor saints Cosmas and Damian, strongly reinforced by Cosimo's visual representations of these saints in altarpieces displayed in public churches and chapels, encouraged citizens to focus not only on Medici intercession in this world and the next, but also to play upon the name of Medici (the doctors), and to represent their role in government as the people's best medicine for the cure of civic ills caused by indecisive leadership. Commenting on the contention aroused by proposals to celebrate the Medici recall from exile on the feast of Cosmas and Damian, a verse by Anselmo Calderoni described his vision in a dream of the Medici and their patron saints. "In 1437, on the first day of May,/ I happened to be in my bed,/ and I began to think about the great outrage/ perpetrated in 33 by some false people/ of my *patria*, wrongfully and sinfully,/mainly against Cosimo and his brother."

Falling asleep, the poet was awakened by two saints. "We have come to say good-day to you,/ so that you should write a speech,/ that everyone might understand with your sounding horn,/ mainly for their consolation/ we have left their father Giovanni,/ who was taken up into heaven by the Almighty./ Already we importuned the king of the lofty regions/ that our feastday might be celebrated each year/ in Florence, free of all deceit./ . . . As you know we are Cosmas and Damian,/ devoted to those brothers, so that we/ pray for them before the good Jesus Christ/ for their great merits throughout your land,/ for aiding churches and hospitals and so many good acts . . . How many maidens have acquired husbands/ with their aid! Widows and orphans/ have been fed and clothed,/ choirs, chapels and other places embellished!/ . . . And whoever seeks to harm them, may he pay/ a great price . . . You know that your land is despoiled every hour/ by envy, avarice and pride,/and its unity every day further eroded,/ because it has taken in all the evil seed,/ I say rebel . . . because the great man, the middling and the small/ are all equals in the honorable kingdom;/ the *popolo* and the commune of Florence are now/ united, pulling together upon a single rope,/ . . . So you should tell your beloved Florence/ that it should make of a good beginning the best possible end . . ."[86]

When the Medici were exiled, the emperor was reported to have observed: "the Florentines have driven out those very *medici* [physicians] of whom they have the greatest need." A year later, after the Medici were restored to Florence, a friend wrote to Cosimo's younger son Giovanni: "I see that our *patria*, our city is cured [*medichata*] and disposed to prosper under the worthy regime which has been established."[87] Around the same time, Palla di Palla Strozzi asked Cosimo to support a petition "which is the medicine to cure these failings." Some time later, the popular poet Giovanni di Maffeo Barberini sent a rhymed recommendation to Cosimo, begging him to apply his medicine or salves to the cruel treatment he had received at the hands of some government officials, and the anthologist and poet Giovanni Pigli complained in his turn of an injury so great that even the Medici saints, Cosmas and Damian, would be hard put to heal it, the same playful phrase that Cosimo himself adopted in an inscription on the flyleaf of Ovid's *Epistolae*.[88] The inclusion of orange fruit in paintings to symbolize the Medici arms, the *mala medica*, also played into these word games.[89] The humanist Marsilio Ficino embroidered them with reference to the fact that his father was the Medici family doctor; just as Ficino the elder had been the physician caring for Cosimo's body, Cosimo was the doctor and medicator of the young Ficino's soul.[90] Marsilio and his generation, steeped in Neoplatonic ideas and images,

and preoccupied with the cosmos, naturally associated it with Cosimo's name. Bernardo Cambini wrote in his verse lament on Cosimo's death that the land had been widowed, since "Cosmo cosmicon" had abandoned the cosmos.[91]

The people of Florence appreciated Cosimo for the merchant he was, as well as the physician his name suggested. According to the apothecary Luca Landucci, "he was called by everyone 'the great merchant'."[92] During the crisis of 1433–4, in the struggle for power between the Mediceans and the families who had traditionally controlled the state, popular opinion suggested strongly that the merchants, represented by Cosimo, should be in charge of government. A butcher named Andrea di Francesco was fined one hundred lire in 1433 for remarking: "If Cosimo were still among us, we should send for him and give him a double stipend instead of exiling him; that would be the lesser evil. This regime cannot survive, and it will not. You will see that before a year has passed things will be different. The merchants should govern, not those [who are now in power] . . ."[93]

The image of the merchant as Florentine hero, implicit in the picaresque tales of Buonaccorso Pitti's *ricordi* concerning his vendettas at home and his ventures abroad,[94] emerges explicitly from popular literary selections in citizens' scrapbooks. Antonio Pucci's trecento love lyric to commerce, "On the beauties of the Mercato Vecchio," appeared in his handbook for popular singers, and found its way into many other anthologies.[95] Popular literature also invoked the precedent of classical Rome to legitimize and ennoble the merchant's profession. The volume that contained Cosimo's poem dedicated to Sforza also included a long account of how merchants took the initiative in the expansion and building of Rome.[96] Even the book of the nun "Suor Ursina," consisting largely of "gems from the sermons of Fra Giovanni da Settimo," began, after an injunction to the merciful Virgin to preserve the copyist from sin, with the unexpected metaphorical conceit that "everyone of whatever condition is a merchant, for nothing can be done without something being sold or bought and thus nothing is so necessary to the world as mercantile trading."[97]

In his verses praising Cosimo, the cleric poet Belcari associated him with the highest ideals of both Church and state – mercantile, Christian, civic, and antique. The Church's doctrine of the supreme virtue of charity offset its traditional condemnation of personal wealth and those who lived off the profits of investment, and helped to reconcile the incompatible elements of Christianity and capitalism. Thus the *Specchio umano* of Domenico Lenzi, who recorded the day to day cost of grain sold at the market of Orsanmichele at the turn of the century, cited verbatim some comments of the poor which combined abuse of the merchants who had driven up prices, with supplications for their help in Christ's name. The communal government, run by merchants, had habitually stepped forward as the savior of the people in the long-standing battle between starving crowds and exploitative traders, maintaining social order in times of scarcity by importing grain from all over Italy and distributing it to the people.[98] After 1434 the regime identified with Cosimo, the greatest merchant of them all, continued this practice with which Cosimo himself was personally associated. An entry for 1450 in the ledgers of the Buonomini of San Martino recorded extraordinary distributions of grain and flour on account of the plague, which were paid for by Cosimo.[99]

The commune's commission to Donatello in the late 1420s to make a gold figure of a woman personifying its collective wealth, the abundance of its prosperity and its charity to its citizens, to be placed atop an ancient column in the city's commercial center, the Mercato Vecchio, shows how effectively the virtues Cosimo represented could be brought together in the public mind through an image (fig. 39). Although Donatello's *Dovizia*, or *Abbondanza*, is now lost, reconstructions suggest that its imagery evoked the Roman state charity instituted by Trajan. Renaissance Florentines knew from reading Dante that Trajan's soul had been saved by such

virtuous acts.[100] As the first work of art since antiquity in which classical forms and ideas were reintegrated, it also served as a reminder that charity in Florence, as in Rome, was funded by its wealthy citizens, on whose continuing prosperity the fulfilment of both Christian and civic responsibilities depended.[101]

Although there is no evidence of Cosimo's direct involvement with the commune's commission, by the time it was made he was among the most influential and visible figures on the stages of government and commerce, as an ambassador and officer of the commune during its wars with Milan and her allies, and as a frequent participant in the proceedings of the powerful court of the merchants (Mercanzia), the main tribunal for regulating the affairs of bankers, traders, and manufacturers. When Donatello and his partner Michelozzo proved dilatory in completing the commission, it was appropriately Cosimo who was chosen by the Priors to write and ask them to return to Florence and finish the work.[102] The statue of Abundance was finally erected on the feastday of San Martino, 1430, and made a considerable and lasting impression on its Florentine audience.[103] Feo Belcari referred to it in his religious play of the late forties, *King Nebuchadnezzar*, as the proof of Donatello's supreme skill as a sculptor. The popular poet Michele del Giogante kept in his house a statuette of Abundance in the figure of a woman, most probably a replica of Donatello's original.[104]

While modern historians might more readily condemn Cosimo de' Medici for his political incorrectness than admire him for his panache, he was clearly an admirable figure in many fifteenth-century terms. This was a culture that accepted hierarchy, and revered authority. The literate Florentine *popolo* respected the dictates of the "authorities," as they called the great writers of the classical and Christian past, the authority of the commune, and Cosimo's *autorità* in their city. The preceding chapters have proposed as a context for Cosimo's patronage and public image, on the evidence of a popular culture demonstrably shared by a large number of patricians and artisans, that civic pride and loyalty to the commune's corporations, and a passionate devotion to the Lord, constituted binding interests between many socially disparate Florentines, even though vast gulfs of wealth and privilege divided the citizens of Florence, and the city's rich exploited its poor, as the commune exploited its dominions.[105]

Many social historians have been *prima facie* sceptical of the suggestion that any bonds of common interest, culture, or association could have spanned such profound economic and social divides. But Florentine society was not simply divided into "the laboring class" and the elite;

39   Florence, Piazza del Mercato Vecchio, before renovation, showing *Dovizia* column at right and church of San Tommaso on northeast corner

nor could these groups, however defined, be equated simply with rich and poor.[106] The creators and participants of popular culture were not the destitute, about whom little more is known than the brute fact of their existence; they were artisans, with a stake, however small, in society, and in the peace with foreign powers and the domestic prosperity the Medici promoted. They were men whose honor and shame were associated with the maintenance of social norms; who, like one beneficiary of the Buonomini of San Martino, would beg their benefactors not to tell their friends and neighbors that they had accepted charity.[107] They were deeply committed to religious beliefs which involved their sharing with the cultured wealthy some basic assumptions about the right ordering of the world.

Of course, the same texts could be read from different points of view. Obviously there were vast areas of experience and perception not shared by the Florentine *popolo* and its patrician rulers. This book focuses on ideas and interests Cosimo de' Medici had in common with his Florentine audience at large, simply because it is these that throw light on the images of his artistic patronage. However, the Medici shaped popular culture not only by the praise they elicited, but also by the protest they provoked. Nowhere is there better evidence of this than in the popular poetry of the artisan class, as it runs the gamut of responses to the Medici and their ilk – idealizing, laudatory, deeply ambivalent, critical, or bluntly hostile. Rage, pain, and shame characterize the plebeian poetry of satire and protest.[108]

Nevertheless, much of the literature, and presumably also the images which appealed to both patricians and plebeians, expressed appreciation of the benefits the Medici conferred on Florence and its citizens. However, while popular literature partakes of the extravagant flattery and praise which was part of patronage relations, there is little trace in Florentine sources of that contented deference to benign paternalism envisaged by some historians as the palliative of pre-modern class hostility. Florentines accepted Medici authority within the framework of their acceptance of the general order of aristocratic patriarchy, unjust but inevitable, because it was God-ordained. It was Christian texts and images of the hierarchies of heaven, such as those commissioned by Cosimo de' Medici, that for many Florentines transformed the perception of patriarchal oppression, a significant theme of popular poetry, into paternalism on the model of the Divine.

★   ★   ★

40   Brunelleschi, Florence, cupola of cathedral

THE FLORENTINE *POPOLO* AS PATRON OF BRUNELLESCHI'S CUPOLA: AN *EXEMPLUM* FOR PRIVATE CITIZENS OF PATRONAGE IN A REPUBLIC

> Florentine intellects are very sharp, and operate strenuously in every area.
>
> (Francesco Filelfo, a humanist scholar from Tolentino, to the cardinal of Bologna in 1432).[109]

This study cannot be more than suggestive in attempting a description of Cosimo's patronage – or that of any other Florentine – in terms of patron's intentions, artists' creativity, and audience response, linked by shared ideals which might be as abstract as an intense admiration for similarly sharp and strenuous intellects (*ingegni*). In particular, the plain man's perspective on images must be painstakingly reconstructed from limited and elusive evidence. There is, however, one major and well-documented fifteenth-century commission of which the Florentine *popolo* were both patrons and audience – the cupola for the cathedral, completed by Brunelleschi in 1436 (fig. 40). A whole range of aspirations common to citizens of the commune, of various social origins and experience, is expressed in the history of its building. Similar aspirations are apparent in the oeuvre of Cosimo de' Medici. The following account of the completion of the cathedral cupola provides a basis for understanding how in both his patronage and his association with the public enterprise of the cathedral building, Cosimo identified himself with communal ideals, which in turn helped to make his own commissions intelligible to his Florentine audience.

41   Andrea di Bonaiuto (da Firenze), *The Church Triumphant*, Florence, Santa Maria Novella, Spanish Chapel, detail

Shared ideas and attitudes apparent in popular poetry and literary compilations are explicitly invoked and elaborated in relation to this enterprise. Since presumably the Florentine populace viewed other important public works in similar terms, the response to the cupola might be seen as the most accessible and clearly articulated popular judgment on works of art and their significance. Even if the response to the cupola were as unique as Brunelleschi's achievement, the evidence relating to it testifies to the enthusiasm and sophistication with which a Florentine audience was capable of responding to a building. The example of the cathedral cupola may also serve as a model for the way in which patrons and artists worked together to express aspirations and ideas that appealed to their audience, whose admiration projected their reputation and fame into an infinite future, an example of the fundamental reciprocity of the patronage process in action in the realm of art.

The cupola commission is only the most ambitious example of a whole body of outstanding work done for corporate and communal patrons such as guilds, the Parte Guelfa, and above all the great public works commission, the Opera del Duomo. Since such corporate groups were answerable to their constituents, and obliged to obtain and record some consensus about their requirements, much of this work is very well documented. The enormous potential of that evidence to illuminate the precise process by which the artistic aspirations of the Florentine people were translated into the works of art that created the Renaissance city has been realized in important work on public commissions, most particularly by Margaret Haines. Public commissions aroused lively and patriotically proprietary interest in large segments of the population, and many wealthy and influential private patrons gained experience as *operai* for corporate commissions.[110] As Haines observed in her imaginative and incisive study of the cupola project, the *chef d'oeuvre* of the Opera del Duomo, the principles of consensus and consultation which governed Florentine politics and society were literally translated into its construction: "in these . . . ties [Florentines found] the strength to promote the most daring projects."[111] This insight brings us much nearer to an understanding of the extraordinary creativity of the early Florentine Renaissance.

After its completion the cupola became closely identified with Brunelleschi. Seen as the product of his "divine intellect," the veritable triumph of Renaissance *virtù*, it immortalized his name in the pantheon of fame alongside those fabled classical creators whose architectural achievements he emulated and outstripped. In his epitaph Brunelleschi was compared to Daedalus, "the legendary craftsman . . . of the ancient world who . . .

invented wings of wax so that man could fly."[112] But the cupola was equally identified throughout its building as the creation of its collective patrons, the people and commune of Florence. It became their icon. Models had been made of the cupola as envisaged in the 1350s, but a fresco painted around 1365 in the Spanish chapel of the church of Santa Maria Novella by Andrea Bonaiuti (da Firenze) pictured a completed cupola of far grander proportions. Andrea's image must surely have helped to impress upon its audience the more ambitious view of the project that was already taking shape in the public mind (fig. 41).

Bonaiuti was one of a committee of master masons and painters who at the request of the Opera came up with a new and much bolder design in 1366. In scrupulous accordance, as Haines pointed out, with the principle of public accountability fundamental to Florentine political institutions (which was also the pre-condition of the acceptance of Cosimo's authority), a model was submitted to the scrutiny first of the leading citizens, and then of the entire populace. In the course of two days, over four hundred citizens of all classes and occupations came to view it. Among them were Brunelleschi's father, the notary Ser Brunellesco Lippi, and several members of the Medici family. The model, which was to remain on public view until the building was completed, was almost unanimously approved by the citizens of Florence, "such that it could be said that the entire commune had passed judgment." They described it in terms of the qualities they most valued in their personal and political lives, committing themselves to construct a cupola which would be of unprecedented weight and size, essentially because it was "more beautiful and more useful and honorable and powerful" than any previously conceived, an enterprise that would bring "honor and glory to the republic."[113]

All this happened before Brunelleschi was even born. His personal achievement was to solve the apparently insuperable technical problem of suspending such an enormous dome above the crossing. Eventually he built, as his fellow architect Alberti admiringly observed, "without the aid of centering or great quantity of wood . . . a structure . . . ample to cover with its shadow all the Tuscan people."[114] Brunelleschi in his building, like Cosimo in his patronage, inserted himself into an ongoing process of corporate creation, and by his personal participation transformed it.

Eager as Florentines were to embrace any proposal that promised a solution to the practical problem they had set themselves (in pursuit, against all reason, of a wildly ambitious ideal), they asserted at the same time their characteristic pragmatism and remained potentially suspicious of

the architect's plan, as they were of Medicean modifications to Florentine government which claimed to represent the interest of the republic. Objections delayed for several years Brunelleschi's definitive appointment as *capomaestro* in sole charge of the construction. Like many of the corporate commissions for the construction and decoration of public buildings which began to grace the city in the early quattrocento, the contract for the cupola was awarded in a contest, announced by the *operai* in 1418. The sheer size of the proposed cupola had defeated attempts to devise a supporting structure over which to build the vault. Brunelleschi, inspired by the achievements of classical architects, insisted that the cupola "could and must be erected without this traditional medieval crutch."[115] His proposal was greeted at first with incredulity, and even derision. He was taunted in verse by Giovanni di Gherardo da Prato, a distinguished Dante scholar, a member of the cupola committee, and an amateur architect who had himself submitted a model for the design, and dismissed as a "miserable beast and imbecile,/ who wants to demonstrate the uncertain to others." Brunelleschi replied: "When hope is given us from heaven,/ O you ridiculous-looking beast,/ we may rise above the corruptible,/ as the Highest Power is the judge." With the bold assertion that "art discovers that which nature hides," he anticipated the celebratory dance, "when my impossible will come to pass."[116]

The exchange between Brunelleschi and his critics, between artist, patrons, and audience, was played out in various characteristic Florentine keys to which popular literature has attuned us. They ranged from lofty idealism, buoyed by faith in the aid of a Creator whose spirit was seen to be mirrored in the artist's creation,[117] through down-to-earth pragmatism − Brunelleschi's erection of the cupola on a tiny scale in a chapel for the church of San Iacopo sopr'Arno helped to persuade some sceptics[118] − to high (or low) comedy. According to his biographer Manetti, the creator of Florence's most sublime architectural monument paved the way for its unimpeded construction by getting his associate Ghiberti "off his back" with an ingenious trick very similar to the one Brunelleschi employed in the joke he played on the fat carpenter in his novella *Il Grasso Legnaiuolo*. One morning Brunelleschi, knowing that no one else could proceed without him, refused to leave his bed. The workmen turned to Ghiberti, who found himself at a loss "because he knew that the organization of the work was Filippo's and had to be followed; however, Filippo kept it to himself as far as he was able, and Lorenzo did not like to ask about it, for fear of appearing ignorant." Ghiberti failed in his independent attempt to make the chain to reinforce the cupola, and although he was retained at an equal salary for three more years, the Opera's next payment to Brunelleschi acknowledged him alone as "the said inventor and supervisor of the building of the great cupola."[119]

However, Brunelleschi's appointment as *capomaestro* of the construction should ultimately be seen as a triumph of faith over fear. Manetti's biography of Brunelleschi evokes the anxiety that mounted with the dome: "Both the danger and the apprehension of the masters and the other men working there constantly increased, because of the absence of trusswork or parapets under them. The height aroused more than a little fear."[120] That, despite all this, Brunelleschi was permitted to persevere and finally to achieve his "impossible" feat, was ultimately due to the faith the Florentine people shared with him in those same values hymned by Cosimo in his poem to Sforza – *ingegno*, *arte*, and the Almighty.

While his experience with the *operai* for the cupola suggested to Brunelleschi that sometimes it was better not to try to explain "your own inventions and actions," he also acknowledged that "the cultivated man grasps what one is saying about a work or a building."[121] As Giovanni Rucellai boasted in his *zibaldone*, Florence was distinguished by men of such "*ingegno* and imagination" as Brunelleschi, Palla Strozzi, and Cosimo de' Medici. Individual distinction flourished in a climate of shared values, expertise, ambition, and pride. Florentines of all grades and occupations identified with the Duomo project, measuring even time in terms of its completion. Events were promised or predicted to occur "before the Dome is covered," and any task that took a long time and was much interrupted might henceforth be described as "l'opera di Santa Liperata" – a task that took as long to complete as Santa Reparata and its cupola.[122]

Cosimo de' Medici was particularly eager to associate himself in the common concern of the Florentine *popolo* with the cupola, and he may have given Brunelleschi some crucial support. The resolution of the architect's difficulties with the Opera was later attributed in a poem by L'Altissimo to Cosimo's intervention: "And if the famous Cosmo de' Medici,/ full of virtue, excellence and intellect,/ a sensible, wise and glorious man,/ had not been his anchor and support,/ there would have been a serious impediment to finishing the cupola,/ because Pippo would have been disdainfully driven out."[123] Whether this tale was true, or merely part of a tendency in the later fifteenth century to credit the Medici with all of Florence's outstanding achievements, Cosimo's reputation for intelligent patronage clearly helped to make such claims both plausible and popular.

As members mainly of the Bankers' Guild, few of the Medici family had served as *operai* for the Duomo before the 1430s. However, both Piero and Giovanni, aged respectively nineteen and fourteen, were admitted in 1435 as under-age members to the Wool Guild responsible for the project, and a number of the Medici family's closest friends and associates were among the *operai* at the moment the cupola was completed. Just three weeks before the consecration ceremony, for the first time since 1392, a member of the Medici family was appointed to this office. He was Giovenco d'Antonio, who owned a woolshop in the San Martino district. Cosimo himself served on a special jury of influential citizens to appraise the design for the lantern in 1436, and strongly associated himself with the completion of the cupola by his prominence at the ceremony of the cathedral's consecration.[124] In this, as in other manifestations of Florentine ingenuity, power, and imagination, Cosimo chose to increase his political capital by reinvesting it in the promotion of the city's interests. However, by contrast with his rebuilding of the church of San Lorenzo or the convent of San Marco, which imprinted the Medici image on Florentine civic space, here Cosimo was only one of a mass of citizens whose collective identity was expressed, over the course of almost a century, in the construction of a cupola to crown the cathedral. It was he who gained luster by his association with this great civic enterprise, as he and his son Piero were to do by their patronage, in cooperation with other individuals and corporate groups, of San Miniato and Santissima Annunziata.

The construction of the cupola was a major contemporary drama, and its consecration a brilliant performance of the culture of its corporate patrons, the people of Florence, in which Pope Eugenius, Brunelleschi, and Cosimo de' Medici assumed the leading roles.[125] The way had been prepared for well over a century for the fusion of sacred and civic in symbols associated with the Florentine cathedral.[126] The church was originally dedicated to Santa Reparata, and many citizens continued to refer in their letters and tax reports to living near, or hearing mass in Santa Reparata, or "Santa Liperata" in popular dialect. However, in 1296 Pope Boniface VIII's legate had given his blessing to a project to rebuild the cathedral and renamed it Santa Maria del Fiore, inviting associations with both the lily of Florence and the papal rose. These innovations seem to have been part of a wider campaign of conscious shaping of civic symbolism, including the republic's identification with David, the lone small force whose valor defeated Goliath and his Philistine armies.

The association of symbols and images of Florence with those of Our Lady, of the lily of Florence, personified by Dantesque poets as a lady, with the lily, symbol of purity, of the Virgin who was her protector, was assisted by the *laudesi* confraternities, dedicated to praise of the Virgin, and then at the height of their popularity. Thus the Madonna del Giglio came to represent the city of Florence herself, and Florentine government was sanctified by its devotion to her. While the Priors' plans for a statue of Santa Maria del Fiore with lily in hand, personifying the commune in the sacred setting of the cathedral, remained unrealized, these images expressing the fusion of corporate civic ideals with sacred obligations saturated popular poetry, and were incorporated by artists into several sculptural programs.

The ceremony of the consecration in March 1436 was thought to have attracted over 200,000 celebrants. These would surely have included almost all of the city's population, which stood at this time around 37,000, and a sizeable proportion of the residents of the surrounding towns and countryside under her dominion.[127] The Chancellor Bruni noted in his *Commentari* that "on the day of the dedication the flocking together of men from the countryside, from the neighboring towns, and from Pisa, the urban multitude was so great that all the avenues and all the roads were filled."[128] While the cupola was not literally, in Alberti's fulsome image, large enough to cover all of them, on this day they all clustered at least in its shadow, in the piazza between the baptistery and the cathedral, and in the surrounding streets, "all excited coming to see the realization and the existence of what was the talk of all the town."[129]

A verse account of the occasion by the shoemaker Giovanni di Cino confirms that the cupola had indeed become in popular eyes the flower of Florence, and a crown for the Queen of Heaven, her city Florence, and Holy Mother Church. Eugenius IV, who made his home in Florence for extended periods of time in the 1430s and 1440s, was about to depart for Bologna to organize the impending church council. In Giovanni's Dantesque image: "But he wants to feed his lamb/ before leaving the beautiful sheepfold." He offered a papal consecration and its attendant indulgences to the Florentine people, who were overjoyed that "he should consent to consecrate their beautiful flower,/ Santa Maria who is called "del Fiore,"/ for the glory of God and for the honor of such a mother,/ and the eternal fame of his Holiness,/ and for his great devotion to sinners . . . / for the salvation of Christianity . . . / to be the giver of such a gift,/ as a consecration by the pope himself."[130]

Quick to observe its symbolic significances, Giovanni praised the choice of the date for this event; 25 March, the Annunciation of the Virgin and the first day of the Florentine new year. "Our Lady chose and wanted March,/ in which was announced such virtue,/ that its disclosure shocked/ such profound humility." On this day

"Three things principally were fulfilled:/ the beautiful name of the church,/ and all the years it took to build,/ and the happy day of our salvation./ Souls awaiting the Sunday of Lazarus/ were ignited in devotion . . ." In Giovanni's mind, even the promise of the season was conducive to the awakening of new devotional life, as Christ raised Lazarus from the dead. Dignifying the event and his poem with reference also to classical celebrations, he compared a bridge or covered walkway some feet above the ground, on which the pope could pass from his apartments next to Santa Maria Novella to the cathedral entrance, not only with the halls of paradise but also with the ancient groves of Helicon and Parnassus, homes of the Muses, where poets were crowned with myrtle and laurel. "It was nine hundred braccia in length,/ more than two braccia high;/ the supports a braccia high, and to add to its grace,/ every six braccia there were columns/ encircled with myrtle, eight braccia high . . . / One seemed to see a new Parnassus or Helicon,/ where crowned already by poetry,/ so much laurel and myrtle was displayed, it seemed a wondrous fantasy,/ to see this great bridge so decorated/ by hangings and tapestries for still more delight."

Giovanni's poem also confirms that the public appreciation of buildings extended to noting the precise specifications of size and design.[131] "Then, arrived whence all beauty was constituted,/ between three *cupole* in a cross and in the middle the one/ of whose size all the world is talking,/ from each of these three there stems another/ five chapels, and from there fifteen altars/ surround the high altar of the tribune./ Its measurements in braccia, to make it clear to every mind,/ are seventy-eight in the corners, and in its lantern/ it is a hundred and fifty high . . ." "To make it clear to every mind," Giovanni went beyond the traditional enthusiasm of the medieval chronicler for facts and figures to suggest some real comprehension of the symmetry and grace of the building's design. Nor did he fail to note that as Eugenius with his retinue reached his destination, he was confronted with what was popularly believed to be Florence's own "antiquity" in the shape of the baptistery. "He passed by San Giovanni and stopping here,/ looked anew at its ornament and wondered/ at such an impressive antiquity standing there." Arrived at the cathedral, the pope descended from the *ponte* "on the first steps of the principal entry," flanked by the newly completed sculptures of the Evangelists John and Luke by Nanni di Banco and Donatello. They had been temporarily installed there for the occasion, as may be seen from an illumination in a contemporary manuscript (fig. 42).[132] Florence's proud patrimony of the arts of the ancients, poetry and architecture, was incorporated in this event "in the most beautiful time that Christians may have," to be stored in the house of memory in the popular mind. The ceremonies over, as Giovanni concluded, "Arrived where he had left his holy memory,/ each man praising the grace he had dispensed,/ departed rejoicing at this high victory,/ rehearsing everything bit by bit."

The real power of images and symbols to create correspondences by which various elements of the Florentine civic world were not just associated, but fused and transformed in their visual translation, appears in the form of the ceremony. The clearest account of this is preserved in a *ricordo* by the young Feo Belcari, in 1436 *scrivano* of the canon chapter of the Medici parish church of San Lorenzo. He deposited his *ricordo* in the archives of San Lorenzo in the interests of the collective memory: "because this seems to me the place in which it will last longer than in any other place." And indeed it is still there.[133]

42   The consecration of Santa Maria del Fiore by Pope Eugenius IV in 1436, Biblioteca Laurenziana, Edili 151, fol. 7v

Many of the links between disparate but intertwined elements of Florentine experience – secular and spiritual, indigenous and foreign, patrician and plebeian, public and private – were embodied in the persons who took part in the ceremony. The pope was attended by Giovanni Vitelleschi, the papal general and a military commander who had intervened in the crisis of 1434 to allow the Medici to return from exile; he was shortly to be consecrated archbishop of Florence. Sigismondo Malatesta was present, as both lord of the papal fief of Rimini, and captain of the Florentine armies. Giuliano Davanzati, as Gonfalonier of Justice, represented the Florentine government, and was knighted by the pope at the beginning of the ceremony. But it was Cosimo de' Medici, who had no official role, who proved the most important Florentine actor in this drama.

Once the participants were inside the cathedral, Guillaume Dufay's music served to raise them to the heights of exaltation. Alberti once described the cathedral as a refuge: "the constant home of temperateness . . . outside, wind, ice, and frost; here inside one is protected . . . outside the heat of summer and autumn; inside, coolness; here you listen to the voices during mass, during that which the ancients call the mysteries, with their marvellous beauty."[134] For the humanist Manetti, describing the consecration, the cathedral became paradise, and Dufay's motet the music of angels.[135] In his *riposte* to Giovanni da Prato, Brunelleschi had spoken of the awe that grows from experience. Beneath the pleasant polyphony of *Nuper rosarum flores* – "lately the flower of the rose came as a gift of the pope" – there rose the refrain: "Terribilis ist locus iste" – this is an awesome place. The hymn addressed the Virgin and her people Florence, but only once did the polyphonic harmonies converge in a single line of melody and song, and that was in audible tribute to the name of Eugenius.[136]

The pope's patronage had provided the music that accomplished the mystery of transporting its listeners to the higher spheres. Dufay, whose motet echoed the harmony and proportion of the cupola itself, was at this time in the service of Eugenius, who also lent his *cappella* of singers to the occasion.[137] But on the very day of the consecration, the pope signed a bull ordering the creation of a school for cathedral singers, which was to be supported by Cosimo de' Medici. It was already flourishing by the time of the celebrations of the church council three years later, and endured for the remainder of Cosimo's lifetime.[138]

At every point in the events of 25 March 1436 the signs of association and cooperation between Eugenius IV and his friend and banker Cosimo de' Medici are evident. Since the pope was the charismatic fulcrum on which this occasion turned, the weight of Cosimo's influence on Eugenius immeasurably increased his own numinous power. On this day in March 1436, scarcely eighteen months after the triumph of his reentry into Florence, Cosimo took center stage at the climax of the consecration. The ceremonies to that point had presented several variations on the theme of mercy and intercession. First the Signoria made it known that they had liberated a number of prisoners, "handing over to God their grave and frequent punishment." The government's release of prisoners was an offering analogous to the pope's charitable granting of indulgences to hasten the liberation of souls from purgatory, and ultimately evoked Christ's liberation of souls from hell on the day of the Last Judgment.[139] As the notary Ser Paolo di Ser Pace da Certaldo explained in his manual of good conduct, describing in the language of patronage the reciprocal economy of salvation, the souls of the dead, like prisoners in life, relied on their relatives and friends to liberate them; they repaid such charity by interceding as *avvocati* for the souls of their benefactors, *raccomandati* in turn by them.[140]

At the conclusion of the mass, the cardinal of San Marco announced the indulgences earned on this special occasion for the remission of the sins of souls in purgatory, "every year six years and six quarantene." Then, as the clerical chronicler recorded, "encouraged later by the pleas of the noble citizen Cosimo de' Medici, he altered that to seven." Cosimo continued to plead for an increase in the treasury of merit upon which Florentines might draw for their salvation, and the bargaining ended in the cardinal of San Marcello's agreement to ten years and ten quarantene, "having already refused this to all the other cardinals and lords of Florence."[141]

This public demonstration of Cosimo's power as an intercessor for the Florentine people figured prominently in Giovanni di Cino's poem, as it did in many other verses written by popular poets. For the shoemaker, Pope Eugenius and Cosimo de' Medici were the joint heroes of the day. Cosimo was the epitome of the Christian patron whose charity alone justified his repatriation. Having described at length how Davanzati "was made a knight, so that human minds/ can scarce imagine such nobility,/ unless the heavens had a hand in it," the cobbler turned to Cosimo. "Similar honors and even great dignity/ were seen in another, so dear to his *patria*/ that he is called worthy of immortality;/ if I am silent regarding his name, heaven will broadcast it; for his wondrous charity,/ he was repatriated in such triumph."

Dufay's motet had climaxed in an invocation of the Virgin as intercessor for the Florentine people: "Through your prayer,/ your anguish and merits,/ may [the people] deserve to receive of the Lord,/ born of you according

to the flesh,/ the benefits of grace/ and the remission of sins, Amen." Cosimo's intercession with Eugenius at the close of the mass to increase the spiritual credit available to the Florentine people linked him to a chain of intercessors culminating in the Virgin herself; it was this "marvelous charity," the spiritual face of his secular patronage, which made him "worthy of immortality" in a higher sense than could his worldly power and fame. Such intercession is the essential subject imaged by Fra Angelico in the altarpiece he painted for San Marco at Cosimo's request.

In the history of the cupola's construction, and at the moment of its consecration, something of the essence of Florentine popular culture in 1436, and of Cosimo de' Medici's relation to it may be captured. Cosimo's major artistic commissions owed their existence largely to the expiatory imperative of charity. As already noted, the commune's similar commitment to charity and restitution was embodied in Donatello's statue of Dovizia, a lady bountiful who had stood since the late twenties in the Mercato Vecchio, the commercial center of the city. Her spiritual counterpart, the Madonna of the lily flower, was

43 School of Verrocchio, *Madonna and Child with Saints Zanobi, Francis, John the Baptist, and Nicola da Bari*, detail, Grassina, Bagno a Ripoli, San Martino dei Cipressi o a Strada

contained in the image of the cathedral crowned by Brunelleschi's cupola. Before the pope arrived on the day of the consecration, Cardinal Corsini had assembled the relics of the saints in the stone reliquary at the altar. But in a sense the whole church, along with its protector, had become a treasury of merit upon which the Florentines could draw, a giant golden reliquary, as it was depicted in the style of Verrocchio some decades later, nestling in the hand of its first bishop, Saint Zenobius (fig. 43).[142]

The *zibaldoni* which acculturated Florentines, educating them to the reception of the ideas and aspirations of great patrons and artists, were at once repositories of popular culture, and indices of its nature and development. Many of the texts relating to Florentine culture and experience which were the context of Brunelleschi's construction of a cupola for the cathedral, as well as those documenting its enthusiastic popular reception, were preserved in *zibaldoni*. Their owners copied the cobbler Giovanni di Cino's poem, the acerbic poetic exchange between Brunelleschi and Giovanni di Gherardo da Prato, the comic tale of Brunelleschi's deception recounted in *Il Grasso Legnaiuolo*, so similar to the ruse which rid him of Ghiberti's interference, and the irreverent verses chronicling the adventures of Geta and Birria in which Brunelleschi was reputed to have had a hand.

The body of texts and precepts conserved in personal *quaderni* encouraged the cultivation of certain habits of mind, most particularly the perception of congruences and correspondences between the verbal and the visual, the worldly and the otherworldly, the classical and the Christian, the individual and the corporate, the sublime and the ridiculous. This culture produced minds that were versatile and flexible, the antithesis of the rigid specialization that now shapes scholars and divides artists, patrons, and viewers into separate objects of study.

Cosimo de' Medici was himself a product of this shared culture. The chapters that follow show how the self he defined in his commissions was constituted by his association with a great variety of cultivated men comprising the circle at whose center the Medici established themselves. When we speak of Cosimo as a patron, this is what we should bear in mind, not simply the narrow issues of the extent of his personal knowledge of Latin, or the expertise of his aesthetic judgment. It is this broader significance of Cosimo's culture, together with his strong impulse to define and express himself as a citizen and a Christian, which accounts for the coherence of his oeuvre, and for the communication and cooperation between Cosimo the patron, and the artists who worked for him, permitting each to realize his aims within the framework of Cosimo's commissions.

III

COSIMO'S RELIGIOUS COMMISSIONS

EXPIATION, CHARITY, INTERCESSION

"THE LIBERAL RICH MAN": CHARITY AND THE PATRON

I turn now to Cosimo's commissions, beginning with the churches and chapels he built or renovated, and the devotional images that adorned them. Historians of art have discussed these at length, interpreting them as works of art, and as part of the artist's oeuvre. Building gratefully upon their expertise and insights, I want to set Cosimo's commissions in the context of the patron's interests and concerns, and those of his audience.[1]

Between the late 1430s and his death in 1464 Cosimo was responsible for rebuilding or redecorating three major religious foundations – the convent and church of the Dominican monastery of San Marco, his parish church of San Lorenzo, one of the city's oldest and largest centers of worship, and the Augustinian church and convent of the Badia at Fiesole. He built also a chapel for the novices at the chief Franciscan foundation in Florence of Santa Croce, and renovated the Franciscan convent of Bosco ai Frati, adjacent to the Medici estates in the countryside north of the city. He had a magnificent chapel made for the Medici palace in Florence, and there were chapels in all the family's country villas. He contributed to the refurbishing of a host of smaller churches and chapels in Florence, Tuscany, and places as far away as Friuli. He commissioned a reliquary from Ghiberti for the Camaldolensian convent of Santa Maria degli Angeli, and altarpieces for the churches of San Marco, Santa Croce, and Bosco ai Frati,[2] as well as for the Medici domestic chapels in Florence and at the villas of Cafaggiolo and Careggi.[3] These commissions made him the major Florentine patron of the Church in his time.

Most of the ecclesiastical foundations to which Cosimo gave his patronage were established well before the beginning of the fifteenth century; they were built, maintained, and frequently refurbished with a mixture of funds from parishes, religious orders, individuals, and the state.[4] Cosimo's gifts to churches followed a long tradition of lay patronage. Florentines and their families had for centuries ensured the commemoration of their souls and asserted a presence in their neighborhoods by renovating or embellishing their local churches, where their generosity was recorded in inscriptions or in the display of family arms.[5]

The ecclesiastical establishment was keen to regulate the nature and degree of lay involvement in churches.[6] At the very beginning of the fifteenth century Giovanni Dominici, general of the Dominican order and an influential spiritual advisor to the Florentine people, addressed a number of works to the laity on moral issues relevant to their lives. Dominici took a conservative line on lay patronage designed to contribute to the donor's salvation. He recommended the rebuilding of churches to charitable laymen, but in accordance with the biblical injunction that true charity should be anonymous, he stipulated that nobody should know whose money was used, and suggested that it was much better to repair old churches than found new ones.[7]

Medici patronage of churches conformed largely to the letter of this last prescription. The architect Filarete observed that the Medici "are all and have been willing and eager to build, and especially in those structures dedicated to religion"; in his praise of this activity he took pains to distinguish in each Medici project between money spent "in riparare" (repair) and "di nuovo fare" (new buildings).[8] However, the scale of Medici renovations at San Marco and San Lorenzo effectively transformed the original structures, and the fame of these building projects was firmly attached to the Medici name from their inception. They were clearly labelled with Medici arms and images, which served as reminders to contemporaries of the family's largesse, and for the information of posterity. By the last decades of the fifteenth century many other patrician families had participated in increasingly self-advertising patronage of churches,[9] but on the map of Florence the measure of Medici ecclesiastical patronage was unmatched (fig. 65).[10]

Modern historians speculating on the motives for Cosimo's extensive patronage of churches have tended to be sceptical about the role of religious feeling, and concerned to distinguish and quantify pious and political

44 Giotto, *Last Judgment*, Padua, Arena Chapel, detail showing Scrovegni presenting a model of the Arena Chapel to angels in heaven

impulses, civic and dynastic interests. To Renaissance patrons, as observed, these were not alternatives. Their patronage simultaneously served "the honor of God, and the honor of the city, and the commemoration of me." Cosimo's patronage of churches expressed a complex amalgam of inherited family obligations, increasing civic prominence, profound involvement with the institutional church, especially the papacy, with which the Medici enjoyed extremely close relations, and personal devotion.[11]

Many scholars have stressed how effectively Medici donations to churches commemorated them and enhanced the honor of the city, and these aspects of Cosimo's patronage are prominent features of his oeuvre. But the importance to the patron of honoring God needs to be grasped more fully. Until very recently indeed the role of ecclesiastical patronage in expiating the sinful acts of the patron and securing his salvation has not been taken sufficiently seriously, particularly in relation to the Medici, whose undeniably powerful political instincts are generally presumed to have been always paramount.[12] The dictum sometimes attributed to Cosimo that "a state is not governed by paternosters" is misinterpreted almost as often as it is cited, by being read out of the context of his having spent a lifetime saying them.[13] In dismissing Cosimo's piety as "conventional in the extreme"[14] historians have failed until lately to realize how far the conventions of late medieval piety and the realities they represented permeated the everday life of the men whose secular fame and political power have attracted their attention. Salvation was the ultimate concern of even the most worldly of Renaissance Christians.

Cosimo's letter of 1463 to the Neoplatonic philosopher Ficino, asking him to come to Careggi with his Orphic lyre and show him the way to happiness through the understanding of God, has often been adduced as rare evidence of a presumed late conversion to an interest in matters spiritual. Although Ficino, son of the old Medici family physician "maestro Fecino," and a familiar of the Medici household since his childhood, may have doctored this letter from the aged Cosimo for inclusion in his collected correspondence, it reflects the real and abiding concern for his soul that is clearly apparent in the earliest records illuminating Cosimo's personal life.[15]

By 1418, when he was not yet thirty, Cosimo's library was full of religious literature, his house of devotional images. If his patronage of churches gathered momentum after his return from exile in 1434, and the rebuilding of San Marco in the mid-thirties was the first of his really notable ecclesiastical commissions, Cosimo's concern with patronage in and of churches had begun at least as early as the mid-twenties, with his involvement in the commission for the tomb of John XXIII in the Florentine

baptistery, and continued with his assumption of his father's commitments at San Lorenzo after Giovanni di Bicci's death in 1429. The chapels and altarpieces he built for the glory of God and the honor of the city also provided him and his family with marvellous images for their own devotion, and gave them unusual access to sacred spaces. Cosimo used the privileges of his secular power and wealth not merely for atonement, but indeed to lay up spiritual treasure in heaven.

His biographer Vespasiano claimed that Cosimo began to rebuild churches in the hope of making restitution for his sins, especially that of usury; like most international bankers he made handsome profits on exchange, which came very close to usury in the eyes of even such subtle urban clerical moralists as Sant' Antoninus and San Bernardino.[16] To this end, like many merchants, Cosimo kept a book which he called "God's account."[17] This has not survived, but Cosimo's grandson Lorenzo referred in his *ricordi* of the state of family affairs he inherited to a bequest to be spent on charity from Giovanni di Bicci to his sons Cosimo and Lorenzo of 179, 221 *scudi di suggello*, "as appears in a record in the handwriting of Cosimo our grandfather in his red leather book on page seven." The obligation to charity was part of the Medici patrimony.[18]

The common notion of "God's account" shows how vividly Florentines conceived spiritual debts on the model of their worldly obligations.[19] Restitution for the sin of excessive profits, seen as usury, was a means of restoring the natural and divine order that making money disturbed.[20] Merchants' accounts with God were not simply conscience money; they served to maintain the proper equilibrium between wealthy and poor, success and salvation. The ingrained imperative of balancing credits with debits shaped devout Florentine merchants' views of the economy of salvation. The building and decorating of churches – patronage to effect the work of God – was a part of charity, the liberality by which sin was expiated. This conception of the charity which Cosimo hoped would balance the sinful weight of his bank's usurious gains at his own final accounting[21] was perfectly imaged in a fresco painted a century earlier by Giotto in the Arena chapel for a Paduan merchant, Enrico Scrovegni. Cosimo, who was often in Padua, would have seen in it a visual model of the reciprocal relation between patronage and salvation. This other-wordly transaction is represented in a scene of the Last Judgment, where heaven extends welcoming hands to Scrovegni as he offers his chapel, supported by a friar, to a bevy of angels; by contrast, sinners below in hell are hanged by their money bags (fig. 44).[22]

The image of this final accounting was very sharp in Florentines' minds. Dante had identified Scrovegni's father among several Florentine usurers "on whom

45　Fra Angelico, *Last Judgment*, detail, Florence, Museo di San Marco

the dolorous fire falls" in the seventh circle of hell, a pouch around the neck of each.[23] The poem attributed to Cosimo imagining the reversal of all natural and familiar phenomena includes a graphically conceived heaven and hell turned upside down: "and hell will be full of joy and glory,/and tempests and tears and loud cries/ will fill the eternal paradise . . ."[24] From the very beginning of their lives in this world, Florentines had before them, in the mosaics of the *Last Judgment* in the baptistery, a quotidian opportunity for the contemplation of their fate in the next (fig. 45).[25] Fra Angelico painted a particularly compelling version of the same subject around 1431, in his panel of the Last Judgment for the church of Santa Maria degli Angeli, where Cosimo went frequently to visit his close friend Ambrogio Traversari, prior of the convent (fig. 46).[26] The compilers of *zibaldoni* inserted here and there in their books, and especially as they came to a close, reminders to themselves and others of this inevitable end. As one poet observed, "Delight and pleasure in the desires of the flesh soon pass away. But sin for ever/ remains, like the faults and evils born of the vice of the flesh that is licentiousness, amen."[27] A *zibaldone* compiled by Michele del Giogante,

46　*Last Judgment*, detail, Florence, baptistery, mosaic

possibly for his Medici friends, began with Giovanni dalle Celle's account of how the world fattens its lovers, like pigs for the slaughter, and how only charity could extinguish and expiate the sins committed in the course of a life laid waste in getting and spending.[28]

Charity, as Saint Paul expounded it, was the highest of Christian virtues: "Though I speak with the tongues of men and of angels, and have not charity, I am become as sounding brass, or a tinkling cymbal . . . And though I bestow all my goods to feed the poor, and though I give my body to be burned, and have not charity, it profiteth me nothing . . ."[29] Charity is the burning link that binds men to each other and to God. In the words of the influential fourteenth-century Florentine Dominican, Iacopo Passavanti, "Charity makes man love God above all things and his neighbor as himself." It was naturally the virtue most lauded and promoted in the pious confraternities to which most Florentine laymen belonged.[30] The benefactors of the Buonomini of San Martino gave to God, as the inscription on the flyleaf of their book of donations proclaims, out of love and fear – "timor domini (fig. 47)."[31] Theirs was not the passive piety often envisaged by many modern historians. Greater wealth enabled men to be more active in their good works, which enhanced their standing before God and man; as Cosimo wrote in a letter to his cousin Averardo, citing a common proverb, "the poor man is never able to do good works." Charity was an important component of Cosimo's reputation, his *fama* as a patron, but it was primarily his key to the kingdom of heaven.[32]

47   Flyleaf of Buonomini collection book with legend "timor domini," Florence, Biblioteca Nazionale, Fondo Tordi I

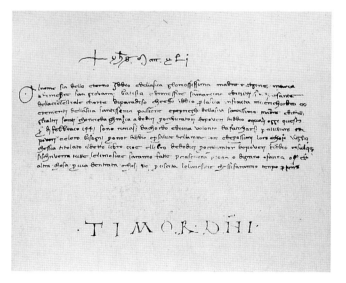

Churchgoers and members of confraternities like Cosimo were constantly reminded of these Christian truths. Michele del Giogante noted in one of his scrapbooks concerning the duty of charity and its power to save: "I say unto you that whatsoever you do unto the least of my brothers you do also unto me . . ." Those who fail to take heed of this injunction "will be sent to suffer eternal punishment, and the just will have life eternal . . . This passage from the Gospel is said on the Monday after the first Sunday of Lent. These were the words Jesus Christ spoke with his own lips to his disciples, according to Saint Mark the Evangelist, on account of which I often bewail my own sins."[33] Feo Belcari contrasted in a pair of widely circulated sonnets the fate of the "rich miser" with that of the "wealthy charitable man." The former he pictured thus: "When he dies and his funeral has taken place,/ Mammon drags him down into the flames/ and feeds them with his corpse clad in the purple." The charitable patrician, however, could take comfort in the knowledge that "whatever his vice or sin or crime,/ alms extinguish it, and endow him with the grace/ to go to God without too great a handicap."[34] As San Bernardino put it, "the rich are necessary to the commune, and the poor to the rich."[35]

The actual mechanism of the expiation of sin through charity operated on the general model of patronage, turning on the reciprocal obligation to merciful intercession assumed by both donors and recipients. As Archbishop Antoninus explained in his widely circulated *Summa Theologica*, a compendium of received, mainly Thomist wisdom, in a passage which evokes, intentionally or not, the Medici style of life: "The Divine Providence, which disposes of everything appropriately, permits some to be lacking in temporal goods, so that in the patient suffering of their poverty they may acquire eternal life. To others he gives an abundance, not in order that they may dissipate it on dogs, falcons, and horses, extravagant clothing, games, banquets, etc. . . . but so that of this property, given to them by God, they should take what they need for themselves, and give the rest to His poor, and by the virtue of charity be received into the eternal tabernacles through the prayers of the poor."[36] Thus, a group of Dominican nuns in Friuli who wanted their convent rebuilt called upon Cosimo – "Mercy, O our Lord, have mercy upon us" – in view of the fame of his "amazing goodness and most extensive charity, for which not only in Italy, but even with the barbarians beyond, you have acquired an immortal name," and promised in return "to pray ceaselessly to the eternal God for your salvation and for the *buon stato* of your house."[37]

As he drew near to death Cosimo did indeed take comfort against his pains and fears from the prayers and devotions of those to whom he had given his charity. He wrote in 1461 to his elder son Piero, himself seriously ill and convalescing at the medicinal baths at Corsina, "we have the help of masses in our honor, and votive offerings, and thus I advise and urge you to make some payment yourself to the holy nuns at Pisa, and to give them alms." Three years later, as he lay dying, Cosimo's wife Contessina wrote to comfort their son that all the clergy of Tuscany were praying night and day for their benefactor.[38]

As I have shown, metaphors ordered the Florentine world; just as patricians built palaces to accommodate their families, they constructed houses of memory to accommodate their learning. Of all metaphors, the patriarchal was the most powerful, providing a means of reconciling the often conflicting claims of family, city, and the Lord, by associating the authority of fathers, patrons, and the Almighty. Charity was an integral part of this scheme. Coluccio Salutati was the humanist chancellor of Florence from 1375 to 1406, and the leader and mentor of the intellectual circles in which Cosimo moved in his youth. The inventory of Cosimo's books in 1418 contains a number of volumes which had belonged to Salutati; the influence of his ideas persisted in his many marginal comments.[39] Salutati pronounced that charity, which "diminished God to the smallness of man through the mystery of the incarnation, elevates man almost to the sublimity of deity through its fruition . . . [charity] alone fosters the family, expands the city, guards the kingdom, and . . . preserves by its power this very creation of the entire world."[40]

The association of these commonly held ideas is implied in Cosimo's act of intercession with the pope to increase the number of indulgences offered on the occasion of the cathedral's consecration.[41] It is spelled out in Branca Brancacci's virtuoso variation on the speech of Christ in the garden of Gethsemane, to invoke the traditional charitable duty of taking mercy upon prisoners and to exhort Cosimo to reverse the sentences imposed by a Medicean Signoria upon their enemies in 1434. "O Lord have mercy upon us . . . blessed are the merciful, for they themselves shall have mercy . . . through your piety and singular grace, my father, I pray that this cup may pass from me: nevertheless, not my will but yours be done." Here the charity of the political patron is represented as an analogue of the divine mercy.[42]

The potency of the patriarchal metaphor in Christian and civic tradition, and its appeal as a means of relating these two fundamental sets of ideals by which all Florentines were shaped, legitimized analogies between authority in this world and the next.[43] The elements of obligation and intercession common to friends, patrons,

and saints helped to fuse their roles in Florentine minds as they had done for Christians since late antiquity, and the specific concepts, images, and structures of patronage that shaped Florentine society further informed their understanding of a *religio amicitiae*. Peter Brown traced the development in late antiquity of this analogy between earthly and heavenly patrons into the perception of the saint as "the very special friend"; in fifteenth-century Florence, patronage relationships served explicitly as the model on which men's perceptions of heaven were based.[44] Paolo da Certaldo, a merchant writing in the late trecento, used his experience of the role of patrons on earth to inform his image of heaven as a celestial court, peopled by patron saints whom he described as *avvocati*, intermediaries with God in the interests of the pious, their *raccomandati*.[45]

The liberality of the Virgin, the supreme intercessor, was an important theme of Archibishop Antoninus's account of liberality and charity, and it found visual expression in the popular image of the Madonna della Misericordia. This image could reflect back on earthly patrons, as when a client wrote to Cosimo that "you are my God on earth . . . never have I wished for anything more in life than to take shelter under the wing of your power and authority."[46] That is precisely the image of the Madonna della Misericordia as represented by numerous fourteenth- and fifteenth-century artists. The painted wooden statue in the Bargello of a large-as-life Virgin, her blue cloak spread to shelter the tiny figures of her devotees clustered beneath its protective shadow, is typical of many objects of devotion to Mary as intercessor (fig. 48). Thanks to his superior artistic skill and imagination, Piero della Francesca's panel for his native Borgo Sansepolcro was able to embody the very essence of the liturgical prayer: "Hail Mary, Mother of God, full of grace . . . pray for us sinners, now and at the hour of our death" (fig. 49).

The mechanism of charity and the cult of patron saints threw a solid bridge across the terrifying abyss that yawned between the protective power of wordly patronage and an analagous but invisible network of protectors and intercessors for souls beyond the grave.[47] Meaning might pass in both directions; in the same spirit as the nuns who, seeking help to rebuild their convent, promised to pray for the preservation both of Cosimo's soul and the power of his family, the rector of the church of San Cosimo in Pisa wrote to Cosimo de' Medici asking for alms to provide for the celebration of the forthcoming feast of Cosmas and Damian, "in return for which those saints will stand before God as intercessors for you, and I continually will pray to him for the preservation and exaltation of your regime [*stato*] as you

48   *Madonna della Misericordia*, fifteenth-century wooden statue, Florence, Bargello

49   Piero della Francesca, *Madonna della Misericordia*, Borgo Sansepolcro, Museo Civico

desire."[48] It is this chain of intercession that is imaged in the altarpiece Cosimo commissioned for the church of San Marco.

IMAGES OF INTERCESSION

Meaning also passed easily in Florentine minds between words and images. Laymen's expressions, in spiritual poems and commissions of devotional images, of their religious conceptions and concerns, their doubts and fears, display the power of their feelings and the sophistication of their grasp of doctrine. Naturally such men, when they commissioned works of art for the glory of God and the salvation of their souls, expected the artists they employed to infuse these images with ideas and emotions so generally shared as to require no explicit repetition in contracts con-

cerned with more tangible considerations, such as time and money.[49] After all, artists, especially those of Brunelleschi's or Ghiberti's caliber, were as well educated in these matters as their patrons. Neri di Bicci, less distinguished as an artist, but perhaps the most widely patronized painter of devotional images of the mid-fifteenth century, was a leading spirit of the confraternity of Sant'Agnese and played a major role in imaging religious ideas in the company's staging of *sacre rappresentazioni*.[50] And obviously it would have been presumptuous indeed of Cosimo to instruct Fra Angelico. At the same time, the majority of men, more skilled in the use of the pen than of the brush or the chisel, often recreated in their words the powerful visual images that gave substance to their ideas and feelings. Images played an active role in shaping Florentines' piety; they did not simply reflect it.[51] These considerations should be kept in mind when turning to Cosimo's commission of religious images.

Contracts with artists show that objects seen in churches or in the homes of friends influenced patrons' expectations of images they commissioned, as they also appear to have influenced poets' visualizations of biblical and liturgical images and metaphors. The importance of images in the experience of churchgoers and worship is cleverly underscored in one of five predella panels of the life of San Niccolò, painted by Gentile da Fabriano for Cosimo's friends the Quaratesi in 1424 (fig. 52).[52] Gentile's depiction of devotional images in his representation of churchgoers bearing witness to the healing power of San Niccolò subtly inserts the artist and the image into the process of communion with the saints, making an important point about the power of the image, both aesthetic and iconic.[53]

Just as the visual sources of artists are an important clue to their creative reshaping of familiar devices to effect new solutions, so the patron's viewing experience in places of worship is likely to have stimulated and influenced his commissions of sacred images, and the audience's knowledge of familiar images their reception of fresh ones.[54] Along with most Florentine patrons of art, Cosimo and his family were frequent churchgoers, particularly at the ceremonial centers of Santa Maria del Fiore and San Giovanni, and at their parish church of San Lorenzo. At least one devotional image for the Medici house clearly demonstrates an appreciation of the development of new themes and techniques already demonstrated by the artist Lippi in a work for another patron, on display in the Medici neighborhood church.[55]

The altarpiece for the chapel of the confraternity dedicated to the Trinity in Santa Maria del Fiore, and Masaccio's fresco of the same subject in Santa Maria Novella, probably served as prime examples to Cosimo of what might be articulated visually on the theme of intercession well before Angelico was ready to paint his altarpiece for the church of San Marco. Cosimo's family was personally affected by the re-siting of the cathedral Trinity early in the century, since it had required the removal of arches furnished by the Medici and Adimari.[56] While representations of the Trinity and of the Virgin as intercessor were common, the cathedral image was unusual in its powerful visual assertion of the hierarchical chain of intercession that linked them (fig. 50).

The line of the Virgin's left hand, at once protecting the flock of faithful sheltering at her feet and presenting them to her son, is linked by strong geometric logic to her right hand, indicating the breast at which she suckled him. The message of this gesture is reinforced by an inscription: "Dearest son, because of the milk that I gave

50 Lorenzo Monaco (attrib.), *The Intercession of Christ and the Virgin*, New York, The Metropolitan Museum of Art, The Cloisters Collection, 1953

you, have mercy on them." This line of argument is continued in Christ's left hand, which gestures towards her, while with his right he displays the wound he suffered for the redemption of man's sin, "a sort of living Man of Sorrows";[57] the plea issuing from his mouth is: "My father, let those be saved for whom you wished that I suffer the Passion." The dove of the Holy Spirit above him sweeps the viewer's eye upward along the line of the right hand of God to the aureole around his head, bright with the stars of heaven. The clear message of the design of this image and its incorporated inscriptions is that men have a direct link to God through the intercession of Christ and the Virgin. This same dialectic between words and the lines of the image is employed by Fra Angelico in his fresco of the crucified Christ with the Virgin and Saint John in the cell at San Marco reserved for Cosimo.[58]

The frequent reflection of vernacular poets on the nature of the Trinity, and the many commissions to artists to represent it, including several examples noted in Neri di Bicci's *Ricordanze*,[59] indicate the extent of popular interest in this theme. As in Angelico's altarpiece for San Marco, a Medici patron is explicitly included in the chain of intercession by Giovanni Betti, a wool manufacturer and contemporary of Cosimo who competed in the Certame Coronario, in a poem he sent to Piero de' Medici: "May the love, the peace, and the good will/ of that immense Divine spirit,/ which descends from heaven and resides in the Divine Trinity,/ bear fruit in you and in your seed:/and from every trouble and harsh judgment/ preserve and relieve you,/ so that through you for the Florentine people/ the eternal clemency may always be invoked:/ and moreover for me may she be an intercessor,/ she who is so fertile and fecund,/ that she may render you holy and make you worthy,/ so that what you desire will be granted to you,/ and what you wish and what you can do will correspond,/ so you may rule and be granted the holy kingdom./ And I of meanest intellect/ pray for your grace,/ that you may accept me as your faithful servant, Giovanni Betti."[60]

The patron also forms part of the chain of intercession depicted in Masaccio's fresco of the Trinity in Santa Maria Novella (fig. 51). Here he remains a spectator of the heavenly exchange,[61] but the artist's *tour-de-force* use of perspective to create the illusion of almost infinitely receding space in a succession of planes links the skeleton and his *memento mori* at the foot of the fresco to the patron and his wife, kneeling just outside the frame, to the figure of the Virgin. She addresses the patron and the viewer in a gesture displaying the sacrifice on the cross of her son to redeem the sins of mankind, disarming the power of death in the example of his own resurrection.[62] God the Father presides over the scene, linked to his son by the dove of the Holy Spirit. Although Father and Holy Ghost are absent from Angelico's *pala* for the high altar of San Marco commissioned by Cosimo, as the Medici are represented by their saints Cosmas and Damian, so the infinite vista of a garden of delights evokes paradise; the chain of intercession linking the patron of the picture to his patron saints and ultimately to his Heavenly Father is similarly an essential message of the image.

DEATH AND THE PATRON

By the mid-1430s Cosimo, recently returned from exile, had acquired both the means and the social stature to encourage him to embark upon a major and very public program of ecclesiastical patronage. However, it was his

anxiety about life after death, his desire to make restitution for his sins, that lent urgency to this enterprise. Describing Cosimo's "great liberality" to the friars of San Marco, Vespasiano stressed the speed, the *diligentia* with which he met their needs, "because he didn't expect to see the completion of the works he had begun since so little time remained to him."[63]

Cosimo was then, by quattrocento standards, an elderly man of forty-seven. Suffering from the congenital and crippling disease of gout from which both his sons and his grandson Lorenzo were to die young, he might well have expected his own death at any moment. Indeed life for the aging and chronically ill in this period was a series of close encounters with death. As early as 1450 Contessina wrote to Piero and Giovanni: "Cosimo has perpetual fever, as he had when you left, and the doctors say it is not gout fever, and you know he is getting on in years, so that one cannot know what may happen from day to day."[64] In fact Cosimo lived on for another fifteen years to be seen in retrospect as "Pater Patriae, 1434–64," the title with which he was honored by communal decree, and which the inscription on his tomb and a medal struck in 1465 have permanently associated with his image.[65]

The powerful emphasis by preachers and poets on the misery and brevity of human life made Cosimo and his contemporaries constantly aware that, in the words of the customary preamble to wills, "nothing is more certain than death, and nothing more uncertain than its hour."[66] In the last years of his life the imminence of death seems increasingly to have colored Cosimo's attitude toward life. Ten years before he died he told Iacopo Guicciardini that "age and illness may be attacking my mind and undermining my spirit."[67] A little later, probably in the early sixties, he wrote to Agnolo Acciaiuoli, his friend and supporter since 1433, of their progressive estrangement: "I bear toward you the same love and affection I always did in the past, and am inclined to do for that brief time that God may permit me to remain here on earth."[68]

Although in the end Cosimo lived far longer than the normal quattrocento experience and his own precarious health entitled him to expect, his commissions should be viewed in the context of his ever-present awareness of mortality. Like the extension of political influence which it accompanied, his patronage was more *ad hoc* than it seems by hindsight; willed, certainly, but patterned, rather than planned in the comfortable assurance of thirty more years remaining to promote his political or dynastic image and to earn the admiration of posterity.

Cosimo's consciousness of mortality was undoubtedly sharpened in mid-life by the trauma of his arrest and exile in 1433. His brother Lorenzo, "out of his mind," as a

51   Masaccio, *Trinity*, Florence, Santa Maria Novella

52   Gentile da Fabriano, *A Miracle of Saint Nicholas*, Washington, National Gallery of Art, Samuel H. Kress Collection

young relative reported, "with fear for Cosimo," expected his enemies would kill him: "Lorenzo has so far been in such a passion of concern for Cosimo, that nobody has been able to say anything to him."[69] Cosimo's closest political collaborator, his cousin Averardo, and Averardo's

son Giuliano, indeed died in exile. Cosimo's mother Piccarda de' Bueri had died in April 1433, about the time he had retreated from factional conflict in Florence into the Mugello in hopes of avoiding the confrontation which led to his arrest that September.[70] Cosimo in fact survived the coup: he succeeded in bribing two of his captors with five hundred florins to arrange his release from prison, and observed in his brief *ricordo* of the experience that "they could have had 10,000 florins and more for my escape from danger."[71] In the same spirit, when a wave of plague engulfed northern Italy in 1430, Cosimo had advised Averardo: "I think you should abandon everything else you are doing and concentrate on saving your own life."[72]

This awareness of the finite nature of human existence is explicitly articulated in the inscription which Cosimo and his brother Lorenzo placed upon the elaborate marble tomb in the old sacristy, built by Giovannni di Bicci in the Medici parish church of San Lorenzo as his burial chapel.[73] Such inscriptions expressed patrons' ultimate fears and aspirations, like the lines on Giovanni Rucellai's Holy Sepulcher tomb embodying his personal hope in the Resurrection.[74] The inscription for Giovanni di Bicci, in fine classical lettering, was unusually fulsome,[75] a valediction in the spirit of Petrarch's *Triumphs*; as fame triumphs over death, so time triumphs over fame. "If services to his native city [*patria*], if the glory of his line and of his generosity to all, were free from dark death, alas, with his virtuous spouse he would live happily for his *patria*, an aid to the wretched and a haven and fair wind to his friends. But since death conquers all, Giovanni lies in this tomb, and you Piccarda, lie there also. Therefore the old, the young, the children, indeed those of every age grieve. Bereft of its parent, the sorrowful *patria* sighs" (fig. 80).[76] The Medici brothers expressed similar sentiments in their letter announcing their father's death to Carlo Malatesta, a *condottiere* of the Florentine commune.[77] The knowledge that death conquers all, particularly fame, and the belief that nothing would be remembered of him fifty years after his own death save a handful of buildings, is a crucial context for the interpretation of Cosimo's building of churches and chapels.[78]

THE MEDICI PATRON SAINTS

Cosimo's first major personal commission was the rebuilding of the Dominican convent of San Marco and its church. The reasons for his decision to begin here in making restitution for his sins will be discussed in the next chapter. This chapter will concentrate on Fra Angelico's frescoes for Cosimo at San Marco, and his altarpiece for the renovated church, together with several other painted altarpieces and panels, commissioned in Cosimo's lifetime, invoking the intercession of the Medici patron saints in the process of salvation.[79]

In direct response to Medici patronage or charity, the convent of San Marco was re-dedicated in 1443 to the Medici family saints Cosmas and Damian as well as its original patron, Saint Mark. The San Marco altarpiece and cell frescoes were apparently among the earliest conceived of a number of images made between the late 1430s and the early 1450s which foregrounded the Medici saints in a manner unprecedented in commissions incorporating patron saints for other Florentine laymen. In relation to the Holy Family, the Medici saints in these images were larger in scale than before, more central to the composition, and played a more important and more active role in the drama of intercession. This was true of Angelico's Medici altarpiece for the Franciscan convent of Bosco ai Frati, of the so-called Annalena altarpiece, perhaps originally for San Lorenzo,[80] of Baldovinetti's altarpiece for Cafaggiolo, of Lippi's altarpiece for the novices' chapel at Santa Croce which Cosimo built in the 1430s, and of many of the frescoes at San Marco. Cosimo's twin brother Damiano had died in infancy, but the patronage of both Saints Cosmas and Damian remained associated with Cosimo. His surviving younger brother, Lorenzo, was represented by his own onomastic saint in their joint commissions, along with the patron saints of their father Giovanni, Cosimo's sons Piero and Giovanni, and of Pierfrancesco di Lorenzo. By the time Cosimo became a patron of art, he was the acknowledged leader of the Medici lineage, and his saintly patrons were recognized as its general symbols.

It is often assumed that the prominence of the Medici saints constitutes a sort of dynastic display similar to that expressed by the inclusion in these pictures of Medici arms and devices. This leads easily to the reading of such images as partly or even predominantly advertisements or claims of the increasing political authority and prestige of Cosimo, his family and friends in Florence. Parallels with the use of saints in princely patronage are frequently adduced to support this reading. However, saints are not, like coats of arms, mere markers of a dynastic presence.[81] By mid-century the Florentine *popolo* identified the Medici closely with their patron saints, who had a distinct and well-elaborated identity in images and in popular poems.[82] The image, as Aquinas taught, recalls the entity; the saints' primary role was to *act*, as intercessors for their namesakes and protégés at the heavenly court, drawing on their behalf upon the treasury of merit they themselves had laid up in heaven through their saintly deeds. As noted in discussion of Feo Belcari's correspondence, in response to the doubts expressed by the mattress-maker Francesco del Maestro Andrea, Belcari reaffirmed the role of the saints in man's salvation: that Christ had conceded "the heights of heaven to our souls,/ by virtue of the credit amassed by the great saints."[83]

The evocation of living men like Cosimo in the images of their onomastic saints served also to enrich their identity through association with the saint's special virtue or spiritual genius.[84] Naming was regarded, according to a biblical tradition familiar to Florentines from both words and images, as a means at once of recognizing and fixing identity.[85] Judaic custom thus forbade the naming of Jehovah. Conversely, the New Testament account of Saint John the Baptist's life, a popular subject for the *predelle* of altarpieces, tells how Zacharias was struck dumb by the Lord for his failure to acknowledge in faith that his aged wife was about to bear a child. His speech was restored when he named – that is, recognized his son John, the Baptist and forerunner of Christ. A name was both identity and destiny. A strong personal identification, not really fostered by the iconic representations of saints made for patrons of previous centuries, was facilitated by the fifteenth-century artist's aim to make visible the real world in lifelike figures.[86] If the Medici adoption of Saints Cosmas and Damian, and their appearance in Medici images, was a conscious strategy, it was one that expressed a variety of common Florentine values, and served a number of ends – spiritual, dynastic, and self-advertising – which cannot easily be distinguished.

Toward the close of the trecento and throughout the fifteenth century – coincident with an enormous rise in the number of pious confraternities and the size of their membership, many Florentines began to abandon traditional family names for their children in overwhelming favor of the names of protective saints.[87] Giovanni di Bicci de' Medici followed this trend when he named his twin sons born in 1389 Cosimo and Damiano, despite the fact that these rather unusual and comparatively obscure saints were not represented in the traditional repertoire of Medici names. The association of Saints Cosmas and Damian, brothers and doctors, with the name of Medici (the doctors) constituted a memorable pun in the quintessential style of Florentine popular culture, with which Medici friends and correspondents, as well as poets and eulogists, played happily throughout Cosimo's lifetime.[88] The adoption of such distinctive names may well have been part of a strategy to consolidate the identity of the Medici family, and to project it publicly with compelling and memorable symbols of the family's presence in the city.[89] Men might naturally look to the *medici* Cosmas and Damian for remedies for the ills of the body social.[90]

The doctor saints were also martyrs from the early Christian period, which by the late fourteenth century had begun to fascinate such humanist scholars of the Bible as Ambrogio Traversari. The influence of Early Christian ideals and symbols is pervasive in the artistic commissions of his friends and pupils, Cosimo and

Lorenzo de' Medici.[91] Early Christian monuments were also a real presence in their lives. Both brothers spent extensive periods of time in Rome, where Giovanni di Bicci de' Medici began his banking business before Cosimo's birth, and members of the family made frequent journeys to deal with the financial and diplomatic business of the branch of the bank attached to the papal court. The church of Saints Cosmas and Damian, one of the most visible and revered monuments of the period of early Christianity in Rome, was an object of their patronage. This may have begun to flag as the century wore on; in an undated letter to Giovanni di Cosimo, the basilica's treasurer, a canon named Piero Pieranimo, invoked the family's past generosity in begging for the aid of Cosimo's younger son:

> I have come to your house [in Rome] time and time again, but have not been able to speak to you.[92] I beg you by the love of God that this holy church be recommended to you, because it greatly needs your help. When Lorenzo de' Medici was in Rome he spent [many] gold ducats repairing the church, then he gave me a chalice and some vestments and a bed for the chaplain, and then he told me that if the church ever needed anything that I should write to you. Well, now we need a missal of whatever value might please you, and a bed for the chaplain and the bell-tower of the church needs repairing . . . and that round *tempietto* near the entrance of the door of Metullus needs repairing before it falls down. I won't write any more; God be with you . . . I beg that when I next come to your house I will receive a reply.[93]

The apse of the Roman basilica, founded by Felix IV, pope from 526 to 530, was decorated with a huge mosaic depicting the apostles Peter and Paul presenting the titular saints to the Redeemer, while the pope offered him a model of the Church (fig. 53; also fig. 44).[94] The inscription spells out the message: "the martyrs, the physicians, and the people have a sure hope of salvation." The mosaic also represented the two parts of the Church, the Western and the Eastern; balancing Felix in the design was Theodorus, a Byzantine saint. In form and style the work was highly unusual for its time. By comparison with the traditional assertion in such images of generalized universal values, this was a strikingly concrete representation, individualized and dramatized particularly in the apostles' compelling gestures of patronage, protection, and intercession, which linked man, the saints and Christ, this world and the next.[95] The main themes of the mosaic correspond closely to major themes in Cosimo's life and patronage, to his close involvement with the council to reconcile the Eastern and Western churches, and to the

53   Late antique lunette mosaic, Rome, SS. Cosma e Damiano

spirit and force of Fra Angelico's dramatic and innovative representation in the San Marco altarpiece of the intercession of Saints Cosmas and Damian with the Virgin and Christ. While it seems that Angelico visited Rome only after the completion of the altarpiece,[96] the Medici could easily have furnished him with a sketch of the mosaic if Cosimo had wished to associate his commission for San Marco with the venerable and famous representation of his ono-mastic saints in the basilica of Saints Cosmas and Damian in Rome.

The Medici associated themselves with many institutions dedicated to Saints Cosmas and Damian, and lavishly celebrated their feastday, which was also observed by branches of the Medici bank throughout Europe. The cult, apparently instituted by Giovanni di Bicci, seems also to have been celebrated by other branches of the family in his time.[97] A letter of 10 September 1436 from the rector of the church of San Cosimo in Pisa, reminded Cosimo that it was his family's custom to provide for a celebration of the feast of Saints Cosmas and Damian in

that city: "I find in a memorandum by my predecessor, and furthermore by public knowledge [*fama*], that your father of happy memory and you yourself have always lent us a hand to subsidize the feast of the glorious martyrs Saints Cosmas and Damian our protectors . . . whose feast will be on the 27th of this present month . . . So that I may prepare a feast for the praise and glory of these saints . . . I beg you to give me some aid with your alms so that these saints may act as intercessors before God for you . . ."[98]

In 1456 the informal council of advisors to the Signoria, the Consulte e Pratiche, considered and rejected a proposal for public celebrations of the feastday of Saints Cosmas and Damian. A poem of 1437 by Anselmo Calderoni, herald of the Signoria, relating how the Medici saints appeared to him in a dream, refers to a similar earlier proposal. His verse was at once a testimony to the popular identification of the Medici with their ono-mastic saints, and a plea to the Florentine people, invoking familiar images and phrases from the *Divine Comedy*, to acknowledge the family's virtues that had already earned them the favor of God and his saints, because they promoted the common good and the unity of the commune.[99] Medici commissions for paintings and frescoes incorporating Saints Cosmas and Damian and the figures of the Magi, with whose cult, centred on San Marco, they also associated themselves, undoubtedly served, and were intended, as effective reminders of the Medici presence and preeminence in Florence. This self-exaltation was in no way incompatible with a desire on Cosimo's part to invoke the intercession of the doctor martyrs on his own spiritual behalf, and of that of the people, in the "sure hope of salvation." Calderoni's poem is evidence of the close association in Florentine minds between personal devotion and public salvation, expressed in images now read often as political in the most reductive sense, although Angelico's San Marco altarpiece shows how completely these concerns could be reconciled in a single powerful image.

Giovanni Morelli may have practiced his devotions before a fairly standard representation of the crucified Christ with the Virgin and Saint John, but a number even of Neri di Bicci's clients, and not always the wealthiest, commissioned personalized images featuring their onomastic saints or others to whom they were specially devoted.[100] Medici commissions were perhaps the most highly developed and clearly articulated expressions of this general impulse. Cosimo and his family furnished themselves at home, as well as in public places, with a plethora of images foregrounding their namesaints in the company of the Virgin or Christ on the cross. Chapter 12 will look more closely at the images apparently made for the Medici house or palace, but it should be noted here that the inventory of the contents of the Medici house completed in 1418, when Cosimo was not yet thirty, suggests that the cultivation of personal virtue and devotion through attention to Christian images as well as texts was an important element of his education. In addition to the many missals and books of offices among the volumes in Cosimo's library, and his copy of the *Lives of Saints Cosmas and Damian*, most other objects in the Medici house had a devotional purpose.[101] These objects are evidence both of the family's active spiritual orientation, and of Cosimo's early intimacy with the visual representation of religious themes. Chief of them was the large veiled altarpiece of Saints Cosmas and Damian in the main *sala* of Giovanni di Bicci's house in 1418. A much later painting by Rogier van der Weyden, the so-called Medici *Madonna*, depicts the Madonna and Child with Saints Cosmas and Damian, Saint Peter, founder of the church which is the only gate, strait and narrow, to heaven to which he holds the keys, and Saint John the Baptist, the forerunner of Christ and patron saint of Florence and all its citizens (fig. 124).[102]

Along with the most practical matters of workmanship, materials, and date due, contracts for altarpieces are often very precise about the identity of the saints to be represented. Chief among the criteria governing their selection were the liturgical function of the image, the references to the dedicatee of the chapel and the church, and if it was destined for a convent, the order to which that convent belonged. The choice of saints appearing in the major altarpieces commissioned by the Medici under Cosimo's direction suggests the confluence of a number of such considerations.

The Annalena altarpiece, apparently the earliest of those commissioned by Cosimo, was painted by Fra Angelico around 1434/5, but probably not for the convent dedicated to San Vicenzo d'Annalena, where it was installed in the 1450s (fig. 54). William Hood very plausibly proposed that it was originally made for the Medici family chapel in the transept of San Lorenzo, dedicated to Saints Cosmas and Damian, and transferred to the Annalena, which was run by a kinswoman of Cosimo's, when the family chapel in San Lorenzo became a reliquary chapel in 1452. This accords with the iconography of the painting, familial as befitted a family chapel, and at the same time referring to the dedicatee and the patron of the church in which it was probably located. The predella panels depict scenes from the lives of Saints Cosmas and Damian. The saints in rather formal *sacra conversazione* are, to the Virgin's right, the doctor brothers; to her left, John the Evangelist, patron of Cosimo's recently deceased father, and of the San Lorenzo sacristy which was his burial chapel. Beside him is Saint Lawrence, patron of the Medici parish church. In the foreground on either side are Peter Martyr and Francis, representing the two major mendicant orders, and often paired in Florentine paintings of this period. Peter Martyr was also the personal patron of Cosimo's son Piero, as Francis was the *onomastico* of his brother Lorenzo's son.[103]

Also by Fra Angelico, and usually dated in the late 1430s, was the altarpiece for the *cappella maggiore* of Bosco ai Frati, a Franciscan convent located on the rural estates of the Medici family, who customarily worshipped there when staying in the Mugello (fig. 55). Its iconography is markedly Franciscan. To the Virgin's right are Saints Francis, Louis of Toulouse, and Anthony of Padua, and the predella depicts members of the order flanking a central panel of the Man of Sorrows. To the Virgin's left are Cosmas, Damian, and Peter Martyr, the patrons of Cosimo, the Medici family, and his elder son. The somewhat surprising opulence of this altarpiece destined for a

54 Fra Angelico, "Annalena" altarpiece, Florence, Museo di San Marco

secluded rural monastery, and the (albeit discreet) references to the Medici arms in the picture, suggest that the
commission had strong personal significance for the
patron, but that he was mindful also of the central role
the image would play in the daily lives and worship of
the Observant Franciscan friars.

Around the mid- to late 1440s Fra Filippo Lippi
painted the altarpiece for the chapel of the novices which
Cosimo endowed at Santa Croce, along with a large
number of commemorative masses for his own soul (fig.
56).[104] In this dynamic *sacra conversazione*, full of movement in the relationship of its figures to the architecture

55 Fra Angelico, Bosco ai Frati altarpiece, Florence, Museo di San Marco

56 Fra Filippo Lippi, altarpiece for Novitiate Chapel, Santa Croce, Florence, Uffizi

and in the flow of their draperies, there are only four participants. The brother physicians Cosmas and Damian
have pride of place on either side of the Virgin, as dedicatees of the chapel and early Christian martyrs. Francis
and Anthony of Padua, friends and brothers in the more
modern mendicant order to which the church is dedi-

cated, form a corresponding pair as in other Medici
commissions.[105] In the predella by Pesellino, a central
Nativity is flanked by scenes from the lives of the four
saints.

While these scenes are all central to the saints' lives and
legends, their selection may also be related to particular

57   Alesso Baldovinetti, Cafaggiolo altarpiece, Florence, Uffizi

themes of Cosimo's personal culture and patronage. Cosmas and Damian are shown at their moment of martyrdom, and in the act of healing the Emperor Justinian, a scene that recalls frequent references in popular literature to the Medici family as the healers of Florence's political ills, and evokes Justinian's image as the personification of classical and Christian traditions of law, justice and good government, as he appears in Dante's *Paradiso*. Saint Anthony is represented in his most graphic and morally didactic act. Preaching at a miser's funeral, Anthony quoted from the Gospel of Saint Luke, 12:32, "Where your wealth is, there will your heart be also," then watched as the miser's treasure chest was opened to reveal his heart inside. This very explicit reference to the

need of the wealthy to redirect their hearts to God and his charity is reinforced implicitly by Anthony's well-known motto which often appears as an inscription in representations of the saint: "But a man dies, and he disappears; man comes to his end, and where is he?" (Job 14:10).[106] These words in turn recall the reference on the inscription ordered by Cosimo and Lorenzo for their father's tomb in the old sacristy to "dark death," which overcame all their father's virtues and pleasures in life.

The last of the Medici altarpieces commissioned in Cosimo's lifetime was for the private family chapel in his villa at Cafaggiolo (fig. 57). It was painted by Alesso Baldovinetti, probably in the early 1450s, and perhaps on the occasion of the birth of Piero's second son, Giuliano.

Saint Julian, not previously part of the iconography of Medici devotional images, appears here for the first time. However, the altar had been dedicated to Saints Francis and Julian when Cafaggiolo belonged to Cosimo's cousin Averardo di Francesco di Bicci, whose son was also named Giuliano.[107] The tone of this *sacra conversazione* is notably personal, relaxed, and rural. The Virgin is seated on a simple wooden chair set on a carpet outdoors; behind her cloth of honor is a variety of carefully depicted trees, and there are flowers in the foreground. To her right, Cosmas and Damian literally converse, by comparison with the several representations in other Medici altarpieces or frescoes of Damian with his back to the viewer, or glimpsed in profile or behind or in the shadow of his brother.[108] Beside the brother physicians, and nearest the Madonna and Child, is Saint John the Baptist.

These saints refer to the Medici family and to Florence, and it is worth noting in view of the heavily politicized interpretation of the personnel of other more public Medici commissions, that this image was destined mainly for family consumption.[109] On the Virgin's left are Lawrence and Julian, the name-saints of the new generation of Piero's sons, Lorenzo and Giuliano. The paired Francis and Peter Martyr, who usually represent the two main mendicant orders, in this case may refer to the dedication of the chapel to Saint Francis, as well as to the sons of Cosimo and his brother Lorenzo, Piero and Pierfrancesco; they are depicted on a much smaller scale, kneeling before the Virgin.[110] The image would seem to combine, in a rather unschematic way, some reference to the onomastic saints of three generations of the main line of the Medici family, their city of Florence, and the mendicant orders of the Church who were beneficiaries of Medici interest and patronage.

Saint Anthony Abbot, who also appears in an apparently contemporaneous domestic devotional image by Lippi for one or other of the Medici houses,[111] is generally regarded as the founder of monasticism. In these two images essentially unconstrained by the iconography of a church or order, Anthony may represent an ideal the patron greatly admired. Two of Cosimo's major commissions were the renovation of the monasteries of San Marco and the Badia, and his personal interest in the monastic ideal in relation to these buildings will be discussed later.[112] Moreover, in 1444 Cosimo had personally helped to locate in an altar in a side chapel of the Romanesque San Lorenzo the relics of Saint Anthony, among others. Additional connotations of Saint Anthony perhaps close to Cosimo's heart were his identification with a crippling illness (he is usually shown as old and bearded and carrying a stick like a crutch with a handle

shaped like a *tau*, an emblem of immortality in ancient Egypt adopted by Alexandrian Christians) and his association with the overcoming of the temptations of the flesh, the subject of a passage Cosimo marked for his attention in his copy of Cassian's *Monastic Institutes*.[113] However, in view of the multivalent associations of saints and their primary role as active intercessors for the faithful viewer, the precise significance to the patron of their appearance in any particular image can only be a matter of speculation.

SAN MARCO: THE FRESCOES

Unlike the paintings incorporating the Medici saints which Cosimo commissioned for other ecclesiastical foundations, the images of Cosmas and Damian at San Marco were made for places not usually accessible to the general public.[114] Moreover, the doctors were included with saints customarily depicted in images destined for a Dominican setting, not only in the community's corporate spaces, some of which, like the chapter room, were open to a select public, but also in the frescoes on the walls of the areas reserved to the cloistered clergy. The private cell for the patron's use was in the less restricted laybrothers' corridor, but even the altarpiece made for the conventual chapel in the church was at least partly hidden from lay worshippers by a rood screen. While this image was the focus of the friars' daily liturgical activity, it was openly displayed to a general Florentine audience once a year, on the feast of Epiphany.[115]

The communities of convents were not as detached from the world as is sometimes assumed. In this very small city, even the cloistered clergy were linked by their families to the restricted and intensely civic-minded circle that directed the city's secular and political affairs. In fact the Dominicans at San Marco came from some of Florence's most influential and distinguished lineages.[116] A broad avenue of personal association joined the convent's cloisters to the world beyond its walls. While the political power of the Medici did not relate to the monastery's main concerns, their personal influence permeated its community. At the same time, the fact that devotional images prominently featuring the Medici patron saints were made for the contemplation of the professional religious, rather than a public more attuned to political innuendo, strongly suggests that their primary function was to stimulate commemorative prayer.

Fra Angelico was one of a group of brothers from the Dominican convent in Fiesole who came to San Marco in 1436, after the convent in central Florence was trans-

58   Fra Angelico, *Virgin and Child Enthroned with Saints Dominic, Cosmas, Damian, Mark, John the Evangelist, Thomas Aquinas, Lawrence, and Peter Martyr*, Florence, Convent of San Marco, east dormitory

ferred to their order. He already had behind him several important commissions from the Dominicans, most notably the altarpiece at San Domenico, and for churches with which the Medici were associated, including the Angeli, for which he painted the *Last Judgment*.[117] Apart from Fra Angelico's qualifications as an artist, as a Dominican he was uniquely equipped to express the particular style of devotion with which the Medici identified themselves in their patronage of San Marco.

The images incorporating Saints Cosmas and Damian served to keep the identity of the convent's patrons constantly before the eyes of its mendicant brothers, the voluntary poor whose vocation was to pray continuously for the salvation of souls. A fresco of the Madonna and Child with eight saints in the east corridor where the friars' dormitories were located is surprisingly sumptuous, revealing perhaps the patron's desire to emphasize his generosity to the convent, and his consequent claim upon

the spiritual services of the friars (fig. 58). This fresco also includes Saint Mark, patron of the church, Saint Dominic, founder of the order, and Saint Thomas Aquinas, who defined so much of its theological orientation. While Saint Peter Martyr was generally favored in Florentine imagery, here he probably served as a reminder of Cosimo's elder son Piero. All the other saints in the fresco were patrons of the Medici family – Cosmas and Damian, Lawrence, and Saint John the Evangelist.

As William Hood showed in his study of Fra Angelico at San Marco, the messages of its frescoes were complex and various. As he observed, in terms of composition and iconography the fresco is "a reprise" of the altarpiece, but in this image for the monks' eyes only there is an intriguing addition to the customary text – "Have charity; preserve humility; possess voluntary poverty," written on the page of an open book which Dominic displays in the altarpiece. Here the text continues: "I invoke God's curse

59   Fra Angelico, *Crucifixion*, Florence, Convent of San Marco, chapter room

and mine on the introduction of possessions into this order." Although Cosimo refrained from leaving property to the convent in his will, he and Antoninus, the convent's prior who later became archbishop of Florence, eventually petitioned the pope to set aside this restriction. Antoninus was an extremely practical churchman who consistently took pains to distinguish between the ideal of communal poverty and the actual demands of the convent's obligations to the real world, including its patron. Since it seems hard to explain why either he or Cosimo would want to make such a statement, Hood speculated that the artist himself may have been responsible for this curious insertion. In any case, the curse is indeed a "symbol of the ambiguity and even irony that lies right at the heart of San Marco."[118] For if the poverty of the Observant Dominicans at San Marco was threatened, this was largely by the charity of the Medici family, to which the inscription and the Medici saints drew distinctly ambivalent attention.[119]

The Medici saints are again prominent in the representation of the Crucifixion that dominates the chapter room, "the heart of the community's moral life, just as the choir was the heart of its spiritual life." As Hood observed, it is elegant, splendid, and in the "luxury and expense of its palette" seldom surpassed in Fra Angelico's oeuvre (fig. 59).[120] The iconography of the chapter room is explicitly Dominican, and the presence here of the Medici saints is at first glance less obtrusive. To the right of the cross is a group of monastic and mendicant saints; to the left are the biblical witnesses to the Crucifixion, the three Maries and John the Evangelist, the Baptist, and Saint Mark displaying his open gospel. Beside him are the patron saints of the Medici patrons; Lawrence, Cosmas, and Damian, the last of these distinguished from all the other figures by his striking mourning gesture as he turns from the scene and covers his face with his hands, just such an expression of human personality as Alberti recommended to the artist to move and involve the

61   Benozzo Gozzoli, *Adoration of the Magi*, Florence, Convent of San Marco, Cosimo de' Medici's double cell

viewer.[121] Once again, it would be perverse to assume that the figure of Damian is intended primarily as a reminder of the wealth and secular power of the Medici family, rather than of its spiritual needs, and the friars' obligation to serve these in respect of Cosimo's charity.

Cosimo was certainly the privileged, if not virtually the only viewer, of the frescoes decorating the double cell set aside for his use. According to the chronicle of San Marco, on the night of his consecration of the church and the unveiling of its altarpiece, Pope Eugenius IV slept, not in the lavishly appointed papal apartments furnished for him at the convent of Santa Maria Novella, but in Cosimo's cell at San Marco. However, its walls at that time were probably still blank. The reservation of a cell for the patron in a religious foundation was itself extraordinary, although not unique; Nicola Acciaiuoli had a similar arrangement with the congregation of the Certosa which he built outside the southern gate of the city at Galluzzo. Nor did Cosimo intrude on strictly cloistered space, since his cell gave off a corridor of rooms probably used by laybrothers – the cooks, housekeepers, and tradesmen who attended to the friars' everyday needs, freeing them for spiritual labor.[122]

The fresco adorning the outer compartment of Cosimo's double cell represents a Crucifixion similar to those found in many other cells (fig. 60). Christ's ribs are clearly visible beneath his pain-wracked flesh, and the blood from the wounds in his feet drips steadily onto Adam's skull at the foot of the cross. The image recalls not only Antoninus's injunction to contemplate in every awful detail the image of the Passion, but also a popular poem celebrating the "Nail of Christ," a miraculous relic conserved in a church at Colle Val d'Elsa. "O sacred, holy and precious nail,/ that pierced the holy feet of the Redeemer/ and with bitter pain/ passed through his bones and his nerves/ . . . Although you are ancient, you reveal yourself/ ever new, appearing to our human selves/ sprinkled and stained with the blessed blood/ by the angel of the Lord."[123]

As in so many other representations of this scene, many of them for private devotion, the Virgin kneels at Christ's right hand, but in place of the customary saints like Mary Magdalen or Mary Cleophas, who appear in the chapter-room *Crucifixion*, Saint Cosmas kneels close at her side. As often, on Christ's left is John the Evangelist; next to him is Peter Martyr. The three male saints depicted here

60   Benozzo Gozzoli, *Jesus Consigning his Mother to Saint John, with Saints Cosmas and Peter Martyr*, Florence, Convent of San Marco, Cosimo de' Medici's double cell

62   Fra Angelico, San Marco altarpiece, Florence, Museo di San Marco

are the patrons of Cosimo and the Medici family in general, of Cosimo's elder son Piero, and of his father and younger son, both named Giovanni. According to the gospel, John the Evangelist was the "beloved disciple" to whose care the dying Christ consigned his mother. An inscription from this gospel, rather like the inscriptions used in the *Trinity* altarpiece for the cathedral, issues from Christ's right side. The words are those Jesus addressed to Saint John and his mother: "Mother, behold your son; son behold your mother." Beneath the inscription, the Virgin turns to Saint Cosmas kneeling beside her. The strong suggestion is that as Christ consigned his mother to John's care, Cosimo is consigned to hers; he and his two sons enjoy her very special protection.[124]

The stark messages of crucifix and skull, a feature of the frescoes for many of the cells at San Marco, are a powerful injunction to penitence. They appeal to the sort of doubts and fears described by the Medici family's close friend Carlo Martelli, meditating upon his faith before a crucifix: "Oh Lord who upon the waves rescued/ Peter who was moved to come to you,/ when he cried out, "Oh Lord, help me,"/ you replied: "Why do you doubt?"/ I turn to you weeping, with pure thoughts,/ with the true love of your promise,/ that you will save me by your grace,/ just as you rescued that poor old man./ Lo, turn your eyes to our cross,/ in which in your name I now renew my faith,/ . . . Lord, I commit myself / to you who are our harbor and salvation . . ."[125]

The frescoes in the two cells, like those on the palace chapel walls, imply a progression; from sacrifice and repentance to atonement and the hope of salvation. On the upper wall of the inner compartment of Cosimo's cell is a lunette-shaped fresco of the Adoration of the Magi (fig. 61). This was probably painted, perhaps as early as 1442, by Benozzo Gozzoli, a first version for the Medici of the subject he depicted so brilliantly in the frescoes for the chapel of their palace some fifteen years later. In the San Marco fresco, as in most other representations of the Magi, the entourage of the wise men approaches literally from the East. Here they wear accurately observed contemporary Eastern hats, which are a notable feature of Florentine images painted after the visit of the Greek delegation to the council of the Eastern and Western churches held in Florence in 1439. The figure with the goatee beard in the Byzantine style is central to the composition; he unites it with his glance toward a figure to the west, while he welcomes a magus from the East. He is holding an armillary sphere, a symbol of astronomy.

Francis Ames-Lewis proposed that the figure to the west is Cosimo, and the venerable newcomer is George Gemistus Pletho, whom Cosimo encountered at the Este court in Ferrara in the early months of the church council. By this time Ferrara was a center of Greek scholarship in Italy, thanks to the efforts of Guarino da Verona, with whom the Medici were well acquainted. Ames-Lewis suggested that Pletho's chief contribution to the education of members of the Medici circle attending the council was not primarily, as is usually assumed, to give them a new knowledge of Platonism, but to introduce to them the text of Strabo's works on astronomy. This subject, together with the related cult of astrology, fascinated many Florentines, and especially the members of the Medici family.[126] The transfer of the council from Ferrara to Florence was a major diplomatic triumph for Cosimo, and several of his subsequent commissions, including the painted ceiling for the old sacristy, the

figures on its bronze doors, and the frescoes in the Medici palace, would seem to reflect the importance he attached to his role in this event.

Hood observed that in shape, composition, and the rich use of color, the Magi fresco resembles more closely than any other in the cells of San Marco the imposing chapter-room Crucifixion. However, other aspects of the fresco "connect it even more deeply with the altarpiece in the church." The Lamentation scene on the predella of the panel for the altar, and the illusionistic crucifix that underscored its eucharistic significance (figs. 62 and 63), are mirrored in Cosimo's cell in the niche set into the fresco, a tabernacle for the reservation of the host. On its back wall is a Man of Sorrows, surrounded by the instruments of the Passion depicted on the returns. In his cell at San Marco Cosimo was therefore able to hear mass in a setting that closely associated his devotions with the liturgical activities of the friars celebrating mass in the church below, before the altarpiece he himself had endowed.[127]

THE SAN MARCO ALTARPIECE: SALVATION, PATRONAGE, AND POWER

Hood's important study sets the images Fra Angelico produced for San Marco at Cosimo's behest, most particularly the altarpiece, firmly in the context of Dominican devotional practice, and especially of the liturgy. He illuminated them afresh in his exposition of what he calls Angelico's "painted prayer."[128] He also discerned, in these representations of the timeless and universal Christian revelation, messages concerning Cosimo's political ambitions so predominant as to suggest that the "grandest messages" of the altarpiece "may have escaped him almost entirely." He saw the Adoration of the Magi in Cosimo's cell as "a personal icon of power and attainment," conjoined with the Corpus Domini to form "totems of Cosimo's political legitimation."[129] These readings are consonant with a long tradition of describing cell and altarpiece in terms of their presumed dynastic and political significance to the Medici family. John Pope-Hennessy called the altarpiece a "Medicean manifesto"; even Susan McKillop, who more than anyone else has drawn attention to the seriousness of Cosimo's religious concerns, described this painting as "central to the formation of the Medici visual vocabulary of power" (fig. 62).[130]

It is impossible on the evidence of the image alone to say what any viewer saw in it. But in the light of what we have learned of Cosimo's concerns with death, sin, and restitution, of his expectation from his patron saints of intercessory powers in heaven analogous to those he himself possessed as a patron on earth, and of the view of the clergy to whom he gave charitable support that there was no conflict in praying for his promotion on earth as in heaven, it seems likely that a concern to secure divine blessing here and hereafter for himself and his family in all their works was a major impulse animating the commission of these images. Angelico's articulation in the altarpiece of the role of the Virgin and other saints in the process of salvation was surely as important to the patron as it was to the picture's Dominican artist and audience. Of course these images are stamped with the impress of Medici identity − of their wealth, power, and pride in lineage − but if they are to be interpreted as "political" statements, as expressions of secular power or aspirations, the concepts of politics and power must be understood much more complexly than they have been to date.

The altarpiece is the most public of Angelico's images for San Marco. At its center is the Virgin enthroned, the Child on her knee, surrounded by angels and saints. Behind her a landscape filled with trees stretches toward a lake and distant mountains. Distinguished from the crowd of attendants by their scale and position, nearest to the viewer and almost at the lower edge of the frame, kneel Saints Cosmas and Damian, chief intercessors before the queen of this heavenly court. Not long before Angelico began this work, Alberti had suggested in his treatise on painting that the artist include someone "who tells the spectators what is going on . . . beckons them with his hand to look . . ."[131] This principle is effectively applied in many Florentine paintings of the period. Here it is Saint Cosmas who mediates between the convocation of saints in heaven and the viewer outside the picture plane whom he addresses with his gaze as he gestures toward the Virgin and Child. His features are not idealized, like those of the other saints: they could be seen as resembling Cosimo's.[132] Whether or no, as numerous letters and poems concerning Medici patronage and intercession attest, as Cosimo's patron saint, Cosmas represented him. Patron and mediator in heaven as Cosimo was on earth, Saint Cosmas was his direct link to the supreme intercessors, the Virgin and Christ, at the heavenly court of a judgmental God.[133]

Right in the Virgin's line of vision Damian, name-saint of Cosimo's dead brother, balances Cosmas in the foreground: he looks directly at the Virgin, his back to the viewer. At the Virgin's right hand are Mark, John the Evangelist, and Lawrence, who stands behind Cosmas at the extreme left of the picture. While the other saints converse among themselves, Lawrence, like Cosmas, looks out at the viewer, appealing to him with his eyes to par-

ticipate in the process of prayer. Like Damian in the chapter-room *Crucifixion*, Saint Lawrence is endowed with a poignant human personality, possibly a reference to the very recent death of Cosimo's beloved younger brother − in 1441, after this picture was planned and not long before it was completed − and to the urgency of the patron's concern at this time with commemorative prayer.[134] This was precisely the function performed almost continuously by the monks of San Marco as they recited the Marian office before the altar at each hour of the liturgical day. Their prayers to the Virgin, a fundamental element of the Dominican observance, served at the same time the patron's spiritual needs, the expected recompense for his charity.

To the Virgin's left are Saints Dominic, Francis, and Peter Martyr. Of the saints represented in the altarpiece, San Marco was the titular saint of the convent, and Dominic the founder of its residents' order. Other saints customarily associated with Dominican altarpieces, for example Aquinas, are absent, their places ceded to the name-saints of the members of the Medici lineage; Cosimo, his brothers Damian and Lorenzo, his father Giovanni and sons Giovanni and Piero, and Lorenzo's sons Francesco and Pierfrancesco.[135] Florentines attuned by such images as Masaccio's *Trinity* and the older *Trinity* in the cathedral to the weight of geometrical shapes in calibrating meaning would have noticed that the figures of Cosmas and Damian literally support the composition, as their devotees did the convent, forming the base of a triangle whose apex is a classical triumphal arch, similar to the one in Masaccio's *Trinity*, crowning the Virgin's throne.[136] The more attentive would have observed the Medici arms decorating the border of the carpet before the Virgin's throne, and the references to the Medici in the signs of the zodiac woven into its fabric.

The drama of intercession is focused on the figures along the strong vertical axis of the picture. The Virgin and Child represent at once the triumph of Christ and his mother in heaven, and the Incarnation by which God the Father sent and sacrificed his only Son to redeem the sins of mankind. Angels at their side hold the instruments of his future Passion, represented in the crucifix at the foot of the throne. The lamentation over the dead Christ by his followers in the central panel of the predella foreshadows the promise of Resurrection, and the restoration of man to the heavenly paradise, the Garden of Eden that was his before the Fall (fig. 63). The latter, visible behind the cloth of honor, is inhabited in eternity by Christ, the Virgin and the saints. Perspective creates the illusion that the crucifix in Angelico's altarpiece belongs not to the heavenly scene of the picture, but to the altar before which this drama of sacrifice and redemption was daily

63   Fra Angelico, *Lamentation*, San Marco altarpiece, predella panel, Munich, Alte Pinakothek

reenacted, in the offering of the Eucharist, the body of Christ, at the celebration of the Mass.

Hood, concerned with the point of view of the artist and his conventual audience, unfolded the complex redemptive message so beautifully articulated by Angelico, arguing that it resonated more richly for the friars than it could for any layman. This may be so, but the themes represented – Christ's Incarnation, Passion, and Resurrection, the mercy of his mother Mary, the treasury of merit accumulated by the saints on which sinners might draw – also preoccupied pious laymen, since their contemplation was the key to salvation for which all sinners strove. Hood's view that Angelico displayed particular skill in perfectly integrating Dominican and Medicean themes and "disguising their incompatibility" stems from an assumption that the meaning of the altarpiece concerning salvation interested only the Dominicans, and only those meanings he saw as relating to Medici dynastic and political ambitions interested Cosimo and his lay audience. All that we know of the religious education and impulses of Cosimo and other devout Florentines would suggest the opposite. In the San Marco altarpiece Angelico integrates not incompatible, but diverse elements; texts, symbols, and spatial relationships constitute an armory of signs decipherable by various members of his varied audience, including both laymen and clergy. The picture sends a special message about the Medici, but it goes both ways; up to heaven with the aid of the friars and through the intercession of the saints, and down to earth to their fellow citizens, invited not only to consider the Medici family's preeminence and power, but also to pray for their salvation.[137]

The main key to the particular spiritual significance of the altarpiece, as Hood demonstrated, is liturgical custom rather than theological writing.[138] The more that is understood of religious belief and practice in the quattrocento, the clearer it is how many of the religious themes imprecisely described as "theological," and assumed to be too esoteric for the average viewer to grasp, were in fact entirely familiar to most Christians from their appearance in the liturgy. As Hood observed, few even of the Dominicans in Angelico's audience would have had much theology at their fingertips,[139] but the liturgy was the very framework of their lives. With the rise of confraternities, laymen too participated freely in paraliturgical rituals. This experience emphasized the central role in Christians' lives of the Mass as a reenactment of Christ's Passion,[140] the climax of his incarnate life with which worshippers identified, particularly through the mediation of the Virgin. As Antonio di Guido wrote in his *Ave Regina*, "For the tears that you shed,/ beneath the cross of death/ when you looked upon Jesus,/ O Virgin, give me comfort . . ."[141]

The inscription on the border of the Virgin's robe is from the *Little Office of the Blessed Virgin Mary*. Dominicans, being particularly devoted to the cult of Mary, recited these words, spoken by Wisdom, at each canonical hour of the liturgical day, in almost "unceasing petition and Marian praise." "As the vine I brought forth pleasant savor,/ and my flowers are the fruit of honor and riches;/ I am the mother of fair love, and fear, and knowledge and holy hope."[142] These words spoke compellingly to the friars of San Marco, but the office was also central to the observances of lay confraternities devoted to the Marian cult, and it was recorded in countless compilations for citizens who expressed their own devotion to the Virgin in spiritual poems and songs dedicated to her praise.

Angelico related the promise of the Seat of Wisdom, the Virgin, specifically to the Medici family through the flowers and fruit of the garden. As well as roses for the rosary, the Virgin, and perhaps also for the pope, there are citrus fruit, symbolizing the Medici arms and, according to Saint Antoninus, signifying the works directed by grace and the fruits thereof.[143] The garden was one of the most fruitful of all metaphors, in Islamic and other cultures beside the Christian. Descriptions of the gardens of both the old Medici house and the palace suggest that both were susceptible of many kinds of symbolic reading. Cosimo also had a similarly lush garden laid out for San

Marco.[144] Piero's wife Lucrezia owned a copy of Antoninus's manual *On Living Virtuously* addressed to her sister
Dianora Tornabuoni, in which the Prior of San Marco
described the soul as a garden which had to be cleared
of weeds, planted with good seed, and cultivated by good
works, in order to produce the sweet fruit that is the
enjoyment of peace and consolation. Cosimo himself is
credited with observing that envy was the weed that
spoiled most gardens, watered by all but the truly wise.[145]

Some of the messages of the San Marco altarpiece may
be lost to us now, but contemporaries could surely read
them clearly, especially with the aid of the inscriptions
and texts. In addition to the verse on the Virgin's robe,
the book Saint Mark holds directly above the head of
Saint Cosmas is open at chapter 6 of Mark's Gospel,
verses 2–8, recounting how Jesus preached in the temple
and sent forth his disciples, "two by two," without money
or possessions, to heal the sick. This passage obviously
refers to the mission of the Dominican order, but may
also be meant as a reminder of the pair of doctors so
prominent in the altarpiece. Their acts of healing, according to the text of *The Golden Legend*, and the life of
Cosmas and Damian, which Cosimo kept in his study, are
celebrated in the predella panels, a radical departure from
previous Dominican predellas that told the story of
the order of preachers.[146] Mindful of puns on the Medici
name, the audience may well have interpreted the
doctors' healing mission to refer also to the Medici role
in Florentine government, a theme of many popular
poems and comments.[147]

This literature of praise for the Medici presumes that
the power and wealth and honor they enjoyed in their
native city were the fruit of divine approbation, the signs
of God's grace due partly to the protective advocacy of
their patron saints in heaven. This helped to make the
Medici themselves powerful patrons here on earth, a connection visibly established in the altarpiece.[148] When he
commissioned it for the church of San Marco, Cosimo
knew it would be seen by a large audience of Florentine
citizens at least once a year, at the feast of the Epiphany
celebrated by the confraternity of the Magi of which he
was a prominent member. Indeed Angelico's painting was
first unveiled on 6 January 1443, when the altar of the
church was rededicated to Saints Cosmas and Damian as
well as to San Marco in the presence of Pope Eugenius,
"with the whole college of cardinals and a great multitude of bishops and other prelates of the church of God
and a great gathering of people."[149] This event clearly
lived long in the memory of those who witnessed it, like
the ceremony of the consecration of Santa Maria del
Fiore in 1436. Similarly, special indulgences were granted
future participants in the annual Epiphany celebration

in Eugenius' bull, "Splendor paternae gratiae," which
ensured that the veneration of the image would continue
to flourish.[150]

Several recent readings of this altarpiece have proposed
more specifically that aspects of Cosimo's patronage at
San Marco, especially the images in the private cell where
he could take communion, and the adjacent balcony from
which after 1450 he could view the friar's liturgical activities before the altarpiece he had endowed, have their
chief precedents in princely practice, revealing princely
pretensions that he dare not express in more practical
political form.[151] This last suggestion makes no sense in
the context of Florentine society and culture. Florentines
read the texts of images and buildings as naturally as they
did the texts of laws or notarial acts. Such "political" messages as they sent were as easily interpreted, and either
applauded or condemned, as were aspects of Cosimo's
behavior in government. He was prized and praised for
his service to the community in his building and decoration of churches, as for his role in Florentine warfare
and diplomacy. He was resented and criticized for the
extravagance of his palace, as he was for his manipulation
of electoral scrutinies and his use of special commissions
(*balie*) to exert ever more direct control over the affairs
of the republic. In interpreting the images of Cosimo's
artistic patronage, we need to take account of the particular nature of Florentine political, civic, and devotional
life, and Cosimo's role in it, and of the complex and
subtle relation in this society between politics, religion
and art.

There is plenty of evidence, not least from his own
letters, that Cosimo worked ceaselessly, through personal
and political patronage, to make himself the most powerful citizen of Florence, and that in doing so he pushed
the republican constitution to its limits. However, there
seems to be no explicit evidence that he aspired to be a
prince, like the rulers of European states or even those of
Italy. His patronage of art is comparable in scale and
extravagance to theirs, but its themes were essentially
those dear to his fellow citizens and patrons in Florence.
Everything that Cosimo said and did, in private letters or
public debate, about politics, himself, and Florence, is
framed in terms of the commune; the opportunities it
offered him, and the constraints it imposed. The city
needed Cosimo's wealth, prestige, and political judgment,
and his fellow citizens allowed him in return to exercise
unprecedented authority in the state. However, Florence
in Cosimo's time remained a republic; he was not its
prince, and he did not rule it. While it endured, the
Florentine republic needed no legitimation beyond its
constitution, and Cosimo's authority could find none in
this context.[152]

The commune as a political form belonged essentially to the classical world; it was an anomaly in medieval Christian political theory, whose imagery did not fit it. The audience of Angelico's altarpiece may have read in it an analogy between Christ's authority over the world and the Medici family's authority in Florence; but the many were not easily translated into one. Notably, Cosimo's contemporary encomiasts preferred to compare him with Plato's wise helmsman of the ship of state.[153] While Florentines saw their city as an analogue of the Heavenly Jerusalem, their Jerusalem was a mercantile republic, and King Herod was an archetype of mankind's enemy.[154] The One in heaven signified many on earth; as a Florentine citizen speaking in a political debate rather awkwardly suggested, "Even as Christ is to be revered as one God, so are you lord Priors . . ."[155] The model of correspondence and congruence between heaven and earth that sprang most naturally to Florentine minds was the pyramid or chain of patronage, linking friends of the friends; at its apex was the Lord of Heaven and earth. While some of his *amici* might describe Cosimo as their "God on earth," most preferred to regard him, like the saints, as their "very special friend."

The only unmistakable messages of images are visual. Many patrons had their onomastic saints included in devotional images. What is extraordinary in the altarpiece Angelico painted for Cosimo is the fundamental place of the Medici saints in its perfectly integrated structure, achieved in the play of vertical against horizontal, the illusion of infinite recession. Many laymen continued until the end of the fifteenth century to prefer the Gothic form of the polyptych in which the saints were segregated in separate compartments of the wooden frame. Under Cosimo's patronage, Fra Angelico was an innovator in using the large, single field of the *pala*, which enabled artists to represent actual people in a unified space with real depth. No other form could have served so well to convey the complex message of this image concerning a chain of intercession linking heaven and earth, the viewer with the Virgin, the continuity between the world outside the frame with which Saint Cosmas mediates, and the celestial court and gardens of paradise located in the realm of eternity.[156] By his fusion of form and content the artist created associations that range, uninterrupted, from reminders of the power of Medici patrons to dispense charity and liberality to the convent and the community it served, to an assertion of their direct connection with their saintly patrons and intercessors, soliciting the liberality of the Virgin in the hope of their own salvation, and that of all Florence.[157]

BUILDING "FOR THE HONOR OF GOD,
AND THE HONOR OF THE CITY,
AND THE MEMORY OF ME"

COSIMO, "PRESERVER OF CHURCHES AND HOLY PLACES"

The last chapter discussed the religious images Cosimo commissioned for churches or chapels, and their relevance to his personal concerns about salvation, a crucial motive for his patronage that has been generally neglected. We saw how these representations reinforced Cosimo's image as a patron able to promote not only the secular ambitions, but also the spiritual welfare of his Florentine supporters, by his charity to the Church and his association with its saints. This chapter will examine the many intertwined interests – of the Medici family, their neighbors, the Florentine citizenry at large, the papacy, and the religious orders – served by Cosimo's most characteristic and conspicuous activity as a patron – building.

This account of the Renaissance patron's point of view began with Giovanni Rucellai's observation that there are two things men do in this world – procreate and build. Also noted was Cosimo's regret that he had not spent more money earlier on building, since he expected that this would be his most enduring memorial. In fact Cosimo, like his father before him, projected himself into the future through both his progeny and his building patronage. The commitments Cosimo inherited from his father, Giovanni di Bicci, shaped his career as a builder of churches. Although there is much less evidence of private patronage in the early years of the fifteenth century, the origins of Cosimo's patronage may be seen in Giovanni's interest in San Lorenzo, San Marco, and Bosco ai Frati.

By the time he died, Cosimo had to his credit a significant body of work which his son Piero helped bring to completion, with further decoration of the Badia, and the erection of his father's tomb in San Lorenzo. Piero and Giovanni followed the pattern of dynastic continuity laid down in the patronage of Cosimo and his brother

Lorenzo, memorializing themselves and their father at the same time. It is difficult – and in many ways inappropriate – to try to distinguish too sharply between commissions for which Cosimo was personally responsible, and those undertaken by his sons in his lifetime. It is inconceivable that Piero would have constructed chapels at San Miniato and Santissima Annuziata except, as Filarete observed "at the wish of his father," just as it is unimaginable that Piero would seriously have diverged, while Cosimo was alive, from the political policies his father spelled out in letters to Piero as his own life drew to its close.[1] Thus, Piero's main commissions for churches are considered here, alongside Cosimo's, in the general context of Medicean building.

A patriarchal drive to self-perpetuation, and a rather austere personal devotion were aspects of Cosimo's identity expressed in his church building program. By the same process as family loyalties and obligations were extended to neighbors and friends in his patronage network, Cosimo's activities as a builder of churches extended outward from his own neighborhood to embrace the city and *contado* beyond it. On Piero del Massaio's map of Florence around 1460, the city is viewed from the north, so that the Medici quarter of San Giovanni appears in the foreground. Picking out, with the mind's eye, the religious foundations which benefited from Medici intervention, it is notable that the main ones are relatively near to Cosimo's palace and other Medici houses lining the Via Largha, from San Lorenzo hard by, then north and east to San Marco and Santissima Annunziata (fig. 65).

Santa Croce by the river, and San Miniato at the top of a hill to the south of the city, just beyond its walls, are outside the Medici territorial and electoral neighborhood.[2] But Fiesole, where Cosimo's younger son Giovanni built a villa, the Medici family helped to renovate the church of San Girolamo, and Cosimo rebuilt the Badia, is set on a hill to the north, overlooking Florence. Just beyond, on the other side of the mountains, is the Mugello, where the Medici family had extensive estates and their villas of Cafaggiolo and Trebbio, and where they rebuilt the convent of Bosco ai Frati, near San Piero a Sieve. The suburban villa of Careggi also lay to the north, off the main road to the Mugello and on to Bologna. In the early migrations into Florence from the surrounding countryside, settlers tended to cluster in the districts of the city nearest the areas of the *contado* whence they had come.[3] In accordance with a similar principle of geographical association, Medici patronage of churches flowed outward from their neighborhood on the fringe of the city center, mainly in the path of their own constant movement between city and countryside.

If, from one point of view, Medici patronage of churches may be seen as the extension of the devotional environment of the family, their friends, and their neighbors, contemporary comments suggest additional perspectives. Filarete described Cosimo's commissions not in terms of any secular or geographical associations, but in relation to the wide range of religious orders which were recipients of his charity. He balanced the building at San Marco for the Dominicans with the considerably less expensive intervention at Santa Croce for the Franciscans. San Lorenzo and the Badia at Fiesole for the Augustinians were mentioned in the same breath, and he went on to note Medici patronage of the Servi at the Angeli, of the Benedictines at San Miniato, and "various places belonging to the Observant friars of San Francesco and of other religious orders, of women and of men, which one sees were built by him in many places."[4] If local foundations such as San Lorenzo and San Marco were closest to the family's hearts, as to their hearth, Medici patronage may well have developed as Filarete perceived it, into the largesse of a great patron extending across the ecclesiastical board into every corner of the city and out into its dominions, as Medici influence and authority in government was extended in the course of Cosimo's lifetime.

The analogous extension of Cosimo's identity as a man and patron of churches, from the domestic and local responsibilities of *paterfamilias* and *padrino* to those of the city's *pater patriae*, is a logical development of the patriarchal ethos that structured the lives and concerns of fifteenth-century Florentines. This ethos was strongly reinforced by a system of Christian beliefs, which incorporated and transcended secular conceptions of patronage in the interests of the institutional church. Florentines also regarded patronage of the Church as the fulfilment of a civic duty to contribute to the good of the commune, for which Cosimo was much praised.[5]

Dante stressed the closely related roles of Church and state in the life of the individual, not only through the entire structure of his epic poem, but in his numerous portraits of the people he encountered in the after-life. Giovanni Dominici set his influential seal on this conjunction in a sermon delivered on Ash Wednesday 1406, enjoining each member of his audience to "defend the *patria* . . . as a true man, a true Christian, a true Florentine."[6] Celebrations of the feasts of the Church, particularly Epiphany and the birthday of the city's patron, John the Baptist, were subsidized by the city, staged by laymen and secular groups, and supported by civic dignitaries; civic triumphs like the capture of Pisa in 1406, or the victory at Anghiari in 1440, were celebrated by church services, and solemnized by the display of miraculous images, like the Madonna of Impruneta.[7] According to Giovanni Rucellai, it was Florence's churches that made her "the most beautiful, the most noble, the finest city in the world, since the Florentines have the most worthy *patria* in all Christendom."[8]

While modern historians debate whether Cosimo's conspicuous patronage of churches was motivated by politics or piety, his contemporaries naturally assumed he could have it both ways. Giovanni Giugni, a Medici partisan and Podestà of Pisa, a city subject to the Florentine state and the site of an important subsidiary of the Medici bank, promised Piero that if Cosimo acceded to his plea to rebuild the church of San Francesco in Pisa, he would enjoy "fame everlasting in this city," and by implication, life everlasting in the heavenly city.[9] At the same time, it would be characteristic of Cosimo to have expressed his own ambivalence on this score in his profoundly equivocal reply, reported by Vespasiano da Bisticci, to the observation of an acquaintance that he must feel confident of salvation in view of his vast charity to the Church. Cosimo supposedly responded: "God knows why I did it; if I did it for glory and the pomp of the world, I will be rewarded according to what I have done."[10]

INHERITED COMMITMENTS, PATERNAL AND PAPAL

An important part of Cosimo's patrimony were the relationships his father had forged with dignitaries of the Church. Cosimo's close personal association with a series of popes, from John XXIII through Martin V, Eugenius IV, and Nicholas V to Pius II, conspicuously empowered him as a patron in the eyes of the Florentine people. The most dramatic example of this was Cosimo's intervention with Eugenius IV to increase the indulgences granted at

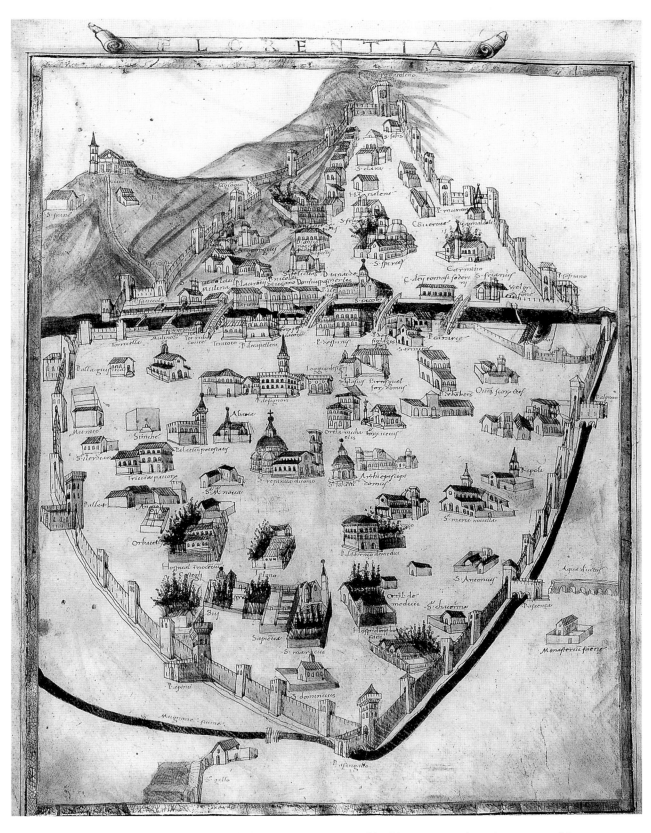

65 Workshop of Piero del Massaio, map of Florence, 1462, Paris, Bibliothèque Nationale, MS Lat. 4802, fol. 132v

the consecration of the cathedral.[11] Although Florence and the Medici were not always to be united in such harmony with the papacy, Cosimo saw his obligations to God, the Church and the pope as very closely related, observing of his support of Pius II's crusade to the Holy Land, "What I have promised to do, I do first for the honor of God, then for the honor of his Holiness, and ultimately for the sake of my own soul."[12] Cosimo's close friend Ambrogio Traversari, prior of the Angeli, once wrote to him that "your devotion to sacred matters will benefit you more than any affairs of public or private business, no matter how zealously undertaken."[13] The sacred matters of interest to Traversari were to include not only Cosimo's building and decoration of churches and chapels, but also his furnishing of a great library of religious texts for San Marco, and later for the Badia, as well as his personal and financial support for the council convened in 1438/9 to unite the Eastern and Western churches.

In a manner analogous to his handling of political issues in communal councils, where, in accordance with Cicero's advice to statesmen, Cosimo took care to build upon the foundation of other peoples' opinions,[14] before he became an independent patron of churches, he chose to associate himself with some notable projects undertaken by others. Toward the end of the second decade of the fifteenth century, he supported the sculptural program for the façade of the oratory of Orsanmichele, built around its miraculous Madonna, and representing the confluence of Florentines' devotional, civic, and artistic aspirations. Cosimo and his father Giovanni di Bicci were major contributors to the financing of Ghiberti's bronze statue of Saint Matthew, commissioned for the niche of the Banker's Guild in 1419; at this time father and son were among the wealthiest and most illustrious members of the guild, and Cosimo was one of four *operai* responsible for the commission.[15] A few years later Giovanni and his son, as executors of Pope John XXIII's will, were responsible for his tomb erected in the Florentine baptistery (fig. 66). This commission was awarded to Donatello and Michelozzo, soon to become Cosimo's most favored artists; the monument itself testifies to the strong links in the early fifteenth century between Florence, the Medici family, and the papacy.[16]

The tomb of John XXIII

Giovanni di Bicci de' Medici seems to have become acquainted with Baldassare Cossa between 1386 and 1397, when he was in Rome establishing the Medici bank. The bank then moved to Florence, and as cardinal legate

in Bologna, Cossa maintained a personal account with it; large sums of money changed hands between the two men, and in his letters to Giovanni, Cossa addressed him as "my most dear friend."[17] Cossa was elected Pope John XXIII in 1410; in 1413 he fled from Rome. His close association with the Medici in the intervening years probably put them at the head of the curial bankers, a position which was confirmed when in 1421 Martin V appointed the manager of the Medici bank at the papal Curia depositary of the apostolic chamber. Thereafter, for the best part of four decades, the Medici were the pope's exclusive bankers, handling most of the enormous financial resources of the Church. Their business with the papal court was the basis of the family's wealth, as their wealth was the basis of their political influence in Florence.[18]

Associates of the Medici bank, headed by Ilarione de' Bardi, accompanied the papal Curia to the Council of Constance; Cosimo was among those to whom the pope issued safe-conducts for the journey.[19] After John XXIII was deposed by the council in 1414, Florence's leading statesmen supported him. He fled, was captured, and then imprisoned in Germany, where Giovanni di Bicci's agent Bartolomeo de' Bardi, soon to be manager of the Medici bank at Rome, went to arrange his release;[20] the ransom of three and half thousand florins was paid through the Medici bank in Venice in April 1419. John died six months later, and Giovanni de' Medici, Niccolò da Uzzano, Bartolomeo Valori, and Vieri Guadagni, four of the most influential members of the inner circle of the Florentine *reggimento*, were named as executors of his will.[21]

Pope John had been particularly popular in Florence, by comparison with his successor Martin V, who inspired the derisive jingle, "Papa Martino/ . . . non vale un quattrino [is not worth tuppence]."[22] The Florentine government sponsored and subsidized John XXIII's spectacular funeral ceremonies, which lasted nine days, and cost three hundred florins. The pope had bequeathed to the city a precious relic – the finger of John the Baptist – to be conserved in the Florentine baptistery. Nevertheless, in fulfilling the pope's wish to be buried there, his executors effected a major coup.[23] The baptistery, believed to be a Roman structure, was the oldest and holiest sanctuary in the city. Athough from the fourteenth century heads of other states, like the doges of Venice, were buried in baptisteries, in republican Florence only three medieval bishops had previously been buried in the baptistery. Their marble sarcophagi were extremely simple, blending harmoniously and inconspicuously with the black and white marble walls against which they stood. When the proposal for John XXIII's tomb was sub-

66   Donatello and Michelozzo, tomb of John XXIII, Florence, baptistery

mitted to members of the Calimala, the international merchants' guild responsible for the baptistery and its decoration, they objected that the tomb would entirely alter the appearance of the sanctuary. After much discussion, Palla Strozzi on their behalf acceded to "a tomb, yes, but plain and straightforward, so as not to intrude into the main area of the church, since it is no mean honor to be buried there at all, and that must suffice."[24]

In the boldness of its design and the brilliance of its execution, the monument eventually produced amply justified Strozzi's apprehensions. In terms of scale, materials, and siting – not to mention style and workmanship – the magnificent tomb made by Donatello and his partner Michelozzo for "John XXIII, quondam Papa" dominated the interior of the building.[25] Located just to the right of the apse, it was framed and supported by two of the massive oriental granite columns which defined the lower order of the architecture. Occupying the whole of the space between them, the monument rose to a height of twenty-four feet. Particularly when picked out by the rays of the sun in early morning, when most Florentines attended church services, the gilded bronze effigy of the former pope set at its mid-point gleamed, in contrast with the monochrome sobriety of the rest of the interior, designed to allow the mosaics in the apse and cupola to command the viewer's attention. In its most distinctive and innovative feature – its incorporation into the architecture of the site – it embodied the fifteenth-century proverbial image of those who increased their own stature by attaching themselves to others already established, like a man who by two successive marriages became "attached to a great column."[26] By the artist's adoption of the symbolism of the Last Judgment that dominated the medieval decoration of the baptistery, the tomb anchored the memory of John XXIII firmly in Florentine minds in the context of compelling symbols of birth, death, and resurrection, at the same time intruding the papal presence into a space otherwise dedicated to corporate religious and civic rites.

It was also strongly associated with Cosimo de' Medici. He was considered by Florentines of the succeeding century, among them Vasari, as its effective patron. Sarah McHam suggested that Cosimo perhaps encouraged the production of such a commanding monument as part of a "carefully disguised tactic of Medici self-promotion."[27] This ultimately unanswerable question of Cosimo's intentions arises again and again. Did the Medici encourage their friends to spend lavishly on enterprises which by association would enhance the Medicean image, while remaining free of such negative implications of self-aggrandizement as might attach to their personal commissions? Did Cosimo's role in building John XXIII's

tomb express more than Florentines' recognition of the value to their city of Medici wealth and influence, and its foundation in the favor of the papal court?

Florentines gladly accommodated foreign patronage to embellish Florence, and many commissions, including those of the Gonzaga at the Annunziata and the Scolari at the Angeli, involved Medici brokerage.[28] Donatello's work for the Opera del Duomo and the guilds was, by the 1420s, so admired that citizens would surely have welcomed any commission giving him an opportunity to do something innovative and impressive. Clearly Cosimo and these two sculptors were seen as a winning team. Cosimo was later named as executor for the tombs of Cardinal Brancacci and the apostolic secretary Aragazzi; both commissions went to Donatello and Michelozzo, and are indebted stylistically to their papal tomb in the baptistery.[29] The nearest prototype for the baptistery tomb was the memorial in Santa Croce for the Bardi del Vernio, Cosimo's wife Contessina's family. If Cosimo is to be credited with transforming the modest proposal approved by the Calimala guild into a major monument, he may have had a role in this resemblance.[30]

Cosimo and Eugenius IV

By the mid-1430s Cosimo and Pope Eugenius had become close personal associates. Eugenius (Gabriel Condulmer) was a native of Venice, where both Florence and the Medici had important ties; Venice had long been Florence's chief ally in the peninsular's almost constant wars, and the city was the site of Giovanni di Bicci's first banking office outside of Florence and Rome. The Medici were firmly established as papal financiers; the managers of the bank in Rome had advanced the expenses for Martin V's funeral and Eugenius IV's coronation.[31] Shortly before his exile Cosimo, anticipating a move against him, entrusted his money to the safekeeping of the Church. In May 1433, three thousand Venetian ducats in coin were transferred from the residence of Ilarione de Bardi, manager of the bank in Florence, and placed in the care of the Benedictine hermits of San Miniato al Monte. Another 5,977 ducats were entrusted to the then Silvestrine convent of San Marco. Cosimo and his brother Lorenzo sold ten thousand florins worth of Monte stock to their branch in Rome, partly to pay off anxious creditors.[32] However, such had been the credit of the Medici bank in papal circles since the late fourteenth century that, according to Vespasiano, "everywhere [Cosimo's] credit increased, rather than diminished; and many in Rome who were his creditors, seeing such largesse, reinvested their money in the bank."[33]

Exiled to Padua, Cosimo, with the support of the Venetian doge, successfully petitioned to be transferred to Venice, where some of the business of the Medici bank could be carried on at its Venetian branch. Threatened by his enemies in Rome, Eugenius IV took refuge in Florence in June 1434, while Cosimo was still in Venice. In September 1434 a pro-Medicean Signoria was drawn from the electoral purses. When the anti-Medicean forces massed in the piazza behind the palace of the Priors, intending to assault and depose them before they could recall Cosimo and his family, the pope sent his legate, the *condottiere* Giovanni Vitelleschi, to intervene. Vitelleschi persuaded the wavering rebels to accept Eugenius's mediation; on their way across town to the papal apartments in the Dominican convent of Santa Maria Novella, the rebel group lost its momentum and deserted its leaders. As the chronicler Cavalcanti quipped, thanks to the pope's *fede* – a verbal play on faith, trust, and bankers' promissory notes – the Mediceans prevailed, and Cosimo was recalled.[34] The papal contribution to this outcome appears to be acknowledged in the honors accorded Vitelleschi; in December 1434 he was made a citizen of Florence and allowed to invest in its funded debt, the Monte, and in October 1435 he was appointed archbishop of Florence, although he held that office only briefly.[35]

The pope stayed on in Florence, which was his base on and off for almost a decade; while he was resident there, his apartments at Santa Maria Novella became the effective center of papal government. The papal quarters were lavishly maintained; the commune commissioned for them from Donatello a sculpture of its emblem, the Marzocco, the lion which stood at the foot of the stairs in the entrance hall. When Piero de' Medici saw the splendid door made for the hospital of San Paolo on the other side of the *piazza* from Santa Maria Novella, he commandeered it for the papal residence; the prior of San Paolo was obliged to commission another.[36] Although Giovanni the cobbler, in his poem on the consecration of the cathedral, spoke of this time in which "Florence rested in the lap of Pope Eugenius," it was Florence in fact who gave the pope shelter. As Cosimo grew stronger in Florence and Eugenius grew weaker in Rome, their interdependence deepened.

The presence of the papal court impinged upon many artistic commissions, particularly those of the Medici, in these years that saw the completion of the cathedral cupola, the rebuilding of San Marco, and the council of the Eastern and Western churches, an event that left its traces on images all over the city. Although by the time

Eugenius left Florence for Bologna in 1443 his relations with Florence and the Medici were cooling, he stayed long enough to reconsecrate San Marco to Saints Cosmas and Damian as well as Saint Mark, and he spent his last night in Florence in the new convent, in Cosimo's cell. The Medici family's profound involvement with the fortunes of the Church throughout most of Cosimo's lifetime cannot be described as essentially financial, political, or personal; Cosimo and his family sustained and were sustained by the body of the Church and its head in many senses which their patronage richly expresses.[37]

IUS PATRONATUS AND BOSCO AI FRATI

Cosimo's interest in the Observant Franciscan convent of Bosco ai Frati, renovated at his expense some time between the late 1420s and the late 1440s, was another legacy of his family's patronage – personal, ecclesiastical, and territorial. His rebuilding of this convent in the Mugello, only a few miles from the Medici villa of Cafaggiolo, redounded to his spiritual credit, but it was also part of the give and take of his patronage as the major landholder of the district around San Piero a Sieve. He gave his support to the convent when he took possession of the surrounding estates.

In the crucible of the so-called War of the Eight Saints from 1375–8, Florentine statesmen like Guido del Palagio learned to defend the secular domain against the incursions of clerical privilege, asserted by the pope. The commune made a committment to lay control of churches by local patrons, who claimed rights over appointments to ecclesiastical offices. While these "rights" were not always strictly in accordance with ecclesiastical law, in practice patrons' wishes in such matters as the election of rectors were usually observed; their charity to local parishes and convents created local interest groups which helped to reinforce *ius patronandi*.[38] Many leading Florentine families exercised such local patronage; the Medici were unusual only in the extent of their sphere of influence. As the fifteenth century progressed, they maneuvered to control appointments to key offices of the Church, as of the state, throughout Tuscany. While the complex relationship between the Medici patronage network, the papacy, and the Church in Tuscany remains to be explored, these connections clearly shaped and found expression in Cosimo's preeminent patronage of churches, both urban and rural.[39]

Since the twelfth century, the Medici family had possessed large landholdings in the Mugello. The main artery of the old Via Bolognese began just outside the city gate

67   Map of
Medici district in
the Mugello

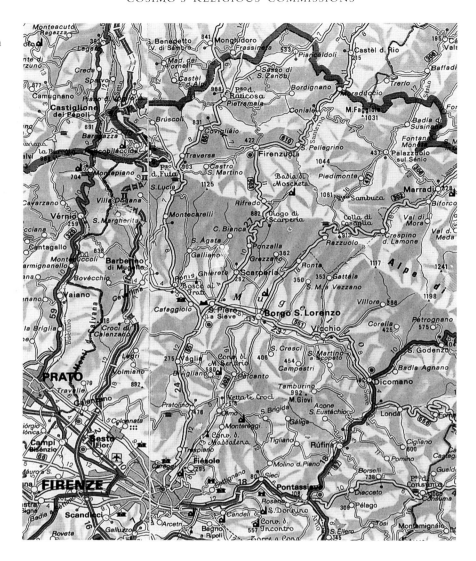

68 (*facing page*)
Michelozzo, San
Francesco al
Bosco (Bosco ai
Frati), San Piero
a Sieve

– the Porta San Gallo at the end of the Via Larga where
the Medici had their houses – and wound northwards
past Careggi lying to the west, through Vaglia and on
into the Appenines. At the junction of the roads to Imola
and Faenza lies San Piero a Sieve, to the east Borgo San
Lorenzo (fig. 67). This triangle was the heart of Medici
territory, marked by the "dwelling, or rather fortress, of
Cafaggiolo," just off the Via Bolognese, and the castle of
Trebbio, overlooking the road north from its perch on
a high hill to the south of Cafaggiolo. Further north are
the communes of Gagliano, Barberino di Mugello, and
Scarperia; to the extreme northeast lies Marradi, on the
border between Florentine territory and the lands controlled by Cosimo's sometime friends, the Manfredi lords
of Faenza. Medici patronage of communal offices was
firmly established in this territory; the most trusted of

their friends regularly held the posts of Podestà and
Captain at Scarperia, Marradi, and Borgo San Lorenzo,
and the Medici name commanded respect and tribute
from the people of these small towns.[40] At the wedding
in 1433 of Francesco di Giuliano, grandson of Averardo,
Cosimo's cousin and then owner of Cafaggiolo, the
young couple received gifts from Ulivieri di Brucolino
of Ghagliano, factor of the estate, and tributes of food
from the communes of Santa Maria a Campiano, San
Piero a Sieve, Bruscholi, Castro, and Ronta.[41]

San Piero a Sieve was the region's market and administrative center, and according to later compilations of the
original records patronage rights over its church passed in
1356 from Giovanni di Ghino d'Alidosio da Caldaia to
the Medici family. In July 1462, Alamanno de' Medici
wrote to Giovanni di Cosimo that

since at this time I have been told that the parish of San Piero a Sieve has fallen vacant, and its *padroni* are the Count Vanni, Bernardo di Leonardo de' Medici and me, and since we have to provide another parish priest as required, I am happy for my part that all and whatever authority I have to carry out this election be delegated to you, for I am absolutely certain that by your intervention the spiritual health of the parish will be taken care of as I am sure you desire . . . may the Almighty preserve you in all happiness . . .

Bernardo's son, Leonardo, bishop of Forlì, became parish priest at San Piero from 1482 to 1528, when he completely rebuilt the church.[42]

Only a few miles west of San Piero a Sieve and a couple of miles north of Cafaggiolo, on the road toward Gabbiano and Gagliano, was the convent known as Bosco ai Frati, for its location in a wooded area (fig. 68).[43] It flourished with the fortunes of the ancient feudal family of the Ubaldini, and passed in the early thirteenth century to the Franciscans. After the Black Death it was abandoned, but at some time in an interval of silence in the records, the brothers adopted the Observant rule, converted perhaps, like so many similar houses, by San Bernardino. According to the convent's chronicle, now lost but consulted by a sixteenth-century copyist, a new phase of its life began "around the year 1420 [when] the Magnificent Cosimo di Giovanni de' Medici . . . bought from the Ubaldini lords, previously *padroni* with authority over the area, many possessions in the Mugello around the convent of San Francesco al Bosco, and became *patrono* of that place." The convent was included "because it was attached to the temporal possessions, although as a spiritual foundation it could not be sold."[44]

Although the villas of Cafaggiolo and Trebbio had their own chapels, Cosimo and his family often chose to worship at Bosco ai Frati. In one of his many letters to Piero, Francesco Fracassini, the factor at Cafaggiolo, wrote that Contessina had ridden over that morning with Giuliano and Lorenzo and the rest of the household to hear High Mass there.[45] An anecdote of Vespasiano's concerns Cosimo's visits to Bosco for spiritual converse; on one occasion, having talked with a particularly learned brother of various matters, he asked as he was leaving if he had a Bible they could consult, "so that they could see the texts they were reconsidering." When the friar said no, he had a portable Bible bought and gave it to the friar the next day, begging him to pray to God for his soul.[46] To the younger generation, the friars were a byword for virtue and obedience. Lorenzo and Giuliano, during a retreat to Cafaggiolo in June 1464 on account of the plague, informed their father: "We arrived here safely yesterday morning . . . Upon our arrival we arranged that Maestro Zanobi's family should go to Gagliano, and we had it made known in the neighborhood that anyone who might go to Florence or any other place where the contagion is should not return here . . . and up to now we have observed your orders so well, that between us and the brothers of Bosco there is very little difference . . ."[47]

The early history of the Medici interest in rebuilding the convent is illuminated by Crispin Robinson's discovery of several important documents. As with the commissions for the tombs of Pope John XXIII and Cardinal Brancacci, and the furnishing of a library for San Marco, the Medici had first become involved with the convent as executors for the bequest of a friend or associate. As early as 1411 the branch manager of the Medici bank in Venice, Giovanni di Francesco da Gagliano, named Giovanni di Bicci and Cosimo as executors of his will, which provided for the testator's burial, and masses to be said "at the place of the brothers of Bosco in the Mugello." Giovanni da Gagliano, as his name implies, was a native of the small town of Gagliano just north of the convent. He may have been a neighbor as well as an employee of Giovanni di Bicci, since the latter declared in his 1427 tax report "a house in Gagliano for my own occupation."[48] Throughout Cosimo's lifetime the Medici continued to own, and to acquire property there, to protect its residents' interests, and to enjoy their protection in return.[49] A certain Piero da Gagliano put so much trust in the Medici that he left negotiations for the sale of his house, which they wanted to buy, entirely in their hands: "and concerning the price, I will leave everything up to

you, since you understand my needs better than I do myself . . . I will be most happy with whatever you do on my account."[50] Piero da Gagliano reappears alongside his Medici friends as one of the major patrons of the rebuilding of Santissima Annunziata.[51]

The provisions of Giovanni da Gagliano's will were implemented by his Medici executors between 1417 and 1419. Money was provided for vestments and repairs to the convent, particularly for the roof, as well as for the commemoration of the donor's soul. A 1416 codicil to his will shows that Giovanni da Gagliano was close to another Medici who was a brother of the Observant Franciscan congregation of San Damiano in Assisi. Fra Romulo de' Medici, encouraged perhaps by his kinsmen's involvement with Bosco through the bequest of their mutual friend, later sought their patronage for his own congregation. Having visited the Medici house in Venice and found the family absent, he wrote to Giovanni di Bicci declaring that "not only I, but all our kin must treat you as a father to be revered." He added that upon seeing at the house a "figure of Our Lady and by her side Saints Cosmas and Damian, I felt myself inspired by God, and wondering whether you [too] were a devotee of these glorious saints, and about how God had granted you the good fortune of temporal possessions."[52]

Giovanni da Gagliano's modest bequest proved insufficient to meet the needs of the friars, and this responsibility was soon assumed by the Medici themselves. Cosimo became *patrono* of the convent when he acquired the land on which it stood in 1420, shortly after Giovanni di Bicci handed over the business of the Medici bank to his elder son.[53] The precise date of his building, and the identity of its architect, are uncertain. According to its chronicler, Cosimo completely rebuilt the convent between 1420 and 1438. Vespasiano, claiming that Cosimo spent 1,500 florins on the work at Bosco ai Frati, seemed to place it after the renovations of San Marco, in the 1440s or 1450s. His reference to the convent may, however, have alluded only to the delivery of a choir book and missals, which his shop supplied to Cosimo, rather than to the building itself.[54] The architecture would seem to confirm the chronicler's earlier date, when the architectural vocabulary of Michelozzo, to whom the building is generally attributed, was being defined in the context of his work at Santa Trinita.[55] Work continued on into the 1440s. Bosco appears in the list of ongoing expenses noted after Lorenzo di Giovanni's death in 1440, and is named in the 1451 division of property between Cosimo and Lorenzo's son, Pierfrancesco. At this time the cadet branch was absolved of all responsibilities for this work, although Lorenzo's name appears together with Cosimo's on books provided for the convent.[56]

The chronicler observed that Cosimo preferred an architectural style "which had a touch of the modern, but was nevertheless appropriate to the Friars, that is, it should not be too sumptuous." Despite the debate about magnificence prompted by Cosimo's patronage at the Badia, this comment might seem an appropriate description not only of Bosco, but also of Cosimo's taste, or of Michelozzo's interpretation of it, at the sites of San Marco and the Badia. At the same time, the plain form of the church was one generally "favored by the Observants because of its simplicity of design, sobriety of space, lack of ostentation, and low cost."[57] A distinctive feature characteristic of Cosimo's commissions is the concern with the garden *loggia* and a well, and the "landscaping" of the site. "Because the wood that the Ubaldini lords gave us didn't seem to him large enough for his purposes, he arranged that the oaks should be allowed to grow around it, where before they were cut back every few years, and he gave to the convent that wood which today seems more sparse than the old one, nearer to the convent, which I believe surrounds it for more than a mile, and he left the use of that wood freely up to the brothers."[58]

The convent's chronicler thought Medici patronage served to increase "the credit of the religion and household of the Observants, and the devotion of laymen," among the primary goals of the Florentine people as expressed in popular religious culture. These achievements were further enhanced when in 1436, on his way to Ferrara, Pope Eugenius "by arrangement of the Magnificent Cosimo . . . came to Cafaggiolo, and because of his love for Cosimo, and because he was very well-disposed toward the household of the Observants, he left orders by word of mouth, which he made known to the district, a great indulgence for visitors to Bosco." San Bernardino added his blessing to the enterprise when he also visited the convent, and in 1449 it was the site of the chapter general of four hundred brothers, to whom Cosimo offered the hospitality of Cafaggiolo.[59]

The Medici paid for the church, with its tower and bell, and the sacristy, dormitory, cloister, and loggia in front of the church. These were liberally adorned with their arms, which also labeled the altarpiece painted for the church by Fra Angelico. San Bernardino's "IHS" monogram decorates the door which leads from the cloister to the sacristy, as it does the ceiling of the Medici palace chapel. Nowhere do the Medici balls appear to such startling effect as on the capitals of the pilasters of the choir, where they replace the customary orders (fig. 69). As Robinson observed, the frieze of *palle* reappears in the apse at San Marco, in the little chapel at nearby Trebbio, and in the first corridor and cloister at Santissima Annunziata.[60] All these buildings are attributed to

69   Bosco ai Frati, detail of capitals decorated with Medici *palle*

Michelozzo. Perhaps in this small feature of design the architect expressed most explicitly his commitment to the perpetuation in stone of his patrons' *fama*.

SAN MARCO

In the period of his early commissions, Cosimo's political influence in the city was great, according to Cavalcanti, on account of the esteem he inherited from his father.[61] It was growing, with the cultivation by Cosimo and his cousin Averardo of a group of partisans whose names were beginning to preponderate in the electoral purses from which the city's major offices were drawn. But alongside Cosimo still towered the figures of such elder statesmen as Bartolomeo Valori, Niccolò da Uzzano, Vieri Guadagni, and Ridolfo Peruzzi; they and citizens like them were also important patrons of art. In addition to the Da Uzzano palace, which preceded that of the Medici as the first great monumental palace of the fifteenth century,[62] major private commissions of the 1420s and early 1430s were made by leading families including the Barbadori, Rondinelli, Carnesecchi, Brancacci, and Strozzi. Brunelleschi designed the Barbadori chapel in Santa Felicita which was the prototype for the Medici old sacristy at San Lorenzo, and Lippi's Barbadori altarpiece, which predated his major work for the

Medici, is generally regarded as indisputably one of the most unconventional and inventive works of its time.[63] Masaccio and Masolino's ground-breaking frescoes were done for the Brancacci family chapel in the Carmine, and Palla Strozzi's commissions for Santa Trinita included Gentile da Fabriano's Magi altarpiece, a model for the succeeding century for representations of the Magi throughout Italy, including those in the Medici palace. The classicizing arcosolium tomb Palla had made *circa* 1423 for his father, Nofri, was imitated in many others of the 1440s and 1450s, among them a group of monuments commissioned by members of the Medici family and their more eminent friends.[64]

The Medici position in the mid-1420s as one of a group of patrons powerful in the *reggimento* seems aptly imaged in Masaccio's now lost fresco of the consecration (known as "the Sagra") of the church of the Carmine in 1422. Partially recorded in drawings from the late fifteenth and early sixteenth centuries (fig. 70), it depicted a group of the city's dignitaries including, according to Vasari, the artists Brunelleschi, Donatello and Masolino, Antonio Brancacci, the original patron of the Carmine chapel, Niccolò da Uzzano, Bartolommeo Valori, and Giovanni di Bicci de' Medici.[65] These last three, along with Vieri Guadagni, had recently served as joint-executors of the commission for John XXIII's tomb.

Valori, were dead. Vieri Guadagni, the Brancacci, and Palla Strozzi, who had acquiesced in the exile of Cosimo and his family in 1433, had been exiled in their turn. Masaccio was dead, Masolino had left Florence never to return. Brunelleschi, nearing sixty, and at the height of his renown, had just completed his cupola for the cathedral of Florence. He had finished the old sacristy, commissioned by Giovanni di Bicci, and Donatello was engaged in its decoration under the supervision of Giovanni's sons. Cosimo, approaching fifty, and driven by an urgent desire to expiate in charitable patronage the sins of a lifetime, turned to Pope Eugenius IV for advice.

Vespasiano, in his account of Cosimo's decision to rebuild San Marco, stressed that in the conduct of his business as a banker and politician, Cosimo had "accumulated quite a bit on his conscience, as most men do who govern states and want to be ahead of the rest." Wishing "God to have mercy on him, and to preserve him in the enjoyment of his temporal goods," Cosimo conferred with Pope Eugenius, who suggested he spend ten thousand florins on San Marco, to lift these burdens from his conscience (fig. 71). The conversation Vespasiano described was clearly a spiritual contract between the two men. When the renovation of the convent was complete, Eugenius issued a bull testifying to the expiatory effect of Cosimo's charity, and the opening lines were inscribed

70 Sixteenth-century drawing after Masaccio, *Sagra*, Folkestone Museum and Art Gallery

71 Michelozzo, Florence, Convent of San Marco, main cloister

Fourteen years later, when Cosimo stood on the brink of his first major independent building commission, most of those elder statesmen and patrons, including Giovanni di Bicci, Niccolò da Uzzano, and Bartolomeo

on the lintel of the sacristy door at San Marco: "CUM HOC TEMPLUM MARCO EVANGELISTE DICATUM MAGNIFICIS SUMPTIBUS CL. V. COSMI DE MEDICIS TANDEM ABSOLUTUM ESSET".[66]

Vespasiano's account also notes the agreement that if Cosimo would pay for the repair of the convent, Eugenius would transfer it from the Silvestrines to the Dominican Observants, which he did in 1436. This transfer was clearly in the papal interest; friars were the only orders who vowed direct obedience to the pope, the official papal theologian was usually a Dominican, and the papal apartments in Florence were attached to the city's main Dominican convent of Santa Maria Novella. The congregation of Observants at San Domenico at Fiesole was flourishing, and its expansion to a city site would increase its influence upon the urban community. In his biography of Eugenius, Vespasiano emphasized the pope's enduring ambition to foster reform of the Church by reimposing the strict observance of their original rule upon communities of conventual friars.

Why would Cosimo be eager to have the convent transferred to the Observant Dominicans? The pope's desire for reform was matched, it seems, by that of many pious lay patrons to associate themselves with it. The Observants, both Dominican and Franciscan, were becoming the main focus of lay patronage by the early fifteenth century. Guido del Palagio, the late trecento statesmen who was an exemplum for devout citizens, especially of the governing class, had been the patron of the first Observant Franciscan house in Tuscany, in a monastery near Fiesole. The construction nearby of the convent at San Domenico to house the Dominican Observants, whose congregation included Antoninus and Fra Angelico, was made possible by a bequest in 1418 from Barnaba degli Agli, whose family was prominent in the religious and devotional life of the city, and closely associated with the Medici.[67] Cosimo's earliest building project was apparently to rebuild Bosco ai Frati, bringing to fruition the hopes of his father's friend from Gagliano; the last example of Cosimo's notable patronage of the Observants was the renovation of the Badia of Fiesole, transferred from the Camaldolensians to the reformed Augustinians in 1440.[68]

The multiplication of Observant congregations was due partly to the impetus of the star preacher of the Observant Franciscans, Bernardino of Siena, whose immense popularity was reflected in references in literary scrapbooks and the widespread use of his distinctive emblem, a sun inscribed with the name of Jesus. The Medici, who used this emblem in their family chapel, were obviously impressed by this emissary for his reformist order. Cosimo was probably familiar with the famous sermons Bernardino delivered in Florence at Easter 1425. The Medici household often promoted the visits of popular preachers, and may well have attended this celebrated event; in any case copies of the sermons

were widely circulated. The convent of Bosco ai Frati had close ties with Bernardino, who was honored in the altarpiece for its church which Cosimo commissioned from Fra Angelico; the family had personally supported Bernardino's canonization, which occurred in 1450, a remarkably short time after his death.[69]

Cosimo's patronage at San Marco was one of many of his projects originating in papal actions, his father's concerns, and civic and neighborhood interests. Giovanni di Bicci, who kept in his bedchamber a copy of some works of Giovanni Dominici,[70] evinced interest in the patronage of San Marco as early as 1418. On 5 January 1419, the eve of Epiphany, which was specially celebrated at San Marco by the confraternity of the Magi associated with the Medici and their friends, Pope Martin V ordered an enquiry into the life of the Silvestrine congregation there.[71] According to documents in the archives of San Domenico in Fiesole, it was the parishioners of San Marco who requested that the convent be given to the Dominicans, because the Silvestrines lived "without poverty and without chastity." The bull Eugenius IV issued in 1436 makes no mention of this issue, referring only to the small numbers of the Silvestrines. An entry in the Deliberazioni of the Signoria and their advisory colleges recorded that the transfer finally took place at the request of the Signoria, on the initiative of Cosimo and his brother Lorenzo.[72]

As at their own parish church of San Lorenzo, so at San Marco the Medici took the lead in promoting the spiritual interests of the wider neighborhood on which their strength as personal and political patrons heavily depended. Medici houses and those of their partisans stretched the length of the Via Larga and its continuation known as the Via Martelli, which led from its opening off the piazza of the baptistery to the piazza in front of the convent of San Marco.[73] The later history of the confraternities which gathered in its church, particularly that of the Magi, confirms their members' commitment to the more rigorous piety of the mid-fifteenth century. The Medici family's patronage of San Marco enhanced their image as patrons of friends, neighbors, and fellow-Christians. This last charge was articulated in an inscription on the great bell Cosimo had cast for the convent, probably commissioned just before his death from Verrocchio: "Christ, the King of Glory, came in peace, and God was made man. The most illustrious man Cosimo de' Medici, son of Giovanni, caused me to be made at his own expense in order that rites might be celebrated for God at appointed times. Glory to God in the highest" (fig. 72).[74]

★　　★　　★

72 Andrea del Verrocchio, bronze bell, Florence, Museo di San Marco

Cosimo and Sant'Antoninus, prior of San Marco and archbishop of Florence

In 1436 seventeen friars were detached from the mother house at San Domenico in Fiesole and took up residence at San Marco; among them were Antoninus and Fra Angelico. The convent frescoes and the altarpiece for the church show how successfully the artist Angelico collaborated with his patron Cosimo; Antoninus's role in Cosimo's patronage at San Marco is more problematic. The two men were precise contemporaries, both born in 1389. Antoninus inherited Dominici's function of guiding spirit of his order; from 1439 to 1444 he was prior of San Marco, and in 1446 he was appointed archbishop of Florence. Through the exercise of these offices, Antoninus became the city's leading practical moralist and theologian. His *Summa theologica* or *Summa historiale*, written around 1450, served as a benchmark of civic morality, but even before its promulgation, his views were familiar to the Florentine public as the basis of his reformist admin-

istration of the Church, and his defence in the courts of its privileges against the encroachments of the state.[75]

The archbishop's decisions on practical matters affecting the Church often touched on questions of the motives and means of lay patronage. His strong interest in the operations of Florentine commerce and trade had led him to comment on the building of chapels and their decoration. His influential writings included important observations on profit, restitution, charity, and liberality, and most particularly on the just wage, the context in which he described and criticized, but did not essentially prescribe, the practice of painters and manuscript illuminators. Unlike Cosimo, who professed himself as capable of judging artists as warriors, Antoninus said that if experts tell us sculptures are good, we must believe them.[76]

Since he was right on the spot while Cosimo was rebuilding, and Fra Angelico redecorating his convent, Antoninus might well have been reflecting on the dilemma of San Marco when he wrote in the *Summa* of "the comfort and sumptuous display" indulged in by Dominican houses: what would Saint Dominic say if he considered their "houses and cells enlarged, vaulted, raised to the sky, and most frivolously adorned with superfluous sculptures and paintings?" Conversely, he also observed in relation to San Marco that "changed conditions" require different responses, and he even conceded that it might be necessary to dispense with the rule of poverty, "since otherwise it would not appear to be possible [for the friars] to maintain themselves." Thus the convent should be built, "not according to the state of the friars, but the state of the city."[77]

A sophisticated economic analyst, Antoninus seems in the end to have come to terms with the paradox of lay devotion in a city like Florence, which was built by, and depended upon, the profits of trade. In the 1460s he even put his imprimatur upon the construction of Giovanni Rucellai's startlingly self-advertising facade for the church of Santa Maria Novella.[78] He was, however, far from being Cosimo's accomplice in the political "indoctrination" of the populace through *sacre rappresentazioni* and other forms of popular religious culture, seeking rather to instil in Florentines the moral principles articulated in his didactic writings.[79] Antoninus's injunctions to the wealthy to support the poor rather than spend too much money on chapels and pomp may have modified the nature of Cosimo's patronage at San Marco. Aside from the rebuilding and redecorating of the convent building, by contrast with most lay patronage, much of Medici generosity to San Marco took the simplest form of direct charity – the daily support of the voluntary poor because they were dedicated to maintaining the spiritual health of the community.[80] The friars of San Marco received from Cosimo six pounds a week for sundry expenses, increased in 1444 to ten, and later to twelve, and supplemented by a variety of recurrent gifts. Lappacini, the convent's chronicler, calculated in 1453 that for the previous decade Cosimo had spent about one gold ducat a day on the friars, who had a direct line of access to the manager of the Medici bank.

Ironically then, it was the issue of support that occasioned Saint Dominic's curse "on the introduction of possessions into this order," so oddly inscribed in Angelico's fresco of the Madonna and eight saints in the convent's east corridor reserved to the cloistered friars.[81] The ever-present conflict between spiritual aspirations and worldly desires, which raged in the heart of every wealthy patron of the Church, was a microcosm of the Church's own dilemma, since patrons inevitably undermined the highest spiritual aims of the Renaissance church, even as they supported its physical existence. In 1455 Cosimo, concerned to secure the convent's future independence of the vagaries of charitable patronage, petitioned Pope Calixtus III for a Bull that would allow the friars to accept and retain property and annual revenues, in contravention of the basic rule forbidding the accumulation of property, by which the reformed Observants had distinguished themselves from the conventual friars. Notably when the government of Florence solicited the pope, its ambassadors were Cosimo's son Giovanni, and Archbishop Antoninus.[82]

The example of San Marco illustrates the difficulty of distinguishing clearly in matters of patronage between politics and piety, between lay and clerical, or individual and corporate interests. The pope, the Mediceans, and Antoninus obviously shared a number of spiritual and civic goals, and often cooperated to establish in Florence some of the order and measure praised in Cosimo's poem as the essential condition of the well-ordered Christian life. The rebuilding of San Marco was the result of their joint exertions, just as the Buonomini of San Martino, the only public charitable confraternity operating at mid-century, was founded with Medicean money and with the blessing of Pope Eugenius and the prior of San Marco.

Other aspects of Medici patronage brought out their sharp points of disagreement with Antoninus. When Giovanni di Cosimo wrote excusing and asking clemency for a friend found guilty of corruption in the exercise of a Church office, the archbishop rebuked him angrily for the excesses of "your friends [who] are all powerful and great citizens, and the Church takes the part of its small and weak wards."[83] Antoninus saw no room for maneuver in a direct conflict between the Medici family's obligations to their *amici* and his own obligations to

Christ's church. An amusing anecdote of Poliziano's may reflect the ambivalence of other exchanges. "Asked by Archbishop Antoninus to support a prohibition against clerical gambling, Cosimo replied: 'Start the ball rolling sooner, by stopping them from using loaded dice'."[84]

The Medici and Michelozzo

Vasari named Michelozzo as Cosimo's architect at San Marco, as well as for the novices' chapel at Santa Croce, the Medici villas at Cafaggiolo, Trebbio, and Careggi, the renovation of Bosco ai Frati, the tabernacles commissioned by Piero for San Miniato and Santissima Annunziata, and Giovanni's villa at Fiesole. He saw the Medici palace as Michelozzo's magnum opus, the supreme expression of his affinity with Cosimo and his distinctive *ingegno*.[85] But of all the architectural projects for the Medici, their friends, and the Church that Vasari attributed to Michelozzo, only Piero's tabernacles, and some other construction at Santissima Annunziata, are documented by contracts or building records.[86] Vasari's attributions, long accepted in the absence of an alternative source, have been shown to be often unreliable in the light of more intensive research on individual works of art, and a more critical comparison of the two very different redactions of Vasari's *Lives* of artists. In describing the achievements of artists in Cosimo's lifetime, Vasari was writing long after the event, and with the patent intention of crafting an image and creating precedents to promote himself as court artist to the sixteenth-century Medici dukes, so there is good reason to accept nothing he says at face value.[87]

In fact, however, there are many documented personal links between Michelozzo and Cosimo, and a number of Medici buildings bear traces of a style identified with the sculptor. While Michelozzo's close relationship with the Medici family does not establish him as the architect of any particular building, it increases the likelihood, in the absence of evidence linking these Medici commissions with another architect, that he assisted in the production of at least a portion of Cosimo's building oeuvre. This association is not undermined by Cosimo's failure to name Michelozzo as his architect, since the patron saw himself as the progenitor of his buildings and others, like his biographer Vespasiano, gave him the credit for them.[88]

Michelozzo's forte as an architect was the integration of new forms with old, just as Cosimo's genius as a civic leader lay in the subtle reworking of traditional elements of Florentine politics into new forms of power and authority. In the terms in which Renaissance men perceived creativity, Vasari's suggestion that Michelozzo, through his familiarity with Cosimo, acquired a special understanding of his patron's *ingegno* makes perfect sense. Michelozzo might well be seen as fulfilling precisely the quattrocento patron's expectation of an architect; to express Cosimo's personal identity and style in the architectural forms of his commissions – to function, in other words, as his architectural *alter ego*.[89]

To implement the grand design of their patron in every sphere was the acknowledged role and duty of all Medici partisans, who swore frequently in their letters to Cosimo and his sons to "uphold you in every word and deed."[90] Michelozzo's correspondence with the Medici family, and his close involvement with several of their households over many years preceding their triumphant return to Florence in 1434, indicate that he was their neighbor, their familiar, and their partisan. The relations of Michelozzo and his family with the Medici are typical of those of successive generations of faithful Medici partisans whose families rose to prosperity from the ranks of artisans and notaries. Michelozzo himself remained a relatively poor craftsman, but his son Ser Niccolò became a Medici protégé, and the story of his rise to wealth and power, crowned by his appointment to the prestigious post of chancellor of the republic, is similar to that of other partisans whose families were promoted by Medici patronage.[91]

Michelozzo established his artistic identity, like many leading sculptors of his day, in the great public projects launched in the first two decades of the century by the guilds, and particularly the Opera del Duomo; these included works for the cathedral, for Orsanmichele, and the baptistery doors. From the early 1420s he seems to have been involved increasingly in enterprises associated with Cosimo de' Medici. In 1425 Michelozzo became Donatello's partner in the workshop awarded the commissions for three great clerical tombs of the 1420s – the Cossa, Brancacci, and Aragazzi monuments.[92] Cosimo played a part in all of these projects as an executor of the wills of their patrons, and in the case of the former pope's tomb, he bore much of the responsibility for the siting and execution of the monument. The rebuilding of Bosco ai Frati begun in the late 1420s is plausibly attributed to Michelozzo. The renovation of the nearby Medici villa at Trebbio, though undocumented and difficult even to date, was probably also begun around this time, and has also been confidently associated with Michelozzo, along with the renovation of the other Medici villas of Cafaggiolo and Careggi, generally assigned to a slightly later date.[93]

The sculptor's tax report of 1427, filed jointly with his brothers, "sons of Bartolomeo di Gherardo, Burgundians," showed him living on the Via Larga where several main Medici households, including those of Cosimo's father Giovanni and of his cousin Bernardo d'Antonio, were established. Two of Michelozzo's brothers had left home, and he largely supported their aged mother and a third brother, Giovanni, who had no trade or position, but was travelling at the time with one of the Florentine galleys bound for Flanders. Of the money Giovanni owed him, Michelozzo wrote: "I have no hope of getting any of it, but I continue to pay his expenses, and if I didn't, he would be in prison." He himself owed back rent for his shop in the Corso to Guglielmo Adimari, and he claimed that the Bankers' Guild still owed him some payment for his role in the casting of Ghiberti's bronze figure of Saint Matthew, made for their niche at Orsanmichele; Cosimo and his father Giovanni were closely associated with this commission. Michelozzo declared that in the partnership formed two years earlier with "Donato di Nichola di Betto Bardi, known as Donatello . . . neither of us has any assets except for the sum of thirty florins." The three tombs were among the work they still had in hand, along with a marble figure for Santa Maria del Fiore. Michelozzo was also working for the Zecca, the Florentine mint.[94]

In 1427 the sculptor, as his brother's guarantor, was summoned before the Mercanzia (the merchants' court) when Giovanni, who had no trade or source of income, failed to pay for a red-lined cape he had ordered and received.[95] Early in 1430 Michelozzo asked Averardo de' Medici, who was Cosimo's cousin, closest friend, and chief counsellor to the Medici party before his death in exile in 1434, to procure a position for Giovanni on the galley captained by Ormanno degli Albizzi.[96] Michelozzo himself was soon engaged in Brunelleschi's scheme to win the war against Lucca by diverting the course of the River Serchio and flooding the city, then under siege by Florentine forces. When supplies necessary to this enterprise failed to arrive, Michelozzo wrote to Averardo asking him to intervene: "I beg you, for the profit and honor of the commune, and of ourselves, to consent to help us." He had already asked Averardo, in a letter written only two days earlier, as his friend and neighbor "to send over to my house and let them know we are all well," adding that he had aquired some profitable personal information for Averardo about which "I would like to be able to speak to you face to face."[97] When Brunelleschi's scheme failed, and the Serchio flooded the Florentine camp instead of the city of Lucca, he and Michelozzo were greatly blamed, and Brunelleschi ceased to be entrusted with important communal offices. However, Michelozzo continued to enjoy close relations with the Medici.

A letter of Poggio Bracciolini to his friend Niccolò

Niccoli confirms that the sculptor was a chosen companion of the Medici family when they fled to Padua in 1430 to escape the plague. Another letter, addressed three years earlier to Averardo in Florence by his son Giuliano, refers to his travels in the Veneto in the company of his own son Francesco, and of Michelozzo.[98] In December 1430 Michelozzo wrote from Padua to Averardo, asking him to arrange with Andrea de' Pazzi, who in the early 1420s had been a junior partner in the Rome branch of Averardo's bank, and was presently, as one of the wealthiest men in Florence, in charge of the city's mint, to keep his position there open, "as I am sure you have done to date . . . The reason for my staying on is a little work I have almost finished, which Giuliano wants to give to one of his friends."[99]

Michelozzo was in attendance at the ceremonies for the wedding in June 1433 of Averardo's grandson Francesco, when tributes of meat and game were delivered by representatives of the villages nearby to the Medici villa at Cafaggiolo, which then belonged to Averardo. Francesco recorded in his diary the details of the associated events in town: "We had a splendid celebration, and we put potted plants around the whole courtyard, and made a decorated structure more beautiful than any that had been built for many years; the sculptor Michelozzo arranged it all."[100] It was probably also for the Medici that Michelozzo made a silver medal of San Tommaso, patron saint of the church of San Tommaso, in the district of the Mercato Vecchio, where Francesco was married and his line of the Medici family were major patrons. Cosimo's line had also lived in this area before moving to the Via Larga near San Lorenzo; he continued to own property in the ancestral district, and to patronize the church well into the mid-fifteenth century.[101] Time spent by Michelozzo with the owners of Cafaggiolo does not confirm that he was therefore involved in its renovation, or that of the nearby villa of Trebbio and the convent of Bosco ai Frati, but it does put him a good deal closer to these enterprises than Vasari's tales of events that occurred a century before he himself was born.

Since there is cause to regard Vasari's traditionally accepted attributions as suspect, arguments concerning Michelozzo's association with particular buildings are obliged to depend on the identification of a distinctive Michelozzan style. As Michelozzo's style may be seen as distinctive, but is generally agreed to be unobtrusive, characterized by the integration of the new quattrocento forms pioneered by Brunelleschi and later Alberti with those of the Florentine and classical past, there remains a great deal of room for maneuver in the definition of Michelozzo's oeuvre. This is particularly the case in the attribution to Michelozzo of the ground-breaking Medici palace.[102] In speaking of the more conservative construction at San Marco, we are probably on safer ground. Vasari's relatively precise and accurate account of this building clearly relies on the chronicles of the convent, although none of these still extant mentions Michelozzo either, and there are no surviving account books relating to the construction. Most architectural historians, however, see Michelozzo's hand in the building at San Marco, along with several other less remarkable Medici commissions in a style generally favored by Cosimo. In the discussions that follow, in the absence of evidence to the contrary, these are assumed to be associated with Michelozzo.[103]

The renovations

Cosimo's renovation of the church of San Marco turns out on closer examination to be less radical than some fifteenth-century comment implies. Only the *tribuna* was rebuilt and enlarged. It contained the choir and pulpits where the brothers gathered daily and at night to say the divine offices before the high altar. After some dispute, the Caponsacchi family ceded their ancient patronage rights over the *cappella maggiore* to Cosimo for five hundred gold ducats, and the citizens of the confraternity of the Holy Spirit who used to meet there were also recompensed for abandoning it.[104] Cosimo's recompense for rebuilding it was the inscription testifying that it would serve to expiate his sins.

The demands of confraternal life, in which Cosimo was much involved, dictated several of the modifications to the refurbished convent and church. The church continued to accommodate the boys' company of the Purification, the company of the Magi, and the artisan confraternity of silk weavers. For the Magi Cosimo built a chapel with a separate entrance to the street, and the silk weavers were given a place next to them, also with outside access. The boys' company, which met at San Marco under the supervision of the general of the Servite order, Ser Mariano Salvini, and of Cosimo's secretary Alesso, had an oratory associated with a chapel dedicated to Saints Cosmas and Damian, to which Cosimo "gave an altarpiece with the figures of these saints painted on it."[105] In 1455 construction of the oratory of the weavers' guild was interrupted because of lack of funds, and the site devolved upon the Magi company, who completed a choir and chapel with Cosimo's aid.[106]

Cosimo's main building work at San Marco consisted of the reconstruction of the living quarters of the monks – their individual dormitories, corporate spaces such as the refectory and the chapter room, and cloisters for recreation and meditation. Rebuilding of the convent began in 1437; work on the church started a year later. According to Vespasiano, Cosimo went most days to hear mass at San Marco and to check with the convent's administrator and record-keeper, Giuliano Lapaccini, on what was needed for the work there. In his chronicle Lapaccini enumerated the benefits of the Medici interventions at San Marco, "among which the library takes pride of place"; he also listed the monks' quarters, including forty-four cells; the pictures painted by Fra Giovanni di Piero de Mugello, "the greatest master of painting in Italy"; the garden, and the drainage and water system.[107]

Particular care was lavished on the creation of a garden much praised by contemporaries. Filarete wrote: "Of the garden I will not speak, but one sees there every rank of fruits, and oranges, and palms and other various plants, and other special things . . . which we will leave aside . . ."[108] It seems to have been similar in the profusion and particularity of its vegetation to the renowned garden of the future Medici palace, and similarly perhaps reflected Cosimo's serious personal interest in horticulture, together with the general Renaissance habit of using the garden as a metaphor to express its cultivator's identity and interests. San Marco's garden with its oranges evoked the arms of the Medici, who imported citrus for their several gardens specially from Naples; it was also an embodiment of biblical passages from the Psalms associated with the Virgin, describing citrus and palms also represented in Angelico's altarpiece.[109] Michelozzo's experience of hydraulics, acquired as assistant to Brunelleschi in his unfortunate Lucchese scheme, found a happier outlet in the sophisticated system for sewerage and irrigation of the gardens at San Marco, extensively documented by the grand-ducal architect who renewed it in 1558.[110]

It was in the library, completed in 1444, that the architect's talents and Cosimo's style of patronage most effectively converged (fig. 64). The library − cool, classical, spare, and graceful, in harmony with Angelico's painting and his strongly articulated sense of space − is the architectural masterpiece of San Marco. The austere character of its design mirrored the character of its patron, as Cosimo's intervention at the convent of the Badia was later to do.[111] The sacred texts with which Cosimo furnished the library expressed his personal concern to propagate the faith, as well as a pleasure in collecting books evident from his youth. The quality of the library also expressed the quality of Medici literary friendships. Cosimo, as the most influential of the group of close friends whom the collector Niccolò Niccoli appointed as his executors, was chiefly responsible for making Niccoli's

legendary classical library the nucleus of his own donation. The library became a gift to the city as well as to the church, since by Niccoli's wish, his books were to be freely available to all Florentine laymen.[112] Thus at San Marco, with the cooperation of his *amici* and the advice of Tommaso da Sarzana, later Pope Nicholas V, Cosimo created for the city of Florence what has been described as its first public library. He brought together under the refurbished roof of San Marco some four hundred volumes, including those specially collected by Lapaccini or produced by Vespasiano's workshop at Cosimo's instruction. In so doing he also brought together with his own interests those of the Church and of the leading citizens of Florence.[113]

Although somewhat to Lapaccini's surprise, Cosimo "left us nothing" in his will, he had provided for the convent's future in characteristic manner by acting as *mezzano* with Pope Calixtus III to enable the convent to be supported by the bequests of others. Calixtus's Bull legitimized bequests already made by several members of the Medici family; in 1436 Maddalena Monaldi, wife of Averardo di Francesco de' Medici, divided her goods between San Marco, San Domenico, and the hospital of Santa Maria Nuova, and in 1449 Itta, wife of Amerigo di Lapo de' Medici, also made a bequest to San Marco.[114] The Medici family's interest in the convent was represented in the display of its arms, which were everywhere at San Marco; on the façade, above and within the *cappella maggiore*, on the biforate windows at the landing of the main stairs, above the door over the night stairs, as a collar around the bell tower (fig. 73).[115]

San Marco was not simply a forum for Medici patronage; it was also the family's refuge − spiritual, financial, and even physical. In 1433, on the eve of their exile, Cosimo and Lorenzo had stored a large quantity of their assets in the convent, where they would be safe from confiscation by a hostile government. On 29 September 1453 an earthquake sent the terrified citizens of Florence fleeing their houses for open ground. Piero de' Medici had himself carried from his house to the garden at San Marco where he felt safe, although as it turned out, the library and north side of the dormitory at San Marco suffered particularly severe damage.[116] Most of all, the Medici hoped to provide at San Marco for the safety of their souls; Lapaccini testified, on account of the thirty-six thousand or so ducats Cosimo had spent on the convent, to "how much we were obliged to pour forth prayers to the Lord God for his soul and the souls of all his descendants."[117]

★   ★   ★

73   Florence, Convent of San Marco, landing of the stairs near Cosimo's cell

SAN LORENZO, PARISH CHURCH OF THE
MEDICI NEIGHBORHOOD

The rebuilding of the church of San Lorenzo in the fifteenth century may be seen as a metaphor for the changing relations in Cosimo's lifetime between the Medici, their partisans, and their neighbors.[118] This would not have escaped the Florentine public, accustomed to seeing metaphors, symbols, and signs all around them. The Medici neighborhood was created by the virtual coincidence of the parish of San Lorenzo and the *gonfalone* (ward) of the Golden Lion (*Lion d'oro*), the administrative district upon which electoral scrutinies and tax assessments were based (fig. 74). Its relation to the Medici party or patronage group was long and close; they were the leaders of a local faction as early as the 1340s. According to Villani, when the nobles took up arms against the *popolo*, "the *popolo* of the quarter of San Giovanni ... chose as their leaders the Medici and the

Rondinelli and Messer Ugo della Stufa, a judge ... and the *popolani* of Borgo San Lorenzo, with the butchers and other artisans, without the permission of the commune, and being altogether about a thousand men ... launched an attack from several quarters ..."[119]

In this society where aspiring individuals and lineages depended heavily upon the protection and patronage of the leading families of their local world, the Medici acted as a magnet for the hopes and ambitions of lesser citizens. Of the identifiable Medici partisans in the late 1420s and early 1430s, shortly before Cosimo's exile, about half lived in the quarter of Saint John, and about half of these belonged to the *gonfalone* of the Golden Lion. Their leaders were members of the Della Stufa, Martelli, Ginori, and Dietisalvi-Neroni families, whose patronage of the main chapels of the new San Lorenzo symbolizes their commitment to a whole range of Medici enterprises. The allocation, construction, and exchange of the chapels was – like other Medicean operations under Cosimo's direction and enjoying the support of his friends – shaped by

74   Map of San Lorenzo and district from Limburger, *Die Gebäude von Florenz*

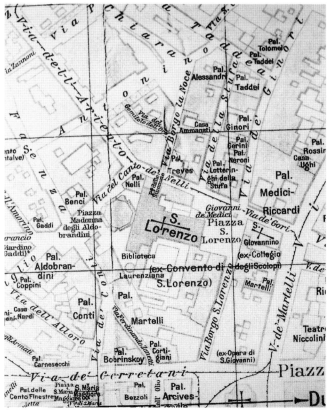

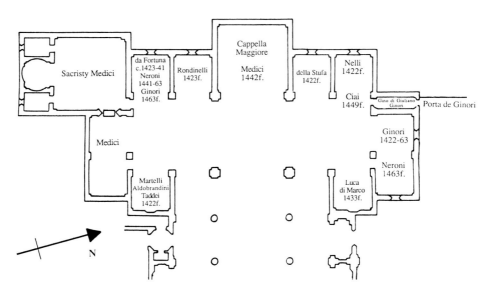

75   Plan of choir and transept of San Lorenzo, Florence,
with chapel patrons, reconstructed by Caroline Elam

constraints and concessions according to the patron's interests. Analogous to other Medici enterprises, like the conduct of the bank and of the party, San Lorenzo's patronage was characterized by cooperation and continuity between the generations of the Medici family (fig. 75).

At San Lorenzo Cosimo fulfilled obligations inherited from his father, as *paterfamilias* of the Medici family, and as patron of many other families of the parish. With the building of the Medici commemorative chapels, prayers of intercession for the souls of all the Medici, past, present, and future, multiplied to a degree unprecedented for any other family.[120] However, the Medici commemorative umbrella extended to cover their friends as well. When in November 1428 Giovanni di Bicci de' Medici instituted canonries and prebends for the chapel of Saint John the Evangelist, better known as the old sacristy, as well as for the adjoining transept chapel dedicated to Saints Cosmas and Damian, he declared that he had built and endowed these chapels, "to augment the Divine cult in the said church and for the salvation of the souls of himself and his relatives and friends."[121] Medici initiatives enabled their *amici* to assume patronage of their own family chapels, honoring their own dynasties and providing for the salvation of their souls.

At the same time, the history of the rebuilding of San Lorenzo reflects the Medici family's growing ascendancy and control over their friends and associates in the ruling group. The scheme to reconstruct the church, dating from at least as early as 1415, was proposed as a parish and neighborhood project by the prior and a group of residents of the *gonfalone*. By 1442 a meeting of sixty-three of the men of the *gonfalone*, most of them members of the Medicean *reggimento*, was happy to hand over complete responsibility for financing the construction of the church to "that great man, Cosimo de' Medici." Various suggestions have been made to explain why Cosimo assumed this responsibility at this time. However, what really seems to require explanation is why he chose to expiate his sins by building first at San Marco, allowing his parish church, of which his father had been the major patron, to remain only partly reconstructed for almost a decade after his return from exile.

Caroline Elam has traced the early history of the rebuilding of San Lorenzo, which sheds fresh light on the relation between the personal and artistic patronage of the Medici family. The *operai* responsible for work at San Lorenzo from the turn of the century were appointed by the syndics of the *gonfalone* of the Golden Lion. After 1416, when a fire destroyed much of the old church, and extensive rebuilding was required, the prior and canons of the church successfully petitioned the Signoria of the city to appoint its *operai*.[122] Throughout this period, whether *operai* served by the authority of the *gonfalone* or of the commune, Cosimo's father Giovanni di Bicci de' Medici was prominent in the building enterprise. In March 1405 he served as one of three syndics to appoint the *operai*; he himself was one of the new *operai* instituted by the Priors for three years in 1416. The families of all five patricians from this group became patrons of the proposed new chapels in the early 1420s. Among Giovanni's colleagues in this office were his close friends and partisans Ugo d'Andrea della Stufa and Nerone di Nigi Dietisalvi-Neroni. The group also included Lorenzo di Andrea, a butcher, Vieri di Andrea de' Rondinelli, and Filippo di Biagio Guasconi. These last two were senior statesmen of the republic in the 1420s; for their role in exiling the Medici in 1433, Rondinelli's son Andrea and two nephews of Guasconi were banished by the victorious Medicean regime in 1434. Before their family chapels could be constructed, the patronage rights passed to other parishioners.[123]

The years 1416–19 were crucial ones for the future of San Lorenzo. Even before the fire, in 1415 the *operai* had planned to enlarge the church to extend westwards into the Via de' Preti, "the little piazza behind the campanile . . . which is inhabited by women of the vilest condition, whose way of life and reputation are not good, and they are for the most part foreigners."[124] In 1417 the chapter of San Lorenzo petitioned the Signoria for permission to level the houses in the way of this expansion, and the commune agreed "to do everything for the defence, maintenance and exaltation of the church." This undertaking was given while Ugo d'Andrea della Stufa, an intimate of the Medici whose ancestor had joined with them in leading the *popolano* revolt of the 1340s, was serving as Gonfalonier of Justice. In 1418 a provision concerning the clearing of the public piazza, justified as a holy work for God, cleared the way as well for the expropriation of private property obstructing the project; it was phrased in terms almost identical to those used by the *operai* at their meeting in 1415.[125] In the autumn of 1422 the offending houses were finally demolished. The ceremony of digging the foundation trench had taken place on the feast day of San Lorenzo, 10 August 1421; the prior and canons, together with the *operai* and the construction workers employed in the building, joined in a formal procession to a point behind the *campanile* and all made a symbolic cut with the spade "where the foundations were to be made."[126]

Elam discovered vital new evidence pinpointing Medicean supporters' assumption of rights to chapels in the report of the archbishop's visit to San Lorenzo in 1422. At that time, relatively few prominent families of the district had become patrons of chapels, although these did include the Ginori and the Rondinelli, and Tomasia Guasconi, widow of Giovanni Rondinelli. Most of the patrons were either priests, or men or women with no identifiable surnames.[127] But among the six *operai* to be appointed in 1422 were members of the Martelli, Masi, and Aldobrandini del Nero families, all close friends of the Medici. By 1423, in addition to the *cappella maggiore* which was the

responsibility of the prior and canons, and the Medici chapel adjoining the sacristy, all eight remaining chapels around the crossing had been allotted. Their patrons came from the immediate neighborhood of the church – Via Martelli, Via Larga, Via Ginori and Piazza San Lorenzo, Via Zanetti and Via Conti. They included the Ginori, Della Stufa, and Neroni-Dietisalvi, who were all sworn friends and partisans of the Medici, Albizzo da Fortuna, and among those closely associated with their opponents, Antonio di Ser Bartolommeo di Ser Nello [Ghetti] and the Rondinelli. The chapel of the *operai* themselves was owned by three families, the Aldobrandini, the Martelli, and the Taddei. This last family, together with Luca di Marco, who founded a chapel in 1433, was not particularly prominent in the political or social life of the city.[128]

A decade later, in 1432, most of the *operai* came from the same families as those of preceding years; several were also past or future chapel-holders. They included a close relative of Ser Nello, Iacopo Aldobrandini, Ugolino Martelli, and Lorenzo di Giovanni di Bicci de' Medici, Cosimo's brother. One newcomer was Niccolò Bonvanni, soon to assume an increasingly important part in the affairs of San Lorenzo. The best-represented family of the minor guilds in the Golden Lion's electoral scrutiny of 1440, the Bonvanni rose rapidly in the course of the next decade into the major guilds, where they gained strong representation. Another new man was the notary Ser Bartolomeo Ciai; his kinsman Ser Ciao was a close associate and supporter of Cosimo and his cousin Averardo de' Medici in the 1420s and early 1430s, and their family was to grow consistently stronger in the scrutinies of the 1440s.[129] The seven *operai* elected for one year by the Signoria in May 1433 included, beside Luca di Marco and Lorenzo dello Stecchuto, five men from the most powerful and influential families, not merely of the district of Lion d'oro, but of the entire city of Florence. They were Cosimo de' Medici and his close friends and partisans Piero Ginori and Lorenzo di Andrea della Stufa, along with Andrea di Rinaldo Rondinelli and Zanobi Guasconi, two of the major supporters of the faction led by Rinaldo degli Albizzi, who less than four months later had Cosimo arrested and imprisoned.[130]

The confrontation between the Medici and their opponents was played out at various sites and venues throughout the city, among them the church of San Lorenzo. By 1433 all the chapels around the crossing at San Lorenzo had been taken, but only Giovanni di Bicci de' Medici had fulfilled his obligations, completing the construction of his two chapels before his death in 1429. Building was at a standstill when in June 1434 the chapter of San Lorenzo convened, "certain men and persons, devoted to the said church, having care and affection for it and having declared themselves wishing in the future to build chapels there for the celebration of the divine offices," and prescribed that all the chapels to be built in the future should conform in their design to those already built by Giovanni di Bicci de' Medici. (This meant that they should incorporate a tribuna and an oculus, and contain square or rectangular altarpieces.) Howard Saalman suggested that these "certain persons" were enemies of the Medici family reluctant to endow chapels under the Medici aegis, but willing to come forward now that Cosimo was "out of town," to preempt a Medici "takeover" at San Lorenzo.[131] Apart from the fact that the chapter's decree explicitly underwrites Giovanni di Bicci's initiatives as a builder, this line of speculation arises from a misunderstanding of the actual political situation obtaining in Florence three months before the Medici were recalled.

Cosimo's friends had kept in constant touch with him since his departure from Florence, reassuring him of their continuing loyalty, and informing him of every move made by his enemies. At the same time, in January 1434 Cosimo himself had patriotically alerted the Signoria to a plot to return him to his native city with the aid of the duke of Milan; his reward was a letter judging that "your irreproachable conduct and your candor deserve commendation and praise."[132] The leading Medici partisans remained faithful and optimistic throughout his exile, anticipating and preparing the way for his speedy return. Thanks to many years of Medici manipulation of the electoral purses, Mediceans continued to turn up in drawings for leading offices.

Lotteringo d'Andrea della Stufa became one of the Priors in March 1434, and in the first weeks of his tenure, the Signoria issued a decree facilitating the continuance of building at San Lorenzo. Referring to a request from "most prudent and zealous citizens," who were much more likely in the circumstances to be friends than enemies of the Medici, the Signoria ordered on 16 and 18 March that the piazza of San Lorenzo should be enlarged by the demolition of a block of buildings between the Della Stufa palace and the church, extending east as far as the Via de' Ginori.[133] On 30 April Ugo di Lorenzo della Stufa, whose father was at that time one of San Lorenzo's operai, wrote to Giovanni de' Medici, Cosimo's younger son who was roughly his own age, noting "all the brotherhood which has existed between us," and informing him of the progress of work at San Lorenzo. "I believe you have heard how our Lotteringo is one of the Signoria, and that the houses opposite ours have been levelled, so that now there is a beautiful piazza in front of the door, so you see how things are proceeding."[134]

By May 1434 the city was bankrupt, and a curfew had to be imposed to prevent armed uprisings, reportedly planned by Cosimo's followers. Although, during the year of Cosimo's absence, the church of San Lorenzo lost some of its privileges as a result of its association with his family,[135] the chapter and canons stood firm behind the Medici and kept them informed of church affairs. The Medici had many friends and clients among its clergy, who over the years included Feo Belcari and Antonio degli Agli,[136] and its major patrons were Cosimo's staunchest supporters. By the time of the meeting of the chapter of San Lorenzo on 3 June, government records and private letters and diaries indicate that the tide was turning against Cosimo's enemies in the *reggimento*. The provisions of this meeting concerning future chapels probably anticipated the imminent recall of those who had played the leading part in the church's rebuilding; this occurred only three months later, at the beginning of September 1434.[137]

While the political upheavals of 1433–4 did not ultimately derail Medicean plans for San Lorenzo,[138] which throughout the crisis enjoyed continuing support from the family's neighbors and fellow-parishioners, political allegiance did apparently affect the ownership of some of the chapels. The succeeding decade saw the gradual extension of the rights and privileges of Medici friends at the expense of those not associated with the Medici, or hostile to them. The *operai* of 1433 had defined the opposing lines of political interest in their persons; on one side were the Medici, Della Stufa, and Ginori; on the other, the Guasconi and Rondinelli. These last two Lion d'oro families, related to one another by marriage, were severely punished in the proscriptions of 1434. In 1446 Bartolomeo di Antonio Nelli, who seems to have declined after the fall of his father-in-law Rinaldo degli Albizzi, sold his house to his brother-in-law, Francesco di Nerone di Nigi Dietisalvi, whose kinsmen were influential and valued allies of the Medici. In 1449 the Nelli were obliged to cede their chapel rights to Bernardo Ciai, from a family of Medici partisans; Bartolomeo Ciai had been an *operaio* in 1432. There is no evidence as to whether politics played a role in the bankruptcy of the heirs of Albizzo da Fortuna, who originally owned the chapel between the sacristy and the Rondinelli chapel in the southwestern corner of the transept, but in 1441 they sold their patronage rights in San Lorenzo to Francesco Dietisalvi.[139]

The experience of the Ginori family, and of the Dietisalvi Neroni, who acquired the Da Fortuna houses in these same years, and who built palaces in the Via Ginori just behind the Medici, exemplified some of the most significant changes over Cosimo's lifetime in the Medici party, in city politics, and at San Lorenzo.[140] When in 1432 the canons of the chapter of San Lorenzo obtained permission from Pope Eugenius IV to wear a special tippet over their heads and shoulders, identical to that worn by the cathedral canons, which many indignant citizens saw as a claim to comparable status for San Lorenzo, it was Nerone di Nigi di Dietisalvi who negotiated with the pope for this privilege. Notably, the representative of the Signoria sent to Rome to contest the award was Biagio Guasconi, who together with his family was exiled after Cosimo's recall in 1434. The privilege was withdrawn early in 1433, not long before Cosimo's arrest and banishment.[141] The incident nicely illustrates the opportunities the Medici family's growing political influence created for Cosimo's cultural and ecclesiastical patronage, but also the concomitant constraints. Cosimo had been unwilling in 1446 to push the candidacy of Dietisalvi's brother Giovanni for the archbishopric, against opposition favoring the more independent Antoninus. In 1462, three years after Antoninus died, Giovanni became archbishop of Florence; by 1463, Dietisalvi was ambassador to Milan, and many Florentines believed the latter's influence at Sforza's court would soon outstrip that of the aged and failing Cosimo.[142]

Throughout Cosimo's lifetime, the Ginori had been unquestioning allies of the Medici in all their schemes, from political promotion to the assembling of the site for their palace. The chronicler Cavalcanti related how, in the first days of September 1433, Piero Ginori, on hearing the news of Cosimo's arrest, "quite fearlessly roamed the city, shouting out, and showing himself to be utterly lacking in wisdom, and in fact quite mad."[143] In the early 1460s, a critical moment for the Medici in maintaining authority over their party, the Ginori were persuaded to relinquish their chapel in the place of greatest honor and prominence at San Lorenzo, adjacent to the Medici sacristy, in favor of Dietisalvi.[144] Three years later, after Cosimo's death, Dietisalvi openly challenged Piero's leadership of the party. When the anti-Medicean conspiracy of 1466 failed, and Dietisalvi was exiled, he lost his chapel altogether, and his elaborate burial monument eventually found shelter in the Florentine Badia.[145]

In 1465 the chapter relinquished to Piero de' Medici permission to allocate all the nave chapels along the north side to whomever he wished; the founders of those chapels were Bernardo de' Medici, Francesco di Piero Ginori, Francesco d'Ubaldo Inghirami (manager of the Medici woolshop in San Martino), Ludovico Masi, and Piero's wife, the devout Lucrezia Tornabuoni. "With this move," as Elam observed, "the Medici family's dominance over patronage at their parish church became complete."[146] However, the predominance in the prestigious

chapels of the transept of the Della Stufa, Ginori, and Martelli, alongside their Medici friends and patrons, is emblematic of the major Medici partisans' original and continuing role in supporting and maintaining the family's rise to power. This was most dramatically demonstrated when Sigismondo della Stufa's resourceful action saved Lorenzo de' Medici from dying alongside his younger brother Giuliano, murdered by their disaffected partisans of the Pazzi family as he stood at Mass before the high altar of the cathedral.[147]

Cosimo as patron of the main chapel, choir, and nave

Cosimo's eventual assumption of sole responsibility for the major rebuilding at his extremely large parish church, one of the four great "quarter" churches of Florence, and the oldest in the city after the baptistery, was a unique event in the history of private patronage in Florence, unprecedented in its sheer scale. In Cosimo's patronage of San Lorenzo, we may see the whole spectrum of the patron's interests and concerns – devotional, dynastic, personal, partisan, and civic (fig. 76).[148]

Cosimo turned to San Lorenzo in the early 1440s, after the building he had commissioned at San Marco was substantially completed.[149] On 20 November 1440 the church's prior, Benedetto Schiattesi, convened a meeting of the council of the gonfalone of Lion d'oro. The neighborhood in both its secular and spiritual capacities came together to discuss the resumption of the church building, and to call for one or more citizens to take over the patronage of the main chapel. At that time the sacristy and the adjacent transept chapel dedicated to Saints Cosmas and Damian constituted a Medici enclave effectively separate from the rest of the church, since renovations of the nave had reached only as far as the seventh bay of the existing structure.[150] As for most other meetings over the preceding decade concerned with the building plans, the group gathered in the sacristy which Giovanni di Bicci de' Medici had built, and in which he was buried. Surrounded by powerful symbols of the Medici family and its achievements, the meeting called for a patron for the church.

When the gonfalone council reconvened with the prior and canons of San Lorenzo on 13 August 1442, Cosimo de' Medici

> asked permission to build the main chapel, which the chapter had already built to a height of about eight braccia at its own expense and with other bequests . . . Provided that the choir and the nave of the church, as far as the original main altar, were assigned to him and

76   Brunelleschi, Florence, San Lorenzo, nave

his sons, together with all the structures so far erected, he would pledge himself to complete that section of the building within six years out of the fortunes that God had granted him, at his own expense and with his own coats of arms and devices, it being understood that no other coats of arms or devices or tombs should be placed in the aforesaid choir and nave, except those of Cosimo and of members of the chapter.[151]

This intervention would finally close the gap between the construction under way and the old Romanesque church it was superseding.

In view of the Medici family's close involvement with San Lorenzo over almost half a century, of Cosimo's conspicuous generosity to the neighboring convent of San Marco, and of his unparalleled standing in the city, he was the obvious candidate to step into the breach. Why,

indeed, had he not done so earlier? The answer may lie partly in the delicacy of the balance of power between Cosimo and his partisans. By 1434 Florence had come to depend on the resources of the Medici bank and the international influence that Cosimo enjoyed as a consequence of his financial and diplomatic activities; the ultimate reason for his recall from exile was probably that he had become indispensable to Florentine prosperity, whereas his enemies were not. However, the decision to recall the Medici was made by the vote of the commune's executive offices and councils, and it was the power of Cosimo's friends in these bodies that effected his repatriation and reestablished his influence over the ruling group. His friends had proven their loyalty in 1434, but only after another decade during which Cosimo acquired firmer control, through a series of reforms, over the electoral processes which kept them in power, could he feel comparatively secure. Even then, he remained beholden to his partisans, dependent upon their continuing cooperation and goodwill.

Meanwhile, he had to tread carefully, respecting the rights and privileges of others; his letters express his constant awareness of this fact. The need for caution in his public patronage was confirmed in his experience at San Marco. If his plan had been to rebuild the convent church completely, he was obliged to abandon it, restricting himself to the renovation of the tribune; even this was accomplished only after negotiation and compensation persuaded other families to renounce their prior patronage claims. Although most of the prominent parishioners of San Lorenzo were Medici friends and partisans, the building of family chapels and the concomitant commemoration of the dead was a sensitive issue. As Florentines were constantly reminded by the texts and images of Petrarch's *Triumphs*, while death soon triumphs over earthly fame and power, eternity triumphs over all. The fate of the soul for all eternity was the issue at stake in the provision of family chapels, where masses were endowed for the commemoration of the dead. As Cosimo's biographer Vespasiano observed: "He acted privately with the greatest discretion in order to safeguard himself, and whenever he sought to attain an object, he let it appear that the matter had been set in motion by someone other than himself, and thus he escaped envy and unpopularity."[152] Possibly Cosimo waited to make his move at San Lorenzo until the manifest need to go on with the building in the interests of all parishioners might incline them to approach him, thus preempting possible resentment or envy when Medici patronage gave them the lion's share of spiritual privileges there.

In the year 1440 several specific events affecting Cosimo's personal and political life may have made his intervention at San Lorenzo seem at once more possible and more desirable. In the spring of 1440 Cosimo's exiled enemies, who had continued to conspire against him with the support of the Visconti duke of Milan, were definitively defeated in the battle of Anghiari, a major turning point in the securing of the Medici regime. Within the city, the scrutiny of 1440 marked an important milestone in the consolidation of the regime's control over the commune's electoral processes. An event of comparable, if not greater significance, was the death of Cosimo's younger brother Lorenzo. This occurred on 23 September 1440, less than two months before the first of the meetings convened by San Lorenzo's prior.

The accounts of the brothers' humanist and clerical friends testify to their strong personal affection, as does the correspondence of the members of their close-knit household, and Lorenzo's frantic concern for Cosimo's

safety while he was under arrest.[153] The striking and poignant portrayal of San Lorenzo in Angelico's San Marco altarpiece suggests a particular and personal commemoration of the very recently deceased Lorenzo. It is likely that the sudden and premature death of his younger brother encouraged Cosimo at once to assuage his grief and to assume his familial responsibilities to the church dedicated to Lorenzo's name-saint; it may also have reminded him of his own mortality. As Susan McKillop pointed out, Cosimo "increased his grasp on the liturgical life of San Lorenzo four days after his brother died. On 31 September 1440 Cosimo subscribed a new Office for himself, his brother, his father and his mother. He gave a *bottega* for the purpose, and the inclusion of his own anniversary Office in the agreement makes clear that by this time his death arrangements were already in his thoughts."[154]

Although Cosimo was not to commit himself publicly to the project for another two years, the ledgers kept by the Medici factor Bartolommeo Sassetti, recording the joint expenses for San Lorenzo and the Medici palace begun in 1445, show that he decided to resume the work at San Lorenzo as early as 1441. Isabel Hyman, who discovered the ledgers, described how in that year stone quarries were opened at Trassinaia; Cosimo also drew a large sum from his private account and deposited it in another in the Florence branch of the Medici bank, "for the many expenses incurred in that year for the work at San Lorenzo."[155] Lorenzo's death necessitated a thorough review of their extensive joint assets; Cosimo may have waited to make his public commitment until this was completed.[156]

The ledger was opened in the names of Saints Cosmas, Damian, Lawrence, and John the Baptist, who personified Cosimo's commitment to family, neighborhood, church, and city, all to be honored in the rebuilding. At the beginning of the fifteenth century, the name Lorenzo was as new to Medici family nomenclature as those of Cosimo and Damiano; its choice perhaps expressed a desire on Giovanni di Bicci's part to associate his family more closely with their parish church.[157] The connection was certainly reinforced by Cosimo's elder son Piero when he named his own son, born in 1449, Lorenzo. Until his untimely death, Lorenzo di Giovanni played a major part in the family's patronage of San Lorenzo. Although the completion of his father's old sacristy was commonly associated primarily with Cosimo, the elder of the two brothers, it was actually carried out and paid for by the family bank in their joint names. This, as John Paoletti has noted, was true of all the commissions popularly attributed to Cosimo before Lorenzo's death. The church of San Lorenzo and the commune combined to honor

Lorenzo with a splendid funeral, attended by the pope and nine cardinals, an appropriate commemoration in view of the Priors' declaration that the building of San Lorenzo honored both God and the city.[158]

Like most of the major building projects associated with the Medici, the renovation of the main body of the church of San Lorenzo is only sparsely documented.[159] While the original design is generally attributed to Brunelleschi, the earliest contemporary testimony associating him with the church occurs more than ten years after the architect's death. In the end, like the patronage of its chapels, the accomplishment of its building proved to be a corporate affair. But while the Medici drew this patronage more and more into their own hands as time went by, it seems the design of the church grew less and less according to Brunelleschi's original plan. Brunelleschi died in April 1446, "before the columns of the naves were even cut from their quarry beds."[160] However, even before his death, there were factors that may have distanced him from the project; his advancing age, his involvement in other projects, and the scale of the enterprise at San Lorenzo, which anyway necessitated the employment of a number of other masters at various times. Eager for a livelier explanation, some have suggested that Cosimo preferred to work with a more malleable architect than the great master; others that Brunelleschi, offended by Donatello's sculptural intervention in the old sacristy at Cosimo's behest, interfering with the purely architectonic values of the architect's design, preferred to work on other projects, like the building at Santo Spirito, whose patrons gave him his head.

The only evidence bearing on Cosimo's view of Brunelleschi's design for San Lorenzo – indeed the only evidence of a direct appeal from an artist to his Medici patrons for arbitration concerning any project – is a letter from Giovanni di Domenico de Gaiole to Giovanni de' Medici of May, 1457. The writer, a far from objective witness, recounted to Giovanni a conversation "in Cosimo's room" in which the other participants included his son Piero, Antonio Manetti, and Antonio Martelli. He claimed that Cosimo asked about the illumination of the tribune, and expressed his opinion that the structure was "two million times as heavy as it ought to be,"[161] and not according to Brunelleschi's intention. More general evidence concerning Cosimo's admiration for outstanding *ingegni* makes it a little hard to believe that he would intentionally have taken the project right out of the hands of Italy's most admired architect, with whose work at the cathedral he had been only too happy to associate himself, even if Michelozzo had served as his architectural alter ego on other projects in which Brunelleschi was not a contender. The ample testimony that exists of the architect's powerful and independent personality makes it rather easier to imagine that after a lengthy period of working closely with Cosimo to complete the old sacristy, it was Brunelleschi who preferred to sever the connection. However, unless or until new evidence is found, this matter remains in the realm of speculation.

THE OLD SACRISTY

Throughout the thirties, while Cosimo devoted himself to San Marco, and the rebuilding of the main part of San Lorenzo was at a standstill, Cosimo and his brother Lorenzo had been supervising the decoration of the old sacristy (fig. 77). Giovanni di Bicci gave the building commission to Brunelleschi shortly after the architect's design of 1419 for the cathedral cupola revealed the remarkable power of his *ingegno*. Unlike many of his peers, the old man lived to see his chapel completed. Building began in 1422, and was finished, according to an inscription incised in the cement of the dome, in 1428. When their father died in 1429, Cosimo and Lorenzo assumed formal responsibility for the embellishment of the interior.[162] The tomb of Giovanni di Bicci and his wife was made by Buggiano, Brunelleschi's adopted son. In view of his work in the 1420s on funerary monuments associated with the Medici, Donatello was a natural choice as the artist responsible for the decoration; the bronze doors, the stucco lunettes above them, and the roundels of the ceiling. All these components of the sacristy are integrated by a unified iconographical scheme suggesting a clear master conception on the part of its Medici patrons, but one necessarily evolved in close cooperation with the architect and sculptors. The figural images represented the themes of death and resurrection, and the major figures of the Church; the prophets, evangelists, martyrs, and apostles. Predominant were the patron saints of the Medici, particularly John the Evangelist, patron of the chapel's patron, and Cosmas, Damian, and Lorenzo, patron saints of his sons, and of the church.

Naturally this masterwork of Florence's greatest architect for the city's major patrons has long attracted the attention of leading art historians. Building on a now substantial body of scholarship, they continue to add information and insights to an understanding of the old sacristy's significance to the Florentine Renaissance, both architecturally and socially. Even more than most Medici commissions, it was immediately acclaimed and emulated. In the course of the succeeding century, at least twenty similar buildings were commissioned by patrons all over Italy.[163] As Manetti's *Life of Brunelleschi* recounted: "the Sacristy went forward before anything else [at San

77   Brunelleschi and Donatello, Florence, San Lorenzo, old sacristy, south wall

Lorenzo] and arrived at a state that aroused the wonder, on account of its new and beautiful style, of everyone in the city, and of the strangers who chanced to see it. The many people constantly assembling there caused great annoyance to the workmen."[164]

However, the building did not arise in a vacuum. Scholars have noted numerous formal prototypes, and Marvin Trachtenberg proposes the interpretive context as "an accelerating if highly regulated competition between Florentine families in the *tre-* and *quattrocento* to build more impressive chapels for their private use and commemoration." Among its precedents were the Strozzi sacristy at Santa Trinita, with its impressive street facade and entrance, and Brunelleschi's Barbadori chapel at Santa Felicita, radical not only in its novel classicizing form, but even more in being the first family chapel to intrude into the main public space of a Florentine church.[165] Notably, the Strozzi and the Barbadori were among the group of wealthy and influential citizens who opposed the Medici, and who after 1434 were vanquished by the Medicean victors, losing their fortunes, their position in the state, and often the palaces and chapels built under their patronage.

Other comparisons locate the old sacristy stylistically in a web of architectural references whose resonances enhance but complicate its reading. Various of its features evoke the Holy Sepulcher in Jerusalem, together with other Christian monuments which it naturally inspired. Among these were the Florentine baptistery, which has been seen as the most immediate source of the *all'antica* aspects of the old sacristy, especially the key feature of the lantern, which resembles that of the baptistery and the tholos on top of the Holy Sepulcher.[166] The siting of Giovanni di Bicci's freestanding tomb in the center, beneath the dome and under a marble vesting table inlaid with a porphyry plaque, also evokes Christ's mausoleum, and the imperial tombs in the Hagia Sophia inspired by it.[167] Modern writers are inclined to read such associations of form and usage with Christ's own tomb as presumptuous, even sacrilegious. To patrons and their audiences of the fifteenth century, as of the fourth, they were part of the constant attempt of Christians to identify themselves as closely as possible with the experience of the Savior; his life, death, and most of all, his resurrection.[168] There is also some evidence to suggest a connection between the repeated use in Florence of the model of the Holy Sepulcher and her citizens' long-held view of their city as the New Jerusalem.[169]

A vision of the form of the Holy Sepulcher was kept alive in the literature familiar to every educated Florentine. There is a detailed description of it in Eusebius's *Ecclesiastical History*, in Cosimo's library by 1418, which may also have inspired the similarities between the Holy Sepulcher and the choir of the new Santissima Annunziata.[170] The influence of early Christian texts and ideas is apparent in much of Cosimo's patronage for San Lorenzo, and Saint Ambrose's injunctions about the burial of martyrs beneath an altar may be reflected in the 1430 contract for Giovanni di Bicci's anniversary office, implying that the vesting table over his tomb functioned in this manner.[171] While some of the stories concerning Florentine expeditions to the Holy Land to see Christ's tomb may document wishes rather than their fulfilment, members of the Acciaiuoli family, who held a fiefdom there from the king of Naples, and were leading Medici partisans between 1434 and 1466, made a pilgrimage to Jerusalem in the 1390s with Leonardo Frescobaldi, whose widely circulated account of their journey piqued the interest of his fellow-citizens.[172] Poggio Bracciolini wrote to his friend Niccoli in 1429 of a friend's planned visit to the Holy Sepulcher,[173] and Giovanni Rucellai reputedly sent to Jerusalem for the exact measurements of the sepulcher upon which his own was to be based.[174] According to Vespasiano, Cosimo was petitioned by a deputation of brothers from Jerusalem to rebuild the ruined mausoleum itself, and indeed paid for repairs and various ornaments, including his arms, through the Venetian branch of the bank. There is further evidence to confirm this tale in the record of the division of property between Cosimo and Pierfrancesco in 1451; the Holy Sepulcher in Jerusalem was explicitly excluded from the obligations of Pierfrancesco's line along with the work at Santa Croce, Santissima Annunziata, San Miniato, Bosco ai Frati and Camaldoli.[175]

Drawing with such inspiration upon fundamental Christian traditions as well as classical forms, and outdoing in this process all its Florentine precedents, the old sacristy was virtually guaranteed to have a tremendous impact upon its audience. In interpreting this impact, and the patron's intentions, as primarily political, some scholars have gone far beyond the considerable evidence of Medici social and political preeminence. Trachtenberg concluded that "the eagerness to participate in a Florentine and trans-Italian discourse of architectural semiosis involving status and power were probably as central to the making of early Renaissance architecture as the undeniably important, exhilarating search for antiquity, beauty, perfection, spirituality, and originality by architects and their backers."[176] This may well be true. It is not, however, true that "within a few years" of the building of the old sacristy "the Medici would impose . . . a north-Italian style of political autocracy [on Florence]."[177] Nor is it possible to justify the claim by John Paoletti that a building, sculpture, or painting "supports, in a barely subliminal manner, Medici plans of rulership which developed so swiftly after 1434."[178]

It seems ironic that art historians should stress a patron's political interests to the exclusion not only of his own and his society's desire for devotional images and places of worship – the "demand" that stimulated the creation or "supply" of most Renaissance art – but also of the skills and imagination of the artisans who responded to it. Why attribute the "daring, pride, and ambition" visible in the old sacristy more to Cosimo than to Brunelleschi, who freely boasted of these qualities of which others accused him?[179] Of course the Medici, like most other private patrons before or after them, "wished to put unambiguous, explicit signs of family possession on their memorial" in the form of arms, inscriptions, and images of patron saints. It does not therefore follow that if "the decorative program initiated by Cosimo and Lorenzo [in the old sacristy] clearly establishes the dynastic continuity of the family's presence in San Lorenzo" it does so also "by extension, in the city."[180] The "richness of architecturally produced meaning,"[181] the complex resonances of the images of the saints, and the use of noble materials combined in the old sacristy to honor not only its patrons, but also God and the city, which Giovanni Rucellai and many other Florentines defined as the joint objects of their patronage.

Many of the above arguments hinge on a distinction between public and private which is not at all supported by the evidence of Florentine ideas and attitudes presented in parts 1 and 2 of this book. Much is made, for example, of "the semiotics of the bronze display,"[182] an "anomalous use of bronze . . . in a private family chapel [which] transforms the space from a family to a quasi-civic structure . . . One might say that with [the old sacristy] doors Cosimo usurped for a private use a project type reserved for public places, just at the time he was gathering the political power of the republic under his private control."[183] But the old sacristy was not a "private" chapel in the sense implied here, any more than Cosimo enjoyed "private" control over the Florentine state. A church and its chapels belonged to the Church. What patrons of family chapels possessed were rights and privileges relating to their use; to their decoration, the display of family arms, the endowment of commemorative masses, and sometimes the burial of the dead. Historians, mindful of the solid display of a family's presence in a church, and the way in which it impressed them upon public awareness, refer for convenience to "private chapels." In fact, families had no actual title to property within a church, by contrast with the family palaces to which they are often compared; wills frequently mention family chapels, but what was bequeathed to heirs was not

land or the building upon it, but a tradition of rights and often onerous responsibilities imposed by the testator. These rights were ultimately contingent upon concessions from the prior and canons of the foundation, the church or convent, which could be and often were renegotiated at their pleasure.[184] Moreover, the old sacristy at San Lorenzo served not only as a burial chapel for the Medici family after they were accorded the privilege of paying for its building. It also played a vital role in the liturgical life of the church, and in its administrative and social functions; it was both the chapterhouse of San Lorenzo's clergy, and the site of their meetings with the parish and the neighborhood.

The building and decoration of churches was by no means viewed as a private affair. Public opinion, as discussed in chapter 11 on the Medici palace, was divided on the magnificence appropriate to the truly private palace, but despite some lingering doubts concerning the intrinsic evils of display, it generally decreed that no extravagance was excessive if it honored the glory of God and his Church. Contemporary comment on Cosimo as a patron of churches, and his association of his family with civic shrines at San Miniato and Santissima Annunziata, suggest that the decoration of the old sacristy may have represented not so much a claim to personal political power, as a demonstration of the benefits Cosimo's immense wealth and commensurate Christian charity might confer upon the commune and its Christian citizens. Moreover, in accordance with the theology of his day, as he neared fifty Cosimo may have judged that the best use of the wealth he had accumulated was to buy his own way into heaven.[185] This is not to dispute the suggestion that Florentine patrons, most notably the Medici, expressed their competition for status in the language of art and architecture. As far as the bronze doors are concerned, the comments of Vespasiano and Filarete imply that this single feature of the old sacristy alone would have made Cosimo de' Medici the outright winner of such a contest.[186] The old sacristy doors were way beyond the means of any other private patron of fifteenth-century Florence, as its citizens would well have known.[187] However, such flaunting of a superiority of means and of taste can in no sense be equated with a challenge to the constitutional authority of the government of the Florentine state.

The same is true of related and misleading suggestions – arising from imprecise borrowing of the terminology of modern linguistics – about the "appropriation," of saints, like symbols, customs, and spaces. The devotional imagery used in the decoration of family chapels like the old sacristy did not "belong" to particular families or institutions.[188] Cosmas and Damian, whose devotees in

Florence were usually friends and relatives of the Medici, if they were not physicians, were mainly identified with Cosimo in the popular mind. However, even these saints were at the same time embedded in a web of alternative associations with doctors, martyrs, early Christian saints, and protectors against illness. The other "Medici saints" – John the Evangelist, Lawrence, and Peter Martyr, were among the central figures of the Christian story. Medici references to civic saints such as Bernard and John the Baptist were matched by those of many other patrons wishing to identify themselves as the proud citizens of the Florentine republic.[189]

Finally, the reflections of Cosimo and his literary friends on death and commemoration show how explicitly the fame and honor for which wealthy and powerful men competed in this world were at once related and subordinated, in familiar Petrarchan terms, to the value of their virtue, and the salvation it earned them in the next. As the popular poet Niccolò Tinucci wrote in a consolatory sonnet addressed to Cosimo shortly after Lorenzo's death: "That worthy fame and valued honor/ which, my lord, renders worthy of memory/ he who virtuously lives, or dies,/ endows our hearts and eyes with hope,/ since we wish him to find comfort in that greater kingdom,/ escaped now from our earthly prison."[190] Cosimo and Lorenzo had made the very same point in their inscription on their parents' tomb.

The tomb

The tomb, finished by Buggiano in 1433,[191] bore two inscriptions. One, as noted in chapter 9, reflected in the same Petrarchan vein on the triumph of death over fame (fig. 78). "If services to his native city [patria], if the glory of his line and of his generosity to all, were free from dark death, alas, with his virtuous spouse he would live happily for his patria . . . But since death conquers all . . ."[192] This elaborate and explicitly classicizing inscription, carved in Roman capitals, is one of several in which Cosimo spelled out the message of his own commissions. It is also a very visible sign that the Medici were in the vanguard of the Florentine elite's interest in classical customs and forms, thanks no doubt to the amount of time that Cosimo, Lorenzo, and Nicola di Vieri de' Medici spent with their humanist friends Poggio and Niccoli. The undated inscription has sometimes been attributed to Lorenzo's contemporary, Poliziano, the most renowned of the Medici family's humanist associates. However, Howard Saalman's suggestion that it was composed by Niccoli, a great friend and admirer of Giovanni di Bicci, seems much more plausible; it is unlikely that

Giovanni's sons would have left bare for thirty years the plaque on the side of the tomb which greets the viewer entering from the church.[193] This inscription represents Giovanni di Bicci as a citizen of his republican patria in the Ciceronian style, as Cosimo represented himself and was represented in the inscription for his own tomb. The image of "dark death" is a common classical topos, and Propertius's Elegies, in Cosimo's library by 1418, contain a striking passage on this theme, very similar in tone to the tomb inscription; this work may also have influenced Cosimo's conception of the patron of art, or Maecenas, whom Propertius describes at length.[194]

In a beautifully observed description of the details of the tomb, John Shearman engaged in no speculation about the semiotics of bronze, but noted that "the centre of each long side rests on a bronze Tuscan column of high classical purity. From each column there grows a cluster of bronze ivy, partly gilded . . . and this ivy seems to grow up and over the edge on each long side to approach the bronze discs with brass palle inset on the tabletop, as if it would invest the Medici arms . . . This evergreen tradition has its roots, of course, deep in classical poetry." Alluding to the tombs of Sophocles and Anacreon, Shearman added that "there is a beautiful elegy of Propertius in which his dead Cynthia begs him to restrain 'the ivy from my tomb, that with aggressive cluster and twining leaves binds my frail bones . . .' It is the evergreen, seasonless nature of ivy, unchanging in frost and sun, that is invoked to express metaphorically the hope of immortality . . . an early expression of that specifically Medicean obsession with eternity and the endless return of the seasons . . ."[195]

While the classicizing tomb speaks of "dark death," Donatello's stucco decorations in the pendentives of the dome represent the light Christ shed on the ancient world. They illustrate the life of Saint John the Evangelist, whose gospel was one of the three books Giovanni di Bicci kept in his room.[196] This text, and the liturgy for the evangelist's feastday, which Giovanni and his sons would have read or heard countless times, is rich in the imagery of light. It records Christ's promise to his followers: "For God so loved the world, that he gave his only begotten Son, that whosoever believeth in him should not perish, but have everlasting life . . . that light is come into the world, and men loved darkness rather than light, because their deeds were evil . . . But he that doeth truth cometh to the light, that his deeds may be made manifest, that they are wrought in God." As Susan McKillop suggested, the office for the feast of Saint John the Evangelist is also a likely source of the iconography of the altar.[197]

The inscription facing away from the entrance to the

78   Andrea Cavalcanti, called Buggiano, tomb of Giovanni di Bicci de' Medici and Piccarda Bueri, Florence, San Lorenzo, old sacristy

sacristy is in more archaic lettering; in content it is similar to traditional Florentine tomb inscriptions. However, it is far more fulsome, and follows the custom of classical Roman citizens in recording the names of the commissioners of the tomb, Cosimo and Lorenzo, as well as its occupants, Giovanni di Bicci and Piccarda de' Bueri. The only obvious precedents in Florence were the memorial plaques of two other outstanding citizens of Giovanni di Bicci's generation, Maso degli Albizzi and Palla Strozzi.[198] Neither the tomb, nor the plaque in the Strozzi sacristy at Santa Trinita is securely dated, and they could have been later than the Medici memorial, but it is much more likely that the Strozzi sarcophagus inspired Giovanni di Bicci's, as the Magi altarpiece in the Strozzi chapel did the Magi frescoes in the Medici palace. Certainly at least four tombs made in the 1440s for other members of the Medici family and their friends were almost exact copies of the Strozzi tomb in its arcosolium setting.[199] In assessing the originality of the Medici tomb in the old sacristy, the weight of differences and similarities with other memorials must be balanced with care. Insofar as the Medici tomb was unique, its difference was one of degree

rather than kind, most particularly in its more genuine and accurate emulation of the classical spirit and its forms.

The altar

The altar of the small chapel within the sacristy, dated by an inscription of 1432, provided for the celebration of a steadily increasing number of commemorative and other masses for the souls of the Medici family endowed after 1429, when Giovanni di Bicci had requested first-class rank at San Lorenzo for the feasts of Cosmas and Damian and of John the Evangelist.[200] The Romanesque form of the altar derived directly from that of the baptistery, with a space in the middle of a front panel opening to an inner compartment. It was decorated with reliefs of the prophets Isaiah, Ezekiel, Jeremiah, and Daniel, holding their identifying scrolls inscribed with passages from their prophecies concerning God's promise to the people of Israel of the coming of the Messiah.

Set in the front panel was Brunelleschi's competition relief for the baptistery doors, depicting the Sacrifice of

Isaac (fig. 20). How the Medici acquired it or when it was installed is not known, but like a painter's signature on a panel or his portrait in a fresco, it served as a personal reminder of the sacristy's builder. The bronze plaque was also a physical link between Donatello's bronze doors and the rest of the decorative scheme, perhaps suggesting an association between these bronze doors in the sacristy and those of the baptistery, one of the city's proudest artistic achievements. The theme underlying the sacrifice of Isaac was in essence that of the whole sacristy; at once the love and reverence which bound fathers and sons, and the obedience to the Lord and his edicts that overrode even this primal bond. It was a story dear to all Florentine hearts and particularly to those of the Medici family; Feo Belcari's later *sacra rappresentazione* of *Abraham and Isaac* was dedicated to Cosimo's younger son Giovanni, and proved to be the most popular of all his plays.[201] Beside its religious and civic connotations, the panel was also something of a collector's piece, which would have increased its appeal to Cosimo and his sons.

McKillop saw in the passages from the books of the four prophets a reference to the Medici exile from their Florentine Jerusalem, and a invocation of divine intervention to guarantee their return to political ascendancy. These passages strongly evoke the prophecies of the city's special destiny which appear in many *zibaldoni* and were to become the focus of Savonarola's message to the Florentines in the last decade of the fifteenth century; they were surely very familiar to Cosimo and his father. Nevertheless, it is impossible to demonstrate that the Medici or their architect conceived a link between such iconographical elements as the twelve apertures of the old sacristy, the twelve apostles, and the twelve gates of heaven, despite the fondness of many Renaissance men, including Brunelleschi, for numerological schema. What we know of what Cosimo wrote or read does not suggest that he was personally interested in such esoterica; the painted ceiling of the small dome of the altar chapel with its precise astrological configuration seems more characteristic of his relatively straightforward interest in the heavens and their signs.

The astrological ceiling of the altar chancel

The ceiling of the chancel has long intrigued students of the Medici and the old sacristy. Painted on it is a night sky with stars and astrological signs whose configuration indicates a particular date. No attempt to identify it has yet been accepted as entirely successful. Once again,

there are classical precedents for such a decoration. There are references to antique vaults painted to look like the visible sky in several classical texts, including Suetonius, in Cosimo's library in 1418. Petrarch's *Africa* refers to an astronomical dome, an idea that caught Alberti's imagination, and which later in the century he was to describe in *De Re Architectura*.[202] At the turn of the fourteenth and fifteenth centuries, the intellectual circle that included Palla Strozzi, Leonardo Bruni, and Roberto de' Rossi, Cosimo's teacher, sponsored expeditions to Constantinople to obtain Greek manuscripts, including Ptolemy's *Cosmographia* or *Geographia*. This atlas of the world greatly advanced the Western understanding of astronomy and also stimulated interest in the related subject of astrology.[203]

Vespasiano described Cosimo as much interested in astrology, "because he was always talking about it with Maestro Paolo [Toscanelli] and with other astrologers, and he believed in it and used it in some of his affairs." Many other Florentines believed in the power of the stars to influence the affairs of men, as may be seen from the references to astrological studies and prophecies in their *zibaldoni*, and from the several occasions on which major civic events, including ceremonies at the cathedral and the palace of government, were scheduled in accordance with favorable astrological indications. Toscanelli was a Florentine physician who became famous for publishing an important astrological treatise in 1446–8, but Cosimo knew him well before that, since they served together as the executors of Niccoli's will of 1430.[204]

The Magi, of course, were wise men whose understanding of scientific magic enabled them to calculate by the stars the time and place of Christ's birth. Francis Ames-Lewis observed that the man at the center of the fresco of the *Adoration of the Magi* in Cosimo's cell at San Marco holds an armillary sphere, the instrument and symbol of astrological and astronomical studies.[205] Saint John the Evangelist, to whom the old sacristy is dedicated, was represented in Byzantine tradition as an alchemist, and even to western Christians his Book of Revelations offered a fertile field for the generation of numerological theories and prophecies.[206] Brunelleschi was also a close friend of Toscanelli, and himself deeply involved with geometrical, numerological, and metaphysical concepts; his architecture depends to a considerable extent on the articulation of number and proportion.[207]

A letter Cosimo wrote to his younger son Giovanni early in 1445 directly testifies to his interest in the study of astrology and its students. With reference apparently to a scholar recommended to him by the Lord of Camerino, Cosimo observed that he has the reputation of being very good in medicine and also in astrology; at the moment there wouldn't be a position for him at the Studio [the university of Florence], because the elections to fill the vacancy for several years to come have already been held. The Lord of Camerino has sent a messenger on his behalf, but if there is nothing to be done about the election, he would like some pretext to be made by which he could receive the scholar's gown to come to the Studio, and this could indeed be done, so let him know this.[208]

With the aid of computer-based astronomical tables, a date of 6 July 1439 at noon was proposed in 1981; another, of 4 July 1442, was suggested after the cleaning and restoration of the fresco in 1985/6. Although technical advances and a clearer vision of the image would seem important, arguments have concentrated largely on identifying a date that was plausibly of major significance to Cosimo and his family. The only event proposed for July 1442 was the visit to Florence of René of Anjou, who arrived in the city on the 15th or 16th of that month. The failure of the dates to match precisely is no real problem; such a symbolic commemoration could equally well focus, for example, on some other point in the delegation's progress toward Florence. Much more important is the fact that everything we know about Florentine custom and Cosimo's caution make it highly unlikely that he would commemorate such an event on the ceiling of his father's burial chapel. All other considerations aside, in view of the volatile nature of the diplomatic balance of power between states, and the paramount importance to any politician, particularly Cosimo, of maintaining flexibility, he would hardly have chosen at a relatively early and uncertain moment in his ascendancy over the Florentine *reggimento* to inscribe the evidence of any political alliance in such a public place. Moreover, while the Medici were generally interested in cultivating ties with the Angevins, a letter from Cosimo to his son Giovanni, written a few months before René's visit, expresses his own serious reservations about the Signoria's proposal of such an alliance.[209]

At any moment some scholar may discover an event of more persuasive significance to Cosimo that occurred on or around 4 July 1442.[210] Meanwhile, 6 July 1439, the date Patricia Fortini Brown suggested is represented on the ceiling, marks an event of indubitable importance to Cosimo, to Florence, and indeed to all Christendom. On 5 July the articles of union between Eastern and Western Christendom, affirming the pope as teacher and father of all Christians, were signed by the Latin and Greek delegates to the council. The following day, 6 July, was declared the Day of Union, and celebrated as a public holiday in Florence; all businesses were closed, throngs of people massed in the streets around the cathedral, and inside it the occasion was marked by splendid ceremonies. The Bull promulgated by the pope to announce this event began with the phrase "Laetentur Caeli"; let the heavens rejoice. It would have been eminently appropriate had Cosimo decided to have represented on the domed ceiling of the altar chapel the position of the stars in the heavens on this day.[211] Nevertheless, the question of the date on the ceiling and its significance to the Medici may well prove to be one of those tantalizing puzzles of history whose solution is lost to us forever.

Donatello's figural decoration

The lunettes beneath the dome over the main space of the sacristy were decorated by Donatello with stucco roundels depicting the four evangelists, and scenes in polychrome from the life of Saint John appear in the pendentives above them (fig. 79). Below the cornice was a frieze of stucco cherubs, and over the bronze doors on either side of the altar there were large stucco reliefs, of Saints Cosmas and Damian on one side, and Saints Lawrence and Stephen on the other. The featured saints were the protectors of Giovanni di Bicci and his sons; as the most direct sources of the message of Christ, the evangelists and the early Christian martyrs were also figures of universal importance to all Christians. One contemporary poet described his view of the chapel: "Looking into the Sacristy,/ every proud man is humbled there./ For here we see imaged the entire Old Testament, and the new as well."[212]

The gospels of the four evangelists were the biblical texts which appeared most frequently in Renaissance libraries and scrapbooks, and Francesco di Altobianco degli Alberti's *terze rime* version of the Gospel of Saint John was particularly popular. And of course the images of Saint John the Evanglist's book of *Revelations* were continually before the public eye in the mosaics of the Apocalypse on the dome of the baptistery. Donatello's representations of the evangelists were distinguished by his characteristic *inventio*, particularly in the virtual personification of their traditional symbols, the lion, the ox, and the eagle. The roses on the pedestal of Saint John's seat may be a reference to Giovanni di Bicci's close and crucial association with the papacy.

The scenes from the life of Saint John were the raising of Drusiana, his martyrdom, his vision on Patmos, and his apotheosis, all concerned with the themes of death and resurrection appropriate to a burial chapel. While the last three themes were treated with stunning originality, in a tour de force of the manipulation of space to great

79   Donatello, *Ascension of Saint John to Heaven*, Florence, San Lorenzo, old sacristy

emotional effect, the raising of Drusiana is clearly based on Giotto's treatment of this narrative in the Peruzzi chapel at Santa Croce, in homage perhaps to the city's most famous artistic son. Cosimo's only specific comment on artists referred to the greatness of Giotto; one small panel attributed to him appears in the inventory of the Medici palace contents in 1492. Cosimo's wife, Contessina, was a Bardi and her branch of the family also owned a chapel frescoed by Giotto at Santa Croce.

Brunelleschi's biographer Manetti launched a tradition that the architect and the sculptor disagreed over the imposition of Donatello's decoration upon Brunelleschi's already eloquent architecture. It has been eagerly embraced by those who find the decorative scheme excessive. Some architectural historians, however, have stressed that what Saalman described as the "numerical niceties" of the architecture in fact support the whole scheme; as he observed, "the Evangelists are given further emphasis (and the three zones of the elevations are subtly interrelated) by the fact that the central consoles under the entablature, the central windows of the sides, the evanglists' roundels and one rib of the melon dome over each of the roundels all lie in the major axes."[213]

Indeed, the most striking aspect of the iconography of the old sacristy is the integration of its various elements, by comparison with earlier family chapels in Santa Maria Novella and Santa Croce, filled with a jumble of individual commissions made over the centuries in various media and styles. This integration is partly a function of the new sophisticated taste for the classical which required patrons to build *ex novo*, and of the wealth that made this possible. The figural decoration follows the progressive revelation of Christianity, unfolded over time according to Scripture; from the four prophets of the altar to the four evanglists of the dome to the four martyrs of the overdoors, the panels of the doors representing a series of apostles and martyrs.

The many associations of the saints most prominently depicted in the old sacristy complicates the question of their function as reminders of their Medici devotees. John Paoletti argued persuasively that this schema, especially on the south wall, which descends from the roundel depicting Saint John the Evangelist over the arch above the altar to the overdoors depicting respectively Saints Cosmas and Damian and Saints Lawrence and Stephen,[214] represents also the genealogical descent of the Medici line from Giovanni di Bicci to Cosimo and Lorenzo, and further to their respective sons Piero and Giovanni, and Pierfrancesco and Francesco, whose name-saints are represented on panels of the bronze doors.[215] The evocation of the patron and his sons was surely a major point of the decorative scheme; the absence of Mariological or Christological imagery is quite striking. Beginning with Abraham and Isaac on the altar panel and passing via Giovanni di Bicci's name-saint to those of Cosimo and Lorenzo, we are looking at a succession of patriarchs and patrons.

The bronze doors

In his wide-ranging discussion of the classical sources of quattrocento artists, Howard Burns drew attention to the possibility "that the Old Sacristy portals are the earliest Renaissance architectural work to reproduce a specific Roman monument . . . in or near the hemicycle of Trajan's Forum."[216] Since Trajan's forum was in the same neighborhood as the basilica of Saints Cosmas and Damian, which Lorenzo, Cosimo's brother, sustained with his patronage, this monument was probably familiar to the Medici brothers; it is known that they studied Roman antiquities in the company of their humanist friends.[217] The doors are usually assigned to the decade between 1434, when the Medici returned from exile, and 1443, when Donatello departed for a long stay in Padua.

80 Donatello, Florence, San Lorenzo, old sacristy, bronze door with martyrs

According to Manetti, they were left until the patrons decided whether they should be be "of wood or some other material."[218]

The door on the left of the altar is usually described as that of the martyrs, since all the figures hold the palm of martyrdom; the one on the right is known as the door of the apostles (fig. 80). The homonymous saints of Cosimo's and Lorenzo's sons can be identified, but only with some difficulty, since their attributes are not all clearly articulated. This might suggest that the doors were intended primarily to represent the Church's honored categories of apostles and martyrs, rather than members of the Medici family associated with these saints.[219] Contemporaries commented on the unusually active postures of the saints; as Eve Borsook remarked, Donatello explored in the panels of the sacristy's bronze doors "all the dramatic possibilities of discoursing figures: greeting, listening, arguing, agreeing, or running past one another".[220] It was in fact the role of saints, martyrs and apostles to point the way for other Christians – to present a view of Christian truths as living, active, and persuasive.

An interpretation of Donatello's saints and martyrs as doing battle for the Church is supported by Filarete's perception of the figures as pugnacious; he thought they resembled fencers or wrestlers rather than holy men.[221] Colin Eisler, exploring the classical concept of athletic virtue, observed that its essence was fortitude, as defined by Aristotle and by Cicero in the *Tusculan Disputations*; Cosimo owned and was familiar with these works. The Neoplatonic patristic writers, incorporating also Saint Paul's frequent references to "the wrestler" and "the boxer," introduced gymnastic imagery into the Christian tradition. The clearest images of athletic combats between virtues and vices, a battle which was also a major theme of popular devotional culture, appear in the writings of Chrysostom, which Cosimo sought out and obtained with Traversari's aid.[222]

San Bernardino employed and further popularized these images in his account of the types of letters by which men might learn. His third category was "vocal letters, invented for those men who desire actively to busy themselves for charity's sake, pleading and discoursing, in order that they may be learned and may teach others; and these excel the first two."[223] Such a view was precisely imaged in the representation of the Ascension play staged in the church of the Carmine, for which Donatello himself designed the stage machinery.[224] The role of the classical orator was similarly didactic and persuasive, a point Cosimo noted in the margin of his copy of Cicero's *Orator*. In 1437 Luca della Robbia was working side by side with Donatello on their *cantorie* for the duomo; later,

81   Luca della Robbia, *Philosophy*, Florence, Museo dell'Opera del Duomo

he borrowed directly from the San Lorenzo doors to represent philosophy – logic and dialectic – in his plaque for Giotto's bell tower (fig. 81), more direct confirmation that viewers read the doors' panels as images of discourse.

Some historians have identified the discourse more precisely as that of the disputing participants of the council called in 1438 to discuss the reunion of the eastern and western halves of the Church. The council was convened in Ferrara, but with Cosimo's encouragement and financial support it moved to Florence in January 1439. The significance of this experience for Florence and its *popolo* was spelled out in the plaque placed on a pillar near the high altar in the cathedral; it makes explicit reference to the contentious debates which characterized the council, announcing its successful conclusion "after long disputations." Ambrogio Traversari, the early Christian scholar who was a close friend of the Medici brothers, played a leading role in these debates. Paoletti pointed out the prevalence of the imagery of fighting in Traversari's descriptions of the council, which would certainly have helped to color Cosimo's view of it, apart from his own impressions.[225] In 1438, before the delegates even convened, Traversari wrote from Ferrara to a friend about preparations for the discussions: "Pray, father (since you are no longer able to fight due to your age), that our Agonotheta is deemed worthy to be granted victory amidst the fighting, and that the only truth that prevails rests with us. Extend like Moses your hand to the hills; we will fight in the plains and the Lord will overcome. Already we have joined in minor battles and have stirred things up in turn, and we are confident they will be conquered using reason and mildness."[226]

Gombrich dismissed Krautheimer's suggestion concerning a reference to the council in Ghiberti's *Solomon and Sheba* panel for the north doors of the baptistery, on the grounds that Renaissance images have no reference to topical events – a demonstrably false proposition – and that the attempt to reunite the eastern branches of the Church with the western was a distant, and in the long run unsuccessful, event.[227] As already observed, this was not the perception of Florentine citizens at the time, who saw this occasion as bringing excitement and renown to their city. Nor was it likely to have been Cosimo's view. His crucial role in the council, which made Florence for a few months the vital heart of Christendom, increased his own importance in the eyes of his fellow-citizens and of the pope; it also increased, in return for a considerable initial outlay, the profits of his bank. It would surely have added to his credit in the ledger he kept for the Lord. Stimulated perhaps by the notable relevance of familiar Christian texts to contemporary events, he might well, wishing to signify in a commission for San Lorenzo his personal commitment to the defence of the Church, have suggested the theme of debate or dispute over Christian truths to Donatello, whose *inventio* took care of the rest.

Apart from the decoration of the old sacristy, the elements of San Lorenzo's design in which Cosimo's interests or patronage are most clearly expressed are the arrangements for his burial before the high altar, and his commission of the bronze pulpits eventually installed in its environs. Since these were conceived and executed at the very end of his life or after his death, concluding his oeuvre, they are dealt with in the final section of the conclusion of this book.

COOPERATING TO HONOR THE CITY, AND THE ORDERS AND CULTS OF THE CHURCH

Most Florentine families' patronage of churches was concentrated in their own special sphere of influence, their residential neighborhood of parish, *gonfalone*, or quarter.[228] The Medici neighborhood was unusually extensive; the Medici family was one of the largest lineages in Florence. Their erstwhile rivals the Strozzi had no less than fifty-four households living in the city in 1427, but the Medici boasted twenty-seven, by comparison with the average family of only half a dozen.[229] These were spread across the ward of the Golden Lion, centred on the parish church of San Lorenzo and extending north to San Marco, and the *gonfalone* of the Dragon, to the east embracing Santissima Annunziata, and to the south, San Tommaso. The conspicuous patronage of Piero di Cosimo at Santissima Annunziata, the parish church of several main lines of Medici resident in the *gonfalone* of Drago, was preceded and accompanied by commissions from other high-profile members of the family from Orlando di Guccio's line. Bernardo d'Antonio de' Medici, leader of the Florentine forces in the victory at Anghiari in 1440, enhanced the Medici aura in the eyes of the populace through his deeds on the field of battle. An important patron at various sites in Florence and the Mugello, particularly of the artist Castagno, Bernardo lived on the Via Larga just north of Cosimo's house, and was also buried at San Lorenzo in a chapel he endowed there.

The Medici role in the patronage of churches has naturally attracted most attention from historians, partly because it was more conspicuous, more extensive and more extravagant than that of any other single family; partly because it is seen as an expression of their increasing predominance in Florentine political life. Either way, the significance of their patronage is distorted by being viewed, as it usually is, primarily from the perspective of an exclusive focus on the Medici. Medici ecclesiastical building was undertaken in the context of an enormous upsurge in private patronage of churches and chapels which preceded their rise to power. Suggestions that the Medici "appropriated" particular sites need to be balanced by an awareness that several Medici interventions occurred as part of larger rebuilding programs involving a number of other patrons, sometimes other prominent members of the Medici lineage, sometimes their friends, whose patronage has been relatively neglected.

San Tommaso

The parish of San Tommaso was the original Medici neighborhood. San Tommaso was a Medici church not because Cosimo took it over in the mid-fifteenth century, but because the houses of so many of the larger lineage were situated in its vicinity. The church stood at the northeast corner of the former Mercato Vecchio, now Piazza della Repubblica (figs. 82 and 39). From the twelfth century the Medici shared the patronage of the

82   Codex Rustici, Florence, Seminario Arcivescovile, fol. 29v,
San Tommaso, church and fresco

tinuing emphasis on his association with San Tommaso is probably, as Paoletti argued, to be linked with the commune's veneration of the patron saint of a Medici family church as a symbol of justice and truth.[231]

Around 1385 a fresco, now lost, was painted above the door to the audience chamber of the Signoria in the Palazzo Vecchio, depicting the Incredulity of Saint Thomas. (The Apostle Thomas, doubting the truth of the Resurrection of the crucified Christ, thrust his hand into the wound in Christ's side to verify the identity of his Lord.[232]) The popular poet Franco Sacchetti wrote the verses placed alongside the image. In his opening lines Saint Thomas urged the viewer to "touch the truth" of the spirit, as he had done, and thus to believe "in the supreme justice in three persons" (the Trinity) who always exalts those "who do right." The principal purpose of Sacchetti's poem was to relate spiritual to secular truth and justice. His verses instructed the Signoria that "your every action/ should consider the good of the commune without fail." If they should "seek the truth, then Justice will follow." They must therefore direct their minds to "the good of the commune," for without this "every kingdom . . . fails." San Tommaso was similarly employed as a symbol of justice in the iconography of other Tuscan palaces of government in the fourteenth and fifteenth centuries, and adopted as a patron by other Florentine civic bodies who wished to represent themselves as serving justice.[233]

These included the Otto di Guardia, the police magistracy, and the Mercanzia, the merchant's court, the chief judicial arbiter of the activities of the guilds, and of the business and manufacturing activities by which so many Florentines were occupied and enriched. Cosimo de' Medici, as we learn from his letters and those of his correspondents, was particularly involved in the business of the Mercanzia, and wielded great influence at its court. The Mercanzia chapel established in the cathedral *circa* 1460 was dedicated to San Tommaso, who was also the subject of Verrocchio's bronze statues for a niche at Orsanmichele, which the Mercanzia bought from the Parte Guelfa in the early 1460s. According to Parte records, the niche was sold to raise money to complete the Parte Guelfa palace, designed by Brunelleschi. Cosimo's elder son Piero was at this time a member of both the Parte Guelfa building committee, and the committee of the Mercanzia responsible for the decoration of their newly acquired niche at Orsanmichele. These corporate commissions would have helped to keep Saint Thomas and his symbolic connotations in the forefront of the public mind, and perhaps to remind people of his association with the Medici. For during his term as Gonfalonier of Justice in January/February 1435, just two

church with the Sizi family; when they died out after the plague of 1348, the Medici apparently remained its only patrons. Several lines of the family, including that of Cosimo's cousin Averardo di Francesco di Bicci, continued to reside in this small inner-city area in the fifteenth century. The wedding of Averardo's grandson Francesco to his Guicciardini bride took place at San Tommaso in June 1433, with most of the lineage and its closest allies and in-laws in attendance, just a few weeks before the young man was exiled to the Veneto along with his elders. Those Medici who had moved away from the district, among them Cosimo and his sons, retained patronage rights over the church because they had property in the parish, including the Medici bank.[230] John Paoletti drew attention to this little considered locus of Medici patronage and assembled a good deal of material relating to the presence of the Medici leaders in their ancestral neighborhood in the 1450s. Cosimo's con-

months after his return from exile, Cosimo had proposed that the feast of San Tommaso be specially celebrated by the commune to mark this occasion. While there was supposedly some objection to his request on the grounds that Cosimo's return was a private matter, and that Florentine feasts were designed to celebrate public victories and procure future grace for the whole body politic, not for a single part of it, the idea was eventually accepted. A law decreed that every year the Sei di Mercanzia and the consuls of the twenty-one guilds must go to the church of San Tommaso to make an offering with "candles or torches lit."[234] Cosimo established another communal feast to celebrate the victory of the Medicean regime over its internal enemies in 1458; this is not recorded as being associated with any particular saint.[235]

Saint Thomas was also the focus of a cult enthusiastically celebrated in Florence and its environs – that of the "Girdle of the Virgin." In one of several apocryphal accounts of the Assumption of the Virgin there was a story parallel to the biblical account of Thomas's incredulity, this time relating to Christ's mother. Absent once again at the crucial moment, and again assailed by doubt, Thomas called upon the Virgin for a sign that she had really ascended. She threw down her girdle. From the twelfth century, the precious relic of the apocryphal girdle was venerated in Prato, now a suburb of Florence, and it became the center of a flourishing cult. This was fueled, no doubt, by the account of the Virgin's gift of the girdle in the life of Thomas in *The Golden Legend*, a story frequently transcribed in popular compilations.[236] In April 1459 Cosimo received a letter from the governors of Prato replying to a letter of his requesting that they give a special showing to the papal and Milanese visitors then in Florence of "the precious girdle of the glorious Virgin Mary"; they acceded to his request.[237]

Cosimo also played at least an incidental part in facilitating the completion of a pulpit to display this renowed relic. In the 1420s Brunelleschi was consulted concerning the design of an outdoor pulpit on the facade of Prato cathedral to display the relic, and in 1428 the commission to make the marble-clad pulpit was assigned to Donatello and Michelozzo. It was to be finished by September 1429, but the work, documented in detail over many years, proceeded excruciatingly slowly. In 1432 Cosimo de' Medici, presumably on account of his close relationship with the two sculptors, was asked to intervene. He sent Giovanni d'Antonio de' Medici, a factor of the Florentine *tavola* of the Medici bank, to see Donatello in Rome, and shortly after, work was resumed. However, not until 1438 was the pulpit sufficiently advanced to permit a ceremony to display the relic.[238] Feo Belcari's well-known reference to Donatello in his *sacra rappresen-*

tazione of *Nebuchadnezzar, King of Babylon,* also alluded to this assignment. When summoned by the king to make his statue in gold, being reputed the greatest of sculptors, Donatello demurred: "I must depart soon because/ I have to do the Pulpit of Prato."[239]

In December 1459, shortly after the reconsolidation of the Medici regime with the institution of the Council of One Hundred, Cosimo exercised his *ius patronatus* in the replacement of San Tommaso's deceased rector Antonio Lenzi by his kinsman Matteo di Iacopo Lenzi; the Lenzi family had long been partisans of the Medici. For the ratification of the election, Cosimo assembled all the living heads of the households of the Medici lineage, no less than eighteen men. He also endowed the church with two prebends; the notarial act was signed in his own house. Paoletti noted that the inventory of the church prepared at the time records numerous fifteenth-century gifts of furnishings by the Medici family, and that Cosimo himself presented the church in 1460 with an altarpiece described in a later inventory as representing Saint Thomas "in the act of receiving the girdle of the Madonna who is depicted hovering in the air above her tomb." The inscription beneath the panel, recording Cosimo's gift as being "in the time that Matteo Lenzi ruled over this seat, 1460" underlines its intention to commemorate the accession of Cosimo's nominee and friend.[240]

In the following century Vasari described a fresco of Doubting Thomas over the door of San Tommaso which he attributed to Uccello. A seventeenth-century observer also referred to the fresco and its particularly public and frequented site in the Mercato Vecchio. He noted an inscription from which he made out the words "India tibi cessit" (India yielded to you).[241] There is in fact a little-remarked contemporary drawing of the fresco in the well-known Codex Rustici, which described and illustrated the city's main buildings; the text dated from 1425, the drawings between mid-century and 1465.[242] Beside his drawing Rustici gave a brief account of the life of Saint Thomas, obviously based on *The Golden Legend*. An important facet of Saint Thomas's image as refracted by this popular text was the saga of his missionary journeys to the East, where he preached the gospel to the Parthians, the Medes, the Persians, the Hircanians, and the Bactrians. He was said to have converted the king of India, and many of his subjects, while designing and building a palace for him. Hence Thomas became also the patron of builders and architects.

The author of *The Golden Legend* repeated Saint John Chrysostom's claim that Thomas had penetrated as far into the Orient as "the lands of the Magi who had come to adore Christ, and that he baptized them and they helped to propagate the Christian faith."[243] There seems little doubt that the fresco was read and commissioned primarily in these terms, if not by Cosimo, then by another member of the family wishing to associate in it two powerful visual symbols cultivated by the Medici, Saint Thomas and the Magi, with images of civic justice and the quest for secular and spiritual truth. Cosimo himself might well have thought of adding resonance to the Medici association with the Magi by building on the tradition of Chrysostom, one of his favorite authors. Just as Thomas baptized the Magi who helped to propagate the Christian faith, so Cosimo, who identified his family with these wealthy but wise men, had helped to propagate that faith when he financed the Eastern delegations to the church council.[244]

John Paoletti, to whom we owe most of the details of Medici patronage at San Tommaso, saw in the San Tommaso ceremonies and commissions "a possible Medici appropriation of civic imagery for . . . a family church . . . merg[ing] family history with city history" and linked to Piero di Cosimo's "supplant[ing]" of Parte Guelfa imagery with that of Saint Thomas as part of the Medici takeover of the Parte Guelfa.[245] The ingredients of his account are fascinating and indeed suggestive of a new phase after 1458 in the relations of the Medici family with the government of Florence which has been recognized and documented by historians of the Florentine constitution, of the Medici regime and patronage network, and of the Parte Guelfa.[246] The gathering of the Medici clan at San Tommaso, the ancestral Medici church, under Cosimo's leadership, emphasizing the strength of the family at a ceremony concerned with spiritual authority, namely the appointment of a rector of a church, recalls Cosimo's performance at the consecration of the cathedral in 1436 and foreshadows similar ceremonial incidents of Laurentian Florence. However, the symbolic associations of San Tommaso for Florentine Christians and citizens preceded Cosimo and his commissions; they could not be simply "appropriated" by any individual, however powerful. Besides, his imagined intentions were only one of the factors affecting the affairs and imagery of the Mercanzia and Parte Guelfa at this time.

Considering these, and the preexisting conjunction of images of the crucified Christ, Saint Thomas and the Virgin of the Girdle within Orsanmichele, Diane Zervas came to a conclusion precisely the opposite of Paoletti's; that Cosimo de' Medici "emulated that conjunction with his altarpiece of the *Assumption with Saint Thomas* for San Tommaso in 1460." The eventual installation of Verrocchio's *Christ with Saint Thomas,* begun in 1467, led to a shift in the Signoria's annual procession, from the church of San Tommaso to the oratory of Orsanmichele,

associating the saint's connotations of justice and good government with the city and its sacred places, rather than with the Medici family and their neighborhood church.[247]

Medici patronage at San Tommaso splendidly illustrates the potential of visual symbols and images to associate, connect, and on occasion fuse the spiritual with the secular elements of Florentine culture. Such fusion is one of the salient features of Cosimo's oeuvre, which illuminates Florentine politics as part of the city's culture, fleshing out its living reality as narrowly political and constitutional studies cannot. The figure of San Tommaso does indeed establish a visual association between the city, the corporation, and the family, but not necessarily a Machiavellian "conspiracy" against the commune – indeed Machiavelli himself judged that the Medici harbored no such plot. The Medici use of such symbolism did not blur the distinctions between these entities; it was effective because no sharp distinctions existed. It was not initially Cosimo, but Florentine popular culture that conflated them.

Santa Croce

In his account of Cosimo's patronage, the architect Filarete made a point of his even-handedness toward the orders of the Church. The frequent pairing in images commissioned by the Medici of Saints Francis and Peter Martyr, while also referring to the family's onomastic saints, perhaps points in the same direction, following the example set in images commissioned by the two great mendicant orders.[248] It may be that Cosimo commissioned a chapel for the novices of the main Franciscan convent of Santa Croce to balance his generosity to the newly founded house of Observant Dominicans at San Marco (fig. 83). Santa Croce also had special significance to Cosimo as a businessman and a partisan politician. The convent was one of a handful of places where he had left money for safekeeping just before he was exiled in 1433, and a chapel built within a decade of his return might appropriately have expressed his appreciation of the convent's past service.

If probably not as Machiavellian as some modern historians represent him, Cosimo was certainly a master manipulator of the political process. His gift may also have anticipated some future service from the friars, since the electoral bags that determined the composition of communal offices, and thus the rise or fall of the Medici regime, were kept at Santa Croce. A letter to Piero from Brother Antonio de' Medici of the convent of Santa Croce, dated 12 June 1469, five years after Cosimo's

death, contains no revelations of electoral gerryman-
dering, but it shows that the friars' privileges did open
the way to their interference in politics. Observing that
he had passed by the Medici palace twice that morning
to visit Piero "as was my duty," but was unable to speak
to him, Antonio referred obliquely to an incident in the
city's foreign relations which he promised that the bearer
of the letter would explain to Piero in full. However, he
did request Piero to pen two lines to the Gonfalonier of
Justice, asking him to communicate to a friar detained in
the Prior's palace Antonio's decision to recommend his
exile, on account of "certain misdeeds in the matter of
holding back letters of the ambassadors of the king of
Naples and the duke of Milan which we were sending
to Venice."[249]

There were other possible rewards for Medici patronage at Santa Croce. The Franciscan church was the
center of the patronage and devotion of a large number
of great old Florentine families, in a district where the
Medici had made no other substantial patronage statement. Its enormous space also invited artisan worshippers
from nearby manufacturing districts like San Martino,
where Cosimo supported a public charity. Services at
Santa Croce were one of the main sources of gifts for the
Buonomini of San Martino, who regularly stood outside
the church soliciting donations after mass or on the occasion of sermons by popular visiting preachers. Extending
to this area of the city a reminder of his civic virtue and
charity, Cosimo could expect in return the goodwill of
many Florentines and also their prayers; the terms of the
endowment of the chapel obliged the monks to say a
mass each week in memory of Cosimo's soul.[250]

However, what Howard Saalman has described as "the
Medici's least lavish ecclesiastical foundation," may well
have sprung from Cosimo's wish to contribute to a joint
effort on the part of various civic agencies, including
the commune itself, to restore one of the city's major
churches after a natural disaster.[251] A fire had destroyed
the dormitory of the convent in 1423, and the building
of the Medici chapel, in conjunction with new quarters
for the novices, was part of a wider campaign of
rebuilding to which the Calimala guild, the commune,
and Cosimo's friend and banking associate Andrea de'
Pazzi also contributed.[252] The merchants' court at which
Cosimo de' Medici was prominent was responsible for
Santa Croce, as the Wool Guild was for the cathedral. It
was the Sei di Mercanzia who disbursed the money collected by the commune to the *operai* of Santa Croce. After
an initial state appropriation to pay for the repairs, collection lapsed while the expenses of war consumed all
the resources of the commune and its citizens. Very little
money was collected until 1434, when payments began

83   Michelozzo, Novitiate Chapel, Florence, Santa Croce

again. By 1436 the new dormitory was substantially completed; in 1439 a specific record of Cosimo's donations
was entered in the *sepoltuario* of the convent: "The chapel
which is at the entrance of the dormitory of the novices
is dedicated to SS. Cosmas and Damian: Cosimo de'
Medici had this dormitory and the chapel and the passage
in front of the sacristy made."[253]

The architect of the Medici chapel is not named, but
it is generally attributed to Michelozzo, with the possible
participation of Bernardo Rossellino. It would thus form
part of the considerable portion of Cosimo's oeuvre
created in cooperation with this Medici friend, sculptor,
and architect. It features the combination of traditional
and Renaissance elements regarded as characteristic of
Michelozzo, and a notable feature of Cosimo's major
buildings, most creatively displayed in the Medici palace.
An intriguing edict of the Signoria of 1448 forbade the
monks to tamper with the existing building: "since it is
known that a large, noble and ample dormitory has
been built by the commune of Florence in the friars'
monastery of Santa Croce, with rooms and other facili-
ties, since there are also other buildings there, and since
the aforesaid friars carry out fresh works every day as
they please, piercing walls and breaking doors between
two rooms, making and widening windows ... which
detract from the beauty, strength and amplitude of the
building."[254]

Historians have wondered whether this was an attempt
to preserve the Medici building plan, or to prevent it

from going ahead, in rather the same way as a large petition signed by the leading citizens of Florence in 1449
was at first thought to be an anti-Medicean protest,
then later revealed as an attempt to shore up the Medici
regime.[255] Pending clarification, the edict concerning
building at Santa Croce may at least be regarded as fascinating evidence of the complex relations between the
Florentine government and various, often autonomous,
bodies existing within the framework of the commune,
among them the guilds, the Mercanzia, the Parte Guelfa,
the orders of the Church, and private citizens and patrons
like the Medici and the Pazzi.

San Miniato

A similar situation of cooperation between private and
corporate patrons existed at San Miniato, under the
purview of the Calimala, or international merchants'
(importers and exporters) guild. In June 1447 the guild
announced that a "great citizen" had offered to construct
an appropriate shrine for the revered cross of San
Giovanni Gualberto, the founder of the Vallombrosan
order. His offer to build a "very imposing and costly
tabernacle" would be gratefully accepted, with the understanding that the only arms to be displayed on it would
be those of the guild – an eagle clutching a bale of
wool.[256] The Medici were unwilling to have their generosity so subsumed under the aegis of the guild, and in
1449 permission was granted Piero de' Medici to display
his own arms in a less prominent place. The avian devices
of guild and patron complement as much as vie with one
another, the modestly sized Calimala eagle being perched
at the apex of the arch of the tabernacle roof, facing the
congregation, and Piero's larger falcon with a diamond
ring in its claw, on a ledge at the rear of the tabernacle,
facing the high altar on the upper storey. The tabernacle
is framed by the mosaic of the apse which depicts, like
the decoration of the old sacristy, the four evangelists,
along with the titular saint of the church, Florence's oldest
martyr, identified as king of the Armenians, whose cults
the Medici supported in their neighborhood and in their
financing of the Armenian delegation to the church
council of 1439 (fig. 84).[257]

In the first edition of his *Lives of the Artists* Vasari had
named Cosimo as the tabernacle's patron; in the second
he named Piero instead. Although by contrast with the
tabernacle for Santissima Annunziata commissioned by
Piero around the same time, the San Miniato *tempietto*
does not bear an inscription, it is just as effectively signed
with Piero's personal *imprese*, including the maiolica tiles
of its roof in the colors of his livery. Similarly, although

Michelozzo's authorship is not documented, as it was at
Santissima Annunziata, most art historians have followed
Vasari in believing him to be the architect.[258]

At San Miniato the Medici commission was again part
of a larger project to refurbish an important church
building. Bernardo Rossellino was entrusted in 1447 with
the repair of the steps that led from the church down
into the crypt, and this work was carried out by members
of his workshop in 1451, the year before the adjacent
tabernacle was completed. The bronze birds perched on
top of the tabernacle were cast by Maso di Bartolomeo
in January 1449. Its extraordinary maiolica roof and
ceiling were almost certainly made by Luca della Robbia,
who was working at that time with Michelozzo and
Maso di Bartolomeo on the doors of the sacristy of the
cathedral. This exquisite *tempietto* fits perfectly harmoniously into the more ancient interior,[259] another instance
of a Medici commission that blends Roman with
Romanesque in the Tuscan style. Moreover, its donation
represents yet another occasion on which Medici took
the opportunity to honor the city's relics of the saints,
especially those of greatest significance to the Florentine
popolo.

Santissima Annunziata

In 1448 Piero de' Medici commissioned another marble
tabernacle, this time to house the miracle-working image
of the Virgin Annunciate, conserved in the church of
Santissima Annunziata. Its mid-fourteenth-century painter
had come to be seen as the very heir of Saint Luke,
believed to have painted the original portrait of the
Virgin, from which all others were seen to be descended.
As Antonio di Meglio prayed to the Madonna of Santissima Annunziata: "Your figure inspiring him who set his
hand to this picture . . ./ I pray it should please you that
such intense devotion/ should not be in vain in its
effect,/ but as if these mercies were asked of your very
essence/ with the greatest fervor,/ there might reside in
your figure the power to intercede . . ."[260]

The cult of this image of the Virgin had been building in intensity throughout Cosimo's lifetime. A letter
of Franco Sacchetti's records that around 1400, "all the
others were abandoned, and everyone rushed to the
Annunciate of the Servi, about which, by one means or
another, they placed and hung so many images that if
the wall had not been recently reinforced with chains, it
would have been in danger of collapsing, and the roof
along with it."[261] The devotees of the miracle-working
image included not only Florentines, but also many powerful and wealthy foreigners who came to the shrine and

84   Michelozzo, tabernacle, Florence, San Miniato

left behind votive images and valuable gifts in gratitude for the miracles the Madonna had wrought. By mid-century, as a verse description of Florence's churches by the Dominican friar Domenico Corella relates, the whole church was crowded with wax votive statues of the sick and wounded, "of kings and powerful lords . . . Often generals, harshly wounded in war, having survived the crisis,/ preserved by the power of this Virgin,/ have dedicated themselves to her, with their horses,/ giving her gifts appropriate to soldiers;/ these are all the fierce leaders of armies/ whom we see sitting astride their enormous horses." The church was a world of itself, wherein the images of the faithful, "on their knees . . . with hands joined and heads bowed," oscillated gently in the movement of air created by the candles lit at matins and vespers. "This hall, containing the likenesses of so many men,/ has the look of a city, where modeled inhabitants dwell/ and, as in real fights, battle lines are drawn/in the correct order in which the battle must be waged,/ so we may distinguish the companies just as sharply/ and closely ranged on either side of the church . . ."[262]

Clearly the Madonna Annunciate was a state treasure, enhancing the fame and virtue of Florence in domestic and foreign eyes; quite as much as, or more than the formal monuments the city had made in the cathedral to its great warriors such as Hawkwood and Niccolò da Tolentino. In 1416 the Signoria took steps to incorporate the cult appropriately into civic tradition. The Priors decreed "that every year in perpetuity, on 25 March, the day sacred to the Annunciation of Mary, there should be a solemn celebration in the church of the Servi, attended by the city magistrates." Pope Eugenius IV, during his sojourn in Florence, also helped to promote the cult. He consecrated the altar of the Annunziata, and in 1441, as part of his program of Church reform, replaced the conventual Servites with a group of northern Italian Observants. In 1444 he issued a bull dispensing special indulgences, "considering the degree to which the *popolo* frequented the church . . . to all those confessed and contrite who came to visit the Virgin's altar in the church and lent a helping hand to its preservation . . ."[263] Prominent among these were the Medici family and their friends and partisans.

The church was enlarged more than once in the fourteenth century, in 1384 on the initiative of Andrea Manfredi, general of the Servites, with the help in particular of one parishioner, "the master carpenter Antonio di Puccio," after whose family of staunch Mediceans Cosimo's partisans in the 1420s were called "Puccini."[264] Around 1440 a major program of rebuilding began, which would include the renovation of the convent and of the church, with a tribune surrounded by seven new chapels,

a new sacristy, an atrium at the entrance, and the magnificent new tabernacle to house the sacred image. In 1444 Michelozzo was put in charge of the program, centered on the tribune, to which the patrons of the church directed their money and their attention, and which the papal indulgence would help to support.[265] In 1445 the Florentine Signoria and its colleges passed a provision transferring from the convent to themselves the right to elect the *operai* for the church of Santissima Annunziata, "considering how great is the devotion of all both here and everywhere for the most glorious mother of God the Virgin Mary, and the veneration of the image or figure of the Virgin Annunciate in the church of the Servites in Florence, and that so many oblations are continually made and so many gifts brought to that church and its chapel." They expressed their desire to maintain and manage the income of the church with the greatest care, "for the fame and dignity of this celebrated church and thus of all the city of Florence, preserving and increasing the cult."[266]

The manifest intervention of the Medici family at this point in the rebuilding of the church, and their provision of a sumptuous tabernacle for the Madonna resemble their participation in a larger program to rebuild and embellish San Lorenzo, in association with other patrons with various ties and obligations to Cosimo, his family, and friends. Once again, although many historians have seen Piero's *tempietto* primarily as an assertion of Medici power and privilege, it represents a variety of elements and impulses inherent in the personal and artistic patronage of the Medici, particularly their response to the groundswell of popular belief and to the prevailing direction of civic feeling.

Many factors likely contributed to the decision of the Medici regime to take control of the celebration of the cult at Santissima Annunziata. The Mediceans were riding high in 1445 after the reform of the electoral scrutinies in 1444 and during Cosimo's term as Gonfalonier of Justice in September–October 1445, a Commission of Eight was appointed to review communal legislation in the interests of the regime. As the Signorial edict declared, the cult at Santissima Annunziata was a matter of great concern to the state, for the sake of the devotion of the city and her people to the Virgin, and for the sake of her reputation in the eyes of the world. A phenomenon of this magnitude required an appropriate response from the city government, and invited its oversight. The church had to be enlarged to accommodate the throngs of devotees, and the consequent building program called for expert and efficient management. The northern Italian congregation of Observants whom Eugenius IV had installed in the convent in 1441 were not favored or trusted by the citizens of Florence, whose rulers had fallen out with the pope in the mid-1440s; indeed shortly after he died in 1447, the commune passed legislation enabling the Conventuals to return.[267]

Cosimo's elder son Piero was among the first group of *operai* nominated by the Signoria in 1445. Just how far the Medicean Signoria was prepared to go to gain control at Santissima Annunziata is indicated by their appointment of two citizens excluded by the laws concerning minumum age requirements for communal officials, and prohibiting more than one member of a lineage from serving at the same time. A committee of Medicean jurists was called in, and agreed that Paolo di Francesco Falconieri, whose family had long been the chief patrons of the church, could be appointed despite the fact that Paolo was not yet twenty-five, and that Piero di Cosimo need not be excluded because Orlando de' Medici, the most eminent Medici parishioner and patron at Santis-

sima Annunziata, had also been elected. Piero was eventually excluded, however, because an essential prerequisite for serving as *operaio* was the patronage of a chapel or tomb in the church. In 1447 he acquired the rights to the chapel for the tabernacle, and in 1453 he was finally elected as one of the *operai*.

The failed attempt to appoint Piero as an *operaio* of Santissima Annunziata in 1445 is of immense interest as one of the most overt attempts on Cosimo's part to exert control over any corporate enterprise, either explicitly political or broadly civic in nature. As such it illustrates both the extent and the limits of his ability to manipulate the Florentine ruling group at this time. Clearly Cosimo wanted to take charge of the management of the building program, and Piero's endowment of the tabernacle was a most effective way of achieving this. However, a closer look at the chapel-holders, and the *operai* appointed by the Signoria between 1445 and 1454, shows that the reins of this project were firmly in Medicean hands, whether Piero was an *operaio* or not. As Diane Zervas observed, Medici family members and partisans dominated this group for the next decade (fig. 85).[268]

Among them was Orlando di Guccio, one of the leaders of the Medici family exiled along with Cosimo in 1433.[269] A banker and wool-trader with a flourishing business in Ancona, he remained prominent in the affairs of the city of Florence and in office-holding, serving as an ambassador to Francesco Sforza and as an envoy in 1451 to the Emperor Frederick III, from whom he received a knighthood. As patron of the sacristy as well as a family chapel, his patronage assumed a similar importance at Santissima Annunziata to that of Giovanni di Bicci at San Lorenzo in the 1420s. His arms appear on the ceiling of the church.[270] He had Bernardo Rossellino make for his own burial chapel a particularly fine arcosolium tomb closely resembling the one for Palla Strozzi upon which Giovanni di Bicci's sarcophagus was also apparently modeled, and Orlando's tomb became itself the prototype for at least five other tombs commissioned in the same period by friends and supporters of the Medici (fig. 87).[271] Along with Bernardetto de' Medici, Orlando was one of Castagno's major patrons. The several chapels for which Castagno painted frescoes after 1450 included Orlando's chapel dedicated to Saint Mary Magdalene.

Another chapel-holder with close ties to the Medici, and who also commissioned Castagno to decorate his chapel, was Piero da Gagliano, Cosimo's friend and neighbor in the Mugello. Piero's compatriot Giovanni da Gagliano, a factor of the Medici bank in Venice, was the original patron of Bosco ai Frati before Cosimo, as Giovanni's executor, took over this responsibility.[272] In

85 Florence, Santissima Annunziata, reconstruction by Beverley Brown of Michelozzo's plan. Begun 1444

3 Florence, SS. Annunziata, Reconstruction of Michelozzo's plan. Begun 1444.

a. Villani Chapel
b. Tebaldi Chapel (after 1464)
c. Antella Chapel
d. Giacomini Chapel
e. Pazzi Chapel
f. Falconieri Chapel
  l. Oratory of the German and Flemish Painters

g. Chapel of the German and Flemish painters
h. Sacristy
i. Romolo Chapel (after 1456)
j. Pucci Chapel
k. Giocondo Chapel

(Although the identity of the original tribuna patrons is known, precisely which chapel the Borromei, Portinari, Rabatta, Rinieri and the *operai* occupied is not known.)

86   Fra Angelico and workshop, *Scenes From the Life of Christ and the Mystic Wheel*, from the silver reliquary cabinet for Santissima Annunziata, Florence, Museo di San Marco

1448 Piero da Gagliano wrote asking Piero de' Medici to serve as his agent in acquiring a piece of property he described as "very convenient in being so near to where you live when Cosimo should want to come to see me," an observation and a request implying a great deal of inti-macy.[273] The bulk of Piero's Florentine property was in the *gonfalone* of Drago, and in 1463 he was buried in his chapel at Santissima Annunziata, adjacent to Piero's taber-nacle, being once more as close to his friends as possible. The chapel was dedicated to Saint Julian, perhaps with some reference to the birth of Piero's second son, Giuliano, and decorated with Castagno's fresco of *Saint Julian and the Savior*.[274]

The chapel of the Pucci family was dedicated to Saint Sebastian; the altarpiece was painted by the Pollaiuolo brothers, who decorated the *sala grande* of the Medici palace. Other *operai* and chapel patrons at Santissima Annunziata included Bernardo d'Antonio, head of a line of Medici prominent in the service of the bank, the Portinari, associates in the Medici bank and Castagno's patrons at Santa Maria Nuova, perhaps by Cosimo's agency, the Benci, long-standing Medici partisans, banking associates and patrons of the church, and even the ubiquitous Ser Alesso Pelli, Cosimo's secretary who appears at so many crucial moments in the execution of schemes dear to Cosimo's heart.

As at San Marco, the former patrons of the church, who were no longer prominent in the city or its government, were at this time effectively ousted by the Servites in favor of the Medici family and their friends. The general of the Servites for most of the period of the

87　Bernardo Rossellino and workshop, tomb of Orlando de' Medici, Florence, Santissima Annunziata

rebuilding was Mariano Salvini, a close friend and associate of Cosimo and his sons in a number of other enterprises.[275] Archbishop Antoninus, who had proved at San Marco that he knew how to cooperate with Cosimo for the benefit of the church, determined the allocation of the last chapels in 1455.[276] Michelozzo, Cosimo's closest collaborator in his building patronage, was the architect of the ensemble.[277] Some of the rebuilding was paid for by Francesco Gonzaga, marquess of Mantua, who was captain of the Florentine army for some time at mid-century, and also Cosimo's close friend and political ally. Cosimo wrote to Gonzaga and persuaded him to divert some of his salary to financing the reconstruction at Santissima Annunziata.[278] Medici patronage at Santissima Annun-ziata was not so much the extension of Cosimo's influence into alien territory, as it is often represented, as its consolidation on what was already Medicean ground. The rebuilding of the Servite church by the Medici and their friends in many ways replicates the situation at San Lorenzo, one of the only five other Florentine churches whose *operai* were appointed by the Signoria.[279]

According to Filarete, Piero commissioned the tabernacle at his father's wish – "con volontà del padre" – because Cosimo was a particular devotee of the Virgin Annunciate (fig. 88).[280] This commission does indeed fit the pattern of Cosimo's expiatory patronage, just as it accords with so much other evidence of his desire to align or associate himself with civic interests and the cultural icons of the Florentine *popolo*. Such impulses were profoundly political, but not simply in the superficial and reductive sense that is sometimes suggested. The Medici *tempietto* to house the miracle-working image of the Madonna, the focus of Florence's most important popular cult, predictably and appropriately inspired more fulsome praise of father and son than any other of their commissions. Feo Belcari, as "the servant and familiar [*famelico*] of Our Lady," expressed his gratitude to Piero that "the columns of the Servi and the ironwork grille,/ with all the other furnishings and decorations,/surpass any other noble building,/ as the fine gentleman does the poor peasant . . ." He rejoiced "that it pleased you to spend such a great treasure/on the chapel of angelic salvation,/which is our path to eternal life."[281]

The Baroque encrustations that later overlaid a more austere classical architecture make it difficult now to imagine the original appearance of the *tempietto*. However, they are in keeping with the original desires of patron, architect and sculptor to spare no effort or expense to construct a fitting monument to the Virgin. This is surely an important context of the inscription "the marble alone cost 4,000 florins," as of the piling up of tribute in the shape of the twenty-one silver lamps that

88   Michelozzo, tabernacle, Florence, Santissima Annunziata

adorned the original structure, and the silver and painted doors that further embellished the reliquary cabinet in which the treasures heaped upon the Virgin were to be kept.[282] Corella's description lingers on the precious materials – marbles, jasper, and bronze – with which the tabernacle was constructed and decorated. While modern art historians have paid more attention to the Renaissance revival of classical forms, the use of such materials was, as Pliny observed, a major passion of antique patrons, and it was shared by their Renaissance successors. For example, Giovanni Rucellai's description of classical and

early Christian Rome dwells mainly on the marble and porphyry monuments, which the Medici were the first private patrons in Florence to emulate.[283]

Like Feo Belcari, Domenico Corella, born in 1403 and for over sixty years a Dominican friar at Santa Maria Novella, saw the Medici family as the Virgin's very special servants, on account of their patronage at San Marco and Santissima Annunziata.[284] His perspective on the latter, both devotional and aesthetic, probably came close to that of most Florentine viewers of the tabernacle, emphasizing the "cost and skill" that distinguished it, and the incorporation of emblems of city and family that lent it significance, so that "in this tabernacle is worthily set the image/ of astonishing power, renowned for many miracles . . ." As he explained, as more and more people flocked to celebrate "this beautiful image of the mother of God the Savior . . . protector of the human race . . ." the inadequacy of the structure of the old sanctuary became clear. "Upon which Piero, showing himself the true heir of Cosimo,/ the custodian and splendor of his house and his city,/ wishing to place her in a worthy setting,/ made this work so fitting for the Virgin./ For, well-composed throughout of snowy marble,/ it outdoes other tabernacles in cost and skill."

He described in detail the vault, supported by four columns adorned with sculpture in the antique style, and the gilded foliage of the lilies of the Virgin, the symbols also of her city Florence, together with the orange fruit that stood for the Medici *palle*: "Many lilies shimmer on green stalks,/ and the symbols of the house of Medici, ripe fruit, grows red." Inside the tabernacle were Michelozzo's font, and a statue of John the Baptist, the city's patron saint. "The holy Virgin's altar, day and night,/ shines with many lamps, replacing gleaming heaven./ Within this hall a beautiful bowl is placed,/ in its wide mouth holding the holy water./ To it black jasper adds its own enrichment,/ and a huge dark marble sphere lends a beauty/ which four smaller orbs duly support./ A small bronze figure of the Baptist completes the work . . . [of this shrine]/ whence thronging crowds obtain the desired atonement . . ."[285]

The Medici tabernacle combined sacred and civic symbols of supreme significance to themselves and the *popolo* of Florence. The votive offerings brought to it were symbols too – of Florence's prized links to the rest of the world, many of them forged by Medici influence. To contain these Piero provided in an adjacent oratory a silver chest closed by a panel painted by Fra Angelico and his workshop (fig. 86). "Of the Virgin's hall I omit to cite the other/ grand treasures that Piero gathered for her./ And for the rich treasures he made new shrines,/ that hold the riches, offered spontaneously/ by kings and famous dukes and powerful tyrants,/ who wished to meet their vow placing them here,/ where there are silver vases, with varied figures./ A panel, painted outside, shelters them inside,/ painted on the front by the Angelic painter named Giovanni,/ not less skilled than Giotto or Cimabue . . . mild in his genius [*ingegno*], honest in his religion."

This Medici commission for Fra Angelico, so admired as a painter of devotional scenes, was eminently accessible to the public, as his work for the Medici at San Marco was not, and surely reveals as much as any other of the paintings the family commissioned about the image they wished to present to the Florentine people. Yet it has received comparatively little attention, perhaps because the iconography is in no sense susceptible of a political interpretation. Piero del Massaio was brought in in 1461 to help implement the scheme for a single shutter, for the greater security of the ex-votos contained in the cupboard.[286] The thirty-five scenes from the life of Christ were painted in the early 1450s, nine being generally attributed to Angelico himself, and others to Baldovinetti, Gozzoli, and Zanobi Strozzi. Particularly striking is the image of the mystic wheel, representing the Vision of Ezekiel.[287]

The theme of Wolfgang Liebenwein's account of Piero de' Medici's patronage at San Miniato and Santissima Annunziata is "the 'privatization' of the miraculous." Stressing the political interests expressed in this patronage, he represented it as a subtle "usurping [of] well-known shrines through the introduction of his arms and *imprese*," and noted the establishment at Santissima Annunziata of "a personal relationship with the miraculous image of the Annunciation . . . already synonymous with civic piety".[288] The last claim is undeniably true, but the sort of sinister calculation and illegitimate intention implied in Liebenwein's account does not seem to capture the spirit of this assumption of responsibility by the Medici and their well-known partisans for the care of a crucial civic shrine, on which they lavished their largesse, to the mutual benefit of themselves and a grateful populace. Insofar as this concerted Medicean patronage constituted a visible statement to other members of the ruling class of their preponderant influence over the city's chief magistracies, this was rather an open secret than a revelation after Cosimo's stint as Gonfalonier of Justice in 1445, and the consequent appointment of a special commission to review legislation affecting the regime.

It may be that the private space above the oratory in which the treasure chest was kept, from which Piero could look down at the holy image and descend into the chapel where it was housed, like Cosimo's private perch on the back stairs above the *cappella maggiore* at San Marco, was created with royal precedents – the *Königlichen Habitus* of the kings of France and Burgundy – in mind.[289] It may also be, as Casalini suggested, that the idea of a pair of rooms from which the invalid Piero could make his devotions to the sacred image in comfort, rather than jostle with the throngs in the over-crowded church, was a happy and convenient inspiration arising out of the physical arrangements for the shuttering of the treasure chest. These, as reconstructed from the *Libro di fabbrica* for the tabernacle, involved the hauling up and down of the shutter with elaborate machinery hidden in the wall, which required the construction of an upper floor in the oratory.[290] Whatever Piero's actual intentions, a building program that so immensely enhanced the devotional opportunities of the Florentine and foreign public can hardly be characterized essentially as "privatization," and whatever the precedents for the construction of cubicles such as Piero's at Santissima Annunziata, in making use of it he can certainly not be described as in any sense a cross between a private citizen and a king.[291]

Santa Maria del Fiore

The cathedral was the very heart and soul of Florence, the focus of civic pride and aspirations, as well as other-worldly hopes and prayers. Like most important religious foundations, it was entrusted by the commune to the administrative custody of one of the major guilds – the Arte della Lana. More than in most Florentine churches, the two-tier corporate management of the cathedral strove to keep the citizens' presence there primarily collective. Some private patrons, among them the Medici, held chapels in Santa Reparata in the early fifteenth century, but the Wool Guild did its best to prevent private burials in the cathedral, accompanied as they were by the display of personal arms and devices. Although it was only partly successful, by and large burial was a privilege reserved to the cathedral chapter and to civic heroes specially honored by the state.[292] The walls of the church were lined mainly with memorials to the defenders of Florence, her military captains, her outstanding poets and musicians, and her learned chancellors. In the course of the fifteenth-century renovations, an ongoing enterprise, chapels were maintained by or allotted to the city's leading corporations, including the guilds, the Parte Guelfa, and the Mercanzia.

The rebuilding and redecoration of the cathedral, whose Renaissance phase began around the middle of the fourteenth century, provided the occasion for the development and display of the talents of the first wave of early Renaissance sculptors and architects – Ghiberti, Donatello, Brunelleschi, Luca della Robbia, and many others. So extensive was the works program at the cathedral that the operai of the Wool Guild in charge of it effectively became the city's "public works" commission. In the course of the fifteenth century, and under the direction of the Medicean regime, like so many aspects of Florentine society and government, the guild moved away from the old corporate forms of organization and toward a more centralized bureaucratic system under the close regulation of the state. In 1441 the traditional republican system of many officials in rapid rotation was altered in favor of only two operai, serving for an entire year. This change also made the office more easily controllable by those outside the guild.[293]

Cosimo built no chapel at the cathedral, and in the fluid and ambiguous circumstances of its later renovation, it is unclear how much influence the Medici wielded or aspired to there. In 1436, on the eve of its consecration, members of the Medici family appeared for the first time among the operai of the Wool Guild; shortly after this, Cosimo himself served on the committee to commission the lantern of the newly completed cupola.[294] In the late 1440s and early 1450s, about the same time as he began to appear as a member of the building committees of the Palazzo della Signoria, the Parte Guelfa, the Mercanzia, and at Santissima Annunziata, Piero de' Medici was consulted about several projects underway at the cathedral, including the design for the main altar.[295] Piero's role as an advisor on public artistic projects considerably increased the visibility of the Medici family in Florentine cultural life, and no doubt their actual influence on the direction of these works. Just what political mileage these activities gained or represented is harder to say. Over the years, an enormous number of wealthy, powerful, and cultured citizens had been consulted by the cathedral operai concerning every aspect of the rebuilding project, and the Medici family's ambitious and distinguished private patronage surely qualified Piero as an expert on various forms of work. He was consulted about the appropriate price for the intarsia doors of the new sacristy at the cathedral;[296] in view of observers' reports that in the Medici palace almost every square inch of wood was elaborately worked, to whom could the operai more appropriately have turned?

On the other hand, the rejection of Piero's proposal for the high altar of the cathedral, and the limitation of his participation in other corporate projects, has reasonably been seen as a rebuff to the family's increasing encroachment on civic ceremonial space, not from the popolo, but by the Church. Archbishop Antoninus had been constantly concerned to limit Medici interference in ecclesiastical matters, and throughout Cosimo's lifetime there was substantial resistance to the family's very real infiltration of the infrastructure of the Florentine and Tuscan church; one indication of this was Cosimo's tentative and unsuccessful nomination in the mid-1440s of his kinsmen and close friends to the Florentine archbishopric.[297] The extension of Medici influence over the Florentine church gathered momentum in the 1450s, with the promotion of the Medici archbishops Donato and Filippo to various key provincial sees, and culminated three decades later in the career of Lorenzo's son

Giovanni as cardinal and eventually pope. But this process met resistance at every step, and was far from complete at the time of Cosimo's death.[298]

Cosimo was able, however, to establish a presence at Santa Maria del Fiore in the less tangible, but highly prestigious sphere of the patronage of music. Music, together with images, was a key element in popular devotion. Singing was the raison d'être of the *laudesi* confraternities, and the expected accompaniment and guide to a spiritual journey. Dante's progress through purgatory was marked by music and passages from the liturgy. Entering purgatory he heard the "Te Deum laudamus," and what he heard "gave me just such an impression/. . . as that we are accustomed to receive/ when singing is accompanied by an organ;/ and now the words are clear, and now they are not."[299] The ancients regarded music as a means of transporting men to the realms of the spirit; when Cosimo invited Ficino to Careggi in order to show him the way to happiness, he asked him to bring his Orphic lyre. Alberti invoked the same view of music as a key to the higher mysteries when he spoke of the services at Santa Maria del Fiore: "Here you listen to the voices during mass, during that which the ancients call the mysteries, with their marvellous beauty."[300] The enchanting singers' lofts for the cathedral were visual expressions of Florentines' high musical and spiritual aspirations. According to the inscription on Della Robbia's *cantoria*, adorned with precisely rendered musical instruments, its depiction of the joys of song and dance was inspired by Psalm 150. We do not know if Donatello's matching piece was similarly intended to illustrate a psalm, as his patrons suggested, but we do know that in an attempt to induce him to accept the commission, he was offered the freedom to decide upon his subject, and, although he seems not to have collected it, more money to outdo Della Robbia's performance (fig. 89).[301]

The Medici family took considerable personal pleasure in music. The organist Antonio Squarcialupi was a frequent companion of their leisure hours *in villa*, and Piero and Giovanni di Cosimo owned a number of musical instruments and manuscripts.[302] Cosimo, whom Vespasiano described as very fond of music – "alquanto se ne diletava" – endowed a *cappella* at San Lorenzo in competition with that of the cathedral.[303] However, the reputation of devotional music in Florence continued to depend upon performances in Santa Maria del Fiore. Pope Eugenius lent his own *cappella* for the occasion of the consecration, but the very same day he signed a bull ordering the creation of a school for cathedral singers. Cosimo became its patron, and it was flourishing by the time the church council took place in 1439. A number of personal letters attest to the Medici family's financial

support and protection of the singers of San Giovanni, who moved between the baptistery, the cathedral, and later Santissima Annunziata, at their Medici patrons' behest.[304] They accompanied the family on a visit to Fiesole, and even traveled as far as Rome, where Piero wrote to Tommaso Spinelli urging him to restrain his cousin Antonio di Lorenzo from evicting the singers from a house provided for them: "and thus you will be the cause of preserving the honor of our city and you will please many people here and particularly me . . . I am sure that I must seem to you too importunate on behalf of these singers, but put it down partly to their way of life, since to maintain themselves they have to feel secure . . ."[305]

The cathedral was a prime theater for civic drama, secular or spiritual; accordingly, Cosimo and his sons attended there, in addition to regular church services, a number of performances which showcased various aspects of Florentine life and their role in it; the consecration, the church council, the Certame Coronario. The city's most influential family had to strut, to stand or to fall, on the city's central stage. Ironically their most memorable appearance in the cathedral was the occasion of the murder of Cosimo's grandson Giuliano by their former partisans, the Pazzi, in league with their previous ally, the pope. Poliziano's account of this tells how an attempt was made to assassinate both Lorenzo and his younger brother, as they stood together at the high altar during the Mass (fig. 90). After Giuliano fell, Lorenzo's friends bundled him into the sacristy to safety. Sigismondo della Stufa, Lorenzo's companion in so many amatory adventures,

89   Luca della Robbia, *cantoria*, Florence, Museo dell'Opera del Duomo

90   Florence, cathedral, interior

a splendid young man and one who from childhood had been attached by bonds of great love and loyalty to Lorenzo . . . quickly climbed a ladder to a lookout point, the organ gallery, from which he could see down into the church, and at once he knew what had been done, for he could see the body of Giuliano lying prostrate. He could also see that those who stood at the doors were friends, so he gave the order to open up; thronging around Lorenzo, they made an armed bodyguard for him and took him home by a side door so that he should not come across the body of Giuliano.[306]

As a man lives, so shall he die. Giuliano's murder may be seen as a counterpoint to Cosimo's triumphant appearance at the cathedral's consecration. The assertion of preeminence invited its challenge on the same ground.

THE BADIA

The renovation of the church and convent of the Badia at Fiesole, begun in 1456, was Cosimo's last major building commission (fig. 91).[307] Its role in his quest for salvation is clear from Vespasiano's testimony that Cosimo "hurried this building along with as much speed as possible, and constantly feared that it would not be done in time." In fact the work remained uncompleted at his death, and although Piero took over his father's patronage, paying for much of the convent's decorative detail, his son Lorenzo did not persist with the project.[308]

Cosimo's patronage at the Badia was part of his lifelong interest in the monastic way of life. His reading in his twenties and thirties of Cassian and Chrysostom indicates that he admired a cloistered virtue.[309] At the monastery of San Marco, his first major building commission, Cosimo had his own private cell. A Milanese priest who saw it was inspired to send Cosimo the gift of a mid-fifteenth-century Milanese manuscript of Prosper's *Concerning the Contemplative Life*; his accompanying explanatory note is bound into the manuscript.[310] A friend of Cosimo's of the order of Monte Oliveto, knowing his inclination toward occasional spiritual retreat, wrote suggesting he set aside for a while his "cose mondane" and come to visit that convent for a breath of spiritual air.[311] The records of the convent of the Badia describe the room that Cosimo reserved there for his own use, "with an entrance hall, study, bed and other comforts, where he would often stay eating and drinking, and talking with the canons as if they were members of his own family, saying that the monastery, built by himself, was not an earthly dwelling place but a heavenly one, inhabited not only by human spirits but by angelic ones."[312]

Cosimo was not alone among Florentine citizens in his admiration for a way of life more spiritually exigent than his own. The humanist Antonio Manetti's *Dialogue on Consolation*, written after one of his sons died, was set in the Certosa, the convent just outside Florence which was built by the Acciaiuoli family in the fourteenth century; Manetti's friend and brother-in-law Agnolo Acciaiuoli had invited him there after his child's death, to seek solace without the dangers of solitude.[313]

The Badia was the only major building commission conceived in the last decade of Cosimo's life, when he was taking an increasing interest in Neoplatonic philosophy, with its strong otherworldly orientation. It was during the mid-fifties that Argyropoulos and other Greek scholars arrived in Florence bringing with them their manuscripts, which they translated for Cosimo's benefit.[314] This was the period of the foundation of the Platonic Academy, whatever its precise form may have been, and of Cosimo's patronage of the philosophical studies of Marsilio Ficino. Cosimo's letter summoning Ficino to Careggi to tell him the way to happiness was written in 1463, the year preceding his death.[315] These well-publicized events are the basis of an impression that Cosimo underwent a spiritual conversion at this time. In fact, they simply marked a new phase, a fresh direction, in the always powerful piety of Florence and its people, among them its leading citizen. In the early 1460s, Cristoforo Landino was reinterpreting Dante and Virgil in allegorical terms, representing Aeneas as moving from

91   Michelozzo, Fiesole, Badia, convent entrance

a world of pleasure through the civil virtues to the con-templative life. Many others besides Cosimo were strongly influenced by these ideas, among them Matteo Palmieri, author of the widely read treatise of the 1440s *On the Civil Life*, who wrote his allegorical poem on its heav-enly counterpart, *The City of Life*, in the late fifties or early sixties.[316]

The foundation of the Badia dated from the eleventh century. Its rebuilding constituted another Medici com-mission for an Observant order to whom it had been recently transferred, this time the Augustinians. Once again Cosimo was casting his patronage net as widely as possible across the orders of the Church. Once again, he was in a sense extending his patronage along neighbor-hood lines, or perhaps extending his neighborhood through patronage. In the district of Fiesole was the Medici villa of Montughi, which they had owned for some time, and Giovanni's new villa on the hill over-looking Florence, not far from the Dominican Observant house and from San Girolamo, where both the Medici and the Rucellai families endowed chapels and altar-pieces.[317] With the completion of Giovanni's villa, Fiesole became another Medici neighborhood, as many of their friends flocked to establish country retreats in this area. Almost all the patrons of the chapels in the new nave of the Badia church were closely associated with the Medici family.

The identity of the architect of the Badia remains a mystery. Most architectural historians discount the possi-bility of Michelozzo's direct participation in the building, although it has something of his general style.[318] It could, however, be seen essentially as a generic church of its period, reflecting the practices of the order and Cosimo's preference for an austere classicism. The convent's abbot, Timoteo Maffei, described himself as having made the renovations "with Cosimo," and Alberto Avogadro's extravagantly encomiastic poem attributed the design of the building to its patron.[319] Perhaps the Badia was the ultimate example of the general fifteenth-century phe-nomenon of a patron acting as *auctor* in the interests of an institution with well-established building traditions, relying on the mason/architect and his building crew and workshop to produce a building that was genuinely the expression of a corporate will. But however much the abbot concerned himself with the project, and contem-poraries like Filarete stressed Cosimo's interest in the practical, no building, it was freely acknowledged, could be erected entirely without expert direction.[320] The architect Brunelleschi, on the one hand, emphasized the extreme difficulty of explaining anything about con-struction to laymen; the patron Francesco Sforza, on the other, denied in a famous letter to the Florentine Signoria that his reputation for architectural expertise should be taken too seriously.[321]

Cosimo's patronage at the Badia provided for some renovation of the interior of the church, while preserving its distinctive Romanesque facade, but as at San Marco it was mainly concentrated on the convent, to which Cosimo added an austere and graceful loggia bearing a muted version of the Medici arms. Within, the elaborately worked *pietra serena* window and door-frames are covered with Medici emblems and *imprese*, many of them dating from the period of Piero's continuation of Cosimo's patronage after his father's death. For Cosimo, an essential aspect of his intervention was the provision of a library similar to the one he created for San Marco. Once again, the contractor for the procuring and copying of books was Vespasiano da Bisticci. A letter he wrote to Cosimo at the very end of 1463 or early in 1464 announced that a copy of Aristotle's *Ethics*, which Cosimo had been eagerly awaiting, had just been completed. The letter itself supports Vespasiano's observation concerning the urgency with which his patron pressed forward on this project. "I lack several copies to finish the books for the Badia of Fiesole, and I went to San Marco, and they said they could not be loaned without your permission on pain of excommunication. So please write a note to the prior to ask him to lend them to me so that I can finish up this work."[322]

It is interesting, in light of the strong Florentine view that the glorification of God justified any expenditure on church decoration on the part of the patron, that historians' discussions of the Renaissance debate about *magnificentia* should have focused on the Badia. This is largely because its abbot, Timoteo Maffei, found it necessary at the time, despite the widespread praise of Cosimo's largesse to the church, to write a dialogue "Against the Detractors of Cosimo de Medici's Magnificence." His central argument, that magnificence is a virtue that motivates the patron to spend his wealth on the construction of monasteries and temples "in the sanctification of the Lord," did not appear to contemporaries, as it has done to Gombrich and other modern historians, as merely a feeble justification of self-interest. The fully-fledged Renaissance form of the debate about magnificence surfaced only in the 1450s, after most of Cosimo's patronage was complete.[323] Before 1450 *magnus* and its derivatives, the adjective *magnificens*, and much more rarely the abstract noun *magnificentia*, are used in ordinary speech to refer mainly to size − to describe, for example, the newly cleared site for the Medici palace. This core sense of the Latin has subsequently been conflated with the modern sense of magnificence, toward which Maffei is reaching for almost the first time. On medals, a major medium of self-advertisement employed by the princes of fifteenth-century Italy, before 1450 *magnus* appears in relation to the stature of a military commander, and notably Alfonso of Aragon's medal of 1448 describing

himself in these terms presents his other chief virtue as *liberalitas*.[324]

In accepting Fraser-Jenkins's dictum, based on Maffei's *Defence*, that Cosimo led the way for the princes of Italy in the expression of magnificence in architecture,[325] and in viewing Cosimo's architectural patronage largely through this prism, apart from undervaluing the aforesaid princes, we have also been led to focus on a classical virtue, or vice, that came to the fore of contemporary minds only in the second half of the fifteenth century. The early Renaissance emphasized the Christian charitable virtue of liberality, which governs most of Cosimo's architectural patronage. By the end of the century, the image of the classical patron had been stripped of the accretions of Christian virtue upon which Archbishop Antoninus had insisted in 1450, in describing the proper liberality and beneficence of patrons towards their friends, including the Church.[326] In the early 1490s it would be possible for the humanist Pontano to write a truly sophisticated treatise on these issues which resecularized the qualities of classical Roman patrons, and distinguished in the patronage of quattrocento princes between magnificence, liberality, beneficence, splendor, and conviviality.[327]

If there were any significant social or political circumstances driving this last great building commission of Cosimo's, they cannot easily be identified. The years in which it was initiated were confused and troubled ones for Florence and the Medici. After Cosimo's personal triumph in establishing the Peace of Lodi in 1454, there followed a period of strong opposition to Medici influence, both in the councils of the republic and on the part of their personal friends and supporters; these years also saw the first decline in the fortunes of the bank, after the death of Cosimo's favorite general manager, Giovanni di Amerigo de' Benci, in 1455.[328] More obviously related to the commission for the Badia were Cosimo's lifelong support of the Church and its more austere cloistered orders, and his growing interest in Neoplatonic philosophy. There are also some signs of a general impulse to set his moral house in order; at this time he gave the use of a house *in perpetuo*, and perhaps in recompense, to Mariotto de' Medici, the kinsman whom he denounced to the Signoria in 1434 for proposing to end their exile with the aid of the Milanese, thus maintaining his civic virtue intact.[329] Moreover, time was running out for the fulfilment of Cosimo's promise concerning his worldly power and possessions: "Only be patient Lord, and I will return it all to you."[330] For all his ambitious and urgent will to power, there runs through Cosimo's life and letters a balancing resignation that "God may allow the best to happen"[331] that is much more than just a form of words.

IV

THE HOUSE OF THE MEDICI

XI

THE PALACE:
MEASURING SELF ON THE URBAN MAP

We decorate our property as much to distinguish family and country as for any personal display, and who would deny this to be the responsibility of a good citizen?

Alberti, *De Re Aedificatoria*.[1]

THE PALATIAL DEBATE

Florentines saw their city as the stage upon which they had to prove their worth.[2] Men defined themselves and their families principally by their participation in public life, and from this they derived honor and fame, which Florentine patricians, like the Romans they claimed as ancestors, valued as life itself.[3] Using language very similar in spirit to that of Cosimo's letters, Gino di Neri Capponi, patriarch of a great old Florentine lineage, and commander of the Florentine army that conquered Pisa in 1406, expressed the patrician concern with public self-measurement in a poem addressed in the first decades of the century to his sons. He urged them in time of plague not to flee the city for the country, "where fame is extinguished and one's good works do not endure./ Honor does not reside in the woods . . . / Worthy men are made in the city,/ nor indeed can he be called a man/ whose measure is not taken there."[4]

The civilized quality of life to be enjoyed in Florence was often measured in terms of the city's abundance of beautiful buildings, which were seen in turn as the index and the evidence of the virtue and resource of its citizens. In 1403 Leonardo Bruni began his *Panegyric to the City of Florence* by describing its buildings. Everyone, he wrote, was amazed that in 1401 Florence was able to prevail over its powerful and resourceful enemy Milan, but their amazement lasted only until they had seen the beauty and magnificence of the city of Florence.

Once they have seen before their eyes such a multitude of works, so many grand buildings, such magnificence and splendor; the lofty towers and marble churches [*templa, cum basilicarum fastigia*], the most superb dwellings, the turreted walls, the multitude of villas, of delights and splendors and embellishments of all these things, at once the mind and opinion of everyone is so changed that they are no longer amazed at the greatest and most extensive achievements of this city, but rather judge it capable of acquiring dominion and sovereignty over all the world.[5]

Around the time Bruni was writing, much of the impression he gained of Florence was created by public buildings, many of which were churches (fig. 93). To consider only one main street in the center of the city, the

93 Iacopo del Sellaio, *Saint John the Baptist*, 1480, detail, Washington, National Gallery of Art, Samuel H. Kress Collection

Via Calzaiuoli presented a truly magnificent face to the visitor. It ran from the piazza of San Giovanni, between the baptistery and the cathedral, on the eastern border of the inner city (delineated by the walls of the ancient Roman town) to the piazza in front of the Palazzo della Signoria, just short of the river; this street was the main axis between the city's spiritual and secular centers. The palace of the Priors was built in the last years of the thirteenth century, around the same time as renovation of the cathedral began. In the last quarter of the fourteenth century a *provvisione* of the Signoria prescribed that the ground floor facades of all the buildings lining the Via Calzaiuoli were to be rusticated in conformity with the appearance of the Palazzo Vecchio. Halfway along this street was the church of Orsanmichele, the grain market loggia walled up in the 1360s to create a sanctuary dedicated to its miracle-working image of the Madonna. The first quarter of the fifteenth century saw the embellishment of the exterior of Orsanmichele with a remarkable group of monumental sculptures commissioned by the guilds, as well as the competition for the design of a series of bronze doors for the baptistery, the decoration of the cathedral's facade, and the beginning of construction of the cathedral cupola.[6]

Private palaces, however, were also seen as contributing to the honor of the city, along with the commemoration of their owners. Gregorio Dati, a silk merchant with a strong interest in Florentine history, gained some personal experience of assessing architecture as an *operaio* of the Silk Guild in the years after 1419, when Brunelleschi built the foundling hospital under its supervision. In his *History of Florence,* Dati described what he saw as the city's major buildings around 1423. His description reveals something of how such a man, of similar education and interests to many later patrician palace builders, "read" the palaces of Florence's citizens as contributions, along with her public buildings, to the enhancement of his *patria*. His claim that "nowhere in the world are there royal palaces that outdo these," puts descriptions of the Medici palace as "fit for a king" in appropriate perspective.[7]

The family palace or enclave of houses had always enshrined the honor and fame of the lineage; Florentine families built, as they did most other things, for "onore e utile" – honor and utility, or profit.[8] The great palace of the Spini dominated the Arno river at the head of the Ponte Santa Trinita, a monument to the family's wealth and power in its thirteenth-century heyday. The later fourteenth century saw the rise of the impressive edifices of the Castellani, Peruzzi, Alberti, Albizzi, and Alessandri families then dominant in Florentine trade and government. As the fifteenth century progressed, in accordance with a growing appetite for conspicuous consumption

and a heightened consciousness of classical precedents for distinguished citizens building distinguished houses, patricians increasingly asserted their stature in programs of church decoration and palace building which imprinted their families' images more effectively upon the urban map. With the institution of the Catasto in 1427, the house in which a man lived was declared exempt from taxation, and so the building of a splendid palace might be seen as an investment for wealthy patricians, although the deduction was the same no matter how much the dwelling cost. At the same time, while many new palaces were constructed in the early decades of the century, building was somewhat inhibited by the fact that wealthy patrician merchants paid out much of their profits in taxes to support the commune's costly wars.[9]

The first of the great monumental fifteenth-century palaces was built some time during the second decade of the century by Niccolò and Agnolo da Uzzano. Niccolò was the wealthy elder statesman of the oligarchic regime, one of the most powerful men in Florence in the 1420s. As Nicolai Rubinstein pointed out, the Da Uzzano palace serves as "a point of reference for the Medici palace," not only as an impressive building belonging to a leading citizen, but one constructed in a very brief hiatus between the commune's constant wars. It was not until the 1440s, when peace was finally concluded with Florence's main foreign enemy, Milan, and the city's internal stability guaranteed by various electoral measures, that "the profits of many patrician merchants were again freed for use in building palaces."[10] The Medici palace was begun in 1445, at the first possible opportunity offered by an improvement in the city's economic and political conditions. Following this example, in the course of the next two decades construction began on at least ten major palaces. By 1470 Benedetto Dei, enumerating the assets of his native city, counted thirty important patrician palaces contributing to the glory of Florence.[11] Building had become, more than ever before, a major means of self-definition and expression, a leading indicator of the culture and stature of its patrician patrons.

Around 1460 Piero del Massaio, a painter and cartographer from the Medici circle, made some maps illustrating his selection of the city's landmark buildings (fig. 65).[12] In his view of Florence from the north, the Medici palace, which constituted after its completion in the late 1450s the most visible expression of the family's preeminence, was prominent in the foreground. The minor impediments of irregular streets and intervening structures were swept away to show it in direct relation to the nearby cathedral and baptistery, dedicated respectively to the Virgin and to John the Baptist, the city's patron saint, and in line with the Via Calzaiuoli that linked this spiritual center of the city to the seat of secular government in the Palazzo Vecchio at its farther end. Del Massaio's placement of the Medici palace on the axis of the Florentine centers of authority represented his sense of the significant rather than strict topographical accuracy, although Cosimo did in fact have a view from the upper windows of his palace down the Via Larga to the cathedral, and beyond it to the crenellated tower of the palace of the Signoria, shown in a Medici manuscript of the late fifteenth century (fig. 94).[13] The other modern private palaces included in Del Massaio's map were those of the Da Uzzano, Lorenzo di Larione de' Bardi, Luca Pitti, Tommaso Soderini, and the Pazzi family, the last four all close associates of the Medici.[14] This building might be regarded as a "palatial conversation" in which the Medici, their friends, and their rivals staked their claims to a particular measure of honor and fame through the construction of monumental private palaces.

Patrons like Giovanni Rucellai saw themselves as the progenitors of palaces as well as of sons, and this connection between the *pater* and the patron was emphasized in the habit of anthropomorphizing cities and buildings, of speaking about them as living beings. Chapter 12 will examine how images on marriage *cassoni* expressed patricians' similarly imaginative associations between the conquests of love and those of war, between begetting sons to fill their houses, the business of the bedroom, and the civic business of preeminent citizens, to create cities full of classicizing buildings, like those erected by the heroes of the ancient world. The image of Cosimo as *padre della patria* was first presented in relation to his building of public churches. Nowhere does it become clearer than in relation to his palace that this patriarchal model of the virtuous as well as powerful citizen was essentially a republican one, derived from Aristotle and Cicero (to whom Rucellai explicitly referred in his *zibaldone*), rather than a predominantly princely one, as many historians have claimed.[15] In the eyes of these classical authors and their Renaissance disciples, a man's patronage honored his own achievement, his family, his role in the community, and the city itself.

Correctly calibrating the balance of these elements was by no means, however, a simple matter. Private palaces were obviously the supreme vehicle for patrician self-expression. By comparison with his building of churches, the patron of a palace was constrained neither by a sense of sin to be expiated and salvation to be achieved, nor by the competing practical and devotional agendas of other families, or of ecclesiastical foundations and their spiritual leaders. The contested issue of how far the individual citizens of a republic ought to attract personal honor

94   View of Florence from the Medici palace, *Laurentii Medices Vita* of Niccolò Valori, Florence, Biblioteca Medicea Laurenziana, Plut. 61, 3, fol. 3r

and fame as the progenitors of architecture became far more exigent in relation to secular than to church building. Cosimo's friends' apologias for the magnificence of his palace were much less confident than for his charitable building of churches like the Badia. As noted, there was a good deal of ambiguity in the popular view of the building of the Medici palace and its reflection on Cosimo's aspirations. The private builder was not without restraint in a physical and intellectual environment where collective needs and social expectations kept the individual's impulses within bounds. "Magnificence" was desirable, but suspect, as it had been in republican Rome, and even Christian "liberality" had to be virtuous, circumscribed by a powerful sense of the decorum which controlled Renaissance representation.[16] Notably the Milanese delegation, among the earliest visitors to the newly completed palace in 1459, chose to refer to Cosimo's magnanimity rather than his magnificence.[17]

The issue of the ideals a private palace should express, clearly crucial to the significance of the Medici palace in its own time, the intentions of Cosimo as a patron and builder, and the public reception of his patronage, was explored and debated at length by patrons, humanists, and the *popolo*. Already in his account of Florence's buildings Bruni had developed the analogy between the physical appearance of the city and the qualities of its citizens; he owed to Quintilian, well known to Florentine readers, the view that "cities are praised after the same fashion as men. The founder takes the place of the parent, and antiquity carries greater authority . . . The virtues and vices revealed by their deeds are the same as in private individuals."[18] This identification of the virtues of the city with those of its citizens was in harmony with the well-known classical view that men and cities were fundamentally interdependent, a view which was widely diffused in Florentine learned and popular culture. Dante had popularized Aristotle's dictum that "man is naturally a political animal," referring to his membership of the polis or city as necessary to humankind; "just as a man need a family, a family needs a neighborhood, a neighborhood needs a city."[19]

Cicero in his *De Officiis*, the most commonly read, summarized, and quoted of the Roman orator's works in Renaissance Florence, invoked the authority of Plato to spell out the responsibilities created by this interaction: "as Plato has admirably expressed it, we are not born for ourselves alone, but our country claims a share of our being, and our friends a share . . ." Debating the question of "what sort of house a man of rank and station should . . . have," he concluded that "as in everything else a man must have regard not for himself alone but for others also, so in the home of a distinguished man, in which numerous guests must be entertained and crowds of every sort of people received, care must be taken to have it spacious"; conversely, "one must be careful too, not to go beyond proper bounds in expense and display."[20] The competing claims on the citizen of magnificence and moderation, frugality and honorable hospitality, had to be carefully balanced in accordance with the classical view, eagerly embraced by medieval Christian scholars and teachers, that moderation in all things was a shining virtue, excess the darkest vice.

Leon Battista Alberti, author of the definitive Renaissance treatise on building, was a cleric, humanist, architect, and close friend of the Medici. Although his *De Re Aedificatoria* was not printed until 1485, the original draft was written much earlier, probably between 1443 and 1452, at the invitation of Lionello d'Este, duke of Ferrara, also an intimate associate of Cosimo and his sons.[21] Alberti's ideas were no doubt circulating in Florence as part and product of Florentine debate about building in the mid-1440s, when construction began on the Medici palace. By this time Alberti had been resident in Florence for a decade, during which he was closely involved with the Medici and their friends. The question of how much magnificence and expense was appropriate to the private builder was becoming an urgent one for patrons and architects, stimulated no doubt by newly favorable economic conditions for building and the conspicuous example of Cosimo de' Medici's patronage of churches.

Alberti addressed at length Cicero's question as to what kind of house was appropriate to a great citizen; his argument, like those of his classical sources, refers to conflicting views and precedents, presenting a sort of dialogue between authorities. He began with the most austere examples of the Greeks, observing that "the best of later generations were faithful to this frugality in works both public and private . . . but then excess gripped almost every one." Conversely as Alberti pointed out, citing the views of Plato, Aristotle, Thucydides, and Cicero, even in the eyes of the Greeks magnificence, arguably a personal vice, was justified as a social virtue. Society began with the family, extending outward toward friends and neighbors to embrace the entire city:

> As Thucydides said, we build great works so as to appear great in the eyes of our descendants: equally, we decorate our property as much to distinguish family and country as for any personal display, and who would deny this to be the responsibility of a good citizen? For both of these reasons, it is preferable to make the parts that are particularly public or are intended principally to welcome guests, such as the facade, vestibule, and so on, as handsome as possible. Although I may think that any excess must be censured, yet I feel that those who spend so much on the bulk of their buildings that they cannot afford to adorn them deserve even greater censure than those who overspend slightly on ornament.[22]

Ultimately the arguments of Cicero and Alberti rested on the interpretation of what was appropriate, or according to accepted decorum, which in turn depended upon the broad consensus of public judgment. The practical message to citizens was further obscured by the fact that Alberti, as much as Cicero, referred in his language and examples to the society of ancient Rome, whose great citizens or senators in many ways resembled the Florentine palace-building patriciate, particularly in their concern with political participation and patronage, and the relation between them. In other ways, of course, their culture was very different; not least because Renaissance civic ideology was infused by Christian conceptions of virtue and decorum, which accepted splendor and display in temples even more wholeheartedly than had the Romans, but who were far more vigorously opposed to the getting and spending of riches on material things, and demanded that magnificence be tempered not just with moderation but also with liberality, the Christian virtue with which it was complexly associated. While later quattrocento humanists such as Pontano were to return to strictly classical, essentially Aristotelian categories in distinguishing sharply between such virtues as liberality, magnificence, and beneficence, in the period of Cosimo's building program they were inextricably intertwined in the public mind.[23]

Cicero's influential observations in De Officiis revolved around an issue implicit in Bruni's comparison between virtuous citizens and virtuous cities: the proper relation between the dignity of the house and the dignity of its owner, the dialogue between the virtue of a man and that of his house. Cicero's chief example illustrating the nature of this issue struck an immediate chord with Florentines' own experience and concerns. The Roman orator related how Gnaeus Octavius was said to have "distinguished himself by building upon the Palatine an attractive and imposing house . . . the construction of this house was thought to have gained votes for the owner, a new man, in his attempts to attain to the consulship." The virtuous exemplum of Gnaeus Octavius was contrasted with the example of Scaurus, the bête-noire of Pliny's tirades against extravagance in his Natural History.[24] Cicero related how Scaurus demolished Octavius's house, and on its site built an addition to his own, pointing the moral that consequently, while Octavius became the first of his family to bring the honor of a consulship to his house, Scaurus, though the son of a very great and illustrious man, brought to the same house when enlarged not only defeat, but disgrace and ruin. His conclusion concerning this rather complicated tale: "the truth is, a man's dignity may be enhanced by the house he lives in, but not wholly secured by it; the owner should bring honour to his house, not the house to its owner," was one which Florentines were to ponder deeply in attempting to define a decorum appropriate to themselves.

In accordance with the Aristotelian ideas expressed earlier by Bruni, Alberti, writing as much for patrons as architects, described the virtues of buildings with words that also referred to the virtues of people; ingenuity (ingegno), dignity, decorum.[25] Alberti stressed that whatever was done must be decens – fitting. Pleasing proportions in a building were those proportionate to the builder's dignity as well as to the dignity of the building.[26] "As generally in public and in private life, so in the practice of architecture, there should be moderation and thrift . . . every form of luxury among the citizens should be eliminated or held in check . . ."[27] The harmony he sought in architecture was as much moral as aesthetic. "Magnificentia" was not just splendor, but also the expression of loftiness of mind, of nobility, majesty, generosity, and artistic greatness, stemming ideally from the skill (ingegno) of the men employed in building.[28] Extrapolating upon a passage of the De Officiis cited also by Giovanni Rucellai in his diary, Alberti declared: "A city should not be adorned more by its buildings than by the glory of its citizens' deeds." Filarete's similar stress in his Treatise on Architecture written in the 1450s, on the importance of matching the dignity of the building to that of the man, shows how far the Florentine debate about building extended beyond any simple equation between magnificence and the exhibition of power. Indeed in an explicit reference to Medici patronage, Filarete observed that Cosimo was a type of private citizen not seen since the era of the Romans, wherein lay the amazing quality of his achievement; this the architect associated primarily with his immense wealth, not with his extraordinary political influence.[29]

Cosimo had De Officiis in his library by 1418, and knew it well; a letter written by his younger son, Giovanni, to Francesco Sforza in 1456, shows that the Medici were very familiar with the debate about the appropriate expression of the measure of a patron's dignity in his building. Cicero's comment concerning a private palace, that "its prime object is serviceableness . . . and yet careful attention should be paid to its comfort and dignity," could have served as a description of the Medici palace. But it was Giovanni Rucellai who most clearly articulated the concerns of the mid-fifteenth-century Florentine patron in relating Cicero's observations explicitly to himself. As so often in this society so reliant upon the authority of the ancients, the reader's and anthologist's interest was piqued by individual exempla of classical virtues and vices. In his zibaldone, Rucellai transcribed and transposed into Florentine terms the example cited by Cicero:

Tulio . . . says that he understands that Gnaeus Octavius, a Roman citizen, obtained the greatest honor by building a most beautiful palace . . . and the aforesaid Tulio, having to write to his son, who was studying in Athens, in order to inspire him to every virtue with the examples of the most virtuous and magnanimous men, said this to him, that is . . . Gnaeus Octavius . . . was made consul of Rome, the first one of his family, on account of his building of a very beautiful palace . . . a palace imbued with great dignity and renown because it embodied good order and measure, and he understood that it was the reason for his acquiring the greatest goodwill and favor with the people."[30]

Writing his compendium of wisdom, like Cicero, for the benefit of his sons, Rucellai recommended to them the example of Gnaeus Octavius who like himself built a palace "full of reputation and dignity." Rucellai's citation of Cicero's example of the reputation and dignity of a palace reflecting on its owner contributes to persuasive evidence that he built his own palace partly to rehabilitate himself in Florentine society and in the eyes of the Medici regime, from which he had long been excluded for his association with his exiled father in law, Palla Strozzi. The extent of his assimilation of the Roman example to the Florentine situation, making it indeed his own, is evident in his definition of the "dignity "of Octavius's palace as consisting in its "good order and measure," the same popular Florentine phrase enumerating the ideal virtues which Cosimo had used in his poem to Sforza. Moreover, by comparison with the simple votes so baldly named by Cicero as Octavius's reward, Rucellai indicated the broader and more subtle conception of support and promotion expected by Florentines of their fellow citizens, in representing Octavius's palace as stimulating "the greatest goodwill and favor in the people," another typically Florentine expression the banker used elsewhere to explain his neighbors' assistance after his bankruptcy in keeping up the appearance of his villa at Quaracchi.[31]

However, it did not escape Rucellai's attention that these classical authorities and exempla testified to the importance of maintaining a balance between the dignity of the builder and that of his building, and to the public function of the palace as the justification of its reputation and the criterion of its measure. Earlier in his *zibaldone*, around 1457, he quoted Cicero's cautionary injunction that "a rich man's house has to receive many foreign visitors and honor them with largesse, or otherwise building an extensive house would dishonor its master."[32] Rucellai's house, like that of Cosimo and those of many other eminent Florentines, did fulfil this important condition. Besides taking pains to point out the public, social, and civic functions of his palace, Rucellai had also noted in his *zibaldone*, immediately after his dictum that man is born to do two things, to procreate and to build: "But San Bernardo says that one ought to build more for

necessity than because one wants to, because by building the desire to do so does not fade but rather grows." His invocation of the impressive authority of Saint Bernard, in the form of a quotation from the extremely well-known letter to Raimondo Manelli erroneously attributed to the saint, reveals the depth of Florentine uneasiness about this vexed question. For this was not just a learned debate between classical scholars and classicizing architects; it was a case in which the impact of classical precedents on Florentine patrons was directly apparent, and one which reveals how far the use of classical forms was perceived as integrally related to the emulation of the classical civic spirit.

While builders such as Giovanni and Cosimo were apparently prepared to shelve their scruples and come down on the side of building for their own and the public benefit, Matteo Palmieri, in his widely read *Vita civile* pointed to its main moral message that "not to the master for the house, but to the house for its master one would wish and ought to give honor . . ."[33] Popular critics were inclined to hold extravagant patrons to a sterner standard. The apothecary Luca Landucci, perhaps with the well-known passage from Cicero in mind, was to observe waspishly of the palace built forty years later by Filippo Strozzi that "it seems that the man should be the master of it, but the opposite is true, that they (our palaces) are the masters of us. This palace will last almost for ever; ask yourself then if this palace has mastered him, and how many others still to come it will master." It may be that the *popolano* Landucci, in noting that this ambitious palace-builder did not live to see his palace finished, "misunderstood the dynastic and personal imperatives that dominated such a man," who looked, in fact, beyond his own lifetime to the completion of his palace by his sons and its endurance as a monument of the family's greatness for all time.[34] Or perhaps he understood them all too well. Since the *popolo* paid close attention to patrician building, the controversy also raged in popular verse. The ideals of civic identity and virtue outlined by Cicero were embraced by a number of ordinary Florentines who felt they had a stake in their society.

Alberti was in close contact with many popular poets, which would certainly have fostered the spread and popularization of his views. Making his case for moderation in both public and private building, Alberti drew attention to the dramatic gesture of more than one Roman citizen who tore down his own house as a protest against extravagance, or out of fear that it might arouse envy.[35] While in his comment on Cicero's tale of Octavius and Scaurus, Rucellai studiously ignored the implied condemnation of those who, like himself, demolished other peoples' houses to aggrandize their own, these exempla and the images they evoked clearly caught the imagination of the plebeian public. Comedio Venuti, not a Florentine, but a notary from subject Cortona, took up this classical precedent and applied it to Cosimo de' Medici, suggesting that he would have done better to emulate Valerius Publicola, "who humble and patient, to acquiesce/in the wishes of a heated and warlike people/ allowed his lofty house to be laid low and pulled down." A poem by Bernardo Cambini, described as being written "in praise of Cosimo," encouraged his readers to see Cosimo as an ornament to his city greater than any Greek or Roman leader. But perhaps not without irony he invoked Lucullus in concluding: "And with great expense and ingenuity/ he built great palaces inside and outside the city,/ so that with their every ornament/ he exceeded Lucullus in magnificence:/ for which yours is the glory, dear Florence."[36]

The chronicler Giovanni Cavalcanti took the argument about palace building out of the realm of classical exempla and placed it firmly in the context of contemporary social comment. He opined that the neighbor of the Medici family who one night smeared blood on the threshold of the palace was almost certainly a butcher, since only butchers were in a position to obtain quantities of blood, and he did so, according to Cavalcanti, in protest against such extravagance in a period of punishing taxation for poorer citizens. In this act, argued the chronicler, the envy generally feared by the wealthy of both classical Rome and Renaissance Florence was explicitly tied to their spending on private palaces, along with a number of other grievances, including Cosimo's support of Francesco Sforza and many citizens' subterranean resentment and suspicion of the hierarchy of the Church.[37]

The multitude of citizens, no less than the plebeian horde, directed their wrath, full of bitterness and inclined to evil-doing, against the more distinguished citizens . . . and united in accursed envy of the infinite riches of Cosimo: for which iniquitous reasons many complained of his magnificent buildings; and many said: In his hypocrisy, full of pride in the church, our purses are emptied to pay for them in the name of taxes . . . And now that there is nothing more to build for the friars, he has begun on a palace, by comparison with which the Roman Colosseum will appear to disadvantage. And others said: Who would not build magnificently, being able to spend money which is not his? And thus throughout the city there was much odious gossip, and everything was turned angrily against Cosimo . . . And they said; We should remember what our fathers told us in the evenings

about the perils in which the Church involves us. And along with these reproaches they added that the coffers of the taxes collected at the gates were being emptied to build Cosimo's house; but they said nothing when this man sustained the Commune with many much greater sums: and by such odd reasoning Cosimo was defamed. Whence under cover of night, his threshold was all covered with blood: about this grievous significance of this there was the greatest murmuring throughout the city.[38]

Notably in describing this vein of popular criticism, Cavalcanti carefully distanced himself from its complaints. Clearly to very many citizens, great and beautiful palaces, like magnificent churches, were ultimately acceptable because they served the common good and the good of the commune; they enhanced the appearance of the city of Florence and its reputation by bearing witness to its citizens' collective virtue. When Giovanni Rucellai went bankrupt in the 1470s, his neighbors helped to maintain the legendary garden at his villa of Quaracchi in acknowledgement of the benefits to the community of the grace and beauty of this spot, apparently animated by that "favor and goodwill" Rucellai hoped, like Octavius, to receive as a result of his building.[39] Filarete described the finished Medici palace as honoring the neighborhood it dominated, and indeed the whole city. Moreover, its building was also an act of liberality, since it redistributed Cosimo's "infinite riches" to the benefit and employment of the needy.[40] And as Richard Goldthwaite calculated, the building of a major palace led to the creation of some two to four hundred jobs for an entire year.[41] As a factor in Cosimo's relations with his fellow-citizens, and his role in the representation of his city, the new Medici palace was on balance more positive than negative.

Nor in this case was the citizen necessarily more honored for the dignity of his palace than the palace for the dignity of the citizen who built it. Shortly after its completion, on the occasion of the visits to Florence in 1459 of Pope Pius II and Francesco Sforza's young son Galeazzo Maria, the traditional processional route taken by foreign guests was altered to incorporate the newly significant pole of the Medici palace on the Via Larga.[42] As the fame of its magnificence spread, it soon became a tourist attraction for all sorts of visitors to Florence.[43] However, despite the novelty of the new palace, its intrinsically fascinating architectural features, and the splendor of its decoration, as we are reminded by Vespasiano da Bisticci's accounts of the lives of many famous citizens of Italy, the attractions of Florence for visitors had always been regarded as consisting in equal parts of her famous citizens and her beautiful buildings. Francesco Giovanni described in his *ricordi* how in February 1452 the Emperor Frederick and the king of Hungary came to Florence and made a tour of the local sites. "Several times he went to look around the district, and especially to Petraia, and to see the chapels and churches, and he went many times to hear mass at the Servi, and similarly he went to see the lions. Then passing along the Via Larga on horseback, he went in to see Cosimo's palace."[44]

The party may have visited the building site of the new palace, which had been cleared in 1444; presumably after eight years of concentrated effort there was something there to see. But the palace the emperor stayed in on that visit was certainly the Medici *casa vecchia*, and although later inventories suggest its precious contents were probably well worth seeing, as Brenda Preyer observed, the old house was large but by no means architecturally distinguished. Obviously Cosimo's status as a citizen dignified his house in an appropriately Ciceronian manner long before he built his magnificent new palace. And while the latter proved to be the last word in Cosimo de' Medici's personal definition of himself, he spent only the very last years of his life there; evidence of extensive renovations to the old house in the 1430s and 1440s and the marked similarity of its accommodations and their comforts to those realized in the new one suggests Cosimo's long-standing interest in making his house as much the expression of his own interests, dignity, and stature as the ideal expression of architectural magnificence.[45]

Some time ago Fraser-Jenkins drew attention to an evolution in the course of the fifteenth century in attitudes to individuals' spending on building. Referring to the debate about "magnificence," he pointed out that between 1436 and 1450 Cosimo de' Medici "was alone in Italy in spending very large sums of money on a series of building projects"; soon many princes, like the Gonzaga and Sforza, were to follow his lead.[46] Chapter 15 will examine more closely the relation between Cosimo de' Medici's patronage activities and choices and those of his princely friends and contemporaries. Meanwhile, however, it should be noted that Fraser-Jenkins's interesting observations were quickly transmuted by other scholars into a claim that "Cosimo led the way for the princes in the expression of magnifience," and then into an assumption that Cosimo's magnificence was therefore "princely" in nature, although Fraser-Jenkins himself stressed the anomaly that Cosimo was neither a nobleman nor a prince: "In all this Cosimo's position is slighty ironical, in that the argument that naturally formed around him in defence of patronage by a private individual as opposed to a prince led to an encouragement to the princes themselves to build."[47] Thanks to the

amount of attention since devoted to demonstrating the "princely" quality of Cosimo's patronage, we are now much better informed about that patronage and about the debate over magnificence. Despite this fact, many historians continue to invoke Fraser-Jenkins and the authorities he cited on Medici patronage; Pope Pius II, not a citizen of Florence or familiar with its civic ideology, and Machiavelli, a Florentine intensely committed to that ideology but not even born until Cosimo had been dead five years. The immense influence of Cicero's argument on Florentine citizens and patrons well into the third quarter of the fifteenth century and many years after Cosimo's death is seldom observed.[48]

Fraser-Jenkins also considered the possibility that the less well-documented Florentine patrons who preceded Cosimo were "conscious of the need to associate themselves with an architectural oeuvre." Bruni's *Panegirico* is evidence of this concern, which has since been observed in a number of other citizens whose patronage will be considered more closely in chapter 15. Of course Cosimo's patronage turned out to be vastly larger in scale and his oeuvre more innovative than any other of his time, but it was not necessarily significantly different in kind from that of other less successful, less powerful, and less wealthy Florentine citizens who had neither the opportunity nor the resources to match him. Since Cosimo's patronage did largely precede that of the princes with whom he is usually compared, for a variety of reasons, many of them serendipitous, the argument that he adopted a princely style is less than entirely convincing. Although Richard Trexler may well be right in part in his assessment of the role of the Medici palace in fostering the family's preeminence in Florence – writing of the visits of foreign guests that "the very essence of this public representation of status and honor was its domestic nature" – there is really no compelling evidence that "Cosimo made the family residence a type of princely *camera*."[49] Conversely, like many other Florentines before and after him, including the Albizzi, Peruzzi, Strozzi, and Rucellai, in the hospitality he extended to both domestic and foreign guests, Cosimo made his palace representative of the highest ideal of the Roman, Ciceronian, and Florentine republican citizen's obligation to his family, neighbors, friends, and ultimately to his city, a worthy expression of their dignity and virtue.

★   ★   ★

PLACING THE PALACE AND ITS PATRON IN HISTORY: THE ARCHITECTURAL FUSION OF FLORENCE AND ROME

Their new urban palace on the Via Larga was the chief measure of the Medici presence in Florence, and the family's major opportunity to articulate an identity which was complexly related to the city and its other citizens. The size of the palace and its architectural innovations expressed and honored the family's preponderance over the rest of the patriciate, while identifying them as building firmly on Florentine tradition. As Brenda Preyer observed, from the second decade of the fifteenth century palace architecture was in ferment, and the Medici palace was a product of this process, but it was also, like the family's position in the city, very special and quite unique: "although one can find precedents for many features, the palace as whole remains a masterpiece of innovation and of synthesis."[50] It fulfilled, indeed, Alberti's prescription for the private palace, that "everything should be measured, bonded and composed . . . so that one's gaze might flow freely and gently along the cornices, through the recessions, and over the entire interior and exterior face of the work, its every delight heightened by both similarity and contrast; and so that anyone who saw it would imagine that he could never be satiated by the view, but looking at it again and again in admiration, would glance back once more as he departed" (fig. 92).[51]

Architectural historians have identified two essential elements in its style; the forms of trecento Florence and those of classical Rome. As in learned and popular literature, so in architecture, these were not always easily distinguishable. Howard Burns pointed out that since architects like Brunelleschi can be shown to have borrowed and assimilated antique forms from every conceivable source, including drawings, illuminated manuscripts, and buildings in various Italian cities, and most particularly from Florentine Romanesque, classical forms by the fifteenth century were integrated, sometimes buried, in the foundations of medieval Italian building. The important change in the mid-fifteenth century was the novelty of the patron's and architect's explicit intention to have their buildings resemble those of ancient Rome. As evidence of the importance of this new perception, Burns cited a comment on the Medici palace by Flavio Biondo, who "almost certainly knew more about Roman topography than anyone then alive, with the possible exception of Alberti":[52] "Whatever private houses had recently been built on the Via Larga must be compared to the work of former Roman princes and certainly to distinguished ones; indeed I myself, who have achieved some measure of fame from my writings, do not

hesitate to state that there are no remains of private princely residences in Rome which display any greater splendor than those." The palace of Cosimo, who in his youth had spent a great deal of time in Rome, studying Roman ruins under the tutelage of Poggio Bracciolini and Niccoli, clearly recaptured something of the spirit if not wholly the letter of the Roman ideals of building.

The Augustan wall of Trajan's forum was probably the direct source for the new rustication. It was not dissimilar to that employed in the building of the Palazzo Vecchio and the associated urban renewal of the area around it, but with its large rounded blocks it gave to Renaissance viewers more of the weathered Roman ruin's appearance of being "in a state of nature." Certainly, on his trip to Rome in 1450 Giovanni Rucellai, another informed patrician patron, in his own mind identified this wall of the forum of Augustus with an ancient palace.[53] The general populace of Florence also recognized the significance of these features, as Isabelle Hyman noted of a poem by Lapaccini describing the similar rustication of the later Pitti palace. "I have seen the building for Luca Pitti;/ some break, some shatter, some strike, some break down/ with shovels, mattocks, spades and entrenching tools,/ in order to surpass the lofty limits,/ that we see in the ancient works of Caesar's time" (fig. 95).[54]

Unlike either medieval or Roman buildings, Cosimo's new palace had a great many windows, which along with the courtyard, garden, and three loggias, may be partly explained in terms of the patron's personal desire for spacious, light, and airy accommodation.[55] The loggia was of course a traditional feature of trecento family palaces and neighborhood enclaves. But by the 1440s and 1450s it had become a rare reference to the past, and was one of the few features of the Medici palace not to be copied in the future, although the almost contemporaneous Rucellai palace formed part of a family ensemble that included a free-standing loggia opposite. The windows of the Medici palace took the form of medieval biforate arches like those of the Palazzo Vecchio and other government buildings, but were adorned with classical ornament (fig. 97). The combined effect has been seen as modern, but not radical, the facade with its windows and rustication presenting a combination of antique features expressive of the classical enthusiasms of the patron and his circle, and Romanesque and Tuscan elements adding up to an impression of a "quasi public edifice."[56] This resemblance might imply a claim on Cosimo's part to quasi-public authority, but it could also be seen as representing an assertion of patriotism in its incorporation of the Florentine trecento ideal of civic building, since Cosimo, as we have seen, was steeped in Florentine civic culture looking back to the trecento as well as forwards in the

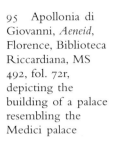

95   Apollonia di
Giovanni, *Aeneid*,
Florence, Biblioteca
Riccardiana, MS
492, fol. 72r,
depicting the
building of a palace
resembling the
Medici palace

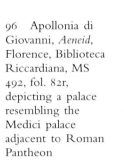

96   Apollonia di
Giovanni, *Aeneid*,
Florence, Biblioteca
Riccardiana, MS
492, fol. 82r,
depicting a palace
resembling the
Medici palace
adjacent to Roman
Pantheon

avant-garde classical enthusiasms of his humanist and artist
friends.

While within, the palace contains a unusual amount of
open space, it also has some fortress-like elements, including the extremely high wall enclosing the garden in the
rear (fig. 102). Only two years after Cosimo's death, in
1466 the palace was prepared for the defence of the
family and its supporters. These defensible elements are
conspicuous in preceding generations of palaces built by
leading citizens such as the Peruzzi, Castellani, and Spini,
and link the Medici palace with the distant Florentine
past as well as with late trecento and early quattrocento
citizens' palaces and the Palazzo Vecchio. Like most of
Cosimo's identifiable concerns, and like his role in government, the palace's architectural associations are both
public and private. Indeed the Medici palace perfectly
exemplifies the family's relation to the city, located complexly between honoring the city and themselves.

Whether or not Cosimo consciously took up a challenge that might have been implied in the words of his
close friend and associate Andrea Bartolini, writing to his

younger son Giovanni from Rome of its buildings: "you
have never seen nor will see more marvellous things,
which it almost impossible to recreate in one's imagination, let alone to build something like them, anywhere,"[57]
there is some evidence that the palace commanded an
important place in the imagination of literate citizens.
The illuminations for the copy of Virgil's *Aeneid* made
by Apollonio di Giovanni, probably for one of the Medici
amici or *parenti*, features a building that looks very like
the Medici palace, alongside such well-known Roman
monuments as the Coliseum and Trajan's column. These
images identify the city built by Aeneas as Rome, while
eliding it with Rome's daughter city, Florence, and its
builders, particularly Cosimo de' Medici, with Aeneas. In
them the boundaries between time and space are dis-
solved to expose the sort of basic associations that characterized Florentine culture, both learned and popular
(fig. 96).[58]

Implicitly this highly personalized palace, in accordance
with the classical analogy between the qualities of men
and cities, personified its owner. When Cosimo's secre-

tary, Ser Alesso, described to Cosimo's son the clearing of its site he referred to the palace as "colui" (he).[59] Expounding his memory scheme, their mutual friend Michele del Giogante illustrated the dependence of the "figure of the will," like the choice of texts to be preserved in *zibaldoni* and memorized, upon an imaginative perception of the relevance of men and objects to oneself. Notably he chose the example of a man and his palace: "Think of this man or woman or thing, of what you would like to do with it . . . or what you would like to see happen to it, whether good or ill . . . like a beautiful palace . . . saying to yourself, if it were mine, I would like to have it all decorated with images and stories in mosaics of gold; if you hate it, you should say, let it be set on fire today rather than tomorrow, so that I may see it reduced to ashes down to the foundations, together with him who had it built."[60]

Similarly, the figure of the owner was evoked by the arms and *imprese* borne by his building. The identification of palaces with persons through their arms was an ancient tradition, and the use of *imprese*, novel in the mid-fifteenth century, was essentially an elaboration by cultured Renaissance patrons on the precedent of family crests.[61] However, the Medici palace identified its owners with arms and devices more numerous, ingenious, and commanding than those incorporated into earlier private palaces. There were, for example, the new freestanding rather than wrap-around arms on the southeastern and garden corners. The first of these thrust itself into the viewer's field of vision at the most striking point of the palace on the bend of the Via Larga. Worked into the fabric of the design, along with the Medici balls, were Cosimo and his sons' personal *imprese*; the diamond ring with three feathers, symbolizing eternity, and often associated on Medici commisions with their motto, "semper," expressing their fascination with the Petrarchan themes of time and eternity. The rose which alternates on the Medici facade with the *palle* and the ring may well inscribe in stone the solid association with the papacy on which much of their fortune was founded, or it could refer to the cult of the Virgin to which Cosimo was devoted (fig. 97). As Preyer pointed out, the significance

97   Medici palace, detail of facade with *imprese*

Piero attached to emblems is indicated in the modification of the *palle* on the palace after the king of France permitted him to use three fleurs-de-lis in 1465.[62] Like the personalized decoration of the courtyard frieze with roundels based on ancient gems in the Medici collection or well known to them (fig. 135), these *imprese* express the patron's delight in the games and conceits of symbolic communication which can be seen in its simplest form in Marco Parenti's design of a belt-buckle for his Strozzi relative. This same pleasure has full play shortly afterwards on the facade of the Rucellai palace; if Alberti was indeed the architect, as seems extremely likely, it can be assumed literally to embody his views on ornament so elaborately articulated in the ninth book of *De Re Aedificatoria.*

In the building of their palace as in many other respects, the Medici were in the vanguard of a culture rooted in the Florentine past and common to many other patrons. As an expression of the patron's interests, the Medici palace seems more exceptional than it is because as Preyer observed, there is simply not enough documentation of comparable cases, especially to connect earlier palaces with their owners and their aspirations. Moreover, the Medici palace is seldom compared with others less remarkable and more obscure, owing to a disproportionate interest on the part of historians in the uniquely successful and well-documented Medici family, and of art historians in the Renaissance of the classical tradition to which it is such a notable contribution. Although individual features of the Medici palace were much copied, it was not the only desirable model, and was never replicated *in toto*. The messages sent by fifteenth-century palace builders, and the qualities their buildings embodied, were as varied as the patrons themselves.[63]

SITUATING THE FAMILY IN THE CITY

The Medici palace located its patron in historical time; in relation to the classical world, and to the civic traditions of Florence, in which its classical heritage played a major part. It also located Cosimo and his family quite significantly in urban space.[64] Much of the effect, and indeed the meaning of a palace depended upon its site. Preyer's studies of Florentine palaces have stressed the primary importance of site as both opportunity and constraint. Builders were limited in the choice of a site by their loyalty to ancestral neighborhoods in which their personal and political influence was rooted, and by the ease or difficulty of effecting transfers of land. In these respects the Medici family was both fortunate and pre-

scient, having moved in the mid-fourteenth century to a less populated district outside the first circle of city walls, where land was more plentiful and the neighbors who became their friends and partisans could be induced to trade in it. As Preyer observed, in its siting and size the Medici palace can be compared only with those of the Castellani and the Spini. In Filarete's opinion, the primary distinguishing feature of the Medici palace was the position which it commanded. "First of all, as is well known, it is at the head of the Via Larga, and I need say no more about how prestigious this is; and on the other side there is a major and most worthy street, and at the head of these still another worthy street, so that on three sides it is bordered by a street."[65]

According to Vasari, Cosimo rejected a model for the palace prepared by Brunelleschi "because it was too magnificent." Finding it difficult to imagine how the palace might have been any more magnificent than in fact it is, some historians have suggested the fear of excessive magnificence might have referred to a proposal by Brunelleschi to turn the facade toward the piazza, unifying it with the church of San Lorenzo, and thus creating an ensemble traditionally the prerogative of civic authorities. This interesting hypothesis might seem partly confirmed by a Medicean manuscript illuminated sometime between 1492 and *circa* 1517, in which the church of San Giovannino on the corner of the Via Larga and the present Via de' Gori, opposite the palace, is swept away to afford a clear view of the building in juxtaposition with San Lorenzo, shown wearing a splendid marble facade which of course it never acquired (fig. 98).[66] However, the issue on investigation proves more complex, the difficulties in the way of such a project greater than at first they might seem, and the rewards rather less.[67]

Moreover, it might be well to consider that the palace in its time – indeed even the cleared but as yet empty site – was judged "a magnificent thing to see" because it conformed to the injunction of Alberti that a palace should turn a magnificent face to the the city which it honored. The actual aspect of the palace, sited on a sharp curve of the Via Cavour – once the Via Larga – is indeed commanding. A worshipper leaving the cathedral and walking toward the baptistery, at the ecclesiastical heart of the city, would have seen the Medici palace directly in his line of vision if he turned his head to the right. In this sense the palace was as the 1460 maps represented it, visually unified with the center of the Florence (fig. 99).[68]

The Medici palace as it stands is usually attributed to Michelozzo, who had cooperated with Cosimo on many projects over the preceding twenty years. However, Brenda Preyer suggested that Brunelleschi was the more

on the main body of the church at San Lorenzo.[70] While it should weigh much less heavily in any calculations than issues of style, Michelozzo's close personal relationship with the Medici, which was to continue into another generation with Lorenzo's promotion of his son Niccolò to the position of Chancellor of the republic, would have been good grounds for Cosimo to choose him, especially in view of his notable ability to translate elements of architectural style into forms in accordance with the wishes of his patron.[71]

Until new documents are discovered, the identity of the architect and the nature of the original plans for the palace must remain open questions. But in whatever direction its facade was formally turned, proximity related the palace intimately to the church of San Lorenzo and to the immediate neighborhood of its parish and the *gonfalone* of the Golden Lion. At same time the palace faced outward toward the city and a more extended neighborhood; north to San Marco which the Medici had made

98 Illumination depicting the Medici palace and San Lorenzo, Book of Hours of Laodamia de' Medici, London, British Library, Yates Thompson MS 30, fol. 20v

99 The Medici palace seen from the piazza of the baptistery, looking north up the Via Larga

likely architect. This view is based on the originality and creative invention of the actual building, which does not really resemble any other securely tied to either Michelozzo or Brunelleschi.[69] Since it was essentially executed after Brunelleschi's death, it might well have been overseen by Michelozzo, or indeed any other architect, and in the process have suffered the same mutations of which Brunelleschi's followers complained in relation to his plans for San Lorenzo. Michelozzo was noted for his adaptations of the signature features of Brunelleschi's designs, and had been working closely with him at the cathedral and the old sacristy in the years immediately preceding the commencement of the palace and the work

their own, and across the Via Larga to the large family enclaves in the *gonfalone* of Drago and the parish of Santissima Annunziata.

BUILDING FOR *PATERFAMILIAS*, *PADRINO*, AND *PATER PATRIAE*

Just as in the rebuilding of the church of San Lorenzo, as important as the relation of the Medici palace in formal terms to antique and Florentine civic traditions, was its relation to the neighborhood, and to the Medici friends and partisans so prominent there. The structure of the palace accommodates an interpretation not only in terms of statements of princely luxury and power, but also the practical requirements of the superior citizen and ultimate patron. The Medici built their palace literally upon the support of *parenti*, *vicini*, and *amici* whose cooperation enabled them to acquire the land that constituted its enormous site. One of the outstanding features of the palace in the eyes of other residents of the crowded city of Florence was its being built from scratch: "it rose from the foundations among the houses that had been bought," as Vespasiano da Bisticci noted in the one sentence of his biography of Cosimo devoted to the Medici palace.[72] Almost all the other palaces of its era, most notably that of Giovanni Rucellai, were created by cobbling together a number of existent houses behind an imposing unified facade. The huge Medici site, assembled over the course of a century with the aid of land sales from kin and neighbors, was a metaphor for the solidarity and coop- eration between the Medici family and their friends. Cosimo's secretary Ser Alesso watched as it was cleared in March 1445, and reported to Cosimo's younger son Giovanni, then in Rome, "It was a magnificent thing to see." He added that another friend "Michelino" would furnish Giovanni with more details. The Medici *amici* were thus literally in on the ground floor of the build- ing of the palace, an enterprise to which they were per- sonally committed, as to all their patrons' concerns.[73]

Richard Goldthwaite was the first to observe that the Florentine private palace "in a sense . . . sums up a civi- lization." Like Burckhardt, he saw that civilization as possessing many of the essential features of the modern world. Goldthwaite's Florence is characterized by social fragmentation, alienation, and rampant consumerism. He used the urban palace as an exemplification of his larger thesis that by the fifteenth century Florentine families were shrinking into nuclear privacy, and that "the privacy of a man's home meant . . . withdrawal from public life" into a world reserved to a tiny nuclear household shaped by women and children. At the same time he saw patri-

cians' oversized palaces as the measure of their individu- alistic and competitive egos.[74] That picture does not match the one that emerges from this study of Cosimo and his culture, nor of his domestic arrangements; although his and Giovanni di Bicci's Catasto reports from 1427 through 1458 claim less than a dozen dependents from three generations of family, they point out that the number of residents of their various houses, the majority of them living in the urban palace, ranged from thirty to fifty. Although most Florentine households were consid- erably smaller than this, the palaces built by the heads of other great and ancient lineages, like the Peruzzi and the Strozzi, could also accommodate astonishly large numbers of servants and retainers. In such cases the urban palace constituted a small community in itself.[75]

While Goldthwaite and others have suggested that such palaces might be perceived less as form than as expres- sions of wealth and magnificence, or as showcases for their contents, the comments of such contemporary observers of society and politics as Marco Parenti and Ves- pasiano da Bisticci represented them rather as places where men met and things happened. F. W. Kent, in his demonstration of the continuing importance of wider family ties in the lives of individuals and their households, showed how much palaces were seen as expressing the identity of the lineage, and functioned as the setting for events of significance to it. In an essay on palaces he assembled a rich collection of anecdote and comment concerning the use and perception of palaces as places where an "ebb and flow" in and out — of neighbors, friends, relatives, and business associates — "dissolv[ed] the boundaries between public and private space."[76] Accu- mulating evidence increasingly contradicts Goldthwaite's picture of the patrician palace as a place where "public life did not penetrate . . . either by way of formal politi- cal functions its owner may have performed for the state, or by way of a highly formalized ritual of upper-class social life" and "that [its] function in a social sense was limited to the immediate family of the owner. His palace isolated him from more distant relatives, whatever pride they may have taken in its splendor, as much as it did from the public."

Nor does it support his claim that the public promi- nence of the Medici "makes them the exception that proves the rule."[77] The social function of the Medici palace constitutes, like most of the family's activities, an extreme example of a common practice. Where Goldth- waite envisaged the palace facade as a clear delineation between public and private space, Patricia Simons's image of the windows by which it was perforated as mem- branes between the worlds within and without takes into account the actual behavior and attitudes of the occupants, such as the well-documented proclivity of women for looking out of windows.[78] Brenda Preyer, focusing on the link between patrons' social activities and the physical fabric of their palaces, saw the constant movement in and out of the Medici palace as orchestrated by "the measured cadences of the inner frames of both openings to the loggia [and] of the central portal" (fig. 101). While the Medici architectural solution represented "a completely new way of handling the transition between the street and the interior" it had precedents in other palaces, and in other buildings by Brunelleschi.[79]

Much of the enormous amount of urban space occupied by the Medici palace had a semi-public function. This was particularly true of the courtyard and the open loggia. The spacious symmetrical courtyard was the most characteristic element of the Renaissance palace; by comparison, medieval palace courtyards were usually small and irregular. There were important precedents for the Medici palace courtyard not only in such public architecture as the Palazzo del Podestà, and in church cloisters, but in the Da Uzzano and Busini palaces.[80] However, the palace also embodied the priorities of the classical architect Vitruvius, and Alberti's conviction that "the principal member of the whole building is the courtyard with its loggias," associated with his view that "a city is no more than a great house; a house is a little city." In the palace, in its exposure to light and opportunities for communication, the courtyard functioned as a miniature piazza.[81] The street loggia, walled up in the early sixteenth century, could be seen as a formalization of the democratic space of the *canto* or street corner space that played such an important part in the life of the city's neighborhoods.[82] The Medici palace was surrounded by such *canti*, includ-

ing one named after Bernardetto de' Medici, adjacent to his house; the Canto de' Medici, outside the church of San Giovannino, where their friends and neighbors watched the progress of the palace building; and the Canto alla Macina on the Via de' Ginori behind the Medici palace and near the Armenian church, from which a group of supporters sent a letter to Lorenzo after his brother's assassination, signed "from the youths of the Canto alla Macina."[83]

Preyer emphasised the unusual character of the Medici palace street loggia at a time when family loggias, so popular in the trecento, were generally going out of style. She suggested that the extraordinary breadth of all the palace's ground floor arches must be related to a desire to make the loggia very open; the ground floor archways were not centred with the windows on the *piano nobile* because the loggia was meant to call attention to itself.[84] Evidence of the usage of loggias, and their function to draw people from the outside in, appears in many contemporary paintings, especially those on wedding *cassoni* (fig. 100). These images show the intonaco walls of the loggia hung with tapestries above benches; in front of these are tables laden with food and drink. They illustrate the use of loggias as described in accounts of formal functions such as the Rucellai-Medici wedding of 1466, or that of Cosimo's grandson Lorenzo at the Medici palace in 1469, when the tables set up for guests occupied all the adjacent open spaces of courtyard, garden, and loggia, according to Marco Parenti's description of this event.[85] While there is no surviving inventory of the Medici palace in Cosimo's lifetime, the one made after Lorenzo's death in 1492 mentions large numbers of benches in the court loggia and in the downstairs rooms

100   Marco del Buono Giamberti and Apollonio di Giovanni di Tomaso, *Story of Esther, cassone* panel, *c.*1465, New York, The Metropolitan Museum of Art, Rogers Fund, 1918

101 (*following page*)   The Medici palace, interior

opening off the courtyard. There were also benches outside the *casa vecchia*.[86] One of Giovanni's friends wrote to him while he was in Naples describing a lovelorn young lady who came every day to sit on a bench outside the palace in anticipation of his return. On one of these occasions, the young *bravi* of the Medici *brigata* profited from the opportunity offered by a thunderstorm to proffer their cloaks and engage her and her duenna in flirtatious badinage.[87]

At the new Medici palace, along with most others built in the fifteenth century, the traditional practice of renting the ground floor space to accommodate shops was abandoned. However, this did not mean that space necessarily became "private." The Medici had only a relatively small *tavola* in the Mercato Vecchio which they had acquired from the Tornabuoni; the inventory made of the old Medici house in 1417/18 indicates that some the business of the family bank was carried on there in Lorenzo's room, which contained a number of account books and papers to do with the bank. Similarly, Raymond de Roover suggested that the ground-floor suite of the new palace, consisting of four rooms next to the loggia – the *sala grande*, *camera* and *anticamera*, which generally functioned as a *scrittoio* or *studio* – was used to conduct the business of the bank.[88]

It also served on occasion to accommodate Cosimo or Piero. As chronic sufferers from the painful and immobilizing illness of gout, both were sometimes obliged to move from their permanent suites on the *piano nobile* down to the rooms adjacent to the loggia to avoid the nuisance of having to be constantly carried up and down the stairs. An anecdote of Poliziano's vividly portrays their problems. "As Cosimo was being carried through his house on a chair by some servants, being about to hit a door, he cried out. One of the servants said, "What is wrong with you? You cry out before anything has happened to you! Cosimo replied: "I need to cry out beforehand: what's the use of crying out afterwards?"[89] Alison Brown suggested that after 1460 Piero's infirmity conveniently served "to deflect the political current from the government palace to his home in Via Larga." When Gonfalonier of Justice in 1461, on account of illness he was exempted for several days from the traditional sequestration of the Priors in their palace, designed to prevent them from contact with other citizens except in public meetings. During this time he in fact received several citizens in his home, one at a time, to examine and draft pending legislation.[90]

If their palace was the most obviously "political" of Medici patronage statements, it speaks most clearly of the politics of patronage. The function of the patronage network was to fulfil the patron's obligations to promote the interests of his *amici* in return for their support, and especially in view of the markedly civic orientation of most patrician patrons, it is difficult or impossible to distinguish here between "personal" and "political" interests. Patronage depended heavily on constant communication. Some of this was effected by the letters on which our knowledge of patronage is largely based, but much more, as the letters suggest, took place face to face. Great patrons such as Cosimo de' Medici were sought out by their friends and clients in the streets and in the churches of Florence; at home in their houses they received a constant stream of visitors. Suppliants besieged them with visits, notes, and gifts. Relatives, friends, and business associates flooded into the palace with help and information relating to the daily conduct of their various business, official or informal, concerning the bank, the state, or simply the conduct of their daily lives, to deliver letters or to read those which others had sent. Cosimo *paterfamilias* shaded imperceptibly in this process into the Medici *padrino*. The most intimate of the family's *amici*, the leading citizens in whose company they had occupied communal offices, the factors of the bank, the scholars and artists whose advice and services they sought, the notaries and secretaries like Michele del Giogante and Ser Alesso, who served as palace factotums, were in effect additional members of the household.[91]

Those who were less familiar, calling to pay their respects or with assurances of their support, hoping to bend the Medicean ear about business of their own, waited outside on the benches set into the walls or lining the loggia. Personal visits to the palace were a duty owed to patrons, and many *amici* apologized in letters if they were unable to come in person, hoping in the future to discuss the most important matters "a bocca."[92] When Galeazzo Maria Sforza met with Cosimo in the palace chapel in 1459, the Milanese party was soon obliged to leave, in order to make way for the crowds of people waiting to see him. Although letters very rarely refer by name to whoever was controlling admission, quite a number of notes were addressed to members of the Medici family informing them that the writer had fulfilled his duty to visit his patron at the palace, only to be turned away, or that he had waited for an unconscionable time, and had finally been obliged to leave to go about his business.[93]

Back in the 1420s the chronicler Cavalcanti had complained that the affairs of the state were discussed less in the palace of the Priors than at the dinner tables of a handful of leading citizens. An assiduous student of fluctuations in the fortunes of pro and anti-Medicean factions in 1466, when the Medici supremacy was challenged by a group of their closest friends, Parenti used

102 (*previous page*)   The Medici palace, walled garden

103 Apollonia di Giovanni, *Aeneid*, Florence, Biblioteca Riccardiana, MS 492, fol. 82v, depicting the fortification of a palace resembling the Medici palace adjacent to Trajan's Column

the number of visitors to their respective palaces as a yardstick of the standing of the protagonists. He described how at one point no one wanted to see Piero de' Medici, where "before everyone used to go to him to consult about public and private affairs . . . his reputation was so reduced at this time . . . [that] few frequented his house." At the same time his chief rival, Luca Pitti, "held court at his house, where the majority of citizens went to confer about the affairs of the state." After the Medici victory the situation was reversed. Pitti, no longer a hot political ticket, *stava freddo*; he cooled his heels "alone in his house, and no one visited him to talk about politics, where once his house was always full of people of every sort."[94]

The Medici palace was built to accommodate the activities not only of the Medici family, but also of their friends and supporters. If necessary, it might also be adapted to repel their enemies. The use of its open loggia conflicted with the implied function of the tall walls around the garden, and the high elevation of the *piano nobile*. Parenti recounted how in 1466 Nicodemo da Pontremoli, the Milanese ambassador resident in the Medici palace and a veteran of many battles, "prepared to defend Piero's house with wooden scaffolding high up over the windows in the manner employed by bombardiers," with a large quantity of stones and other weapons for fighting, and how he occupied the streets around the house with armed footsoldiers. Luca Pitti's supporters made similar preparations, and the two houses became "virtually two fortresses, each guarded by its own men."[95] This appears to be the scene represented in Apollonio di Giovanni's *Aeneid* depicting a palace resembling the Medici's fortified with structures at the junction of the *piano nobile* with the ground-floor rustication (fig. 103). Another account testified that Cosimo had in

his house at the time of the crisis and *parlamento* of 1458, "so many arms and cross-bows as to be worth a fortune, and such that I believe no other man in Italy has so great a number." This estimate would seem to be confirmed by the enormous quantities of arms listed in the inventory of the palace made in 1492. Even in 1418, in the old house headed by Cosimo's father Giovanni di Bicci, there were large quantities of arms for practical as well as ceremonial use, particularly in Cosimo's suite.[96] The open loggia was walled up in 1517, perhaps because it was redundant, but more likely because it made the palace too vulnerable to forced entry.[97]

Demolishing the houses of vanquished enemies was traditionally a visible sign of the redistribution of power on the Florentine political scene. In the era of constant conflict between Guelfs and Ghibellines, the houses of the Uberti were leveled to make way for the building of the Palazzo Vecchio. At the end of the trecento Sacchetti still saw the destruction of private houses in these terms, just as Michele del Giogante fantasized, when he thought of a man he disliked, about the destruction of his palace.[98] In this same spirit, although literally more constructively, the new wave of palace-building which followed in the wake of the Medici initiative threw up several monuments to the competitive ingenuity of individual builders which express the flattery of imitation. The subsequent palace-building activities of other patricians suggest they indeed saw the Medici palace as something against which to measure themselves, not only for the sake of stylistic imitation or innovation, but also in the spirit of Gino Capponi's injunction to his sons to acquit themselves with honor upon the social and political stage.

The Medici palace invited the partial emulation of partisans such as the Pazzi or the Neroni. The Pazzi palace was part of a whole patronage program, including a

104   Florence, Pazzi palace

105   Florence, Santa Croce, Pazzi chapel

chapel modeled on San Lorenzo's old sacristy built for the church of Santa Croce which imitated but also competed with that of the Medici (figs. 104 and 105). In this case there is even less concrete evidence than usual concerning the patron's precise intent, but it is not unreasonable to infer in their building something of their growing rivalry with the Medici for the business and support of the papal court, the increasing estrangement of the two families after Cosimo's death, and its culmination in the attempt on the lives of Lorenzo and his brother Giuliano.[99] Dietisalvi Neroni's challenge to the Medici followed more swiftly on the heels of the erection of his palace with its *sgraffito* facade, and that of his brother Nigi – a miniature imitation in its heavy rustication of the neighboring Medici palace from a family whose political resources lay less in palatial statements

than in their growing influence outside Florence, especially at the court of Milan, Florence and Cosimo's major ally (fig. 106).[100] The Rucellai palace has been seen as a concrete attempt to build upon the newly established relations of that family with the dominant Medici, an alliance which promised to take them in a new direction after decades of ostracism associated with Rucellai's prior ties to the exiled Strozzi family. It was also the assertion, however, of a passionate and informed patron of building of the value of a very different style, of the elegant appropriation of consistently articulated classical forms rather than a claim to association with the grandeur of classical and civic tradition (fig. 178).[101]

Ten important surviving palaces were built in the twenty years after 1445, while Cosimo himself was still alive. They belonged to the families of the Rucellai,

106   Florence, Nigi di Nigi Dietisalvi-Neroni palace

107   Florence, Strozzi palace

Lenzi, Strozzi, Pitti, Ridolfi-Guidi, Spinelli, Dietisalvi Neroni, Nigi Neroni, Gianfigliazzi, and Boni-Antinori. We must await the decoding by an expert of the architectural meaning they bore for their builders and for the Florentine audience, but as Preyer's studies have already shown, the conjunction in Florentine palace builders of great wealth with notable political power was in the quattrocento almost exclusive to the Medici. The patrons of most of these palaces constructed in the two decades after the Medici palace was begun were not in fact men of visible political ambition or even influence in the city, a fact that must surely modify any conception of the civic conversation inherent in palace building as primarily political.[102] As Preyer observed, Cosimo's palace was so flamboyant that it is difficult to reconcile it "with the usual observations on Cosimo's prudent use of

patronage for political reasons."[103] Cosimo was personally responsible for the exile of the mighty Strozzi clan, but there is little evidence that they had previously competed with him in his pretensions to power in government. The Strozzi may have derived some satisfaction from the fact that the palace built by Filippo in the early 1490s, thirty years after Cosimo's death, when his family was finally readmitted to Florence after six decades of exile and political discrimination, was described by the duke of Ferrara as even "prouder than Lorenzo's own," (fig. 107).[104] In Preyer's judgment the impact of the Medici palace on some others, like the Strozzi, may be obvious, but this is less true of the Rucellai or Boni-Antinori, or of the subtler manner in which the Medici example underlies the palaces of the Pazzi and Gianfigliazzi. Her observations cast important doubt on the reductionist

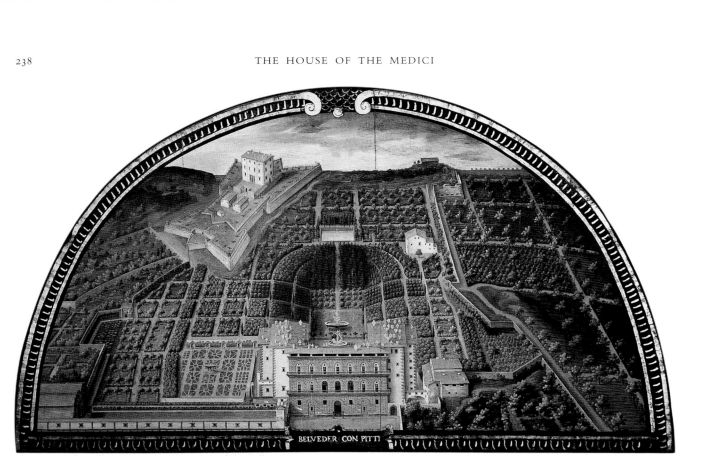

108   Giusto Utens, Pitti palace before addition of extra bays, Florence, Museo di Firenze com' era

interpretation of Medici choices simply as due to political considerations.

The Pitti palace was the one building clearly linked with its owner's explicit political ambitions, and his challenge to Medici supremacy in 1466. Pitti made a blatant pitch for the dominant position in the city, not only in his leadership of a conspiracy against Piero de' Medici but also in the selection of the site for his palace. It was set upon the highest ground within the city walls, and Pitti cleared an enormous area in front of his original seven bay palace to enhance its impact (fig. 108). His actions were explicitly read by his fellow-citizens as a naked claim to power, and his anti-Medici party of the mid-1460s was named "the party of the hill." The Signoria, in its *provvisione* to allow Pitti to acquire the last of the land he had been accumulating between 1451 and 1458, expressed its belief, in accordance with the prevailing Ciceronian view, that it was

reasonable for him to want to build in order "to house his family comfortably, according to his station." As in the *provvisione* permitting the clearance of the piazza alongside San Lorenzo to allow for the rebuilding of the church, the communal justification of the necessary demolition of other peoples' houses was that only low people lived there, "a disgrace to the city." On these grounds the commune agreed to sell Pitti the land cheap.[105] As the palace was begun in 1458, it is quite possible that Pitti obtained his privilege and some tolerance for his grandiose plans as a trade-off for his support of the Medici in the parliamentary crisis the regime suffered in that year.[106] Eventually, Luca Pitti lost his bid to challenge the Medici, and with it all the power and position he had won with their support. The Medici family's takeover of Pitti's palace, after they were installed as Dukes of Florence in 1534, might be seen as the perfect palatial riposte.

XII

ACCOMMODATING THE PATRON

"THE COMFORT OF HIS ACCOMMODATIONS"[1]

When Galeazzo Maria Sforza visited Florence in 1459, one of his counselors, Niccolò de' Carissimi da Parma, wrote to Francesco Sforza describing to the father his son's tour of the Medici palace:

> the aforesaid count, together with the company, went on a tour of this palace, and especially of its noblest parts, such as some studies, little chapels, living rooms, bedchambers and gardens, all of which are constructed and decorated with admirable skill, embellished on every side with gold and fine marbles, with carvings and sculptures in relief, with pictures and inlays done in perspective by the most accomplished and perfect of masters, down to the benches and all the floors of the house; tapestries and household ornaments of gold and silk; silverware and bookcases that are endless and innumerable; then the vaults or rather ceilings of the chambers and salons, which are for the most part done in fine gold with diverse and various forms; then a garden all created of the most beautiful polished marbles with various plants, which seems a thing not natural but painted.[2]

Carissimi's description conveys some sense of the density and intensity of decoration in the new Medici palace, created by the splendid sum of the objects listed in the inventory Piero compiled after his father's death in 1464.[3] The whole palace was a work of art; even the garden did not simply grow, but was cultivated, as Cosimo had promised to love his friend Francesco Sforza, "con arte e ingegno, ordine e misura" – with artifice and ingenuity, order and measure.

In accordance with Cosimo's dictum that Florence was a city of "commerce, literature, and leisure," the profits of the Medici bank, of which the lion's share in every partnership went to Cosimo and his sons, paid for the palace, which was estimated by some contemporaries to have cost around 100,000 florins.[4] The family held their commerce with their business associates and political supporters more and more within the walls of the palace, as

the health of Cosimo and his elder son declined, and their share in the *stato* increased. The need to accommodate these visitors seems to have been a factor influencing its design.[5] The Medici family house was also decorated for the pleasurable pursuit of leisure, enhanced and refined by what the family learned from the literature with which their houses and their minds were richly stocked, for the play of friendship and self-cultivation. These are the themes of Alberti's *Della Famiglia*, a work that envisaged and described the ideally civilized life, whether at the courts of Naples and Rome, or in the patrician houses of the author's native republic. Filarete's comment on Cosimo's dwelling was that "he has neglected nothing which would add to the comfort of his accommodations."[6] Although these were indeed princely, and Giovanni Rucellai thought them fit for a king,[7] such similes sought to characterize the lifestyle of this extraordinarily wealthy family, rather than their literal political pretensions. Pope Pius II, for example, commented that Cosimo was as rich as Croesus,[8] and Carissimi observed that it would cost Duke Francesco Sforza a pretty penny to equal or surpass the Medici palace, as he undoubtedly would wish to do when he saw it.[9]

When Cosimo spoke in the 1450s of the Florentine pursuit of *otium*, along with *negotium* and *litteras*, he meant the leisure of "freedom from commerce and public business" – the major occupations of the Florentine merchant-patrician – to cultivate the mind and soul through learning.[10] His phrase expresses the mid-fifteenth century ideal of the educated Florentine elite, with its positive view of leisure derived from the Greeks, particularly from Plato and Aristotle. The Romans had tended to see *otium* as idleness, a vice opposed to the virtue of action. However Cicero, Cosimo's favorite writer, and the Roman who spoke most frequently of *otium*, associated it with well-earned peace and tranquillity after a period of war and strife – such as Cosimo might have hoped to enjoy in the late 1450s, after helping to negotiate the Peace of Lodi, which in 1454 put an end to decades of Florentine wars against Milan and her allies.[11] The concept of *otium* is related here to the Renaissance opposition between *res publica* (matters of the public domain) and *res privata* (everything that falls outside it). Florentine patricians and their palaces were not private in the modern sense of secret and secluded, but rather personal, pertaining to the individual, his family, and his lineage, as distinct from the communal and corporate interests of government and guild.

The type of the house of memory constructed by the Medici family's friend and follower, the poet-accountant Michele del Giogante, perfectly expressed the educated Florentine's sense of a home as a dwelling-place for the mind as well as the body.[12] The proliferation of objects in the Medici palace was clearly part of the great fifteenth-century expansion of domestic consumerism chronicled by Richard Goldthwaite, but his characterization of this in Henry James's words as "the empire of things" inappropriately associates late nineteenth-century values with Renaissance Florence.[13] The relationship between personal experience, education, and taste, and the acquisition of objects which this phrase implies, is modern, and the reverse of that which obtained in the fifteenth century. Taste was not shaped by what one might happen to own or procure; art, or skill and *ingegno*, rather crafted an environment in a style which appealed to the cultured community and its patrons.

Contemporary descriptions of the contents of the Medici palace were not simply literal: they employed many of the conventions of ekphrasis, the rhetorical form appropriate to the praise of worthy things, that which is *degna*.[14] They stressed not only the fine quality of the materials employed, but "the powers of mind which gave them form."[15] The author of the *Terze Rime* praised the products of "so many sculptors' skill and inventiveness [*ingegno*],/ of all sorts of metal work and intarsia,/ of wondrous architecture and paint-brushes . . ." Cosimo's was the integrating intellect, not merely in theory, but by virtue of the command of detail which he brought to the implementation of all his patronage, including that of building; he was in close touch with the overseers of his works and aware of the importance of "sculptors and masons . . ." in any construction.[16]

There being, in the words of the *Terze Rime*, "nothing in the world more an earthly paradise than this," the Medici palace was the perfect setting for the entertainment of noblemen like Pope Pius II and Sforza's son, and for the exercise of noble minds. The *Terze Rime* notably began with an account of Cosimo in terms of Christlike virtues, including the charity, liberality, or magnanimity that had made him the patron already of numerous ecclesiastical foundations. The sophistic rhetoric of these ekphrases strove to match not only the architecture they described, but also the quality of the builder's mind, because a citizen's house, as Cicero decreed, should adorn its owner's virtue rather than constituting it.[17]

Randolph Starn, in his account of the marquess of Mantua's Camera degli Sposi, offered some interesting suggestions as to how the very viewing of a Renaissance room elaborately decorated with iconographically complex images of antique or Christian themes constituted a demanding intellectual exercise, offering patrons an opportunity for the rehearsal of the learning necessary to conceive and to appreciate such programs.[18] The members of the Medici circle, including Cosimo himself, who had poked about in the ruins of Ostia with his friend Poggio, were acquainted with the decoration of Roman houses and villas through literary descriptions as well, as may be seen from Matteo Palmieri's citation in his *Della Vita Civile* of Juvenal's views on proper house management, and in his imitation of the antique custom of installing an ancestor portrait over the entrance to his house.[19]

In his dialogue *On Nobility*, Poggio Bracciolini presented his protagonists, including Cosimo's brother Lorenzo, as involved in a discussion of the relation of possessions to personal nobility. Niccoli proposed that in addition to virtue, the noble man possesses "the courtyards full of statues, the colonnades, the theaters and public entertainments, hunting parties, and other things by which we enhance our reputation; these things make men famous, and thus bestow nobility." The Lorenzo character's reaction to Poggio's house was at once ironic, amused, and appreciative of the learned collector.

> He smiled at my treasures . . . with the remark: "Our host, having read that illustrious men of old used to ornament their homes, villas, gardens, arcades and gymnasiums with statues, paintings and busts of their ancestors, to glorify their own name and their lineage, wanted to render his own palace noble, and himself too, but having no images of his own ancestors, he acquired these meager and broken pieces of sculpture, and hoped that the novelty of his collection would perpetuate his fame among his own descendants."[20]

In the Medici palace, style, taste, function, and family tradition were inseparable. The function of its decoration was first to accommodate and please those who lived in it. The Medici household, consisting primarily of Cosimo, his sons, and their wives and children, was a large but close domestic unit that expressed the continuity and cohesion of the line over three generations. The palace was designed also to impress those who saw it with the nobility and honor of the builder's lineage, and to perpetuate his fame. These ambitions and interests, as classical as they were Florentine, were often most appropriately realized in classical forms. In this way the house and its contents expressed the identity of the inhabitants and their associations with one another, as well as the family's relation to the antique past, to the present and the future state of Florence, and to the world beyond it.

There is no surviving documentation of the objects in the Medici palace in Cosimo's time to compare with the inventory of his father Giovanni di Bicci's house, made in 1417/18. In 1456 and again shortly after Cosimo's death, in 1464/5, Piero made a list of his personal possessions, chiefly the books and precious objects he had collected, household items of gold and silver, as well as valuable tapestries and linens and other items of cloth and clothing. The next extant account of the contents of the palace and the rooms in which they were kept was compiled after Lorenzo's death in 1492, almost thirty years after Cosimo died. So what little is known of the paintings and sculptures in the Medici palace so admired by Carissimi and other observers in the late fifties and early sixties must be painstakingly reconstructed. In all but a handful of cases it is unclear precisely when the individual items listed were commissioned and by whom, but if few of the objects in the palace by the date of Cosimo's death can be certainly identified as his personal commissions, Cosimo was the patriarchal builder of his palace, and everything in it was ultimately, if not immediately, part of his oeuvre.

"PER NON DIVISO": FAMILY VALUES AND THE USE AND DECORATION OF DOMESTIC SPACE

The principle underlying Florentine laws of inheritance was not primogeniture, a divisive system that consigned many of the younger sons of northern European families to the army or the Church, as alternatives to the management of property, but rather partible inheritance, largely through the male line. This fostered a solidarity of interest between all the sons of a family, united in a determination to maintain the patrimony of the lineage intact. Florentines took very seriously advice such as Gino Capponi's in his *Ricordi* to his sons: "hold on to the house in Florence at any cost."[21] It is not uncommon to read in wills and tax reports of individuals owning "two-seventeenths of a tower" or "three-elevenths" of a plot of land, but no matter how small the fractions that belonged to each property-holder, the ancestral home was preferably to remain inviolate, "per non diviso."[22]

Apart from the period of his residence in Rome in the 1390s, Cosimo's father lived originally in the ancestral Medici district around the Mercato Vecchio, in the parish of San Tommaso. The houses in the Via Larga that he and his sons were to occupy had belonged to the line of Conte di Foligno de' Medici. In 1349 this line of the Medici family acquired nine of the twenty parts of "a palace in the Via Larga," and in 1361 they obtained the last eleven parts; five years earlier they had bought a house that they described in the mid-fifteenth century as "adjacent to our palace." With the failure of Conte's direct line, this parcel of dwellings passed by 1401 to Iacopa, widow of Cosimo's grandfather Averardo, "detto Bicci." Cosimo's grandmother, who lived nearby the estate in the Via Larga, bequeathed to the fourteen-year-old Cosimo and his younger brother Lorenzo, the "casa vecchia," which was to be described in 1417/18 as belonging to their father Giovanni di Bicci. In the further consolidation of their property, by 1446 at latest, the *casa vecchia* and the houses immediately to its north and south were incorporated into a single unified dwelling, probably created some time before construction began in 1445 on the new Medici palace.[23] Speculations differ about when the latter was ready for Cosimo and his sons to move in, but it may have been as early as 1456.[24]

Regarding the decoration of the palace, many art historians tend simply to assume that it expressed a major difference in style and taste between Cosimo and his sons, following the lead of Ernst Gombrich in his brilliant, but often no more than suggestive essay, "The Early Medici as Patrons of Art."[25] Gombrich conceived their familial relations in terms of modern competitive individualism, or of a generational cycle set in the narrow context of the accumulation of wealth, as in nineteenth-century tales of rags to riches which inspired such family sagas as Galsworthy's of the Forsytes. Thus he imagined a marked difference between the sensibility of Cosimo, under whom the bank reached its zenith, and his heirs, born to wealth, assuming them to be anxious to assert their own ideas and artistic taste. But fifteenth-century Florentine lineages in no sense fit this Victorian bourgeois model. While most of the Medici family's numerous households in the fourteenth century lacked negotiable wealth and the prestige of participation in communal politics at the highest level, since the end of the thirteenth century they had been respected, and even feared, as a family who played a major role in the life of the commune, and especially of its *contado*. The first Medici Prior to serve in the government of the *popolo* did so in 1293, only ten years after the establishment of this office. Foligno di Conte de' Medici in the 1370s could look back nostalgically on the prosperity of a family that he feared was in decline. However, only a decade later another branch, that of Cosimo's ancestors, would create the basis for a future commercial empire on the foundations of the banking company of yet a third line, that of Messer Vieri di Cambio de' Medici.[26]

The differences in the patronage of art and architecture undertaken by Cosimo, Piero, or Giovanni were manifestations not of first or second generation wealth and power, and certainly not of generational conflict, but of personal diversity developing over several generations, along with Florentine Renaissance culture, out of a shared dynastic ideal, within the firm framework of the patriarch's authority. This is similarly true of every aspect of Medici patronage; personal, political, literary, or artistic.[27] The quality of Medici life was a product of cooperation and continuity across the various branches of the lineage and down through the generations of its single most successful line, as well as between individuals within that line's mid-fifteenth-century household. Florentine sons did not rebel, or even react, against the values of their fathers, except in very rare and patently traumatic cases.[28]

Popular poets such as Feo Belcari hymned the ideal relation between Cosimo the father and his sons, Piero and Giovanni, most notably in the dedication to Giovanni of the sacred play of *Abraham and Isaac*, an exemplary father and son. The private letters of the members of the Medici family, particularly those written by or about Cosimo, Piero, and Giovanni, show how closely their relationships actually conformed to these generally admired Florentine and Christian ideals. Medici friends and supporters addressed their appeals to any one or all of the family, seen as a community that included the living and the dead in an unbroken continuum. For example, the priest Piero di Sozzo, rector of the church of San Cosimo in Pisa, wrote asking Cosimo de' Medici in 1436 for patronage for alms for which he was renowned "by public fame," and because he had been told by his precedecessor that "the blessed memory of your father and you had always lent a hand in subsidizing the feast of the glorious martyrs Saints Cosmas and Damian, our protectors."[29] Another wrote to Giovanni di Cosimo "although you don't know me I remind you in the name of the revered Cosimo and the blessed soul and famous memory of Lorenzo . . ."[30]

The descendants of Giovanni di Bicci expressed their aspiration to live "under one will"[31] quite literally, by refusing to make formal testaments. Lorenzo, Cosimo's grandson, wrote in his *Ricordi* concerning Cosimo's father, Giovanni di Bicci, who died on 20 February 1428/9: "He would not make a will, and left property to the amount of 179, 221 *scudi di suggello* . . ." Cosimo's cousins Averardo, his son Giuliano, and Francesco di Giuliano di Averardo died intestate, as did his brother Lorenzo, by intention. His elder son Piero wrote to his own sons Lorenzo and Giuliano on 26 July 1464, a few days before Cosimo's death: "He said he would make no will, not having made one whilst Giovanni was alive, seeing that we were always united in true love, amity, and esteem."[32] Giovanni, Cosimo's younger son, had predeceased him the previous year, also intestate, and indeed

not even emancipated at the age of forty-one. As Lorenzo observed, "Giovanni, our uncle, on whose intelligence and virtue Cosimo greatly relied, so that he greatly lamented his loss," died on 1 November 1463, in our house in Florence, without making a will, because he had no children and was under parental tutelage. But all his last wishes were faithfully carried out."[33] While the absence of formal wills probably gave the family a financial advantage, by keeping the division of an inheritance out of the hands of the communal officials who oversaw these matters, it seems that the Medici of Bicci's line in the fifteenth century assumed the identity of their interests and put their faith in family trust.[34]

As far as their patronage was concerned, the Medici dealt with artists as they did with the everyday demands of other friends and business associates. As the sons grew up and their father grew old, more of the actual business was entrusted to Piero and Giovanni, but they operated under Cosimo's direction, and even in the very last months of his life, old and ill as he was, he never completely relinquished the reins. Giovanni di Bicci had retired from the banking business in 1420, confiding the care of his affairs to his sons Cosimo and Lorenzo. Cosimo followed his example in 1451, leaving as partners in the bank on the one hand Pierfrancesco, his brother Lorenzo's son, and on the other his own sons, Piero and Giovanni. The faith of these *capi famiglia* in the next generation was in accord with the general Florentine view that the relationship of fathers and sons was one of seamless continuity, as the younger generation took the place of the elder in the cycle of life. Sons "became" their fathers at a certain point, caring for them as fathers did their sons.[35] The attitudes Cosimo adopted and lived by were taken up and preserved by his son Piero, whose address as Florence's newly elected Gonfalonier of Justice in 1465/6, a year after Cosimo's death, is couched in terms of values almost identical to those expressed in his father's letters to him.[36]

There was, as Gombrich observed, some division of artistic labor between Cosimo, and Piero and Giovanni, in conformity with quattrocento perceptions and customs, and corresponding closely to their division of labor in the administration of the bank and their response to partisans' patronage requests. The father dedicated himself to the patriarchal generation of austere buildings, while the sons' portion was chiefly to see to their extravagant decoration. Nevertheless, while most Medici building in his lifetime is essentially attributable to Cosimo, Piero had his *tempietti* and Giovanni his own villa, in whose building his family and many of their friends also took an active interest.[37] Giovanni predeceased Cosimo, and Piero outlived him by a scant five

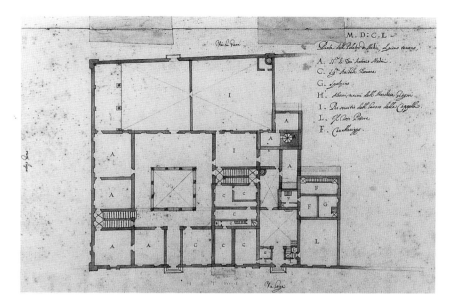

109 The Medici palace, plan of ground floor, 1650, north at right, Florence, ASF Guardaroba Mediceo, 1016

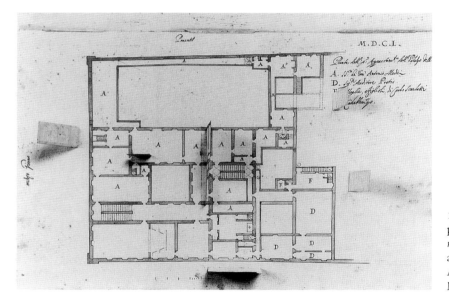

110 The Medici palace, plan of *piano nobile*, 1650, north at right, Florence, ASF Guardaroba Mediceo, 1016

years, hardly long enough to launch a building program of his own, even had he not by then been virtually physically immobilized. At the same time, while the very small number of extant letters concerning domestic paintings and the decoration of the palace was addresssed to Piero and Giovanni, Cosimo commissioned and personally oversaw the enormous quantity of painting and decoration at San Marco in the 1440s and early 1450s, and was responsible for numerous altarpieces, both public and domestic.

Per non diviso was also the principle that dictated the design of the palace, and the residential arrangements

within its walls. These consisted of a series of separate suites, comprising bedchamber, anteroom, and study, with interconnecting rooms (figs. 109 and 110). This plan envisaged that Cosimo's grown sons and their families would continue to reside under his roof, as Cosimo and Lorenzo and their young children had remained with Giovanni di Bicci. The members of larger Florentine lineages like the Medici could not literally all conform to Alberti's ideal prescription, that when kinsmen passed from the personal world of the palace to the public world of the streets it should always be through a single door.[38] However, three generations of Medici, including Cosimo, his wives and children and those of his brother Lorenzo, and his childrens' children, were to come and go in his last years through the impressive portals of their palace on the Via Larga.[39] The premature death in 1463 of Cosimo's younger son Giovanni followed closely on that in 1459 of Giovanni's five-year-old son Cosimino, in whose company the aged Cosimo and his wife Contessina had taken such delight. These bereavements allegedly wrung from the patriarch a lament at the sudden emptiness of a palace so recently prepared to accommodate all his descendants: "This is too large a house for so small a family . . ."[40]

The chronically ill Cosimo and his sons were house-bound for extensive periods during the years after they moved into their new home. Giovanni and Piero both inherited the family complaint of uricaemia, of which Cosimo's grandson Lorenzo was to die at the relatively early age of forty-three. In 1459 Francesco Sforza's son Galeazzo Maria reported that Cosimo had to be carried into the chapel where he transacted much of his daily business, secular as well as spiritual. Alessandro de' Gonzaga wrote from Florence to his father, the marquess of Mantua, on 24 June 1461:

> And I went there to visit Cosimo who gave me a most gracious welcome, finding him sitting in his room with his two sons, all three afflicted with gout; he only a little, and Piero his elder son was not suffering at the time, but they were all seated as if they could not move from that position, nor could they ride, and they had to be carried to and fro. Giovanni, the younger son, although he too has gout is not yet so lame, so that on the feast of Corpus Christi he carried the baldachino through the city, but the following night he had gout in one foot and in a hand, so that I found him with his father sitting as I described above. And indeed after this visit when I came to Cosimo wishing to see his house, he told his son Giovanni to come with me because he was no longer in pain, and so although he had to hold on to Guidone with his arm around his neck and limping, he absolutely insisted that he wanted to go around the house with me, except when it came to going up or down stairs, apologizing that he could only walk on the flat."[41]

To men so frequently confined to the house, or even to a single room, the domestic environment would have assumed an importance even greater than it possessed in the eyes of most Florentines. This understanding illuminates Filarete's reference to Cosimo's concern with "the comfort of his accommodations," and his memorable description of Piero being carried into his study to revel in the pleasure of his possessions. Their fearfulness for the precariousness of one another's health, which, beyond business or politics, is the main thread running through the letters between members of the family, also increased the cohesion of a household united in intimacy and affection.[42] For all the power of Medici financial, political, and dynastic ambitions, their correspondence expresses most strongly the importance of close personal relationships with immediate family, friends, and household, a circle that was in every sense the center of Cosimo's life and identity.

FILIAL PIETY: THE MAINLY DEVOTIONAL WORKS OF ART IN COSIMO'S HOUSE

Tradition and continuity in domestic display: the Medici inventories of 1417/18 and 1492

Despite the quantity of "sculptures in relief, with pictures and inlays done in perspective by the most accomplished and perfect of masters," which the Milanese Carissimi saw in the Medici palace in 1459, there are no contracts or accounts relating to the decoration of Cosimo's palace. Only Benozzo Gozzoli's frescoes for the chapel are documented in correspondence between the painter and Cosimo's elder son Piero. Nor has any inventory come to light that lists all the works of art in the Medici house or the palace between 1418 and 1492. However, the inventory of the palace contents made after Lorenzo de' Medici's death in 1492 constitutes a rough guide to works probably commissioned by Cosimo or his sons for their home.[43] Items attributed to such artists as Botticelli and Bertoldo, who flourished after Cosimo's death, can obviously be excluded from a list of his putative commissions.

The works of artists who predeceased Cosimo or died very shortly after him, including Angelico, Lippi, Domenico Veneziano, and Donatello, were most likely acquired in his lifetime. All the Medici assembled collections of beautiful and valuable objects, but with one or two possible exceptions, it does not seem to have been the custom to collect the works of contemporary Florentine artists. The palace contained at least one Giotto in 1492, and Piero di Lorenzo acquired a Cimabue, but these were literally "collector's pieces" by the long-dead fathers of Renaissance art. All the evidence suggests that patrons preferred works of art made to their own very precise specifications in terms of subject and even style, and the Medici family were particularly in the habit of "customizing" their commissions with personal and family symbols and devices.[44]

However, the impulse to "modernize" the domestic interior was as yet in its infancy. Since these customized works were repositories of Medici family traditions, and the artists who produced them were the outstanding representatives of the city's artistic Renaissance, they remained on display in the palace throughout Lorenzo's lifetime.[45] Brenda Preyer and James Draper remarked that Cosimo's grandson, having inherited the Medici palace already filled with decorative objects, was obliged to live in an environment created largely by his father and grandfather. He assembled a brilliant personal collection of small and exquisite objects made of precious metals and stones, which he kept in his *camera* and his study, but he was limited as a patron of contemporary artists in part because the Medici palace was already a museum of Medicean iconography.[46]

The evidence of the inventory of 1492 suggests Lorenzo's interest in preserving this, testifying to the priority of continuity in the objects on privileged display. The two main showrooms of the palace were the *camera di Lorenzo* on the ground floor and the *sala grande* on the *piano nobile*. In Lorenzo's *camera* were the great showpieces the Uccellos and the tondo of the Magi, attributed in the inventory to Angelico, although considered by modern art historians as as much or more the work of Lippi. The tondo was four and a half feet in diameter, "with the frame around it decorated with gold, and depicted there Our Lady and Our Lord and the Magi who come to make their offering, by the hand of Fra' Giovanni"; valued at one hundred florins, it was the single most expensive painting in the palace. However, the major element in the decorative scheme was a spectacular installation that may have wrapped around two adjacent walls, consisting of "six pictures with gilded frames above the *spalliera* and the *lettuccio*, 42 *braccia* long and 3½ *braccia* high, painted, that is three of the Rout of San Romano and one of battles and dragons and lions and one of the story of Paris by the hand of Paolo Uccello, and one by the hand of Francesco di Pesello, depicting a hunt, 300 florins."[47] In the main room on the *piano nobile* was the similarly epic Hercules cycle by the Pollaiuolo brothers, a work dated to 1464 on the authority of Antonio Pollaiuolo himself, and almost certainly commissioned by Piero. There was also an image of Saint John by Castagno, for which the artist's death in 1457 provides the *terminus ante quem*.[48]

In the bedchamber attached to the main room on the upper floor, also described as the "camera di Lorenzo," alongside Lorenzo's later selections were various objects of enduring familial significance, including the *desco da parto* depicting the Triumph of Fame commissioned for his birth, the marble busts by Mino da Fiesole of his parents Piero and Lucrezia, and an Ascension by Donatello. The other birthtrays were by Masaccio and his half brother, Lo Scheggia.[49] The *anticamera* of Lorenzo's bedchamber contained more works from the artistic giants of Cosimo's era; a Deposition by Angelico, Donatello's marble *quadro* of the Madonna and Child, and another by him of the same subject in bronze. Also attributed to Donatello was a low-relief marble in perspective with "lots of figures" surrounding Saint John. There was a pair of saints (Jerome and Francis) by Pesell[ino] and Lippi, and another piece by "Pesello," now identified as Domenico Veneziano's tondo of the Magi. There were portraits of two of Cosimo's closest allies among the *condottieri* of his time, Sforza and Gattamelata, by an unnamed Venetian artist. A Crucifixion with three figures by Giotto could have been acquired at any time before 1492.

There had been continuity as well between the accommodations of the new palace completed in the later 1450s, and those of the complex of older houses on the Via Larga, from which the family moved some time after 1456. This is particularly seen in the design and function of the gardens, and the similar arrangements of three suites for the patriarch and his sons on the *piano nobile* (figs. 111 and 112; cf. figs. 109 and 110). Many of the objects that decorated these suites of rooms were probably transferred from the old house.[50]

Historians have focused so exclusively on the palace that some have assumed its completion in the late fifties to be the *terminus post quem* for many of the works associated with the Medici, most notably the Uccellos and Donatello's bronze *David*. But, in fact, contemporaries had considered the old house quite a showpiece as well. A Neapolitan delegation of 1452 went out of its way to take a tour of its more remarkable features. The *Terze Rime* written after 1459 "in praise of Cosimo and his sons" dwelt mainly on the new palace, but their author also observed of Cosimo and the *casa vecchia* that "Three quarters or more of his father's house/ in Florence he rebuilt with rooms so divine/ that all the beauties of others were devalued;/ nor did any man, dead or alive/ ever see in this land a building so beautiful/ as that constructed by this distinguished citizen." If it is difficult to distinguish from the cursory descriptions of the 1492 inventory which of the objects listed there originated in Cosimo's era, it is impossible to establish which of them came from the *casa vecchia*. However, referring to the generally accepted dating of works in terms of the development of their artists' personal styles, it seems that their number may have been quite large.

The vast majority of the images in the new palace commissioned by the most avant-garde of Florence's patrons were devotional. There was a great quantity of only generically described crucifixions, and Madonnas

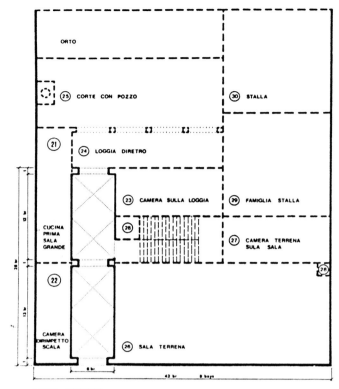

ORTO

25 CORTE CON POZZO

30 STALLA

21

24 LOGGIA DIRETRO

CUCINA
PRIMA
SALA
GRANDE

23 CAMERA SULLA LOGGIA

29 FAMIGLIA STALLA

28

27 CAMERA TERRENA
SULA SALA

22

CAMERA
DIRIMPETTO
SCALA

26 SALA TERRENA

28 AGIAMENTO

31 BELOW VOLTA PICCOLA

32 BELOW VOLTA GRANDE

28

6 br

42 br   9 bays

PIANO TERRENO

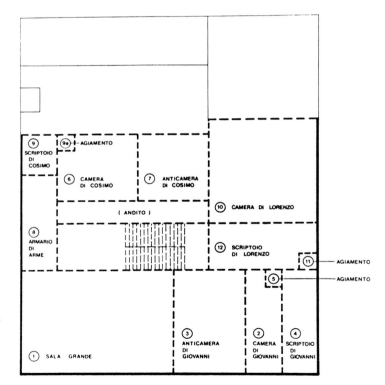

9 SCRIPTOIO DI COSIMO

9a AGIAMENTO

6 CAMERA DI COSIMO

7 ANTICAMERA DI COSIMO

10 CAMERA DI LORENZO

(ANDITO)

8 ARMARIO DI ARME

12 SCRIPTOIO DI LORENZO

11 AGIAMENTO

5 AGIAMENTO

1 SALA GRANDE

3 ANTICAMERA DI GIOVANNI

2 CAMERA DI GIOVANNI

4 SCRIPTOIO DI GIOVANNI

PIANO NOBILE

111 and 112
Medici *casa vecchia*,
plan of ground
floor (*top*) and of
piano nobile (*right*)
as reconstructed
by Howard
Saalman

with unnamed saints, some of which may have dated back to the days of Cosimo's father, Giovanni di Bicci. Such pictures were part of Cosimo's youthful environment, which can be re-created from the inventory of 1417/18.[51] In Giovanni di Bicci's *camera* was a single image of Our Lady in a shuttered tabernacle, and the quintessential familial object, "a little birthtray for Monna Nannina," as his wife Piccarda de' Bueri was affectionately called. There was also a small gilded box containing one hundred black rosary beads and ten of gilded silver, a string of 140 large coral beads, a talisman of the infant Christ wearing a coral, a protective amulet, and an *Agnus Dei* of gilded silver. Giovanni kept three books in his bedroom, all of them devotional.[52]

In the *camera* of Cosimo was "a panel of Our Lady in a tabernacle with two painted shutters, with a veil of silk in front of it," and a small terracotta figure of Our Lady, "*una tavoluzza* in which is painted a Crucifix," and "a wooden tabernacle inside which is Our Lord as an infant wearing a dalmatic of blue velvet and a shirt and the other garments of a deacon."[53] In the *anticamera* there was a birthtray; neither the artist nor the painted subject was named. The adjacent study contained more devotional objects; a panel with the figure of Our Lady and other "ancient figures," a phrase which might have referred either to classical antiquities or to the figures accompanying Our Lady in a work of some considerable age. There was also "a panel on which is depicted the Passion."[54] The *camera* of Cosimo's brother Lorenzo contained "a panel of Our Lady with a silk veil and curtain [*cortinazza*] painted with two large images of San Lorenzo."[55] In the ground-floor *camera* opposite the stairs was a panel of Our Lady, equipped with shutters which could be closed, and in another room a panel of the Crucifixion.[56]

In the main *sala* on the *primo piano* there was an altarpiece depicting the fraternal doctor saints, "covered with a sheet."[57] These sacred images were normally covered, presumably because it was considered inappropriate to expose them to casual viewing in rooms with functions other than the devotional.[58] In 1421 Giovanni di Bicci had been granted the relatively rare papal privilege of a portable altar, a privilege accorded the following year also to Cosimo and his wife Contessina.[59] Successive generations of Medici were able to hear mass before chapel-niches in their house, well before they became one of the very few Florentine families of the mid-fifteenth century to have a separate chapel in their palace. The doctor saints were also depicted in every known altarpiece for a public church endowed in Cosimo's lifetime. There is no mention in the 1492 inventory, however, of any image of Saints Cosmas and Damian. As observed in chapter 9,

several letters addressed to Piero at the very end of Cosimo's life suggest perhaps a waning of interest in this family cult, initiated in Giovanni di Bicci's generation and explicitly tied to Cosimo himself. By 1492 the only surviving domestic image of Saints Cosmas and Damian appears to have been in a room described as having belonged to Giovanni di Bicci's wife, Monna Nannina, in a country house at Montughi, near Fiesole.[60] The saints most heavily represented in the Medici palace at Lorenzo's death were John the Evangelist, patron of Cosimo's father and younger son; John the Baptist, the city's patron saint; and Jerome, whose cult became increasingly popular throughout Europe in the second half of the fifteenth century.

Our limited view of Giovanni di Bicci's patronage may reflect as much a limitation of the evidence and the customs of his time as his own inclinations as a patron. The record of his personal possessions is unfortunately obscured by the fact that the page reserved for the description of his study was never filled, leaving a blank between the contents of his *camera* and that of his elder son Cosimo.[61] What evidence remains of his public patronage suggests that Giovanni was an innovative patron in the terms and style of his period. Although only in the very last years of his life did Giovanni outstrip other Florentine patricians in affluence or influence as his son Cosimo was to do, his burial chapel, the old sacristy at San Lorenzo, at least equalled in boldness and imagination any of Cosimo's subsequent building for Florentine churches. The old sacristy was well under construction by 1427, when Giovanni became Florence's second wealthiest taxpayer. Since the practice of private citizens assuming responsibility for major building in public spaces like churches gathered momentum only toward the end of the second decade of the fifteenth century, Giovanni di Bicci was well in the vanguard of this movement. He had also served as an executor for a series of highly original tombs built by Donatello and Michelozzo in the 1420s, and as one of the preeminent patrons of the commission by the Banker's Guild in 1419 for Ghiberti's statue of Saint Matthew for Orsanmichele. His contemporaries' view of him as an outstanding patron is preserved in Masaccio's *Sagra* of 1423, where he appears as one of the small group of the city's most distinguished patrons and artists (fig. 70).[62]

The earliest art historians – Antonio Billi, the Anonimo Magliabechiano, and Vasari – attributed to Giovanni di Bicci some interesting secular domestic commissions; unfortunately none of them survives. According to Vasari, Dello Delli, a leading specialist in painting and decorating furniture and rooms, and above all "in making the most graceful small paintings" painted for "Giovanni de'

Medici the entire furnishings of a room."[63] This claim gains plausibility from the fact that an aged Delli lived on into the mid-quattrocento, and his work probably lasted into Vasari's own lifetime. Moreover, a note by Giovanni di Bicci's contemporary Ridolfo Peruzzi in his Catasto report of 1433 records that he had paid eight florins to "Dello di Nicholò [Delli], painter." The artist painted for the bedchamber of Ridolfo's newly married son, Bonifazio, "a picture of a woman and many other things in the house."[64]

Giovanni di Bicci was also reputed to have commissioned from Lorenzo di Bicci, father of Neri, a cycle of *uomini illustri* or famous men. This was a popular subject based in the trecento on Petrarch's *De Viris Illustribus*, and later drawing on Suetonius's text of the same name. In the early fifteenth century it found favor with several private patrons outside Florence, and around 1385 a group of famous Florentine figures accompanied by inscriptions written by the chancellor Salutati had been commissioned for the smaller hall of the Florentine palace of government. Early Florentine humanists such as Petrarch and Salutati supported the city's traditional claims that Florence was a second Rome by observing that she had citizens as worthy as the Romans. This important humanist and civic theme, much emphasized in Giovanni di Bicci's middle age and his sons' youth, and later illustrated by Castagno for the villa of Cosimo's friends the Carducci, probably contributed more to Cosimo's image of himself than Neoplatonic notions of the philosopher king and Maecenas applied to him by humanists in the

last years of his life (fig. 113).[65] Cosimo's sons were also interested by this subject. His illegitimate son Carlo was involved in the recovery of a manuscript of Suetonius's *De viris illustribus* for his half-brother Piero's collection, and Giovanni di Cosimo commissioned from Desiderio da Settignano a group of twelve Caesars taken from that text for his study, either in the Florentine palace or at his villa in Fiesole.[66]

The works of art likely to have been commissioned by Cosimo himself for the old house or the new palace between the mid-1420s and his death in 1464 may most clearly reveal his personal taste and concerns. Unlike the works made for churches, where the interests of the orders and their congregations entered into the choice of image and sometimes of artist, along with questions of setting, liturgical function, and general decorum, within the walls of the patron's palace his own interests determined his choices. It is therefore significant that the artists favored by the Medici to furnish their domestic images – Donatello, Angelico, and Lippi – and the subjects they were asked to depict, are nearly identical with those responsible for Cosimo's major public commissions for San Marco, San Lorenzo, and Santa Croce. Although patrons of such wealth and education might be expected to choose the very best artists Florence had to offer, it is also notable how precisely the Medici family's most personal choices coincided with popular taste.

Donatello was by general acclaim the city's most gifted sculptor, rated even more highly than Ghiberti, who won such fame for his participation in the landmark public

113   Andrea del Castagno, *Uomini Illustri*, Florence, Uffizi

114 Donatello, *Banquet of Herod*, marble relief, Lille, Musée des Beaux-Arts

project of the baptistery doors. Most lists of the century's greatest painters included Angelico, Lippi, and Domenico Veneziano (the last did no public work for Cosimo, but painted several pieces for the palace). It has often been observed that these artists did their best work for the Medici, but only recently, with the expansion of a rather rigid art historical canon of excellence that excluded from really serious consideration all but the major protagonists of the classical revival, has it been suggested that painters such as Angelico, Uccello, and Lippi also did their most intellectually demanding work for Cosimo and his sons.[67] The Cosimo emerging from this study, a man fascinated and drawn by a "variety of intellects," is further illuminated by a closer viewing of the variety of paintings and sculpture of outstanding quality with which he surrounded himself at home.

★　　★　　★

Donatello

Donatello takes pride of place, by virtue of both the number and the importance of his works for Cosimo de' Medici. The seemingly infinite variety of Donatello's *ingegno* would probably disincline many art historians from describing some of its particular products as definitely "better" than others. However, it is generally agreed that his bronze figures of David and of Judith slaying Holofernes, discussed at length later in this chapter, are among his most remarkable creations. Although these are not included in the 1492 inventory, other evidence points strongly to their Medici provenance. By the time of Cosimo's death, or very shortly thereafter, the *David* was the centerpiece of the Medici palace courtyard and *Judith and Holofernes* occupied a corresponding position in the garden. These works, directly in the visitor's line of vision as he entered the palace through its main door, would have been the "establishing image" of the

115   Donatello, *Ascension with Christ Giving the Keys to Saint Peter*, marble relief, London, Victoria and Albert Museum

Medici and their style of life. While the large bronzes dominated the main areas of public traffic and private recreation, Donatello's devotional *quadri* and tondi of marble and bronze were displayed in the living rooms, adding to the highly tactile quality of an environment lavishly decorated with carved and gilded furniture and intarsiated woodwork.

In the 1450s Giovanni commissioned three works from Donatello for his villa at Fiesole.[68] In the urban palace in 1492 were a marble *tavoletta* of "Our Lady with the child clinging to her neck" and another of gilded bronze of "the Virgin with the child on her arm."[69] There was also a more complex marble piece in low relief, depicting Saint John, "with many figures . . . and other things in perspective . . . by the hand of Donato"; most recent writers have identified this with the *Banquet of Herod* now in Lille (fig. 114).[70] Yet another marble image by Donatello, framed in wood, depicted in low relief "an Ascension." This John Pope-Hennessy identified with the work in the Victoria and Albert Museum in London usually described as *Christ's Consignment of the Keys to Saint Peter* (fig. 115). He further suggested that the relief originally formed part of a larger whole, the decorative scheme for the Brancacci family chapel in Santa Maria del Carmine. The theme of the chapel's frescoes is the acts of Saint Peter, but the crucial scene of Christ's consignment to him of the keys of the church and the kingdom of heaven is absent from the ensemble. Observing that an independent pictorial relief of this type would have been an anomaly in the early fifteenth century, Pope-Hennessy rested his argument on its subject, on an iconographical comparison between Donatello's relief and

Masaccio's frescoes, and on a document of 1426, when Masaccio was at work on the Brancacci chapel, recording the transfer of part of his payment for the frescoes to Donatello.[71] Some scholars have been inclined to agree with his suggestion; some have not. Joachim Poeschke, for example, pointed to the format of the work — a markedly elongated rectangle — and that it was intended to be viewed from below, "which would indicate that [the Ascension] was conceived as a predella."[72] The Brancacci were exiled when the Medici returned to Florence in 1434, and by 1436 Antonio, the chapel's patron, had abandoned his enterprise. Cosimo might easily, Pope-Hennessy suggested, have acquired the relief at this time.

This hypothesis has intriguing implications. It must be kept in mind that Lorenzo may have acquired some of the Donatellos in the Medici palace after the deaths of Cosimo and Donatello in the mid-1460s. Available evidence indicates that the only compelling reason for a patron to acquire the work of one of his favorite artists at second hand would be if the artist were dead, and no more of his work would be forthcoming. Lorenzo might have "collected" this piece. But why would Cosimo have wanted it when Donatello could have produced another like it to his own precise specifications? To imagine that he acquired the work simply because he admired it, or that Donatello refused to replicate it, may seem reasonable nowadays, but it is out of mid-quattrocento character. Cosimo was Donatello's major private patron, and patronage, as we have seen, involved claims and obligations to personal service in the production of art as in other areas. Nor were artistic objects yet regarded purely as "works of art." However, Florentine custom had for centuries decreed that the victorious leaders of factions should have the right to acquire at nominal cost the property of their defeated enemies, and indeed many Medici *objets d'art* were sold off after the family's expulsion from Florence in 1494. Often exiles' houses had been taken over and torn down to make way for buildings erected by the victors, as in the thirteenth century the palace of the Priors was built upon the site of the former houses of the rebellious Uberti. If Cosimo did indeed end up with a piece of his enemies' proudest possession, their much admired family chapel, this would be a novel variation on a traditional theme transposed into the new key of the rivalry of patricians in the acquisition of art.

Pope-Hennessy also proposed that Donatello's source for the unusual combination in his relief of the rather rare subject of the consignment of the keys with the more commonly represented Ascension was the play for the feast of the Ascension presented annually in the church of the Carmine, which housed the Brancacci chapel. There is a growing body of evidence of artists' use of the performative arts as a source of images for more formal and permanent works, and since Donatello himself designed the elaborate machinery necessary to create the much-admired effect in the Carmine play of Christ's ascension into heaven, this seems a plausible suggestion.[73] Donatello was to use this image again to great effect in his San Lorenzo pulpits, which might imply that it particularly appealed to Cosimo (fig. 190). Similarly, if the marble relief of Saint John "with many other figures in perspective" was in fact the Lille piece, it reproduced the dramatic highlight of Donatello's earlier depiction of the Banquet of Herod for the font of the baptistery in Siena, a work with which Cosimo would also have been familiar. Both these pieces display to the highest possible degree the particular appeal of the form of low-relief sculpture, of which Donatello was the acknowledged master, and to which Dante likened the terraces of purgatory, the better to stimulate his readers' imagination to reach out from the well known to the unknown.[74]

Most Donatello scholars agree that these reliefs are relatively early works. The *Ascension* has been dated to the mid-1420s, partly because of its presumed association with the Brancacci chapel; Pope-Hennessy described it as "the finest of Donatello's *stiacciato* carvings." The *Banquet of Herod*, considered by Poeschke as "probably [Donatello's] subtlest work in marble, a bas-relief filled with exquisite nuances and delicately contrasting values," is generally attributed to the years 1433–4, a moment of acute importance in Cosimo's career. The relief is seen as "an exemplary instance of a *storia* as the Early Renaissance understood the term," and is usually, if variously,

associated with Alberti's observations on narrative in the *Della pittura* of 1435.[75] As it concerned the martyrdom of Saint John the Baptist, the patron saint of Florence, its subject was of particular significance to Florentine patrons, and especially to the Medici. Most writers see this as perhaps the earliest example of an independent work, a "showpiece" for the private consumption of a connoisseur, like the later bronze *David*. Artur Rosenauer would see it as a gift from Donatello to Cosimo after his return from exile, with the aim of securing the commission for the later, and stylistically related, roundels in the old sacristy. His suggestion is largely fanciful, but there is in Donatello's relations with his friends and patrons a possible parallel in his appreciative gift to his doctor Chellini of the bronze cast of the Madonna and Child (fig. 37).[76] Whatever the precise circumstances of the Medici family's acquisitions of these two reliefs, their particular characteristics display not only the brilliance of the artist, but also a discriminating appreciation on the part of the patron or owner of the pieces, which is absolutely in keeping with what we have learned of Cosimo from his general culture and his particular patronage choices.

Fra Angelico

Half a dozen pictures in the Medici palace in 1492 are attributed to Fra Angelico. The Dominican, who was at once one of Florence's most renowned artists and a member of the congregation of San Marco when Cosimo de' Medici assumed the patronage of that convent, was a natural, indeed almost inevitable choice to paint the new Medicean altarpiece for the convent's church, and to work out the program of frescoes for the monastery's communal rooms and individual cells. The appearance of such a large number of his works in the Medici palace implies a more particular preference on Cosimo's part for this artist, who died in 1455. Contemporaries, describing the qualities of Angelico's painting, suggested that his particularly inspiring devotional images were the expression of his personal devoutness. Cristoforo Landino, a member of Lorenzo's inner circle, characterized Angelico's style as "very precious, devout and rich, with the utmost fluency."[77] A fellow Dominican from Santa Maria Novella, Fra Domenico Corella, spoke of "his many virtues;/ mild in his intellect [*ingegno*], honest in his religion . . . above other painters, to him deservedly/ was given one grace, of rendering the Virgin,/ as we see from the graceful form of the divine Annunciate,/ which is often painted by his hands."[78] None of the paintings in the Medici palace is described as an Annunciation, but Angelico's mastery of the art of "painted prayer" would

116   Fra Angelico, *Deposition*, Florence, Museo di San Marco

surely have appealed to a patron as devout himself as Cosimo de' Medici.[79]

In the *anticamera* to the bedchamber of the main suite on the *piano nobile* were two works by Fra Angelico – a small tondo of "Our Lady" and a wooden *tavoletta* approximately four *braccia* wide, on which were depicted various stories of the Holy Fathers. There was also a rectangular panel of Christ on the cross surrounded by nine figures. The often imprecise descriptions of works of art in domestic inventories suggest that the compilation of these lists was sometimes left to people inexpert or unconfident in identifying and describing images. From such generic descriptions as these of Angelico's three paintings, which specify no distinguishing details, not even of the sacred personnel of the scenes in question, it has not been possible to identify them with any of the artist's known works.[80] The *tavoletta* "depicting Our dead Lord, being carried to his tomb by many saints" has been tentatively associated with the *Deposition* now in the museum of San Marco (fig. 116).[81]

There was a very large work "in the passage at the head of the stairs that go to the chapel . . . a canvas on which is painted the Nativity of Our Lord and with the Magi on horseback on their way to make him an offering, 7 braccia long and 5 braccia wide, 5 florins." Another work by Angelico described as "a *colmo* for use as an altarpiece, 2 braccia long and 1⅓ braccia high, framed and gilded, on which is depicted the story of the Magi, by the hand

of Fra Giovanni, 60 florins," was kept in what is described as "the little chapel on the way up to the roof." It was valued at the very large sum of sixty florins.[82] This item may help to account for Carissimi's reference in the plural to "chapels" in the Medici palace in 1459.[83] Perhaps the Angelico altarpiece was the second of three known domestic altarpieces for the Medici in the fifteenth century, supplementing or possibly replacing the one dedicated to Cosmas and Damian described in the inventory of the *casa vecchia* of 1417/18, and preceding the Adoration altarpiece painted around 1459 by Lippi for the chapel of the new palace. The work is certainly further evidence of Cosimo's increasing identification of the Medici family with the image of the Magi, which culminated in the frescoes for the new palace chapel. A progression from the altarpiece imaging Cosmas and Damian to that of the Magi to Lippi's new mystical altarpiece of the Adoration with the Trinity, and including Saints Bernard and John the Baptist, interestingly charts the evolution both of Florentine devotional art, and of Medici taste across the century.

Angelico's paintings in the Medici palace were images for private contemplation and devotion, designed to encourage the viewer to an appreciation of God's redemptive gift in the form of his incarnate Son, of the infinite mercy of the Virgin as mediator between mankind, the Son and the Father, and to an identification with Christ's suffering for man's sins, to which all devout Christians were constantly exhorted in sermons and devotional literature. It seems that for most of Cosimo's lifetime and long beyond, it was the art of Angelico and Lippi that most inspired the Medici family's devotion. William Hood suggested that "works of art helped fifteenth-century Florentines to know who they were";[84] if many of the objects in the Medici house defined them primarily as citizens, Angelico and Lippi helped the Medici to know themselves as Christians.

The Lippi-Angelico tondo of the Magi

The most remarkable item associated in the inventory with Fra Angelico was "a large tondo with a gilded frame, depicting "Our Lady and Our Lord and the Magi offering their gifts, by the hand of Fra Giovanni." It was valued at the positively astronomical figure of one hundred florins, the most expensive single painting in the palace. Despite the inventarist's attribution to Angelico, this picture has been confidently identified with the magnificent tondo in the National Gallery in Washington, for which Filippo Lippi now shares much of the credit with

117   Fra Angelico and Fra Filippo Lippi, *Adoration of the Magi*,
Washington, National Gallery of Art, Samuel H. Kress Collection

Angelico or his assistants (fig. 117). Opinions vary widely about the respective contributions of these two distinctive artists, as about the painting's probable date, although most recent accounts place it in the 1440s or 1450s. Jeffrey Ruda's is to date the most extensive analysis of the picture, and he presented the most elaborate hypothesis concerning its genesis, proposing that Fra Filippo began the picture in the 1430s, and worked on it sporadically into the 1450s with an assistant trained by Fra Angelico. While Ruda's account of this highly intellectual composition in the context of his profound study of Lippi is technically compelling, in view of all that is known of patrons in general and the Medici in particular, it seems rather implausible that Cosimo would have commissioned in the 1430s such an expensive and elaborate representation of a favorite subject, and then been content to wait twenty years for one of his most favored artists to deliver it.[85]

While many scholars have stressed the opulence and appeal of the decorative elements of this brilliantly colored and gilded work, and the interest of the symbols with which it is laden, Ruda saw it as the most elaborate of the "sermon-like" panel paintings that Lippi produced in the 1440s and 1450s, culminating in the mystical "wilderness" altarpiece made for the chapel of the Medici palace around 1459. He also presented it as an ideal example of a work that does not directly illustrate a biblical or liturgical text, but rather serves as a "framework . . . for the various associations brought to bear by individual viewers." In his view, the Medici *Adoration* "is a narration studded with optional symbols," in which the artist "seems to use groups of established sacred metaphors with no single textual source."[86] An exploration of attitudes to images in Florentine culture and particularly in the circle around the Medici strongly supports this view of what Renaissance people brought to and saw in images, and what patrons and artists expected of each other and of their audience.

In his analysis of the *Adoration*, as exemplifying the analogy between the ways in which sacred paintings and sermons communicated with their audience, Ruda suggested that the imagery of the mountain draws on Psalm 71:2 – "the mountains shall bring peace to the people, and the little hills, by righteousness" – but does not precisely reflect it, referring to other sources "as a sermon may gather quotations and paraphrases to enrich its discourse." For example, the peacock signified resurrection because of Saint Augustine's remark that its flesh did not decay after death. The symbol of the peacock appears in various other Medici images, particularly in manuscripts; Giovanni di Cosimo adopted it as his personal emblem. As Francis Ames-Lewis observed, the Medici use of the peacock derives explicitly from patristic rather than courtly or heraldic sources.[87] Similarly, the falcon that hunts the pheasant is the emblem of the faithful who always return to their master, a symbol expounded by Saint Gregory and adopted by Piero de' Medici as his personal device. The dog in the foreground is an ancient symbol of fidelity, and may represent, in lieu of a signature, the artist of the Dominican order, the "Domini canes" or "watchdogs of the Lord."

The infant Christ holds a pomegranate, an ancient symbol of immortality associated with the annual return of spring and the rejuvenation of the earth. Beside the gate, a rounded Roman arch, there is a cypress, an ancient funerary sign that may point specifically to death and rebirth, whereas the Gate of Heaven usually refers simply to Mary and the Incarnation. The mysterious semi-nude figures opposite may represent death and rebirth through the sacrament of baptism, for which they are undressed, and which is commemorated in the liturgy of the Epiphany. The ruins on which they stand came to signify in fifteenth-century art the destruction of the pagan world at the birth of Christ, as expressed in a passage from the Gospel of Saint Luke, 2:34: "Behold, this child is set for the fall [*ruinam*] and rising again [*resurrectionem*] of the many in Israel." Iacopo da Voragine, author of the widely read and copied *Golden Legend*, explained this prophecy, as Ruda pointed out, in terms very close to the imagery of the Washington tondo. He compared weak mankind to leaning walls that may fall into ruin, and God to a mountain or rock of support, while Christ is the sign who appears over a mountain that represents the world. "In the *Adoration*, followers of the Magi look up to what may be this sign" – metaphorically, the star – "while Jesus sits upon Mary and Mary on rock, which is Christ, the rock of salvation, and the 'cornerstone' of the Psalms, of Isaiah's prophecy, and of the gospels of Matthew and Luke."[88]

The *Magi* tondo is an extremely original work made, like most other objects in the Medici palace, for an audience both devout and sophisticated. It is essentially, according to Ruda's description, "an exceptionally rich illustration of Epiphany themes," which were the focus of Medici patronage and devotion at San Marco.[89] Among these are the Incarnation and the Eucharist, closely related to Epiphany in the popular mind, as seen in the works of Florentine poets discussed in chapter 8. Moreover, liturgically the Feast of Epiphany on 6 January, celebrating the redeeming Incarnation, commemorated not only the Adoration of the Magi, but also the Baptism of Christ by Saint John, the patron saint of Florence, and Christ's transformation of water to wine for the Marriage at Cana, a miracle that was the antetype of the Eucharist. These themes are explicitly associated in the Christmas and Ephiphany offices by a passage from Saint Gregory's eighth homily: "Today the Church is joined to the divine Bridegroom, because Christ washes away its sins in the Jordan; the Magi bring wedding gifts, and the wedding guests rejoice at the water made wine."[90]

The very shape of the tondo enriches its meaning, since the circle is an ancient emblem of the macrocosm, the entirety of creation. It complements the role of the kings as representatives of the community of the faithful and the Universal Church, embodied in all its diversity in the variety of figures of every status and occupation, just as the Magi represent in their persons the three ages of men; youth, maturity, and old age. There is a similar play on the circle and eternity in the familiar Medici emblem of the diamond ring, particularly when accompanied by the motto "semper," as it is in the frescoes of the Magi in the Medici chapel, the visual analogue of the play of popular and humanist poets on Cosimo's name – "Cosmos, Cosmicon" and its associations with universality. These central themes reappear in the last of Cosimo's putative commissions, the design for his tomb marker. At the same time, the circular form invites a composition swirling with movement, in the rhythmic pull of the progression of figures around the edge of the frame.

In the *Magi* tondo we have a commission attributed to the Medici, and probably, in view of its iconography and date, to Cosimo himself, which in its conception expresses not only the intellectual force of the artists but also the sophistication of the patron. In the variety and richness of its symbolism, it conformed to the early Renaissance ideal of painting articulated by Alberti, and appealed to viewers as cultivated as Cosimo de' Medici and his family and friends. But since the resonance of its imagery depends not upon the exegesis of obscure texts, but on a combination of quotidian sources which were part of devout Florentines' daily experience – the liturgy, the gospels and writings of the prophets, the commentaries on these by such popular authorities as the church fathers, and the author of a favorite handbook of Christian information, the *Golden Legend* of Iacopo da Voragine – this painting would have been eminently accessible to the simplest of Christian viewers. Moreover, the addition to the Christian symbols that gave the picture its primary meaning of others originating from antiquity would have interested the many viewers of this period, both simple and sophisticated, concerned with the parallels between Christian and classical culture that preoccupied Renaissance viewers with some knowledge of humanist texts, or even those who had acquired, through the digests of such literature in popular compilations, some smattering of classical culture. The tondo is filled with images of universal significance to Christians, learned or otherwise, but at the same time it is endowed with special significance for its putative Medici patrons, since Cosimo and his sons made so many of these symbols their own – the Magi themselves, the falcon and the peacock, the circle of the globe and of eternity.

★　　★　　★

Domenico Veneziano

Many objects rich in Medici symbolism have appeared and reappeared already in the course of this account of Medici patronage – the San Marco altarpiece, the fresco in Cosimo's cell, Piero's *tempietti* for San Miniato and Santissima Annunziata, the facade of the Medici palace – and others have yet to be discussed; Donatello's bronzes, the illuminated manuscripts commissioned by various members of the family, the frescoes of the Medici palace chapel. The closest comparison to the Lippi/Angelico tondo in terms of imagery and symbolism is with another tondo for their domestic contemplation, depicting the Magi, and attributed in the 1492 inventory to "Pesello."[91] The attribution to "Pesello" of more than one painting in the Medici possession in 1492 reveals a confusion on the part of the inventarist between Giuliano Pesello, an artist who flourished in the fourteenth century, and his grandson and pupil Francesco di Pesello, known as "Pesellino," an admired contemporary and co-worker of Domenico Veneziano, to whom modern art historians confidently attribute the tondo in question, now in Berlin (fig. 118). A comparison between these two Magi tondi illustrates not only the strength of the Medici interest in this subject, but also the subject's versatility for purposes of representation. The style and content of the tondo by Domenico Veneziano suggests that its function in family eyes was as different from the Lippi/Angelico tondo as this was from Angelico's painting of the Magi which served the Medici as an altarpiece before the building and decoration of the chapel in the palace.

Domenico's tondo is described by Helmut Wohl as "an astonishing fusion of northern Italian and Netherlandish achievements with those of Florence . . . the most brilliant of his surviving paintings." While the datings suggested by historians on stylistic grounds alone span three decades, from the late 1420s to the late 1450s, Rab Hatfield observed that the Greek-style headwear worn by two of the figures in the background is found in Florentine paintings only after the church council of 1439. Wohl suggests that other elements of the painting were also related to the council and its importance to the Medici, and proposes the earliest possible date after it occurred, *circa* 1440.[92] By comparison with the Lippi/Angelico tondo this is a plainer, although not necessarily simpler, composition. As Wohl observed, it is built up on a quadratic grid and perfectly illustrates Alberti's exposition of perspective. The train of followers bringing up the rear of the three wise men, although disappearing in both works into the distance to imply infinity, is nevertheless reduced by Domenico, by comparison with the varied multitude of the larger and more elaborate tondo,

118   Domenico Veneziano, *Adoration of the Magi*, Berlin, Staatliche Museen Preussischer Kulturbesitz, Gemäldegalerie

representing "all the nations" of the biblical phrase, essentially to a smaller and more aristocratic group occupying
the foreground.

By comparison with the Lippi/Angelico landscape
crowded with figures set in or against a variety of buildings, Domenico depicted empty though carefully culti-

vated fields, and pastures upon which the sheep of the
biblical narrative are safely grazing. Apart from the partial
representation of the manger in the foreground, only a
few distant castles and and houses dot the hills sloping
down to a lake where white-sailed craft bob on the
waves. Although writers earlier in this century identified

the landscape as that of Lake Garda, near where Domenico grew up, it is generally agreed that few if any early Renaissance landscapes represent actual places, although some of the essential features of the customary composites recall elements of particular sites.[93] In this case the castle, slightly off-center where the convergence of the hills on the very line of the horizon draws the viewer's eye,[94] is not entirely a generic one. With its rather squat crenellated tower that widens at the top and overhangs the main structure, protected by a ditch and surrounded by walls, in front of which are a cultivated *prato* and grazing land, it suggests an idealized combination of Cafaggiolo and Trebbio. These villas, on the Medici estates on the plain from which the Appenines rise to the north toward Bologna, are explicitly described in successive tax reports of the late twenties and thirties by Cosimo and his cousin Averardo, the previous owner of Cafaggiolo.[95]

Only a couple of miles distant from this main villa is the family castle of Trebbio, perched on the top of a very steep hill. It was used particularly as a hunting lodge by Cosimo's sons in their youth, and later by their cousin Pierfrancesco di Lorenzo to whom this property passed in 1451. Domenico's tondo depicts the sort of aristocratic hunt in which the young Medici men participated with their patrician and princely friends. Where the attack of the falcon upon the pheasant in the Lippi/Angelico *Adoration* seems purely symbolic, and unrelated to the rest of the picture's action, in Domenico's, the figure on horseback at the extreme left is a falconer, who has just released the attacking falcons.

Representations of the Magi offered ideal opportunities for the inclusion of portraits of the patrons and their friends.[96] It seems very possible that the man at the center of the group of Magi, standing slightly behind them, as if presenting them to the Holy Family, and to the viewer, and associated with the falconer or master of the hunt by his identical dress, portrays Piero de' Medici, the putative patron of the picture. He still holds his falcon, Piero's personal emblem, and a symbol, as noted, of the faithful who always return to their heavenly master. As Wohl observed, this young man's features generally resemble those of Piero as delineated in the certain portrait of his marble bust by Mino da Fiesole; he seems to be about the same age as Piero in 1440 – in his mid-twenties – and his figure may be read as less robust than the others, with reference to Piero's physical frailty. The same partial degree of resemblance to his established portrait might be discerned in the apparently younger figure to "Piero's" right, dressed in an elaborate brocaded jacket and holding the crown of the oldest Magi, who prostrates himself to kiss the Christ child's foot. This could be Piero's brother Giovanni, five years younger, whose personal emblem was

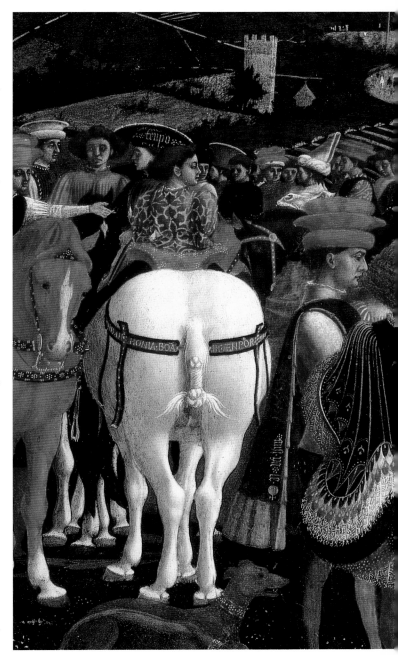

119 Domenico Veneziano, *Adoration of the Magi*, detail of fig. 118

the peacock, which perches on the roof of the manger with its resplendent tail pointing directly down to "Giovanni."[97] The hunting theme is further elaborated in the two hunting dogs near the falconer, one of whom, like the watchdog of the Angelico/Lippi tondo, remains alert, while the other rests, as if after strenuous activity. It may also be emphasized in the repetition of the attack in the sky in one on the ground at the very front of the picture, where another of nature's little murders is taking place.

The four mottoes inscribed upon the trappings of the horses and the dress of the members of the cortège are extremely unusual in a fifteenth-century religious painting (fig. 119). They are not of course entirely unique; the Medici motto "semper" appears prominently on the bridle of the horse ridden by the figure identified as Piero, at the head of the procession in Gozzoli's frescoes in the Medici palace. Two of the mottoes of the tondo also refer to time, as Piero's son Lorenzo's personal motto – "le tems revient" – was later to do: the Italian "tenpo," inscribed on the hat of a figure near the falconer, and the Latin "Ho[m]nia bo[n]a in tenpor" (all good things in time), on the trappings of the adjacent horse. The other two mottoes in French: "ainsi va le monde" (so the world goes), on the cloak of the figure with the fantastic hat standing next to the horse, and "grace fait die[u]" (grace is from God), on the border of the jacket worn by the figure behind and between "Piero" and "Giovanni," are often seen as belonging to the "late medieval milieu of chivalry."[98] This may, as Wohl suggested, be a cultural context of the passion of the younger Medici for the hunt, as it was of their interest in the joust. But the four messages of this tondo, together with a central symbolism not so much heraldic as early Christian, add up more compellingly to a vision like that of Petrarch in his *Triumphs*, of the passing in time of worldly love and pleasure, and man's ultimate progression, through the grace of God, toward that greater good which is eternal. Matteo de' Pasti was about this time preparing a representation of the *Triumphs* for Piero, whose particular interest in Petrarch and the *Trionfi*, the first of the many elaborate manuscripts he commissioned, is discussed at greater length later in this chapter.

Although no concrete evidence has yet been unearthed concerning the patron of this picture, and some of the clues to his identity mentioned above could equally point to Cosimo, he was almost certainly a Medici, and most likely Cosimo's elder son Piero. Not the least of the reasons for believing this is the impression that the tondo is a young man's picture, representing, in addition to the primary devotional theme of the Adoration of the Magi, the strong sub-theme of the pleasures of courtly or country life, depicting a group of young men who, while engaged in one of their favorite pastimes, are caught up in the action of the Christian story. Rather than in "chivalric," or "courtly," terms, which here refer to no more than the costumes and pastimes of aristocratic leisure, this work might be described as a combination of

the recreational and the devotional, in which the human aspects of the Magi story are emphasized as much as the divine.[99] As often observed, such interweaving of sacred and secular preoccupations, emblematic of the very life of the Christian man, seemed perfectly appropriate to this society, especially if they could be linked with an intellectual elegance and spiritual integrity similar in spirit to that of Petrarch's *Triumphs*.

The camel in the stable is a relatively new and exotic touch which appears earlier in the prototype for Adorations in this period, Gentile da Fabriano's altarpiece painted in the early 1420s for the Strozzi. Along with the bearded retainers and the black stable-boy, it evoked the East, which was also the setting of the lives of Cosimo's patron saints, as depicted most notably in Angelico's predella for the San Marco altarpiece, finished in the early 1440s. Even more notable is the variety of headwear in the distinctive Eastern conical or cylindrical forms. Florentines were fascinated by their Greek visitors' hats, which are featured in many images after 1439. Even the Virgin's headdress suggests the conical headwear displayed in its purer form in the group clustered around the white horse.[100]

A wealth of evidence shows us the myriad ways in which the church council brought this exotic world to the forefront of Florentines' minds, as seen in so many of the images of this period, particularly those associated with the Medici. Wohl made a strong case for some specific reference in this picture to the council which both Cosimo and Piero attended, as bankers to Pope Eugenius, in Ferrara in 1438, and the following year in Florence. As appears from a series of documents dating from the mid-1430s, Cosimo took the initiative in proposing Florence as an alternative site, and when an outbreak of plague obliged the group to move from the more politically neutral Ferrara, he almost singlehandedly financed the transfer.[101] The council was the occasion for the young Piero to assume his first serious diplomatic and business responsibilities on the Medici behalf, and as such was a major milestone in his life, which he might well have wanted to commemorate in an image he commissioned. While the references to time seem more general to the Medici than specific to the council, the tondo could well be read as the depiction of a an imagined – or even a real – hunting excursion in 1439, in which the members of the Eastern delegation to the council were the main protagonists.

Stylistically the painting seems most indebted to Masaccio, Masolino, and Pisanello, a Veronese artist with whom Domenico worked between 1426 and 1432 on the frescoes for St. John Lateran in Rome. Pisanello was for some time resident at the court of the Marquess of

Ferrara, along with his compatriot Guarino da Verona. The court humanists Guarino and Bartolomeo Fazio considered him the epitome of the perfect painter. In this respect too, the council may have influenced the particular character of the tondo. There is a good deal of evidence that during their extended stay in Ferrara, Piero de' Medici and his father were much impressed and influenced by the culture of the highly cultivated Este court. Piero in particular took the opportunity to study with Guarino, and the delightful *studiolo* he created in the new Medici palace was probably modeled on that of Ercole d'Este, who installed the first of the elegant Renaissance *studioli* in his palace in Ferrara and at his country house, Belfiore.[102]

Wohl suggested that the vogue for Pisanello led Piero to commission Domenico to paint a piece in his style, and pointed to a number of borrowings from Pisanello's works, including the fact that the model for the boy in the brocade shirt mounted on the white horse is the reverse of Pisanello's famous medal of the Eastern emperor John Paleologus. He proposed that the two artists may have met again in Florence in 1439 while Pisanello was there to make the medal. But if, as others believe, the medal was made in Ferrara in 1438, a meeting there of Piero, Pisanello, and Domenico is also plausible, since Piero and Pisanello were in Ferrara, and Domenico might well have detoured there on his way to Florence from Perugia, where he had been working on some frescoes in the Baglioni palace.[103]

Domenico Veneziano, who died in 1461, is the most obscure of those whom contemporaries considered the greatest artists working in Florence in Cosimo's lifetime.[104] Only twelve of his works survive, none is documented, and they are datable only by style. Nevertheless, he may be identified as one of the handful of artists most favored by the Medici; from his letter to Piero di Cosimo in 1438 soliciting a previous commission — albeit one apparently rejected, at least initially — from the Magi tondo, and from two other rather unusual and wholly secular works described in the 1492 inventory. One was "a small *colmo* with two shutters" in which was depicted a head of a lady, "by the hand of the master Domenico from Venice."[105] The second was a painting on cloth of "a figure seated in a tabernacle, half nude, holding a skull, by the hand of the master Domenico da Vinegia, colored in oils, and simulating marble." Creighton Gilbert suggested that the figure represented Vanitas, which seems very likely. Although it must have been done late in Domenico's life, his death in 1461 is the *terminus ante quem*, suggesting a particularly early interest on the part of Cosimo and his sons in the sort of allegorical representation which only later in the century became commonplace.[106]

Fra Filippo Lippi

The Medici commissioned several images of Saint Jerome, whose cult flourished in the climate, both learned and penitential, of Florentine piety. "A painting with a gilded frame depicting a Saint Jerome and a Saint Francis" tentatively identified with an extant work, was attributed to Fra Filippo Lippi and Francesco di Pesello (fig. 120).[107] It was the latter to whom the compiler of the inventory assigned the Domenico Veneziano tondo, and who is generally supposed by art historians to have painted the predella for Lippi's Medici altarpiece in the novices' chapel in Santa Croce. "A little *colmo*, with a gilded frame, on which is depicted Our Lady seated with the Child on her arm, with two little angels at her feet," was also described as being "by the hand of Francesco di Pisello, 10 florins." The only other work attributed

120 Fra Filippo Lippi, *Saint Jerome in Penitence*, Altenburg, Staatliches Lindenau-Museum

121   Fra Filippo Lippi, *The Annunciation*, London, National Gallery

to Lippi was "a wooden *colmo*, depicting a nude figure sleeping in a hammock with two clothed figures with some grand houses, by the hand of Maestro Filippo."[108]

However, since Lippi was probably in fact the chief author of the marvelous Magi tondo, as well as of the important public image of the Madonna and Child in *sacra conversazione* with the Medici saints at Santa Croce, he was obviously a more important member of the small circle of artists particularly favored by the Medici than the works noted in the inventory would suggest. It was Lippi whom Giovanni chose, apparently at Cosimo's behest, to paint the altarpiece which the Medici presented as a diplomatic gift to their new ally, the king of Naples, in 1457. This commission was very important to the patrons. At the time, Lippi was busy working on some frescoes for the cathedral of Prato, but he was temporarily released from that commitment in order to do the triptych for Naples. The king was delighted with the finished product, and Giovanni and Cosimo were clearly pleased with Lippi.[109]

Further evidence of the Medici family's predilection for his work are the two lunette-shaped panels, now in London, of the Annunciation and seven saints. All the saints were onomastic protectors of the Medici family (figs. 121 and 122). The emblem of the diamond ring with feathers prominently displayed on a capital at the center of the *Annunciation* panel also marks these matching works indubitably as a Medici commission. The panels were probably intended originally to be hung above

doors, but whether in the new palace or the old house, for the pleasure and edification of Cosimo's household, or that of his nephew Pierfrancesco, is not clear. First closely investigated by Martin Davies, these works have recently been reexamined by Francis Ames-Lewis and John Paoletti, and by Jeffrey Ruda. Lippi's authorship of the panels has never been doubted, but opinions about their date have varied, from very early in Lippi's career to the late 1450s. An evolving appreciation of the artist's work supports a late date, which would coincide with the completion of the Medici palace. Although a number of objects originally in the old house were transferred to the new palace, overdoors would probably have been designed specifically to fit the architecture and the decorative scheme. On the other hand, Ruda plausibly suggested that the appearance of Pierfrancesco's onomastic saints in key positions at either end of the intercessory tableau might imply that he commissioned the picture around the time when he married and became the major occupant of the *casa vecchia*. However, there is no other evidence of Pierfrancesco using the emblem of the diamond ring with feathers which was developed primarily by Piero di Cosimo.[110]

Proposals to identify the patron based on the identity and order of the seven saints have been mutually contradictory, and remain problematic. A study of dedications to saints in personal diaries and compilations of literature, account books, and the notarial acts of business companies, suggests that the Medici, like many Florentines, were

122 Fra Filippo Lippi, *Saints Francis, Lawrence, Cosmas or Damian, John the Baptist, Damian or Cosmas, Anthony Abbot, and Peter Martyr*, London, National Gallery

devoted to a variety of saints for reasons that are not always clear. Modern attempts to account for the inclusion, exclusion, or placement of saints in paintings are fraught with difficulty, since there is little explicit evidence of how individuals chose and related themselves to particular heavenly protectors. For example, we do not know whether John the Baptist could occasionally stand in for John the Evangelist, the patron of Giovanni di Bicci and his grandson, or Peter the Apostle replace Peter the Martyr, patron saint of Piero di Cosimo, as saintly representatives of Giovanni or Piero in Medici images. What we do know of personal devotion to onomastic saints would suggest the substitution in images of saints merely of the same name to be quite irrational, but the visual evidence does sometimes seem to point in the opposite direction.[111] The appearance of their onomastic saints in Medici family commissions for chapels or altarpieces is obviously connected to commemorative masses for the souls of the family dead; their presence in images relates as well to family genealogies and represents in a sense the visual equivalent of family *ricordi*. But beyond their role in the collective devotion of the lineage, the onomastic saints of the Medici family were all important figures in the history of Christianity, endowed by history or legend with a variety of associations of significance to all Christian worshippers.[112]

Whoever actually commissioned the lunette panels, they are evidence of Lippi's popularity in Medici circles at mid-century, an appreciation also reflected in the number of works commissioned from him by Medici *amici* (discussed in chapter 15).[113] Ruda observed that the lunettes are very close in style to Lippi's altarpiece for the palace chapel. If they too formed part of the original furnishings of the palace, they would constitute further evidence of the family's lively appreciation of Lippi's experiments in the brilliant use of atmospheric color and his extraordinary treatment of light, begun in other and probably earlier representations of the subject of the Annunciation with which Cosimo would have been familiar. These included altarpieces for two of his closest friends and business associates; for the Martelli in the San Lorenzo chapel of the *operai*, adjacent to that of the Medici, and for the Benci at the convent of the Murate, which Giovanni d'Amerigo, one of the four partners of the Medici bank with Cosimo and Lorenzo between 1435 and 1441, had established in 1439.[114]

Ames-Lewis, in an interesting comparison between the Medici Annunciation lunette and the Annunciation panels made for the Benci, and also those perhaps for the Florentine Signoria, pointed to the lavish use of rich materials, vibrant colors, and brilliant detailing and decoration characteristic of other commissions attributable to Piero de' Medici. He further suggested that the seven saints panel carries a strong message "about the dynastic relationships between the two major branches of the family, and about the future succession of family leadership and inheritance of Medici family power." He referred in support of this argument to "quasi-narrative" gestures in other Medici images possibly pointing to a genealogical succession; the "Annalena" altarpiece, and the crucifixion fresco in Cosimo's cell at San Marco. John Paoletti saw similarly significant references in the decoration of the south wall of the old sacristy. Several contributors to the volume on Piero de' Medici edited by Andreas Beyer and Bruce Boucher observed that such references are much more marked in Piero's commissions than in Cosimo's. There is no need, however, to make a sharp distinction between "dynastic" and "devotional" elements in such images, since a familial succession was an integral part of domestic devotion.[115]

The Medici family's taste for Fra Filippo Lippi's work demonstrably survived the succession of generations. The artist died while working on some frescoes in the cathedral of Spoleto, and he was buried there. Lorenzo de' Medici was sufficiently appreciative of Lippi, and in particular of his innovative treatment of color, that twenty years later he had a funerary monument erected to the artist on which he inscribed these lines: "Here I am brought, Filippo, painting's fame,/ to nought unknown my wondrous grace of hand./ With craftsman's fingers I gave color life,/ and fooled the living with its long-awaited voice./ Nature herself by my expressive figures stilled/ confesses me the equal of her arts."[116]

The Medici, Florence, and Flemish artists

Renaissance art historians, particularly those interested in Lippi and Domenico Veneziano, have long speculated about the influence on this group of Italian painters, and on their patrons, among them the Medici, of major Flemish masters such as Van Eyck and Van der Weyden. Since there is little evidence of direct contacts, some scholars are inclined to believe that Flemish styles were transmitted to Italy by the handful of works dispatched to Italy on commission or as diplomatic gifts. Vasari wrote about a number of Van Eyck's works sent to various Italian notables in the 1450s, most particularly to the king of Naples, and of one that he had seen in Florence among the possessions of Lorenzo de' Medici.[117]

There are in fact a couple of items attributed in the 1492 inventory to Flemish masters. One, the "head of a French lady" was assigned to "Pietro Cresci da Bruggia." Another was carefully described as "a *tavoletta* from Flanders on which is painted a Saint Jerome in his study, with a cupboard representing many books in perspective, and a lion at his feet, a work of Maestro Giovanni of Bruges, colored in oils, in a *guaina*." This painting, small and precious enough to be enclosed in a protective box, was valued at thirty florins. It has been identified with a work

123   (?)Petrus Christus, *Saint Jerome in his Study*, Detroit, The Institute of Arts, City of Detroit Purchase

now in Detroit, possibly a copy of Van Eyck, by a pupil, perhaps Petrus Christus (fig. 123).[118] Whether a diplomatic gift, a Medici commission, or a later acquisition, the style of the work would have appealed to the family's appreciation of exquisitely detailed workmanship apparent in their collections of precious objects and illuminated manuscripts, and their fondness for intarsia.

A Madonna and Child with Saints Cosmas, Damian, John the Baptist, and Peter the Apostle, now in Altenburg, is generally attributed to Rogier van der Weyden and dated after 1454. Its heavenly personnel, and a shield bearing the *giglio* of Florence, identify it fairly clearly as a Medici commission. It has the colors of Piero's livery – white, green, and violet – although these were also

124 Rogier van der Weyden, *Madonna with Saints Cosmas and Damian, Peter and John*, Frankfurt am Mein, Städelschen Kunstinstitut

more generally associated with the theological virtues (fig. 124). The humanist Bartolomeo Fazio recorded that Van der Weyden was in Italy in the jubilee year of 1450, when he admired some frescoes in the Lateran in Rome by Gentile da Fabriano. Describing Rogier as a pupil of Van Eyck, Fazio specified several works the Flemish master made for Italian patrons, including a picture shown to Ciriaco D'Ancona, a Medici agent and intellectual advisor, in Ferrara in 1449. There was also a triptych with the Fall on one wing, and a donor on the other, and in Genoa a picture of a woman in a bath with two youths observing her. None of these has been identified with any surviving work.[119] In May 1458 Alessandro Sforza,

lord of Pesaro, returned from an eight-month journey to Flanders, including Bruges, bringing with him a portrait and two other pictures assigned to Rogier and recorded in Alessandro's grandson's collection at Pesaro in 1500. One of these works was probably the Crucifixion with saints and angels and with a donor in armor and conspicuous Sforza devices, now in Brussels (fig. 172).[120]

The so-called Medici *Madonna* might have been commissioned during Rogier's brief trip to Italy, but there is no evidence of this, nor that it was ever in the Medici palace. Erwin Panofsky thought its style intentionally Italianate, but suggested that Saints Cosmas and Damian have the features of two Burgundian courtiers, who also appear in other works by Rogier. Martin Davies was convinced that the shield on the (incorporated) frame, bearing the Florentine lily rather than the Medici *palle*, suggested a commission for a public, rather than a domestic setting.[121] However, it seems possible that the city's arms served simply to mark the patrons as Florentine nationals in a commission from a foreign artist, or that the painting was intended perhaps for a setting outside Florence or even Italy, where the Medici arms would have been less readily recognized. Foreign artists of Florentine commissions normally identified themselves in their signatures by their place of origin, as did Florentine artists working abroad. The picture is rather small for public display, only twenty-one inches by fifteen.

It would, however, have been a perfectly appropriate size for a devotional image for a business office. Neri di Bicci's workshop book records the commission of such images for shops as unpretentious as that of a Florentine barber. The two blank shields flanking the central escutcheon bearing the lily most obviously suggest a marriage, but they might have been incorporated in a work made to mark the occasion of a different partnership, a new business alliance forged between two Florentine families under the aegis of the Medici company. One possibility is the appointment of Giovanni di Cosimo in 1455 as manager of the Medici bank, after the death of Giovanni de' Benci. This was a major event, necessitating the redrawing of all contracts between the Florentine branch of the bank and its subsidiaries. The latter included the all-important branch at Bruges, which held the key to Medici trade in English woolen cloth, necessary to maintain the balance of payments between Italy and the Low Countries. A new agreement was drawn up in 1455 with Agnolo Tani, the future patron of Memling's triptych, *The Last Judgment*, who was manager at Bruges from 1449 to 1464, and his assistant Tommaso Portinari, who took over after Tani's death as manager from 1464 to 1480, and upon his return to Florence commissioned the Van der Goes altarpiece, *The Adoration of the Shepherds* now in the Uffizi.[122]

The handful of non-devotional images in the Medici palace inventory of 1492 indicate the avant-garde nature of Medici taste. Of particular interest, in addition to the heads and figures mentioned above, are the studies of Florentine buildings. In one room was "a wooden picture, depicting a perspective view, that is the palace of the Signoria with the piazza and loggia and great houses around as it is." Since perspectival cityscapes did not really come into fashion until after Cosimo's death, this image probably belongs to the Laurentian period, along with two other representations of buildings kept in the room described as belonging to Bertoldo, Lorenzo's favorite

artist-in-residence. These were "a wooden picture depicting the Duomo and San Giovanni," and "a canvas depicting the palace of the Signoria."[123]

Cosimo's curiosity about the world beyond the walls of Florence was early evidenced in the "beautiful globe" or book of maps he kept in his room in the *casa vecchia* in 1418, and in the inclusion of globes of the earth and the heavens in various images he commissioned, among them the armillary sphere represented in the fresco of the Magi in his cell at San Marco, and the orb in Christ's hand in the altarpiece for the convent's church. The family's horizons continued to expand in the course of the fifteenth century, and by the early years of the sixteenth the Medici were the owners of one of the finest collections of maps in Europe. The many maps – of Spain, Italy, and the Holy Land – already in the palace by the time of Lorenzo's death, may perhaps have constituted the nucleus of this collection.[124]

There were also two painted portraits, apparently a pair, of two of Cosimo's major military allies, the *condottieri* Francesco Sforza and Gattamelata, the work of a Venetian artist.[125] They may have been commissioned by Cosimo as a mark of respect for these men, or presented to him as a gift, or ordered by Lorenzo to honor his grandfather and his allies. Their presence in the Medici palace does suggest something of the same interest in heroes of the battlefield as Donatello's bronze *David*, Cosimo's collection of armor, and the Uccello panels of the Battle of San Romano.

UCCELLO'S *BATTLE OF SAN ROMANO*: COSIMO, THE COMMUNE, AND WARFARE: IMAGES OF FAME AND DEFAMATION, PUBLIC AND PRIVATE

Art-historical opinion has always been divided over the distinctive qualities of Uccello's three huge battle panels, now dispersed among the galleries of London, Paris, and Florence. They are virtually the only surviving examples of their genre. Although representations of battles were common enough in northern Europe, they seem to have been less so in Italy, especially in a domestic context; none of the comparable commissions made later by Cosimo's *condottiere* friends – Sigismondo Malatesta's *Triumphs*, or the Pisanello *Tournament* for the palace of the marquess of Mantua – represented actual battles, although there were models for Uccello's work in battle scenes on Roman triumphal arches with which he was familiar.[126] Yet Vasari claimed that battle pictures by Uccello were still in the sixteenth century to be seen in the houses of many great Florentine families, most particularly those of the Medici and the Bartolini. "In the house of the Medici

125   Paolo Uccello, *The Battle of San Romano*, London, National Gallery

he painted in tempera on cloth some stories of animals, in which he always delighted, and in order to do them well he studied them very carefully." In Gualfonda, "in the garden there that used to belong to the Bartolini, and in a terrace, there were four stories by his hand on wood, all about war; that is, horses and armed men with the most beautiful accoutrements of that period; and among the men portrayed were Paulo Orsino, Ottobuono da Parma, Luca da Canale, and Carlo Malatesta, lord of Rimini, all captains general of that time."[127]

Once again, there are no contracts or correspondence attesting to these commissions and their patron or patrons. On the basis of the above passage, scholars were first inclined to connect the extant panels with the series belonging to the Bartolini, long since disappeared. Then at the beginning of the twentieth century, the inventory of 1492 came to light, containing the passage cited in full at the beginning of this chapter describing an installation, 42 *braccia* long and 3½ *braccia* high, in the Camera di Lorenzo, comprising six pictures: "three of the Rout of San Romano and one of battles and dragons and lions and one of the story of Paris by the hand of Paolo Uccello and one by the hand of Francesco di Pesello, depicting a hunt." Ever since, the extant panels, always

confidently attributed to Uccello, have been identified with the scenes of the Rout of San Romano in the Medici house at the time of Lorenzo's death. Although there is considerable controversy concerning the date of the panels, on the basis of their subject, a battle which took place during the Florentine war with Lucca in June 1432 of which Niccolò da Tolentino was the hero, and more recently, of the more precise dating of the armor they depict, the London and Uffizi panels are increasingly assigned to the late 1430s, that in the Louvre more rarely and tentatively to the early 1440s. For the last hundred years or so, Cosimo de' Medici has therefore been the presumptive patron of these works (figs. 125–27).

In 1999 Outi Merisalo published another important document concerning Lorenzo de' Medici's possessions, this time the records of a commission of 1495 set up to consider the claims of hundreds of Florentine citizens to Medici property, largely in respect of unpaid debts, after the expulsion of Lorenzo's sons, Piero and Giovanni, from the city. In the favorable circumstances of the abandonment of their ancestral palace and its goods by the exiled Medici, most of the petitioners were successful in pressing their claims, and large quantities of valuable objects, such as silver and tapestries, were sold to satisfy alleged obligations. Several claims asserted that *objets d'art* apparently identifiable in the inventory of 1492 belonged originally and rightfully to people other than the Medici; Michelangelo Buonarroti and David del Ghirlandaio were among those who successfully requested the restitution of such works.[128]

In a forthcoming study of Medici "political and patriotic" commissions, most particularly the Donatello bronzes, Francesco Caglioti draws attention to the complaint of Damiano Bartolini, considered by the commission on 30 and 31 July 1495, that "some histories [*istorias*]" had been taken by Lorenzo de' Medici from his home "by force."[129] On the first morning, Iacopo Marsuppini testified on Damiano's behalf, but his claim was not accepted. After the additional testimony of Mariotto di Antonio Carnesecchi and Galeotto de' Martelli, it was decided on the second day that one and a half of three histories should be restored to Damiano, and that if he wished to purchase the rest, Rinieri di Niccolò Giugni and Girolamo Martelli, the officials representing the commune, should deal with this matter; what Damiano did then, we do not know.[130]

A fuller account of the incident on the second day described how Andrea Bartolini and his brother Damiano possessed various property in common, "among other things a certain history called 'The rout of the tower of San Romano' or 'The rout of Niccolò Picino.'"[131] Some years earlier Andrea had given his half of the history to Lorenzo de' Medici. Lorenzo then demanded that Damiano should hand over the portion belonging to him as well. Damiano produced letters between himself and his brother, then resident in Milan as an agent of the Medici bank there, in which Andrea attempted to persuade Damiano to accede to Lorenzo's request, but Damiano perservered in his resistance. He transferred the history from the Bartolini country villa at Santa Maria a Quinto to his house in town, from whence it was removed against his will by Lorenzo with the aid of some laborers and the renowned woodworker Francione, an intimate Medici friend and partisan. Galeotto Martelli testified to having been present when Lorenzo sent for the history. Andrea Bartolini was unable to contest his brother's claim or tell his version of the story, since at the time of the hearing he had already been dead for ten months. Francione had died only five days before.[132]

This fascinating tale requires further investigation. The proceedings of 1495 unfortunately tell us nothing of the original patron of the three paintings in question, nor their whereabouts in the half century between their presumed commission and Lorenzo de' Medici's alleged seizure of the works, which according to evidence assembled by Caglioti probably took place in the late 1480s. Nor does the document provide an entirely clear warrant

for the natural assumption that the three histories in question were all of the Rout of San Romano and identifiable with the three panels we know today; the above examination of the inventory of 1492 showed that the correlation between works described there and those now extant was limited and uncertain. It is in the nature of claims to invite contestation, and indeed in 1512, when the Medici returned to Florence, they issued a proclamation ordering all who were in possession of any of the family's goods which had been sold to declare them; as the writer of a contemporary diary records, "they got back an enormous number of things." Vasari's testimony of 1568, that he saw paintings by Uccello including animals in the Medici palace, might refer to the extant panels; certainly the Medici inventory of 1598 puts representations of the Battle of San Romano back in the palace by that date at latest.[133]

The Bartolini claim obliges us to reconsider our view of Cosimo's oeuvre, since it opens up several new possibilities concerning the patronage of these works. The first, and most obvious, is that the panels were commissioned between the late 1430s, and around 1450, not by Cosimo de' Medici, but by the Bartolini, and remained in their hands until Lorenzo's seizure of them in the late 1480s. In this case their most likely patron would be Lionardo Bartolini, father of Damiano and Andrea, who played a part, albeit a relatively minor one, in the war against Lucca, whose father and uncle were patrons of frescoes and an altarpiece by Lorenzo Monaco in the family chapel in Santa Trinita, and who himself ordered an altarpiece from Filippo Lippi, although the work may not have been executed for him, owing to intervening commitments on the part of that somewhat unreliable artist.[134]

Lorenzo's dramatic raid on the Bartolini house goes far beyond his well-known propensity for putting pressure on his friends to obtain things he wanted, as he obtained from Giovanni Rucellai the site for his villa at Poggio a Caiano, and apparently from Andrea Bartolini his half of the Uccello *istoria*. It requires some explanation, beyond his documentable predilection for images of battles, animals, and jousts.[135] We might find this, perhaps, in the immense significance to his own family's history and traditions of the war with Lucca. Cosimo was the Florentine citizen who indisputably played by far the largest part in financing and directing the war against Lucca, and his grandson would naturally have been eager to display famous representations of this event in the family palace. Cosimo's fascination with warfare and warriors, clearly apparent in his personal letters, is visibly documented in his notable but so far unremarked collection of armor described in the inventory of the *casa vecchia* of 1417/18, predating the well-known collections of his sons and grandson, and the representation of his younger son Giovanni in antique armor in the mid-century portrait bust by Mino da Fiesole. These objects, to be discussed later in this chapter, illustrate a continuity of interest in matters military across three generations which is at once historical, dynastic and aesthetic.

A second possibility is that the claim submitted to the commission of 1495 represented an opportunistic attempt, on the part of the Bartolini, to get hold of some Medici property they had long admired and envied. A third scenario, less straightforward but nevertheless intriguing and absolutely consonant with the behavior of Florentine exiles and with many other events in this dynamic and uncertain phase of the city's history, characterized by constantly shifting allegiances and interests on the part of the Florentine elite, might be that the Medici were indeed the patrons and owners of the histories described in the inventory of 1492, and that Damiano Bartolini laid claim to them in 1495 to save them from sequestration. If he had not made his claim, the *istoria* of San Romano would probably have shared the fate of other objects in the Medici palace, including most notably Donatello's *David* and his *Judith and Holofernes*, as well as Lippi's altarpiece incorporating Saint Bernard. These works were judged by the officials of the revived republic later that same year to represent important symbols of its history, values, and ideals, and on these grounds were confiscated for display in public places, never to be returned to their original owners. As it is, there is no mention of the Uccello battle panels in the acts of sequestration.[136]

There spring to mind many cases over the centuries in which friends remaining in Florence cooperated and connived to defend the property of exiles through various legal fictions and ruses. A prime example is that of Giovanni Rucellai's protection of his father-in-law Palla Strozzi's assets by actions which appear on the surface to be evidence of his exploitation of them, a situation clarified only after years of archival digging by F. W. Kent.[137] The decisions of the 1495 commission considering claims were rendered prima facie problematic by the fact that at least half of its members were men close to the exiled Medici, including their former factor Francesco d'Agostino del Chegia, acting as agents for the exiles.[138] As a factor of the Medici bank in Milan, Andrea Bartolini was extremely close to Lorenzo and in constant correspondence with him,[139] and the association between the two families can be traced back at least as far as Piero's friendship with Lionardo Bartolini, who in the 1440s gave a dinner in his honor at which they were entertained by one of their mutual protégés among the singers at San Martino.[140]

A fourth possibility is that if, as Vasari claimed, the Medici and the Bartolini were Uccello's major patrons for domestic decorations involving battles and animals, both families might have had a part in the commission of the three extant panels, although none of the latter really matches Vasari's description of the works he saw in either family's house. It is usually assumed that the panels we know were painted as a matching set; however, a number of scholars, particularly those expert in quattrocento armor, are inclined to believe that they were not. While the armor depicted in the London and Uffizi panels belongs to the late 1430s, only a few years after the Battle of San Romano was fought, the armor represented in the Louvre panel is different and could help to date the painting as late as the 1450s.[141] Moreover, the London and Uffizi panels represent the attack of Niccolò da Tolentino, the hero of the encounter in Florentine eyes, against the Lucchese forces, and the subsequent rout of the enemy. Other scholars have remarked upon the slight redundancy to this central narrative of the Louvre panel, which memorializes another skirmish and another *condottiere* present at the encounter, Micheletto Attendolo da Cotignola.[142]

Lorenzo's determination to obtain Damiano's portion of the pictorial inheritance of the Bartolini brothers, having already obtained Andrea's, might be explained by the works in question all depicting the Rout of San Romano. However, this cannot be assumed on the basis of the 1495 document alone. Although three *istorias* are mentioned, only one *istoria* is described as concerning the Rout of San Romano, or rather of the Milanese condottiere Niccolò Piccinino. An alternative hypothesis which would account at a single stroke for the slightly anomalous subject of the Louvre panel and its possibly later date, as well as Lorenzo's eagerness to acquire at least one of the Bartolini "histories," might suggest that his grandfather, Cosimo, had indeed commissioned the two panels referring directly to his friend and ally Niccolò da Tolentino's role in the action, in which Niccolò Piccinino, mentioned in the claim of 1495, did not take part.

Lionardo Bartolini, conforming to the pattern of almost all post 1434 commissions by friends of the Medici, of emulating or competing with their patrons' innovations only after a slight interval,[143] might perhaps have followed Cosimo's example with a similar representation featuring Micheletto Attendolo, intended to form part of a series of famous *condottieri* in battle scenes which Vasari described in the sixteenth century as being in the Bartolini villa at Gualfonda, including one of Paolo Orsini, one of the captains at the Battle of Anghiari in 1440, which did accomplish decisively "the rout of Niccolò Picino." Lorenzo might well have coveted these

126   Paolo Uccello, *The Battle of San Romano*, Florence, Uffizi

scenes, so closely related to those he owned, in order to fill out the ambitious installation that Francione is believed to have made for his Medici patrons; this would certainly have given the artist a vested interest in procuring the components of the ensemble. The other two purloined histories could well have been the other two Uccellos displayed in the Medici palace in 1492, whose subject matter also made them desirable elements in a series generally dedicated to histories and the representation of animals in battle.[144]

However, in view of the preoccupation, described in previous chapters and discussed at greater length below, not only of Cosimo de' Medici, but of many other Florentine patricians, and indeed of the Florentine people in general, with the waging and representation of war, quite a number of citizens, especially those closely involved in the conflict with Lucca, would have had good cause to commission such work. Such interests and concerns are certainly their essential context.[145]

The question of the patronage and ownership history of the three known Uccello battlepieces can only be resolved by the discovery of further documentary evidence, together perhaps with more extensive work on the archaeology of the objects which might furnish valuable clues about the dating and the relation of the panels to one another. Meanwhile, since much of the evidence presently available would lead us to believe that while Cosimo was by no means the only plausible patron of Uccello's San Romano panels, he was nevertheless, in the absence of compelling evidence to the contrary, by far the most likely patron of a cycle that so precisely embodied his personal interests and concerns, that evidence deserves closer scrutiny at this point.

"Togas and arms"

Representing the genius of men in battle,[146] one of "the variety of *ingegni*" that Cosimo most admired, the Uccello battle panels constituted a decorative domestic illustration of an almost obsessive interest in the details of strategy and combat in the field, the subject of so many of Cosimo's personal letters. The battle of San Romano, fought in June 1432, was the first victory won by the Florentines in the war against Lucca, begun in 1429, in which Cosimo and his cousin Averardo played a very large part. Uccello's panels foreground the role at San Romano of Niccolò da Tolentino, a Florentine military

127 Paolo Uccello, *The Battle of San Romano*, Paris, Louvre

captain who was an immensely popular hero of that time, and whom Cosimo in his *Ricordi* called "my very great friend."

Renaissance writers, like their classical predecessors, framed the issue of immortality in terms of the ancient topos of letters and arms. Tracolo da Rimini, a poet who hoped to become famous by "attaching himself to the great column" of the Medici dynasty, began a verse adumbrating a well-known theme of Cicero's, and addressed to Giovanni di Cosimo: "Which garland is greenest and more worthy,/ that of him who follows Mars or Apollo? . . . Since my heart, which desires only fame,/ having been intent on one or the other,/ was ceaselessly occupied in gathering up its fruit,/ advise me, for I am inclined entirely/ to entrust my ship to your fair wind/ to guide it in the happiest path." Feo Belcari replied on Giovanni's behalf: "Both togas and arms are worthy parts,/ decreed by Him who speaks to us in thunder and lightning/ to preserve the virtuous republic,/ and without them liberty is lost./ The counselor employs his intellect to advise you/ of everything to your benefit, and by his speech the warrior/ is spurred on, so that he never spares himself/ until the force of the enemy is dissipated./ Often the first with patriotic speech,/ he so prepares the *patria* and its

rulers [*reggimento*],/ that without a blow being struck, the enemy is destroyed."[147]

This is an almost perfect description of the Medici family's role in the republic's defence, and of Cosimo's relationship to the *condottieri* who fought for Florence. In fact, as a citizen of a merchant republic Cosimo had no option but to assume the toga, since he had no mandate to bear arms. In fact, although the topos proposed these as alternatives, given that so much classical poetry and prose sang the praises of the warrior – Hercules, Hector, Aeneas, Caesar – arms and learning were naturally associated in Florentine, as in Roman minds. Dante thanked his teacher Brunetto Latini for his lessons in "how man makes himself immortal"; by studying the literature of the past.[148] Following such advice, as noted in chapter 4, Cosimo learned from the classical works in his library a good deal about war and its strategies.

In his copy of Caesar's *Commentaries* he noted the great general's dictum concerning the importance of knowing your enemy. Sallust had debated whether strength or intelligence were more effective in warfare; Cosimo may well have pondered this question with the Roman historian's aid, since he owned two copies of the *Jugurtha* by 1418, and his young cousin Francesco was to cite Sallust's views as he reflected on the Medici family's misfortunes while living in exile in Cosimo's household in Venice.[149] Cosimo, keen to aquire a more expert undertanding of warfare, borrowed a copy of Frontinus's *Strategemata* from the notary Anastasio Vespucci. There is a note to this effect in Latin, signed by Cosimo but probably written on his behalf by Leonardo Bruni, then chancellor of the Florentine republic: "I recently received from you Frontinus's book on warfare, which satisfied my desire to know something about its ordering and discipline . . ."[150] The chancellor's own writings on warfare and the knightly class, especially the *De Militia*, were influential in the city's ruling circle.

Cosimo already knew very well, according to advice he had noted in Cicero's *Orator*, how "with patriotic speech," as counselor and diplomat, to persuade the *reggimento* of the republic to order the *patria* in what he considered its best interests. His contribution to a session of the Consulte e Pratiche in 1455 indicates that his advice on when and how to invoke the genius of the warrior to conserve the commune's liberty was generally followed by his fellow citizens. Feo Belcari observed in another verse addressed to Cosimo's elder son Piero that "he who wants to adorn his brow/ with glory which outshines all others/ seeks to acquire honor through just wars."[151] For thirty years Cosimo did precisely that; his was the part of Apollo, and on his judgment depended the fame of the disciples of Mars; their praises sung by Orpheus, their figures immortalized by Apelles, as in the panels and frescoes of Uccello and Castagno which preserved the memory of soldiers like Niccolò da Tolentino.

Florentine preoccupation with warfare and warriors: Cosimo's role in communal conflicts and diplomacy

As another leading patron of the arts, Giovanni Rucellai, wrote in his *zibaldone*: "Our city was involved in war and its great expense for thirty years, that is from 1423 to 1453."[152] These wars were one of the factors that fostered the ascendancy of the Medici family over their fellow oligarchs in the 1420s. Some of the driving force behind Cosimo's manipulation of the electoral system was clearly his conviction, expressed in his many letters to his cousin Averardo, that the Medici were far better suited than any of their fellow patricians to give direction to the state, and particularly to the conduct of the wars against Milan and Lucca; they proved this true in practice.

In addition, as director of perhaps the most profitable bank in Christendom, Cosimo was in a unique position to lend the commune (and its *condottieri*) vast sums of money to pay for these wars. Cosimo and his closest friends and business associates head the list of the Ufficiali del Banco constituted at this time to rescue the commune from its financial difficulties with shrewd advice and large personal loans.[153] Cosimo's banking operations had also created for him an extensive network of powerful contacts and supporters outside Florence, among them the pope, who ruled over several states which were important military powers, and various *condottiere* princes like the Gonzaga and Malatesta. Cosimo's exile in 1433 was a backhanded acknowledgment of his potential power in these respects; his recall a recognition that Florence could not do without him.

As noted in chapter 8, the Medici recall provoked a charge from the popular poet and barber Burchiello that the republic had been sold to the highest bidder. Some verses written by Bernardo Cambini, a friend and neighbor of the Medici from the parish of San Lorenzo, read like a response to this charge, although they were written at least a decade later.[154] They echo a persistent voice from public debates of the early thirties, which can also be heard in a letter of Piero Guicciardini to his friend Matteo Strozzi, destined for exile after the Medici return. In Guicciardini's opinion, in truth the Florentine people yearned for "the discipline of the rod" (*la fermezza del bastone*).[155]

In an ode to Cosimo Cambini built on this image of the baton of authority presented to the commune's *condottieri*, and incorporated the opening phrase of Burchiello's denunciation: "O Florentine *popolo*, you do not understand/ what a Timon guides you toward salvation,/ maintaining you in peace and liberty;/ and if you would open and widen your mental eyes,/ and direct your gaze virtuously and without wrath,/ you would see your highest needs,/ and the calamity/ in which you would find yourself, without the remedy/ of Cosimo, that famous and distinguished/ citizen of yours, who with love and sound sense/at your slightest nod/ would amend that which the *popolo* and the comune/is not able to do, to pull together on a single rope." With this point Cambini picks up the motto of the thirteenth-century commune, cited by Dante and imaged in Lorenzetti's frescoes, an image also evoked in similar poems, including Antonio di Meglio's celebration of the Medici recall.[156]

Cambini suggested that the time was past when corporate cooperation could preserve the commune. Like the humanist Lapo da Castiglionchio, who employed the image of the careful steersman, taken from Plato and popularized by Cicero, to characterize Cosimo's conduct toward the commune during his exile of 1434, Cambini argued that a single strong man was needed to chart its course through the dangerous shoals of later fifteenth-century war and politics. "Now think a little about foreign wars,/ to be provoked by great power and evil counsel,/ by peoples strange, and crude and barbarous/ . . . were it not for that supreme/ vessel of wisdom, faith and love,/ who provides for you with his money and advice/ . . . you have someone to correct you,/ with his wise actions . . . without laying down the law [*sanza dar norma*]/ . . . "God has provided for you well, as with a monarch . . ." Cosimo, however, resembled not contemporary kings and princes but the more acceptable heroes of Greek democracy and Roman republic: "as for Athens the good Solon,/ and the great Lycurgus in Lacedemonia,/ and Trismegistus among the Egyptians,/ acquiring neither profit nor gain,/ behaving rather like your son,/ a new Numa Pompilius,/ sterner toward his *patria* than Mucius/ or Regulus or Curtius;/ therefore give thanks to the prime Mover/ who has allowed to you such a shining splendor."

Diplomacy was Cosimo's special gift or genius. He mobilized all his disciplined energies, his entrepreneurial skills, and his international contacts to advance the interests of the commune through negotiation. Often mistrustful and even scornful of appearances, when Cosimo was summoned in 1428 while on business in Padua to serve as ambassador to Venice, he sent home to Florence for his ceremonial armor in order to cut a more impressive figure on the commune's behalf.[157] Cosimo expended large sums to help support Florentine wars, but he negotiated constantly for peace. When this was finally established for an extended period by the Treaty of Lodi in 1454, it was thanks to Cosimo's inspired diplomacy, together with the efforts of his friend Francesco Sforza. Such achievements were acknowledged explicitly in his recognition as Florence's most authoritative citizen during his lifetime, and his memorialization as *pater patriae* after his death. The communal decree according him this final honor spoke of how "he conducted himself in war and in peace to the fullest and ultimate benefit of the republic . . . and always sought with all possible piety to preserve and aid his *patria*, and to augment its glory . . ."[158]

Cosimo's first direct experience of warfare dated from 1406. At the age of seventeen he was one of a group of young patricians held as hostages while terms were arranged between Pisa and its conquerors, Florence and her *condottiere* Muzio Attendolo, Francesco Sforza's father. In these negotiations he had been a pawn, but with time Cosimo became as adept at diplomacy as he was at chess, moving his pieces adroitly on the territorial checkerboard of Italy.[159]

Cosimo also made important friendships which benefited the commune in the arena of war and diplomacy. The rulers and *condottieri* of Renaissance Italy were a tight-knit group; Michael Mallett observed that of the 170 or so leading captains in the fifteenth century, over 60 per cent came from only thirteen families, most notably the Sforzeschi and Bracceschi, the Orsini and the Colonna. They were closely connected to one another by service together in the field, and often by marriage as well.[160] Thanks to the Medici bank's network of operations throughout Italy, and especially in Rome, most of these men were also associates and *amici* of Cosimo de' Medici. For example, Gattamelata, the warrior immortalized in Donatello's equestrian monument, had an account with the Medici bank, and wrote several letters to Cosimo, observing "how much goodwill there is between us."[161] Cosimo's relationship with the Orsini, a family of Roman *condottieri*, predated by half a century its cementing with the marriage of Piero di Cosimo's son Lorenzo to Clarice Orsini in 1469.[162]

Carlo Malatesta was the lord of Cesena, and served the commune of Florence as captain of war; Leonardo Bruni wrote a letter of consolation on behalf of the Signoria to his wife and children after his death in 1429. Bruni may also have written the letter addressed six months earlier to Carlo by Cosimo and Lorenzo de' Medici, on the occasion of the death of their father Giovanni, appealing to and confirming the friendship between the two families. A reply to the Medici letter in the name of Carlo Malatesta was composed by Pier Candido Decembrio, then secretary to the duke of Milan. This interesting exchange involving both letters and arms shows how closely these two aspects of the classical and Renaissance worlds were intertwined.[163] Sigismondo Malatesta, lord of Rimini, was also a close friend of Cosimo's, and in his capacity as captain of the Florentine forces in 1436, attended the consecration of the cathedral. Also present on that occasion was Giovanni Vitelleschi, captain of the papal forces; it was he whom the pope sent to intervene in 1433 with the anti-Mediceans wishing to prevent the Priors by force of arms from recalling Cosimo. Later in 1436 Vitelleschi returned to Florence to serve as its archbishop.

The most important of all these associations for Cosimo and for the commune, as observed earlier in several contexts, was the alliance with Francesco Sforza, the greatest of the "uomini di nome," as Cosimo called the *condottieri*.[164] Sforza, acclaimed as a hero by the Florentine populace as well as its leading citizen, was the scion of a dynasty of *condottieri*. His cousin Micheletto Attendolo also played a notable role in Florentine affairs, and was Niccolò da Tolentino's co-commander at the Battle of San Romano. Sforza's father Muzio Attendolo, from an influential and warlike Romagnuol family, was employed by the Florentines in 1402, and was one of the commanders who conquered Pisa for Florence in 1406. After the fall of Pisa, he took service with Niccolò d'Este of Ferrara. He joined the army of the papal-Angevin-Florentine alliance against Ladislas of Naples, and became the principal architect of the celebrated victory of Roccasecca over the Neapolitans in 1411. After he drowned in 1424, his son Francesco held the Sforza companies together.[165] Sforza acted as consultant to the Florentine Signoria on military matters in the late 1420s and early 1430s, when a correspondence began between Sforza and Cosimo which was to last the length of their lives.[166] When Sforza became duke of Milan, his secretary Nicodemo Tranchedini, from Pontremoli, was dispatched to Florence as envoy to the Signoria, and moved into the Medici palace.[167]

Cosimo's particular interest in warriors and warfare may have distinguished him, but it also linked him to the Florentine *popolo* and his fellow patricians. Giovanni Cavalcanti recounted an anecdote of the renowned English *condottiere* Sir John Hawkwood, who fought for Florence in the late trecento; that he was once obliged to tell a Florentine statesman giving him advice about a battle to "go and make cloth and let me manage the army."[168] While Cosimo's appreciation of military issues was outstanding, many Florentine merchant statesmen showed themselves eager to take an active part in warfare, and *pace* Hawkwood, quite a few became expert in the conduct of war by their frequent service as commissioners to *condottieri* in the field.[169] Although Florence posed, and even persisted in seeing herself in the image of David, the beleagured little defender of liberty against the tyrannical princely Goliaths, in fact throughout the fifteenth century the Florentine state pursued an aggressive imperialistic policy dedicated to the domination of Tuscany.[170] As Giovanni di Iacopo Morelli accused his fellow patricians during the deliberations of 1430 that led to the Florentine war against Lucca, "You create war, you lead us into war, you suckle those nourished by war. Florence has never been without war, and she never will be, until you cut off the heads of four of your leading citizens every year."[171]

Just before his death in 1420, Gino di Neri Capponi, an elder statesman of the ruling group and a veteran of the conquest of Pisa, composed some *ricordi*, a patrimony of wisdom to bequeath to his sons. In Capponi's *Ricordi*, concern for his own fame, the honor of the family, and the conduct of the state are as closely intertwined as they are in Cosimo's letters. Like these, many of Capponi's maxims relate to the conduct of war; for example, he declared that "the Commune of Florence will maintain its authority so long as it stands sword in hand against foreign powers . . ."[172] Gino's son Neri took his father's advice, and played a leading part, alongside Cosimo's cousin Bernardo d'Antonio de' Medici, in the defeat of

the Medici enemies and their Milanese backers at Anghiari in 1440. The Capponi presided, as Cosimo's arch-rival Rinaldo degli Albizzi observed, over a huge patronage network, strongly supported by their bellicose provincial allies, the Cancellieri of Pistoia, and the *condottiere* Niccolò Fortebracci.[173] Rinaldo himself had urged the war on Lucca, arguing for a display of force, to which "all just and effective law is amenable . . . Only the sword is competent to judge; you have access to force, and authority over the militia."[174]

War was also, as we saw from the program of performances at San Martino, a great spectator sport of the Florentine populace. Both patricians and plebeians relished tales of the exploits of military heroes past and present, from Hector and Charlemagne to Tolentino and Sforza. Contemporary *condottieri* could themselves be seen as star performers on the Italian public stage. As the humanist Guarino da Verona wrote from the Este court in Ferrara in 1446: "One must feel sorry for this generation in many ways, but amid so much that is bad, one factor above all emerges upon which we may congratulate modern times; they have had the good fortune to witness a revival of the long lost art of warfare; foreigners have for some time been dispensed with, and Italy has had a more than adequate fund of military talent of her own."[175]

The Medici and the commune's monuments to its condottieri

Representations of soldiers and battles were rooted firmly in formal traditions for imaging fame and defamation, triumph, and defeat. A renewed enthusiasm in the Renaissance for the history of the ancient world, with its emphasis on *res gestae*, on the deeds of great men which brought them fame and glory, gave a humanist imprimatur to the profession of arms. Just as poets praised equally togas and arms, so pictorial cycles of *uomini illustri* honored soldiers as well as scholars. The princes of Italy customarily had themselves commemorated, in life or after their death, in private palaces or in public places, by a variety of military monuments; they struck medals bearing their profiles, which they circulated to their friends and allies; they had portraits painted of themelves in full ceremonial armor; they were glorified in equestrian statues on the Roman model. As Wendy Wegener observed, Cosimo was closely associated with the princely patrons of every important military monument of the mid-fifteenth century.[176] However, none of these was a suitable model for an image of warfare commissioned by a citizen of a republic.

In the Florentine republic the visual representation of soldiers was governed by a different decorum. What was celebrated was not the achievements of an individual, but the glory of honorable warfare in the interest of the city and its people. The imaging of war was the province, not of particular persons, but of the commune. However, Cosimo and the Medici family seem to have been closely associated with communal monuments made in the mid-fifteenth century to honor Florence's leading *condottieri*.

The Florentine *popolo* expressed its admiration for its *condottieri*, as for its leading humanists, theologians and poets, with splendid public funerals and commemorative monuments in the cathedral. A program of cenotaphs and tombs was proposed in the 1390s. The plan for Hawkwood's monument was first outlined in the Deliberazioni of the Signoria and its colleges in 1393, a year before his death. This unprecedented proposal to honor a still-living soldier was made with reference to the "magnificent and faithful actions redounding to the honor and magnificence of the Florentine republic on the part of the said lord Giovanni . . ." The monument "to be decorated with stone and marble . . . as much for the magnificence of the commune of Florence as for the honor and perpetual fame of the said lord Giovanni . . ." but was subsequently shelved; Agnolo Gaddi and Giuliano d'Arrigo (Pesello) were commissioned to paint a fresco in Hawkwood's honor in December 1395.[177] Thirty years later, in July 1433, the Opera del Duomo, in accordance with its customary procedure, announced a competition for a grand monument to Hawkwood.[178]

No explanation is offered in the documents relating to the commission as to why a new monument was to be made, and in a sense, none is needed. The amount of Florentine attention and resources devoted to warfare in the first half of the fifteenth century eminently justified, and indeed required, the memorialization and idealization of its heroes. The decades intervening since Hawkwood's death had produced few unambiguously honorable warriors for Florence. Conversely, in July 1433 the commune had something it needed to celebrate, having just signed a peace with Lucca and her Milanese allies that ended almost four years of expensive and inconclusive hostilities.

Hawkwood's image was one the rulers of Florence wanted to keep before the public eye. The Englishman had died in 1394, when Cosimo was only five years old, but the rehearsal of his deeds in poetry and song kept his memory alive in the public mind. He appeared in one of Sacchetti's much read *Trecentonovelle*; and his amenability to the commune's orders and his splendid funeral at the commune's expense were described in a popular poem still copied and recited in the mid-fifteenth century.[179] At

that time Cavalcanti, in his classicizing treatise on great statesmen and soldiers, represented Hawkwood as indispensable to Florence, "no less for the defence of our liberty, than to the offense of our enemy . . . This excellent man went almost every morning to confer with our war committee [*Dieci*]; and as often as not it was he who gave them advice rather than they who advised him. This was only possible because he was so solicitous of our well-being."[180] Florentine problems with foreign mercenaries throughout the early decades of the fifteenth century had made Hawkwood a classic exemplum of the sort of military leadership Florence sorely needed.

Less than two months after the competition was announced, Cosimo was exiled by an anti-Medicean faction of the ruling elite led by the Albizzi. After one brief and difficult year in power the latter were exiled in their turn. The commission for the Hawkwood monument was again put on hold, and only finally awarded some three years later, in May 1436. This was just two months after the splendid ceremony of the consecration of the cathedral that marked the effective completion of Brunelleschi's cupola. The Hawkwood commission was made, with the request that it be expedited for the honor of the commune, during the term of office of Cosimo's cousin Giovenco d'Antonio de' Medici, who was appointed as one of the *operai* of Santa Maria del Fiore three weeks before its consecration, on the first day of March, 1436. In view of this, and of Cosimo's manifest interest in both Florentine warriors and the decoration of the cathedral, it is likely that he lent his support to the implementation of the scheme for the Hawkwood monument.[181] However, the initiative to revive it was taken while the opposing regime was in the ascendant, and it would no doubt have been realized under the aegis of the Albizzi faction, had they been victorious instead. Rinaldo degli Albizzi and his son Ormanno, like Cosimo and his cousin Averardo, had served their city in the war against Lucca with diligence and passion, and all had identified themselves publicly with a patriotic devotion to honorable warfare. Bruni's treatise on this subject, the *De Militia*, was dedicated to Rinaldo degli Albizzi, who was himself a knight.[182]

The commission was awarded to Uccello and completed within an astonishingly short time – just one month. The patrons promptly pronounced it unacceptable, and ordered it to be destroyed, "because it is not depicted as it should be."[183] This intriguing rejection was neither explained nor justified; a week after they condemned the fresco, the *operai* ordered Uccello to paint it again. The second version was approved, and the salary Uccello eventually received took account of his having done the work twice. The final version has been

128   Paolo Uccello, *Sir John Hawkwood*, Florence, cathedral

129   Andrea del Castagno, *Niccolò da Tolentino*, Florence, cathedral

described not only as "the first true Renaissance equestrian monument," but also as "one of the incunabula of systematic perspective construction," and its effect would have been even more startling in its original position higher up on the wall, seen from a lower viewing point which would have heightened the effects of foreshortening (fig. 128).[184]

Twenty years later the commune commissioned from Castagno, who may have been Uccello's pupil,[185] a matching fresco memorializing Niccolò da Tolentino, similar in its imposing size and in its simulation of an equestrian monument, but this time one in marble rather than bronze (fig. 129). The dating, sequence, and relation of these communal images of warriors and warfare to Uccello's domestic panels has been much debated.[186] Bernardetto de' Medici, a soldier himself and a close friend of Niccolò da Tolentino, was Gonfalonier of Justice in 1455 when Castagno, who had previously worked for both Bernardetto and Orlando de' Medici, was commissioned to paint the picture of Tolentino.[187] It seems likely either that Uccello was chosen to paint the cathedral fresco because of his performance in the domestic panels, or that these were commissioned because the patron was impressed by the painting he saw in the cathedral. Certainly their patriotic subjects, their artists, and their associations with the Medici constitute a strong link between these works. However, their very particular relevance to Cosimo's strong personal interest in warfare has not been sufficiently appreciated.

★   ★   ★

Cosimo, Niccolò da Tolentino, and the war with Lucca; a very personal engagement

Where once art historians unfamiliar with Florentine history were puzzled by the patron's choice of what they saw as an obscure battle and an unlikely hero, now ample evidence has been assembled to explain the importance of San Romano and Niccolò da Tolentino in fifteenth-century Florentine eyes, and to show how closely Cosimo and his family were identified with this key engagement and its popular hero. The disastrous war against Lucca, originally intended to exploit the success of some border raids by Niccolò Fortebracci, then in Florentine employ, began in December 1429. Vast sums were levied in taxes to meet its enormous expense, as other *condottieri*, among them Micheletto de Attendolis, Sforza's cousin, and originally the Florentine Captain General, threatened to change sides if their exorbitant demands were not met. Milan and Siena joined the alliance against Florence, and the Visconti duke Filippo Maria lent Lucca the leading Milanese *condottiere* Niccolò Piccinino, who in 1424–5 had fought for Florence against the Visconti, as well as briefly Francesco Sforza, who had previously served the Florentines as a military advisor.

Florence saw the integrity of her defences, and even her very territory, as seriously threatened; as the commissioners reported from the field precisely a year after the war began, "Now it is no longer a matter of obtaining Lucca, but of preserving our own state."[188] The reputations of every leader of the ruling elite became hostage to the war effort, and in the pursuit of elusive success, many were in fact tarnished. Even Brunelleschi, revered for his design of the cathedral's cupola as a "divine intellect," was temporarily disgraced when his scheme to divert the Serchio river to flood Lucca failed, and the encampment of the Florentine army laying siege to the city was inundated instead.[189] After three and a half years the engagement at San Romano in June 1432 was the first Florentine victory of the war, and even there, the story spread that Niccolò da Tolentino, appointed the previous month to replace Micheletto, was saved by a hair's breadth from the disastrous consequences of a reckless assault when Micheletto arrived at the last moment to relieve him.[190]

In the climate of feeling prevailing in Florence, Tolentino was extravagantly acclaimed for having restored the city's fortunes. As one popular poet sang: "O triumphant Florence, deck yourself out,/ rejoice in eternity, glorious people,/ for you have the bold and brave and powerful/ new Mars for your faithful star,/ that is, your Tolentino, whom all the world calls/ more than others famous, by virtue of arms,/for it is he who returns victorious,/ so that your glory is exalted and renewed./ You need fear no more the eagle or the viper,/since your reason and his expertise take care/of all those who have wrongly attacked you,/demolishing and casting down your enemies . . ."[191] Even the relatively austere Giovanni Rucellai, who took no active part in the war, wrote in retrospect in his *zibaldone* of San Romano that the rout of the enemy camp by Tolentino and Micheletto, "our captains and *condottieri* . . . was considered the greatest and best news that the commune of Florence ever had, for our finances had been greatly depleted by the long war, and if on the contrary we had been routed, we would have been driven off."[192]

In the months following the battle, both Tolentino and Micheletto de Attendolis were made honorary citizens of Florence, and Averardo de' Medici wrote to Micheletto: "My sweet companion, let my writing renew the great faith I have in you and the great love I bear you; and above all the others I would like you and Niccholò to be famous and victorious . . . and soon you will have more wealth than you could want and in addition to this the hearts of the men of this city, which you should not value less, but consider of the greatest importance."[193]

The official representatives of the commune were quick to join in the chorus of praise, and to score it in accord with the main themes of civic interest and ideology. On the first anniversary of the battle, or rather on the feastday of the city's patron saint, 24 June 1433, Leonardo Bruni, chancellor of the republic and chief architect of Florence's image in its wars against Milan, delivered an oration honoring Tolentino from the *ringhiera*, the public platform outside the palace of the Priors. As Randolph Starn and Loren Partridge observed, this showed just how much the unpopular and ultimately unresolved war with Lucca still needed to be reconciled and re-presented to the Florentine people. This fact is further confirmed by the appearance of the oration in many personal compilations around mid-century, along with a treatise by Bruni with the revealing title: "A work written in defence of the people of Florence since certain calumniators have condemned the enterprise of the war with Lucca undertaken by the said Florentine people."[194]

Speaking of the Battle of San Romano, Bruni declared: "On that day it may truly be said that the health of this city began to recover from its long and wretched sufferings, and that it regained vigour and enlightenment, learning and hope."[195] Tolentino was praised in terms practically identical to those that had supposedly distinguished Hawkwood: he "deserved even higher honor than the philosopher," since arms are necessary to defend "life, liberty and everything dear to man." Inverting

Cicero's well-known phrase "Cedant arma togae, concedat laurea laudi," Bruni declared that "to the sublime and glorious exercise" of the discipline of arms, "all other human endeavours render honour . . . Learning, literature, eloquence, none of these is equal to the glory won in battle."[196] In the councils of the late 1440s Cosimo de' Medici was also to refer to warfare as a matter of the defence of liberty; indeed a play on both Cicero and Bruni might be discerned in Cosimo's speech to a Pratica of September 1448. On that occasion he questioned whether the Florentine contest with Ladislas of Naples was in fact "a struggle for liberty" in which "no expense ought to be spared."[197]

Bruni's epideiectic rhetoric and his praise of classical monuments to military heroes set the stage for the later monument to Tolentino. He appealed to his listeners' familiarity with the analogy between verbal and visual rhetoric when he argued in his oration "that the statues of valiant men declare that the practice of arms is the most excellent . . ." and indeed pointed to the ancient monuments to generals like Romulus, Camillus, the Scipios, and Caesar "as visual proof of the excellence of their achievements."[198] Uccello's panels, like the encomia for Tolentino, represented him as riding to the rescue of the republic's liberty, to the defence of which Cosimo was dedicated.

However, the Medici family's personal stake in the war with Lucca had been greater than that of most Florentine citizens. Rinaldo degli Albizzi and Neri Capponi had been its most vociferous advocates, and both played leading roles in its conduct. Cosimo, although pessimistic about its outcome – in October 1430 he wrote to his cousin Averardo: "It doesn't seem to me that the affair of Lucca is going to turn out as successfully as expected, which I regret"[199] – committed himself to its direction. As he told Averardo in 1429: "It seems to me that although we did not favor this undertaking, seeing that the matter has reached the point where the honor of the commune is involved, that everyone must give it every possible support . . ."[200] Cosimo was a member of the Ten of War for extensive periods of time in its crucial phase, and he negotiated the ultimate peace.

Averardo de' Medici, as a commissioner in Pisa, was much nearer to the field than the officials in Florence, and dedicated all his energies to victory. Cosimo's dozens of letters to his cousin between 1429 and 1432 are taken up with the details of the combat and Averardo's everyday negotiations with its *condottieri*.[201] Averardo's son and three sons-in-law, Alamanno Salviati, Antonio di Salvestro Serristori, and Giannozzo Gianfigliazzi, advised him on occasion to refuse office; the latter wrote to him in 1431: "By God I know that you take upon yourself too many

discomforts and too much hard work. It is a fine thing to carry out the business of your commune faithfully, but you must still be willing to look after your health and I beg you to do so."[202] Niccolò Tinucci, a devoted friend and Medici partisan, wrote to Averardo once that he found him so depressed at the Florentine setbacks that until things improved, "I couldn't have hoped with all the savors of Damascus or Capri to have restored your appetite." Averardo himself confessed to his son Giuliano in December 1431: "I am driven half mad by not being able to do any good."[203]

He exhorted his fellow patricians in a *pratica* of 1430: "We must not be sparing with our wealth, lest this should threaten the success of our cause: we must employ all the men and captains we need."[204] Cosimo agreed; as he wrote to his cousin in September 1431: "We have begun to pay the captain's chancellor and by tomorrow this will amount in cash and in promises to ten thousand florins, and the other foot soldiers and cavalry will receive their pay right away. But if for lack of money we cannot do this as promptly as we need to, and time passes without any results, then the proverb that the poor man can never achieve anything good will be proved true." This maxim might well have been the motto for Cosimo's life.[205] The Medici and their friends were as good as their word; while their loans to the commune were at high interest, they invested heavily in what seemed at the time an improbable victory, and the fragmentary financial records suggest that Cosimo lost money rather than profiting from these loans. Serristori, Averardo's son-in-law, his partner Andrea Pazzi, and Cosimo himself both financed and directed the war as Ufficiali del Banco, an emergency office created to cope with the monetary crisis.[206]

Quite a number of historians and several of Cosimo's contemporaries suggest that his truthful boast that he paid the troops of the commune out of his own pocket – he was the state's largest creditor for 27 per cent of the total amount it borrowed – was in fact a claim that he personally commanded the loyalty of their Captain General, Niccolò da Tolentino. Cavalcanti put into Rinaldo degli Albizzi's mouth a speech justifying Cosimo's arrest on the grounds that in the recent war Cosimo had given "untold loans and payments to soldiers" like Tolentino, hoping to make himself tyrant of the city.[207] There is no doubt that it was his leading role in the Lucchese war that made Cosimo de' Medici the leading citizen of Florence and indispensable to its government, but there is no evidence to support any allegations of conspiracy. Indeed Cosimo's private letters demonstrate quite the contrary; despite a characteristic caution that led him once to advise Averardo that "we should not attempt to be among the Dieci this time: partly to give a share to others, and furthermore because it seems to me that considering the divisions within our city, this group can't do very well,"[208] ultimately Cosimo put all his skills and resources at the service of the commune.

However, it is certainly true that by the time Cosimo de' Medici went to Ferrara to negotiate the peace with Lucca and its Milanese allies in May 1433, Tolentino had become his intimate friend and supporter, along with several other major military commanders in the peninsula. There are numerous letters dating from the 1420s from Cosimo, his brother Lorenzo, and his cousins Averardo and Bernardetto d'Antonio, testifying to their intimacy with Tolentino. In the inventory of gifts presented to Lorenzo during his service as the commune's ambassador to Venice and Milan in 1429/30, there is listed "a straw hat, very fine," from Niccolò da Tolentino. Around the same time, Vanni de' Medici wrote to Averardo that he hoped to obtain a position in the service of the marquess of Ferrara or of Modena through Tolentino's influence.[209]

When in September 1433, less than two months after the signing of the peace with Lucca, an anti-Medicean Signoria arrested Cosimo, they immediately contacted the Captain General to express the Priors' anxiety that he should understand the reasons for their action.[210] As Cosimo wrote in his *Ricordi*: "My brother Lorenzo in the Mugello and my cousin Averardo in Pisa were notified . . . likewise my very great friend, Niccolò da Tolentino . . . [who] having heard how things stood, proceeded on the morning of the 8th with all his company to Lastra, with the intention of raising a rebellion in Florentine territory."

The Signoria ordered Tolentino to return at once to Pisa, where he was stationed. According to Cosimo, Bernardetto de' Medici, who had served with him in the field, was exempted from the proscriptions against the Medici family out of respect for, or rather fear of Tolentino. "The Captain and Lorenzo were advised not to stir up a revolt, which might be the occasion of my coming to harm, which they accepted, and although those who gave this advice were relatives and friends, and acting with good intentions, it was not good advice, because if they had gone ahead, I should have been free, and those who were the occasion of my plight would have been destroyed."[211] However, once his banishment became law, Cosimo went obediently into exile, and when approached by the Milanese with offers of aid, refused them, declaring that he would return to Florence only as he had left it, by order of the Signoria.[212]

Tolentino retained the baton of Captain General of the Florentine forces under the the anti-Medicean regime, and was sent to fight an engagement at Castel Bolognese,

where he was captured by the Milanese *condottiere* Niccolò Piccinino in August 1434, a month before Cosimo's recall from exile. Although their commander was in prison, Cosimo continued to enjoy the protection and support of Tolentino's company, who stationed themselves outside the Medici house in Florence while a *parlamento* of the people was summoned to grant authority to a Balìa to reform the state, recalling the Medici and banishing their opponents instead.[213] In March 1435 Tolentino died, still a prisoner of the duke of Milan.[214] Tolentino's body was brought back to Florence and buried in the choir of the cathedral with the greatest possible honor; in the process no less than 2,567 pounds of wax were consumed. Pietro Pietriboni described his magnificent funeral. He first lay in state in the baptistery, surrounded by twenty servants all dressed in black, with thirty torches. A ceremony in front of the palace of the Priors was attended by the representatives of the pope and various kings, as well as all the major Florentine dignitaries and a large body of citizens. Finally he was interred in Santa Maria del Fiore.[215] Thus the subject of the Battle of San Romano, and Niccolò da Tolentino's role in it was eminently appropriate to represent the Medici family's civic pride, as well as their patriotic personal involvement in the war with Lucca. Similarly, on a much lesser scale, a pair of *cassoni* apparently made for the Capponi family probably commemorated Neri's role in the Battle of Anghiari in 1440.[216]

Inventorying the battlefield; playing with the possibilities of perspective

It is clear, however, that Uccello's three enormous pictures were designed for the personal pleasure of the patron. Their tone is very different from that of the classicizing rhetorical statements about the commune's requirements of warriors made by the pair of frescoes for the cathedral. As Partridge and Starn pointed out, the San Romano trilogy is more medieval than classical; less descriptive of nature, than a narrative of meaning. Uccello created for his patron a painted history, not merely of three phases in a particular battle, but a narrative of warfare whose rhetoric parallels the many written accounts of *res gestae* collected in the libraries of Cosimo and his elder son Piero. Uccello's pictures reveal perspective to be "a laboriously artificial construction."[217] In the tension they create between illusion and artifice, so troubling to modern critics, they represent precisely the virtues Cosimo celebrated in his poem dedicated to Francesco Sforza, Tolentino's successor as his friend and ally, and the commune's Captain General; they are the epitome of "art, ingenuity, order and measure." Over-shadowed by historians' concern with the anti-classical elements of Uccello's work, with its "disturbing charm," at best "an interpretation of classicism more Romanesque than Roman,"[218] the particularity of this commission has been insufficiently stressed. The scenes of San Romano bespeak a profound and intimate fascination on the part, not only of the artist, but also of the patron, with the objects and mechanics of warfare.

As Starn and Partridge observed, these are a visual representation of "the endless detail of war." They are "the quartermaster's dream or nightmare," an inventory of the battlefield: "the armorer's rivets, the fittings on the horses, the blacksmith's horseshoes and horseshoe nails are all accounted for."[219] De Robertis drew attention to the play in popular poetry with the form of the mercantile inventory, the accounting mentality of the Florentine run riot. In his images of war Uccello was very much concerned with the numbers — of "horses and knights (at least 35), foot soldiers (20), shields (5), lances (20), halberds (4), crossbows (9), trumpets (4) . . ."[220] So too was Cosimo in his letters. He wrote to Averardo as commissioner in the field in August 1431: "150 florins have recently been paid out, as you will be advised in a letter from the officials, and if you want to keep account, you will have over there 600 footsoldiers, 50 from the district, 300 bowmen and cavalry . . . and moreover when our people arrive you can let some peasants go, and they are also sending some stonemasons and bricklayers, so you will be able to wage a decent war . . ."[221]

Cosimo was a connoisseur of good warfare, and the "huomo di nome," the star of the battlefield, was someone he admired and appreciated, even when he fought on the opposing side. He once wrote to Averardo recommending to him the example of their enemy, Niccolò Piccinino, in providing for his troops far more ingeniously than the Florentine commissioners, including his cousin. "We saw what Niccolò Piccinino did last year, that he was still engaged in the campaign when winter came and he had no money; and at one point he had to go to Staggia and then Arezzo and then immediately from Arezzo into Lombardy; and although you could say that there are few who are his equals, we will see what the Sienese troops who are over-running our entire *contado* will do, and they are less than 500 cavalry and nine renowned leaders." By contrast the Florentine commander Micheletto de' Attendolis

has two thousand enlisted cavalry without the other troops and altogether in three months you have gone four miles. I know that he who holds the banner must proceed with caution, but there is no need to be so

careful that you achieve nothing. Worrying about the Lombard troops who are two hundred miles away seems to me a vain concern, because you will always hear about whoever is advancing toward you in time to withdraw; and I also think that you are very ill advised about the movements of the enemy, not only those in Lombardy but also those in Tuscany, and the first concern of those desiring an honorable outcome should be to know about the enemy.

This last adage was a piece of advice taken directly from a passage of Caesar's *Commentaries* marked by Cosimo with a "nota bene" in the margin of his copy.[222]

Cosimo's cousin Bernardetto de' Medici had been an eyewitness of the Battle of San Romano, assisting Luca degli Albizzi, a Medici partisan who was dispatched as special envoy to Tolentino's camp in May 1432. If texts describing the details of the battle were needed, there were plenty circulating in Florence and available to patron and painter.[223] But clearly Uccello's images do not explicate any one or combination of these. What they represent, as Starn and Partridge astutely recognized, is "a collective inheritance of heroic deeds and noble gestures," woven into a narrative, with the aid of "simplifying formulas which aid and acclaim memory as they had done when the epic was a chant or song . . . Uccello's formal patterning has its analogue in the language and the syntax of the epic style."[224]

This is precisely the style of representing history to which performances at San Martino had accustomed a Florentine audience, and indeed the *Song of Roland* at Roncevalles, compared by Partridge and Starn with Uccello's representations of San Romano, was in fact a favorite of the *cantori in panca*, as it was of the artist Benedetto da Maiano, who owned a copy of the history of Charlemagne's wars. "You would have seen, that day, the earth bestrewn . . . many spear shafts sundered, broken in two . . . men dead and wounded and bleeding,/one lies face up, [another] face down." A horse rears "quick and spirited,/ his hooves high-arched, the quick legs long and flat,/short in the thigh, wide in the rump, long in the flanks,/ and the backbone so high, a battlehorse! . . . The country round is wide . . . helmets shine . . . high pitched trumpets sound, their voices clear . . . thundering the pursuit."[225] The artist's role as shaper of the pictorial narrative is ingeniously asserted in the shield in the Florence panel, a masterly conceit of perspective representation. It bears a scroll or pennant with Uccello's name on it — "Pauli Ugieli opus," — "a tool and token of deeds done," the artist's own *res gestae* (fig. 126).[226]

Starn and Partridge further suggested that in the commission of a work like Uccello's, "the citizen . . . was cast as the impresario and connoisseur of the action which he, not the soldier, had the wherewithal to produce, and the power to consign to fame or to oblivion."[227] Cosimo's letters confirm that this was precisely how he saw his own and his fellow patricians' role. Indeed, if there is a governing or explicating text for Uccello's panels it could be Cosimo's exhortation to Averardo on the battlefield to have faith in his own discrimination, in war as in art: "Although we do not have the expertise in feats of war of those who practice it continually, nevertheless, seeing what others do, we are able to judge who does it better. I believe that although you are not a great painter, nevertheless you would judge the figures of Giotto to be better than those of Balzanello."[228]

Vasari referred to Uccello as "the most delightful and fanciful talent in the art of painting since Giotto." Paul Barolsky, taking up this aspect of Uccello's work, observed the endless possibilities in these panels for amusement and diversion.[229] Surface patterns of color play against perspective, narrative against rhetoric, one point of view against another (figs. 130 and 131). As Cosimo was noted for the ambiguity of his speech, Uccello was remarkable for the ambiguity of his perspective effects, employing not the single-point perspective of Brunelleschi and Alberti, but as Franco and Stefano Borsi suggested, integrating the possibility of an oblique with a perpendicular vision, which varied according to the movements of the observer or of his eye, allowing for his emotional and psychological participation.[230] Play, as we have seen, was an important element in Florentine popular culture. Here the pleasure of artist and patron in such play is conflated, as love and war were conflated in other domestic images for *cassoni* and *deschi da parto*, through metaphors like the one for making love: "to break a lance."

Uccello's "geometric naturalism and realistic geometry"[231] play off art against nature. Reality and representation are set against one another like the action played before the scenery on a painted curtain.[232] There is play as well between the battle and the tournament; the horses and men on foot in the background are depicted in the fields as though on a checkerboard. What Borsi and Borsi described as a "sort of material transfer between the depicted object and the depiction itself," the building up of substance on the painted surfaces with pastiglia and encrustation, like "a colossal miniature,"[233] amounts to a play between painting and decoration, seen in so many objects in the Medici palace, including Gozzoli's frescoes for the chapel, and the ubiquitous intarsia work.

What must have been the epic sweep of the original scenes is somewhat spoilt by the cutting down of the panels to fit a new setting, signaled by the amputated standards. But what remains is a patchwork of arms, devices, and trademarks. *Mazzocchi*, the trademark of the student of perspective, are everywhere. There is Tolentino's fantastic damask hat; his device of the Solomon's or Gordian knot; the oranges, perhaps standing for Medici *palle*; a hint of ring and feathers in the Paris panel; a detail of the mythical unicorn, and a myriad of the plumed helmets, decorated harness, and pennants with which the *cassoni* in Cosimo's *camera* and *studio* were filled. Cosimo's collection of elaborately decorated arms and armor for ceremonies and jousts, described in the inventory of the *casa vecchia* in 1417/18, is the corollary of the collection of objects depicted in Uccello's panels.[234]

Medici interest in images of fame and defamation

While there is every good reason why Cosimo should have commissioned the paintings representing Niccolò da Tolentino's victory of 1432, there might seem to be even better ones for his preferring the Battle of Anghiari, won by Florence in 1440. The fact that the Uccello panels represent San Romano might suggest that they were completed before 1440, or it might contribute to an argument the Cosimo was not their patron.[235] Conversely, insofar as the Florentine victory at Anghiari marked the definitive defeat of the rebellion of exiled Medici enemies assisted by the Milanese, it was a major triumph both for Cosimo and the commune. It was hailed as such in a series of celebrations marked by the illumination of various public buildings, including Brunelleschi's newly completed cupola. The relief felt by the citizens of Florence was particularly immediate and personal, since the incursions of Milanese soldiers into Tuscan territory, raiding and ravaging the countryside, had terrified them.[236]

By 1440 Francesco Sforza had detached himself from the Visconti and begun to make his play for the lordship of Milan, with the support of Cosimo de' Medici and the Florentine state. In the spring of 1440 the Milanese *condottiere* Niccolò Piccinino, vanquished in Lombardy by Sforza, who had liberated Verona and Brescia from Visconti rule, attacked northeast Tuscany. He had with him Rinaldo degli Albizzi, and indeed took the Mugello as far as Torre a Vaglia. Piccinino enjoyed the support of the counts of Poppi, who invited him into the Casentino. Sforza offered to come to Cosimo's aid there, but in the end Florence relied on its citizen commanders. These were Cosimo's friends and allies Neri Capponi, Bartolomeo Orlandini, and Bernardetto de' Medici, with the help of Sforza's troops under a Roman lieutenant from the Orsini family, Lorenzo de' Medici's future in-laws. They defeated the Milanese and the Florentine rebels

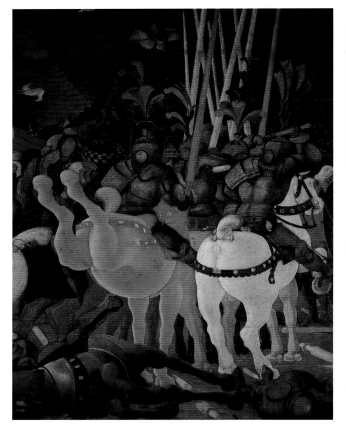 

130   Paolo Uccello, *The Battle of San Romano*, detail of fig. 126   131   Paolo Uccello, *The Battle of San Romano*, detail of fig. 126

near the town of Anghiari, in the territory of the counts of Poppi, in June 1440.[237]

The verses written by the commune's herald Anselmo Calderoni in celebration of their victory suggest that Florentines had seen this battle almost as a crusade. They gave thanks to God for confirming the rightness of Medici leadership and its alliance with Sforza against Milan. "O Lord, we praise you, all of us singing,/ together with your Mother the glorious Virgin,/ and praising all the apostles/ and especially the great Baptist/ with all the court of heaven/ portrayed in the form of a white rose,/ since it is the day when he who opens the portals/ of Paradise admits the Florentine people,/ who were victorious by just Fortune/ against the evil Niccolò Piccino/ and his followers; for they were never safe/ until he crossed the Appenines." The heroes of the day were "Neri di Gino, the sovereign commander/ in whom the other paladins fitly put their faith,/ then the honest captain of the Orsini/ and Bernardo de' Medici along with him,/ who held the standard in his hand . . . And all honor to the

men of Sforza,/ who enforced the triumph of the Holy League,/ pursuing and driving out the men of the duke."[238]

Anghiari soon became the subject of a number of images of fame and defamation. The painted panels of *cassoni* made around this time represented the *res gestae* of living patricians on the Florentine battlefields of Pisa and Anghiari in terms identical with battles fought by the Romans and Gauls in the ancient world. Anghiari was the battle assigned to Leonardo da Vinci – specifically the episode of the fight for the standard, held by Bernardo de' Medici – when he and Michelangelo were commissioned in 1504 by the restored republic to paint matching frescoes for great hall of the palace of the Signoria. The victors of this battle were to be enshrined in that hall of fame, just as in 1440 the vanquished had been depicted in infamy on the walls of the Palace of Justice by Andrea del Castagno, henceforth known as "Andrea degli Impiccati," the painter of the hanged men. Traitors to their country, among the sinners consigned by Dante to the deepest circles of hell, were customarily depicted in public places hanging upside down, as may be seen from the handful of drawings of them that survive.[239]

On 19 October 1455 the Signoria and its colleges deliberated that in view of the honor and glory he had brought to the commune, Niccolò da Tolentino should be commemorated with a large painting resembling that of Hawkwood, "as soon as possible."[240] Once again, no explanation was offered for the commemoration at this particular moment of a hero twenty years dead. There were long delays in the realization of many projects of the Opera del Duomo. However, the Signoria's commission at this time might reasonably be related to Bernardetto de' Medici's tenure as Gonfalonier of Justice.

In view of the challenges of the mid-fifties to the Medici regime, 1455 was as good a time as any to put before the Florentine people an image of the role of the Medici and their friends in the wars whose success had paved the way for the peace. The choice of Castagno as the artist seems natural enough in view of his patronage by Bernardetto and other members of the Medici family at Santissima Annunziata,[241] and his conclusion of the series of mid-century monuments to Florence's wars might have appeared as the depiction of an appropriately happy ending by the author of the *pitture infamanti* of those defeated at Anghiari. It is perhaps piquant to observe that while the commune was obliged, for lack of finance, to commemorate its heroes with *faux sculpture*, Cosimo and his sons could afford the real thing in Donatello's magnificent bronze monuments to civic virtue made for the courtyard and garden of the Medici palace.

HEROES CLASSICAL, CHRISTIAN, AND CIVIC: DONATELLO'S *DAVID* AND *JUDITH AND HOLOFERNES: THE LABORS OF HERCULES*

Most of the commissions clearly attributable to Cosimo were for the building and embellishment of churches and chapels. Although naturally the themes of their decoration were Christian, Medici church buildings and images also made major stylistic contributions to the revival of antique forms and the classicizing spirit that characterized the early Florentine Renaissance. In the decoration of the Medici palace, the family's fascination with the antique had free reign, and finds its most remarkable expression in two bronze statues by Donatello, the centerpieces of the courtyard and garden of the new palace at the time of Cosimo's death in 1464.

The subjects of the statues were two biblical exemplars of fortitude and patriotic virtue – David, who slew the Philistine Goliath, and Judith, who to save the Hebrew people from oppression beheaded the Philistine general Holofernes (figs. 132 and 133). The compelling dramas of this pair of Christian heroes were represented in forms heavily indebted to classical inspiration.[242] Moreover, like many of the legendary masterpieces of antique art, these statues were cast in bronze. In the classical world the use of bronze, an extremely expensive material requiring great skill in its handling, conferred a special dignity and nobility on works of art, as readers of Pliny, among them Cosimo and his friends, well knew. In the early Renaissance large bronze sculptures were reserved to the monuments of *condottieri* and princes, like the equestrian statue of Gattamelata in Padua, or in republican Florence to the commissions of the commune or the guilds or other corporate bodies, such as the Parte Guelfa's *Saint Louis of Toulouse* for Orsanmichele.[243] The appearance of these two statues in the Medici palace was therefore extraordinary, and opens up a whole new perspective on Cosimo and his patronage oeuvre.

There are no documents directly concerning the commission of the Medici statues. Questions of their date and patronage have long preoccupied scholars of the field. Closer attention recently accorded inscriptions originally attached to the works, included in miscellanies of humanist literature, the Latin equivalents of the vernacular scrapbooks surveyed in part 2 of this study, has served to clarify the terms in which they were presented to their contemporary audience, as well as to confirm their association with the Medici and their significance to the patron as symbols of the patriotic defence of liberty against tyranny. However, the interpretation of the terms "liberty" and "tyranny" remains problematic, along with the precise dating of each of these works, and the question of whether they were commissioned by Cosimo or his elder son Piero.

The last two issues, however interesting, are tangential to the main aims of this study; to consider the commissions of Cosimo's household in his lifetime, and the light they shed on Medici interests and concerns. Nor can information unearthed in the exploration of those themes add much to any understanding of these particular objects in terms of their cultural and textual context, which has already been intensively studied from almost every possible point of view. Moreover, while in most works commissioned by Cosimo and his sons the elements of meaning relating to function, clearly visible in religious commissions, are most revealing of the patron's concerns, in these objects, which are difficult to classify in terms of function, the artist's invention transcends any obvious patronal agenda. Consequently the following account,

132 Donatello, *Judith and Holofernes*, Florence, Palazzo Vecchio

133 (*right*) Donatello, *David*, Florence, Bargello

concentrated on the *David*, is intended mainly to set these statues within the framework of the particular interests of Cosimo and his audience, to consider the variety of ways in which they might have been viewed, and to suggest what new light their presence in the courtyard and the garden of the Medici palace might throw on perceptions of Cosimo's patronage.[244]

Of the two works, the *Judith* is slightly less problematic, from all points of view. Although aesthetically among Donatello's most challenging pieces, it is generally agreed to have been cast at the earliest in the late fifties, its primary subject is obvious, and its message about civic virtue was spelled out in an inscription on its base: "Kingdoms fall through luxury, cities rise by virtues. Behold the neck of pride severed by the hand of humility." A second inscription added by Piero, probably in the mid-1460s, reasserts the Medici family's identification with the republic, and the defence of its liberty. It seems also to refer to the unsuccessful challenge around that time to the Medicean regime. It reads: "The salvation of the state. Piero de' Medici, son of Cosimo, dedicated this statue of a woman both to liberty and to fortitude, whereby the citizens with unvanquished and constant heart might return to the republic."[245]

The name Holofernes was translated in medieval textbooks glossing the biblical story as "he who weakens the fatted calf"; thus representations of him often signified "that particular power of the Devil by which Man was first tempted and seduced: Incontinence, or Luxuria." Extrapolating on this theme are three reliefs of Bacchanalian scenes on the pedestal, illustrating the subjugation of this vice. The subject of Judith and Holofernes, like that of David, usually occurred in a religious cycle, and this was the first time it was used as an individual figure in a secular setting.[246] Whatever else the work might signify, it was clearly intended to convey a moral message generally matching that of the bronze *David*, like its location in the Medici garden, corresponding to *David's* setting in the courtyard.

The origins, date, import, and even the identity of the *David*, on the other hand, have been hotly contested by almost every authority on Renaissance bronzes and Donatello's oeuvre.[247] On grounds of style and of the handling of the bronze,[248] the work has been dated anywhere between 1430 and 1460, and even proposed as the posthumous casting of a Donatello model by another artist.[249] Its patronage has been attributed to Cosimo, to Piero, or to a hypothetical third party, perhaps a communal agency, from whom the Medici subsequently acquired it.[250] Arguments center on whether it was done before, after, or during Donatello's absence from Florence in Padua from 1442,[251] on whether it was made specifi-

cally for the courtyard of the new palace, or acquired while Cosimo and his family still lived in the old Medici house, on when and by whom were made the base and column on which it originally stood, which was crucial to its original impact.[252]

These are issues concerning which various persuasive but conflicting suggestions have been offered, and the consequent arguments may never entirely be resolved. The relatively recent association of an inscription with the *David*, and its attribution to Gentile Becchi, resident priest in the Medici palace and humanist tutor to Lorenzo and Giuliano, has made an important contribution to clarifying the meaning the object bore for its patron and other contemporary viewers. Its inscription read: "The victor is whoever defends the fatherland. God crushes the wrath of an enormous foe. Behold! a boy overcame a great tyrant. Conquer, O citizens!"[253] This is an explicit reiteration of the traditional symbolic significance of David to the citizens of the Florentine commune, rooted in the image of the biblical warrior and statesman of the Psalms. Donatello's marble *David*, made for the Operai del Duomo in 1409, and transferred in 1416 to the Palazzo Vecchio, bore a similar inscription: "To those who fight strongly for the fatherland, God lends aid even against the most terrible foes."[254] However, there remains ample room for disagreement about how the statements concerning liberty and tyranny affixed to Donatello's two statues might be fitted into prevailing views of the Medici and their role vis-à-vis the Florentine state.

A focus on the establishable connotations of the figure of David in the eyes of the Florentine *popolo* provides the most reliable evidence of how the Medici *David* was seen by its patron and audience. They were familiar with both the narrative of the battle of David and Goliath recorded in the book of Samuel, and as noted in relation to Castagno's painted processional shield representing this narrative (fig. 17), with the image from the Psalms, recited constantly in confraternities, of the Lord as David's and Israel's deliverer and shield.[255] In the early fourteenth century Dante had made David a symbol of fortitude, the Christian analogue of the pagan Hercules, who also appears frequently in both public and private contexts, including that of the Medici palace.[256] By the beginning of the fifteenth century the image of the biblical David, earlier represented primarily as a prophet, had come to epitomize for Florentines a patriotic virtue, the heroic defence of the liberty of a small republican commune against larger more centralized states better equipped for warfare.[257]

In the increasingly sophisticated humanistic climate of the early fifteenth century, Florentines had made ever more elaborate use of classical symbols and parallels between their own society and that of Greece and Rome, seeing Florence, like Athens and Rome before it, as the bastion of republican civilization. The role of judicious warfare in the heroic defence of Florentine liberty was the constant theme of Florentine humanist publicists like Bruni, and Florentine statesmen like Cosimo.[258] In the context of Florentine experience well into the 1450s, the liberty of Florence referred to her independence as a sovereign state. The tyrant was any of the predatory Italian powers seeking to swallow up as much of each other's territory as they could, particularly Milan and its Visconti duke. When Cosimo defined his native city as one in which commerce and literature could flourish with leisure, he was speaking in a council debate in the mid-1450s, shortly after his negotiation of the Peace of Lodi, on the apportionment of expenses for war. He argued that Florence's rulers could now spend more of their time and money on cultivating the arts of peace, because after decades of war the essential condition of the city's liberty was assured.[259]

Since Cosimo had long played a leading role in the commune's defence, at any time from the later 1420s it might have seemed to him, and to others, entirely appropriate to have commissioned for his own palace a visual symbol of the victory of the virtuous citizens of Florence over vicious foreign force.[260] Later in the century, when the foreign threat subsided and Lorenzo de' Medici more freely identified the interests of the Florentine state with his own, opponents of this appropriation of power, including Alamanno Rinuccini and Donato Giannotti, cast the Medici in the role of tyrants of Florence who had destroyed the liberties of her ancient republican constitution. In 1494 defenders of a revived republic expelled Lorenzo's sons; they then raided the Medici palace and carried off to the palace of the Signoria a large number of works of art incorporating civic symbols. These included the altarpiece in the Medici chapel representing the patrons of the city and of the Signoria, Saint John the Baptist and Saint Bernard, as well as Donatello's two statues.[261] The contemporary message of these actions is unmistakable, but its relevance to Cosimo's patronage and the statue's political connotations at least thirty years earlier is questionable.[262] The civic and republican symbolism of the bronze statues of Judith and David is as likely to represent the commemoration of Cosimo's loyalty and service to the Florentine state, as a claim of personal authority and power over it.[263]

A study of popular culture helps to reveal the variety of meanings that any image or symbol might bear. There persisted in the context of the liturgy, of confraternal ceremonies and vernacular compilations, the powerful image of David as author of the Psalms, an exemplum of divinely inspired wisdom and virtue. As such, he is cited extensively in Saint Bernard's much-read *Steps of Humility*, as well as by fifteenth-century religious writers, among them San Bernardino, and Sant' Antonino in his manual for living a virtuous life addressed to Dianora Tornabuoni, the sister of Piero's wife Lucrezia, who also owned a copy of this tract. Two manuscripts made for Piero de' Medici from the 1460s oddly juxtapose very different images of David by illustrating the penitential psalms with illuminations loosely based on Donatello's bronze.[264]

David was also an archetype of the exile, and the Medici family's exile from Florence in 1433 was undoubtedly one of the more significant and enduring of the life experiences of Cosimo and his sons.[265] It was natural to men of this period to relate their tribulations to those of the Old Testament sages and prophets, Job being only the most obvious example. Additionally, the humanist-educated youth of the Medici family documentably identified with the exemplary exiles of the classical world. His young cousin Francesco di Giuliano di Averardo was moved by reading Juvenal's *Satires* to compare Cosimo's situation to that of Hannibal, obliged by his fame and conquests to flee his *patria*, and end his days abroad.[266] The image of the triumph of David also evokes the turn of Fortune's wheel which returned the Medici to Florence in 1434. The fickleness of Fortune and the triumph of Fame, equally transient, were themes at the forefront of the minds of many Florentine patricians, and frequently represented in the art they commissioned.[267]

A number of iconographical interpretations of the *David* focus on more esoteric ideas, which might be associated with either Cosimo or his sons on the basis of the works in their libraries. David's sensuality has been plausibly associated with the revival of interest in Epicureanism in Florence during the 1420s and 1430s, after Poggio Bracciolini's rediscovery of Lucretius's *De Rerum Natura* in 1418, and the reformulation of his ideas in Lorenzo Valla's *De voluptate* of 1431. The copy of Lucretius listed in Piero's inventory of 1464 was probably made for Cosimo some time after 1429, since it was a direct copy of Niccoli's transcription.[268] Another work owned by the Medici and related to the humanist enthusiasm for Lucretius was Panormita's *Hermaphrodite*, presented to Cosimo de' Medici in 1425 and passed on, with the progressive addition of ever more splendid illuminations, to his son and grandson.[269]

Homoeroticism, a major theme of Panormita's work, is an obvious context for Donatello's *David*, not in relation to the personal sexual predilections of either patron or

artist, but in view of the fact that an appreciation of the physical beauty of young boys was a notable element, not only of the culture of contemporary Florence, but also of the classical sources of its artistic and literary Renaissance. It is inconceivable, as some writers have argued in adducing the limited if suggestive evidence of Donatello's homosexuality, that an artist could have imposed this sort of personal expression on a patron's conception of a work of art, particularly such an expensive and conspicuous commission. It is perfectly plausible, however, that Cosimo found the figure's homoerotic appeal quite acceptable, as he did Panormita's text.[270] Nor do the solemn civic and moral messages of the bronze *David* preclude a homoerotic subtext. The naturalness with which Florentines accepted the juxtaposition of the sacred and the profane is apparent from the contents of hundreds of *zibaldoni*, and perfectly expressed in Bocaccio's comic euphemism enthusiastically repeated by the cleric/humanist Poggio and other fifteenth-century raconteurs, describing a priest aroused by a beautiful young girl: "He experienced the resurrection of the flesh."[271]

Plato's writings, particularly the *Symposium*, have been proposed as a likely inspiration for particular elements of

134 (*above*) Donatello (attrib.), *Bust of a Youth*, Florence, Bargello

135   Florence, Medici palace, courtyard, roundels based on antique cameos

Donatello's work, suggesting the triumph of spiritual over physical love. From the mid-1450s Cosimo was increasingly fascinated by Neoplatonic ideas, and Ficino's famous translations of Plato for Cosimo were completed in 1463-4. However, a Platonic reading of the *David* does not necessarily imply a late dating for the work. As James Hankins observed, Plato's ideas were influential in Florence much earlier in the century, often through the intermediacy of other classical texts. For example, Rinuccini described Cosimo as quoting from memory the well-known *Dream of Scipio*, "in which Cicero reproduces Plato's argument in the Phaedrus for the immortality of the soul."[272] Bruni made a Latin translation of the *Phaedrus* owned by Piero which was probably done for Cosimo. A passage on the soul from this work has been identified as the source of a medallion from *The Bust of a Youth* attributed to Donatello, and based on a cameo first recorded in the inventory of the collection of Cardinal Pietro Barbo, later Pope Paul II (fig. 134).

Such antique objects were also important visual sources for the *David*. The scene on Goliath's helmet appears to be a Triumph of Love, based on an antique sardonyx cameo which also belonged to Barbo in 1457, eventually becoming part of the Medici collection. The cameo was also used as the prototype for one of a group of roundels based on antique gems decorating the frieze of the Medici palace courtyard. There is ample and growing evidence of the strong interest of Donatello, his fellow artists, his Medici patrons, and their humanist friends, in antique gems and Renaissance plaquettes modeled on them, dating from as early as the 1420s (fig. 135).[273] These gems were frequently loaned, exchanged, and circulated, often as collateral for debts.[274] Francesco Caglioti, suggesting that the similarity between the *David* and a famous Augustan bronze nude, also a psychological study, has been underrated, proposed that Donatello's work might be seen as a sort of "moralizing Spinario." He also observed that it belongs, like Donatello's *Dovizia* for the Florentine commune, to a small group of objects emulating the antique custom of mounting statues of exemplary figures or individuals on columns.[275]

This Medici commission for Donatello perhaps brings into play the popular love of ambiguity and equivocation shared by Florence's greatest patrons and artists, particularly Cosimo and Donatello. Both men were reputed by popular tradition to be given to ingeniously indirect expressions of their attitudes and ideas. A contemporary raconteur observed how Donatello, wishing to convey that the sculptor Lorenzo di Bartoluccio (Ghiberti) was indeed "a small star beside his sun," made imaginative use of the latter's recent sale of an unprofitable property called Lepricino. Asked what was the best thing Lorenzo had ever done, meaning which of his sculptures, Donatello responded smartly, "Selling Lepricino."[276] Cosimo's friends and enemies concurred in ascribing to him an infuriating and intentional ambiguity, from Filelfo's complaint that he was "the sort of person who pretends to be, and pretends not to be all things," to Nicodemo da Pontremoli's observation that "When Cosimo explains what he has in mind he only uses complex and ambiguous words and sentences."[277] The Medici *David* interweaves a variety of themes central to the experience of patron and artist and that of the Florentine *popolo* – civic, military, biblical, heroic, and homoerotic – in a manner that is subtle, intricate, and perhaps ultimately and intentionally gnomic.[278]

Donatello's *David* is an immensely complex and original work whose sources may be suggested but not securely identified in a variety of esoteric texts and images known to Cosimo and his friends. More than any other single commission, it confirms the sophistication of Cosimo's interests and tastes, further developed by his sons in the 1450s and 1460s, but flourishing already in the circle of humanists and artists with which Cosimo surrounded himself in his early manhood and maturity. It is the quintessential product of a longterm collaboration between Donatello's creative *ingegno* and the intelligent patronage of Cosimo and his family, and in consideration of the patron's oeuvre, more perhaps than any other of Cosimo's commissions, it brings us inexorably back to the role of the artist. Embodying perfectly the patron's impulses to self-representation, his preoccupations with civic and Christian virtue, triumph, and fame, articulated through familiar symbols of Florentine culture, the bronze *David* is at the same time uniquely and absolutely Donatello's. It shames the desire to apportion creative credit, to invoke the opposition of patron and artist, by demonstrating the futility of attempts to distinguish in such remarkable works between bold intention and brilliant realization.

The Florentine Hercules, a classical analogue of the Hebrew David

By the beginning of the fifteenth century Hercules was almost as popularly associated with the Florentine commune as Mars and John the Baptist, and he appears in a number of contexts familiar to Cosimo and his descendants. Hercules was adoped in 1281 as an emblem of the Signoria in its seal, described by Gregorio Dati in his *Istoria di Firenze* written over a century later; it was meant "to signify that Hercules, who was a giant, overcame all tyrants and evil lords as the Florentines have done."[279]

A much-copied poem, among those memorized half a century later by Benedetto Dei, described the great snowfall of 1406, when the populace came out into the streets to build figures of snow in all sorts of shapes, including that of Hercules. Perhaps Luca Landucci had this in mind when he described a similarly rare snowfall in January 1494, when Piero di Lorenzo de' Medici supposedly commanded Michelangelo to build a Hercules of snow in the courtyard of the Medici palace.[280] Hercules is a major figure in Seneca's *Tragedies*, which were in Cosimo's library by 1418. As a symbol of strength and fortitude, his image was also elaborated in the learned literature of the Renaissance; Petrarch opened his list of famous men with Hercules, and Salutati, in his work *On the Labors of Hercules*, made Hercules an emblem of virtue. The image of Hercules at the crossroads represented life's crucial choice – downhill to pleasure, uphill to virtue. Rinaldo degli Albizzi invoked a comparison of the Florentine populace to a new Hercules, ready to overcome all tyrants, in actual political discussion in the early decades of the fifteenth century.[281]

Petrarch's *De Viris Illustribus* both marked and occasioned a renewed interest in the Labors of Hercules, which were represented on the *campanile*, on the Porta della Mandorla of the cathedral sometime in the 1390s, and in later commissions for private patrons. The hero's exploits were depicted in the style of antique sarcophagi and coins on a pair of *cassoni* for a Ginazzi-Boni marriage, and Tommaso Spinelli, a Medici bank factor, used the image of Hercules and the lion in the decoration of his palace.[282] This was perhaps in emulation of the enormous Hercules cycle made for the Medici. Now lost, the three huge paintings on cloth framed with gold dominated Lorenzo's room on the *piano nobile*, as the Uccello battle pieces did his room on the ground floor. Each six braccia square, they represented Hercules killing the Hydra, strangling the lion, and wrestling Anteus. According to the inventarist, "all these labors of Hercules are by the hand of Pollaiuolo."[283]

This is confirmed by a letter of 1494 in which Antonio Pollaiuolo referred to having painted these pictures with his brother in the Medici house in 1460: "It is thirty-four years since I did those labors of Hercules that are in the great room of his [Piero di Lorenzo's] house, which my brother and I did between us." They probably resembled in style the two small panels by Pollaiuolo now in the Uffizi (fig. 136).[284] Art historians have connected the Hercules theme with the interests of Piero di Cosimo and his son Lorenzo, who later adopted Hercules as a personal emblem; Landino, in his *Conversationes camaldulenses*

136   Antonio Pollaiuolo, *Labors of Hercules*, Florence, Uffizi

was to represent Hercules as an exemplum of the active life and civic virtue in Lorenzo's circle. No such associations are documented in Cosimo's life and writings, but the adoption of this republican symbol, like that of David, was very much in accord with his view of his family's relation to the commune.

DECORATING AND COLLECTING: CONTINUITY AND CHANGE

There is a widespread tendency among historians to represent Piero as the master of the Medici palace at the time it was completed, arising largely from the uncritical acceptance of Ernst Gombrich's suggestion that Piero was probably responsible for most of its decoration, and depending mainly upon miscontructions of vague and encomiastic contemporary comment.[285] Informed observers painted a different picture. Filarete, for example, described the Medici palace in his *Trattato*, completed after Cosimo's death in 1464 and dedicated, after the demise in 1466 of his main patron, the duke of Milan, to Piero de' Medici. He praised Piero's contributions to the beauty and magnificence of the palace, but gave the essential credit for its splendor to Cosimo, observing that "he has neglected nothing which would add to the comfort of his accommodations."[286]

Preoccupied as always with business and politics, and weakened by age and illness, Cosimo no doubt left many of the details of decoration, including the documented supervision of the chapel frescoes, to his sons, who were expert assessors of *objets d'art*. It is difficult to distinguish between the commissions of father and sons, who clearly cooperated to create the domestic environment they shared. For the purposes of this study it is also unnecessary. The main point to be made about the palace decoration in relation to Cosimo's oeuvre is that the texture and quality of Medici domestic life, in all its sophisticated opulence, must be seen as illuminating an important but relatively unexplored aspect of Cosimo's supposedly austere personality and patronage; his extravagant enjoyment of the leisure to which he saw his city as dedicated.

Following Gombrich, many scholars of art have continued to contrast Cosimo's austere architectural commissions for churches such as the Badia with Piero's jewel of a study and the glowing tapestry of Gozzoli's frescoes for the palace chapel, adducing these works as evidence of a sharp generational and temperamental conflict of taste between Cosimo and his elder son.[287] Insofar as this interpretation ignores the crucial issue of the respective functions of these disparate objects, and is predicated upon a thoroughly modern model of familial relations which is demonstrably inappropriate to the quattrocento, it has tended to mislead rather than to enlighten.

Nor, however, is it appropriate to regard Cosimo's sons as mere appendages of their father, as many historians have done, perhaps because Giovanni, the younger, predeceased him, and Piero, the elder, survived him by only five years. The period between Cosimo's death in 1464 and Piero's in 1469 is often seen as an insignificant interval between the era of the astute and authoritative Cosimo and that of his charismatic and cultivated grandson Lorenzo. Closer attention to Cosimo's sons has recently been rewarded by the discovery of new material that begins to illuminate their lives and patronage interests. Giovanni died six years before Piero, and since as the younger son he lived less in the public and political spotlight, much less evidence of his activities survives. However, after 1455 he was general manager of the Medici bank, he served the republic in civic magistracies and as an ambassador for Florence and the Medici at the

courts of their foreign friends, and he was an educated patron and collector. His building and decoration of his own villa at Fiesole offers some real insight into his character, taste, and interests, and the way in which he embodied many aspects of the ideal of the cultivated Florentine merchant envisaged by his father.[288]

A more precise and extensive consideration of the whole of Piero's patronage oeuvre, departing from a less subjective view of "good taste" and of the direction of development previously considered appropriate to quattrocento art, led Francis Ames-Lewis to articulate some more subtly distinctive characteristics of Piero's commissions. On the basis of his probable role in the decoration of the *sala grande*, including the Pollaiuolo brothers' Hercules panels, Alison Wright described Piero as a discerning and innovatory patron whose taste can hardly be dismissed as *nouveau riche*. Similarly, Shelley Zuraw pointed to the marble busts he commissioned from Mino da Fiesole as evidence of Piero's sophistication as a patron far in advance of his contemporaries. Other scholars assessing his distinctive achievements as a politician and a patron, particularly after his father's death, stressed his purposeful extension of Medici power and privileges through his activities in the political arena, and by symbolic statements in his patronage for public places.[289]

Some of the distinctive characteristics of Piero and Giovanni's patronage might most sensibly be related to change and development in Florentine artistic preoccupations and norms, and to the considerable difference in education and cultural experience between father and sons. Cosimo's literary education, like that of many of his contemporaries, was largely acquired in informal colloquies with humanist friends. Piero studied formally with various tutors, including the humanist and chancellor of the republic Carlo Marsuppini, and more briefly with the great Renaissance educator Guarino da Verona in Ferrara. In Florence he associated closely with leading intellectuals like Alberti, who testified that Piero had read all of his extremely subtle and complex works. Giovanni's correspondence with a variety of learned friends reveals him as even more attached than his elder brother to literature and learning, and Lorenzo de' Medici described his grandfather Cosimo as relying greatly upon the virtue and intellect of his younger son.[290]

In accordance with their education, and with the accelerating tempo of artists' adoption of classical forms and themes, the patronage and collecting of Cosimo's sons expresses an interest in the antique that was more developed and more esoteric than their father's. Mino da Fiesole's marble portrait busts of the brothers are the first known Renaissance examples of a popular antique genre (figs. 137 and 138). The *cassone* now in Philadelphia, made

137 Mino da Fiesole, Piero de' Medici, marble bust, Florence, Bargello

138 Mino da Fiesole, Giovanni de' Medici, marble bust, Florence, Bargello

between 1440 and 1460, bearing the Medici and Bardi arms and plausibly identified as one of the many painted chests described in Medici inventories as containing the personal possessions of Cosimo and his wife Contessina, is decorated simply with a classicizing wreath of laurel and orange fruit surrounding a shield bearing the eight red *palle* and the red and gold stripes of the Bardi arms; on either side of the wreath are a diamond ring and the motto "SEMPER" (fig. 139). By contrast, the representation of the story of Cupid and Psyche on a pair of *cassoni* made for Piero's wedding to Lucrezia Tornabuoni presumes, as Luisa Vertova observed, a program so esoteric it could only be devised and appreciated by the most learned and sophisticated of patrons (fig. 140).[291]

Piero and Giovanni belonged to the generation responsible for the proliferation of domestic possessions and decorations, in contrast with the more austerely furnished households of the late fourteenth and early fifteenth centuries. By comparison with the *casa vecchia* in Giovanni di Bicci's day, or in Cosimo's middle years, the pictures and hangings and household goods acquired for the new palace were conspicuous for the richness of their mate-

rials and decorative ornament. However, the decorative themes of even the most luxurious rooms of the Medici palace – the *camera terrena, the sala grande* and the chapel – were those traditionally associated with the family, or expressive of Cosimo's essential interests as defined by his commissions for public places. The Medici set an example for other citizens in the comfort of their accommodations, outstripping their competitors in the quantity and luxurious quality of their domestic goods, although from the mid-fifteenth century, other Florentine families too were devoting more attention, and a higher proportion of their resources, to the more splendid decoration of their domestic environments.[292]

Also particularly relevant to the perception of Piero's patronage is the difference of personal and political experience from father to sons. Piero and Giovanni did not represent a second generation of Medici prosperity, as is sometimes suggested; their grandfather Giovanni di Bicci had long been extremely wealthy when he died the richest man in the city in 1429. They did, however, represent a second generation of power; of the undoubted supremacy of the Medici family over all the other wealthy

and cultivated patrician houses who had once been their
equals or superiors. While Cosimo up to the age of forty-
five was not yet even *primus inter pares*, but rather still one
of several scions of old and distinguished families hotly
contesting primacy in the political and cultural arenas,
Piero, born in 1416, was less than twenty years old when
the regime's recall of his father in 1434 acknowledged
the Medici as the leading family of Florence. At Cosimo's
death, thirty years later, a partisan wrote to Piero on
behalf of a group of Medici friends and supporters:
"We want to be fathers to you as we were brothers to
Cosimo." But already men many years Piero's senior were
accustomed to acknowledge his superior authority with

139 (*right and below*)   *Cassone* with Medici and Bardi arms,
Philadelphia, Museum of Art: Gift of Mrs. William E. Helme

140 (*bottom*)   *Cassone* panel, *Cupid and Psyche*, Berlin, Staatliche
Museen Preussischer Kulturbesitz, Gemäldegalerie

the honorific title, "Carissimo come padre" (most dear, like a father).[293]

It is true that at the tender age of seventeen Piero experienced the trauma of exile, when the family's very survival seemed in doubt, and it is unlikely that he ever forgot this lesson in the impermanence of political pre-eminence. On the other hand, by the time he died in his early fifties, he had behind him thirty years in which Medici authority had seldom been seriously questioned. The regime was briefly threatened in the mid-1450s, but the Mediceans emerged from these uncertainties in 1458 into comparative security. When in 1466, two years after Cosimo's death, some of their chief partisans again challenged Medici leadership, Piero responded with a show of force and cunning that outmaneuvered his opponents. Despite occasional threats, of which the Pazzi conspiracy of 1478 was the gravest, Piero's son Lorenzo, born in 1449, passed his whole life in the enjoyment of his family's ascendancy; possibly this, as much as any other aspect of the evolution of the Florentine political and social world, accounts for his bolder and more explicit expressions of Medici superiority in wealth and influence, and of his aspirations after 1469 to an authority incompatible with genuine republicanism.

The extension of Medici authority over the Florentine state from the early 1470s is well documented in public and private archives; the situation in the last five years of Piero's lifetime is much less clear. Many scholars have perceived in Piero's artistic commissions, even more than in those of Cosimo, an analogous expression of political pretensions they interpret as "princely." However, the same problems arise in deciphering the "messages" of Piero's patronage. There is still no clear match between Piero's artistic commissions and his activity in the political arena, and it is illegitimate and unwise to read the obvious ambitions of the late Lorenzo back into the still inchoate and volatile relations obtaining some fifty years earlier between Piero, his aging father, their patrician rivals, and the Florentine state.

Like the political evidence, the products of Piero's artistic patronage do, however, suggest a gradual movement away from Cosimo's careful expressions of his superiority over his fellow citizens, in the direction of more arrogant and aggressive assertions of Medici wealth and power. This progress seems to have been sharply accelerated by Cosimo's death and the accompanying challenges to the putative heirs of his position, both as patron and statesman. Conversely, in its general direction the patronage attributable to Piero in his father's lifetime shows him continuing along the same broad course as Cosimo, whether in diplomacy or domestic politics or art. The speech Piero delivered as Gonfalonier of Justice

in 1461 reiterated the ideals of citizen unity which Cosimo had striven to maintain by his lifelong insistence on consulting "cives non mediocres" in the implementation of his personal and partisan policies. Piero also relied and built upon his father's fundamental alliances with Milan and the papacy, without which he would probably not have survived the conspiracy of 1466.[294]

Piero's early public patronage followed in the well-trodden paths established by other eminent citizens, honoring the austere Florentine saint Giovanni Gualberto at San Miniato, as the Strozzi had at Santa Trinita, and at Santissima Annunziata promoting the city's most popular cult, that of the Virgin Annunciate, to whom his father was especially devoted. At San Tommaso he or Cosimo dignified not only their family's ancestral neighborhood, but the saint who for his association with justice and truth had been adopted as the patron of the governors of the commune. Within the Medici palace, it was probably Piero who added Hercules and Judith and Holofernes to David as emblems of the liberty and justice defended by the Florentine *popolo*. Piero's patronage is part of the continuum of Cosimo's, and occurred within the context he established, even while it gradually altered that context with its growing boldness in the expression of personal and familial interests in the public sphere. This was an elusive process, and Piero was an elusive figure; though assuredly he did nothing in Cosimo's lifetime that was not "according to the will of his father,"[295] he was clearly evolving a will of his own which had much freer reign after Cosimo's death.

The comfort of Cosimo's accommodations

While the decorative arts have traditionally been dismissed as "minor," patrons took a major interest in them, and they furnish vital clues to the interests that determined a patron's spending. The Milanese Carissimi, describing the palace, recorded the dazzling impression created by every detail of ceilings, floors, walls, and benches, with their tiles and tapestries and gilding and intarsia.[296] Unfortunately these are long since gone. Some sense of the Medici palace interior can, however, be recreated from these descriptions and from the inventories of personal and household effects.[297]

Father and sons shared a taste for luxury in their surroundings. The furnishings of the palace included an enormous quantity of expensive goods; tableware of silver and gold, linens of fine fabrics elaborately embroidered with pearls and threads of silver and gold. Cloths, carpets, and tapestries, many of Flemish manufacture, and decorated with designs of figures, animals, birds, arms, devices, and the hunt, covered walls and floors, softening surfaces already embellished with carving, intarsia, coffering, tiles, pictures, and sculpture. Piero's apartments in particular contained a wealth of stuff; sheets, towels, shirts, handkerchiefs, pillowcases, tablecloths, and napkins, all of silk or linen richly worked. Bedcovers were decorated with the Medici arms and the device of the diamond ring with feathers; bedheads were painted with figures and the family arms, like the one represented in the bedroom of the Virgin in Lippi's overdoor, *The Annunciation*. Objects were wrought in every precious material – not only silver and gold, but also brass, glass, crystal, porcelain, ivory, and ebony. They were decorated with coral and a variety of precious stones – chalcedons, rubies, pearls, and even diamonds.[298]

All the Medici men and their wives, from Giovanni di Bicci through Cosimo and Lorenzo to Piero and Giovanni di Cosimo, were fashionable dressers. The many decorated trunks and chests in their bedrooms and antechambers were filled with clothes and luxury items such as buttons of pearl, handkerchiefs embroidered with gold, and velvet and gold and pearl encrusted pillows.[299] A list of possessions that on one occasion accompanied Cosimo and his brother Lorenzo and their families to Pisa, where they were establishing a *filiale* of the bank, indicates what was considered a basic minimum of clothing and personal effects. In addition to his books, Cosimo carried with him a couple of breastplates, his huge silver and gold clock, his crystal goblet, and a "unicorn horn."[300] By the time Piero compiled a list in 1456 of his own personal effects, their quantity and quality were dazzling. Piero's clothing included brocade and velvet tunics and cloaks lined with fur, and his wife Lucrezia's velvets and brocades and taffetas were embroidered with silver and gold; she also had a large quantity of belts and purses in brocade, silver, and gold.[301]

Marco Parenti painted a vivid picture of the opulence of a dinner in the Medici palace on the occasion of Lorenzo's wedding to Clarice Orsini in 1469.[302] Descriptions of similar occasions during Cosimo's lifetime, for example the banquet given at Careggi for Francesco Sforza's son Galeazzo Maria ten years earlier, convey a similar sense of luxurious living and elaborate entertaining. A memorable feature of the dinner for Sforza was singing and dancing, as it was at many more informal gatherings described in family letters. The renowned organist Antonio Squarcialupi was a frequent guest at the country villas of Trebbio and Cafaggiolo, and Piero and Giovanni's correspondence contains numerous references to their exchange of new music and songs with friends such as Rosello Roselli and the younger Della Stufa. Bagpipes were played at the celebration in honor of

Sforza; similarly Pierfrancesco had written to Piero in 1443, when he was barely thirteen years old, asking his cousin to send some bagpipes to Trebbio because "a lot of women" were coming the following Sunday.[303] Piero's inventories of 1456 and 1464/5 list a number of musical instruments for the use of the family or their familiars at play, including lutes, pipes, violas, and two Flemish organs. There are also letters addressed to both Giovanni and Piero concerning the sale and purchase of musical instruments.[304]

Cosimo's dancing days were long over by the late 1450s, but according to Vespasiano he diverted himself playing chess; several boards and sets of men are mentioned in the inventories, and Michele del Giogante gave Cosimo a book of chess games.[305] Other items testifying to pastimes of leisure and pleasure included hunting equipment – nets, snares, and gloves for handling falcons and dogs[306] – and armor and weapons for jousting. Despite their physical infirmities, all the men of the family had at some time partaken in this aristocratic ritual, and household inventories from 1418 to 1492 contain long lists of expensive equipment lavishly decorated with personal and family devices.

Cosimo's collection

A fundamental distinction between objects created by commission, and those collected or found, is maintained by the art historian concerned with the Renaissance artist's achievement, and the patron's role in it. However, the patron's personal taste may be easier to identify in objects collected rather than commissioned, since their form is unaffected by the concerns of artists or audience. Little has so far been written of the objects collected by Cosimo, many of them absorbed into the collections of his sons and grandson, which far outstripped his own. However, the objects in his possession indicate that his interests were along similar lines to those later more fully developed by his descendants, and may have laid the foundations for them. Most of the decorative objects in Cosimo's quarters in Giovanni di Bicci's house were devotional. He owned a number of small precious objects, several of them religious; these included a small silver cross decorated with pearls, a breviary embroidered with pearls and precious stones, two "branches of coral with a setting of silver" and "a gold chain with a small cross of jasper." Also in his study were various gold, silver, ivory, and enamelled objects, a "carved crystal goblet with a silver stem," which reappears among the possessions of Piero and Lorenzo, and "a large piece of crystal to serve as a night light."[307]

In addition to these objects, Cosimo's rooms housed a large collection of armor and weapons, consonant with his lively interest in the conduct and accoutrements of war and military display. Since hardly any examples of armor survive from Florence in Cosimo's lifetime, Uccello's panels, in which the painter conscientiously represented the armor and weapons of the first half of the fifteenth century, are the best indication of the appearance of the objects in Cosimo's collection (figs. 141 and 142).[308] While armor was an important category of the large range of expensive items owned by Piero, Giovanni, and Lorenzo di Piero, apart from books, arms were the major component of Cosimo's personal possessions. Unlike Piero's armor, Cosimo's was not clearly categorized in the inventory under items for ceremonial, jousting, or fighting use. All the Medici men seem to have kept some fighting armor near at hand, like their friend Michele del Giogante who hung his on a hook at the entrance to his house.[309] A good quantity of functional armor and weapons seems to have been stored in Cosimo's suite, as opposed to the armories maintained in both the *casa vecchia* and the new palace. However, the precious materials of which many pieces in Cosimo's collection were made, and their elaborate decoration, suggest that they were intended for civic ceremonies or jousts. In a letter to his nephew Pierfrancesco in 1458, Cosimo dismissed the pastime of jousting as "frivolous" unless the honor of the commune were involved.[310] However, he clearly knew quite a bit about its conduct, and the amount of decorated armor he owned in 1418 suggests that he himself had certainly jousted in his virtually undocumented youth.

First noted, and most distinctive, were "a shield decorated in relief with arms and crest, a helmet with a crest upon it, two Damascan bows with quiver and arrows, two new Turkish scimitars, and a pair of andirons." The coupling of armor with other decorative metalwork suggests these were collector's items; Piero's inventory of 1456 included two whole pages of Damascene ware.[311] Although the Florentines' fascination with the East was to increase after the council of 1439, already in 1418 the finely wrought weapons of the infidel were highly prized.

A triple-locked chest at the foot of Cosimo's bed contained, among other cloths and clothing, materials for jousts or other ceremonies calling for heraldic trappings. Besides four yellow cloth covers decorated with the Medici arms, perhaps for horses, there were no less than eight garments made of yellow cloth to be worn over armor, and two "in the antique manner," all "with arms all over them." A large number of ceremonial flags, also decorated with the Medici arms, included a large one

"with arms and crest," "a standard decorated with an angel surrounded by clouds," two small cloth standards "painted for riding with," a banner for a foot soldier, five square flags and a trumpeter's banner.[312] Another trunk contained helmets and a sword "with a sheath of red velvet, decorated with silver." There was a matching beaver helmet, also covered with red velvet and decorated with silver, with a silver crest upon it in the shape of a dog, weighing six pounds eight ounces. There was also a helmet decorated with silver, with a crest in the form of a gilded eagle, two more helmets covered with red velvet, and a horse's headguard with silver plume.[313]

There was nothing but armor in the *anticamera*. Several of these items, like the breastplate covered with black velvet belonging to Giovanni di Bicci and two velvet covered breastplates of Cosimo's, also seem intended for ceremonies or jousts. But some of this armor was obviously functional, like the three polished steel helmets for common footsoldiers stored in a wooden cupboard, along with three pairs of new steel armguards, two steel shoulder pieces, two pairs of metal gloves, more steel helmets (one of them painted), three pairs of steel saddles and harness, a fighting dagger, and a box with a small hammer, pliers, and other tools for maintaining armor. In another box underneath the cupboard were eight sets of embossed steel body-armor; two more of iron, four pairs of steel greaves, two steel throat-pieces, a horse's breastplate; two dozen bits; and assorted other pieces, including two large swords.

The place described as "the armory above Cosimo's study" contained a similar variety of arms, many of them decorated. In addition to a pair of leather greaves with spurs for jousting, there were half a dozen sets of saddle and harness, a Milanese hat-shaped steel helmet, two basin-shaped helmets, one covered with black velvet and the other with cloth, without chainmail for the neck, a number of breastplates covered with damask and suede, and painted steel helmets and hats, one red and yellow, probably heraldic colors. There was also a considerable quantity of weaponry, some of it decorated; perhaps for the hunt, very possibly for defence. This cache included ten more pairs of armguards, three new and seven used; three helmets and a steel breastplate, all with mesh attachments to cover the neck, and a foot-soldier's steel helmet; there were also bows of wood and steel and quivers, pikes, swords, spears, and lances, twenty-five javelins, and more than a hundred assorted missiles. Finally, on a storage shelf up under the roof there was a painted shield picturing a young girl, and a large number of painted lances.[314]

Apart from the items recorded in the 1417/18 inventory, Cosimo was reputed to have collected other precious objects in his youth and early maturity. In his diary

141   Paolo Uccello, *The Battle of San Romano*, detail of fig. 127

of the late 1440s, Ciriaco d'Ancona, a famous scholarly antiquarian whom Cosimo sent to the East to collect information about that world and objects belonging to it, described a tour he took of the collections of the Medici circle in Florence around 1433. "In the company of Carlo Aretino [Marsuppini], having seen his choice library, with the ancient coins and images, they saw the representations of the priest of Lupercal carved by Pyrogoteles out of an agate gem on a seal, and of Mercury with his winged sandals in a bronze image, and many precious objects of the same type, belonging to Cosimo, a man of abundant wealth, and in the possession of Donatello and Nencio [Ghiberti], noble statuary and many things both old and new, images constructed by them out of bronze and marble . . ."[315] Cosimo had been involved in the sale of John XXIII's collection of jewels, although whether as a collector or a broker is not clear. It is probable that the items remembered by Ciriaco were

acquired in the 1420s, when the discovery of ancient manuscripts and the collection of *objets d'art* began to gather real momentum. But the origins of the collector's impulse may perhaps be discerned in the handful of precious objects in Cosimo's possession by 1418.

Poggio Bracciolini's letters and dialogues suggest that Cosimo and Lorenzo learned about connoisseurship from their humanist friends Poggio and Niccoli, an impression explicitly confirmed by Vespasiano's testimony.[316] Poggio, Bruni, and Traversari all sent the Medici medals, coins, and cameos. Niccoli had once owned the famous Diomedes chalcedon, used as the basis for the design of one of the roundels in the frieze of the Medici palace courtyard; appropriately the gemstone ended up in Lorenzo di Piero's collection.[317] Vasari also claimed to have seen in the Medici palace an ancient marble *Apollo and Marsyas* belonging to Cosimo and restored by Donatello or Verrocchio.[318]

142   Paolo Uccello, *The Battle of San Romano*, detail of fig. 126

Collections of succeeding generations

Lorenzo's acquisition of the Farnese cup, valued in the inventory of 1492 at 10,000 florins, compared with the estimated cost of 100,000 florins which his grandfather Cosimo paid for the construction of the entire Medici palace, puts the collections of his forebears in the shade, although also in sharper perspective.[320] However, the collecting of earlier generations does shed important light on the context of their patronage. Just as Lorenzo received some of his education in taste from his tutor, Gentile Becchi, we learn from their letters that Piero and Giovanni solicited their humanist tutors' and friends' opinions and assistance in assembling the collections of antique coins, medals, marbles, precious metalwork, and gems begun in their youth.

They also relied on the entire structure of Medici business and patronage association in acquiring items of value and beauty from all over Europe. Employees of the far-flung branches of the bank assisted them especially in purchasing tapestries. These, along with a wide variety of commodities from jewels to almonds, were an important part of the late medieval venture trade, and the Medici

143   Dioskourides, *Apollo, Olympus, and Marsyas*, cameo, Naples, Museo Archeologico Nazionale

One of only two works of art Ghiberti described in his *Commentaries* was a gem: "I set in gold a cornelian the size of a nut, on which three figures had been carved most beautifully by a very excellent ancient master. They were as perfect as anything I have ever seen in *intaglio*." A prize of the collecting enthusiasm of Cosimo and his circle in the 1420s, this work, a miniature *Apollo and Marsyas*, seems to be identifiable with a piece belonging to his grandson Lorenzo. It was one of his five most valuable gems, valued at one thousand florins: "A large cornelian with three figures carved in more than half relief, one naked and standing upright, with a lyre in his hand, with a nude figure kneeling at his feet, the other an old man seated with his hands behind him bound to a tree, without backing, transparent, set in gold," (fig. 143).[319]

★　　★　　★

144   *Studiolo*, Ducal Palace, Gubbio, New York, The Metropolitan Museum of Art, Rogers Fund, 1939

brothers imported them to sell to others, as well as to decorate the splendid new family palace. The web of Medici patronage was also woven or reinforced through the acquisition and exchange of *objets d'art*.[321] This point was made by Caroline Elam with reference to Lorenzo and his relations with the rulers of foreign courts. Although these customs cannot be documented so dramatically or even precisely for an earlier period, Lorenzo's diplomatic gifts were clearly a development of the patronage practices of Cosimo's day. The portraits of Gattamelata and Sforza may well have fitted into this category, and the panel Giovanni di Cosimo had made by Lippi for the king of Naples certainly did.[322] Modeled on their business and diplomacy, the family's cultural relations were also national and international.

Although the accumulation of decorative objects enhanced the whole environment of the family palace, personal collections were kept in the studies adjoining each man's bedchamber. The Medici studies were among the earliest of the Renaissance *studioli* dedicated to the display and rehearsal of learning, and to the pleasures of the connoisseur; Medici patronage was by no means exclusively a show for the benefit of others. The room in

the *casa vecchia* specially decorated by the painter Dello Delli was probably Lorenzo's study; all that is known of Cosimo's study in 1418 is that it contained a large collection of books, and that it was considered, on account of its intarsiated woodwork, the showpiece of the old house. Of Cosimo's study in the new palace nothing is known. A description of Giovanni's study as more than rivaling his brother Piero's in its opulent and inventive decoration may refer either to the urban palace or to his villa at Fiesole, along with the known commissions from which its contents can be partially reconstructed.[323] Apart from the chapel, Piero's study was the most elaborately decorated, admired, and described room in the Medici palace. It may have been modeled on the Este *studioli* in their palace in Ferrara, and at their country villa of Belfiore; like Piero's study, these were both destroyed. However, the spectacular intarsia wood panels depicting perspective compositions that illusionistically enlarged Piero's tiny room inspired the decorations of Federigo da Montefeltro's *studioli* at Gubbio and Urbino in the 1470s, both of which have survived. The former in particular, recently restored, re-creates the aspect of the lost showpiece of the Medici palace (fig. 144).[324]

According to the author of the anonymous *Terze Rime*, Piero's study was entered by: "A door so artfully worked that I believe/ it must be true relief, and covered with intarsia./ Then we go into the triumphal and luxurious study,/ designed with such ingenuity and order and measure,/[325] that it seems the picture of an angelic celebration,/ covered with intarsia and paintings/ in perspective and sublimely worked/ with a great mastery of architecture./ There are many ornately decorated books/ and vases of alabaster and chalcedon/ mounted on gold and silver./ And everything there is beautiful and fine,/ brought to complete perfection/ by nature and by human intellect."[326]

This obviously idealizing account is confirmed and balanced by Filarete's extremely precise description, which allows us to identify some of the objects the study contained. A small room about ten feet by eight, it was "embellished most fittingly with books and other worthy objects . . . with a most elaborate tiled pavement and coffered ceiling."[327] It also contained a group of glazed figures by Luca della Robbia, "the admiration of all who saw them." Opinion is divided on whether these can be identified with the *Twelve Labors of the Months* now in the Victoria and Albert Museum, but it seems highly likely that they can (fig. 145). Piero was the patron of Della Robbia's first major commissions in painted terracotta, the vaults of the tabernacles for San Miniato and Santissima Annunziata. The depiction of the tasks of the agricultural seasons marked by astrological signs in the roundels expresses something of the same interest in astrology and the passage of time seen in the painted ceiling of the San Lorenzo sacristy chapel, as well as the whole family's pleasure in participating personally in such labors at their country villas.[328] Other decorations of the study included "a head of the duke of Milan in a silver setting," and various coins, cameos, and rings depicting the heads of Domitian, Vespasian, Hadrian, Camilla, Persephone, the Medusa, and the stories of Daedalus, as well as rosaries and sacred images.

Everything in Piero's study was exquisite, testifying to his particular pleasure in fine workmanship. When the marquess of Mantua visited Piero, "who was in bed . . . owing to gout . . . he was shown coins, cameos with various carvings, vases and many beautiful jewels."[329] Thanks to Ames-Lewis, quite a lot is also known of about the appearance and shelving of Piero's rich collection of illuminated manuscripts which Filarete testified he "liked to spend time with, having himself carried into his studio . . . they seemed to him like a mass of gold."[330] Having invested an enormous amount of time and money in procuring these manuscripts, Piero liked to tell over his treasures, the miser's hoard of the chronic invalid.

In their collections of books, pictures, and precious objects that decorated the palace, as in many of their commissions for public places, the members of the Medici family expressed their consciousness of the distinction and continuity of the lineage, its image in the eyes of the Florentine people, and its location in historical time and urban space, all intertwined and articulated with civic and Christian symbols and themes. A strong sense of history places Cosimo's household in the continuum of family and city, the classical and Christian past, and an eternity of hoped-for salvation. Cosimo's sense of history was fed and supported by his familiarity with a variety of texts from Cicero to the Scriptures. Piero's collection of books and manuscripts displays the development of that interest in history, as in the cognate themes of narrative and the passage of time.[331]

For many Florentines, including Cosimo and his sons, Petrarch's *Triumphs* was probably the text that best related secular and Christian history, the word and the image. This work, described in Piero's inventory of 1456 as a "Book of the work of Petrarch, the *Triumphs*, first illllustrated and illuminated, written by pen," was the first of the many beautifully illuminated manuscripts he commissioned; it belongs to the early 1440s. The initial folio was decorated with the Medici arms, the *palle*, set within the diamond ring symbolizing eternity, intertwined with three feathers resembling those of the ostrich, a bird associated with the Resurrection, representing the three

145 Luca Della Robbia, *February*, terracotta roundel, London, Victoria and Albert Museum

146 Scheggia, *Triumph of Fame*, birthtray, New York, The Metropolitan Museum of Art, Purchase in memory of Sir John Pope-Hennessy: Rogers Fund, The Annenberg Foundation, Drue Heinz Foundation, Annette de la Renta, Mr. and Mrs. Frank E. Richardson, and the Vincent Astor Foundation Gifts, Wrightsman and Gwynne Andrews Funds, special funds, and Gift of Mr. and Mrs. Joshua Logan, and other gifts and bequests, by exchange, 1995 (1995.7)

theological virtues, with their colors of red, white, and green; faith, hope, and charity.[332]

Bernardo della Casa, in a poem described by the author as "written in front of a work of Petrarch's, the book being richly decorated," was inspired by Petrarch to an almost Keatsian vision of beauty and truth: "First see what I am, you who read me,/ and how beautiful I am; gaze at me bit by bit,/ my letters and pages decorated with gold,/ and look if you have seen my equal in beauty./ And then in my first sonnet read/ what I speak of in rhyme . . . understand it . . ."[333] Petrarch offered his readers warrants both metaphorical and literal for the pursuit of beauty and truth. He wrote in his own will of the extraordinary and educated pleasure of owning a Giotto: "whose beauty the ignorant do not understand, but whose skill astonishes experts"; in *Of the Varieties of Fortune* he confessed impulsively: "I love pictures and painted tables."[334]

These objects offered educated patricians the immense pleasure of ingeniously conflating Christian, classical, and dynastic themes, as did the panels of *cassoni* and painted birthtrays. The *desco da parto* ordered by Piero for Lorenzo's birth depicting the Triumph of Fame was both an affirmation and a prediction of the destiny of his dynasty (fig. 146).[335] In this world of learning and imagination, a Cosimo or a Piero de' Medici could see himself, surrounded by armed retainers, represented as another Aeneas, laying the foundations of a newly civilized Florence in the image of Rome. In the gaily colored illuminations of Apollonio di Giovanni's Riccardiana Virgil, made in Cosimo's lifetime for a patron apparently from the Medici circle, the building of the Medici palace was depicted side by side in an imaginary city with Trajan's Forum and the Pantheon. Retainers bearing bows, swords, and pikes, like those stored in Cosimo's *cassoni*, and resembling the soldiers who populated the backgrounds of Uccello's panels, defended it with ready arms.[336]

A CULTIVATED LIFE: GARDENS AND VILLAS

Gardening was one of the fruitful occupations Cosimo pursued in his leisure hours, free of the business of banking and government, encouraged perhaps by the example of the Roman philosopher and statesman Cato, of whose *De Re Rustica* he owned one of the few extant copies.[337] Cosimo's biographer Vespasiano observed that except for chess, he never played games. He preferred the worthier, because more productive, pastimes of tending the vines and gardens cultivated at all his estates, as also at the major sites of his public patronage, like San Marco and the Badia.[338] We noted the Milanese description of the palace garden as "all created of the most beautiful polished marbles with various plants, which seems a thing not natural but painted."[339] Less familiar to historians is the elaborate garden attached to the *casa vecchia*, a few doors north along the Via Larga, where Cosimo and his sons had previously lived.

The relatively recent discovery of a "notebook of expenses for the garden of Cosimo and Lorenzo de' Medici" reveals that between January and March 1432, the brothers had constructed there a *hortus conclusus*, surrounded on four sides by a high wall which divided the garden from the main courtyard of the house. Within, it was subdivided into three distinct spaces. "The little garden of the well" included a paved courtyard, and its centerpiece was an elaborate construction surmounted by a gilded *spiritello*; the role played in the ensemble by water is apparent from the piping underneath the pavement, not

dissimilar to the elaborate irrigation system installed in the garden at San Marco, and showing the influence on Italian gardens of this period of medieval Byzantine and Arab gardens. The other two notable areas were "the little garden of the *melarancie*" (this fruit stood symbolically for the golden balls of the Medici family arms), and "the little rose garden," roses being a central element of medieval garden symbolism and associated with the Virgin.[340]

This space Cosimo at least partially re-created in the garden behind his new palace, closed off on two sides from the street by crenellated walls more than twenty feet high. Where Richard Goldthwaite saw Cosimo and Lorenzo's one thousand braccia of garden wall as "a means of achieving privacy, designed to keep others out," some might see these walls as creating a special interior space, rich in symbolism, and replete with delights for the recreation of mind and body.[341] Cosimo's suite in the new palace overlooked the garden (fig. 112), while his elder son Piero occupied the rooms at the front of the palace facing the Via Larga.[342] Bulst argued that this disposition of space symbolized Cosimo's cession of pride of place and authority over family affairs to his elder son, but in fact Cosimo's retirement from business was more formal than real. While Giovanni di Bicci retired from the bank and some other duties in favor of Cosimo in 1420, the inventory of his house around this time shows that his father continued to occupy the front rooms, while Cosimo was established, as he was in the new palace of the 1450s, in a suite adjacent to the garden. Perhaps Cosimo simply took great personal pleasure in growing things, as Vespasiano claimed.

The restoration of the Medici palace garden at the beginning of this century, in accordance with the literary description of it in the anonymous fifteenth-century verses known as the *Terze Rime,* makes it now more, rather than less difficult to reconstruct what it was actually like. But a description of the festivities in the courtyard and garden of the palace on the occasion of Lorenzo's wedding in 1469 furnishes some more objective, because incidental, evidence of its layout. The adjacent spaces of the inner courtyard and the external garden functioned as a single ensemble, visually connected by the prospect through the archways between them, and by the correspondence of Donatello's bronze *David*, as the centerpiece of the courtyard, with his *Judith and Holofernes* at the center of the garden.[343] Along the south wall was a three-bay loggia which could be entered by a door from the southwest room of the *pian terreno;* on the west wall there was a hanging gallery with a walkway at the level of the *piano nobile.*

The garden was carefully planned for the leisure and pleasure of its residents and their guests, and its plants and decorations presented to the viewer a variety of images and symbols. An imaginative encomium by the humanist Avogadro described elaborate topiary in the shapes of elephants, other animals, and a ship. While his poem appears to be largely fanciful, there exists a very down-to-earth description by their owner of trees clipped into similar shapes in the gardens of the Rucellai villa at Quaracchi. The author of the *Terze Rime* described the Medici garden's floral delights: "A dance is there, as gentle as one can say,/ of jasmine, violets, roses and lilies,/ and flowers blue, yellow, white and red."[344] Lilies stood for Florence, roses for the Virgin, violets for humility and the infant Christ. Young Sforza's chaperone Carissimi included in his description of the garden in 1459 the Milanese devices and arms cut in new planted grass, the Sforza adder with the *palle* of Cosimo, as testimony to the flourishing friendship between the two families.

In addition to this floral profusion of Medici interests, associations, and symbols, a garden offered to the cultivated viewer the pleasure of contemplating its traditionally understood intellectual and spiritual significance. A garden quintessentially signified Eden, evoking at once man's happy state before the Fall, and the site of his temptation from which sprang human pain and sorrow; correspondingly, it symbolized the Virgin Mary, the *hortus conclusus* by whose fruitfulness man would be redeemed and returned to the garden of paradise. Dante finds a garden at the end of his path through both *Purgatory* and *Paradise*, first the earthly paradise inhabited by Adam and Eve, and at last the "celestial rose which is the image of the Virgin."[345] In the garden, virtue triumphs over vice, a message underscored in the Medici garden by the bronze figures of David and of Judith and Holofernes. Judith, prefiguring the Virgin, is represented as virtue prevailing over the vice of Luxuria.[346] David was the citizen patriot who triumphed over the foreign tyrant. These explicitly political messages to the Medici guests cultivated the Medici family's image of themselves as representing the civic virtues of the defence of the republic and its liberty against both foreign aggressors and domestic conspirators.[347]

If the garden of the Medici palace was as eloquent a statement of Medici interests and concerns as the edifice itself, a similar fusion of functionalism and the taste for diversion was evident in the family's rural villas. "The Renaissance villa," about which so much has been written in an attempt to establish a typology, is by general consensus a phenomenon of the late fifteenth and early sixteenth centuries. The first real Renaissance villa built by the Medici was at Poggio a Caiano, begun by Lorenzo almost thirty years after his grandfather's death, and indeed not finished before his own demise in 1492.

However, the country villas of merchant patricians had played a major and many-faceted role in Florentine life and culture from at least the middle of the fourteenth century, as literary accounts from Boccaccio's *Decameron* to Giovanni Gherardi's *Paradiso degli Alberti* attest. Where the urban palace was designed to "take the measure" of a man in the city, in the less public and more expansive setting of his rural villa there was more room for recreation, as well as for the serious business of cultivating a source of agricultural produce (most quattrocento villas, even Poggio, were also productive farms) and a reliable territorial base in times of urban stress and conflict.[348] As Amanda Lillie observed, attempts to distinguish the Medici villas to fit preconceived typologies distort the evidence of what the family actually did there; all the Medici rural retreats served various combined functions, although each had its particular emphasis.[349]

Florentine villas were traditionally sites for the enjoyment of fresh air and rural pursuits, of leisure and friendship, the essential elements of a classical ideal of which fifteenth-century patricians were highly conscious. Alberti wrote in his *De Re Aedificatoria* of "the decorum of the town house and the pleasing qualities of villas; a city building requires dignity, a villa delight." Alberti had earlier written much more personally in a brief comment on *Villa*, reflecting bitterly perhaps on the lost "Paradiso degli Alberti": "Buy your villa to nourish your family, not to give pleasure to others."[350] An oft-invoked Virgilian topos decreed that the patrician should work on his own estate, especially tending the vines. In the case of the Medici, this was more than a literary convention; Cosimo and his sons really did so. And although the neoclassical ideal of bucolic pastimes stimulated the building of villas in the later fifteenth century, Florentines had always sought refuge from the heat of Florence in August in a period of *villeggiatura*. Reminders of the originally rural origins of the inhabitants of the city existed not only in the extensive country properties of patricians like the Alberti, Rucellai, and Medici, but also in the "piece of land" somewhere in the country noted in their tax reports by an extremely high proportion of all property-owning Florentines.

Until the very end of the fourteenth century, when Averardo and Cosimo's father Giovanni, the two surviving sons of Francesco, *detto* Bicci, established important banks in Rome, the power of the Medici family and the quality of their image derived chiefly from their position as extensive landholders in the Mugello. The villas of Cafaggiolo and Trebbio, and their surrounding lands, had been in the Medici family's possession for generations (figs. 147 and 148). On the occasion of the first detailed inventory of property for the new tax assessment

147   Giusto Utens, Cafaggiolo, Florence, Museo di Firenze com'era

148   Giusto Utens, Trebbio, Florence, Museo di Firenze com'era

149   Michelozzo, Careggi, Medici villa

of 1427, both were described by their owners as "forti-fied houses," serving the dual purposes of administering the adjacent land and defending it.[351] Cafaggiolo at this time was owned by Averardo; it passed to Cosimo with the extinction of Averardo's line, by 1443 at latest. Trebbio passed out of Cosimo's hands, and into those of his dead brother's son Pierfrancesco, after the division of their joint property in 1451. During the 1430s and 1440s, Cosimo's immediate family owned three main villas; the castle of Trebbio, nearby Cafaggiolo, at the center of the exten-sive Medici estates, and Careggi, much nearer Florence, and purchased by Giovanni di Bicci only in 1417 (fig. 149).

All three villas were originally fairly rude country houses, but since the cultivated pastimes of the owners *in villa* required the appropriate physical and architectural setting, they were renovated, probably by Michelozzo, between 1420 and 1450. All were modified in varying degrees with the addition of classical architectural fea-tures. But they all – particularly Trebbio and Cafaggiolo – retained some features, however superficial, of the defensive appearance appropriate to a still untamed coun-tryside. The loggia at Careggi, which bespeaks a more lit-erally "civilized" way of life, probably postdated Cosimo's era. Although when visiting Cafaggiolo or Trebbio the family often attended services at San Francesco al Bosco, all three villas had their own chapels. Out in the coun-tryside a private chapel indubitably offered its owners more than mere cachet; clearly immediate access to the

sacraments was one of the family's vital concerns.[352] The evidence of letters and diaries sheds a good deal of light on the Medici family's use of villas, and may even illu-minate the issue of the dating of renovations, particularly to Cafaggiolo. For example, the family letters reveal that Averardo, its owner before 1434, was a much more polit-ically important and cultured character than is generally realized. Michelozzo in the 1420s was as much or more Averardo's intimate than Cosimo's, and may very well have refurbished this center of Medici family life in the Mugello to the former's requirements well before Cosimo acquired the property.[353]

Cafaggiolo was a large farming complex with its own hamlet of laborers' houses. The tax reports in which Cosimo and his father assessed the value of their Mugello produce and the costs of its transportation all the way to the city serve to show how much was grown there, and what precise command these urban bankers had over every detail of the agricultural economy. Planting and harvest, loans of seed to laborers and the maintenance of their houses, their personal problems and foibles, their marriages and deaths, figured largely in the lengthy cor-respondence between Cosimo and his factors, who reported regularly to their employers in Florence. In 1464 the factor at Cafaggiolo showed Lorenzo and Giuliano, aged respectively fifteen and eleven, around the estate, instructing them in various practical matters they were expected to master.[354] They went to church at Bosco ai Frati with the members of the rural community, of whom they would soon become the masters. Trebbio, perched on the top of a nearby hill, was more a hunting lodge with a kitchen garden and a few surrounding fields and vineyards, although the tower of the castle served a serious defensive purpose in affording a clear view of any danger approaching from the surrounding towns, or along the main road linking Florence with Bologna and the north.[355]

The different entertainments provided for their guests there suggest the different styles of the three rural villas. Pope Eugenius slept at Cafaggiolo several times on his way north; in 1436 en route to Ferrara, when he pro-mulgated an indulgence for visitors to Bosco ai Frati, and on his journey to Bologna in 1443, after consecrating the rebuilt church of San Marco. In 1449, when Bosco was the site of the chapter general of the Franciscans, Cosimo reputedly offered the hospitality of Cafaggiolo to four hundred friars.[356] Cafaggiolo was the destination of most of the family's extensive summer stays in the country, although the much nearer Careggi was more favored by Cosimo as he grew older. As numerous family letters attest, Trebbio was popular for youthful musical and hunting parties hosted by Piero and Giovanni in the

1440s, and later by Pierfrancesco, along with such other bloodsports as the pursuit of beautiful young women. However, a letter of September 1446 from Ser Alesso at Trebbio to Piero, back in Florence, describes the horticultural pleasures enjoyed there by his elders. The secretary reported that Cosimo and Contessina were well and happy, and also very busy, burning off and cleaning up in preparation for winter: "We are cutting back the wooded areas of the park, and looking forward to the feastday [presumably the traditional family celebration of Cosmas and Damian on 26 September] like children . . ."[357]

The almost suburban villa of Careggi was the site for "visits of state" – it was there that Cosimo and his sons entertained the pope and Galeazzo Maria Sforza with singing and dancing in 1459 – and for the cultivation of more self-consciously intellectual pleasures. There Cosimo received Ficino, to whom he had given a neighboring house associated with the young scholar's "Platonic Academy," and it was there that he reputedly read demanding religious texts, among them Gregory's *Moralia*. However, it was also there that he went to let off steam by staking the vines – a suitably metaphorical gesture – after Giovanni had greatly displeased him by his behavior during a visit to Naples.[358] Careggi was also the scene of Cosimo's final hours; he died there in August 1464. Perhaps the single picture in the room described as "the *camera* which was Cosimo's" in 1492, "a canvas, depicting Our Lord Jesus Christ crucified upon the cross with the Virgin Mary at his feet with other saints," rather similar to the image in Cosimo's cell at San Marco, already hung there at the time of his death.[359]

The villa built at Fiesole by Cosimo's younger son Giovanni was different and original, in that it was his personal creation, and obviously much of its *raison d'être* was its spectacular view of Florence (fig. 150). This gave rise to the quip attributed by Poliziano to Cosimo that he preferred the view from Cafaggiolo, set in the center of the Medici estates, because everything he could see from it, he owned; this was not true of the view from Fiesole, which looked over the city of Florence.[360] It has also encouraged a view of the Fiesole villa itself from a peculiarly modern perspective – as a place for Giovanni to escape from his family and its traditions, without practical function, and lacking any local ties. As Amanda Lillie pointed out in a very subtle assessment of the significance of Giovanni's villa, "all of these observations are as much wrong as right."[361] The real interest of the building's highly original architectural design lies in its very successful integration of the various functions of the villa, including the provision of hospitality for Giovanni's friends as at Trebbio, the cultivation of intellectual life as at Careggi, and even the cultivation of the land, as at Cafaggiolo.

150   Michelozzo, Fiesole, Medici villa

The villa at Fiesole was declared in Cosimo's 1458 Catasto report as Giovanni's personal possession. But in its creation, on which he lavished so much of his time and attention, he had quite a lot of help from his friends and family. On occasions when Giovanni was ill, Piero went to oversee the building. There are detailed discussions in letters from the *amici* of their collective efforts to solve the problems encountered in the earthworks to shore up the steep hill, and in the rather complicated irrigation of the garden.[362] The filling of the house with objects of beauty and distinction – books, instruments, antique sculpture – was also a corporate affair. Donatello, who had been one of Cosimo's favorite artists before Giovanni was born, did some of the most important decorative work.[363] Bartolomeo Serragli, the dealer who for decades had furnished Giovanni with objects for his collection, wrote to him in October 1453 offering his services again and suggesting that Giovanni should "think a little about the villa at Fiesole, before it is finished."[364] Six months later Giovanni Rossi told Giovanni de' Medici that Serragli was going to Naples in eight days' time to send on a lot of things "which we want for Fiesole"; these included "*melarancie*, lemon trees," and other plants for what was to prove one of the most impressive of the Medici gardens.[365]

Indeed, the creation of Giovanni's villa fulfilled a variety of impulses toward cultivated leisure evident in the decoration and renovation of all of Cosimo's properties, where the functional was embellished with grace and style. Like all of these, Giovanni's villa was also closely integrated with its surrounding district. Alessandro Gonzaga wrote to his father from Florence on the feast-day of John the Baptist in 1461: "Tomorrow I am going to dine at a palace belonging to Cosimo's son Giovanni up on the mountain of Fiesole three miles from here, where there are several places dedicated to the religious and among them an abbacy of canons regular at which I understand Cosimo has done some excellent building . . ."[366] Cosimo's patronage at the Badia was making Fiesole a Medici neighborhood, and Giovanni's own patronage there of the convent of San Girolamo reinforced the family's presence on the hill overlooking Florence.[367] Giovanni's young friends also followed him up the hill to Fiesole, building or renting their own properties, or simply visiting, seeking "to enjoy the cool when they want to take the country air." Bartolomeo Scala described to Filelfo how once he "set out in the afternoon for Fiesole, where Giovanni was rusticating, absorbed in his building," and spoke to Scala of his plan to have Filelfo "undertake the work of interpreting Petrarch's poems."[368] The joys of the cultivated life to be lived *in villa* are gracefully celebrated in these lines by Francesco Scambrilla: "Every man may spend some time there resting,/ some days of peace, some hours of tranquility,/ some quiet nights there in some villa,/ enjoying the breezes along his joyful path . . ."[369]

XIII

THE CHAPEL IN THE HEART OF THE PALACE:
A MICROCOSM OF MEDICI PATRONAGE

*Spiritual and social connotations of the Medici chapel
and its Magi frescoes*

Many writers have offered ideas and insights about the
chapel, especially since its recent restoration, which
should be brought together and viewed within the larger
context of Cosimo de' Medici's patronage oeuvre (fig.
151). The chief theme of the chapel's decoration is the
Journey of the Magi. The biblical account of the three
wise men from the East, in later legend transformed into
kings,[1] who saw the star in the sky and followed it to
Bethlehem where it shone above the manger of the
newborn Christ child, provided a perfect metaphor for
the spiritual journey of the wealthy and powerful toward
true devotion, the submission of the kings of the earth
to the supreme authority of the word of God, incarnate
in his Son. The story of the Magi presented this basic
and familiar spiritual lesson in progress from pride to
humility, from preoccupation with the things of this
world to acknowledgment of the infinity of the next,
in a vivid and appealing manner that adapted itself
splendidly to the forms in which spiritual lessons were
customarily expressed and absorbed in this society. The
journey of the Magi became an extremely popular
subject of performances in pageants and elaborate pictorial images throughout the Middle Ages in many
European countries.[2]

The general popularity of the Magi is an indispensable
context of the Medici family's special devotion to them.
It is often suggested that Cosimo consciously asserted his
pretensions to increasing control over Florence through
the medium of this popular story.[3] That may well be so,
but we really do not know. Certainly he participated, clad
in princely robes – a cloak of cloth of gold or fur – in
Florentine processions reenacting the Magi's progress
from Jerusalem, located in the baptistery, or later the
palace of the Signoria, up the Via Larga past the Medici
palace to the convent and church of San Marco, which
represented Bethlehem. The complex at San Marco had

been greatly enhanced by Cosimo's conspicuous generosity, and in his renovations Cosimo took care to foster
the devotion of the confraternities accustomed to meet
there, particularly the company of the Magi, for whom
he built a new chapel.[4] After 1434 the Medici were
indelibly and almost exclusively associated in their native
Florence with this popular cult; they commissioned
numerous other representations of the Magi, including
the fresco in Cosimo's cell at San Marco and several
paintings catalogued in the inventory of the palace of
1492.[5]

However, the worldliness the Magi embodied consisted
as much in their wealth as in their regal power; they were
the patrons of merchants, travelers, and knights as well as
of kings.[6] The spiritual significance of the Magi story was
the opposite of a justification of earthly rule; at Epiphany
the wealthy and powerful of this world knelt before the
King of Heaven. In Florence, if the Magi bore a "political" message, the three kings and their followers were as
likely to be seen as expressing the realities of the Medici
partisan regime, as to represent the Medici family as putative princes. The portraits of Medici *parenti* and *amici* in
the retinues on the east and west walls of the chapel were
reminders of the role in the Medici rise to power of their
partisans and foreign allies, and most of the Florentine
Magi images of the mid-fifteenth century not attributed
to the Medici were commissioned by their friends,
apparently in tribute to their Medici patrons.[7] Donato
Acciaiuoli, in a letter to Lorenzo in 1468, described the
Medici-dominated confraternity of the Magi, which met
at San Marco and comprised a good number of the most
distinguished citizens of Florence, not as their devotional
kingdom, but as "la Repubblica de' Magi."[8]

The frescoes in the chapel, completed around 1459, just
five years before Cosimo's death, were the culmination of
his long association with the cult of the Magi. They may
be seen as imaging his own spiritual journey as a wealthy
and powerful man, who enjoyed, as Vespasiano observed,
"great authority in the city," but who in his gifts to the

Church made offering as the Magi did to the Christ child, a "sacrifice with heart, word, and work" that acknowledged the ultimate authority of Christ, the one true Lord who alone holds out the glittering prize of eternal life. As the devotional literature so familiar to Cosimo and his fellow Florentines instructed, this was the final goal on which man should center himself, just as at the heart of the splendid Medici palace stood its chapel, a small, architecturally self-contained casket filled with the jewels of the craftsman's art.[9]

Cosimo's was almost the first chapel to be constructed for a private palace in Florence.[10] As well as being the devotional center of the palace, the chapel was also the center of Cosimo's social and diplomatic life in his last years, although the injunction in an inscription once displayed in the chapel that "the profane crowd" should not set foot in it implies an expectation that those who did would respect this consecrated place.[11] It could be entered either from a private room to the east, or from the grand staircase on the west, serving as the site for the ceremonial reception of individuals and the audience of public delegations, as well as the place where the family heard mass or retired for private prayer and meditation. The visit of Galeazzo Maria Sforza in April 1459, not long after the palace was completed, and before the walls of the chapel were adorned with Benozzo Gozzoli's frescoes, begun in the summer of that year, produced an unusually rich record concerning its usage.

When the young Sforza arrived at the Medici palace, he was received by Cosimo in the chapel. As he wrote to his father, Cosimo's old friend Francesco Sforza: "I went to see the magnificent Cosimo, whom I found in his chapel, no less ornate and beautiful than the rest of the house . . . He embraced me with great generosity and affection, and almost weeping with happiness and tenderness, said that in all his life he could never have been more pleased by anything, since wishing above all to see your Excellency, seeing me he seemed to see you." According to the boy's chaperone, Carissimi, "he was then obliged to leave because of the multitude who arrived wishing to see the aforesaid magnificent Cosimo."

Later in the day, Galeazzo Maria returned to find Cosimo "in the same chapel from which he was unable to move"; at this point in his life, being virtually immobilized by illness, he chose to spend much of his time in his spiritual retreat.[12] Since there was a priest resident in the household, he probably heard mass there every day. Certainly on six of the fifteen days of his stay in Florence, Galeazzo Maria attended mass in the Medici chapel; he also went to services in other locations of particular civic and religious importance, including Santissima Annunziata, the baptistery, and the pope's apartment

in Santa Maria Novella.[13] To the young Sforza, the Medici chapel seemed no less than "an earthly paradise." To an anonymous popular poet, known as the author of the "*Terze rime* in praise of Cosimo de' Medici and his sons and of the honors done . . . to the son of the duke of Milan and to the pope on their visit to Florence," the chapel was "so ornate/ that it has no equal in all the universe,/ so well prepared is it for the worship of God./ And he who looks at it carefully from every side/ will say that it is the tabernacle of the Divine Three . . . ," the Trinity to whom it was dedicated.[14]

The confusion or conflation of the secular and spiritual apparent in the uses of the chapel, as in the associations of the Magi whom Cosimo made his own patrons and exempla, invited comment from Nicodemo, the Milanese ambassador, as he watched the citizens of Florence flocking to the Medici palace to declare their allegiance to Cosimo in 1458, after the resolution of an extended challenge to the government of the Medici regime: "It was as if [Cosimo] were holding a church dedication [*sagra*] at home."[15] The fresco cycle and its culmination in Lippi's altarpiece, stressing, with Saint Bernard's presence, contemplation and withdrawal into the wilderness of penance, expresses the essence of Cosimo's personal piety and charity, symbolized similarly in his withdrawal to a cell at the convent of San Marco, where the Dominicans continued the Cistercian devotion to Mary that was Saint Bernard's major contribution to popular religious observance. Cosimo could, however, be seen as incorporating these cults into his own domestic life in a manner that some Florentines might have felt to be as inappropriate to an individual citizen as staging a church dedication at home. Nicodemo's observation implies no such adverse judgment, but it seems to be implicit in the removal, after the expulsion of the Medici in 1494, of the chapel furnishings, the altar, and its altarpiece to the palace of the Signoria, a site where the blending of sacred and secular was legitimized by the divinely sanctioned mission of the Florentine republic.

Conversely, the style of piety that stressed intense emotional and imaginative identification with Christ and his earthly experience, so strongly expressed in the texts and images surveyed in this study, fostered associations that might seem profane to modern scholars, but were a natural consequence of the quattrocento tendency to frame and even recast personal experience in terms of Christian symbolism and allegory. The meeting between Cosimo and the young son of his major supporter and ally, the duke of Milan, certainly constituted a ceremonial reaffirmation of the crucial diplomatic ties between Florence, the Medici, and the Sforza. But whereas many historians classify this occasion simply in the category of

151   Florence, Medici palace, chapel

"political" acts, an example of Cosimo transacting the business of the state in his own private palace, the perceptions of the protagonists of this encounter were clearly more complex. In the passage from his letter to his father cited above, Galeazzo Maria stressed the elements of personal patronage, obligation, and affection in the relationship between Sforza and Cosimo, who embraced the son with the love he felt for the father. The attendant Carissimi noted the crowd of supplicants seeking audience with their patron Cosimo, but his comment on the meeting between Cosimo and the young Sforza associated it primarily with one of the great Christian images of encounter, the presentation of "our Lord, Jesus Christ" to Simeon, "a man just and devout," at the temple, with all its implications of divine approbation of both parties. As Carissimi wrote to the duke, Cosimo gave Galeazzo Maria his blessing, and "I really believe that he went on to say, 'Now let thy servant depart, O Lord our Father,' as Simeon did at the presentation at the altar."[16]

The intensely decorated small space of the chapel is filled with images laden with symbolism, which art historians in their ekphrases have noted and variously interpreted. The aim of this chapter is not to offer a derivative account of these observations, nor to make amateurish additions to them, but rather to note when and how these interpretations are supported and enriched by what we have learned from other evidence of Cosimo's interests and concerns. It is also to suggest that whatever the conscious intentions of the patron animating this grand design, or the precise significance of particular details of the images rendered by the artists who realized it, these are fused in a whole that expresses the unity of Cosimo's identity as a Christian, citizen of Florence, and patron of art. The chapel frescoes in particular are the product of a cohesive, if many-faceted devotional vision articulated by the artist in close consultation with his family of patrons,[17] their imagery and symbolism embracing the play of sacred and secular in the Medici universe.

Among the earlier representations of the Magi to which Gozzoli's frescoes owe formal debts, especially important is Gentile da Fabriano's altarpiece for the Strozzi family chapel in Santa Trinita (fig. 153).[18] Before the Medici, the Strozzi had associated themselves with the Magi; both lineages, like many others throughout Europe, saw the wise and wealthy monarchs from the East as appropriate symbols of their familial identity. However, the Magi themes in the Medici chapel are articulated with explicit attention to a number of quite particular interests of Cosimo and his sons, among them an extreme pleasure in the opulence of domestic decoration, a delight in "the variety of *ingegni*" (in this case the painter's ingenuity in depicting a cavalcade of men and animals and

scenes), a fascination with the exotic east as Florentines had observed it in the dress and customs of the members of the Eastern delegation at the church council in 1439, Cosimo's participation in agricultural and country life at his villas of Cafaggiolo and Trebbio, and his sons' addiction as youths to the chase.

Fra Filippo Lippi's altarpiece, at once the visual focal point of the chapel and the destination of the cortège that winds around its walls, images both the Trinity of Father, Son, and Holy Ghost, and the Incarnation of God, through the action of the Holy Spirit, in his Son born of the Virgin Mary (fig. 163). These themes have appeared in other Medici commissions. The conspicuous presence in the altarpiece of Saint John the Baptist, patron of the city of Florence, and Saint Bernard, patron of its governing magistracy, expresses the strong Florentine interest in these saints and their writings, and evokes Cosimo's lifelong personal identification with, and devotion to, the governance of his native city. The Medici devotion to the Magi cult might also be seen as paying indirect homage to their chief allies, the Sforza of Milan, since it was to Milan that Saint Eustorgius, the early Christian bishop of that city, first brought the bodies of the Magi for burial.[19]

The chapel decoration and its themes

The palace chapel was probably built between 1450 and 1455; Harriet Caplow remarked that it repeated some favorite motifs that Michelozzo had used in the tabernacle-chapel at Santissima Annunziata.[20] Almost no natural light penetrated the chapel at the heart of the palace; it was illuminated only by torches and candles, which picked out the brilliance of silver and gold, not just in the coffered ceiling and the frescoes on the walls, but also the gold outlining of the architectural members, and the highlights of stonework painted white in imitation of marble. Much of the chapel's original visual effect thus consisted in the gleaming decorative details that "reverberated" in the dimness. (Vasari complained in the sixteenth century that the chapel was so dark he could not see the portraits well enough to describe them.)[21] However, contrasts of light and dark were symbols central to the perceptions of good and evil, knowledge and ignorance, life and death. A *luogo tenebroso* set the mood of the Magi's awareness of the length of the journey yet to be accomplished by sinful man, his salvation still in doubt. In 1459 Cosimo was, if hardly "in the middle of our life's journey," still certainly in the "dark wood," an image imprinted on every educated Florentine's mind by the opening lines of Dante's *Commedia*, and which may have helped to inspire the wilderness setting of the Nativity of the altarpiece.

The wooden coffered ceiling was gilded and painted in blue, red, green, and white – the colors of the sky and of the three theological virtues, faith, hope, and charity, as of Piero de' Medici's livery. It was carved with geometrical shapes and flowers, especially roses, associated both with the Virgin and with the pope (fig. 154). The chancel ceiling was dominated by the emblem of San Bernardino, the flaming sun, surrounded by the emblems of the Medici family; a gilded garland of red, white, and green feathers held together by pairs of silver and gold diamond rings, symbolizing eternity, and at the four corners diamond rings threaded by ribbons bearing the motto "SEMPER". The theme of endurance, of secular or of spiritual faith, was further elaborated in the cornice worked with a design of rings, fusaroles, and palms. The palm, in the ancient world a symbol of military victory carried in triumphal processions, was adopted by the early church as the emblem of Christ's victory over death, and became the sign of a martyred saint. In the minds of Renaissance men, filled with the literature and images of both classical and Christian cultures, such symbols resonated equally with secular and spiritual significance.

The pavement was exquisitely worked in polychrome marble, reminiscent of the Florentine baptistery (fig. 152), but also of early Christian basilicas in Rome, the imperial chapel in Constantinople, and the pavement of Saint Mark's in Venice.[22] Such Cosmatesque pavements were familiar to the Medici from their years spent on business in the Eternal City and in Venice, where Cosimo resided for most of his year in exile; an interest in their use in the East may have been fed by the reports furnished to Cosimo from cultural emissaries such as Benedetto Dei and Ciriaco da Ancona. Geometric symbolism is a major feature of the Medici chapel pavement. Alberti in his comment on the decoration of sacred buildings observed that "lines and figures which regard music and geometry will make the spirit inclined to worship." The relationship between the centre, the circle, and the regular polygons signified the mystery of the division of one into many, the essence of the Trinity, a symbolism deriving from Neoplatonism through Christianity, Judaism, and Islam. The same symbolism recurs in Cosimo's tomb marker in San Lorenzo (fig. 188).[23] The red, white, and green of the stones were the traditional colors of mosaic decoration in Florence, but like those of the ceiling they evoked the theological virtues and Piero's use of them in his livery. At the center of the floor was a porphyry disk, like the one on the vesting table in the old sacristy. These disks were used in antiquity, and later

152   Florence, baptistery, pavement

in Byzantine buildings, to mark the position of important persons who were often, but not always, emperors or kings. In early Christian buildings they customarily referred to the presence of the body of Christ, the focus of the Medici chapel altarpiece and the goal of the Magi procession.[24]

The altar of the chancel, lost in the late fifteenth century, was of red marble; its walls were inlaid with geometric designs incorporating various Medici emblems – the balls, diamond rings, and feathers. Gozzoli began the frescoes on the chapel walls in the summer of 1459, and finished them by December; Lippi's altarpiece was probably in place by then. Last to be completed, possibly between 1470 and 1475, were the intarsiated wooden

153   Gentile da
Fabriano, *Adoration of
the Magi*, Florence,
Uffizi

choir stalls attributed to Giuliano da Sangallo.[25] These
were richly carved with Medicean arms and devices, and
with symbols of the city of Florence, the cross of the
popolo and the lily of the commune. The combination of
these symbols, especially in the representation on one seat
of the lily of Florence encircled by the Medici diamond
ring, could equally signify pretensions to domination or
promises of preservation and protection. The choir stalls
and the intarsia door of the right sacristy are among
the few surviving examples of this virtuoso and labor-
intensive form of decoration so lavishly applied to the
surfaces of the original Medici palace.

There is a key to the reading of the elaborate symbolism of the Medici palace chapel in a collection of
inscriptions, which also includes the inscriptions for
Donatello's *David* and his *Judith and Holofernes*, recorded
and probably written between 1460 and 1470 by Gentile
Becchi.[26] Becchi was a learned prelate who from 1454
lived in the Medici palace as tutor and companion to
the young Lorenzo and Giuliano, and probably served
as the family's resident priest.[27] The inscription for the
Medici palace chapel explains the significance of the
component parts of its decoration and their relation to

the whole. Cristina Acidini suggested that this text once
appeared in front of the altar on a plaque that was
removed when the chapel and its furnishings were plun-
dered after the expulsion of the Medici in 1494. Signs of
damage to the pavement can be seen at this spot. Such a
plaque would certainly be consistent with Cosimo's fondness for labeling his commissions with messages indicating their meaning. Although Becchi, who was dependent
on Medici patronage, was a somewhat extravagant
encomiast of the family in his Latin poetry in praise of
Cosimo, which greatly exceeded the patriarch's more
sober representations of himself, it is likely that in composing an inscription to be placed in their private chapel
the humanist accurately represented the family's perceptions of it. Certainly he saw the Magi company through
Medici eyes, and was eager to assist it on their behalf.
Even before one of its members, Filippo Martelli,
apprised Lorenzo of an appeal drafted by Becchi in 1467
concerning an indulgence for "your confraternity," Becchi
himself was able to inform Cosimo's grandson that he had
obtained this privilege.[28]

The titulus of the inscription was in prose: "In
Cosimo's chapel, there are firstly the Magi, secondly the

angels singing, thirdly Mary adoring her newborn child, painted so that visitors to the chapel should come to make sacrifice with heart, with words, and with deeds." These virtuous actions may be conceived as corresponding to, and intended to expiate, the three ways of sinning, in thought, word, and deed, expounded by Saint Jerome in his *Commentary on Ezekiel*. Cosimo owned several works of Saint Jerome, and this may have been among them; the formulation was in any case common currency in devotional circles.[29] The verse distych reads: "The gifts of the kings, the prayers of the supernal spirits, the mind of the Virgin, are the sacred things in this temple. Let the profane crowd not set foot in here." This trilogy of meaning is echoed in the three Magi and their three gifts, and the three persons of the Trinity, represented in Lippi's painting. The inscription suggests a unified conception of the frescoes and the altarpiece, and a reading that begins not with the altar, but with the Magi, setting forth to accomplish the sacrificial deeds of their spiritual journey.

154   Florence, Medici palace, chapel, ceiling

Patrons and artist

For some decades scholars have followed Gombrich in expressing surprise – and disappointment – at the Medici embrace in Gozzoli's frescoes of the supposedly retardataire International Gothic style at the height of the Florentine antique revival. Closer study of the diverse currents of quattrocento artistic style has suggested, as William Hood observed, that such pigeonholing terms have little meaning in practice.[30] They fail to take account of the complexity of influences on artists, and ignore the cross-fertilization of traditions resulting in work neither purely Gothic nor purely antique; "neither ancient nor modern." Anna Padoa Rizzo proposed that part of the modernity of Gozzoli's Medici palace frescoes lay in their very sumptuousness, often seen as a throwback to the courtly styles of northern Europe, but arguably just as much an expression of the growing later fifteenth-century taste for elaborate domestic decoration.[31] The influence on the frescoes of performative art, a major element in the visual experience of both patron and artist, of theatrical representation on which one-point perspective could not be imposed, may have increased the artist's emphasis on the imaginative, illusory, magical aspects of the scenes, independent of more formal representational traditions.[32]

The Medici association with Benozzo Gozzoli began at San Marco. As Angelico's chief assistant there, Gozzoli was almost certainly responsible for the fresco of the Magi in Cosimo's cell (fig. 61). Although the mood of the San

Marco Magi fresco was infinitely more austere, in its incorporation of an Eastern sage, and in its vibrant palette, it prefigured the palace chapel frescoes.[33] Gozzoli also worked on the San Marco altarpiece and the painted shutters for the treasure chest at Santissima Annunziata.

A series of frescoes depicting the Journey of the Magi for Florence's major patrons was a marvelous commission indeed for any artist. This was a theme that lent itself to the display of the painter's talents. It contained all the elements that Alberti had enumerated in his influential treatise on painting, written in 1435, describing the narrative (*historia*), "the most important part of the painter's work . . . in which there should be every abundance and beauty of things; we should take care to learn to paint well, as far as our talent allows, not only the human figure but also the horse, the dog and other living creatures, and every object worthy to be seen."[34] The chapel frescoes gave Gozzoli the opportunity, in his splendid fulfilment of the Albertian requirement of *varietà*, to vie with the Magi tondo for the Medici attributed to his masters Angelico and Filippo Lippi, as well as with renowned renditions of this theme by earlier giants on the Florentine artistic scene, most notably Lorenzo Monaco and Gentile da Fabriano.

When it came to the decoration, as their correspondence shows, his Medici patrons expected Gozzoli to work, like their other friends and clients, in close consultation with the family, and indeed, like the best of their *amici*, the painter implemented the Medicean design with imagination as well as good faith. His devoted service to the Medici and his strong sense of self are both expressed in at least two and perhaps three self-portraits in the frescoes. In one he placed himself appropriately in the train of the family's retainers, boldly labelled by the name on his cap: "BENOZZ DI LE . . ." (fig. 157).[35]

Gozzoli's letters concerning the chapel frescoes were addressed to Piero. The scant remaining evidence indicates that Cosimo's elder son was responsible for the overseeing of this commission, as for many other of the adornments of the new palace. As noted, the palace was not just the residence of the Medici family; it was the embodiment of the identity of the lineage, and the vehicle for its self-expression. Consequently, there is no meaningful distinction to be made on the basis of the chapel decoration between the patronage of Cosimo and of his sons. As Rab Hatfield pointed out, it makes no sense to speak of "Piero's chapel . . . the chapel was no more Piero's than anyone else's in the family . . . it was part of the building, and if it belonged to anyone, it belonged to Cosimo."[36] There is no need to wonder, as Gombrich did, "what old Cosimo may have thought of this work by Fra Angelico's favourite pupil";[37] whatever was in the palace was surely there by Cosimo's wish or consent.

Exotic influences, real and imagined: the church council and Magi images in Medici commissions and in Florentine processions and performances

Gombrich dismissed a nineteenth-century tradition that the frescoes of the Journey of the Magi, which begin on the east wall of the Medici chapel (fig. 156), literally represented the arrival of the emperor and patriarch of Byzantium in Florence for the council of the eastern and western churches in 1439. He did so on the grounds that the frescoes were painted twenty years after this event, which in the end failed to achieve its goals.[38] Other scholars have pointed out that the figures of Balthazar and Melchior are not in fact portraits of the emperor and the patriarch. There is considerable evidence in other commissions by Cosimo, most notably at San Lorenzo, that the church council long remained vivid in his mind as one of the high points of his service to Church and commune. However, in the chapel decoration no real attempt is made, by comparison with Gozzoli's fresco of the Magi in Cosimo's cell at San Marco, or with the scenes for the predella of the San Marco altarpiece in which Gozzoli also had a hand, at a convincing representation of Eastern figures or settings. Where the San Marco predella depicts Lysias in full Eastern dress (fig. 155), along with camels amidst desert sands, in the chapel

155   Fra Angelico, *Saints Cosmas and Damian before Lycias*, predella panel of San Marco altarpiece, Munich, Alte Pinakothek

frescoes we see a thoroughly Tuscan landscape, peopled essentially by familiar faces and figures clad in Florentine dress, however fancy.

Nevertheless, viewers have been struck by the exotic impression of the whole, as well as those touches intended to evoke some sense of the distant kingdoms from which the Magi came. Some riders at the very ends of the cortèges wear Eastern headdress and have dark complexions, as do Balthazar and the black bowman in attendance on the train of Cosimo and his sons, and there are a leopard, a monkey, and several camels in the procession of the eldest Magus, Melchior (figs. 156, 159 and 160). Such elements, many of them already present in Gentile da Fabriano's Magi altarpiece of 1423, became more pronounced in Florentine paintings as the century proceeded; some, like genuine Eastern headgear, only appear after 1439. The Florentine interest in Greek culture dates from at least the beginning of the century, when a group of patricians began to offer their patronage to Greek scholars, and the attempt to imagine Christian realms far distant in time and space was a feature of Magi and related processions and performances long before the church council. However, the presence of the council delegates both sharpened Florentine appetites for more precise knowledge of the exotic East whence the legendary Magi had come, and stimulated Florentine imaginations concerning these remote regions. When, in January 1439, the Medici household offered its hospitality to Palaeologus, emperor of the Greeks, he may well have seemed to them the living embodiment of the legendary wise man and prince from the East.

In addition to the Greeks, other Mediterranean Christians to the east of Rome, including the Armenians, Copts, and Ethiopans, sought unity with the Roman Catholic Church at this time. The historic accord of 5 July 1439 included only the Greeks and the Russian bishop, but Pope Eugenius was also in contact with Christian communities in India and Egypt, and sent his Franciscan representative in Africa letters of recommendation to present to the emperor of the Ethiopians. The papal delegate was graciously received by the patriarch of the Copts, who dispatched a turbaned delegation to Florence, but communication with Ethiopia proved effectively impossible.[39] However, some evidence of the extent to which Ethiopia captured the imagination of the Florentines is the letter attributed to the legendary Ethiopian bishop and king Prester John, circulating in Florence around this time. It was copied by Michele di Nofri del Giogante into his most important personal compilations. A letter of 1441 to Giovanni di Cosimo from Ser Alesso, Cosimo's secretary and household factotum, gave news of an embassy to Prester John.[40] Cosimo provided financial assistance for the attempted union with the Indians and the Ethiopians, as is known from a document dated 11 May 1442, recording a payment from the Medici bank of 51 florins, 25 soldi, "for the expedition to the Indians and Jacobites," and continuing diplomacy after 1439 led finally to the union of the Coptic Church with Rome on 4 February 1442.[41]

We have seen how closely images from art, life, and literature informed one another, and that performances particularly inspired the *invenzione* of artists. The procession on the walls of the palace was probably constructed in Gozzoli's imagination from a combination of pictorial models for representing the Magi, and the observation of a variety of actual processions and performances. Outstanding among such events in the artist's lifetime were the splendid ceremonies enacted during the Council of Florence, when he was at the impressionable age of eighteen or so, and the festivities in April 1459 for the visit of Pope Pius II and of Galeazzo Maria Sforza, which occurred just before he began work on the chapel's decoration, and would still have been fresh in his mind. More explicit visual models were available in representations associated with the Magi, including the annual parade of floats for the feast of the city's patron saint, and the elaborate performances of the company of the Magi at San Marco in which the Medici played major roles.[42]

The Journey of the Magi served the Medici well as a personal icon because the related devotional cult could incorporate a number of occasions of special significance

to Cosimo and his family. At the re-dedication on 6 January 1443 of the Medici-renovated church and convent of San Marco to Saints Cosmas and Damian as well as to Saint Mark, Angelico's new altarpiece was revealed to the public for the first time, as it would be henceforth at each Epiphany, a ceremony bringing with it the benefit to the attendant congregation of special indulgences decreed by Pope Eugenius IV. This added a new Epiphany event to San Marco ceremonial, which already featured the biennial or cinquennial performance of the Magi festival. Epiphany was also the date traditionally associated with the baptism of Christ by Saint John. Since Piero di Cosimo's elder son, Lorenzo, was conveniently born on 2 January, he associated himself with Epiphany by celebrating his birthday a few days later, on 6 January.[43] Such coincidences were obviously symbolically very satisfying. In the 1470s and 1480s the sermons addressed by Lorenzo's intellectual friends, among them Ficino, Landino, and Giovanni Nesi, to the congregation of the company were to connect the mission of the Magi, by means of Platonic correspondences, quite explicitly to liberality and charity. However, this association, implicit in traditional observance, had long since been articulated more simply in the words and deeds of Antoninus and Cosimo, who cooperated in founding the charitable confraternity of San Martino and in fostering the cult of the Magi centered on the powerful symbolism of the gift.[44]

The first record of the "festa de' Magi" at San Marco, which housed a replica of the manger, is from 1390. In 1408 the commune officially recognized the cult and made the Sei di Mercanzia, the merchants' tribunal, responsible for their own and the guild consuls' Epiphany offerings of candles at San Marco. A levy on Jewish merchants subsidized the devotions of their Christian brothers, "for the honor and glory of God and his most holy Trinity, and then for the fame of the city, and the consolation and joy of all citizens."[45] Cosimo was a powerful figure at the court of the Mercanzia by the mid-1420s, as his earliest surviving letters reveal. In 1419 the regime, suspicious of confraternities' potential function as centers of political conspiracy, had suspended their activities, but by 1426 the Magi confraternity was operational again, and in June 1428 it contributed a remarkable processional float to the San Giovanni day celebrations. Six months later, at Epiphany 1429, the Compagnia staged an elaborate all-day performance.

In 1435, just after the Medici family's return from exile, Cosimo could well have been among the *festaiuoli* of the Magi whom the blind poet Niccolò Cieco enjoined to fulfil their duties in unity. "Let the high-flown beginnings and vague deliberations/ be silenced, O lord captains,/

and fertile minds and wisdom and experienced hands/ take the great arrangements into their care./ And may full faith be given to those who know,/ nor their sane counsel be rejected."[46] Niccolò's poem indicates the extent of popular interest in the festival; at the same time, given his sway over the audiences at San Martino, he would have made a first-rate mouthpiece for the desires and aspirations of the *festaiuoli* themselves. In 1446/7 this body certainly included Giovanni di Cosimo and Michelozzo.[47] A letter to the poet Burchiello from Rosello Roselli, also a popular poet and close Medici companion, relayed to him several messages from Giovanni di Cosimo, including an injunction: "Be sure to line up every detail for the feast of the Magi, as you want to involve Michelino [as the sculptor Michelozzo was known in the Medici circle] with [making] the float . . ."[48]

In December 1450 Cosimo's wife Contessina wrote to her son Giovanni that their friend Messer Rosello had procured for Cosimo a fine cloak "of marten and sables" in the Polish style; he also sent a pair of gloves, and "a fish-tailed cap" a yard long. She observed that "when we need to stage the Magi procession again, these will give my cloth of gold a bit of a rest."[49] The Polish cloak represented the insertion of a genuinely Eastern, in fact Armenian, element into the Medici Magi pageant. The Armenians, including those from Poland, had been invited to the church council, and their expenses were paid by Cosimo and Lorenzo de' Medici,[50] who took a special interest in the Armenians and in their plays and performances. Well before the council, this community was already a notable presence in Florence, owing to the importation of slave and other labor from eastern Europe. Pope Eugenius's "Decretum Concerning the Armenians," of November 1439 affirmed the contested number of the sacraments as seven, but allowed the Armenians freedom in the celebration of their feasts, and put an end to the Western abuse of baptising, and then keeping fugitive Armenian slaves.[51] Cosimo and Lorenzo de' Medici manumitted a number of slaves at this time, and the company of the Armenians, which met in the church of the Armenian monks in the Medici parish of San Lorenzo, was one of the very select number of religious organizations chosen by Cosimo to take part in his last rites.[52]

A letter of 1439 from Lorenzo de' Medici to his elder brother Cosimo reveals the extent of the family's involvement with urban and rural workers in the celebration of festivals relating to the Magi and the fantasy kingdoms of the East, centred on the Armenian church in their neighborhood. Writing from the villa of Trebbio, Lorenzo advised Cosimo that "the bearer of this letter is Dumbo [Becchone] our laborer." Ser Alesso was to be instructed to

> hunt up a cloak in the Greek style for Dumbo and send him as an ambassador to the emperor on behalf of the king of Armenia, and make sure he is advised properly about it. The parish priest of San Ghavino hasn't let me know much, so that I don't know what is needed for the festivals; if I know, I will provide it. You would do well to come to the aid of your Persian who wears her hair in the Greek style at the very feet of the brothers of San Francescho dell'Osservanza [Bosco ai Frati]. She was the most beautiful thing in the world and we were utterly taken with her.[53]

The performance to which the letter refers was probably part of the San Giovanni parade, in which the Armenian church was also responsible for the Resurrection play. The 1439 procession was especially splendid and made a tremendous impression on the visitors from the East. The Russian bishop Abram de Souzdal left a long and enthusiastic account of it, and a member of the Greek delegation remarked particularly on the performance of the Magi.[54]

The Armenian company called its district the "Land of the King of the Millstone" (della Macina), one part of a festive hierarchy of noble kingdoms, dominated by the Compagnia de' Magi, and including Egypt, Ethiopia and Nubia, Arabia, Sheba, India, both the Medias, and Armenia. A comment in the chronicle of Giovanni Villani suggests that these fantasy kingdoms dated back at least to the early fourteenth century.[55] The hierarchy of the festive kingdoms also mirrored aspects of real life in Florence. Just as the Armenian kingdom of the millstone was dominated by the Magi under Medici patronage, so was the working-class district of the same name. This was the Canto alle Macine, "the corner of the millstones," at the intersection of the present Via Guelfa and Via de' Ginori, not a hundred yards from the Medici palace. It was here that a group who identified themselves as "the youths from the Canto alle Macine" gathered after the Pazzi conspirators' assassination of Giuliano de' Medici, Cosimo's younger grandson, in 1478. They described their pursuit of the conspirators as far as the Porta San Gallo, in a letter to Lorenzo assuring him of their undying loyalty, and their readiness to put this to the test of arms whenever he might need them.[56]

Further evidence of the role of the Magi in a play between fantasy and reality is provided by a letter from the Compagnia de' Magi to the Compagnia di San Bartolomeo (Bartholomew was the disciple of Christ responsible for establishing Christianity in Armenia) concerning preparations for some forthcoming pageants. The letter was found in one of Giovanni Pigli's several compilations, completed around 1469.[57] Pigli entertained John Palaeologus at his villa at Peretola in July 1439; his brother Gerozzo was then head of the London branch of the Medici bank. The letter in question was written in 1481, a year after Pigli's death, and seventeen years after Cosimo's; however, it testifies to the elaborate historical and symbolic framework in which these festivities were set, not least in the manner in which it is dated, "5110 after the Flood." It was sent from "Guaspar, Baldassar et Melchior," the three Magi,

> by the grace of almighty God princes and deputies in the oriental parts, etc . . . to the most devout and illustrious princes, governors and protectors of the most excellent kingdom dedicated to the holy college which under the glorious name of the apostle Bartholomew journeys to the Italic parts in the splendid city of Florence . . . We notify your illustrious Lords that to the thrones of our possessions, your actions are acceptable and indeed most gracious, and have aroused in us the greatest benevolence . . . We should like to have been able to present ourselves personally with all ceremony, but because we are occupied in transforming our kingdoms – and expecially Egypt, Ethiopia and Nubia, Ar[a]bia, Sabea, India, Madja etc. and Armenia, it has been impossible to give ourselves this pleasure . . . so we send to you with all haste a solemn embassy, from which you will understand more fully our fervor . . . Written in the oriental parts near those regions bordered by the equator in the year of the flood 5110.[58]

While the Magi frescoes in the Medici chapel are far from being a literal representation of the Council of Florence, they certainly represent the imaginative identification of the Medici with these Eastern potentates, of which the family's major role in the church council seems to have been both a cause and an effect.[59] This perspective on the Medici attachment to the image of the Magi, emphasizing the part played by fantasy and imagination in the service of religious devotion in their adoption of the Magi as an "icon," is an important corrective to attempts to interpret this essentially, and reductively, in terms of their supposed pretensions to rule over Florence.

The Magi on Medici territory: incorporating family and friends

The decoration of the Medici chapel constitutes a continuous narrative. On the walls to the east, south, and west are depicted the cortèges of the three Magi. On the north

wall is the altar with Lippi's representation of the Nativity, the goal of their journey, flanked by frescoes of angels rejoicing while the shepherds watch over their flocks in the fields. The scenes of the Magi are related, as Becchi's inscription noted, by an elaborate system of correspondences of three, a traditional use of numbers as symbols, keys, and memory devices which sermons and compilations of devotional literature have made familiar. Proceeding from east to west, on a journey through life and time to eternity, Caspar, Balthazar, and Melchior represent respectively Asia, Africa, and Europe; youth, maturity, and age; morning, noon, and evening; spring, summer, and autumn. Each scene is depicted predominantly in colors of white, green, and red, the colors of the three theological virtues. The three Magi bear the three gifts of gold, frankincense, and myrrh. The plethora of symbolic significances of these gifts as enumerated by Iacopo da Voragine in his popular work, the *Golden Legend*, indicates the propensity of the medieval and Renaissance mind to enrich its perceptions of simple signs by multiplying their meanings almost endlessly.[60]

The journey begins with the Medici family, as they start out, appropriately on the east wall of the chapel, on a road winding down from a crenellated fortification at once reminiscent of Cafaggiolo and Trebbio and of trecento representations of Jerusalem, where the Magi were summoned to an audience with Herod before going on to Bethlehem (fig. 156).[61] The castle is one of several devices in the frescoes that serve to locate the Medici family in alternative time and space, both real and ideal. They are depicted not as Magi, but as following in their footsteps, as Saint Bernard enjoined all Christians to follow the steps indicated by the Holy Trinity, proceeding by humility and charity to the revelation of truth in Glory.[62] Comparison with authenticated portraits does not support traditions that the youngest, golden-haired magus represents Lorenzo, the mature and dark-complexioned Balthazar on the south wall John VIII Palaeologus, emperor of the Greeks, or the elderly Melchior the patriarch of Constantinople. The three Magi are ideal types who may stand, among many other things, for the three generations of Cosimo's family; Lorenzo, Piero, and the patriarch himself. The actual, clearly individuated portraits of the family and their relatives and retainers appear in the cortège following in the train of the young Caspar (fig. 157).

It is hard to be entirely confident of the identification of individuals in a period when genuine portraits were comparatively rare, and often taken from death-masks in extreme old age. Cristina Acidini's recent proposals, considering earlier suggestions in the clearer light of the restored image, and in the contexts of the protocol of

156   Benozzo Gozzoli, Florence, Medici palace, chapel, east wall

processions and portraits and our knowledge of the Medici familial circle, are generally plausible (figs. 158 and 159).[63] Cosimo, mounted on a mule which could be seen as a symbol of humility, often adopted by abbots and popes, but which family letters record was also an animal members of the family rode on their journeys around the countryside and between Florence and their villas,[64] is flanked by his sons Piero, Giovanni, and the illegitimate Carlo. The son of Cosimo's Circassian slave, Carlo is clearly distinguished by his dark skin, and by his exotic features and headdress.

Behind the principal members of the family, in the front row to the left of them, are their principal allies; the young Giangaleazzo Maria on a horse bearing the devices of the Sforza of Milan, and beside him Sigis-

mondo Malatesta, lord of Rimini, and once captain of the Florentine forces, encountered earlier in real life at Cosimo's side at the consecration of the cathedral in 1436. Behind them, in the second row of portraits, are the youthful sons of Piero, Lorenzo and Giuliano, and Cosimino, son of Giovanni di Cosimo, who died at the age of seven in 1461, just two years before his father. Alongside these may be Giovanni di Francesco Tornabuoni, brother of Lucrezia, Piero's wife, and head of the Rome branch of the Medici bank. In the center of the third row of the Medici *familia* of friends, relatives, and retainers, is the artist.

The portrait of the patron on this wall may be the only one made in Cosimo's lifetime, although scholars have discerned likenesses of Cosimo and his wife Contessina

157 Medici palace, chapel, east wall, detail of portraits

158 Diagram of east wall of Medici palace, chapel, with portraits as identified by Cristina Acidini: 4 Cosimo de' Medici; 2 Piero di Cosimo; 16 Giovanni di Cosimo; 3 Carlo di Cosimo; 5 Giangaleazzo Maria Sforza; 6 Sigismondo Pandolfo Malatesta; 10 Lorenzo di Piero; 13 Giuliano di Piero; 8 Cosimino di Giovanni di Cosimo; 15 Giovanni di Francesco Tornabuoni; 18 Benozzo Gozzoli

159 Diagram of west wall of Medici palace, chapel, with portraits as identified by Cristina Acidini: 21 Neri Capponi; 23 Bernardo Giugni; 24 Francesco Sassetti; 25 Agnolo Tani; 27 Nerone di Nigi Dietisalvi; 28 Roberto di Niccolò Martelli; 33 Luca Pitta

in the panels of Donatello's San Lorenzo pulpits, and of Cosimo in a fresco by Uccello.[65] Gozzoli's portrait precedes by half a dozen years the well-known medal struck after Cosimo's death to commemorate the commune's conferring on him the title of *pater patriae*, on which most subsequent images of him depend. Like this honorific title and the medal's inscription, Cosimo's appearance here in a composite portrait of the Medici *parenti*, *amici*, and *vicini* represents an essential element of his role in his Florentine world, imaging an identity as much collective as individual.

In a corresponding position on the west wall opposite, scholars have tentatively identified portraits of a number of Medici associates in the essential enterprises of their bank and their political party (figs. 159 and 161). Among these are Neri Capponi, Nerone di Nigi Dietisalvi, Luca Pitti, and Niccolo Soderini. Neri Capponi, as the leader of a powerful patronage network of his own, centered on Pistoia, was more independent of the Medici than most of those described as their *amici*, but when Capponi died in 1457, Cosimo wrote to Piero praising this elder statesman and urging his son to honor him.[66] Dietisalvi, Pitti, and Soderini, among the Medici family's staunchest and most active supporters for four decades from the 1420s to the late 1450s, were the party's chief brokers and lieutenants. In this capacity they became, not entirely unnaturally, the chief conspirators against Piero when, two years after his father's death, continuing Medici authority over the party Cosimo had created was challenged. Another putative portrait is that of Roberto Martelli, who remained a pillar of the party and of the Roman operations of the bank; his face was particularly familiar to Gozzoli, since he was Piero's agent overseeing the execution of the frescoes and communicating directly with the artist.[67] We may also see here the likenesses of Francesco Sassetti, previously head of the branches of the Medici bank at Geneva and Lyons, but recently recalled to Florence, and Agnolo Tani, director of the important office at Bruges from 1450 to 1465.[68]

In quattrocento Florence, fresco portraits served the same function of memorializing the lineage as the rarer surviving contemporary panel portraits of ancestors.[69] Acidini observed that Benozzo Gozzoli is seldom included in considerations of the evolution of Florentine portraiture, although in fact in his work for the Medici he was in the vanguard of important artistic advances. His Magi frescoes record the early influence, more highly developed in later Florentine portraitists such as Ghirlandaio, of the Flemish masters whom the Medici admired and collected.[70] This familiar, domestic style was appropriate to the depiction of a domestic unit, particularly as domestic affairs and affections were such a

major concern of Cosimo and his sons throughout their lives.[71]

By contrast Caspar, the "Lorenzo" magus framed by the laurel, is an idealized figure. In the laurel's symbolic promise of renewal, the lineage and its aspirations flower, and they shine forth in the glittering trappings of Piero's horse, whose bridle is decorated with the Medici emblem of the diamond ring enclosing the *palle* with three feathers, and their related motto, "SEMPER" in golden letters. Cosimo kept highly decorated ceremonial armor for horses in his *anticamera*, and in Lorenzo's time the Medici had frequent dealings with a *bottega* that specialized in horse-trappings, which would explain Gozzoli's painstaking representation of these in the chapel frescoes, and in his diagrams showing the *giornate* of the decoration.[72] The headdresses of Caspar's companions resemble those worn at the joust staged in 1459 for the visit of Pius II and Galeazzo Maria Sforza: "Every participant wore a *piannella*/ encircled by a garland like a *mazzocchio*,/ beautifully decorated with silver *scaglie*/ and with golden feathers rising from it,/ bright and shining like a star."[73]

The tapestry-like effect of the frescoes matches the actual tapestries, brocades, and hangings, many imported from the great northern textile center of Bruges with the aid of employees of the Medici bank there, which furnished the rooms of the Medici palace, and were more luxurious and far more expensive than the paintings so highly prized today. The wealth and dignity of the family is displayed in the gorgeous costumes of all the Magi and their trains, dressed in fur-trimmed velvets and brocades encrusted with pearls, jewels, and gold thread, like the garments stored in their houshold *cassoni* and described in the inventory of Piero's possessions in 1456, or in letters and other records of important items of dress such as those worn by Cosimo in the Magi procession, or the guests at Lorenzo's wedding in 1469. Particularly splendid is Caspar's belt, decorated with rubies, sapphires, and pearls, and fastened with a silver buckle, like several such belts in Piero's wardrobe.[74] Details of dress also constitute a vehicle for the artist's display of his technical virtuosity and his capacity for invention in the variety of colors, textures, and visual special effects; as the son of a tailor, Benozzo was especially fitted for this task.[75] In view of the speed with which the chapel frescoes became a model subject for miniaturists, they probably had access to the chapel and the opportunity to copy Gozzoli's design while he was still at work on it. Given the emphasis on textures, much of the detailing had to be done *a secco*, which led to Gozzoli's unusual and innovative combination of painting on a dry surface with traditional fresco techniques.[76]

The sumptuous cortège winds down a steep hill

through sharp ravines perforated with caves and punctuated with lush thickets. The journey represented in the frescoes closely resembles the family's descriptions in their letters of numerous actual journeys between Florence, the curative baths they frequented, and the country villas where they spent so much of their time. For example, as Cosimo wrote to Piero while he was taking the waters at Bagno a Corsina in 1461:

> I got your letter of the 5th, from which I understand you were thinking of leaving on the morning of the 12th and taking the road to Pisa, and that I should send mules and horses to collect you, and this will be done; and the men to lead the train and the chests and another three mules will be with you Saturday night or Sunday morning; either Arighetto or I will send you eight pack animals, six for you, so that two remain for the three men who brought the train, that is Arighetto and a servant of Nicodemo [the Milanese ambassador], and another boy who was in the house who will return on foot or on the mule for Matteo, whom we can't have because his son was in the Mugello.[77]

The Medici landholdings in the Mugello fostered the family's fourteenth-century reputation of being "wild men" from the mountains; they were also an important basis of their power and patronage in the fifteenth century. Cosimo's sense of his patriarchal responsibilities extended far beyond his immediate family to embrace the many members of his various extended households in the countryside as well as the city. He declared in his tax report of 1458: "There are fifty mouths to feed in our family, including the villas and Florence, and we also employ forty-one retainers, amounting to more than 400 florins a year." The factors of the estates surrounding these villas were among the Medici familiars, as acknowledged by their attendance at Cosimo's funeral.[78] We may see in the rustic types bringing up the rear of the family cavalcade the individualized features of the actual, if unidentifiable Medici retainers whose births, marriages, deaths, and working arrangements are endlessly discussed in letters to Cosimo and his household from the factors at Trebbio and Cafaggiolo.[79] James Draper, who also remarked that these retainers were an intimate part of Medici existence, distinguished portraits of the Medici staff as well as the family in Domenico Veneziano's Magi tondo, and in the tray decorated with the Triumph of Fame for Lorenzo's birth in 1449 (figs. 119 and 146).[80]

Where in earlier, smaller images of the Magi by Lorenzo Monaco, Gentile da Fabriano, and in the Lippi/Angelico tondo, the countryside is essentially background for the figures, establishing the narrative of the journey, here it is a distinctive presence. Despite the generally abstract and geometrical design of Gozzoli's landscape, in his attention to detail the artist may also offer, in what Diane Cole Ahl suggested "may have been the most extensive study of landscape in Italy from its century," a schematized portrait of the countryside to which Cosimo was deeply attached.[81] Vespasiano described how he was "extremely well informed about agricultural matters, and talked of them as if he had never done anything else . . . and when the peasants came to Florence he asked them about the district where they came from and its produce . . ."[82] Ser Alesso once wrote to Giovanni from Cafaggiolo informing him that grain for sowing had been loaned to the laborers, and that they were waiting for his arrival to begin slaughtering the pigs.[83] When angry and disappointed in his younger son Giovanni, Cosimo sought solace in rural chores at Cafaggiolo. Gozzoli's trees are meticulously described and elaborately pruned according to the rather outré fashion that apparently persisted in Tuscany until the early years of this century.

On the southern wall, although it has been badly damaged, the countryside is depicted in the opulence of high summer, an opulence matching that of the central figure of Balthazar, attended by his pages in procession bearing the gift of frankincense to salve the future wounds of Christ (fig. 160). Balancing the cultivated countryside to the left, with its neat fields, fortified towns, castles, bridges, and farmers' houses, are the wilder woods to the right, which continue on around the southwest corner beside the door. This section of the fresco was transferred from its original position in the seventeenth century to make way for the construction of a staircase, and was considerably "restored" in the process. Here, with the figures of youths bearing crossbows, begins the hunt which is a major theme of the west wall depicting the train of Melchior, the oldest magus (fig. 161).

Hunting was a passion of the youthful Medici *brigata*, first of Cosimo's sons Piero and Giovanni, and later of their younger cousin Pierfrancesco. They kept plenty of equipment for themselves and their horses in the Medici palace, and perhaps more at the *castello* or hunting lodge of Trebbio where they spent much of their time.[84] Hunting, horses, and dogs are the subject of numerous letters to and from the men of the Medici family. Guglielmo da Sommaia wrote to Giovanni in Rome in the spring of 1445 that if he were to respond adequately to his friend's latest letter: "I'd have to write a whole book, because when I got your letter I seemed to see you yourself, hearing of the delight you took in that hunt . . ."[85] A couple of years earlier another close friend, Giovanni Vespucci, who was then Podestà at Arezzo, was

160 Benozzo Gozzoli, Florence, Medici palace, chapel, south wall

obliged to refuse Giovanni's invitation to a hunt at
Cerbaia because the Captain of the city was making his
ceremonial entrance that day. But since autumn was one
long round of hunting parties, he suggested that "if you
decide to come here after the Cerbaia hunt . . . tell me,
and if I know for certain you are coming to hunt game
. . . we'll have a good time for fifteen days, and bring
whatever company you want."[86]

The heavenly goal

Moving on to the chancel on the north side of the
chapel, from earthly to heavenly happiness, Gozzoli

framed the Nativity with scenes on the strips of plaster
flanking the altar niche of the shepherds watching over
their sheep, as yet unaware of the miracle of the birth of
Jesus. His quotation of antique sources in the figures of
the shepherd and the ox, as in the horses of the Magi
cavalcade, adds resonance to the scene as a last reminder
of the pre-Christian world regarded by fifteenth-century
Florentines as an intellectual and moral preparation for
the coming revelation of Christ.[87]

On the west and east walls of the chancel, angels
mediate between humanity and heaven. With subtle
attention to the niceties of doctrine that so preoccupied
the correspondents of Feo Belcari, Benozzo represented
the gradual metamorphosis from pure spirits to anthro-

161 Benozzo Gozzoli, Florence, Medici palace, chapel, west wall

pomorphic figures, from seraphim to cherubim, as the angels descend to earth.[88] According to the tripartite scheme Becchi described for the chapel, while the Magi offer their gifts of deeds to the newborn Christ, the angels offer up words in the form of their songs of joy and celebration. These allude to the Gloria in the liturgy of the Mass, from which comes the inscription in the aureoles about their heads: "Gloria in excelsis deo/ et in terra" and "Adoramus te/ glorifica[mus te]." The source of this passage is the Gospel of Saint Luke, 2:24; the evangelist attributes to the angels who sang on the holy night the words: "Glory to God in the highest, and on earth peace and good will toward men." This is a key passage in the *sacre rappresentazioni* enacted in Magi pageants, not only in Florence, but also in Milan and northern Europe; groups of young boys played the part of the angels singing the Gloria.

The angels in their brilliantly varicolored robes move gracefully, as in many fifteenth-century images, in the steps of a dance, in harmony with the Medici patrons' interest in the symbolic significance of dancing, and their personal pleasure in this pastime.[89] Whether in accord with the patrons' corresponding interest in music,[90] or with the painter's concern for accuracy, the songs they sing are identifiable fairly precisely as Gregorian chant, performed without the scores indispensable to polyphony, and led apparently by the angel on the west wall in the rose and blue shot-silk robe, with his sharply pointing right hand (fig. 162). On the east wall is the angelic soloist, who was believed to have begun the singing on the night of the Nativity, and whose role is performed in the liturgy by the priest. He is the central figure in the group of three, dressed in the stole of a deacon in the Medici colors and decorated with golden shields bearing the Medici arms.[91] Behind the heavenly choir on the west side of the chancel, a city within its walls nestles in the curve of a hill. Gozzoli's city is ideal rather than real, a renunciation perhaps by patron or artist of any temptation at the end of the Magi's spiritual journey to identify them too closely with the worldly environment from whence they came.

The garden of paradise is certainly an image of the ideal, the *locus amoenus* so celebrated in Florentine literary circles, from the fictive site of Bocaccio's *Decameron* and the *Paradiso* of the Alberti, to the Orti Oricellari, as the setting in which the intellect might soar to infinite heights. According to contemporary descriptions, the garden of the Medici palace also relates to this ideal.[92] In Gozzoli's Garden of Eden are many birds, including a peacock, a palaeochristian symbol of resurrection that recurs in fifteenth-century representations of the Adoration of the Magi and most particularly in the tondo

Lippi had painted previously for the Medici. Here it bears the motto "Regarde moi" (Look at me), the personal emblem of Giovanni de' Medici. A partridge is also discernible, and a parrot recalls the talking bird described by Pliny as a symbol of eloquence. The Medici inventory of 1492 included, along with a copy of Pliny, objects decorated with parrots, a symbol later adopted by Lorenzo and appearing in numerous illuminated manuscripts of his library, accompanied by the motto "Non le set qui non l'essaye" (Nothing ventured, nothing gained).[93]

The garden is full of roses and others flowers suitable for the garlands of honor being prepared by a young boy in the heraldic colors of white and vermilion, the colors of the shields of the commune of Florence with its lily, of the Parte Guelfa, and of the cross of the Captain of the Florentine *popolo*. The cypresses, trees completely dry at their center, may symbolize the opposition between the death of the soul, or sin, and the spiritual *vita nuova* offered to mankind by the Incarnation of the son of God.[94] A palm tree, whose branches proclaim the martyrs of the Church, is prominent in the background of the scene on the west wall.

On the wall behind the altar, once adorned with the symbols of the four evangelists, the theme of the decoration of the old sacristy at San Lorenzo, only the eagle of Saint John and the angel of Saint Matthew remain against the background of the night sky. Nothing survives of the star that guided the Magi to Bethlehem. Perhaps it appeared where there is now an oculus, recalling the oculi of the old sacristy with their bronze grilles in motifs of stars and rays. Certainly the wall behind the altarpiece would seem the proper position for the star; not, as is sometimes proposed, the ceiling bearing Saint Bernardino's monogram, which is in fact a sun.[95]

The altarpiece

Or perhaps the star is the Virgin herself. For the Magi have now arrived at the end of their journey; the contemplation of the Christ child, the God incarnate of Lippi's altarpiece, adored by his Virgin mother (fig. 163). As joyously as Gozzoli's painted angels, a poem by Cosimo's friend Francesco d'Altobianco degli Alberti, sent on 21 October 1450 to their mutual friend Poggio Bracciolini, announced the Incarnation and its significance to sinful mankind. "The word is made flesh, O ungrateful mankind!/ Woe to those who, for their sins,/ are deprived of eternal pleasures!" Such eternal pleasures are imaged in Gozzoli's frescoes, just as the grave and silent wonder of the heavenly witnesses to the

162   Benozzo Gozzoli, Florence, Medici palace, chapel, chancel, west wall

miraculous birth pervades Lippi's altarpiece. "God incarnate has come to dwell among us,/ from whose glory proceeds our salvation,/ we saw the sign just now in the heavens;/ whence all tongues are silenced/ and the most sublime intellects fail/ in rendering the gratitude owed/ to the Father for so gracious Firstborn." The poet's conclusion: "Almost the whole of glory and good/ appear to us, and we see every design [*disegno*] fulfilled,/ which is full of grace and truth" resonates with the experience of a lifetime of viewing images like this altarpiece.[96]

Jeffrey Ruda rightly stressed that the likely inspiration for Lippi's altarpiece is not a single text, but many sources, too complexly intertwined to be effectively disentangled.[97] The same is true of the seamless web into which are woven both the interests and concerns of the patron, so clearly identifiable in this image, and the creative problems with which the artist was preoccupied at this point in his career, together with the solutions he proposed in this and other related altarpieces painted around the same time. The public and private, the sacred and secular themes of the painting appear in various texts, both verbal and visual, which were part of the common stock of Florentine popular culture.

Among these were the *Revelations* of Saint Bridget of Sweden, circulated widely in pious circles throughout Europe in the late fourteenth century and included in a number of compilations made in mid-fifteenth century Florence.[98] Bridget envisioned the Christ child lying not in a manger, but on the plain ground, adored by his mother kneeling humbly before him. Her vision was probably one component with which artists such as Lippi reformulated the Nativity into something that might alternatively be described as an Adoration or an Incarnation. Lippi painted several altarpieces around mid-century depicting this type of Adoration, not inside the traditional stable, but upon the bare earth of a mountain wilderness.[99] Many of the saints who commanded the most devoted following in fifteenth-century Florence had retreated into the wilderness to do penance. They included the Magdalen, who appears in Lippi's similar, slightly earlier altarpiece for the convent of the Annalena, directed by Cosimo's goddaughter; Jerome, whose cult was particularly celebrated in Florence, and who appears in various images commissioned by the Rucellai and the Medici, among others; John the Baptist and Bernard of Clairvaux, both saintly protectors of the city of Florence also appearing in the Medici chapel altarpiece. The Baptist replaces Saint Bernard as the central saint in an almost identical altarpiece by Lippi for a cell dedicated to Saint John at the hermitage of Camaldoli, founded in the eleventh century by Saint Romuald. The Camaldoli picture was commissioned, according to the convent's records, by Cosimo's wife Contessina de' Medici shortly after her husband's death, and the celebration of the cult there was continued by Piero di Cosimo (fig. 164).[100]

Lippi, like his contemporary Domenico Veneziano, seems to have made quite precise use of the text of Fra Domenico Cavalca's *Vulgarization of the Lives of the Holy Fathers*. Cavalca's writings were among the most popular of all devotional works in the compilations of ordinary Florentines. Marilyn Lavin observed in her studies of the young Baptist, San Giovannino, that Cavalca's life of Florence's patron saint was the sole source for the narrative in which the boy Saint John saw the newborn Christ; this account also invoked Saint Bernard's approbation of the Baptist. Cavalca's work was once attributed to Feo Belcari, and was clearly the source of the latter's "Representation of when San Giovanni was visited in the desert by Christ," which he sent to Cosimo's son Giovanni. Piero di Cosimo's wife, Lucrezia Tornabuoni, wrote a life of Saint John the Baptist in *ottava rima*, which owes much both to Cavalca and to Belcari, and envisages Saint John's penitence in the desert while still a young boy, amidst serpents, scorpions, and flowers as depicted in Lippi's altarpiece.[101]

In the complex picture Lippi painted for the Medici chapel, all that remains of the traditional Nativity picture are Mary and the Christ child. The angelic chorus, still present in Lippi's Annalena *Adoration*, appears in the Medici chapel on the frescoed walls of the chancel, as do the shepherds watching over their flocks. They are replaced in the altarpiece by God the Father, looking down on the Incarnation of his Son, irradiated by the golden light of the Holy Spirit. A banderole held by John the Baptist spells out the message of sacrifice implicit in the Incarnation: "Behold the lamb of God, behold Him who taketh away the sin of the world." The Mystic Lamb, described by Saint John the Evangelist in his Apocalpyse, was depicted above the original portal of the chapel; placed on the sacrificial altar, he is accompanied by the seven golden candlesticks and the seven seals that must be broken before the coming of the millennium (fig. 165). These images were especially familiar to Florentines from the final cantos of Dante's *Divine Comedy*, as well as from translations of the Scriptures in vernacular books.[102] In Lippi's picture the Baptist, a child of seven or so, points to an axe in the stump of a felled tree, which may be intended to recall a sermon of Saint John calling for repentance, as reported by Saint Luke, 3:7–9: "And now also is the axe laid unto the root of the trees: every tree therefore which bringeth not forth good fruit is hewn down, and cast into the fire."[103] The handle of the axe, immediately beneath the Baptist's feet, bears the signature of the artist, who thus inserts himself into his innovative image.

The figures are skilfully integrated by the use of color and *chiaroscuro* into this landscape, which sets the tone for their somber contemplation. Like the chapel as a whole, the altarpiece in particular evokes echoes of the *selva oscura*, in which Dante found himself at the beginning of his poetic journey, an allegory of the human condition deprived of the divine light. At the same time, the appearance of Saint Bernard recalls Dante's foretaste in the last *canto* of *Paradiso* of the vision of the Trinity in the blinding light of revelation. Approaching his journey's end, Dante encounters Saint Bernard, who mediates between him and the Virgin, the special object of Bernard's devotion. Since she herself is the mediatrix between her son and mankind, Saint Bernard urges the poet: "Now to that face which most resembles Christ lift up that gaze; its radiance alone can grant to thee power to look on Christ . . ."[104] Bernard's "Salve Regina," part of a sermon on the Song of Songs, was the anthem of *laudesi* confraternities dedicated to the praise of the Virgin, and is echoed in Dante's invocation in the first lines of his final *canto*: "Virgin Mother, daughter of thy son,/ lowly and exalted more than any other creature."[105]

Devotional confraternities dedicated to the Virgin associated her with Saint Bernard through this memorable scene from the *Divine Comedy*, recalled in later images of the Virgin inspiring Saint Bernard's treatise, "Homilies in Praise of the Virgin Mother." As David Clark pointed out, in a painting of this subject by Lippi's son, Filippino, Bernard's book is open at the page on which is written: "As a star sends out its ray without detriment to itself, so did the Virgin bring forth her Child without injury to her integrity . . . she is therefore that glorious star, which, according to prophecy, arose out of Jacob, whose ray illumines the entire earth." These lines are from one of the most famous of all passages from the writings of Saint Bernard, included in the Roman breviary; his exhortation to "look to the star, call upon Mary."[106] The hymn *Ave Maris Stella*, attributed to Saint Bernard because of these allusions, was sung from as early as the ninth century at Vespers on most feasts of the Virgin Mary, and is cited by Iacopo da Voragine in his account of the Epiphany to explain part of the significance of the star: "I am the root and stock of David, the bright and morning star."[107]

Saint Bernard, whose works were among the most frequently copied vernacular texts, was perhaps the most popular medieval writer, exemplum, and saint. Cosimo owned a volume of vernacular translations of "the ecclesiastical writings of Saint Augustine, Saint Bernard, and various others," and in the library he gave to the Badia at Fiesole were three volumes of Bernard's works, including the *Sermons on the Nativity*, the *Sermons on the Song of Solomon*, and the *Steps of Humility*.[108] In addition to the devotional texts which appear to have inspired aspects of the iconography of the altarpiece, Saint Bernard was noted also for his sermons and letters on the good government of the family and of the state. The account of his life in the *Golden Legend* associated him with the calming of civil strife and the reconciliation of cities with the Church. Perhaps for this reason he was the patron saint of the Signoria; the cornerstone of their chapel dedicated to him was laid in the Palazzo Vecchio in 1298.[109] The anniversary of Bernard's death, 20 August, was one of the city's half dozen major feastdays, and in the first half of the quattrocento celebrations marking this day grew to such an extent that in 1452 the Signoria issued a decree limiting the display and expense allowed on this occasion.[110]

Bernard was also closely connected in Florentine minds with the doctrine of the Trinity, on which he had written extensively. Ambrogio Traversari, Cosimo's close friend and intellectual mentor, had presented Pope Eugenius IV, on his elevation to the papacy, with a dedication copy of Saint Bernard's treatise on the Trinity, *De Consideratione*. The Trinity was the chief point of theological dispute between East and West at the Council of Florence in 1439, and a preoccupation of many ordinary Florentines, like the scissor-maker who questioned Feo Belcari on its nature. Compelling images of the Trinity were to be found in such public places as the church of Santa Maria Novella and the cathedral. A copy of Ambrose's treatise *On the Trinity*, containing notes by Niccoli and one perhaps by Cosimo, and coupled with ten dialogues of Plato translated into Latin by Ficino for Cosimo, was included among his gifts to San Marco's library.[111]

The vision of the Trinity is the revelation, at the apex of the elaborate symbolic system of threes, toward which the Magi have been progressing. Three was the eternally perfect number, one and indivisible. As Iacopo da Voragine, quoting Saint Bernard, observed in his explanation of the significance of the feast of the Nativity, the Lord's birth serves us by humbling our pride. Christ's remedy for man's threefold malady — his birth unclean, his life perverse, his death perilous — was that "his birth cleansed ours, his life put order in ours, his death destroyed ours."[112] The close connection between the subject of Gozzoli's frescoes of the Magi and that of Lippi's altarpiece depicting the Incarnation is clearly made in a poem by the star performer of San Martino, Antonio di Guido, who had so impressed the young Galeazzo Sforza, a few months before these frescoes were painted, with his recital at a Medici dinner. Antonio reminded his audience that the Magi were revered because they recognized the miracle of the incarnation of God the Father in his Son, through the grace of the Holy Spirit vouchsafed to the Virgin. "I contemplate the holy Magi from

163 Fra Filippo Lippi, *Adoration of the Child*, Medici chapel altarpiece,
Berlin, Staatliche Museen Preussicher Kulturbesitz, Gemäldegalerie

the east,/ taking note and leaving their kingdoms,/ following the gleaming star/ which announced to them the word made flesh,/ and offered him incense and myrrh and gold/ . . . offer your heart to the King of Heaven,/ like the Magi struck by the holy star."[113]

The Magi thus progress in their journey from the worldly pride and magnificence embodied in their brilliant train, to the austere revelation in the wilderness of the wisdom of penance. God led them to Himself, says the author of the *Golden Legend*, quoting Chrysostom, "thereby extending to all sinners the hope of pardon." Here, as Saint Bernard explained, "the wise men give up their wisdom in order to become wise."[114] The third gift to Christ imaged in the chapel, after the hearts of the Magi and the songs of the angels, is according to Becchi the heart, mind, and soul of his mother, the Virgin Mary.

164 Fra Filippo Lippi, *Adoration of the Child* (Calmaldoli altarpiece), Florence, Uffizi

165 (*below*) Benozzo Gozzoli, *Mystic Lamb*, Florence, Medici palace, chapel, entrance

Arrived at their goal, the Magi do indeed call upon the star, the Virgin, as Saint Bernard suggested, on their own behalf and of all those who follow in their path: "Hail Queen of Heaven, o pious Virgin!/ For the sake of the offerings of gold, myrrh and incense,/ which with such immense joy/ the Holy Magi brought to your Son,/ O fount of humility, mother Mary,/ whose mercy when I consider it/ revives my spirit and my senses entirely,/ and hope cancels out all woes,/ O my refuge, O my only comfort,/ O my happiness, o my good, o my joy,/ may it please you to see that severe justice/ is not arraigned against me,/ that grace from heaven is not denied me." Another Florentine poet, Antonio di Meglio, took up Bernard's theme: "O benign mother, full of grace,/ I beg you by the star/ that shining guided and led the Magi / to your hut . . . / Virgin holy and pious,/ dissolve these ancient knots,/ make of my thorns roses, lilies and violets . . ."[115]

Each highly significant element of the altarpiece is firmly locked in its place within the whole. There are two witnesses to the Incarnation; Saint Bernard, whose presence adds resonance to the image of the Virgin and to the representation of the Trinity, and Saint John the Baptist. The mountain, the axe, and the stream are symbols generally associated with Saint John's Baptism of Christ, which was thought to have taken place at Epiphany.[116] At the moment of his baptism the Trinity appeared; the dove descended and the Lord's voice was heard from the heavens saying, "This is my beloved son, in whom I am well pleased." There are precedents for the pictorial conjunction of these themes; for example, Christ's baptism was depicted by Domenico Veneziano, another favorite artist of the Medici, in his *Saint Lucy* panel, which also includes the Trinity. In the Medici altarpiece, the patrons of the city and its rulers constitute in addition a reminder of Cosimo's close personal identification with Florence.[117]

In paradise, Dante recognized the charity of Saint Bernard in vouchsafing him, while still living, a glimpse of eternal peace. Lorenzo Benci, a relative of the Medici bank manager Tommaso, who addressed a moving sonnet to Cosimo on the occasion of his son Giovanni's death, also wrote a meditation on the Nativity and the Incarnation. These he represented as God's charity to man, both *amicizia* and *caritas*, beginning: "Oh how great is your charity/ to us in your coming to demonstrate to us/ the highest truth, the child incarnate!" His poem was prefaced in compilations with the rubric: "Lorenzo di Giovanni di Taddeo Benci wrote this *lauda* on the coming, or rather the birth, of our lord Jesus Christ, who for our salvation put on human flesh. He wrote it in the year 1435, on the night of Christmas Eve."[118] Similarly,

the canon Leonardo Dati had observed in his contribution to the 1441 poems on *amicizia* that God's was the only true love and friendship: "The great Master and Supreme Monarch/ became incarnate man, real and suffering,/ to restore the error of our primal seed./ O human race, however reprehensible,/ gathered with me in your little boat; / this is the true good, the certain hope from another."[119]

Charity was the meeting point of the worldly and the spiritual. God's charity served as an example to man. Cosimo's charity to the confraternity of San Martino provided "the good wine that slakes our thirst," in Belcari's phrase referring to the Florentine poor. The water that slakes spiritual thirst springs from Lippi's mountainside, through the charity of the Lord, as in Isaiah's prophecy: "When the poor and needy seek water, and there is none, and their tongue faileth for thirst, I the Lord will hear them . . . I will make the wilderness a pool of water, and the dry land springs of water. I will plant in the wilderness the cedar . . . I will set in the desert the fir tree and the pine."[120]

The gifts the Magi brought were not only gold, frankincense, and myrrh, but also charity and humility in their hearts, offerings which the confraternal followers of the Magi sought to emulate. These were themes that preoccupied Cosimo de' Medici, in his life and his patronage, and were articulated in the sermons of members of the Magi company written shortly after his death. One of the earliest of these to be recorded was delivered by Cristoforo Landino, Lorenzo's close friend and a leading Dante scholar, and referred to that immense "I say not liberality, but charity of the creator to his creature . . ." Cosimo's cousin Bernardo d'Alamanno de' Medici addressed at a meeting of the Magi company the subject of the Crucifixion, enjoining his *confratelli* "to follow to the best of our capacity the traces of our venerated fathers, protectors and advocates . . . the Magi; to behave like them at the most joyful Nativity of the Son of God, departing from the regions of the orient . . ."[121] In the 1480s Giovanni Nesi linked the journey of the Magi with Ficino's tenets about the nature of divine love. Ficino himself composed a Latin sermon, *De Stella Magorum*, which may never have been delivered to the confraternity, but strongly influenced Renaissance views of the Magi.[122] Nesi argued that many of the mysteries of Christ can be deduced through astrological principles, just as the star led the Magi to him at his birth. The star envisaged by Nesi is illuminated principally by Charity who, descending "in the breasts of the Holy Magi, will lead them to . . . the fiery gates of the New Jerusalem"; there, filled with "cognition and fruition," they would live "in happy eternity."[123]

V

THE PATRON AS "AUCTOR"

XIV

PATRONS AND THEIR ARTISTS:
"THE VARIETY OF GENIUS"

THE PATRON'S ROLE IN THE PRODUCTION OF ART

The purpose of this book has been to reconsider the body of works of art commissioned by Cosimo de' Medici, viewing them as a coherent whole, constituting the patron's oeuvre. The concept of an oeuvre characterized by the recurrence of certain themes presupposes a relatively high degree of interaction and communication between the Medici and the artists who worked for them, and we turn now to consider this exchange.

The nature of the relations between patrons and artists in Florence has been much misunderstood, and the role of the patron concomitantly both under- and overrated. If many art historians have deprecated the contribution of the patron to the production of great works of art, very few historians of fifteenth-century Florentine society and politics have paid much attention to art and artists, and most do not consider images as texts on a par with written documents. At least one social historian has managed to belittle all parties to the artistic exchange. Anthony Molho, citing Kenneth Clark's observation in relation to the patronage of the seventeenth-century Habsburg emperors of "how enormously important artists were to the great princes of the day, and how, in return, the princes' ideologies dominated the artists," suggested that we should "pursue the same question in the context of Florentine art in the late '300 and '400 . . . to see how artists and intellectuals served the purposes of their Florentine patrons (who to paraphrase Machiavelli's reference to Zanobi Buondelmonti and Cosimo Rucellai were princes in all respects but in name), to delineate the ways in which the ideology of their employers dominated their own work." The other side of this Marxist/functionalist coin is Molho's surprise that "the bonds of clientage and tensions of class antagonism were largely absent from the relations between artisans and patrons in Florence."[1]

In considering Cosimo's artistic commissions in the context of Florentine society and culture, a good deal of evidence has been accumulated concerning two major points which are sharply relevant to these issues. The first is that, contrary to the assumptions underlying push–pull arguments positing ignorant artists instructed by the patrons' learned advisors, or artistic geniuses making masterpieces out of the bumbling prescriptions of aesthetically insensitive patrons, artists in fact shared with patrons and their audience a broad culture, comprising the fundamental elements of the Christian and classical traditions, which provided a basis for effective exchange between artists and their often more formally educated patrons. The second is that rather than artists and patrons being mutually uncomprehending or hostile strangers linked only by the work in hand, the many social venues in which they had the opportunity to meet provided a context within which artists were admired and recommended, commissions were made, and the work was carried out. Medici artists were advised, consulted, supported (and often harassed) by the family and other members of their patronage network.

The themes of this chapter are communication, cooperation, collaboration, and above all, the reciprocity of the patronage exchange between patrons and their artists. The last word, however, must surely go to the artist. The patron's directive role did not detract from the ability of gifted artists at once to fulfil and to transcend his expectations; indeed, it was this latter ability that compelled the admiration of the sophisticated Florentine audience whom patron and artist addressed.

Putting arguments ex silentio in perspective

The most insistent claims that patrons had very little to do with the production of art rest on the supposed absence of evidence to the contrary. Few aspects of fifteenth century experience are as well documented as we would like. Ernst Gombrich rightly stressed the importance of envisaging artists and patrons as "living people in concrete situations";[2] unfortunately, this is easier said than done. I have tried wherever possible to give a sense of the texture of social contacts and relationships between patrons and artists, but since the vast majority of personal exchanges in this face-to-face society were verbal rather than written, they have naturally left no trace in records. Despite the comparative richness of Florentine archives, these document only a tiny fraction of actual occurrences, and they contain only such records as survived the passage of time.

Nevertheless, many art historians argue *ex silentio* that there was little creative communication between patrons and artists.[3] Part of the problem lies in unrealistic expectations about the quantity and quality of records we might expect to find, and what sort of things they might be expected to say. As observed, the personal letters and contracts between patrons and artists, upon which art historians have chiefly relied for information, are primarily functional documents; not, in fifteenth century eyes, appropriate forums for expressing aesthetic preferences.[4] Moreover, just as historians are untrained in formal analysis of paintings or buildings, many art historians are unfamiliar with techniques developed by historians to "squeeze, tease, and press" the maximum informational yield from the evidence that does exist. Often the most basic questions are not addressed – for example, to whom precisely were letters sent, and when? Where were they sent from, and where to? What else was going on at that time in the artist's or the patron's life that might color their allusions to the work of art? The questions asked of documents must be framed not simply in terms of what we want them to tell us, but of what they were intended to say. It is sometimes claimed that excessive attention to the "social facts" of the context of a work of art detract from, rather than enhance our appreciation of it. That may be true for some viewers, but artists' letters to their patrons have much to tell us about their aspirations and intentions, and what they say cannot be interpreted in a social vacuum.[5]

Owing to misunderstandings of the language of letters or overlooking the context of meetings in which corporate contracts were generated (whether, for example, they were official or informal gatherings, and at what stage of the proceedings toward a commission), the situations these documents describe are often misrepresented.[6] Writers quite convinced of the explanatory value of such distinctions as those between artists as "modern" or "old fashioned," corresponding implicitly to "major" and "minor,"[7] may fail to note essential distinctions between the needs and procedures of different types of patrons; corporate and individual, cloistered clergy or laymen, the customized commissions by discriminating patrons from eminent artists, and the customers of workshops dealing in mass production. Too often the *modus operandi* of princes and their accompanying "humanist advisors," are automatically attributed to the citizens of the Florentine republic, where exchanges between humanists, artists, and their patrons were of a much more informal nature.[8] Most importantly, too many art historians focus on random searches in archives for evidence of programs for works of art, instead of considering the modes of thought fundamental to this society which shaped the production of images.[9] A combination of the rigid application of preconceived categories on the one hand, and an insufficient precision about manifest social and personal distinctions on the other, contributes to a constant attempt to maximize the patron's interest in function, usually arbitrarily defined as self-advertisement, and to minimize his personal and aesthetic concerns. The documentation that exists of relations between the Medici and their artists in Cosimo's lifetime presents a more subtle and complex picture.

ARTISTS IN THE MEDICI PATRONAGE NETWORK: THE LETTERS

Despite the problems and limitations of the evidence, there is still quite a lot of material bearing on the Medici family's relations with their most favored artists. Many of these were clearly close and enduring, both embracing and embraced by the extensive network of Medici friendship and patronage. This is perhaps the most important of many reasons for rejecting anachronistic attempts to distinguish between *clientelismo* and *mecenatismo* where Cosimo's contemporaries did not do so. The behavior of patrons and artists toward one another, and particularly their speech, cannot be understood properly except in the context of the patronage obligations and expectations by which most activities in this society were framed.[10]

Artists employed the vocabulary of patronage, and operated within its structures. Like businessmen, craftsmen, shopkeepers, and politicians, they sought out patrons. Patrons recommended artists to other patrons; artists recommended one another. Cosimo's network of communication kept him informed concerning artists' movements and their achievements, just as he kept track of politicians, merchants, and *condottieri*. Artists' continuing relationships with many members of the Medici family and their friends over several generations might in some ways be seen as the group's "collective patronage," since often quite a slice of the patronage network would be activated in the production of important works of art; in procuring materials, sorting out practical problems, with oversight, payment, and delivery.

Letters, as observed, were the coin of patronage. They identified the Medici family's friends and the terms of their friendship, not only by pledges of loyalty and obligation, but through their language and forms of address.[11] The fact that these forms are often misunderstood has led to some very misleading assumptions about the attitudes of artists to their patrons, and vice versa. Writers commonly describe artists' letters as "humble," or ingratiating."[12] Pope-Hennessy referred to Lippi's "insinuating letter of 1457" to Piero (in fact addressed to Giovanni; while this study suggests that members of Cosimo's family cooperated closely in their patronage, our understanding of the latter is not advanced by a common assumption that they were entirely equivalent and interchangeable). Gombrich's influential essay on the patronage of the early Medici set the tone for such comments, in observing of a letter from Lippi to Piero, written after the patron had refused to accept a panel he had painted: "It is a real tear-jerker in the best tradition of begging letters . . . No wonder that, despite Browning, Cosimo felt he had no time to deal with such artists." Gombrich also suggested that Domenico Veneziano addressed his famous letter of 1439, soliciting the commission for the San Marco altarpiece, to Piero because he did not dare to write to Cosimo directly.[13] This may have been so, but in fact a great many Medici clients, soliciting favors of all sorts, wrote either to all the major members of the family in a sort of scatter-shot barrage of their defences, or first approached the sons to intercede with the father, on the model made familiar by the habit of approaching the Virgin, herself man's chief intercessor with her Son, via her court of intermediary saints.

Rab Hatfield, in a review of David Chambers's widely used book of documents concerning patrons and artists, complained appropriately of the meaning of the texts being distorted by the editor's gratuitous and condescending comments. One concerning a letter by Mantegna described the artist as "querulous"; another drew from Leonardo's petition to his patrons concerning the *Virgin of the Rocks* the inference that its patrons were "philistines."[14] Fraser Jenkins, citing two letters appealing to Cosimo for money for building, from the confraternity of the Florentines in Venice and from Francesco Barbaro, observed alternatively a "lack of respect in both of these letters which suggests that the money was being demanded in the light of past obligations, rather than being begged for," and that Cosimo may have created "a situation in which patronage was expected."[15] Reciprocal obligation was indeed the cement of patronage, artistic as well as personal and political, and while letters lacked the binding force of contracts, they were seen as similarly creating and testifying to the parties' expectations.

More recently, sophisticated studies of complex artistic personalities, such as Jeffrey Ruda's of Filippo Lippi, have included more careful and less anachronistic readings of their letters. Where Creighton Gilbert saw Lippi's note to Giovanni de' Medici about the altarpiece he had commissioned as a gift for the king of Naples as "mixing obeisance and familiarity, competence and chatter," Ruda discerned in Lippi's determination to make his point "obeisance only lightly dusted over hard bargaining."[16] His Medici patrons obviously took no offence at the artist's tone, since they commissioned at least five of Lippi's later works. Vasari's biography represents Lippi as very difficult to get on with, and certainly the documentable facts of his life suggest that he might not have been the most amenable or reliable of his patrons' servants. However, Vasari also garnished his tale with an anecdote designed to mythologize the artist and to demonstrate that great patrons valued great talent over good manners. He claimed that Cosimo, when asked why he put up with Lippi's behavior, replied: "Rare geniuses in their excellence are heavenly forms, not carters' donkeys."[17]

Filippo Lippi

Lippi's letters to the Medici and their friends, like those of other major artists, are of interest particularly because they illuminate the ways in which artists shaped and appealed, as well as responded, to the traditional social expectations of patronage relationships. It should be noted that when Lippi protested Piero's rejection of his work in 1439, he was already known as the author of the so-called Tarquinia *Madonna*, probably painted for Giovanni Vitelleschi, who had been archbishop of Florence in the mid-1430s, and the imaginative altarpiece for the "conspicuously lavish" Barbadori chapel in the sacristy of Santo Spirito, which was probably already on show and causing quite a stir.[18]

Fra Filippo's letter to Piero of 13 August 1439 was written in reply to one from his patron, itself elicited by a previous communication from the artist. It had taken thirteen days to reach him. It is not clear whether Lippi meant that the delay or the content of the letter, "has injured me greatly," but as Ruda observed, Lippi's note is extremely familiar, by comparison with Domenico Veneziano's friendly but punctilious self-recommendation to Piero the previous year.[19] It lacks a salutation or signature, those crucial elements of recommendations which established the terms of the relationship of the writer to his putative or actual patron. Their omission in this case strongly suggests that the writer was either confident or indifferent, or both, about his personal standing with his patron. Writing from Florence to Piero at the villa of Trebbio, the artist was contemplating a trip which seemed to be a major reason for his objection to Piero's suggestion that he hold on to the panel, "which by God I don't like."[20] Such a strong and frank statement was rare, even between such intimates as Cosimo and his cousin Averardo; Cosimo took some care to couch his criticisms of Averardo's behavior in self-deprecating language that deflected some of their real force.[21]

The supposedly craven plea to Piero adducing his poverty and the nieces he had to marry off is more likely to have been an astute appeal to the universally accepted obligations of the wealthy to the major objects of society's charity; the clergy, the sick, the poor, widows, children, and marriageable girls. Lippi pressed all the charitable hot buttons here, in reponse to a claim by the wealthiest man in Florence that "you cannot give me a penny." The artist then suggested he might call at Piero's house for a handout, at least of bread and wine, on account. This was a common custom of the poor, but it was seen as the cause of such great shame to decent working men that Cosimo founded a confraternity of professional charity workers to save the faces of the needy by soliciting on their behalf. While to speculate about what the letter might reveal of Lippi's character or his mood when he wrote it is to venture onto shaky ground, the proposal of an artist who was well known for his excellent work in a city that revered its famous artists, and sought after as an arbiter by distinguished foreign patrons such as the cathedral chapter of Padua, to come begging in person at the Medici kitchen door, might rather be read as theatrical – even farcical – than ingratiating.[22] Lippi's subsequent introduction, in the guise of a request for a recommendation from Piero, of a reference to the rewards he anticipated for accepting the patronage of an unidentified "marquess," reinforces the impression that the artist is playing craftily upon a whole range of accepted expectations of patrons of reputation, in order to shame Piero into behaving better. This would be very much in the spirit of the behavior described in writings by and about Brunelleschi, Donatello, and other members of the Florentine artistic fraternity.

The next written evidence of the relations between Lippi and his Medici patrons is a series of letters of 1457 concerning a panel commissioned by Giovanni di Cosimo as a diplomatic gift to the king of Naples (figs. 167 and 168). In the meantime, Lippi had painted, among other major works, the *Annunciation* for the chapel in San Lorenzo belonging to the Medici family's close friends, the Martelli; the Medici altarpiece for the novices' chapel at Santa Croce; and probably a substantial portion of the great Magi tondo later displayed in the main *sala* of the Medici palace. He was soon to embark upon the Medici overdoors depicting the Annunciation and the seven saints, as well as the altarpiece for the palace chapel. A letter of 20 July 1457, from Lippi in Florence to Giovanni at Fiesole, is prefaced by the affectionate and respectful, but casual salutation, "Charissimo e magior [most dear and superior] etc." The artist announced that "I did what you instructed me concerning the panel, quite precisely in every detail. The Saint Michael is thoroughly finished, down to the silver and gold on his armor and also the wings. I just checked with Bartolomeo Martelli, who said that concerning the gold and whatever is needed, he would speak to Ser Franciescho, and that in everything I should do what you want, and then he reproached me greatly for having done wrong by you."[23]

In 1457 Bartolomeo Martelli, one of the group of brothers who by this time were the mainstay of the Medici bank's management, was a partner of its Pisan branch. He acted as a broker for many of the Medici patronage transactions, not only with artists, but also with their business associates, political partisans, and foreign friends. Members of his family also served as *operai* of San Lorenzo, and commissioned Lippi's *Annunciation*, so innovative in its use of color and light to create effects of spatial illusion, to adorn their family chapel there.[24] In writing to Giovanni, Lippi responded very forcefully to Martelli's charge.

> Now then, Giovanni, I am here to be your slave in all things, and so indeed I shall be. I have had fourteen florins from you, and I wrote to you that the expenses would amount to thirty, and that this would be because of the beauty of the ornaments. I beg you for God's sake to entrust Bartolomeo Martelli with responsibility for facilitating this work, so that if I need anything to get on with it, I can go to him and he will see to it, and I will defer to him in the matter, and I have told him that he should be the guarantor between you and me, and he says he is happy about that and would like to do it, and that I should hurry you up and write to you about it, and if you want to do this you should, since I am stuck because I have no more gold or money to pay the gilder. I beg you not to leave me like this; I haven't done anything for three days waiting for you here.

Lippi was clearly very confident of his craftsmanship, and keen to get on with his work, while also wanting to please his patron in every possible way. Having set Giovanni straight on these issues, he proposed in the second half of the letter a simple settlement, of the thirty florins

167　Fra Filippo Lippi, *Saint Anthony Abbot*, Cleveland, Cleveland Museum of Art, Leonard C. Hanna, Jr., Fund, 1964.151

168　Fra Filippo Lippi, *Saint Michael*, Cleveland, Cleveland Museum of Art, Leonard C. Hanna, Jr., Fund, 1964.150

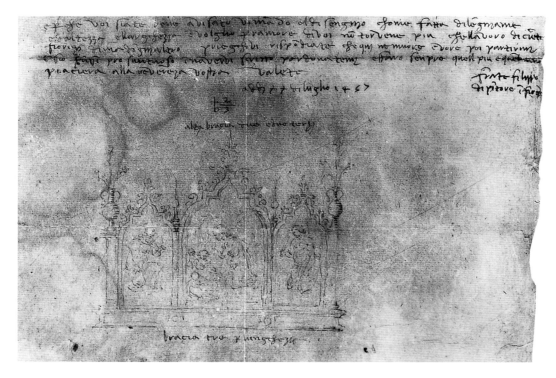

169   Fra Filippo Lippi, letter to Giovanni de' Medici, Florence, ASF, MAP, VI, 255 (formerly 260)

owed so far, plus sixty more for everything remaining to be done, as Martelli has suggested, to avoid bothering his patron again. In return he promised to have it all done within the month. If Giovanni felt the finished product was not worth the price, Lippi would be content with whatever he decided to do. For his patron's information in the meantime, he sent a drawing (sketched underneath the message) of the triptych in its elaborate wooden frame (fig. 169), expressing his wish "for love of you" not to ask more than a hundred florins for the whole thing. He begged, in conclusion, for some reponse: "for it is killing me here and I want to leave, and if I have been presumptuous in writing to you, forgive me, and I will always do what pleases your reverence in all things great and small. Farewell." The concluding salutation – *Valete* – was one used by relative equals to express their companionship in the classical idiom. Lippi's definition of separate but equal competences for himself and his patron is an important feature of his letter; he also referred familiarly to Martelli as "Bartolomeo." Lippi's words are at once firm, friendly, direct, courteous, and confident. There is perhaps a hint of irony, although this last is difficult to gauge. The letter might also, as others have suggested, be interpreted as expressing outrage or impatience, but that is not my impression.

In any case, this letter was not the end of the matter. A week after the projected deadline for completion of the work, Giovanni, then at Cafaggiolo *in villa,* as was the custom of patrician families in August, received another communication about it. This came from Ser Francesco Cantansanti, his secretary and factotum, in Florence. The project, by his own admission, was "killing" Lippi, and although Cantansanti had stood over him for an hour the previous Saturday evening, "to make him work," and had returned the night before he wrote to hurry him up, more still remained to be done. "Matters," Cantansanti added, "have been made worse by the rent." Bartolomeo Serragli, the art dealer based in Rome who had procured a number of objects for both Piero's and Giovanni's collection, and was apparently responsible for the payment and delivery of this work, had been deputed "to move this affair along"; if he failed, Cantansanti promised to try again himself, adding, "But you see what danger the man is in!"

Nine months later, in May 1458, Giovanni wrote to Serragli in Naples, responding to the dealer's account of the reception of the altarpiece by the king, who was very pleased with it. The count of Ariano also wanted a similar work for himself, and Giovanni instructed Serragli to take the drawing back to the artist and arrange for him to make a copy, which Giovanni thought he could probably be persuaded to do if the count were not in a hurry, "especially now that Fra Filippo has gone back to Prato." There he would have been reunited with his mistress, an Augustinian nun, who about this time seems to have given birth to their child, the future artist Filippino Lippi. As Ruda suggested, this may well have been the "error" to which Serragli referred as having caused some amusement at the Neapolitan court.[25] The exchange of letters over the altarpiece documents Lippi's close association, both professional and personal, with a number of the Medici *amici,* whose speech and actions express a combination of affection, amusement, and exasperation at his personal behavior, along with their respect and admiration for his art.

This commission was obviously very important to the Medici and their friends, both within Florence and beyond it. In 1456 Fra Filippo was working on a mural cycle for the commune of Prato. Although the project was already behind schedule, the city magistrates released Lippi to do the altarpiece for the king of Naples, apparently as a result of Giovanni de' Medici's intervention.[26] After a decade in which Florence had seen Naples as a major threat to her liberty, in 1455 the two powers had become partners in the League of Italy, which established peace, or at least brought an end to war. This context makes the Medici family's gift to Alfonso of a triptych by an admired Florentine artist, featuring the saints depicted on the triumphal arch at his castle in Naples, a highly strategic and politicized one.[27] Giovanni's letter to Serragli of 27 May 1458 confirms this impression. Having noted with satisfaction how pleased the king was with Lippi's work, Giovanni went on to comment on what he had heard of Serragli's conversations with the king, including the latter's favorable response to Cosimo's message, "from which Cosimo and I derived the greatest pleasure, because we have an intense desire to see these differences resolved." Alfonso had refused to include Genoa in the peace agreement of 1455, and the "differences" to which Giovanni alludes were apparently the continuing conflict between Genoa, supported by the king of France, and the Neapolitan king and his ally the duke of Milan, with which the rest of Giovanni's letter is concerned.

In a letter written ten years later by Lippi to Lorenzo di Piero, in September 1468, the positions of supplicant and patron are reversed. It is Lorenzo who has asked a favor of the artist-monk, and Lippi, as firm in this matter as in the supervision and pricing of his work, apologizes to the nineteen-year-old, who by that time had a considerable patronage clientèle of his own, for being unable to support his candidate for an ecclesiastical preferment.

This letter[28] is unusually explicit evidence of the fact that personal, political, and artistic patronage all operated within the same social framework and involved the same personnel. The last word on Lippi's relations with three generations of Medici is the monument Lorenzo had made for him twenty years after his death in Spoleto in 1469, and the inscription which concludes: "Nature herself by my expressive figures stilled/ Confesses me the equal of her arts."[29] The quantity of outstanding work the artist did for the family and its friends is perhaps, however, a more enduring monument to his membership of the Medici patronage network for more than thirty years.

Domenico Veneziano

What little is actually known of the life and work of this Venetian-born painter, much admired by his contemporaries, indicates that he was trained mostly in Florence and Rome. His first major Florentine commission has been assumed to be a frescoed tabernacle made for the Carnesecchi family, set on a street corner known as the Canto de' Carnesecchi, opposite the church of Santa Maria Maggiore, where the family had a chapel. The centerpiece of the tabernacle was a *Madonna and Child,* including also the Father and the Holy Spirit; much damaged and now much restored, it is usually dated in the early to mid-1430s. Bernardo di Cristofano Carnesecchi was a partisan of Cosimo de' Medici before 1434, and after the Medici rise to power was conspicuously favored in Medicean scrutinies.[30]

By 1437–8 Domenico was in Perugia, painting some frescoes for the palace of its Baglioni lords. In 1439 he was again in Florence, at work on the Portinari chapel at Sant' Egidio, and it was probably around this time that he painted the Medici *Adoration of the Magi.*[31] A letter he wrote to Piero de' Medici in Ferrara, dated 1 April 1438, has been the subject of a great deal of speculation and comment, much of it arising more from historians' preconceptions about artists and patrons than its actual text. Piero, at this time only twenty-one, was not "the leading patron in Florence," and this letter certainly does not support the contention that Cosimo always left the details of dealing with artists to his sons. Nor is it "obsequious" in its address.[32] The language and epistolary conventions employed by Domenico are identical to those used by hundreds of others, either Florentines or foreigners, writing to the Medici. "Spectabilis et generose vir" (notable and magnanimous man) was the form of greeting most often used in letters between the members of the Medici family and their closest friends, along with the shorthand reference to "le debite rechomandacione" (the usual recommendations), being taken as read. The brief concluding identification of the writer as "lo vostro fidelisimo servitore" (your most faithful servant) signifies little more than "yours faithfully" or "yours sincerely" do today.[33]

It is obvious from Domenico's letter that he and Piero already knew one another quite well. They may have met in Florence in the mid-1430s, or, as Ames-Lewis suggested in his study of Domenico's relations with the Medici, perhaps they met earlier in the artist's native Venice, where the Medici spent most of the year of their exile, from late 1433 through 1434. After the family's recall to Florence in September of that year, Piero stayed on in Venice to acquire an education in banking under the expert supervision of Antonio Martelli, manager of the Venice branch. Piero also spent time in Ferrara in the 1430s; he was there in 1435, and again in 1438, when Cosimo and both his sons were attending the church council in their capacity as papal bankers.[34] Domenico's repeated expressions of concern for Piero's health were obviously more than mere convention; the reference to his own – "I can tell you that by the grace of God I am well, and eager to see you well and happy; and time and again I have asked after you" – suggests they had not met for some time before Manno Donati told Domenico that he could reach Piero in Ferrara. Domenico made the usual self-deprecatory allusions to his own "more lowly condition" and the common assurances of "the perfect and sincere love I bear for you, and all yours;" these phrases appear in numerous letters to the Medici from friends writing similarly "for pleasure and to discharge my duty . . . considering how attached and obliged I am to you." Already the friendship of these two young men – Domenico was some half-dozen years the elder – was established, and its obligations acknowledged by both parties, so Domenico was writing to ask a new favor.

The "sincerity" or otherwise of this complex of sentiments so basic to quattrocento friendship and patronage is really not at issue. This was a very standard set of expectations upon which the artist sought to build in a very standard way, in requesting his contemporary Piero's help to secure the commission for an altarpiece he had heard was to be made by Piero's father, Cosimo. Perhaps the most interesting information contained in this letter is that when a patron wanted to generate a really important work of art, he let it be known. The public discussion of such a major private commission re-created the circumstances of the public commissions awarded by competition, stimulating an artist like Domenico to put himself forward as persuasively as he could. That meant first of all securing the support of a personal inter-

mediary – in this case Piero – and begging him "insofar as a servant may his master, that you should be good enough to exercise your skills [of intercession] in my aid and favor"; the resulting work would redound to Piero's honor if "by your mediation . . . I should paint it." Intercession and mediation greased the wheels of patronage in this society, and many Medici commissions, as we have seen, required the facilitation of their friends. All parties stood to benefit from this exchange. Confident of his own abilities, Domenico promised Piero that "you will receive honor by what I do . . . I would hope with God's help to show you wonderful things."

The Venetian artist also knew how, as Rudolf and Margo Wittkower observed, to market his product in a competitive environment.[35] Envisaging the formidable competition of Fra Angelico and Fra Filippo, he pointed out how much work they already had in hand, and specified as a case in point the latter's Barbadori altarpiece, also much talked about in circles of artists and patrons. He sensibly canvassed the possibility that, "if the work should be so great that Cosimo should decide to give it to several masters," he might have at least some part in it. In responding to the patron's expressed desire for "a magnificent work" Domenico represented his own desires as perfectly complementary, as indeed they were: "If you knew how much I want to make some famous work, and especially for you, you would certainly support me in this." His words emphasize the reciprocity of relations between patron and artist, the mutual obligation and cooperation that were the key to all patronage relations, and perhaps also to the particularly favorable conditions in which Florentine artists could express their creativity.[36]

Cosimo had other plans for the San Marco altarpiece, for which Fra Angelico was for many reasons the most natural contender. However, the response Domenico requested from Piero surely came in the form of at least two commissions for the Medici and their friends within the next year. Both Wohl and Ames-Lewis saw a close connection between the award to Domenico of the major commission to fresco the Portinari chapel at Sant' Egidio, and his Magi tondo for the Medici. Ames-Lewis, who believed that Cosimo was largely responsible for implementing the Portinari commission, suggested the tondo might have been a trial run for this work; Wohl saw the sequence of the works and the causes of their commission as reversed. Either suggestion is perfectly plausible, given the very close relationship between a number of Medici commissions and those of their friends, and in both works the patron's influence is rather evident.[37] Of the handful of Domenico's extant paintings, among the most remarkable is the main panel of an altarpiece, dated in the mid-1440s, for the Florentine church of Santa Lucia de' Magnoli. The church in the via de' Bardi was under the patronage of Niccolò da Uzzano before his death and his family's subsequent disgrace for his opposition to Cosimo de' Medici. Although no evidence has been found to confirm the suggestion that Cosimo had a role in the commission's award to Domenico, and little is known about the later patronage of the church, the pro-Medicean Capponi took over the Da Uzzano palace just down the street from it; other Mediceans may well have assumed responsibility for the patronage of the church, as they filled the gaps left by a number of anti-Medicean patrons active before 1434.

Matteo de' Pasti

The letter addressed by Matteo de' Pasti to Piero in 1441, concerning the young man's personal commission of a representation of Petrarch's *Triumphs*, is perhaps the most straightfoward of artists' letters to the Medici. The text and the theme on which the work was based were close to the patron's heart; the work itself has been identified by Ames-Lewis as the first important manuscript commissioned by Piero for his magnificent collection.[38] Matteo's letter from Venice is brief and to the point, announcing that "since I have been in Venice I have learned something that couldn't be more appropriate for your work." This proved to be a new technique for painting on ground gold "like any other color, and with it I have started to enrich it, so that you have never seen the like." Describing enthusiastically in detail what he had already done with "the ladies" in the *Triumph*, presumably of Love, he begged Piero "urgently to send me your notion of the others so that I can visualize them, and if you like, I will send you these." He apparently enclosed a sketch with the request to Piero to "complete it as you wish, and if you like it, send me word to do the other one of Fame, for I have the concept, except that I don't know whether you want the seated woman in a short gown or in a mantle, as I would like." He particularly called upon Piero "to let me have something to see." This letter is clear testimony to the liveliness and precision of the verbal and visual exchange between patron and artist over the application of materials and techniques recommended by the latter, and concerning the subject matter, chosen by the patron, but well known also to the artist, who had his own ideas about it. As Matteo continued of the *Triumph of Fame*: "For the rest I know all that is to go into it, that is, the chariot drawn by four elephants." The issue in question was Piero's personal preference concerning whether the ancillary figures following should be "shieldbearers and girls, or famous men of the past," obviously a choice between previous models for the representation of the *Triumphs* known to both patron and artist. While the artist also apologized for something he had done, or not done, the main points which emerge from Matteo's letter are that he is enthusiastic about the commission and his technical discovery, eager to please his patron in every last detail of a project where details mattered, and confident in his ability to produce "something you never saw in the world before."[39]

Benozzo Gozzoli

The letters which tell us most about the patron's role in the supervision of a commission are those exchanged between Benozzo Gozzoli, Piero de' Medici, and his agent Roberto Martelli, concerning the frescoes for the Medici chapel, painted in 1459. Once again the artist, as Fra Angelico's assistant for the altarpiece and the frescoes at San Marco, was already well known to the patron.[40] According to the convent's chronicler Lapaccini, Cosimo closely oversaw the work at San Marco, leaving the accounts to others, but calling in daily at the convent to attend mass and to see how all the work was coming along. Gozzoli has been identified as the author of the frescoes in Cosimo's personal cell, including a representation of the Magi, which was also the subject of the palace frescoes. While Piero's supervision of these has been adduced as evidence that he was also their patron, it is more likely that the subject and the artist were Cosimo's considered choice, as a result of his experience with Gozzoli at San Marco, and because the chapel was the centerpiece of Cosimo's palace. This commission is viewed by many art historians as Gozzoli's masterpiece, as it was by many contemporaries.[41]

On 10 July 1459 Gozzoli wrote to Piero at Careggi acknowledging receipt of his patron's letter via Roberto Martelli, who as manager of the main branch of the Medici bank at Rome was the man chiefly responsible at this time for disbursing the money for Medici charitable and other personal projects. He may also have been the patron of a marble *David* and a *San Giovannino* once attributed to Donatello.[42] Dispensing with pleasantries and preamble Gozzoli began: "I have heard that you don't like the seraphim which I have made; they are quite appropriate. I did one in a corner among some clouds, of whom you see nothing except the tips of his wings; and he is so hidden, the clouds cover him in such a way that he doesn't spoil anything, but rather enhances the beauty . . . I have done another on the other side of the altar, but hidden in the same way." Perhaps Piero had seen the seraphim before he left to spend the summer at Careggi, but the patron's absence from Florence, the artist's precise description, and his later request that Piero should come to see the work before it was finished suggest that Piero might only have heard about them from a member of his household or a friend. Justifying his own judgment, and seeking support for it, Gozzoli observed that Roberto Martelli, "saw them and said they were nothing to make a fuss about." He undertook, however, to conform entirely to his patron's wishes: "I will do what you tell me to; two little clouds will take them away."

Piero's objection to two half-hidden seraphim shows how close a watch he was keeping on the work, even if through the eyes of his agents. Gozzoli's response shows how seriously he took his patron's reaction: "I would have come to speak to you, but this morning I began putting on the azure and can't leave; it is very hot, and the glue spoils in an instant." He added: "I think that in the coming week I shall have covered all the area I can reach from this scaffolding, and I think you should come and look at it before I take the scaffolding down . . . I have gone on with the work as far as I can; what I don't do will be left for not knowing." Rather than self-deprecation, this last phrase seems in context to allude to his waiting upon Piero's verdict, and to the considerable demands of the task: "God knows that nothing weighs on my mind more than this; and I am continually looking for ways to do something which will satisfy you, at least in the main." His signature is both austere and commonplace: "I recommend myself to your magnificence. Your servant, Benozzo di Lese, painter in Florence."[43]

Three days later Martelli wrote to reassure Piero, apparently without reference to any further exchange between patron and artist; perhaps on his own initiative, perhaps at the artist's request. "I gave the painter the letter and saw those two little cherubs that he painted among some clouds, which in my opinion don't look bad there, and he will leave them there until you get back, for angels can always be painted. I gave him two florins for the colors; he says he doesn't need anything else for now; he is doing this work diligently and serving well." Martelli referred to the figures generically as "cherubim," while Gozzoli had spoken more precisely of seraphim; the latter's particular role in the heavenly order was of some interest to theologians of the day, and Martelli's suggestion that angels might be substituted for seraphim might imply that these distinctions were the issue.[44] Martelli's letter, seeking rather to inform than to contest the patron's view, reinforces the impression that Piero had not actually seen the figures himself. It appears that when he did, he deferred or conceded to the artist's judgment,

since in recent restorations of the frescoes it was discovered that the figures were not painted over in the quattrocento.[45]

Discussion of this correspondence has focused on the patron's objection to the seraphim, which has been adduced quite inappropriately as evidence of the low status of artists. In fact, like other artists' letters to the Medici, Gozzoli's testify to the freedom of communication between patron and artist. The latter was very ready to defend his own actions and judgments, but he was also eager to have Piero's approval. His later letters, of 11 and 25 September, both report upon his progress, and express his urgent wish that Piero, apparently still summering at Careggi, should see and pronounce upon his work. The first of these letters was addressed to "Amicho mio singhularissimo" (my most particular friend), a form of address common among intimate equals, like the simple signature "your servant." Gozzoli referred to a previous letter in which he had requested payment of forty florins to cover his expenses. "My idea was to ask you for nothing until your magnificence had seen what I had done." But as he observed, now is the time to buy grain, and need constrains him. He also asks Piero to send to Venice for the azure, and explains that "the brocades and other things" (the extravagantly worked and gilded portions of the pictures) will be done before the figures. His second letter later in September announces a bargain on a huge quantity of gold, worked in Genoa, that he has come by via someone "who I think is a servant of your Pierfrancesco"; he asks for the money to close the deal quickly. Again he speaks of his intention of visiting Piero: "I wanted to come last Sunday to see you, but I was intimidated by the weather . . . it seems to me a thousand years since your magnificence was here to see if you like the work."[46]

Gozzoli's correspondence with Piero testifies to an artist's expectation of his patron's close interest in the details of his work, and the patron's exercise of careful supervision, whether in person or through the intermediacy of relatives and friends.[47] The artist's pride in his own craft and his solution of the technical problems described in his letters is further expressed in the self-portraits he included in the Medici palace frescoes. In the most prominent of these, the artist appears appropriately among the retinue of the Medici family's friends and retainers (figs. 156 and 166). The Medici patronage network continued to include, promote, and protect Gozzoli in the years that followed.[48] Two years after the Medici chapel was completed, Benozzo received the commission for the altarpiece of the Confraternity of the Purification, who met in an oratory at San Marco built by Cosimo, and whose chapel was dedicated to Saints

Cosmas and Damian, as was the previous altarpiece, which had been donated by Cosimo.[49]

Gozzoli's relationship with the Medici family, like Lippi's, endured over three generations. In 1467 he wrote to Lorenzo di Piero di Cosimo to thank him for his intervention with the vicar of Certaldo on behalf of an assistant of his, who had been accused of stealing three bedsheets. Addressing Lorenzo as "My dearest in Christ, after infinite recommendations, etc.," Benozzo proceeded to give him a full report on the matter, observing that "nothing like this has ever happened to me with him; we have been in many and various places, and he was always most true. Perhaps God has allowed this scandal to occur for some good purpose." He concluded by thanking his patron in terms common to so many recipients of Medici favors, with the assurance that "I shall consider this as having been done for me. To offer myself to you or anything that I can do seems to me superfluous, for I belonged to you and your house before this incident occurred . . . Jesus Christ be with you always."[50]

Other artists in the Medici patronage network

As in other activities, Medici friends and relatives usually followed their leaders, patronizing artists favored by Cosimo and his sons. However Castagno, who painted only one work noted in the inventory of the Medici palace in 1492, seems originally to have been the protégé of Bernardetto de' Medici, for whom he did work in Florence and in the Mugello. Castagno also received important commissions from Orlando de' Medici and other Medici friends and partisans, including the Carducci and Piero da Gagliano.[51] He established his reputation with the commune's commission of *pitture infamanti* of its enemies defeated at the battle of Anghiari in 1440. Bernardetto de' Medici, who was one of the victorious Florentine generals, might well have been behind the award of this commission to Castagno, as for the fresco of Niccolò da Tolentino for the cathedral, which was commissioned while Bernardetto was Gonfalonier of Justice in 1455. John Spencer's study of *Castagno and His Patrons* presents Castagno's oeuvre as the joint product of the artist and a group of patrons at the center of the network of friends and relatives bound together by the personal and political patronage of the Medici family.[52]

Medici business associates played a prominent part in the family's acquisition and commission of precious objects, particularly the many tapestries in the Medici palace. These were mostly imported from Flanders, which was the center of the industry, and the site of the Bruges branch of the Medici bank. In the late 1440s and 1450s several members of the staff of the bank in Bruges or in London assisted Giovanni in procuring, commissioning, and shipping these elaborate and expensive works of art. In 1453, he ordered a six-piece set from a weaver in Lille representing Petrarch's *Triumphs*, and in 1459 another set from the same master depicting seven figures enthroned, probably the Virtues or the Liberal Arts. Gerozzo de' Pigli, a partner in the Bruges branch, assured his patron that in commissioning these he had dealt in his name "with the greatest master of the land" who "had well grasped the intention of his client."[53] Simone Nori, who was manager first in Bruges and then of the London branch, supervised the commission in Bruges of a set of three *spalliere*, three *banchali*, and a dozen cushions, all of which were stolen while the Florentine galleys carrying them were docked in London in October 1460; in 1462 Tommaso Portinari of the Bruges branch suggested ordering an identical series to replace them. All Bruges flocked to see another magnificent pair of *spallieri* they had made for Giovanni, before these were dispatched to Florence.[54]

In 1448 Fruosino da Panzano, also an employee of the bank, wrote to Giovanni from Bruges reporting upon his visit to the fair at Antwerp, "where I looked for what you had commissioned me to get . . . I found nothing I thought would serve your purpose . . ." He had rejected a tapestry depicting the story of Samson, because it was too large for Giovanni's room and "I didn't like the subject, because there was a great quantity of dead people in it, and I thought it was just the opposite of what one would want for a bedchamber . . ." Observing that "all those who want a better than average work have it done to order," he suggested that Giovanni send him the measurements and the story he wanted, "and I'll have it made by the best master that can be found."[55]

Even this handful of well-known letters concerning the Medici family's acquisition of works of art paints a richer picture of the relations between patrons and artists when considered together, and in the context of a broader view of Medici patronage as a system of social organization. Over the last several decades art historians have unearthed quite a lot of new material, and it is likely that more evidence remains to be discovered or more fully explored. For example, recently Alison Wright observed the considerable evidence for the close relationship of Antonio and Piero Pollaiuolo with the Medici, pointing to at least ten surviving letters referring to their work which reveal Medici connections of some kind.[56]

In addition to the letters from artists of major works, long since extracted from the Medici correspondence, there are quite a number of letters addressed to the Medici by craftsmen describing obscure commissions, but close personal relationships. Iacopo di Biagio, a wool-trimmer who was one of the administrators of the charitable confraternity of the Buonomini of San Martino, founded with the support of the Medici and their friends, wrote to Giovanni di Cosimo at Careggi in June 1449. He recommended the bearer of the letter, one Giuliano di Santi, a carpenter "who did the scaffolding and the structure at Cestello, and I agreed with him that he should get 20 lire for all his expenses; he has served us well . . ."[57] An armorer wrote a letter to Giovanni, unfortunately undated, in which he addressed him affectionately as "Giovannino" (my little Giovanni), as well as "charo mio magiore" (my dear superior), expressing his delight that a breastplate he had recently made for Giovanni had pleased him, but adding that he would have liked to see him try it on before he finished chasing the inside; he offered to make the journey to Florence if Giovanni would provide him with a mount.[58]

Giovanni d'Angelo d'Antonio, who described himself as a painter and a lute-player, wrote to Giovanni in 1451 from Camerino, regretting that it was so long since he had fulfilled his duty of coming to see him, but observing that he had written many times: "I don't know if they gave you the letters, I believe not, since I have never had a reply." This was perhaps understandable, since the burden of the painter's letter was to propose, "if your Magnificence has not taken a wife," Batista, the thirteen-year-old daughter of the lord of Fabbriano, who was perhaps his patron and employer. Extolling her beauty and the size of her dowry, he declared that "all that I need to bring this about is the inspiration." Reminding Giovanni of their trip together to the baths of Petriolo, when Giovanni had lent him three ducats and Piero four, he promised to return them to whomever Giovanni should nominate, and sent his recommendations also to "your father and your mother Madonna Contessina."[59]

While his attentions, along with those of dozens of others daily pressed upon the Medici family, were apparently unwelcome, some artists were friendly enough with their patrons to secure by their mediation personal favors for others much more socially distinguished than themselves. In 1451 an impoverished Francesco di Bivigliano degli Alberti, hoping for Piero's help in marrying off his daughters, invoked Piero's affection for his favored miniaturist Filippo Torelli, calling upon him as an intermediary. Torelli's workshop was responsible for Piero's first splendidly illuminated manuscript of Petrarch's *Triumphs*. Alberti was godfather to a son of the artist, who had a farm "a stone's throw away from me, and we chat a little every day when he is there . . . and since he is a very dear friend of yours, he tells me he has spoken to you, and that you responded graciously that you would like to help me, for which I thank you very much."[60]

THE ARTIST'S EXPERTISE AND THE PATRON'S CHOICE

The correspondence between leading patrons like the Medici, the Malatesta, the Gonzaga, and the Sforza, recommending artists to one another and seeking each other's advice on artistic projects, is well known. But as much work may have come the way of artists through their links with one another. A number of those who received commissions from the Medici had been pupils, assistants, or partners of other artists who had worked for the family. Gozzoli was Angelico's assistant; Castagno perhaps Uccello's pupil. Michelozzo had partnerships with Ghiberti, Donatello, and Luca della Robbia.[61] Giovanni di Bicci's tomb in the old sacristy was probably entrusted to Brunelleschi's adopted son Buggiano in deference to the architect.[62] Artists helped to guide and educate the patron's taste in other ways. Several of the artists who worked for the Medici had art collections of their own, or acted as brokers helping to create the Medici collections. Ciriaco d'Ancona commented on Donatello's and Ghiberti's collections in the same breath as those of Cosimo and Marsuppini.[63] Letters to Piero and Cosimo from such friends and family as Bartolomeo Serragli and Carlo de' Medici, Cosimo's illegitimate son, testify to their search for antique heads for the younger Medici, but their only documented purchase of an ancient figure was from Bernardo Rossellino in 1455. Giovanni also acquired thirty fine silver pieces from Pisanello's antique coin collection a few days after the artist's death.[64] There are references to at least two cases of Donatello's assessing antiques for the Medici and their friends.[65]

The lively exchange of information between patrons and artists and between artists themselves played some part in shaping the patron's choices. Chapter 8 introduced a world of artists whose friendships and cooperation, born presumably of workshop associations, balanced the vigorous competition for which they are better known.[66] Information about Cosimo's proposed commission for the San Marco altarpiece led to Domenico Veneziano's later work for the Medici. His friends wrote to apprise Ghiberti of the contest for the baptistery doors.[67] Artists knew one another and each other's work very well; Angelico, Lippi, and Domenico Veneziano served together in Perugia as judges of murals, and as a Milanese painter observed of Mantegna, "among painters it is always known by whose hand any painting is, especially when it is by the hand of any established master."[68] Patrons would certainly have been attentive to artists' assessments of one another, not only in the arbitration they often requested, but also in observations like Alberti's, in dedicating the Italian text of *Della pittura* to Brunelleschi, discerning in him "and our great friend the sculptor

Donatello and in the others" – Ghiberti, Della Robbia, and Masaccio – "a genius for every laudable enterprise in no way inferior to any of the ancients who gained fame in these arts."[69] Masaccio's *Sagra*, and Uccello's panel depicting outstanding artists, represent a similar assessment of their fellows artists.

The patron's choice of artist was probably influenced by a combination of the factors considered here, together with the practical issue of who was available at the time the work was needed. Like Lippi when Giovanni wanted to commission a gift for the king of Naples, an artist might be out of town, or occupied with other commitments; Lippi and Donatello often seemed to have more work than they could manage, and their patrons had to persuade them to set aside other commitments, and to pursue them until they completed their commissions. Beyond these more pedestrian concerns, Florentine patrons, and particularly the Medici, were interested in the distinctive *ingegno* of their artists, the particular "fantasia" by which they were governed.[70]

Some years before the humanist Landino described the special qualities of Florentine artists along lines inspired by Pliny, the citizen chronicler Giovanni Cavalcanti demonstrated the extent of an ordinary man's perception of what made some artists special.[71]

> There are as many different human creatures as there are stars in heaven; as these are, so are the human creatures. And thus human inclinations [*voluntà*] are as different from one another as are the influences stemming from the nature of the stars. And so there was a different inclination in Pippo di Ser Brunellesco than in Lorenzo di Bartoluccio [Ghiberti], and a different imaginative faculty [*fantasia*] in master Gentile [da Fabriano] than in Giuliano d'Arrigo [Pesello]; and thus as the inclinations are different, so are the *fantasie* and the skills in men, and similarly there is a great diversity of skills that springs from the diversity of genius [*ingegni*].

After mid-century there developed a more sophisticated vocabulary for describing and indeed conceiving of art and artists, out of which grew the artistic theory of the High Renaissance. But already in Cosimo's day, individual style was explained in terms of the variety of *ingegni*, which Cosimo was said to admire, of God-given talents or creative intellects partaking of that of the Creator himself.[72]

The *Elegies* of Propertius, in Cosimo's library by 1418, instruct his patron Maecenas in appropriate consideration for his artists' particular abilities. Addressing Maecenas as "knight sprung from the blood of Tuscan kings," the poet protests his inappropriate demands: "Why dost thou launch me on so wide a sea of song? Such spreading canvas suits not a bark like mine . . . All things are not meet alike for all men; from different heights the palm of fame is won." The examples adduced by Propertius are all of artists: "'Tis Lysippus' glory to mould statues with all the fire of life; Calamis, it seems to me, boasts the perfection of his carven steeds; Apelles claims his highest glory from his painting of Venus; Parrhasius asserts his place by his miniature art . . . the Jove of Phidias arrays himself in a statue of ivory; the marble in Triops' city gives Praxiteles glory." This passage constitutes a virtual program for the patron's oeuvre which is almost precisely applicable to Cosimo himself; it could well have been a blueprint for Cosimo's pursuit of the "variety of *ingegni*."[73]

THE MAJOR PARTNERSHIPS: DONATELLO AND MICHELOZZO

Donatello and Michelozzo, partners with one another and their patron, might be seen as the bookends of Cosimo's personal oeuvre. They also stood at opposite ends of its spectrum. Donatello's reputation as a genius has endured the test of time; Michelozzo's has not. Documentation concerning either artist's work for Cosimo is limited, but while Donatello's connection with Cosimo's commissions seems relatively clear, the assumption that Michelozzo was his patron's right-hand man in building is more speculative. This difference may well be related to the patron's distinction between buildings, regarded primarily as his own productions, and other patronage. Conversely, while only a few fragments of evidence illuminate Donatello's personal relations with his Medici patrons, Michelozzo's own letters place him firmly within the Medici patronage network.[74] If Michelozzo was indeed the architect of most of the Medici buildings attributed to him, and might literally be seen as Cosimo's *alter ego* in their creation, Donatello and Cosimo apparently had an affinity of temperament. Vespasiano described Cosimo as "a very great friend of Donatello,"[75] and Poliziano's anecdotes about the two men's reported repartee suggest they had quite a lot in common. The artist's response to a beggar asking for alms "for the love of God," that he would give "not for the love of God, but because you have need of them," resembles Cosimo's comment on his own charity as reported by Vespasiano, that God knew why he had given it, and if for his own aggrandizement, he would be rewarded accordingly. Despite such stories, Cosimo's character remains opaque; similarly, one of most plausible comments about Donatello is that he was "molto intricato."[76]

Donatello's great gifts enabled him to interpret Cosimo's interests brilliantly, while of all the Medici artists

170   Giotto, *Last Judgment*, Padua, Arena Chapel, detail showing Scrovegni presenting a model of the Arena Chapel to angels in heaven

he seems to have been least trammeled by them. Another major patron, Lodovico Gonzaga, observed of Donatello that he had "a mind constituted in such a way, that whatever did not come from him, it was no use hoping for."[77] In other words, Donatello's patron could only draw upon his artist's creativity; he could not control it. Indeed, Donatello's work for Cosimo might seem to constitute a satisfying match between Florence's greatest patron, and the man often considered the city's greatest artist in Cosimo's lifetime, saving the architect Brunelleschi. Insofar as the main themes of Cosimo's patronage were civic and religious, Donatello was well equipped to realize them visually. Most of his early commissions were from corporate groups within the Florentine commune, like the Opera del Duomo and the guilds; most of his patrons outside Florence were ecclesiastical, among them popes and cardinals, the cathedral at Siena, and the church of the Santo at Padua. The Medici, indeed, were almost his only consistent private patrons. Joachim Poeschke has suggested that Donatello's work, however admired, was really too radical for the general taste, which if true would imply something very interesting about Cosimo.[78] Conversely, by contrast with most princes' support of the artists they retained, the Medici did not offer Donatello enough work to keep him securely in Florence. Cosimo several times served as a broker between Donatello and his other patrons; at their request he pressed the sculptor to complete the statue of Abbondantia for the Mercato Vecchio, and the pulpit for the cathedral at Prato.[79]

The two men were almost precise contemporaries. Donatello was born around 1386, some three years earlier than Cosimo. Cosimo died in 1464, Donatello two years later. Donatello was the artist for the two earliest important commissions with which Cosimo was involved; the tomb of Pope John XXIII in the Florentine baptistery, and the decoration of the old sacristy at San Lorenzo. He was also the recipient of Cosimo's last commission, for the bronze pulpits in San Lorenzo, and he may have had a hand in the design of Cosimo's tomb. Certainly he successfully petitioned the Medici family for permission to be interred alongside Cosimo, as the records of the church and the present plaque attest.[80]

Relations between Cosimo and Donatello were not restricted entirely to the elevated realm of artistic creation. Donatello was also the recipient of the personal patronage of the Medici family, although less willingly than most of their friends and clients, if Vespasiano's tale

171   Giorgio Vasari, *Brunelleschi and Ghiberti Presenting a Model of San Lorenzo to Cosimo*, Florence, Uffizi

recounting his refusal to accept Cosimo's present of a length of red cloth intended to make him look more respectable is true.[81] Like Michelozzo, Donatello also had ties with Averardo de' Medici, and an account with his bank in 1424.[82] In 1433 he was renting a house from Cosimo, according to the latter's Catasto report.[83] Two years later, payment of his debt to the bank of Cosimo and Lorenzo was enforced by the court of the Mercanzia; he also owed money to Nicola di Vieri de' Medici and their close friends the Carducci. In 1454 Piero sent on to the artist in Faenza some possessions which had been stored at Careggi.[84]

The patron's conception of his oeuvre was the framework within which the artist created the elements of his. Michelangelo's experience with Pope Julius II, involving the substitution of the Sistine chapel ceiling commission for that of an elaborate marble tomb, is an extreme example of the artist's creativity operating triumphantly within the patron's constraints. Most of Cosimo's commissions seem rather to have represented a reciprocity of inspiration and self-expression between himself and the artists who worked for him. H. W. Janson's repudiation of the notion of a "Medici cycle" in Donatello's

oeuvre perhaps reflected a concern common to many historians of art, that stressing the patron's contribution might diminish that of the artist.[85] But why should it, when both were so well served? Cosimo's commissions for Donatello superbly illustrate both the range of the patron's interests and the artist's apparently infinite capacity for invention.

Their cooperation may have helped to sow the seeds of a shift in perceptions of patronage and the role of artists. Although much has been said of this development, it is very hard to pin down. Cosimo's patronage might, however, be seen as a halfway house between that of the Paduan merchant Enrico Scrovegni, represented in the early trecento *Last Judgment* of Giotto, his artist at the Arena chapel, and Vasari's mid-cinquecento image of his idealized vision of Cosimo's patronage at San Lorenzo. In the former, the patron presents his commission to a bevy of angels as his passport to the Kingdom of Heaven. In the latter, the patron is surrounded, "not by angels but by artists"; Donatello and Michelozzo look on while Brunelleschi and Ghiberti present a model of the church, represented as their creation, to Cosimo, Florence's ultimate "maestro della bottega" (figs. 170 and 171).[86]

172   Rogier van der Weyden, follower, *Crucifixion with Saints and Angels and Donor,*
Brussels, Musée des Beaux-Arts

XV

THE PATRON'S CHOICE:
PRINCES, PATRICIANS, PARTISANS

CHOICE AND INTENTION

In a comment on the nature of knowledge and the history of ideas, abjuring any personal interest in the individual oeuvre, Michel Foucault astutely observed how the historian who explores the creation of such an oeuvre almost inevitably is drawn into the quest for elusive intention.

> [The] archaeology [of knowledge] is not ordered in accordance with the sovereign figure of the oeuvre . . . It does not wish to rediscover the enigmatic point at which the individual and the social are inverted into one another . . . does not try to restore what has been thought, wished, aimed at, experienced, desired by men in the very moment at which they expressed it in discourse . . . to recapture that elusive nucleus in which the author and the *oeuvre* exchange identities . . . It does not claim to efface itself in the ambiguous modesty of a reading that would bring back, in all its purity, the distant, precarious, almost effaced light of the origin . . .[1]

Over and over again in the preceding pages, the question of what Cosimo intended his patronage to convey to the audience for his artistic commissions has arisen in discussion of the literature interpreting the resulting works of art. This is largely because many art historians are convinced that Cosimo consciously and quite calculatedly used art as propaganda, to promote public awareness and acceptance of his increasing political power.[2] Finding the evidence adduced in support of such arguments often unconvincing and almost always inconclusive, I have tried as far as possible to describe more neutrally the close relation between Cosimo's commissions and the themes – civic, familial, devotional – with which he and his Florentine audience most strongly identified themselves. Whereas the term "propaganda" assumes that the patron manipulatively "used" art to convey messages about power, I have tried to show how Cosimo's

power was inevitably part of the personal identity he expressed in his artistic commissions, and that art was a natural vehicle for its expression. At the same time, since Cosimo's identity is indeed inseparable from his own and others' perceptions of the power he exercised over the Florentine state and its citizens, a consideration of how this might have played out in his commissions is essential to an understanding of his oeuvre.

It seems to me that Cosimo's intentions are ultimately unrecoverable, along with the precise dialogue between object and viewer which is part of the "message" of a work of art.[3] If his commissions are to be read in some sense as "power statements," then Cosimo's role in Florentine political life must be understood more complexly than it usually is. One approach to these questions that can be simply documented is to examine Cosimo's particular and distinctive choices from among the variety of possibilities open to the Renaissance patron, comparing and contrasting them with the patronage choices of his fellow-citizens and his princely friends. While not enabling us to "bring back, in all its purity, the distant, precarious, almost effaced light of the origin" of his commissions, the choices they represent may allow us to infer something of their function in Cosimo's eyes and those of his audience.

The patron's choice was not as open as at first it might seem, even where, as in Cosimo's case, money was no object. The choices in question in this chapter – of medium, materials, site, theme, symbolism, and scale of patronage – were heavily circumscribed by social conventions. For example the building of a private palace in the republican city of Florence was governed by a strict decorum, to be violated by the patron only at the peril of public criticism, which, if Cosimo's purpose in building were mainly political, would rather have defeated it.

Since the essential issue is whether Cosimo's patronage was "civic" or "princely," and what that might mean, the discussion that follows focuses on the following questions. Within the broad categories of private or public, secular or devotional, what seem to have been the particular "models" for Cosimo's commissions? Did they in fact emulate the commissions and styles of princes, either ancient Romans or Renaissance Italians? How did Cosimo's patronage differ from that of his princely friends and contemporaries? What was practically possible/impossible for a citizen of a republic without a prince's command over his physical and social environment? How do Cosimo's commissions compare with those of other wealthy and influential Florentine citizens, both before the Medici gained the political advantage in 1434, and after, when their patronage, political and artistic, often shaped the behavior of their fellow-citizens?

THE EXTENT AND LIMITATIONS OF COSIMO'S POLITICAL POWER IN FLORENCE: WAS IT IN FACT "PRINCELY?"

This was unclear even to contemporaries. Many of the Medici family's Florentine *amici*, requesting tax relief or asking for a particular office, assumed that these were in the gift of their Medici patrons and their leading partisans. Andrea Sertini, seeking the advancement of a friend, wrote asking Giovanni di Cosimo in 1434 "to be good enough to gild the pawn [*pignere . . . la pedina*] a little, as you can . . . for every small favor that he obtains, apart from those from Manno Temperani and Martino dello Scarfa, who wish him well more than they do Christ himself, you are the cause of bringing him to light . . ."[4] In a letter to Giovanni a decade later Niccolò Bonvanni, in pursuit of an ecclesiastical preferment, referred to "what Chosimo said to me about this when he was in my room," observing "that everything seems to depend upon you." And in 1448 Niccolò Popoleschi, writing to Piero from Cortona where he was Captain of the city, that he had heard "you are doing a new scrutiny of the external offices" concluded: "I beg you as strongly as I can that in this first round of votes you should arrange with your friends that things go in my favor, as I know you know how to do, insofar as this is consonant with justice . . ."[5]

The heads of other states, accustomed to regarding Cosimo as an equal in business and diplomatic dealings, often assumed that his domestic powers were also equal to theirs. When Pius II enjoined Cosimo to see that Florence contributed to the proposed crusade against the Turks, his response, "I am not a prince and cannot dispose of these things as if I were," seemed to the pope merely an excuse for his limited support. Similarly, when Francesco Sforza expressed dissatisfaction with Florence's refusal of financial aid, Cosimo replied that "a republic

cannot be run in the same way as a despotic regime."[6] Nicolai Rubinstein suggested that "Cosimo liked to emphasize his private status at Florence when this was convenient to him, but that "there was probably some wishful thinking in the attitude of Italian rulers" who would have found it far easier to deal with a Florentine despot than "negotiating with a republic whose policy might change overnight with a change of government, and whose proceedings were necessarily far less secret." Moreover, the vague observations about Florentine government by foreigners suggest they knew little more of how this actually functioned than many modern historians of society and art uninterested in the minutiae of Florentine constitutional arrangements, and the extent and limitations of their manipulation by Cosimo. Cosimo's power indeed depended upon his *modus operandi* remaining obscure.

The passage of time further muddied the waters. Cosimo's grandson Lorenzo, exploiting the influence of his friends in key offices, continued to consolidate the power of the state in his own hands, and was accused with greater frequency and more justice of being the prince of Florence in all but name.[7] From the 1530s the Medici dukes enjoyed a title to rule by authority of the Habsburgs, who had conquered large parts of the peninsula; behaving like princes ceased to be a cause for criticism.[8] But in the nineteenth century the heat of nationalism that inflamed all Europe colored Florentines' views of their distinctive past. This was especially true of the Renaissance, the city's moment of greatest glory. Looking back to the republican commune and the nascent national patriotism of pre-Renaissance figures such as Petrarch, writers saw Cosimo de' Medici as the man who betrayed these ideals. This image of the Medici penetrated Anglo-Saxon, and especially American culture, at its nineteenth-century liberal roots. As Mark Twain wrote in his influential *Innocents Abroad*: "We saw Dante's tomb in that church [Santa Croce] also, but we were glad to know that his body was not in it; that the ungrateful city that had exiled him and persecuted him would give much to have it there, but need not hope to ever secure that high honor to herself. Medicis are good enough for Florence. Let her plant Medicis and build grand monuments over them to testify how gratefully she was wont to lick the hand that scourged her."[9]

Such Risorgimento passions, enshrined explicitly in the writings of the great Italian archivists who laid the basis for the modern history of the Italian Renaissance, left their traces in both Anglo-Saxon and Italian historiography. Writing in the 1890s of a Medici supporter, the literary scholar Francesco Flamini derided the "relatives of Cosimo and . . . his gutless lackey."[10] Toward the middle of this century, the battle against fascism in Europe reinforced the revulsion of historians against tyranny in the remote past. Edgar Wind envisaged the Medici and their protégé Ficino as "infus[ing] the merchant tyranny of Florence with . . . Platonic poison," through a reading of classical philosophy that underwrote the depotism of a prince. Eugenio Garin's variation on this theme was to suggest that otherworldly Platonic humanism, as promoted by the Medici, distracted the remainder of the Florentine oligarchy from the business of politics, lulling the rest of the patriciate into acquiescence in their "rule."[11]

Many historians now are convinced that in everything he did Cosimo was implementing a master plan to make himself prince of Florence. Paola Ventrone, for example, described the Magi festivals as "revealing the royal ambitions that the Medici unconsciously cultivated from the very beginnings of the establishment of their hegemony."[12] John Paoletti spoke for many other scholars in concluding that "[Cosimo's] use of individual commissions as a means of social and political control is now a commonplace in discussions of his patronage."[13] In arguments like these, often unsupported assumptions about Medici intentions and ambitions are joined and justified with a modern conception of "propaganda," shaped in the twentieth century by the experience of communism and fascism, but with little establishable relation to early fifteenth-century modes of thought.[14]

Implicit in this discussion are some highly debatable visions of the nature of quattrocento Italian princes, the terms of their rule, and how they were regarded in the Florentine republic. For some time past, scholars of urban government and Italian regionalism have observed that the real differences between the everyday functioning of republics and principates in Italy were much smaller than "propagandists," past and present, would have us believe. The fundamental economic give and take between city and countryside underlay and outlasted the rise and fall of city governments or *signori*, and many princes of Italian states were large landholders turned *condottieri* who in the fourteenth and fifteenth centuries won back their territories from the urban republics by force of arms and became princes. In view of the persisting claims of urban agencies, and beyond these, the ancient pretensions of the papacy and empire to authority over Italy, variously intertwined with the ambitions of foreign dynasties such as the Angevins or the Aragonese, these princes' "titles" to a power essentially imposed upon the populations of cities were a motley and uncertain lot, by comparison with those of some long-standing hereditary rulers of other European states like England and France.[15] These latter at least could plausibly invoke a title, however contested, to an authority delegated by God, long recognized as legiti-

mate by medieval political theorists.[16] The more research that it is done on principates, particularly those of the Este of Ferrara, the Gonzaga of Mantua, the Malatesta of Rimini, the Angevins and Aragonese of Naples, and especially the upstart Sforza of Milan, the clearer it becomes that the roots, the reality, and the image of princely power differed markedly from state to state. But in most of them, although a prince had immeasurably more power than any citizen of a republic, however influential, the relatively recent or precarious claims of the ruler necessitated that he consult and respect alternative and preexistent authorities in his city in a manner not entirely dissimilar to the way in which the Medici were obliged to operate in Florence.[17]

Richard Trexler's book on *Public Life in Renaissance Florence* performed the inestimable service of drawing attention to the social meaning of images and their role in Florentine civic and political life. At the same time his account of the Medici family's self-presentation, and their use of images to increase their personal influence or power, was based on some seriously faulty premises. For example, he suggested that Florence embraced the Medici because their image promised to legitimate a state, often compared to a ship, that was a "tawdry skiff adrift among princely galleons."[18] This reworking of a traditional metaphor perverts Florentines' actual views of contemporary princes, most of whom were mercenary soldiers and many of whom had fought in Florence's employ. When they won they were hailed as heroes for their exploits on the battlefield, but they were ultimately the servants of the Florentine state and its Priors, whose authority Florentines compared only to that of God. Gregorio Dati observed that the power of the Priors was "great without measure," and that unlike the duke of Milan, who was merely mortal, the Florentine commune was immortal. His view was based on no lesser authority than Roman law, since Florentines believed their city had been founded and granted her liberties and government by Rome. By contrast, Florentine popular poets counted Sforza among the age's most famous self-made men. The duke of Milan was partly Cosimo de' Medici's creation, and if hardly his creature, was seen, and represented himself in diplomatic and personal letters to Cosimo, as the dutiful and respectful son of an older and wiser father.[19] Florentines may have felt from time to time that they needed a prince to defend their interests more resolutely in an increasingly authoritarian world, but while it endured the Florentine republic needed no legitimation beyond its constitution, and the authority of the Medici family could find none in this context.[20]

Cosimo did not control or "rule" Florence, however much he influenced its government, and whatever his ultimate ambitions might have been. This is clear from Rubinstein's careful study of actual political and constitutional arrangements, on the basis of a wide range of governmental and especially electoral records, over the period of Medici ascendancy, 1434–94. He emphasised and documented the constraints of the constitution, as well as the opportunities it offered the Medici for manipulation. I find that the family's personal correspondence, and particularly Cosimo's letters, which previously have not been systematically studied with this question in mind, supplement Rubinstein's picture with abundant evidence of Mediceans' tireless attempts to increase their political influence, and to implement their friends' requests for favors, but also of the opposition that often frustrated these aims. The evidence unearthed in these two bodies of sources, public and private, suggests that Cosimo, in his quest for ever greater influence over the affairs of state, encountered numerous obstacles in the way of its extension, necessitating constant effort on his part to surmount them.[21]

Whatever his supplicants chose to believe, Cosimo could not simply appoint people to office, requisition money for projects he favored, or have his wishes enacted into legislation. Both public and private records show that he was obliged to pursue these ends with the aid of his partisans in a roundabout way, respecting the constitution and the opinions of the *principes civitatis* (the leading citizens).[22] Rubinstein showed that Cosimo's political power was established and increased largely by ingenious modifications of the electoral system. The major offices of the republic were filled by a complex process originating in the nominations and votes of neighborhood committees, and culminating in the extraction of names from the electoral bags. We know that, as their personal patron, Cosimo exercised immense influence over many of his neighbors in the Medici *gonfalone* or ward. We know that the Accoppiatori, the officials in charge of the crucial business of filling the electoral bags and drawing out the names of those who were to serve, were always among his most trusted partisans. We do not know just how far Cosimo could go in controlling the whole process.

For example, the multiplication of electoral bags in the first few years after Cosimo's recall resulted in a situation where between 1434 and 1440, only three names were seen to be drawn from the purse for the republic's leading official, the Gonfalonier of Justice.[23] So whoever was drawn was bound to be acceptable, perhaps even a foregone conclusion. Cosimo himself was Gonfalonier just after his recall from exile, serving for the first two months of 1435, while the government dealt with the punishment of his enemies. He held this office again early in 1439, in the months in which the church council, by his own

arrangement, was transferred to Florence, making the city for some months the stage upon which the chief drama of the Church was enacted, attracting the attention of all Christendom. It would seem, then, that on sufficiently important occasions, the results of elections could effectively be guaranteed by Cosimo and his friends.

Conversely, while for long periods the ruling group acquiesced in these obvious electoral ploys to maintain Medici power, from time to time they were vigorously opposed. This opposition is documented in the records of the Florentine councils and in letters between Cosimo and his friends and family, which testify to their interest in maintaining restrictive practices, but also to their realization that this could not be done in open defiance of the wishes of influential members of the patriciate. While a majority of the ruling group seemed willing to accept the extension of these electoral "safeguards" in the 1440s, when foreign wars and consequent economic crises argued for the importance of continuity in the regime, after the signing of the Peace of Lodi in 1454, many citizens saw no further reason to accept them. Between 1454 and 1458 protests in the councils, some anti-government uprisings in the city, and even the disaffection of formerly loyal partisans demonstrate that the Medici grip on power remained tenuous. Cosimo's continuing influence was contingent upon the family's fulfilling the expectations of partisans whose cooperation was essential to the manipulation of the constitution; he was thus ultimately dependant upon those whom he appeared to control.

In 1458 the Medicean patriciate traded a concession to the opposing financial interests of the general populace, reviving the more equitable tax system of the Catasto, in return for a modification of the system of councils that would allow them to consolidate support for other legislation they favored. However, the success of some attempts by the Medici family and their regime to increase their bureaucratic control over important communal agencies like the Parte Guelfa was counterbalanced by a growing movement within the Medici party to contest the leadership of the aging Cosimo and any attempt by his son Piero to succeed him. It culminated in 1466 in a conspiracy against the Medici led by a group of their most prominent partisans, from which Piero emerged victorious largely by a combination of luck and the crucial support of the Milanese.[24] The Medici reaction to these events is revealed in their correspondence, which shows how seriously Cosimo and his leading partisans took these challenges, how discontented many of their *amici* were becoming, and with what subtlety and caution Cosimo thought it necessary to move against his opponents. Vespasiano's observation that Cosimo made a point of never seeming to initiate any action, but rather appearing to respond to the wishes of others, is confirmed in the numerous letters in which Cosimo intructed his friends to maneuver as best they could, in procuring offices or passing legislation, but in the process to consider and consult the leading citizens, and to avoid opposing the declared interests of others.[25]

Many writers assume that Cosimo's maneuverings were part of a carefully calculated long-term political strategy. In fact there is no documentation of this in public records, nor, more importantly, in private letters; these are concerned with immediate advantage. Such a strategy can only be inferred by reading backwards from the evidence of the family's ultimate success. Similarly, it is often argued that Cosimo used his artistic commissions to make political statements which he did not dare to articulate in any other form. Since Florentines read visual texts as naturally as verbal ones, it makes no sense to assume that any "political messages" in Cosimo's artistic patronage would be any more subtle or ambiguous or acceptable than his overtly political actions, or that art could constitute an instrument of "political and social control" which he was unable to assert in government or legislation. Throughout Cosimo's lifetime Medici influence in Florence seems to have been increased gradually by an intelligently opportunistic response to such possibilities for the family to assert its leadership as presented themselves on the civic scene. It is within this framework that Cosimo's patronage choices might more realistically be viewed.

COSIMO'S COMMISSIONS AND THOSE OF HIS PRINCELY FRIENDS: COMPARISONS, CONTRASTS, CONNECTIONS

A growing interest in the patronage of the princes and courts of quattrocento Italy has begun to redress the imbalance of an excessive focus on Florence. General studies as well as monographs now provide a broader context for the evaluation of Florentine patrons' interests and achievements. A proper comparison of Cosimo's commissions with those of his princely contemporaries is far beyond the scope of this book and the competence of its author.[26] However, a few general points may be made. References to the "princely" examples followed by the Medici are notably vague; some writers cite precedents in French or German royal practice, which have not been shown to be in the forefront of Florentine minds at this time, and certainly not in Cosimo's.[27] Others, particularly with regard to the use of porphyry, point to the customs of popes and Roman emperors, to whose authority the merchant Medici of republican Florence

could hardly have harbored serious pretensions. Sometimes "princely" is simply an adjective attached to the use of materials such as marble and bronze, whose great value associated them with the Renaissance or Roman nobility. In fact, in the ancient world such materials were widely employed, by the testimony of Pliny and much to his disgust, by many citizens of the Roman republic.[28] If we are to talk about princely patronage, we need to consider what that really meant in fifteenth-century terms.

While Renaissance princes of classical enthusiasms and education, among them the Este, Malatesta, and Gonzaga, used Roman symbols to associate themselves with classical rulers, such analogies could simply not be made by citizens of a republic.[29] Florentine citizens, influenced by their reading of Roman historians, did include in their domestic decoration images of emperors, for example the marble heads Giovanni di Cosimo had made for his study, but it may be unwise to ascribe to such commissions a precise political consciousness. Although Florentine humanist scholars and some citizens after 1400 were sharply aware of the ideological distinction between empire and republic, and this was reflected in some informed artistic commissions, many creative artists, particularly Donatello, seem to have quoted from classical precedents mainly according to the demands of the human dramas they were depicting, rather than the politics of the period from which their prototypes derived. In Cosimo's lifetime the archaeological interest in Roman artifacts was still in its infancy. Collectors such as Poggio, Niccoli, and the Medici brothers appear to have been avid for any remnants of the admired antique, and political ideology did not enter into their comments on their trophies or their negotiations with dealers.[30]

The most practical models for any pretensions Cosimo might have had to authoritarian government, as for artistic commissions which could have expressed them, were those of contemporary rulers. Culturally and even politically, the republics and the principates of the peninsula had much in common, and many Florentine citizens cultivated relations and exchanged ideas with the heads of foreign states. By the early quattrocento members of the Acciaiuoli, Alberti, Cavalcanti, and Strozzi families had held major office at the Neapolitan court under its Angevin rulers, laying the basis for an appreciation of courtly culture and strong personal loyalties and ties that endured far into the century. However, in the realm of art, until some years after Cosimo's death, other Italian patrons more often emulated Florentine commissions, and Florentine artists, beginning with Giotto, went to work for them. In the mid-fifteenth century the Strozzi preceded the Medici in introducing Florentine artists to Naples.[31] At the same time foreign princes, especially those who had served the city as mercenary captains, were influenced by Medici patronage and became significant patrons of Florentine projects, for instance the Gonzaga at Santissima Annunziata.[32]

By the mid-fifteenth century, by virtue of his leading role in Florentine government and diplomacy, Cosimo enjoyed closer relations than most of his fellow citizens with the heads of other Italian states. He numbered among his friends and correspondents, in many ways part of his personal patronage network, the Bentivoglio lords of Bologna, the Ordelaffi of Forlì, the Manfredi of Faenza, the Montefeltro of Urbino, the Malatesta of Rimini, the Este of Ferrara, the Orsini of Rome, the Sforza of Milan, the Gonzaga of Mantua, and from time to time the kings of France and Naples, although the latter were often allied with the opposition to the league with which Florence was aligned.[33] More than any other Florentine citizen, Cosimo's personal wealth enabled him to embark on patronage projects on a scale similar to those of his princely friends, where most Florentine citizens could not have afforded them. So how, generally speaking, did their commissions compare?

Most early Renaissance princes seized power by military conquest. Some had once been feudal overlords of the territories they annexed; some had previously established a local base for their authority as vicars of the pope or representatives of the emperor or other lords. The Roman heritage revived in the Renaissance was replete with military images, both republican and imperial. Most princely patronage incorporated and emphasized the symbols with which warriors, classical and contemporary, were naturally associated, but many Italian rulers further sought to legitimize and ennoble their conquests with reference to the comparable exploits of the legendary heroes of Rome. This process has been described in relation to the Malatesta, the Este, the Sforza, and the Gonzaga, using, among others, the example of medals made for ceremonial purposes and as gifts to promulgate the freshly coined heraldic images of their authority.[34] The only medal commemorating Cosimo was struck by the authority of the commune after his death, and it bore the republican legend, most closely associated with the Roman republican statesman Cicero, of "pater patriae." When Cosimo ordered images of warriors, what they commemorated (like the cycles of *uomini illustri* or the frescoes of *condottieri* commissioned by the commune for the cathedral) was the virtue of military valor, an antique and Renaissance topos, and the honor of the republic, which could pertain only indirectly to his own.[35]

Although the identification between most Italian princes and their people was nothing like so solidly established as in the great European kingdoms, the patronage displays even of petty Italian princes were devised and read in light of the fact that the honor of a people was identified with the honor of their prince. While Cosimo managed to identify himself in the Florentine popular mind quite closely with republican aims and ideals, it was the republic, not he, that continued to embody Florentine identity, because the legitimate title to power and rule resided with its Priors. Although republican citizens and princes used similar classical and Christian symbols in their patronage, their significance in context was often very different. Studies, particularly of Milanese and Mantuan patronage, have emphasized princely preoccupations with legitimizing and defending a title to rule, and with establishing the succession of a lineage, a concern outweighing even the interest in military insignia.[36] Since the Medici had no putative title to rule, a succession in the princely sense was impossible, and so the celebration of a dynasty had a different meaning in the Florentine context. Even as their power increased at the expense of that of other ancient and distinguished lineages, all the Medici could do, as first Cosimo's and then Piero's death became imminent, was to enlist the continuing support of their foreign allies, and appeal, in the case of their Florentine friends, to the continuity naturally inherent in the patronage relationship, with its emphasis on the identity between generations of a patriarchal family. To achieve this, Cosimo did not need to create a princely image, and insofar as his grandson may have begun to do so, it proved ultimately unacceptable. While the republican framework of their power remained unchallenged the Medici had only to justify their predominance within it. When their actions began to challenge the maintenance of the republic itself, it was their authority that was overturned.

The twin themes of the identification of the honor of the polity with that of the prince, and the legitimation of a title maintained chiefly by the reality of conquest and its images, determined the forms of the most significant princely patronage, however much republican citizens and princes may have borrowed from one another in domestic or church decoration. Lorenzo's entourage is sometimes referred to as a court, but a comparison with the hundreds of domestic retainers considered necessary to the maintenance of the honor of his contemporary Galeazzo Maria Sforza, duke of Milan, puts that perception in more realistic perspective.[37] It is similarly impossible to compare a warrior prince's defensive castle to a citizen's palace. However the latter might be adapted to the street scrimmages of urban uprisings, it could certainly not be used, like the Castello Sforza, as a major symbol of the patron's dynasty and its identification with his city. The most memorable commission made by the Aragonese kings of Naples during Cosimo's lifetime was their Roman triumphal arch, a patronage choice not open to a Florentine merchant patrician. The same is true of the equestrian monuments made by the Sforza, Bentivoglio, Colleoni, Serego, and Sanguinacci.[38] The medals struck by Roman and Renaissance rulers, and the profile portrait modeled on their form, were alien to Florence in Cosimo's day.[39] Piero and Giovanni de' Medici were the earliest patrons of the classicizing portrait bust, and Giovanni had himself fancifully depicted in antique armor, but unlike the medal, this Roman form was not specific to soldiers or rulers, and Cosimo, by contrast with almost all his princely friends, refrained from commissioning any official portrait of himself.

Much princely patronage, like that of the Este at Ferrara, the Montefeltro in Urbino, or the Sforza in Milan and later Vigevano, involved large-scale urban renewal. This depended upon the ability to build and renovate at will, itself a demonstration of a prince's right to dispose of his territory. As Caroline Elam pointed out in her study of Lorenzo de' Medici and the urban development of Florence, all citizens' building, even that of the Medici, was modest compared with the transformation of Pienza, Vigevano, and Ferrara by princes and popes, partly because citizens "lacked the dictatorial powers necessary for compulsory purchase and demolition."[40] In Cosimo's time, when the Florentine state decreed the desirability of clearing away part of the *piazze* adjoining the public church of San Lorenzo to make way for its expansion, described as a major civic benefit, the pertinent laws were nevertheless concerned to justify the demolition of private houses, even those of the poor, the dissolute, and foreigners. When Luca Pitti, shortly before his almost-successful attempt to replace Piero as leader of the city's partisan regime, cleared the *piazza* in front of his new palace to enhance its effect, buying up properties and then tearing them down, he aroused a good deal of hostility, showing just how far even powerful citizens were expected to respect the rights of others.[41]

The close relations of the Este of Ferrara with Cosimo and his sons, and the possible influence of Este precedents on Medici patronage, have already been considered.[42] Otherwise, the princely patron perhaps closest to Cosimo and to his experience, one who was actually commissioning comparable work in Cosimo's lifetime, was Sigismondo Malatesta. A comparison of their patronage reveals elements both of similarity and difference. The Malatesta were lords of several cities of the Marches, including Pesaro and Rimini. Sigismondo's title to power over Rimini derived from his appointment as papal vicar, but even so, his government has been described as in fact a dependent partnership between councils, officials, and the

lord, official documents and laws referring to the "prince and the commune" together as the final authority.[43] In his capacity as a captain of the Florentine forces, Sigismondo was a frequent visitor to the city. He was part of the ceremonial party at the consecration of the Florentine cathedral, and dedicated a portion of his salary to the patronage of Santissima Annunziata; he was also one of the first to visit the newly completed Medici palace, along with Pope Pius II and Galeazzo Maria Sforza, in 1459, and his portrait appears in the chapel frescoes painted later that year. Thirty years earlier, he had sent a letter of consolation to Cosimo and Lorenzo on the death of their father, and Cosimo's close friend and partisan Agnolo della Stufa arranged in the mid-1450s for Filippo Lippi, an artist much favored by the Medici circle, to paint a picture for Sigismondo.[44] Several generations of Malatesta also shared the Florentine predilection for popular poetry; a number of the verses they wrote are transcribed in Florentine compilations, and Lorenzo sent collections of Florentine popular verse to Naples and Milan.[45]

Sigismondo's rebuilding of the church of San Francesco might be compared with the Medici intervention at San Lorenzo. The new foundations of the church at Rimini were laid in 1450 by Alberti. San Lorenzo by that time had been under reconstruction for some decades, beginning with the old sacristy and the transept chapels. The building of the main church soon departed from the original plan by Brunelleschi, whose classical sources were eclectic, whereas Alberti was in the forefront of a rapidly advancing archaeological interest in classical building, and he closely supervised the construction of San Francesco. Some of the major differences between the two buildings arise from these circumstances.[46] But the differences in the memorialization and representation of the patrons were much more closely related to the fact that one was a prince, while the other was a citizen of a republic.

Like the Medici at San Lorenzo, the Malatesta had been earlier associated with San Francesco, where they had a family chapel. Helen Ettlinger suggested that Sigismondo's building, rededicated to his patron saint, was less the despotic self-commemoration of a tyrant than it is represented. Its associations were also civic and religious, since it was a votive offering in gratitude for Sigismondo's survival of the Italic Wars between Florence, Venice, and Sforza on one side, and the Visconti, Naples, and the pope on the other. Sigismondo himself had secured the victory for the Florentines and their allies by switching sides and defeating Alfonso of Aragon at Piombino in 1447. His votive dedication appears on the medal by Matteo de' Pasti struck to commemorate the new building, and buried in its foundations, as well as being distributed to Malatesta friends and allies.[47]

No such personal symbols were built into the foundations of San Lorenzo; the first cuts were made by the
church's *operai*. The facade of San Francesco bears the
patron's name and dedication in large Roman capitals,
like those recording Giovanni Rucellai's gift of the facade
of Santa Maria Novella, also by Alberti, some twenty years
later. The correspondingly explicit Medici inscription at
San Lorenzo appears, much less prominently, in the old
sacristy on Giovanni di Bicci's tomb, and it foregrounds
its occupant's deeds and virtues as a citizen, a father, and
a patron of his friends. While Cosimo had the old sacristy decorated with stucco images of the patron saints of
his immediate ancestors and descendants, Sigismondo's
plan for the facade of San Francesco centered on a tomb
for his ancestor, admittedly the focus of a popular local
cult, in an extraordinary display of related personal,
dynastic, and Christian themes.[48]

The epic poem entitled *The Hesperis*, written by Sigismondo's court poet and celebrating him as the builder of
San Francesco and the hero who saved Italy from the
foreign invader in the person of Alfonso of Naples, like
the similar epics emulating the Aeneid written for the
Este (the *Borsiad*) and the Sforza (Filelfo's *Sforziad*), is very
different in its pretensions from the popular poems in
praise of Cosimo and Piero and their patronage of
Florentine churches.[49] And where the Medici *impresa* of
the diamond ring, used in connection with Cosimo
himself only on the palace, could be seen as taking up
the religious implications of Petrarch's *Triumphs*, of time
and eternity over fame, Sigismondo stamped on San
Francesco his personal device of the elephant, also a

symbol associated with Petrarch and fame, but derived
from the triumphs of Roman soldiers. Piero della
Francesca's 1451 fresco for San Francesco, of Sigismondo
Malatesta kneeling before Saint Sigismund, may perhaps
be compared with Fra Angelico's altarpiece for San
Marco, unveiled in 1443. The latter prominently features
the Medici saints, but Saint Cosmas invites the Florentine citizen viewers to join the chain of intercession culminating in the Virgin, and the *pala* is a *sacra conversazione*
in which a large group of saints, in addition to the protectors of the Medici, is engaged (fig. 62). In Piero's
fresco, the armor-clad Sigismondo appears alone with his
dogs before his patron saint, who is also a king; the donor
is the sole and direct link between the earthly and the
heavenly kingdoms (fig. 173).[50]

A pair of roughly contemporary pictures by Rogier
van der Weyden and a follower of his, the first made for
the Medici, the second for the Sforza (probably Alessandro, lord of Pesaro, rather than Francesco's line), invite
a similar comparison. Where the small Medici panel features Saints Cosmas and Damian, Saint Peter, who stands
for the Church, and Saint John the Baptist, patron of
Florence, and is adorned with the lily of the republic
(fig. 124), the much large Sforza panel shows the donor
himself, dressed in full armor, kneeling at center stage
before the cross; Sforza arms and devices are liberally scattered around him (fig. 172).[51] Cosimo's closest friend and
ally was Francesco Sforza; as Evelyn Welch has shown,
early Sforza patronage was much more circumscribed by
civic and ecclesiastical rights and precedents than has previously been supposed.[52] However, Francesco's patronage
does not provide a very useful point of comparison with
Cosimo's, because it effectively began with his investment
with the lordship of Milan in 1450, by which time most
of Cosimo's commissions had already been made.

173   Piero della Francesca, *Sigismondo Malatesta Kneeling before
Saint Sigismund*, fresco, San Francesco, Rimini

FLORENTINE PRECEDENTS FOR COSIMO'S PATRONAGE

What, then, were the major models for Cosimo's commissions? Most of them, as we have seen, had their foundations in the patronage of his fellow citizens. Because
private patronage blossomed only in the third or fourth
decade of Cosimo's life, and the earliest years of the fifteenth century saw a great explosion of work commissioned by the Florentine commune and its guilds, most
of the artists employed by Cosimo had learned their trade
and made their reputations with commissions in the styles
and forms that appealed to the Florentine *popolo* in
general.

Moreover, while Cosimo's patronage was indeed unique and remarkable, it has been made to seem excessively so by fact that it is usually considered in splendid mid-fifteenth-century isolation, rather than in its proper context of the work that was done in Florence between 1400 and 1434. Cosimo's was not the first monumental palace of the early Renaissance; that was constructed for a political opponent, Niccolò da Uzzano and his brother, around 1417. Giovanni di Bicci's was not the first sacristy to double as a family burial chapel; that was built by Palla Strozzi at the behest of his father Nofri in their neighborhood church of Santa Trinita. Nor was it the first self-contained chapel within a church, which was made by Brunelleschi for the Barbadori at Santa Felicita. Cosimo's decoration of the old sacristy was not the first decorative program for a family chapel in the innovative style of the early Renaissance; that was created by Masaccio and Masolino for the Brancacci family at Santa Maria del Carmine. Cosimo's building patronage of the Dominican convent of San Marco had precedents in that of the degli Agli at Fiesole, and the Acciaiuoli at the Certosa outside the city. It was not Cosimo who commissioned the first major Florentine image of the Magi; this was the altarpiece painted for Palla Strozzi by Gentile da Fabriano. Most of these patrons were men of wealth, influence, education, and originality, from whom much more might have been expected – until the political confrontation of 1433/4 resulted in an overwhelming Medicean victory, and they were exiled or ruined.

Beyond these immediate precedents there was a long tradition in Florence of wealthy and powerful families financing great patronage projects, both secular and ecclesiastical; a whole enclave of Peruzzi houses defined by the enormous archway bearing their arms at the entrance to the piazza that bears their name; the complex of Alberti houses with their tower and public loggia on the same street; the commissions of the Peruzzi, Alberti, and Bardi at the nearby Francisican quarter church of Santa Croce, where their family arms marked their patronage of chancel and sacristy as well as private chapels painted by Giotto himself. Across town at the Dominican quarter church of Santa Maria Novella, the wife of Mainardo Cavalcanti, grand seneschal of Naples, built the sacristy, and the wealthy Guidalotti the imposing and grandly decorated Spanish chapel.

Cosimo's line of the Medici was as conscious as any Florentine family of precedent and tradition, making their marriage alliances with the ancient clans of the Bardi, Cavalcanti, and Spini.[53] Medici partisans measured themselves against their patrons, artists quoted their masters, and the pattern of Cosimo's early patronage suggests that he may thereby have measured his triumph over Palla

174 Pietro Lamberti, tomb of Onofrio Strozzi, Florence, Santa Trinita, sacristy

175 Bernardo Rossellino and workshop, tomb of Giannozzo Pandolfini, Florence, Badia

Strozzi, who had been by far his greatest rival in the early thirties in prestige and personal influence, although not in political expertise. In addition to the Strozzi sacristy, their association with the image of the Magi,[54] and Palla's library, there is a striking similarity between the tomb Palla built for Nofri in the sacristy at Santa Trinita and Cosimo and Lorenzo's tomb for Giovanni di Bicci, an almost identical sarcophagus placed beneath a vesting table rather than set in an arch (figs. 174 and 178). The arcosolium form of Nofri's tomb was precisely replicated at Santissima Annunziata around 1450 for Orlando de' Medici by Bernardo Rossellino, who subsequently made copies, some of them virtually identical, for a group of Medici friends and partisans including Giannozzo Pandolfini, Filippo Inghirami, Francesco and Nera Sassetti, and Neri Capponi (figs. 87 and 175).[55]

EMULATION, COMPETITION, AND EXCHANGE IN THE PATRONAGE OF COSIMO'S FELLOW-CITIZENS

Caroline Elam proposed the notion of meta-patronage to describe the tendency of men of lesser wealth and influence to follow the trends set by leaders of patronage, both personal and artistic, and particularly by the Medici.[56] This is another subject that can hardly be considered adequately here, but it is relevant to an attempt to assess the relation of Cosimo's oeuvre to others that themes and forms used by the Medici, like the arcosolium tombs and representations of the Magi, and elements of the design of their palace, were often adopted by their close friends and followers. At the same time, the range of genres, forms, and even images of real significance available to any patron was relatively restricted by tradition – civic, classical, and Christian; hence too much should not be read into apparent borrowings and quotations.[57] Some of these were clearly flattery by imitation, extreme cases perhaps being those of the Alessandri altarpiece by Lippi, featuring the Medici saints Cosmas and Damian (fig. 176), and Archbishop Filippo de' Medici's replications in Pistoia of Cosimo's palace and elements of his church patronage.[58] Later in the century Medici portraits in Magi images in particular served to associate the patrons of the pictures with their personal patrons, the Medici. These remarks should however be balanced with the observation that between the patronage of the Medici and their friends there are examples of influence and exchange going both ways, and that given the commonality of their culture and concerns, it is really far-fetched to imagine that patrons like the Pazzi and the Rucellai were incapable of devising patronage programs of their own

176 Fra Filippo Lippi, *Madonna and Child with Saints*, New York, The Metropolitan Museum of Art, Rogers Fund, 1935

without Cosimo's advice or even direction.[59] Some of this patronage probably represented a coincidence of interest; for example the Quaratesi had offered to pay for a facade for Santa Croce, but were turned down because they wanted to put their arms on it, before Cosimo apparently suggested that they turn to San Salvatore instead, taking over his obligations there.[60] Sometimes the Medici may not so much have set new fashions in patronage then slavishly followed, as paved the way for others by managing to discern and stay just ahead of a developing trend, an ability which was very much the hallmark of Cosimo's political genius.

Cosimo's very close association with the Portinari patrons of the frescoes at Sant' Egidio bears on the role of friendship in shaping artistic patronage. This work by Domenico Veneziano and Castagno, dated *circa* 1439 and now destroyed, has been seen as the most important fresco cycle to be painted in Florence after Masaccio's Brancacci chapel. It also, as Ames-Lewis observed, sounds very much like a pictorial record of Cosimo's persecution and triumph.[61] The church of Sant' Egidio, in the hospital of Santa Maria Nuova, was founded by Folco Portinari, father of Dante's Beatrice. His fifteenth-century descendant Folco was patron of the family chapel after 1420, and manager of the Florentine *tavola* of the Medici bank. An apparently accurate description by Vasari of the lost frescoes depicting the marriage, and the dormition of the Virgin, refers to portraits not only of Folco and his family, but also of Bernardo Guadagni, Gonfalonier of the Signoria that exiled Cosimo in 1433; of Rinaldo degli Albizzi, his chief enemy; of Messer Bernardetto de' Medici, "Conestabile de' Fiorentini," Cosimo's soldier cousin who was exempted from the ban against the Medici because of his friendship with Niccolò da Tolentino, then captain of the Florentine forces; and the Medici party lieutenant Puccio Pucci.

When Folco Portinari died in 1431, leaving three sons aged ten, four, and three, all of whom eventually held positions of trust and authority in the Medici bank, Cosimo took them into his own house. Letters from the thirteen-year-old Pigello to Giovanni, who was precisely his own age, and written when the Medici were exiles in Venice, show they were close friends, and that Pigello had just joined the bank as an office boy "to help out in raising my brothers and sisters."[62] Ames-Lewis speculated that since the Medici themselves had no chapel suitable for frescoing, and Pigello Portinari was very young to have authorized the commission made in 1439 (he was then eighteen), that Cosimo probably initiated the project and took the opportunity to have created "a Medicean cycle" comparable to that in the Brancacci family's chapel. Be that as it may, it seems that a family very close to the Medici and strongly under their influence, personally as well as politically, chose to commemorate a key incident in the Medici family's and their own experience unusually explicitly, in their charitable and devotional patronage of a major and particularly public chapel.

A COMPARABLE FLORENTINE OEUVRE: THE PATRONAGE OF GIOVANNI RUCELLAI

At various points in reviewing Cosimo's commisions, reference has been made to the similar themes and sources of the patronage of Giovanni Rucellai. Throughout this study Rucellai, with his eloquent formulation of the satisfaction he derived from his patronage of art and architecture, serving "the honor of God and the honor of the city and the commemoration of me," has himself served as the most articulate spokesman for the patron's point of view.[63] Giovanni was loquacious where Cosimo was taciturn, and his remarkable *zibaldone* makes him unusually accessible to the historian, whereas Cosimo, despite his prominence in a wealth of both public and private record, remains relatively remote. On almost every point common to their patronage oeuvres, Rucellai spelled out

what can only be painstakingly inferred and reconstructed from the evidence of Cosimo's actions.

The lives and fortunes of the two men were closely intertwined, although in terms of temperament and personal life experience Rucellai and Cosimo present a sharp contrast. Giovanni suffered political persecution by the Medicean regime for almost three decades after 1434, "sospetto allo stato" (suspect by the state) on account of his intimacy with his father-in-law Palla Strozzi. His acceptance by the regime was both signaled and effected by the marriage in 1466 of his elder son Bernardo to Piero de' Medici's daughter Nannina, although a letter of Cosimo's from 1461, soliciting his nephew Pierfrancesco's opinion of the proposed match, makes it clear that he canvassed the alliance only because, for one reason or another, "there are very few choices."[64] Briefly "honored, esteemed, and well-regarded," Giovanni was soon to find himself again "struck down by fortune" in the bank failures of 1474.[65] For all of these reasons, Rucellai may cut a rather more sympathetic figure in modern eyes than the relentlessly successful and obdurately silent Cosimo.

The unique financial and political success that distinguished Cosimo from all his fellow patrician patrons helped to distinguish his artistic patronage as well, making it unrivalled in terms of extravagance, scale, and retrospectively at least, of social and political significance. However, in most fundamental ways, Cosimo de' Medici and Giovanni Rucellai, and their patronage oeuvres, were closely comparable. Both men were leading members of old patrician families, both were extremely wealthy merchant bankers, both were strongly committed to the Christian life and the support of the Church. Both, above all, were men not learned, but rather intelligent and informed products of a wide-ranging Florentine culture, which both richly expressed in their outstanding patronage of the arts. The meaning of a patron's "oeuvre" in this period is clarified by observing the distinctive nature of each man's patronage, within the framework of a broadly similar social agenda, and a common cultural repertoire from which each patron made his individual choices. At the same time, some more extreme readings of Cosimo's patronage as political propaganda are put in perspective by the extraordinary visual statements of Rucellai's tomb and his facade for Santa Maria Novella, commissions of a man whose life and writings preclude their interpretation as claims to power.

In an imaginary portrait of the early sixteenth century, Rucellai is shown surrounded by his most important projects (fig. 177). These were his palace, the family loggia opposite, the Albertian facade of his quarter church, Santa Maria Novella, his tomb in his parish church of San Pancrazio, which was a replica of the Holy Sepulcher in

177   Anon., *Imaginary Portrait of Giovanni Rucellai*, Florence, Rucellai Palace

Jerusalem, and his *zibaldone*. This last was written largely, in circumstances similar to so many other personal compilations, while he was staying in Castel San Gimignano to escape the plague in 1457; it was intended, like most other *ricordi* or *zibaldoni*, to instruct his sons in those things "which I believe will be useful to them."[66] The palace was begun around 1452; the loggia in 1463.[67] The sepulcher, planned from 1448, was probably completed by about 1467. The facade for Santa Maria Novella was underway by April 1461, and according to its inscription was completed in 1470.[68] Rucellai's patronage oeuvre was much smaller than Cosimo's, was perhaps cut short by his bankruptcy, and was neither preceded by that of a wealthy father nor followed by that of affluent sons.

The nature of their major patronage, of churches, chapels, tombs, and a family palace, was however very similar. So was its place in their lives' trajectories, in relation to their age and wealth. Born in 1403, Giovanni died in 1481; fourteen years younger than Cosimo, he outlived him by seventeen years, surviving more than a decade into the regime dominated by Cosimo's grandson, Lorenzo. The earliest commissions associated with Cosimo were inherited from his wealthy father; his own major projects, from San Marco to the Badia, were undertaken in the twenty years between 1436 and 1456, from his mid-forties to his mid-sixties. Giovanni Rucellai's father died when he was a child; his first major commission, the rebuilding of his family palace, began shortly

after 1452, when he was in his mid-forties and soon to become the third richest man in Florence, after Cosimo and the manager of the Medici bank. His patronage proceeded with the personal and financial cooperation of his exiled father-in-law Palla Strozzi, who had been the wealthiest man in Florence in 1427. Giovanni's last major work was completed, some twenty years after his palace was begun, when he was sixty-seven.[69]

Both men thus conformed to the broad pattern of Florentine patrician patronage, analogous to patrician marriage patterns, and in accordance with the perception that there was a time for getting and a time for spending, as Giovanni observed.[70] Both waited to build, as many patricians waited to procreate, until they had amassed a sufficient fortune to make liberality both possible and necessary, and had met the particular personal challenges posed by Fortuna.[71] Rucellai articulated this analogy, only implicit in the actions of Cosimo and others, with the observation that "there are two principal things which men do in this world: the first is to procreate: the second is to build."[72] As to getting and spending, he declared the latter to have been by far the more pleasurable.[73] Although Cosimo expressed regret to his friend Vespasiano that he had not begun his building program twenty years earlier, this was on account of the fame rather than the pleasure he might thus have enjoyed; concerning Cosimo's satisfaction in spending the testimony of others, such as Filarete, that he spared nothing to ensure the comfort of his accommodations, and the evidence of the luxurious appointments of the palace itself must suffice.

The two men adopted very different stances toward the public world. After decades of political exclusion or subordination on account of his connections first with the Strozzi, and then with the Medici, Rucellai advised his sons "to leave politics to those who enjoy them."[74] Cosimo continued his avid pursuit of banking and political interests to the bitter end, although by Vespasiano's testimony he aimed at last to return if not all, then certainly a large portion of his gains, ill-gotten or no, to the Lord, by means of charitable building. While Rucellai committed himself simply to "pious works" in return for Palla Strozzi's permission to make use of his assets,[75] Cosimo stressed his urgent need to expiate the sins accumulated in a lifetime of political and financial profiteering.

★   ★   ★

Giovanni's buildings and their decoration in the context of the patron's reading and viewing

In their related studies of Rucellai as patron, Brenda Preyer and F. W. Kent painted a convincing picture of a man whose palace was in many ways a response to Cosimo's, begun less than a decade earlier; a bid to call attention to himself and his own achievements with a palatial statement of distinctive style and grace. The Medici palace owed much of its impact on contemporaries to having been built *ex novo*, unlike most others in the city, and to its enormous and commanding site. The restricted site of the Rucellai palace, on a very narrow street, precluded a visual impact dependent on mass and weight, the salient features of the Medici palace (fig. 92). The Rucellai palace facade, persuasively attributed to Alberti, seduced the viewer instead with the virtuosity of its surface patterns (fig. 178).[76] There are several other signs of competition between the two families played out in their patronage – in Rucellai's gift of an altarpiece depicting Saint Jerome for the Hieronymite convent at Fiesole, already the recipient of Giovanni di Cosimo's patronage, to which the Medici soon added their own image of Jerome, and in the pressure subsequently exerted by Lorenzo on Giovanni to hand over the prized site at Poggio a Caiano, where the Medici constructed the beautiful Renaissance villa Rucellai might have hoped to build himself.[77]

Somewhat at odds with their own accounts of Giovanni's many-faceted experience, both Kent and Preyer suggested that in hiring the brilliant and intellectual Alberti, Rucellai inadvertently procured a rather better building than he quite deserved.[78] However, it is unlikely that the patron was unaware of the artist's reputation for originality when, or if, he awarded Alberti his commissions. Although the latter was only occasionally in Florence he was, as noted, a highly visible presence on the Florentine scene, if not for examples of his art or architecture, then certainly for his writing about it, and his participation in such cultural events as the Certame Coronario. Moreover, as Kent observed, Giovanni's close acquaintance included many other men with an expert interest in classical literature and art.[79]

Rucellai's *zibaldone* reveals him not as an original thinker – he was, after all, a businessman, not an intellectual – but one quite directly influenced in his patronage by his wide and carefully considered reading. For example, while others conventionally debated the relevance of Ciceronian prescriptions to Cosimo's building, Giovanni thoughtfully related these precepts to himself, subtly weighing the perils of the envy excessive extravagance might attract against the evidence that in classical

178   Leon Battista Alberti, Florence, Rucellai palace

Rome, to which Renaissance Florence was heir, beautiful buildings which did honor to the city conferred upon their owners the "greatest goodwill and favor" (*grandissima benivolenzia e grazia*) of their fellow citizens, which Rucellai so highly valued.[80]

Preyer pointed to the imprecision of Giovanni's comment on the finished palace, which was certainly not that of an expert in architecture, such as several of the Medici were considered to be; in this regard she also observed his awkward additions to the facade as designed by the architect. Conversely, Rucellai expressed his satisfaction in its "order and measure," criteria of excellence carefully inserted into his quotation of Cicero's text, which both literally described the facade's most distinctive features, and praised it in the terms most Florentines, including Cosimo de' Medici, most admired in men and works of art.[81]

The testimony of his *zibaldone* also suggests the strong influence on Giovanni's building patronage of his practical visual experience, a relation that can only be hypothesized for Cosimo and most other patrons. It is obvious from the long entry in his *zibaldone* describing the "beauties and antiquities of Rome" that he went there in the Jubilee year of 1450 for the spiritual benefits of the pilgrimage.[82] The indulgences to be earned depended on his spending fifteen days in Rome during which he attended every morning its four major churches (San Piero, San Paolo, San Giovanni Laterano, and Santa Maria Maggiore). But he chose to spend his afternoons systematically visiting literally "all the ancient buildings and worthy things in Rome," and his evenings writing up his impressions of them.[83] Rucellai's notes are much more precise and informed than the comments of his predecessor Gregorio Dati on Florentine buildings.[84] Some of his observations reflect the preoccupations of the Christian tourist, happy to be treading where the saints had trod. His interest in measurement no doubt reflected the habits of mind of the merchant "good at the rule of three" whom Baxandall imagined and Kent was able to document.[85]

However, clearly Giovanni was excited by his encounter with classical architecture, and his own taste in buildings can be closely related to his expressed interests in the antique. Imagining the time "when the Romans ruled the world," and distinguishing Brunelleschi as one of Florence's four greatest citizens because he was "the reviver of antique building in the Roman style," he took pleasure in enumerating the distinctive features of ancient buildings for himself.[86] He noted the numbers and spacing of the columns and the arches by which they were joined, in effect their "order and measure," as well as the details of capitals, cornices, and architraves with their friezes of foliage.[87] Such pilasters and capitals were to constitute the major feature of the facade of his palace. Nor was he unaware of the classical conquest of perspective and illusion, which related to the ascending orders of his own palace facade, remarking of Trajan's column that it was "of marble and adorned with scenes of his victory and was made with such skill that the figures at the top and in the middle seemed to be the same size as those at the bottom, though in fact they were much larger."[88]

The buildings Giovanni admired most were churches of the late antique or early Christian period. His chief interest in them was less in the classical forms that fascinated Renaissance architects, than in the use of marbles,

of porphyry, serpentine, and granite, in mosaics and pavements, and also in objects of bronze. He thought the mosaics of Santa Costanza the most "gracious and charming . . . not only in Rome but in all the world," with their "many spirits cruising around in different ways."[89] His descriptions of these suggest that Florentines who, like Cosimo and his brother Lorenzo, spent extended periods of time in Rome, were powerfully impressed by these archetypal and seductive examples of the use of valuable stones. The preeminent role played by marbles on the facade of Santa Maria Novella and in Giovanni's Holy Sepulcher tomb, although characteristic of Alberti's architecture and associated with Florentine Romanesque, was surely related also to the taste for this type of decoration which Rucellai acquired in Rome.

The commissions in which Cosimo expressed a similar taste are inevitably seen as statements of power and pretensions to rule, as scholars speculate at length on the political implications of Cosimo's use of porphyry in a manner similar to that of Byzantine emperors.[90] However, as Pliny noted in condemning it, the extravagant use of marbles constituted a positive craze of builders in the last decades of the Roman republic.[91] Few historians discern in Giovanni's tomb and his facade for Santa Maria Novella a self-assertion – in terms of site, materials, theme, symbolism, and scale – quite as remarkable as any statement made by Cosimo's building. The frieze below the pediment at the Dominican church bears an inscription in enormous gilded Roman capitals, "I, Giovanni Rucellai, son of Paolo, made this in the year 1470" (fig. 179).[92] Inscriptions in the classical style were also a specialty of Alberti's, but the patron as well as the artist was sharply aware of the major Roman precedent of the Pantheon, of which Giovanni observed, "a private citizen called Marcus Agrippa had this made" (fig. 180).[93] As Kent remarked, Archbishop Antoninus gave permission for this extraordinary display of self-advertisement in opposition to his own well-known views on that subject, since Rucellai's inscription was quite as bold as Sigismondo Malatesta's on the facade of Alberti's San Francesco at Rimini.[94]

Giovanni's ecclesiastical patronage, unlike Cosimo's, has been appropriately viewed in the context of civic charity and Christian piety. Patronage of the Dominican church, whose convent was the site of the papal apartments which also provided hospitality for other distinguished visitors to the city, honored God and the city as well as commemorating its patron. San Bernardino's emblem of the sun, one of the most compelling Christian symbols of the day, appears at the center of the pediment, as it does on the ceiling of Cosimo's palace chapel.

The tomb Rucellai built for himself has also been

179 Leon Battista Alberti, Florence, Santa Maria Novella, facade

180 (*below*) Rome, Pantheon

taken at face value as expressing his aspirations to personal salvation; its precise replication of the Holy Sepulcher has not attracted the imputations of megalomania read into the much less explicit associations with the Holy Sepulcher of the tomb built by Cosimo and Lorenzo in the old sacristy for their father Giovanni di Bicci.[95] Giovanni's tomb and its inscriptions are an extreme expression of a common Christian impulse to associate oneself with the hope of resurrection implicit in the tomb from which Christ rose on the third day after his crucifixion. The first inscription, on the frieze beneath the cornice of the temple, comes from the Gospel of Saint Mark, 16:6, and reads: "YHESUM QUERITIS NAZARENUM CRUCIFIXUM, SURREXIT NON EST HIC. ECCE LOCUS UBI POSUERUNT EUM" (You seek Jesus of Nazareth, who was crucified: he is risen; he is not here: behold the place where they laid him). The second, on a plaque over the entrance to the tomb, is more explicit: "Giovanni Rucellai, son of Paolo, caused this chapel,

181   Leon Battista Alberti, Rucellai Holy Sepulcher, Florence, San Pancrazio

similar to the Sepulcher in Jerusalem, to be made in 1467, in order that he might pray for his own salvation from that place whence the resurrection of all with Christ was accomplished" (fig. 181)[96]

Once again the concrete sources of Giovanni's inspiration are documented in his *zibaldone*, in his description of a Roman chapel, the Sancto Sanctorum, "adorned with marbles, porphyry, and mosaic," where he observed that the quantity of pardons granted a visitor was equal to those earned at the Holy Sepulcher in Jerusalem. Some time after the completion of Rucellai's tomb, the pope issued a bull of indulgence to those who might visit it, thus attracting to Rucellai's burial place a constant flow

of prayers for its occupant's soul similar to that which Cosimo planned for himself at San Lorenzo.[97]

Whereas the works in Cosimo's palace bear silent witness to his distinction as a collector, Giovanni articulated his impulse to "collect" what was best of the art for which his native city was distinguished, advertising to his sons and to posterity that "we have in our house many objects, sculptures and pictures of intarsia and mosaic, by the hand of the greatest masters who have worked up to the present time, not only in Florence but in all Italy . . ."[98] The only extant images attributable to Rucellai's commission are the frescoes, now nearly destroyed, in the *altana* of his palace, originally a covered terrace on the roof.[99] Their themes, like Uccello's battle scenes, were rather unusual ones for a private house, including a "Thebaid" illustrating scenes from monastic life more customarily seen in convents. Its literary source was Saint Jerome's life of Saint Paul, possibly known to Giovanni from Cavalca's *Vulgarization of the Lives of the Holy Fathers*; this appears in a number of quattrocento *zibaldoni*.[100] There was also a representation of the Virgin's appearance to Saint Bernard, patron saint of the Signoria, who figures prominently in the altarpiece for the Medici palace chapel.

The remainder of the frescoes consisted of scenes from the life of Joseph, which Roberto Salvini suggested may represent at once the exaltation of the mercantile life with which both Giovanni and Joseph were occupied, and the latter's triumph over adversity, enduring the repeated blows of ill fortune until the Lord himself restored his fortune.[101] This would be in harmony with Giovanni's preoccupation with Fortune, as notable as Cosimo de' Medici's with warfare. On the other hand, the story of Joseph's casting into the pit and his later release was usually regarded rather as a prefiguration of the Entombment and Resurrection of Christ. As Salvini pointed out, Joseph was the subject of a popular *sacra rappresentazione*; it appears in the earliest known codex of these plays, dated 1464/5. Although merchants figure prominently in the *dramatis personae*, they are hardly the heroes of the story, since they sell Joseph to Potiphar, and the moral pointed in the last verse is not so much Joseph's triumph over adversity as that: "If one of us should stray from virtue/and fail to properly enhance the divine glory,/you are enjoined to pray for us to God,/that he should pardon us, and grant you the desire to do good."[102]

The attention given to gardens adjoining Medici buildings, at Cosimo's *casa vecchia* and his new palace, as well as for the monastic foundations he patronized – San Marco, Bosco, and the Badia – testify to the patron's pleasure in their cultivation. Giovanni expressed similar delight in a vivid description of the gardens at his country villa at Quaracchi. These were a famous showplace and site for the diversion of his friends and neighbors, among them the Medici. A mutual friend, Giuliano della Luna, described to Giovanni di Cosimo a visit to Quaracchi in August 1439, which featured boating on the Arno and a picnic accompanied by plenty of wine. Giovanni himself paid a visit to the estate a couple of weeks later, and after the marriage between the two houses, the Medici family were frequent guests.[103] The personal fantasy according to which Giovanni Rucellai governed himself, in the phrase used by Cavalcanti and Machiavelli, was freely articulated in the plants in his garden. He applied his reading of Cicero to the conduct of his life and the construction of his palace, and Cicero appears in person in the topiary hedge at Quaracchi, along with dragons, centaurs, camels, jousters, philosophers, a pope, and some cardinals.[104] Giovanni's description of the delights to be savored at Quaracchi resembles Michele del Giogante's mental walk around his house for the memory treatise he compiled, and indeed Rucellai's *zibaldone* included a section entitled "How to commit things to memory."[105]

In its cultivated sense of possibilities for aesthetic and sensual pleasure Giovanni's description is more than just a merchant's inventory. He reflected that among the hedgerows, walls, and borders there was one "which has fifteen steps, one above the other, each step modeled and pruned to distinguish it from the next, in such a way as to give great pleasure to the eye and consolation to the body," as the "many other sweet-smelling herbs give to the human senses." He also spoke of a path which led from the pergola directly down to the Arno, "so that when I am sitting at table in the dining room I can see the barges passing opposite me along the Arno," and the tree he had placed at the head of the path so that "we of the household and of the district" may rest in its shade, since "no stranger ever passes by without pausing at least a quarter of an hour to look at the garden." Another path was bordered by red, white, and flesh-colored roses, "composed and ordered in the form of terraces, which look so beautiful in the season when they are in bloom, that I cannot convey with my pen the pleasure which the eye takes in seeing them . . . and so many other things so well ordered and composed and well-proportioned."[106]

Despite all this, Giovanni Rucellai, like Cosimo, has often been damned with the faintest of praise pointing to the "conventional" piety and the derivative and superficial culture he brought to his commissions. This study has attempted to show that an appreciation of visual experiences and images might exist without the intellectual originality and verbal articulateness assumed by many modern historians to constitute essential evidence of its presence. This was particularly so in view of the Renais-

sance reverence for the authority of verbal and visual texts, particularly those of antiquity. Merchant patricians could seldom rise to a professional level of expertise in writing or scholarship or architecture. But most great Renaissance patrons, among them Giovanni Rucellai as well as Cosimo de' Medici, were both educated and reflective, and these qualities of mind were reflected in their commissions.

Cosimo's faith in eternity and Giovanni's preoccupation with Fortuna; the impress of individualism upon these patrons' oeuvres

Rucellai's *zibaldone* is perhaps the most personal, reflective, independent, eloquent, and highly structured of the hundreds of similar compilations surveyed in this study.[107] The often obscure sources of the precious fragments of past wisdom that make up this mosaic have largely been identified by Alessandro Perosa, one of the small number of modern scholars familiar enough with Renaissance popular culture to recognize them.[108] They included Petrarch, Boethius, Aristotle, the Florentine chroniclers Dati and Buoninsegni, and the medieval *Fior di virtù*, texts most Florentines, from soapmakers and saddlers to Giovanni's peers in wealth and social distinction, among them Cosimo, relied upon in reflecting on their civic, mercantile, and religious experience, reconciling Christian and classical ideas not in humanist, but rather in moral terms. Perosa documented in detail the process by which Giovanni accumulated this wisdom and then applied it to the problems and preoccupations of his life.[109]

Rucellai and his *zibaldone* are distinguished by the degree of his preoccupation with the common concern about the vagaries of Fortune and how the goddess might be mastered. Directly addressing his sons Pandolfo and Bernardo, he expressed his hope that he might help them by instructing them on the difference between Fortune and chance, "so that you may understand whether good sense and prudence and good conduct in man can resist the accidents of Fortune or not." He asserted his own belief that "most times the wise man can defend himself against these," provided that he considers the issues carefully enough, and seeks the right advice. Giovanni recommended to his sons the course that Cosimo took so often in his letters: "with all the decisions you have to make in your life, those of moderate as well as those of great importance, you should examine them very carefully and closely, turning them upside down and inside out in your mind . . . and if you do this and conduct yourself in this way, you will rarely have to bemoan your fortune."[110] In the fashion of so many of our compilers, he then transcribed eight folios of opinions on the matter drawn from various authorities, beginning with Boethius, and invoking also the accepted expertise of Aristotle, Petrarch, Dante, and Seneca in their well-known works on this subject, balancing at length the pros and cons in the manner of a medieval commentary.[111]

Rucellai went further than most of his contemporaries in his search for an understanding of Fortune, personally soliciting the opinions of various esteemed contemporaries, most famously Marsilio Ficino, from whom Cosimo de' Medici and many other Florentines from his circle sought advice on moral and spiritual questions. Ficino concluded in his reply, which was widely circulated and reproduced in many later anthologies, that "following along the lines of the things discussed above we will draw near to the secret and divine mind of Plato, our prince of philosophers, and we will finish the letter with this moral maxim: that it is good to combat fortune with the arms of prudence, patience and magnanimity; it is better to retire and flee from such a battle . . . it is best to make peace or a truce with fortune, adjusting our will in conformity with hers . . ."[112] The import of his words, drawing on the fundamental precepts of classical and Christian morality that guided most Florentines, is identical to that of the lines from the penitential Psalm 37:4 transcribed on the flyleaf of his *zibaldone* by the soap-maker Antonio di Guido: "Accord your will with that of God/ And he will fulfil your every desire."[113]

Ideas did not have to be original to shape the lives and actions of Renaissance patrons and writers, and images charged with highly personal significance were frequently generated in a shared culture and enjoyed in common. Among the many popular writings on Fortuna produced in the circles in which Rucellai moved was one by Bonaccorso Pitti, who made the same allusion as Giovanni to being struck down by fate: "I think that he who judges wisely,/ when he is struck down by Fortune,/ will declare himself moved by her/ not to take the safer path."[114] A vivid image of Fortune as a ship in full sail appears in a poem by Rosello Roselli, a close friend of Giovanni di Cosimo de' Medici and perhaps a guest at Quaracchi, expressing his despair, "Since Fortune has led my fragile craft/ into a sea surrounded by a thousand rocks,/ and I can see no shelter . . . and she who was my faithful guide and true star/ does not care for me but harms me ever more,/ as I try to take cover under her beautiful sail."[115] All Florentine merchants were dependent upon the city's fleet of galleys for their trade; the loss of their investment in merchandise when ships were wrecked or captured by pirates was a common and expected occurrence, and a ship was therefore a perfect metaphor for a gamble with fortune.[116]

Visual and verbal images reinforce one another as clues to patrons' priorities. Just as the vocabulary of Cosimo's personal letters reflects his preoccupations as much as their content, so Rucellai's prose is laced with references to navigation which evoke, like the communications of other similarly cultured Florentines, Platonic metaphors of the ship of state then popular. As noted in chapter 2, Lapo da Castiglionchio's dedication to Cosimo of Plutarch's *Life of Themistocles* in 1435 compared him to "the vigilant and careful steersman [who] fears nothing, but bravely takes on the tempest . . ."[117] Cosimo also used the verb *navicare* to refer to particularly delicate negotiations, but not as often, as explicitly, or as vividly in relation to Fortune as Giovanni. The latter brought his treasured *zibaldone* to its conclusion with the observation that of very many of his accomplishments, "one might say that I achieved them in a time of adversity, since I have been not accepted but suspected by the government for 27 years, that is from 1434 to 1461; so that I have been obliged to navigate very carefully and without making mistakes."[118]

In view of such passages, Aby Warburg assumed the *impresa* of the ship in full sail, incised on the facade of Giovanni's palace, the loggia, and Santa Maria Novella, to be the patron's personal conceit (fig. 182).[119] However, as Brenda Preyer has pointed out, quite a number of other patrons impressed the diamond ring or the sailing ship upon their commissions. As she demonstrated by her masterful reconstruction of the building history of the palace, the *imprese* on its facade are not an appropriate basis for its dating, as some historians tying Giovanni's use of the diamond ring to the Medici – Rucellai marriage in 1466 have imagined. Ames-Lewis's study of Medicean devices revealed how limited and elusive is the evidence concerning their use and sources, especially so early as the 1440s and 1450s.[120] Moreover, as Perosa observed, the quattrocento use of the sailing ship to represent Fortune, replacing the traditional medieval symbol of the wheel in constant motion, was an imaginative idea, and produced an appealing image, whoever its originator.[121] The significant point is surely that like the ideas to which such devices refer, the weighty and universal concepts of Fortune and Time and Eternity, the number of compelling symbols was limited. What is interesting is the fact that particular patrons embraced particular *imprese* and used them to personalize their commissions.[122]

There was room for the patron's *inventio* as Marco Parenti demonstrated, in the placement or combination of common visual symbols. Volker Herzner observed that the form of the Este sailing ship was very different from Rucellai's; the vertical object at the center of the former, in place of a mast, being in fact a column on a stele.[123]

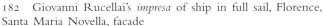

182   Giovanni Rucellai's *impresa* of ship in full sail, Florence, Santa Maria Novella, facade

183   Rucellai *impresa* and coat of arms, Florence, Rucellai palace, courtyard

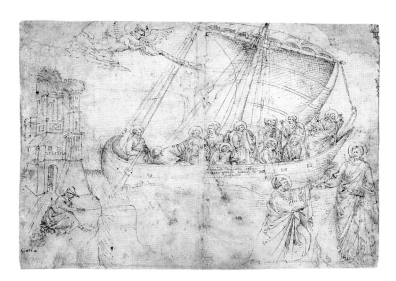

184   Parri Spinelli, *La Navicella*, copy of a mosaic by Giotto on wall of Old St. Peter's, Rome, New York, The Metropolitan Museum of Art, Hewitt Fund, 1917

Both Herzner and Preyer commented upon the considerable difference between the ship in the roundel in the Rucellai palace courtyard, in which a naked female figure, presumably the goddess Fortuna, stands before the mast, and the highly stylized device, in which the large curved sail is dominant, on the palace and church facades (fig. 183). While the ship on the roundel resembles the Este *impresa* in its general form, and is similarly presented in a heraldic context, it is perhaps worth noting that the surviving fragment of Giotto's *Navicella* mosaic for St. Peter's

in Rome, stylized and sometimes reversed, is a closer visual parallel for Rucellai's facade *impresa* than other Renaissance versions of the device (fig. 184). It may be that Giovanni's encounter with this work, much copied by artists, of immense significance to Florentines for its association with Giotto, and to Christians for its message that faith might overcome all obstacles, was the immediate source of the Rucellai *impresa*. Rucellai admired the mosaic on his visit to Rome, noting "on one facade of the courtyard the ship of the Apostles, with sail and rudder, in mosaic; a thing so fine that it is said to be by the hand of Giotto." It was also the only modern work that Alberti, Giovanni's architect, singled out for praise in his *Della pittura*, describing "the boat in which our Tuscan painter Giotto represented the eleven disciples struck with fear and wonder at the sight of their companion walking on the water." Moreover, the general image of a *navicella* and the metaphor it evoked was made familiar to all Florentines, among them particularly Alberti, by Dante's use of it in the first *terzina* of his *Purgatorio*: "To cross the water better hoist your sails/ O little boat of my intellect,/ and leave behind you the cruel sea."[124]

If Rucellai was attracted to the sailing ship as a metaphor for the unpredictability of Fortune, Cosimo and his sons were preoccupied with symbols of endurance and immortality (the diamond ring, the falcon, the peacock).[125] The Rucellai and Medici emblems represent different and characteristic personal choices from a common repertoire of images and ideas (fig. 185). The same is true of their patronage oeuvres. A comparison of the body of artistic work commissioned by Cosimo de' Medici with that created by Giovanni Rucellai's patronage strongly supports the thesis of this study that patrons created oeuvres comparable to those of artists, being similarly a visual expression of what they saw and read and experienced. Patrons' oeuvres, like those of artists, were unified and distinguished by particular problems and themes. At the same time, this comparison demonstrates that Medici patronage, however special, was not unique, even within the city of Florence. In terms of his choices of artists, subjects, and forms, Cosimo's patronage oeuvre was closely related to the bodies of work commissioned by other citizens with whom he shared a common culture.

Consequently, Rucellai's explicit comments on his own choices may illuminate similar aspects of Cosimo's patronage that remain unstated. Indeed, apart from his reference to the long period of adversity which he was obliged to navigate with such care, the concluding paragraphs of Rucellai's *zibaldone*, written in 1473, might have described the themes of Cosimo's life and patronage as much as his own:

> There is a popular saying that in a good life there is a good death . . . I am most happy . . . that our city, having been at war and incurring heavy expenses for thirty years, that is, from 1423 to 1453, and wishing in my time to see a long, happy and secure peace, have been granted this grace by God in my old age, that we have achieved a tranquil peace . . . In the business of banking and being a merchant I have been very fortunate through the grace of God . . . never having done anything else for fifty years until now but earning and spending . . . all the aforesaid things have given and give me the greatest happiness and the greatest pleasure, since they related in part to the honor of God and to the honor of the city and to the commemoration of me.[126]

185   Medici and Rucellai *imprese*, Florence, Rucellai loggia, facade

CONCLUSION

AN OEUVRE DEFINES ITS PATRON: COSIMO'S VISIBLE IMAGE

Only have patience with me Lord, and I will return it all to you.

Cosimo de' Medici.[1]

THE PATRON DEFINES HIMSELF IN RELATION TO HIS WORLD

This book has proposed that Cosimo's patronage of art be seen as part of his self-definition through a variety of actions; it has attempted to reassemble the patron as the integrated subject of his own activity, rather than the object of academic attention fragmented by too many disciplinary boundaries. The body of Cosimo's artistic commissions – his oeuvre – sheds important light on the relation between his life and patronage, and the culture and experience of his society. Gathering together the threads of this enquiry, a number of issues emerge as particularly interesting or problematic, deserving of more attention or further investigation.

Cosimo and the republic

There is much evidence in Cosimo's patronage to support the judgments of contemporary political pundits like the chronicler Cavalcanti, at once one of Cosimo's keenest admirers and his sharpest critics, that Cosimo "always sought to put the interest of the Commune above everything else, and used to say: 'Nature teaches us that for the sake of preserving the whole, the part must consider itself of no importance.'"[2] Machiavelli, similarly torn between respect and resentment of the Medici family, and writing with the benefit of hindsight, while considerably after the event, averred that he did not recognize in the Medici "any ambition . . . contrary . . . to the benefit of the commune."[3] Cosimo's private letters offer abundant evidence of his apparently unceasing efforts to increase the scope of his financial and diplomatic activi-

ties, of his influence and control over his patronage group of *parenti* and *amici*, and thus ultimately of his ability to direct the policies and conduct of Florentine government. But whether from choice or necessity, he envisaged that government as a republic, with himself as its leading citizen, protecting and promoting its interests as he protected and promoted those of his lineage, and of his friends and associates. Florence needed leadership in moments of crisis; Cosimo took charge of the republic's affairs because he could, and because he believed that he could handle them better than anyone else. Clearly he took pleasure in his power and predominance, on occasion rather unpleasantly it would seem. But that is about all that we can say. If he secretly schemed to become first Caesar and then Augustus in Florence, as some of his encomiasts envisioned him in the very last decade of his long life, he left no clearly legible trace of this ambition.

Cosimo's obvious ambition to take charge as fully as possible of his native city could eventually have been framed in a variety of alternative constitutional arrangements. Of all the communes that flourished in the twelfth and thirteenth centuries, Florence in the fifteenth century was one of the few remaining republics. Until overcome by the external force of foreign invasions, Florentines resisted the drift to one-man government to which other important cities had long since succumbed. The blueprint for an intermediate solution lay close at hand in the example of Venice, Florence's oldest ally and for much of the quattrocento, her citizens' most admired practical political ideal. Under the Medici, a numerically expanded but in substance increasingly static Florentine *reggimento* came more and more to resemble the Venetian hereditary patriciate. After the expulsion of the Medici, the city experimented with a Gonfalonier for life who resembled the Venetian doge. If Cosimo had any long-term political strategy, which is debatable, it may well have lain along these Venetian lines. However, by the time Cosimo died, the political balance in the peninsula had definitively tipped in favor of hereditary principates, and soon even these would be swallowed up in the expansion of the nascent nation states that overran Italy at the end of the quattrocento. Whatever Cosimo intended or imagined, he could hardly have planned for this last intransigent obstacle to his own and Florence's autonomy, one which was to catch such master political strategists as Machiavelli and Guicciardini by surprise, even as it overtook them.[4]

Politics, power, and ideology

In his brilliant construction of Italian Renaissance society, appropriately entitled *Power and Imagination*, Lauro Martines nevertheless insisted on so close and causal a relation between politics and ideas as ultimately to deny the real power of his own and Renaissance men's imagination. The way in which ruling classes draw upon culture as a source of power is so complex that it might better be described plainly as a mystery. As Jackson Wilson summed up Rhys Isaac's account of the aristocratic polity of colonial Virginia: "The great planters had wealth, and wanted more. They had power, and wanted more. And they had some of that seeming capacity to get their way without the overt and direct use of money or force, that apparent authority which nowadays gets called hegemony."[5] The contribution of Christian teaching to the acquiescence of the Florentine *popolo* in Medicean hegemony is customarily dismissed by Marxist social historians as merely masking the underlying reality of social conflict, when in fact it constituted the language, the terms, the very framework, of social exchange. In this society which thought in terms of "orders" rather than class, inequality and injustice in the distribution of wealth and power were seen as a God-ordained characteristic of the social order, not a symptom of disorder to be set to rights by social protest.

Some of the most high-flown contemporary praise of Cosimo is couched in the language of the patriarchal metaphor, characterizing the virtuous governor as an image and surrogate of God on earth. The son being "a mirror and image" of his father, Cosimo was to his friends and dependents a "second God" whose commandments his "sons" should "fearfully and reverently obey." To his cousin Orlando, Cosimo was "my God on earth," as his grandson Lorenzo was to his partisans "my savior after God." Peter Brown's insight that the cult of the saints, "the very special friends," created an unbroken chain of association between the protection and authority of earthly fathers, friends, and patrons, and those who dwelt in heaven, is fundamental to understanding the quality of political patronage and the government built upon its

relationships in Mediterranean societies, from antiquity through the Renaissance to the present.[6] This mode of thinking has been marginalized by modern political theory, which arose on mainly northern European, post-Reformation foundations. Insisting on the individual's direct relation to authority and the Word, and removing the sanction of the saints for a society of orders, the Protestant Church provided no model of the function of mediation, which had been the cement of pre-modern Catholic society.

Cosimo and the classical and Christian exempla of virtue

Florentines assessed the quality of patrician patrons like Cosimo de' Medici and Luca Pitti and Giovanni Rucellai not so much by comparison with the princes of other contemporary states, but against the idealized and exemplary citizens of ancient Rome, and in terms of the virtues traditional to the wealthy and fortunate Christian merchant. Learned and even merely literate Florentines, by means of the texts they recovered and preserved, whether in large libraries or small scrapbooks, heard and heeded the advice of classical Roman philosophers or the Christian fathers as clearly as that of their neighbors on the Florentine streets.

Filarete, a Florentine citizen who worked for a Milanese prince and was familiar with the function as well as the decorum of both polities, measured Cosimo's patronage explicitly against that of the most renowned citizens of the Roman republic, and concluded that his special virtue lay in being not a great lord, but a Christian merchant. Filarete praised Cosimo for reviving the antique civic virtues, just as Alberti had praised the Florentine artists who worked for the Medici – Brunelleschi, Michelozzo, Donatello, Ghiberti, and Della Robbia – for reviving the skills of ancient artists.

> For not for a very long time, perhaps never, had there been a private citizen such as he. Let us leave aside the ancient Romans like Lucullus, Agrippa, Milo, and the others who made great and magnificent buildings; they may be considered as kings and great lords by virtue of their government of the republic, for often they ruled over huge provinces, from which they obtained enormous treasure, so that we cannot call these great men private citizens, but great lords. But he [Cosimo] lived only like other citizens and merchants, and without any greater privileges than the other private citizens of the city of Florence,[7] so that it contributes greatly to his praise, considering that with such a

humble and communal and civil way of life, he acquired such fame and reputation, and that he earned by his industry as a merchant such infinite riches. Of which he disposed not as many perhaps would have done; but rather, in appreciation of the benefits he had received from God, for the glory of the city of Florence, and the benefit of the many, he has spent and spends every day. Being so grateful to God for granting him such goods, he shares them by the grace and love of God with many who are needy, and with those who by their industry and actions and virtue have earned a share in them. And of that which he has been seen to spend, daily over a long period of time, the witness is the churches and places of the religious repaired by him or built from scratch; which we may see to have been done by him at no small expense.[8]

The cosmopolitan character of Cosimo's world

In the mid-fifteenth century, the Medici bank had branches or affiliates in Rome, Venice, Naples, Milan, Pisa, Genoa, Perugia, Siena, Bologna, Ferrara, Geneva, Lyons, Avignon, Montpellier, Bruges, London, Barcelona, Cologne, and Rhodes.[9] Cosimo kept in close personal contact with most of them. As the apothecary Luca Landucci observed, "the whole world called him 'the great merchant,' for he did business throughout the civilized world. One could make no more favorable comparison than to say, 'He seems like a veritable Cosimo de' Medici,' which is virtually to say, that no richer or more famous man existed."[10]

Cosimo ruled over a financial empire of importers and exporters; of credit, cash, goods (from alum to almonds), and ideas. He and his sons imported Flemish tapestries, antiquities from Rome (illegally), and the Damascene ware of the Islamic east. The Medici factors in Bruges, to whom he wrote regularly, absorbed the influence of Flemish culture and brought it back home when they retired.[11] The cosmopolitan adventurer Benedetto Dei, who traveled to Greece and the Middle East in the Medici pay in search of information, diplomatic intelligence, and ideas, described Medicean Florence in 1460 as a cultural magnet which attracted the visits of princes and popes, and had orchestrated the international council of the Western and Eastern churches, which included delegates from Greece, Russia, Armenia, India, and Ethiopia. After 1434 Cosimo de' Medici presided over these visits and partook in the extension of Florentine mental horizons which they effected. Dei, for example, described one spectacle staged in the Piazza della Signoria where men

confronted wild beasts from whom they were protected by a *palla*, an ingenious mechanical device in the shape of a ball, which was also the device of the Medici arms. Whether this superlative symbolism was intentional or not, as Dei observed, this "was a marvellous thing, and most ingenious, and had never before been made in Italy." It had been copied by a citizen "who had seen it in the country of the Sultan."[12] Who knows how many of Cosimo's ideas, like the Solomon's knot on his tomb, in the Eastern and Islamic tradition of non-figural imagery, had their origins in his contacts with cultures far beyond that of his native Florence?

The ambiguity of Cosimo's image

Alison Brown, introducing a collection of essays on *Language and Images of Renaissance Italy*, astutely observed that "the fascination of fifteenth-century Florence, like Augustan Rome, lies in its lack of clarity." Employing metaphor in the manner of Renaissance writers, she suggested that the "opaque images in Plato's cave . . . usefully remind us how ambiguous and opaque [was] the world and language of Renaissance politics"; how easily its expressions "can be read in opposing ways."[13] Ernst Gombrich on several occasions reflected on the unwisdom of either uncritically accepting or sceptically rejecting the image of the Medici presented by contemporary adherents and associates. In 1960 he began his renowned essay on "The Early Medici as Patrons of Art" with Bruni's aphorism "aliud historia, aliud laudatio" (history is one thing; praise is another). In a later piece he added, however, that "it would not serve our purpose if the somewhat sycophantic tone of court historians, past or recent, provoked the modern historian into an attitude of sceptical debunking."[14] In his introduction to a volume of studies of Cosimo, suggesting that most historians "would like to penetrate the clouds of incense for a glimpse of the real man behind the myth," he cautioned them with a citation from Montaigne's essay, "On the Inconstancy of our Actions": "Even good authors are wrong to insist on fashioning a consistent and solid fabric out of us. They choose one general characteristic, and go and arrange and interpret all a man's actions to fit their picture."[15]

The "real man behind the myth of Cosimo" may well be illusory.[16] While Dorothy's little dog Toto pulled aside a curtain to reveal the mighty Wizard of Oz as merely human, and relatively unremarkable, the fact remained that his manipulative effects of sound and light had the power to inspire real awe and action in the pilgrims from Kansas to the imaginary land of Oz. Cosimo's importance consisted essentially in what he seemed to be. Perhaps it is time to abandon the common metaphor of a "facade" behind which there is assumed to be an actual and establishable truth to be discovered concerning Florence and the Medici. The republican constitution and Medici manipulation of it were equally essential elements of Florentine political life; one was not necessarily more "real" than the other. The search for "the real Cosimo" arises partly from the moral strain in history, based ultimately in the classical tradition. However, for all his romantic reverence for the wisdom enshrined in the experience of the ancients, one of the main contributions of Cosimo's compatriot and near-contemporary Machiavelli to a modern view of history was his recognition that ambiguity, contradiction, and concealment are inherent in human character and behavior. In his own words, "I smile, and the laughter does not pass within me: I burn, and the burning does not show outside."[17]

The culture of the Florentine *popolo* elevated *double entendre* to an art form. A penchant for opacity and double meaning is a documented trait of Cosimo's which suggests that the ambiguous significance of much of his patronage was intentional, as well as a consequence of our inability to reconstruct its specific referents.[18] Fluidity of meaning is also inherent in the use of metaphor and symbol, as acknowledged in the proliferation of commentaries on Renaissance texts, whether verbal or visual. Dante's *Commedia* and its "keys" which appear in so many Renaissance libraries, including Cosimo's, are archetypal of Florentine ways of seeing and representing the world.

"The honor of God, the honor of the city, the memory of me": an integrated life

Confirming the accuracy of Giovanni Rucellai's articulation of the patron's motives, Cosimo's life and patronage, viewed as a whole, is full of associations, correspondences, and the coming together of related people and ideas. The integrity of his experience stems from a way of seeing the world that bound its fragments together as coordinated parts of a divine plan, which gave pleasure and reassurance, and was reflected in human aesthetic designs.

Although the ingredients of Cosimo's and Florentine culture came from a variety of sources separated by time and space, the precedents for the themes and even the forms of Cosimo's political authority and artistic patronage are mainly to be found within the walls of his native city. Like any other Florentine citizen, Cosimo's chief responsibilities were to promote the interests of family, friends, and neighborhood, the state and the Church. The themes of his patronage were therefore those most dear to the Florentine *popolo* whose culture he shared and promoted. He was everything they wanted the most powerful and visible Florentine to be: a great merchant, a slaker of the thirst of the poor, a preserver of churches and holy places, a patron and protector in this life, and their intercessor, through his ecclesiastical patronage, with the patron saints of the next.

He was learned enough in classical and Christian culture to be willing and able to express himself with sophistication in these terms, and to appeal to a Florentine audience educated to appreciate this expression. He was informed enough about art and artists to seek out, through his network of associates and connections, those painters, sculptors, and architects who would commemorate him through the sheer quality of their work. His precise choices indicate that his personal preference was for generally classicizing architecture, sculpture, and painting, but that he was concerned most of all with finding the appropriate form and artist for each commission, since he admired artistic virtuosity in all its manifestations.

THE MEDICI AND FLORENCE: CONTINUITY AND CHANGE

A lot of what is said about Cosimo, especially about his pretensions to be a princely ruler of Florence, stems from reading his grandson's behavior, and the much altered state of Laurentian Florence, back into Cosimo's own time. There is a tendency, given the eventual metamorphosis of the Medici family into princes on the pan-European model, after the republic came to an end, to assume that this was the planned and inevitable course of events. No historian would make inferences about the affairs of Europe or America in the 1950s on the basis of evidence relating to the last decades of the twentieth century; it is similarly inappropriate to leap across thirty or forty years in describing the more distant affairs of Renaissance Florence.

In attempting to understand who people are, and why they behave as they do, and what this behavior might mean, it is always appropriate to push our enquiries back to the beginnings of their lives, and the experience that shaped them. What is illegitimate and bad history is reading backwards into the characters and events of any age the attitudes and developments of a later one in which they never participated. The temptation to do so is made greater in the case of Medicean Florence because the attitudes and actions of Lorenzo are so much more clearly documented than Cosimo's, both in official records and in Lorenzo's own highly articulate and reflective writings; moreover, even in the quattrocento, retrospective perceptions of Cosimo were framed by the values of the Laurentian age. Similarly, Cosimo's idealized memory, incorporating the idea of a "cosmos" of universal order, was from the beginning invoked to justify Lorenzo's authority and its extension.[19]

Continuity and change in Cosimo's lifetime

Cosimo's self-definition in patronage was an ongoing project. His oeuvre, like that of most artists, focused on a handful of central themes or problems, but like the artist, the patron too evolved, in responding to new ideas and opportunities arising in the course of his lifetime. For example, devotion and expiation are fundamental themes of Cosimo's patronage, but over the years their expression altered, coming to reflect specifically what he learned in his middle years from the early Christian orientation of sophisticated Florentine piety, influenced by humanism, and the enrichment of his devotional vocabulary in his last years by the infusion of Neoplatonism into the Florentine religious and philosophical tradition. These currents of thought left their traces, above all, in the design of Cosimo's tomb.

Conversely, although accounts of Cosimo's "piety" often focus on the last decade of his life, and some even assume that he was suddenly "converted" from worldliness in his declining years, in fact Cosimo's religious concerns, like most of Florentine popular culture, were rooted firmly in trecento traditions. Florentines' chosen guides on the road to salvation were Dante, the supreme chronicler of the spiritual journey, and Petrarch, who began to recover for Renaissance Christians in its original form the classical moral literature of Cicero and the Stoics, and who renewed their interest in Augustine, the great saintly witness of men's inner conflict between worldliness and spirituality. Salutati and the Augustinian Luigi Marsili carried this tradition forward to the end of the fourteenth century, the period of Cosimo's early youth.[20] In terms of his religious education, Cosimo de' Medici was fundamentally a late trecento man whose horizons expanded with those of his city, in the new century of the early Renaissance.

From Cosimo to Lorenzo: a shifting scene

In fact in the last decade of Cosimo's life, the relationship between Florence and the Medici underwent impor-

tant changes, which are crucial to tracing the trajectory of Medici power across the fifteenth century but not particularly germane to this book, concerned as it is with the preconditions of Cosimo's patronage and his major commissions, which were all accomplished or at least conceived by that time. It seems best to tread lightly in reference to these complex and confused years about which too little is yet known. In the mid-1450s, many of the conditions, political, economic, and diplomatic, that obtained throughout most of Cosimo's life, were coming to an end along with it. The most obvious of these was prosperity of the Medici bank, which underlay all Cosimo's achievements. Raymond de Roover located the beginning of its decline precisely in this period, coinciding closely with the decline of Cosimo's health and powers, and the weakening of the cohesion of the Medici party, upon whom unity was reimposed only by fresh and more extreme constitutional measures.[21] A full century lies between Cosimo's birth in 1389 and his grandson Lorenzo's death in 1492. When Cosimo was born, Florence was unambiguously an oligarchy. By the time Lorenzo died it was a city with many of the characteristics of a princely court, in which the republican constitution had been modified to serve the ends of Lorenzo and his intimates, and the expulsion of Lorenzo's sons was required to restore it.[22]

These developments are beyond the scope of this book, but Lorenzo's own retrospective comments on the lives, aspirations, and achievements of his father and grandfather serve at once as an assessment of Cosimo's legacy to the later fifteenth century, and to capture something of the nature and quality of the changes that were taking place at the time of Lorenzo's accession to power. The essential issues are emphasized in the italicized passages of the following extracts from Lorenzo's *Ricordi*.[23] Around 1471 Lorenzo wrote of Cosimo's recall from exile:

On September 29, 1434, *the Council of the Balìa revoked the sentence of exile*, to the great joy of the whole city and of almost all Italy, and here [in Florence] he lived until his last day as *head of the government of our Republic*. Cosimo our grandfather, a man of exceeding wisdom, died at Careggi on August 1, 1464, being much debilitated by old age and by gout, to the great grief not only of ourselves and of the whole city but of all Italy, because he was most famous and adorned with many singular virtues. He died *in the highest position any Florentine citizen ever attained at any period*, and was buried in San Lorenzo. He refused to make a will and forbade all pomp at his funeral. Nevertheless, all the Italian princes sent to do him honor, and to condole with us on his death; among others His

Majesty the king of France commanded that he should be honored with his banner, *but out of respect for his wishes our father would not allow it.* By public decrees he was named *Pater Patriae*, and the decree and the letters patent are in our house.[24]

Cosimo, in his account of his recall from exile in his own *Ricordi*, had stressed that he owed his rehabilitation, along with all that prosperity and authority he enjoyed, "to the good will and shrewd operations of my friends [*gli amici*]."[25] As Lorenzo's narrative continues into the years beyond Cosimo's death, there is a shift away from the republican terms in which Cosimo saw himself and was seen. This was apparent in the ambivalent behavior of former Medici partisans, and in his grandson's growing preoccupation with the princes of Europe and their perceptions, and with the visible honors accorded his house.

After his death much sedition arose in the city, and especially our father [Piero] was persecuted out of envy. From this sprang the Parliament at the change of government in 1466, when Messer Agnolo Acciaiuoli, Messer Dietisalvi, Niccolò Soderini and others were exiled, and the state was reformed. In the year 1465, His Majesty King Louis of France, out of regard for the friendship between our grandfather, our father, and the house of France, decorated our escutcheon with three golden lilies on an azure field, which we carry at present. We have the patents with the royal seal attached, which was approved and confirmed in the Palace with nine beans [that is, the Signoria's vote to approve its acceptance was unanimous].

In 1469, Lorenzo's father Piero also died.

He would not make a will, but we drew up an inventory and found we possessed 237,988 scudi . . . He was much mourned by the whole city, being an upright man and exceedingly kindly [Cosimo he had described rather as "wise"]. The princes of Italy, especially the principal ones, sent letters and envoys to condole with us and offer us their help for our defence . . . The second day after his death, although I, Lorenzo, was very young, being twenty years of age, the principal men of the city and of the state came to us in our house to condole with us on our loss and to encourage me to take charge of the city and of the state, as my grandfather and my father had done. This I did, though on account of my youth and the great responsiblity and perils arising therefrom, with great reluctance, *solely for the safety of our friends and of our possessions. For it is ill living in Florence for the rich unless they rule the state.*

While concerned to maintain and protect the family's friends or partisans, Lorenzo no longer attributed the authority he enjoyed to their operations, seeing this rather as a God-given reward for virtues such as the immense amount of the family's charity, made possible by its wealth.

Till now we have succeeded with honour and renown, *which I attributed not to prudence but to the grace of God and the good conduct of my predecessors . . .* I find that from 1434 till now we have spent large sums of money, as appears in a small quarto note-book of the said year to the end of 1471. The sums noted down are incredible. They amount to 663,755 florins for alms, buildings, and taxes, let alone other expenses. But I do not regret this, for though many would consider it better to have a part of that sum in their purse, I consider that *it gave great honor to our state*, and I think the money was well expended, and am well pleased.

However perceptions of patronage changed across the century, the conviction that it was an essential component of civic and patrician virtue endured.

COSIMO'S VISIBLE IMAGE

The suggestion that the body of Cosimo's commissions be regarded as an oeuvre, cognate to that of the artist, was intended not simply as a conceit which might conveniently serve as a thread to bind this book together. It springs from a profound conviction not only that the objects produced by Cosimo's commissions might be better understood in the context of a clearer picture of their patron, but also that Cosimo's patronage of art has been comparatively neglected in attempts to understand him. So far the evidence of visual and verbal texts has been juxtaposed in an attempt to illuminate Cosimo's artistic commissions by placing them in the context of Cosimo's personal experience, and viewing them within the terms of Florentine political, social, and cultural life. The time has come to deduce from the objects he commissioned something more of the patron himself. How does a close study of his artistic oeuvre modify or alter the traditional picture of Cosimo de' Medici which emerges from his more commonly studied activities as banker, statesman, and leading citizen of fifteenth-century Florence?

★   ★   ★

The traditional image

I have derided the conventional image of Cosimo as a "gouty old banker,"[26] because this phrase is usually intended not so much to describe, as to delimit. Nevertheless, initially and fundamentally, Cosimo de' Medici was an enormously talented and successful businessman who made a fortune in international banking. In the pursuit of this activity he became an immensely powerful figure in his native city, and the same shrewd calculation and bold initiative that made him rich made him powerful as well. De Roover described Cosimo as "a *condottiere* of men," running his bank like a miniature state.[27] Cosimo believed that he was better at running things – banks, military campaigns, the state – than anyone else around him, and very often he was proved right. Certainly more Florentines seem to have agreed with him than resented and opposed his undermining of the reality of republican oligarchy. It was Cosimo's bank that gave him the international contacts – with popes, the princes of Italy, and heads of state from an even wider world – upon which his success as a diplomat and strategist in Florentine interests depended. Intelligence, confidence, personal presence, and access to innumerable resources made Cosimo an outstanding patron to his partisans. As De Roover pointed out, the Medici bank began to decline under Cosimo's less able successors because "entrepreneurs must go forward or fall backward; they cannot simply stand still."[28]

Cosimo extended his control over the functions of Florentine government as he expanded his business empire and diversified into investments all over Europe. As his lifetime saw the heyday of the bank, arguably it also witnessed the heyday of Medici power in Florence, when the the goals of the Medici family and those of the Florentine people meshed as well as they were ever to do. Although under Lorenzo Florentine government became more centralized, and Medici control of it much tighter, the balance of harmony and prosperity, in the state as in the bank, was already tipping toward economic depression and discontent with the family's failure to meet its partisans' expectations. Where Cosimo died honored as father of his country, his great grandsons, shortly after their father's death, were driven out of it in disgrace.

These aspects of his experience have long been the main components of portraits of Cosimo, based largely upon the public records and business accounts documenting his successes as a banker and politician. Thanks to the objects that remain from Cosimo's extensive patronage of art, his city's greatest glory, and to his biographer Vespasiano's emphasis on his support of the literature and learning that defined the Florentine Renaissance, in even the briefest biography some space is always accorded Cosimo the man of culture. However, more often than not, these other aspects of Cosimo's life are tacked on to what is defined as his "core identity" as a man of affairs, in the manner of accomplishments required of prominent men in highly civilized societies. We can do better than this on the basis of what we now know of Cosimo's artistic commissions, as much more than a pastime to round out the cultivated man, but rather a natural and inevitable expression of his many-faceted identity, and of the Florentine culture that shaped it.

Looking beyond the palace

Just as biographers have tended to focus on Cosimo's business and political activities as his "essential" and most "significant" contributions to history, so, by analogy, for art historians the Medici palace has constituted the core of his image, viewed as an expression of Cosimo's wealth and power and preponderance in his native city. Perhaps this is why so much of the comment on Cosimo's other patronage is refracted through this lens. But looked at in their own right, his other commissions expand our view of Cosimo far beyond this central image, drawing attention to other equally vital aspects of his life and personality.

Sin and salvation

What Cosimo's other building shows most clearly is his desire to achieve expiation of his sins through the support of the institutional church, and particularly to support the institution of monasticism much revered by Florentine laymen as an ideal of Christian perfection beyond them personally, but to which they wanted to contribute in some concrete way. Charity and its rewards in commemorative prayer were the nexus between patronage and personal salvation. Cosimo's use of the sacred spaces he created for his own devotions can be interpreted in various ways, but their existence points unmistakably to the importance of such devotion in Cosimo's personal life. The same is true of the plethora of devotional images which he placed in public chapels and with which his impressive and fashionable palace was packed, many of them personalized by his attachment to the family cults of the doctor saints Cosmas and Damian and to the Magi, the exempla of virtue for wealthy and powerful Christians.

Art and current affairs

Cosimo's patronage also indubitably demonstrates that within the austere and demanding framework of Christian and classical conventions and forms, Renaissance patrons clearly chose to express their involvement with current issues and causes. Among the most notable of these for Florence and for Cosimo was the convening in their city of the council of Eastern and Western churches, and the presence in their midst for much of 1439 of the delegates from a variety of exotic places. Cosimo's investment in this event – politically, financially, and personally, as a leader of men and a Christian – was immense, as may be seen from the imagery of so many of his commissions dating from this period and long after it.

The art of war

Similarly, Cosimo's essential role in Florentine politics as a diplomat and military strategist, among the chief preoccupations of his life and his personal letters, along with his personal pleasure in military images and symbols, finds visual expression in his collection of armor and weaponry, and more sublimely, perhaps in the great trio of Uccello's painted panels depicting the victory of Florence, and its captains Micheletto and Niccolò da Tolentino, at the Battle of San Romano during the war with Lucca. If Cosimo was indeed their patron, these objects and images would have dominated his living space, first in the *casa vecchia* and then in the more elaborate decorative schema of the new palace. Whether or no, it may well be that his service as advisor to the commune and its commanders on warfare was the aspect of his career in which he took the most immediate pleasure and pride.

Cosimo, "optimus cive"

Comparing Cosimo's commissions with those of other wealthy Italian patrons points up their civic and patriotic themes. The personal interests so vividly imaged in Cosimo's patronage were interests he shared with the Florentine *popolo*. To those who considered him to be the mirror of the perfect merchant and virtuous citizen, his so-called private commissions of works of art appeared in fact as contributions to and in the public interest. His patronage of churches was perceived as conducing to the salvation of the body politic and its members, his commemoration of the church council and the victories of *condottieri* who fought for Florence as celebrations of the interests and achievements of the Florentine

people. Looking at Cosimo through the lens of these artistic commissions, he appears less the tyrannical and power-hungry propagandist of his dynasty's aspirations to rule the city, than the exemplum of the virtues on which Florence was founded and to which its citizens subscribed.

The Medici and the Magi

The Journey of the Magi was a metaphor for the quest of all wise wealthy men for salvation. Given the number of representations Cosimo had made of this subject, it might well be described as a personal or family icon. However, those who interpret its appearance primarily as an "assertion of Medici political power" are ignoring the many and complex resonances of this theme both within the Florentine tradition and beyond it.[29] Its first really memorable visual representation in Florence was commissioned not by the Medici, but by the Strozzi family, and it was always, and continued to be, an immensely popular theme in northern Europe. The universal significance of the story of the Magi was to affirm the submission of worldly to spiritual power and authority. Whatever the effect of Medici participation in Magi pageants and performances, notably all the permanent images of the Magi commissioned by the Medici in Cosimo's lifetime were essentially for private or domestic contemplation. This theme also presented a brilliant opportunity for an artist's *inventio*, of which the Medici artists Angelico, Lippi, Gozzoli, and Domenico Veneziano took the fullest advantage.

What precisely any image or symbol meant personally to Cosimo we cannot know. However, a letter of the Compagnia de' Magi to the company of San Bartolomeo would seem more likely than most modern constructions to point us in the right direction. "In assemblies for contemplation summoned by men we ought principally to attend to ordering our days, which fly away faster than arrows, under virtuous auspices, occupying ourselves always in praiseworthy acts and works worthy of fame; and thus we make our memory eternal and immortal, than which nothing is more blessed and which we mortal men should desire above all to do."[30]

The Medici saints: patrons, protectors, and intercessors

The Medici saints, who apart from the Virgin and Child are the main protagonists of the *sacre conversazioni* represented in all the altarpieces commissioned by Cosimo and his family to adorn Medici chapels in public churches, appear as spiritual patrons of the family and intercessors on their behalf with the Virgin, the Father and the Son. They serve at the same time as reminders of the Medici family's own role as secular patrons, and even spiritual brokers for their Florentine friends and clients. Such an identification is most explicitly achieved in Cosimo's lifetime in his participation in the consecration of the cathedral. This performance displayed Cosimo's notable talent for coining not only pithy phrases, but also telling images. These themes are articulated with particular brilliance and clarity in Fra Angelico's altarpiece for the church of San Marco, rebuilt under Cosimo's patronage in the 1440s.

The force of this image rests partly upon the Florentine assumption of a natural relation between the structure and hierarchy of patriarchal authority in heaven and that upon earth, justifying and even sanctifying the whole extensive complex of patriarchal relations implied in the perception of Cosimo, in his own and others' eyes, as at once *paterfamilias*, *padrino*, and *pater patriae*. Cosimo commissioned no secular images spelling out more specifically these related roles, but the commune was to do so when it coined, shortly after his death, the medal bearing his portrait and the honorific title it bestowed upon him, "pater patriae," together with the legend "pax et libertas," which acknowledged his part in stabilizing the city and the relations between the Italian states (figs. 186 and 187).

The memorialization of Cosimo's patriarchal image

The strands of which Cosimo's civic image was woven were pulled together visually in the performance of his funeral rites and other ceremonies attending his death.[31] On 26 July 1464 Piero sent a letter to his sons Lorenzo and Giuliano at Cafaggiolo:

I wrote to you the day before yesterday how much worse Cosimo was. It appears to me that he is gradually sinking, and he thinks so himself . . . Yesterday morning, he left his bed and had himself carefully dressed. The priors of San Marco, of San Lorenzo, and of the Badia of Fiesole were present. He made his confession to the prior of San Lorenzo and then heard mass, and he spoke the responses as though in perfect health. Then being asked the articles of faith, he repeated them word by word and made his confession and took the Holy Sacrament with more devotion than can be described, having first asked pardon of all present. These things have raised my courage and my hope in the Almighty; although according to the flesh I am sorrowful, yet seeing the greatness of his soul and

186 and 187 *Cosimo de' Medici, Pater Patriae*, medal, obverse and *Florence Holding an Orb and Triple Olive-branch*, reverse, *c*.1465, Washington, National Gallery of Art, Samuel H. Kress Collection

how well disposed he is, I am in part content that his end should be thus.[32]

Through thirty years of expiatory patronage Cosimo had been preparing himself for this end, and when it came, his son and the priors of the great churches whose greatest patron he had been – San Marco, San Lorenzo, and the Badia – were with him as he intended.

Cosimo had specified some of the details of his own funeral ceremony. He wanted only these three sets of canons and priests, and neither more nor less wax torches than were used at an ordinary funeral. "This he ordered," wrote his son Piero, "with his last breath; saying that alms-giving and other good works ought to be performed while alive, as he had done, and were then of more use." Notwithstanding Cosimo's characteristic deathbed homily, Piero added: "I, wishing to pay my filial debt to paternal piety, did what was requisite on account of those who remained, ordering alms and masses, as follows in this book."[33]

Both the coherence and the extensive nature of Cosimo's patriarchal world appear in the arrangements for his funeral, burial, and commemoration. The network of Cosimo's patronage had radiated from the center of his household. Its members were constantly in motion between Florence and the Medici villas at Careggi, Cafaggiolo, and Trebbio, where they were frequently joined by relatives and friends. The household drew into its orbit the various factors of these estates, and of the Florentine *tavola* of the Medici bank which operated out of Cosimo's home on the Via Larga. There resident sec-retaries, tutors, and doctors came and went, as did foreign visitors and diplomats, and the Florentine friends who were the family's most faithful partisans. In his tax return of 1458 Cosimo had estimated the number of mouths he had to feed as regularly around forty or fifty. His son Piero recorded the names of forty-five members of "the household" to whom he gave mourning clothes for Cosimo's funeral.

Where his father's mourners had all been male kinsmen, Cosimo's funeral broke with tradition to incor-porate the women of his wife's family, and most of the regular residents of the Medici rural as well as urban dwellings – those who had lived in Cosimo's lifetime under his roof and his protection. Beside his sons, grand-sons, and nephew, and their wives, daughters, servants, slaves, and widows, the mourners included his wife's female relatives, the factors of the Medici rural estates, a steward, a barber, and the family doctor. Mourning was provided for several scholars – the canon Gentile Becchi, resident priest in the palace and tutor to Cosimo's grand-sons Lorenzo and Giuliano, Ser Francesco Cantansanti, Piero's secretary, and Bartolomeo Scala, who had lived for some years in the *casa vecchia* as Pierfrancesco's secretary, and was to be appointed chancellor of the republic in 1465. Also included in the funeral party was Nicodemo da Pontremoli, ambassador in Florence from the duke of Milan, Cosimo's closest foreign friend and ally; he had

resided in the Medici palace for more than a decade before he died in 1466.

If the clergy who attended Cosimo's funeral repre-sented the immediate devotional neighborhoods of the Medici family, then in the distribution of dowries to widows and the liberation of prisoners in accordance with Cosimo's will, together with the celebration of com-memorative masses in no less than fifty-three churches, Cosimo's posthumous pious patronage embraced the entire city. Piero's arrangements also included masses to be celebrated at the various branches of the Medici bank at Rome, Venice, Milan, Bruges, Geneva, London, and Avignon, so that Cosimo might be remembered in death as he was maintained in life, by the efforts of the employees of his bank.

The unique position Cosimo had come to occupy in a republic in which he held no constitutional title to power was recognized in a communal decree of March 1465 honoring him posthumously as *pater patriae*. This title, derived from republican Rome, clothed Cosimo in the Ciceronian civic virtues he had admired and striven to emulate all his life.[34] In the words of the communal edict, Cosimo "conferred upon the Florentine republic innumerable benefits in times of both war and peace, and always with absolute piety preserved his *patria*, aiding and augmenting it with his concern for its greatest profit and glory; and up to the very last day of his life he conducted himself in all things as befitted the most excellent man and citizen, governing it with every care and concern and diligence as a *paterfamilias* does his own house, with the greatest virtue and benevolence and piety . . ."[35]

In representing Cosimo as the ultimate exemplum of the virtuous citizen, this encomium invoked Cosimo's *beneficia*, most commonly associated in the fifteenth century with the favors and support a man rendered his friends and clients, and his *pietas*, the sacred duty and loyalty owed by the virtuous Roman citizen to parents, children, country, and the gods. Cosimo himself had used very similar language to refer to his own father in the inscription on Giovanni di Bicci's tomb.[36] The Florentine Signoria with these words acknowledged that Cosimo's influence and power in the city were firmly grounded in the familial and communal traditions that chiefly shaped its history and its quattrocento life, fostering and legiti-mating the extension of the patriarchal governance of household and lineage to the affairs of the Florentine state.

There is no way of knowing how far the image of Cosimo as *pater patriae* was one that he himself created or promoted. There is no evidence to confirm the asser-tion that Cosimo had long before his death "encouraged his friends to regard him as pater patriae," although we know they had long done so.[37] Belcari's sonnets of the 1440s and 1450s incorporated this idea, a theme also prominent in the elegies for Cosimo composed by a number of popular poets. Bernardo Pulci referred to his "virtù paterna disciplina integra,"[38] and another poet's reflections at this time on the appropriate subjection of the son to the "carità" of his father further clarify the patriarchal context in which Cosimo's power in Florence is to be understood.[39] The ideal of a *pater patriae* was reiterated by Lorenzo on the funerary monument he had made for his father Piero and uncle Giovanni. It would seem that Cosimo and his descendants really did want these to be the last words on their lives.

EPILOGUE: "RETURNING IT ALL TO THE LORD": COSIMO'S TOMB IN SAN LORENZO

Cosimo's final commemorative commission, among the most eloquent articulations of his visible image, was his tomb in San Lorenzo. Piero's note that as Cosimo lay dying he "reminded me of his often expressed desire to be buried in San Lorenzo" seems somewhat superfluous, in view of all his father's previous arrangements, and was presumably rhetorical. Piero's description of the funeral concluded with the observation that Cosimo "was buried in the church of San Lorenzo in the earth, in the sepulcher ordered by him."[40] The form and location of Cosimo's tomb underlined his position as patron of the church and its parishioners, but expressed above all his urgent aspiration to salvation, to union with God after death. His body was placed in the vault beneath the floor at the very center of the crossing, his tomb the symbolic focus and support of the church that was the center of the spiritual life of his family and his partisans, who had rebuilt and embellished it in classic Renaissance style over the course of his lifetime. A porphyry plaque marking the site of the tomb below is set in the pavement directly before the high altar (fig. 188). The inscription on it reads: "Cosmus Medices Hic Situs Est Decreto Publico Pater Patriae. Vixit Annos LXXV, Menses III Dies XX" (Here lies Cosimo de' Medici, by public decree Father of his Country. He lived seventy-five years, three months and twenty days).

Cosimo's burial monument lies outside the mainstream tradition of fifteenth-century tombs, and its salient features have been the subject of much scholarly speculation.[41] Unlike the monuments which the Florentine state ordered to commemorate its great writers and humanists, churchmen, and military captains, it boasted no effigy, and no obvious religious symbols. The final disposition of Cosimo's remains was delayed while the Signoria deliberated on the question of his tomb, but eventually they acceded to his own wishes, and on 22 October 1467 his body was transferred to its present resting place. The simplicity of the burial marker, and the modesty of the black and white marble tomb in the crypt, affirm the message recorded by Piero from Cosimo: "he said he did not want to make any will . . . and that when God should decide to do something else with him, he did not want any pomp or show at his funeral, and as he had said to me at other times in his life, he reminded me where he wanted his tomb in San Lorenzo, and he said all this with such order, and with such prudence, and with such great spirit, that it was marvellous . . ." Piero added that Cosimo specifically requested a "modest burial"; his father's frequent calls in the counsels of the republic for consultation with other citizens, both eminent and modest, puts this wish in its proper political perspective, along with Cosimo's reported remark to Vespasiano da Bisticci that after death, "I know I shall not wear the crown of laurel more than any other citizen."[42]

However, as Janet Clearfield pointed out, the position of the tomb and its marker, connecting it with the high altar and the daily consecration of the Eucharist, a place traditionally reserved for saints and relics, is overwhelmingly its most significant feature.[43] Thanks to Cosimo, the high altar was the repository of some important early Christian relics. His personal interest in these was earlier expressed in his commission of a bronze reliquary from Ghiberti to hold the relics belonging to Ambrogio Traversari's convent of Santa Maria degli Angeli, which were those of the early Christian martyrs Protus, Nemesius, and Iacintus.[44] The Medici chapel dedicated to Saints Cosmas and Damian became a reliquary chapel in 1452, and Lippi's San Lorenzo *Annunciation*, customarily described as an altarpiece, may have been painted on two panels comprising the doors of a reliquary cabinet for the chapel.[45] On the night of Saint Martin, 11 November 1444, Cosimo led a search by torchlight at San Lorenzo for the relics of Saint Mark of Rome, Saint Concordia and Saint Anthony Abbot. They were found in the altar of a side chapel of the Romanesque edifice, identified by their inscriptions, and shortly after this date, Saint Anthony Abbot began to appear as a participant of the *sacre conversazioni* depicted in Medici altarpieces. When the new high altar of San Lorenzo was consecrated on 9 August 1461, the relics were transferred there, on the eve of the feast of Saint Lawrence, following a great procession through the city led by Taddeo Gaddi's famous standard of the *popolani*, which later hung from the cupola of the church. Cosimo subsequently established this procession as an annual custom.[46]

188   Andrea del Verrocchio, tomb marker for Cosimo de' Medici, 1464–5, Florence, San Lorenzo

As Clearfield observed, Cosimo's decision to be buried in front of the altar could be seen as exceedingly pretentious, as it was by Flavio Biondo, who remarked that the whole of San Lorenzo thus became Cosimo's burial chapel. Alternatively it might be interpreted as an expression of humility, placing Cosimo in a public location from which no votive masses were sung for him, mass being said there for the benefit of all the clergy of San Lorenzo and its congregation, by contrast with interment in a family chapel marked by more extravagant personal and dynastic display. Certainly the position of the tomb testified to the decedent's piety, considering the spiritual benefits to be derived from proximity to the celebration of the Eucharist and the bones of the holy martyrs. Nor were the services at the high altar without personal significance to Cosimo. In 1462, in the face of unanimous

opposition from the prior and canons of San Lorenzo, and following his donation of a large silver cross for the new high altar, he had instituted a votive Mass of Our Lady, who was closely associated with tombs and burial in her role as intercessor at the Last Judgment, to be sung there in perpetuum by twelve young clerics from the college he had endowed. This occurred each morning at dawn, at the canonical hour of lauds, celebrating the moment of the sun's rise, and symbolizing resurrection and new life.[47]

The most telling evidence of Cosimo's concern with his own and his family's salvation has been assembled by students of the liturgy at San Lorenzo.[48] By the time Cosimo died, each Wednesday, the day special indulgences for visitors to the church and the weekly market in the piazza outside drew the largest number of worshippers to

San Lorenzo,[49] was set aside for the anniversary services for his father. On Mondays, an office of the dead was celebrated for Giovanni di Bicci, his family, and the souls of his friends, the church's benefactors, as well as all those buried in the crypt. In addition to the weekly masses for his father, his brother and his mother, Cosimo endowed a votive mass for his own soul three hundred and sixty-five days a year. He also included his friends and neighbors in his spiritual largesse, providing in addition a weekly mass for the dead of the entire parish.[50]

Much of the considerable literature on Cosimo's tomb is shaped by the perception of Cosimo as primarily concerned to impress his wealth and power upon the Florentine people.[51] Several scholars emphasize the special connotations of the materials used in the tomb marker, composed of a few large slabs of white marble, and red and green porphyry, cut in geometric patterns and defined with bronze, according to antique techniques of inlay rather than those of medieval incrustation. Andreas Beyer took this argument much further in seeing the marker as part of a pattern of the "insistent application of porphyry roundels" – in the chapel of the Medici palace, in the old sacristy, and at the San Lorenzo crossing – linked to Byzantine court ceremony. "Orchestrated consistently if subtly by Piero, the introduction of this imperial style led ineluctibly to the presentation of the young Lorenzo de' Medici as an occidental *Porphyrogenetos*, 'born to the imperial purple.'"[52]

While inclined to accept the "princely" implications of the Medici use of porphyry, Susan McKillop acknowledged that its use in Cosimo's tomb marker might be related either to Christological or princely iconography, since such markers were used in the early Christian world to honor not only emperors, but more importantly, the body of Christ. She suggested that its immediate inspiration was close to home, in the porphyry disks in the pavement of the Florentine baptistery, directly beneath the Crucifixion mosaic on the ceiling (fig. 152), and in St. Peter's in Rome, to mark the position of participants of the papal liturgy and coronations; similarly, the rota in the altar table over the tomb of Cosimo's father "marks the place where the Corpus Domini is honored, and his own body beneath it in *imitatio Christi*."[53] Suzanne Butters's masterly study of the use and working of precious materials in the sixteenth century puts the Medici use of porphyry in perspective, describing it as a material generally used in classical, Christian, and medieval contexts to do honor to emperors, to Christ, and to the saints and their relics.[54]

The design of Cosimo's tomb brought together in an unusual way various elements of the religious culture of his native city which had particular personal significance to him. As Irving Lavin observed, chief of these was the early Christian tradition, so strong in Florentine humanist circles, and transmitted to Cosimo through the writings and teachings of his close friend Ambrogio Traversari.[55] The incorporation of antique and early Christian elements in Cosimo's tomb and the associated pulpits he commissioned were in keeping with Florence's view of herself, enshrined in the *Chronicle of the Origins of the City* written around 1200, as a new Christian Rome, succeeding the old pagan one.[56] The two bronze pulpits now situated in the nave of the church mark "a return to the long obsolete custom of reading the Epistle and the Gospel of the Mass from a pair of ambos," a tradition exemplified in the early basilicas of Rome. The pulpit illustrating the scenes of the Passion is on the left as we face the altar, those following the Passion on the right, apparently representing "the passing from death to resurrection through the operation of the Eucharist at the altar."[57]

According to Manetti's *Life of Brunelleschi*, Cosimo persuaded the architect to enlarge the *cappella maggiore* to hold the choir he had originally intended to put in the crossing. This enlargement was underway by Brunelleschi's death in 1446, and was probably intended to make room for Cosimo's burial at the crossing.[58] Another feature of the schema was the orientation of the altar in the early Christian manner, *versus populum* (facing the congregation), and also facing Cosimo's tomb.[59] The dome of the crossing, with four gigantic stucco sculptures of the evangelists, now lost, that stood in niches at the transept ends, can also be seen as integral to the design of the tomb. Later centrally planned Renaissance churches were to revive this early Christian symbolism of the dome of heaven, also a likely connotation of the similar placement of Giovanni di Bicci's tomb directly under the dome of the old sacristy. The circle in the square of the tomb marker mirrors the dome directly above it, and according to Howard Saalman Brunelleschi used the crossing square "as the modular unit from which he derived the elevation of the crossing itself," as well as the plan of the entire building." In light of Cosimo's complaint that what was built after Brunelleschi's death was too heavy and dark, Lavin suggested that the original project likely anticipated Brunelleschi's great innovation at Santo Spirito, "a drum with windows above to provide truly celestial illumination."[60]

Elements of the site refer to the early Christian concern to reconcile Christianity with Platonic philosophy, and to the aim of the council of 1439 to restore the ancient unity of Christianity itself. Lavin concluded that "Cosimo was interred in a setting that related him to a rediscovered heritage and an auspicious future in the

Christian universe," in a manner similar to the way in which the "long, increasingly self-conscious tradition of Florentine historicism . . . defined the city's religious, political and cultural nature through what can only be described as a mystical transfer of identity from the past to the present."[61] This perception of the significance of the setting of Cosimo's tomb is in harmony with the argument of this book that in his patronage Cosimo sought to identify himself and his family with the Florentine civic ethos, and to locate them in significant historical time as defined by the shared culture of the Florentine *popolo*. The archaeology of the sources of the tomb recalls Jeffrey Ruda's sense, in relation particularly to the Magi tondo made for the Medici by Fra Angelico and Fra Filippo Lippi, of the way in which paintings, like sermons, relied less for their meaning on particular texts, than on perceptible reference to a whole complex of

familiar cultural assumptions. I have argued that patrons and artists also communicated and cooperated on the basis of this shared culture, which makes it unnecessary for historians to search for programs and "humanist advisors" as conduits for sophisticated ideas, and inappropriate to focus on apportioning credit for creativity to either patron or artist.

This is particularly so in relation to Donatello's pulpits for Cosimo, his lifelong friend and patron, which deal with the themes of death and the promise of resurrection. Donatello, having petitioned to become a Sienese citizen, so that he might "live and die in Siena," working on the cathedral there, returned suddenly to Florence around 1460, perhaps to work on the design of Cosimo's memorial.[62] The unfinished pulpits were to be Donatello's last, most complex and challenging work. Shortly after Cosimo's death the artist obtained permission from the

189 (*facing page*)
Donatello, *Christ before
Pilate and Caiaphas*,
Florence, San Lorenzo,
bronze pulpit

190   Donatello, *The
Ascension*, Florence,
San Lorenzo, bronze
pulpit

Medici family to be interred alongside him; two years later Donatello was buried very close to the pillar in the crypt which was finally to hold Cosimo's remains. At the very beginning of Cosimo's career as a patron Donatello had worked with him on the tomb of Pope John XXIII, and he lay beside his patron at the end. The bronze pulpits, the last objects that owed their existence to their joint authorship, contribute more perhaps than any other to our sense of the highly individual *ingegno* of each man, and the richness of their collaboration.

There is some controversy concerning the identity of those who worked on the pulpit panels: which ones are wholly or mainly by Donatello's hand, how they were originally intended to be assembled, and even whether they were really designed as the panels of two pulpits, as Cosimo's biographer Vespasiano testified, or rather as parts of a free-standing tomb or altar that was never made.[63]

There is little disagreement about the boldly, even daringly original composition of many of these scenes, viewed, like those of a sacred play, from a point well below the action, and crowded with overlapping figures spilling over the edge of their frames (fig. 189).[64] Viewers have admired the brilliant and uniquely personal interpretation of images from antique sculpture, for the very different dramatic and expressive purposes of these contrasting scenes of Christian tragedy and triumph. The Janus-faced messenger to Pilate seems literally "torn between convenience and compassion" (Fig. 190);[65] the dying Meleager of classical sarcophagus reliefs is transmuted into Christ at the very moment of his resurrection, wearily breaking free of his winding sheet and of the bonds of death (fig. 191).[66]

The personal relevance of these events to the patron may be underlined in portraits of Cosimo and his wife

191   Donatello, *The Resurrection*, Florence, San Lorenzo, bronze pulpit

in the *Lamentation over the Dead Christ* (fig. 192).[67] As in the fresco of the Crucifixion in Cosimo's cell at San Marco, where Christ's consignment of his mother to the care of Saint John, the beloved disciple, is extended to embrace Saint Cosmas, here Cosimo and Contessina partake in the grief of the biblical protagonists over the body of the dead Christ beneath the cross, and bear living witness to his sacrifice. In John Pope-Hennessy's opinion Donatello's pulpits, representing "his last thoughts on the central theme of Christian iconography," reveal "the working of a fervid, highly personal, dramatic imagination, which has no equivalent in Western art before the Passion etchings of Rembrandt".[68]

On the pier in the crypt in which Cosimo was buried is a simple triple cross, the sign made over the eucharistic chalice, symbolizing the Trinity, and thus the Resurrection (fig. 193). Dante alluded to this in his reference to his pilgrimage taking "the way that links four

circles with three crosses." The device on Cosimo's tomb marker above the crypt is a cross in a circle, signifying the promise of salvation in eternity. It is based on the Christian cosmology of Isidore of Seville, relating the human microcosm to the macrocosm of the universe, a Neoplatonic notion expressed in the poets' play on Cosimo's name, "Cosmos Cosmicon."[69] It is also an unending knot, a symbol used by Niccolò da Tolentino in his insignia, which appear in the Uccello panels in the Medici palace (fig. 125), and one that figured prominently in the chief sources of Florentine popular devotion; the *Canticle of Canticles*, sung at the services of devotional confraternities, and Dante's *Divine Comedy*.[70] These familiar texts were nevertheless able to bear the weight of the most sophisticated theological exegeses of the age, and their meaning was further elaborated for Cosimo by the Neoplatonic humanists whose studies he supported in the hope of learning from them "the way to happi-

192   Donatello, *The Lamentation*, Florence, San Lorenzo, bronze pulpit

ness."[71] Representing the impediments to salvation, the knot had been the symbol of Solomon's legendary wisdom and a common motif in early Christian mosaic pavements, where it represented an imperial cross.[72] As Ficino explained in a letter to Cosimo apologizing on behalf of Lorenzo Pisano for the theologian's delay in finishing the commentary on the *Canticle of Canticles* which Cosimo had commissioned from him, "the more that the knot of Solomon is involved, the greater the task of explanation."[73]

Solomon's knot is the sign that appears to Dante as he stands on the threshold of paradise. The humanist and Dante scholar Cristoforo Landino, another member of the Medici circle of intellectuals, in his *Commentary* on *Purgatorio* interpreted this knot as "the obligation remaining to be met by those who have a debt of punishment yet to pay to God."[74] It was probably with the very last lines of *The Divine Comedy* in mind, full of the symbolism of light that animated his decoration of the old sacristy, that

193   Tomb of Cosimo de' Medici, Florence, San Lorenzo, crypt

Cosimo chose the final image with which to symbolize his spiritual aspirations and to stamp his memory on the mind of posterity. In the last *canto* of *Paradiso*, the knot reappears in the poet's beatific vision of the form of the universe. Encouraged by Saint Bernard, whose own vision is recalled in the altarpiece of the Medici palace chapel, Dante raised his eyes to "the eternal light."

> Within its depths I saw gathered in,
> bound by love in a single volume,
> the scattered leaves of all the universe,
>
> substance and accidents, and their relations,
> almost fused together in such a way,
> that what I speak of is one simple flame.
>
> The universal form of this knot
> I believe I saw, because more fully,
> saying this, I feel myself rejoice . . .
>
> As the geometer who dedicates everything
> to squaring the circle, and does not find it,
> trying to figure the principle he lacks,
>
> so was I at this new vision:
> I wished to see how the image
> coincided with the circle, and how it dwelt
> therein . . .
>
> At this point my powers failed before this lofty
> fantasy; but already my desire and my will moved
> together, like a wheel that is equally moved
>
> by the love that moves the sun and the other
> stars.[75]

"The memory of me"

Much of this book has been dedicated to demonstrating that Cosimo did indeed care about the glory of God and the honor of the city. That he cared about "the memory of me" is never disputed. Cosimo and his contemporaries understood that his memory would live most fully, not in his achievements as a banker and politician, but in the works of art he had made, and particularly in his buildings, which would remain long after he was gone, but not forgotten. Historians of art, responding to the beauty and distinction of the objects artists created at Cosimo's behest, have comparatively neglected his role as patron in their creation. This book was designed to redress that imbalance. Without Cosimo's interests and initiative these objects would not have existed, and we cannot fully appreciate them without understanding him.

But obviously works of art cannot be read simply as translations by the artist of the patron's desires. This is the final reason why we cannot speak confidently of Cosimo's artistic commissions as expressions of too particular aspirations and intentions on his part. At the vital intersection between the patron's concerns and the artist's creativity the former are transmuted and transcended by the latter. Visual texts cannot easily be deconstructed, and unlike historians' reconstructions of the past, they have a weight and substance and form of their own that endures. They exist. The objects of Cosimo's patronage belong to our world as well as to his. That is why they matter to us. Cosimo was quite right; ultimately, it is because he was a remarkable patron of artists that still, after half a millennium, we remember him.

APPENDIX

A LIST OF WHAT APPEAR TO BE POPULAR MISCELLANIES COMPILED FROM THE PUPILLI RECORDS

Selected items from Christian Bec's transcriptions of the Pupilli inventories, recording the contents of the libraries of average Florentines, being those which by their description would seem to be *zibaldoni* or *quadernucci*. From *Les Livres des Florentins (1413–1609)*, 149–90, discussed above, page 79, and note 97.

1413, Ser Piero Grisi, "2 libri umiliari"; 1413, Messer Rinaldo, "popolo San Biagio, uno libro di forma di stormenti, uno libro in charta di chavretto, non si sa il nome"; 1413, Messer Nicholò Guasconi, "uno libro di novelle, di lettere antiche, coverto d'assi, uno libro in volgare chiamato la Fiorita"; 1413, Giuliano di Tomaso Branchacci, "Pistole e Vangieli, in volgare, sermoni, in volgare"; 1413, Bernardo di Giorgio de' Bardi, "Novelle di Boccacio, 3 libricciuoli di cantari"; 1414, Filippo di Piero Rinieri, "uno libro di Marcho Polo di Vinegia, un libro con Apochalisse [and the letters of St. Paul]"; 1414, Bartolo Biliotti, a large library of twenty-two volumes, many standard religious works, including one of "sermoni in volghare"; 1420, Papi di Beninchasa, "uno libro si chiama Troiano, in volghare"; 1420, Iachopo d'Ubaldino Ardinghelli, "uno libricciuolo di Santi"; 1421, Bartolo di Schiatta Ridolfi, "Aesop, più quaderni di stratti di legiende"; 1421, Bartolomeo di Giovanni de' Rossi, "uno libro di chantari"; 1423, Piero Teci [Teri?], "uno quaterno di cose si chiama Segreto, vechio e tristo"; 1423, Giovanni di Giovanni, "uno libretto con coverte di carta pecorina, di canzoni e assempri"; 1423, Nero di Bardo Altoviti, "uno libro di chantare in francescho"; 1425, Francesco di Giovanni Chavalieri, "uno libro della Chanticha a di Salamone"; 1425, Piero d'Aghostino Martini, "uno libro chiamato Sochorso di poveri, salmi penitenziali, libro d'asempri"; 1425, Sertini, Tomaso di Bartolo di ser Tino, "uno libro di chantari"; 1425, Niccholò di Meser Ghuccio, a large library of thirty-four books, including Cicero's *De Amicitia*, Sallust, Terence, Lucan, Boethius, Virgil, Statius, Seneca, Ovid, Dante, and "uno libro da chantare, Esopo"; 1425, Michele di Giovanni del Chiaro, "Vita di San Francesco, Isopo, uno libro di storie in volghare"; 1425, Simone di Bartolo Chambrini, "v libri di legiende"; 1425, Pagholo di Ghuglielmo, only one book, the "Fiore di Virtù"; 1425, Jachopo Vecchietti, "Libro dello specchio della Croce, in volgare, libro di rimette, in volgare, III libri di novelle, in volgare"; 1425, Benedetto di Filippo, "uno libricciuolo di storie"; 1426, Piero di Giovanni Bandini Baroncelli, "piu scartabegli di chantari"; 1426, Messer Iachopo Nicholi, "libretto . . . Domine n'è in furore"; 1426, Giovanni del Chiaro, "ii libri di storie, più quaderni di cronache, uno libraccio di cose romane"; 1426, Francesco di Ser Andrea, "libro tratta di santi Padri, Vita di Christo, Boezio in volgare, Libro della Schala di San Bernardo"; 1426, Giovanni di Giovanni, "uno libraccio di quaderni 2, di fatti d'asempro d'un chavaliere menato da' dimoni e altro che fu un libretto vecchio, di forma quasi come d'uficio di donna [that is, small and portable], scrittovi drento e' 30 gradi di san Girolamo, uno libretto un pocho minore che saltero, di lettera di forma scritto di Lode della Vergine Maria, in rima, libricciuolo di salmi penitenziali, un libretto di chanzone e asenpri" [altogether ten books, many devotional, all small and portable, which sounds as if it may have been the library of a singer/entertainer or leader of a confraternity]; 1427, Iachopo Guidetti, "uno libro di chanzoni morali e sonetti e altro in fogli mezani" [cf. two compilations owned by the Guidetti, Laur., Plut. 90, supr. 103, Ricc., 1317], "uno libro e uno quadernuccio di sonetti e altro, Virgilio, Aeneid"; 1429, Messer Matteo Castellani, "sette quinterni di chronacha, in charta pechorina" [identified by Bec as Villani, see ch. 5, n. 74]; 1429, Filippo d'Arrigho Arrigucci, "uno libro di storie, in volghare"; 1429, Ser Giuliano di Betto Ferravecchio, a book of a Podestà, "quaderni di Statuti, uno libro di Regemine [Aquinas or Aegidius Romanus?], uno libro degl' Ordini della Giustisa"; 1429, Iachopo d'Anichino Ricchardi, "più quaderni d'uno Passionario, uno libro di charta di banbagia . . . di Troia, uno libro . . . che chomincia: Voi che ascoltate in rime . . . ;" 1430, Giovanni di Ghuido di Michele Ghuiducci, "libro di Storie di Santi Padri, istoriati, e Ninfale"; 1430, Giovanni di ser Pietro Ciantellini, one of the largest libraries listed, mostly devotional works, perhaps a cleric? Approximately thirty books including one on chess, "Degli Scachi"; 1430, Matteo di Bartolomeo Tanaglia, "Centonovelle, Dante, Corbaccio"; 1430, Gabriello di Messer Bartolomeo Panciatichi, "2 messali begli, uno libro in volghare . . . detto libro di Vertù," also Virgil, Dante, and "uno libro in volghare, di legiende, in chavretti, di san Giovanni e sancta Doratea . . . uno prolagho sopra Quintiliano, in chavretti, in vol-ghare," also the life of Sancto Franciescho, "quattro libri grandi, in volghare, in fogli reali di banbagia, iscritti di mano di Ghabriello, choverti d'asse, cioè la Bibia, e la Vita di Giobo, e' fatti di Troia e altre chose"; 1430, Giovaniello di Giovanello Adimari, "uno libro di leggiende, in francioso," and one of stories from the Bible, and another Troiano, "un libro di storie, un libricciuolo di leggienda"; 1431, Giovanni Moregli, "uno libriccino da donna con choverte di velluto verde, con affibiatoi, uno libro detto e' Fioretti di san Franciescho, uno libro di Vangieli, uno libro de' Soliloqui di santo Aghostino, in volghare," another selection from the Evangelists, "libricciuolo de' Fioretti della Bibbia," a book on medicine, a fragment of a Livy Decade and "uno libro di Vangieli e Pistoli."

ABBREVIATIONS

Journals

AB	*Art Bulletin*
AHR	*American Historical Review*
ASI	*Archivio storico italiano*
BM	*Burlington Magazine*
Del. erud. tosc.	*Delizie degli eruditi toscani*
GSLI	*Giornale storico della letteratura italiana*
JAMS	*Journal of the American Musicological Society*
JHI	*Journal of the History of Ideas*
JIH	*Journal of Interdisciplinary History*
JMH	*Journal of Modern History*
JSAH	*Journal of the Society of Architectural Historians*
JWCI	*Journal of the Warburg and Courtauld Institutes*
JMRS	*Journal of Medieval and Renaissance Studies*
Mitteilungen	*Mitteilungen des Kunsthistorisches Instituts, Florenz*
RQ	*Renaissance Quarterly*

Archives and Archive Collections

ASF	**Archivio di Stato, Firenze**
CS	Carte Strozziane
Cat.	Catasto
CP	Consulte e Pratiche
Conv. Soppr.	Conventi Soppressi Religiosi
CS	Carte Strozziane
Delib. Sig. e Coll.	Signori e Collegi, Deliberazioni
MSS	Manoscritti
MAP	Medici avanti il Principato
Not. antecos.	Notarile antecosimiano
Provv., Reg.	Provvisioni, Registri

BLF	**Biblioteca Medicea Laurenziana**
Acqu. e Doni	Acquisti e Doni
Ashb.	Ashburnham
Conv. Soppr.	Conventi Soppressi
Laur.	Fondo Laurenziana
Plut. supr./inf.	Pluteo, supra/infra

BNF	**Biblioteca Nazionale, Firenze**
CS.	Carte Strozziane
Magl.	Magliabechiana
Pal.	Palatino

BRF	**Biblioteca Riccardiana**
Ricc.	Fondo Riccardiana

Vat. Lat.	**Vatican Library, Fondo Latino**

With reference to letters

s. f. (*stile fiorentino*) indicates that a date is given according to the Florentine calendar, which began the New Year on 25 March, the feast of the Annunciation. Dates between 1 January and 24 March are alternatively indicated thus: e.g., 1434/5.

s. a. (*senza anno*); year not given

s. d. (*senza data*); undated

Numbers after citations of published works refer to pages, after manuscripts to folios, r (recto) and v (verso).

NOTES

Introduction

1   This way of looking at paintings and their patrons proposed by Baxandall in *Painting and Experience*, and his suggestion, 2, that "a work of art is the deposit of a social relationship," invited more sophisticated studies of the role of patrons in the production of works of art. However, many assessments of patrons and their commissions continue to focus on relatively superficial considerations; see the literature cited below. John Hale observed in his general survey of *Italian Renaissance Painting*, 19: "Patron, painter, public: an understanding of Renaissance art involves them all," but as yet the role of the audience in this three-way dynamic has received little attention.

2   On art as problem solving, see Gombrich, "Leaven of Criticism." On the concept of style as the sum of an artist's solutions, see Ackerman, *Essays in Theory*, 3–19, especially 16: "in using an image of style . . . to establish orderly relationships among works of art, we follow the path of the artist . . . accepting or altering certain features of the arts around him . . . A style then may be thought of as a class of related solutions to a problem – or responses to a challenge." On the sort of demands a Renaissance work of art made on its audience, see Shearman, *Only Connect*, and below, ch. 1; for evidence of the ability of the Florentine audience to meet these demands, pt. 2. Hood, *Fra Angelico at San Marco*, 302, n. 3, presented his study as part of "a growing body of work interpreting Italian religious art in a strongly historicized reconstruction of the intended audience's expectations." For other examples of studies setting works in their social and functional context, see Belting, *Image and its Public*; Goffen, *Piety and Patronage*.

3   By Randolph Starn, in a preliminary version of his article, "Seeing Culture," addressed to the Renaissance Society of America at its 1988 conference in New York. Warnke, *Court Artist*, xv, observed the limitations of an approach that concentrates on the wishes of two individuals, artist and patron, and the "human relationship" between them: "if there were no more to it than that, art history would perforce be reduced to a series of double biographies."

4   Diane Zervas noted in *Brunelleschi and Donatello*, 4: "Attempts to understand the relationship between patrons and the type of art they commissioned in Florence during the early *Quattrocento* must be undertaken with caution; they are viewed with scepticism by some art historians, and by others with alarm or straightforward disbelief." On this see also below, n. 34.

5   This usage came into currency in late nineteenth-century France. However, the essential meaning of the word *oeuvre*, according to the authoritative contemporary *Dictionnaire de L'Académie Française*, was simply "ce qui est fait, ce qui est produit par quelque agent . . . e.g., oeuvres de Dieu, de la nature . . ." The modern French *Encylopaedia universalis*, 12, 13–18, distinguishing oeuvre and non-oeuvre, is notably critical of the traditional literary or artistic usage and image. While the most recent edition of the *Oxford English Dictionary* continues to privilege a particular assocation with an artist's work, *Webster's Dictionary* favors the more pragmatic emphasis on a simple body of work. Even if we restrict the implications of the term to those envisaged by a specialist group of art historians, the similarities between artist's and patron's oeuvre outweigh the differences. However, these should certainly be borne in mind. I am grateful to Katherine Weil-Garris-Brandt for her trenchant and stimulating criticisms, and to David Alan Brown for his constructive suggestions and helpful clarifications. Brown's "Leonardo and the Ladies" is an account of an artist's oeuvre which serves as an exemplary reminder of the serious implications of extending the aesthetic connotations of an oeuvre from the artist to the patron.

6   Art historians have generally been more inclined than other historians to spread their methodological nets widely in search of any information relevant to a given object. Conversely, they have tended to compartmentalize the art of a period and obscure the coherence of the patron's choices by their insistence on privileging major artists and genres in their studies. On the importance of the minor arts and collecting in revealing the patron's interests and tastes, see below, pp. 287–99. For an overview of Cosimo's choices of artists and commissions from the patron's point of view, below, chs. 14 and 15.

7   Pts. 3 and 4.

8   Pt. 1.

9   Ch. 15.

10   Pts. 1 and 2. The resulting picture of Cosimo's oeuvre consists not of a series of confident causal connections, but rather of a pattern of behavior or interests which has meaning where individual works or acts do not; it is constituted by the juxtaposition of a variety of information relevant to the problems or objects under discussion. This method of argument was largely developed by anthropologists such as Clifford Geertz, who called it "thick description"; see Geertz, various.

11   The phrase appears in a marginal note to the original manuscript of a letter believed to be addressed to Piero Soderini's nephew Giovan Battista in 1506. For translation and comment see Bondanella and Musa, *Portable Machiavelli*, 62. See Starn, op. cit., for an exploration of one patron's fantasy, that of the Gonzaga duke of Mantua.

12 Below, ch. 14.

13 *Complete Poems*, 24.

14 Gilbert, "Archbishop on the Painters," 84, articulated this assumption, which underlies the work of many art historians.

15 See below, pts. 1 and 2.

16 See particularly pt. 2, and ch. 9.

17 Below, ch. 2.

18 The oeuvre of Giovanni Rucellai, a particularly eloquent spokesman for the patrician patron's attitudes, is often invoked for comparison, and is examined more fully in ch. 15.

19 On the role of reception and criticism in "constituting" a work of art see Baxandall, *Patterns of Intention*.

20 *Trattato* 2, 683.

21 Hyman, "New Light on Old Problems," "Notes and Speculations," and *Fifteenth-Century Florentine Studies*.

22 *Zibaldone*, cit. Kent, "Making of a Renaissance Patron," 13: "Due cose principali sono quelle che gl'uomini fanno in questo mondo: La prima è lo 'ngienerare: La seconda l'edifichare"; also n. 8 for Giannozzo Salviati's repetition of this formula in his *zibaldone*, begun in 1484.

23 See *Trattato*, trans. Spencer, 1, 16–18: [building] "is nothing more than a voluptuous pleasure, like that of a man in love." As Welch observed, *Art and Authority*, 145: "Filarete created a virtual family out of the patron-father, architect-mother and the building-child." See also Alberti, *On the Art of Building*. On these palaces and their patrons, see particularly the work of Brenda Preyer, various.

24 The fact that architecture has an inescapably functional dimension has helped to force some reassessment of the relative roles of patron and artist in the genesis of buildings. There is a growing body of literature addressing the question, "Who was the architect of a Renaissance building?" See, for example, Pellecchia, "Patron's Role"; also her review of Morselli and Corti, *La chiesa di Santa Maria delle Carceri*; Kent, "*Più superba*"; Brown, "Enthusiastic Amateur"; Goldthwaite, *Building of Renaissance Florence*. On Cosimo as "architect," see below, p. 213.

25 See, for example, Douglas, *Natural Symbols*; Geertz, *Interpretation of Cultures*. For a general critical exploration of the Western aesthetic see Freedberg, *Power of Images*, especially 436–8. He called for a reconsideration of "the whole insistence in Western art theory . . . on the radical disjunction between the reality of the art object and reality itself . . . What clouds our perception is exactly the compulsion to establish whether an object is art or not, and whether it belongs in a museum or not . . ." Important studies of how function affected the form of Renaissance objects include Trexler, "Sacred Image"; Sinding-Larsen, *Iconography and Ritual*; and Van Os, *Art of Devotion*. An increased consciousness of practical function has perhaps contributed to a growing interest in artists' workshops, on which the pioneering and still major work is Wackernagel, *Florentine Renaissance Artist*; see also Thomas, *Painter's Practice*. For a recent comment on artist's workshops and patronage see Bullard, "Heroes and Their Workshops"; for discussion of the issues she raised, and of the practical relations between artists and patrons, see below, Ch. 14.

26 "Magnifici viris Cosmo et Laurentio Mediceis autoribus," *Cronaca*, in Morçay, "La Cronaca del convento," 11.

27 See below, p. 360.

28 On this see especially Baxandall, "Patrons Efficient and Patrons Final." For a historically authentic account of the patron as privileged viewer, see Starn, "Seeing Culture."

29 *Generation of Animals*, 1, 21, cit. and discussed by Horowitz, "Aristotle and Woman." See also Simons, "Art of Viewing."

30 *Painting and Experience*, 152.

31 See, for example, Greenstein, *Mantegna and Painting*, and Woods-Marsden's review: "Greenstein gives the artist center stage, and all decisions are seen as his and his alone."

32 For a discussion of the different perspectives of historians of society and of art which bear on these questions, see the papers of the symposium ed. Alpers, "Art or Society: Must We Choose?" Davis, "Gifts of Montaigne," 32, represents the historian's response to the question: "finally we *do* choose in the sense that we each want to explain something different: the art historian, a picture or sculpture, an artist's oeuvre, a visual genre or its impact: the social historian, a set of events, cultural, economic or political connections, a social genre or an actor in one of these settings." For an art historian's reaction to the "use" of art to illuminate society see Baxandall, "The Bouguer Principle." Insofar as his essay offers a *reductio ad absurdum* of the view that art "reflects" society, he is clearly correct, and his conclusion springs inevitably from his premise, 40, that "society" is not a collection of individuals but a "complex of institutions through which an individual finds a relation to a collective." Naturally it is difficult to relate this abstraction to his definition of a work of art as "a class of physical objects and the mental states associated with them." The present book, like so many others, is greatly indebted to Baxandall's earlier work, as the foundation and point of departure for enquiry into many of the issues it addresses. In *Giotto and the Orators*, Baxandall drew attention to the importance of the language in which art was described, although mainly by learned humanists and clerics. In *Painting and Experience* he raised the question of the "cognitive skills" Renaissance patrons brought to the appreciation of art, although he felt that "this sort of explanation is too speculative to have much historical use in particular cases," and he did not pursue these themes. This book pursues them in more pedestrian ways, concentrating on the responses of individuals to particular commissions, on the language of less learned patrons and their popular audience, and on the personal, intellectual, and religious understandings and presuppositions they brought to the viewing of works of art.

33 Below, ch. 14; for a more theoretical discussion of the creative part played by the patron see Baxandall, "Patrons Efficient and Patrons Final." David and Rebecca Wilkins also observe in their introduction to a group of esays entitled *The Search for a Patron*, 3, that patrons need to be seen as more than "those who bankrolled fortunate artists or as individuals who fortuitously achieved fame because they selected the 'right' artist." Price, "Effect of Patronage," is particularly concerned with "the patron's intellectual involvement in the artistic process," 6.

34 See below, ch. 15, for some comparison of Cosimo's patronage choices with those of other important Florentine and Italian patrons. Haskell's major work on patronage, *Patrons and Painters*, avoids the exploration of any patterns in patronage, which the author associates with the "attempt to 'explain' art in terms of patronage"; he similarly eschewed generalizations "about the relations between art and society." Cf., however, the introduction to his more recent work, *History and Its*

Images. On patronage as process, involving interchange and evolution, see Burke, "Social History of Art"; Simons, "Art of Viewing."

35   For the use of this simile in relation to later Medici political patronage see Kent, "Lorenzo as 'Maestro della bottega'." Bullard, "Heroes and Their Workshops," took up the issue of agency in Florentine patronage, arguing that the patron's role in shaping culture, and particularly the role of the Medici, has been overrated at the expense of their political clients and of those who worked in the artist's *bottega*. This is certainly true. The "heroic" image of the patron created in the nineteenth century is to some extent a construct, and the language of patronage is certainly not to be taken at face value; on this see also Kent, *Fathers and Friends*. However, the picture of Renaissance patrons at the pinnacle of a hierarchy of authority, either personal or familial, is painted from reliable Renaissance sources. Moreover, notions of hierarchy based on Christian rather than classical precepts emphasize, rather than diminish, the value of participants at all levels, stressing the social and spiritual benefits of cooperation within a divinely ordained and stratified framework; on this see in general below, pt. 2, and in particular the discussion of the role of the poor in charity, ch. 9. Lack of evidence as much as lack of interest helps to explain historians' relative neglect of patrons' partisans and artists' workshops. On the contribution of friends and family to Cosimo's achievement, see below, passim. For an insight into the operations of Verrocchio's workshop when the young Leonardo was working there see Brown, *Leonardo da Vinci*.

36   See Martindale, *Rise of the Artist*; Janson, "Birth of Artistic Licence"; Warnke, *Court Artist*, ch. 1. On artists' self-portraits, Krautheimer, *Ghiberti*, 9–10, discussed Ghiberti's portrait and Filarete's signature on the bronze doors of St. Peter's in Rome. There are only four previous examples of artists' portraits on bronze doors; two of artists shown kneeling to patron saints, and two with their tools. Ghiberti and Filarete were pioneers in reviving the self-advertising precedents of ancient art, known to the Renaissance through such sources as Plutarch's description of bald Phidias. For Ghiberti's concern with immortality, see Gilbert, "Ghiberti on the Destruction of Art." For Benozzo Gozzoli's several self-portraits in the Medici chapel frescoes see below, ch. 13.

37   Francis Ames-Lewis observed "the difficulty of persuading biographical details about patrons to yield indications of their attitudes and interests, and of relating these constructively with the works made . . . for those patrons." See his review of four important monographs: Pope-Hennessy, *Luca della Robbia*; Wohl, *Domenico Veneziano*; Horster, *Castagno*; Lightbown, *Donatello and Michelozzo*, 343.

38   As Curtius, introducing his monumental guide to the origins of *European Literature*, remarked: "Specialization without universalism is blind. Universalism without specialization is inane," ix. On the inherent illogicality of binary oppositions, see La Capra, *Re-Thinking Intellectual History*; also White, *Content of the Form*. Modern Renaissance scholarship has been driven largely by the impulse to verify or refute the main propositions of Jacob Burckhardt's imaginative but impressionistic essay, *The Civilization of Renaissance Italy*, which indeed captured much of the spirit of creative achievement in the fifteenth century. On the relation of current Renaissance scholarship to the agenda set by Burckhardt see particularly Starn, "A Demand for Art";

Cohn, "Burckhardt Revisited." It is easy to become embroiled in the contrasts and oppositions by which the father of modern Renaissance scholarship identified the movement from a "medieval" to a "Renaissance" sensibility, characterized by the triumph of the individual over corporate institutions; of reason, human values and the state over religion and the transcendant. However, by now most subtle scholars have so nuanced Burckhardt's broad brush strokes that his portrait of the Renaissance is as inappropriate a model for historians as the work of his contemporaries, the impressionist painters, would be for modern artists.

39   On the role of space, place, and significant civic centers in Florentine emotional and ritual life see particularly Trexler, especially "Sacred Image" and *Public Life*; also Muir and Weissman, "Social and Symbolic Places." On the importance of establishing and maintaining a distinct identity in parish, *gonfalone*, and physical neighborhood, see Kent and Kent, *Neighbours and Neighbourhood*, and below, especially chs. 10, v, and 11. Literature on the personal records of Florentine patricians addresses the issue of identity; see particularly Starn, "Francesco Guicciardini"; Price Zimmerman, "Confession and Autobiography"; Kent, *Household and Lineage*; Najemy, *Between Friends*. Family *ricordi* and *prioriste* bore witness to participation in the city's past, while citizens associated themselves with the classical past through the reading and application of the lessons of its literature; see below, ch. 4 and pt. 2. These impulses were linked in the legend of Florence's Roman foundation; on this see below, ch. 5.

40   On the interaction of these traditions in shaping Florentine identity see Brucker, *Renaissance Florence*, 101; for a particular example see Kent, "Michele del Giogante's House of Memory."

41   In his *Renaissance Self-Fashioning*, Stephen Greenblatt formulated a concept which has proved extremely fruitful in engendering a more subtle approach to the prominent patron's agenda, too often seen simply in terms of power. However, it is important to distinguish between the imaginative self-fashioning of literary figures, with whom Greenblatt mainly dealt (his model is nicely applied to Renaissance Italy by Diana Robin, *Filelfo in Milan*), and the less free and self-conscious self-definition of patrons such as the Medici, strongly shaped by the practical contexts of government and society in which they operated.

42   Rubin, *Vasari*, critically reevaluated Vasari's *Lives of the Artists*, which helped to create this long-lived image. Nourished by nineteenth-century realities and representations, it still maintains a hold on the popular imagination. On Vasari see also below, especially pp. 27, 175. For a modern scholarly study of the "artistic temperament" in the Renaissance, see Wittkower and Wittkower, *Born under Saturn*.

43   The patron's taste is often advanced in explanation of sudden and marked changes in an artist's style; for a compelling argument along these lines, see Ruda, "Style and Patronage." However, such changes may as well be the product of the artist's choices. Ames-Lewis, "Donatello's Bronze *David*," pointed out some weaknesses of the prevailing developmental concept of artistic style, and the circularities it may involve; for this same point, made also in relation to Donatello, see Caglioti, "Donatello, i Medici e Gentile Becchi." On the patron's taste as reflected in his choices, see below, ch. 15.

44   Rosenberg, *Art and Politics*, 4.

45 See particularly Verdon, "Environments of Experience and Imagination," 5, and below, especially chs. 5 and 7–9.

46 On this last see below, pp. 153–5; on the popularity of these writers, pp. 84, 86; on their likely inspiration of the Medici chapel altarpiece, ch. 13.

47 *Opera a ben vivere*, pt. 3, 149. There are similar injunctions by Giovanni Dominici, cit. Lesnick, "Civic Preaching" and "Dominican Preaching." Such passages strongly challenge Charles Hope's absolute distinction between image and *istoria*; see especially his "Religious Narrative," and the discussion below, ch. 7. On the relation of image to *istoria*, see alternatively Belting, *Likeness and Presence*, 351. He argued that Italian panel paintings have "a rhetorical activity of their own . . ." They "no longer kept the distance typical of narrative painting but . . . became narrative themselves, either by engaging in an internal dialogue among the figures represented or opening an external dialogue with the viewer . . . whom they were addressing." Similarly Shearman, *Only Connect*, 33, observed in relation to Verrocchio's bronze group, *Christ and Saint Thomas*, made for the niche of the Mercanzia at Orsanmichele, that the spectator, encouraged by sermons and spiritual exercises "to think, as he read, what it was like to be *there*, and *then*, in that very space and time in which the miracle occurred . . . finds himself in the position of the other Apostles . . . to say that Verrocchio's subject is completed only by the presence of the spectator in the narrative, is to realize that the relationship between work of art and spectator is now fully transitive." On the nature and consequences of attention to art see Gaston, "Attention and Inattention." The decorum governing visual representations of Christ precluded a literal translation into images of a description of the Passion as horrific as Antoninus's. However, the scenes of the Passion on the pulpits for San Lorenzo commissioned by Cosimo from Donatello, a master of the physical representation of the accidents of emotion, capture the essence of such a vision; see below, pp. 380–82.

48 A comparison of household inventories (see especially Lydecker, "Commitenza artistica per la casa" and "Domestic Setting of the Arts") suggests the number of such images in the Medici household was unusual; on these see below, pp. 244–64, iii, and Spallanzani and Bertelà, *Libro d'inventario*; Spallanzani, *Inventari Medicei*. However, many patrician households possessed secular as well as devotional images; see Neri di Bicci, *Ricordanze*, and below, pp. 111–15. Lineage portraits, like those in the National Gallery of Art, Washington, D.C., *Catalogue of European Paintings*, and lost cycles of *viris illustribus*, such as Giovanni di Bicci de' Medici commissioned, see below, p. 248, were important early examples of domestic secular art.

49 On this widespread pre-modern view, see Greenblatt, *Shakespearean Negotiations*, 65. Curtius, *European Literature*, 92, discussed the role of nature as commentator in the Scriptures. On Florentines' reading, below, pt. 2.

50 *Institutio* XI, iii, 67, cit. Spencer, "*Ut Rhetorica Pictura*," 42.

51 Note, however, Starn's caution, "Seeing Culture," that princes do not simply use art, they are used by it; cf. Woods-Marsden, "How *Quattrocento* princes used art."

52 On patronage in Florence, and the personal nature of politics, see particularly Brucker, especially "Structure of Patrician Society" and *Renaissance Florence*; Kent, *Rise of the Medici* and *Fathers and Friends*; Klapisch-Zuber, "Parenti, amici, e vicini"; Kent and Simons, *Patronage, Art and Society*.

On *stato* as a personal attribute, Rubinstein, "*Stato* and Regime." Alessandra Strozzi, *Lettere*, 443, spoke of the Parenti who "anno un po' di stato"; cf. Lorenzo de' Medici, *Ricordi*, cit. below, pp. 371–2.

53 For an analysis of this language, see Kent, *Rise of the Medici*, pt. 1, especially 83–5; *Fathers and Friends*.

54 Below, pp. 175–7 and 343–5. On the elasticity of the Medici household and the number and variety of those who were part of it, below, ch. 11; Kent, *Fathers and Friends*.

55 On artists' contracts see Glasser, *Artists' Contracts*; Chambers, *Patrons and Artists*; Wackernagel, *Florentine Renaissance Artist*. On legal contracts in general see Kirschner, "Monte delle doti," and Kuehn, *Law, Family, and Women*. For business contracts see De Roover, *Rise and Decline*, and Goldthwaite, "Medici Bank"; for marriage contracts, Klapisch-Zuber, "Les rites nuptiaux." On relations between the Medici family and their artists see below, passim, and particularly ch. 14. See also Ames-Lewis, "Domenico Veneziano and the Medici"; Draper, *Bertoldo*; Foster, "Donatello Notices"; Spencer, *Castagno and His Patrons*.

56 On the form and function of personal letters and their role in Medici life and patronage, see Kent, *Rise of the Medici*, passim, and *Fathers and Friends*; on Cosimo's letters, below, ch. 2. These letters contain clues concerning attitudes to everything from eating to art, but not in the explicit vein of the sort of self-conscious literature which later became a natural vehicle for such comment. On the rise of this literature in the eighteenth century, see Darnton, "Readers Respond to Rousseau." Cf. the epistolary collections of Renaissance scholars, which were reflective, moralizing, and memorial; see, for example, Ficino, *Letters*; Robin, *Filelfo in Milan*; also the much more informal, but still carefully crafted letters of Poggio Bracciolini to Niccoli, ed. Gordan, *Two Renaissance Book Hunters*. Machiavelli's *Letters*, although often casual in tone, are highly self-conscious in their representation of self and their ploys to persuade others to action; see Najemy, *Between Friends*.

57 For collections of artists' letters see Gaye, *Carteggio*; Milanesi, *Nuovi documenti*; also translations in Chambers, *Patrons and Artists*, Gilbert, *Italian Art*. Tax reports are also valuable; see, for example, Mather, "New Documents"; and "Documents Mostly New"; Corti and Hartt, "New Documents."

58 The most vigorous spokesman for this widely held view is Creighton Gilbert; see his various writings, especially *Italian Art* and "What Did the Renaissance Patron Buy?" and a discussion of this position below, ch. 14. Hankins, "Platonic Academy," put forward a typical argument *ex silentio*, based on the formal collection of encomiastic and consolatory letters put together by Bartolommeo Scala for Piero after Cosimo's death, that the academy was not a major project of his; in fact, Renaissance correspondents simply do not write about a whole range of matters modern historians think important.

59 For a rarely explicit articulation of the common misconception that words, even those uttered in an alien context, are clearer than images or actions, see David Herlihy's comment on the ethnographic method of Klapisch-Zuber, *Women, Family and Ritual*, in his introduction to that volume. Unfamiliarity with fifteenth-century letter forms leads to frequent misrepresentations in the translations and introductory comments of Chambers, *Patrons and Artists*, and of Gilbert, *Italian Art*; see Rab Hatfield's comment on Chambers in his review,

630–31. The letters of Fra Angelico, Gozzoli, and Domenico Veneziano have often been misunderstood; for alternative readings see below, ch. 14.

60 For examples see below, especially chs. 10 and 12.

61 See Weissman, various, and particularly "Taking Patronage Seriously." In reaction against this trend, other scholars have exaggerated the weaknesses and limitations of such comparisons: see, for example, Molho, "Il Patronato a Firenze" and "Patronage and the State in Early Modern Italy."

62 Felix Gilbert made the pointed observation that Florence was not a Mediterranean village in a review of Trexler, *Public Life*, Cohn, *Laboring Classes*, and Carmichael, *Poor and the Plague*, which he entitled "The Other Florence," not perhaps perceiving the considerable relevance of these studies to "high culture," cf. below, pt. 2. Ironically, he entitled his review of Richard Goldthwaite's *The Building of Renaissance Florence* "The Medici Megalopolis."

63 See particularly Kent and Simons, *Patronage, Art and Society*, 2, 4–5, and ch. 16. Ianziti, "Production of History," 299–300, called attention to the clarity of this distinction in modern Italian and French to suggest that historians might usefully exploit the ambiguity of the English word "patronage." However, as his own study of Sforza's humanist secretary Simonetta shows, the connection between the elements of *mecenatismo* and *clientelismo* in their relations was a fact of Italian society at the time, not the product of a modern play with language. On this, see Rubinstein's review of the volume; as he observed, 706–7, problems are created not by "this ambiguity of the word patronage," but by failing to make the appropriate links between *clientelismo* and *mecenatismo*. Cf. Robertson's review, "*Cui Bono?*" 570–74; she mistakenly took Ianziti's distinction to imply that "the Renaissance Italian would here have distinguished two quite different activities; the promotion of the client-artist or otherwise as *clientelismo*, and the commissioning of works of art as *mecenatismo*;" for the application of this view see her own *Alessandro Farnese*, 5, and Willette's review. Kettering, "Patronage in Early Modern France," citing Ianziti, assumed this distinction to be generally accepted by "historians of the Italian Renaissance," and went on to pose the questions in relation to early modern French cultural patronage; "Did cultural patronage differ significantly from political patronage? Do the same models of behavior apply?" 843–4. Even Bullard in her stimulating revisionist essay "Heroes and their Workshops," adopted this anachronistic distinction, 187, showing how an excessive concern with academic models and distinctions may obfuscate rather than illuminate the past.

64 The abstract nouns *patronato* and *padroneggio* appear very infrequently in Cosimo's lifetime, and refer usually to ecclesiastical preferments or to the protective role of saints. Giorgio Vespucci referred to the Three Magi as "nostri patroni," cit. Hatfield, "Compagnia de' Magi," 133. I know of no reference to *mecenatismo* in this period. Only in the last years of his life was Cosimo even likened to Maecenas, the famous Roman patron of the arts; see Brown, "Humanist Portrait of Cosimo." In his *Trattato dell'architettura*, promulgated shortly after Cosimo's death, Filarete, probably influenced by the rather different language of the Milanese court where he resided, used *padrone* to refer to a patron of art. Cf. Gombrich, "Early Medici as Patrons," 36, for the phrase used by the artist Cennini as he implored his fellow consuls

in the Arte della Lana not to vote against Lorenzo's wish and turn "patronum artis Laurentium" into an enemy. For the evolving language of patronage in Lorenzo's time, including the use of *padrone*, see Kent, "Lorenzo as 'Maestro della Bottega'."

65 Brucker, *Renaissance Florence*, 101, identified these as the key elements in Florentine culture. For the distinction between classical and Christian moral views of the world, and its consequences for the reception of literature and perceptions of art, see especially Curtius, *European Literature*. On mercantile values, see Bec, *Les Marchands écrivains*; on their infusion into Cosimo's speech, below, ch. 2. For feudal elements persisting in Florentine patronage see Kent, *Fathers and Friends*.

66 On this see below, ch. 15. For a rather different perspective on the nature of taste, see Goldthwaite, *Wealth and the Demand for Art*, 243–8. Personal aesthetic preferences for individual styles do not emerge from the early Renaissance vocabulary for speaking about artistic commissions. However, this is more likely a limitation of language and convention than aesthetic response; see Baxandall, especially *Giotto and the Orators*; also Kemp, "Equal Excellences." When the patron's decisions about commissions and artists to execute them are assessed in the light of all his interests and associations there appear to be some choices which, as Hope argued in "Artists, Patrons and Advisors," are best explained in terms of what we call personal taste.

67 On the relevance of collecting to an understanding of the patron see below, pp. 292–9. Cosimo's grandson Lorenzo expended more of his money and passion in the collection of antique gems than he did on the patronage of contemporary artists, and Cosimo's sons Piero and Giovanni each assembled considerable collections of antique medals and busts, most now lost, beginning in their youth. See Gombrich, "Early Medici as Patrons"; Fusco and Corti, "Medici as Collectors." Fifteenth-century monetary valuation of objects serves as an index of their worth to patrons; in many cases this differs greatly from the modern. Painting was comparatively cheap. In contrast, monumental bronzes were as prized in the fifteenth century for the skill they demanded and the cost they entailed, as they are today. This Renaissance view was probably influenced by Pliny's remarks on antique art; see *Natural History*, especially bk. 35. On fifteenth-century criteria of value, see Baxandall, various, especially *Painting and Experience*.

68 Any discussion of Medici artistic patronage must begin by acknowledging a profound debt to Ernst Gombrich's brilliant if brief essay, "The Early Medici as Patrons of Art," first published in 1960 and reprinted in *Norm and Form*. Many of Gombrich's original insights have been confirmed by the great quantity of subsequent research on the Medici family and their commissions. However, some of his impressions need to be nuanced or revised in the light of new research.

69 For a comparison between Medici patronage and that of other citizens and of princes, see below, ch. 15. When Florence was the almost exclusive focus of Renaissance studies it seemed that the Medici led the way for the princes of Italy in the expression of magnificence; see Fraser-Jenkins, "Theory of Magnificence." Now the picture appears more complex.

70 See below, pp. 355–7.

71 See Kent, *Rise of the Medici*, ch. 5, and below, p. 355. Gregory, "Palla Strozzi's Patronage," argued strongly that this was not

consciously "political," just as I argued that the Strozzi did not particularly challenge or oppose the Medici rise to power.

72 See Rucellai, *Zibaldone* 1, 121. For a discussion of this trinity of motives for patronage see Baxandall, *Painting and Experience*, also Kent, "Buonomini di San Martino." For Giovanni's patronage, and a comparison with Cosimo's see below, pp. 357–66; also the essays, *Zibaldone* 2, by F. W. Kent, "Making of a Renaissance Patron," Preyer, "Rucellai Palace," and Perosa, "Lo Zibaldone."

Chapter 1

1 Vespasiano, *Vite* 2, 191–2. Cf. Giovanni Rucellai's very similar comments, discussed below, ch. 15.

2 Patrician patrons like Cosimo were intensely involved with contemporary intellectual and religious issues and with the events of war and politics, which along with their personal experience shaped the identity they expressed in their commissions of art. Gombrich spoke for a number of art historians in deprecating the significance of such interests when he declared categorically that "the monumental art of the Italian Renaissance is generally concerned with great and universal themes and . . . it is a mistake to look in such works for topical allusions," *Topos and Topicality*, 2. However, recent more interdisciplinary research has uncovered so many likely topical allusions in Renaissance art that it is implausible to argue that they are all imaginary. The themes of art are indeed universal, but Renaissance men discerned the manifestation of universal truths in every particular of their lives, producing precisely such multiple "levels of meaning" as Gombrich decries. See below, especially pt. 2.

3 "La cara e buona imagine paterna," Dante, *Inferno*, xv, 83. The poet referred here to another teacher and mentor, Brunetto Latini. His phrase struck a profound chord in Florentine hearts; Rinaldo degli Albizzi, for example, repeated it in describing how, at a moment of crisis, his dead father's "cara e buona imagine paterna" appeared to him in a dream to offer counsel, *Commissioni* 3, 76, cit. Kent, *Household and Lineage*, 303. As Kent observed, Rinaldo's note about his dream may have been inspired by Cicero's *Dream of Scipio*, from which Cosimo was heard to quote; below, p. 402, n. 20. Classical literature often gave added resonance to personal experience, as may be seen from the writings of many well-read and articulate Florentines; see below, pt. 2.

4 See particularly Kent, *Household and Lineage*.

5 On these themes see below, particularly chs. 2, 9 and conclusion; also Kent, *Fathers and Friends*.

6 Kent, "I Medici in esilio," *Rise of the Medici*, passim.

7 For the employees of the Medici bank, see De Roover, *Rise and Decline*, passim.

8 See Kent, *Household and Lineage*, ch. 1, on the developmental cycle of the Florentine household, and Gino Capponi, *Ricordi*, for one prominent example of a father's injunction to his eldest son to hold onto the house; "E nelle divise tu, Neri, voglia la casa di Firenze e non guardare il pregio," XIX, 36.

9 See Saalman and Mattox, "First Medici Palace."

10 See Piero's account of the funeral, MAP, CLXIII, discussed below, conclusion; see also the comments of Strocchia, *Death and Ritual*.

11 This is the major point of Paoletti's "Fraternal Piety"; on their roles in the bank see De Roover, *Rise and Decline*.

12 On Traversari see below, especially chs. 3 and 13 and pp. 379–80.

13 Below, chs. 11 and 12.

14 Below, pp. 220–24.

15 Below, ch. 12. Cf. Hatfield's suggestions concerning the Stoic and Epicurean strains in the decoration of the Medici palace, "Some Unknown Descriptions," 245–6. See also Spallanzani and Bertelà, *Libro d'inventario*; Spallanzani, *Inventari Medicei*; Dacos et al., *Il tesoro di Lorenzo*; Fusco and Corti, "Medici as Collectors."

16 Lavin, "Renaissance Portrait Bust"; Schuyler, *Florentine Busts*; Zuraw, "Medici Portraits."

17 Gombrich, "Early Medici as Patrons." Evidence from several articles in Beyer and Boucher, *Piero de' Medici*, tends to confirm this suggestion. On the chapel and its frescoes, below, ch. 13 and 14, pp. 339–41; see also particularly Acidini, *Chapel of the Magi*, and Cole Ahl, *Benozzo Gozzoli*, ch. 3.

18 On this question, see below, ch. 12, especially pp. 239–44.

19 Brenda Preyer also sees Cosimo's patronage as archetypal in relation to the Medici palace; see "L'architettura del palazzo."

20 For this common testamentary formula see, for example, the will of the artist Luca della Robbia, 1470, in Pope-Hennessy, *Luca della Robbia*, 91.

21 *Vite* 2, 177.

22 For example, Hankins, "Platonic Academy," 147, declared that "Cosimo's Christian piety was conventional in the extreme," although he never discussed Cosimo's devotional practices or the religious significance of his commissions.

23 On this see below, pt. 2, particularly chs. 5 and 9. Florentine religious life has been greatly illuminated by recent studies of confraternities by Weissman, *Ritual Brotherhood*; Henderson, *Piety and Charity*; and the essays in *Christianity and the Renaissance*, ed. Verdon and Henderson, especially Verdon's introductory essay, "Environments of Experience and Imagination." This properly stresses that religious culture "is more than a subcategory of the history of ideas," and that for Renaissance Florentines, "traditional Christianity was the matrix of experience," 3–5.

24 Litta, *Famiglie celebri*, Medici; Pieraccini, *La stirpe dei Medici*, 14. Some scholars are sceptical of the existence of Cosimo's brothers Damian and Antonio; see particularly Paoletti, "Donatello's Bronze Doors," 68, n. 17. There are indeed some inaccuracies in Litta's genealogies, and no other source concerning these sons of Giovanni di Bicci has yet come to light. However, in my own extensive use of Florentine genealogical records presently housed in the BNF, most of them later abstractions from now unidentifiable fifteenth-century manuscripts on which Litta's work was based, chance confirmations from various quattrocento *fondi* have shown the antiquarian to be generally very reliable. On the genealogies of the Medici and their friends, see Kent, *Rise of the Medici*, especially pt. 1, 1. Florentine families customarily preserved the memory of the children who died in infancy through their names; see Klapisch-Zuber, "Le nom refait"; Kent, *Household and and Lineage*, 46–7. As seen from naming patterns revealed in *ricordi*, for example Gregorio Dati's diary, this was particularly the case when children died too young to leave other traces of their brief sojourn here.

25 This last suggestion was made by Hood, *Fra Angelico at San Marco*, and is discussed below, ch. 9.

26 On the "very special friend," see Brown, *Cult of the Saints*. On the Medici and the cult of saints, below, ch. 9. On the San Marco altarpiece, pp. 155–9.

27 Below, pp. 244–64. This pair of panels may have been commissioned by Cosimo's nephew, Pierfrancesco.

28 On the Medici chapel, see below, ch. 13; on the Medici and the Magi, see especially Hatfield, "Compagnia de' Magi."

29 Spallanzani and Bertelà, *Libro d'inventario*, and below, pp. 244–64.

30 On Cosimo's Cassian, see De La Mare, "Cosimo and His Books," 138; BLF, Laur. Plut. 16, 31. On his interest in monasticism, see below, especially p. 37 and ch. 10, passim.

31 Viti, *La Badia Fiesolana*, cit. Hood, *Fra Angelico at San Marco*, 320. On the Badia see below, pp. 212–14.

32 See Gaston, "Liturgy and Patronage"; McKillop, "Dante and *lumen Christi*"; below, pp. 378–9.

33 Vespasiano, *Vite* 2, 195. On patristic studies in Florence see Stinger, *Humanism and the Church Fathers*; on Cosimo's connections with Christian humanists and patristic scholars like Traversari, ibid., and below, ch. 3; on the expression of these interests in Cosimo's patronage, below, especially pp. 379–80. Lavin, "Donatello's Bronze Pulpits"; Paoletti, "Donatello's Bronze Doors."

34 On this see below, pp. 197–200.

35 Below, pp. 138–41, 190–91.

36 On these themes in Medici patronage see below, ch. 12; on *otium*, see Vickers, "Leisure and Idleness." On play and pleasure in the life of the Florentine patrician, see Alberti, *Della famiglia*, and Kent, *Fathers and Friends*. Poggio Bracciolini, *De Nobilitate*, described Lorenzo di Giovanni de' Medici's pleasure in patronage and collecting, discussed below, ch. 12. On visual play, see Panofsky, *Meaning in the Visual Arts* and *Studies in Iconology*; Barolsky, *Infinite Jest*. On play as a social act, Huizinga, *Homo Ludens*; Heers, *Fêtes, jeux et jouts*; Bakhtin, *Rabelais*; on play in Florentine popular culture, below, pt. 2.

37 *On Painting*, especially bk. 2.

38 See Brunelleschi's comment on this issue in a conversation recorded by Taccola, published Battisti, *Brunelleschi*, 20–21.

39 *Vite* 2, 193.

40 On Uccello's panels and on Cosimo's interest in warfare and the objects and images associated with it see below, pp. 264–81.

41 Below, pp. 281–7.

42 Below, pp. 193–4.

43 Below, pp. 380–82. On Cosimo and Donatello, see below, pp. 343–5. Janson, *Donatello*, rejected the concept, first advanced by Lanyi, of a Donatello "Medici cycle," but much recent research suppports it. See particularly Paoletti, "Donatello's Bronze Doors"; Lavin, "Donatello's Bronze Pulpits."

44 See below, particularly pp. 175–6, 343.

45 On this last see Brown, *Bartolommeo Scala*, 17, and below, pp. 297–9; on Cosimo's books, ch. 4; on Piero's, pp. 296–9.

46 See his letter to Piero published by Milanesi, "Lettere d'artisti," 78–9. The English translation in Chambers, *Artists and Patrons*, 94–5, is accompanied by a misleading commentary; see alternatively Gilbert, *Italian Art*, 6, and Ames-Lewis, "Matteo de' Pasti."

47 See Ventrone, *Le Tems revient*, 155–6. On birthtrays and their significance see Callman, *Apollonio di Giovanni*; Cole Ahl, "Renaissance Birth Salvers"; Bellosi and Haines, *Lo Scheggia*.

48 *Inferno* 15, 85. A high proportion of compilations of popular

literature included the *Trionfi*, as well as extracts from the *Divine Comedy* or commentaries on it; see below, pp. 81–2.

Chapter II

1 *Detti piacevoli* 57, no. 174.

2 These are conserved in the Archivio di Stato, Florence (ASF), in the *fondo* Medici avanti il Principato (MAP).

3 ASF, Cat.; the most informative surveys were in 1427, 1442, and 1458. On the nature and use of these records see the major work by Herlihy and Klaspisch-Zuber, *Les Toscans et leurs familles*, abridged in English as *Tuscans and their Families*, and Kent's review; also below, ch. 5.

4 The definitive study of the Medici bank is De Roover's *Rise and Decline*. See also his "Cosimo de' Medici come banchiere," and Goldthwaite, "Medici Bank."

5 These have been most fully exploited for the early decades of the fifteenth century by Brucker, *Civic World*. Rubinstein, *Government of Florence*, makes extensive use of these sources from 1434 to 1494. See Kent, *Rise of the Medici*, for an analysis of these records between 1426 and 1434.

6 See particularly ASF, Signori, Commissioni e Legazioni, Missive. Guasti published many extracts from these archives for the period 1420–40 in his edition of Albizzi, *Commissioni*. They are also discussed by Brucker and Rubinstein, op. cit., and Clarke, *Power and Patronage*.

7 See below, especially ch. 4, and pt. 2. See also particularly Brown, "Humanist Portrait of Cosimo." For the works in Cosimo's library, De La Mare, "Cosimo and His Books"; Hankins, "Cosimo de' Medici as a Patron." The most extensive account of popular literature relating to the Medici is Flamini, *La lirica toscana*; see also the published collection of popular poetry by Lanza, *Lirici toscani*, and Tanturli's essay, "Ambienti letterari fiorentini."

8 This study refers to some 150 of his letters, mainly in ASF, MAP; see also Milan, Biblioteca Ambrosiana, MS Z 247 sup.; Paris, Bibliothèque Nationale, Fonds italiens. There are autographs scattered across the world, in libraries from that of the Society of Antiquarians in London to Pomona College, California, but I know of no other extensive collections of Cosimo's letters.

9 Of course the private correspondence touches on many other themes, and there are in addition, in various *fondi* of the Florentine state archives, letters written to and by Cosimo, often along with other citizens, in his capacity as a public official.

10 On these issues see below, particularly chs. 3, 4, and 11.

11 See below, for example, pp. 343, 369–70. Cosimo's letters show him chiefly as a strategist in business and politics, and as a dedicated family man. These concerns are related to his patronage of the arts, but do not occasion direct comment on it.

12 *Vite* 2, 167–211. Gutkind, *Cosimo de' Medici*, still the definitive biography of Cosimo, took the tone of his portrait from Vespasiano, whose picture of Cosimo he confirms with additional evidence. Recent accounts of Cosimo recontextualize rather than add to this account; see Hale, *Pattern of Control*; Field, *Platonic Academy*.

13 *Vite* 2, 183: "un dì, sendo io in camera sua . . ."; 198: "giunto in camera sua . . ." The easy quality of his relations with the Medici is also apparent from a brief note to Cosimo of 1464,

published Ullmann and Stadter, *Public Library*, 14, and his
letters of the late 1450s to Piero; see Cagni, *Vespasiano*,
139–42.

14 He was particularly critical of the victorious Medici regime
for exiling Palla Strozzi, whom he greatly admired; see his
life of Cosimo, *Vite* 2, 174, and the *Proemio* to his lives of
the various Strozzi, ibid., 2. On humanist panegyrics of
Cosimo, which multiplied after about 1450, see Brown,
"Humanist Portrait."

15 *Vite* 2, 175: "Non mi distenderò in molte cose che si potreb-
bono dire, iscrivendo questo per via di ricordo, lasciolo fare
a quegli che volessino iscrivere la vita sua"; 211: "Solo ho
fatto infino a qui quello che io ho fatto per via di ricordo
quello di lui ho veduto et udito da persone degne di fede.
L'altre cose le lascio a quegli che si voranno afaticare a
scrivere la vita di sì degno cittadino . . . In quello ho scritto
ho messo la propria verità, secondo l'ho o udita o veduta,
non levando né agiugnendo nulla del mio."

16 Kramer, "Literature, Criticism and Historical Imagination,"
29, on Dominick La Capra and Hayden White's insights
into problems of historical explanation. Cf. the tone of confident understanding assumed by Field in his mini-biography
of Cosimo, *Platonic Academy*, ch. 1.

17 These issues preoccupied Herodotus and Thucydides, and
are still much debated. Elements of the nineteenth-century
positivist view of history as the uncovering of "wie es
eigentlich gewesen war" survive in current writing. For a
rejection of this "authorial voice" and a fresh discussion of
the logical status of narrative explanation see particularly La
Capra, *Re-Thinking Intellectual History* and *History and Criticism*; White, *Content of the Form* and *Tropics of Discourse*, especially 46–7: "There is no such thing as a *single* correct view
of any object under study but . . . *many* correct views, each
requiring its own style of representation." One practical
response to such reflections has been to admit and even to
embrace the fictive nature of a good deal of historical explanation. Consequently historians, like creative writers, may
feel freer to offer narratives designed to "portray the ambivalent interactions of opposing tendencies in life and thought";
Kramer, "Literature, Criticism and Historical Imagination,"
119. For some examples, see Darnton, *Great Cat Massacre* and
particularly Davis, *Fiction in the Archives*. Cf. La Capra, "Is
Everyone a *Mentalité* Case?"

18 *De Officiis*, bk. 1, vi.

19 *Vite* 2, 192. See also Gombrich, introduction to Ames-Lewis,
Cosimo 'il Vecchio,' 2, on Cosimo's actions and their relation
to our perception of his character: "the public image of
Cosimo, as it has come down to us, must owe at least a much
to the situation in which he found himself as it did to those
innate dispositions we would call his 'character.' " On action
as text see Ricoeur, "Model of the Text: Meaningful Action."

20 See Robin, *Filelfo in Milan*, 40.

21 Bk. VI, 19–21. Renaissance and classical reflections on the
question may not have been connected in this case; according to Lee, "*Ut pictura poesis*," 201, Aristotle's *Poetics*, strangely
neglected in the early Renaissance, was not available in Latin
translation until 1498.

22 Several dozen of the secretary's vivid and informative
personal letters survive in MAP; they will appear as the
subject of a separate study. Cosimo's domestic letters fall
into two main groups: the long early letters to his cousin
Averardo, from the late twenties and early thirties, almost

all autographs, and his letters after 1434 to his sons Piero
and Giovanni, most containing practical instructions about
domestic, diplomatic, business, and political affairs, many in
Cosimo's hand, but more in Alesso's. On messengers, see
MAP, II, 14.

23 See below, ch. 4 and pp. 295–6.

24 Concerning the variety of ways in which projected images
of self may be related to the actor's own perceptions and
intentions, see Goffman, *Presentation of Self*.

25 On Cosimo as the product of the particular culture of the
Florentine *popolo*, see below, pt. 2; for the popular image of
Cosimo's desirable qualities, see especially pp. 117–21.

26 MAP, VI, 48, to Averardo, 20 March 1427/8: "Or tutto questo
è uno indovinare; aspettereno di vedere il cierto"; MAP, II,
30, 18 March 1429/30, "si può più tosto inmaginare e indovinare che giudichare o prendere partito."

27 See Gadol, *Leon Battista Alberti*, 225.

28 MAP, II, 38, 123; III, 145.

29 MAP, II, 123; III, 145; VIII, 200.

30 MAP, IX, 227, Cosimo to Giovanni in Milan, 26 Aug. 1457;
II, 87, 95: "io none fo quello chonto fanno quasi tutti
glialtri".

31 MAP, IX, 561, on calculating the number of horses needed
for Giovanni's return from the Mugello to Florence.

32 MAP, II, 308, to Averardo, 31 Jan. s. a.

33 MAP, II, 387, to Averardo, 29 Nov. 1430; below, pp. 117–21.

34 Machiavelli to Francesco Vettori, 9 April 1513, *Lettere*, 124,
239–40: "la fortuna ha fatto . . . e mi conviene ragionare dello
stato." Machiavelli, by contrast with Cosimo, explained his
obsession with politics as a consequence of his ignorance of
the wool or silk trade, of income and expenditure.

35 See, for example, MAP, II, 100, 113, 143, 223; III, 145; IV, 77.

36 "Honore della casa . . . honore della ciptà," MAP, III, 452.

37 MAP, II, 170: "Il chomune avesse et verghongia et danno, et
ingienansi in quanto possono questo abi a seghuire, che è
chativa chondizione d'uomo. Parmi nonostante questa inpresa
non ci sia piaciuta, veduto la chosa essere e ridotta in luogho
dove interviene l'onore del chomune, per ciaschuno si deba
dare ogni favore possibile et chosì fo in quello posso qua e'l
simile chonforto te benchè sono certo non bisogni."

38 MAP, II, 101.

39 Copy, ASF, CS 2a ser., 136, 26 Nov. 1454. I wish to thank
Alison Brown for drawing my attention to this letter. It
shows the typical Florentine usage of the term "private" in
opposition to "public"; the "private" passions to which he
referred were the interests of various political factions. Cf.
the quite different modern interpretation of this dichotomy,
discussed above, introduction.

40 This conviction was shared by community leaders sympathetic to the Medici. Ambrogio Traversari, a noted classical
and biblical scholar, and general of the Camaldolensian order,
observed of the republic after Cosimo's exile: "We are in a
worse way since Cosimo [was exiled] . . ." Stinger, *Humanism
and the Church Fathers*, 30–31. See also the testimony of
popular poets, below, ch. 8.

41 See originally Molho, "*Pater Patriae or Padrino?*" His characterization became the point of departure for arguments about
Cosimo's role in the exploitation of the working classes by
Cohn, *Laboring Classes*, and Field, *Platonic Academy*. I have
adopted this modern conceit of referring to Cosimo as a
"Godfather" (*padrino*) because most English readers are
familiar with this concept and with those other terms –

paterfamilias, *pater patriae* and patron – whose common linguistic root underlines their fundamental relation, which I have stressed in my characterization of Cosimo. However, in the fifteenth century *padrino* referred to the literal godfather acquired at baptism; on the role of actual godfathers as patrons see Klapisch-Zuber, "Compérage et clientélisme."

42 See, for example, the well-known letter of Ficino to Lorenzo praising Cosimo, *Letters* 1, 136, as "a man surpassing others in prudence, dutiful towards God, just and magnanimous towards men, in himself even-tempered, full of care for his family, yet watching even more carefully the affairs of state; a man who lived not for himself alone, but for God and his country . . ."

43 See, for example, the classic feminist work by Lerner, *Patriarchy*; also the subtle and influential studies of the English working classes by E. P. Thompson, especially "Patrician Society, Plebeian Culture."

44 See Rubinstein, *Government of Florence*; Kent, "Dynamic of Power"; Clarke, *Power and Patronage*; Phillips, *Memoir of Marco Parenti*. This opinion was summed up by Pope Pius II, Aeneas Sylvius Piccolomini, *Commentarii* 1, 150: "sed populi excellentem virtutem omnes oderunt: invenenti sunt qui tyrannidem Cosme ferendam negarent."

45 Addressing a meeting of the Consulte in 1429, Lorenzo Ridolfi declared: "Just as we should adore one God, so you, Lord Priors, are to be venerated above all citizens, and those who look to others are setting up idols, and are to be condemned," CP 48, 51r. On these themes see Kent, *Fathers and Friends*; also below, chs. 8 and 9.

46 On Medici friends in government see Rubinstein, *Government of Florence*, and Kent, *Rise of the Medici*.

47 Ricc. Frullani, 1212; I thank Alison Brown for drawing my attention to this letter.

48 Aquinas, *De Regimine Principum*, 1, 4, cit. McKillop, "Dante and *Lumen christi*," 262; see also 291–301 on the commune's conferral of the title *pater patriae* on Cosimo. For Belcari's sonnet describing Cosimo as "padre della tua patria," see below, p. 118. The humanist Francesco Filelfo, who for many years was bitterly hostile to the Medici, also used the title in a letter to Cosimo; see Hankins, "Platonic Academy," 149–50. "*Liber de Regimine Principum*" is no. 55 in the 1417/18 inventory of Cosimo's books; see De La Mare, "Cosimo and His Books," 126; she suggested the work could be either Aquinas or Aegidius Romanus. On Cosimo and charity see below, ch. 9.

49 Foucault, in such studies as *Archaeology of Knowledge* and *Madness and Civilization*, observed the politicized nature of all objects of study. On the other end of the methodological spectrum, Geertz, *Interpretation of Cultures*, and "Blurred Genres," demonstrated the close interaction between politics and culture, an insight which Richard Trexler applied most fruitfully to Florence in his various studies of the political significance of ritual and drama. The possibilities and the problems presented by these approaches are discussed below with reference to many particular studies of aspects of Cosimo's oeuvre.

50 See Vespasiano, *Vite* 2, 167–8: "Cosimo di Giovanni de' Medici fu d'onoratissimi parenti et prestantissimo cittadino, et di grande autorità nella sua republica"; 195: "era uomo d'autorità"; 209: "né ignuno fu che avessi ardimento di parlare per la autorità sua." In Florentine parlance, power depended on the ability to act effectively in relations with others; hence the terms for magnates, whose actions overrode others – *prepotentes* – and the poor – *impotenti*, who were unable to act effectively at all. On the relation between *auctorità* and *amicizia*, see the popular sonnet, "Certe auctorità di molti valenti huomini," BNF II:II:81, 176v, ff. Vespasiano's choice of this noun is very significant in indicating the nature of Cosimo's role in Florentine society. Paoletti, "Familiar Objects," saw Lorenzo's declaration in 1481, twenty years after Cosimo's death, that "Io non sono signore di Firenze ma cittadino con qualche auctorità," as an example of "the ambiguous nature of Medici meaning," referring to the "double role of citizen/authority," 80, 102, n. 3. But Lorenzo spoke the literal truth. Moreover, as Rubinstein explained in his account of "Cosimo *optimus civis*," especially 7, *auctoritas*, understood by Florentines in the sense established by Cicero, was the quality by which the ideal citizen, or senator, exerted his influence, by contrast with written law; such citizens were "emphatically, not single rulers."

51 See, for example, the role he played in the consecration of the cathedral, below, pp. 126–7. His public intervention with Pope Eugenius to obtain more indulgences for the Florentine people on this occasion was one of the more ingenious displays of his political influence and power as a patron able to protect the interests of Florentines in this world and the next. The incident perfectly illustrates what Trexler meant when he observed in the introduction to his edition of the *Libro Cerimoniale*, 9: "What modern writers still like to call 'mere ritual' seemed to the Renaissance the very essence of public order, foreign relations, eternal salvation and personal identity."

52 In his *Political Letters*, Dante denounced Florence while making it clear that as far as his own personal happiness and comfort were concerned, there was nowhere on earth that he would rather be. See also Starn, *Contrary Commonwealth*, on Florentine exiles and their estrangement from their native city.

53 MAP, v, 690, cit. and discussed by Kent, "I Medici in esilio," 20.

54 Laur., Plut. 16, 31, 92; see also De La Mare, "Cosimo and His Books," 140.

55 Kent, *Rise of the Medici*, 309; "I Medici in esilio," 20–21.

56 ASF, Signoria, Missive, published Fabroni, *Magni Cosmi* 2, 87. Some years later Cosimo may have been moved to compensate Mari for the effects of his stern civic virtue in the thirties. See below, p. 214.

57 Roscoe, *Lorenzo de' Medici*, 411. This document was published in the eighteenth century by Fabroni, *Magni Cosmi* 2, 97–101; he cited an earlier antiquarian's description of the work "levato da un libro di propria mano di Cosimo de' Medici, dove scriveva i suoi ricordi d'importanza; e fu levata detta copia da Luigi Guicciardini." Cosimo was recalled by the Signoria of September 1434, which consisted almost entirely of his friends – "tutti i buoni cittadini," as he called them. That their names were drawn from the electoral purses was hardly fortuitous; for several years previously the committees entrusted with filling the purses had been stacked with Medici partisans, thanks to the maneuvering of the Medici party and its friends. See Kent, *Rise of the Medici*, ch. 5, and Rubinstein, *Government of Florence*, passim.

58 Machiavelli, *Istorie fiorentine*, 66; cf. Najemy, "Machiavelli and the Medici," especially 566–71, who argued that this was not Machiavelli's meaning. It is true that Cosimo's entourage

entered Florence inconspicuously by night, at the Signoria's request, but his whole journey from Venice, as his *ricordi* and other sources represent it, was a triumphal progress; en route he was greeted and hailed by rulers of various states including the Este and the Malatesta. On the frescoes and their likely inspiration in actual processions, see below, ch. 13.

59 On the statue and its inscription see below, pp. 283–4. Many art historians have been troubled or confused by Cosimo's use of republican imagery; see, for example Griffiths, "Uccello's *Battle of San Romano*." This is largely because they are influenced by an image of Cosimo essentially shaped by the moral judgments of a modern commitment to liberal democracy. The Risorgimento clothing of Cosimo in wolf's garments, as a despoiler of the republic, is still influential, despite recent revelations of the intricacy of the actual arrangements of Florentine government. Many questions about Medici artistic patronage have been framed, and indeed circumscribed, by too simplistic a view of Cosimo and Florentine government, and too narrow a definition of politics and power. On these issue see below, especially ch. 15 and conclusion.

60 Hankins, "Cosimo as a Patron," 86–7. On the steersman in classical political thought, see Brown, "Platonism in Fifteenth-Century Florence," 384–8; on Lapo's reasons for dedicating this work to Cosimo, see Celenza, "Parallel Lives."

61 "Nel tempo ch'egli erano a confini/ poteron ritornar per torte vie:/ non vollon mai, come buon Fiorentini," Lanza, *Lirici toscani* 1, 357. Not everyone agreed with this view of Cosimo. Among the most eloquent of his critics was the popular poet Burchiello; for his verses denouncing the Medici as tyrants see Lanza, *Polemiche e Berte* 1972, especially 192–4; for his later amicable relations with them, below, p. 49.

62 MAP, VIII, 200, to Piero, 1449/50: "mosterrai quanto schrivo a Ruberto, et di lettere ho auto più sue lettere; et per essere malato non gli ò potuto fare risposta perchè la febre anchora no' m'a lassato, et il chapo non mi serve chome bisognierebbe"; V, 623, 1449: "la testa non mi serve a ffare risposta . . ." Cf. Alessandra Strozzi, who also found writing hard work; see, for example, *Lettere*, no. 53, 476.

63 The Renaissance analogy between art and war illuminates Cosimo's interest in both, and is expressed and explored by Machiavelli in his treatise, *L'arte della guerra*.

64 "Io non dicho per riprendere né per insegnare, che non è mia usanza né mio mestiere; ma più la speranza mi conferma in sull'openione mio, e tu veggio ti stai in sul tuo, e a questo modo seguireno l'autorità di ser Muccio;" *mucciare = fare beffe*.

65 See, for example, MAP, II, 30, 34, 100, 101.

66 See, for example, *Inferno* 2, 7, ff: "O Muse, o alto ingegno, or m'aiutate. . ." Classical writers such as Quintilian and Cicero, whose works were very popular in Florence, were also concerned with *ingenium* and *inventio* in discussions of rhetoric; see Curtius, *European Literature*, 296. Florentines adopted the classical usage of *ingegno* to praise the achievements of artists and writers, paradoxically to liberate the geniuses of their own times from the tyranny of classical precedent. On the nature of the originality implicit in this term, its use by humanists, and their debt to Cicero, see Smith, "Originality and Cultural Progress." See also Quint, "On ingegnio," 434, cf. Cicero, *De Oratore*, I, 38, 173; Proctor, "Quaedam Particula Perfecti."

67 Rucellai, *Zibaldone*, 54–5; see also Gombrich for Ghiberti's use of *ingegnai*, "Renaissance Conception of Artistic Progress." Smith, op. cit., explored the importance of this conception to Renaissance thinking; see also her *Architecture in the Culture of Early Humanism*. Concentrating exclusively on architecture, she assumed that this emphasis on *ingegno* arose largely from the reading of antique sources, whereas in fact it was used in popular speech in relation to every area of Florentines' activity.

68 See especially D'Ancona, *Origini del teatro italiano* 1, ch. 9.

69 Toscan, *Carneval du langage* 4, 1707.

70 *Vite* 2, 200, 204. The mutual admiration of one another's *virtù* was one of the bonds of reciprocal friendship between cultured men; see Cicero, *De Amicitia*, and a Renaissance application of this text in Alberti's protestations of friendship to Piero de' Medici, which appear in the dedication to him of an Italian version of *De Uxoria, Opere volgari* 2, 303. Alberti described Piero as "studioso di lettere e virtù," hoping "vederti in tempo alla patria nostra simile al padre tuo Cosmo, uomo virtuosissimo e a me amicissimo, pregiato e utilissimo cittadino, da cui la nostra republica per tuo consiglio e fortuna di dì in dì più riceva autorità, dignità e amplitudine . . ."

71 Published by Lanza, *Lirici toscani* 2, 55–6. The attribution to Cosimo derives from one of two manuscript copies of the verse, Vat. Lat. 4830. In the other, apparently a later copy, Laur., Segnani 4, the author is not named, and the name of Giovanni Peruzzi is substituted for that of Francesco Sforza as the dedicatee. The form is a common one; there are several similar examples published by Lanza. I am most grateful to Suzanne Branciforte for drawing this poem to my attention. On adynata and the upside down world of opposition, a topos Virgilian in origin and familiar to the Middle Ages, see Curtius, *European Literature*. It is likely that Cosimo was the author of another verse, or rather a note in verse, addressed to Michele del Giogante. See Flamini, *La lirica toscana*, 689; Laur., 41, 34, 86v; Magl. II:II:40, 118r, "Michele il nostro cavalier ci e' portò . . ."

72 See below, pp. 292–3. The involvement of eminent Florentines in warfare, as *commissari* to *condottieri* on the battlefield, is well documented; see particularly Brucker, *Civic World*, Albizzi, *Commissioni*, and Mallett, various, especially *Mercenaries and their Masters*. It has seldom, however, formed part of the traditional picture of the urban republican citizen.

73 On jousting, see Cosimo to Pierfrancesco, MAP, II, 452, 17 March 1459.

74 His name was Magnolino; see Vespasiano, *Vite* 2, 195. Michele del Giogante, a poet and compiler of popular literature, noted in one of his *zibaldoni*, Ricc. 2735, 171r, old numeration, that on 22 November 1437 he had sent Cosimo from Castel San Giovanni "un libretto di partiti di schacchi . . . il perchè rispondendomi adì 28 detto assai grazioso e cche l'avea a ricordo . . ." On the symbolic significance of the chess-game in the Renaissance see Simons, "Check (Mating)."

75 MAP, V, 441, Cosimo to Giovanni di Cosimo, 24 June 1442.

76 For the analogies Florentines drew between these areas of activity see Kemp, "From 'Mimesis' to 'Fantasia'," and below, pt. 2.

77 Cit. Gombrich, "Renaissance Conception of Artistic Progress," 7. The pairing of *arte e ingegno* was a commonplace for describing works of art. Cosimo and his circle might have

derived it directly from Cicero, or via Petrarch, whose work was the chief model for popular poets, and who became an arbiter of Florentine taste; see below, p. 81. Baxandall, *Giotto and the Orators*, 51, described this as one of Petrarch's "anthology formulas," worn "threadbare" by the early fifteenth century. While this may be true in relation to the development of creative criticism, most men actively ordered and measured their world in terms of such accepted values, as Baxandall went on to show in his discussion of the language of the humanists which, translated into Italian, was adopted into popular speech, ibid., 8–20; see also below, ch. 3. One coupling of *arte e ingegno* in popular speech appears in the favorite game of double-entendre: *ingegno* signified sex in general, while *arte* stood particularly for the anus or sodomy; see Toscan, *Carneval du langage* 4, 1663. Like many commonplaces, this one conveyed real and live meaning in many contexts to ordinary people unable to characterize their views in more original ways. Moreover, in this world in which classical culture was held up as the standard by which all achievement was to be measured, the commonplace or topos was often a conscious tribute, in the spirit of Bernard of Chartres's disclaimer in the twelfth century that "moderns" were "but dwarves standing on the shoulders of giants" in relation to the ancients; cit. Southern, *Making of the Middle Ages*, 211. Cf. Marsuppini, below, ch. 3. Modern classical scholars seem suspicious of the "genuineness" or "sincerity" of feelings and attitudes expressed in borrowed phrases, which are the staple of popular culture in any age; see, for example, Gombrich, "Classical Topos," 173. Such topoi constituted an effective shorthand to evoke a whole history of related responses to art. The description of realistic sculpture as appearing to "breathe and speak" satisfactorily expressed the response of viewers from ancient Rome to Renaissance Florence, and the latter, strongly influenced by humanism, naturally relied on the classical formulation. Petrarch borrowed phrases from Pliny, *Natural History*, XXXV, to praise classical sculpture, of which he himself was a knowledgeable enthusiast and collector, observing that he admired the art of the ancient sculptors because "they transform the mute and senseless substance so that it seems to breathe and speak and they sometimes represent the passions of the soul so that matter which can feel neither joy nor grief seems to be smiling and grieving," *Epistolae* IV, 2, cit. Holmes, *Florentine Enlightenment*, 227. Ancient authors were invoked because they effectively expressed contemporary responses with the added weight of authority accumulated over centuries. At the same time, as Holmes observed of a fifteenth-century reference to Pliny, "the humanist is adopting from classical art a critical standard which is clearly related to the novelties of Donatello and Masaccio," cf. below, ch. 3. These issues are sharply relevant to our discussion of the content of popular culture, below, ch. 6, and of popular response to art, ch. 8.

78 For example, Burckhardt's representation of the state as a work of art, *Civilization of the Renaissance*, pt. 1, is a metaphor arising out of fifteenth-century usage, like Machiavelli's reference to the Art of War. See also Greenblatt, *Shakespearean Negotiations*, introduction and ch. 1, and Gombrich, "From the Revival of Letter"; he shows that Brunelleschi's reforms of architecture and Niccoli's reforms of orthography were related in being similarly symptoms "of an increasingly critical attitude towards tradition," 82.

Chapter III

1   Gombrich, "From the Revival of Letters," 71.

2   On *istoria* and *invenzione* see Alberti, *On Painting,* especially 14–15; also Greenstein, "Alberti on *Historia*." The classical sources of these concepts were Cicero and Pliny, *Natural History,* bk. 35. The latter text circulated in Florence after Poggio's rediscovery of an antique manuscript in 1429; see Gordan, *Two Renaissance Book Hunters,* LXXIV, 148, and LXXVII, 153. Leonardo Bruni later acquired Salutati's copy of Pliny, ibid., 332. In 1421 the Signoria granted Brunelleschi a patent for a conveyance to be used on the River Arno, observing that he was "vir perspicassimi intellectus et industriae et inventionis admirabilis," Gaye, *Carteggio* 1, 547–8. Among the early examples of much-admired artistic *invenzione* were the baptistery doors, especially Ghiberti's *Solomon and Sheba* panel, Donatello's *Saint George* for Orsanmichele, and Masaccio's *Trinity* in Santa Maria Novella.

3   See, for example, Starn, "Seeing Culture", also below, ch. 15.

4   See particularly Hope, "Artists, Patrons and Advisors," 293–343; also Gilbert, *Italian Art,* introduction and comments on documents, passim.

5   Hope, "Religious Narrative." On Iacopo da Voragine's *Golden Legend* see below, pp. 97–8. This handbook obviously influenced many artistic representations, but it was only one of many popular sources of information concerning the saints, and by no means the most sophisticated.

6   Gilbert, *Italian Art,* 113.

7   For an exploration of these interactions in particular city neighborhoods see Kent and Kent, *Neighbours and Neighbourhood;* Eckstein, *District of the Green Dragon.* For the operation of such associations in the organization of a charitable institution see Kent, "Buonomini di San Martino."

8   See, for example, Smith, "Originality and Cultural Progress," 311–13.

9   Hankins, "Platonic Academy," pointed out that the philosophy in which Cosimo was most interested was not in fact mid-century Neoplatonism, cf. Field, *Platonic Academy,* but the moral philosophy of Aristotle and Plato transmitted via Cicero, the stuff of Bruni's translations in the early decades of the fifteenth century. On the intellectual climate of this time, see also Hankins, *Plato in the Italian Renaissance.*

10 Holmes, *Florentine Enlightenment,* 97. Holmes's vivid account of this learned world has been insufficiently applied to an understanding of the Medici circle and their patronage. On the Medici as a focal point of popular culture, see Tanturli, "Ambienti letterari fiorentini" and Lanza, *Lirici toscani,* passim; also below, pt. 2.

11 Much effort was expended by this group in following up the manuscript discoveries made by Poggio at the time of the Council of Constance; see Holmes, op. cit., 82–3, and Gordan, *Two Renaissance Book Hunters.*

12 *Vite* 2, 193, 203; also 168: "ebbe bonissima peritia delle lettere latine, così delle sacre come de' gentili."

13 See, for example, Field, *Platonic Academy,* 13: "As to Cosimo's interactions with the world of ideas, little can be said." See also below, ch. 4.

14 On Marsili see below, pp. 86–7; see also Giovanni Gherardi da Prato's *Paradiso degli Alberti,* set in the 1380s. On Traversari see his *Hodoeporicon,* and Stinger, *Humanism and the Church Fathers;* on the *Orti Oricellari,* Gilbert, "Orti Oricellari" and *Machiavelli and Guicciardini.*

15 *Vite* 2, 169.

16 Martines, *Social World.*

17 *Hodoeporicon,* 162, ff.

18 See below, ch. 4, for patristic works in Cosimo's library; on San Lorenzo, pp. 183–97 and 377–84. For Traversari's possible influence on Florentine art see Stinger, *Humanism and the Church Fathers,* and "Tempio degli Scolari."

19 *Vite* 2, 200.

20 MAP, XIV, 467; also De La Mare, "Cosimo and His Books," 143, no. 23.

21 Vespasiano, loc. cit., and De La Mare, op. cit., 133.

22 Zippel, "Niccolò Niccoli," 121; Hankins, "Cosimo de' Medici as a Patron," 94.

23 Krautheimer, *Ghiberti,* 138–9, 147–8, and below, p. 377.

24 Rao, "Ambrogio Traversari al Concilio"; also Gill, *Council of Florence; Eugenius IV,* and *Personalities of the Council.*

25 Below, pp. 196–7, and ch. 13.

26 *Vite* 2, 200; on Rossi, see Martines, *Social World.*

27 See Kent, *Rise of the Medici,* appendix 1.

28 On Lorenzo at the Studio, see Holmes, *Florentine Enlightenment,* passim. While the Medici failed to offer sustained backing to the Studio between 1434 and 1472, when it was transferred to Pisa (Brucker, "Civic Debate"), in the years immediately before and after 1434 Lorenzo was a prominent figure there. See below, n. 30, and Tratte, 80, 430r. The Studio officials of 1436–55 included Lorenzo and Cosimo's sons Piero and Giovanni, as well as several of their close relatives and partisans, among them Antonio di Salvestro Serristori, Agnolo Acciaiuoli, Luca Pitti, Alamanno Salviati, and Agnolo della Stufa. On the Florentine Studio before the Medici rise to power see Brucker, "Florence and its University." For a list of lecturers at the Studio, Park, "Florentine Studio."

29 On Marsuppini, see Martines, op. cit.

30 Filelfo claimed that the Medici conspired to assassinate him, in order to clear the way at the Studio for Marsuppini; see Zippel, "Il Filelfo a Firenze," 215–53, and Robin, *Filelfo in Milan,* 17–45.

31 *Francisci Philelfi Epistolarum Libri,* 12r–v, cit. and trans. Holmes, *Florentine Enlightenment,* 99.

32 See Zippel's comment, "Il Filelfo a Firenze," and the letter published by Ricci, "Una consolatoria inedita."

33 On Niccoli, see Zippel, "Niccolò Niccoli"; Vespasiano, *Vite* 1, 225–42; Martines, op. cit., and Holmes, *Florentine Enlightenment,* passim, especially 92–3. For a recent reassessment of his reputation and abilities, see Davies, "An Emperor without Clothes?" On Niccoli's library, Ullman and Stadter, *Public Library.*

34 Zippel, op. cit., 95.

35 Martines, op. cit., 116.

36 Ullman and Stadter, op. cit., 292–9; for the documents, including Niccoli's wills, ibid., 304, ff.; also Zippel, "Niccolò Niccoli," 152–3. For the building of the library, see below, p. 178; on Sacchetti, below, especially pp. 105–6, 198.

37 On Alesso's role in the Medici household, at SS. Annunziata, and in the Medicean funded confraternity of the *Buonomini,* see especially pp. 16, 47, 207, and 457, n. 268.

38 MAP, VII, 292; Ullmann and Stadter, op. cit., 13.

39 Besides the references to the Medici in this correspondence, trans. and ed. Gordan, *Two Renaissance Book Hunters,* there are three vernacular letters in Poggio Bracciolini's *Opera Omnia.* Two were addressed to Cosimo, and one to Giovanni di Bicci (IV, 213–15, 611–13, 647). See also Poggio's letter of consolation to Cosimo during his exile, comparing him to various unjustly treated Roman heroes, *Epistolae* V, 12.

40 Gordan, op. cit., XV, 61. On Nicola di Vieri's learning and patronage, and his close relations with Cosimo, see Kent, *Rise of the Medici,* and below, ch. 15.

41 Gordan, op. cit., XXX, 88–9.

42 On these manuscripts of Cosimo's see De La Mare, "Cosimo and His Books," and below, ch. 4. Poggio also borrowed Cosimo's copy of Plutarch's *Lives,* Gordan, op. cit., LXXVII, 153.

43 De Roover, *Rise and Decline,* 63–4, 422.

44 Gordan, op. cit., LIV, 119–21.

45 Gordan, op. cit., XL, 113–15.

46 On Giovanni's tomb, see below, pp. 141, 190–91; on Cosimo's interest in inscriptions, below, passim, especially p. 190.

47 Poggio appears to have been less informed on current than on classical affairs; for Cosimo's important role in the commune's wars before 1434 see above, ch. 2, and below, pp. 264–81.

48 Gordan, op. cit., XXXIII, 91; De La Mare, op. cit.; on the Bardi, Bec, *Les Livres des Florentins,* passim, and below, ch. 6, passim, for the Bardi family's role in popular culture.

49 The term he uses here is *patronus;* see the discussion of patronage terminology above, p. 8.

50 Gordan, op. cit., LXVI, 136–7. See also Bracciolini, *Opera Omnia* IV, 213–5; 611, 613, 647, letters to Cosimo and Giovanni di Bicci.

51 See below, ch. 4, and above, ch. 2, on Cosimo's exile.

52 Gordan, op. cit., LXVIII, 138–9. This is a typical humanist consolation, cf. Antonio Manetti's rejection of these formulae in the face of the loss of his son, Banker, "Mourning a Son"; McClure, "Art of Mourning." See also Cosimo's distinctive inscription on his father's tomb, below, pp. 141, 190–91.

53 Gordan, op. cit., LI, 116.

54 Gordan, op. cit., XC, 183.

55 Ibid., LXXVII, 152–3. See also below, p. 248, on Cosimo's father's commission for his house of a representation of *uomini illustri.*

56 Holmes, "How the Medici became the Pope's Bankers." According to Vespasiano, *Vite* 1, 170, Cosimo also went to Constance in 1414. This is very likely, since at that time he was in charge of the operations of the Rome branch of the bank. There is no corroborating evidence of Vespasiano's account of the trips to Germany and France after the council ended.

57 See below, pp. 164–6.

58 See Vespasiano, *Vite* 1, life of Nicholas V, and 2, 167–211, life of Cosimo. On the pope's advice concerning the library, see also Ullmann and Stadter, *Public Library.*

59 MAP, II, 62, 27 Nov. 1427. Cosimo wrote to Averardo that "this morning the priors dismissed the chancellor . . . A lot of explanations are being put forward, but I think it's probably hatred and enmity rather than anything else." Giuliano de' Medici announced to his father Averardo, MAP, II, 65, 3 Dec. 1427, that "ieri mattina fu eletto Messer Lionardo d'Arezo cancielliere . . . a anchora andare pe' consigli, ma a ciaschuno piace tale electione."

60 Hankins, "The Humanist, the Banker, and the *Condottiere.*"

61 See below, ch. 4.

62   On this see Rubinstein, "Florentine Constitutionalism," cf. Hankins, "Cosimo de' Medici as a Patron." Cosimo's personal patronage embraced Bruni's family; see MAP, XI, 159, 20 Feb. 1438, Carlo Bonciani, Captain of Arezzo, to Cosimo, Gonfalonier of Justice in Florence. Bonciani was responding to a recommendation of Cosimo on behalf of "uno parente di Messere Lionardo vostro cancielieri di certo offitio el quale lui disiderebe avere in questa città . . ."

63   See Kristeller, *Iter Italicum* 1, 89. For example, Alberti's *Della tranquillità dell'animo*, composed in 1443, is a dialogue between Nicola de' Medici, Alberti himself, and Agnolo Pandolfini, the son-in-law of Cosimo's cousin Averardo. It is set in the cathedral of Florence, beneath Brunelleschi's newly completed dome. See Alberti, *Opere volgari* 2, 107–83.

64   On the dialogue, see Marsh, *Quattrocento Dialogues.*

65   Cit. Holmes, *Florentine Enlightenment*, 79.

66   On Vasari see particularly Rubin, *Vasari*; also Gombrich, "Vasari's *Lives* and Cicero's *Brutus*." Vasari's presentation of the patron, less interesting in his view than the artist, is necessarily rather at odds with the patron's presentation of himself. As historical evidence, his mid-sixteenth-century testimony concerning persons and events a century earlier must necessarily be considered rather weak. There are also serious textual problems posed by the different versions of his *Lives*. This is not to deny his unique value as the earliest historian of Renaissance art. Modern art historians have depended heavily on his work for clues concerning particular artists and works of art, and in following these have produced a huge and valuable body of critical comment and evaluation bearing on the reliability, the strengths, and the limitations of his *Lives* to which this study cannot add. For all these reasons I have made use of his testimony concerning the circumstances of commissions and relations between patrons and artists only when there is no other evidence, and then with extreme caution. I have used his work mainly for anecdotes which, like collections of *facetiae,* properly pertain to the realm of image-making. On Vasari and the image of Michelozzo see below, p. 175.

67   The long and distinguished list of the latter includes the sculptors and stonemasons from the stone-quarrying region in the hills just north of the city, among them Desiderio da Settignano, Benedetto da Maiano, and the Rossellino brothers; Andrea from the Mugello town of Castagno, and of course Leonardo, from the small town of Vinci by the Arno, downstream from Florence.

68   On Brunelleschi, see below, pp. 81–2, 116, 122–4, and Zervas, "Brunelleschi's Political Career." Some decades later, Michelangelo wrote poetry in the popular mode of humor and irony, describing the discomforts of painting the Sistine ceiling and the charms of his mistress, who with shining skin like snail's trails would turn the pope's heart to custard; see Buonarotti, *Complete Poems,* 165–6. On the education of artists, and their role in popular culture, ch. 6, passim, pp. 115–17, and ch. 14.

69   More informal, quotidian associations between artists and the community are discussed below, pp. 116–17.

70   See Kent, *Rise of the Medici*, 128.

71   See Gorni, "Storia del Certame Coronario"; Bertolini, *De vera amicitia,* for the texts of the contributions, and for their relevance to Florentine perceptions of contemporary friendship and patronage, Kent, *Fathers and Friends.*

72   See below, ch. 15.

73   *On Painting*, 34. Christine Smith, "Originality and Cultural Progress," advanced an elaborate explanation for this dedication of a work on painting to an architect, but it is much less "puzzling" than she suggested if we concentrate our attention on the realities of artistic production and personal relations in Florence, rather than emphasizing formal divisions between genres of artistic activity.

74   *Opere volgari* 2, 302–5.

75   See particularly Haines, *Sagrestia delle Messe*, introduction; also Holmes, *Florentine Enlightenment*; Lightbown, *Donatello and Michelozzo*. See also below, especially ch. 8, for the evidence of popular response to works of art.

76   For example, Donatello was at work on the Porta della Mandorla from 1391 to 1423; a number of sculptures were made for the facade and the buttresses of the dome, including Nanni di Banco's *Isaiah* and Donatello's *David*. The latter was completed 1408–9, and in 1416 was removed and transferred to the Palazzo della Signoria. Work proceeded on statues for the *campanile,* some by Donatello, between 1416 and 1425. For documents concerning particular commissions, see Poggi/Haines, *Il duomo di Firenze.*

77   Ricci, "Una consolatoria inedita"; see also Holmes, *Florentine Enlightenment*, 228.

78   For the text and a comment see Gilbert, *Italian Art*, 163–5, cf. Holmes, *Florentine Enlightenment*, 234.

79   Gombrich, *Topos and Topicality*, 8–9.

80   Krautheimer, *Ghiberti*, 180–8, cf. Gombrich, op. cit.

81   See Gombrich, "Renaissance Conception of Artistic Progress," 5. Aurispa wrote to Traversari on 15 March 1430: "I have the siegecraft with me and so, if the sculptor could give me in return that ancient Virgil you have in your monastery and the perfected copy of Cicero's Antoniana, recently discovered, I shall send the Athanaeus." See also Stinger, "Tempio degli Scolari."

82   For the general similarities and particular differences between Florentine amateur humanists and foreign-born professionals, see Martines, *Social World.*

83   *Epistolae,* IX, 2, cit. Holmes, *Florentine Enlightenment*, 235.

84   See Zippel, "Niccolò Niccoli," 90, 110, for the tensions between Bruni and Niccoli; for other coruscating exchanges between the humanists in this circle, see Camporeale, "Poggio Bracciolini contro Lorenzo Valla."

85   *Vite* 2, 237.

86   Guarini, *Epistolario di Guarino* 1, 39–40. See also Gombrich, "Revival of Letters," 71–82.

87   Gordan, op. cit., LXXXV, 167–70; see also Holmes, op. cit., 189–90.

88   See Zippel, op. cit., 110; Gutkind, *Cosimo de' Medici*, 228.

89   Gordan, op. cit., LXXXIV, 167; Fabriczy, "Nanni di Miniato," 74–6.

90   See below, p. 294.

91   See Haines, "L'Arte della Lana," especially 272–3; also 267–8, describing how in 1427, when the canons of the cathedral asked Pope Martin V to revoke John XXIII's bull of 1413 entrusting it to the Arte della Lana, objecting that this body consisted of "homini mechanici, lanini, e tessitori," Giovanni di Rinaldo Gianfigliazzi, then Florentine ambassador to the Curia, had to point out that they were in fact an entrepreneurial elite to whom this responsibility had long been entrusted; "degni, idonei e veri Guelfi."

92   Haines, *Sagrestia delle messe*, is an account not simply of the

decoration of this sacristy for the cathedral, but more broadly of the institution of the Opera del Duomo and its functions, which conveys a fine sense of the texture of corporate patronage in this period, relating the Florentine community's traditions and ideals to religious, artistic, and patronage practices. See also Zervas, *Brunelleschi and Donatello*, especially introduction, and *Orsanmichele*. Cf. Goldthwaite's contrast of the activities of the "private sector" with an *opera* which was atypical because run by the state, *Building of Renaissance Florence*, and Elam's comment on this, "Conspicuous Construction." Besides Orsanmichele and the baptistery doors, major commissions handled by committees of *operai* included the Innocenti, a foundling hospital begun by the Silk Guild in 1421, SS. Annunziata, and the palace which the Parte Guelfa began to rebuild around 1420. On the *operai* for the Annunziata see Zervas, "Quos volunt"; on the Parte Guelfa, their palace, and Donatello's statue *Saint Louis of Toulouse* for their niche at Orsanmichele, her *Brunelleschi and Donatello*. See also Haines, various, especially "L'Arte della Lana," on the involvement of guilds and their patrician leaders in public patronage. The Calimala Guild was responsible for the baptistery, San Miniato al Monte and Santa Croce. The Silk Guild had charge of city hospitals, as well as the *loggia* and *palazzo* of Orsanmichele. Goldthwaite, op. cit., 90–97, points out that lay building committees were a classical, but not a medieval institution.

93   "più ricco . . . più adornanza," Haines, *Sagrestia delle Messe*, 126–8.

94   Gilbert, "Earliest Guide," 37. The story continues that one of them made a mistake in the molding, an example perhaps of the sort of incident that contributed to Brunelleschi's derogation of some citizen "experts" in his conversation with Taccola, below, p. 440, n. 121. See below, p. 186, for Giovanni di Gaide's account of urgent consultations with Cosimo about the design of San Lorenzo after Brunelleschi's death.

95   Haines, op. cit., 127; on Capponi's private patronage see Kent, *Household and Lineage*.

96   Zervas, "Brunelleschi's Political Career," 636, and below, p. 275.

97   Vasari-Milanesi, *Vite* 2, 159, and Gilbert, *Italian Art*, 27; for the relevant documents see Poggi/Haines, *Il duomo di Firenze*, 333, ff.

98   Gilbert, op. cit., 29–30. A similar case of arbitration occurred when in 1458 Federigo Federighi, patron of the tomb of his uncle Bishop Benozzo Federighi, accused Luca della Robbia of not having installed the tomb in the church of San Pancrazio as agreed. This case was heard by the court of the Mercanzia; see Corti and Hartt, "Documents Concerning Luca della Robbia's Federighi Tomb," 31.

99   *Painting and Experience*, pt. 2 and 109; see also Jayne, "Choreography by Lorenzo," on Botticelli's *Primavera* and the dance.

100 See, for example, his *Ricordanze*, 25. The Cambio guild's contract with Ghiberti for the *Saint Matthew* specified that it be at least as big as the *John the Baptist* which he had done for the Calimala guild; see also Chambers, *Patrons and Artists*, 43.

101 See also below, p. 279.

102 It appears in the inventory of Lorenzo's possessions made in 1492, after his death. The date of its acquisition is of course unknown. See below, p. 244.

103 *Vite* 2, 203.

Chapter IV

1   MAP, XIV, 467, Cosimo to his son Piero, s. d.

2   Cit. Rubinstein, "Cosimo *optimus civis*," 16–17.

3   Brown, "Humanist Portrait," 192.

4   *Vite* 2, 168; cf. above, ch. 3. Despite his ultimately adverse judgment of Cosimo's intellectual abilities, Hankins, "Platonic Academy," 146, concluded that "it does not seem possible to doubt" this claim.

5   Field, *Platonic Academy*, 10–11; see also his deprecating reference to "Cosimo's 'introspective phase' . . . when late in life Cosimo began to question commonly accepted worldly values . . . " 3, and especially n. 2. He dismissed the judgment of Vespasiano on the grounds that he was "not especially learned himself."

6   Hankins, "Platonic Academy," 146. Cosimo was nowhere near as learned as most of the citizen humanists discussed by Martines, *Social World*, but his primarily practical concerns did not disqualify him from a literate interest in ideas. Cf. Hankins, op. cit., 156: "the picture . . . of Pletho kindling enthusiasm for metaphysical speculation within the breast of the shrewd and practical middle-aged banker . . . is implausible in the extreme." Field, *Platonic Academy*, 150, cites Hale, *Florence and the Medici*, 27: "According to the humanist Niccolò Tignosi, Cosimo's wisdom was as natural to him 'as flying to a bird, leaping to panthers, racing to horses and savageness to lions.' The absurdity of applying such comparisons to a gout-ridden old banker is obvious." Why illness, age, or business acumen should be inimical to intellectual enthusiasms is not clear to me.

7   See Bec, *Les Livres des Florentins*; Ciappelli, "Libri e letture," and below, ch. 6. See also Holmes, *Florentine Enlightenment*.

8   On this see Fanelli, "I libri di Messer Palla"; Fiocco, "La biblioteca di Palla Strozzi."

9   Spallanzani, *Inventari Medicei*, 79.

10 MAP, XIV, 467.

11 MAP, VII, 329, "forzeretto degli armati."

12 Connell, in his review of *I Ceti Dirigenti*, 369–70, pointed out that the date on the first folio of what has long been known as the inventory of 1418 was originally 1417, later amended to 1418. When he published the inventory Spallanzani, acknowledging Connell's observation and pointing in his introduction, *Inventari Medicei, xiii–xv*, to internal evidence which shows that it was largely compiled in 1417, adopted this date. As Connell and Spallanzani suggest, it seems likely that the amended date of March 1418 refers to the completion of a revision. A close examination of the manuscript, MAP, CXXIX, 54r–78v, suggests that pages were headed with the names of rooms, and their contents filled in later; in the case of Giovanni di Bicci's study, the contents were never added and the rest of the page was left blank. Several emendations and additions, some involving books, were made in the same hand as the amended date on the first folio. In these circumstances it seems most accurate to refer to the inventory as that of 1417/18, and to describe Cosimo's books listed there as being in his possession "by 1418," as I have done throughout this book.

13 See "Cosimo and his Books," and Spallanzani, op. cit., 20–23. It would have been impossible to write this chapter on Cosimo's reading before the appearance of De La Mare's landmark study. I am also particularly grateful to Francis Ames-Lewis, the editor of the volume *Cosimo "il vecchio"* in

which her article appeared, for kindly making available to me the advance proofs of the book so that I could pursue my own investigation of the manuscripts annotated by Cosimo, based on her citations and guided by her observations.

14 "Cosimo and his Books," 116. Sabbadini, *Le scoperte de' codici* I, 183, spoke of "quell'intelligente raccoglitore che fu Cosimo de' Medici." The inventory of 1417/18 was first published by Pintor, "Libreria Medicea," who also remarks on the distinction of Cosimo's collection.

15 Above, ch. 3.

16 See Wind, "Platonic Tyranny," 494, of Ficino: "che egli fosse stato il primo ad infondere questo particolare veleno platonico nella tirannia mercantesca di Firenze . . ." Garin, *L'umanesimo italiano*, took up the implications of this view in contrasting Platonic and civic humanism. His thesis was at once modified and disseminated by Martines, *Social World*.

17 These are the major questions posed by Field, *Platonic Academy*, especially introduction and ch. 1. He saw Florentine society not in its own terms, but through the lens of Gramsci's theories. Hankins, although his approach to the "Platonic Academy" is very different from Field's, is similarly anachronistic; he argued, 152, that Cosimo would hardly have entrusted a major cultural initiative to Ficino, "a dreamy, twenty-nine-year-old medical school dropout"; cf. Field, op. cit., 27, "nearly every humanist . . . was a law-school dropout." Cf. Davies, "Marsilio Ficino," 785, on Ficino's career as student and lecturer at the Florentine Studio. Ficino was already a student of logic there in 1451, and continued to study philosophy and medicine throughout the fifties; he was still described as a student of philosophy at the Studio in 1462.

18 Rucellai, *Zibaldone* I, 117. Hankins, "Cosimo de' Medici as a Patron," 89-90, proceeding from the assumption that all the acts of powerful men are explicitly calculated, as distinct from recognizing that they naturally have political significance, suggested that Cosimo supported and participated in humanist studies partly to impress his partisans who were educators and notaries, and pursued learning because the personal virtue it emphasized had "political implications." Cosimo had better reasons for acquiring a knowledge of the great works of classical and Christian literature, and patricians were not in the habit of shaping their personal lives to please men infinitely inferior to them in social status and dignity. Conversely, the admiration for classical values and virtues that patrons shared with scholars and educators, including those they employed as tutors or secretaries, was indeed a notable element in their friendship, as may be seen from the verses on friendship written for the Certame Coronario. On the association of friendship, learning, and pleasure, see Alberti, *Della Famiglia*, which drew heavily on Cicero's *De Amicitia*, a staple of Florentine patrician libraries. Cf. Field, op. cit., 33, that Florentine patricians "learned from the humanists the definition of friendship" only after mid-century, and even then found "little of its reality in their own class."

19 See below, n. 69 and ch. 5.

20 Brown, *Bartolommeo Scala*, 36; Panormita, *Hermaphrodite*, preface. Alamanno Rinuccini recalled Cosimo quoting from Cicero's *Dream of Scipio* as if he were reading it, *Lettere ed orazioni*, 62. We do not know how well Cosimo knew Latin, since he wrote nothing in that language; nor did he cite Latin authors in his letters, which were primarily concerned with

practical issues; see above, ch. 2. Field, op. cit., 11, can only speculate as to whether, if Cosimo read Gregory the Great's *Moralia* as Vespasiano claimed, in "only" six months, he was "plodding through the original or an Italian translation." Hankins, "Cosimo de' Medici as a Patron," 74-5, expressed the opinion that he did not read Latin, but in "Platonic Academy" he decided that Cosimo was "widely read in Latin literature and able to follow spoken Latin," 145-6.

21 See below, pt. 2; also Weissman, *Ritual Brotherhood*, 100.

22 See Grafton and Jardine, *From Humanism to the Humanities*, introduction. The "present-minded pieties" they sought to unmask, among them that "the rise of the classical curriculum and the downfall of scholasticism [represented] the natural triumph of virtue over vice" were also the pieties of the humanists' fifteenth-century audience. Cf. Proctor, "*Studia Humanitatis*," especially 815-16, on common quattrocento views of classical learning: "The original humanities offered confidence in a self, one's own self: they held out the hope that the deep and ongoing study of Roman, and to a lesser extent Greek, literature, history and moral philosophy would give people the strength of character to withstand the blows and guiles of Fortune, and, if they aspired to positions of leadership, the wisdom and virtue necessary to rule their own lives and the lives of others." While Proctor rested his argument against Grafton and Jardine on principle, since "there is no way to prove that [while studying grammar] . . . students would not also have been moved . . ." by tales of classical tragedy and heroism, the evidence assembled below in chs. 5 and 6, from personal literary compilations and private letters, makes it perfectly clear that they were. For a more subtle and complex view of humanism as "an educational program for the ruling classes," see Martines, various, especially *Power and Imagination*, ch. 11.

23 Below, pp. 70, 81-2; see also Cosimo to Ficino, Ficino, *Letters* I, I.

24 Juvenal, *Satires*, X, 346-9. On Francesco and the letters in which he cited classical authors see Kent, "I Medici in esilio," 24-5, n. 74, and MAP, V, 703, 693. Cf. Manetti's rehearsal of his classical and Christian learning in an attempt to console himself for the death of his child; Banker, "Mourning a Son."

25 MAP, CLXIII, 41b, published Rochon, *La Jeunesse de Laurent*, 47, n. 12. This letter is discussed below, p. 375.

26 Sabbadini, "Storia e critica di alcuni testi," 329.

27 Laur., Plut. 16, 31, 78v. De La Mare, op. cit., found no notations in any manuscripts copied for or acquired by Cosimo after about 1420, apart from Seneca's *Epistles* and Aristotle's *Ethics*. On the acquisition of learning and libraries early in life, see Bec, *Les Livres des florentins*.

28 Some of the books described as being "in Cosimo's study" in 1417/18 could have belonged to his brother Lorenzo, or been owned in common with him. There are no literary manuscripts listed in the inventory of Lorenzo's study; only "più libri et lettere del bancho di Giovanni sopra lo scriptoio," Spallanzani, op. cit., 31. However, there are gaps in this inventory, and although all the brothers' formal assets were jointly owned, books were considered personal property, like clothing. De La Mare observed, op. cit., 119, that Francesco Barbaro presented the dedication copy of *De Re Uxoria* to Lorenzo on the occasion of his marriage in 1416, and Cosimo later had a copy made for himself. Cosimo's autograph notations in his manuscripts help to identify his particular concerns; a strong impression of Lorenzo's personal

culture emerges from the comments of his intellectual friends; see above, ch. 3.

29 Below, pp. 78–9. The inventory of Palla Strozzi's books in 1431, published Fanelli, op. cit., contained 277 volumes, of which many were in Greek; he had been a pupil of Chrysoloras at the turn of the century.

30 Op. cit., 119. Gombrich, "From the Revival of Letters," has traced the underlying relation between the humanists' concern for the revival of antique calligraphy and Renaissance artists' revival of antique forms. Piero's library was particularly notable for the number of volumes he had specially copied and beautifully decorated by the finest humanist scribes and the best illuminators; see the detailed descriptions in Ames-Lewis, *Library and Manuscripts of Piero*; also below, p. 297.

31 On these see Bolgar, *Classical Influences*; Bec, *Les Livres des Florentins*.

32 De La Mare, op. cit., 19. An eleventh-century manuscript of Tacitus was brought to Florence in the second half of the fourteenth century by Boccaccio or Zanobi da Strada, and came into the possession of Niccoli by 1427 at latest, ibid., 122, no. 17.

33 A number of Cosimo's manuscripts bore annotations in Niccoli's hand, ibid., passim.

34 Rutherford, "Antonio da Rho." As Julian Brown pointed out to me, the occasional use of Lactantius as a Christian name which I observed in the scrutiny lists of 1433, ASF, MSS 555, is an extremely early indication of increasing Renaissance interest in this early Christian writer. As a tutor to Constantine's son, he could be seen quite literally as a bridge between antique and Christian learning.

35 On this see below, pp. 86–7.

36 De La Mare, op. cit., 133.

37 Ibid., 127.

38 See Vespasiano, *Vite* 2, 194. The Virgilian topos was very popular at the time; on topoi see Curtius, *European Literature*. But see also MAP, v, 597, Alesso to Giovanni di Cosimo in Rome, 12 April 1445; ibid. 605, 7 May 1445. On Cosimo's general interest in rural pastimes, see MAP, vi, 300, Nov. 1457, Cosimo at Cafaggiolo to Giovanni at Careggi, informing him that they were waiting for his arrival to slaughter the pigs, but if he did not return, they would do it themselves. Meanwhile, he should lend some grain to the *contadini* for the sowing. On the Medici gardens see below, pp. 299–300.

39 Cf. Field, op. cit., 11.

40 Only three volumes, all devotional works, were listed in the 1417/18 inventory of the contents of Giovanni di Bicci's *camera*; see Spallanzani, *Inventari Medicei*, 6. However, not only was the inventory of his study missing, but Giovanni, who was then over sixty, may already have passed on his library to his sons, as Cosimo later did in part.

41 On the exchange and circulation of prized manuscripts see Gordan, *Two Renaissance Book Hunters*; MAP, xiv, 467, cxxix, 62.

42 See De La Mare, op. cit., 131; Ullman and Stadter, op. cit., 22. On Guarino's possible influence on Medici domestic commissions, see below, pp. 258–9; for early Christian themes in Cosimo's patronage, see, for example, pp. 186–97.

43 For the history of Piero's collection and its relation to Cosimo's, and to the library of his younger brother Giovanni, who died in 1463, see Ames-Lewis, *Library and Manuscripts of Piero*. On the bequests of libraries and manuscripts in general, see Bec, *Les Livres des Florentins*.

44 A number of volumes which originally belonged to Cosimo passed to San Marco; see De La Mare, op. cit., passim. The *Moralia* of Saint Gregory, which Vespasiano tells us Cosimo once spent six months reading, appears in the 1417/18 inventory of Giovanni di Bicci's house, but is missing from the list of 1465. Cosimo's early library, as has often been observed, was particularly strong in moral philosophy, and above all in the works of Cicero; he continued for many years to acquire new editions of this author's works, but none of them appears in Piero's inventory of 1465. This is published by Spallanzani, op. cit., 139–61; for an earlier transcription and extensive comment see Ames-Lewis, op. cit.

45 Laur., Plut. 36, 28, 58v: "Io di quale virtù non so' tanto più forte che io ti possa rag[i]onare niuno mio fatto/ imperciò che tu inpalidisti sì tosto che niuno medicho midirebbe di quale malati[a] tu sentisi/ più che Piero che Giovanni che è pure aghuto che m'incresche . . . " If the inscription is indeed by Cosimo, it would give comfort to those convinced that he did not read Latin with ease. I wish to thank Gino Corti for his suggestions concerning the reading of this extremely difficult passage, of which neither of us succeeded in deciphering the remainder.

46 On Piero's special interest in history see Ames-Lewis, op. cit., 44–5.

47 On this see Hankins, "Cosimo de' Medici as a Patron."

48 Modern scholars tend to disagree about these. Hankins, op. cit., emphasized the eclectic nature of Cosimo's interest in ancient philosophy, pointing out that Platonic ideas, often derived from Cicero, balanced the traditional communal preference for Aristotle even in the early years of the fifteenth century. Field, op. cit., represented Cosimo as a late, if superficial convert to the Platonism that came to prevail in learned circles after the fall of Constantinople and the influx of scholars and manuscripts from the East.

49 See below, chs. 9 and 10.

50 See below, ch. 11, on the "civic" theme in the architectural ideas of Alberti and Filarete, and the relevance to the virtuous citizen builder of Cicero's *De Officiis*, explicitly invoked by Giovanni Rucellai.

51 Cf. Francesco di Giuliano di Averardo de' Medici's relation to himself of the classical exempla, cit. above, n. 24, particularly that of Hannibal, obliged by his fame and conquests to flee his *patria*, ending his days in exile.

52 Hankins, op. cit., 75.

53 See, for example, De Cossart, *Antonio Beccadelli*, and Hankins, op. cit.

54 Panormita's presentation manuscript is Laur., Plut. 34, 54, pt. 1. On Cosimo's jokes, see Brown, "Wit and Wisdom." On double-entendre, especially in Lorenzo di Piero's poetry, see Toscan, *Carneval du langage*. On the possible relevance of the homosexual elements of Florentine culture to Donatello's *David*, see below, pp. 284–5. Like Donatello's work, Panormita's *Hermaphrodite* was sophisticated, urbane, and heavily indebted to classical models. The *Hermaphrodite* was also explicitly homoerotic and misogynistic, but it was taken very seriously as a virtuoso imitation of Martial.

55 From my own reading of Cosimo's autograph letters, written in a hand which is extremely difficult and varies considerably from time to time, I could not with absolute confidence

identify these marginal marks as his. Dr. De La Mare's experience of books and book hands is formidable, and in view of other evidence I have seen of the use and marking of books, below, ch. 6, I am happy to rely upon her expertise. She is preparing a study on the content of the passages Cosimo marked for particular attention which will undoubtedly be illuminated by her immense knowledge of early Renaissance books and texts; my own brief summary meanwhile simply indicates the general relation between Cosimo's reading, his main interests, and the themes of his artistic commissions.

56 Other versions of the sign, in the form of dots or balls on a shield surmounted by a cross, are reproduced on the title-page of De Roover, *Rise and Decline* and Grunzweig, *Correspondance de la filiale*, xlv–i.

57 See also De La Mare, op. cit., 138.

58 Laur., Plut. 16, 31, 75v, 78v, 217r, 224r.

59 Ibid., 277v; cf. his observations in his *Ricordi*, op. cit., and Vespasiano's comments on Cosimo's moral vigilance, discussed above, ch. 2. See also the *Detti piacevoli* attributed to him by Poliziano.

60 162r, ff, 252v. This interest could have some relevance to Cosimo's illegitimate son by a Circassian slave. He and Lorenzo later freed such a slave by an act of manumission, below, p. 314. However, the fathering of one illegitimate child is hardly evidence in this period of gross dissipation. See Origo, "Domestic Enemy," and for some particular references to Medici slaves, Spencer, "A Note on Slavery."

61 Laur., Plut. 16, 31, 218v, 277v. For Cosimo's aphorisms on envy, see Vespasiano, *Vite*, and Brown, "Wit and Wisdom."

62 Conversely, the marginal mark in Cosimo's copy of Priscian simply notes a grammatical point, and his notation of Horace's *Epistles* seems to acknowledge a witticism turning on the impossibility of writing poetry in a city.

63 Laur., Plut. 79, 4, 14, ff.

64 Laur., Plut. 79, 19, 7v. Bruni's translation was made in 1420; see Hankins, op. cit., and Griffith, Hankins, and Thompson, *Humanism of Leonardo Bruni*. Cosimo married Contessina de' Bardi in 1413; Piero was born in 1416, Giovanni in 1421. Presumably on account of its perceived relevance to Florentine issues and experience, the *Economics* became extremely popular; see Soudek, "Fifteenth-Century Humanistic Bestseller." For the use of familial analogies by Florentine statesmen in council debates, see Brucker, *Civic World*, and Kent, *Rise of the Medici*, 284; for example, Giovanni Minerbetti went so far as to suggest that the communal budget should be managed from month to month, like that of the household, since "the tailor cuts his coat to suit his cloth." For these themes in Aristotle's works and in Dante's, below, p. 50 and 411, n. 79; see also Matteo Palmieri, *Della Vita civile*, especially ch. 9.

65 Laur., Plut. 45, 32, 71r; cf. Vespasiano, *Vite* 2, on Cosimo's hierarchy of virtues; also Brown, "Wit and Wisdom."

66 Laur., Plut. 68, 13, 22r. See also above, ch. 2, and below, pp. 278–9.

67 Laur., Plut., 50, 32, 57r; Rubinstein, *Government of Florence*, passim.

68 As De La Mare observed, op. cit., 138–9: "Would someone who was only interested in the outward appearance of his books, and who was building up a library of new humanistic books merely because it was the fashion, have hunted down second-hand copies of an expensive text (like Livy)

that he already owned because it had been made by a favourite scribe, Giovanni Aretino, or have acquired for himself so many second-hand manuscripts – precious for their texts but not at all showy – from the library of Coluccio Salutati?"

69 There is a rapidly growing literature in the new sub-discipline of "reading practices." See especially De Certeau, *Writing of History* and *Practice of Everyday Life*; Chartier, *Cultural History* and especially *Order of Books*, 1, on "the transience of reading, an activity that rarely leaves traces." Chartier distinguished between three tasks of the historian of books; an analysis of the texts, the history of books and their production, and "the study of practices that seize on these objects and these forms in a variety of ways and produce differentiated uses and meanings." He called on the reader, 7, "to reject this dependence that relates gaps in cultural practices to *a priori* social oppositions . . . [like] dominant and dominated or between the elites and the people . . . ," observing the reductive nature of a history of the book that "ignored the process by which a text takes on meaning for those who read it." See also Chartier's "Leisure and Sociability," on reading aloud in the sixteenth and seventeenth centuries. With reference to Renaissance practices see Grafton and Jardine, various, and Hankins, *Plato*, 118, ff., for a typology of formal reading in the Renaissance, which distinguishes between meditative, doctrinal, scholastic, imitative, allegorical, critical, and aesthetic. For more informal reading practices in fifteenth-century Florence see below, chs. 5, and 6.

Chapter V

1 Among the early proponents of this view were the authors of essays in Lytle and Orgel, *Patronage in the Renaissance*; see also Woods-Marsden, *Gonzaga of Mantua* and "How Quattrocento Princes Used Art." Orgel's *Illusion of Power*, related to Roy Strong's English studies, which have influenced many students of Renaissance Italian patronage, is not entirely appropriate as a model for the situation of most Italian princes, either of Church or state. Their authority, although much more clearly defined than Cosimo de' Medici's in Florence, was nevertheless more ambiguous than that of northern monarchs. Along with the rather complex case of Venice, Florence and the other Tuscan republics – Siena, Prato, and Pistoia – offered the major opportunities for civic, corporate, or citizen patronage in the first half of the fifteenth century. Leading Florentine artists such as Donatello and Michelozzo did some of their most important work in these cities; see particularly Lightbown, *Donatello and Michelozzo*. However, Florentine artists since Giotto had also worked for princes and popes, and after 1450 such major figures as Lippi, Angelico, Leonardo, and Michelangelo worked in a courtly setting. On this milieu, see particularly Warnke, *Court Artist*. Some recent studies that address the expression in artistic commissions of the identity and aspirations of politically prominent patrons in a variety of polities include Hersey, *Aragonese Arch*; Waddy, *Seventeenth-Century Roman Palaces*; Fortini Brown, *Venetian Narrative Painting*; Robertson, *Alessandro Farnese*. Of the studies of Medici patronage that emphasize its expression of political aspirations and power see particularly the work of McKillop and

Paoletti, and McHam, *Looking at Italian Renaissance Sculpture*, introduction.

2 Holmes, *Florentine Enlightenment*, established this point in his detailed discussion of the interaction between the ideas of intellectuals and educated citizens, and the innovations of artists. Among the many others who have stressed the high concentration of major patrons in Florence is Kenneth Clark, who in his popular television series *Civilization* attributed Florentine preeminence in the arts to the constant encouragement of the "most intelligent group of men who ever governed a state": episode 5, "Man the Measure of all Things," BBC-TV. See also the sociological study of Kempers, *Painting, Power and Patronage*, who found "the dynamics of Florentine patronage . . . were quite unique," 183.

3 This recent reorientation of early modern history is so marked that it hardly requires documentation. Particularly significant formulations of the major questions relating to popular cultural preferences include: Burke, *Popular Culture*; Thompson, "Patrician Society, Plebeian Culture"; Ginzburg, *Cheese and the Worms*; Darnton, *Great Cat Massacre*; La Capra, "Is Everyone a *Mentalité* Case?" The trend is less pervasive in Florentine studies, with a few exceptions, most notably in the work of Trexler, Cohn, and Weissman. See also the comments of Kent and Kent, *Neighbours and Neighbourhood*, especially introduction. On popular acclaim of Florentine artists, Donatello's reputation is evident in his appearance as the greatest living sculptor in Feo Belcari's *sacra rappresentazione, Nabucodonosor, Re di Babilonia*, cit. Janson, *Donatello*, 111–12. The significance of this reference to him has become clearer in the context of recent studies of theatrical representations; see Newbigin, various, and Barr, "Music and Spectacle." On Brunelleschi's popular reputation see Haines, "Brunelleschi and Bureaucracy"; also Battisti, *Brunelleschi*; Tanturli, "Ambienti letterari fiorentini"; Saalman, *Cupola*, especially documents, and below, pp. 82, 116, 122–3.

4 Foucault, "Archaeology and the History of Ideas," 135–40, entered an eloquent plea for the study "not of literature, but of that tangential rumour, that everyday, transient writing that never acquires the status of an *oeuvre*, or is immediately lost: the analysis of sub-literatures, almanacs, reviews and newspapers, temporary successes, anonymous authors . . . all that insidious thought, that whole interplay of representations that flow anonymously between men; in the interstices of the great discursive monuments, it reveals the crumbling soil on which they are based."

5 See, for example, Molho, "Brancacci Chapel," 69: "I would suggest that if there is any unity in the frescoes of the Brancacci Chapel it is to be found in the thematic cohesion which binds all scenes into one large propaganda statement on behalf of papal primacy in the administration of ecclesiastical affairs." See below, passim, for many other examples, and especially ch. 15, for a general assessment of the view of Renaissance art as propaganda.

6 See the studies of Ambrogio Lorenzetti's frescoes of *Good and Bad Government* in the town hall of Siena, particularly Rubinstein, "Political Ideas in Sienese Art"; Baxandall, "Art, Society and the Bouguer Principle"; Skinner, "Artist as Political Philosopher;" Starn and Partridge, *Arts of Power*; Greenstein, "Vision of Peace."

7 "Art, Society, and the Bouguer Principle," 40. See also the other contributions to the symposium for which this paper was written, cit. above, introduction, n. 32.

8 Bullard, "Heroes and their Workshops," 197, also observed this assumption of historians focused on the biographies of great men.

9 Grendler's studies of early modern education, "Schooling in Western Europe" and *Schooling in Renaissance Italy*, necessarily focus on a later period for which evidence is more abundant. In a brief comment in the latter work on Florentine schools before 1480, 71–4, he queried Villani's statistics of 1338 and suggested more plausible figures for the early fifteenth century, based on comparisons with better-documented Venice.

10 The fundamental study of the Catasto is Herlihy and Klapisch-Zuber, *Les Toscans et leurs familles*, which provides a demographic profile of the city of Florence and its inhabitants. The size of Florence's urban population altered relatively little over Cosimo's lifetime. It grew from *c*.37,000 at the time of the first Catasto in 1427 to *c*.45,000 in 1480; see also Brucker, "Economic Foundations," 8. Dal Poggetto, *L'Oreficeria*, published the occupational breakdown of all those who filed reports, taken from the machine-readable edition of the Catasto compiled by Herlihy and Klaspisch-Zuber. This provides no direct evidence about literacy, since the study was based not on the original *portate* submitted by citizens, but on the Catasto officials' redaction in their *campioni*.

11 For evidence from the Catasto of the wide diffusion of literacy among the working masses, including wool-washers and dealers in secondhand clothes, see particularly Elio Conti, *L'imposta diretta*, and Gene Brucker, "*Popolo Minuto*," *Documentary Study*, and "Voices from the Catasto." In this last work Brucker observed, 17–18, that "most Florentine lower guildsmen were able to read, write and keep accounts, skills that distinguished them from the majority of salaried workers. Their tax returns are a rich source for studying the levels of literacy and numeracy in this society." He also cited examples of the numerous citizens who boasted at the bottom of their declarations, "I have drafted this return with my own hand," as well as those who, like Meo di Biagio, transcribed a return for an illiterate friend or neighbor "because Maso di Miniato [a cloth weaver] cannot write." The signature of a cook, "Io Piero di Fruosino o rechato la sopra detta iscrita," Cat., 28, fol. 344, is reproduced here as it appears in his *portata*, the words all run together. F. W. Kent and Dale Kent, who used the *portate* extensively in their studies, *Household and Lineage, Rise of the Medici*, and *Neighbours and Neighbourhood*, found that most heads of households wrote their own returns; those who had others write out their reports usually added their own signatures. On Pennuccia, the dealer in feathers, see Kent and Kent, *Neighbours and Neighbourhood*, 114. For discussion and reproductions of other Catasto reports see also De Angelis et al., *Civiltà fiorentina*, 229–45.

12 See Verde, *Lo studio fiorentino* 3, 1011–1202, and passim, and Grendler, *Schooling in Renaissance Italy*, especially 102–3 for particular examples.

13 On the form and content of these books see below, ch. 6. While Lorenzo, Cosimo's grandson, promoted and contributed to vernacular literature in the popular style, which persisted long after the end of the fifteenth century, the period of its most widespread and socially diverse appeal

seems to have coincided closely with Cosimo's lifetime (1389–1464), from the last decade of the fourteenth century to the third quarter of the fifteenth. Flamini, *La lirica toscana*, is the classic study of Florentine popular literature, published more than a century ago. The most frequently copied popular poems are in Lanza, *Lirici toscani*. His two, very different editions of *Polemiche e berte*, 1971 and 1989, contain the texts of many works in the satirical style of poets such as Burchiello and Stefano Finiguerra, known as "Lo Za." See also the studies of De Robertis, especially "L'esperienza poetica," and Tanturli, especially "Ambienti letterari fiorentini"; also Branciforte, "Poetry as Document" and *Ars poetica rei publicae*.

14 An important exception is Lauro Martines's body of studies of vernacular poetry and *novelle*, and his *Power and Imagination*, in which he used popular poetry to show how, in the society of the early Italian communes, politics, and culture were similarly shaped by citizens' imaginative perception of the nature of power. See Martelli, "Appunti sulla poesia volgare," 713–14, for an account of more recent literary studies of this genre.

15 Grendler commented on the similarly diverse content of the curricula of vernacular schools, and the close correlation between the texts used in these schools and those most often included in the earliest printed books; see "Schooling in Western Europe" and *Schooling in Renaissance Italy*, especially 72–8, 304–5; on artisan education, 102–7; on vernacular religious texts, 279. He made the interesting observation, 305, that Dante, Boccaccio, and Petrarch were not normally taught in schools; see 143, 203. See also Bec, *Les Livres des florentins*, 383–91.

16 Below, this chapter, and pp. 120–21. See Franceschi, *I lavoratori fiorentini*, on the density of social relationships between wool-workers of various levels of skill, and with other artisans and laborers who worked crowded together in the city's major wool trading and manufacturing areas, particularly the *piazze* of San Martino and the nearby districts of the Mercato Nuovo and Porta Rossa. Their shops were crucial centers of the exchange of information and ideas.

17 On the intricate relation between the main texts and leading proponents of this movement, and the corpus and authors of a more generally plebeian or *popolaresco* culture see below, chs. 6–8, and Branciforte, "Poetry as Document," especially 4–7. Just as there is not one homogeneous "popular culture," but rather a body of texts popular in several circles that overlap with those of learned vernacular and Latinate elite culture, see below, ch. 6, there are significant gradations within the plebeian world of Renaissance Florence in economic prosperity, literacy, social visibility, and political influence. The important studies of the laboring classes by Samuel Cohn and also Richard Trexler generally lump together unskilled workers and artisans without discrimination; on this see below, pp. 120–21. On the need for clearer distinctions between the gradations of unskilled laborers and the many skilled workers in Florence's wool manufacturing industry, see also Stella, *La Révolte des Ciompi*, and Franceschi, *I lavoratori fiorentini*.

18 See Ginzburg, *Cheese and the Worms*, also the critical assessment of La Capra, "Cheese and the Worms." For Florence's Menocchios, see below, ch. 6. Their compilations might perhaps be used as the basis for a quantitative study of Florentine popular literature; to identify more systematically the texts most frequently copied would yield very significant

information about popular tastes and interests. At the same time, as Ginzburg observed, op. cit., xxii, titles "do not themselves furnish unequivocal data." Recent studies of reading practices, amongst them Darnton's "Readers Respond to Rousseau," cf. above, p. 404, n. 69, support Ginzburg's contention that whereas almanacs, books of piety and lives of saints may appear "static, inert, and unchanging to us," the manner in which they were read, including the interjection into the text of "the prevalently oral culture of those readers . . . modifying it . . . reworking it . . ." is of vital importance. The rubrics in which compilers justify the inclusion of particular texts and explain the circumstances in which they were produced are invaluable evidence of this process.

19 For an attempt to describe and account for the arbitrary nature of this usage in a single case, that of the chronicler Giovanni Cavalcanti, see Kent, "Importance of Being Eccentric."

20 The particularity of Florentine sources puts a whole cluster of difficult questions concerning the nature of popular culture in a different light. The earliest learned studies of a "popular culture," defined by folklorists of the seventeenth and eighteenth centuries, tended to explain the overlap between popular and elite cultures in terms of opposing alternative "trickle-down" or "percolate up" theories of the transmission of ideas. On this see Burke, *Popular Culture*, pt. 1, and Ginzburg, op. cit., preface to the Italian edition. Scholars still tend to defend the blanket applicability of one or other of these models, albeit in more sophisticated versions, but the Florentine evidence suggests a much more complex interaction between social groups and ideas in a society where literacy is widespread. Recently, the focus of historians' methodological attention has shifted toward identifying plebeian voices, whether in rural France, Germany, and Italy in the Renaissance, or in modern Russia and the Mediterranean basin, in non-literary records. Of many such studies see particularly Gurevich, *Medieval Popular Culture*, and Gellner and Waterbury, *Patrons and Clients in Mediterranean Societies*. Florentine scholars have applied the insights of ethnographic approaches, emphasizing the eloquence of social custom, ritual, and images as well as words. See especially Trexler, Weissman, and Klapisch-Zuber, various; also the anthropological studies of Geertz; Douglas, *Natural Symbols*, and Silverman, *Three Bells of Civilization*. Adversarial sources – legal records, court proceedings, and prosecutions – have been exploited to illuminate their objects in many classic studies of popular culture, including those of Carlo Ginzburg and Natalie Davis, following in the *annaliste* tradition of Emmanuel Le Roy Ladurie and Jean Imbert. Gene Brucker and Samuel Cohn have used criminal records extensively to describe the attitudes of the Florentine laboring classes. However, those who use such adversarial sources observe the difficulties of having to read them "against the grain," since they present both the artisan world view and its protagonists while on trial. Because of the high rate of literacy in Italian towns, particularly Florence, the availability of much more literary, as opposed to ethnographic and legal evidence of popular ideas, presents the historian with different problems and opportunities. Diaries and personal compilations of favorite readings offer more fulsome and positive evidence of artisan attitudes. The devotional literature of Florentine artisans has given Newbigin, Barr, Blake Wilson and Henderson insights into the quality of popular religious

feeling, of which we see a very different face in the records of many northern European post-Reformation societies, where religious conflict and heresy were prevailing issues. Thus Florentine records do not primarily support the emphasis of Foucault and his followers on "exclusions, prohibitions and limits," nor justify the question, *Archaeology of Knowledge*, xvii, as to "whether popular culture exists outside the act that suppresses it." Ginzburg, op. cit., xv, observed that "in the past historians could be accused of wanting to know only about the great deeds of kings . . . today . . . more and more they are turning toward what their predecessors passed over in silence, discarded, or simply ignored. 'Who built Thebes of the seven gates?' Bertolt Brecht's 'literate worker' was already asking. The sources tell us nothing about these anonymous masons . . ." Florentine sources do throw some light on the Brechtian question, as Goldthwaite's *Building of Renaissance Florence* has shown, and so does the artisan literature described below.

21 Like Renaissance humanists, many modern academics privilege the testimony of their fellow scholars of the past, as of the present, and regard the representatives of what they see as degraded forms of high culture with some disdain. Brown, *Cult of the Saints*, 28, cited the not untypical observation of a leading classical historian, A. H. M. Jones, *Later Roman Empire*, 2, 963, concerning the cult of saints: "Such silly stories had no doubt always been believed by the common herd, but it is a sign of the times that a man of the intellectual eminence of Augustine should attach importance to them." The loose association of "popular culture" with modern mass culture has added to its disrepute. On the essential quality of the latter as a commodity whose marketing makes it quite distinct from any pre-modern variety, even the so-called "popular" culture imposed from above after the spread of printing, see La Capra, "Is Everyone a *Mentalité* Case?" 77–9. Scribner, "Is a History of Popular Culture Possible?" summarized some of the essential questions raised in the vast literature on the problematic nature of the study of popular culture focusing on printed material; many of these do not apply to the individual handwritten compilations that are the basis of this study.

22 On this event, and for the text of Alberti's *protesta* against the judges, see Bertolini, *De vera amicitia*.

23 *Facetiae*, LXXXIII, 203.

24 Bruni, *Dialogues*, in Thompson and Nagel, *Three Crowns of Florence*, 36. Lorenzo de' Medici also raised this issue in his *Justification of the Commentary on his Sonnets*, ibid., 134–47. Bruni was an Aretine whose working life was divided between the service of the international papal court and his employment as chancellor of Florence. On his relations with the Florentine political and intellectual elite, see above, ch. 3; on his life and experience in general, Baron, *Crisis*; Martines, *Social World*, and Griffiths et al., *Humanism of Leonardo Bruni*.

25 The regular post of lecturer on Dante at the Studio was held in Cosimo's lifetime by various luminaries of the Florentine literary scene; see Park, "Florentine *Studio*," and below, passim. Some readings were held in the cathedral because more space was needed to accommodate the audience; for these gatherings, see Schalk, *Das Publikum*; also Zervas, *Orsanmichele* 2, 186.

26 Laur., Plut. 90, and inf. 47, 119v–120r: "Veduto già di molti piazze/ per diverse città ma di vicini/ vorà cantare lasciando

l'altre razze./ Bella mi pare quella de' Perugini . . . E posson dire nonne maggior/ che richordarsi del tempo filice dolore/ sì chome dise il nostro buono auttore [Dante] . . ."

27 On San Martino see Flamini, *La lirica toscana*; Becherini, "Un canta in panca," "Poesia e musica." Singers presumably stood up on a ledge set in the wall of the church a few feet above the ground to accommodate those waiting outside the building for services. Such benches were built into the walls of many churches as well as private palaces in the Renaissance. On this see below, ch. 11.

28 On one occasion the performer known as "L'Altissimo" sang for five days in succcesion; see below. Originally performances were staged mainly on Sundays and feastdays. On the latter see Iacopo da Voragine, *Golden Legend*, and De Roover, *Rise and Decline*, 184–6, who noted that the holidays prescribed by guild statutes left only 275 workdays each year.

29 Flamini, op. cit.; Becherini, op. cit. D'Accone, "Note sulle compagnie," especially 109–14, suggested that the power of these traditional popular performances was such that they probably served to retard the development in Italy of the more complex musical traditions of the north, and to account for the paucity of written musical manuscripts in this period. On music and performance in Florence see Barr, various, and Wilson, *Music and Merchants*.

30 Laur., Conv. Soppr. 109, 49r (SS. Annunziata).

31 On the personnel of the Florentine entertainment establishment, see Flamini and Becherini, op. cit.; Lanza, *Lirici toscani*, and below, pp. 48–50, 78. On the heralds, Trexler, *Libro cerimoniale*, and Branciforte, *Ars poetica rei publicae*.

32 See Renier, *Strambotti e sonetti dell'Altissimo*. The singer's most famous poem was described as "La Rotta di Ravenna cantata in S. Martino di Firenze all'improvviso dall'Altissimo poeta fiorentino, poeta laureato, copiata dalla viva voce da varie persone, mentre cantava," ibid., xii. The manuscript breaks off suddenly with the note: "Here some stanzas are missing, the last ones, because the poet was so inspired at the conclusion that the pen or the memory of the man who was taking this down could not keep up with him," Burke, *Popular Culture*, 67. The peak of l'Altissimo's career came after Cosimo's death, but a comparison of his material with that of the singers of Cosimo's youth shows that he continued to work in substantially the same tradition as they. He seems to have been little influenced by a new culture arising around Lorenzo de' Medici's "court" and incorporating some of the elements of traditional popular culture into a much more elitist context; see Newbigin, "Piety and Politics."

33 Renier, op. cit., xi: "Terren senza patron, sasso smurato . . . / statua bieca, hedifitio che cada,/ fronte senza capel, virtù secreta,/ corpo senza alma, cultor senza biada,/ pigro artigian, banchier senza moneta,/ ricco senza ordin, senza stil poeta,/ sarei, benigni uditor, senza voi/ nel far principio, nel mezzo et dapoi./ Tromba d'argento con suono importuno,/ arbor colmo di foglie senza frutto,/ nobil pittura posta in loco bruno,/ femmina con bei panni et volto brutto,/ . . . monarca al nome, al dominar niente,/ angelo al nome, furia all'eccellentia,/ buoni e discreti auditor sare'io,/ non havendo favor dal sommo Iddio:/ perchè da lui deriva la cagione/ dell'instinto che in versi mi fa dire,/ et dipoi voi, che amate l'opre buone/ lo riferite altrui, per far fruire/ questa virtù, che piace a più persone./ Così molti mi

vengono a udire,/ ma lo havere io di voi le banche piene/ nè da me, nè da voi, non pende o viene." For Cosimo's poem, see above, ch. 2.

34 Ibid., xvii.

35 See Martines, especially "Politics of Love Poetry;" also his *Society and History in English Renaissance Verse.*, and Branciforte, "Poetry as Document."

36 Renier, op. cit., xvii. On topoi of modesty see Curtius, *European Literature*, 83–5.

37 Renier, op. cit., xviii.

38 He refers here to the *Città di vita*, which Palmieri did not allow to be promulgated in his lifetime, and which was later condemned for its heretical content by the ecclesiastical authorities; see Rooke's introduction to Palmieri, *Libro del poema chiamato Città di vita.*

39 Ibid., xix–xx.

40 On this theme see Auerbach, *Mimesis*, especially ch. 7.

41 Renier, op. cit., xv.

42 L'Altissimo's verse is full of powerful visual images, and whereas he used words to paint his vast gallery of characters, his son Cristofano became an artist, and gave a face to several of the major figures on the scene of popular poetry. He painted portraits of Leon Battista Alberti, Luca Pitti, and, most notably, Burchiello. These portraits were posthumous, drawn not from life but from his imagination, buttressed perhaps by earlier images now lost. On this family see Haines, "Artisan Family Strategies."

43 See Lanza, *Lirici toscani* 1, 202–7: "Canzon' morale del detto messer Niccolò, dove pon' quello che dee fare il servo verso il suo signore e così il signore verso il servo." The reciprocity of spiritual services between rich and poor encouraged an acceptance of differing stations and conditions; see, for example, the statutes of the Florentine company of Santa Brigida, Laur., Ashb. 460, 48r, cit. Weissman, "Brothers and Strangers": "Blessed are the poor, for paradise will be theirs . . . the poor in this world need the rich for the sustenance of food for the body but in the other life the rich will need the poor for the sustenance of their souls . . ." Unbuttressed by such doctrines, secular loyalties might prove insufficient to maintain the cohesion of a traditional world. E. P. Thompson noted in his classic study of "Patrician Society, Plebeian Culture," exploring the ambiguous effects of the physical proximity and practical social bonds linking the dominant and subordinate classes in pre-industrial England, that the Reformation "left a remarkable dissociation between the polite and the plebeian culture," 393. Neglecting the capacity of religious belief to cement society in the fifteenth century, many scholars of popular culture assume that it was necessarily alternative or "in opposition," a verbal or dramatized threat to the social or religious orthodoxy of the dominant elite on the part of a hostile and subversive underclass. As Carlo Ginzburg acutely observed, such studies of popular culture are often "politically" motivated; moved, that is, by a desire to redress the injustice of centuries of historical neglect by turning attention to the losers instead of the winners of history. This is patently a concern of the Florentine studies of Cohn, Molho, and Field, among others. Of course there were also vigorous manifestations of hostility between the privileged and the deprived in the popular culture of Renaissance Florence, and its main texts and leading protagonists were expert in the literary subversion of ideal images; see particularly Lanza, *Polemiche e berte*. The

social grievances expressed in popular poetry are discussed at much greater length in Kent, *Fathers and Friends.*

44 On the wool industry see Hoshino, "L'arte della lana"; De Roover, "Florentine Firm of Cloth Manufacturers"; Goldthwaite, *Building of Renaissance Florence*, 42. On the number and variety of workers associated with the Florentine wool trade see Dal Poggetto, *L'Oreficeria*, 101–17.

45 MAP, XVI, 174, Tomaxo di Nicholò to Piero de' Medici in Pisa, 11 March, 1465. He seems to have been press-ganged: "sichè voi fati molte lemosine a Dio, se voi facti questo, che fati conto di chavare una anima fora delo inferno, e sempre io mentre che io viva sarò vostra bono schavo e servidore . . ." This rare example of the use of the term *patron* to mean the boss of the *bottegha* indicates the technical sense to which its meaning was restricted, like *patronus*, referring to the holder of patronage rights over churches or chapels. See the discussion of patronage terminology, above, introduction, v.

46 *Cronica* 1, iv: "E chiamaronsi Priori dell'Arte; e stettono rinchiusi nella Torre della Castagna appresso alla Badia, acciò non temessono le minaccie de' potenti."

47 See the reconstruction of Desideri Costa, *Chiesa di San Martino*, especially 24–30.

48 Appropriately enough, in view of the strong emphasis in popular poetry on satire and ribaldry, while Saint Martin's primary association was with charity, he was also the patron saint of humor, although this aspect of his persona was more fully articulated in England and Germany than in Florence. On this see Walsh, "Martin of Tours," who points out that the role of the beggar in Saint Martin's story provides an opportunity for grotesquerie in its representation. See also Toschi, *Invito al folklore*, 372–8, for the continuing Italian tradition of celebrating the eve of the *festa* of San Martino on 11 November as a mini-carnival, characterized by drinking, feasting, and the public denunciation of those who contravened the community's laws of acceptable social and moral behavior. The *festa* of San Martino marks the beginning of both the invernal cycle and of the vintage. According to a traditional proverb, "Per San Martino – si spilla la botte del buon vino." Saint Martin was the patron saint of the vintners, who had his image painted on the pilaster at Orsanmichele assigned to their guild *c.*1380; see Henderson, *Piety and Charity*. Surely Feo Belcari had this in mind when in his poem praising Cosimo and Piero's charity, he alluded to Cosimo's "good wine [which] slakes our thirst," below, n. 55. Alternatively Branciforte, *Poetry as Document*, 20, saw an allusion here to the Mass. These associations of wine with devotion and festivity are not necessarily incompatible. I am grateful to Dr. Walsh for the reference to Toschi's work.

49 See Kent, "Buonomini di San Martino"; on the dedications, Desideri Costa, *Chiesa di San Martino*, 98. It seems unlikely that this was the essential reason Cosimo chose it as the locus of his public charity, but the coincidence of its earlier identification with the Medici patron saints must have been pleasantly fortuitous. The church of San Martino may have become the headquarters of the Buonomini because the general shift of popular devotion away from nearby Orsanmichele, and an increasing emphasis there after the initiation of the sculptural program of 1411 on guild competition in artistic self-advertisement, suggested the need for a new charitable center in this crowded inner-city district of woolworkers. On these developments see Henderson, *Piety and Charity*, ch. 9, and Holmes, *Florentine Enlightenment*, ch. 6.

50 Beneficiaries at San Martino were less than usually the customary charitable targets, widows and orphans. They included a notable number of young artisans, fathers of families who withdrew from the rolls of those to whom the company gave bread as soon as they were able to earn it again for themselves. On the confraternity and its beneficiaries see Spicciani, " 'Poveri vergognosi' "; Kent, "Buonomini di San Martino"; Henderson, *Piety and Charity*, 388–97; Zorzi Pugliese, "Good Work of the Florentine 'Buonomini' "; see also Trexler, "Charity and the Defense of the Urban Elites" on the confraternity's very different character after 1470. The sources – three books containing information on the constitution, officers, beneficiaries and benefactors – are BNF, Fondo Tordi, 18, 1–3, and the archive of the still extant company of the Buonomini di San Martino. I wish to thank the *confratelli* for allowing me to consult their confidential records.

51 BNF, Fondo Tordi, 1, especially 1r, 63; also Kent, "Buonomini di San Martino." These names may be compared with biographies of major Medici partisans in Kent, *Rise of the Medici*, passim, and the names of the most influential citizens of the regime, Kent, "*Reggimento*." For Florence's wealthiest citizens in 1427, see Martines, *Social World*. On the Medici and their business associates, De Roover, *Rise and Decline*.

52 See Kent, "Buonomini di San Martino," 58–60. Alesso is a key figure of the Medici circle, whose appearance in various contexts, such as the consignment of Niccolò Niccoli's library to San Marco, above, p. 25, or the apportionment of patronage rights at Santissima Annunziata, below, p. 207, signalled a Medici presence, and the representation of Cosimo's interests. Many of the personal letters of the 1440s written by Cosimo and his wife Contessina were in Alesso's hand. See above, ch. 2. On Ser Alesso see also Kent and Kent, "Two Comments of March 1445"; Zervas, "Quos volent."

53 The Medici contributions continued to be recorded in the name of Cosimo's bank, described simply as "the bank," after his death.

54 That is not to say that their perceptions of society and charity were the same. This confraternity offers an illuminating example of how false it is for historians to feel compelled to construct a single, authoritative account of any particular institution or phenomenon. cf. above, ch. 2, n. 17. I am presently preparing a study emphasizing different and sometimes irreconcilable perspectives on the confraternity, as seen from the point of view of its Medici patrons, its clerical sponsors, Archbishop Antoninus and Pope Eugenius IV, its benefactors from various strata of society, both lay and and clerical, its administrators, mostly lower middle-class and artisan members of a tight-knit charitable and devotional establishment, and finally its working-class beneficiaries.

55 Lanza, *Lirici toscani* 1, 227. For Belcari's life and works see Newbigin, various, particularly *Feste D'Oltrarno*, especially 27–8. On Belcari and the Medici see below, this chapter, and p. 118. Belcari's *ricordo* for the church of San Lorenzo contains the most detailed description of Eugenius IV's reconsecration of the cathedral after the completion of Brunelleschi's dome in 1436; below, p. 126. On the close relation between Lucrezia Tornabuoni's devotional interests and the Medici palace chapel altarpiece, see below, ch. 13; for her writings, *Poemetti Sacri*.

56 On this see particularly Henderson, *Piety and Charity*. For the praise of Cosimo's charity by other popular poets, see below,

pp. 117–19; on his own perception of its role in his salvation, ch. 9.

57 BNF, Fondo Tordi, 3, 27v. Two of the Buonomini were shoemakers, who were particularly well represented among popular poets; one of these was also a recipient of the confraternity's charity, ibid., 13r. The present *confratelli* of the Buonomini request that scholars consulting their archives maintain the confidentiality to which they are committed, and not reveal the names of beneficiaries of the confraternity's charity.

58 See Renier, op. cit., xvii. In canto 67 of the *Reali*, L'Altissimo acknowledged the "uditor degni, uditor singular,/ che purch'io canti in versi questa historia,/ mi sovvenite coi vostri denari . . ."

59 MAP, XVII, 108, 24 May 1454; the quatrain appears also on the first folio of the compilation of literature celebrating Sforza's 1450 victory which Michele del Giogante made for Piero de' Medici; see below, pp. 53, 73.

60 On this issue see below, this chapter, and chs. 6–8.

61 For a detailed description of the repertoire, see Flamini, op. cit., 155–7; Rajna, "Cantare dei cantari"; Graf, "Il Zibaldone attribuito ad Antonio Pucci." There are at least two codices of the Pucci *zibaldone*; BNF, Magl. XXIII, 135, and Ricc., 1922. The contents of the latter include the book of Marco Polo da Vinegia, interesting testimony to the fifteenth-century Florentine taste for Eastern exotica, cf. below, pp. 90–92, and ch. 13.

62 On Florence's citizen humanists see Martines, *Social World*, and more irreverently, Bracciolini, *Facetiae*, LXXXIII.

63 The implications of the existence of this office and its tranformation in the early fifteenth century, especially for the development of Florence's civic self-consciousness in the Renaissance, her relations with the princely courts, and the growth of the art of diplomacy, have yet to be fully explored. Trexler, *Libro cerimoniale*, was the first scholar of this century to see the importance of the herald's office; he interpreted its significance as an attempt on Florence's part to compete with courtly life and ceremonies; for an alternative view see below, ch. 15. Branciforte, *Ars poetica rei publicae*, is the first monographic study of the herald's role, the incumbents of the office, and their literary production.

64 When Antonio di Meglio became ill, Anselmo Calderoni was elected as his substitute, presenting himself as "miles araldus," a title he earned in the service of Guidantonio Montefeltro, duke of Urbino. Branciforte, op. cit., clarified many of the misundertandings of previous scholars arising from the fluid and ill-defined nature of the post. She noted, 90–91, that before 1417 Antonio had no title, being described in payment records simply as "eletto a dir chanzone alla mensa de' nostri Signori . . ." After 1417 he was designated "Cavaliere di cortte." During this same period, that is, the end of the first and beginning of the second decade of the quattrocento, Zanobio di Landino, called Berardino, is described as "buffone e famiglio del palagio del popolo di Firenze e giocholatore de Signori"; he was paid much less than the heralds, who were obviously regarded as serious poets. I have adopted Branciforte's usage of the adjective *popolaresco* to describe the populist culture of a socially mixed group of Florentine poets.

65 See Trexler, *Libro cerimoniale*.

66 Laur., Redi 184, Mano di Giovanni da Prato, 139r–40r. On

the herald as part of the Signoria's *familia* see Brucker, "Bureaucracy and Social Welfare."

67   See Branciforte, op. cit, especially 147.

68   On Calderoni's poem ibid., especially 133–57, and below, p. 280.

69   See Branciforte, op. cit., especially 154–67. Much of this repertoire was copied into personal compilations. See, for example, Laur., Redi 184, for the songs of "Benuccio barbiere, canta per la Signoria"; Laur., Conv. Soppr. 109, 89v–92v, for the "tre virtù della S. messa del nascimento di Maria" by "Maestro Antonio che chanta in San Martino"; Ricc., 2732, Iacopo Borgianni, *zibaldone*, 90v, "Frottola di Messere Antonio di Matteo di Meglio Kavaliere araldo della Signoria di Firenze fatta in certi divisioni de' Signori . . ." This poem, published Lanza, *Lirici toscani* 2, 90–94, enjoins the Priors to harmony.

70   On Burchiello, see Watkins, "Il Burchiello"; Lanza, *Polemiche e berte 1972*, especially 192–3; MAP, v, 401; ibid. x, 378. A profound ambivalence, the product of close contact and constant exchange, rather than the distant and intractable hostility pictured by some modern historians, seems to have characterized relations between patricians such as the Medici and the articulate poor, like Burchiello, and ingenious insult was the stock-in-trade of popular poets. Typical of this is a crack at Burchiello by Messer Rossello Rosselli, a crony of the younger Medici, which aims glancing blows at class, homoeroticism, and clientage, using San Martino as a byword for luxury cloth: "Ma fa' che non lo inganni:/ dirai che 'l panno fu di San Martino／ di quel che tu facesti al masculino," Lanza, *Lirici toscani* 2, 451. Ambivalence was certainly the hallmark of Michele del Giogante's relations with his patrons, see Kent, *Fathers and Friends*.

71   On this see Flamini, op. cit.; Becherini, op. cit.

72   This letter is published in full by Buser, *Die Beziehungen der Mediceer*, 347–8; see Becherini, "Un canta in panca," for comment. Sigismondo Malatesta was also present on this occasion, so that the literary topos of the association of the heroic virtues of poets, princes, and military commanders was literally embodied in Cosimo's guests; on this topos, see below, p. 269, and for its relevance to the respective artistic oeuvres of Cosimo and his princely friends, ch. 15.

73   *Diario*, 3. Poliziano wrote in a Latin epigram entitled "De Antonio tusco extemporali poeta" of Antonio di Guido, cit. Branciforte, *Ars poetica rei publicae*, 167, "Tuscus ab othrysio Fabiane, Antonius Orpheo／ hoc differt: homines hic trahit, ille feras." This appreciation was not, however, universal. For a rather different view of his performances in the semiserious and obscenely vituperative tradition of poets' rivalries, or *tenzoni*, see the sonnet of Antonio di Cola Bonciani, "per maestro Antonio canta in panca," Lanza, op. cit., I, 324: "O puzzolente e velenosa botta; di mastro Antonio, imperio singulare di tutti i vizi e di tutto il mal fare,／ ne' qual hai fatta tuta persona dotta,／ tu se' cagion d'aver guasta e corrotta／ Firenze, se ci se' lasciato stare,／ e dopo cena reci, per cenare,／ per gran golosità di cosa ghiotta.／ E per adempier tua ingorda gola,／ un vil fattor non ti sarebbe bacco,／ bavalischio scorreto, ingrato e reo.／ Semiramis tu terresti a scuola,／ soddomitando il tuo merdoso sacco,／ ch'avanza di superbia Capaneo.／ Che malan ti dia Deo,／ porco, gagliofo, scelerato mulo,／ ch'eserciti la bocca equal ch'l culo."

74   On the popularity of this item on the Florentine's reading list, see particularly De Angelis, *Civiltà fiorentina*, 236, citing

Doffo di Nepo Spini, Ricordanze, CS 2a ser., 13, 50r, 59v: "Prestai a Giovanni di Scolaio degli Spini, il 16 ottobre 1428, la mia cronicha di Giovanni Villani in due volumi"; also Ciappelli, "Libri e letture," 274. Francesco Castellani, aged twelve when his father died in 1429, inherited seven books, including two chronicles, one of which was Villani's. In 1469 he lent his "Chronicle of Giovanni Villani" to Boccaccino Alamanni. For the inventory of the books of Messer Matteo Castellani, see Bec, *Les Livres des florentines*, 166–7; these included "sette quinterni di chronacha, in charta pechorina."

75   The Florentine republic resembled the Greek and Roman republics enough to encourage its citizens' strong identification with the classical world. On the legend of the Roman foundation of Florence see Rubinstein, "Beginnings of Political Thought," tracing the evolution of these ideas in Dino Compagni's history and Dante's epic poem. For the humanist emphasis on the republican nature of Florence's Roman heritage and its relevance to contemporary concerns, see particularly Baron, *Crisis*; Wilcox, *Development of Florentine Humanist Historiography*. See also Skinner, "Vocabulary of Renaissance Republicanism"; he stressed the continuity of republican language and ideals from the early communes of the twelfth and thirteenth centuries, boosted by the scholastic reliance on Aristotle in the mid-thirteenth century, to Petrarch and Bruni, who promoted interest in other major sources of republican ideology, particularly the works of Cicero and Sallust. On the popularity of these writers, see below, p. 83. The extent to which these ideas permeated citizens' conceptions of Florentine history is indicated in the first entry of Benedetto Dei's year-by-year chronicle of Florentine history, *Cronica*, 110: "72 anni fu posto Firenze inanzi che Christo venisse in Santa Maria e fu posto da Ciesere e da Ponpeo e da Marino e d'Albino, cittadini romani e nimici de' Fiesolani."

76   Modern scholars have continued to insist on measuring Florentine republicanism by modern standards, although as Jones, "Communes and Despots," and Bueno da Mesquita, "Place of Despotism," pointed out some time ago, the Florentine republic was not a democracy. Nevertheless, in 1427 about one in four of every adult males, including over three hundred artisans, might participate in the city's government by being eligible to hold major office. And however the odds and the consequences of exercising office were altered by Medicean modifications to the electoral system after 1434, Florentines continued to enjoy a very high degree of participation in government, by comparison with other contemporary states. For the figures from electoral scrutinies see Kent, "*Reggimento*"; Rubinstein, *Government of Florence*. Whereas other medieval communes had become principates by the fifteenth century, Florentine political life also remained popular in the sense of being constitutionally based on the *popolo*, as it had been since the late thirteenth century, when Florentine merchants and artisans asserted the equality or superiority of the self-made man over the magnates, the feudal blood nobility. For an interpretation of this movement, manifested in the establishment of the government of the guilds in 1260, and the Ordinances of Justice of 1293, excluding the magnates, see Martines, *Power and Imagination*; Najemy, "Guild Republicanism." For L'Altissimo's extrapolation of the same themes in his performances at San Martino, see above. Cosimo de' Medici and his fellow mer-

chant patricians may have replaced the feudal magnates, against whom the guilds of the *popolo* once united in self protection, as the most powerful threat to the integrity of the republic, but the guilds, which were the foundation of the Florentine polity, continued to play a role in it, however diminished; see Najemy, *Corporatism and Consensus* and "Linguaggi storiografici sulla Firenze." More importantly, as Najemy also observed, "Dialogue of Power," especially 278–84, the government of the ruling elite in the fifteenth century was shaped and modified by the popular ideology embedded in the institutions of Florentine government. He stressed the importance of persisting ideas "of consent and representation as the foundation of legitimate republican government, of officeholding as a public trust, of the supremacy of law, and of the delegated quality of all formal power; fictions all, to be sure, but ones that deeply affected the political style of the Florentine elite, modifying the means and forms of its power," 278. On these issues see also Weissman, "Commentary, Politics and Conflict." The present study of Cosimo de' Medici's patronage of art shows how profoundly Cosimo's actions and the image he projected were shaped by this popular ideology and opinion.

77 A series of biographies of virtuous Florentine politicians compiled by Giovanni Cavalcanti, dubbed by its editor the "*Trattato politico-morale*," demonstrates how firmly this connection was implanted in the minds of politically conscious citizens. On this work see Grendler, introduction to her edition, and Kent, "Importance of Being Eccentric," 131.

78 Weinstein, "Myth of Florence," traced the growth of these ideas from their origins to their flowering in Savonarola's Florence at the end of the quattrocento, in a vision which blended Rome and Jerusalem as elements of the Florentine heritage and destiny. The Book of David was one of the sources of these prophecies invoked by fourteenth-century religious leaders such as Giovanni dalle Celle. One of many prophecies ascribed to Saint Bridget of Sweden, but clearly of fifteenth-century Florentine origin, envisions Florence arising anew from her struggle with Milan, in a Joachimite-style prophecy drawing on Revelation 35; see Magl. VII, 1081, 12–15; 56–7. It is easy to see how in this context Cosimo might be regarded as a contributor to Florence's most glorious destiny, though as the idea of a mythical Florentine cultural empire developed, the Medici came to be regarded as antithetical to its triumph. Savonarola's ideas were widely embraced in Florence by citizens of all classes; see Polizzotto, *Elect Nation*. For the widespread popularity in Cosimo's lifetime of the works of Giovanni dalle Celle and Saint Bridget, see below, pp. 86–7; for their relation to Cosimo's patronage below, passim, especially chs. 9 and 13.

79 *Inferno*, XV; see also Davis, "Brunetto Latini e Dante," *Dante and the Idea of Rome*, and "Topographical and Historical Propaganda"; D'Entrèves, *Dante as a Political Thinker*. For the development of a Florentine "urban ethos" on the basis of these ideas, see Holmes, "Urban Ideology" and *Florence, Rome*. Apart from Dante's writings and comments on them, which were the items most frequently copied into personal compilations, other works which had informed the evolution of the commune and its institutions circulated widely in Cosimo's lifetime. Leonardo Bruni, chancellor of Florence from 1427 until his death in 1444, completed the translation

of Aristotle's *Ethics* in 1416 and his *Politics* in 1437. The Aristotelian view of the relation between household and society, domesticity and politics, is elaborated in the *Economics*, then attributed to Aristotle, translated by Bruni and presented to Cosimo in 1420 with his own commentary. On Bruni, Cosimo, and Aristotelianism see Rubinstein, "Florentine Constitutionalism"; Hankins, "Cosimo de' Medici as a Patron"; Griffiths et al., *Humanism of Leonardo Bruni*. Summaries and epigrams of the "Philosopher" appear in many compilations. Dante's *Convivio*, also a popular work, had built upon a passage from the *Politics* describing the natural need to extend the biological union of husband and wife to embrace successively the wider family, the neighborhood, and ultimately the polis, the Ciceronian and Florentine *res publica*, since as "the Philosopher says . . . 'man is naturally a political animal,'" IV, 4, cf. *Politics*, 1, 2. Thanks, perhaps, to Florentines' familiarity with these texts, the Florentine understanding of "political" never became entirely detached from the Aristotelian sense of *polis*, implying the acts of the collectivity of the residents of a city. In council debates in the mid-fifteenth century, citizens invoked Aristotle's authority in arguing for a humane administration of the republic, and the adoption of the *via media*, "'Aristotelico more'"; cit. Brown, "City and Citizen," 95; she also referred to an interesting cross-gendering of the metaphors of *patria* and parents. Archbishop Antoninus assumed Florentines to be sufficiently familiar with the Aristotelian dictum that "man is naturally a political animal" to play upon this phrase in asserting in his spiritual letters that "man is naturally a spiritual animal," *Lettere*, 144. These ideas are crucial to Cosimo's conception of his own role in Florentine society and others' perception of its expression in government and in artistic patronage; see below, especially conclusion.

80 See Cosimo's letters, above, ch. 2. For similar sentiments in the letters of other statesmen, among them Rinaldo degli Albizzi, see *Commissioni*, and Kent, *Rise of the Medici*, passim. On the public records, ibid.; Rubinstein, *Government of Florence*; Brucker, *Civic World*.

81 "Ma tutti per comune/ tirassero una fune/ di Pace e di ben fare/ che già non può scampare/ terra rotta di parte . . ." *Tesoretto*, 175–80, quoted in a poem by Anselmo Calderoni, in Lanza, *Lirici toscani* 1, 358.

82 See Brown, "Platonism in Fifteenth-Century Florence," 388.

83 See below, pp. 88–90.

84 See Watkins, *Humanism and Liberty*, for comment and extracts from humanist writings on this subject, particularly Bruni's *History of Florence*. See also Baron, *Crisis*; Rubinstein, "Florentine Constitutionalism," "Florentina Libertas," and Gino Capponi, *Commentari dell'acquisto di Pisa*, written in the first decade of the fifteenth century; also below, pp. 88, 276.

85 On this see below, pp. 62, 283.

86 In March 1448 Cosimo supported the imposition of a tax to finance war with Alfonso, King of Naples, asserting that "if this is a bitter drink, it has to be swallowed in the defence of liberty." By September, when it appeared that a war would be hard fought, but peace could be secured by a payment to the king, he argued: "If this were a struggle for liberty, no expense ought to be spared . . . but if peace could be had with little expense, it would be foolish to obtain it with greater sacrifices. Nor is it shameful for the republic to make some concessions to the king, as long as its liberty is safe;

especially as this city is dedicated to commerce, literature, and leisure," translation and original Rubinstein, "Cosimo *optimus civis*," 16–17. This was not just a statement for public consumption; Cosimo's private letters express a similar view; see above, ch. 2. See also his secretary Ser Alesso Pelli's classicizing gloss, in a letter to Cosimo's younger son Giovanni, on a recent Florentine military and diplomatic victory: "Sine timore de manu inimicorum nostrorum liberati serviamus . . . ," MAP, v, 418.

87 On the *David*, see below, pp. 281–6.

88 On Cosimo's interest in warfare, see above, ch. 2, and below, pp. 264–81. For popular interest in matters military, see the chronicles and diaries of Del Corazza, Dati, Landucci, and Cavalcanti, op. cit., representing a wide social range of Florentine citizens. This interest is reflected in popular compilations, below, pp. 88–90.

89 Renier, *Strambotti e sonetti dell'Altissimo*, xxv–xvi. Franco Sacchetti's *Rime*, an influential collection of poetry and songs compiled in the latter half of the fourteenth century, contained a number of songs similarly concerned with the battles of the French nobility.

90 De Roover observed, *Rise and Decline*, 184–6, that the wool industry depended on foreign markets, and was therefore particularly sensitive to war, which often led to unemployment; this might also help to account for their interest.

91 See above, ch. 2.

92 See Mallett, *Mercenaries and their Masters*, for an account of Florentine relations with the great quattrocento military captains.

93 See below, pp. 88–90.

94 Cosimo was traditionally viewed as the architect of the Peace of Lodi, which was indeed the high point of his diplomatic career; see Gutkind, *Cosimo de' Medici*, and Ady, *Lorenzo de' Medici*. More recent studies revealing the problems faced by the Medicean regime in the 1450s (described by Rubinstein, *Government of Florence*, though exaggerated by Field, *Platonic Academy*), and exploring Sforza's part in the politics of the peninsula (see especially Ilardi, "The Banker-Statesman and the Condottiere-Prince"), have led to a more balanced view of Cosimo's role. On Florentine interest in Sforza's career, as evidenced in popular poetry, see Flamini, *La lirica toscana*, 128–36, 161ff.

95 Lanza, *Lirici toscani* 2, 690–91.

96 On this see Paoletti, "Banco Mediceo"; on Sforza symbols in the Medici garden, below, p. 300. By 1456 Piero owned a cameo "with the head of Francesco Sforza"; see Spallanzani, *Inventari Medicei*, 94.

97 "Come sono stato per infino a qui buon figliuolo et servidore di quella excielsa Signoria, così delibero al presente essere, et molto maggiormente in futuro ò a essere sempre presto e pronto et apparecchiato di mettere lo stato, uomini, giente, danari et la persona in beneficio et conservazione et amplificazione dello stato loro, come potranno vedere per effetto," BNF, Magl. xxv, 676, 3v; on this compilation, see below, p. 73.

98 MAP, v, 623: "Voi arete sentito chome i Milanesi anno chiamato il chonte per Signiore e per ducha che è suta ghran novella; qui se n'è fatto ghran festa et ghran dimostratione perchè genneralmente è piaciuto a ciaschuno et anchora perchè qui a schripto lettere piene di tanta affectione et amore et con tale sommessione di parole che ogniuno è chontentissimo d'ogni sua essaltatione; chredo che hora si

doverebbe fare più facilmente quello che pareva a Nostro Signiore si dovesse fare; et dal chanto nostro si cercherà et farassene ogni opera possibile. Idio per sua ghratia metta buona pacie per tutto."

99 BNF, Magl. xxv, 676, 3; Feo Belcari also composed an elaborate sonnet for the occasion, published and discussed by Flamini, op. cit., 133–4. The popularity of Sforza's victory in 1450 may have owed something to Florentines' detestation of their long-standing enemies, the Visconti dukes of Milan. As one compiler of a literary anthology commented: "La Signioria di Milano debba tornare nelle mani de' discendenti di Sforza/ et non debba di poi essere a Bischonti mai più Signiori," Ricc., 1088, 43v.

100 Flamini, op. cit., 132–6.

101 Michele del Giogante, introducing the poem in his compilation for Piero, cit. above, n. 99. Iacopo Donati also wrote a poem in praise of Sforza; see Lanza, op. cit., 2, 588.

102 Lanza, op. cit., 2, 55–6, and above, ch. 2. Note the evocation of the later Medici motto *semper* in the key last word of the penultimate line: "che io non ami continovo e sempre,/ Francesco Sforza, sopra ogni altra cosa."

103 There are some notable exceptions to this general neglect. Devotional groups in the Veneto have long interested scholars for their impact on early Catholic reform; see for example Matheson, *Cardinal Contarini*, also Bornstein, "Giovanni Dominici, the *Bianchi*, and Venice," an important new study of this movement. Weinstein's work on *Savonarola and Florence* raised the crucial question of what prepared the way for the Dominican's enthusiastic reception in Florence. Becker, *Florence in Transition*, and Kristeller, "Lay Religious Traditions," drew attention to the influence of lay piety on Florentine civic and literary circles. On the Florentine church in the mid-fifteenth century, see now Peterson, various, and on Savonarola and the ruling class, Polizzotto, *Elect Nation*.

104 Weissman, *Ritual Brotherhood*, added the confraternity to the number of corporate institutions recognized as playing a vital role in Florentines' lives. Henderson, *Piety and Charity*, is the major recent systematic study of confraternities in Renaissance Florence; as he observed, 7, the confraternity exemplified "the interpenetration of the secular and sacred in the private and public life of the late medieval republic." See also the classic study of Meerssemann, *Ordo fraternitatis*; Weissman, "Importance of Being Ambiguous," "Taking Patronage Seriously," "Sacred Eloquence," and "Brothers and Strangers"; Henderson, "Penitence and the Laity," "Le confraternite religiose"; Verdon and Henderson, *Christianity and the Renaissance*; Eisenbichler, "Le Confraternite Laicali" and *Crossing the Boundaries*. For studies of performance and theater, see below, particularly notes on pp. 415–17.

105 See Henderson, *Piety and Charity*, 438–42, for Varchi's estimate of confraternity membership, probably based on the census of 1527, and the obstacles in the way of arriving at a precise figure; see also Weissman, *Ritual Brotherhood*, especially ch. 2. In the first half of the fifteenth century, the regulations of most brotherhoods prohibited their members from joining more than one confraternity. However, some citizens documentably belonged to several such organizations, and this practice increased after 1470.

106 See particularly Weissman, "Brothers and Strangers"; also Henderson, op. cit., pt. 2, on confraternal charity, and the growth of confraternal hospitals in the fifteenth century.

107 See especially Kristeller, "Lay Religious Traditions," 101–2, and "Marsilio Ficino as a Man of Letters"; also Becker, "Aspects of Lay Piety." Weissman, op. cit., and Wilson, *Music and Merchants*, offer particularly evocative descriptions of confraternal activities drawn from the records of meetings; Hatfield, "Compagnia de' Magi," published a number of sermons delivered by lay brethren.

108 *Ritual Brotherhood*, especially 118–19. While this analysis throws invaluable light on the social composition of one of the few confraternities for which extensive information survives, Weissman's findings are affected by the limitations of the categories drawn from his records. Florentines naturally identified themselves by membership of guilds or their affiliates, a classification that was the basis of the whole system of communal government and the organization of labor. However, the categories of textile workers – independent *sottoposti* or even some dependent *sottoposti* – included men very diverse in wealth, education, social standing, and opportunities for political participation. This is even truer of the broad categories of tradesmen and craftsmen. Apothecaries such as Luca Landucci, of modest income, were poles apart from the wealthy handlers of spices and drugs, or dealers in fur and leather. Notaries, although often professionally associated with judges, were, along with most doctors, closer in social standing to many craftsmen or shopkeepers. Finally, the category of those who did not identify themselves in terms of an occupation at all was likely to range from those who had no skills, and lived on the margins of society, through solid citizens who identified themselves more in terms of family than trade, to nobles and rentiers who were outside the system of the guilds. These patterns of Florentine usage, which defy scholarly attempts at classification in modern social terms, are apparent in many key sources of record, including particularly lists of eligibles for office (Tratte) and transcripts of council meetings (Consulte e Pratiche); see Kent, *Rise of the Medici* and "*Reggimento*." See also below, p. 77.

109 Weissman, op. cit., especially 68–74, and "Cults and Contexts."

110 Some did, of course, and the anxiety to expiate past sins no doubt increased with age; *laude* and *canzoni morali* testify to the impulse to repentance. On the prevalence of explanations of Cosimo de' Medici's patronage in terms of last-minute conversion, see below, p. 132.

111 Weissman, op. cit., especially 129 ff., 154–60.

112 On these and their role in Florentine ceremonial life see especially the company of the Purification, below, pp. 59, 66.

113 Wilson, op. cit., 35. Henderson's fundamental checklist of companies, *Piety and Charity*, 443–74, classifies them as one or the other, and his discussion treats them separately according to function; indeed part of his argument, tracing change in forms of piety and charity between the thirteenth and the sixteenth centuries, concerns the increasing predominance in the fifteenth century of penitential companies over *laudesi* groups. Naturally the studies of confraternities concerned with performance (Newbigin and Barr, various, also Wilson) lend weight to this distinction. At the same time Weissman, *Ritual Brotherhood*, 58, pointed out the difficulty of making sharp distinctions between *laudesi* and flagellant groups, and the importance of similarities in their spiritual experience, although his social and geographical analysis of their membership points also to some important differences; below, this chapter.

114 The performances of *sacre rappresentazioni*, like the persistence of the *laudesi* and the foundation of boys' companies, were particularly characteristic of lay piety in Florence, by comparison with other Italian cities; see Henderson, op. cit., 72–3.

115 On the *laudesi* companies, see D'Accone, "Le Compagnie dei Laudesi" and "Alcune note sulle Compagnie"; Barr, *Monophonic Lauda*, "Music and Spectacle," and "Singing Confraternity," and particularly Wilson, op. cit., who set them skilfully in their social context, and showed how perfectly their activities expressed the essential values of urban life. See also Henderson, op. cit., especially appendix, for the fullest list of these companies. D'Accone, "Le Compagnie dei Laudesi," especially 254, 258–60, discussed the singers they employed in the first two decades of the fifteenth century. The first of these groups, founded in 1244, became the Compagnia di San Piero Martire, meeting in Santa Maria Novella. For the singers of San Zanobi, ibid., 266–8; on Orsanmichele, 274–8. See also Cattin, "Contributi alla storia della lauda." D'Accone, "Alcune note sulle Compagnie," discussed the importance of oral tradition and improvisation in the music of the early fifteenth century.

116 Weissman, op. cit., 49; D'Accone, "Note sulle compagnie," especially 92. The singers of San Zanobi in 1470, ibid., 99, were all artisans; weavers, dyers, fullers, a lantern-maker, and a maker of spectacles. Companies competed for audiences. The most distinguished artists performed in the early fifteenth century at Orsanmichele, around the corner from San Martino; the fourteen-year-old Antonio Squarcialupi was already playing the organ at Orsanmichele in 1431, and he was still there in 1450; ibid., 102–4.

117 Wilson, op. cit., 70–73; Henderson, *Piety and Charity*, 78.

118 See Wilson, op. cit., and Barr, *Monophonic Lauda*, for the function and incorporation of *laude* into the framework of the liturgy.

119 Wilson, op. cit. There was a *laudesi* company attached to every major church in every quarter of Florence: in Santa Croce, Orsanmichele and Santa Croce; in San Giovanni, San Zanobi (the cathedral) San Bastiano, SS. Annunziata, San Marco and San Lorenzo; in Santa Maria Novella, San Piero Martire at Santa Maria Novella and the singers of Ognissanti; in Santo Spirito, Sant'Agnese (the Carmine), San Frediano, and Santo Spirito.

120 D'Accone, "Alcune note sulle Compagnie"; Barr, *Monophonic Lauda*; Wilson, op. cit.

121 Wilson, op. cit., 67–70. More is known of the music of the second half of the fifteenth century; see particularly Barr, op. cit., introduction, especially xi; as she observed, the entire corpus of surviving monophonic *laude* in the vernacular with musical scores consists of only two manuscripts. This is partly due to the fact that oral transmission was the principal practical mode of dissemination. See also Wilson, op. cit., especially chs. 2 and 3. On the Laudario of San Gilio, ibid., 63–6; also Henderson, *Piety and Charity*, 87. The majority of manuscripts that preserve fifteenth-century *laude* in musical settings were associated with the Veneto; the possible impact of Venetian traditions on Florence is discussed by Wilson, 167–76. On the close relation between *laude* and images, see below, pp. 104–6.

122 See also below, p. 71. See Wilson, op. cit., 165–6, on the *cantasi come*.

123 See below, ch. 9, pp. 135–6, and fig. 49.

124 On processional and miraculous images see particularly Trexler, "Sacred Image."

125 Neri di Bicci, *Ricordanze*, 21; Wilson, op. cit., ch. 5, especially 209.

126 Museo del Bigallo, Florence; see also Orlandi, "Il vii centenario della predicazione di S. Pietro Martire," especially 55–8. In the last decade of the fifteenth century the Buonomini di San Martino commissioned frescoes for their oratory of the prescribed acts of charity, painted by a follower of Ghirlandaio; see Spicciani, "Poveri vergognosi." Several confraternal images are reproduced in Henderson, *Piety and Charity*.

127 See below, pp. 105–6, and fig. 32.

128 Poggi/Haines, *Il Duomo di Firenze* 1, cvi–cix; Wilson, op. cit., 198.

129 BNF, Magl. VIII, 1282, 45r; Rubinstein, *Government of Florence*, 119, and Henderson, *Piety and Charity*, 156.

130 In the mid-thirteenth century 80 per cent of confraternities were *laudesi*, but after the middle of the fourteenth, flagellants increased at their expense, and constituted 46.7 per cent of all companies between 1440 and 1460; Henderson, op. cit., 41–2. Of the 90 confraternities known to have been active in this period, 10 were *laudesi*, 42 flagellants, 4 charitable, 11 were boys' companies, 14 artisan associations, and 10 engaged in miscellaneous devotional activities.

131 See Wilson, op. cit., 35.

132 Below, pp. 247, 259, and fig. 120.

133 Below, pp. 84–5.

134 Weissman, *Ritual Brotherhood*, 85–6.

135 On this cycle see *Golden Legend*, 1, 3, and below, pp. 97–8.

136 Henderson, "Penitence and the Laity," 240–41. The evening service was modeled on Compline, the morning one on Matins. On *lauda* singing in disciplinary companies see Barr, *Monophonic Lauda*, 24–6.

137 Cit. Weissman, op. cit., loc. cit.; see also Lanza, op. cit., 1, 386–8.

138 Weissman, "Sacred Eloquence," 257; Henderson, *Piety and Charity*, 113.

139 Henderson, "Penitence and the Laity," 243.

140 Weissman, *Sacred Eloquence*, 261; see also Bernard of Clairvaux's sermon on the grief of the Virgin at Calvary, cit. above, p. 6. The surviving fifteenth-century texts date mainly from the 1470s and 1480s, although lay sermons were a part of confraternal life throughout the fifteenth century.

141 Above, pp. 6–7; below, ch. 7, especially p. 97, on "imitatio Christi."

142 See below, pp. 153–5, and fig. 60.

143 Wilson, op. cit., 108. On faction in Florence before 1434, and its association with confraternities, see Kent, *Rise of the Medici*, introduction and ch. 3; on the Medici, their partisans, and San Lorenzo, ibid., ch. 1, iv, and below, pp. 179–83. See Wilson, op. cit., 216–7, for the ban of 1419 which excepted "any confraternity which is newly established with the license and consent of the Lord Priors." On Florentines' suspicion of meetings, see Guasti's comments in Albizzi, *Commissioni*, 3; Rubinstein, *Government of Florence*; Henderson, "Le confraternite religiose." Successive regimes were wary of the extensive interest group of the patrician lineage, especially when it was large; at the turn of the fifteenth and sixteenth centuries the Rucellai were forbidden even to attend church together; see Kent, *Household and Lineage*. At the other end of the social scale, prohibitions against confraternities were related to the desire to prevent their use as labor organizations, De Roover, *Rise and Decline*, 184–6.

144 See, for example, the letter of the organist Antonio Squarcialupi to his Medici friends, MAP, VIII, 131; also MAP, XVI, 67. The confraternity to which he belonged, probably the Zampillo (see below, ch. 13) was about to appoint new officers, through a system of drawing by lot analagous to that of the commune, which had proved so susceptible to Medicean manipulation. He informed Piero di Cosimo that "tonight the opposition party is going to enter through a certain place in the courtyard which leads into the company's rooms and hold a council of war there." Piero responded by sending round maces, shields, and retainers. The Zampillo met in the church of Santa Trinita, which before 1434 had been a major sphere of influence of the Medici rivals, the Strozzi; later in the century it became closely associated with the heavily Medicean company of the Magi; see Hatfield, op. cit. Ugo della Stufa wrote to Giovanni de' Medici in Rome in 1445, MAP, V, 571, that the *brigata* of his young friends was enjoying themselves at Trebbio, where Squarcialupi could not be restrained from playing his organ at all hours of the day and night, and the young men could talk of nothing but the confraternal elections. The popular poet, cleric, and notary Messer Rosello, another of Giovanni's cronies, was elected one of the captains of the Compagnia di San Zanobi on 9 April 1445.

145 Domenico di Niccolò Pollini wrote in his Ricordanze, cit. Rubinstein, *Government of Florence*, 119, that the confraternity of San Piero Martire was committed to promoting the welfare of its *confratelli* in every way, including "any mundane need, for example, because of a lawsuit or some other trouble" and also to support those "weak in the scrutiny."

146 Henderson, op. cit., 420.

147 In 1444 the regime tightened its control over elections to the republic's highest offices; at the same time proscriptions against its enemies exiled in 1434 were renewed, and still more citizens were banished or deprived of the right to hold office. A law of 1444 prohibited the participation in confraternities of the *veduti*, those whose names had at one time or another been drawn out of the purses containing the names of citizens eligible for the Tre Maggiori. The membership of the highly popular confraternity of San Girolamo was halved as a result of this law; see Henderson, *Piety and Charity*, 141–2. In the mid-fifties, the regime confronted its most serious challenge during Cosimo's lifetime; prohibitions against confraternities were issued in 1455, and again in 1458, when the Mediceans reasserted control with sweeping legislation enacted by a *parlamento*. Some companies were closed down for six to eleven years. On anti-confraternal legislation and its effects see Rubinstein, op. cit., passim; Weissman, *Ritual Brotherhood*, 117. See also Trexler, *Public Life*; Henderson, "Le confraternite religiose."

148 See Trexler, "Charity and the Defense of the Urban Elites."

149 BNF, Fondo Tordi, 1, i.

150 Saalman, *Bigallo*, 6–9; Poggi and Supino, "La Compagnia del Bigallo"; Henderson, *Piety and Charity*, 67–70, 354–9; Park, *Doctors and Medicine*. See also Passerini, *Storia degli stabilimenti di beneficenza*, 793–6; Orlandi, "Il vii centenario della predicazione di S. Pietro Martire," especially 55–8.

151 See Achenbach, "Iconography of Tobias and the Angel."

Alessandra Strozzi, when she heard of the sinking of a Florentine galley in Flanders while her younger son Lorenzo was at sea, prayed "che l'Agnol Rafaello l'accompagni," *Lettere*, no. 29, 282.

152 See Orlandi, op. cit., loc. cit.; also Henderson, op. cit.

153 On charity, see below, ch. 9.

154 David Peterson suggested in a personal communication that Cosimo's ecclesiastical patronage served "to legitimate power already acquired by identifying with existing (and emerging) strains of public religious sentiment."

155 See below, p. 177. The weavers may eventually have been displaced to premises on the Via San Gallo to make way for the expansion of the Magi in the 1450s. I thank Daniela Lamberini for this suggestion.

156 Kristeller, "Lay Religious Traditions," 108–11. Most of the evidence relating to the Magi company's spiritual life dates from the period after Cosimo's death; see Hatfield, op. cit.; also Henderson, op. cit., 461, for its transformation from festive to flagellant company. On Cosimo's personal contribution to the confraternity of Sant'Agnese on 20 November 1440, to help pay for its Ascension play, see ASF, Conv. Soppr., Sant'Agnese 24, 8r.

157 On the sermons see Lesnick, "Civic Preaching," 209: on Del Corazza's diary, see also below, pp. 81–2.

158 See, for example, MAP, V, 514. See also Cosimo to Piero, XVI, 333, concerning an imperial visit: "Messer Francesco da Padova dovra avere concessione da Roma di predichare della pace se n'anno voglia come Ruberto scrive, avisa quando altro va di nuovo."

159 See below, pp. 102–4.

160 Below, ch. 7. Although Machiavelli is better known for the cynicism of his *Prince* or the ribaldry of plays such as *Mandragola*, he was also the author of an "Exortatione alla penitenza"; see Henderson, *Piety and Charity*, 437.

161 BNF, II: IV: 250. Like many artists in the Medici circle, the musician was himself a patron and collector. On Squarcialupi's collection of luxurious manuscripts of sacred music, particularly polyphonic choral works, see Guenther, "Unusual Phenomena," 87–118; Becherini, "Antonio Squarcialupi e il Cod. Mediceo-Palatino 87."

162 See Hope and Gilbert, various, discussed below, p. 96.

163 The work of Ludovico Zorzi and Paola Ventrone, various, rightly stresses the complexity of this process; see also Pacciani, "Immagini, Arti." My purpose here is simply to underline the extent of popular interest and participation in public theater, and its general role in accustoming a large popular audience to the visual representation of religious and political themes.

164 Richard Trexler, in a series of studies, particularly *Public Life*, raised scholars' consciousness of the importance of the previously neglected role of ritual in Florentine lives. Subsequently a good deal of imaginative and illuminating research has addressed this theme; see notes below. Sources from criminal records to private diaries testify to how Florentines saw the streets and *piazze* of their city as the natural setting for social theater. For example, Benedetto Dei, *Cronica*, 37v–39r, listed in succession the streets of the quarter of Santo Spirito where he lived, the *piazze*, and the major festivals celebrated in the city. Cf. Trexler, "Florentine Theater."

165 Dati's account is published with comment in Guasti, *Le feste*, 4–8. On thirteenth- and fourteenth-century descriptions of city life by the Milanese friar Bonvesin della Riva and by

Giovanni Villani see Lopez and Raymond, *Medieval Trade*, 60–74.

166 Rossi, "Le lettere di un matto," 113–15.

167 Cf. the poem of 1407 entitled "La festa di santo Giovanni Batista che si fa a Firenze," Guasti, op. cit., 9–17. The author described at length the goods displayed in shops on particular streets, and dwelled lovingly on the details of women's dress and on the devices decorating various floats. This poem appears in several manuscripts, along with items including a watercolor diagram for calculating the dates of movable feasts; see, for example, Magl. VII, 375.

168 Guasti, op. cit., 7. The presence of such paraphernalia in churches, among them SS. Annunziata, below, pp. 202–4, is seldom taken into account in assessing the visual impact of permanent monuments, like Piero de' Medici's tabernacle or John XXIII's imposing tomb in the baptistery; on the latter see below, pp. 164–6, and fig. 66.

169 The triumphal cart was an essential feature of illustrations of Petrarch's *Trionfi*, and no doubt its frequent appearances in ceremonies and paintings informed one another. On the illustrations of manuscripts of the *Trionfi* see below, p. 76; on images of the *Trionfi* commissioned by the Medici, pp. 297–9, and fig. 146.

170 While this point is originally Trexler's, his extensive account of the San Giovanni festivities, *Public Life*, 240–62, interprets them in relation to a rather different view of Florentine civic life than the one presented here. See also Newbigin's comment on Palmieri's description, *Nuovo corpus*, xxviii–xliv, and Chrétien, *Festival of San Giovanni*. Palmieri's account is published in Guasti, op. cit., 20–23.

171 See Trexler, *Libro cerimoniale*, and his introductory comments.

172 There are similar descriptions by Dati, *Istoria*; Buoninsegni, *Storie*; Pietrobuoni, Priorista, BNF, Conv. Soppr. C.4.895; Dei, *Cronica*; Landucci, *Diario*; also in many narrative poems published by Lanza, *Lirici toscani*.

173 *Diario*, 20–21.

174 Ibid., 21.

175 The marble for the base of their tabernacle was sold to the armorers' and swordsmiths' guild by the workshop of the cathedral in 1417; see Janson, *Donatello*, 23. For the early appearance of Saint George in the San Giovanni parade, see Gori, *Le feste fiorentine*, 20; this figure was particularly noted by a Greek observer of the annual celebration in 1439, Newbigin, *Nuovo corpus*, xxvii. For the poem by Grazzini addressing the statue as "my beautiful Ganymede," see Janson, *Donatello*, 24.

176 See particularly Ventrone, "Thoughts on Florentine Fifteenth-Century Religious Spectacle" and "La Sacra Rappresentazione"; also Zorzi, "La scenotecnica brunelleschiana" and "Figurazione pittorica e figurazione teatrale." Fabbri et al., *Luogo teatrale*, especially introduction, emphasized the uniquely creative possibilities of perspective in theater.

177 On the objects in Cosimo's *camera* and his *studio* in 1418, pp. 292–3; on Neri di Bicci's workshop book, pp. 110–15; for his inventory of the property of the Sant'Agnese confraternity, Newbigin, "Ascension Plays," document 2, and *Feste D'Oltrarno*, 67–79.

178 See Trexler, "Sacred Image" and *Public Life*. Pope Pius II vividly described a Corpus Christi procession of 1462 in Viterbo, not unlike those in Florence, published Gilbert, *Italian Art*, 213–15. Each of the cardinals was allotted a section of the city to decorate. The pope had constructed a

tabernacle containing an altar "adorned with tapestries . . . and . . . many wonderful things . . . In a nearby room there were cloths or tapestries woven in silk, wool and gold, representing ancient tales and portraits of famous men." Among the cardinals' decorations were precious objects of gold and silver, statues, and *tableaux vivants* representing episodes from the life of Christ, elaborated in song and music.

179 Painted on leather, the figure is similar in style to the series of famous men and women that Castagno painted for the Villa Carducci, now displayed in the Uffizi Gallery, Florence. The classical model has been identified as the Niobid group, not widely known until mid-century; see Bober and Rubinstein, *Renaissance Artists and Antique Sculpture*, 35. See also Haitovsky, "Source of the young David," and Barolsky, "Castagno's *David*." The subject, and the evidence concerning Castagno's career and patrons, point overwhelmingly to a commission for display in Florence. Spencer, *Castagno and His Patrons*, 133, suggested that Orlando de' Medici, a major patron of Castagno's, may have commissioned the shield for ceremonies associated with the visit to Florence in 1451/2 of the Holy Roman Emperor Frederick III, when Orlando was knighted. On this see Trexler, *Libro cerimoniale*, 71–3. As Barolsky observed, viewers would naturally have associated this image with David's metaphor of God as the shield of salvation.

180 These might differ from one manuscript to another. See the different directions concerning dancing for *Abraham and Isaac*, in D'Ancona, *Sacre rappresentazioni* 1, 59, cf. Laur., Ashb., 539, 127r: "Di poi danzano un pocho onestamente e infine uno angelo licenza ognugno diciendo la infrascritta stanza cioe . . . Andate in pace . . ." There are clearly important differences between the traditional representations staged by the *laudesi* in local churches, the plays by Belcari and his associates based on a strong textual tradition, and the mobile performances which were set in the context of processions. Newbigin, "Word Made Flesh," 362, observed that plays performed between 1430 and 1478 "are conceived for performance in at least four different contexts"; they "are quite different in their use of space, narrative, language, and spirituality" from later *sacre rappresentazioni*, among them many based on Belcari's texts. In the introduction to her new edition of *Sacre rappresentazioni*, Newbigin drew attention to elements of similarity and continuity between various and evolving types of play, and argued that the procession performances included spoken texts. A fragment of evidence confirming this is appears in Magl. VII, 1168, 171r: "Sonetto di Piero de' Ricci a Re di 'Raona Napoli; parla uno ghiogante ane perlla festa di San Giovanni." See also Newbigin, *Feste D'Oltrarno*, appendix 1, for the texts of three of Belcari's important plays. Ventrone, various, sees a great disjunction between the various types of performance.

181 See especially Newbigin, "Word Made Flesh"; also Barr, "Music and Spectacle."

182 See below, ch. 13.

183 Hatfield, "Compagnia de' Magi," 112–13, 146. In the trecento Bethlehem was located in the baptistery, but some time between 1390 and 1429 it was moved to the Priors' palace, which almost doubled the length of the parade route, and perhaps also served to underline the commune's contribution to the staging of the festivities. On provisions for the festival in 1429 and 1446, see *Signori e Collegi, Deliberazioni*, published Fabriczy, *Michelozzo*, 93–4. The document of 1446,

22v, listed Michelozzo, along with Cosimo de' Medici, among the members of the company responsible for organizing the festivities.

184 These were installed *c*.1487.

185 D'Ancona, *Sacre rappresentazioni* 1, 41; for the elaboration of this theme, below, pp. 101–2. The second gate was hearing, and in addition to the recitation of the text, Belcari's audience had their "intellects nourished" by the singing of *laude* as indicated in the direction, 55: "Isaac porta il coltello in mano, e laudando Dio giù pel monte, va cantando così . . ." See also Becherini, "La musica nelle 'sacre rappresentazioni,'" and Smith, "References to Dance," including the stage directions, which show that dancing made an important contribution to the effect created by *sacre rappresentazioni*, for example, in expressing joy at the conclusion of the ordeal of the protagonists of *Abraham and Isaac*, above, n. 180. Brunelleschi, a designer of stage machinery for *sacre rappresentazioni*, imagined in his famous riposte to Domenico da Prato's scepticism about the viability of his cupola design the "celebratory dance" which would ensue when his scheme, derided as impossible, "should come to pass"; see below, pp. 123 and 485, n. 86. Filarete's famous signature on his bronze doors for St. Peter's, Rome, incorporates an illustration of such a dance.

186 Genesis 22: 11–12.

187 Newbigin, "Il testo e il contesto dell'*Abramo e Isaac*," makes a rather different point in comparing the narrative of Belcari's play to that of visual representations of the scene. The text translated here is taken from the combination of several partial manuscript redactions she published, among them D'Ancona, *Sacre rappresentazioni* 1, 41–59, the fullest published version. As Newbigin, 17, observed, much of the play's significance derives from the correspondence between Old and New Testaments represented by the analogy between Abraham and Isaac and God the Father and God the Son, an important example of the sort of symbolic reading of ideas and images to which Florentines were accustomed; on this see below, p. 96. For the significance to Florentines of reflections on fathers and sons, as evoked by this panel when installed in the old sacristy, below, pp. 191–2; also 194. On iconographic links between plays and paintings see also Newbigin, *Feste D'Oltrarno*, especially 16–18.

188 On these see particularly Newbigin, "Word Made Flesh" and Barr, "Music and Spectacle"; their texts and staging are the subject of Newbigin's *Feste D'Oltrarno*. The earliest description of the Ascension play is by Pietroboni in 1422, but Sacchetti in his *Trecentonovelle* made reference to such a play at the Carmine, and as early as 1425 there are entries concerning expenses for these performances in the account books of Sant Agnese; Barr, op. cit., 377–8. The customary reference to the company of the Holy Spirit as "il Pippione," symbolized by a white dove, is typical of the mixture of reverence and punning familiarity with which many Florentines spoke of matters of faith; for other examples, see below, ch. 6, passim.

189 See Newbigin, *Feste D'Oltrarno*, 7–12, on the question of whether the performance took place in SS. Annunziata, as generally assumed from Souzdal's reference to the "large church dedicated to our purest Mother of God," or at San Felice in Piazza, as was customary. That sacred plays literally brought the scripture to life is the theme of Newbigin's "Word Made Flesh." The purpose of the play is "to create real space somewhere between the unreal-because-intangible

world of God and the unreal-because-imperfect human world," ibid., 365–6.

190 For a discussion of Souzdal's descriptions see Newbigin, *Feste D'Oltrarno*, 1–21. Until recently, as she observed, 3, scholars have had to rely on an "Italian translation of a German translation of a seventeenth-century redaction of the fifteenth-century Russian text" published by D'Ancona, *Origini del teatro italiano*, 1, 246–53; see Danilova, "La rappresentazione dell'Annunciazione," for the significant points lost in translation. I rely here on Newbigin's new translation into English from the modern edition of the Russian text with Latin translation, 3–7, 60–63. See Ventrone, "L'eccezione e la regola," 427–30, for recent challenges to the attribution of this text.

191 For the high valuation of artifice as a quality of art, see Baxandall, *Painting and Experience*, pt. 3. On the machinery for the construction of the *cupola* see Battisti, *Brunelleschi*, ch. 8; on Brunelleschi's stage machinery and the likelihood that it was in use by 1422, Blumenthal, "Newly Identified Drawing of Brunelleschi's Stage Machinery"; Pochat, "Brunelleschi and the 'Ascension.'" Barr, op. cit., 382, discussed the inventory of Sant'Agnese's property made by Neri di Bicci, listing the items needed for the play and the uses to which they were put. See also her "Renaissance Artist," and below, p. 115. Newbigin, "Ascension Plays," reconstructed the function of the stage and its props.

192 On this see Olson, "Brunelleschi's Machines of Paradise."

193 On the music in this representation see Barr, "Music and Spectacle," 388–97. She also observed, 380, the striking parallel with the action of the liturgy of Ascension Day when, "after the reading of the Gospel, the paschal candle, which has been lit since the Easter vigil as a visible reminder of Christ's physical presence among mortals, is extinguished." Cf. also the description, above, p. 57, of the symbolism of light and dark in the services of penitential confraternities.

194 "La rappresentazione dell'Annunciazione," 173–6. See also Ciseri, "Spiritualità e spettacolo," for the opportunity these plays offered Florentines to play the dual role of participants and spectators of festivals both popular and sacred, experiencing the "sacralità dello spettacolo e spettacolarità del sacro," 455.

195 Ventrone, op. cit., loc. cit.

196 See below, p. 115.

197 On Piero del Massaio and his map, see below, ch. 11. For artists involved in the Ascension representation, see Barr, "Music and Spectacle," and "Renaissance Artist."

198 MAP, VIII, 136, cit. Hatfield, op. cit., 136–7.

199 See MAP, XI, 268, discussed below, ch. 13; also Ventrone, "Esperienze dello spettacolo religioso," 93.

200 Above, p. 47. One of the sources of the play as performed in Florence was Chyrsostom's homily on the Ascension, with which Cosimo was probably familiar, since he owned a collection of Chrysostom's homilies; see Hankins, "Cosimo de' Medici as a Patron," 75.

201 See Newbigin, op. cit., 363, and below, pp. 177, 340–41.

202 See Morçay, *Saint Antonin*, 473–4.

203 For these views see especially Ventrone, "Thoughts on Florentine Fifteenth-Century Religious Spectacle," 407–8. See also, however, her more recent study, "Lorenzo's 'Politica Festiva,'" which concludes, 115, that "Lorenzo's 'politica festiva' was less demagogical in character than it might at first sight have seemed," and refers in retrospect, 106–7, to

public spectacles which were "basically popular in origin and tradition," being nurtured by confraternities, guilds, and neighborhoods, and *sacre rappresentazioni* "fostered by intellectuals and churchmen such as Feo Belcari and Antonino Pierozzi, and followed with great interest by Cosimo de' Medici, with the aim to give children of boys' companies rhetorical training." See below, pp. 102–4, on Belcari's role in popular education, and p. 175, for the archbishop's swinging criticism of Giovanni di Cosimo's attempt to promote his partisans at the expense of the church, and Rubinstein, *Government of Florence*, 98, for Antoninus's public denunciation of open voting that would have favored the Medici party in 1458. See p. 102, for his comments in the *Summa* on art and errors of doctrine. The performance of the Ascension play of 1439 may be described as propaganda insofar as it seems to have been modified to reinforce the Western church's point of view concerning those aspects of the doctrine of the Trinity which constituted the major bone of contention with Eastern visitors and critics. See Ventrone, "L'eccezione e la regola" and below, ch. 13.

204 See Newbigin, "Piety and Politics."

205 This passing observation by Barr, "Music and Spectacle," 387, indicates how thoroughly such unsupported assumptions permeate the general literature that is the context of her specialized research.

206 On the origins of a general movement away from guild corporatism in the late trecento, see Najemy, *Corporatism and Consensus*; also Brucker, *Civic World* and "Bureaucracy and Social Welfare"; Brown, "Florence, Renaissance, and Early Modern State."

207 *Music and Merchants*, introduction and ch. 6, especially 1, 4, 6, 142–3. The first professional singers were nearly all artisans; see appendix 3. The earliest explicit references to lay polyphonic singers at Sant'Agnese occurred in 1442, ibid., 23, and they were identified as a furrier, a butcher, and two boy singers. Wilson will argue in a forthcoming study that "the extraordinary *quattrocento* culture of the Florentine *improvvisatori*, as well as the interrelated traditions of *lauda* singing and the civic *trombetti*, were manifestations of a relatively large and pluralistic environment that continued to nurture and articulate traditional republican ideals, and to do so through practices that were rooted in a Florentine past that was being mythologized by prominent Florentines like the Dominican Giovanni Caroli . . . All three were rooted in improvisatory modes (including memorization techniques) that made possible the spontaneous and affective performances required in popular public spaces. That all three continued to thrive in quattrocento Florence, despite the advent of an imported polyphonic culture that tended to undermine them in other cities, is a sure vital sign of the city's traditional civic culture." I am grateful to Blake Wilson for his permission to cite this personal communication. On the singer Niccolò Cieco's memory scheme, see below, pp. 91–3.

208 Signori e Collegi, Deliberazione, cit. Fabriczy, *Michelozzo*, 94. A similar phrase was used by the companies of Sant'Agnese and San Felice in their requests to the Signoria for aid; see Newbigin, "Word Made Flesh," 374, n. 30, cf. Giovanni Rucellai's much-quoted dictum.

209 A point also emphasized by Barr, op. cit., 397. Several of these early plays were written by members of the artisan class; the herald Antonio di Meglio collaborated with Feo Belcari on the Day of Judgment play, and the *Festa del vitello sagginato*,

the first Florentine Prodigal Son play, was written by the leader of the boys' company of the Purification, Piero di Mariano Muzi, a pursemaker. See Newbigin, op. cit., 363.

Chapter VI

1   Speaking in the Consulte e Pratiche of March 1448, cit. Rubinstein, "Cosimo *optimus civis*," 16–17.

2   Morpurgo, *I manoscritti*, surveyed some 3,800 manuscripts in the Riccardiana, of which the first 1001 are works in Greek, Latin, or oriental languages. His comparatively detailed description and index of nos. 1002–1700 made it possible to include their contents as general evidence of literary preferences, and easy to select a sample of compilations for closer examination. Along with formal books, like most of those in Cosimo's library, the Laurenziana also houses a number of very interesting scrapbooks. In the Biblioteca Nazionale there is an enormous quantity of these, relatively little explored by modern scholars; it is difficult to identify the most important from the very general information in inventories. Therefore the discussion which follows is based largely on the Riccardiana manuscripts, with the addition of those books in the Laurenziana and Biblioteca Nazionale identified by literary scholars as crucial to the study of popular culture, and particularly those owned or compiled by key figures in the circle that created it.

   Most datable manuscripts belong to the first three quarters of the fifteenth century, which coincides with Cosimo's lifetime. A good many others were produced in the last quarter of the century, during the lifetime of his grandson Lorenzo, but manuscripts compiled after 1470 are excluded from this survey, in accordance with the aim of the book to distinguish clearly the culture of Cosimo's era from that of Lorenzo; see below, ch. 15 and conclusion. The number of surviving works from the early years of Cosimo's life, the later fourteenth century, is relatively small.

   The sample of manuscripts considered here includes 140 from the Riccardiana, 30 from the Biblioteca Nazionale, and 30 from the Laurenziana. Comments concerning the popularity of particular texts refer to this sample. References to the number of copies of particular texts reviewed are made for the reader's information. These numbers are not useful statistically, since they represent random observation, and over-represent works in Morpurgo's index of Riccardiana 1002–1700. Impressions conveyed by these numbers are notably conservative; there are many more unexamined manuscripts in the Laurenziana and Biblioteca Nazionale.

   All compilations from the Riccardiana are from the main *fondo* (Ricc.) The *fondi* of the Biblioteca Nazionale cited here are the main *fondo*, under which many manuscripts from the Strozziane collections were reclassified after the original inventories were made (BNF), the *fondo* Magliabechiana (Magl.), and the *fondo* Palatino (Pal.) The Laurenziana *fondi* cited are Acquisti e Doni (Acqu. e Doni); Ashburnham (Ashb.); Conventi Soppressi (Conv. Soppr.) Laurenziana (Laur.); Redi; Segnani (Segn.); Strozzi; Tempi; and the *fondi* indicated by the system of shelving or *plutei* (Plut.). Transcriptions from compilations have been edited as little as possible to preserve the flavor of the originals, which derives in part from eccentricities of grammar, spelling, usage of words, and orthography.

3   See Schama, *Embarrassment of Riches*, 20, cf. below, notes 28–31, on compilations written in the Stinche. On the "political" potential of printed popular works see the general remarks of Burke, *Popular Culture*; for a particular example of such use of early Reformation printed pamphlets in Germany, Scribner, *For the Sake of Simple Folk*. The anthologies printed in Florence in the last years of the fifteenth century and the early years of the sixteenth drew on a repertoire similar to that of earlier copyists of manuscripts; see Grendler, "Renaissance Popular Books." It may be that like *ricordi,* compilations of popular literature were the product of a configuration of persons, education, and traditions particular, though probably not unique, to Florence. However, it seems likely that the printed anthologies published in other northern Italian cities, most notably Venice, were preceded by manuscript collections similar to those surveyed here. For a description of some similar, though not identical sources from the Veneto, see Grubb, *Provincial Families*, and his comment, 216, that: "Even in the most sympathetic treaments of spiritual life . . . subaltern groups emerge as essentially passive receivers of messages and audience of ritual. On the contrary, as the Venetian memoirs abundantly demonstrate, devotional writers, preachers, and organizers of ritual provided raw materials from which lay people constructed personalized religious views. Compilers had available a large and growing corpus of patristic and medieval wriings, sermons, popular texts, and learned treatises . . . they selected among their sources and so were active agents in shaping their devotions," cf. below. Florentine authors overwhelmingly predominate in Florentine compilations, but at least seven of them feature the poems of several generations of the Malatesta; Malatesta, Sigismondo, and Pandolfo. See also Ricc., 1103, and Morpurgo's comments, op. cit., 113; this manuscript includes work by Lorenzo Moschi, Antonio della Foresta, Antonio da Ferrara, Pandolfo Malatesta, and a Lombard work about the *Conte di virtù,* in addition to the usual Florentine staples, such as Petrarch's *Trionfi*. The Venetian Giustiniani was some-times included in Tuscan compilations, often as the only foreigner.

   Duffy, *Stripping of the Altars*, based his observation of the depth and breadth of Everyman's knowledge of religion and the liturgy on a corpus of English manuscript anthologies, apparently much smaller in number than the Florentine sources (he noted some fifty surviving from the fourteenth and fifteenth centuries), but very similar in their mixture of personal and business records, practical information, and popular literary selections, especially moral and devotional texts; see particularly introduction, and 68–84. The *Common Place Book of the Fifteenth Century,* ed. Toulmin Smith, which was found at Brome, contains a play about Abraham and Isaac; cf. above, p. 63, on Belcari's play of that name. Another English book which notably resembles its Florentine counterparts was compiled by Robert Reynes, a rural artisan of the village of Acle; see Louis, *Commonplace Book of Robert Reynes.*

4   On compilations, see Kristeller, "Lay Religious Traditions," "Marsilio Ficino as a Man of Letters," and *Iter Italicum*; Tanturli, "Codici di Antonio Manetti," "I Benci Copisti" and "Ambienti letterari fiorentini." It would be false to distinguish too precisely between copies of individual works, books containing several selections on a single theme — for example, Dante's poems, Bruni's life of the poet, and the *Con-*

fessione attributed to Dante – and anthologies of a wide variety of material. However, it should be noted that some individual texts were schoolbooks, or books acquired by chance or bequest; these may throw light on what Florentines knew, but are perhaps less revealing of what they were strongly interested in. Some of the texts in popular compilations were drawn from the either the Latin or the vernacular school curriculae in Italy in the later fifteenth and sixteenth centuries as described by Grendler, *Schooling in Renaissance Italy*, especially chs. 5 and 10. Of the former, he observed: "Renaissance Latin schools taught a small number of texts. This was in sharp contrast to the wonderfully ambitious programs of study prescribed by humanist pedagogical theorists." Extracts from these texts appear in translation in vernacular compilations. Cicero's *Epistolae ad familiares* was the text for rhetoric; his letters appear constantly in translation in *zibaldoni*. Terence, Horace, Valerius Maximus, Ovid and Caesar were also major Latin school texts; quite a few compilations contain Latin tags and *exempla* from these authors, and the last two appear frequently in translation. Virgil was used to teach poetry, and there are many informal copies of the *Aeneid* in Florentine libraries; however, the poet is only infrequently invoked as an *exemplum* in vernacular compilations. Of the vernacular curriculum, Grendler pointed out that it "emerged from the practical experience and lay culture of the Italian merchant community of the later Middle Ages. It developed without any guidance from above"; see "Schooling in Western Europe," 782–4. Among the works most often chosen for use in vernacular schools was Aesop's *Fables*, an immense favorite with compilers; conversely, Dante, Petrarch, and Boccaccio, whose works dominate the selections in most scrapbooks, were not part of the school curriculum. Also used in schools were Cavalca's devotional works, very popular with compilers, and Boethius's *Consolation*, of which there are a number of individual copies in Florentine libraries; anthologists often invoked Boethius as an *exemplum* of wisdom, and copied selections from the *Consolation*. Other school texts which appear in part or whole in compilations include the *Meditazione della vita di Cristo*, a number of chivalric romances, and various memory schemes, including Quintilian's and the *Ad Herennium* erroneously attributed to Cicero. On these see below, pp. 91–3.

5 *Zibaldone* 1, 2; see also Kent, "Making of a Renaissance Patron," and Perosa, "Lo Zibaldone"; below, ch. 15.

6 *Cronica*, 140. See also Ciappelli, "Art, Memory and the Family."

7 "Buono iscrittore, e buono abachista, e buono ragioniere," ibid., 47; in this work, the phrase "correvano gli anni" introduces most new entries. See also Dei, "Lista dei Personaggi"; Phillips, "Benedetto Dei's Book of Lists"; Frati, "Cantari e sonetti." Dei, born in 1417, had close personal links with key figures in the circle of popular poets: his brother Miliano married Papera, the daughter of Feo Belcari, and his brother Bernardo's wife was Bartolomea, a daughter of Goro di Stagio Dati. On these figures see below, passim. In Dei's list of letters received "in quarant'anni di tempo," were communications from Cosimo, Piero, Lorenzo, and Antonio de' Medici.

8 On the familial origins of Florentine records, see particularly Gilbert, *Machiavelli and Guicciardini*; Rubinstein, "The *Storie fiorentine* and the *Memorie di famiglia*"; Starn, "Francesco Guic-

ciardini"; Phillips, *Guicciardini: The Historian's Craft;* Kent, *Household and Lineage.*

9 BNF, II: II: 81. The author of this book was probably the son of Antonio di Ser Lodovico della Casa, from a family of notaries, who was a friend of the Medici in the 1420s; see Kent, *Rise of the Medici*, appendix 1 and passim. The contents included the poems of the herald Calderoni, the moral letters of the Vallombrosan Giovanni dalle Celle, poems by Dati, Davanzati and Alberti on friendship from the *Certame Coronario* of 1441, Chancellor Bruni's letters to Sforza and in defence of the Florentine war against Lucca, Filelfo on liberty and liberality, vulgarizations of various classical texts, and a letter of Saint Bridget to the women who served in the hospital of Santa Maria Nuova. Cf. Ricc., 1126, flyleaf, which specifies the line of the copyist's descent: "Questo libro è di Zanobi di Benedetto di Charoccio degli Strozzi et suorum decendentium da lato d'Iacopo." It remained in his line for at least two more generations; the next owner was Piero di Zanobi Strozzi, and after him, Antonio di Zanobi di Charoccio Strozzi. Cf. Ricc., 1546, 87v: "Questo libro ène di Piero di Ghuccio di Giovanni e sua dicendetti," and a similar comment by another of the Strozzi, Ricc., 1126; also Ricc., 1582, 147r: "Questo libro è scritto per Piero di ser Nicholò di Ser Verdiano, a chontenpracione di sé e di sua famiglia . . . 1458."

10 Ibid., 182r: "Nella volontà dela carne tosto passa via el diletto el piaciere./ Ma il pecchato in etterno rimane et simile e difetti et mali."

11 On this phenomenon, see also Grendler, *Schooling in Renaissance Italy*.

12 Ricc., 1556.

13 "Quelli che sono alletterati dovrebbono bene mettere la loro chura ne' buoni exempli – ciò che qui è scritto, sono tucte veritadi e sperience di veri e buoni exe[m]pli," Ricc., 1088, 3r. His was certainly an edifying selection, including Aesop's *Fables*, the *Vendetta di morte di Cristo* and a *lauda*, "Atte richorro Vergine Maria," 69r–70v, by "Dolcibene buffone." Also transcribed were the trecento poems of Dante, Guido Cavalcanti, Petrarch, Boccaccio, and Sacchetti, in accordance with the view that poetry was one path to truth and virtue.

14 Ricc., 1388, 181r: "dando refrigeramento nelle tributiatione e menomandolarci."

15 Ibid., 1185B, 52v.

16 Ashb. 539, 1r: "Questo libro si chiama libro di chonsolatione e da chonoscimento perchè ssi possono chonsolare choloro che delle tribulationi del mondo si sentono gravati ed amonimento a choloro chesono in rea via d'umiliarsi e chonvertisi chonsiderando il malvagio stato e pessima chonditione a che sono dati in questo mondo, e da chonforto e vigore a choloro chesono buoni di megliorare per quella speranza che mostra del guidandone."

17 Ibid., 80r: "Comincamento del mio trattato sarà al nome di Dio del quale cogedato hottimo e ogni dono perfetto che discende dal padre de' lumi di quanto amore e di quanta diletione la mia carità di padre a me la tua sugiezione di figluolo a pena te lo potrei dire a male una guisa nominare voglendo io al tenpo mio informare di vostri chostumi e dello amore e dela diletione di Dio e del prossimo e daltre chose e dalla forma della honesta vita ad amaestrarti . . ." On Belcari's *Abram e Isaac* and his dedicatory verse to Giovanni de Medici, see below, p. 192.

18 Cf. Darnton's account of the motives and choices of readers in eighteenth-century France, "Readers Respond to Rousseau."

19 Tempi, 2, 59r. See also Rosello Roselli's book, Ricc., 1088.

20 See, for example, Ricc., 1605: "Written in the hand of the said Giovanni Amici in the year 1454"; ibid., 1577, 50r: "Belonging to Giuliano di Giovanni de' Bardi, and copied in his own hand in the year 1416"; ibid., 1315, 69v: "Questo libro iscrisse Franciescho d'Iachopo di Gianni speciale a Merchato Vecchio, popolo di San Lorenzo, a dì primo di dicienpre 1378"; it contained works of Domenico Cavalca and of Saint Gregory. See also ibid., 1115, 224r, begun by Guido di Ser Francesco Ghuardi in 1448; ibid., 1689, 74v: "Written by the hand of the unfortunate Buono di Marcho del Buono Filippi Marchi . . . 1426."

21 Ricc., 1057. It later passed to the leather-worker Matteo di Bartolo, and later still to Giuliano de' Ricci.

22 Ibid., 1537, 247v–248r.

23 Above, p. 48.

24 Ricc., 1361, 109.

25 The first folio is dated July 1394; on the reverse of the 305th folio is written in words borrowed from the liturgy: "Dad deus laudamus te te dominum confitemur Compiuto di scrivere qui venerdi adi xxviiii di decenbre 1396 il dì di santo Tomaso di conturbia per Antonio di Guido Berti saponaio acchi i messere domenidio faccia grazia alla fine sua e a tutti i fedeli Xpiani Amen." See also below, p. 78.

26 Ricc., 1071; this miscellany was later acquired by Antonio da San Gallo, who made the index in his own hand.

27 Niccolò Davanzati transcribed his own book, Ricc., 1251, 87v, in the castle of Figline where he was Podestà in 1473; Gualtiero Biliotti had his notary write his (1355) while he was Captain of Pisa in 1422.

28 "Per rifrigerare e dare luogo alle mie passioni, e da quelle farmi lontano quanto era possibile, per obbliare le perverse e sì malvage genti, e le loro conversazioni, ellesi di scrivere della divisione de' nostri cittadini," Istorie fiorentine, 3. On Cavalcanti, and the ways in which his prison experience shaped his chronicle, see Kent, "Importance of Being Eccentric."

29 Ricc., 1543, written 1453, see fols. 27v, 39v, 1042, dated 1468.

30 Ibid., 1524, containing Piero di Crescenzi's Dell'Agricoltura; on the last folio is written: "Voi che leggete, chon divotione/ Porgete prieghi al sommo creatore/Che chi lo scripxe traggha di prigione."

31 Ibid., 1133, "Iacopo di Coccho Donati Ex Stinchis," dated Florence, 22 June 1451.

32 Ibid., On this obscure and unfortunate member of Cosimo's family see also below, p. 79.

33 Ibid., 1577, 50r: "O tu che mi legi, fa' che non mi chegi, però ch'io son Donatto/ a chi m'a chopiatto . . ." On Donatus's grammar see De La Mare, "Cosimo and His Books"; cf. the similar "Cicerone," which has passed into general usage.

34 Ricc., 1608. BNF, ii: xi: 35 is a book of laude very similar in size and shape, also with pages dog-eared from use.

35 Lanza, Lirici toscani 1, 383. Bernardo di Ser Iacopo della Casa had held an important public office in 1391. In 1433 the small Della Casa family was divided between loyalty to the Medici and their enemies; one member was exiled, another wrote a letter pledging his support to the Medici. See Kent, Rise of the Medici, appendices 1 and 2, and passim; also above,

n. 9, on the quaderno of Lodovico d'Antonio, notary to the Signoria, and probably the son of the Medici partisan Antonio di Ser Lodovico Della Casa. On Piero de' Medici and his books, see below, p. 297.

36 See BNF, Magl. iv: 250; also Ricc., 1088, 27r. See also below, pp. 73 and 79, for this "libricciuolo" of Piero.

37 Ricc., 1591, index and 16r.

38 Number codes were in regular use at least as early as the 1450s, and later employed in the correspondence of Lorenzo de' Medici's youthful brigata to refer not only to confidential matters of business and politics, as their elders had done, but also to very explicit accounts of their sexual adventures; see Rochon, La Jeunesse de Laurent, 132–3, especially n. 380. Cf. Ricc., 1142, where a line of letters is incised in a large rough hand across the tops of the pages. On Geta and Birria see below, p. 82.

39 Index, Ricc., 1591. The noun here is storie, which refers to both visual and verbal narratives. Ibid., 1052, is another compilation which ranges from the sublime to the ridiculous, including moral precepts from Cato, a treatise on the Holy Mass, the Credo attributed to Dante, two laude, the ternario of Niccolò Cieco to Eugenius IV, the Legend of Santa Cristina, Meditations on the Life of Christ, The Virtues of the Holy Mass, and finally the lewd and irreverent carnival songs of the Ubbriachi. On these see Lanza, Polemiche e berte.

40 Nor was there always a marked social difference between copyist and commissioner. In 1458 Nichola di Ser Dino di Nichola dell'Arte della Lana finished a book of commentaries on Dante and Boccaccio "a stanza e pitizione de Lazero di Michele di Piero da Varna del popolo di San Piero Ghattolino," hoping that "piacea addio che per a tempo e con santà lungha ne possiano comincare e finire degli altri, chon salute dell'anima e del corpo," Ricc., 1028, 241r. Cf. also Ricc., 1021, copied in 1462 by Piero Buoninsegni for the Albizzi family.

41 Ibid., 1098, especially 177v.

42 Ibid., 2815.

43 On this see Mauss, The Gift; Davis, "Gifts of Montaigne," and on Medici supporters' gifts to their patrons, Kent, Fathers and Friends; also the example above, ch. 2, n. 74, of Michele del Giogante's gift to Cosimo of a book of chess games, which his patron assured Michele would not be forgotten in the future.

44 For this see above, p. 47; below, ch. 7.

45 Magl. xxv, 676, 1r, flyleaf: "O famoso Piero mio di Cosme figlio,/ questo mio libricciuol ch'è tuo lo chiamo,/ perchè 'l Forte fatto è per tuo consiglio/ chè sai sognando di servirti bramo,/ con certe agiunte qual vedrai ch'i' piglio/ col tempo aute donde noi sappiamo,/ là dove sempre germinò tal fonte,/ palese all'universo non ch'al Conte." See also the inscription: "Questo quadernuccio o fatto cioè più scritto che fatto a stanza di Piero mio più che maggiore di Coxme de' Medici, andò a Milano adì 27 detto." On this compilation, see also above, n. 36, cf. Michele's compilation for his own use, Ricc., 2735, discussed below, this chapter. His dedicatory poem to Piero is published by Lanza, Lirici toscani 1, 672.

46 Ricc., 1563, 46–159; the rest of the manuscript is in another hand. On Baldovini, and the abbot of San Pancrazio's commission from Neri di Bicci of a picture of San Giovanni Gualberto including his own self-portrait, with many

other saints, see the artist's *Ricordanze*, 26–7, and Kent and Kent, *Neighbours and Neighbourhood*, especially ch. 5. On Giovanni and Pandolfo Rucellai see ibid., also Kent, *Household and Lineage* and "Making of a Renaissance Patron." On the Medici tabernacle for San Miniato, below, p. 202, and fig. 84.

47 Ricc., 1333, 1r–v. The dedication reads: "A Pandolfo Ruciellai in Domino salutem," but Pandolfo's name has been substituted for the original. This is no longer clearly discernible, but the family name appears to be Rucellai, and the first name could be Giovanni. The writer explained: "Le spiacevole occupationi e grave cure del secolaresco vivere non mi lasciano, come vorrei, conducerre a debito fine la cominciata opera . . ." Then after the index he continued, 14r: "Quantunque a me et a molti altri tu sia degno exempio, singulare lume, splendido spechio del vivere honesto, et ripieno non solamente della temporali, ma delle spirituali richeze; niente di meno più volte di richesto me, huomo sanza lingua e in ogni parte povero, che alcuna cosa ti scrivi delle maravigliose cose di Dio ne' nostri tempi dimostrate, et della doctrina et exempli di coloro che in questa nostra parte anno sanctificato . . ." See also Morpurgo, *I manoscritti*, 392, on the name of the dedicatee. Cf. Benedetto Dei's assessment of Pandolfo, published Corti, "Lista dei personaggi." Baldovini's book for Rucellai includes Petrarch's *Rime e Trionfi*, and his *Sonetti*, with the usual selection of *rime varie*, many of them devotional, including "Ave pastor della [tua] sancta madre," 94v–104v.

48 Magl. VII, 104, especially 4v, 57r. The names of the donor and the dedicatee of this book may not be the original ones; Betti's verse recommendation was copied in many collections, and he may have used it himself more than once. A later account of the assassination in 1478 of Giuliano de' Medici, when Sigismondo della Stufa played a heroic part in defending Lorenzo, is appropriately added to this volume. On portraits in Magi pictures as tributes to Medici patrons see below, ch. 15. The best-known examples belong to a later period; see Hatfield, *Botticelli's Uffizi "Adoration,"* and Borsook, *Mural Painters*, on the Sacchetti chapel in Santa Trinita; also Simons, *Portraiture and Patronage*.

49 See Kent, *Household and Lineage*, 274.

50 See Morpurgo, *I manoscritti*, index. The custom of keeping a *zibaldone* seems to have become popular in the later fourteenth century. Those books not dated by the author may sometimes be dated by the contents; for example, Magl. VI, 1121, contains the "Terze rime," cited below, passim, see index; portions of it must therefore have been compiled post-1460. Since that text is followed by a lengthy encomium to Piero, it was most likely copied before or just after his death in 1469. See also Ricc., 1939, dated Morpurgo, op. cit., 1443–6, and signed "Zibaldone di cose di Domenicho di Giovanni." Its list of contents is typical of this period: 1r, "Comincia illibro di Nicchodemo del nostro Signiore Yhu Xpo . . ."; "Tulio [Cicero] ai romani"; Bruni's letter to the Aragonese ambassadors; a list of the names and biographies of popes, a long comment on Eugenius IV; Niccolò di Francesco della Luna's poem on *amicizia* from the Certame Coronario of 1441; an entry entitled "Trionfo d'amicizia" by a doctor of laws, presumably named by analogy with Petrarch's six Triumphs; Petrarch's *Trionfi* and other works; Niccolò Cieco's poems, several *laude;* seven psalms; selections from Dante and Aesop.

51 There are among the Riccardiana compilations about a hundred such manuscripts. Morpurgo, op. cit., and Lanza have also identified a number of "apografi sicuri" (copies from an original manuscript). For a list of some compilations classified in these categories, see Lanza, *Lirici toscani* 1, 17–20.

52 Careful examination and caution are required before attributing any given entry to the choice of the owner or copyist identified on the flyleaf or elsewhere; see Morpurgo, *I manoscritti*, passim, for examples of multiple compilations bound together between a single set of covers.

53 Ricc., 1377, flyleaf.

54 Ibid., 1591, had five owners between the fifteenth and seventeenth centuries; see flyleaf, 175r, 217r–v. The first sent his book in 1462 to the workshop of Verrocchio to be illustrated, see below, p. 76, and inscribed his comments on each text in the margins in a large, rough, and uncontrolled hand, like those of the least educated filers of tax reports in the Catasto rolls. He used a thick nib and plenty of ink. The fanciful arms sketched on the first folio have not been identified. On fol. 47v there is an entry in another hand: "+1474, adì 6 di dicembre 1474, la quale addio per suo grazia piacci comendarlli." Subsequent marginal comments are in the same mid- to late fifteenth-century hand; its owner identified himself thus: "Trovasi al presente è questo dì xxx di maggio 1480 cassiere de banco de' Rabatti ed già stato mesi xxxviii." After him came a gentleman seeking his fortune at the papal court in 1480, and then "Pierfrancesco detto l'annebbiato [the frostbitten] nell' Accademia della Crusca." The book then passed to another member of this learned literary society dedicated to the preservation of the Italian language: "Simone di Giovanni Berti, cognominato lo SMUNTO" (the disreputable), whether on account of his taste for the ribaldry of *Geta e Birria* or for other reasons unknown. He bought the book on 13 October 1628, for 2 lire. Cf. Redi, 184, described as "Smunto's book."

55 Ricc., 1022, 204r: "Conperòllo da Bernardo del Nero, Bernardo di Andrea di Lipacio de Bardi, e suo è. Chostòlli fiorini 5, 8 di giugno l'anno 1451." This seems a rather high price, and if accurate may bear on the comparative value of books and pictures; Domenico Veneziano's Magi *tondo* for the Medici cost only 12 florins; on this, see below, pp. 255–9, and figs. 118–19.

56 Ricc., 1057.

57 "Tu che con questo libro ti trastulli,/ deh fa' che con le galle non s'azzuffi/ guardato da lucern' ed a fanciulli," Ricc., 1577, 50r; cf. ibid., 1275, last folio. Other owners were content with a more straightforward plea that borrowers return their books; e.g., Ricc., 1052: "Questo libro è di Francesco di Nicholò di Teri di Lorenzo Teri fiorentino: chi l'achatta lo rendi."

58 Ricc., 1275, flyleaf: "Detto libro chonperai io Antonio Ghuidi cimatore in Portarossa da detto Iacopo de Lione, lire otto; funne mezzano Giovanni di Iacopo da Brucanese, che fa gl'occhiali in Borgho San Lorenzo, sì chi l'acchatta sì lo renda a me, Antonio di Christofano detto, e guardilo da' facungli e da llucierne."

59 Pal., 54, flyleaf: "Sempre si dicie che uno fa male a cento,/ benchè a me non paia il dovuto/ peruno inganno ch'io o ricevuto;/ seghuire intendo tale ordinamento./ Prestai a uno e dico molto mi pento,/ uno libro. Et quando e l'ebbe assai tenuto/ e de provo ch'e me lavea renduto./ Dichè diciò mi convenne star contento/ de nonmi chieggia niuno

imprestanza./ Acciò che non mi avengha come suole/ ch'io perda il libro et ancho l'amistanza,/ ma pure se dicio fforzare mi vuole/ arrechi in be' si facta ricordanza/ che tener faccia in pie le sue parolle./ Chi non vo sanza schuole/ che niuno affari più alle mie spese/ che sia villano et io allui cortese."

60 On Cosimo's loans of rare manuscripts not only to his humanist friends, but also to a barber, see MAP, VII, 254. Astorgio Manfredi, wrote from Faenza to Piero in 1442, asking for a loan of "vostro canzonario delli sonetti del Petrarca per fare quello accoppiare . . . e diciò non ne dubitate niente . . . et cusì senza acuno fallo ve sarà restituito . . . ," MAP, XVI, 20.

61 "Se tu piacessi alchuno, chopisene uno," Ricc., 1577, 50r. This compilation consisted of the version of Ovid's *Epistles*, "Ridotte in ottavo rima da Domenico da Montecchiello," which was also Cosimo's famous schoolbook, perhaps he took his own advice and borrowed the text for translation from his Medici relative by marriage. Cf. Pal., 214, whose copyist described his discovery in someone else's book of an item he then added to his own compilation. It was a poem by Simone di Ser Dini da Siena dedicated to Giovanni Colonna in 1408; "sichome io scriptore Iacopo di Nicholò ho trovato scripto in uno Dante di sua mano il quale dice n'andò a donare al sopra detto Ianni Colonna . . ."

62 Plut. 90, inf. 35, 1; "Questo libro si è d'Alessandro Cerretani e suorum amicorum."

63 See Ricc., 2729, 2734, 2735. Lotteringhi also wrote BNF, Pal. 215. His handwriting is so similar to that of Michele del Giogante that it is almost impossible to tell them apart. On problems of identification, see Flamini, *La lirica toscana*, 243; Tanturli, "Ambienti letterari fiorentini." On Ricc. 2734 see Bacci and Della Lega, "Di Michele di Nofri del Giogante."

64 Van Eyck's personal motto was "als ich kann." On representation as a devotional act, see below, pp. 105–6. Davis, "Books as Gifts in Sixteenth-Century France," 72, also notes the medieval belief "that copying manuscripts was a meritorious and godly act (rubrication was compared to the blood of martyrs) and lending a manuscript an act of mercy . . . a belief that property in a book was as much collective as private."

65 Ricc., 1431, front flyleaf, dated 1469.

66 Ibid., 1689, especially 74v.

67 Ibid., 1254.

68 Ibid., 1023, flyleaf: "Et priega a Ddio che a ciaschuno che lo leggerà conceda . . . [partially erased]": 171v: "Qui scrissit scribat et semper cum domino vivat. Qui scripxit hunc librum colocetur in Paradisum. Anima scriptoris superni lettetur amoris." Cf. Ricc., 1364, transcribed by Ser Lamberto di Goccio Lamberteschi, who concluded his work in 1464: "Laus Deo: pregate Idio per me," 233.

69 See, for example, Ricc., 1577, a book transcribed for his own use by Giuliano di Giovanni de' Bardi in 1416, decorated with initial As and Os colored in pen and ink and playfully filled with little faces. For a list of manuscripts with miniatures, sketches and illustrations see Morpurgo, *I manoscritti*, 62–4.

70 Ricc., 1091, 225v, the portrait preceding Petrarch's sonnets. Biffoli's book also included Petrarch's and Dante's moral dicta, some *fioretti* of Boccaccio, a rhyme about the liberal arts, and Dati's *Sfera*.

71 Ricc., 1205. His book is a portable size *vocabolario italiano– latino*; its most appealing entry is the definition of *zabaione*: "epulum ex ovis et vino," 173r. For patrician family arms see also Magl. VII, 1120; this *libroncino* with charming illuminations is a copy of "L'armeggeria che fece Bartholomeo Benci composta per Filippo Lapaccini, 1473," and bears a particularly elaborate shield with crest. Ricc., 1021, Petrarch's *De Utriusque Fortuna* bears on the first page the Albizzi family's illuminated arms, and a fine initial with the figure of Petrarch in doctoral robes, crowned with the poet's laurel wreath and with his book in hand. Ibid., 1102, a much plainer manuscript with colored initials, contains Petrarch's *Trionfi* and *Canzoni* and the same treatise on fortune. The owner is unnamed. Ibid., 1137, "di Giovanni Battisti Doni," including Petrarch's *Canzoni* and *Trionfi*, bears a shield awaiting arms; ibid., 1534, a copy of books 1–10 of Villani's *Cronaca*, has those of the Guadagni, gilded and illuminated. Ibid., 1154 (see also Morpurgo, op. cit., 177) has colored initials, red rubrics, one gold rubric, and the shield of the Visconti/Sforza dukes of Milan. This manuscript is one of the few to include sonnets from all over Italy, some of them Milanese, and some poems by Malatesta and Sigismondo Malatesta.

72 Ricc., 1124. Cf. ibid., 1128, a volume of Petrarch's *Trionfi* and *Canzoni*, together with Bruni's *Life of Petrarch*, heavily decorated with ribbons, *putti*, animals, and the crowned shield of the Baldinotti arms.

73 This is sometimes attributed to his son, Francesco, Neri di Bicci's Landlord; see below, p. 104. The manuscript is Ricc., 1114. It seems to contain three different collections subsequently bound together. The first part appears in Morpurgo's and Lanza's lists of *apografi sicuri*. It consists almost entirely of fifteenth-century poems, although it begins with Petrarch and a "Pistola del Boccaccio." On fol. 10v there is a sketch garlanded with laurel and red flowers, and another version of the shield.

74 On the illustrations of Petrarch's works and the poet's attitudes to art see D'Essling, *Pétrarque, ses études d'art*; on the *Triumphs*, see also Carandente, *I Trionfi*, and Eisenbichler and Iannucci, *Petrarch's Triumphs*. On these themes in Medici artistic patronage, below, pp. 297–9.

75 See, for example, Ricc., 1109. The first selection, the *Inferno*, begins with a beautifully illuminated initial containing a portrait of Dante. The arms at the bottom of this page are unidentified.

76 Ricc., 1103, 10r: "In po/tans passa le gran pluie." The sketch appears on the verso of the last page of Petrarch's sonnets, ending, "O lasso a me diciera senpre el foco/ che tenpo chol pianto in chui ghiaccio . . ." Other selections include the verses of Antonio di Meglio and Antonio Pucci. Morpurgo, op. cit., 113, dated this first part of the compilation to the beginning of the fifteenth century. Laur., Conv. Soppr. 122, which includes the same treatise on fortune and various vulgarizations of Cicero's works, is also rather originally illustrated.

77 On painters' representations of the Trinity, see below, ch. 9. Ricc., 1392 contains Saint Catherine's "Dialogo della Divina Providenza," and a sketch, 5v, of "S. Caterina in cielo, in atto di adorare la Trinita e in terra un cardinale inginocchiato." Ibid., 1122, Ser Piero di Buonaccorso's volume, includes Dante's works and a memory treatise built around the figure of Santa Quaresima, elaborately sketched; on the treatise see also below, this chapter, p. 91. Ibid., 1309, 1r, has a fine illuminated portrait of John the Baptist, Florence's patron saint,

with the Quaratesi arms; see also 82v: "Finita è lla leggienda di Santo Giovanni Batista scritta per me Giuliano di [Quaratesi]; finita adì x di dicenbre, a ore 20." A copy of the revelations of Saint Bridget, ibid., 1397, 1r, has a large initial with the figure of San Bruno, holding in his left hand a wheel; 2v, a portrait of Christ, and 46v, "Santa Brigida e il demonio." On the popularity of this last work and its likely influence on the altarpiece of the Medici chapel see below, vi, and ch. 13.

78 Ricc., 1052; see also Morpurgo, op. cit., 47–8, Kristeller, *Early Florentine Woodcuts*, and cf. the northern European post-Reformation pamphlets in Scribner, *For the Sake of Simple Folk*. The manuscript images relate graphic depictions of corpses to the hope of resurrection through Christ and the saints. Particularly notable is a full-page image of Christ rising from the tomb with leaves of blood sprouting from heart and hands, 89r. Although not a direct illustration of the penitential psalms transcribed earlier in the volume, this image is very much in harmony with their tone: "Domine Dio non mi riprende nel tuo furore o nella tua ira non mi choregiere abbi misericordia di me," 11r.

79 One manuscript compilation containing this work, Ricc., 1071, passed to Antonio San Gallo; two other manuscripts owned by San Gallo, Laur., Conv. Soppr. 109, and Ricc., 1132, contained the *Trionfi* of Petrarch which inspired so much decoration. Dati's own book, Ricc. 1023, is an illustrated comment on Dante. Other illustrated manuscripts of the *Sfera* include BNF, II: IX: 137, belonging to "Tomaso di Tomaso." It also contained works of Boccaccio, and Manetti's tale of the trick Brunelleschi played on "Il Grasso."

80 Ricc., 1591. On these illustrations, see Brown, *Leonardo da Vinci*, p. 176, n. 25. The enormous discrepancy between these drawings and the quality and style of those attributed to Verrocchio suggests perhaps that even a major workshop might include, along with apprentices who would eventually become distinguished masters like Verrocchio's pupil Leonardo da Vinci, some hacks to cater to the simpler needs of the general populace. On the genre of "populist" art, particularly from the Finiguerra workshop, of which Giovanni Rucellai was a patron, see Maso Finiguerra, *Cronaca Illustrata*, British Museum, London; also Cropper et al., *Florentine Drawing*, especially Whitaker, "Florentine Picture Chronicle," 181–96; Petrioli Tofani, *Il disegno fiorentino*. These sketches suggest that artists as well as patrons regarded popular literature as a distinct genre with its own conventions; see also below, ch. 8. Cf. Ricc., 1129, which is decorated with a rich frieze incorporating the Della Stufa arms, and contains six large illustrations of the *Trionfi* in the very different, more "courtly" style of Apollonio di Giovanni, as seen in the Riccardiana *Aeneid*; on this below, p. 299.

81 Ibid., 175r: "Tutto chuesto libro è paghato: chostò lire dieci. Chostò lire tre e mezo la dipintura a[n]dre' del verrochino esta a chapo a via ghibellina; lire sette e mmezzo chostò la scrittura, a paghare piero de' rici. Paghossi detti danari a dì 12 di ferraio 1462 (s. f.). Chosta più la leghatura, e che ci arrogierai di più." Tanturli, "Ambienti letterari fiorentini," 127, and n. 27, identified the illustrations of Aesop and *Geta e Birria* in Magl. XXI: 87 and Ricc., 2805 as by the same hand; indeed the manuscripts are almost identical, although the drawings in these last two are perhaps of lesser quality. Also eloquent of the contemporary valuation of this book is its passage through the hands of six subsequent owners, includ-

ing two members of the seventeenth-century Accademia della Crusca. One of them, "Lo Smunto," also acquired Ricc., 2805; see above, n. 54. Better documented transactions between the various parties involved in making books are described by Brown and De La Mare, "Bartolomeo Scala's Dealings with Booksellers."

82 See particularly the account of the five layers of Florentine society as defined by Guicciardini in his comment on the scrutiny of 1494, published Rubinstein, *Government of Florence*, 318–25. See also the letters of Alessandra Strozzi, concerning prospective partners for her children, and on the same theme Phillips, *Memoir of Marco Parenti*. For the useful formula that social position depended upon a combination of family name, wealth, old blood, and civic participation, see Martines, *Social World*; for its fruitful application, Brucker, various, especially *Florentine Politics and Society* and *Renaissance Florence*; also Kent, "*Reggimento*" and *Rise of the Medici*.

83 For a lively evocation of the texture of this world and the daily experience of its inhabitants see Brucker, *Giovanni and Lusanna*. On the relative status of various guilds see Doren, *Le arti fiorentine*; Najemy, *Corporatism and Consensus*; Dal Poggetto, *L'Oreficeria*. The system of craft affiliates attached to professional guilds defies simple social classification; for example, apothecaries were associates of the major guild of doctors, as notaries were of the major guild of judges.

84 On Iacopo, son of the dyer Borgianni di Mino, see his compilation, Ricc., 2732; Kent, "Lorenzo di Credi"; Rossi, "L'indole"; Flamini, *La lirica toscana*, 319. Borgianni was a consul of the Arte degli Oliandoli in 1443, and in 1477 Iacopo was a member of the Otto della Guardia.

85 On the vulnerability to fire and loss of artisans' possessions, including works of art they commissioned, see below, p. 111. Lanza, *Lirici toscani*, includes the work of some hundred writers, half of whom were active mainly after Cosimo's death. Most poems which appear frequently in important compilations appear in Lanza's collection, but there are hundreds of other compilations which he did not consult; see his preface on manuscripts used, 1, 17–22.

86 On these poets' relations see particularly Lanza, *Polemiche e berte*, 1989 edition. Mariotto Davanzati sent a verse to Antonio Manetti "In Morte del Burchiello"; Betto Busini greeted the news of Burchiello's death with the lines: "Or piangi Marte nella tua Tessalia,/ e pianga Orfeo e spezzi la sua cetra,/ e per dolor Cupido la faretra,/ e Vener bella avampi le su' alia,/ perch'egli è spento un gran lume in Italia . . ." Lanza, *Lirici toscani* 1, 337, 353, 440. On Burchiello, see also above, p. 49; below, p. 118.

87 On the relevance of this view to the issues of class conflict, Cosimo's image, and the reception of his patronage, see below, passim, and especially chs. 8 and 15, and conclusion.

88 "Chi non può quel che vuol,/quel che può voglia,/ ché quel che non si può foll'è volere./ E quell'uom dico saggio da tenere/ che da quel che non possa il voler toglia./ però ch' ogni diletto nostro o doglia/ sta in sì o no saper poter volere/ . . . E però tu lettore di queste note,/ se vuoi vivere in pace e adio servire,/ voglia senpre volere quel che tu puote," Ricc., 1254. See Lanza, *Lirici toscani* 2, 133, for the text and some manuscripts in which it appears, in different variants. Given here is the standardized version from Lanza, except for the last two lines, taken from Antonio's manuscript. See Lanza also for Niccolò Cieco's extremely popular verse on the stations of life, their responsibilities and duties, 1, 202–7.

89 "Achorda il tuo volere con quel di Dio,/ e adenpierassi ogni tuo desio." The psalm actually reads, 3: "Trust in the Lord" and 4: "Delight thyself also in the Lord, and he shall give thee the desires of thine heart." On confraternal rituals and the liturgy, see above, pp. 54–7.

90 Cf. above, p. 70.

91 See, for example, the inventory of Palla Strozzi's library, Fiocco, "La biblioteca di Palla Strozzi"; also the inventory of Piero de' Medici's books in 1456, Spallanzani, *Inventari Medicei*. See also Vespasiano on Cosimo's San Marco and Badia libraries, and his turning to Pope Nicholas V for expert advice on the decorum of classification, *Vite* 2, 183. On the major effect of decorum on Renaissance behavior, Gaston, "Attention and Inattention," and below, ch. 11. Field, *Platonic Academy*, 11, noted the Italian popular and devotional literature in Cosimo's 1418 library, but exaggerated the quantity in deprecating the significance of his much larger Latin collection.

92 On Giovanni Gherardi da Prato, a major contributor to Florentine vernacular culture, see his *Paradiso degli Alberti*; also Lanza, *Polemiche e berte*, 1989 edition, and below, p. 123.

93 Del Lungo, "Un Pensiero a Dante," 450–7, re-told a story from a letter of Manetti, which he reprinted, 456–7. Lorenzo was thought to be the first to have the idea of recovering Dante's bones from Ravenna, but according to Manetti, Benedetto Dei was sent by Cosimo to treat with Ostasio da Polenta only a few years after the lord of Padua had refused the Signoria's request that Dante's remains be returned to Florence.

94 Identified by De La Mare, "Cosimo and his Books," 125, as Alexander de Villa Dei.

95 See Morpurgo, passim; Bandini, *Supplementum*, XI, Bertolini, "Censimento dei manoscritti della *Sfera*." De La Mare, op. cit., 126, no. 63, suggested perhaps it was a globe, but this seems unlikely, as it appears as part of a list of books, whereas the many other objects in Cosimo's study were listed separately. See below, pp. 292–4. Note also the books presented to Cosimo, listed in Hankins, "Cosimo de' Medici as a Patron," 75, including translations of Saint Ephraem of Syria's sermons and of Saint Chyrsostom's homilies, presumably including the one on the Ascension that inspired the Sant' Agnese *sacra rappresentazione*; see above, pp. 64–5.

96 Piero's inventories of 1456 and 1465 also include a number of devotional and popular vernacular titles; see Spallanzani, *Inventari Medicei*.

97 On Florentine libraries see Bec, *Les Livres des florentins*; also Verde, *Lo studio fiorentino* 1, especially appendix, and "Libri tra le pareti"; Ciappelli, "Libri e letture"; Tanturli, "Benci Copisti"; De La Mare, "Library of Francesco Sassetti." Verde's notices of Florentines' vernacular books, including those owned by families important for their patronage of the arts and their relations with the Medici, such as the Della Stufa, 8, and the Portinari, 11, are mainly from the end of the century. Only one library with more than thirty volumes passed through the hands of the Pupilli between 1413 and 1453; see Bec, 20–21. But their records may reflect a particular and rather limited sample of Florentine property; see Ciappelli, op. cit. Most Florentines owned at least a few books, which as Bec observed constituted "un fond commun de livres-lectures-connaissances," 22–3. By his count, there were at least "779 ouvrages, dont 654 répertories." The total included nine Greek authors, 150 Latin, 219 works on reli-

gion, 185 medieval authors, 91 technical works, and at least 125 works were not identified. Translated into percentages, religious works constituted 28.11 per cent of the total, medieval authors 23.74 per cent, Latin 19.25 per cent, Greek 1.15 per cent, unidentified 16.04 per cent, technical 11.68 per cent. Notably most of the collections in the Pupilli records belonged to patricians with family names. The major titles noted in Bec's summary correlate closely with Grendler's lists of school texts, the volumes in Cosimo's library, and the most popular texts in our sample of informal books. For a selection of items from Bec's transcriptions of the inventories which by their description seem to be *zibaldoni* or *quadernucci*, see appendix 1.

98 See below, Appendix. Cosimo's collection also included some schoolbooks, among them "Prospero et Cato, Arrighetto," dismissed by the compiler of the inventory as "da poco a fare," and the *Epistles* of Ovid.

99 See De La Mare, "Shop of a Florentine 'cartolaio' in 1426," especially 239. The few texts he stocked, some of them secondhand, were almost all schoolbooks, grammars, vocabularies, prose and verse texts, and *alfabeti*. There were also a few texts used by notaries, some liturgical and devotional books, a medical text, the book of Marco Polo, and a number of saints lives and popular tales in verse and prose in the *volgare*, including Boccaccio's *Teseida* and *Filostrato*.

100 See also above, p. 73.

101 Ricc., 1037, "Chiose sopra Dante"; the hand is fifteenth century and it is signed on fol. 2, "Io Antonio di Raffaello . . ."; the arms of the Medici, sketched in ink, appear on fols. 147r and 182v. Ricc., 1150, is a Boccaccio with Medici arms; the name Andrea "lamentire" appears on fol. 1. Laur., Plut. 40, 48, has a later binding covered with Medici arms, and the signature, 88r, "Iacobus Vespucius scripsit." Scala's book for Lorenzo, the Collectiones Cosmianae, Laur., MS 54, 10, is mostly in Latin; on this see Brown, "Humanist Portrait" and *Bartolomeo Scala*, 40–41. Laur., Redi 184, is one of several compilations collected by "Lo Smunto." One fascicle seems addressed to Lorenzo; see particularly the verse 92v: "Laureo segno trionfale/ al signore desto libro il nome segna/ viva virtù che dentro al suo cor regna,/ resplendiente il fa et in mortale . . ."

102 See, for example, Ricc., 1114, a compilation of well-known early fifteenth-century material, including, 204v, the sonnet "I' cercho libertà con grande affanno"; 171v, "Morale del Maestro Nicholò ciecho mostrando l'esaltatione del buon servidore"; 204v, "Sonetto di Rossello adiritto a Giovanni di Cosimo mostrandosi innamorato con molte varie voglie"; 205r, "Risponde al soprascritto sonetto Bernardo d'Alamanno de' Medici"; 175r, "Niccholò Tinucci a Cosimo, Quantunchè e' vi fie inanzi a gli ochi tolta"; 199v, "Antonio di Meglio al Conte Francesco"; also Belcari's sonnet praising Cosimo and Piero's patronage at the Annunziata, and Andrea delle Sargie, 195v, "Spirito supremo pien' di gentilezza . . . A Piero di Cosimo a laude di Franscesco Sforza ogi duca di Milano . . ."; 204r, "Ben disse al mio parer Quintiliano." For Michele's other compilations, see below, p. 91.

103 Andrea's book is Ricc., 1042; Ser Piero's ibid., 1122, entitled the "Quadraiesima"; on this see also above, p. 79.

104 Ricc., 1098. Rosello claimed in the index that his book contained "Sonetti 316, Canzoni 29, Sestine 9, Canzonette 8, Madriali 2 = 364." On folio 107v he punctuated two verses with the announcement, "hac die sepultus dominus Leonar-

dus aretinus," thereby dating that entry to 1444; see 177r for the original date, and a later date, Jan. 1435, crossed out. On Rossello's friendship with Giovanni and Piero see Rossi, "L'indole"; see also 151v for three sonnets he addressed to Piero which apparently refer to the latter's lady love, not his wife Lucrezia: "Se Lucretia fu simile a costei,/ La qual porti nel cor con pura fede,/ sanza mancho veruno il ver si crede,/ pur chi vuol ch'ella stia fra gli altri."

105 See above, p. 48, for Pucci's book. See Ricc., 1185 A, for his poem "Belezze di mercato vecchio," and San Bernardo, "Pistola del ghovernamento e chura della famiglia 37r–38v"; below, p. 207, for the Pucci family's cooperation with the Medici in patronage at Santissima Annunziata.

106 Ricc., 1577, 50r. On the Bardi role in the Medici bank see De Roover, *Rise and Decline*. Giuliano's book contained the "pistole di Ovid," a common school text "volgharizatto in rima per messer domenicho da montechieso." He adorned it with little sketches in the initials, and concluded, 49v, "Finitto libro referamus grazias xpo." Cosimo also owned a copy of this text, annotated in his own hand; see above, ch. 4.

107 Tanturli, "Benci copisti"; see also Ricc., 1088, and especially 33r, "Canzone di Tomaso Benci."

108 Laur., Tempi, 2.

109 BNF, Magl. VII, 1120; on Filippo Lapaccini, see below, p. 104; on Giuliano, pp. 175, 178.

110 Giuliano's book is Ricc., 1524. For the 1457 Ricci rebellion see Rubinstein, *Government of Florence*, 89; Buoninsegni, *Storie*, 110; CP 54, 155r–v, 7 Sept. 1457; Cohn, "Character of Insurrection." For Piero's poem describing beaten and starving Florentine troops making their weary way back home from Rome, see Lanza, *Lirici toscani* 2, 371–6: "Fratel, se tu vedessi questa gente/ passar per Banchi tutti sgominati,/ co' visi magri, gialli e affummicati,/ diresti dell'andare ognun si pente . . . Sì si vergognan che passan di notte;/ vannosi inginocchiando per la fame,/ trottando e saltellando come botte . . ." A close friend and correspondent of Cosimo and his sons (see, for example, MAP, V, 302, 324, to Averardo in Ferrara, 1430; ibid., 328, 331, to Lorenzo di Giovanni, 1437–8; ibid. VI, 34, 39, 51, 71, 79, to Giovanni di Cosimo, 1447–8; ibid. XVI, 64 to Piero, 1448), he may have been alienated by the failure of the Medici family to alleviate his own straightened circumstances, of which he spoke in his letters. The stories of these Ricci shed interesting light on patrician association with populist ideology and culture.

111 BNF, Pal., 214; Laur., Plut. 90, inf. 47.

112 "Se già prigione, o morte non mi tiene . . . ," ibid. Cf. Morporgo's assumption that the portion of the *zibaldone* written in prison belongs to someone else. Among Iacopo's other selections, appropriate to his circumstances, is a verse of Dante, on the front flyleaf: "O figliuol' mio, non il gustar del' legno/ è suto la cagion di tanto exilio,/ n'a solamente oltrepassar' il segno," introduced by the description, "immoderata miseria est maxima crudelita." Also included are poems by Burchiello, Dante's *Inferno*, and a sonnet, 37r, apparently written by the compiler, "in Pistoia 8 Feb. 1467, essendo in detto tempo Podestà in detto luogo." There is a prayer of San Sebastiano, and the "Epistola di Monna Brigida," (Saint Bridget). There is also the story, 66r, of one Iacobus de Parmentorio and his experience as a merchant in Turkey in 1444. Ricc., 1080, a "collectio litterarum, epistole e dicerie," contains Petrarch's "Epistola a Niccolò Accaiuoli," and letters of Giovanni dalle Celle, Guido del Palagio, Luigi Marsili, and

the pseudo-Bernard to Raimondo; it is identifiable as Iacopo's because the hand is the same as that of other books which he signed.

113 Ricc., 1309; on San Salvatore, see below, pp. 107 and 434, n. 11.

114 Laur., Plut. 40, 43. Although unsigned, the appearance, at the end of this volume of Petrarchan works in a formal hand, of her own remarkable poem, not found in any other *zibaldone*, mourning her husband and written in an informal hand, creates a strong presumption that the manuscript was hers; see also Bandini, *Catalogus*.

115 Ricc., 1431.

116 Magl. VII: 104, cf. above, p. 108. The last *terzina* of a rhymed recommendation addressed to Piero de' Medici is emphasized by Betti's use of ink of a color constrasting with the rest of the text: "Et me d'infim' ingegno,/ per tuo benignità priego ch'accepti/ el tuo buon servo me Giovanni Betti," 57v. See also the inscription, 1v: "Incominciai el proemio del Migliaio di ghiribizi composti per Gioanni di Zanobi di Manno [Betti] et mandati al savio et discreto giovane Gismondo d'Agnolo di Lorenzo di messer Andrea della [Stufa] ciptadino fiorentino"; Sigismondo's name is written over that of a previous owner, now almost illegible, but apparently also a Della Stufa.

117 Ricc., 1444, I, 20r, "finita in die palmarum 1436." The manuscript comprises four *fascicoli*, probably of separate origin, the first three apparently written in Cosimo's lifetime; I, 1–23; II, 24–51; III, 52–56. The third of these sections ends: "1460, questo libro è di Giovencho di Lorenzo dalla Stufa," and includes the rule of San Girolamo in Latin and *volgare*, the rule of San Agostino, and "Dottrina di vita spirituale."

118 Ricc., 1129. See also Ricc., 1396, owned by Giuliano d'Agostino Nesi, another member of this Laurentian circle prominent in the San Marco company of the Magi, below, ch. 13.

119 "Isforzasi la presente scritura accò che chon dileto facca utilitade," Ricc., 1185.

120 Grendler, *Schooling in Renaissance Italy*, ch. 10, especially 304–5. His suggestion that since vernacular schools taught what they pleased, the absence of the "three crowns" perhaps indicates they were less popular in vernacular culture than those works that presented "simple didacticism and human interest" is not supported by the evidence of popular books. The evidence of the Pupilli records shows that large numbers of patricians owned texts of Dante and quite a few of Boccaccio, but not Petrarch. On the other hand, in popular compendia, Petrarch's poetry was the most frequently copied.

121 On the Dante lecturers employed by the Studio, see Park, "Florentine *Studio*," 280–8. From 1422 to 1426, Messer Giovanni di Gherardo da Prato read Dante's *Cantilene morales*, *La Commedia*, and "sua canzone morale"; from 1429 to 1430 there were lectures on Dante "diebus festivis" by Frater Antonio di Cipriano da Arezzo, of the *frati minori*. Filelfo read Dante as lecturer on rhetoric and poetry from 1429, and from October 1431 he lectured on Dante and moral philosophy. Messer Lorenzo di Giovanni da Pisa, canon of San Lorenzo, lectured on Dante "diebus festivis," from 1431 to 1432, and after 1434 he lectured on Dante and theology. For readings at Orsanmichele see Zervas, *Orsanmichele*, 186 and n. 22.

122 One or more *cantiche* of the *Commedia* often constituted a volume by themselves. Selections from the *Rime* were too numerous to make an accurate count. In a group of some

150 Riccardiana manuscripts containing selections from Dante's works, twenty include the credo attributed to him. Dante and Petrarch were often paired; see, for example, Ricc., 1392, a book written by Piero di Nicola di Iacopo Aiuti di Reggiolo, Florentine notary, 17 June 1445. It contains Bruni's *Lives* of Dante and Petrarch, along with Saint Catherine's illustrated "Dialogo della Divina Providenza." Other characteristic manuscripts include Ricc., 1127, copied in 1417 by Amato *lanaiuolo*, containing Petrarch's *Trionfi* and Dante's *Rime*; ibid., 1115, "di Guido di Ser Francesco Ghuardi, scritto di suo mano a dì xvi de marzo 1448 [s. f.]," including the *Commedia*, Iacopo Alighieri's "Divisioni della Commedia," and Bosone da Gubbio's "Capitolo sulla Commedia"; ibid., 1047, consisting entirely of Dante's *Commedia*. The copyist of this, perhaps a member of a confraternity, concluded with some Latin phrases gleaned presumably from religious services: "Finito liber isto referamus gratia Christo. Qui schrissitt ischribatt senper chun Domino vivat. Vivatt in celis senper chun Domino felis. 1 Lug. 1465," 224r. Ricc., 1043 includes the *Convivio* and a vulgarization of *De Monarchia*; see especially 125v: "Finito il Chonvivio di Dante poeta fiorentino, che è lla disposizione di tre delle sue chanzone; l'altre lasciò, che nne restò a sponere vi. Et scritto per me Pierozzo di Domenicho d' Iachopo de Rosso, e finito questo dì 21 di maggio 1461." Ricc., 1094 is written in three different hands, apparently from the early, middle and late fifteenth century; the third part, which in the following century became the property "di Giovanni di Francesco dell' Fede, chostagli soldi dieci, addì 26 di febraio 1561, da uno rivenditore"; it contains Dante's *Paradiso*, letters of Luigi Marsili to Guido del Palagio, Dante's "Epistle to Henry VII," and a "Diceria di Dino Compagni a papa Gio XXII."

123 For this see Lanza, *Lirici toscani*. San Gallo's book is Laur., Conv. Soppr. 109. This notably plebeian and patriotic collection was transcribed at least in part by Zanobi di Federico Ghori in 1459, and also included, among other things, an illustrated version of Dati's *Sfera*, works by Niccolò Cieco and Leonardo Bruni, the *canzona morale* "fatta per Maestro Antonio che chanta in San Martino a Francesco degli Alberti sopr'al ghoverno," "Dormi giustinano," and "Morale fatta per Maestro Antonio da Bacherato barbiere fu e ora chanto in pancha sopra la disperatione." For manuscripts containing the *Trionfi*, see Ricc., 1032, 1091, 1099, 1102, 1108, 1114, 1124, 1125, 1126 (belonging to Zanobi di Benedetto di Charoccio degli Strozzi "et suorum"), 1128 (arms of the Baldinotti family), 1131 (Orsola Orlandi), 1132, 1133 (Iacopo di Niccolò Cocco-Donati), 1137 (Giovanbattista Doni), 1139 (Buonaccorso Adimari), 1140 ("Questo libro è di Piero Peruzzi: chi l'accatta lo renda, acciò con furto non s'aprenda," containing Petrarch's *Canzoni* and *Trionfi*); 1142, 1146 (Daniello di Piero Betti). Also of particular interest is a book belonging to a woman, Ricc., 1135, 172r: "Questo libro è di Mona Chatherina di Benvento Aldobrandi vedova, chiamato Chanzoniere del Petrarcha, chon ghratia."

124 See, for example, Ricc., 1020, "I rimedi dell'una e dell'altra Fortuna," written 1462 by Piero Boninsegni (his name in code) for the Albizzi family.

125 Manuscripts with selections from Boccaccio's works include Ricc., 1061, 1062, 1088, 1114, 1139. How fully Florentines internalized Boccaccio's *Centonovelle*, and how his style seemed the natural vehicle for the description of youthful diversions and amatory experiences, is apparent in a letter

from Braccio Martelli to the young Lorenzo, MAP, XXII, 28. "Caro mio Lorenzo . . . narrarti quello che è seguito di poi la partita tua . . . ho più tosto voluto per questa lettera darti qualche amaro piacere che tacere questa nostra felicità . . . sappi adunque che domenica sera dapoi cena. 5.2.6. andorono a chasa. 16. et quivi insino a quello hora stettono . . . Hor quivi quello che seghuì nonchè io giovane indocto et inexperto sanza alcuna facultà di scrivere, ma il fonte d'eloquentia Giovanni Bocchaccio divino narratore di simili chose non sarebbe abastantia . . . Gli ochi nostri non sostenevano tanto isplendore. Le mani tanta delicatezza tocchando tremevano, et stupefacti i sentimenti non facevono il loro officio. Che dirò io dello angelico canto anzi della celeste harmonia. Qual cierte o quali syrene già il ballare venustissino, le honeste acchoglientie, gli atti e le parole humanissime mi pare superfluo ad te optimo chonoscitore di quelle scrivere. Chosì passamo la felice sera . . ."

126 Lanza, *Lirici toscani* 1, 421; cf. 327, Branca Brancacci's image of Dante's *Inferno*. Francesco degli Alberti hoped God "prestagli ingegno all'opra ornata e pregna," ibid., 78.

127 Ibid. 1, 29. Cf. *Paradiso*, 33, cit. below, conclusion, iv. See also Michele del Giogante, in Lanza, op. cit., 1, 667, invoking Petrarch's "vaga stella."

128 BNF, II: IX: 137.

129 "Il grasso legnaiuolo" is published along with Manetti's *Vita di Filippo Brunelleschi*, ed. De Robertis and Tanturli; see also Martines, *Italian Renaissance Sextet*, and below, p. 116. While historians attribute the work to Brunelleschi's biographer Antonio Manetti, who transcribed the tale, quattrocento copyists ascribed it to Brunelleschi, its chief protagonist, and it soon became part of his public persona. For the architect's possible contribution to *Geta e Birria*, see especially BNF, II: II: 39; Michele del Giogante, the copyist of this collection, observed that "tiensi che Filippo di Ser Brunellesco anche fosse in compagnia del detto." Martines, 254, counted at least five different versions of the "Grasso legnaiuolo" in fourteen manuscripts. One of these is Ricc., 1396, owned by Giuliano d'Agostino Nesi of the Magi confraternity. Part 1 of this manuscript was "scritto negli anni Domini 1447 a dì 20 Oct.," 54r, and includes a "Formulario di Dicerie"; fols. 84–140 belonged to Giuliano Davanzati, "detto il Gabellato"; his nickname was a Florentine pun about being taxed. His compilation included Bruni's oration to Niccolò da Tolentino and the *Fior di virtù*. This section is followed by the "Novella del Grasso legnaiuolo," 142r–8r; pt. 4, 135v, concludes: "finis del primo bello punicho, oggi questo dì 23 di luglio 1489." Ricc., 1142, dated 1472, contains "il Grasso legnaiuolo" and Petrarch's *Trionfi*. The verse exchange between Brunelleschi and Domenico da Prato is published in De Robertis and Tanturli, op. cit., 21–2. According to Tanturli, "Ambienti letterari fiorentini," the only compilation in which these verses appear is Magl. VII, 1168, 87r; this also contains poems by Burchiello, Orcagna, Calderoni, Michele del Giogante (a sonnet addressed to Lucrezia, wife of Piero di Cosimo de' Medici), and Antonio di Meglio, "non si voglia più che si possa," above, p. 78. On this genre see Rochon, *Formes et signification de la "beffa"*; Guerri, *La corrente popolare nel Rinascimento*; on the related genre of facetiae, Bowen, "Renaissance Collections of *facetiae*."

130 On *Geta e Birria* see Lanza, *Polemiche e berte*, 1989 edition. The manuscripts in which this work occurs include Ricc., 1142, 1592; this last was copied c.1463 by Ser Piero Galeotti

"notaio da Pescia," who believed the work was translated from the Latin by Boccaccio, 43r–76r. See also Laur., Plut. 90, suppl. 103, and BNF, II: II: 39, compiled by Michele del Giogante. In three manuscripts, Magl. XXI, 87, Ricc., 1591, and ibid., 2805, *Geta e Birria* is coupled with Aesop's *Fables* and copiously illustrated; see above, p. 76. On the *burle* against the humanists see Pullini, *Burle e facezie*, and Lanza, op. cit., both editions. See also Bakhtin, *Rabelais*, 19–20, on the role of play in reducing the elevated and serious to the mundane through comedy. This is the key to the *charivari* world-turned-upside-down, where Florentine clergymen and scholars were often the butt of popular humor, and the rituals of religion and the triumphs of poets were effectively mocked.

131 "Rising before daybreak, I prepare the birdlime and go out with such a bundle of birdcages on my back that I look like Geta when he returned from the port with Amphitryon's books . . . ," *Letters*, translated Bondanella and Musa, 64. On Machiavelli and *Geta e Birria*, see Najemy, *Between Friends*, 215–40. The work is a Tuscan *rifacimento* of a thirteenth-century neo-Latin comedy, *Geta*, by Vitale de Blois, adapted from Plautus' *Amphitruo*. Vitale's *Geta* was still being used as a school text in the fifteenth century, and went through four printed editions in Machiavelli's lifetime; see Avesani, *Quattro miscellanee medievali*, 7–17.

132 See, for example, Ricc., 1591, 217r, 182r. The idea of this work obviously owes much to Dante's *Inferno*. Stefano was probably related to Maso Finiguerra, an artist who did a great deal of work in the popularizing style; see above, p. 76. For the texts and commentaries on Lo Za's poems see Lanza, op. cit.

133 On Burchiello see Lanza, op. cit., both editions, and for the texts of his poems 1972, 367–86; Pullini, op. cit.; Gutkind, "Burchelliana," and Watkins, "Il Burchiello." I should like to thank Professor Watkins for sharing various insights, and encouraging me to pursue the question of the role of popular literature in the culture of the Florentine elite. Compilations with extensive collections of Burchiello's verse include Ricc., 1109, Laur., Plut. 40, 48, with a binding bearing the Medici arms, and Plut. 40, 47, dated and attributed IV, and 63v: "Scriptus per me Michaelem Niccollai de Vulterris in die sabbati hora vigesima prima comincio sexta die martii, 1461." On fol. 13r, dated 1465, is a particularly splendid example of the barber poet's *burle e baie*: "Mandami uno nastro da orlar dicchieri e tanto vento ch'io empi una pala,/ duo sonagli et duo gieti da ffarfalla/ e un cappel di paglia da sparvieri,/ e venti buchi di fichi sampieri/ pel mio farsetto che disdia galla,/ un arista mi salta et una mi balla,/ che sa che qua si mangon volentieri,/ Et alquanti scoppretti di panelle,/ tanto della mia prima anco mi preme/ per amar pisa colle suo castelle,/ e più mi manda un cortocin di seme/ di ramerin di quel che far frictelle,/ che sulle ciocchi paion diademe,/ Ella risposta insieme/ contredici coltella da tagliare/ per risquittire duo agnoli daltare . . ." The line referring to "un capello di paglia da sparvieri" is quoted by Ser Alesso Pelli, Cosimo's secretary, in a letter of the 1440s to Giovanni di Cosimo, MAP, V, 341. This manuscript also includes, fol. 124, a sonnet on poverty; *Geta e Birria*; Sonetto di Filipo di Ser Brunelescho, Panni alla Burchia"; Antonio Araldo, "non si voglia più che si possa" and the sonnet addressed by Michele del Giogante to Lucrezia, wife of Piero de' Medici. BNF, II: IV: 250 contains Burchiello's "O umil popolo," 51, and a "sonnetto mandato a Antonio [Squar-

cialupi] quando tolse a fare gli orghani di gra' grandeza in santa Riperata," 61. Other poets explicitly modeled their work on Burchiello's: see, for example, the "Sonnetto burchiellesco" of Michele del Giogante, BNF, Pal. 54, or Niccolò di Cieco's extremely popular verse, Ricc., 1091, 108r–9v, "O misera, isfacciata, al ben dispetta . . ."

134 Ricc., 1088, 3r: "Quelli che sono alletterati dovrebbono bene mettere la loro chura ne' buoni exempli – ciò che qui escritto sono tucte veritadi e sperience di veri e buoni exepli." Cf. Grendler, op. cit., 159, citing the much later case of the Sienese professor who urged his students to compile notebooks of notable sentences. Other edifying selections include Petrarch's *Canzoni*, the "Vendetta di morte di cristo," and works by Sacchetti, Guido Cavalcanti, Boccaccio, and Dante, as well as the devotional poem "Atte richorro Vergine Maria," 69r–70v, by Dolcibene, *buffone*. On the Renaissance treatment of classical figures, see especially Wind, *Pagan Mysteries*; Seznec, *Survival of the Pagan Gods*. Virgil's *Eclogues* were Dante's warrant for viewing him as a prophet of Christian truth, and thus an appropriate guide to the afterlife; Salutati's *Epigrams* for the Palazzo Vecchio stressed parallels between classical and Christian figures, as did cycles of *uomini illustri*. On Hercules and David in the Florentine tradition, see pp. 281–7. Ricc., 1202 contained the Life of Hercules, a comment on Ovid, and Columella's agricultural treatise, also owned by Cosimo; see Lord, "*Ovide moralisé*," for examples of the pairing of the account of creation in Genesis with that of Ovid's *Metamorphoses*.

135 On Aesop's *Fables*, see Curtius, *European Literature*, passim; Grendler, *Schooling in Renaissance Italy*; Mardersteig, in his introduction to Esopo, *Favole*. Alberti used them in his *Dinner Pieces*; Leonardo and his master Verrocchio, whose workshop made the illustrations for selections from Aesop in at least three compilations, above, p. 76, both owned copies of the *Fables*; see below, pp. 116–17. They were obviously a source for many of the moral tales and fantasies recorded in Leonardo's *Notebooks*, as well as a number of his drawings. Banfi, in his account of the Aesop manuscript tradition, *Favole*, op. cit., especially 21, observed in Tuscan translations a typically "accentuata intonazione popolaresca."

136 See, for example, the contents of Ricc., 1591, and above, pp. 76–7. Ibid., 2805, and BNF, Magl. XXI, 87, illustrated apparently by the same hand, are similar in content; the latter also contains a number of poems by Burchiello. Magl. VII, 375, consists mainly of Aesop's *Fables*, the watercolor table for calculating dates of *feste*, and Pope Innocent III's recipe of herbs sent to the abbot of San Paolo in Pia, 61r. See also Ricc., 1185; ibid., 1600.

137 Ricc., 1591, 85v. The cockerel naturally loves things less precious than the stones, which also signify "lo frutto della scienza." Cf. the compiler's comment on the fable "Del topo e della ranocchia." "Spiritualmente s'intende le bestia delli grandi orecchi li semplari religiosi. I quali perchè sieno di medesimo abito, e d'una medesima ubbidienza e prendono ardire di troppo domesticho parlare, contro a loro maggiori dell'ordine e contro a ogni altra persona . . ." Cf. Ricc., 2805.

138 Discussed above, pp. 46 and 408, n. 43. See also Banfi, in Esopo, *Favole*, op. cit., on the significance of the different selections from the Aesop repertoire favored in different places and periods, and Ricc., 1185, cit. above, p. 70, for Leonardo Carnesecchi's observation that the greatest truth may lie in the humblest objects.

139 BNF, II: II: 81, 176v. Cf. Ricc., 1088, 60r, for a digest of fourteenth-century vernacular moral *exempla* drawn from Franco Sacchetti, Guido Cavalcanti, Boccaccio, and Maestro Paolo dell'abbacho.

140 On school curricula see Grendler, op. cit. At least six manuscripts contain extracts from *Catiline* and *Jugurtha*, the texts quoted by Cosimo's cousin Francesco di Giuliano di Averardo to reinforce his resolution to resign himself to exile; above, p. 34. Seneca's *Epistles*, *Sentences*, and especially his "Trattato delle 4 virtù morali," were frequently cited.

141 This work appears in half a dozen Riccardiana manuscripts; see, for example, Ricc., 1519–20, 1553. See below, p. 248, for Giovanni de Bicci's commission of a cycle of *uomini illustri*.

142 Ricc., 2729, 44 v: "sofferente nella sua non debite o non possibile volontà tinta." In a sample restricted to books begun before Cosimo's death in 1464, there are few extracts from Plato's actual works, although a couple of anthologists use the *Epistole* and the *Timeo*. Nor was Pliny yet widely circulated, although one book cited the "Storia naturale epitomata."

143 For the texts of the contributions to this competition, see Bertolini, *De vera amicitia*.

144 Ricc., 1603. His book also included works of the humanist Leonardo Bruni, among them his letter to the Lord of Mantua, and his oration in praise of Niccolò da Tolentino.

145 Laur., Segnani, 4.

146 See Morpurgo, op. cit., index, and especially Ricc., 1546, 87v: "Questo libro ène di Piero di Ghuccio di Giovanni e sua v. dicendetti," including the *Consolation* and commentaries on it. Cf. ibid., 1547: "Questo Boetio è di me Cione d'Urbano da Lactaia in Ravi," dated by the entry, "Lo re Alfonso in questo tenpo stava a campo a Pionbino." See also Laur., Ashb. 539, belonging to Albizzi, above, pp. 70–71. For attitudes to Fortuna after 1450, and the replacement of the Boethian wheel of fortune popular in the Middle Ages with new symbols, see below, pp. 363–6, on Giovanni Rucellai's patronage.

147 Ricc., 1255, last folio. More than twenty Riccardiana manuscripts contain extracts from Augustine's sermons; also copied were his "Epistole a San Cirillo," and his disquisitions on the Psalms, on the joy of the elect, and the pains of the damned. See also Ricc., 1329, "Scripto per me Michele di Sictii del Buonconsiglio Sitii 1459," containing works of Saints Augustine, Jerome, and Bernard, and also of Cavalca. For Cosimo's copy of the *City of God* see De La Mare, "Cosimo and His Books," 149, no. 51.

148 Ricc., 1444, finished by Giovanni della Stufa on Palm Sunday 1436, passed to Giovenco di Lorenzo dalla Stufa and including the "Regola di San Girolamo" in Latin and Italian, the "Regola di San Agostino," and his *Dottrina di vita spirituale*.

149 Ricc., 1361, 1445: "Questo libro è di Giovanni di Zanobi Amadory chalzaiuolo, ciptadino fiorentino, el quale scrisse di sua mano; e chonpiessi di scrivere a dì vii del mexe di marzo negli anny della 'ncarnatione del nostro Signore Ihesu Christo mccccxliiii. Priegasi che a chi fuss' prestato lo renda." Its contents also included an extract from Eusebius.

150 For these see below, p. 262; on the expression in Cosimo's patronage of his interest in early Christian ideas, below, pp. 379–80. On Cosimo's copy of Saint Jerome's works, see De La Mare, op. cit., 126; on the saint's growing cult, Rice, *St. Jerome in the Renaissance*.

151 Ricc., 1364, fol. 233: "Finito il libro 14 Jan 1464 a ore xx Ser Lamberto di Gocco Lamberteschi cittadino fiorentino Laus Deo; pregate Idio per me." There are briefer extracts in Ricc., 1274, and ibid., 1436. On Cosimo and Saint Gregory's *Moralia*, see above, p. 402, n. 20.

152 See Morpurgo, op. cit., index.

153 For the *Meditations*, see particularly Ricc., 1376, belonging to the Baroncini family, especially 144r–152v. Half a dozen Riccardiana manuscripts include Bernard's *Meditation on the Passion of Christ*. See especially ibid., 1261, for Bernard's "Esposizione della Cantica canticorum di Salamone," finished 27 Oct. 1451, unsigned.

154 At least seventeen Riccardiana manuscripts, as well as a number from other libraries, contain the letter to Count Raimondo Manelli, together with various genuine works of Saint Bernard. Among the earliest of these manuscripts is the trecento 1185A, 37r–38v. See also, for example, ibid., 1156, 1185. Ibid., 1080, belonging to Niccolò Coccho Donati, also includes the correspondence between Giovanni dalle Celle, Guido del Palagio, and Luigi Marsili, see below. Ricc., 1429, is an extremely interesting collection of mainly devotional works, "Schritti et chopiati per mano della Benedetta, donna di Piero d'Antonio Niccholi, fatti nel 1464 a dì venti di marzo," 56v, which includes along with the Bernardine letter the *Consolation* of Boethius, Saint Augustine's sermons, "I perdoni di Fiesole," Dante's credo, the "grazie che l'uomo riceve udendo la messa," some poems by Belcari, and his *sacra rappresentazione Abraam e Isaac*, together with Cicero's "Epistola di Lentulo" and "tre ternati e un sirventese." See also BNF, xxxv: 21: 34, which also contains Bernard's "Orazione sopra il Crocefisso."

155 See below, ch. 13.

156 See Ruda, *Fra Filippo Lippi*, 33, 169–73, pls. 94, 95; also catalogue, no. 35.

157 Below, pp. 281–6.

158 See Psalms 38:1; 51:1. A dozen or so Riccardiana compilations contain the penitential psalms; see, for example, 1052; also 1939, which includes the "Sette Salmi di Davit" along with Aesop's *Fables*, *Opere Romani*, and works by Saint Bridget.

159 See Morpurgo, op. cit., index, under these various heads, including Alberti's "S. Gio Evangelista in terze rime." See also Ricc., 1309, 82v, "Finita è lla leggienda di Santo Giovanni Batista scritta per me Giuliano di [Quaratesi]: finita adì x di decembre 1458, a ore 20."

160 For the *laude* of Iacopone da Todi, see, for example, Ricc., 1431, dated 1469, inscribed front flyleaf: "Questa si è la vendetta di Christo, la quale a schritto Luigi di Donato di Pagholo di meser Pagholo Ruciellai." It also includes a millenarian prophecy. See also BNF, Pal. 54, a mostly devotional collection. Ibid., II: VII: 4, a much-thumbed volume, contains mainly *laude*, along with "Una confessione bella" and the "Contasto di Vivo e Morto." For transcriptions of various holy offices, see Morpurgo, op. cit., index; the copies of *laude* are too numerous to count.

161 On the genre of confession, see Price Zimmerman, "Confession and Autobiography." He analyzes the formal system of introspection designed for confession, leading to the individuation of sin, and observes its application to more secular ends in the "coherent interpretation of the self from a particular viewpoint in time," 121, that characterizes genuine

autobiography as distinct from memoirs, journals, diaries, and other forms of generally "autobiographical" literature. On Cosimo's "account with God," see below, p. 132.

162 See below, ch. 7.

163 One compilation also included his *Seconda somma*; see Ricc., 1335, owned at the turn of the century by Baccio Valori; ibid., 1430, containing only his confession. Ibid., 1403, "Libro di Mona Ginevra donna che fu d'Antonio Mattei," consisted of Antoninus's "Meditazione della vita di Gesù Cristo"; for this, see also ibid., 1377; the entry is dated 1446. See also ibid., 1508, containing his *Tratatello dei sette sacramenti*, *Trattato dei peccati mortali*, *Trattate delle scomuniche*, and *Trattato sui dieci comandamenti*.

164 Ricc. 1052, cf. above, pp. 76 and 423, n. 78. Teri's section of this book is undated, though the content and handwriting suggest it was written no earlier than the third quarter of the fifteenth century. Woodcuts were made in Florence from the early years of the century, but these are probably much later.

165 Below, pp. 98–100. Morpurgo's index alone, op. cit., notes forty-one prayers.

166 Ricc., 2729, 108v; see also BNF, Pal. 215. "Alletto, alletto menavo l'anima e'l chorpo adio;/ la do perchè la dia a San Giovanni, che / l'asegni e che la ghuardi che 'l nimicho nollanghanni, nollanghanni./ E poi la dia a San Michele, che la pesi et/ guardi bene, e lui po' la dia a San Piero che/ la metta nel regno del cielo, ammen." "Una altra pure per dire quando vai alletto; nel mio letto me n'andai Gieso Xpo;/ vi trovai Gieso Xpo e San Salvestro che cci facion' questo letto,/ e anchor San Aghostino fece chon sette chandele acese e chon sett'agnoli di Dio/ tutti dintorno alletto mio, amen."

167 Laur., Segnani 4, 91, 106r, prayers; 1r: "Io Chanbio da Chastello, studente sopra gli autori . . ."; 104r: "Finis Deo gratias Amen ne' Anno Domini 1433 In Pisa in San Gorgio nella roccha questo dì xxiii di giugno."

168 See BNF, II: VII: 4, 4v: "Misericordia pacie e charità te dimandiamo dolce Signior Giesù." The poem begins: "Mosso da santa pazzia,/ vo' narrar la vita mia . . . Udite matta pazia/della stolta vita mia;/ io degli anni quaranta/ spero menar vita santa,/ acquistata ò virtù tanta/ che veder non si potria,/ mosso da santa pazia,/vo narrar la vita mia." "Misericordi pacie e charita /te dimandiamo dolce Signior Giesu . . . prendi la croce che ttu puoi portare . . . ciaschuno amante che ama el signore/ vegna alla danza cantando d'amore,/ venga danzando tutto inamorato . . ." I wish to thank Joyce Treble for sharing this reference with me. Cf. BNF, Magl. VII, 375, 16v; "Prendi la crocie chettupuoi portare . . ."; 18r, "Ciaschuno amante che ama el signore/ vegna alla danza cantando d'amore,/ venga danzando tutto inamorato . . ." See also Ricc., 1251, containing a prophecy of Iacopone, his "Udite matta pazzia", a verse by Belcari, and "Pistole ed Evangeli per tutto l'anno", signed and dated: "Finito il detto libro, a dì 18 di febraio 1472 (s.f.) per me Niccolaio di Giovanni Davanzati, ed è mio; e scrissilo nel chastello di Fegghine, e ffinilo a ore 17".

169 Cf. Rosello Roselli's contrast of "delightful life" with "horrid death," Lanza, op. cit., 2, 434–9.

170 On the momento mori, see also Masaccio's *Trinity* (fig. 51); on Cosimo's concern with death, below, pp. 138–41.

171 This piece is relatively common; see, for example, BNF, II: VII: 4, where it appears with "una confessione bella" and Iacopone's "Udite matta pazia/della stolta vita mia . . . ,"

above, n. 168. See also ibid., II: IV: 250: "Quando talegi huomo dal tiera/ va e poni mente alla sipultura,/ id ivi poni il tuo contemplare/ e pensa bene che tu dei tornare/ in quella forma che tu vedi stare/ l'uomo che giace in fossa scura./ Or' mi rispondi, huomo soppellito,/ se desto mondo se tosto gita;/ ove sono i drappi da d'ieri vestito,/ adorno ti veggio di molta bruttura . . . O fratel mio de' non mi ripugnare,/ chollo mio fatto atte puo giovare./ Quando i miei parenti mi vennono aspogliare/ da uccilliccio mi feciono vestitura./ O vai lo capo cosi pettinato/ concui t'agussasti che l'ai coi fa pelato/ fa acqua bollita chela chosì raschiato,/ nonti fa bisognia altra raschiatura./ Questo mio capo che avea si biondo/ è caduto ne la carne e capegli dintorno;/ non ne lo pensava quando io era al mondo,/ quando portavo grillande in altura./ Ove son gli occhi così inamorati,/ che della lor forma mi paion cavati/credo chegli vermini glitanno mangiati;/ del tuo ngoglio non ebbono pagura,/ questi miei occhi con chiogia gratando/ inverso le donne sempre peccando,/ lasso dolente che tratto megliano,/ gli occhi divorati ella mia sguardatura."

172 See Grendler, op. cit., Morpurgo, op. cit., index.

173 See, for example, Ricc., 1397, including an illustrated figure, 46v, of "S. Brigida e il demonio"; also ibid., 1251, 1258, 1345, 1939.

174 Marilyn Lavin drew attention to the influence of Cavalca's writings on pious Florentines in her analysis of the sources of Lippi's altarpiece for the Medici chapel, "Giovannino Battista"; see also below, ch. 13. Among the more interesting of the numerous compilations in which they are appear are the following. Ricc., 1315: "Questo libro iscrisse Franciescho d'Iachopo di Gianni speciale i' Merchato Vecchio, popolo di San Lorenzo, a dì primo de' dicienbre 1378, in dì 30." This includes *Lo specchio della Croce* and Cavalca's sonnets, as well as his vulgarization of a *Dialogue* of Saint Gregory. Ricc., 1273 contains the *Meditazione della Vita di Cristo* and *Lo specchio di peccati*; on the flyleaf is inscribed: "Questo libro è di monna Antonia donna di Cristofano di Lionardo Rondinelli." See also Ricc., 1274, dated 1443: "Questo libro è di Giovambatista d'Attaviano Doni proprio." The index lists Cavalca's *Trattato della pazienza* with the comment, 1r: "A ditestazione e biasimo dell' ira, meritiamo di ghodere cho' llui nell' sua etterna gloria. Qui est benedittus." There follows a "descrezione dei dici chomandamenti," with the explanation: "Et perciò che'l Nimicho, lo qual venne per nostro maestro d'umiltà e di pazienza, Qui est beneditus . . ." Ricc., 1328 contains Cavalca's *Specchio della mondizia del cuore e della pura confessione*, Giovanni Dominici's "Predica del sabato santo orazione latina," and the text of an indulgence of Pope Giovanni XXIII. The copyist noted, 31v, that his book was finished in 1444 "per Ser Piero di Niccolo da Reggiuolo a Giovanni di Miniato"; at one time it belonged to Niccolò Bargiacchi. Ricc., 1317 is dated 1451 on the flyleaf: "Questo libro è di Ghidetto di Francescho Ghuidetti"; it subsequently passed to Francesco di Lorenzo Guidetti, then Agnolo di Lorenzo Guidetti. Its contents include Bono Giamboni, *Della Miseria dell' Uomo*, Domenico Cavalca, *Trattato delle 30 stoltizie*, and various other religious and moral tracts, among them a rare work of Brunetto Latini, *Piccola dottrina del parlare e del tacere*, 67r–70v, from his *Tesoro*. Ricc., 1329, "Scripto per me Michele di Sictii del Buonconsiglio Sitii 1459," includes Saint Augustine's sermons, San Bernardo, *Meditazione sopra il*

pianto S. Girolamo, and his *Trenta gradi della scala celestiale*; also *I perdoni di Fiesole*, Cavalca's *La medicina del cuore*, the *Leggenda de' dicimila martiri*, a *Meditazione sopra l'albero della Croce*, Origen's *Omelia sopra La Maddalena*, and finally Leonardo Bruni's *Lives* of Dante and Petrarch. Ricc., 1376, dated 1478, "Scritto per me Baroncino di Giovanni Baroncini," and passed to other members of the family, cousins, and their sons, was entirely devotional. It contained Cavalca's *Specchio della Croce*, the *Disciplini spirituali*, Saint Bernard's *Meditazione sopra il pianto di nostra donna* (subtitled "stava presso alla croce di Yhesu la madre sua"), and three sermons of Saint Augustine, "Della morte, della vita, del Giudicio." Ricc., 1436, another largely devotional book with no date or name, included Cavalca's vulgarization of Saint Gregory, his *Trenta stoltizie* and the *Disciplini spirituali*.

175 Among the manuscripts including these selections are Ricc., 1156; BNF, II: II: 39; ibid., II: II: 81; ibid., II: I: 102; ibid., XXV. 9. 650, formerly Magl. 650. See also Ricc., 1080, Niccolò Coccho Donati's book; ibid., 1090, written apparently in three different fifteenth-century hands, one of them belonging to Giovanfrancesco di Andrea *calzaiuolo*, the others later; ibid., 1094, also by three different quattrocento hands, containing Dante, *Paradiso*, Marsili to Guido del Palagio, Dante's *Epistle to Henry VII*, and a "Diceria di Dino Compagni a papa Gio. xxii." On the flyleaf: "Di Giovanni di Francesco della Fede; chostagli soldi dieci, addì 26 di febraio 1561, da uno rivenditore."

176 See Pitti, *Cronica*, 38. The Pratese notary Ser Lapo Mazzei wrote to his friend Francesco Datini in 1398, when Cosimo was nine years old: "è stato tratto Gonfalon' di Compagnia; dico di Guido, tutta la città se n'allegra; perchè istima che dove e' fosse, non si potrebbe far male," *Lettere* 1, 204. In the early fifteenth century Guido del Palagio's name was still familiar to Florentines like the diarist Del Corazza. Del Palagio preceded Cosimo as a patron of monasteries, and particularly the Observants: he settled the first Observant Franciscan house in Tuscany in a monastery near Fiesole; see Rubinstein, "Lay Patronage and Observant Reform," 64. Like Cosimo, Guido wrote a poem, a patriotic address to Florence comparing her with Rome, strongly influenced by Dante and Petrarch.

177 On this group of friends and correspondents, see Flamini, *La lirica toscana*, 307–8; also Kristeller, "Marsilio Ficino as a Man of Letters," 107–8; Becker, "Aspects of Lay Piety," 523–4, *Florence in Transition* 2, 179–81; Brucker, *Florentine Politics and Society*, 301–3; also Gherardi, *Il Paradiso degli Alberti*, introduction and passim. On Marsili's books in Cosimo's library, see above, ch. 4. Giovanni dalle Celle's letters were published by Sorio in 1845 and entitled *Lettere del Beato Don Giovanni*; see especially no. 14, cit., 1375; see now also Giovanni dalle Celle-Luigi Marsili, *Lettere*, for the correspondence between the Vallombrosan and Marsili. On Giovanni see also Cividali, "Il Beato Giovanni dalle Celle." His correspondents, like those of Feo Belcari fifty years later, comprised a wide social range, including Giorgio Gucci and Donato *correggiaio*.

178 Below, p. 118; on civic piety see particularly Baron, "Franciscan Poverty and Civic Wealth"; Weinstein, "Myth of Florence" and *Savonarola and Florence*; Polizzotto, *Elect Nation*.

179 For Cosimo's reading, see above, ch. 4; see also below, pp. 212–14, on his building of the Badia.

180 Giovanni dalle Celle, *Lettere del Beato Don Giovanni*, 17, 1; cf. 18, 20, 25. Among the vulgarizations of Latin moral texts

181 On Lodovico's book see above, p. 83.

182 See below, p. 359. On the altarpiece see Rice, *Saint Jerome in the Renaissance*, and Meiss, "Scholarship and Penitence," 134. Giovanni dalle Celle also drew heavily on Saint. Bernard; see Sorio's edition, *Lettere del Beato Don Giovanni*, for example, 13, 23, 25, cf. Bernard of Clairvaux, *Letters*, 396. Saint Bernard was also represented in Medici commisions, for the Medici palace chapel, and for Giovanni's hermitage of Vallombrosa; see below, ch. 13. The Vallombrosan order was dear to the hearts of many eminent Florentines, including the Strozzi and Rucellai parishioners of Santa Trinita and San Pancrazio; see Kent, "Making of a Renaissance Patron," and Kent and Kent, *Neighbours and Neighbourhood*. For other images of Jerome in the Medici palace, below, p. 262.

183 See also below, especially ch. 7.

184 See, for example, Laur., XL, 47; Ricc., 1301, 1328.

185 For this see below, pp. 102–4. For Belcari's poems and the manuscripts in which they appear see Lanza, *Lirici toscani*, 2; for his plays and a complete account of their manuscript tradition see Newbigin, *Nuovo corpus*; Belcari, "La Rappresentazione quando . . ." Belcari's own book is Ricc., 1608, inscribed on the flyleaf: "Rendimi a Feo di Iacopo di Feo Belcari." Some compilations containing large numbers of Belcari's sonnets are Laur., Red. 184; ibid., 181; Ashb. 539. See also Plut. 90, sup. 96, 181r–190v; Magl. VII, 690.

186 For the laud, see Laur., Redi, 121, 28v. For Bernardino's sermons see, for example, Ricc., 1264, ibid., 1939; this also contains "Sette salmi di Davit pro festa fatti in versi sono belle cose . . . Pistola per Lentulo, Pistola di S. Bernardo a Mesere Ramondo, Signiore del castello di Sancto Ambruogio"; see also 90r: "Come Xpo giudicha i benedetti a vita etterna e maladetti allo inferno . . ." On the Medici and San Bernardino, below, p. 171.

187 See below, pp. 155–9, and fig. 62.

188 Ricc., 2729, 44r, 37r-v.

189 See Ricc., 1254. For extracts from *The Golden Legend* see, for example, Ricc., 1390, of Giovanni Cherichi, "cittadino fiorentino," who also translated the extracts from the Latin. Ricc., 1276, included various other saints' legends, and ibid., 1301, also contained some sermons of Dominici. Ibid., 1476 consisted of a copy of Iacopo da Voragine's chapter on Advent, an extract from Cavalca's *Specchio di Croce*, Saint Bernard's *Trattato della conscienza*, the *Sette omelie* of Saint Gregory, and various *Morali*. Ricc., 1388, belonging to Mario Guiducci, was entirely taken up with Iacopo da Voragine's work. The legends of the saints were the literature of Christ's friends and emulators; the tract known as the "Vendetta della morte di Cristo" dealt with his enemies. This anti-Semitic tale illuminates a climate in which Jews were obliged to subsidize Christian plays and processions, including that of the Magi. They were also forced to take on the indisputably usurious transactions avoided by Christian bankers; on banking and taxation regulations affecting Jews, and the Medici regime's treatment of them, see De Roover, *Rise and Decline*. For the *Vendetta*, see, for example, Ricc., 1088, 59v–61v; ibid., 1431, dated 1469, flyleaf: "Questa si è la vendetta di Christo, la quale a schritto Luigi di Donato di Pagholo di meser Pagholo Ruciellai," with the plea, "O tu che llegi, priegha Idio per me pechatore."

190 His grandfather Cacciaguida, whom he encounters in heaven, voices Dante's deepest feelings about his native city. See *Paradiso* XXV, 130–35: "A così riposato, a così bello/ viver di cittadini, a così fida/ cittadinanza, a così dolce ostello,/ Maria mi diè, chiamata in alte grida,/ e nell'antico vostro Batisteo/ insieme fui Cristiano e Cacciaguida." See also Benvenuti Papi, "I culti patronali," 100, on the impossibility of separating the Florentine and the Christian: "La 'nazione' fiorentina era privilegio sancito all'atto dall'immersione battesimale in San Giovanni."

191 These verses, among those particularly memorized by Benedetto Dei, below, p. 91, are discussed below, pp. 125–6. See also Antonio degli Agli's poem to Eugenius, and other accounts of the cathedral consecration, loc. cit.

192 See, for example, Laur., Redi 184, 94r; published by Lanza, *Lirici toscani* 1, 651.

193 For this last, see BNF, II: II: 39; Ricc., 1074, 1080; Laur., Segnani 4, 104v: "Pe' risturare a chiunque giace nello penion' falsa che Fiorenza/ non si difenderà dal suo nimico prima per avere co' virtuosi pace,/ dimosterrò con tutta mia potenza/ le ragion chiare di questo che dicho./ Ne mai del vulgo voglo essere amico,/ ma continuamente suo rubello/ mentre che vivo et così son disposto,/ ritornando a proposto/ vo' chiarire a chi a fermo cervello/ come la mia città ogni percossa/ può sostenere et vincere ogni possa." On Niccolò da Tolentino, his role in the affairs of Florence and of Cosimo de' Medici, and poems and orations in his praise see below, pp. 275–6. For a number of *zibaldoni* containing Bruni's address to Tolentino, see Morpurgo, op. cit., index. Ricc., 1074, contains a typical selection of this sort of material. Its late fifteenth-century owner was Carlo Altoviti, "canonico fiorentino"; the material apparently transcribed by an earlier owner, whose name on the flyleaf is completely cancelled, included Bruni's oration to Tolentino, Manetti's oration to Bernardetto de' Medici, Bocaccio's "epistola a Messer Pinto de Rossi," and his letter to Francesco Bardi, Petrarch's letter to Nicola Acciaiuoli on good government, Bruni's "opera in difesa del popolo," the pseudo-Saint Bernard letter to Raimondo Manelli, Sforza's letter of March 1449 to Sigismondo Malatesta after he took Milan, and Sforza to Neri Capponi and Cosimo in reply to theirs of December 1449. It also includes one of the earliest examples of this patriotic military genre, "Orazione di M. Stefano Porcari, Romano, capitano di Firenze quando prese la bacchetta." See also BNF II: II: 81, 60v, della Casa's compilation; BNF, Magl. VIII, 1370, 12, including the oration to Porcari and an "Orazione del dare il Bastone a M. Gismondo Malatesta;" Laur., Plut. 90, sup. 89.

194 See above, pp. 53–4; also especially Ricc., 2732.

195 See, for example, Ricc., 1088, 43v; for Antonio di Meglio's sonnet, Lanza, op. cit., 2, 83. See Hans Baron, *Crisis*, for the thesis that the conflict with Giangaleazzo was the crucible in which the republican ideology of early Florentine humanism was forged.

196 See, for example, Ricc., 1176, 31v, "Lettera della Signoria Fiorentina ai Pisani 1405"; at the time this entry was written, the compilation appeared to belong to Giovanni Gherardi [da Prato]. On his major role in the production of Florentine popular culture, see above, n. 196. See also Ricc., 2729, 44ff, entries on Siena, Piombino, Mantua, Faenza, Bologna, Ferrara, Naples, Perugia, Lucca, and Genoa.

197 See, for example, BNF II: II: 40; ibid., II: II: 81; ibid., Pal., 215;

Ricc., 1078, 1080, 1090, 1105, 1156, 1396, 1491, 1603, 1619, 2729, 2983; also above, n. 191. For a discussion of these manuscripts, Lanza, op. cit., introduction; Flamini, op. cit., especially 315–53.

198 Ricc., 1095, especially flyleaf and 101r; Flamini, op. cit., 351–3. See also de Blasi, *Libro de la Destructione de Troya*.

199 On this last see Rubinstein, *Palazzo Vecchio*, especially 52–3.

200 On these visits see *Libro cerimoniale*, ed. Trexler, especially 74–5; also BNF, II: II: 81. Trexler's thesis, *Public Life*, that Florentine public ritual developed out of a need to compensate for feelings of shame and inferiority to princely states is not supported by the literature of the *zibaldoni*. On Cosimo's personal relations with these princes and a comparison of their patronage choices with his, see below, ch. 15.

201 See Alberti, *Della Famiglia*, especially pt. 1; Vespasiano, *Vite* 2; Alessandra Strozzi, *Lettere*; Phillips, *Memoir of Marco Parenti*.

202 See above, pp. 48–9; also BNF, II:II:81; II:II:39; Pal. 216, for these works by leading performers at San Martino, such as Niccolò Cieco, Antonio di Guido, Antonio *barbiere*, Cristoforo, Calderoni, and Giovanni da Prato. See also Lanza, *Lirici toscani*.

203 Ricc., 2729, 40r: "Dice e narra Valerio libro quarto chapitolo primo d'uno che piangneva la morte del nimicho suo perochè avea chonosciuta la vita sua esser hutile alla republicha cioè al ben chomune . . ."

204 See, for example, Laur., Conv. Soppr. 109, 18v; Lanza, op. cit., 1, 169, ff.

205 See BNF, Magl. VII, 375, 61r, for the sonnet against taxes; Lanza, *Lirici toscani* 2, 208–9. See also Molho, "Brancacci Chapel," and below, ch. 15.

206 Ricc., 2815; Lanza, *Lirici toscani* 2, 661. See also, for example, Ricc., 1317, and Laur., Plut. inf. 47, f. 120: "Trionfal ciptà bella fiorenza/ o sito allegro vago dolce giocondo . . ."

207 On this, and on Cosimo's interest in cartography, see below, p. 264. According to Lippincott, "Art of Cartography," this was one of the few areas of scientific endeavor in which Florentines were preeminent; a thirteenth-century illuminated copy of Ptolemy's *Geographia* was left by Manuel Chrysoloras at his death in 1415 to Palla Strozzi, and became the source of all such maps in Italy. See also Edgerton, "Florentine Interest in Ptolemaic Cartography." Ptolemy's *Geografia* was translated into Latin by Iacopo d'Angelo in the first decades of the fifteenth century. The maps were copied by Francesco di Lappacino and Domenico di Lionardo Buoninsegni, Vespasiano, *Vite* 2, 375–6. In 1469 a pupil of Landino's, Francesco Berlinghieri, whose family managed the Medici woolshop in San Martino, translated Ptolemy's work into Italian verse; see Butters, *Triumph of Vulcan*, 35–6. On Strabo and the studies of Pletho and Toscanelli see Larner, "Quattrocento Renaissance in Geography." For examples of the *Sfera* in Florentine manuscripts see BNF, II: II: 81, 47v; ibid., II: IX: 137, 10v–21r; ibid., Pal. 215 (Sandro Lotteringhi, Michele del Giogante), 1r: "Queste sono 144 stanze dette mappamondo maravigliosamente belle e buone e liggiadramente detta fatte per Ghoro di Stagio Dati nostro famoso cittadino."; See also Bertolini, "Censimento dei manoscritti della *Sfera*," and Ricc., 1091, 40r–59v (Benedetto Biffoli); 1106, 1163, 1185 (pt. 2 belonged to Lionardo Carnesecchi). Laur., Conv. Soppr. 109, 51r, is illustrated rather in the manner of the ceiling of the *scarsella* in the sacristy at San Lorenzo ceiling; this book belonged to Antonio da San Gallo. The *Sfera* was sometimes attributed to Goro's kinsman, the cleric and popular poet

Lionardo; see, for example, Plut. 90, sup. 103, "La Sfera di Fra Lionardo di Stagio Dati." A "mappamondo, bello" appears in the inventory of Cosimo's *studio* in 1417/18; on this and on Cosimo's interest in cartography, see below, p. 264.

208 On the council and its effects on Florentine culture and Cosimo's outlook, see below, chs. 10 and 13 passim. Although Frescobaldi's account of his journey has been found in only one compilation, references to it in other literature suggest that it was well known. For Frescobaldi's poems and his "Terra santa," or "viaggio al santo sepolcro," see *Viaggi in Terra Santa*, and Ricc., 1030, which also includes Simone Sigole's "Viaggio al Monte Sinae." On Florentine interest in the Holy Sepulcher, below, p. 188. Ricc., 1133, written by Iacopo di Coccho Donati while in prison from June, 1451, contains an account of the Turkish persecution of Italian merchants just before the fall of Constantinople.

209 See BNF, II: II: 39; also II: I: 102 and II: IV: 195, put together by Manetti; ibid., II: II: 102. See also Ricc., 2729, 1475; along with the letter of Prester John to Frederick of Rome, this last manuscript contains the "book of Sidrach concerning the duties of friendship." Ricc., 1279, is full of items revealing a fascination with the east. See also Laur., Plut. 90, sup. 89, containing the "Pistola mandorono turchi al papa, 1349;" beside the Roman date for each entry the writer also gives "l'anno di maometta." Burchiello wrote a sonnet to Rosello Roselli alluding to the Fables of Ovid and the Ethiopians, Lanza, *Lirici toscani* 2, 453. See also Ser Alesso Pelli to Giovanni di Cosimo, MAP, XVI, 371, and below, ch. 13.

210 On compilations rich in selections from Ficino see Kristeller, "Marsilio Ficino as a Man of Letters." For recipes and cures, see for example, Laur., Segnani 4; Ricc., 1159, 65r–72r, Morporgo, op. cit., index, and Tanturli, "Codici di Antonio Manetti."

211 *Cronica*, 139–41. See Frati, "Cantari e sonetti," for identifications of various obscure selections from this list. See also Phillips, "Benedetto Dei's Book of Lists," for some interesting suggestions about the nature of Dei's memory.

212 Magl. VII, 375, 61r.

213 *Letters*, trans. Gilbert, 139–44. Cf. Curtius, *European Literature*, on "Dante and the Book," 526.

214 Ricc., 1402, also 1122. See also BNF, Pal. 54, 1–5v; the unidentified copyist of this memory treatise explicitly attributes it to Cicero. See also Laur., Plut. 90, inf. 47, 106v.

215 See, for example, Ricc., 1159, 12r, "Cicerone della memoria artificiale," attributed originally to Aristotle's *Ethics*; the book is in Michele del Giogante's hand and belonged to Michele Grazzi. It also contained a vulgarization of the *Rosarium odor vite*, a compendium of wise sayings of the ancients, organized under categories for memorization.

216 BNF, Pal. 215; published Lanza, *Lirici toscani* 2, 671. Cf. the reference in a poem by Feo Belcari addressed to Mariotto Davanzati, ibid., 2, 217, to "L'immenso ingegno e l'etterna memoria . . ."

217 Ricc., 2374, 28r–29v, new numeration.

218 *Ad Herennium* 3, 16–24; Cicero, *De oratore* 2, 86, 351–4; Quintilian, *Institutio oratoria* II, 2, 17–22. See also the comments of Bergmann, *Roman House as Memory Theater*, especially 225.

219 *Art of Memory*, 109.

220 Petrarch's remarks in his *Secretum*, which took the form of a dialogue with Saint Augustine on the model of Augustine's own *sortes Biblicales* in the garden, recounted in *Confessions*, VIII, are an example of "regarding books as personal sources

whose function is to provide memorial cues to oneself, divine influences being able to prophesy through the images of letters on the page just as they are during sleep through the images written in the memory," Carruthers, *Book of Memory*, 163.

221 See Pardo, "Memory, Imagination, Figuration," especially 47–8; Kemp, "Visual Narratives, Memory, and the Medieval *Esprit du Système*."

222 Ricc., 2734, 30r–32r.

223 "Perchè ella sta senpre parata a tutte le ydioma;" for this second half of the tract, Ricc. 2734, 30r–32r.

224 Concerning the particular significance of Michele's choice of example, see below, p. 227.

225 Allen, *Mysteriously Meant*, viii–ix.

226 "Marsilio Ficino as a Man of Letters," 2. On the structuring of sermons for memorization, see Origo, *World of San Bernardino*, 39–40; for Antoninus's analyses of images, above, pp. 6–7; below, p. 102.

227 Cit. Baxandall, *Painting and Experience*, 46.

228 This translation of metaphorical language is characterized alternatively as *ut rhetorica pictura*, or *ut pictura poesis*; see below, pp. 104–6.

229 Op. cit., 3, xvi, xxi. 34. For a brilliantly articulated example of the imaginative use of images along the lines suggested in these passages, eliding play, dream and rite, see Klapisch-Zuber, "Holy Dolls."

230 For a transcription and discussion of Michele's list of 100 places in his house and their associations, see Kent, "Michele del Giogante's House of Memory."

231 *History and its Images*, ix. See also Hood, "Creating Memory."

232 Cf. Starn, "Seeing Culture."

Chapter VII

1 A basic work on this subject is Douglas, *Natural Symbols*. For some recent writing relevant to specific questions discussed below, see Freedberg, *Power of Images*, and Nash, "Art and Arousal"; these authors offer constrasting opinions on whether the power of images may be derived from a "primitive cognition" that perceives them as alive (Nash, 568–9), an issue that arises most sharply in relation to religious images. On images and their role in religious life, see Hans Belting, *Image and its Public*, and *Likeness and Presence*, which incorporate important work on this subject particularly by French, Italian, and German scholars. See also Scribner, various, especially "Popular Piety and Modes of Visual Perception." On modes of attention see Starn, "Seeing Culture"; Baxandall, *Painting and Experience*, 152: "A society develops its distinctive skills and habits, which have a visual aspect," to which "pictorial style gives access"; he commented on Piero della Francesca's "gauged sort of painting," Angelico's "preached sort of painting," and Botticelli's "danced sort of painting," cf. Jayne, "Choreography by Lorenzo." In a review of Baxandall, Middeldorf summed up his subject as "a body of cognitions common to a society that included patrons and artists," 204–5.

2 See particularly Van Os, *Art of Devotion*. The texts he invoked to illuminate his images are fragments of the liturgy, or devotional works generally popular in Europe in this period; the Florentine images and popular poetry compared below have an added advantage of being very closely linked in terms of

time, place, and even persons, since some poets were also patrons and friends of painters; see below, ch. 8. For some indication of the current view of attempts to relate religious ideas and images as highly problematic, see Cassidy, introduction to *Iconography at the Crossroads*, 3–15. He referred to a growing mistrust of the search for texts as keys to images, in the style of Panofsky and even Warburg, 6. While observing that it is easy to sneer at "disguised symbolism," he contended that "insofar as hidden meanings, mysteries and prophecies are an essential essential part of Christian belief" and that which remains to be revealed, this is not so silly. On the other hand, he suggested, 8, that "the search for a moral or for some profound intellectual significance in images . . . has less to do with the medieval and Renaissance view of art than with the prevailing modern view that the function of art is to express emotions and ideas or subtleties of Christian doctrine."

3 See Wilson, *Music and Merchants*, 19–28, for an excellent account of the way in which sermons created *devotio*. "A mendicant sermon typically began with a brief scriptural reference (*thema*), usually the source of an image or key word, then proceeded to develop distinctive levels of meaning through recourse to *distinctiones* (or *divisiones*), different senses of a term contained in scripture. Preachers had recourse to *distinctio* collections, alphabetized word-lists which linked a repertory of key scriptural words to their divere interpretations among various *auctoritates*, and made possible the ready amplification of an image or word through simile," 22.

4 See above, pp. 6–7.

5 Gilbert, *Italian Art*, 145–6; "Subject and Not-Subject," 207; see also Dominici, *Regola del governo*. Gilbert's collection of documents and his comments on them reflect a determination to maximize the initiative and role of the artist in the conception of a work of art, to minimize that of the patron, and generally to simplify the meaning of the object. Quite a lot of Charles Hope's writing addresses a similar agenda; see especially "Artists, Patrons and Advisors," "Altarpieces and the Requirements of Patrons," and "Religious Narrative." Cf. below, ch. 14, on patrons and artists. Dominici was born *c.*1356, and died *c.*1419 in Buda; see Salvi, introduction to *Regola del governo*. Although his Lenten sermons of 1399 were remembered as legendary for some decades after his death, Dominici's attitudes to images as expressed in his *Regola* of 1403 were way out of date by mid-fifteenth century; cf. the infinitely more sophisticated observations of Antoninus about that time, although the archbishop praised his Dominican forerunner's *Libro d'amore di carità* in his *Summa theologica*, essentially and paradoxically because it was written in the *volgare*.

6 Both Gilbert and Hope tend to confuse doctrine with theology; see especially the latter's three articles cit. supra. Obviously one shades into the other, and a few of Belcari's correspondents did address theological issues, see below, pp. 102–4, but most popular compilers recognized their interests as doctrinal rather than theological; even Antoninus's famous *Summa* frequently bore in his lifetime the adjective *historiale* rather than *theologica*.

7 Antoninus, *Lettere*, 33–5.

8 Sinding-Larssen, *Iconography and Ritual*; see also Ringbom, *Icon to Narrative*; Van Os, op. cit.; Miles, *Image as Insight*. These scholars of objects related to liturgical activities have written at length on the absurdity of regarding images as detached from religious observances.

9 "Altarpieces and the Requirements of Patrons," 535–6. Cf. Iacopo da Voragine, *Golden Legend*, especially introduction and prologue, on the conception of revelatory or salvational history as independent of historical time. This is exemplified in the chapter on "The Passion of the Lord," 1, 208–9, concerning the unity of time in which the sin of Adam and the Passion of Christ occurred. Biblical narratives painted in contemporary Florentine settings image the timeless revelation and continuous manifestation of central Christian truths, in daily life as in the sacrifice of the Mass. Similarly, donor portraits may be meant and seen "to exist on a different plane of reality from the heavenly figures," Hope, 551, but these planes were not separated into separate categories of heaven and earth, "because their union with the saints was a beatific vision the living had not yet seen." As Verdon, "Environments of Experience and Imagination," 3, observed, from the first the Church presented Christ as "something . . . that we have heard, and we have seen with our own eyes, that we have watched and touched with our own hands; the Word, who is life . . . made visible (1 John 1:1–2)"; he added that "devices such as linear perspective and correct anatomical rendering made sacred history a credible extension of the viewer's individual experience."

10 "Altarpieces and the Requirements of Patrons," 535–6, 547, and especially 544: "Most altarpieces are reflections of devotion to the Virgin and the saints, not to Christ." Such propositions would have made no sense at all to a Florentine audience. Hope acknowledged here his debt to Gilbert's introduction to *Italian Art* and "extrapolated" on Gombrich, *Symbolic Icons*. 13–17, 26–30, asserting that "great art" makes no serious reference to contemporary persons or events, and decrying the discovery by art historians of "hidden meanings," ignoring the fact that many of these, as Kenneth Clark pointed out, would have been "perfectly open and obvious to men from the Middle Ages down to the late eighteenth century," introduction to Hall, *Subjects and Symbols*, vii. Gombrich in turn suggested in his introduction to Hope's "Religious Narrative" that "Dr Hope's conclusions invite revision [downwards] of our estimate of the theological learning of the laity, and more generally, of the potential of works of art as bearers of complex doctrinal ideas." Hope's conclusion that "there is no hint in any document of the period, so far as I know, that people wished to express or sought any deep theological message in altarpieces," ("Altarpieces," op. cit., 554) seems based on the absence from the contracts he analysed of the sort of exegesis of the nature of the Incarnation or the Trinity such as filled men's prayers, poems, and the liturgy in which they were steeped. It may be true that as Middeldorf observed in his review of Baxandall's *Painting and Experience*, "we have only the scantiest and vaguest utterances on works of art from the period," and are "forced to rely on ingenious reconstructions" of contemporary attitudes. No one now can see into Renaissance minds, but it seems bizarre of Hope to suggest he can do so better without the encumbrance of too much "detailed research into the sources and documents" from which actual attitudes might be reconstructed. There is much more and much better evidence illuminating these than Middeldorf implied or Hope assumed. For example, in relation to the latter's dismissal of recent interpretations of Masaccio's Brancacci chapel frescoes invoking the context of contemporary debates on the Catasto, it is at least possible to show that when at least one

Florentine citizen discussed this tax in a government debate, he associated it with tax paid to Caesar in mind. See Brucker, *Civic World*, 483, n. 47, Rinaldo degli Albizzi, CP 47, fol. 51, 1426: "Et Cesar, ut tributa haberet, unite machinam universam describere fecet: et per hoc clare apparet utilem viam Catasti."

11 Ricc., 1309, 1r: "Nonne intendo d'entrare in chosì somma alteza, ma voglio dire della sua vita, meditandola e pensandola piccholo e grande, e chi legge si pongha mente alle mani che sella mente fusse di viata a meditare la vita di Xpo e pensare di lui piccholo e grande, e della morte e della resuresione e della grolia sua nome, da lasciare questa però che pensare di lui, amore di lui ene l'utima parte; e questa di Messere San Giovanni sì facciamo per dare ricreazioni alle menti inferme, edè una chotale opera fanculesca; sicchè queste anime fanculli n'abino una letizia ispirituale chosì aparino di meditare e entrare alla vita di Xpo e della Donna Nostra suo madre, e se troveranno letizia in pensare la vita de' santi in chotali chosì fanciulesche, quanto maggiormente penseranno la vita di Xpo dove ene tutta perfezione; e vezzando la mente a queste meditazioni bassette sapranno poscia entrare a pensare le gran chose de' santi, et chosì enteranno a pensare Messer Giesu Xpo che afatti i santi suoi chosì buoni. E queste chose non sono provate damme se non quam che si dice chose che sieno aprovate per lla chiesa. Ma dilettomi di pensare chosì, e se di voi diletta di pensare più chose o per altro modo potetelo fare e potetevi trastullare chome vi piace, ispezialmente di chostui chella chiesa fa fessta della sua nativitade . . ." In the first initial was a portrait of the Baptist, painted and gilded, and the Quaratesi arms, cf. 82v, "Finita è lla leggienda di Santo Giovanni Batista scritta per me Giuliano di [Quaratesi]: finita adì x di decenbre 1458, a ore 20." Quaratesi was the patron of the altarpiece for San Niccolò by Gentile da Fabriano, whose predella panel illustrates the role of images in worship in church; see below, p. 137, and fig. 52. He took over from Cosimo the patronage of San Salvatore al Monte, right next to San Miniato al Monte, which was already the site of Medici patronage; see below, pp. 80, 356.

12 Origo, *World of San Bernardino*, 121, Sermon XLIX, "De Christiana religione."

13 Particularly sophisticated, for example, is the account of the Resurrection which incorporates the exegesis of Saint Augustine, among the exponents of doctrine most admired by the Florentine *popolo*; see 1, 216. On Saint Augstine, see *Golden Legend* 2, 116–32; on Saint Peter, 1, 340. For extracts from this work in compilations, see Morpurgo, *I manoscritti*, index.

14 See, for example, Ricc., 1301. What the copyist noted as significant in Iacopo's work is not only information concerning the saints, but phases in the liturgical year representing the unfolding of the revelation, like the "avvenimento del Signore": "Abiamo adunque potuto comprendere tutte le chagioni del santissimo Avento, e'l modo preso nella presente lettura e sposiçione del Giudicio secondo che tratta il Sancto Vangelo, del quale vedremo la lettera con alquante exposiçioni brievi . . ." This is also a framework within which large-scale decorative programs for chapels, like the Brancacci chapel or the Medici old sacristy, can fruitfully be read.

15 Lanza, *Lirici toscani* 1, 189–90. Antonio's imagery here owes much to Saint Bernard and the ideas on which Lippi's Medici altarpiece draws; see below, ch. 13.

16 Below, p. 263.

17 See below, p. 156; Baxandall, "Bartholomeus Facius on Painting," 92–5. He drew here on Plutarch's "pictura poema tacitum." "Simonides calls painting wordless poetry and poetry verbal painting," but both are "representing vividly emotion and character." He also invoked Horace's recommendation that poetry should move the hearer and drew an analogy with painting through a term used by Quintilian – *figuratus* – which associates verse with a metaphor from the visual arts. See *Institutio Oratoria*, II, xiii, 8–11: "It is often expedient and sometimes also becoming to make some change in the traditional arrangement, in the same way as in statues and paintings we see variation in dress, expression and attitude. For when the body is held bolt upright it has little grace; the face looks straight forward, the arms hang down, the feet are together and the work is stiff from head to toe. The familiar curve and, if I may call it such, movement, gives a certain effect of action and animation. For the same reason the hands are not always disposed in the same way, and there are a thousand different kinds of expression for the face . . . Rhetorical figures, whether of thought or of speech, produce the same effect of grace and charm. For they introduce a certain variation of the straight line and have the virtue of departing from ordinary usage." Baxandall pointed out that this sequence of associations would have come easily to a Renaissance audience familiar with these texts – Alberti, for example, built on it in his treatment of variety in painting. He noted, 97, Alberti's only mention of a modern work in *De Pictura*: "Also praised is the Navicella in Rome, in which our Tuscan painter Giotto has portrayed the eleven men stricken with fear and astonishment at seeing their companion passing over the wave, each so revealing in his face and whole body the mark of an agitated soul, that an individual emotion is manifest in each figure." Notably Giovanni Rucellai went to see the *Navicella* on his 1450 pilgrimage to Rome, and was much impressed by it; perhaps he had Alberti's view in mind; see below, p. 366.

18 Edgerton, *Pictures and Punishment*, 47–50, pls. 11, 12; on iconoclasm, see also Freedberg, *Power of Images*, and Trexler, especially "Sacred Image."

19 *Painting and Experience*, 109. His pioneering work on responses to works of art centered on learned commentators who express, as he observed, "the Latin point of view . . . the ascendancy of language over experience," *Giotto and the Orators*, 46. He is somewhat ambivalent on the question of ordinary people's ability to respond to art. While pointing out that a resort to commonplaces probably signals a failure more of words than of feeling, he gave limited attention to popular responses which are less than original.

20 See Trexler, *Public Life*, for a perceptive account of Morelli's spiritual crisis, to which the following paragraphs are indebted. This passage had gone unnoticed in a source long adduced as evidence for many other subjects, particularly the nature of social relations; see, for example, Kent, *Rise of the Medici*. For an account of the tensions inherent in social relations which also makes insightful use of Morelli, see Weissman, *Ritual Brotherhood*.

21 *Ricordi*, 71. See Branca, introduction, for an account of Morelli's reading and personal culture.

22 *Ricordi*, 477–91, especially 477–8.

23 Ibid., 479–81.

24   These phrases are from the *Salve Regina*, which Morelli recited earlier; see 483–7.

25   See Branca's note, 490; in Hebrew, according to Saint Jerome, Giovanni means "Dominus gratia eius;" therefore Giovanni = gracious, cf. Dante, *Paradiso* XII, 80–81. The writer drew parallels between earthly and heavenly patronage; on this, see below, pp. 135–6. Notably his prayers followed the pattern of the liturgy.

26   Cf. the compiler's prayer to defend himself from the "Enemy" aroused by that prayer, above, p. 85.

27   The parrot was also a symbol in Michele del Giogante's memory treatise, on which, see above, pp. 91–3. Branca noted, 507, n. 2, that the bird, common in quattrocento iconography, sang in "uno iscoperto luogo, isterile e sanza frutto," recalling the deserts to which saints and martyrs retreated, frequently represented in images of Saints Jerome and John the Baptist.

28   Op. cit., 185. On the fundamental nature of father–son symbolism for Florentines, see below, ch. 9.

29   Cf. Hope, "Religious Narrative." For the quattrocento significance of "honoring the saints," to secure their intercession to obtain the mercy of God, see *Golden Legend*, All Saints, 272–80, below, ch. 9; also, Johnson, "Sculpture and the Family."

30   The verse continues: "The Ear is second, with the attentive Word/that arms and nourishes the Mind," BNF, Magl. VII, 744, 1v, cit. most effectively by Baxandall, *Painting and Experience*, 153. See also the same author's comment, *Giotto and the Orators*, 17, on "the ease with which [the classical system of language] brought intersensory metaphor into play."

31   1 Corinthians 14:12: this passage continues: "now I know in part; but then shall I know even as also I am known."

32   "Nam quod legentibus scriptura, hoc idiotis praestat pictura cernentibus, quia in ipsa ignorantes vident quod sequi debeant, in ipsa legunt qui literas nesciunt; unde praecipue gentibus pro lectione pictura est," cit. Van Os, *Art of Devotion*, 157; 173, n. 1.

33   Ibid., loc. cit., and n. 2.

34   Ibid., 162. In this sense, the lay viewers of the frescoes commissioned by Cosimo for San Marco were perhaps not as divorced in sensibility from the monks as Hood implies; see below, pp. 155–9.

35   *On the Education of Children*, 34–5; see also the extract in Gilbert, *Italian Art*, 146. We may note here something of the pre-Reformation clergy's jealousy of their privilege of interpreting the Scriptures, one which Florentine members of lay confraternities were already beginning to usurp.

36   Cited and discussed by Hope, "Altarpieces and the Requirements of Patrons," 560, 571, n. 54, taken from San Bernardino, *Opera Omnia* 3, 282. Origo, *World of San Bernardino*, 258, observed the importance of distinguishing between the sermons reported by others and those written out by Bernardino himself in Latin; of the latter, the Lenten course *De Pugna spirituali* is now considered spurious. On the emblem and the trial see Origo, op. cit., 120. The monogram was viewed as the visible symbol of God, being the abbreviated Greek form of his name, cf. below, ch. 9, on the significance attributed to names and their recognition. The Church saw Bernardino's encouragement of people to kneel before the monogram as heresy; he was tried in 1426/7, but acquitted. In 1431, several Dominicans, including Bartolomeo Lapacci, kinsman of the chronicler of San Marco during the period of Cosimo's patronage, wrote pamphlets against him; as late as 1438 the issue was reexamined during the Council of Basle. The response to Bernardino's emblem by patrons of chapels was not to delete the arms that represented their family names, but rather to add to them the name and device of Christ; an obvious example is the placement of the monogram on the ceiling of the Medici palace chapel.

37   However, to make simple moral points Bernardino drew the attention of his audiences to Lorenzetti's frescoes *Good and Bad Government*, and commented on Simone Martini's *Annunciation*; see Gilbert, *Italian Art*, 146–7.

38   Op. cit., ch. 182, "The Dedication of a Church," 2, 385, ff.

39   See Rubinstein, *Government of Florence*, 91, for Antoninus's opposition in 1458 to the open ballot in the councils which the Medici favored, as "against natural reason"; he affixed a proclamation stating his argument to the doors of the cathedral. See also Vespasiano's *Life* of Antoninus, *Vite* I, 161; the archbishop put up notices in all the churches that votes should be given secretly, on pain of excommunication.

40   See the selections from Antoninus's *Summa theologica*, published Gilbert, *Italian Art*, 48; also Summa pt. III, tit. 8: "Sulla condizione di mercanti ed artigianis [cap. 4, sez. I: viii] . . . De architectis seu aedificatoribus huiusmodi . . . Post factum etiam factum de mercede, si negligenter operaretur, ut citius expediret, malum esset. In hac arte periti fuerunt sancti quattuor Coronati . . . [x] De carpentariis seu lignaiolis . . . " The issue here is the amount of labor that goes into producing the effect of intarsia, "ornatum seu ostentationem," rather than the utility and permanence of the work. "Qui vero ligna secant, quum multum laborant, digni sunt mercede bona, fideliter operando. Hujus artis fuit Joseph Mariae sponsus. Dicit enim Chrysostomus in sermone de Epiphania, quod fuit carpentarius . . ." This most frequently cited passage refers, as Gilbert admitted, to particularly naive representations of subjects such as the Trinity, whereas the paintings on this theme by major Florentine artists were notably extremely sophisticated; see also Gilbert, "Archbishop on the Painters." As Rouse and Rouse pointed out, "St. Antoninus . . . on Manuscript Production," the archbishop's comments are made chiefly with reference to minor artists engaged in manuscript illumination; hence the reference to monkeys or dogs chasing hares which were common embellishments of illuminated initials or friezes.

41   However, Gilbert, "Saint Antonin de Florence et l'art," offered some examples of his influencing commissions for churches.

42   Op. cit., 75; see also Spencer, "Ut rhetorica pictura," 26. The italics here are mine.

43   Belcari's service in communal office also reflects his image as moral guardian; in the late 1450s he served as one of the Conservatori delle Leggi, and was also among the Ufficiali della Notte entrusted with the extirpation of homosexuality. On this see Rocke, *Forbidden Friendships*. Antonio degli Agli was another of those clergymen close to the Medici who wrote popular poetry and participated in the spiritual education of the Florentine *popolo*; see below, pp. 107, 182.

44   Lanza, *Lirici toscani* 1, 214, "Antonio calzaiuolo a Feo Belcari."

45   Ibid., 219; see also ibid., Benedetto Busini, 221: "O nuovo Orfeo e con sì dolce cetra/ e con l'armonizzanti alte ragioni,/ sonora tromba alla salute nostra . . ."

46   Antonio di Guido to Feo Belcari, ibid., 215.

47   Ibid., 215–16.

48 Ibid., 217; on early attempts to represent the Immaculate Conception in images, see Gallizzi, "Immaculate Conception."

49 Lanza, op. cit. 1, 225.

50 Ibid., 214; cf. Ricc. 1114, 195v.

51 Ibid., 230–31.

52 *Istorie fiorentine*, bk. v, ch. 9, also Kent, "Importance of Being Eccentric"; Lanza, op. cit., 232–3, 233–4.

53 "Che rinnovar' mi fa l'antico amore," Lanza, op. cit., 234, cf. Dante, *Purgatorio* xxx, 39: "d'antico amore sentì la gran potenza."

54 Ibid., 234.

55 Although mainly concerned with the effect on art theory of Horace's dictum "ut pictura poesis," Lee, in his article of this title, offers a number of vivid examples of how fifteenth-century writers connected these two arts in their minds. A very simple and concrete example of a popular association between language and image, an aid to meditation and the penetration of holy mysteries, is the figured poem; on this see Cook, "Figured Poetry." Such poems were popular in compilations; see the manuscripts written by Rossello Rosselli, and especially Ricc., 1098.

56 Notably Landino's translation of Pliny was among the first books to be printed in Italy, in 1476, which suggests a strongly felt need for this work.

57 See Spencer, "Ut rhetorica pictura." On Fazio see Baxandall, "Bartholomeus Facius on Painting"; and Gilbert, *Italian Art*, 176, for the translation of the passage cited.

58 See Gilbert, *Poets Seeing Artists*, 28–9; *Purgatorio* x, 28–33: "Lassù non eran mossi i piè nostri anco',/ quand'io conobbi quella ripa intorno,/ che, dritta, di salita aveva manco,/ esser di marmo candido, e adorno/ d'intagli sì che non pur Policreto,/ ma la natura lì avrebbe scorno."

59 See also below, p. 381.

60 Ames-Lewis and Bednarek, *Decorum in Renaissance Narrative Art*, 7; *Purgatorio* x, 34–45; also Edgerton, "'How Shall this be?'" For Bernardino's sermon see Gilbert, *Italian Art*, 146–7, and Carli, "Luoghi ed opere d'arte" on Bernardino's references to art. On this theme see also Procacci, "Come gli artisti leggevano Dante."

61 *Rime*, 480, 483. On the Bianchi, see Henderson, *Piety and Charity*, 51–4; Bornstein, "Giovanni Dominici, the *Bianchi*, and Venice." On the decoration of Orsanmichele, and Sacchetti's role in it, Henderson, op. cit., 227–31; Zervas, ed., *Orsanmichele*, chs. 7 and 8. The tabernacle was built by Orcagna (Iacopo di Cione) in 1369/70, with the aid of the Bankers' Guild. See also Cohn, "Franco Sacchetti." With the aid of the verses Cohn reconstructed the content and sequence of the frescoes.

62 Hood described the devotional images painted by Fra Angelico for Cosimo de' Medici at the convent of San Marco as painted prayer; see "Fra Angelico at San Marco: Art and the Liturgy," and below, pp. 149–59.

63 Below, p. 260, and fig. 121.

64 See below, p. 137, and fig. 50.

65 See Rubinstein, *Palazzo Vecchio*, 51–2; Sacchetti, *Rime*, 285, 270. Rubinstein compared these patriotic messages to the incriptions on the Lorenzetti frescoes in Siena; see above, fig. 15; below, fig. 38. Cf. Salutati's "Epigrams of the famous Men placed in the smaller hall of the Florentine Palace." On these see Hankey, "Salutati's Epigrams"; Rubinstein, op. cit.; Laur., Conv. Soppr. 79, 102v–4r; below, p. 198.

66 Lanza, *Lirici toscani* 2, 120–3, including the comment of the compiler of the Vatican manuscript: "capitolo del detto messer Antonio fatto a laude della gloriosa Annunziata di firenze, nel quale dispone el vangelio di santo Luca." Cf. below, pp. 207–9, and fig. 88.

67 Ibid., 1, 120; see also Antonio di Meglio's other verses, 126, 140, those of Antonio di Guido, 188–9, 191–2, and Matteo Scambrilla, ibid., 2, 468.

68 Cit. Arasse, "Annonciation/énonciation," 5; see also the comments of Didi-Huberman, *Fra Angelico*, 42–3.

Chapter VIII

1 Readers should consult the index for other references to those named below.

2 On the life and writings of this interesting and eccentric figure, see Minnich, "Autobiography of Antonio degli Agli."

3 See Gombrich, introduction to the Selwyn Brinton Lecture given by Charles Hope at the Warburg Institute, 1986, "Religious Narrative," 804–18. Recently Gombrich has repudiated some products of a tradition, associated with the Warburg, of which he himself was a pioneer and master. This might be seen a reaction against what he called the "modish exaggeration" of this method, or even as a perverse manifestation of the extraordinary flexibility of mind which has made him such a lively scholar of this arcane field.

4 Cf., for example, Lanza, *Lirici toscani* 1, 298, Bernardo Biffoli: "Io ho pieno di fantasia il cervello." Parenti's note was first published by Sale, "An Iconographic Program"; for translation and comment see also Gilbert, *Italian Art*, 112–14.

5 Cf. above, pp. 96 and also 91–3.

6 Borsook, "A Florentine *Scrittoio*," 91.

7 For Parenti's patronage of Domenico Veneziano see Wohl, "Domenico Veneziano Studies." See Borsook, "Documenti relativi alle cappelle di Lecceto," on Parenti's involvement with the great *lettuccio* that Filippo was having made for the king of Naples by Benedetto da Maiano. Sale described Parenti's business letters to his mother-in-law Alessandra Strozzi as "disappointing," since "they betray none of his intellectual and philosophical interests," cf. Gilbert, op. cit., loc. cit. But why would they?

8 *Italian Art*, 113; italics mine.

9 See Gilbert, op. cit., of Landucci, 217, and Chambers's interpretation, *Patrons and Artists*, 207, of Leonardo da Vinci's complaint that his patrons did not understand the technical demands of his work.

10 On the importance of adding to a picture of the production of art in Florence the numerous "non-canonical" commissions, produced in circles best described as "artigianale-artistico" and recorded in relatively unexploited records such as the Catasto, see Guidotti, "Pubblico e privato, committenza e clientela"; he described a number of such objects.

11 See *Cult of Remembrance*. According to Cohn's limited sample of data from testaments up to 1425, such commissions were most numerous in Arezzo, Perugia, and Florence, and in the third quarter of the thirteenth century. The author's conclusion concerning "the rise of patrician cultural hegemony in the Renaissance" which "paralleled changes in political control," pushing artisans out of the art market, as out of the political process, 278–9, arose from assumptions about the nature of Renaissance society which have yet to be tested for the fifteenth century, on the basis of an appropriately

wide range of evidence. His stimulating study represents not the end of enquiry into the important subject of artisan patronage of art, but rather the beginning.

12   Ibid., 244–5.

13   Ibid., 22.

14   Ibid., 215.

15   Ibid., 238, cf. below, pp. 183–4, on the provisions of the Medici donations to San Lorenzo. See also the *Priorista* of Francesco di Tommaso Giovanni, BNF, Magl. xxv, 379.

16   Cohn, op. cit., 23; below, n. 49.

17   On the continuity of the shop over the generations, and its customers, see Frosinini, "Il passagio di gestione." On Neri de Bicci, his workshop practice, and his relation to quattrocento stylistic developments, see Thomas, *The Painter's Practice*.

18   Notably Neri di Bicci was not mentioned in Giovanni Rucellai's list of the major artists who had worked for him, *Zibaldone* 1, 24.

19   See Neri di Bicci, *Ricordanze*, and on his relations with the neighborhood, Eckstein, *District of the Green Dragon*. The last entries in this workbook belong to 1475, but more than half the commissions recorded in it were made by 1464. In keeping with the concern of this study to distinguish carefully between evidence relating to Cosimo's lifetime and what came after his death, the examples cited here are mainly from the first decade of the *ricordanze*.

20   *Ricordanze*, 224.

21   Ibid., 116–17.

22   Ibid., 222, 225.

23   Ibid., 162–3, 172. The saints included Bernardo's own patron and the patron of the church. The commission is identified with a work in the Musée Jacquemart-André in Paris. A note on payment, 299–300, includes a fuller description of the piece and associates "Mona India," the patron's sister, in the commission, delivered in August 1467. She was also associated with the commission for an Assumption identified as the picture now in the church of San Leonardo.

24   Ibid., 145.

25   *Ricordanze*, 25–6; on this work, now in the National Gallery of Canada, Ottawa, see Thomas, "Neri di Bicci's *Assumption of the Virgin*."

26   *Fra Filippo Lippi*, 33–4, 524–6, document 11.

27   *Ricordanze*, 313.

28   Ibid., 193.

29   Ibid., 130–31.

30   Ibid., 96.

31   Ibid., 290–91; Samuel H. Kress collection, Denver Art Museum, *Catalogue* 28. The same patron ordered a tabernacle of Our Lady in 1466, 285–6. On the Medici tondi, see below, pp. 252–9, and figs. 117, 118; Olson, *Florentine Tondo*, especially ch. 7.

32   Ibid., 236–7.

33   Ibid., 68–9.

34   Ibid., 56–7, 28 April 1456; Lanza, *Lirici toscani* 1, 263–4; see also Antonio di Guido's poem to Batista Salviati, ibid., 181.

35   Ibid., 174. Historians have been slow to identify and consider the role of dealers in the Florentine art market; see now, however, Fusco and Corti, "Giovanni Ciampolini."

36   For a breakdown of Neri's customers by trade see Santi's introduction, xxii–iii. Their range was not as wide, however, as he suggested, since his statistics include the sculptors and woodworkers with whom Neri cooperated professionally to produce objects for other patrons, as well as tradesmen who appear in Neri's *Ricordanze* on account of their personal business with him.

37   Ibid., 13, 15 Mar. 1453/4; "io Neri di Bicci tolsi a dipignere da Lorenzo funaiolo al Ponte Rubachonte degli Alberti, uno tabernacholo fuori della porta a San Miniato a Monte a uno suo podere, nel quale ò fare la Nostra Donna e quattro Santi da lato a suo modo [it is not clear whether he means the saints are to be painted as they usually are or as Lorenzo explained he wanted them] e dipigniere il tetto e gli sportegli di detto tabernacholo . . ." There is a structure on the corner of a house just outside the Porta San Miniato with a much-overpainted figure of the Madonna and Child which is now unrecognizable as belonging to Neri di Bicci, but the Virgin is set on a throne with a high baldachino which is part of the typology of the artist's works at that time.

38   Ibid., 113: "Richordo che a detto dì dipinsi e rende' dipinto a Francescho donzello de' Signori una testa di dama grande chome natural cholorita e ornata d'oro fine a nostre ispesa acetto che d'azuro . . ." The work cost one *fiorino largo*.

39   See particularly Haines, "Artisan Family Strategies."

40   See Callmann, *Apollonio di Giovanni*, and below, pp. 297–8.

41   For this see ibid., appendix 1. The list was transcribed by an antiquarian of the Strozzi family in the eighteenth century; it is possible that he was interested only in great families and ignored the names of other patrons.

42   *Ricordanze*, 167–8, Sat. 22 Aug. 1461: "Richordo che detto dì rendei a Domenicho da Prietasanta sarto uno descho da parto dipinto a mia ispesa." He received in return "una ciopa nera achonciò alla Ghostanza mia donna insino a dì [. . .] di giugno 1461; ànne dato a dì 8 di novembre 1461 la chucitura di dua mantegli verde bruni e' quali chucì a Lorenzo e Tonio mia figliuoli: per tuto l. [. . .]; ànne dato a dì 21 di novembre 1461 la chucitura e fornitura d'una ciopa di mostavoliere per me per sotto el mantello e la chucitura d'uno mantello per me monachino per tuto."

43   Ibid., 175.

44   Ibid., 15–16.

45   See Kent, "Michele del Giogante's House of Memory."

46   *Ricordanze*, op. cit., 204, 213; payments were made by Piero d'Antonio *battiloro* and Nofri di Filippo *chalzaiuolo*; "E de' dare la detta Mona Lionarda e gli altri per dipintura d'uno dosale dipinsi per l'altare dove istà detta tavola." The work was identified, in Milanesi-Vasari 2, 80, with one in the church of San Niccolò Oltrarno. The appeal of this subject may have derived from the well-known Trinities painted earlier in the century and prominently displayed in the cathedral and at Santa Maria Novella. Bartolomeo Cederni, a relatively wealthy and eminent patron, also ordered a Trinita for the Badia in 1461; see *Ricordanze*, 167, cf. below, ch. 9; on Cederni see Kent, "The Cederni Altarpiece by Neri di Bicci."

47   *Ricordanze*, 107: "uno artefice dell'arte della pittura buono . . ." Cf. 292–3, for another commission where the same arrangement was made for arbitration, involving Zanobi Strozzi and Alesso Baldovinetti acting for Bishop Bartolomeo de' Lapacci, prior of San Romolo.

48   Ibid., 43: "San Sebastiano orante per la compagnia delle Convertite, insegna in panno."

49   Ibid., 319, 398. Another barber whose shop was right next door to Neri's apparently had better luck; see 124–5, Wed.

10 Oct. 1459: "Vergine Maria fatta per Giovanni barbiere mi sta da lato a bottega . . . Richordo ch'el detto dì vendei a Giovanni di . . . barbiere in Porta Rossa a llato a mia botegha 1a meza Vergine Maria di gesso, cholorita, messa d'azuro e d'oro e ornata chon una ghocciola da pie' . . ."

50 Ibid., 128, cf. the similar specifications of Francesco di Cristofano, *calzaiuolo*, 401–2.

51 Ibid., 224–5. This is identified with the *Virgin and Child with Saint Lawrence* in the Berenson collection in Villa I Tatti.

52 Ibid., 96.

53 Ibid., 127; it cost one *fiorino largo*.

54 Ibid., 108, 117: "Richordo ch'el detto dì tolsi a fare al Machetta chalzolaio alla Parte ghuelfa uno cholmo da chamera, cioè una vergine Maria di gesso di pocho rilievo leghata in legniame in questo modo, cioè all'anticha, cholonne da llato, architrave, fregio e chornicione e ghocciola da pie'a tute mia ispesa d'oro e d'azuro e d'ogni altra chosa acetto legniame . . ."

55 Ibid., 180. Cf. the representation of this last scene in a predella identified with another Neri di Bicci commission of the Annunciation in 1470 by Thomas, "Neri di Bicci's *Young St. John the Baptist.*"

56 See Pope-Hennessy, *Study and Criticism of Italian Sculpture*, 82, and "Interaction of Painting and Sculpture." See also, for example, Neri di Bicci, *Ricordanze*, 186, concerning a relief by Desiderio da Settignano.

57 *Ricordanze*, 24.

58 Ibid., 75–6, 29 April 1457: "volvi drento Santo Zanobi e Santo Friano quando si visitano e dua altre figure, da ogni lato una . . ." The work is from the ex-collection Hurd of New York. Cf. *Ricordanze*, 139, 18 March 1459/60, concerning a "Dosale di Zanobi bottaio" for the altar in the church of San Frediano: "in sul quale feci una opera domaschina biancha e di più altri cholori e cho molte pignie d'oro e di sopra fe' un fregio cho certe meze fighuze e cholla frangia e da lati dua pendenti d'azuro chon fogliami d'oro, drentovi l'arme sua . . ."

59 Ibid., 134–5: "Richordo ch'el detto dì missi d'oro fine a Tomaso Finighera orafo 10 sole intagliato e razato intorno di rilievo messo da ogni parte; è di grandeza di 2 in tra 3 . . . e a detto dì lo riebe."

60 Ibid., 156; cf. 165: "Cholmo da chamera vendè a Giusto orafo . . . Richordo che più dì fa tolsi da Giusto di . . . orafo in Vachereccia a cholorire uno tabernacholo da chamera drentovi una meza Vergine Maria di gesso e leghata in detto tabernacholo, messo d'oro fine in certi luoghi e in d'ariento e d'azuro di Magnia fine e cholorita la Nostra Donna e ornata tuta d'oro fine . . ."

61 Ibid., 23–4. This encounter may have led to Neri's further work with Del Massaio, a well known mapmaker and designer favored by the Medici; see below, fig. 65. Cf. ibid., 53; Neri returned to Del Massaio a "rilievo grande di Gesso," with the Virgin and Child, the Holy Spirit, and below it in letters of gold . . ."

62 On this see Franceschi, *I lavoratori fiorentini*, ch. 6, and above, ch. 5, passim; also the plaques illustrating various trades on the bell tower of the Florentine cathedral.

63 Above, p. 65; see also Pacciani, "Brunelleschi e la Magnificenza." Neri di Bicci's inventory of the Sant'Agnese company 1466/7 is transcribed by Newbigin, "Ascension Plays," document 2.

64 Kent, "Lorenzo di Credi," 83.

65 Dei, *Cronica*, 82–3; Memorie Istoriche, fols. 19, 21, 44f, 49, published Gilbert, *Italian Art*, 181–4, under the heading "A poet of Florentine statistics." On workshops see Wackernagel, *Florentine Renaissance Artist*, 184ff; Carnesasca, *Artisti in bottega*; Bullard, "Heroes and Their Workshops."

66 *Life of Brunelleschi*, 34.

67 See Martines, *Italian Renaissance Sextet*, ch. 6. The story is firmly rooted in Florentine literary and social experience. Based on Boccaccio's popular tale of Calandrino, it incorporates many salient facts of actual life, such as the role of debtor's prison in facilitating contacts between patricians and plebeians; on this see also Kent, "Importance of Being Eccentric." There is a reference to the workshop of someone called "il grasso" in the piazza behind the cathedral in Michelozzo's tax report, published Mather, "New Documents," 229. For the close match between the details of such humorous and satirical tales about real Florentines, and evidence from other records concerning their actual lives and associations, see Piovano Arlotto, *Motti e Facezie*, and Kent and Lillie, "The Piovano Arlotto: New Documents." On the general authenticity of this genre, see Martines, "Italian Renaissance Tale as History."

68 See Neri di Bicci, *Ricordanze*, 105, 225, for his rental from the sons of "Andrea che dipigne delle sargie, *materassaio*."

69 "E seggo a mensa a tavola ritonda,/ guernita d'un grembiul da dipintore;/ suvi catini ov'io non truovo fonda," Lanza, *Lirici toscani* I, 201. For the sonnet to Michelozzo, see ibid., 206: "Quantunque al vostro elevato, alto ingegno/ l'infime rime mie non sien conforme,/ non vo' però dal mio proposto tôrme:/ supplico ben che non vi sieno a sdegno./ Vorre' saper se destinato segno / o pianeta del ciel può sottoporme/ alle 'nsidie d'Amore, inique e inorme,/ o se si può, chi vol, fuggir suo regno./ Perch'è novellamente atteso al varco,/ fra li balcon d'una vicina e' miei,/ la rete ov'i' provai già grave incarco;/ né di suo forze unquanco temerei,/ per quantunque ver me spiegassi l'arco,/ se non fusse el bel viso di costei."

70 See Lanza, *Polemiche e berte*, 1972, for Orcagna; for the family connections between poets and artists, 1989, 271–2. Stefano Finiguerra "detto lo Zà," was the son of Tommaso, who was probably the brother of the *orafo* Antonio, father of the celebrated engraver Maso. Ser Alesso Pelli's father was also a painter. See also Haines, "Artisan Family Strategies." See Onians, "Brunelleschi: Humanist or Nationalist?" for the association of Brunelleschi's "Tuscan" architecture with popular *volgare* culture. On Brunelleschi as a poet, see Tanturli, introduction to Brunelleschi, *Sonetti*, 5: "Non dunque poeta a tempo perso, il Brunelleschi, ma sonettista al momento opportuno. In quest'uso il sonetto è tutt'uno con la situazione presupposta, che quanto più si condensa in quel breve giro, tanto più di energia dà allo scoppio a catena delle allusioni e dei sensi molteplici . . . L'effetto si esalta, non per un semplice raddoppio della spazio, ma per un moltiplicarsi delle possibilità allusive, come un gioco di specchi, nella tenzone, che infatti al movente occasionale, reale o almeno pretestuoso, è condizionata."

71 Giovan Antonio Faie, a chemist from fifteenth-century Lunigiana, described the multitude of "persone che brigano ala botega," cit. Franceschi, *I lavoratori fiorentini*, ch. 6; see also Lanza, *Polemiche e berte*, 1989, ch. 5, on Burchiello's shop. For the community of artists on the Corso degli Adimari see Procacci, "Di Iacopo di Antonio"; for the *gonfalone* of Vipera,

around Borgo SS. Apostoli, see Bernacchioni, "Botteghe di artisti e artigiani."

72 See Chellini, *Ricordanze*, especially 25–6, 31–3, 47–8, 199, 218. Chellini's original cast is now in the Victoria and Albert Museum, London. See Pope-Hennessy, "Madonna Reliefs of Donatello"; Radcliffe and Avery, "Chellini Madonna"; Janson, "Giovanni Chellini's *Libro* and Donatello." See also Schulz, "Tomb of Giovanni Chellini." For Girolamo da Imola's commission from Neri di Bicci, see Neri's *Ricordanze*, 345.

73 Covi, "Four New Documents," 99. For Leonardo's books see Kemp, *Leonardo da Vinci*, 247ff, and "Commentary 3."

74 Laur., Conv. Soppr. 109.

75 Gilbert, *Italian Art*, 42–7.

76 Carruthers, *Book of Memory*, 343.

77 On this argument see Kent, *Rise of the Medici*, especially 105–6. On Cavalcanti see also Kent, "Importance of Being Eccentric"; for his comment, *Istorie fiorentine*, 4.

78 Cf. Brown's similar point about humanist praise, "Humanist Portrait of Cosimo."

79 On Cosimo's role in the commune's wars, see below, pp. 268–81.

80 Above, pp. 59–60.

81 See Watkins, "*Il Burchiello*," 39–44, for text, translation, and comment.

82 Lanza, *Lirici toscani* 2, 87–90.

83 Below, pp. 126–7.

84 See below, pp. 155–9, on the San Marco altarpiece.

85 Lanza, op. cit., 1, 222, 227. This view of Cosimo was not merely the product of encomiastic rhetoric. See MAP, v, 650, 11 Nov. 1440, Gometius, camaldolensis Ordinis generalis, "ex Abatia Rotis." Complaining to Cosimo of "alchuna molestia sopra l'altra," squeezed by taxes and "stretti per la fortuna delle guerre passate in Casentino ch'è rubbata la casa e tolte le ricolte dai inimici et dagl'amici insino a mettervi fuoco," Gometius asked Cosimo to bring the plight of his house to the attention of the Signoria, "o di chi l'a da ffare," since, "veramente Cosmo nostro non abbiamo altro refugio che a voi . . . che se l'aiuto vostro non ci soccorre andiamone in profondo et noi e quel sancto luogo."

86 Lanza, op. cit., 1, 356–8; the poet is borrowing heavily from Brunetto Latini's speech in Dante's *Inferno*, xv, as well as Latini's own *Tesoretto*. A law of 1435 decreed the celebration of the Medici recall on the feastday of San Tommaso; see below, pp. 198–9. It is not clear whether the feast of Cosmas and Damian was proposed as an additional, or an alternative day of celebration. Nor is the whole weight of Anselmo's elaborately allegorical verse entirely clear; beside the passage cited, there are others which seem to imply some criticism of the Medici.

87 "Vegho la nostra patria, la nostra città medichata e ata a prosperare durante il buon ghoverno principiato," MAP, v, 653, Malpiglio d'Antonio di Malpiglio Cicioni to Giovanni di Cosimo in Venice, 20 Nov. 1434, cit. Molho "*Pater Patriae*, o *Padrino*?" 8. The emperor's comment is recorded by Francesco di Giuliano de' Medici in a letter to his father, ibid. v, 703, 1433.

88 Above, ch. 4. Strozzi's letter is MAP, xi, 150, 11 Jan. 1434/5; for Barberini's poem, Lanza, *Lirici toscani* 1, 689–91; 2, 265. Pigli was an indefatigable compiler of vernacular works, with at least five important collections to his credit; see above, ch. 6. He was also a great burlesque poet. For a possible early

example of a play on the Medici name see Kent, *Rise of the Medici*, 248.

89 On the Medici arms see McKillop, "L'ampliamento dello stemma mediceo."

90 Letter to Cosimo, *Letters* 1, 1; see also his preface to his translation of Plotinus, cit. Hankins, "Platonic Academy," 144–51.

91 Lanza, op. cit., 1, 372–3. "Cosmo cosmicon cosm' ha derelitto,/ e ritornato a ornar quella parte/ che infuse in lui tanta scïenza e arte,/ per la cui morte il secol resta aflitto./ O infilici antichi, che iscritto/ poetizando avete tante carte,/ vostr'opere son tutte invano sparte,/ perché 'l più degno fa più degno il ditto! Riman la terra lacrimosa e mesta,/ vedova intenebrata, avendo person/ chi la teneva in pace e'n fama vera./ Ma rallegrisi tutto l'universo,/ ché, se lasciata ha qui l'umana vessta,/ l'alma trïonfa alla suprema spera."

92 *Diario*, 3.

93 Cited Brucker, *Civic World*, 506.

94 See Brucker, *Two Memoirs*; see also the editor's introductory comments.

95 See, for example, Ricc., 1185.

96 Laur., Segnani, 4; the extract is described as being from the "Libro Imperiale di Cesare," concerning the "reggimento di quattro mercatanti Romani."

97 Ricc., 1387, 1r: "Omnia iudicia eius in chonspetto mio e iustizia eius non repulit ad me et ero inmachulatus chum eo conobservabo me abi iniquitate mea prius. Ogni persona di qualumque condizione e merchatante che niente potrebbe stare sanze vendere o comperare niuna cosa è tanto necessaria al mondo quanto la merchatantia . . ." Cf. 131r: "Et breviter omnis creatura ad eum comperata defettum habet, quia infiniti ad infinitum nulla est proportio. Deo Gratias, amen."

98 See Henderson, *Piety and Charity*, 275–80; 292. An important underlying purpose of the confraternity's public charity at Orsanmichele was to ensure that the poor did not attack the persons or property of those better off, in their desperate search for sustenance, ibid., 296. See Calderoni's poem on this theme, Lanza, op. cit., 1, 344. For discussions in the Consulte e Pratiche about grain distribution, see Brucker, *Civic World*, passim.

99 BNF, Fondo Tordi, 3, 65v.

100 See *Paradiso* xx, 43–8.

101 Wilk McHam, "Donatello's *Dovizia*," observed that it "might be seen as embodying an argument in favor of individual wealth." See also her comment, related to this work, in "Public Sculpture in Renaissance Florence," 149, on the "the Renaissance's rediscovery of the dynamic power, known in antiquity, of a public monument to crystallize interpretations of cultural identity in visual form, and to influence the citizenry's perception of them." On the crucial relation of the issue of civic wealth to the development of the Renaissance state, see Baron, various, particularly "Franciscan Poverty and Civic Wealth," and Brown, "Hans Baron's Renaissance." On the form and significance of this important lost work of Donatello, see also Wilkins, "Donatello's Lost *Dovizia*"; Haines, "La Colonna della *Dovizia*"; Pope-Hennessy, "Donatello and the Bronze Statuette."

102 McHam, "Donatello's *Dovizia*," 19–20.

103 San Martino was the patron of the harvest festival marked by its celebration of plenty, and the conspicuous consumption of food and wine by popular revellers; on these events see Wilkins, op. cit., 401–5.

104 For Belcari's reference to Donatello, below, p. 199; for Michele's replica, above, p. 113.

105 On these issues see particularly Herlihy and Klapisch-Zuber, *Les Toscans et leurs familles.*

106 For examples of a general failure in the literature describing Florentine society to distinguish between the working or laboring classes and artisans, see Cohn, *Laboring Classes,* "Character of Insurrection," and Molho, various. Molho, "*Pater Patriae* or *Padrino?*" assumed that class conflict inevitably and absolutely divided this society: "I would suggest that the principal characteristic of Florentine life throughout the *quattrocento,* during and following Cosimo's career, was the cleavage which rent political and cultural manifestations into experiences perceived and assimilated differently by the rich and the poor," 9. However, the dissident group he described, 14–15, as all "members of the working class," the supposedly alienated segment of society, consisted in fact of a carpenter, a painter, two weavers, a wine seller, a messenger, a cook, a resident or employee of a communal brothel, a goldsmith's assistant, a cobbler, and a *sensale,* in fact not the unskilled poor, but all artisans or their social equivalent. Such men we have seen in chs. 5 and 6 to have had a strong commitment to a culture and morality they shared with the most affluent citizens. Cf. Trachtenberg, *Dominion of the Eye,* who read and interpreted the significance of civic space almost exclusively in terms of the power and domination of the political and economic elite. He notably excepted from consideration "the vitality of religious life" as an important theme "of marginal importance to this book," and denounced analyses of Florentine society which posit the existence of elements of civic harmony for their "undervaluation (or suppression) of important strata of the historical process, severe problems of class conflict, psychologically and ideologically acute strategies of rule and identity construction, and other multidimensional sociological and political phenomena with sharp edges," as the products of an "archival positivism" which is really "a mask for political conservatism," an "idealizing strategy" that "tends to ennoble an elite class (which this scholarship obsessively admires)," 1–3.

107 Kent, "Buonomini di San Martino," 65.

108 This face of Medici patronage and its reflection in popular poetry is discussed at greater length in Kent, *Fathers and Friends.* On this theme see also Martines, "Love and Hate in Renaissance Patronage"; for the disjunction in art between the actuality of poverty and its perception and representation, Riis, "I poveri nell'arte italiana." However, the hierarchies of power and responsibility were not necessarily or always resented by those lower down the social ladder. As Giovanni Bacci once wrote to Giovanni di Cosimo: "Io non te voglio più dire quello che più volte a tutta casa vvostra per noi e stato decto. Sì non che a voi sia la fadigha del chomandare et a noi con fedeltà amore e charità de' obedire . . ." MAP, VII, 2, Bologna, 1438, March 26 to Giovanni di Cosimo in Ferrara.

109 "Nam ingenia florentina acerrima sunt, et in omnen partem strenua," Zippel, "Il Filelfo a Firenze," 215.

110 On the Opera del Duomo see Poggi/Haines, *Il duomo di Firenze,* and Haines, various, especially *Sacrestia della Messe* and "Brunelleschi and Bureaucracy"; also "La Colonna della *Dovizia.*" I am most grateful to Dr. Haines for making available to me before publication her work on the Arte della Lana, San Zanobi, and the Piazza di San Giovanni. On *operai* and the commissions of the Parte Guelfa, see Zervas, various, especially "Quos volent" and *Brunelleschi and Donatello.* Her introduction to this work, especially 7, makes valuable comment on the interaction between patrons and artists in these commissions, and on the distinction between corporate and communal commissions. For an excellent introductory survey of the latter, see Holmes, *Florentine Enlightenment.*

111 Haines, "Brunelleschi and Bureaucracy," 125.

112 Hyman, *Brunelleschi in Perspective,* 1. For a digest of contemporary comments on Brunelleschi, including those of Matteo Palmieri, Flavio Biondo, and Archbishop Antoninus, see Saalman, *Cupola,* 11.

113 Haines, op. cit., 107; 105–6. On the use of these same adjectives in relation to other important aspects of Florentine life like friendship, patronage, political office, etc., see particularly Kent, *Fathers and Friends.*

114 *On Painting,* prologue, 35.

115 Haines, "Brunelleschi and Bureaucracy," 112. For details of the competition, ibid. 108–20; also Saalman, *Cupola,* p. 249.

116 "Pauper animal ed insensibile,/ che vuoi lo 'ncerto altrui mostrar visibile . . ."; "Quando dall'alto ci è dato speranza/ o tu ch'hai efigia d'animal resibile,/ perviensi all'uom, lasciando il corrutibile,/ e ha da guidicar' Somma Possanza," Brunelleschi, *Sonetti,* 21–2. This pair of verses is a prime example of the *tenzone,* the acerbic poetic exchange which was one of the favorite forms of popular poetry; on Giovanni Gherardi da Prato, see Lanza, *Polemiche e berte,* 1989, ch. 8. See also Saalman, "Giovanni di Gherardo da Prato's Designs Concerning the Cupola."

117 On the creative claims of the quattrocento artist see particularly Jarzombek, *On Leon Baptista Alberti*; Greenstein, "Alberti on *Historia*"; Leonardo da Vinci, *Notebooks.*

118 Haines, op. cit., 113, and Saalman, op. cit., 137.

119 "Detto inventore e governatore della muraglia della magiore cupola," *Life of Brunelleschi,* ed. Saalman, 94; Haines, op. cit., 116.

120 Haines, op. cit., 116; Manetti, *Life of Brunelleschi,* 84–5.

121 Reported conversation with the architect Mariano Taccola, in Battisti, *Brunelleschi,* 20–21.

122 This was the phrase Marco Parenti used to refer to the making of a belt-buckle for Filippo Strozzi; see Sale, "Iconographic Program," 298. See also the anonymous sonnet cited by Battisti, *Brunelleschi,* 326, satirizing clerical habits and predicting the collapse of one congregation into chaos "before the dome is closed." The Florentines' pleasure in civic buildings and personal identification with them persists to the present day. I once knew an old lady of at least seventy who worked in a greengrocers' shop in the district of Santa Croce. Her entire family had emigrated to Australia and settled in an unlovely area near Melbourne called Werribee, the site of a sewage farm. When I asked her why she had returned alone to live in Florence without the support and protection of sons and grandsons she replied, "I missed the Palazzo Vecchio."

123 Renier, op. cit., 24. This opinion is also recorded in Vasari-Milanesi, *Vite* 2, 345–6; its provenance remains uncertain.

124 See Arte della Lana, 39, 6v–11v, 42r–44r, especially 11v. I am grateful to Margaret Haines for providing me with a copy of these records. Fantino di Giovanni de' Medici was an *operaio* of the Arte della Lana in 1392. Giovenco de' Medici's com-

panions in this office in 1436 included Lorenzo di Andrea di Messer Ugo della Stufa and Giovanni di Coccho Donati, both from families whose members daily frequented the Medici house on the Via Larga; see below, p. 234. On Giovenco see De Roover, *Rise and Decline*, 174, and Kent, *Rise of the Medici*, 55; a factor of the bank, he was personally close to Cosimo, who helped to arrange his marriage in 1428. From 1434 to 1443 the bankers of the *operai* were Neri di Domenico Bartolini and Bartolomeo Orlandini; see Saalman, *Cupola*, documents, 272a; on the latter's close relationship to the Medici, Kent, op. cit., pt. 1. From the early thirties, Cosimo's immediate family began to extend their guild membership beyond the Bankers' Guild, the Cambio, in which Cosimo was matriculated in 1420. He joined the Silk Guild in 1433, and his sons Piero and Giovanni were admitted to the Wool Guild in 1435, at the ages respectively of nineteen and fourteen. Piero had been a member of the Cambio since 1425 and Giovanni since 1426. Piero joined the Silk Guild in 1436, and the Calimala in 1439; see De Roover, op. cit., 20. For the development of the relationship between the Opera and the Arte della Lana, see Saalman, op. cit., and Haines, op. cit.

125 On the drama of the construction see Haines, op. cit., and particularly Saalman, *Cupola*, especially 11–16.

126 On these themes see Bergstein, "Marian Politics." She observed the schematic representation of the component parts of the commune and its authorities, secular and spiritual, in the assignment of chapels. The republic was represented in the dedication to Santa Maria del Fiore, the Church in the main chapel of San Zenobius, its founding bishop; the Parte Guelfa, a traditionally pro-papal group of the city's elite, in the chapel of Saint Anthony [of Padua], and the guilds, nine of which took apostles as their patrons, were collectively represented by the Arte della Lana whose banner was the Agnus Dei. The baptistery in the piazza opposite the west end of the cathedral was the exclusive province of the city's original patron saint, Saint John.

127 This estimate is taken from Feo Belcari's account of the event, published by Saalman, *Cupola*, documents, 276, no. 286. While presumably an exaggeration, the figure indicates the observer's sense that almost everyone in the city and its environs was in attendance.

128 *Commentarii*, cit. Holmes, *Florentine Enlightenment*, 142.

129 Cambi, *Istorie*, XX, 179.

130 Lanza, op. cit., I, 683–7.

131 See also, for example, Dei's list of features and measurements in Cronica, 108–9.

132 See Munman, "Evangelists from the Cathedral of Florence."

133 "Perchè mi pare luogo dove più lungamente durerà che in altro luogo"; Saalman, *Cupola*, documents, 286; the archival reference is Laur., Archivio di San Lorenzo, no. 2210.

134 *Profugiorum ab aerumna*, 80–81.

135 Prefatio, Biblioteca Apostostolica, Vat. Lat., 1603, 4v, ff; Hatfield, "Compagnia de' Magi," 146.

136 See Dufay, *Opera Omnia*, XXVII, 106–7. I thank William F. Prizer for this point and for his advice on music in this period. Dal Corazza, *Diario*, 292, noted the pope's gift the preceding Sunday, "la domenica della rosa."

137 On the papal singers see D'Accone, "Music and Musicians," especially 115–16. Warren, "Brunelleschi's Dome," argued that the mathematical correspondence between music and architecture is so complete that Dufay must have consulted Brunelleschi on the proportions of the cupola in order to create "a sounding model of Brunelleschi's architecture," 92. This idea has not found favor with architectural historians, who stress the *ad hoc* elements in its construction, and the musicologist Charles Brewer concluded, "Defrosted Architecture," that the basic design principles of architecture and music before the mid-fifteenth century were incommensurable. I want to thank Jessie Anne Owens for drawing this discussion to my attention. See also Wright, "Dufay's *Nuper Rosarum Flores*"; he described an "architectonic design," 396, based on number symbolism relating it to the temple of Solomon as a paradigm for the universal church and its union with the Virgin.

138 Seay, "Fifteenth-Century Cappella," 45–55; D'Accone, "Singers of San Giovanni." The most famous organist of his time, Antonio Squarcialupi, had taken up a permanent position at Santa Maria del Fiore shortly before its consecration. He also enjoyed the patronage and support of the Medici family, and was to perform for them often in the following decades, not just on state occasions but also in informal gatherings at the Medici villas of Trebbio and Careggi. See D'Accone, "Antonio Squarcialupi," 3–24. Becherini, "Relazioni di Musici Fiamminghi," published extracts from the Medici letters referring to Squarcialupi; see also above, p. 211.

139 See Belcari, op. cit. The analogy between Christ as liberator of souls from hell, and the liberation of prisoners, was similarly elaborated by Branca Brancacci in his letters to Cosimo after 1434; see below ch. 9, and MAP, XII, 189; see also his poem addressed to Astorgio II Manfredi, lord of Faenza, who eventually nominated him as an apostolic notary, Lanza, *Lirici toscani* I, 327. Another letter addressed to Cosimo in 1439 referred to Cosimo's ability to liberate prisoners as "resurrecting the dead," MAP, XI, 253.

140 Cit. Wilson, *Music and Merchants*, 15; for the passage in its original Italian see Weissman, *Ritual Brotherhood*, 48.

141 Belcari, op. cit.

142 On the transfer of the relics, see Benvenuto Papi, "Un momento del concilio."

Chapter IX

1 My accounts of these commissions naturally draw upon information accumulated in the art historical literature, but unless specific citations indicate otherwise, observations about objects are my own. I have generally avoided aesthetic judgments I am unqualified to make; however, occasionally I have cited such judgments as might contribute materially to a sense of the likely impact of a work on its audience.

2 Also the altarpiece at the convent of the Annalena, which was not its original location; Hood, *Fra Angelico at San Marco*, suggested it was made for the Medici chapel in San Lorenzo, see below, p. 144, and fig. 154.

3 For the Medici domestic altarpieces see below, p. 252.

4 See Brucker, "Monasteries, Friaries and Nunneries."

5 Some major examples are the Bardi and Peruzzi, patrons of Giotto in Santa Croce, the Acciaiuoli and Altoviti in SS. Apostoli, the Capponi and Frescobaldi in Santo Spirito, the Strozzi and Federighi in Santa Trinita. For details of this patronage see Paatz, *Die Kirchen*, Richa, *Notizie istoriche*.

6 Brucker, op. cit.

7 See Trexler, "Charity and the Defense of the Urban Elites."

8 *Trattato*, 2, xxv, 693, 684–5.

9 Most notably Giovanni Rucellai, whose self-advertising façade for Santa Maria Novella, and Holy Sepulcher tomb in San Pancrazio, made bolder and more explicit claims than any Medici commission; see below, pp. 360–62, and figs. 179, 181.

10 On their building at these sites see below, ch. 10.

11 Gombrich, in his biography, *Aby Warburg*, 171, noted and concurred with Warburg's early insight, now often overlooked, of the importance to "worldly-wise Renaissance merchants" of "the religious aspects of patronage"; a telling example is his observation that even the inclusion of family portraits in frescoes was "less an act of religious indifference or profanity – as it had appeared to nineteenth-century scholars – than a resumption of those religious practices of wax *voti* . . ."

12 The outstanding exception to this neglect of spiritual and liturgical considerations governing Medici patronage is the work of Susan McKillop on San Marco, San Lorenzo, and the Badia. See her "Dante and *Lumen Christi*," also "He shall build a house." I am primarily indebted to her for most of my observations about the Medici and the liturgy at San Marco and San Lorenzo. On these issues see also Hood, *Fra Angelico at San Marco*; Gaston, "Liturgy and Patronage," Ringbom, *Icon to Narrative*; Sinding-Larssen, *Iconography and Ritual*. The findings of important studies of Florentine religious confraternities by Weissman, *Ritual Brotherhood*, and Henderson, *Piety and Charity*, have not yet been sufficiently integrated into the art historical literature on Cosimo's commissions.

13 Savonarola made this dictum memorable (although Benedetto Dei, the great amanuensis of Florentine gossip, attributed it to someone else) by seizing upon it as a saying of "mad and evil men; of tyrants"; see Weinstein, *Savonarola and Florence*, 147, cf. Gutkind, *Cosimo de' Medici*, 123. In fact, the bedrooms and studies of Cosimo and his sons contained an enormous number of *paternostri* made of precious materials such as ivory and coral; see below, p. 292.

14 See, for example, Hankins, "Platonic Academy," 147.

15 Ficino, *Letters* 1, 1. On Cosimo's "conversion" see, for example, Field, *Platonic Academy*, 3–4. As additional evidence, Field adduced a rather uncritical reading of Ficino's preface to his translation of Plato's "On Death," addressed to Piero de' Medici shortly after Cosimo died. Here Ficino appeared to claim credit for Cosimo's recent conversion to an interest in the other-worldly: "Cosimo began to deplore the misery of this life, and he so inveighed against the errors of mortals that he called death a gain." Notably Ficino admitted that Cosimo "aspired already to celestial beatitude" and "said acutely and elegantly many things in contempt of life." For the topos of Cosimo's late conversion see also Hale, *Florence and the Medici*; Hankins, "Platonic Academy." On Ficino's familiarity with the Medici household see MAP, v, 301, Ser Alesso Pelli to Giovanni de Medici. See also above, p. 391, n. 56, p. 401, n. 5. Most humanists wrote or revised their personal letters with an eye to publication; on this, see Robin, *Filelfo in Milan*; and Bullard, "Marsilio Ficino and the Medici."

16 On their theories see De Roover, "Two Great Economic Thinkers"; on Medici banking practices, his *Rise and Decline*.

17 See Borsook, *Companion Guide*, 208, on "il conto di Messer Domeneddio," a vivid expression of Florentine merchants' perception of God and their relation to him.

18 *Ricordi*, 158–9. On the Medici perception of their patrimony, see Kent, *Fathers and Friends*.

19 Wilson, *Music and Merchants*, discussed the influence of this "arithmetical mentality" on the hearing and saying of *laude*, an "opportunity to earn spiritual credit against . . . long standing penitential debt." While this is an important insight, his characterization of the *laudesi* companies as "a sacred business run for the purpose of earning shared spiritual debts" may be a little misleading. On the intense spirituality expressed in many laymens' poems, see above, especially ch. 7.

20 The Aristotelian view that money, unlike animals, was not alive and could not multiply, was adopted by most major Christian theologians and most notably Aquinas. On the doctrine of usury and its effects on the business world, see De Roover, *Rise and Decline*, especially 10–14. Le Goff, *Birth of Purgatory* and *Your Money or Your Life* explored in general how normal business activity made merchants morbidly conscious of their sins and the need for expiation either here or in purgatory, either personally or through the prayers of others.

21 The calculation of the sum of Medici charity included "alms, buildings, and taxes"; see above, n. 18.

22 See Borsook, *Mural Painters*, 8. On the Arena chapel's message to merchants see Derbes and Sandona, "Barren Metal and the Fruitful Womb"; Kohl, "The Scrovegni in Carrara Padua." McKillop, "He shall build a house," also noted this image and suggested that the Arena chapel may have influenced Cosimo's patronage at San Marco. In the 1420s and 1430s Cosimo was several times in Padua, Verona, and Venice to attend to business. In 1430 he went to the Veneto to escape the plague, and in 1433 he was exiled to Padua, where he spent some time before the Signoria allowed him to move to Venice.

23 *Inferno*, XI, XVII, especially 46–75.

24 "E pien di gioia e gloria fia lo 'nferno,/ e di tempesta e pianti e alte grida/ sarà ripieno il paradiso eterno," Lanza, *Lirici toscani* 2, 55–6.

25 I owe this observation to David Peterson.

26 On this work, see Pope-Hennessy, *Fra Angelico*, 192.

27 BNF II: II: 64, 27r: "Nella volontà dela carne tosto passa via el diletto el piacere. Ma il pecchato in etterno/ rimane et simile e difetti et mali che del vitio della carne, cioè della luxuria nascono amen." Cf. ibid., 182r.

28 BNF, Magl. 650, 1r–v: "come l'acqua spegne il fuoco, così la limosina, il peccato." On Giovanni dalle Celle, see above, pp. 86–7.

29 1 Corinthians, 13:1, 2.

30 Henderson, *Piety and Charity*, ch. 1.

31 BNF, Fondo Tordi, 1, 1r.

32 MAP, IV, 221. On the relation between the virtues of charity, liberality, and magnificence, see below, pp. 134–6. Women, being without wealth of their own, were often denied the opportunity to exercise the virtue of charity on their own behalf. Saint Antoninus stressed in his *Opera a ben vivere* addressed to Dianora Tornabuoni that she should give no alms, except out of her own dowry, without the consent of her husband, "a ciò che credendovi voi far bene non incorriate in male." She could, however, be generous in her "mental disposition," like the poor man who "if he had the means, he would dispense it abundantly and reasonably . . ." Cf. Alessandra Strozzi, reflecting on imminent death, that the most urgent bequests were those for "the good of the soul,"

since this "is the most important thing I have," *Letters*, ed. Guasti, 275–6. On Cosimo's *fama* as a charitable patron, see Belcari, in Lanza, *Lirici toscani* 1.

33 Ricc., 2734, 13v–18v.

34 Ibid. 1, 212: "quando muor che s'ordina l'essequie,/ Mammona giù di foco gli fa il talamo,/ e su si mette il corpo in tra la porpora/ . . . Qualunque vizio, over peccato o crimine,/ la lemosina spegne, e porge grazia/ d'andare a Dio sanza troppo discrimine."

35 Cit. Trexler, "Charity and the Defence of the Urban Elites," 68.

36 Cit. Spicciani, "Poveri vergognosi," 123. This passage was not written until 1450, but of course the Thomist elements were received wisdom, and many of the basic principles emphasized by Antoninus had already been articulated in his administration of the Florentine church and his rulings in ecclesiastical courts. See Peterson, various. Popular poems interpreted the teachings of the Church as articulated in sermons and didactic writings addressed to the laity. In his *Summa*, Antoninus explored as length the associations and distinctions between charity, liberality, and restitution. Liberality, for example, is discussed under the head of justice, charity under mercy. For the relevance of this concept of liberality to Florentine perceptions of Medici patronage, see below. I am most grateful to Peter Diehl, my research assistant at the Getty Center for the History of Art and the Humanities, who with his far firmer grasp of the language and concepts of medieval theology was my guide through the thorny thicket of Antoninus's *Summa*.

37 MAP, XII, 168.

38 Cosimo to Piero, 8 Oct. 1461, MAP, XVII, 306: "noi esiamo aiutato e chonorazioni e chonboti e chosi chonforto te afar fare o ragioni e quelle sante monache da pisa effarloro una limosina . . ." This is an unusually explicit reference to the motives behind charity and its expected rewards.

39 Above, ch. 4.

40 Cit. Trinkaus, *In Our Image and Likeness* 1, 75–6.

41 Above, p. 127.

42 MAP, XII, 183. The use of the biblical passage is of course not without irony and irreverence, means by which popular poets and aphorists characterstically assimilated contradiction into order. Weissman, *Ritual Brotherhood*, 47, cited examples to illustrate the concept of "divine patronage," showing how "just as patronage lay at the heart of the late medieval social system, so the imagery of patronage lay at the heart of Florentine systems of spiritual exchange." Expounding the analogy between purgatory and prison Paolo da Certaldo, *Libro di buoni costumi*, 101–2, urged his readers to say masses for the souls not only of relatives and friends but also of strangers. "Imagine that you were in prison and were abandoned by relatives and friends, and no one ever came to visit you – how would you feel if someone you did not know came to visit you and free you from prison – how would you feel? Thus it is for abandoned souls." This parallel underlay the Signoria's liberation of prisoners which matched Pope Eugenius's concession of indulgences on the occasion of the consecration of the cathedral in 1436; see above, p. 127.

43 On the ideology of the Florentine lineage of male descent, see Kent, *Household and Lineage*. See Kent, *Fathers and Friends*, on the resonances of the father image in late medieval Christian texts.

44 See Brown, *Cult of the Saints*, especially 59. On this whole world view, see also his *Society and the Holy*. Kent, "Maestro della bottega," 14–16, also observed an increasing tendency to conflate earthly and heavenly patronage in Laurentian Florence.

45 The conception of the *raccomandati di Dio* is reflected in the name of a Sienese confraternity, the Raccomandati di Gesù Cristo; for this see Henderson, *Piety and Charity*, pls. 3 and 5. On the language of patronage and its extensive possibilities, see Kent, *Fathers and Friends*. Another notable example of the assimilation of otherworldly relations to Florentine social patterns, in the application of the vocabulary of *amicizia* as patronage to the friendship of Christ, is Donato Acciaiuoli's sermon on the Body of Christ to the Magi confraternity in 1468, published Hatfield, "Compagnia de' Magi," appendix. See also several of the poems recited as part of the Certame Coronario, noted passim. For the relation of the ultimate Enemy, the Devil, to Florentine perceptions of personal enemies, prominent in the lists of Benedetto Dei, *Cronica*, op. cit., see the prayers discussed above, p. 85.

46 MAP, XIII, 27, cf. the similar language used with reference to the Priors, cit. Kent, *Rise of the Medici*, 242: "As we should adore one God, so you, Lord Priors, are to be venerated."

47 Saint Catherine, whose revelations strongly influenced the late trecento papacy and a significant group of the Florentine ruling elite, claimed that God himself explained to her that the sin of Adam had opened a deep gulf between earth and heaven, filled with the turbulent waters of mortal life, but then he had thrown a bridge across these waters – the crucified Christ. See Hood, *Fra Angelico at San Marco*, 110; Becker, *Florence in Transition*, 2, 56–60.

48 MAP, XII, 168.

49 The instructions in testaments concerning the form of commemorative works of art were similarly spare; see Cohn, *Cult of Remembrance*.

50 See particularly Barr, "Music and Spectacle," and above, p. 115.

51 Above, chs. 5–8. For some reflections on the role of images in lay worship, see Verdon, "Le Spirituel vécu." Banker, *Death in the Community*, presented a case study from another community to compare with the Florentine experience.

52 Cosimo conceded patronage rights at San Salvatore al Monte in Oltrarno to the Quaratesi; see Pellecchia, "First Observant Church." Guidotti, "Pubblico e privato, committenza e clientela," 539, noted references in the Catasto of 1427 and 1431 to payments by Francesco d'Andrea Quaratesi to Attaviano di Giovanni for the tabernacle of the altarpiece for the *cappella maggiore* at San Niccolò Oltrarno.

53 For a brilliant account of the function of pictures within pictures see Foucault's essay on "Las Meninas," *Order of Things*, ch. 1.

54 On the artist's eclectic use of sources within the range of his experience in relation to the conscious revival of antique precedents; see Burns, "*Quattrocento* Architecture and the Antique"; Greenhalgh, *Donatello and His Sources*; Bober and Rubinstein, *Renaissance Artists and Antique Sculpture*. Similarly Sperling, "Donatello's Bronze 'David'," argued plausibly that the Medici commission was partly inspired by Cosimo's viewing (in fact not once, as she suggested, but many times in the course of his official business) of the marble *David* made by Donatello for the cathedral facade and transferred

to the palace of the Signoria. For other examples relating to Medici commissions, below, especially ch. 12.

55 See Ruda, *Fra Filippo Lippi*, on the patronage of the Martelli.

56 Poggi/Haines, *Il Duomo di Firenze* 1, 201–2, doc. 1004, 1397; on this work see particularly Meiss, "An Early Altarpiece."

57 The phrase is Meiss's, ibid., 306. The "double intercession" was a theme widely disseminated in popular literature, including an account attributed to Saint Bernard, and the *Speculum Humanae Salvationis*, composed in the early fourteenth century and circulated throughout Europe.

58 Below, pp. 153–5, and fig. 60.

59 Above, pp. 111–15.

60 Lanza, *Lirici toscani* 1, 269.

61 On this, see Verdon, "Environments of Experience and Imagination," 31.

62 Verdon, op. cit., 26–7, saw the cross as a "ladder, standing on the ground with its top reaching to heaven (Genesis 28:12; John 1:51), just as in the fresco the vertical beam connects the upper and lower zones of the composition." Jesus "did not cling to his equality with God, but . . . became as men are . . . was humbler yet, even to accepting death . . . on a cross (Philippians 2:6–8)." Others have observed that the artist situated this Christian lesson in humility beneath a magnificent coffered vault that some viewers would immediately have identified as a Roman triumphal arch, so that, as Rona Goffen suggested in "Masaccio's *Trinity*," death was visibly swallowed up in victory. On this fresco see also Dempsey, "Masaccio's *Trinity*."

63 *Vite* 1, 180.

64 MAP, LXXX, 7, cit. Maguire, *Women of the Medici*, 202. Pieraccini, *La Stirpe dei Medici*, published a digest of Medici letters referring to the family's constant crises of health, many of them near misses with death. The average life-expectancy of this period was less than thirty years; see Herlihy and Klapisch-Zuber, *Les Toscans et leurs familles*. Herlihy discussed the Renaissance ages of man and perceptions of aging in "Veillir à Florence"; see also Carmichael, "Health Status of Florentines" and *Plague and the Poor*. On illness as an element in shaping the Medici family identity see below, p. 244.

65 See below, pp. 375–7, and figs. 186, 187.

66 See Cohn, *Cult of Remembrance*.

67 "La età et infirmità mi po'offendere et nello intellecto e nel farmi manchare l'animo . . ."ASF, CS, 2a ser., 136, 126, Nov. 1454.

68 Copy in CS, 1a ser., 136, 122, undated, but before Giovanni di Cosimo's death in November 1463.

69 MAP, v, 697, 10 Oct. 1433, Francesco to his father Giuliano d'Averardo, cit. Kent, "I Medici in esilio," 14–15; also v, 699, 700. See also Ambrogio Traversari's affectionate anxiety for the Medici brothers' safety, *Hodoeporicon*, 168–73. Lorenzo di Piero wrote in his *Ricordo*, 158, "our grandfather Cosimo was imprisoned in the Palace, and in danger of losing his head."

70 Pieraccini, op. cit., 14; on Cosimo and Averardo see Kent, "I Medici in esilio," *Rise of the Medici*, and *Fathers and Friends*.

71 *Ricordi*, 410.

72 MAP, II, 371.

73 See below, pp. 190–91, and fig. 78.

74 Below, ch. 15. Cf. also the tomb of Cosimo's friend Sigismondo Malatesta, captain of the Florentine militia in the 1430s, at Rimini, Ettlinger, "Sepulcher on the Facade."

75 See also Paoletti, "Donatello's Bronze Doors," and cf. the Bardi Cherichini tomb in the porch of Santa Felicita.

76 "SI MERITA IN PATRIAM SI GLORIA SANGUIS ET OMNI LARGA MANUS NIGRA LIBERA MORTE FORENT VIVERET HEU PATRIAE CASTA COM CONIUGE FELIX AUXILIUM MISERIS PORTUS ET AURA SUIS OMNIA SED QUANDO SUPERANTUR MORTE IUVENIS HOC MAUSOLEO TUQUE PICARDA IACES ERGO SENEX MOERET IUVENIS PUER OMNIS ET AETAS ORBA PARENTE SUO PATRIA MOESTA GEMIT." For the text of the inscription see Richa, *Notizie istoriche* 5, 37–8. I wish to thank Mr. Nicholas Goodhue for his advice on the translation. For the Medici family's particular interest in Petrarch's *Triumphs* see below, pp. 297–8.

77 Hankins, "The Humanist, the Banker, and the *Condottiere*," 67–9. "Neque enim ea sapientia sumus ut mortem tam optimi, tam cari ac benefici parentis sine moerore et lachrimis ferre possimus. Nam si unquam summo amore immortalibus in filios beneficiis aliquis pater lugendus fuit, nemini mirum videri debet si tam cari genitoris obitu moveamur . . . Qua consuetudine domestica fuerit famulorum moeror, qui eius decessum non secus ac parentis luxerunt, intelligi licet. Neque vero eum senectus morosum ac difficilem reddiderat, non vires animi debilitaverat, sed ea gravitate, ea iocunditate erat, ut eum tota domus summa caritate complecteretur. De vigore autem animi dicere pretermittimus: in promptu enim omnibus est quo consilio, qua cura, qua integritate omnia rei publice obiret munera. Quanto vero officio amicis navaret operam, moerore funeris indicatum est." Hankins suggests the letter was actually written by Bruni; perhaps he also composed the inscription on the tomb, but Niccoli is a more likely candidate; see below, p. 191.

78 See Vespasiano's account of Cosimo's patronage, *Vite* 2.

79 My perception of these works owes much to the wealth of information and insight in Susan McKillop's account of them, "He shall build a house," as well as to William Hood's sensitive reading of them as expressions of Dominican devotion, *Fra Angelico at San Marco*.

80 Hood, op. cit., cf. Ames-Lewis, "Fra Filippo Lippi's S. Lorenzo *Annunciation*."

81 An unfortunate impression arising from comments such as Paoletti's in "Donatello's Bronze Doors," 48, of the San Marco and Annalena altarpieces: "In these paintings, the brothers used a specific saintly stand-in to mark their presence and their generosity."

82 Above, pp. 118–19.

83 Lanza, *Lirici toscani* 1, 214–15.

84 See Herlihy, "Tuscan Names."

85 Several passages from Genesis and Deuteronomy turn, for example, on the significance of Jacob's naming of his sons.

86 Kemp, "From '*Mimesis*' to '*Fantasia*,'" suggested that Renaissance realism generally works against symbolism. See, however, Barolsky, "Naturalism and the Visionary Art," 63: "The history of Italian Renaissance art as it is currently written is still so weighted with matters of style, or naturalism, that it insufficiently attends the visionary character of such illusionistic devotional art, which is the mimetic means to a spiritual end . . . all . . . devotional images were intended . . . to direct the devout beholder's gaze toward a realm ultimately beyond what can be seen corporeally in nature, to the divine truth, which can only be apprehended (as the church fathers taught) with spiritual eyes." In any case, attempts to find the features of Cosimo in representations of his patron saint Cosmas miss the point of the nature of the

identification between the two; Saint Cosmas did not have to bear Cosimo's features in order to recall him.

87 Herlihy, op. cit., 573: "For all of Florentine Tuscany in 1427, of the fifteen leading names that account for half the male population, thirteen point to a celestial sponsor." As he observed, Saint Antoninus, in his discussion of baptism in the *Summa theologica*, advocated the use of saints' names, "not the names of pagans, such as Pyramides or Palamides, Lancelot and of that sort."

88 Above, p. 119.

89 Such a deliberate strategy is particularly suggested by the fact that Cosimo was actually born on 10 or 11 April, but celebrated his birthday on 27 September, the feast of Saints Cosmas and Damian. This was a much more radical shift than Lorenzo's moving his official birthday from 1 January to 2 January because of the octave of Santo Stefano; see McKillop, "Dante and *Lumen Christi*," 255.

90 For the vigor of this metaphor in late medieval culture see Najemy, "Republic's Two Bodies"; also the memory treatise of Michele del Giogante, above, pp. 91–3. Cosmas and Damian were two of a number of saints, including Roch and Sebastian, invoked as protectors against disease. This certainly made them sharply and personally relevant to the Medici family, chronic sufferers from the debilitating and crippling disease of uricaemia, or gout. This is the major theme of Pieraccini, *La Stirpe dei Medici*.

91 On Traversari's relations with the Medici brothers see above, ch. 3; on these commissions below, especially ch. 10.

92 This was a common complaint of seekers of Medici patronage; see Kent, *Fathers and Friends*.

93 MAP, VII, 113, to Giovanni di Cosimo, s. d.

94 Cf. Giotto's depiction of Scrovegni presenting his church in heaven, in the Arena chapel, above, fig. 65.

95 In the view of Budriesi, *La Basilica dei SS. Cosma e Damiano*, 138, "in nessuno degli antecedenti possibili o presunti il gesto patrocinante assume quella prepotente evidenza; mai si stabilisce far personaggi un legame di così alta intensità drammatica . . ." Cosimo's interest in the culture of early Christianity is clearly expressed in other commissions; see below, ch. 10 and conclusion. As Krautheimer observed, *Rome*, 91–7, the mosaic in SS. Cosmas and Damian is the last great representation of character in Early Christian art before the Byzantine conquest; he noted in particular the illusion of space and the monumentality of the figures. See also Matthiae, *Mosaici medioevali*.

96 See Pope-Hennessy, *Fra Angelico*, 28.

97 Below, p. 170.

98 MAP, XII, 168, Prete Piero di Sozzo, rectore della chiesa di S. Cosimo, Pisa, to Cosimo in Florence, 1 Sept. 1436. There are many other letters documenting the family's devotion to the cult of these saints. See Ross, *Lives of the Early Medici*, 62, for Cosimo's letter to Giovanni at Careggi about the forthcoming celebrations. See MAP, V, 342, Ser Alesso from Florence to Giovanni in 1438: "Piero e tu che trovandovi a Pisa e avendo qua la festa di San Cosimo in sabato ci tractasti molto bene, forse stimavate che di quella si facesse come di natale che si mangia della carne venendo in tal di gran facto fuse/so non mandasti nulla e sai che facemo una grande invitata come sai e usanza e la mattina più di una hora e mezo indugiamo il disinare dicendo stiamo a vedere se giungono aspecta il corbo . . ." Just a few weeks after Cosimo's death, Matteo di Ser Giovanni, the factor at Cafaggiolo,

wrote to Piero at Careggi that he had just returned from Pistoia and "ho domandato il turcho si ssera ordinato nulla per la festa de santi Chosimo et Damiano la quel è giovedi che viene . . . se voi volesse si faciesse l'usato provederei domani il bisogno quello si suole dare loro e questo." Bread and wine were sent to the friars of Santa Croce and wine and silver to the frati of San Benedetto, a gift to the Armenian friars and a large offering of food and wax for a mass and vespers to San Marco. See Trexler, "Martyrs for Florence," 300, n. 21, for Ficino's reference to the Medici family celebrations; Foster, *Lorenzo de' Medici's Villa*, 414, n. 350, for Niccolò Michelozzi's letter to Lorenzo concerning Saint Cosmas's day.

99 See above, pp. 118–19.

100 For Morelli, see above, pp. 99–100. Neri's *Ricordanze* document the same identification with his onomastic saints on the part of Zanobi *botaio* as seen in Medici images of Cosmas and Damian; see also Cohn, *Cult of Remembrance*, for evidence that patronage as a projection of identity and power beyond the grave was not restricted to the powerful.

101 Below, p. 247.

102 See below, pp. 263–4, and fig. 124; on the 1417/18 inventory also Lydecker, "Commitenza artistica per la casa."

103 On this work see particularly Hood, *Fra Angelico at San Marco*, 102–7. Ames-Lewis, op. cit., suggested that the new image for the Medici chapel was perhaps the *Annunciation* by Lippi, usually assumed to be the altarpiece for the Martelli family chapel. He proposed that the painting was originally divided into two separate panels for the doors of a reliquary cupboard, rather similar to the Medici commission of a painted screen for the reliquary cupboard for Santissima Annunziata by Angelico and Baldovinetti. Richa, *Notizie istoriche*, 44–9, listed the San Lorenzo relics including those of Cosimo, Damian, Lawrence, Peter, and Ambrose. See also Paatz, *Die Kirchen*.

104 On this work, see particularly Ruda, *Fra Filippo Lippi*, cat. no. 32, 414–17.

105 See below, this chapter, and ch. 12.

106 See Hall, *Subjects and Symbols*.

107 ASF, Diplomatico, Famiglia Medici, 90, 139.

108 Most notably in the San Marco altarpiece, the chapter-room fresco, and the Annalena altarpiece.

109 Visitors to Cafaggiolo included figures as distinguished as San Bernardino and the pope, but foreign and domestic dignitaries were by this time usually entertained at the more conveniently situated Careggi.

110 The chapel may also have come under the jurisdiction of Bosco ai Frati, the Observant Franciscan convent only a few miles away.

111 Below, pp. 260–61, and fig. 122.

112 Below, ch. 10, passim.

113 Above, ch. 4. There are important references in Cosimo's commissions to early Christian figures and practices of major interest in Medicean cultural circles (see especially below, conclusion), and a well-known sermon by Archbishop Antoninus (cited above, p. 96) testifies to Florentines' familiarity with the *tau*.

114 This is a major point of Hood's study, op. cit.

115 On this see particularly McKillop, "He shall build a house," n. 59, also Hood, op. cit.

116 See Brucker, *Monasteries, Friaries and Nunneries*.

117 Angelico may already at this time have painted the Annalena altarpiece for the Medici for its original location. The

following account of Angelico and the frescoes is much indebted to Hood's account, op. cit.

118   Ibid., 260.

119   On this see also Rubinstein, "Lay Patronage and Observant Reform."

120   Hood, op. cit., 167, 186.

121   The iconography of the *Crucifixion* is predominantly Dominican; seventeen portraits of prominent members of the order appear in roundels at the base of the lunette. However, it is notable that the group of saints represents a particular selection from the usual Dominican repertoire, Hood, op. cit., ch. 8, and that it includes figures with particular Florentine and frequently Medicean associations: Peter Martyr, Anthony Abbot, Bernard of Clairvaux, Romuald, founder of Camaldoli, and Giovanni Gualberto, founder of Vallombrosa. Cf. below, passim; see index.

122   Hood, op. cit., 241.

123   Lanza, *Lirici toscani* 2, 254. The author was Don Pellegrino da Castiglion Fiorentino. Obviously a pro-Medicean patriot, he also wrote the poetic response to the famous "Lamento del Conte di Poppi"; ibid. He is probably the Peregrinus Monacus who wrote to Giovanni di Cosimo from Podio Bonitio, MAP, VII, 179, s. a. Oct. 12.

124   The text is John 19:26–7. Such an inscription is rather old-fashioned for Florence in the mid-fifteenth century, although it was quite common in northern European centers such as Bruges. Patrons' efforts to identify themselves with the participants in Christ's Passion are not, as is sometimes suggested, sacrilegious claims, but rather a devotional duty encouraged in the fifteenth century. On this, see above, ch. 7; below, pp. 360–62.

125   Lanza, op. cit. 2, 39, an incomplete transcription from Magl. VII, 1091.

126   Ames-Lewis, "Early Medici and their Artists," 108–10. Although there is no visual evidence for comparison, we know that Pletho was a distinguished old man of eighty in 1438. Ptolemy's *Geografia* was available in Florence by 1395, and was translated into Latin under the title *Cosmografia* in 1410; Piero de' Medici owned a set of Ptolomaic charts. In relation to the Medici interest in astrology, Ames-Lewis also noted the astrological designs on the carpet of the San Marco altarpiece and the ceiling of Piero's *tempietto* in San Miniato al Monte. See also below, pp. 192–3, on the astrological ceiling of the chancel in the old sacristy at San Lorenzo. On Pletho's influence on Cosimo see also Hankins, "Platonic Academy" and Woodhouse, *George Gemistus Plethon.*

127   See Hood, op. cit., 250. After a door was opened onto the staircase linking the dormitory to the church in the 1450s, he could also have observed their activities from a position on the landing; see McKillop, "He shall build a house."

128   Op. cit.; also "St. Dominic's Manners of Praying" and "Fra Angelico at San Marco: Art and the Liturgy."

129   *Fra Angelico at San Marco*, 252.

130   Pope-Hennessy, *Fra Angelico*, 25; McKillop, "He shall build a house."

131   *On Painting*, 77.

132   For this suggestion, see Orlandi, "Beato Angelico," 70–72, and Berti, *Fra Angelico*, 37.

133   As Paoletti observed, "Fraternal Piety," 213–14, Cosmas and Damian adopt the kneeling position traditional to donors rather than saints in a *sacra conversazione*. On the other hand,

they upstage the main patron saints of the church, Dominic and Mark. The image thus conflates the concepts of donor and patron.

134   Hood, *Fra Angelico at San Marco*, 110, observed "the still-moving pathos" of this face. McKillop, "Dante and *Lumen Christi*," noted that Lorenzo's death was the occasion when Cosimo embarked on his extensive endowment of commemorative masses at San Lorenzo; see below, p. 185.

135   Of course the saints who are represented also have meaning in the contexts of Dominican observance and of the mendicant orders. Dominic and Francis are often paired, as by Dante, to represent cooperation rather than competition between the orders. Of the six saints in the altarpiece who were namesaints of the Medici family, two, Lawrence and John the Evangelist, also had special significance to the Dominicans and appeared in the polyptych painted in 1402 by Lorenzo di Niccolò that Angelico's altarpiece replaced. Miller, "Medici Patronage," offered more elaborate and extensive readings of the multivalent symbols of the image to suggest their rich significance to the Medici. She noted, for example, the representation of the crucifixion of Cosmas and Damian in the predella in juxtapostion with that of Christ at the foot of the *pala*, but acknowledged it is not clear what might be "the implications of this linkage," ibid., 7.

136   See above, p. 138, and fig. 51.

137   In fact the importance to Cosimo of his charity to San Marco in making restitution for his sins is explictly spelled out, as McKillop observed, in an inscription from a papal bull over the door of the main chapel leading to the sacristy: see below, p. 172. See Vespasiano, *Vite* 2; McKillop, "He shall build a house," 8; also Richa, *Notizie istoriche* 7, 124, and Caplow, *Michelozzo* 2, 535. The bull was in fact anticanonical, because canon law required restitution to the person aggrieved; see De Roover, *Rise and Decline*, 12 and 410, n. 19. Antoninus stressed this point in his *Summa*, but seems in practice to have been more flexible in accepting charitable donations.

138   On this feature of altarpieces see also Sinding-Larssen, *Iconography and Ritual*, Van Os, *Art of Devotion*.

139   On the limited theological education of the clergy see also Brucker, "Monasteries, Friaries and Nunneries."

140   Henderson, *Piety and Charity*, 113, 123. On the significance of the Eucharist in late medieval culture see Rubin, *Corpus Christi*.

141   Lanza, op. cit., 1, 189–90. Cf. Del Corazza, *Diario*; the significance of every gesture of the sacrifice of Mass and of the procession of Corpus Christi was impressed upon his mind. See also John Bossy, "The Mass as a Social Institution," a catalytic ritual which fused its participants in the experience of *communitas*. On this see also Rubin, op. cit., especially introduction, 8: "In the language of sacramental religion the most disparate experiences were articulated . . . all acting and enacted through its use."

142   Apocrypha; see McKillop, op. cit., 14; the translation is by Miller, op. cit.

143   This basic lesson about charity appears constantly in the literature, learned and popular, with which Cosimo was familiar. See Antoninus, *Summa*, IV, title 15, ch. 26, iii, 3c; IV, title 5, ch. 21, 290c; also McKillop, "He shall build a house."

144   Below, pp. 178, 299–300.

145   Vespasiano, *Vite* 2, 209–10.

146 Hood, op. cit., 100.

147 Above, p. 119. One of the predella scenes depicted Damian accepting payment for his services, and Cosmas repudiating it, signifying that liberality is the essence of charity. Saint Lawrence was also revered as a deacon of the early church who charitably distributed its possessions to the poor. Other readings have been suggested which may or may not have have sprung naturally to the minds of Cosimo's contemporaries; for instance, in the passage following the verses displayed in Saint Mark's book is the observation that "a prophet is without honor in his own country," which could be a subtle reference to the Medici exile.

148 See also the observations of Ringbom, *Icon to Narrative*, on the altarpiece as a charismatic object connected with the donor. An indication that altarpieces associated with the Medici were seen as Cosimo's property appears in a letter from the "Priores, popoli et comunis Cortonae" to Cosimo, 26 Dec., 1438, MAP, XI, 198. The letter thanks him for sending them the Lorenzo di Niccolò *tavola* taken from San Marco after it was replaced there by Angelico's *pala*, and sees the work as his direct gift, "la quale cosa essendo stata accepta e grata nel conspecto dell'omnipotente Dio e del glorioso Messer San Domenico, meritamente induce noi universalmente a laudare e a exaltare la Vostra Magnificenza, e fia la decta opera pia per la Vostra Nobilità usata a perpetua gloria e fama della Vostra persona." Lapaccini, chronicler of the convent of San Marco, described the altarpiece alternatively as having been given to the brothers of Cortona through the agency of the then prior, Frate Cypriano, "who had the arms or insignia of the Medici family and their name attached to it," Morçay, "La Cronaca del Convento," 12.

149 Ibid., 16–17. As Trexler noted, "Sacred Image," the power of images was often enhanced by their being seen only rarely. An intention to restrict the impact of images to moments of conscious contemplation appears, for example, in the use of veils to cover them in private homes like those of the Medici. However, while Hall stressed that the rood screen obscured the visibility of altarpieces and frescoes on the walls of the apse, see " 'Tramezzo' in S. Croce," "Ponte in Sa. Maria Novella," in the latter study she conceded, 169, that "the opening in the center of the choir screen would have provided a view of the altarpiece from the nave, at least from the northern end of the nave reserved for the male laity." Miller, *Major Florentine Altarpieces*, 78–81, 159, observed that in the case of the San Marco altarpiece features in the composition aided in projecting the image – the order and symmetry of the composition, the triangular form, the manipulation of one-point perspective, focusing attention on central figures, and the general clarity and cohesion of the work.

150 The Bull is dated 7 Jan. 1443; see Morçay, op. cit., 17.

151 See particularly Hood, Paoletti, McKillop, op. cit. McKillop observed at the same time that there were precedents for the "viewing balcony" in Scrovegni's Arena chapel, in Nicola Acciaiuoli's Certosa, and in the doge's access to San Marco in republican Venice. None of these patrons was a prince, although there were also plenty of princely antecedents of this custom.

152 McKillop suggested, op. cit., 8 ff., that the altarpiece represents "the congruence between the mystical body which is the church . . . and the mystical body of the state as expounded in medieval political theory in the Thomist tradition." But this theory referred explicitly to princes, and was part of the development of a doctrine of their rule by divine right. As she acknowledged, the model of the *corpus mysticum* was applicable only with difficulty to the commune, and while Cosimo owned a copy of *De regimine principum*, which might have been either Aquinas's or Egidio Romano's work, all the evidence suggests that his political education derived not from this isolated medieval treatise, but from the large number of classical republican works, particularly those of Cicero, which he owned and annotated.

153 See Brown, "Humanist Portrait of Cosimo," and above, ch. 2.

154 By the same token, Gregorio Dati's God was the ultimate *maestro*, not the supreme monarch.

155 Kent, *Rise of the Medici*, 22. The speaker was surely conscious of the play here between individual and collectivity, the latter represented in the Aristotelian notion of the common good. See above, p. 50.

156 As McKillop observed, op. cit., 4; she also suggested that this new form is ideally suited to express familial, as opposed to individual identity. On the form of the *pala* see particularly Gardner von Teufel, "Die Erfindung der Renaissancepala" and "From Polyptych to Pala"; also Gardner, "Altarpieces, Legislation and Usage," and Humfrey and Kemp, *Altarpiece in the Renaissance*.

157 Cf. Goffen's similar observations, "Masaccio's *Trinity*."

Chapter X

1 For a fuller discussion of these questions, and of differences in style and taste between Cosimo and his sons, see below, pp. 287–91. On continuity and change in the political policies of Cosimo and Piero see Rubinstein, *Government of Florence*, pt. II; Kent, *Fathers and Friends*; above, ch. 2.

2 On the partial and complex coincidence of parish, quarter, and *gonfalone*, the electoral unit, see Kent and Kent, *Neighbours and Neighbourhood*.

3 Plesner, "L'Emigration de la campagne à la ville."

4 *Trattato*, 685.

5 Above, pp. 181–2.

6 Lesnick, "Civic Preaching," 212.

7 See, for example, above, p. 61. See also Trexler, various, especially "Sacred Image" and *Public Life*.

8 *Zibaldone* 1, 65–6.

9 MAP, XVI, 327, 5 Nov. s. a. Giugni's language links spiritual with worldly rewards. While *fama* refers to worldly renown, *sempiterna* pertains essentially to the hereafter; this usage was well known to Florentines from Dante's *Divina Commedia* and Saint Gregory's *Moralia*, a favorite text of Cosimo's. Cf. also Giugni, MAP, VIII, 168.

10 *Vite* 2, 191.

11 Above, p. 127.

12 Above, ch. 2.

13 Stinger, *Humanism and the Church Fathers*, 155.

14 Above, ch. 4.

15 See Chambers, *Patrons and Artists*, 42–4. Cosimo's cousin, Averardo di Francesco, was one of the four consuls of the guild also named in the contract.

16 On the tomb see Lightbown, *Donatello and Michelozzo*, and McHam, "Donatello's Tomb of John XXIII"; the latter's

interpretation of the work in its social context informs the following account.

17 For their correspondence, see MAP, I, 208–15. These ties were cultivated and maintained by the next generation; Giovanni Cossa wrote from Naples to Cosimo de' Medici, July 21 1439, XI, 573: "Magnifice frater honorande . . . Io non cesserò mai non solo per me, ma per mey parenti et amici continuo invocare el favor vosstro dove me bisognarà . . ."

18 See Holmes, "How the Medici Became the Pope's Bankers"; De Roover, *Rise and Decline*. In 1422 Martin V conceded a portable altar to Cosimo and his wife Contessina, and created Giovanni di Bicci count of Monteverde, although he never assumed the title; his younger son Lorenzo was made papal scutifer. See De Roover, *Rise and Decline*, 51; Saalman and Mattox, "First Medici Palace," appendix IX. The close relationship between the papacy and the Medici lasted throughout most of Cosimo's lifetime, when the bank was at its apogee. There was a brief interruption in the later part of the pontificate of Eugenius IV, when the Spinelli were appointed papal bankers between 1443 and 1447, and toward the end of Cosimo's life, when a Sienese banking firm briefly held this position under the Sienese Piccolomini pope Pius II.

19 See above, ch. 3.

20 For Bartolomeo de' Bardi's sophisticated cultural and intellectual interests, and his close friendship with Poggio Bracciolini and Niccolò Niccoli, above, loc. cit.

21 Cossa at one point had stayed in Giovanni di Bicci's house; see Canestrini, "Documenti relativi alla liberazione," 429 ff. According to Pieraccini, *La Stirpe de' Medici*, 12 (no archival citation), Averardo wrote to Michele Cossa, the pope's brother, that since almost no assets remained to Baldassare, the Medici family had to build the baptistery monument at their own expense. See also Pellegrini, *Sulla repubblica fiorentina*, documents. On the leaders of the *reggimento* at this time see Kent, *Rise of the Medici*.

22 Flamini, "La lirica toscana," 72. See also the comments of Bartolomeo del Corazza, *Diario*, above, pp. 61, 88.

23 On the broader implications of the site, architectural frame, and form of this monument see particularly McHam, "Donatello's Tomb of John XXIII."

24 Herzner, "Regesti Donatelliani," 69.

25 The inscription, which cleverly blurs the issue of Cossa's legitimacy and deposition with a reference to his being defunct, may be one of several examples of ingeniously ambiguous inscriptions for objects associated with Cosimo; see below, passim.

26 See Ricc., 2729, 107r, "colonna e sostegno."

27 Op. cit., 156. As she observed, this was Donatello's first tomb, and the only one he was to build in Florence; its innovative features made an enormous and lasting impact on funerary sculpture.

28 Below, this chapter, p. 470, n. 162, and ch. 15.

29 See Lightbown, *Donatello and Michelozzo*.

30 Cosimo and his in-laws were quite close. See, for example, MAP, XII, 141, 13 Oct. 1435, Sozzo de' Bardi de Vernio to Cosimo, Vernio to Florence; the letter, addressing Cosimo as "Hon. et char. ut pater," is a recommendation on behalf of a friend: "vi piaccia per amor mio farlo quanto fareste per me propio." Cf. MAP, XX, 525, Vernio, 17 Sept. 1469, Gualterotto de' Bardi to Lorenzo, a recommendation for "un mio nipote Don Pelegrino monacho dell'ordine di Badia a Coltibuono . . . E se mai faciesti chosa alchuna in mio favore, prieghovi che a questa volta non mi manchate a mettere e a gli infiniti oblighi o con esso voi . . ."

31 Holmes, "How the Medici Became the Pope's Bankers," 378.

32 De Roover, *Rise and Decline*, 54–5.

33 *Vite* 2, 173. Cosimo also observed in his *Ricordi*, 102, that the Florentine enemies who exiled him in September 1434 hoped that while he was away in Venice, the Medici bank in Florence and in Rome might fail. That this effect was averted he attributed to the action of his friends, many of them associated with the Church.

34 Cavalcanti, *Istorie fiorentine*, 310. For a fuller account of these events see Kent, *Rise of the Medici*, especially 331–5. Cosimo described Vitelleschi in his *Ricordi*, loc. cit., as "an intimate friend."

35 On this "warrior prelate" see Law, "Giovanni Vitelleschi."

36 Goldthwaite and Rearick, "Michelozzo and the Ospedale di San Paolo," 234. For the contract with Donatello for the Marzocco see Janson, *Donatello*, 41.

37 On this theme see particularly Holmes, "Cosimo and the Popes."

38 Brucker, "Urban Parishes"; Bizzocchi, "Patronato politico e giuspatronati."

39 David Peterson's forthcoming study of the Florentine church in the time of Antoninus will fill an immense gap in our understanding of this process. On Medici family patronage rights at San Lorenzo and San Tommaso in Florence, see below.

40 See ASF, MAP, *Inventario* 1, passim.

41 *Ricordi*, MAP, CXLVIII, 30r–33v. The factor at Cafaggiolo "donò uno ghrato [*granato*: bellows] legato in ghambo d'oro."

42 MAP, XVI, 110. Cf. MAP, V, 494, Jan. 1444/5, from Gualandi Latera to Giovanni di Cosimo asking to be made *piovano* of San Giovanni in Mugello.

43 The following account, particularly of the patronage of Bosco, is heavily indebted to Robinson, "Cosimo de' Medici"; see also his *Cosimo de' Medici's Patronage*. On the renovations, see especially Ferrara and Quinterio, *Michelozzo*; on the church see also Siebenhüner and Heydenreich, "Die Klosterkirche S. Francesco." In 1420 "Mariano de Florentia" estimated that in central Italy there were no more than 200 Observant friars occupying 30 convents, but by the time of Bernardino's death in 1444, there were 230, Robinson, "Cosimo de' Medici," 182.

44 Fabriczy, "Michelozzo di Bartolomeo," 70–71. This account from the convent's records is confirmed by Cosimo's father, Giovanni di Bicci, in his tax report of 1427, Cat. 49, 1140r–41r; 1156r: "anchora o più boschagli e in più luoghi nella selva de' frati dal boscho." On the Medici family's continuing patronage after Cosimo's death, see MAP, XVI, 230, 25 April 1467, Francesco Fracassini, Cafaggiolo, to Piero, concerning some local business with the church and a decision involving the "magiore dell'ordine de' frati minori."

45 MAP, XVII, 642, published Rochon, *La jeunesse de Laurent*, 49.

46 *Vite* 2, 202–3.

47 MAP, XVI, 153, Lorenzo and Giuliano, Cafaggiolo, 7 June 1464, published in Lorenzo de' Medici, *Lettere* 1, 3–4. Maestro Zanobi di Betino was a factor of the Medici farms around Cafaggiolo.

48 Cat. 49, 1140–41r: "una chasa per mia habitatione et alchun' altre chasette che sono a mio servigio di granai et celle . . ."

Cf. Giacomo di Michele Turi of Scarperia, who in 1439 appointed Cosimo and his brother Lorenzo executors of his will, which designated 500 florins for the construction of a chapel in the church of San Barnaba in Scarperia. If this were not possible, he stipulated that the legacy was to be transferred to Bosco, Robinson, op. cit., 187.

49 When in the early months of 1440 the countryside around Cafaggiolo was threatened by the Milanese troops sweeping south toward Florence, and the lives of the Medici family were in serious danger, one Cristofano da Gagliano wrote to Cosimo in Florence: "The men of this commune have got together, and seeing that there is nothing here that can be defended, they have decided to go over to your place . . ." Giving Cosimo a list of what they would require, he begged "that you will do whatever they want you to, letting you know that by God they will with the very best will defend that place . . . so that nothing is lacking to be able to attack those who want to give you trouble, and when they present themselves to you, be pleased to see that they are provided for, and you will find they will serve you well," MAP, XI, 234, 23 March 1439/40. A few years later, Cosimo wrote from Florence to Giovanni, then "in Mugello," that having consulted "the men of Gagliano," he was convinced that a man from the town who was under threat of torture from the Vicar of the District was being undeservedly persecuted. He told Giovanni that he would have a word with the Ufficiali del Sale who initiated the victim's arrest, and if there proved to be nothing more in the matter than there appeared, he would speak to the Vicar himself, to see that the man was not molested further, ibid., V, 399, 1441.

50 Ibid., XVI, 332; also XI, 552, Piero da Gagliano, 17 June 1448, from Naples to Piero in Florence.

51 Below, pp. 205–7.

52 MAP, I, 218, cit. Robinson, op. cit., 192–4.

53 Cf. Ferrara and Quinterio's assumption, op. cit., 165, that Cosimo's intervention must have occurred after Giovanni's death.

54 Robinson, op. cit., 87–8.

55 Caplow, Michelozzo 2, 590–93.

56 Brown, "Radical Alternative."

57 Robinson, "Cosimo de' Medici," 189.

58 Fabriczy, op. cit., loc. cit.

59 Ibid., 70–71.

60 Op. cit., 189; they are also on shields placed over the entrances to the altar chapel and apse, as well as on two of the entrance loggia's capitals. On the palle here and in other buildings by Michelozzo, see also Siebenhüner and Heydenreich, II, 388, ff.

61 Istorie fiorentine, 25, 56–7; the partisan letters to Cosimo invoking the admired memory of his father confirm this judgment, see Kent, Fathers and Friends.

62 Below, ch. 11.

63 See Gardner von Teufel, "Lorenzo Monaco, Filippo Lippi," 176. On the Barbadori chapel see also Battisti, Brunelleschi; Saalman, Brunelleschi: The Buildings; Trachtenberg, "On Brunelleschi's Old Sacristy,".

64 Below, pp. 205, 355.

65 See Joannides, Masaccio and Masolino, catalogue, 13.

66 On the pact and the inscription see McKillop, "He shall build a house"; Richa, Notizie istoriche 7, 124; Caplow, Michelozzo 2, 535; De Roover, Rise and Decline, 12, and 410, n. 19; Vespasiano, Vite 2, 177–8.

67 On these figures see above, pp. 86–7, 107. Rubinstein, "Lay Patronage and Observant Reform."

68 Below, pp. 212–14.

69 On Bernardino's visit to Bosco, above, p. 171; on the Bosco altarpiece, above, pp. 144–5, and fig. 55; on Bernardino's monogram on the Medici chapel ceiling, below, ch. 13, and on his canonization, Origo, World of San Bernardino, epilogue.

70 Spallanzani, Inventari Medicei, 6.

71 This year also saw the first move to suppress confraternities suspected of political conspiracy; see above, p. 58.

72 Ferrara and Quinterio, Michelozzo, especially 186. See also the testimony of Giuliano Lapaccini, chronicler of San Marco and the overseer of the building, Cronaca. Gatti, "Comune Studio Libertatis" observed that an earlier intervention by the commune at San Marco, to repair damage to the roof in 1427, referred to the aid given the Florentines by the Venetians and the need to honor the Venetian patron saint, San Marco, in the name of a shared concern with liberty. On Venice as a political model for Florentines see below, conclusion, p. 367.

73 On the residence patterns of the Medici family and their neighborhood partisans see Kent, Rise of the Medici, pt. 1, ii, iv. Bernardetto de' Medici's house was on the corner of the modern Via Guelfa, still labeled "Canto Bernardetto de' Medici." Caroline Elam, "Il palazzo nel contesto della città," 45, suggested Cosimo may have envisaged the Via Larga as a "Medici street."

74 "+CRISTUS REX GLORIAE VENIT IN PACE ET DEUS HOMO FACTUS EST+VIR CLA[RISSIMUS] COSMUS MEDICES IO[HANNIS] F[ILIUS] ME SUIS IN PENSIS FACIUNDUM CURAVIT + UT STATUTIS TEMPORIBUS SACRA DEO CELEBRENTUR GLORIA IN EXCELSIS DEO+". On the bell see Butterfield, Verrocchio, 11–12, cat. 2; also Carocci, "La campana di S. Marco." On one side of the bell is a roundel containing a Virgin and Child with angels and the inscription "Ave Maria Gratia Plena Dominus Tecum." On the opposite side is a roundel with Saint Dominic surrounded by angels and the inscription "S[an]c[tus] Dominicus Ordinis Predicatorum Fundator." In the same spirit as Ficino's declaration to Cosimo that he had two fathers, Cosimo and Plato, Saint Dominic is honored as the spiritual father of the convent, Cosimo as its physical progenitor.

75 On Antoninus see particularly Orlandi's classic study, S. Antonino; also Peterson's recent "Archbishop Antoninus" and various articles. Brucker, Giovanni and Lusanna, gives a vivid account of the archbishop's practical effect on Florentines' lives.

76 See above, p. 435, n. 40.

77 For this last observation, and the similar remark by Castello Quaratesi concerning his project for the new church of the Franciscan Observants of San Salvatore al Monte in reponse to protests against its excessive magnificence that he "did not intend to build it according to the status of the friars, but according to what was suitable to the city," see Rubinstein, op. cit., 68.

78 See below, p. 360.

79 On this issue see above, p. 66. In Peterson's judgment (personal communication), Antoninus's "brief and unsuccessful challenge to the Medici in 1458 . . . indeed his episcopate as a whole . . . served as a foil that underscored the retreat from reform in the Laurentian period and laid the ground for Savonarola." See also Peterson, "Archbishop Antoninus"; Trexler, "Episcopal Constitutions of Antoninus."

80 Rubinstein, op. cit., 66, and above pp. 134–5.

81 Above, pp. 150–51.

82 Ferrara and Quinterio, op. cit., loc. cit., and 280. As Rubinstein pointed out, op. cit., 66, there were similar interventions in favor of Observants by *signori* like the Gonzaga and the Este, but Cosimo was obliged to work through the Signoria.

83 MAP, VI, 208, Antoninus to Giovanni di Cosimo de' Medici, 8 Dec. 1456: "Le scuse che fai per le lettere tua del'amico dello excesso suo non tolgono sufficientemente la cagione giusta e ragionevole della sua captura, però che qui occasionem damni dat, damni quoque dedisse videtur. Lui è stato il principale per cui aiuto e favore è stato rubata la pieve . . . Ignorantia non può pretendere . . . Et pertanto indarno t'afaticaresti a venire qua per questa facienda. Et avegnadio che Bernardo Gherardi e Agnolo della Stufa m'abino pregato per la sua liberazione e non meno tu. In iudiciis personarum acceptio non est habenda. Tutti siete potenti cittadini e grandi ella chiesa tiene e luogo del pupillo picolo e debole . . . Et parvum et magnum audietis, dicie Idio."

84 *Detti piacevoli*, 25.

85 Vasari–Milanesi, *Vite*, 4, 433.

86 For the documentation and tentative chronology of Michelozzo's life and works, see particularly Ferrara and Quinterio, *Michelozzo*; also Fabriczy, "Michelozzo di Bartolomeo."

87 On Vasari's work and his personal agenda see Rubin, *Vasari*. For the notably different versions of the *Lives* of 1550 and 1568, and their textual traditions, see the essays in Garfagnini, *Giorgio Vasari*. Vasari's description in his biography of Michelozzo of the renovations at San Marco with reference to significant landmarks of his own lifetime suggests how far he saw Cosimo's patronage as a prelude to that of the Medici dukes he served; see, for example, Vasari-Milanesi, *Vite*, 4, 440. See also Preyer, "Michelozzo and Vasari."

88 See above, introduction and ch. 2.

89 This is essentially the thrust of the arguments of Gombrich, "Early Medici as Patrons," and Procacci, "Cosimo de' Medici e la costruzione."

90 On patronage obligations and terminology see Kent, *Rise of the Medici* and *Fathers and Friends*.

91 On Michelozzo's friendship with the Medici see Kent, *Rise of the Medici*, especially 70, 78. Bartolommeo Scala rose from the post of secretary to Cosimo's nephew Pierfrancesco di Lorenzo in the 1450s to become chancellor; see Brown, *Bartolommeo Scala*. For further comment on the Medici and Michelozzi, see below, ch. 14; for other upwardly mobile Medici partisans, see, for example, this chapter, pp. 205–7.

92 On this partnership see Lightbown, op. cit., and Caplow, "Sculptors' Partnerships."

93 The dating of work on these villas has long depended far too heavily on a presumed correlation with Cosimo's ownership. As Ferrara and Quinterio also observed, op. cit., 179, if Michelozzo were responsible for the renovations at Cafaggiolo, Averardo was just as likely to have been his patron. Concerning Careggi, an anecdote of Vespasiano's named a "maestro Lorenzo" as the man appointed to carry them out; this would not preclude a design by Michelozzo, ibid., 250. On the Medici villas see also below, pp. 300–04.

94 All Michelozzo's extant Catasto reports are published by Ferrara and Quinterio, op. cit., 37–45; for the citations above see especially 37–8.

95 Ibid., 33.

96 MAP, II, 201, 11 Feb. 1429/30, published Ferrara and Quinterio, op. cit., 33–4. He mentioned having already spoken to Averardo when he was in Pisa, and asked him "più volte, se achadesse chostà che voi potessi dare qualche inviamento a Giovanni mio fratello, l'avessi a ricordo, e così credo arete auto." When Andrea de' Pazzi was one of the sea consuls, he had appointed his *garzone* Matteo to the position of *sottoscrivano*; now that Matteo was otherwise engaged, Michelozzo hoped his own brother might inherit the position, "o se altro vedete potere faccia per lui." Almost all of Cosimo's personal letters before 1434 are addressed to Averardo, with whom he discussed every aspect of his personal business, the family's relations with its partisans, and the military and diplomatic affairs of the Florentine commune, with which Averardo was also closely involved. See above, ch. 2 and below pp. 273, 276–7; also Kent, *Rise of the Medici*, passim, and on Averardo and his family, Kent, "I Medici in esilio."

97 MAP, II, 354, 5 May 1430; ibid., 352, 1 May 1430. On the full social and partisan significance of such requests, see Kent, *Fathers and Friends*.

98 MAP, II, 399, 27 Dec. 1427. Vasari's unconfirmed claim that Michelozzo accompanied Cosimo when he was exiled, first to Padua, and then to Venice, may rest on a confusion with the earlier Paduan trips; on this, and Poggio's letter, see above, ch. 3.

99 MAP, II, 400, 27 Dec. 1427, published Ferrara and Quinterio, op. cit., 34. Confident that he could rely on his Medici friends to protect his position at the mint, Michelozzo saw his service to them as his most compelling obligation. Although his employment at the Zecca was interrupted by frequent absences, it continued for another twenty years, ibid., 17, 425–9. On Andrea de' Pazzi, his wealth, and his relation to the Medici and their banking enterprises see De Roover, *Rise and Decline*; Kent, *Rise of the Medici*; Molho, *Florentine Public Finances*.

100 *Ricordi*, MAP, CXLVIII 30, 32r–33v.

101 Below, pp. 197–200.

102 For a strong challenge to the accepted attribution of this building to Michelozzo see Preyer, "L'architettura del palazzo."

103 See particularly Ferrara and Quinterio, op. cit., 185–96; also Hood, *Fra Angelico at San Marco*, and McKillop, "He shall build a house."

104 Ferrara and Quinterio, op. cit., 188. The patronage of the Caponsacchi had previously been usurped, with the complicity of the Silvestrines, by Agnolo di Ghezzo della Casa. His nephew Bernardo was exiled by the pro-Medicean Balìa of 1434, Kent, *Rise of the Medici*, 356. It is intriguing to speculate whether the interference of others' patronage rights in the Medici plans might have played a role in the transference of the convent to the Dominicans. See Lapaccini, *Cronaca*, 12, for the convent's view; anxious no doubt to avoid the implication that patronage at San Marco could simply be bought, its author declared that Mariotto freely ceded his rights to Cosimo and Lorenzo who "recogoscentes liberalitatem dicti Mariotti gratis sibi obtulerunt et donaverunt ducatos aureos quingentos."

105 Archivio di San Domenico di Fiesole, cit. Morçay, "La Cronaca del convento," 15–16. The account continues: "Et detto Cosimo a messa in tenuta negli anni del inc[arnatione] di signor Giesu Cristo 1444 a dì 29 di Giugno, cioè el dì di

sancto Piero et san Paulo, et fece et fecesi una solempne processione con tucti e frategli di detta schuola vestiti di biancho e fecesi dare le chiavi del sopradetto luogo. . . ." See also Lapaccini's comment on Alesso, ibid., 16: "notario florentino, qui multum domum suam [Cosimo] frequentabat . . ."

106 Ferrara and Quinterio, op. cit., 193–4.

107 Lapaccini, *Cronaca*, op. cit., 14.

108 *Trattato*, 2, 690.

109 See below, pp. 299–300, on the Medici palace garden. On the association of the Medici arms with citrus fruit, McKillop, "L'ampliamento della stemma mediceo."

110 Ferrara and Quinterio, op. cit., 192; on Michelozzo's hydraulic and military engineering in general, ibid., 105–21.

111 See particularly Caplow's evocative description of the library, *Michelozzo* 2, 540, and her observation, 541, that in general, "The most notable aspect of the convent-church compound is its simplicity. Even in the smallest details Michelozzo is concerned only with the essential . . ."

112 On the library and Niccoli's relationship to Cosimo, see above, ch. 3.

113 See Rubinstein, op. cit., 39, 70: "During the general chapter of the Dominican order held at Santa Maria Novella in 1414, Simone da Cascina observed, "There is no great family in the city of which we have not had members among our brethren."

114 Ferrara and Quinterio, op. cit., 194.

115 For a full list see McKillop, "He shall build a house"; also Lapaccini, *Cronaca*.

116 The building was repaired by Michelozzo in 1459; see Caplow, *Michelozzo* 2, 540. Cosimo at the time was staying at Cafaggiolo.

117 *Cronaca*, op. cit., 23–4. In addition to the feasts of Ephiphany, Mark, and Cosmas and Damian, the convent particularly celebrated that of Piero's patron, Saint Peter Martyr.

118 See Elam, "Cosimo de' Medici and San Lorenzo"; Kent, *Rise of the Medici*, pt. 1, 69–71.

119 *Cronica*, iv, 45. On the nature and functions of neighborhood see Kent and Kent, *Neighbours and Neighbourhood*; on the Medici neighborhood, Kent, *Rise of the Medici*, pt. 1, iv.

120 On this see Gaston, "Liturgy and Patronage"; McKillop, "Dante and *Lumen Christi*," and below, pp. 378–9.

121 Saalman, *Brunelleschi: The Buildings*, doc. 28, 5r, MAP, CLV, cit. more fully Blumenthal, "Science of the Magi," 11. The Pucci family endowed commemorative masses to be said in their chapel at Santissima Annunziata for Cosimo and his sons.

122 Elam, "Cosimo de' Medici and San Lorenzo," 109; what follows relies heavily on her account. See also her "Site and Early Building History."

123 Elam, "Cosimo de' Medici and San Lorenzo," 163ff. Molho, "*Pater Patriae* or *Padrino*," 26, noted that of thirteen meetings of the *gonfalone* of Lion d'oro, 1399–1427, Giovanni was present at nine, and was always listed among the very first in attendance. On five of the six occasions during those years that syndics were appointed to supervise the collection of back taxes and their confiscation from debtors, Giovanni was one of them; see ASF, Notarile Antecosmiano B 742, 11r–12r, 16 May 1399; M 265, 1404–17, 4th bundle, 69r–70r, 20 Nov. 1412; M 546, 1421–6, 102r–v, 10 June 1425; 137r–138r, 8 Aug. 1426; B 748, 133r–v, 23 March 1404/5. On the building program and its *operai* see also Saalman, *Brunelleschi: The Buildings*, ch. 4.

124 Cianfogni, *Memorie istoriche*, 1, 263.

125 Published Ginori Conti, *Basilica di San Lorenzo*, 234–6: "Et quia ecclesie huiusmodi corpus cum cappellis, sacristia, et aliis opportunis ex posteriori parte extendi per longitudinem debet brachii sexaginta quinque, et per latitudinem centumdecem in ordine Cappellarum, et infra spatia antedicta pars cuiusdem vie, que dicitur la via de Preti, in qua, multis respectibus, continue habitare dignoscitur gens conditionis depresse, fame non comendabilis, nec vite, et ut plurimum, aliene nationis, et quedam plateuncula post campanile ipsius Ecclesie, et alia ad Commune Florentie pertinentia includentur; et etiam quia sunt alique parve domus ad privatos spectantes, qui, si repugnantes essent concepto operi multum nocere possent cunctorum bonorum residuo ad ipsum capitulum pleno iure pertinenti: et quod ipsi hoc tam sanctum opus Deo, atque mundo, vestreque Dominationi honorabile, atque devotum, ad perfectionem non posse deducere dubitantes quin ymmo, ut designatum est, sine vestre Dominationis suffragio non valeant, deliberaverunt . . ."

126 See Cianfogni, op. cit., loc. cit., also Saalman, op. cit., 112. These *operai* included three chapel-holders; Vieri Rondinelli, Ugo della Stufa, and Giovanni de' Medici.

127 Elam, op. cit., 162, and appendix A.

128 Ibid. On the political affiliations and fortunes of the *operai* and chapel-holders see Kent, *Rise of the Medici*, passim, and especially appendices 1 and 2.

129 Elam, op. cit., especially 178–80. See Rubinstein, *Government of Florence*, 66, for the changing representation of Lion d'oro families in the electoral scrutinies of the forties, when rebuilding of San Lorenzo was resumed. Those most heavily respresented were the Medici, Masi, Aldobrandini del Nero, Ginori, Martelli, Dietisalvi-Neroni, and Della Stufa. On the Ciai, see Kent, op. cit., passim. Zanobi [di Niccolò di Zanobi?] Bonvanni wrote to Lorenzo de' Medici, MAP, xx, 151, Dec. 1465: "Et perchè io mi trovai distante al non poterti a bocha parlare chon fede e chon amore istimo essere a la presenza ed io insieme con tutta la mia chasa sempre per la chasa vostra s'a metere lavere e le persone . . . bixogna aumentare tutti e li amici vostri e fedeli antichi . . ."

130 For these figures see Elam, Rubinstein, Kent, op. cit., also Kent, "Reggimento."

131 The record of the meeting, ASF, Not. Antecos. M 273, ins. 1, 32r–v, is published with comment by Ruda, "Building Programme at San Lorenzo," and Saalman, "San Lorenzo: The 1434 Chapel Project," especially 363; also Hyman, "Notes and Speculations."

132 Published Fabroni, *Magni Cosmi* 2, 87.

133 ASF, Sig. e Coll., Deliberazioni, ordinaria autorità, 34, 16r–v, 18r–19v. See particularly 16, 18 March 1433/4, cit. Hyman, "Notes and Speculations," 106–7. Since the demolition was to occur under the direction of the "*capomaestro* and masters and other workmen on the building and at the Opera del Duomo," Hyman credited Brunelleschi, as *provveditore* at the Duomo, with the plan for clearing the piazza in Cosimo's absence. But as Margaret Haines kindly pointed out to me, Brunelleschi was *provveditore* for the cupola project only, and the demolition is not recorded in the archives of the Opera. The clearing of the San Lorenzo piazza was probably in accordance with the intentions of all those involved in building at San Lorenzo, particularly Giovanni de' Medici.

134 MAP, v, 358, cit. and correctly redated by Hyman, "Notes and Speculations," 108.

135 Bizzocchi, *Chiesa e potere*, 93–4.
136 On these two see above, chs. 7 and 8. Neither, however, was a signatory to the June docment; see Ruda, op. cit., 361. See also MAP, XI, 391, Biagio, "pievano in val di Sieve, s. d. to Cosimo: "Mi conposi con Misere Gioanni priore pasato di Sancto Lorenzo e con i sindechi del confalone che di novanta fiorini io dovevo pagare al confalone ne pagasse dodice fiorini . . ." He paid these dues to Messer Giovanni, who subsequently died. The new prior "non mi vole amettere questa compositione e gratia mi fece el priore con gli sindeci pasati; anti mi ha facto pignorare e tore le masaritie dela pieve in modo che sto in su la paglia per la quale cosa humilmente vi prego che voi faciati che elo priore mi renda le mie cose . . . concedendo voi gratie limosine infinite a multi e varii homini el quali molte volte non hanno la povertà e bisogno como io, el quale so' fidelissimo amico e servitore dela casa de' Medici e ano sapete quanta fedeltà e amore vi portava mio padre ultrache ancora siamo consorti de' e Medici . . ."
137 See Kent, *Rise of the Medici*, 297–339.
138 The most notable effect of this conflict on the urban fabric of the district occurred when Cosimo's disgruntled enemies, on their way to meet with the pope at Santa Maria Novella, decided to vent their frustration by setting fire to the houses of the Martelli as they passed by San Lorenzo. Cosimo's young cousin Francesco di Giuliano di Averardo wrote to his father: "Messere Rinaldo [degli Albizzi] e Ridolfo [Peruzzi] e tutta la brighata chapitorno a chasa Ugholino Martegli e volo[n]lo ardere in chasa. E se non che fu sochorso d'Antonio di Ser Tomaxo [Masi] e da que' Ginori, e da la Stufa, l'arebono fatto." The moment of crisis in 1434 made these *operai* and chapel-builders at San Lorenzo the chief target of Cosimo's enemies, and the Medici family's most active defenders. In 1393 the Martelli had joined with the Medici in an attempted coup against the Albizzi-led regime. By 1434 this single household of nine brothers was the mainstay of the Medici bank at the papal court in Rome, and of the Florentine *tavola*. During the Medici exile, Roberto Martelli ran the bank from Venice, and was responsible for Piero's early training in business affairs. He was a major figure at the church council in 1439, and later, as head of the Rome branch where he had been a factor since 1424, carried out most of Cosimo' personal financial transactions, including his dispensation of charity and payment for some of his patronage. The Pisa branch of the bank was managed by Ugolino Martelli, that at Venice by Alessandro Martelli. The Martelli remained the constant companions and consultants of the Medici well into Lorenzo's lifetime. See, for example, MAP, V, 123, 143, 446, 588; XVI, 237. On the Masi and the Medici, ibid., V, 591.
139 Elam, op. cit., especially 171; Kent, *Rise of the Medici*, especially ch. 5; see also Saalman, *Brunelleschi: The Buildings*, 161–2.
140 On the Dietisalvi Neroni at San Lorenzo, see Elam, op. cit., especially 171. On the palaces of Dietisalvi and Nigi di Nerone, below, p. 236, and fig. 106. On the Ginori chapels see Elam, "Site and Early Building History," appendix II, "The Ginori Chapels in S. Lorenzo and the Porta de' Ginori, 183–5.
141 See Holmes, *Florence, Rome*, 171; Bizzocchi, "Patronato politico e giuspatronati," 98. Bizzocchi suggested that Cosimo did not pursue this matter after his return to Florence

because by that time he was concentrating on the cathedral itself; on the Medici presence there, see below, pp. 210–12.
142 On Giovanni's ecclesiastical career, see Peterson, "Episcopal Election"; for the family's changing role in Florentine politics, Rubinstein, *Government of Florence*, passim.
143 *Istorie fiorentine*, 279–80. The Ginori lived then on the street that now bears their name, just behind the Medici houses facing the Via Larga, and thus practically on their patrons' doorstep. Giuliano Ginori wrote to Cosimo's cousin Averardo in May 1432, rejoicing that "the friends really have the wind in their sails, and are navigating in all waters," MAP, V, 201. The Ginori also cooperated with the Medici to help them acquire the land on which to build their new palace; see Hyman, *Fifteenth-Century Florentine Studies*.
144 Elam, op. cit., 173, and fig. 6. It should be noted that Gino di Giuliano Ginori, at the behest of his father Antonio, had constructed three doorways at the entrance to the church on the north side, adjacent to their new chapel, so the arrangement may not have been altogether detrimental to their interests.
145 On Dietisalvi's later career see Kent, op. cit., 131–2, 327–8, and Rubinstein, *Government of Florence*, pt. 2, and "La confessione di Francesco Neroni," 386. On his monument in the Badia, Gilbert, *Italian Art*, 34–5.
146 Op. cit., 175–6.
147 The Della Stufa remained close and faithful friends of the Medici throughout the fifteenth century, as one generation succeeded another, and their correspondence serves nicely to nuance the tone of Medici relations with their neighbors, sometimes assumed to be crudely coercive. There are numerous letters from Ugo della Stufa to Giovanni, written in the 1430s and early 1440s when Cosimo's younger son was still in his late teens and early twenties. They were part of the same *brigata* of young men who spent time together not only in town, but also "in villa" in the Mugello. Ugo wrote from Scarperia to Giovanni when his friend was in Florence on business, MAP, V, 355, and from Florence to Giovanni in Trebbio, VII, 101, 29 May, s. a., in response to Giovanni's invitation to join him there: "Charo mio Giovanni. In questo punto a ore 20 o circha ho ricieuto una tua pichola lettera et per essa inteso voresti venissi costí questa sera. Et però vorei fussi posibile di mettere l'alie per far cossa ti fussi in piaciere, posto qui ci abia alchuna facienda, ma questa facienda grande ci avessi la lascierei istare per venire a essere apresso di te . . ." In 1445 when Giovanni was in Rome, Ugo wrote to him describing the diversions of the *brigata*, ibid., V, 571: "questo solo per ricordarti che venendone il caldo nonè più costà da volere dimorare . . . Noi siamo quagiù, et non domandare con quanto diletto stiamo, hora la facciamo a Romolo, hora a Bivigliano, fugiendo e pensieri più potiamo. Antonio [Squarcialupi] ancora cogli organi ci da piaciere asai, che sono forniti quegli di quesuso, et altro non voresti udire che comantaci; non si può soperire alla volontà d'Antonio di sonare quando glia tra manno . . ." In another note he thanked Giovanni for the *ballata* he had sent the *brigata* from Rome, MAP, IX, 148. Once he wrote to Giovanni at Careggi, ibid., VII, 103, s. d.: "Mi pare mill'anni che non ti ho veduto," hoping that "sanza mancho ti verò Domenicha a Santa Re[parata]." Cf. Giovenco della Stufa to Giovanni, ibid., V, 525, 5 June 1444, "nel porto di Livorno," describing his voyage in one of the Florentine galleys, and how bad weather took them to Brest in Brit-

tany, where they had to stay twenty-five days. Antonio della Stufa also wrote to Giovanni while he was taking a cure at the baths, ibid., v, 4, sending greeetings and recommendations to Cosimo, Piero and Pierfrancesco, "e a tutta la brigata," and on another occasion, ibid., v, 53, 1442, 9 July, Florence to Bagno: "A questa brighata pare loro mill'ani che tu torni perchè pare essere loro mezzi issimariti e vogliono venire al Trebio a iucellare agli starnoni." A third letter acknowledges news of Giovanni from another partisan and parishioner of San Lorenzo, ibid., v, 401: "Domattina va Maso Pitti al bagno e dicie ne vorrà menare di qua il Burchiello . . . facci avere uno bullettino da' Dieci . . . Da Simon Ginori o'nteso il buono tenpo avesti a Chalenzano . . ." However, the relations of these local partisans with their patrons were not all frivolity. When Antonio was vice-vicar of the Mugello he wrote, ibid., v, 318, 14 Jan. 1439/40, that he had been glad to hear from Giovanni about the appointment of new *accoppiatori*, "ch'è suto buona lezione," since they would be keeping the purses "in mano a questo modo usato" for another year.

148 On this, see among others, Elam, Saalman, op. cit. For the foundation of San Lorenzo, see Cianfogni, op. cit., 42, ff. Santa Trinita, however, preceded San Lorenzo as "the first basilical church in Florence wholly surrounded by family chapels along its side aisles as well as at the head of the transept to either side of the main chapel," Saalman, *Brunelleschi: The Buildings*, 109. As the focus of the Strozzi family's sphere of influence in their neighborhood and parish, it serves in some sense as a precedent for the Medici at San Lorenzo, see below, ch. 15.

149 Work in some areas, like the decoration, went on much longer; some of the frescoes were painted as late as 1450, see Hood, *Fra Angelico at San Marco*.

150 Saalman, op. cit., 115–16.

151 Cit. and trans. Gombrich, "Early Medici as Patrons," 42. Previously the main chapel, transept, and nave had been reserved to the prior and canons: they continued to receive burial in the church under the area for which Cosimo became responsible. See also Saalman, op. cit., loc. cit.

152 *Vite* 2, 192.

153 See above, pp. 19, 138–41.

154 "Dante and *Lumen Christi*," 272–3. See also Gaston, "Liturgy and Patronage"; Gombrich, "Early Medici as Patrons," 42. Cf. Giovanni di Bicci's concern in 1427 with the completion of his burial chapel, the old sacristy; see Cat. 49, 1159v: "E piu maestà d'incharicho el muramento principiato in San Lorenzo dove fo chonto mi bisogni spendere anchora fiorini tremila o più e quali o diliberato non mi dovendo rimanere altretanto di finirlo se adio piacerà . . ."

155 Hyman, *Fifteenth-Century Florentine Studies*, 302–6; also "Notes and Speculations," 98, n. 3. In her view, "The announcement and notarized document of August 13, 1442, were no more than confirmations of a responsibility already engaged." See also MAP, VIII, 156, Bartolomeo Sassetti to Giovanni di Cosimo, Florence to Petriolo, 26 March 1446.

156 Lorenzo died, like most of the Medici, intestate, and Cosimo observed concerning the very limited inventory of their joint possessions made at that time, excluding business assets and Monte investments, that "because of his many public and private commitments and because of the multiplicity of his business operations and uncertainty about [their] debts and credits and possessions and rights, he was incapable of giving

or adding any more definite possessions to the said inventory at the moment," MAP, 161, 5v–7r. Over the next three years Cosimo sorted out his situation, adding various Monte holdings and other credits, including the estate of his cousin Francesco di Giovanni di Averardo, who also died intestate, in 1443. For details of the Medici finances and the ultimate division of Cosimo's estate with Lorenzo's son Pierfrancesco, see Brown, "Radical Alternative."

157 On family naming strategies, see above pp. 141–2; see below, p. 247, for the fact that in devotional images in Giovanni di Bicci's house in 1418, San Lorenzo was as well represented as Saints Cosmas and Damian.

158 See Paoletti, "Fraternal Piety"; also Gaye, *Carteggio* 1, 128, on Lorenzo's funeral; also Cianfogni, op. cit., 1, 36, 42; 2, 398–403.

159 On the major renovations of the nave see particularly Herzner, "Zur Baugeschichte von San Lorenzo"; Saalman, *Brunelleschi: The Buildings*, ch. 4.

160 Hyman, "Notes and Speculations," 101. In 1449 the nave superstructure was only lately completed, and payments for the roof were still being made in 1450. Saalman speculated, "1434 Chapel Project," 363, that Brunelleschi may have been out of the picture after Giovanni di Bicci's death in 1429, but presented no evidence for this.

161 Gaye, *Carteggio* 1, 167–9; see also Gombrich's comment on the issue, "Early Medici as Patrons."

162 Saalman, *Brunelleschi: The Buildings*, 112–13. In the early twenties at least one document had referred already to construction at San Lorenzo as the "fondamenti di Cosimo"; conversely, the master mason Filippo di Giovanni reported in his tax return of 1427 that he was working with "other masters who were his companions" in the "building for Giovanni de' Medici in San Lorenzo."

163 See Trachtenberg, "On Brunelleschi's Old Sacristy." The following discussion, and my appreciation of the old sacristy, owes much to his study and his ekphrasis of the building. See also the essays ed. Gurrieri, *La Sacrestia vecchia di San Lorenzo*, and Baldini et al., *Brunelleschi e Donatello nella Sagrestia*.

164 Manetti, *Life of Brunelleschi*, 106; Trachtenberg, "On Brunelleschi's Old Sacristy," 9.

165 Ibid., 16; see also his analysis of these and other important examples of Strozzi, Bardi, Castellani, Baroncelli, Peruzzi, and Rinuccini patronage. The Peruzzi and Cavalcanti paid for the sacristies respectively of Santa Croce and Santa Maria Novella.

166 See especially Saalman, *Brunelleschi: The Buildings*, 128, 132, following Krautheimer, *Early Christian and Byzantine Architecture*; also Burns, "*Quattrocento* Architecture and the Antique." For the popular view of the baptistery as Florence's own "anticaglia," see the poem of Giovanni *calzaiuolo* for the cupola consecration, above, pp. 125–6. Other suggested models include churches at Rome and Padua, and various Eastern influences.

167 The Barbadori chapel and the old sacristy embodied this ideal long before Alberti built his tomb for Giovanni Rucellai; on the former, see above, pp. 171–2.

168 Above, ch. 7, cf. Saalman, op. cit., 132, 141.

169 McKillop, op. cit.

170 See De La Mare, "Cosimo and His Books," 112, no. 15; Lang, "Programme of the SS. Annunziata." See also Rosenthal, "A Renaissance 'Copy' of the Holy Sepulchre," 2, ff.

171 McKillop, op. cit., 264–5; also Battisti, *Brunelleschi*, 354, n. 12.

172 Above, p. 90. Another possible source of Florentine knowledge of the Holy Sepulcher was Rustichi's illustrated "Dimostrazione dell'andata e viaggio al Santo Sepolcro e al Monte Sinai compilato da Marco di Bartolmeo Rustichi, orafo di Firenze circa l'anno 1425"; for this see Gilbert, *Italian Art*, 224.

173 Gordan, *Two Renaissance Book Hunters*, 148–9.

174 Preyer and Kent in Rucellai, *Zibaldone 2*, were inclined to be sceptical of this claim, but the evidence collected in this study of Florentine relations with the East suggests that it was not implausible.

175 See Brown, "Radical Alternative," 84–5; Vespasiano, *Vite 2*, 180–81; De Roover, *Rise and Decline*.

176 Op. cit., 32.

177 Ibid., 17. Nor would most historians agree that the oligarchical regime after 1382 consisted of only "a dozen influential families." See Najemy, *Corporatism and Consensus*; Brucker, *Civic World*; Kent, "Reggimento," *Rise of the Medici*; Rubinstein, *Government of Florence*.

178 "Donatello's Bronze Doors," 68.

179 Why can the "expanded decorative program" imposed upon the superb architectonic articulation of the old sacristy "only have resulted from the rising ambitions and demands of increasingly self-confident, insistent patrons?" See Trachtenberg, op. cit., loc. cit.. Might not the opportunity offered by Donatello's readily available genius have had something to do with it, along with the need for the figural images characteristic of fifteenth-century Florentine piety, with its emphasis on the image as a heuristic or mnemonic device to aid in prayer, contemplation, and identification with the exemplars of the Christian revelation?

180 Paoletti, op. cit., 49.

181 Trachtenberg, op. cit., loc. cit..

182 Op. cit., 21.

183 Paoletti, "Donatello's Bronze Doors," 51–2, also 58. In a later article Paoletti amended his definitions; see "Fraternal Piety," 201: "Given the multiple functions of the Old Sacristy – family burial chapel, sacristy, and, most likely, chapter-house as well – it is impossible to view it exclusively as either a private or a public space." However, he continued to stress ownership: "yet the family iconography . . . clearly designates the space as one in which the Medici family had legal property rights," an inaccurate claim taken up by other writers to bolster a "public and civic" versus "private" distinction.

184 For example, Cosimo had to negotiate to obtain patronage rights at San Marco which had previously "belonged" to other families; this was a long and complex process, involving the pope's transfer of the convent to a new order, and substantial compensatory payments from Cosimo to the previous patrons before they ceded their rights "of their own free will," see above, p. 177 and 450, n. 104. Similarly, the Tornabuoni struggled for many years, against the chapter and the previous patrons, to obtain patronage rights over the *cappella maggiore* at Santa Maria Novella; see Simons, *Portraiture and Patronage*.

185 Cf. above, p. 134.

186 Filarete paid tribute to them in his own bronze doors for St. Peter's in Rome, which he completed in 1445; see Westfall, "Chivalric Declaration." Renaissance practice, conscious of antique customs as described by classical writers like Pliny, decreed that bronze was reserved for important commissions, which made those that used it all the more impressive.

187 No other patron disposed of such great wealth, or more importantly, assets so readily available. Palla Strozzi, by contrast, although once the richest man in Florence, had, as a large investor in land, serious problems of solvency, by which the Medici banking moguls were at this time quite untroubled. See Kent and Kent, *Neighbours and Neighbourhood*, ch. 2. Protesting that he was unable to pay his taxes in 1423, and referring to the expenses of building the chapel to commemorate his father, Strozzi explained that because he could not instantly liquidate the assets tied up in land, he was very short of cash. See also Kent's study of Rucellai, *Zibaldone 2*, for Strozzi's tangled financial affairs after his exile in 1434, which created the opportunity for his son-in-law, Giovanni Rucellai, to finance his patronage with Strozzi's aid.

188 "It is worth noting that the saints the Medici selected as monastic references also had civic meaning and may suggest a deliberate appropriation of imagery belonging to other groups in the society, comparable to Cosimo's assimilation of political powers," Paoletti, "Fraternal Piety," 218, n. 58. Similar points are made by Saalman, Hyman, op. cit.

189 See above, pp. 111–15, for commissions from Neri di Bicci, including, for example a *tavola* for a large tabernacle with the Madonna and Child and Saint John the Baptist, *Ricordanze*, 285; see also below, ch. 15.

190 Casotti, *Prose e Rime*, 332: "La degna fama e reputata onore,/ che, Signor mio, fa di memoria degno/ chi virtuosamente vive, o more./ Ne presti più la fone agl'occhi il core/ ch' e' voler sollevarsi a maggior Regno,/ uscire quinci d'esto carcer fuore." My reading of this verse assumes a very different relation between fame, honor, virtue, and salvation from that assumed by Paoletti's observation, "Fraternal Piety," 219, that "the propagandistic purpose of the commissions [of Cosimo and Lorenzo de' Medici], the issue of personal salvation aside, was clearly recognized and delineated in a sonnet addressed to Cosimo by Niccolo Tinucci."

191 The sarcophagus may well have been installed before the decree of exile banished the brothers from Florence for a year in September 1433, since Brunelleschi's tax report for that year refers to it as finished. The vesting table on top of it was in place by 1459. It is mentioned in a document recording a canons' meeting of that year; see Saalman, *Brunelleschi: The Buildings*, 132. Beck, "Alberti and the Night Sky," 14, suggested that several documents concerning celebrations in "the new sacristy" in May 1439 and January 1440 may indicate that the decorations were substantially completed by that time.

192 Cf. above, p. 141.

193 *Brunelleschi: The Buildings*, 140; see also above, ch. 3, for Poggio's comments on Giovanni di Bicci's death in a letter to Niccoli, and for Niccoli's close relation to the Medici.

194 While Dante's *Inferno* was a place of lively torment, Propertius's "pale portal closes on the world of shadow" where "no prayers may open the gate of darkness"; *Elegies*, IV, xi.

195 *Only Connect*, 10–16, especially 15–16. My own, more pedestrian connection between the inscription and Propertius's *Elegies* was made before Shearman's aptly titled essays appeared. These nicely illustrate the greater richness of interpretations of Renaissance objects by the few modern scholars, certainly excluding myself, as familiar with classical culture as fifteenth-century artists and their patrons. Although Shearman was less interested in patrons, he did make the interesting suggestion, in view of the similarities between

Giovanni's sarcophagus and Donatello's tomb for Pope John XXIII, that it was "perhaps to be recognized and interpreted positively as a token of the clientage of the Medici to Cossa," 13, cf. above, this chapter, pp. 164–6, and fig. 66. On the association of Cosimo and his sons with symbols of time and eternity see below, passim, especially p. 258, and fig. 119 and ch. 13.

196   See Spallanzani, *Inventari Medicei*, 6.

197   See John 3:16–21. The Gospel of Saint John opens with the image of Christ as the Light of the World. The Evangelist described John the Baptist as sent "to bear witness of the Light . . . He was not that Light, but was sent to bear witness of that Light. That was the true Light, which lighteth every man that cometh into the world . . ." John 1:6–9. This imagery of light served to link the two Saints John in medieval minds; see Iacopo da Voragine, *Golden Legend* 1, ii; cf. below, n. 200. See also McKillop, "Dante and *Lumen Christi*," 270, n. 107: "To you, judges of men and true light of the world, we tell in prayer our hearts' desires; hear your supplicants' words./ You shut heaven's gates and with a word undo their bolts; give the word of command, we beg you, for us sinners to be undone from our guilt . . . That when Christ comes again at the end of time to be man's judge, He may graciously call us to possess eternal joy."

198   See Paoletti, "Donatello's Bronze Doors," 59, ff. For the plaque Palla Strozzi ordered for the tomb of his father Nofri, see Davisson, "Iconology of the S. Trinita Sacristy," 315. It bears two of Palla's coronets with two palm fronds inserted in each, flanking the family coat of arms and the motto "le bel e le bon." There is also a plaque on the sacristy wall: "AN. MCCCCXXI. HANC CAPPELLAM SANTIS HO/NOFRIO ET NICOLAO DED/CATAM TESTAMENTO CLARISSIMI VIRI HUNFRII PALLE DOMINI /IACOBI DE STROZIS MAGNUS /EQUES PASSA EIUS FILIUS/ PER CELEBRATIONE QU/OTIDDIANARUM MISSARUM/ ET DICTORUM SANCTO/RUM FESTO QUOTANNIS/SOLEMNITER CELEBRANDO/DUOBUS MILIBUS FLORE/NORUM . MONTIS COMMUNIS/DOTAVIT ITS UT NEMO/PRAETER, DESCENDENTS/ IN EA SEPELLIRI /POSSINT." The inscription for the Medici tomb read: "COSMUS ET LAURENTIUS DE MEDICIS V.CL IOHANNI[S] AVERARDI F. ET PICARDAE ADOVARDI .F. CARISSIMIS PARENTIBUS HOC SEPULCRUM FACIUNDUM CURARUNT OBIIT AUTEM IOHANNES X. KAL. MARTIAS MCCCCXXVIII. PICCARDA VERO XIII KAL. MAIAS QUINQUENNIO POST E VITA MIGRAVIT."

199   See Schulz, *Bernardo Rossellino*, and below, pp. 205, 355.

200   A new contract was signed 21 Jan. 1430; for this and other comments on the sacristy altar see McKillop, op. cit., 266–71, especially 270, n. 107, 271, n. 112.

201   See above, p. 118. That Giovanni di Bicci was apparently one of the judges of the competition for the baptistery doors, Avery, "Early Medici and Donatello," 73, might help to explain its presence in the Medici chapel if not to confirm Vasari's story that Brunelleschi gave the competition panel to Cosimo.

202   See Fortini Brown, "*Laetentur caeli*," especially 177. Beck, "Leon Battista Alberti and the 'Night Sky,'" believed the painting was done by Alberti, an interesting and plausible suggestion, although no confirmatory evidence has yet come to light.

203   See Edgerton, "Florentine Interest in Ptolemaic Cartography," especially 275–80; above, p. 90.

204   See above, p. 25.

205   Discussed above, p. 155, and fig. 61; below, ch. 13.

206   Blumenthal, "Science of the Magi," 2–3, suggested that the sacristy "was designed as an Athanor, or cosmic oven, with the *vas insigne electionis*, or vessel in which the alchemical Mercury would be created. This in turn would transmute common man into divine spirit and produce the "m = perfect man" as a member of the Medici family. He would be the long-awaited Great Monarch, ruler of the new Golden Age." There seems to be no evidential warrant for this hypothesis.

207   See Saalman, *Brunelleschi: The Buildings*. The Pazzi chapel at Santa Croce has a similar scheme and and also an astrological painting.

208   MAP, IX, 557. In the last decade of his life, Cosimo may have pursued his interest in astrology informed by Ficino's studies in Neoplatonic and Hermetic philosophy. See Kaske, "Twelve Gods of the Zodiac"; Copenhaver and Schmitt, *Renaissance Philosophy*.

209   MAP, V, 441; also Fabroni, *Magni Cosmi*, 2. 164–5 for a letter from Agnolo Acciaiuoli to Cosimo of January 1442/3 showing that while René of Anjou continued to court the friendship of influential Florentines in Cosimo's circle, they greeted his overtures with caution. Cf. Trexler, *Public Life*, 429, for the honors paid the Angevin visitors in 1454. For this proposal see Lapi Ballerini, "Celestial Hemisphere," "Gli emisferi celesti della Sagrestia Vecchia e della Cappella Pazzi," "Considerazioni a margine del restauro della 'cupolina.'" There is no other example in Cosimo's commissions of any reference to political alliances. The use of roses which might be read as papal symbols some ten years later on the facade of Medici palace was comparatively safe politically, as a papal connection would always seem in some sense desirable. The only reference to Francesco Sforza, the major ally of Cosimo's career, was the very transient tribute of representing his arms in the vegetation of the palace garden.

210   Lavin, "Donatello's Bronze Pulpits," 15, pointed out that the date 4–5 July 1442 identified by Lapi Ballerini is only a month before Cosimo formally agreed to be the patron of San Lorenzo, a decision actually made some time earlier; this event would indeed be an appropriate one for commemoration. Moreover, Feo Belcari's sonnets to the Medici invoke Giovanni's birth-sign, Gemini, in the ascendancy on this date, and the poet Commedio Venuti, who replied on Giovanni's behalf, referred to Belcari as "Tu buon poeta e ottimo cosmografo." See Lanza, *Lirici toscani* 1, 223–4.

211   Cf. also Ames-Lewis, op. cit. Fortini Brown, op. cit., further suggested that the date recorded by the fresco linked Cosimo's family to "Florentine millenial expectations of political and religious leadership." In this connection she observed that the vines and lilies on the marble choir screen may be more than funerary symbols, recalling the prophecy of Fra Antonio da Rieti of 1422, discussed by Donald Weinstein as part in the early fifteenth century of "the myth of Florence"; see "Myth of Florence," 34–6: "the Florentine lily is seen putting out ever more beautiful branches, flowers and leaves until it covered all of Italy . . . the Pope would fly to the protection of the lily, that is, of Florence." While there is no reference in Cosimo's letters or papers to these prophecies concerning the destiny of Florence, they are often mentioned in popular literature, and if there was one myth to which the pragmatic Cosimo could subscribe it might be this. Conversely, given the chapel's explicit focus on the iconography of Giovanni di Bicci's patron saint, John the Evangelist, in the roundel above the altar whose form is echoed in its cupola, a reference to some event in the life of the chapel's patron might seem *prima facie* more plausible.

212 Cit. Fabriczy, *Brunelleschi* 1, 252, "Ricordo di firenze dell'anno MCCCCLIX di Autore Anonimo," published in full in *Rerum Italicarum Scriptores* II, 725: "In San Lorenzo entrai Martir grazioso/ e mai non vidi tanta dignitade./ Tutto il mio cuore qui prese riposo/ non già di panni, o di fiori adorno,/ ma di un bel sito di un muro prezioso./ Quivi guardando io intorno intorno,/ pietre conce di tale adornamento,/ che Policleto n'avrebbe iscorno [a reference to Pliny];/ molto è adornato il duro pavimento,/ e 'l tetto tutto luce d'oro fine;/ non vidi mai di si bello fornimento./ Finestre grandi vidi e piccoline/ di vetro laborate si gentili,/ non mostra manufatte ma divine./ A questa chiesa non trovo simile./ Guardando poi nella sua Sagrestia,/ ogni superbo vi diventa umile./ Qui affigurato par, che tutto sia/ intero il Vecchio, e 'l nuovo Testamento;/ meglio adombrato non credo, che sia,/ mai non mi sazirei di starvi dentro,/ non vidi intagli, e tarsie mai migliori,/ di marmi un desco di gran valimento."

213 *Brunelleschi: The Buildings*, 133.

214 The *Golden Legend* describes Stephen's martyrdom and the legend that when Lawrence's bones were brought to Rome, Stephen rolled over in his tomb to make room for them. They were henceforth regarded as "brother saints," like the actual brothers Cosmas and Damian, perhaps by an analogy between sharing a tomb and sharing a womb, the terms in which Florentines graphically envisaged the fraternal relationship. See, for example, Cavalcanti, *Istorie fiorentine*, 310, who marveled that in the partisan conflict of the early 1430s, Luca degli Albizzi could side with Cosimo de' Medici rather than Rinaldo with whom he had shared a womb.

215 This is the main point of Paoletti's "Donatello's Bronze Doors."

216 "Quattrocento Architecture and the Antique," 285; "an almost identical pedimented portal, with freestanding Ionic columns, is drawn by Giuliano da Sangallo, whose note indicates" its location. McKillop, op. cit., 270–71, suggested that the doors resemble the portals of the Holy Sepulcher as represented in medieval ivories.

217 Above, pp. 142–3.

218 *Life of Brunelleschi*, 108–9.

219 Paoletti, op. cit., 49, found it "hard to explain away" the "redundancy" that the only identifiable figures on the martyr's door are the same four as on the overdoors. Like the "confusion" he also discerned here, this problem may stem partly from a rather strained attempt to define the sacristy figural program as dynastic to the effective exclusion of other considerations. Grayson, "Composition of L. B. Alberti's *Decem libri*," 156, pointed out that these "generic saints and martyrs . . . conform to the type used on doors in Italy from the early Christian period," offering as example San Paolo fuori le mura in Rome. The bronze doors of a sacristy are a different case from the panel paintings for private chapels and domestic use, which do seem to have a dynastic function.

220 *Companion Guide*, 233.

221 His characterization probably derived from Alberti's prescription, *On Painting*, that "a philosopher, when speaking . . . show modesty in every limb rather than the attitudes of a wrestler," 73.

222 Eisler, "Athlete of Virtue," 82–5, especially 84. Chrysostom's images Eisler described as evoking "the most vivid scenes of the experience of the palaestra and the gymnasium, the stadium and the hippodrome," fleshing out "the athletic ref-erence in the writings of his favorite author, St. Paul. It is Paul . . . who represented to Chrysostom the athletic ideal – Paul the wrestler, the 'boxer.'"

223 Cit. more fully above, pp. 101–2.

224 See above, ch. 5, pp. 63–4.

225 Op. cit., 66–7: "Donatello's pugnacious figures parallel in their poses the Traversarian characterization of the participants of the Council." See also Stinger, *Humanism and the Church Fathers*, especially 221. As not only the leading citizen of Florence, but also the pope's banker, Cosimo would certainly have attended some of the sessions himself.

226 Ceccioni, *Studi storici sul concilio di firenze*, clxxxii.

227 See below, ch. 13.

228 See Kent, *Household and Lineage* and "Making of a Renaissance Patron," particularly on Giovanni Rucellai; for his oeuvre, see below, pp. 357–64.

229 See Kent, "*Reggimento*."

230 On Francesco's wedding see Kent, *Rise of the Medici*, 64–5; also "I Medici in esilio." On Medici activity at San Tommaso see Molho, "*Pater Patriae* or *Padrino*," 26, n. 46; ASF, Notarile antecosmiano M 569, 1458–60, 106r–109v, 112r–113r, 114r–117v, 120r–121r. See Brucker, "Medici in the Fourteenth Century," for their move away from this district. For Cosimo's tax report of 1442, Cat., 622, fols. 594–632, especially 597v, for his property in the parish of San Tommaso, including part of several houses and *botteghe* and the bank.

231 See Paoletti, "Ha fatto Piero con voluntà del padre"; also Rubinstein, *Palazzo Vecchio*, especially 50–52.

232 John 20:19–29.

233 See Rubinstein, op. cit., loc. cit; Paoletti, op. cit., 230–32; above, pp. 105–6, for Sacchetti's poems.

234 Paoletti, op. cit., 249–50, n. 75. See also Dorini, "Il culto delle memorie Patrie," 20; Sframeli, *Il centro di Firenze restituito*, 370.

235 See Trexler, op. cit., 423, n. 15: also ASF, Provv., 152, 242r–243v, 14 Sept. 1460.

236 The cult was also important, as Lightbown observed, *Donatello and Michelozzo* 1, 230–31, because it buttressed the doctrine of the bodily Assumption of the Virgin, "dear in the Middle Ages to popular devotion and to the Franciscans, but vehemently opposed by the Dominicans." Antoninus expressed doubts about the tradition, but "discreetly separated the authenticity of the story from that of the Virgin's girdle," observing "that it may with piety be believed that her Girdle is on earth; it is said to be at Prato and is there exhibited to the people."

237 MAP, XI, 537.

238 Ferrara and Quinterio, *Michelozzo*, 173–6; see also the documents in Janson, *Donatello*, 108–18.

239 Cited Janson, *Donatello*, 111–12.

240 Paoletti, op. cit., 247, n. 58; MAP, CLV, 45r. On the Lenzi, see Kent, *Rise of the Medici*, 320.

241 Paoletti, op. cit., 248–9, especially notes 68, 71.

242 See Brown, "Patronage and Building History," 72, 137, n. 32; Paoletti, op. cit.; Borsi, *Paolo Uccello*, 334–6.

243 1, 35.

244 See below, ch. 13.

245 Op. cit., loc. cit.

246 Rubinstein, *Government of Florence*, described the establishment of the new Council of One Hundred in 1458, in response to the challenges to the Medici regime in the preceding several years, as "the consolidation of the regime." He and other students of the dissension within the Medici party

leading up to the conspiracy of 1466 regard 1458 as a watershed. See particularly Clarke, *Power and Patronage*; also Phillips, *Memoir of Marco Parenti*, for Parenti's account of this period. Brown, "Parte Guelfa," especially 120, shows how the Medici takeover of the Parte in these years marked the beginning of the consolidation of the bureaucratic state under much closer Medici control.

247 See Zervas, *Orsanmichele*, 211–19, especially 218. She pointed out that while the Parte Guelfa and its Angevin Saint Louis were appropriate symbols of civic freedom and liberty during Florence's wars against Milan, the alliance of its new Sforza duke with Florence after 1450 altered this situation. Moreover, it made "good symbolic sense," 213, for a Parte Guelfa convinced that its dignity was damaged by a continuing association with the guilds at Orsanmichele to sell its niche to the Mercanzia, the court with judiciary authority over the guilds, which after 1420 seems to have replaced its former patron Saint Zenobius with Saint Thomas, symbol of civic justice. On the Mercanzia's probable patronage of the Saint Thomas chapel in the cathedral after 1444, see Paoletti, op. cit., n. 47. For an important reevaluation of Verrocchio's work, one that views the Mercanzia's commission of *Christ and Saint Thomas* as a result mainly of Medici influence and propagandistic intentions, but emphasizes that its ultimate interest lies elsewhere, in "its interpretative and aesthetic character," see Butterfield, "Verrocchio's Christ and St. Thomas"; *Verrocchio*, ch. 3, especially 63, and notes 51–3, stressing also Chrysostom's influential exposition of the Incredulity of Saint Thomas as an allegory for the sacrament of communion.

248 On this see Hood, *Fra Angelico at San Marco*, ch. 3.

249 MAP, xx, 498: "Vi gravo facciate per vostra parte due [versi] al gonfaloniere della giustitia si degni far dire al quel frater ch'è in palagio anno sostenuto vada con mia autorità a stare per due anni o tre in exilio per certa cattivita facta di lettere ritenute delgli inbasciadori del re di Napoli e del Ducha di Milano quali mandamo da Vinegia chome pienamente a bocha dalla portatore di questa sarete informato." Richard Trexler pointed out how effectively the "trust function" of the clergy was made to serve political ends; see his "Honor Among Thieves."

250 ASF, Diplomatico, S. Croce, 31 Jan. 1456/7.

251 See Saalman, *Brunelleschi: The Buildings*, 227. The figures given by Vespasiano for Cosimo's building expenses are as follows: for the novices' chapel, the income on fl. 8000 of Monte shares at 3.75 per cent, by comparison with Bosco ai Frati 15,000, San Marco 40,000, San Lorenzo 60,000, and the Badia 70,000. On the desirability of looking at the well-known commissions of famous individual patrons like Cosimo in the broader contexts of civic and workshop activity see Bullard, "Heroes and their Workshops."

252 On the Medici building at Santa Croce see Ferrara and Quinterio, *Michelozzo*, 200–4; on its attribution to Michelozzo, Vasari-Milanesi 2, 442; on its association with the Pazzi and their chapel, Saalman, *Brunelleschi: The Buildings*.

253 Saalman, op. cit., 224.

254 Gaye, *Carteggio* 1, 558; see also the comment by Gombrich, "Early Medici as Patrons," 44.

255 See Pampaloni, "Fermenti di riforme democratiche," cf. Rubinstein, *Government of Florence*, pt. 11.

256 For this document, and on the tabernacle in general, see Pope-Hennessy, *Luca della Robbia*, especially 239.

257 On San Miniato see Leonardi, "San Miniato: Il Martire e il suo culto"; on the church in general, Gurrieri et al., *La Basilica di San Miniato*; on the Medici and the Armenians, below, ch. 13.

258 For these attributions and divergent opinions see Ferrara and Quinterio, *Michelozzo*, 243–5, 301, especially nn. 1, 2.

259 See also the comments of Liebenwein, "Die 'Privatisierung' des Wunders," 273.

260 Cf. above, p. 106, for fuller citation and comment; also Wazbinski, "L'Annunciazione," 534–5.

261 Cit. Mazzoni, *I Bóti della Ss. Annunziata*, 21.

262 Sacchetti, cit. Mazzoni, op. cit., loc. cit.

263 Cits. Ferrara and Quinterio, *Michelozzo*, 305, n. 4. These acts were part of a broader program of reform including San Marco, the Badia at Fiesole, and the Badia a Settimo di San Bernardo di Cestello; see Vespasiano, *Lives* 1, 11.

264 Ferrara and Quinterio, op. cit., 214, 190, n. 4: on the Puccini, see Cavalcanti, *Istorie fiorentine*, 4–5; on the Pucci family, Kent, *Rise of the Medici*, especially 106–8; 118–9; 122–3.

265 The clearest account of the program in general is in Ferrara and Quinterio, op. cit.; see also Teubner, "San Marco in Florenz"; Brown, "Patronage and Building History," and on its patronage Bulman, "Artistic Patronage at Santissima Annunziata."

266 ASF, Provv. Reg., 136, 243v–4r, 17–23 Dec. 1445, cit. Zervas, "'Quos volent'," appendix 1, 473–5.

267 Zervas, op. cit., 406; on the political situation at this time, Rubinstein, *Government of Florence*.

268 See Zervas, op. cit., for the names of the *operai*. A letter to Piero from Mariano Salvini, prior of the convent during the renovations, shows how closely he consulted the Medici and their friends. "Iacopo Villani iersera tutto mi disse. E faremo lui, Ser Alexo e io quanto stimeremo sia la volonta di Dio e la tua. In ogni modo io ti priego noi possiamo seguire l'anticappella insino alla volta inclusive, acciò che alla tua tornata per G. Giovanni la vegga adorni di panni dorazo etc. E avisami quando o dove o in Firenze o a Chareggi io n'abi per hora di tempo a starmi techo, che stamattina ordinamo in co.[mpagnia]? che ogni mattina insino alla tornata, tre di noi dichano certa orisone per non stieno vote. Feo Belchari perfetto huomo e Arrigo Arrigucci ti si raccomandano. 26 April. Frater Mariano." MAP, xvi, 316.

269 See Kent, *Rise of the Medici*, passim. In 1451 Orlando held land in the Mugello jointly with Cosimo. The fullest biography of Orlando is by Spencer, *Castagno and His Patrons*, 49–56. Spencer also gave a detailed account of Castagno's commissions at Santissima Annunziata from several Medicean patrons; ibid., 42–69.

270 Ferrara and Quinterio, op. cit., 218.

271 By April 1445 Orlando had also assumed responsibility for the new sacristy; ibid., 216. On Orlando's tomb see Schulz, *Bernardo Rossellino*; the other tombs were commissioned by the Pandolfini, Inghirami, Sassetti, Castellani, and Capponi; on these see also below, ch. 15.

272 See above, v; Robinson, "Cosimo de' Medici," and Spencer, op. cit., 62–9.

273 MAP, xi, 552.

274 On this and other chapels see Ferrara and Quinterio, and Spencer, op. cit. Spencer suggested, 65–6, that Piero's dedication of the chapel, and the naming of his second son Giuliano in 1459, may have been made in deference to his friends and patrons. Piero de' Medici's second son, born in

1453, was named Giuliano, as was Averardo di Francesco di Bicci's son. The chapel at Cafaggiolo, which passed when Averardo's line was extinguished to Cosimo's, was dedicated to Saints Francis and Julian.

275 Salvini was prior of Santissima Annunziata from 1447 to 1448 and from 1452 to 1453. He later replaced Filippo de' Medici as bishop of Cortona. He recorded his long conversations with Piero de' Medici in his *Dialogus de origine ordinis servorum*. He cooperated closely with Medici in various enterprises, including their charitable building at Fiesole. See MAP, XVI, 318; also ibid., VII, 46, asking Giovanni di Cosimo to "lend a sympathetic ear to the bearer [of this letter] . . . hear him in charity, and help him insofar as is just, not only him but all the oppressed, as is very pleasing to God, and I swear to you faithfully that God and Our Lady will help you to prosper."

276 Ferrara and Quinterio, op. cit., 85, doc. 18, 1455/6.

277 Op. cit., 213–34. Michelozzo's contribution included aspects of the church, particularly the tribuna, the library, and the convent. Alberti took part in a later phase of the rebuilding. See also Brown, Bulman, Lang, op. cit.

278 Ferrara and Quinterio, op. cit., 63, doc. 8.

279 See Zervas, op. cit., 406. The other Florentine churches administered in this way were the cathedral, San Lorenzo, Santa Croce, and Santa Trinita.

280 *Trattato*, 2, 691.

281 Lanza, *Lirici toscani* 1, 222, 227; see also above, p. 118. The representation of Cosimo as the savior of beleaguered ecclesiastical foundations was not merely the encomiastic rhetoric of the poet. See also MAP, V, 650, 11 Nov. 1440, Gometius, Camaldolensis Ordinis Generalis, "ex Abatia Rotis"; he complained to Cosimo of "alchuna molestia sopra laltra," being squeezed by taxes and "stretti per la fortuna delle guerre passate in Casentino che rubbata la casa et tolte le ricolte dai inimici et dagl'amici insino a mettervi fuoco." He asked Cosimo to bring the convent's plight to the attention of the Signoria, "o di chi l'a da ffare . . . veramente Cosmo nostro non abbiamo altro refugio che a voi . . . che se l'aiuto vostro non ci soccorre andiamone in profondo et noi e quel sancto luogo."

282 Gombrich, "Early Medici as Patrons," 48, observed of the inscription on the tabernacle – "the marble alone cost 4,000 florins" – that it was "truly astounding," and "worthy of remark by those who still believe that this type of announcement was invented by American tycoons." Suggesting "how far in works of these kinds the patron rather than the artist expressed himself," he saw the inscription as evidence mainly of crass self-advertisement.

283 See also below, pp. 377, 379–80.

284 His comparatively unknown comment is published and translated in part by Gilbert, *Italian Art*, 148–52; for the same extract in the original Latin see Gilbert, *L'Arte del Quattrocento*, 176–8. Corella was one of a number of well-educated and civic-minded clerics on good terms with the Medici, like archbishop Antoninus, Belcari, Lapaccini, Alberti, and Degli Agli. Gilbert saw Corella as "exceptionally modern" in naming so many artists; this is more likely a consequence of his familiarity with them owing to his particular personal interests and social position.

285 As Gilbert observed, Corella's description of this lost work of Michelozzo is the most detailed we have. The Dominican draws particular attention to the orbs, a symbol of Christ's

universal kingdom that appears in other Medici commissions, including the San Marco altarpiece and the Magi fresco in Cosimo's cell, as an armillary sphere. His account of the glories of Florentine churches nicely balances aesthetic admiration with the concerns of the devotee. For example, he admired the statues of saints in the niches of the four facades of Orsanmichele, among them some works that were to change the face of fifteenth-century sculpture as well as of the city. But he saw the interior of the oratory, "where shines the image of the holy mother of God," set in a late trecento tabernacle by Orcagna, as far more beautiful and significant. Moving on to the baptistery which he described in Dantesque locution as "the temple of Mars, now of John the Baptist," he mentioned not only the unprecedented achievement of the bronze doors by Ghiberti, "a work which will forever honor his intellect . . . so that his name will shine forth wherever there are men of excellence . . ." but also the familiar mosaics and polychrome floor in the early Christian style, and "the bronze casket that holds Pope John." This tomb by Donatello and Michelozzo, like Michelozzo's font for the Annunziata and the wax votive figures in churches, are rarely mentioned in contemporary comments, although Filarete briefly described the *voti* of Santissima Annunziata, vivid in his mind perhaps because he himself had donated one of them.

286 On the reliquary cupboard see primarily Casalini, "L'Angelico e la Catterata"; on the painted scenes see also Pope-Hennessy, *Fra Angelico*, 217–18. Art historians attempting to reconstruct the order of the scenes had originally envisaged a pair of doors, but Corella refers to a single panel, and in fact the chest was closed by an enormous shutter hoisted up and down by a series of pulleys. On this see also Ferrara and Quinterio, op. cit. Michelozzo and Angelico worked closely together here as at San Marco; notably Angelico represented several of Michelozzo's buildings in his paintings; see Caplow, *Michelozzo* 2, 541–2.

287 See Pope-Hennessy, *Fra Angelico*.

288 Beyer and Boucher, *Piero de' Medici*, introduction, xix; Liebenwein, "Die 'Privatisierung' des Wunders."

289 Liebenwein, op. cit., especially 266–70.

290 Casalini, op. cit., 106–7.

291 A possible corrective to the impression that the Medici were entirely occupied at Santissima Annunziata with portentous assertions of their political presence or power to privatize the miracles of the Madonna, exists in a letter written just two years after Cosimo's death to the young Lorenzo in Rome from one his cronies, Sigismondo della Stufa, MAP, XX, 198, 29 March 1466. Lamenting that lately he had seen no fine women, either in San Miniato or Fiesole or Santa Gaggia, whose charms he might report to his friend, he described one whom he had met in the church of Santissima Annunziata on the eve of the Virgin's feast. "Ma bene è vero che la vi[gi]lia della donna . . . la riscontrai in sul lastricho de' Servi che pareva confesso e tutto contrito di sua peccati senza fuco alcuno che non vedessi mai si bella cosa con quella vesta nera e il capo velato con que soavi passi che pare che le prietre e le mura gli faccino riverentia quando va per la via io non voglio dir più avanti per non ti fare peccare in questi dì santi . . ."

292 On the management of the Opera del Duomo and the patronage of the cathedral see Haines, *Sagrestia delle Messe* and "Arte della Lana," 269; the guild was determined that the

cathedral "non doveva diventar teatro dello sfoggio della committenza privata." Among a handful of families who in the later fifteenth century had memorial chapels in Santa Maria del Fiore were the ancient house of the Inghirami, associates in the Medici bank; on them see De Roover, *Rise and Decline*. See also Cosimo's tax report, Cat. 622, 1442, 597v, for a previous Medici family foundation in the cathedral, in the name of Giovanni di Bicci's father; the donation had been supported by the proceeds of two *botteghe*; "dotammone l'altare della chappella di san Francesco che è in Santa Liberata dove metteremo uno chappellano."

293 Haines, "Arte della Lana," 273, ff.

294 The manner in which those members of the Medici family who happened to be members of the Wool Guild were mobilized to serve as *operai* at the time of the cathedral's consecration is some indication of the readiness of other members of the lineage to serve Cosimo's interests. On this episode, see above, p. 124.

295 On this, and on Piero's membership of civic building committees see Paoletti, "Ha fatto Piero con volontà del padre," 114–15; Zervas, 'Quos volent'; Poggi/Haines, *Il duomo di Firenze*, docs. 1192, 1194, 1196, 1198.

296 Haines, *Sagrestia delle Messe*, 138, 296–7.

297 See, for example, p. 486, n. 25.

298 On the very eve of Piero's demise, a certain Dietaiuti wrote to him from Rome, 30 April 1469: "E s'è finalmente obtenuto ben che con grandissima difficultà per la contradictione ciè suta facta da alchun de' nostri el padronegio dell'arcipresbiterato della chiesa cattedrale. Attendo all spaccio della bolla," MAP, XVI, 289. Precisely what sort of patronage was involved, and for the cathedral of which city, is not clear. Niccolò Bonvanni wrote to Giovanni di Cosimo, 17 Feb. 1444, MAP, VI, 498, asking Giovanni to procure him a canonicate at Santa Maria del Fiore; what this indicates about Medici influence at the cathedral of Florence is not clear either.

299 *Purgatorio* IX, 142–5; on this passage see Sanesi, "Maestri d'Organo," 171.

300 See above, p. 126, for this passage in full; for Cosimo's letter, Ficino, *Letters* 1, 1.

301 For the document, see Herzner, *Regesti Donatelliani*, 14 Nov. 1433; I thank Margaret Haines for further information on this. The *cantoria* bears a striking resemblance to an antique sarcophagus at Ostia. According to Saalman, *Cupola*, doc. 133, Luca della Robbia and Donatello were working on the *cantorie* in early 1435. The twelve apostles were painted on the choir balustrade for the occasion of the consecration; see Belcari's account of this, op. cit., and Saalman, docs. 275, 286.1.

302 See below, p. 292; for the inventory of Medici possessions; for their relations with Squarcialupi, below, p. 414, n. 144.

303 *Vite* 2, 193.

304 On the cathedral musicians see D'Accone, "Singers of San Giovanni"; "Music and Musicians." Of the personal letters, see particularly Dufay's letter to Piero di Cosimo, published D'Accone, "Singers of San Giovanni," 319; also MAP, XVI, 317. The writer of this last was Iacopo di Biagio, a cloth trimmer and leader of a boys' confraternity that took part in 1454 in the annual procession to celebrate the city's patron saint. He wrote asking Piero for alms for the cathedral singers to whose society he belonged, specifically to pay to pay the salary of one Hubertus, "quia multum idonius est et humilis et in arte nostra bene expertus," who was needed as the feast

of San Giovanni was coming up. Iacopo was a partner with Francesco Berlinghieri, one of the benefactors of the Buonomini di San Martino, in the Medici silkshop in that district. The shop provided vestments for Sant'Antonino after his election as archbishop; see Orlandi, *S. Antonino*.

305 The letter to Spinelli is from the Spinelli archive, box 24, folder 557, cited Jacks and Cafarro, *Tommaso Spinelli*, appendix to ch. 5, doc. 4, dated 13 July 1458, Careggi. Tommaso replied promising to do his best the very same day.

306 Poliziano, *Pazzi Conspiracy*, 176–7.

307 For the evidence of Medici participation in the renovation of the convent of San Girolamo at Fiesole, see Ferrara and Quinterio, *Michelozzo*, 234–8. On Cosimo's and Piero's contribution to rebuilding the church of San Girolamo at Volterra, ibid., 355–8. See also Robinson, *Cosimo de' Medici's Patronage*, ch. 3; as he observed, the latter was not a Medici building. The work was originally commissioned by the commune of Volterra; when they ran out of money, the priors of the church appealed to Cosimo for help. A later inscription acknowledged the aid of both Cosimo and Piero and recorded that work was completed on 10 November 1465.

308 *Vite* 2, 183. On the Badia see Borsi et al., *La Badia Fiesolana*, especially Borsi, "Badia Fiesolana: Culture and Architecture"; also Belluzzi, "La Badia Fiesolana."

309 Chrysostom's *Adversus vituperatores monasticae vitae* was translated into Latin by Ambrogio Traversari between 1418 and early 1421, and copied specifically for Cosimo in a cursive version of the humanistic hand. See De La Mare, "Cosimo and His Books," 146.

310 Ibid., 148. Following the text, on a leaf apparently written by the original scribe, is a letter addressed to Cosimo by Giacomo Becchetti, and dated Milan "quarto idus februarii." Becchetti also asked Cosimo to have a copy made from this manuscript for the archbishop of Florence, whom he venerated for his great learning and sanctity.

311 MAP, XI, 696, s. d. to Cosimo from Antonio da Bargha, "visitatore del ordine di Monte Oliveto": "Sono qui a Santa Lena . . . Se non sete troppo ocupato ci serebbe grato che anchora voi ci venisi et anchora se sete ocupato, è buona alcuna volta interrumpere gll'afanni mondani et respirare in Domini."

312 Cit. Hood, *Fra Angelico at San Marco*, 320.

313 See Banker, "Mourning a Son"; on the use and patronage of the Certosa, Chiarelli and Leoncini, *Certosa del Galluzzo*.

314 See Hankins, "Cosimo de' Medici as a Patron," for the list of such works dedicated and presented to him in these years.

315 Ficino, *Letters* 1, 1. On the Academy, see the divergent views of Field, *Platonic Academy*, and Hankins, "Platonic Academy."

316 See Field, "Cristoforo Landino's First Lectures"; Palmieri, *Città di Vita*.

317 See above, n. 307, and below, p. 304; Rice, *St. Jerome in the Renaissance*.

318 Ferrara and Quinterio, *Michelozzo*, 385. Caplow, *Michelozzo*, argued on stylistic grounds that he was probably an advisor. Fabriczy, *Brunelleschi*, published portions of the "Ricordi della fabrica," which identifies the *muratori*, but not an architect.

319 See Avogadro, "De religione et munificentia Cosmi Medices"; Gombrich, "Early Medici as Patrons," and "Alberto Avogadro's Descriptions of the Badia"; Procacci, "Cosimo de' Medici e la costruzione." There are scraps of evidence to indicate that Cosimo had some real understanding of building. Just after Sforza became duke in 1450, he wrote

to Cosimo asking him for a plan of Santa Maria Nuova on which to model the Milanese hospital, and two subsequent letters on this question were addressed to Giovanni. See Gaye, *Carteggio* 1, 194–5; also Spencer, "Dome of Sforzinda Cathedral." When in 1444 the priors, among them Bartolomeo Michelozzi, father of the architect, decided to renovate the council hall, Cosimo was one of three *operai* put in charge, along with Neri Capponi; see Rubinstein, *Palazzo Vecchio*, 3, 24.

320   On the typology and architectural language of the Badia see Belluzzi, "La Badia Fiesolana." On the architect and his role in the production of a building see Goldthwaite, *Building of Renaissance Florence*, especially ch. 7; also Hollingsworth, "Architect in Fifteenth-Century Florence." On the question of craftsmen acting as architects, Elam, "Conspicuous Construction," 1335, pointed out that no *muratore* as opposed to *scarpellino* ever became an architect in the fifteenth century, although "the tradition of the architect as a designer has a long history in Florence."

321   See Brunelleschi's conversation with Taccola, published Battisti, *Brunelleschi*, 20–21; on patrons consulting one another, see also below, p. 342.

322   Cagni, *Vespasiano da Bisticci*, 153–4.

323   See above, n. 319; Maffei, op. cit., especially 166; Gombrich, op. cit., and Thomson, *Renaissance Architecture*. However, the degree of magnificent display appropriate to rulers in secular building was already a hot topic in the trecento, as Louis Green observed, "Galvano Fiamma, Azzone Visconti."

324   See Hill, *Corpus of Italian Medals*; Hersey, *Aragonese Arch*. See also Green, op. cit., 101–5; all the usages he cited, but one, of derivations of magnificence are adjectives, not nouns, and Azzone makes a specific connection between greatness, war, magnificence and expiation in devotional building.

325   See Fraser-Jenkins, "Theory of Magnificence," and below, ch. 11, for a fuller discussion of his observations.

326   See above, pp. 134–5.

327   Pontano, *I trattati delle virtù sociali*; especially 161–2; 174. The real moral point is "la giusta misura." So re-classicized and therefore secularized is Pontano's treatise that he actually spoke of "pietà verso gli dei" and "superstizione," 189. Welch, "Theorising the Decorative Arts," also noted how much Pontano's essays, although related to one another conceptually, are *pièces d'occasion*, their content affected by the very different recipients to whom each was addressed.

328   See De Roover, *Rise and Decline*, 71.

329   ASF, Notarile antecosmiano, A 376, 1463–6, new numeration, 89v–90r. On 8 Dec. 1463, there was notarized, in the house of Cosimo de' Medici in the *popolo* of San Lorenzo, the donation to Marioctus Medicis of a house *in perpetuo* "which cannot be revoked on grounds of ingratitude or anything else."

330   Recounted by Fontius in his *zibaldone*, Ricc., 907, 14.

331   "Idio ne lasci seguire il meglio."

Chapter XI

1   On the Art of Building, 291.

2   Trexler, especially in *Public Life*, was the first historian of Florence to describe its citizens' lives in terms of public theater, of self-presentation in public and private rituals. This model of social behavior was persuasively presented and applied by anthropologists like Clifford Geertz, various, especially *Interpretation of Cultures*, and sociologists like Erving Goffmann, *Presentation of Self*, and Berger and Luckmann, *Social Construction of Reality*. It was earlier embraced by students of the northern Renaissance courts; see, for example, Strong, *Art and Power*; Orgel, *Illusion of Power*. More recently it has been fruitfully developed by Florentine historians of performance, music and ceremony; see below, pp. 415–17.

3   On office-holding as the chief criterion of social distinction in Florence see above, p. 77, and below, p. 423, n. 82.

4   Lanza, *Lirici toscani* 1, 381. I thank William Connell for drawing this verse to my attention long before I became familiar with the corpus of popular poetry. Capponi's emphasis on the virile quality of public life in the city, an important theme in the arguments of Cicero, Alberti, and others concerning the virtue of building, is underlined by a lament put into the mouths of the Piacenzan women raped by Sforza's soldiers in Filelfo's *Sforziad*, II, 699–707: "Ah woe, nature or god has dealt us a sad fate – our being the female race . . . Our nature has nothing unusual in it which can be displayed in public. And so, we are looked upon and we bear our slavish yoke deservedly." I thank Diana Robin for this passage and her translation. See also Simons, "Renaissance Palaces, Sex and Gender," for the exploration of gendered metaphors for building and their illumination of the perception of female roles. Filarete spells out the relation between patron and architect in terms of that between man and woman; see above, p. 5. The view that the city makes men, the country beasts, is a common topos of Renaissance writers which is both modified and elaborated in the course of the fifteenth century, particularly in discussions on building and civic behavior. On the view that only certain affairs are appropriate to the city see the letter of Maestro Matteo da Fucecchio, "frate minore ministro di Toschana," MAP, VII, 136, Prato, to Giovanni di Cosimo de' Medici; he wrote concerning an issue he spoke to Giovanni about on Sunday in the church of Santa Maria Novella because "queste non som cose senon da boscho e da strada e non di farle in Firenze."

5   *Panegirico*, 27–9.

6   Responsibility for public building was largely divided between the guilds, who took responsibility for particular enterprises, and the government which, for example, gave direct subsidies to the building of the cathedral, and to the construction of the Dominican church of Santa Maria Novella and the Franciscan church of Santa Croce; see Goldthwaite, *Building of Renaissance Florence*, introduction. For the building boom of 1414–23, a long period of peace after incessant wars, see Rubinstein, "Palazzi Pubblici." On Orsanmichele see Zervas, *Orsanmichele*.

7   *Istoria*, 182. Cf. the observation of Pope Pius II which is the basis of Vasari's comment on the accommodations of the Medici palace, Vasari-Milanesi, *Lives*, 4, 434: "tutte quelle comodità che possono bastare non che a una cittadino privato, com'era allora Cosimo, ma a qualsi voglia splendissimo ed onoratissimo re." That this was a wild exaggeration is apparent from a comparison even with the accommodations of the upstart duke of Milan, Francesco Sforza: see Welch, *Art and Authority*. Dati's Florence is essentially a "working model," in the tradition of so many medieval citizens' proud descriptions of the beauties and

amenities of their native cities, including Bonvesin della Riva's description of Milan, and Giovanni Villani's four-teenth-century account of Florence. This genre of praise of cities stresses, like Bruni's humanist *Panegirico* imitating Aelius Aristides' *Panathenaicus* of the second century A.D., that the architecture of a city is the best evidence of its citizens' abilities. Gilbert, "Earliest Guide," appropriately drew attention to the interest and value of Dati's description, but wrenched it out of context to present it primarily as an aesthetic response to individual buildings, suggesting its author favored old-fashioned secular buildings over the modern ecclesiastical ones which occasioned the great architectural breakthroughs of the early Renaissance. Dati's account does include expressions of pleasure in architecture that enhances the visual quality of the Florentine environment, like the bridge of the Ponte Vecchio and the design of the Palazzo Vecchio, and it is civic pride that focuses his attention (Gilbert, 40–41). His description of these buildings would indeed have have served the purpose of a guide to visitors such as those described by Bruni. But it is functional, rather than aesthetic, governed primarily by the significance of the buildings to the operation of civic life, and by envisaging the physical paths by which the citizen passed naturally around his city. From the mills on the periphery that provide the power to grind the city's grain and to effect the various processes in the cloth manufacture which is the city's major industry, he proceeded along the logically laid out arteries of main roads and bridges to the heart of the city – its palace of government topped by a tower whose bells set the rhythms for its daily life, sounding the hours and summoning the citizens to councils. Adjacent are the auxiliary organs of government and the buildings that enshrine their power – the criminal courts, palace of justice and of the Captain, custodian of the peoples' rights, and nearby a courtyard housing twenty-four lions, live symbols of the republic. Past the Zecca where the city's currency – the lifeblood of its commerce – is minted, and to the treasury that controls the flow of funds, he proceeded logically down the main axis of the Via Calzaiuoli that joins the secular to the sacred center of the city, the great piazza of the baptistery, and the cathedral facing it, pausing on the way to describe the glories of the church of Orsanmichele containing the city's major miraculous image of the mid-trecento, the Virgin and Child. He moved on to the baptistery mentioning its octagonal shape and the mosaics for which it was famous, but not its supposed classical origin, and thence to Santa Reparata to describe the continuous work of embellishing it. Other churches are noted in terms of the orders to which they belong. Closely following the customary medieval pattern, Dati then enumerated the number of monasteries and hospitals. Although among these was the Innocenti, whom he served at the time as an *operaio*, he did not single this out for special mention. His detailed description emphasises the hospitals' functional aspects – the underground cellars to store the year's vintage, the wells pumping perfectly fresh water up to the very tops of the houses. When he came to the beautiful villas of the surrounding countryside he stressed that not an inch of land lay uncultivated, which is why this is the most fruitful countryside in the world. Cf. Benedetto Dei's later description of Florentine palaces *c*.1470, which was similar in content and spirit, beginning "memoria sia tutta Italia e dappoi a tutto il christianesimo della signoria e possa e groria che a'nno e tenghono li Fiorentini in Toschana," ASF, Manoscritti, 119, 29r. Gilbert dated the section of Dati's *Istoria* he dubbed "the earliest guide to Florentine architecture" *c*.1423.

8 For the frequent use of this common formula see Rubinstein, op. cit., passim, and Cosimo's letters, above, ch. 2. On the significance of family palaces to their owners, see especially Kent, *Household and Lineage*. The Spini palace and the Peruzzi enclave (see Kent and Kent, "Self-Disciplining Pact") are examples of enduring family monuments. Politically disgraced families in medieval Florence were defamed by the destruction of their houses; see Villani, *Cronica* VIII, 26, for the example of the Uberti.

9 Rubinstein, "Palazzi Pubblici," especially 29–33, cf. Goldthwaite, op. cit., 15.

10 Op. cit., loc. cit. See also Goldthwaite, "Il contesto economico del palazzo fiorentino." Preyer, "'Chasa overo palagio'" believed that the Da Uzzano palace could have been begun as early as 1411. Rubinstein, op. cit., 32, argued that the timing of the building of the Medici palace indicates a strategic political calculation; peace with the Visconti duke of Milan was concluded in 1441, and the battle of Anghiari in 1440 marked the victory of the governing regime of Florence and of the Medici over their Milanese and Florentine enemies; in 1443 a league was concluded between Florence and Venice against Milan, and in 1444 a Balìa was voted in for five years. He saw it as no coincidence that in 1444 the Balìa assigned 6,000 florins for renovations of the Palazzo Vecchio. He also argued that Manetti, in his account of the Medici rejection of Brunelleschi's plan and his regrets that Brunelleschi was unable to build any great private palaces, failed to realize that no one was building them for two decades before the architect's death.

11 Dei, op.cit., loc. cit.

12 See particularly Paris, Bibliothèque Nationale, MS Lat., 4802, 132v.

13 See Elam, "Il Palazzo nel contesto della città."

14 The shop of Cosimo's friend the bookseller Vespasiano was also represented.

15 On Rucellai's *zibaldone*, see also below, pp. 357–66.

16 See Gaston, "Attention and Inattention."

17 Below, p. 239; for the text of the Milanese comment see Hatfield, "Compagnia de' Magi," appendix. Cf. Maffei, *In magnificentiae Cosmi Medicei Florentini detractores*, 166, where he gave Aquinas as his source for the use of the noun.

18 Cit. and comment by Smith, *Architecture in the Culture of Early Humanism*, 179.

19 *Convivio*, IV, 4. Citing Aristotle, *Politics*, I, i–ii, it is Dante who inserts the neighborhood into the schema of the concentric circles of man's sociability.

20 Bk I, 6, 231; ibid., 38–9, 143.

21 See especially Grayson, "Composition of L. B. Alberti's *Decem libri*," on the date and dedication of this work. Alberti rebuilt his own parish church at Gangalandi, in the environs of Florence.

22 *On the Art of Building*, 291.

23 Cf. above, pp. 117–19.

24 See particularly bk. XXXVI, 88; XXXVII, 171–5, where he denounced the excessive use of precious stones as "oriental splendor." Owing to the immense interest of scholars like

Poggio in the *Natural History*, above, ch. 3, the general educated public was made aware of its existence and some of
its precepts even before Landino's famous translation of 1473.

25 On this see Rykwert, introduction to *On the Art of Building*,
    and Smith, op. cit. The latter's argument concerns the use of
    rhetoric in the visual arts to entertain and persuade in the
    first half of the fifteenth century, by comparison with its
    more ideal forms in the second. Alberti's sources were Aris-
    totelian rather than Platonic, concerned with architectural
    allegories of virtue.

26 *De Re Aedificatoria*, 780–81: "placere quae pro cuisque dig-
    nitate moderentur . . ."; 784–5: "quod eximia cum dignitate
    coniunctum sit . . . ," by contrast with the villa, which
    enshrines pleasure; see below, ch. 12.

27 Ibid., 778–9: "Apud maiores nostros video prudentissimis et
    modestissimis . . . vehemeter placuisse cum in caeteris rebus
    et publicis et privatis tum hac una in re aedificatoria fru-
    galitatem atque parsimoniam, omemque luxurien in civibus
    tollendam cohercendamque putasse . . ."

28 Ibid., 778.

29 *Trattato*, 189, ff. Filarete embellished the Ciceronian and
    Albertian ideas on which he builds in speaking of "lo orna-
    mento della città, dentro e di fuori, si può vedere in diversi
    luoghi: le case, e' palazzi in varii luoghi si vede, e massime
    quello che è nella città sopradetta, quanto che si magnifico
    e degno tacerò per al presente," ibid., 683–4.

30 On Rucellai's citations of Cicero see Preyer, "Rucellai
    Palace," and below, p. 488, n. 81.

31 This argument is persuasively made by both Kent and Preyer,
    Zibaldone 2. Preyer, 203–4, observed Rucellai's addition to
    Cicero of "good order and measure" as evidence that he was
    applying the passage to his own house and experience. As
    Kent observed, 54, n. 2, the entry comes not long after the
    ricordo of 1464 and his account of Quaracchi. Cicero's phrase
    is both more cryptic and more austere: "praeclaram . . . et
    plenam dignitatis domum." Where Cicero spoke only of the
    votes Gnaeus Octavius received after he built his house,
    Giovanni Rucellai represented the palace as inspiring " nel
    populo grandissima benivolenza e grazia," a phrase he used
    elsewhere to express his social aspirations. The most awkward
    element of the story, which Rucellai ignored, was surely the
    reference to Scaurus's demolition of Octavian's house to
    extend his own, a charge that could certainly be brought
    against most Florentine palace builders including, most
    notably, both Giovanni Rucellai and Cosimo de' Medici, and
    later Luca Pitti. It was explicitly leveled against Giovanni by
    one of his own kinsmen whose house he had demolished to
    build his palace and who hoped that Giovanni's house would
    fall down in its turn; see Kent, *Household and Lineage*, 242–3.

32 Kent, "Making of a Renaissance Patron," 84, from *Zibaldone*,
    23v. In fact Rucellai made two references to *De Officiis*; in
    1457, 23v, and 1464, 63v., cit Kent, 55.

33 194. For these citations and comments on them see Kent,
    op. cit., 52, and Preyer, op. cit., 184.

34 Kent, "Palaces, Politics and Society," 50; Landucci, *Diario*, 62.

35 *On the Art of Architecture*, 291. Octavian was his exemplum of
    the man who was so upset by over-extravagance in building
    that he demolished a villa "which was too lavish," 292. Cf.
    780, for Valerius who pulled down his house on a hill, and
    rebuilt it on the flat so as not to arouse envy.

36 Lanza, *Lirici toscani* 1, 223, 362.

37 This lingered long after the War of the Eight Saints. As Gino

Capponi wrote in his *Ricordi* to his sons in 1420: "Have no
truck with the priests, except for the purposes of taking the
sacraments, for they are the scum of the earth," XIII, 35.

38 Cavalcanti, *Istorie fiorentine*, Polidori ed. 2, 210–11.

39 *Zibaldone* 1, 23.

40 *Trattato*, 2, 683–4.

41 "Il contesto economico." He calculated the median cost of
    a palace at 5–10,000 florins, roughly the entire capital of a
    large wool or silk manufacturing business. The cost of the
    Medici palace was estimated at *c*.100,000 florins, so it cer-
    tainly represented a major redistribution of wealth.

42 See Trexler, *Public Life*, on the alteration of processional routes
    over time; also Testaverde, "Ingressi Trionfali," 329, on how
    the route taken by Pius II and Sforza in 1459 "comprovano
    un sostanziale mutamento nella vita pubblica fiorentina con-
    temporanea che, in termini spettacolari e nell'ottica dei per-
    corsi celebrativi, si giustificano anche in uno spostamento
    significativo dell'attenzione verso un nuovo polo; il palazzo
    Medici di Via Larga . . ." While the pope stayed in his offi-
    cial residence at Santa Maria Novella, Sforza "acconciosi lo
    palazzo maggiore di Cosimo dei Medici."

43 See, for example, MAP, XIII, 221.

44 Ricordanze, ASF, C.S. 2a ser., 16 bis, 14r–v; the lions may
    have been the live ones kept by the Signoria or various
    representations of the Marzocco in their palace or at the
    papal apartments.

45 See Saalman and Mattox, "First Medici Palace."

46 "Theory of Magnificence," especially 162. In fact major pro-
    jects of the Malatesta and the Este were already in the works,
    and the Neapolitan monarchs had been building in a differ-
    ent, more military genre since the early 1440s. As Fraser-
    Jenkins admitted, 169, "These events are too close to one
    another in time and too varying in character to be seen as
    a connected sequence, but they do document a clear change
    in taste either side of the mid-century."

47 Ibid., 169–70.

48 With the notable exceptions of Kent and Preyer, op. cit. For
    the ultimate judgment of Machiavelli, born 1469, on the
    Medici regime, see below, p. 367.

49 *Public Life*, 425.

50 Preyer, "L'architettura del palazzo," 60. What follows on
    palaces in general and the Medici palace in particular is
    heavily indebted to Preyer's published work, and also to our
    many discussions of these issues from which I have learned
    such a lot. See also Hyman, *Fifteenth-Century Florentine Studies*
    and, "Notes and Speculations"; Sinding-Larsen, "Tale of
    Two Cities." On Florentine architectural traditions and the
    antique, see Burns, "*Quattrocento* Architecture and the
    Antique"; Trachtenberg, "What Brunelleschi Saw."

51 *De Re Aedificatoria*, bk. 9, ix.

52 "Quid quod privatae aedes suae [Cosimo's] recens in via lata
    extructae, Romanorum olim principum et quidem prima-
    riorum operibus comparandae sunt: quin ego ipse, qui
    Romam meis instauravi scriptis, affirmare non dubito nullus
    extare privati aedificii principum in urbe Romana reliquias,
    quae maiorem illis aedibus prae se ferant operis magnificen-
    tiam," Burns, op. cit., 273, translated Hyman, *Fifteenth-Century
    Florentine Studies*, 205. Burns regarded the Palazzo Medici as
    a good example of a building "whose intended all'antica
    character is no longer very obvious, for example its biforate
    windows are only modernisations, that is antiquisations of
    a common medieval type."

53 *Zibaldone* 1, 75–6; Preyer, "L'architettura del palazzo," 65. On rustication see especially Sinding-Larsen, op. cit., 190. A Roman writing on noble architecture in 1510 observed that Cosimo was the first to use the example of Trajan's forum – that is, the Augustan wall – in the decoration of his palace; see Weil-Garris and D'Amico, "Renaissance Cardinal's Ideal Palace." On Florentine perceptions of ancient Roman architecture in the early quattrocento see also Gombrich, "From the Revival of Letters," 80.

54 Cit. Hyman, op. cit., 62; see also 156–60 on the "archaeological character" of the *bugnato rustico*. The rustication of the facade is certainly an impressive statement, and could perhaps seem overbearing, as Kent suggested, citing Mary McCarthy's comment, "Palaces, Politics and Society," 56. However, this is essentially a modern perception. Florentines were accustomed to heavy rustication since the Signoria ordered *bugnato* facing on the ground floor of all major buildings in the renewal of the urban center. It was more the sophistication of its cutting, the use of worked stone on all three floors, and the size of the corner site that made the Medici palace special. It also bore what Hyman described as a "respectful but creative relationship to the trecento tradition epitomized by the Spini and Castellani palaces, the only previous palaces with the siting or size to create such an impression," ibid., 60. The heavy cornice seems explicitly intended to evoke an ancient form; see Preyer, op. cit., 13.

55 See also below, pp. 299–300.

56 Preyer, op. cit., 60–61. She referred to antiquity the semicircular arches that frame the ground-floor openings and the windows on the upper floors; with the exception of the Palazzo Vecchio, previously arches had been pointed or segmented. Other features found previously in public buildings only were the biforate windows and the cut stone from top to bottom.

57 MAP, v, 468, Nov. 1442, cit. Kent, op. cit., 51.

58 On the tantalizing questions associated with the identification of these buildings and the possible patron of this manuscript, see below, ch. 12, 299.

59 MAP, v, 509, partly published by Kent and Kent, "Two Comments of March 1445."

60 See Kent, "Michele del Giogante's House of Memory."

61 On *imprese*, see Ames-Lewis, "Early Medicean Devices"; also *Library and Manuscripts of Piero*. For their use on Florentine private palaces, Goldthwaite, *Building of Renaissance Florence*, 86. For a precise account of those built into the fabric of the Medici palace, see Preyer, op. cit.

62 Ibid., and on the rose, 63. Her tentative suggestion seems much more persuasive when considered in the context of the family's relationship with the papacy, which was fundamental to the interests of both in the first half of the fifteenth century; see above, pp. 162–7. The pope's golden rose was presented to the city and its citizens on the occasion of the consecration of the cathedral, which emphasized the coincidence of symbolism in the dedication of the church, Santa Maria del Fiore, to the Virgin, whose emblem was also the rose; see above, p. 126, below, p. 227.

63 Preyer's corpus of work on Florentine palaces put the Medici palace in perspective in terms of tradition and innovation, and provided the basis for a comparison with other Florentine palaces both earlier and later. See particularly her "Chasa overo palagio," on Alberto di Zanobi's palace in the Via dei Neri, *c.*1400, and its relation to palaces past and future, especially those of the Cavalcanti, *c.*1390 and the Da Uzzano, begun by 1411; also "Two Cerchi Palaces in Florence," *Palazzo Corsi-Horne* and "Florentine Palaces and Memories of the Past."

64 On the significance of space and place in Renaissance cities, see Muir and Weissman, "Social and Symbolic Places."

65 *Trattato*, 2, 696.

66 See Hyman, "Notes and Speculations"; Krinsky, "View of the Palazzo Medici." The Medici Pope Leo X announced plans to put a facade on San Lorenzo late in 1515.

67 Preyer and particularly Elam, "Il palazzo nel contesto della città," especially 44–6, have pointed to the problems involved in demolishing a consecrated church, the expense of a three-sided facade, and a misunderstanding of apparently supporting documents relating to the demolition of the piazza in front of San Lorenzo. On this see also Elam, "Cosimo de' Medici and San Lorenzo." Her observation that the hypothesis concerning a proposed unification with San Lorenzo depends on a view of urban planning more modern than Renaissance is compelling. The whole story of Brunellechi's rejected model seems likely to be a fabrication of his biographer, Manetti, who sharply regretted that Brunelleschi never built a private house; see *Life of Brunelleschi*, 98. The proposed Barbadori palace, for example, was preempted by the family's exile; other Brunelleschi projects remained uncompleted or were not finished according to his design. By the time the site was cleared for the Medici palace, the architect was a very old man, self-declaredly weary, and occupied elsewhere, particularly in the rebuilding of Santo Spirito.

68 Via de' Martelli, the south end of Via Larga between Via de' Gori and the piazza of San Giovanni, was rather narrower in the fifteenth century, probably about as wide as the present Borgo San Lorenzo. However, the modern enlargement seems to have occurred on the northeast side, so that the palace would have been visible from the piazza as it is now; see Preyer, op. cit., and Elam, op. cit.

69 The nub of her argument is that "no other work connected with Michelozzo shows such richness and inventiveness, and in none is the design so calculated, so tight, so resolved," op. cit., 67.

70 Preyer noted that the courtyard columns with their elaborate Corinthian capitals follow a format designed by Brunelleschi for San Lorenzo; Cosimo's tax reports, discussed by Hyman, "Notes and Speculations," 102, show that during 1445, 1446 and early 1447 he was still buying up and trading properties in the neighborhood with the intention of demolishing them to create a larger site for the palace.

71 Cf. above, pp. 175–6.

72 *Vite* 2, 189.

73 See MAP, v, 509. Kent and Kent, "Two Comments," suggested on the basis of a reference in a letter of Bartolommeo Sassetti, accountant and paymaster for the Medici building on Via Largha and at San Lorenzo, to "Michelino del Ghiogante," ibid., 412, that "Michelino" can probably be identified with this accountant/poet whom we have seen to be so close to the Medici and so interested in building; on Michele see passim, especially chs. 5 and 6. However, Michelozzo, generally accepted as the architect of the palace, was also a Medici friend and correspondent, see above, pp. 175–7, and the same diminutive was sometimes applied to him. On the assembling of the site, Hyman, "Notes and Speculations"

and *Fifteenth-Century Florentine Studies*, especially 85. In 1427 Giovanni di Bicci owned seventeen houses, as did his sons in 1433. Between 1443 and 1446 eight new houses were purchased or traded to the Medici expressly to be demolished to build the palace; altogether twenty-one or twenty-two houses were torn down to accommodate it.

74 "Florentine Palace," especially 1011, 998, 996–7, 1009. Goldthwaite's interpretation of Renaissance society in general and its palaces in particular has been widely debated and criticized, but his studies of these structures and most recently their building have established much of what we know about the Renaissance palace. See particularly *Building of Renaissance Florence*; also "Building of the Strozzi Palace."

75 See, for example, Giovanni's report of 1427, Cat. 49, 1159v: "Siamo in chasa otto chome apresso danno . . . E stimate alla spesa ci chonviene tenere e di parenti e di forestieri a bisogna molto magiore numero dimessi e chosì molte magiore somma che fiorini cxii . . . che tra in villa e in Firenze chontinuamente si può ragione siamo bocche trenta o più . . ." For Cosimo's similar estimates of the size of his household see below, p. 376.

76 "Palaces, Politics and Society," 59. See also his *Household and Lineage*. Cf. Goldthwaite, "Building of the Strozzi Palace," 110–11: "Even as a monument to its builder's dynastic ambitions it was not designed in anticipation of having to accommodate in any way a growing lineage . . ."; also "Florentine Palace," 988, where he spoke of the patrician palace's "aloof presence . . . a new world of privacy." How much privacy could there be when Marco Parenti could push his way in, despite the protests of a servant, to Piero de' Medici's bedroom while he was sleeping? See Phillips, *Memoir of Marco Parenti*, 134, for Parenti's report to his mother-in-law, Alessandra Strozzi, on his efforts to see Piero to argue her son Filippo's cause on the occasion of the visit of the son of the King of Naples: "And I went with them right to Piero's chambers; and because he was sleeping, they were on the point of leaving him, since no one dared to disturb him. But I was so insistent that in the end the servant was sent back in and woke him."

77 "Florentine Palace," 989.

78 "Renaissance Palaces, Sex and Gender," 59; cf. Goldthwaite, *Building of Renaissance Florence*, 103.

79 Preyer, op. cit., 64. A major concern of her most recent work is to link social activities to the physical fabric of Florentine palaces. See particularly "Planning for Visitors at Florentine Palaces."

80 Hyman, *Fifteenth-Century Florentine Studies*, 188–92.

81 See Saalman, "Palazzo Communale in Montepulciano," 193, 197, 204, for a discussion of these views which "expressed a new style that was less radical than the *meaning* of that style."

82 It was remodeled by Michelangelo *c.*1517.

83 Kent and Kent, "Two Vignettes."

84 Op. cit., 60.

85 BNF, II: IV: 324, 108r; Rucellai, *Zibaldone* I, 28–34. On representations of loggias on *cassone* panels see Hyman, *Fifteenth-Century Florentine Studies*, 156–60; for a selection of such images see Schubring, *Truhen und Truhenbilder*.

86 See Spallanzani and Bertelà, *Libro d'inventario*; Spallanzani, *Inventari Medicei*; Preyer, "Planning for Visitors at Florentine Palaces."

87 Giovanni di Cosimo's appeal seems to prefigure that of his nephew Lorenzo.

88 De Roover, *Rise and Decline*, 19; Hyman, op. cit., 154; Spallanzani, *Inventari Medicei*.

89 *Detti Piacevoli*, 192, cit. and comment by Brown, "Wit and Wisdom," 97.

90 "Piero's Infirmity and Political Power," 9–10.

91 This extended Medici household is the subject of a chapter of Kent, *Fathers and Friends*. See also, for example, Lapaccini, *Cronaca*, 16, for a description of Ser Alesso as "notario fiorentino, qui multum domum suam [Cosimo] frequentabat . . ." See also MAP, v, 424, Matteo di Ser Giovanni in Trebbio to Giovanni in Florence, describing how Ser Alesso reported the response of the crowds in the piazza to the latest political news; other letters refer to friends like the Martelli delivering news and letters to the palace.

92 On the duties of the visit, see Kent, op. cit.; on the importance of face-to-face encounters in political negotiation, Phillips, *Memoir of Marco Parenti*, especially pt. 2.

93 See below, p. 306.

94 Phillips, op. cit., 208; Parenti, *Cronica*, BNF, Magl. 25, 272; also cit. Kent, "Palaces, Politics and Society," 62–3.

95 Cit. Kent, op. cit., 64; cf. Nicodemo's letter to the duke of Milan, 8 Aug. 1458.

96 See Buser, *Die Beziehungen der Mediceer*, 401; Spallanzani, *Inventari Medicei*, and below, p. 293.

97 Cf. Hyman, *Fifteenth-Century Florentine Studies*, 177.

98 See above, p. 92.

99 On Pazzi patronage, see Saalman, *Brunelleschi: The Buildings*, ch. 5. His speculations exemplify the serious problems of trying to be more precise about the patron's intention without the support of more explicit evidence.

100 On Dietisalvi Neroni see Rubinstein, *Government of Florence*, passim; for the identification of his palace as the present Gerini-di Montauto, and the Neroni palace as that built by Nigi, see Preyer, *Palazzo Corsi-Horne*, 56; for the latter, see Benigni, *Palazzo Neroni a Firenze*.

101 For a fuller discussion of Rucellai and his palace see below, pp. 359–60.

102 On these palaces see Preyer, "Chasa overo palagio"; cf. Kent, "Dynamic of Power," for the notion of a palatial conversation conceived in 1986 in much oversimplified terms.

103 "L'architettura del palazzo," 64–5.

104 See Kent, "Più superba." For a comparison of Strozzi and Medici patronage, see below, p. 355.

105 "Allogiare la sua famiglia comodamente, secondo la sua qualità," cit. Morandini, "Palazzo Pitti," 35; see also 44, n. 9. Pitti's palace was a more radical departure from Florentine tradition than Cosimo's; Machiavelli observed that never before had a private citizen of Florence built himself a dwelling in royal isolation from his neighbors on top of a hill.

106 See Heydenreich and Lotz, *Architecture in Italy*, 41.

Chapter XII

1 Filarete, *Trattato*, 2, 697.

2 Hatfield, "Some Unknown Descriptions," appendix 2, 246.

3 See Spallanzani, *Inventari Medicei*, cf. the much fuller listing made after Lorenzo's death, Spallanzani and Bertelà, *Libro d'inventario*.

4   For estimates of its cost see Hatfield, op. cit., 235. Vespasiano's estimate was 60,000 ducats, *Vite* 2, 189.

5   See Preyer, "Planning for Visitors at Florentine Palaces." For an alternative view of the Medici palace decoration as designed to address visitors in more specifically political terms see Crum, "Retrospection and Response."

6   *Trattato*, 2, 697. See also Bulst, "Die Ursprüngliche Innere Aufteilung," 394, on how the house, apartments, garden, and *loggia* "forma sopratutto un unità estetica, che fin dall'inizio non concedeva molto alle necessità pratiche." Somewhat before 1468, less than a decade after they moved in, the family found it necessary to add some more modest functional areas to the west and north – kitchens, stalls, and rooms for work and servants.

7   Cf. the *Terze Rime* published Hatfield, op. cit., 247–8: "nonn è imperio o re che gli abbia tali."

8   *Commentaries*, 88.

9   Cit. Hatfield, op. cit., 245.

10 On the history of the usage of *otium* and its changing meaning, see Vickers, "Leisure and Idleness."

11 In fact the mid-1450s proved to be a time of quite serious challenges to the Medici regime; see Rubinstein, *Government of Florence,* ch. 5.

12 Above, pp. 91–3.

13 See "Empire of Things"; also *Building of Renaissance Florence,* especially 424–5.

14 Cf. above, p. 220.

15 Hatfield, op. cit., 247.

16 See MAP, IV, 77, to his cousin Averardo in 1431 on their employment on the battlefield.

17 Hatfield, op. cit., 245–6, characterizes the architectural rhetoric of the Medici palace as Epicurean rather than Stoic, an opposition he extended to the style of Michelozzo as opposed to Brunelleschi, Abbot Suger versus Bernard of Clairvaux.

18 "Seeing Culture."

19 136; cf. the letter of Poggio to Niccoli, in Gordan, *Two Renaissance Book Hunters,* 167–8. According to Coffin, *Villa in the Life of Renaissance Rome,* the Renaissance knowledge of Roman villas was mainly literary.

20 Watkins, *Humanism and Liberty,* 143, 150; see also 122–3.

21 XIX, 36.

22 See Kent, *Household and Lineage,* 48–54, 135–49.

23 Hyman, *Fifteenth-Century Florentines Studies,* 44 n. 8, 238; Carl, "La Casa Vecchia"; Bulst, "Die Ursprüngliche Aufteilung." See also Foligno de' Medici's *Libro di Memorie,* iv, Jan. 1374.

24 Preyer, "L'architettura del palazzo"; cf. Hyman, "Notes and Speculations," 99; the last entries in the Medici Palace/San Lorenzo ledger are in 1453.

25 See, for example, Bulst,"Die *sala grande* des Palazzo Medici"; Tönnesmann, "Zwischen Bürgerhaus und Residenz."

26 See De Roover, "Gli antecedenti del Banco Mediceo," on the first successful Medici banker, Messer Vieri di Cambio (1323–95), and the role played by his bank in the establishment of Giovanni di Bicci's. On the fourteenth-century history of the Medici see Brucker, "Medici in the Fourteenth Century." In the late 1370s and early 1380s, Cambio's branch of the family played a significant role in the revolt of the Ciompi, the rebellious laborers of the wool-working industry, when his nephew Salvestro di Alamanno became one of its leaders. In the 1390s members of the Medici family

were involved in plots against the regime; one was executed in 1397, and in 1400 most of the lineage was barred from holding public office for twenty years. The sons of Bicci and the descendants of Messer Veri were excepted.

27 It was also true of the business of the bank. While Cosimo officially retired in 1451 in favor of his sons, and partnerships were henceforth drawn up in their names, the Medici correspondence with factors shows that Cosimo was giving instructions and receiving reports up until a few weeks before his death. See, for example, Grunzweig, *Correspondance de la filiale* 1, passim.

28 On the father–son relationship see Kent, *Household and Lineage,* 45–8, 99–117; for some colorful examples of the traumatic consequences of its breakdown, Brucker, *Documentary History,* 62–6.

29 MAP, XII, 168, 10 Sept. 1436: "la buona memoria del vostro padre et voi avere sempre posto le mani in subsidio della festa de' gloriosi martiri San Cosma Damiano nostri protectori . . . che veduto che la chieza co' detti santi la festa de' quali sarà adì 27 del presente mese per cagione dellagucita et malignità del tempo et delle sue ricolte et fructi per modo manchata che assai debile ricordo fare se ne può. Acciò che alaudedulio et gloria de' detti santi pio su linemente detta festa io fare possa vi degnate in acto de lemozina farmi qualche aiuto aranno detti santi dinanti di dio intercessori per voi, et io di continuo lo pregherò che lo stato vostro conservi et exalti come desiderate dat. Pisa."

30 Ibid., V, 445, 27 Jun. 1442, Agnolo di Ser Bartolomeo dei Ridolfi. See also ibid., XI, 27, 19 Feb. 1434/5, to Cosimo, Gonfalonier of Justice.

31 Alberti, *Della famiglia,* 192: "Sotto uno volere stiano le famiglie."

32 See below, pp. 371–2.

33 Simons, "Two Rucellai Altarpieces," suggested that Giovanni remained in legal tutelage to Cosimo because of his father's preternatural determination to control his sons; the evidence presented here does not support that view.

34 With the conspicuous exception, as Alison Brown has pointed out, of Lorenzo di Giovanni's son Pierfrancesco after he came of age; see "Radical Alternative," especially 85. Notably he remained in the *casa vecchia* when the rest of the family moved to the new palace. Lorenzo's *Ricordi,* 158, betray some irritation at Cosimo's determination to give Pierfrancesco more than he thought his due in the division of family property in 1451. "Lorenzo de' Medici, brother of Cosimo our grandfather, quitted this life at Careggi on September 20, 1440, aged about forty-six, at the fourth hour of the night, and would not make a will; Pier Francesco, his son, was his sole heir. The property amounted to 235,137 *scudi di suggello*, as appears in the said book kept by Cosimo on p. 13, which amount Cosimo kept for the use and benefit of the said Pier Francesco, and for Piero and Giovanni, his own sons, until they were of proper age . . . On December . . . 1451, the said Piero Francesco being of age, we divided the property according to the arbitration of Messer Mannello degli Strozzi, Bernardo de' Medici, Alamanno Salviati, Messer Carlo Marsuppino, Amerigo Cavalcanti, and Giovanni Serristori, by whom a liberal half of our possessions was assigned to him, giving him the advantage over us and the best things. The deed was drawn up by Ser Antonio Pugi, notary, and at the same time we gave him an interest of one-third in our business, whereby he gained much more than we did as he

had no expenses." Pierfrancesco's comment on these expenses for Cosimo's various charitable buildings, that "we do not want them on our backs, because our father never wanted them," may not have been accurate, since the major Medici commissions before his death in 1440, including those at San Marco and San Lorenzo were made in the joint names of himself and Cosimo. It does, however, suggest that he shared his younger cousin Lorenzo's general resentment of the failure of previous generations to demarcate more clearly their financial interests.

35 See Kent, op. cit., 45-8.

36 See Rubinstein, "Piero de' Medici," cf. above, ch. 2.

37 Below, pp. 303-4.

38 *Della Famiglia*, 192: "a me mai piacque questo dividere le famiglie, uscire e intrare per più d'uno uscio; né mai mi patì l'animo che Antonio mio fratello abitasse senza me sotto altro tetto." The gated enclave of the Peruzzi family houses grouped around an oval piazza was an alternative solution for a large family which graphically illustrates how Florentines remained loyal to this aspiration; on this see Kent and Kent, "Self-Disciplining Pact."

39 See Preyer, especially "Chasa overo palagio," on other palaces built in the early fifteenth century for pairs of brothers, including the Da Uzzano and the Busini.

40 Machiavelli, *Istorie fiorentine*, bk. VII, Ch. 6. Cf. Pulci's consolation to Cosimo on Giovanni's death, MAP, VIII, 205, and Cosimo's own comments, Rochon, *La jeunesse de Laurent*, 47, 143.

41 Portioli, *I Gonzaga ai Bagni*, 43-4.

42 Pieraccini, *La stirpe de' Medici*, made an exhaustive study of this subject, based on the Medici correspondence; for an extensive discussion of the Medici household and its domesticity see Kent, *Fathers and Friends*.

43 Vasari described various works by major artists which he claimed to have seen in the Medici palace; some of these attributions are demonstrably false, but others constitute clues to likely commissions. Of particular importance here is the strength and reliability of Vasari's earlier sources: on these see Murray, *Index of Attributions*.

44 Some of the objects listed in the inventories can be identified with known works; see below for examples.

45 A few of the less outstanding *objets d'art* with which the palace overflowed were put away in *cassoni* or consigned to the servants' quarters, see Spallanzani and Bertelà, *Libro d'inventario*, passim.

46 See Draper, *Bertoldo*, introduction; Preyer, "Lorenzo de' Medici and Questions of Style and Time."

47 Spallanzani and Bertelà, *Libro d'inventario*, 11-12; for the appearance of the reframed ensemble in the "camera di Lorenzo," see Borsi and Borsi, *Paolo Uccello*, 216.

48 On this see Spencer, *Castagno and His Patrons*.

49 Spallanzani and Bertelà, op. cit., 26. This room also contained a large number of elaborate decorative objects, including intarsiated and gilded furniture, four pieces of mosaic, and various marble figures. In Giuliano's room, 72-80, was the *cassone* by Lo Scheggia depicting the scene of Lorenzo's first joust, a picture of the Terrasanta, a bronze *Hercules and Anteus*, and in a cupboard in an *anticamera* to Giuliano's room "uno desco da parto drentovi una schermagli di mano di Masaccio."

50 For speculation concerning Uccello's panels in this regard, see Joannides, "Paolo Uccello's 'Rout of San Romano,'"

Gebhardt, "Some Problems in the Reconstruction," cf. alternatively Caglioti, *Donatello e i Medici*.

51 The following citations from the 1417/18 inventory are from Spallanzani, *Inventari Medicei*, transcribed from MAP, CXXVIII, 54v, ff. On household objects and furniture see also Lydecker, "Commitenza artistica per la casa" and "Domestic Setting of the Arts"; Schiaparelli, *La Casa Fiorentina*.

52 Spallanzani, op. cit., 4-7. The books, 6, were the legend of Santa Margherita, a sermon of "fra Giovanni," possibly Dominici, and the books of the evangelists in *volgare*. Also illuminating of Giovanni's domestic and devotional concerns were, 6, "una cintola da fare e fanciulli et una candela dal Sipolco venne," the latter perhaps a sacred souvenir from the Holy Sepulcher.

53 Ibid., 11-12, 19. Paoletti, "Familiar Objects" took this last to be a holy doll, such as described by Klapisch-Zuber, "Holy Dolls." However, the reference to "uno tabernacolo di legno, entrovi uno bambino Nostro Signore con dalmatica indosso di velluto azzurro et camisce et altro habito da diacono" by no means necessarily implies a separate set of clothes as he assumed, 84, nor that the figure as well as the tabernacle was made of wood. Neri di Bicci's *Ricordanze* refer to both sculptured figures and paintings as frequently set in tabernacles; see, for example, 313.

54 Ibid., 19-20.

55 Ibid., 24; Lorenzo also had "a beautiful intarsiated bed."

56 Ibid., 42, 44.

57 Ibid., 35.

58 See Trexler, "Sacred Image," on the rituals of access to the numinous powers of sacred objects.

59 See below, ch. 13.

60 Spallanzani, op. cit., 65. These saints do, however, appear in the new sacristy at San Lorenzo, decorated by Michelangelo; see Verellen, "Cosmas and Damian."

61 See MAP, CXXVIII. The heading for Giovanni's study appears at the bottom of fol. 56v; 57 is missing, 58r-v are blank, and 59r begins with the contents of Cosimo's *camera*.

62 See above, p. 164.

63 Vasari-Milanesi, *Vite 2*, 148-9. Paoletti, "Fraternal Piety," suggested the decoration, including "giostre, torneamenti, cacce, feste ed altri spettacoli fatti ne' tempi suoi," may have been for Lorenzo's room; see also Pellegrini, *Sulla repubblica fiorentina*, documents, 17.

64 In 1433 Ridolfo Peruzzi came into possession, apparently after his brother Berto's death, of the entire "palagio dela mia abitazione"; see Kent and Kent, "Self-Disciplining Pact," 351, and Cat. 451, 287-303v, especially 296, 99, 300.

65 On the latter, see particularly Brown, "Humanist Portrait of Cosimo"; cf., however, the account of Maecenas in Propertius's *Elegies*, which Cosimo owned by 1418, above, p. 190, and below, p. 343. On the Palazzo Vecchio *Uomini Illustri*, see Hankey, "Salutati's Epigrams"; Rubinstein, "Classical Themes." Over half of the twenty-two of Salutati's famous men were the same as Petrarch's; there were also another five poets associated with Florence, including Dante, Boccaccio, and Petrarch, whose biographies had appeared in Filippo Villani's *Chronicle*. See Rubinstein, 30: "The programme for the Palazzo Vecchio constitutes a compromise between Salutati's Petrarchan classicism and Florentine patriotic tradition as reflected in Filippo Villani's work." The frescoes in the *saletta*, the smaller of the Palazzo Vecchio halls, still existed in 1461; on this see Rubinstein, *Palazzo Vecchio*, and a letter by Sac-

chetti, Laur., Conv. Soppr. 79, 102v–4r, ed. Hankey, "Salutati's Epigrams." On the Carducci frescoes, see Spencer, *Castagno and his Patrons*; Gilbert, "Castagno's Nine Famous Men and Women." See also Joost-Gaugier, "Poggio and Visual Tradition: *Uomini Famosi*." For later, non-Florentine representations of these themes see Joannides, *Masaccio and Masolino*.

66 For the latter, see below, p. 296; on the Suetonius, Rossi, "L'indole," 36.

67 See particularly Hood, *Fra Angelico at San Marco*; Ruda, *Fra Filippo Lippi*; Cole Ahl, *Benozzo Gozzoli*.

68 On these see Lillie, "Giovanni di Cosimo"; Caglioti, "Donatello, I Medici, e Gentile de' Becchi."

69 Spallanzani and Bertelà, op. cit., 33: "Segue nell'antichamera di detta chamera: Una tavoletta di marmo, di mano di Donato, entrovi una Nostra Donna chol banbino in chollo f. 6 . . . Uno quadro di bronzo dorato, entrovi la Nostra Donna chol banbino in braccio, chornicie ador[n]o, di mano di Donato f. 25."

70 See Pope-Hennessy, *Donatello, Sculptor*, 132–6; Poeschke, *Donatello and His World*, 302. Rosenauer, *Donatello*, 158–61, hypothesized that stylistic elements of this work suggest a precedent for the old sacristy tondi depicting the life of San Giovanni and that this may have been a demonstration piece soliciting the commission.

71 See Spallanzani and Bertelà, 33; Pope-Hennessy, "Donatello's Relief," 37–46, especially 40; *Donatello, Sculptor*, 123–9.

72 Poeschke, op. cit., 388–9; cf. Rosenauer, op. cit., 388.

73 Above, pp. 64–5.

74 Cf. Janson, *Donatello*, introduction, and Procacci, "Poets' Views of Artists."

75 Poeschke, op. cit., 302–4; he viewed this work as an exemplum of Alberti's ideas on *storia*, though before the fact, c.1433/4. Cf. Pope-Hennessy, op. cit., 132, for the opinion that although highly accomplished, this work is weaker than the *Ascension* and the subject is treated less realistically than in the bronze relief on the Siena font. He concluded, 333, n. 18, that the piece was a didactic exposition of perspective and narrative, planned by Alberti and completed by Desiderio da Settignano c.1460.

76 Above, p. 116; Rosenauer, op. cit., 161; Poeschke, op. cit., 394.

77 Cit. Ruda, *Fra Filippo Lippi*, 309.

78 Gilbert, *Italian Art*, 152.

79 See Hood, "St. Dominic's Manners of Praying." Didi Hubermann, *Fra Angelico*, 64, made a similar point in his exposition of the "epistemological relationship between description and illusion" in Angelico's paintings.

80 Spallanzani and Bertelà, op. cit., 33: "uno tondo chon una Nostra Donna, picholo, di mano di Fra' Giovanni f. 5"; 80: "una tavoletta di legname di br. 4 incircha, di mano di Fra' Giovanni, dipintovi più storie di santi padri f. 25"; 93: "una tavoletta quadra, dipintovi per mano di Fra' Giovanni uno Cristo in croce con 9 figure datorno f. 12." By contrast with the stocktaking of 1492, Piero de' Medici's inventories of his own personal possessions, mostly precious objects and books, are described with great care; perhaps he supervised or even dictated the descriptions himself.

81 Spallanzani and Bertelà, op. cit., 33: "una tavoletta, dipintovi il Nostro Signore morto chon molti santi che lo portono al sepolchro, di mano di Fra' Giovanni f. 15"; see Ruda, *Fra Filippo Lippi*, 98.

82 Spallanzani and Bertelà, *Libro d'inventario*, 23, 78.

83 Above, n. 1.

84 "Creating Memory," 158.

85 For the description in the inventory, see Spallanzani and Bertelà, op. cit., 12; see also Ruda, op. cit., ch. 5, catalogue 47, and appendix 1. Some indication of the complexity of the issues of date and authorship is that Pope-Hennessy's 1952 edition of *Fra Angelico* describes the work as done in the 1440s by Fra Filippo, strongly influenced by Fra Angelico; the second edition of 1974 places the picture in the 1450s, begun by Angelico and completed by Lippi. On the frequency with which patrons litigated against artists for lateness in completing work, a problem which particularly affected Fra Filippo Lippi, see Ruda, passim, and especially documents; also below, ch. 14. Although Ruda argued convincingly in many cases that Lippi was an artist particularly concerned to please his patrons, and he presented a great deal of valuable material on the friar's relations with them, his natural focus on the artist and his work tends to exclude a consideration of the actual dynamic between patron and artist, and he did not address this problem in relation to the Washington tondo. The evidence pointing to a Medici commission is very strong.

86 Op. cit., 210–15. Cf. his similar comment on the chapel altarpiece, and Lavin's "Giovannino Battista," below, ch. 13. On Lippi in his religious context, see Holmes, *Lippi the Carmelite Painter*.

87 Ruda, op. cit., 213; Ames-Lewis, "Early Medicean Devices."

88 Ruda, op. cit., 215; see also *Golden Legend* 1, 78–83.

89 Op. cit., 210; also 119: "It presents a wider range of incident than virtually any other panel painting of the early to middle fifteenth century, other than panels of the Last Judgment."

90 Ibid., loc. cit. Notably Lorenzo chose to celebrate his birthday, actually on 1 January, on the feastday of Epiphany because of the richness of its symbolic and religious resonances; see Rochon, *La Jeunesse de Laurent*, 59. On the significance of the tondo form and its classical precedents, see Olson, *Florentine Tondo*.

91 Spallanzani and Bertelà, op. cit., 33: "Uno tondo alto br. 2, entrovi la storia de' Magi, di mano di Pesello, f. 20."

92 *Domenico Veneziano*, 122. The discussion that follows is heavily indebted to this study. Domenico's oeuvre is largely undocumented.

93 Wohl, op. cit. See also Gozzoli's Magi frescoes, which represent a largely fanciful landscape.

94 See Wohl's graphic figure 9.

95 See Giovanni di Bicci's tax report of 1427, Cat., 49, 1144r: "In mugiello . . . Un luogho adato di fortezza per mia abitazione chon più maxerizie a uxo della chaxa . . . luogo detto a trebio con ortto, prato, cortte, e con due pezzi di vignia in presso, fo a mia mano, che l'uno si dicie la vignia del chanciello a pie dell'ortto, l'altro si dicie il posticcio." Domenico depicted a terraced slope below the main gate of his castle; in its elaborately walled aspect it resembles more the description of Cafaggiolo in MAP, LXXX, 406–9: "Uno habituro grande hedificato a ghiusa di fortezza con fussi murati intorno et chon antimuri et chon due torri entrovi 4 cholombaie . . ."

96 For some notable examples see Wohl, 71; also Hatfield, *Botticelli's Uffizi "Adoration."*

97 According to Ames-Lewis, "Early Medicean Devices," 131–4, the peacock is not known to have been used by Giovanni until later in the 1440s. However, the framework for dating Domenico's opus is as conjectural as our knowledge of *imprese*; this picture could belong to the late 1440s, or it could

be an early example of Giovanni's usage of the peacock symbol.

98 Wohl, op. cit., 71.

99 For a very different view of the manner and meaning of the depiction of the countryside in this work, see Brock, "Sguardo pubblico, privato e intimo." Adopting "un approccio prossemico," 552, Brock discerned the signs in Domenico's painting of "l'appropriazione materiale e simbolica dello spazio extra-urbano da parte dei gruppi urbani dominanti," 554.

100 Wohl, op. cit., 72 cited Vespasiano da Bisticci's expression of the Florentine belief that "the Greeks in fifteen hundred or more years never changed their costume." Other notable illustrations of Greek hats include the Magi fresco in Cosimo's cell.

101 See particularly the essays in Viti, *Concilio di Firenze*.

102 On the Medici in Ferrara and Piero's *studiolo* see below, vii, and ch. 13.

103 A letter of Paolo Giovio to Duke Cosimo a century later is not very persuasive evidence that the medal was made in Florence in 1439, but it seems quite possible that Domenico, who wrote to Piero at the beginning of April 1438 from Perugia where he painted the frescoes in the Baglioni palace, and a year later received his first payment for work on the frescoes of Sant Egidio in Florence, passed by Ferrara perhaps to renew in person his request to Cosimo and Piero for some really important Florentine commission.

104 See Baxandall, *Painting and Experience*, pt. 3, for these assessments, and below, for Domenico Veneziano's inclusion in a trio of arbitrators with Lippi and Angelico.

105 Spallanzani and Bertelà, op. cit., 72: "Nella chamera che risponde in sulla via chiamata la camera di monsignore, dove sta Giuliano . . . un colmetto con dua sportelli, dipintovi dentro una testa d'una dama, di mano di maestro Domenico da Vinegia f. 8."

106 See Spallanzani and Bertelà, op. cit., 71; Gilbert, "Archbishop on the Painters"; Wohl, op. cit., 24. As Wohl pointed out, "colorito a olio" refers specifically to the Flemish style of painting, which may bear on the vexed question of whether Domenico Veneziano did work extensively in oils, as he was reputed to have done for the now lost frescoes for San Egidio. Wohl also raised the question of Flemish influence on Domenico, cf. Ruda's discussion of the same issue in relation to Lippi.

107 Ruda, *Fra Filippo Lippi*, catalogue 15, 382–4.

108 Spallanzani and Bertelà, op. cit., 33, 72, 70.

109 On this commission, see below, pp. 334–7, and figs. 167–9; for the negotiations with Lippi's Prato patrons see Ruda, *Fra Filippo Lippi*, document 21, 536–7.

110 The panels do not appear in the inventories of either household's possessions; for those of Pierfrancesco's line see Shearman, "Collections of the Younger Medici." For discussion of the panels see Davies, "Fra Filippo's Annunciation and Seven Saints"; Ames-Lewis, "Fra Filippo Lippi's S. Lorenzo *Annunciation*" and "Art in the Service of the Family"; Paoletti, "Fraternal Piety"; Ruda, op. cit., catalogue 50a, b, 199–203.

111 On this question see Paoletti, op. cit., and Ames-Lewis, "Art in the Service of the Family," 219, n. 23 for a Medici bank contract of 1427, MAP, CLIV, 154, 1, also noted by Paoletti: "Al nome sia del'onipotente iddio e della chroliosa madonna santa maria e di tutta la chorte del paradiso e di beato miss santo giovanni batist evagelista e di beato miss santo michele agnolo e del beato miss santo iacopo apostolo e del beato miss santo andrea e del beato miss santo tomaso e de beato miss santo chosimo e di beato miss santo ilarione e di madonna santa maria madelena e della beata santa chaterina e di madonna santa lucia e di tuta chorte del paradiso . . ." The Bardi family were partners to this agreement and their namesaints included Ilarione and Andrea; their parish church was Santa Lucia dei Magnoli. Paoletti followed Ames-Lewis in reading "santo giovanni battista evangelista" as evidence that the two Saints John were seen as optional alternatives, but it seems to me in view of the orthography of the passage that the reference here is a contracted one to both saints; Giovanni di Bicci's patron, the Evangelist, and the Baptist, who represented the city of Florence. The inclusion of the latter is especially likely because so many of the bank's dealings were with foreigners. Similarly, cf. Ames-Lewis, 219, n. 24, it seems less likely that John the Baptist and the Apostle Peter, in Van der Weyden's Medici *Madonna*, are substitutions for Piero's patron, Peter Martyr, and Giovanni's Evangelist, than that they represent Florence and the Church in a commission perhaps associated with the bank; see below. The introduction of Saint Anthony Abbot, and occasionally Saint Anthony of Padua into Medici artistic commissions around the middle of the century, also invites some explanation. Saint Anthony is included in the dedication to Piero's 1456 inventory, Spallanzani, op. cit.: "Al nome sia dell'omnipotente dio et della sua gloriosa madre madonna sancta maria sempre vergine et di miss. sancto giovanbatista et di miss. sancto Lorenzo et di miss. sancto Cosimo et di miss. sancto Damiano et di mess. sancto Antonio et di mess. sancto Piero martire et di mess. sancto Francescho et di mess. sancto Giuliano et universalmente di tuta l'altra celestiale corte di paradiso allore laude et gloria et reverentia . . ." Anthony of Padua appears in Medici paintings around 1450, shortly after the discovery of his relics at San Lorenzo, which may be significant. Ames-Lewis, op. cit., observed that in the *Seven Saints* panel there is a dead tree behind him, as there is behind Damian; both saints may refer to Cosimo's long dead brothers, Damiano and Antonio; the latter's saintly protector was presumably Saint Anthony Abbot.

112 Cf. above, pp. 193–4, on the figural decoration of the old sacristy. On portraits and memory, see also Johnson, "Sculpture and the Family."

113 Particularly notable is the Alessandri altarpiece, in which Cosmas and Damian, both protecting and towering over the tiny donors, evoke at once earthly patrons and patron saints; see Ruda, *Fra Filippo Lippi*, catalogue 39 and below, p. 356, and fig. 176.

114 Ibid., catalogue 22a, b; 29, 115–26, 159–63, also Holmes, "Giovanni Benci's Patronage." On the Martelli and Benci in the Medici bank, see De Roover, *Rise and Decline*, especially 56.

115 See Ames-Lewis, "Art in the Service of the Family," especially 212; Paoletti, "Fraternal Piety"; Beyer and Boucher, *Piero de' Medici*. The concept of a "dynasty" proposed in such arguments is sometimes mistakenly assumed to relate specifically to princely successions or their equivalents, but in fact the term "dynasty" refers more generally to any family's perception of itself as an ongoing entity.

116 See Ruda, op. cit., 43.

117 On Florentines and Netherlandish paintings see particularly Nuttall, "Early Netherlandish Paintings in Florence".

118 For both works see Spallanzani and Bertelà, op. cit., 51; for the second Baldesi, *Jan van Eyck*, 87–8.

119 See Baxandall, "Bartholomeus Facius on Painting." On the basis of possible evidence that Rogier was influenced by Angelico's panel from the predella of the San Marco altarpiece of the Lamentation for Christ, it has been suggested that he passed through Florence. However, the compositional similarities between Angelico's panel and Rogier's *Deposition* seem rather general. There is also a record of payment to Rogier via Bruges for various pictures for Lionello d'Este, died 1450. There is no evidence that he did any work in Italy.

120 See Campbell, *Van der Weyden*; Musée des Beaux Arts, Brussels, *Catalogue*.

121 See Davies, *Rogier van der Weyden*, 212–13; Panofsky, *Early Netherlandish Painting*; see also Paoletti's comment on this work, "Donatello's Bronze Doors," 51, 68.

122 On the history of the Bruges branch of the Medici bank see De Roover, *Rise and Decline*, ch. 13 and esp. 325.

123 Spallanzani and Bertelà, 18, 22.

124 Ibid., 6: "Nella sala grande in su detta loggia . . . Uno quadro dipintovi una Italia; Uno quadro di legno dipintovi la Spagna . . ."; 27: "Nella camera grande di detta sala, detta camera di Lorenzo . . . Uno colmo di br. 2½ dipintovi la Spagna, f. 8 . . . ; 6, "Terrasanta," in the "camera grande terrena di Lorenzo."

125 Ibid., 33: "Uno colmo di br. ii ½ chon dua teste al naturale, cioè Francesco Sforzo et Ghattamelata, di mano d'uno da Vinegia f. 10."

126 See Hale, *Artists and Warfare*, especially 153–5; on the Malatesta *Triumphs*, 80, also 157ff; on Pisanello's *Tournament* of 1447, 55; on Piero della Francesca's True Cross frescoes, c.1460, another type of representation of warfare within a religious cycle.

127 Op. cit., 2, 208, 213. He described the Bartolini group of pictures as having been damaged and very badly restored: they were repainted by Giuliano Bugiardini, "che piuttosto ha loro nociuto che giovato."

128 Merisalo, *Le collezioni medicee nel 1495*, especially 60, 89; Caglioti, *Donatello e i Medici*, ch. 6.

129 Merisalo, op. cit., 55: "multototiens se doluisse sibi fuisse per vim de domo suo sumptas nonullas istorias"; for the second day's proceedings, see 56. See particularly Caglioti, op. cit. I wish to thank Dr. Caglioti most warmly for his extreme generosity in allowing me to consult the proofs of his book while I was correcting the proofs of this one.

130 Merisalo, 56: "Item deliberaverunt quod restituatur Damiano Bartolini de tribus storiis 1a ½ et si aliam partem emere voluerit, sit remissus in Raynerium et Ieronimum . . ." The passage is cited as transcribed and modified by Caglioti, op. cit., 270.

131 "inter alia una certa storia che si dice 'La rotta della Torre a San Romano' sive 'La Rotta de Nicolo Picino.'"

132 Caglioti, 270. For a revised transcription of the text, see ibid., 271: "dictam storiam tunc conduxit ruri a Qunito a[d] domum sue habitationis . . . dictus Galeottus . . . dixit esse presentem quando dictus Laurentius misit pro dicta storia. Quapropter dictos Sindacos . . . declaraverunt dimidiam dicte storie fuisse restituendam dicto Damiano, qui sua, et alia dimidia, si dictus Damianus eam et eas vellet, sibi vendatur per Raynerium de Giugnis et Ieronimum de Martellis pro eo pretio prout eis videbitur."

133 On the flood of objects returned to the Medici, see Horne, "The Battle-piece by Paolo Uccello," 122, and Caglioti, op. cit.; on the Medici inventory of 1598, Horne, 123–4; on the Uccellos in the Medici palace in the mid-sixteenth century, Vasari-Milanesi 2, 208.

134 Although in his exploration of the implications of the 1495 document Caglioti canvasses a number of possibilities and offers several interesting hypotheses about the possible patronage of the Uccellos, his essential view, referring successively to the *Ercole* of Michelangelo and Uccello's, San Romano cycle, is that "Per un capolavoro perduto che viene oggi ad arricchire in modo definitivo l'ormai ideale museo mediceo della *Florentina libertas*, eccone invece uno, tuttora superstite, che ne sortisce inappellabilmente, procurando un piccolo terremoto bibliografico"; ibid., 269.

135 Ibid.; see also above, p. 245; Kent, "Lorenzo de' Medici's Acquisition of Poggio a Caiano."

136 On the confiscation of the Donatellos, see below, p. 267, and Caglioti, op, cit., 273. On the turmoil of the period post 1494 to the end of the republic, see Stephens, *Fall of the Florentine Republic*; Polizzotto, *Elect Nation*; Butters, *Governors and Government*.

137 See Rucellai, *Zibaldone* 2, "Making of a Renaissance Patron."

138 Merisalo, op. cit., xii–xiii.

139 See Del Piazzo, *Protocolli del carteggio di Lorenzo*; ASF, *Medici avanti il Principato, Inventario*. These letters are certain now to be scrutinized with the utmost care, and may yield further information. The Bartolini archive is presently under investigation by Dr. Caglioti; on this see Ridolfi, "Le lettere dell'archivio Bartolini Salimbeni."

140 See above, p. 48. Lionardo does not appear to have been one of Cosimo's early partisans. His brother, Niccolò, was exiled in 1458, which might alternatively have given the wider family a grudge against the Medici, and a motive for laying claim to their property. On the political fortunes of the Bartolini, see Rubinstein, *Government of Florence*, 123n, 143n.

141 Gebhardt, *Paolo Uccellos "Schlacht"*, "Some problems," and Roccasecca, *Paolo Uccello*, especially 24–7, are in agreement in seeing the Florence and London panels as a diptych and the Louvre panel as distinct, but they disagree on the issue of which came first. Far more authoritative on the armor is Boccia, *Le armature di Paolo Uccello*. On armor see also below, p. 293.

142 See below, p. 275.

143 See below, ch. 15. Medici partisans' patronage included not only domestic decoration like Castagno's *Uomini Illustri* for the Carducci, following c.1450 the cycle commissioned, according to Vasari, by Giovanni di Bicci de' Medici for the *casa vecchia* decades earlier, but also the Pazzi chapel begun in the 1440s and based, like so many others, on Brunelleschi's old sacristy, completed in the late 1420s and itself a reworking of the chapel of the Barbadori exiled in 1434; palaces from mid-century onward that emulated or rivaled that of the Medici; tombs of the 1440s modeled on that of Orlando de' Medici which drew on the arcosolium form first employed in the 1420s by the exiled Strozzi; altarpieces commissioned in the 1440s and '50s by the Martelli and Lionardo Bartolini from Filippo Lippi, following the innovative *pale* produced by Fra Angelico in the late '30s and early '40s for the Medici, and among them the altarpiece for the Alessandri family which foregrounds the Medici saints, Lawrence, Cosmas, and Damian, possibly with reference to Ginevra Alessandri's marriage to Giovanni di Cosimo in 1453. In the extravagance of their domestic decoration and the ambitious

nature of their domestic commissions, however, the Medici far outstripped any other family of the mid-fifteenth century; see Lydecker, "Domestic Setting of the Arts."

144 Vasari might have been referring to these or to still other paintings when he claimed that Uccello "in casa de' Medici dipinse in tela a tempera alcune storie di animali," op. cit., 2, 208. On the physical alterations to the panels, see Caglioti, op. cit.

145 On the possibility of an official or corporate commission, see Caglioti, op. cit., 275.

146 Starn and Partridge, "Representing War," 33.

147 Lanza, op. cit., 1, 221–2. Belcari concluded with a compliment to the poet: "Quell'altro non può mai essere indutto/ a fama eterna, se 'l dolce istrumento/ d'Orfeo non canta con sua melodia."

148 *Inferno*, xv, 85. On the topos of arms versus learning and the Medici image, see Gombrich, "Golden Age."

149 See Kent, "I Medici in esilio," 24; on Florentine absorption of classical literature, Wilcox, *Development of Florentine Humanist Historiography*.

150 See Hankins, "The Humanist, the Banker and the *Condottiere*," 65: "Frontini librum de re militari nuper a te mihi dono missum, quum voluptati meae satis fuerit eius ordinem ac disciplinam cognovisse, ad te nunc honesta de caussa remitto. Satis tibi gratiarum habeo, si tanti viri, quod mirum in modum cupiebam, de ipsa militia tuo munere sententiam cognoverim; nec sane tua apud me benevolentia ullo munerum testimonio eget; nihil enim aut auctoritatis aut facultatis apud me est quod a te alienum esse velim." Cosimo may have had the book copied while it was in his possession; a copy of the *Stratagemata*, together with Vegetius, *De re militari*, was among Piero's books, inherited from Giovanni di Cosimo; see Ames-Lewis, *Library and Manuscripts of Piero*, 259, catalogue no. 22.

151 Lanza, op. cit., 1, 224.

152 *Zibaldone* 1, 122. Rubinstein, "Palazzi Pubblici," 27, discussed the enormous expenses thereby incurred.

153 See Molho, *Florentine Public Finances*; Kent, *Rise of the Medici*, ch. 4.

154 The poem is undated, but Cambini was born only in 1424; for the text and a biographical note see Lanza, op. cit., 1, 359–61.

155 ASF, CS, 3a ser., 132, 295, 19 Mar. 1429/30.

156 Lanza, op. cit., 1, 361–3; above, p. 118.

157 MAP, v, 147.

158 See below, p. 376. See Rubinstein, *Government of Florence*, especially 132–3, on Cosimo's outstanding reputation for the conduct of war and diplomacy.

159 For Cosimo's appearance in the Dieci di Balìa, the war commission, at crucial moments from 1427 on, see Kent, *Rise of the Medici*, passim; Rubinstein, op. cit., especially appendices.

160 See Mallett, *Mercenaries and their Masters*, 209.

161 For these letters, and details of Cosimo's relationships with other Italian *condottieri* and princes see below, ch. 15, iii.

162 Mallett, op. cit., 206, ff. Florence had a famous *condottiere* of her own. Filippo Scolari, known as Pippo Spano, came from an old Florentine noble family, but went to Hungary at the age of thirteen as an apprentice and bookkeeper for a Florentine merchant firm. He then entered the service of King Sigismund and fought against the Turks. Florentines were welcomed at his residence at the Hungarian court, and he brought Masolino there to work on his chapel. Scolari

was a collector of manuscripts, and supported with his patronage the rebuilding by Brunelleschi of Ambrogio Traversari's convent of Santa Maria degli Angeli.

163 For the Medici letter, see Hankins, "The Humanist, the Banker, and the *Condottiere*." The Medici brothers wrote a similar letter to their close friend Romeo Foscari, the doge of Venice; see Kent, op. cit., ch. 5.

164 MAP, iv, 246.

165 Mallett, op. cit., 76–9.

166 Some of Sforza's letters to Cosimo are in ASF, MAP, passim. The largest body of their correspondence is in Milan, Biblioteca Ambrosiana, Archivio Sforzesco Ducale. Some letters relating to their relationship are published in Fabroni, *Magni Cosmi* 2, and translated by Ross, *Lives of the Early Medici*, 34–8; see especially the letter from Lorenzo de' Medici while ambassador to Ferrara for the Ten of War to his brother Cosimo asking him to mediate between Sforza and the pope. See also MAP, v, 370, Ser Alesso Pelli to Giovanni di Cosimo de' Medici. For an interesting analysis of the relations between the two men see Ilardi, "Cosimo de' Medici and Francesco Sforza."

167 On Nicodemo Tranchedini, see Massai, "Nicodemo da Pontremoli," especially 135–6. Tranchedini also had a house in the environs of Florence at Canto alla Paglia, and a villa at San Martino a Montughi, near the Medici property there. He was born in 1411 of a father who was captain of various military companies, and joined Sforza's service when he became Lord of Pontremoli in 1433; Nicodemo himself became Sforza's secretary. Their correspondence, much of it concerning Cosimo, is conserved in Paris, Bibliothèque Nationale, Fonds Italiens, and partially published by Buser, *Die Beziehungen der Mediceer*.

168 *Istorie fiorentine*, ed. Polidori, 488.

169 See Brucker, *Civic World*, especially 450–500; Mallett, *Florentine Galleys*; Molho, "Note on the Albizzi"; Palla Strozzi, *Diario*.

170 See Herlihy and Klapisch-Zuber, *Les Toscans et leurs familles*; Brown, *Under the Shadow*; Connell, "Clientelismo e Stato Territoriale." Pisan rage and resentment against Florence generated a good deal of satirical verse; see Lanza, op. cit., passim.

171 *Ricordi*, 73, 86.

172 *Ricordi*, 1, 34.

173 See Kent, *Rise of the Medici*, 201, 264.

174 Ibid., 217. See also Albizzi's *Commissioni*, and his letters published by Molho, "Note on the Albizzi."

175 Cit. Mallett, *Mercenaries and their Masters*, 209–10.

176 "'That the practice of arms is most excellent.'" See also her "Mortuary Chapels of Renaisance Condottieri." The following discussion of Florentines images of war owes much to these works and to our correspondence in the early 1990s.

177 Poggi/Haines, *Il Duomo di Firenze* 2, 123, doc. 2052, 22 Aug. 1393. For the original plan, see Borsook, *Mural Painters*, 76. Plans for eight marble monuments were promulgated by public decree between 1393 and 1396; see also Poggi/Haines, op. cit., 123–5. Coluccio Salutati, chancellor of Florence from 1375 to 1406, and author of the inscriptions for the series of *uomini illustri* in the Palazzo Vecchio, was probably a leading spirit behind this project. Subsequently the commune's failure to obtain the bones of some of those to be commemorated, together with a lack of money, led to changes in personnel and the decision to use paint instead of marble. The more ambitious monuments actually made included

those for Cardinal Corsini, c.1422, then Hawkwood in 1436, Marsili in 1439, and Dante in 1465. A marble monument for Niccolò da Tolentino was proposed in 1435, but in 1455 he was commemorated with a fresco matching Hawkwood's. On 5 April 1400, a general prohibition was issued against private tombs above floor level in the cathedral. Monuments commissioned by the commune or the Arte della Lana were exempt, but in fact no above-ground tombs were made after this date. Hawkwood's remains were buried in the floor; see Wegener, op. cit., 132.

178 Poggi/Haines, op. cit., 124, doc. 2054, 13 July 1433.

179 For this see Borsook, *Mural Painters*, 75. It appears in Benedetto Dei's list of 1473 of prose and poetry he had committed to memory; see above, p. 91. For the long delays between proposals for cathedral works and their execution, see Haines, *Sacrestia delle Messe*, cf. Wegener's concern, op. cit., to explain the revival of interest in Hawkwood forty years after his death.

180 *Trattato politico-morale*, 124.

181 See ASF, Arte della Lana, 39, 11v. On Giovenco d'Antonio, see De Roover, *Rise and Decline*, 174. The more explicit speculations concerning Cosimo's intervention by Borsi and Borsi, *Paolo Uccello*, are not supported by any evidence.

182 See Bayley, *War and Society*, for the text and comment.

183 Poggi/Haines, op. cit., 124, doc. 2058, 28 June 1436. The other documents relating to the commission are as follows: 124, doc. 2056, 26 May 1436: "detur expeditio dicte sepulture pro honore dicti communis et prefate opere." 124, doc. 2057, 30 May 1436. 124, doc. 2059, 6 July 1436; doc 2060, 31 Aug. 1436: "A Pagholo di Dino . . . degli uccegli, dipintore, l. LXIV p. per suo faticha e prezzo di dipignere due volte la persona e chavallo di messer Giovani Aghuto pello adreto chapitano generale del chomune di Firenze nella chiesa magiore di Firenze."

184 See Meiss, "Original Position of Uccello's *John Hawkwood*."

185 On this question see Spencer, *Castagno and His Patrons*, 3–4.

186 The link between these works, and with the *pitture infamanti* of the Medici enemies defeated at Anghiari in 1440, discussed below, is the main subject of Wegener's detailed study of the objects and their subjects. In "'That the practice of arms is most excellent,'" 130, she argued that "these works, all representing military leaders and displayed in more or less public settings, were first and foremost vehicles for a political message." For a sophisticated discussion of the rhetoric of images and the representation of war, with particular reference to Uccello's panels, and a number of penetrating and imaginative insights into these works, see Starn and Partridge, "Representing War."

187 On Castagno's many earlier commissions for the Medici and their friends, particularly Bernardetto de' Medici, see Spencer, op. cit.

188 ASF, MSS, 315, c.16.

189 See Zervas, "Brunelleschi's Political Career." Cavalcanti, *Istorie fiorentine*, ed. Polidori I, 328, recounted how "some of our fantastical spirits, among whom was Filippo di Ser Brunellescho . . . advised, and with their false and misleading geometry . . . demonstrated that the city of Lucca could be flooded; and they drew this so effectively with their bad arts that the silly masses were led to cry out . . . we touch with our hands what these theorists draw for us, but you others wish the war to go on and on, so as to ensure that you will remain in power forever!" The affair was satirized in at least

two verses attributed to Burchiello, full of obscure references to Florentine people and places, including the working-class districts of San Pier Gattolino and San Martino, cit. Battisti, *Brunelleschi*, 373–4.

190 See Cavalcanti, *Istorie fiorentine*, 246–7. Luca degli Albizzi, the Florentine commissioner in the field, told a different story; for the details of this see Partridge and Starn, op. cit., esp. 50–51.

191 Antonio di Meglio, Ricc., 2971, published Lanza, *Lirici toscani* I, 131; see also Flamini, *La lirica toscana*, 88–9; he attributed the work to Francesco d'Altobianco degli Alberti. The wolf refers to Siena, the viper to Milan.

192 *Zibaldone* I, 47.

193 MAP, CXXXVII, 24, 11 Aug. 1432, cit. Starn and Partridge, op. cit., 57, and n. 53. See also Buoninsegni, *Storie*, 45; the pair were presented with cermonial gifts by the republic, including pennants, shields, vestments in brocade, and helmets like that carried by Tolentino's page in the panel by Uccello now in London.

194 See Morpurgo, *I manoscritti*, index, 62, 69, 76, 87, 100, 124, 190, 439, 582, 588, and especially Laur., Plut 90, sup. 89. For the *Difesa*, see above, p. 88; on Bruni and the image of Florence see also Baron, *Crisis*.

195 Cit. Wegener, op. cit., 159.

196 Ibid., 153. Holmes, *Florentine Enlightenment*, 154, observed that Bruni's oration for the funeral in 1426 of Nanni Strozzi, both a member of a great Florentine family and a *condottiere* in the service of the city, was also very similar to his speech to Tolentino.

197 Cit. Rubinstein, "Cosimo *optimus civis*," 16.

198 Wegener, op. cit., 155. Eight of the twelve generals he mentioned were celebrated by Plutarch; on the Hawkwood monument's debt to this recently discovered manuscript, see Borsook, op. cit., loc. cit. On Bruni's belief in the importance of military captains see also Wilcox, *Development of Humanist Historiography*; Griffiths, et al., *Humanism of Leonardo Bruni*. On the rhetoric of praise and blame see also McManamon, "Continuity and Change."

199 MAP, II, 371.

200 Ibid., II, 170.

201 Some fifty or so of Cosimo's letters to Averardo in these years are conserved in the *fondo* MAP. Patrician involvement in Florence's wars is generally extremely well documented. Guasti's huge three-volume edition of the official reports from camp, the *Commissioni* of Rinaldo degli Albizzi between 1426 and 1433, is supplemented by scores of letters to or about Rinaldo from other protagonists in the conflicts, including the Medici. Luca degli Albizzi's report on his service for the state on the Florentine galleys in the late 1420s and early 1430s, published in Mallett, *Florentine Galleys*, includes a detailed description of the encounter at San Romano. Neri Capponi wrote his *Commentaries* on the acquisition of Pisa, in which his father Gino played a leading role, and his *Commentaries* on Italian affairs from 1419 to 1456 includes a narrative of the action at San Romano. For a much fuller list of sources for the war with Lucca, see Wegener, and Starn and Partridge, op. cit.

202 MAP, IV, 6, cf. III, 112, from Ser Ciaio: "Meglio voglate ad altri che a voi proprio, che è una pazzia."

203 MAP, V, 684, 3 Dec. 1431; ibid., II, 186, 7 Feb. 1429/30.

204 CP, 49, 26r.

205 MAP, IV, 221: "Abbiamo cominciato addare danari al

cancellaria del capitano e domane lo contereno tra danari e promesse insino in fiorini dicemilia, et così subito daren' agli altri dappie e da cavallo. Ma se'l manchamento del danaio non si può fare a tempo chome bisognierebbe, et così il tempo passa sanza fare frutto, e verificasi il proverbio ch'el povero huomo non può mai fare bene."

206   See Molho, *Florentine Public Finances*, 176–8; Kent, *Rise of the Medici*, especially 285.

207   *Istorie fiorentine*, 267.

208   MAP, II, 371, 21 Oct. 1430.

209   See Spallanzani, *Inventari Medicei*, 167; MAP, V, 639. On the close relations between Averardo de' Medici and Micheletto de' Attendolis see Kent, op. cit., Starn and Partridge, op. cit., Guasti, op. cit. The fact that Tolentino's code name, revealed in a letter of Neri di Gino Capponi to Matteo Strozzi, 24 Jan. 1431, ASF, CS. 3a ser., 112, 197, was apparently "Eros" is intriguing, and Niccolò Tinucci warned Averardo in 1432 of the danger of associating too closely with Micheletto on account of some "indecent" poems he had written: "To tell you the truth, it is deemed far too great a shortcoming that you have spent so much time with him, and yet you are unable to say whether he is a man or a woman; I would therefore do everything possible to clarify this, and may the smoke fly wherever it will," cit. Rocke, *Forbidden Friendships*, 43. Starn and Partridge, 54, suggest there was a "male romance" between them, but their friendship seems as likely in the circumstances to express the intoxicating excitement, akin to that of love, felt by Florentine patricians like the Medici and Capponi in waging war. The language of Averardo's letter to Micheletto cited above n. 175: "Chompare mio dolce, ripigliate el mio scrivere da gran sicurità che 'o in voi e da grande amore ch'io vi porto," is fulsome but not unusual in letters between *amici*; on this see also Martines, "Love and Hate in Renaissance Patronage."

210   The letter, along with other related documents, is published by Gelli, "L'esilio di Cosimo," 157.

211   *Ricordi*, 97; see also Gutkind, *Cosimo de' Medici*, 77.

212   Kent, op. cit., 309–11.

213   *Ricordi*, op. cit., loc. cit. The Medici stayed in touch with Tolentino's family; see MAP, V, 320, 21 Mar. 1438/9, a letter from Cesena to Giovanni di Cosimo, "In Ferraria al banco de' Medici." The writer had been in camp near Cesena with Cristofano and Giovanni da Tolentino and wanted to know if they were interested in selling a horse which they sent to the camp; he sent his recommendations to Cosimo, Piero, and their factor Antonio da Pescia.

214   Contemporary speculation that he was murdered seems more plausible than that concerning Cosimo's possible role in his death, supposedly to represent himself as the sole leader and savior of Florence. Promulgated largely by Cavalcanti, these speculations are discussed in detail by Wegener, op. cit., 152.

215   Poggi/Haines, op. cit., 2, 128–9, doc. 2072, extract from Pietriboni's *Priorista*. See also Strocchia, *Death and Ritual*; BNF, Conv. Soppr. 4, 195; Wegener, op. cit., 151–3.

216   See below, n. 239.

217   Starn and Partridge, op. cit., 33.

218   Borsi and Borsi, *Paolo Uccello*, 9. See also Pope-Hennessy, *Uccello*, especially 28; he saw the artist as torn between "two imperfectly reconciled visual traditions and two incompletely synthesized attitudes to art."

219   Voltaire's phrase, cit. Starn and Partridge, op. cit., 33; see also n. 1.

220   Ibid., 40–41; De Robertis, "L'esperienza poetica."

221   MAP, IV, 77: "Di nuovo s'è soldato fiorini 150, chome per lettera dall'uficio sarai avisato, e se s'abi ne fare chonto, arai costì fanti 600, forestieri 50, arcieri e cavagli 300 . . . a però quando vegnente la brighata potrei dare licenzia a de' paesani, e più vi si manda maestri di scharpello e di chazuola, sicchè potrete fare buon ghuerra . . . " This letter also makes rarely explicit reference to an expectation of "gloria" as Averardo's reward for bringing about a Florentine victory.

222   MAP, IV, 246: "Noi vedemmo la sperienza di Niccolò Piccinino l'anno passato, che di verno e sanza danari sempre stette in hopera; et in uno punto quando bisognio s'andò da Stagia, Arezo et chosì poi di subito d'Arezo in Lombarda; et perchè potresti dire de' suoi pari ci sono pochi, noi vegiamo quello che fanno le genti de' Sanesi che schorrono tutto il nostro chontado, et non sono 500 chavalli e nove huomo di nome . . . [Micheletto de' Attendolis] a dumila chavalli di chondotta sanza l'altre genti et in tutto in tre mesi siete iti quattro miglia. Chonoscho che chi tiene il segnio tiene lui bisognia sia chauto, ma non bisognia però avere tanto righuardo che non si faccia nulla. Temere della genti di Lombarda che sono di lungi dugento miglia mi pare timore vano, perchè sempre chi venissono in qua n'arebe sentore attempo si potrebbe ritrarre; et anche mi pare voi siate molto male avisati delli andamenti de' nimici, non solo di quelli di Lombarda ma di quelli di Toschana, et la principale parte ad volere honore chredo sia sentire del nimicho." On Caesar's *Commentaries*, see above, ch 4.

223   On these texts see Griffiths, "Uccello's *Battle of San Romano*"; Starn and Partridge, op. cit., especially 50–51 and 59, n. 6. Neri Capponi, author of the account in *Commentari*, col. 1177, 43, xvii–xxvii, was a close friend of the Medici, as was Luca degli Albizzi, who gave a full account of the battle in his report from the field, cit. Starn and Partridge 50, 61–2; see also Mallett, *Mercenaries and their Masters*, 181. Matteo Palmieri's *Annales*, crediting Tolentino with the strategic ingenuity that won the battle, and exalting it as a great republican victory against tyranny, were in Piero's library by 1456.

224   Op. cit., 43–4.

225   *Song of Roland*, ll. 1656–7, 3386, 3388, 1490–93, 3305–10; partially cit. Starn and Partridge, 42. Charlemagne was a key figure in Florentine history and civic tradition, being credited with the second founding of the city and the rebuilding of the walls, to which one of Salutati's epigrams for the Palazzo Vecchio refers: "Karolus Magnus. Rex ego gallorum karolus cognomine magnus/ Perdomui gentes longobardosque tirannos/ Nactus et imperium mea te Florentia muris/ Fortibus armavi romanis civibus auctam," cit. Hankey, "Salutati's Epigrams," 364–5. Starn and Partridge cited several examples of the medieval battlepieces available to Uccello, 43; the persistence of interest in these subjects into the fifteenth century is also illustrated by their appearance in *cassoni* panels. See Callman, *Apollonio di Giovanni*, plate 207, for the notable similarity between the *Battle of Pharsalus* and Uccello's three panels; also Schubring, *Truhen und Truhenbilder*.

226   Starn and Partridge, op. cit., 40; see also Parronchi, *Paolo Uccello*.

227   Ibid., 57.

228   MAP, IV, 246: "Benchè non abiamo quella sperienza de' fatti dell'arme che a chilli praticha chontinuamente, pure nonè che veduto quello si fa per gli altri nonsi possa giudicare chi

facci meglio; chredo tu no sii um buono dipintore et pure
giudicheresti che le fighure di Giotto stessono meglio che
quelle del Balzanello." Neither I nor anyone else I know has
been able to identify Balzanello; Cosimo may have confused
him with Buffalmacco, or the name may well be one of those
verbal jokes in which Florentines delighted, since *balzare*, "to
dance," also signifies in popular parlance "to have inter-
course"; see Toscan, *Carneval du Langage*, lexicon.

229 *Infinite Jest*, ch. 1.

230 Op. cit., 154.

231 Noted by Borsi and Borsi, op. cit., 206. Starn and Partridge
also remarked on his "arbitrary geometrical constructions and
forms-within-forms – circles, chords of circles, ellipses, rec-
tangles and so on," op. cit., 40.

232 Pope-Hennessy, op. cit., 19, observed that "the background
has no spatial reference to the episode in front . . . the composition resemble, scenes played before a drop curtain;" this
was of course an effect familiar to Florentines from *sacre
rappresentazioni*.

233 Op. cit., 212.

234 On Cosimo's collection of armor, see below; on the physical
alterations to the panels, see above, n. 144.

235 The studies by Wegener and by Partridge and Starn, op. cit.,
follow recent scholarship in suggesting a date for the Medici
panels before 1440. See particularly Gebhardt, *Schlacht von
San Romano* and "Some Problems of Reconstruction."
Boccia's precise assignment of the armor to the 1430s, "Le
armature di Paolo Uccello," indicates, although it does not
necessitate, an earlier date.

236 See Cavalcanti, *Istorie fiorentine*, especially 362.

237 On the battle of Anghiari see Mallett, op. cit., Wegener,
op. cit., Neri Capponi, *Commentari*, op. cit., 1193–5.

238 Lanza, *Lirici toscani* 1, 346–8: "Versi fatti per messer Anselmo
Calderoni quando fu rotto Niccolò Piccolino in laude del
magnifico conte Francesco." See also Leonardo di Piero
Dati's Latin verse on the battle of Anghiari, cit. Lanza, 1, 397.

239 For the *cassoni* panels with military subjects made in the
workshop of Apollonio di Giovanni, and their patrons, see
Callmann, op. cit., especially appendix 1. See Callmann and
Schubring, op. cit., for the opus of "the Anghiari master." The
Anghiari *cassone*, *c*.1443, was one of a matching pair; the other
cassone panel depicted the victory of the Florentines at Pisa.
Although the arms are obscured, this pair was most probably painted for the Capponi, since Gino di Neri had been
the major Florentine commander at Pisa, as his son Neri was
at Anghiari. On the battle commissions for the Signoria in
1504, see the documents in Chambers, *Patrons and Artists*,
87–8. The resolution of the Great Council concerning
Leonardo's cartoon and fresco was drawn up on 4 May 1504,
by Niccolò Machiavelli, then chancellor to the Signoria. On
Castagno's *pitture infamanti*, see Edgerton, *Pictures and Punishment*; Ortalli, *La pittura infamante*, and for Andrea del Sarto's
preparatory drawings for such pictures, Shearman, *Andrea del
Sarto* 2, 320–21. Defamatory images were regarded as a powerful instrument of revenge for betrayals of the state. When
Piccinino left Florentine service for that of the duke of Milan
in 1425, the Florentines chose to regard his act as treasonous,
and a *pittura infamante* was displayed in Florence. Piccinino
protested to the duke of Milan, who demanded that the
offending image be removed, but the Florentines replied:
"Concerning the depainting of Niccolò Piccinino, we marvel
that you would require it, or anyone consent to it. For it

would set the worst example and give cause to the captains
to be lacking in faith and not concerned for their honor."
See Wegener, op. cit., 144, for this episode, the removal of
the painting in 1430, and the payment to Piccinino at that
time of back wages owed him by the commune of Florence.

240 See Poggi/Haines, op. cit., 2, 129–30, doc. 2074.

241 See above, pp. 205–7.

242 The precise nature of Donatello's debt to classical art is much
debated. For example, Greenhalgh, *Donatello and his Sources*,
stressed the sculptor's classical models, while Dixon, "Drama
of Donatello's David," minimized the importance of such
influences. Most scholars emphasize the individual nature of
Donatello's classical borrowings and the personal genius by
which he transformed them; see particularly Pope-Hennessy,
Donatello, Sculptor. For a checklist of antique works known
to Donatello and others see Bober and Rubinstein, *Renaissance Artists and Antique Sculpture*. On the relation of the
David to the *Spinario* see Caglioti, "Donatello, I Medici, e
Gentile de' Becchi," III, 36–7.

243 Both of these works were by Donatello.

244 The literature on these two works is extensive; see footnotes
below and bibliography. Herzner, "Regesti Donatelliani,"
published the corpus of Donatello documents; Caglioti, op.
cit., pts. I–III, has republished many of those relating to the
Judith and the *David*, including the inscriptions, along with
an exhaustive account of the previous literature.

245 Sperling, op. cit., 219. This translation of the second inscription, which appears with slight variations in different manuscripts and whose meaning has been much contested, is by
Nicolai Rubinstein, and is informed by his peerless understanding of fifteenth-century political terms in the context of
their actual usage. See his account of the events of 1466, *Government of Florence*, pt. II. Some alternative translations are predicated upon very particular views of Medici motives and
intentions, and often erroneous assumptions about the family's
relation to the state. See the examples in various languages
cited by Caglioti, op. cit. I, n. 36. He reviewed the manuscripts
in which the two inscriptions appear and a letter of condolence addressed to Piero after Cosimo's death in 1464 referring to the first of them, 14–20. While these compilations of
poetry and letters throw valuable light on Florentine learned
culture, and on the interest in Cosimo's commissions, most of
them were made much later than the statue and were governed by their own conventions; they are much less reliable
evidence of the patron's views and identity than Caglioti suggested. His conclusion that Piero commmissioned the *Judith*,
while plausible on other grounds, is not really advanced by
this evidence; see also Brown, "Humanist Portrait of Cosimo,"
on the considerable gap between Cosimo's own limited claims
to power, in harmony with the views of his fellow-citizens,
and the exaggerated encomia of a poet such as Gentile Becchi,
dependent upon Medici patronage.

246 See Parronchi, *Donatello e il potere*, 23.

247 On these controversies see particularly Ames-Lewis,
"Donatello's Bronze *David*" and "Donatello's Bronze David
Reconsidered"; Caglioti, "Donatello, I Medici, e Gentile de'
Bacchi"; Dixon, "Drama of Donatello's David"; Herzner,
"David Florentinus"; Janson, *Donatello* and "La Signification
politique"; Pope-Hennessy, "Donatello's Bronze David" and
Donatello, Sculptor; Schneider, "Donatello's Bronze *David*" and
"More on Donatello's Bronze *David*"; Sperling, "Donatello's
Bronze *David*" and Spina Barelli, "Note iconografiche."

248   See especially Pope-Hennessy, "Donatello's Bronze David," cf. Janson, *Donatello*.

249   Paoletti, "Bargello David."

250   Janson, "La Signification politique."

251   See especially Pope-Hennessy, "Donatello's Bronze David."

252   Vasari attributed the base to Desiderio da Settignano; modern opinion has been sharply divided on this question. See particularly Parronchi, op. cit., Pope-Hennessy, op. cit., Caglioti, op. cit., III.

253   This and other inscriptions for Medici commissions contained in a book of poems and epigrams by Gentile Becchi compiled between 1460 and 1470, now in the Bodleian Library, was published by Grayson, "Poesie latine di Gentile Becchi," in 1973. Sperling, op. cit., especially 218–19, first used the inscription, which she observed in Ricc., 660, 85r, to reassess Donatello's work. However, her inferences about the dating of the epigram and the statue to 1428 are not acceptable, either on philological grounds or in terms of her arguments about the work's supposed relation to Cosimo's participation in the commune's wars. Just as Acidini, *Chapel of the Magi*, ch. 1, used Becchi's epigram on the Medici chapel to illuminate its meanings (see below, ch. 13), in reemphasizing Becchi's authorship of the inscription Caglioti, op. cit., especially II, has established its importance as an indication of how the Medici meant the work to be seen. See also his pt. 1, 14–16, on the slight variation between Ricc., 660 and Laur., Acquisti e Doni, 82, on the one hand, reading "frangit immanis deus hostis iras," and on the other Bodleian, Lat. Misc. e 81, "frangit iniusti deus hostis iras."

254   Janson, *Donatello*, 198.

255   Above, p. 52, and fig. 17. Butterfield, *Verrocchio*, 27–31, has recently reiterated the importance of this broader and more ancient political significance of David, whom Ambrose and Theodosius had represented as a symbol of just government by divine approbation. See also Herzner, *David Florentinus 1*, 90, ff.

256   Ettlinger, "Hercules Florentinus"; Ames-Lewis, "Donatello's Bronze David Reconsidered," 141.

257   This is clearly implied in the inscription attached to the marble *David* in the Palazzo Vecchio, which is echoed by the inscription for the Medici bronze *David*; see Rubinstein, *Palazzo Vecchio*, 55–6; Donato, "Hercules and David," especially 91. On this element in Florentine civic thought see Baron, *Crisis*; for its application to the *David*, Hartt, "Art and Freedom"; Janson, "La Signification politique." See also Hughes, "Representing the Family," especially 72–4, on the "replication of the exemplary person," a common-sense context for the representation of civic saints and heroes.

258   See Bruni, *Laudatio*, and Baron's comments on this, op. cit.

259   On these issues see above, pp. 88, 276.

260   Cf. the insistence of Sperling, op. cit., on the work's relation to the conflicts of the late 1420s and that of Herzner, "David Florentinus. II," that the *David* is an allegory of Medicean peace after the defeat of the Milanese and Florentine exiles in 1440.

261   See below, ch. 13.

262   For a recent, more subtle interpretation of the *David* in terms of "foreign versus domestic tyranny," see Crum, "Donatello's Bronze David," especially 448: the "Medici . . . sensitive to charges of tyranny . . . might well have commissioned the *David* and had its inscription composed in an effort to demonstrate, despite a high level of fraudulence, their commitment to republican liberty in Florence."

263   If we assume that the sculpture and its inscription refer to the defence of Florentine liberty in warfare, rather than to internal political arrangements, the evolution of Medici power ceases to have any putative relevance to its dating; it is not a question of what the Medici *dared* to do when, as is often argued. The extravagant use of bronze is probably the most daring aspect of the commission. Caglioti and Gasparotto, "Lorenzo Ghiberti," 16, assigned the work to *c.*1435–40, a dating to be justified at length in a fourth part of "Donatello, I Medici e Gentile de' Becchi," announced as forthcoming in *Prospettiva*.

264   Ames-Lewis, "Donatello's Bronze David Reconsidered," 142.

265   On this see particularly Winter, "Paradox and Parallel"; Butterfield, *Verrocchio*, loc. cit.

266   Kent, "I Medici in esilio," 42.

267   These are the terms in which Poggio represented Cosimo's exile in a letter to Niccoli; see Gordan, *Two Renaissance Book Hunters*, 193; see also Lapo da Castiglionchio and Ambrogio Traversari on the Medici exile as a reversal of fortune. See also below, pp. 363–6, on Fortune and the patronage oeuvre of Giovanni Rucellai.

268   Spina Barrelli, "Note iconografiche," especially 29. Valla's *De Voluptate* was supposedly inspired by a real conversation in Rome around 1427 between Leonardo Bruni, Niccolò Niccoli, and Antonio Beccadelli, called Panormita, all members of the Medici circle of intellectuals. Spini Barelli dated the *David* to this period and saw Niccoli as responsible for its iconography, 32.

269   On this manuscript see above, ch. 4; De La Mare, "Cosimo and His Books," 151–2; Ames-Lewis, *Library and Manuscripts of Piero*, 383, and "Donatello's Bronze David Reconsidered," 146. Pope Eugenius IV and San Bernardino both condemned the work, but the suggestion that Cosimo burned his copy was obviously a figment of later, overheated imaginations. Cf. De Cossart, *Antonio Beccadelli*, 10–11.

270   Rocke's study of the records of the Ufficiali della Notte, *Forbidden Friendships*, confirms the involvement of an unexpectedly large proportion of the Florentine population, both patrician and plebeian, in homosexual activity. Several writers have sought to justify the sensuality of the figure in alternative terms; see Fehl, "On the Representation of Character," 301–2, that the biblical David took off the armor Saul gave him; Dixon, "Drama of Donatello's David," 6–7, that he danced naked and joyous before the ark of the Lord; Pope-Hennessy, "Donatello's Bronze David," remarking the supportive function of the wing of Goliath's helmet that caresses David's inner thigh. Janson, *Donatello*, saw the bronze *David* as "not a classical ephebos, but the 'beautiful apprentice'"; Schneider, "Donatello's Bronze *David*" and "More on Donatello's Bronze *David*," not only assumed the artist's homosexuality as the foundation for the work, but also speculated that Cosimo had "an interest in, if not an inclination towards, homosexual practices." Concerning Donatello's homosexuality, see Jean Toscan, *Le Carneval du langage*, 1178–9, for a convincing reading of the well-known anecdote from Poliziano about Donatello and his apprentice "laughing" at one another, as a euphemism for sexual exchange. Shearman, *Only Connect*, 26, acknowledged the homoerotic nature of the relationship between the tri-

umphant David and his victim, locating it implicitly in a general social context where such a relationship would be familiar and readily recognizable, and explicitly in the more directly apposite context of the artist's solution of the problem of narration, as "an extraordinarily imaginative way of establishing the identity of David, the beloved," this meaning of David's name being the sort of thing that would be noticed by Renaissance spectators, as distinct from the preoccupations of modern art historians. Pope-Hennessy, "Donatello's Bronze David," 125, dismissed all such considerations out of hand, as "aberrant nonsense"; he scathingly rejected the "tarring" of "that cautious, devout figure Cosimo il Vecchio," as "unhistorical . . . thinking [which] left a little trail of slime on a great work of art." Since no evidence has as yet been unearthed concerning Cosimo's sexual life (the fathering of one illegitimate child is hardly significant in this respect), speculation about his sexual proclivities is quite unhistorical. However, while sexual innuendo plays no part in the anecdotes purporting to describe Cosimo's character, even he was credited with one joke about homosexuality. Once when he was in the piazza, a man described as "mad" turned to his companion, a well-known pederast, and said to him, "Bugger Cosimo!" Cosimo swung round and said, "Why not bugger him, since he'd enjoy it!" Poliziano, *Detti Piacevoli* 49, no. 134. On this anecdote, and the status of other such tales as evidence of culture or character, see Brown, "Wit and Wisdom."

271 For this tale and suggestions about what it tells us of the Renaissance *mentalité*, see Steinberg, *Sexuality of Christ*, 199–203; Davis, *Fiction in the Archives*, 31. Cf. Butterfield, *Verrocchio*, 243, n. 37, for a different view.

272 Brown, *Bartolomeo Scala*, 38. For Platonic or Neoplatonic interpretations of the *David* see particularly Ames-Lewis, "Donatello's Bronze David Reconsidered" and "Donatello's Bronze *David*." On the circulation of Platonic ideas, see Hankins, *Plato*.

273 On these see particularly Caglioti, "Lorenzo Ghiberti"; also Dacos, *Il Tesoro* I, 158; Schneider, "Donatello's Bronze *David*," 215; Ames-Lewis, "Donatello's Bronze David Reconsidered," 143. On the roundels, see Wester and Simon, "Die Reliefmedaillons." On the complex tradition of quotations of antique images by artists and patrons like the Medici and the Este see Sheard, "Antonio Lombardo's Reliefs." On Cosimo's collecting, see below, pp. 292–4.

274 See Fusco and Corti, *Lorenzo de' Medici, Collector*.

275 "Donatello, i Medici, e Gentile de' Becchi," III, 36–7.

276 Poliziano, *Detti piacevoli*, 33, no. 42.

277 Filelfo, cit. Hankins, "Platonic Academy" 35, n. 31; Nicodemo, cit. Massai, "Nicodemo da Pontremoli," 135, recounted by Simonetta, Sforza's court historian.

278 For this view, see Ames-Lewis, op. cit.; also Pope-Hennessy's observation, op. cit., 126, that "as always in Donatello, the classical sources of the figure are synthesized in a naturalistic vision which obscures their origin . . . and the resulting imagery is ambiguous for the simple reason that it is highly personal . . . unorthodox and inexplicit." Contemporaries described Donatello as "molto intricato"; see below, p. 343.

279 *Istoria*, 126, ff.

280 Ettlinger, "Hercules Florentinus," 119–21. Vasari claimed that Michelangelo, in his grief at Lorenzo's death in 1492, carved a giant Hercules four braccia high.

281 Ettlinger, op. cit., 123; Witt, *Hercules at the Crossroads*.

282 Jacks and Cafarro, *Tommaso Spinelli*, forthcoming.

283 Spallanzani and Bertelà, *Libro d'inventario*, 26.

284 For the letter, see Gilbert, *Italian Art*, 18. The small panels can also be linked by their provenance with the Medici, and may once have decorated a piece of furniture in the palace; see Ettlinger, op. cit., 129.

285 See, for example, Bulst, "Die *sala grande* des Palazzo Medici," who went beyond his very solid architectural evidence to make this argument mainly on the basis of the *Terze Rime*. See also Gombrich, "Early Medici as Patrons."

286 *Trattato*, 2, 697.

287 On this see also above, pp. 241–3. This view, first proposed by Wackernagel, *Florentine Renaissance Artist*, 237, n. 40, and reinforced by Gombrich, op. cit., 46, n. 8, 51, n. 2, has also been accepted by most students of Medici patronage, rather on the authority of these scholars' general distinction than any particular evidence adduced in this case.

288 See below, pp. 303–4. Until very recently, the only study focusing on Giovanni's interests, education, and collecting was Rossi, "L'indole." See now Lillie, "Giovanni di Cosimo."

289 For all these studies see Beyer and Boucher, *Piero de' Medici*, particularly Ames-Lewis, "Art in the Service of the Family"; Wright, "Piero de' Medici and the Pollaiuolo"; Zuraw, "Medici Portraits." Black, "Piero de' Medici and Arezzo," showed that Piero assumed on behalf of the Medici an authority in Arezzo previously wielded by Pitti; Böninger, "Diplomatie im Dienste der Kontinuität," argued that Piero's role in Ferrara and with Francesco Sforza was much more high-profile than Cosimo's. On Piero's patronage of art, see also Caglioti, *Donatello e i Medici*.

290 See above, p. 242. On Cosimo's education, see above, ch. 3; on Piero's books, see below, pp. 297–8.

291 See Vertova, "Cupid and Psyche"; Du Bon, "Medici Cassone."

292 See Goldthwaite, "Empire of Things" and "Building of Renaissance Florence"; Lydecker, "Domestic Setting of the Arts"; Schiaparelli, *La casa fiorentina*. One particular example for comparison with the Medici is the inventory of Marco Parenti's domestic possessions assembled after his marriage, discussed by Lydecker; see also Phillips, *Memoir of Marco Parenti*, ch. I. Giovanni Rucellai's account of his villa at Quaracchi also bears witness to the comfort, grace, and beauty of its accommodations and his pleasure in these; see below, pp. 362–3.

293 For an analysis of the addresses of these letters see Kent, *Fathers and Friends*.

294 See Rubinstein, *Government of Florence*, 127–8.

295 See above, p. 207.

296 On intarsia see Haines, *Sacrestia delle Messe*; Raggio and Wilmering, *Studiolo from the Ducal Palace*.

297 For the inventories of the *casa vecchia* of Giovanni di Bicci in 1417/18 and those listing Piero's possessions in 1456 and 1465, see Spallanzani, *Inventari Medicei*. The inventory of the palace after Lorenzo's death in 1492 is published by Spallanzani and Bertelà, *Libro d'inventario*; see also Dacos, Heikamp, and Grote, *Il tesoro di Lorenzo*. See also the earlier transcriptions and comments by Müntz, *Les Collections des Médicis*, and *Les Précurseurs de la Renaissance*; also Lydecker, "Domestic Setting of the Arts." A few domestic objects survive; in the British Museum there is a Hispano-Moresque lustreware vase, *c.*1465, with the Medici arms on one side and Piero's diamond ring and feathers on the other; see also Goldthwaite, "Italian Renaissance Maiolica."

298 Ibid., passim, for example, 122–3.

299 Spallanzani, *Inventari Medicei*, 24, 48. On dress in this period see particularly Frick, "Wedding and Conventual Trousseaux."

300 Spallanzani, op. cit., 72–5. This was in fact the tusk of a sea-mammal, the narwhal, commonly assumed to be the horn of a unicorn; see Welch, *Art and Society in Italy*, 39.

301 On cloth and high-cost clothing see Goldthwaite, *Building of Renaissance Florence*, 42ff. Garments in precious materials embroidered with gold, silver, and pearls were also an investment, appropriate to cloth merchants from a cloth manufacturing town.

302 BNF, II: IV: 324, 108r. Previously thought to be the work of Parenti's son Piero, this account has recently been reattributed to Marco. See Parenti, *Lettere*, introduction of the editor, Marrese, and appendix.

303 Cit. Brown, "Radical Alternative," 82; see also Pieraccini, *La stirpe de' Medici*, 1, 150.

304 These included an organ, MAP, v, 157; see also Spallanzani, *Inventari Medicei*, especially 128.

305 Ibid., 159. Michele del Giogante noted in one of his *zibaldoni*, Ricc., 2735, 171r, old num., that on 22 November 1437, he had sent Cosimo from Castel San Giovanni "un libretto di partiti di schacchi . . . il perchè rispondendomi adì 28 detto assai grazioso e cche l'avea a ricordo . . ."

306 Spallanzani, op. cit., 129.

307 Ibid., 23; see also 19, *anticamera*: "Un chorno d'osso da tenere [da voria] in tavola, fornito d'ariento dorato con pietre; Una choppa da cristallo intaglata chon piedistallo darïento [this re-appears in the inventories of Piero and Lorenzo]; Uno oriuolo di ferro stagnato paragino picolo appicato di fuori a l'armario." *Studiolo*, 22: "Una chonfectiera d'ariento dorata e smaltata; Una chonfectiera picchola d'ariento dorata; Uno orciuolo d'ariento dorato et smaltato. Una choppa di christallo in su tre piedi, fornita d'ariento smaltato, lavorato alla tedescha, chol choperchio simile, pesa lib. 6, vale f. 150 [also in Lorenzo's study, *Libro d'inventario*, 35]; Un chorno d'osso da tenere in tavola, fornito d'ariento dorato con pietre."

308 See above, especially pp. 277–9. Cosimo transported his books in a trunk which he described, presumably with reference to its decoration, as the "forzeretto degli armati," MAP, XIV, 467, cit. above, ch. 4. Information about armor in the first decades of the fifteenth century is very limited, by comparison with what is known about it in Lorenzo's day. I wish to thank Mr. Stuart Pyhrr, Curator of Arms and Armor at the Metropolitan Museum of Art, New York, for his help on this subject and his advice concerning the identification of items in Cosimo's collection. On armor see Cardini and Tangheroni, *Guerra e guerrieri*; Boccia, "Le Armature di Paolo Uccello"; Boccia, *Armi Difensive*; Gebhardt, "*Schlacht von San Romano*"; Scalini, "L'armatura fiorentina." The Pupilli records from which Scalini's information is drawn do not evoke a clear picture of early armor, but as he pointed out, 108, Apollonio di Giovanni's *cassone* panel picturing a joust of 1439 matches Piero de' Medici's descriptions of his armor in 1456. Cf. Del Corazza on jousting armor in 1406, above, p. 61.

309 See Kent, "Michele del Giogante's House of Memory," 33; also Granato, "Location of the Armory in the Italian Renaissance Palace."

310 MAP, II, 452, to Pierfrancesco di Lorenzo de' Medici in Trebbio. "In Firenze adì 17 di marzo, 1458, Chosimo de' Medici. Questo dì ho avuto una tua lettera et inteso quanto mi schrivi sopra'l fatto del tuo chavallo, avendo inteso della giostra si debbe fare per la venuta del chonte Ghaleazzo, et chome aresti il pensiero et volere giostrare se io me ne chontentassi. Io non chredetti tu fussi in tal pensiero, avendoti sentito dire più volte in non avere pensiero più a giostrare, et per queste chagione non chredevo avessi di bisognio del chavallo, et anchora mi pareva non fosse da entrare in questa spesa per te al presente; pure se ttu te ne chontentassi io sarò chontento a quello vorrai tu. Quando tu non diliberassi giostrare che chredo sarebbe migliore diliberazione et tu volessi mettere uno giostrante in champo mi piacierebbe, ma vorrebbe esser ciptadino et persona da bene et più tosto di chasa nostra che altri per honore della chasa, et chrederei che uno di que' figliuoli di Chambio fosse buono a questo servigio et che uscisse di chasa tua et sarebbeti ghrande honore et saresti schusato a volere il chavallo per te. Ma quando tu non giostrassi tu per non volessi questa brigha nè questa spesa per mettere uno giostratore in champo, bisogna chettu presti il chavallo tuo a questa giostra che non si adoperando te ne seghuirebbe charicho ghrande, avisandoti chesse ci fusse chavalli ci sarebbono xx giostratori, e per averne s'è schripto a tutti i signiori dattorno insino al Re Ferando perchè questa è festa della chomunità et fassi per honore della ciptà et non per altre leggieri chagioni come s'è chostumato più volte. Il papa verrà a mezo Aprile. Il chonte Ghaleazo ci sarà prima, sicchè ti conforto achonciare quanto più presto puoi, perchè volendo giostrare o mettere uno in champo non bisogna perdere tempo et rispondimi quello che diliberi di fare. Ne altro per questa. Xpo ti ghuardi in Firenze adì 17 di marzo 1458."

311 Spallazani, *Inventari Medicei*, 17–18; for Piero's Damascene ware, 117–19.

312 Ibid.

313 Ibid., 17.

314 Ibid., 18–20; 35. These last items were probably for use in a tournament like the one described by Bartolomeo de' Benci, above, p. 80, or the joust staged in 1459 for the visit of Pius II and Galeazzo Maria Sforza, described by the author of the *Terze Rime*: "Every warrior wore a helmet/ encircled by a garland like a *mazzocchio*,/ beautifully decorated with silver scales,/ and with golden feathers rising from it,/ bright and shining like a star." Such a headress seems to be illustrated in that of the attendants of the youngest Magi in the Medici chapel, at the junction of the east and south walls.

315 See Gilbert, *Italian Art*, 207–8; also Smith, "Cyriacus of Ancona's Seven Drawings of Hagia Sophia."

316 See Vespasiano's lives of Cosimo and of Niccoli for a description of the latter's collection; Zippel, "Niccolò Niccoli," especially 102–3.

317 Wester, *Die Reliefmedaillons*, 34, said Filarete sold it to the patriarch of Constantinople; he sold it to Pope Eugenius's doctor, and it passed eventually to Lorenzo. Cf. Ghiberti, *Commentari*. These accounts tell slightly different stories. Ghiberti's description relates to the effect of light on the gem, which he had seen in Niccoli's collection; see Niccoli's will, and Holmes, *Florentine Enlightenment*, 229.

318 Müntz, *Les Collections des Médicis*, 5, cf. Fusco, *Medici as Collectors of Antiquities*; on this see now Caglioti, "Due 'restauratori.'"

319 For Ghiberti's account see his *Commentari*; also his Catasto report, published Krautheimer, *Ghiberti*, 399, doc. 154. See also Spallanzani and Bertelà, *Libro d'Inventario*, 39: "Una chorgnuola grande con tre fighure intagl[i]ate di chavo e più che mezzo rilievo, una parte gnuda et ritta, chon una lira in mano, con una fighura ginochioni gnuda a' piedi, l'altra testa di vechio a sedere cholle mani dirieto leghato a uno albero, sanza fondo, trasparente, leghato in oro." For the complex history of this work see Caglioti and Gasparotto, "Lorenzo Ghiberti."

320 Spallanzani and Bertelà, op. cit., 36: "Uno corno d'unichorno lungho br. 3½ stimiamllo f. 6000 . . . Una schodella di sardonio e chalcidonio e aghata, entrovi più figure et di fuori una testa di Medusa, pesa lib. 2 once 6, f. 10,000."

321 On the Medici dealings in the venture trade see De Roover, *Rise and Decline*. Their correspondence shows that they procured tapestries and books for the Manfredi of Faenza, among others. Bartolomeo Serragli, whose wife Lena was a member of the Pucci family who had provided the Medici with some of their most reliable support since the 1420s, was an art dealer who often assisted Piero and Giovanni. In 1451 Serragli was absolved from the general ban of exile imposed on his family since 1444, and wrote to Giovanni shortly before he died in 1458 asking him to procure for him a seat on the Signoria; see Corti and Hartt, "New Documents," 156 ff. Procuring ancient objects was one of the services various *amici* competed to offer their patrons. Serragli sent dozens of letters to Giovanni de' Medici in the 1450s, explaining to him in one from Rome, MAP, VIII, 361, 31 Oct. 1453: "You know how much I would like to find some ancient object for you, and have not given up hope, but to date I haven't found anything, because I don't have many contacts here." Leonardo Vernacci, he continued, "has many of them in his hands, but doesn't want to give them to me; he says he wants to give them to you himself." Serragli wrote that he wanted to alert Giovanni, lest the objects slip through his fingers; they included the *Mark Antony* and the *Hercules* he had mentioned in his letter sent four days before. Some of the reason for his concern was undoubtedly that the trade in ancient Roman objects was illegal, because exporting them was forbidden. As Giovanni Tornabuoni wrote to Piero in 1462: "I am waiting for a carrier [to Florence], and I will send you the Hercules when the pope leaves . . . It cannot be done without danger; these Romans keep a sharp eye on these things. I will do my best," MAP, CLXXI, 324, 30 April 1462.

322 See Elam, "Art and Diplomacy"; below, pp. 334–7.

323 See below, pp. 303–4.

324 On all these studies and the sequence in which they were built, see Liebenwein, *Studiolo*. On Piero's, see especially Bulst, "Die *sala grande* des Palazzo Medici," 384–5. Diomede Carafa, a Neapolitan courtier and friend of Lorenzo, recreated Piero's *studiolo* in his own palace c.1467, based on a painted copy he had the Strozzi obtain for him; see Borsook, "A Florentine *Scrittoio*," especially 92. On the *studiolo* at Urbino, see Cheles, *Studiolo of Urbino*; Raggio, *Studiolo from the Ducal Palace*.

325 A repetition of the theme of Cosimo's poem to Sforza, above, ch. 2.

326 See Hatfield, "Some Unknown Descriptions," appendix 1.

327 Cit. Bulst with comment, op. cit., 390.

328 On the roundels, see Pope-Hennessy, *Luca della Robbia*;

Ames-Lewis, "Art in the Service of the Family." Similar images appear in a *Breviarium Romanum* which was the most highly valued of all Piero's manuscripts in the 1464/5 inventory, and the most richly decorated by far to survive from his library. For each month there is a border decoration, contained within a frame of two diamond rings, of small scenes representing mythological gods and signs of the zodiac; see Ames-Lewis, *Library and Manuscripts of Piero*, 358–9.

329 Portioli, *I Gonzaga ai Bagni*.

330 See Filarete, *Trattato* 2, 686; also Ames-Lewis, *Library and Manuscripts of Piero*, especially 31–8 on the bindings colored according to subject, and the catalogue of manuscripts, 233–361, describing the decoration and illumination of each work.

331 See Ames-Lewis, op. cit., especially 7–9, 289, 93, 302. Apart from an extensive range of classical histories headed by Livy and Plutarch, Piero owned his own copy of Bruni's *History of Florence*, which had been presented to Cosimo, Bruni's *De temporibus suis*, and the dedication copy of Matteo Palmieri's work of the same name.

332 Spallanzani, *Inventari Medicei*, 49. See also Ames-Lewis, op. cit., 336–7; the manuscript is Petrarch's *Canzoni e Sonetti, Trionfi*, Paris, Bibliothèque Nationale, MS. Ital. 1471, done in the workshop of Filippo di Matteo Torelli, on whom see below, p. 342.

333 Lanza, *Lirici toscani* 1, 383, cf. above, p. 72.

334 Cit. Baxandall, *Giotto and the Orators*, 60. His inspirational effect is apparent in the praise and emulation of his work in so many *zibaldoni*, and Palla Strozzi bought a villa at Monselice near where Petrarch had lived and died, a gesture, Amanda Lillie suggested, of secular piety from a man forcibly cut off from Florence and her traditions; see her "Memory of Place," 208.

335 For the *desco da parto* see Spallanzani and Bertelà, *Libro d'inventario*, 27. Bellosi and Haines, *Lo Scheggia*, 10, remarked the compositional similarities between Scheggia's *Triumph of Fame* birthtray and Domenico Veneziano's Magi tondo. Lorenzo himself became quite a talented poet in the Petrarchan vein; among much other literature on this, see Kennedy, "Petrarchan Figurations of Death in Lorenzo de' Medici's Sonnets."

336 See Virgilius, *Opera, Bucolica, Georgica*, and *Aeneis*; Kallendorf, "Cristoforo Landino's *Aeneid* and the Humanist Critical Tradition" and *In Praise of Aeneas*; Field, "Manuscript of Cristoforo Landino's First Lectures on Virgil."

337 De La Mare, "Cosimo and his Books," 127. Piero owned a copy also of Columella's agricultural treatise; see Ames-Lewis, *Library and Manuscripts of Piero*, 227, catalogue no. 39.

338 *Vite* 2, 194–5.

339 Above, i.

340 See MAP, CXXXI; Carl, "La Casa Vecchia," 39, n. 40. For the Medici palace gardens see MAP, CLXXXVI, 38, esp. cc. 339–40, and ibid., CXXXI.

341 *Building of Renaissance Florence*, 103.

342 Bulst, "Die *sala grande* des Palazzo Medici," fig. 1, 91, also "L'uso e trasformazione"; Saalman and Mattox, "First Medici Palace."

343 On the details of the design of the garden, and their role in its integration with the palace, see particularly Looper, "Political Messages in the Medici Palace Garden."

344 Hatfield, "Some Unknown Descriptions," 234.

345 *Purgatorio*, XXXII; *Paradiso*, XXXII; Looper, op. cit., 260–61. See

also Watson, *Garden of Love*, for the literary and visual traditions linking gardens with both earthly and spiritual love.

346 Above, p. 283, and *Paradiso*, XXXII, 10, where in the garden of Dante's celestial rose, Judith is seated directly under the Virgin, as noted by Looper, op. cit., 263.

347 Looper's contention, 225, that this republican message is balanced by "strong princely overtones. . . . to cast Cosimo in a princely light" in the garden's layout and iconography, is more assumed and asserted than demonstrated.

348 Foster, *Lorenzo de' Medici's Villa*, observes that Poggio a Caiano was a working farm, and even had a model dairy. Giovanni di Bicci's and Cosimo's Catasto reports detail the produce from their estates. Cosimo retired to the Mugello for some months in 1433 when he sensed a coup in the offing.

349 "Giovanni di Cosimo." On the Medici villas see particularly Ackerman, "Sources of the Renaissance Villa," 8, and *Villa: Form and Ideology*, ch. 3. For the architectural history of these villas and the relevant documents, see Ferrara and Quinterio, *Michelozzo*. On their landholdings and relation to the neighboring *contado* see Casali, "I passaggi di proprietà." See also Diana, "Interventi Medicei in Mugello"; Natali, "Cosimo il Vecchio, la campagna e due tracce michelozziane." For a more detailed account of villas see Lillie's study of the Strozzi and Sassetti properties, "Florentine Villas."

350 *Villa*, 359; *De Re Aedificatoria*, 790–91.

351 See above, p. 257.

352 For the chapel furniture at Careggi and Cafaggiolo in 1465, including rich vestments and altar cloths, see Spallanzani, op. cit., 159–61.

353 On this see also Ferrara and Quinterio, op. cit., 179.

354 MAP, XVI, 153, in Lorenzo, *Lettere* 1, 3–4, cit. above, p. 170.

355 For descriptions from the Catasto see above, p. 467, n. 95.

356 See above, p. 171.

357 "Attendiamo rimandare questi boschi del parcho, e anchora disideriamo la festa come i fanciulli . . . ," MAP, XVI, 69, 3 Sept. 1446; see also V, 451.

358 See above, p. 35.

359 See Spallanzani and Bertelà, op. cit., 141.

360 Poliziano, *Detti Piacevoli*, 25, no. 3.

361 "Giovanni di Cosimo," 191. On Giovanni's villa see also Bargellini and De La Ruffinière, "Sources for a Reconstruction of the Villa Medici"; Ackerman, *Villa: Form and Ideology*.

362 See, for example, MAP, IX, 146, from Giovanni Macinghi in 1455, on the complex arrangements for the provision of water; also ibid., 139, on the fact that these were proceeding well, and CXXXVII, 68, on the occasion when a wall collapsed.

363 See Foster, "Donatello Notices in Medici Letters."

364 MAP, VIII, 336.

365 Ibid., V, 722, 9 Apr. 1454.

366 Portioli, *I Gonzaga ai Bagni*, 44.

367 On this see Lillie, op. cit.

368 Brown, *Bartolomeo Scala*, 17–18.

369 Lanza, *Lirici toscani* 2, 479.

Chapter XIII

1 Iacopo da Voragine, *Golden Legend* 1, 79.

2 See particularly Trexler, *Journey of the Magi*; also "Magi Enter Florence"; Trexler and Lewis, "Two Captains and Three Kings."

3 The earliest and most extreme statement of this view is by Trexler, *Public Life*, 424: "The festivity of the Magi commented on the economic wealth of the city, asserted its citizens' noble character, and, over the years, established the royal pretensions of its leading family." See also below, n. 24. Conversely the same author, in his later extensive studies of the Magi, above, n. 2, painted a more complex picture. Writing of another Medici chapel, designed by Michelangelo for San Lorenzo's new sacristy, he identified its "central iconographic content" as the Journey of the Magi and their Adoration of the child; see "Two Captains and Three Kings," 124. He saw it as offering "a vivid contrast between the darkness of time and the light of eternity in the form of an almost Petrarchan progression from wordly to spiritual triumph . . . As the captains live through their family, the spirit of that family lives because Christ has risen," 123. This would seem to me the major message also of the palace chapel. On other Magi images in the palace, see above, especially p. 252. As Hatfield observed, "Compagnia de' Magi," 137, no representations of the Magi appear in the inventory of Giovanni di Bicci's house in 1418, suggesting that the Medici attachment to the Magi was developed by Cosimo around or after the 1420s.

4 See above, p. 177.

5 Above, p. 155, and fig. 61, also p. 252.

6 See especially Hatfield, op. cit., 108; Trexler, various.

7 See particularly Hatfield, *Botticelli's Uffizi "Adoration."*

8 Hatfield, "Compagnia de' Magi," 139.

9 This simile is Acidini's; see "Chapel of the Magi," 7. Although the description of the chapel that follows is my own, it is indebted to her vivid ekphrasis as well as to her technical expertise as supervisor of the recent restorations. Hatfield, "Cosimo de' Medici and the Chapel," argued that the altarpiece is not literally the goal of the procession, nor the focus of its attention. The cortège of the oldest Magi winds away up the hill and "no one is looking at the star." However, as Acidini observed, the compositional problems of concentrating a cortège spread over three walls on the sole focus of the altar would have been considerable. It seems to me undeniable that the spiritual message of progress is a powerful one, and the suggestion that the frescoes and the altarpieces were not necessarily connected in the mind of patron and artists seems implausible in view of the importance to Cosimo of this chapel, the attention lavished on the ensemble, and the general sophistication, even intellectualism, of the other religious commissions of the last decade of his life.

10 On the papal dispensation to allow Giovanni di Bicci de' Medici to have a portable altar, which would permit the celebration of mass in his house, and the several images which might have served as part of an informal "chapel," see above, p. 247, ff. For the text of a similar dispensation for Cosimo and his wife Contessina, see Saalman and Mattox, "First Medici Palace," appendix VI. Olivieri de' Cerchi had a chapel in his house in the 1290s; see Cole Ahl, *Benozzo Gozzoli*, 88.

11 See below, n. 28, ff.

12 The passages from these Milanese letters, partially published by Magnani, *Relazioni private*, xiv, were first cited and discussed by Hatfield, "Some Unknown Descriptions."

13 Hatfield, "Cosimo de' Medici and the Chapel," 228.

14 BNF, Magl. VII, 1121. The poet continued with an appraisal of its style: "L'altare v'era parato molto herile,/ d'argiento et

15 Cit. Rubinstein, *Government of Florence*, 132, and ff. Although Rubinstein spoke of "observers" it is important to note that the comment was made in a private dispatch of Nicodemo to Sforza, conserved in Paris, Bibliothèque Nationale, Fonds Italiens, MS 1588, 114r.

oro et velluto et brocchato,/ sanza pare nel moderno o nel senile," that is, timeless; see Hatfield, "Unknown descriptions," 248, on the use of "senile" interchangeably with "antico."

16 Noted by Hatfield, "Cosimo de' Medici and the Chapel," 226. The author of the *Terze Rime* also reported, 39, that Cosimo uttered these words. The context of this comment in the biblical account, Luke, 2:26, is that it was revealed to Simeon "by the Holy Ghost, that he should not see death, before he had seen the Lord's Christ."

17 For an analysis of their correspondence see below, pp. 339–41.

18 See initially Gombrich, "Early Medici as Patrons," 50, and figs. 76–8. While there is a pattern in the patronage of the Medici lineage suggesting a desire to emulate and outdo the commissions of their most distinguished rivals, the Strozzi (see below, p. 355), the interpretation of these borrowings in terms mainly of Cosimo's "thirst for competition" (Acidini, "Procession of the Magi," 40) should perhaps be modified by the observation that Gentile's altarpiece served as a model for most artists' representations of the Magi in the quattrocento. There are also notable similarities between Gozzoli's frescoes and Domenico Veneziano's earlier tondo for the Medici, see above, pp. 252–9, and figs. 117 and 118.

19 Iacopo da Voragine, *Golden Legend* 1, 82. The relics were supposed subsequently to have been moved to Cologne, but the Milanese remained among the most ardent observers of their cult. See Trexler, various.

20 *Michelozzo* 2, 549–50.

21 Acidini, "Chapel of the Magi," 15.

22 On the pavement see particularly Bartoli, "Neoplatonic Pavement," 25–8.

23 On this see below, pp. 382–4.

24 See above, p. 188. The most eloquent argument for a secular and "political" significance for the porphyry rota in the Medici chapel is advanced by Beyer, "Funktion und Repräsentation," especially 154; he argued that when Cosimo received his guests in the chapel he "must" have stood on the porphyry circle, and that in doing so he must also consciously have emulated Byzantine court ceremonial. He referred to Déer, *Dynastic Porphyry Tombs*, who suggested that the implications of the twelfth-century Hohenstaufen use in their Sicilian kingdom of porphyry rotae are primarily monarchical, and only secondarily liturgical, 137. However, Déer also noted that the early Christian use of porphyry rotae was "without monarchical implications, despite the closeness to imperial forms of display; nor is it specifically papal in the later sense of the word," but rather "a consequence of the great Constantinian revolution whereby the church of the martyrs became the church of the empire," 136. In the absence of any evidence of Cosimo's actual beliefs, it seems more likely to me that Cosimo was following early Christian custom than harboring imperial ambitions. Butters observed in her definitive study of the Medici use of porphyry in the sixteenth century, *Triumph of Vulcan*, 122, that the porphyry roundels in the pavement of the Medici chapel are adequately justified by the presence of

Christ in the altarpiece and in the Magi procession. On these questions see also below, pp. 382–4.

25 Acidini, "La cappella medicea attraverso cinque secoli," 89–90.

26 Acidini, "Chapel of the Magi," 11–15, drawing on Grayson, "Poesie latine di Gentile Becchi," gave a full account of the inscription for the chapel which appears in several manuscripts; see above, p. 283, and below, p. 473, n. 245, p. 474. n. 253.

27 He was appointed as priest to the church of San Giovannino, opposite the Medici palace, in 1450; for this and other details of his relations with the Medici see Rochon, *La Jeunesse de Laurent*, 31ff.

28 Hatfield, "Compagnia de' Magi," 123, 151–2; Filippo Martelli in Rome to Lorenzo: "Abbiamo spedito una indulgenzia per la Vostra compagnia, 'ssendo il disegno dato per messer Gentile . . ." For Becchi's encomiastic verse, see Brown, "Humanist Portrait of Cosimo."

29 On the works of Saint Jerome in Cosimo's library see De La Mare, op. cit., 126, 142. On popular vernacular copies of his works, above, p. 84.

30 Hood, "State of Research," 176.

31 "Benozzo Gozzoli's Oeuvre," 358. Similarly, one might perceive in the play of surface decoration in the Pazzi chapel not a dilution, but rather a modernization of the powerfully architectonic values of Brunelleschi's early buildings like the Medici old sacristy.

32 Ibid.; Cole Ahl, *Benozzo Gozzoli*, ch. 5.

33 For a general comment on the San Marco Magi fresco, see Hood, *Fra Angelico at San Marco*, 250; for Ames-Lewis's proposal that Gemistus Pletho was the figure at the center of the composition, above, p. 155.

34 *On Painting*, 93.

35 On Gozzoli's relations with the Medici, below, ch. 14, ii; for his self-portraits, see Cole Ahl, ch. 3, 96–8; Acidini, "Medici and Citizens," 367–8.

36 "Cosimo de' Medici and the Chapel," 222.

37 "Early Medici as Patrons," 49.

38 See Gombrich, op. cit., loc. cit. On Medici commissions which seem to refer to the Council, see above, pp. 192–7. For the historiography of the Council of Florence and some new proposals to associate the frescoes with this event, see Crum, "Roberto Martelli, the Council of Florence," See also Deimling's observation, "Meeting of the Queen of Sheba," 20, that the aims and undertakings of the council of East–West union took on new significance after the fall of Constantinople in 1453; this is surely apparent also in Pius II's call for a new crusade in the early 1460s.

39 Gill, *Eugenius IV*, 134, 150.

40 See BNF, II: I: 102; II: II: 39, flyleaf: "Questo libro è di me Michele di Nofri del Giogante ragioniere da Firenze, scritto il forte di mia mano nel 1453 et 1454"; 104–106: "Cose maravigliose del Pressto Giovanni." Ser Alesso, MAP, V, 418, wrote: "Scrissiti come frater Alberto fu mandato dal Presto Giovanni . . . ambasceria di questo Giovanni e da molti signoria d'India et di non so chi dal Cairo che si conclude molta ragione . . . e anno partito 2 anni avorie di tanto lungo paese vengono . . . grande exaltazione da nostra sede per tutta questa setimana . . ." The Laurenziana library contains a number of Ethiopian manuscripts apparently acquired around this time; see, for example, Gaddi, 230, for liturgical books

and "sacre orazioni e preghiere che si practicano nel paese degli Abissini . . ."

41 Hofman, *Kopten und Aethiopier auf dem Konzil*; Gill, *Personalities of the Council*, 63.

42 The popular imagination harbored a vivid image of Ethiopians: the Sienese preacher Fra Filippo described in his sermons the miserable deaths of usurers, taken away by "men black as Ethiopia, dark and terrible beyond all imagining," Heywood, *Ensamples of Fra Filippo*, 140. The following observations concerning the Magi company owe much to Hatfield's classic study, "Compagnia de' Magi."

43 Ibid., 137.

44 On this see Mauss, *Gift*; Davis, "Gifts of Montaigne"; Kent, *Fathers and Friends*.

45 Hatfield, op. cit., 109–10.

46 Lanza, *Lirici toscani* 2, 211.

47 Fabriczy, "Michelozzo di Bartolomeo," 94, lists the *festaiuoli* from ASF, Signori e Collegi, Deliberazioni, 65, 24v, Nov./Dec. 1446.

48 Fabriczy, op. cit., 93.

49 "Messer Rossello ha arrecato a Cosimo una bella ciopa a la polacca di martore e zibellini e uno pajo di guanti e uno dente di pesce [che] è lungo un' braccio; ché abiendosi a fare più la festa de' Magi, queste cose daràno un po' di risquitto al mio drapo a oro," MAP, VIII, 136.

50 Gill, *Eugenius IV*, 132–3.

51 Gill, *Council of Florence*, 305–10. To commemorate the accord, a medal was struck depicting Eugenius, Saint Peter, Palaeologus, and the Armenian patriarch. Pope Eugenius also commemorated the church council with an inscription on the bronze doors for St. Peter's in Rome, made by Filarete; see Gill, *Eugenius IV*, 64.

52 For the slave trade in general, see Origo, "Domestic Enemy"; on the Medici slaves, Spencer, "Note on Slavery." Cosimo had an Armenian slave, who was the mother of his illegitimate son Carlo. She may have been among those to whom Cosimo and Lorenzo gave their freedom at this time.

53 "Achattate una cioppa alla ghrecha a Bechone et mandatelo per imbasciadore allo'mperadore per parte del re d'Armenia, et ghuardate s'ebbi aviso dacciò. Il piovano da San Ghavino non m'a fatto molto, sicchè io non so di quella s'abbia di bisognio per le feste; sello saprò lo provedrò. Voi fareste bene a venire a socchorrere questa vostra persa che a i chapelli alla ghrecha a pie de' frati di San Franceschо dell'Osservanza. Era la più bella chosa del mondo et vanne infummo," MAP, XI, 268. The letter had begun: "La pportatore di questa sarà Bechone nostro lavoratore il quale a dato moglie a Marcho suo fratello: ordina a Ser Alesso lo meni al notaio dell'arte del chambio et facali confessare l. 50 de' danari d'Averardo; questa è una di quelle fanciulle che rimase sola in champo litardi." This may be one of the many cases of Medici charity given in the form of dowries donated to marry off poor girls. On the working-class district of Campo Litardi and the involvement of its residents in radical politics see Cohn, *Laboring Classes*; Trexler, "Neighbours and Comrades." The nickname "Becchone," meaning stupid or "thick," was popularized by Boccaccio's *Centonovelle*, 73:21, 75:9, and taken up in the fifteenth century by the popular satirical poet Burchiello. In his letter Lorenzo went on to discuss the seasonal work of the estate at Trebbio, which Gozzoli represented in idealized form in the chapel frescoes, observing,

among other things, that "le lignee faremo mandare poi che ssi potrà innanzi la richolta." Cosimo and Lorenzo not only oversaw, but sometimes participated in agricultural work at their country villas.

54 Hatfield, op. cit., 113.

55 See Trexler, *Public Life*, 401–7; Hatfield, "Compagnia de' Magi," 120–21, 148.

56 See Kent and Kent, "Two Vignettes," 259.

57 BNF, II: IV: 128, 37v–38r. On Pigli's other compilations see above, pp. 104, 119.

58 Hatfield, op. cit., 148.

59 On this see also above, pp. 193, 196–7; also Bizzocchi, "Concilio, papato e firenze"; Pontani, "Firenze nelle fonti greche del Concilio"; Zaccaria, "Documenti e Testimonianze Inedite," relating to the council.

60 See Acidini, "Procession of the Magi," 41, for a schema of these correspondences of threes; also Iacopo da Voragine, *Golden Legend* 1, 83.

61 On such portraits of buildings in paintings see Ackerman, *Villa: Form and Ideology*, 62.

62 Bernard of Clairvaux, *Steps of Humility*, especially ch. 7, "Quomodo Sancta Trinitas hos tres veritatis gradis in nobis operetur," 161–2.

63 See her chapter, "Medici and Citizens," on which the following discussion of portraits is largely based, and Hatfield, "Cosimo de' Medici and the Chapel"; for an earlier view, see Langedijk, *Portraits of the Medici*.

64 See Cosimo's letter to Piero at Bagno a Corsina, MAP, XVII, 306, cit. also below, n. 77. In September 1468 Francesco Fracassini, factor at Cafaggiolo wrote to Piero, ibid., XVII, 642: "Ier mattina Mona Chontessina, Lorenzo e Giuliano cholla brigata di chasa adarono a chavallo al luogo de' frati al Boscho e quivi udirono la messa grande, che si disse innanzi alla tavola mandaste di San Giuliano dinanzi alla quale i frati avevano horevolmente parato . . . Mona Chontessina chavalcò la mula di Lorenzo et maravigliasi di sè parendole riuscire più gagliarda non credeva . . ."

65 See Saalman, "A Cosimo Portrait?" and Gebhardt, "Ein Porträt Cosimo de' Medicis"; also below, pp. 381–2. Gombrich, "Early Medici as Patrons," 50, drew attention to a head of Cosimo in a manuscript of Aristotle, *Opera varia*, Laur., Plut. 84. 1, 2r, dated to the third quarter of the fifteenth century.

66 MAP, VI, 300.

67 See below, pp. 339–40; on the Martelli family and their role in Medici affairs see also above, pp. 179–83, and below, p. 452, n. 138, and Crum, "Roberto Martelli, The Council of Florence."

68 Acidini, "Medici and Citizens," 367–8; De Roover, *Rise and Decline*.

69 There are several examples of such panels, of uncertain attribution, in the National Gallery of Art, Washington, D.C.; see its *Catalogue of European Paintings*.

70 "Medici and Citizens," 363.

71 See above, ch. 12, esp. pp. 241–4; also, for example, MAP, VI, 300; VIII, 200.

72 Padoa Rizzo, "Benozzo Gozzoli's Oeuvre," 362.

73 Cit. Acidini, *Chapel of the Magi*, 126.

74 See Spallanzani, *Inventari Medicei*, and above, pp. 291–2.

75 On this see Cole Ahl, *Benozzo Gozzoli*, 92.

76 Padoa Rizzo, op. cit., 358–9.

77 MAP, XVII, 306.

78 For Cosimo's tax report, MAP, LXXXIII, 598r; on the funeral, see below, conclusion, pp. 375–7.

79 On the Medici villas, see pp. 300–04. Giovanni di Cosimo was godfather to a son of Matteo, factor at Cafaggiolo, MAP, V, 319, 446. A major example of Cosimo's concern with the affairs of this rural community is his defence of an unjustly accused man from Gagliano, discussed above, ch. 10, p. 170. The Medici and their friends intervened in an attempt to solve a worker's problems on another occasion in 1450, when a man was beating up his wife; Piero was asked to arrange with the girl's father to remove her from her husband's house by stealth, and take her to a priest, MAP, XVI, 46.

80 See his *Bertoldo*, a study of an artist and member of the Medici household.

81 *Benozzo Gozzoli*, 88; as she observed, Gozzoli does not appear in major studies of landscape like that of Turner, *Vision of Landscape*, because these are concerned with the avant-garde naturalism of artists like Leonardo.

82 *Vite* 2, 194.

83 MAP, VI, 300.

84 See above, ch. 12, pp. 302–3.

85 MAP, V, 587, 17 April 1445, written "in Firenze nel palagio de' Signoria" to Giovanni in Rome. Cf. ibid., 390, 11 Aug. 1440, Lorenzo de' Medici from Trebbio to Giovanni di Cosimo in Florence, advising him that he had sent to Guido Bonciani for one of his dogs.

86 Ibid., 487, 6 Nov. 1443. See also Brown, "Radical Alternative," on his enthusiasm for hunting.

87 Acidini, *Chapel of the Medici*, 257, pointed out that "features from two well-known antique prototypes, which were familiar through numerous copies, are combined in the stance of the hooded old man: the crossed legs are taken from Scopas's *Pothos*, and the cudgel on which he supports himself from *Hercules at Rest*."

88 See Acidini's comment, ibid., 264–7, on the angels which concerned Piero and his agent Martelli, cf. below, ch. 14, pp. 339–40, on the correspondence between patron and artist relating to these figures.

89 As Baxandall observed, *Painting and Experience*, pt. 1, dancing was an element of quattrocento experience which viewers brought to looking at paintings. This was particularly true of Gozzoli's Medici patrons, many of whose letters describe the dancing at family entertainments. Luca della Robbia's *cantoria* for the cathedral (fig. 89) is a particularly vivid sculptural representation of dancing, and for a demonstrable example of the Medicean application of dancing to painting see Jayne, "Choreography by Lorenzo."

90 Piero's library contained a number of musical manuscripts, and the exchange of songs is also a frequent subject of letters.

91 Cf. the representation described in the 1417/18 inventory of the Medici house, of Saint Lawrence dressed as a deacon, in which capacity he distributed charity to the poor; see above, ch. 12, p. 247; also Paoletti, "Familiar Objects."

92 See above, ch. 12, p. 300.

93 Spallanzi and Bertelà, *Libro d'inventario*, 43, 59.

94 Acidini, op. cit., 340.

95 For the range of speculations concerning the star, ibid., 267. On Bernardino's device, see above, ch. 7, pp. 101–2. It also appears in later Medici manuscripts, see Krinsky, "View of the Palazzo Medici." On Medici interest in San Bernardino see above, passim, and especially p. 171.

96 Lanza *Lirici toscani* I, 122; cf. Lorenzo Benci, ibid., 254: "Oh, quanto è grande la tua carità . . ."

97 *Fra Filippo Lippi*, 224–30. Among these were also the well-established visual traditions of representing elements of the iconography, particularly of Saint Bernard. On this see Dal Prà, *Bernardo di Chiaravalle nell'arte italiana*; Lesher, "Private and Public Images of Bernard of Clairvaux."

98 Above, pp. 86, 87.

99 See Ruda, op. cit., ch. 6. Lavin, "Giovannino Battista" and "Supplement," first drew attention to the influence of the *Revelations* of Saint Bridget and Cavalca's *Life of St. John the Baptist* on the iconography of this painting.

100 On this see ibid., 230–32.

101 Lavin, "Giovannino Battista."

102 See especially John, 5:1.

103 Lavin, "Giovannino Battista."

104 *Paradiso*, XXXII, 85–7.

105 Ibid., XXXIII, 1–2.

106 "Filippino Lippi's 'The Virgin in Spirit,'" 176.

107 *Golden Legend* 1, 82.

108 De La Mare, "Cosimo and his Books," 126, inventory of 1417/18 no. 49. On the books for Fiesole, see Hatfield, "Cosimo de' Medici and the Chapel," 241, n. 94; Bandini, *Supplementum* 11, iii, cods. 75–7.

109 See *Golden Legend* 1, 103–5; on Saint Bernard and the Signoria, and on his writings most frequently copied by Florentines, above, p. 84.

110 Strozzi, "Adoration of the Child," 29. See above, p. 112, for Abbot Salviati's commission for Neri di Bicci of an altarpiece with Saint Bernard.

111 De La Mare, op. cit., 153, no. 76, Laur., San Marco 626. For Feo Belcari's correspondent, see above, p. 104, below, p. 436, n. 53; on Florentine Trinity images in paintings and poems, pp. 137–8, and figs. 50, 51.

112 Op. cit., 1, 42.

113 Lanza, *Lirici toscani* 1, 191.

114 *Golden Legend* 1, 79, 83.

115 Lanza, op. cit., 2, 120–23.

116 *Golden Legend*, op. cit., 1, 78: "On the feast day of the Lord's Epiphany four miracles are commemorated . . . On this day the Magi adored Christ, John baptized him, he changed water into wine, and he fed five thousand men with five loaves." The last two miracles are associated with charity.

117 Cf. Cole Ahl's comment, op. cit., 85, that "Cosimo's appropriation of Bernard and the Baptist for the altarpiece of his chapel was not a coincidence; it signified his role as *de facto* ruler in Florence and that of the Palazzo Medici as the true seat of power." This claim goes against the grain of her iconographical exegesis based on the biblical and devotional texts to which the panel clearly refers. It is a good example of the extent to which art historians have come to accept the need to frame Cosimo's commissions in political terms, whether or not this accords with their own more precise iconographical readings of these works.

118 Lanza, *Lirici toscani* 1, 254; for Tommaso's consolatory poem, ibid., 149.

119 Ibid., 1, 406. Cf. Iacopo Cocco-Donati's *lauda* to the Virgin, ibid., 587.

120 Cit. Ruda, op. cit., 228.

121 Cit. Hatfield, "Compagnia de' Magi," 157.

122 See Buehler, "Marsilio Ficino's *De Stella magorum*."

123 Hatfield, op. cit., 134–5.

Chapter XIV

1 "Art and Society in *Quattrocento* Florence"; see also Trevor-Roper, *Princes and Artists*.

2 "From the Revival of Letters," 71.

3 This point was most insistently made by Creighton Gilbert in his introduction to *Italian Art*, and in his comments on the documents which are editorialized to support the author's thesis that artists on the whole were creatively independent of their philistine patrons. Because Gilbert made available to a general public much fascinating and often little-known material, illuminated by his insight and expertise on many issues other than patronage, his book has had a strong influence on art historians in training, which is unfortunately reflected in the work of many writers. His recent revisiting of the issue of the relations between patrons, artists, and works of art, "What Did the Renaissance Patron Buy?" is a more nuanced account, but based essentially on the same "commonsense" preconceptions about where we might expect to find evidence on these questions and what it should say, almost entirely divorced from the specific structures and presuppositions of pre-modern societies.

4 See, for example, Gilbert's comment on medals, op. cit., 109: "Surprisingly, since they must have had great interest for the rulers who were often portrayed in them, there is scarcely any evidence of attitudes to them." Surely their widespread manufacture and distribution to friends and allies as gifts of friendship and patronage, along with their use as votives buried in the foundation of buildings like the Tempio Malatesta, is testimony enough. Where and in what context would we expect a written statement? Cf. Hope, "Artists, Patrons and Advisers," 328; he invoked "the familiar observation that contemporary art is little discussed in early Renaissance literature, and that most humanists – at least in the fifteenth century – seem to have taken little interest in the subject. Either they thought it unworthy of serious consideration or regarded it as an autonomous activity best left to specialists."

5 The most obvious example is that of the correspondence between Benozzo Gozzoli and the Medici, discusssed below. All Gozzoli's letters to Piero about the chapel frescoes, written over a period of at least two months crucial to the work's completion, were sent to Careggi. This suggests that Piero spent the summer there, and that his information about the work was second-hand, a suggestion strongly supported by the content of the letters. That would shed a very different light on the exchange between patron and artist, which is usually described in terms of an assumption that Piero frequently inspected the work going on in his own palace. There are of course some very careful analyses of artists' letters and other related texts; see, for example, Ames-Lewis, "Domenico Veneziano and the Medici."

6 For example Gilbert, op. cit., 114–16, adduced as evidence of the patron's lack of interest in the subject matter of visual representations and their "levels of symbolism" the proceedings of a meeting of the Pistoian priestly confraternity of the Holy Trinity, called to ratify their resolve to commission an altarpiece, and to discuss ways of financing it. Naturally this preliminary meeting was concerned primarily with these two essential points; the fact that when the members moved to a discussion of the content they could not agree suggests not indifference, but rather a strong concern on the part of these ordinary parish priests with the particular message of the image. Its central element was the Trinity, to which the group was devoted, and an image whose levels of symbolism were much more complex than most other subjects commonly represented in devotional paintings. Nevertheless, many ordinary men were anxious to grasp this doctrine; see above, p. 481, n. 111. As usual at such business meetings, more complex matters were delegated to a sub-committee, in this case of two men, including "the venerable religious master Filippo di Ser Giovanni."

7 On the meaninglessness and circularity of some of these distinctions see particularly the cogent observations of William Hood, "State of Research."

8 The figure of the patron's advisor, a real enough presence at courts such as that of the Este of Ferrara in the 1440s, where the humanist Decembrio was an early and explicit interpreter of this role, is a largely mythical one when imported into the Florentine scene at this time. Cf. Chambers, review of Lytle and Orgel, *Patronage in the Renaissance*. Observing disparagingly that "patronage is a fashionable subject," 316, he urged that "the artist's own formal considerations and informedness need to be contrasted with the follies of learned advisors." His major example of artists' disregard of their patrons is Donatello, almost unique in his notorious and glorious independence; most of his commissions, apart from those for the Medici, were for various ecclesiastical institutions in Prato, Padua, and Florence. Apart from clergymen, probably not particularly learned, but not foolish either, where, in these contexts, were the "learned advisors?" For a sophisticated model of the roles of patron, artist, and advisor applicable to courtly contexts see Settis, "Artisti e committenti."

9 Gilbert's collection of documents, also published in their original language, and his *Poets Seeing Artists' Work*, have, despite his comments, contributed much to providing a basis for such an understanding. For example he cited in the latter, 194–5, the Paduan poet, Strazzoli, speaking in the voice of an ill-formed image of Christ: "those who see me laugh, and do not pray,/ making game of my ill-formed effigy,/ which wipes out reverence among the people"; the image concludes his lament with the hope that Bellini "will make me more human, more divine." Such a vivid perception of images by men other than artists is not unique, but rather fundamental to the traditions of popular poetry.

10 Once again, we have more evidence for Lorenzo's ties with the artists who worked for him than for Cosimo. Even so, preconceptions about patron–artist relationships and a limited grasp of Florentine cultural conventions have distorted the reading of this evidence. For example, it is only very recently that James Draper radically reconsidered the relationship between Lorenzo and Bertoldo, who lived in the Medici palace. Bertoldo's famous letter to Lorenzo about "stews," previously assumed to refer to his enthusiasm for cooking, has finally been understood as an allusion to very different interests, made in the parlance of populist humor and *double entendre* in which both the artist and his patron were well versed. See Draper, *Bertoldo*.

11 Bullard, "Heroes and Their Workshops," also makes the important point that the language of patronage is complex, highly conventionalized, and does not always mean what it seems to. However, rather than suggesting that "language does not always accurately reflect experience" I would say

that usually it does, but not always directly, or on the most obvious level. For a detailed analysis of Medici patronage letters and their language see my forthcoming *Fathers and Friends*.

12 Gombrich, "Early Medici as Patrons," 47, of Domenico Veneziano; cf. Ames-Lewis of the same artist, "Domenico Veneziano and the Medici," 67.

13 Gombrich, op. cit., loc. cit..

14 Hatfield, 630–32; Chambers, *Patrons and Artists*, 118, 207. Such arbitrary and anachronistic interpretations of documents deprived of their complex contexts precludes their use to genuinely advance understanding of either patrons or artists, or of their relations.

15 "Theory of Magnificence," 164–5.

16 Gilbert, *Italian Art*, 7; Ruda, *Fra Filippo Lippi*, 38. Ruda also struck a nice balance between under- and overhistoricizing the paintings, acknowledging the testimony of the artist's letters that the background of his life intruded into the foreground of his work, affecting the way he handled his patrons and his commissions, but observing that in the paintings themselves there is no trace of his personal troubles.

17 Cit. Ruda, op. cit., 348.

18 Ibid., 26–7.

19 Lippi's letter, MAP, XVI, 8, was first published by Gaye, *Carteggio* I, 142; a more accurate transcription is provided by Ruda, op. cit., doc. 6, 520, and discussed and reproduced in a photograph, 27–9. For Domenico's letter, see below.

20 "Che perdio ò male." Storing valuable work and materials was a problem for peripatetic artists; Lippi had once left with Neri di Bicci quite a large quantity of gold until he needed it; see the latter's *Ricordanze*, 24–5.

21 See, for example, above, pp. 276–7.

22 Notably the artist had not applied for any of the charitable gifts of vestments available from the Carmine, his own convent, since shortly after the first mention of his work as a painter, in 1431/2; see Ruda, op. cit., 514.

23 For the letters concerning the Naples commission see Gaye, *Carteggio* I, 175–81; Ruda, op. cit., doc. 21, 536–8.

24 On Martelli see De Roover, *Rise and Decline*, 277; for the painting, Ruda, op. cit., 117.

25 Much speculation has been devoted to the cause of what Caroline Elam neatly described as the not infrequent "Homeric laughter" of aristocrats about their social inferiors. See "Art and Diplomacy," 813–15,

26 Ruda, op. cit., 36.

27 See Elam, op. cit., Ruda, op. cit., 194–9; Bentley, *Politics and Culture in Renaissance Naples*, ch. 1.

28 Ruda, op. cit., doc. 29, 545.

29 Ibid., 43.

30 See Wohl, *Domenico Veneziano*, cat. 1, 114–17; on the Carnesecchi, Rubinstein, *Government of Florence*, 10, and Kent, *Rise of the Medici*, passim.

31 Wohl, op. cit., especially ch. 1.

32 See Gilbert, *Italian Art*, 4–5, for comment and translation; also Pope-Hennessy, *Luca della Robbia*, 42. The letter was published by Gaye, *Carteggio* I, 136–7; a more accurate transcription is offered by Wohl, op. cit., 340.

33 Clients really wishing to impress their patrons resorted to much more extreme language, signing themselves as "schiavo," "creatura," or even "cane"; see Kent, *Fathers and Friends*.

34 Ames-Lewis, "Domenico Veneziano and the Medici"; De

Roover, *Rise and Decline*, 247–8. See also MAP, XIV, 3, 467.

35 *Born under Saturn*, 34.

36 The exercise of arbitration, to decide the price of a work of art or assess the fulfilment of the contract, was also modeled on the mediation or "mezzanità" which held patronage structures together. See, for example, Michelozzo's Catasto report, published Mather, "New Documents," 228, on the arbitration concerning the price of the Aragazzi tomb: "una sepoltura per a Monte Pulciano di messer Bartolomeo da Monte Pulciano Secretario di Papa della quale nonno pregio s'è fatto senonchè quando illavorio serar' fornito sì di stimare per amici comuni potea esser di maggior spesa o di minore che non si stimava prima . . ." The same process occurred when the patron rejected the finished product; see, for example, Kennedy, "Documenti inediti su Desiderio"; Frate Andrea Rucellai was appointed to act "chome mezzano della famiglia et huomini della chasa de Rucellai." The numerous references to arbitration in Neri di Bicci's *Ricordanze* indicate that it was not necessarily adversarial, but rather often built into the process of producing a work of art.

37 On this see also below, pp. 179–83; on Sant' Egidio, Ames-Lewis, op. cit., especially 86; on Domenico's Magi tondo above, pp. 255–9, and figs. 118, 119, and especially Wohl, *Domenico Veneziano*, 69–75, and cat. 4, 120–3.

38 "Matteo de' Pasti." The letter was published by Milanesi, "Lettere d'artisti," 78–9, and republished by Ames-Lewis; it appears in translation and with comment by Gilbert, *Italian Art*, 6. According to Acidini, "Chapel of the Magi," the new technique of applying powdered gold was also employed by Gozzoli at the chapel.

39 Cf. Gombrich's comment, "Early Medici as Patrons," 47: "De' Pasti clearly knew how to appeal to Piero, with his tale of powdered gold and his qualms about including old men in his picture. We find the same preoccupation with the pleasing and the magnificent in a letter which the Medici agent Fruoxino addressed to Piero's brother Giovanni from Bruges in 1448."

40 See especially Cole Ahl, *Benozzo Gozzoli*, ch. 1.

41 Gozzoli's work for many important patrons like the companies of the Purification and Sant' Agnese suggests that his contemporaries associated him with his master, Fra Angelico. When the company of the Purification specified in their 1461 contract with him that he should "operarsi in modo che detta dipintura exceda ogni buona dipintura infino a qui facta per detto Benozzo, o almeno a quella si possa debitamente equiperare," they probably had in mind the Medici palace chapel, which it would have been difficult to exceed; see also below, n. 48. For this document see Cole Ahl, op. cit., 277–8.

42 See Janson, *Donatello*, 21–3, 191–6, cf. Civai, *Dipinti e sculture in casa Martelli*. Most Donatello scholars now attribute these works to other artists. On the Martelli and the Medici see above, pp. 179–83, and below, p. 452, n. 138; also Crum, "Roberto Martelli." The letters of 1459 regarding the Medici chapel are reprinted in Cole Ahl, op. cit., 276–7.

43 "Ellavoro i'ò seguito quanto posso" recalls Van Eyck's motto: "Als ich kann."

44 Cf. above, p. 320, and below, p. 481, n. 88.

45 Acidini, "Choirs of Angels," 265; see also Grote, "Hitherto Unpublished Letter," 321.

46 This last expression "mi pare mill'anni . . ." is very common

in the letters of the *brigata* of young friends of Piero and Giovanni, and later of Lorenzo; see above, p. 452, nn. 138, 147, for examples from the letters of della Stufa and Martelli.

47 Anecdotes about Donatello going to extraordinary lengths to avoid such supervision, locking himself in his workroom, and covering his sculpture with cloths (see, for example, Poliziano, *Detti Piacevoli*, no. 44, 33), suggest that Gozzoli was the norm and Donatello was, as in many other ways, exceptional. Patron oversight is documented in a number of cases. The executors of Francesco Datini's will consulted with one another on some frescoes for his house and asked the artist for a drawing; Francesco's widow Margherita invited the painters to dine at her own table; see Gilbert, *Italian Art*, 108–9. Banker, "Sassetta Altarpiece," documented the continuing oversight of the iconography of this commission, and during the construction of the Tempio Malatestiana in 1454, the patron, the architect Alberti, and Matteo de' Pasti, supervisor of the building, exchanged and pored over Alberti's designs for the facade; see Borsi, *Alberti*, ch. 5. Both Piero and Giovanni de' Medici worked closely with Manetti in the building of Giovanni's villa at Fiesole; see Lillie, "Giovanni di Cosimo and the Villa Medici," 195.

48 See Padoa Rizzo, "Benozzo Gozzoli's Oeuvre," 358; Cole Ahl, op. cit., 81.

49 Above, p. 177. In 1453 the confraternity was subsumed under the adult confraternity dedicated to Saint Jerome, who along with Saint Francis was depicted in the new altarpiece; on this, see Cole Ahl, op. cit., 112–19.

50 The invocation of Christ's name in the address and signature imparts an egalitarian tone to the letter, and suggests perhaps that the two men were brothers in one of the several religious fraternities to which Lorenzo belonged, possibly that of the Magi. I have found no examples of these expressions in letters to Cosimo, although they are often signed with the more formulaic: "xpo vi ghuardi."

51 See Spencer, *Castagno and His Patrons*, and above, pp. 205–7, on his work for this group at Santissima Annunziata.

52 Castagno described himself as "servitore ed obbligato alla casa de Medici," ibid., 104.

53 Grunzweig, *Correspondence de la filiale*, 31.

54 See Lillie, "Giovanni di Cosimo," 192; Grunzweig, op. cit., 26–31, 78–83, 94–5, 98–103; De Roover, *Rise and Decline*, 144, ch. 13, especially 325–33.

55 Gaye, *Carteggio* 1, 158–9. Patrons' personal tastes obviously varied widely. Astorgio Manfredi, lord of Faenza, wrote to Giovanni concerning some hangings (*cortine*) the Medici were importing for him, MAP, XI, 36, 29 May 1454, requesting that "li faciate fare a quello magistro che fece la hystoria de Sansone . . ." There is apparently only one surviving tapestry bearing the Medici arms, dating from the late fifteenth century, in the Cleveland Museum of Art: see Asselberghs, *Les Tapisseries flamandes*, plate 8 and comments.

56 "Piero de' Medici and the Pollaiuolo," 129. A reference to the brothers' authorship of the Labors of Hercules cycle for the Medici palace occurs in Antonio's letter of 1494 to a member of the Orsini, Lorenzo's wife's family; see Gilbert, *Italian Art*, 17–18.

57 "El quale fece el palcho e'l monte a Cestello," MAP, VIII, 219.

58 Ibid., VII, 204.

59 Gaye, *Carteggio* 1, 161–3.

60 MAP, XVI, 88, 5 March 1451/2. On Torelli see also Ames-Lewis, "Matteo de' Pasti," 351, *Library and Manuscripts of Piero*, passim. Torelli also worked for Cosimo; see De La Mare, "Cosimo and his Books," 133. Several of the less eminent Medici *amici* were connected with the world of art and architecture; Ser Alesso's father Matteo was a painter (Cat. 62, fol. 277r–v) and his letters indicate that he had some expertise in building, in which Michele del Giogante was also very interested; see above, pp. 92–3, 230; below, p. 463, nn. 60, 73. For the really close friendship between Manno Temperani and Apollonio di Giovanni see Kent and Kent, *Neighbours and Neighbourhood*, 150, 167–8. Temperani entrusted to Apollonio the painting over his own marble tomb of "whatever seems appropriate . . . to him . . . as a kind and beloved friend in the home of the said testator," and the artist in turn made Temperani's son his principal heir.

61 See Caplow, "Sculptors' Partnerships," especially 164–73; also Beck, "Networking in the Renaissance."

62 Gilbert, op. cit., 40, pointed to an interesting but failed attempt by Verrocchio to bequeath to his assistant and executor Lorenzo di Credi his commission for the Colleoni monument: "I leave the work on the horse begun by me to him to be finished, if it please the illustrious Doge of Venice, and I humbly beg the government of the Venetians that it may see fit to allow the said Lorenzo to complete the work, since he is qualified." Verrocchio's will, dated 1488, left Lorenzo all his belongings in Florence and Venice, except his two houses in Sant' Ambrogio, which he left to his brother Tommaso.

63 Above, p. 294, and Krautheimer, *Ghiberti*, 422, describing particularly Ghiberti's cameo ring. See also Bober and Rubinstein, *Renaissance Artists and Antique Sculpture*.

64 See Carlo de' Medici's letter to Giovanni, Gaye, *Carteggio* 1, 163. See also Bober and Rubinstein, op. cit., 35; Caglioti, "Bernardo Rossellino a Roma"; Rossi, "L'indole."

65 Above, ch. 3. See also Haines, "Artisan Family Strategies," for a commission by Maso Finiguerra.

66 See also Wackernagel, *Florentine Renaissance Artist*; Thomas, *Painter's Practice*; Carnesasca, *Artisti in Bottega*; Procacci, "Compagnie dei Pittori," and the suggestions of Bullard, "Heroes and Their Workshops."

67 See Gaye, *Carteggio* 1, 148–55.

68 Gilbert, op. cit., 32.

69 *On Painting*, 34.

70 On this see Kemp, "From 'Mimesis' to 'Fantasia,'" and "Equal Excellences," especially 10; Procacci, "Compagnie di pittori," 20.

71 *Istorie fiorentine*, ed. Polidori, 2, 499. For Landino's account, Baxandall, *Painting and Experience*, pt. 3.

72 On Petrarch's contribution to the formation of such theories, and Ghiberti's use of *ingegnai* see Gombrich, "Renaissance Conception of Artistic Progress"; also Krautheimer, *Ghiberti*, xix. On the relevance of *ingenium* to a later, more developed artistic theory, see especially Kantorowicz, "Sovereignty of the Artist," 356.

73 *Elegies*, bk. 3, ix, 1–16.

74 Above, pp. 175–7.

75 *Vite* 2, 193.

76 Cited Pope-Hennessy, *Donatello, Sculptor*, 12.

77 "Un cervello facto a questo modo; che se non viene de li non li bisogna sperare"; cited Pope-Hennessy, op. cit., loc. cit. The latter's gloss on this somewhat obscure observation was: "He moved in the direction in which instinct told him

that he should go, with an obstinate, solipsistic self-concentration that in his own time was unique."

78 *Donatello and His World.*

79 For these and other examples of Cosimo's ubiquitous presence in the artist's practical life see Herzner, "Regesti Donatelliani."

80 On the tomb in the crypt, see below, p. 382.

81 *Vite* 2, 194.

82 Janson, *Donatello*, 89.

83 Cat. 470, 521, cit. Hyman, "Notes and Speculations," 108. Cosimo listed among his properties some houses on the corner of the Via Larga and Via de' Gori, an inn and a cluster of *chasette*, including "una chasa nella quale si solea fare albergho et due chasette allato chon chorte poste in detto popolo presso al canto della via largha le quali abiamo apigionate a donato intagliatore, et daccene l'anno di pigione fiorini cinque."

84 See Beck, "New Notices for Michelozzo;"

85 See *Donatello*, 83; also Ames-Lewis, "Donatello's Bronze *David* Reconsidered," 147.

86 This last expression, discussed by Kent, "Patron-Client Networks," 279–80, was popularly used with reference to Lorenzo di Piero di Cosimo's dominance of the state; it was employed by Benedetto Dei *c.*1470. Cf. Bullard, "Heroes and their Workshops," on similar ways of conceptualizing quattrocento politics, business, and art. The view that patron and artist were each *maestri* in their own *botteghe* was used to justify the artist's independence in an anecdote of Poliziano, *Detti Piacevoli* 33, no. 42: "Mandando più volte il Patriarca per Donatello, e non vi andando egli, al fine pur sollicitato, rispose: 'De' al Patriarca che io non vi vo' venire, ch'io son così Patriarca nell'arte mia, come esso sia nella sua.'" On the painting of the artists and their patron Cosimo, executed by M. da Faenza to a design by Vasari, see Allegri and Cecchi, *Palazzo Vecchio e i Medici*. Artists' signatures and self-portraits testify to their developing individualism as the fifteenth century wore on. Medici artists who followed this trend include Benozzo Gozzoli, who incorporated his self-portraits in the Medici palace chapel frescoes, Lippi, who signed the axe in the chapel altarpiece, and Uccello who autographed the shield in one panel of the *Battle of San Romano*. Particularly interesting is the explicit distinction in the inscription on Piero's *tempietto* in Santissima Annunziata: "Piero di Cosimo de' Medici fece fare questa hopera et Pagno di Lapo da Fiesole fu el maestro chlla fe MCCCCIIL." See also King, "Filarete's Portrait Signature," 297–9, on Filarete's signature on the bronze doors of St. Peter's in Rome, which "takes the extraordinary form of a narrative showing himself and his assistants linking hands in a dance and holding their chiselling and sculpting tools. The sculptors issue from a gate on the left, upon which is chiselled the artist's signature," cf. Brunelleschi's reference to a celebratory dance when the cupola should be completed, above, p. 123.

Chapter XV

1 "Archaeology and the History of Ideas," 139–40.

2 See above, especially pp. 155–9, 186–90.

3 This message is illuminated, but not circumscribed by the patron's intentions; see Baxandall, *Painting and Experience*, for one perspective on this dialogue, and the same author's *Patterns of Intention* for another that is very different, but not as incompatible as at first it might seem.

4 "Volere pignere un pocho la pedina chome potrai . . . che ogni picolo favore che egli arà oltre a quel di Manno Temperani e di Martino delo Scharfa, ch'egli vogliono meglio che a Christo, tu saria chagione de aluminarlo," MAP, V, 521, 21 May 1444.

5 Ibid., v, 498, 17 Feb. 1444/5; XVI, 42, 10 Oct. 1448: "Ti priegho quanto m'è possibile che a que' primi partiti aoperi in mio favore cogliamici tuoi e come son cierto saprai quanto t'è posibile con onestà aoperare . . ."

6 See Rubinstein, *Government of Florence*, 128–9.

7 See especially the essays in Garfagnini, *Lorenzo il Magnifico* and *Lorenzo de' Medici*, and Mallett and Mann, *Lorenzo the Magnificent*.

8 See Hale, *Florence and the Medici*, ch. 4; Cochrane, *Forgotten Centuries*.

9 Ch. 24. Since Dante's life's mission was advocating the restoration of imperial authority, and he wanted to put an emperor back in the saddle to subdue unruly Italy, Twain's choice of villain versus hero here is somewhat perverse. Perhaps his real problems with Florence were personal. Failing to find his way back to his hotel one night and unable to speak Italian and so seek directions, he concluded: "my experiences of Florence were chiefly unpleasant. I will change the subject."

10 "Suo sviscerato servitore," *La lirica toscana*, 287.

11 Wind, "Platonic Tyranny," 90; Garin, *L'umanesimo italiano*; see also Martines *Social World*, introduction.

12 "*Le Tems revient*," 22, 21–53. Cf. however, her more recent judgment, "Lorenzo's 'Politica Festiva,'" 106–7, on the "unequivocal and unhistorical representation of Lorenzo as an absolute monarch."

13 "Invisible Images of Control," 99.

14 The very different meanings of tyranny and liberty in Renaissance and modern contexts have been extensively explored in discussions of Hans Baron's thesis in his *Crisis*; see above, ch. 5.

15 See below, p. 410, n. 76.

16 See Ullmann, *Principles of Government and Politics*.

17 See particularly Lippincott, "The Neo-Latin Historical Epics," and on Milan, Welch, *Art and Authority*. Welch, "Italian Courts," commented on some problems confronting historians of the Italian courts, particularly the question of whether the study of princely families can be considered as coterminous with the study of their cities; see especially 27. See also Dean, "Lords, Vassals and Clients in Renaissance Ferrara," and "Commune and Despot."

18 *Public Life*, 279. Cf. the critical comments of Rubinstein, review of *Public Life*, and Najemy, "Linguaggi storiografici," 151–9. Noting the strength and persistence of a corporate civic ideology through the fifteenth century, Najemy observed, 151: "Quei fiorentini che parlavano questo linguaggio di sovranità popolare e collettiva e lo applicavano al loro stesso ordinamento politico – ed erano molti – non avevano alcuna ragione di temere che tale ordinamento fosse illegittimo, mancasse di affidabilità o fosse in qualche modo inferiore al governo dei principi."

19 See above, ch. 2; cf. Rubinstein, *Government of Florence*, 132, n. 5, Nicodemo da Pontremoli to the Duke of Milan: "infinite fiate me habiate comandato che sempre e in omne caso

obedisca Cosimo non altramente che vostro padre . . ." On diplomatic relations between Cosimo and Sforza see also Fubini, "Appunti sui rapporti diplomatici."

20　Rubinstein, op. cit., 89, was moved to suggest that Trexler seemed willing to canvas any theory of Florentine perceptions of politics and power save the explicit testimony of informed citizens of the time. Trexler is not alone in this. Paola Ventrone, having noted Cosimo's remark in a letter to his nephew Pierfrancesco that the joust held on the occasion of the visit of Galeazzo Maria Sforza and Pope Pius II was important because it reflected on the honor of the commune, MAP, ii, 452, 17 March 1459, went on to argue by appeal to the anonymous, encomiastic, and fanciful "Terze Rime" that the ceremony was in fact a homage to Medici family; see Ventrone, "La sacra rappresentazione," cf. the *Terze Rime* published in part by Hatfield, "Compagnia de' Magi," appendix 1.

21　See Rubinstein, *Government of Florence*, and for the evidence of the letters, Kent, *Rise of the Medici* and *Fathers and Friends*.

22　Rubinstein, *Government of Florence*, 24, 131: Cosimo agreed with previous speakers in a *pratica* that the election of the Signoria by lot should be restored, provided that "principes civitatis in hoc concordes essent." See also Rubinstein's exposition of the Ciceronian connotations of Cosimo's standing as leading citizen, "Cosimo *optimus civis.*"

23　Rubinstein, op. cit., 37.

24　On these events ibid.

25　Ibid., 129, for citation and comment. A good example is his response to the vacancy of Florence's archbishopric, described above, p. 183. Letters revealing his caution in the promotion of his partisans are discussed at length in Kent, *Fathers and Friends*. Rubinstein's account, op. cit., ch. 5, of the challenges to the Medicean regime and its consolidation in 1458, describes Cosimo's reluctance to give his open support to the Parlamento and to call for Sforza's military assistance. In 1455 he rejected the duke's offers of help with the explanation that the situation in Florence was "not as dangerous as he understood was believed" in Milan; see particularly 90, 102–3, 132–3. Although dissension within the ruling group persisted, and Pius II noted that after 1458 "there were some who asserted that Cosimo's power was intolerable," 128, most leading citizens seemed anxious at all costs to avoid the internal disunity so damaging to the regime, 133. Regardless of Rubinstein's judicious and amply documented analysis of the complex political situation of this period and Cosimo's ambivalent attitude to proposed solutions of military and judicial intervention, a number of scholars have recently relied in preference on the more lurid but largely unsubstantiated account of these years in Field, *Platonic Academy*; see especially 28–33. His interpretation depends heavily on Niccolò Machiavelli's claim, made almost seventy years after the event, that after 1458 government in Florence was "unbearable and violent," which Field freely translated as "a virtual reign of terror." It should be noted that in addition to approving electoral revisions, the Parlamento gave the Otto di Guardia extraordinary powers to deal with the enemies of the regime, among whom Girolamo Machiavelli was prominent; see Rubinstein, op. cit., 103, 109. Field's account has been invoked by some art historians as the foundation of a series of "cantilevered hypotheses" concerning Medici control and its supposed expression in Cosimo's patronage of art; see, for example, Crum, "Roberto Martelli,

the Council of Florence," especially 412–15; it is also cited by Cole Ahl, *Benozzo Gozzoli*, 82–3, although notably it plays only a limited part in her careful analysis of the Medici chapel frescoes in terms largely of the artist's achievement.

26　Mallett, *Mercenaries and their Masters*, observed that many *condottieri* were cultured men, interested in learning as well as arms; see also his "Notes on a Fifteenth-century Condottiere and his Library." For a broad picture of patronage in Italian Renaissance cities see Welch, *Art and Society in Italy*, and Paoletti and Radke, *Art in Renaissance Italy*.

27　Although Cosimo was the recipient on occasion of letters from the French royal house and English kings (see, for example, MAP, xi, 202, Henry VI, King of England, Windsor, 26 Aug. 1440, to Cosimo, Florence), the city's closest royal contacts were with the Angevins and the Aragonese of Naples. Cosimo was extremely wary of the latter, as of the overtures of René of Anjou; see above, p. 193. After his death, his son Piero and grandson Lorenzo felt themselves honored by the privilege of adding the French fleur-de-lis to their arms; see below, p. 372.

28　*Natural History*, especially bk. xxxvi–vii, cit. above, ch. 11, n. 24. Lorenzo de' Medici, who cited Pliny in his *Commentary* on his Sonnet xx, mindful perhaps of such extravagant patronage, which was largely beyond his own means, observed that Florentines who seem rich would have been poor in Roman society, *Opere scelte*, 259.

29　As Gombrich observed, "Golden Age."

30　See above, ch. 3 and p. 295.

31　See Warnke, *Court Artist*; Borsook, "A Florentine *Scrittoio.*" The Strozzi arms were derived from those of the queen of Naples, who knighted Palla, her court banker, in 1415. Nanni degli Strozzi, exiled in the Ciompi revolution of 1378, became a *condottiere* and a military captain at the court of the Este of Ferrara; Bruni delivered his funeral oration in 1428.

32　See Woods-Marsden, *Gonzaga of Mantua*, especially ch. 5. In 1449 Lodovico donated a substantial portion (1,200 florins) of his unpaid back stipend as Florentine captain-general to the building, in honor of his father, of the tribuna of Santissima Annunziata in Florence; on this see also Brown, "Patronage and Building History." In 1450 the stonemason Luca Fancelli was sent to Mantua by Cosimo in response to Lodovico's request for an architect with Florentine training. Between 1450 and 1452 Lodovico tried unsuccessfully to get Donatello, then in Padua, to create an *arca* in honor of Mantua's patron saint, Saint Anselmo. Only seven sculptures, now lost, were finished. In 1454 Baldovinetti worked on a canvas of the Last Judgment that Lodovico had originally commissioned from Castagno.

33　Of the very large number of letters addressed to Cosimo and his sons from these lords see, for example, Antonio Galeazzo Bentivoglio, MAP, xi, 53, 15 Jan. 1435, Sant'Agata to Cosimo in Florence. Bentivoglio wrote to seek assurances that his faith in their friendship was justified. Although he knew Cosimo to be very busy, "nientemanco non credo che be' dementicate me, nè le cose pertenente a la conditione e l'essere mio, perchè son zerto me amate singularmente e poi conforme al stato vostro." Cf. Antonio Ordelaffi, Forlivii dominus, ibid., xii, 140, to Cosimo, 12 Oct. 1435: "Magnifice frater compaterque carissime. Io contenuamente ho informatione da Misser Nofrio mio ambasciatore de quanto per la M V se vene adoperato ne li fatti mei, deli quali ve ne sono obligato immortalmente, pregandovi instantissimamente vogliate perserverare de bene in meglio . . ." See also ibid., XII, 163, Ordelaffi to Cosimo and Lorenzeo, 25 Oct. 1435: "Magnifice frater et compater carissime. Cum securta domesticamente ricorro ala M V a gravarvi spesso ne li mei bisogni de quelle cose cedeno più ali vostri commodi . . . pregandovi vogliate continuare ali mei favuri suso le altre mie facende como fatto haviti per lo passato . . . semper a tucti li beneplaciti de la MV paratissimo . . ." Guidantonio Manfredi wrote to Cosimo from Faenza, ibid., XII, 146, 15 Oct. 1435: "Spectabilis nobilisque vir tanquam frater . . ." recommending the bearer, "et etiam a quanto per mia parer ve dixa li davate quanto a me proprio piena fede." Guidantonio Montefeltro, "de Urbino e de Durante conte" thanked Cosimo for a loan, "preghandove pigliate sigurta de me come vedete la piglio çempre de voi che me serà più caro essere da voi rechesto et satisfarve che in nelle mee recheste essere satisfacto da voi . . . ," ibid., XII, 153, 19 Oct. 1453. On Medici relations with the lords of Faenza see Boucher, "Florence and Faenza at Mid-Century."

34 See especially Woods-Marsden, op. cit., on the Gonzaga; also "How *Quattrocento* Princes Used Art." The latter is concerned with Pisanello's medals, a form developed in Ferrara for Leonello d'Este, and widely used by the Este, Malatesta, Gonzaga, and others from 1443. They incorporated personal devices that would later become *imprese*, among them Sigismondo Malatesta's use of his castle as an attribute after 1451.

35 See above, ch. 12, pp. 269, 272–4.

36 See Woods-Marsden, *Gonzaga of Mantua*; Bentley, *Politics and Culture in Renaissance Naples*; and on Milan, Welch, *Art and Authority*, especially 192.

37 Welch, op. cit., 310, observing that the style of life and the customs of the court rather than its decorations were the criteria by which the Milanese people measured their prince's greatness, described the court and retinue of Francesco Sforza and his wife Bianca Maria. It consisted of over four hundred persons in 1463, by comparison with the fifty mouths Cosimo had to feed, between his Florentine palace and his country villas. Cf. ibid., 213; after his visit to Florence in 1459, when he was received by Cosimo in the Medici palace chapel, Galeazzo Maria remarked how unsuitable this small private space was for large crowds, and how quickly the group had to leave to make room for others. His own new chapels were dramatically larger; "not spaces for private prayer and contemplation but areas of public performance."

38 On these see Wegener, "Mortuary Chapels"; she commented, ch. 2, on how far the Medici of Florence stand outside of this tradition.

39 The first notable private Medici medal was to commemorate Lorenzo's escape from assassination in the Pazzi conspiracy of 1478, and the memory of his brother Giuliano, who was murdered.

40 "Lorenzo de' Medici and the Urban Development," 43.

41 Above, pp. 181, 238.

42 See, for example, pp. 238–9, 296.

43 See Jones, *Malatesta of Rimini*, 369, especially n. 114.

44 See Neri di Bicci, *Ricordanze*, 24–5, 1 Feb. 1454/5; also above, pp. 126, 316, and fig. 156, also index.

45 See, for example, Ricc. 1100, 1103, 1154; Flamini, *La lirica toscana*, 317.

46 For example, the Greek inscription for the church was in fully developed classical form, and dedicated to Immortal God and the City (*polis*) not San Francesco; see Lavin, "Antique Source." On the Tempio in general see Hope, "Early History."

47 See Ettlinger, "Sepulcher on the Facade." The medal was inscribed: "Praeclarum Arimini Templum Anno Gratiae voto fecit MCCCL"; the facade: "Sigismundus Pandulfus Malatesta Pandulfi filius voto fecit anno gratiae MCCCCL."

48 See above, pp. 190–91; Ettlinger, op. cit.

49 See Lippincott, "The Neo-Latin Historical Epics"; cf. above, pp. 118–19.

50 See Lavin, "Piero della Francesca's Fresco of Sigismondo"; cf. above, pp. 155–6.

51 On the Medici panel, see above, pp. 262–4; for the Sforza panel, Brussels, Musée Communale, *Rogier van der Weyden*; for comment see Davies, *Rogier van der Weyden*, 206–8.

52 See "Process of Sforza Patronage," *Art and Authority*, x: "When I began this book I too believed that this study would illustrate how visual propaganda supported ducal hegemony . . . but . . . the records of the cathedral and hospital of Milan . . . do not illustrate clear signorial supremacy; they offer, instead, a more confused and often conflicting story of tensions, collaboration and consensus between the ruler and those he or she ruled." There are some scraps of evidence concerning exchanges over patronage between Francesco Sforza and Cosimo, Florence and Milan. Just after Sforza became duke in 1450, he wrote to Cosimo asking him for a plan of Santa Maria Nuova on which to model the Milanese hospital, and two subsequent letters on this matter were addressed to Giovanni. When his son's entourage visited the Medici palace in 1459, one of its members remarked that the father would surely wish to follow Cosimo's example in domestic decoration. In 1460 Sforza responded to a request of the Florentine Signoria for advice concerning the "nuova cittadella" they proposed to build at Pisa, since they had seen a drawing of Milanese fortifications brought back to Florence by Antonio Manetti. Declaring himself less than expert on these matters, Sforza suggested they should go to see the works themselves, because this was the only way to ascertain the precise measurements. However, he did observe, in view of their faith in his opinion, and his love for them, that he had spoken to Manetti to give them a better idea; he also suggested, perhaps implying that a lesser show of force was appropriate to a republic, that they might want to make the Pisan *cittadella* simpler. See Gaye, *Carteggio* 1, 194–5; Spencer, "Dome of Sforzinda Cathedral."

53 Giovanni di Bicci's mother was a Spini; his sons Cosimo and Lorenzo married respectively into the Bardi and Cavalcanti families.

54 This was not restricted to Palla's very public altarpiece for the sacristy at Santa Trinita. One of two pictures Alessandra Strozzi considered selling in 1460, when she needed cash, was of the Three Magi; the other depicted a peacock, often part of the Magi scene. A third picture, the Holy Face, was the miraculous image of Christ's face left on Saint Veronica's handkerchief when he wiped his brow with it on the way to Calvary; this she wanted to keep "for it is a devout figure, and beautiful"; see Gilbert, *Italian Art*, 117–18.

55 On these see Schulz, *Bernardo Rossellino*, ch. 7, especially 65. There is some dispute as to the sequence of the tombs made for Palla Strozzi and Giovanni di Bicci, although the balance of opinion tends to see the Strozzi tomb as earlier; see Saalman, "Strozzi Tombs in the Sacristy of Santa Trinita," especially 149–55; cf. Davisson, "Iconology of the S. Trinita

Sacristy." See also Jones, "Palla Strozzi e la Sagrestia di Santa Trinita."

56 See particularly "Lorenzo de' Medici and the Urban Development."

57 See, for example, Butterfield, *Verrocchio*, on the typology of tombs, which depended fairly strictly on the position and occupation of the deceased.

58 For the Alessandri altarpiece see Ruda, *Fra Filippo Lippi*, 429–32. He dated the painting between the mid-1440s and the mid-1450s; Ginevra Alessandri married Giovanni di Cosimo de' Medici on 20 Jan. 1453. Francesco Sassetti's villa at La Pietra, a town palace transposed into the countryside, is based on the Palazzo Medici and is only slightly smaller than it; see Lillie, "Humanist Villa Revisited," 207–11; for other quotations from the Medici palace, see above, pp. 235–8. The Portinari chapel in Milan was one of many replicas of the old sacristy; see Trachtenberg, "On Brunelleschi's Old Sacristy"; Bernstein, "Florentine Patron in Milan."

59 Howard Saalman insisted on such a relation, on the basis of little or no evidence, in various studies; see "Strozzi Tombs in the Sacristy of Santa Trinita"; review of *Giovanni Rucellai ed il suo Zibaldone*, II; and on the Pazzi chapel, *Brunelleschi: The Buildings*, ch. 5. Trachtenberg has similarly argued that the Pazzi in building their chapel at Santa Croce sought at once to emulate and "erase" both Brunelleschi and the Medici, because they were assailed by "the anxiety of influence," a phrase coined by the literary critic Harold Bloom to refer a very different, indeed almost contrary impulse. This suggestion is at odds not only with the fundamental assumptions governing Florentine social relationships, but also with the evidence of the identity of interest between the Pazzi and the Medici in 1442, when plans for the chapel were initiated. It took another thirty-six years for the tensions inherent in the relations between Florence's greatest patrons and their chief brokers to manifest themselves in the Pazzi conspiracy.

60 See Pellecchia, "First Observant Church."

61 "Domenico Veneziano and the Medici." The following comment is based upon his study.

62 See De Roover, *Rise and Decline*, 262, 387; also MAP, V, 284, 297, 298; CS., 3a ser., I, 51. Tommaso di Folco was manager at Bruges, 1465–80; Pigello ran Milan, 1453–1468, and was succeeded at his death by his brother Accerito, 1468–78. Their uncle Giovanni Portinari was manager of the Venice branch, 1417–35; he died in that office. Another uncle, Accerito, worked for the bank in Florence and Naples until his death c.1427.

63 As indeed he was characterized by Brucker, *Renaissance Florence*, 125–6. In his introduction to the group of studies comprising the second volume of *Giovanni Rucellai ed il suo Zibaldone*, Nicolai Rubinstein wisely cautioned that Rucellai should not, however, be seen as typical of his class, but rather "as exemplifying its richly diverse contribution to the civilization of Renaissance Florence," 5. These studies, particularly those by F. W. Kent, Alessandro Perosa, and Brenda Preyer, are the indispensable foundation of any discussion of Rucellai, and the account that follows is heavily indebted to them. For Giovanni's much-quoted phrase see *Zibaldone* I, 121.

64 MAP, II, 480, 26 Nov. 1461: "et quello è el maritare la Nannina, che esaminando quello ci è da ffare ci è scharsi partiti, chi per uno rispetto et chi per un' altro; pure bisog-niando fare il meglio che ssi può, ci adriziamo a uno figliuolo di Giovanni Ruciellai, et perchè queste chose non si possono tenere per la lungha, rispondi di tuo parere . . ." "onorato, stimato e righardato . . . perchosso dala fortuna . . ." For these evocative phrases with which Rucellai described his life's experience, and Kent characterized its phases, see *Zibaldone* I, 120–22, and passim.

66 *Zibaldone* I, 2.

67 Preyer, "Rucellai Palace," 202–7.

68 On this see Kent, "Making of a Renaissance Patron," 58, 65.

69 Preyer, op. cit.; Kent, op. cit., especially 33; the major theme of the latter's study of Rucellai is the ingenious reconstruction of the cooperation between Rucellai and Palla Strozzi, to finance Giovanni's building program.

70 He noted a dictum ascribed to Seneca that "il giovane debba attendere a guadagnare e aquistare, e il vechio debbe godere usando quello ch'egli à aquistato nella giovaneza"; *Zibaldone*, unpublished, 25r, cit. Kent, op. cit., 52.

71 On the demographics of patrician marriage see Herlihy and Klapisch, *Les Toscans et leur familles*, ch. 14.

72 *Zibaldone*, unpublished, 83v, cit. Kent, 13.

73 *Zibaldone* I, 121. He cited the popular saying "che'l ghuadangnare e lo spendere sono del numero de' grandi piaceri che gl'uomini piglino in questo mondo," concluding that "anchora sia maggore dolcezza lo spendere che il ghuadangnare."

74 *Zibaldone* I, 42. Kent, op. cit., 31, suggested that Giovanni's relative indifference to politics "cannot perhaps be wholly attributed to his own harsh experience." Cf. Gregory, "Palla Strozzi's Patronage," for a similar characterization of Rucellai's father-in-law as relatively apolitical.

75 Kent, op. cit., 47.

76 For an expert comparison of the Medici, Rucellai, and other contemporary palaces see Preyer, "Rucellai Palace," 202–3.

77 On Rucellai and Medici patronage of San Girolamo, see Rice, *St. Jerome in the Renaissance*; on Rucellai's sale of the land at Poggio a Caiano, Kent, "Lorenzo de' Medici's Acquisition."

78 See Preyer, 204. Kent, "Making of a Renaissance Patron," 50–51, suggested a possible "gap between the character of Giovanni Rucellai, who was not an educated man, and the sophistication of the buildings he commissioned"; however, he adds that "the size of the gap can easily be exaggerated."

79 Op. cit., especially 44–7.

80 See *Zibaldone*, unpublished, 63v, cit. Kent, op. cit., 39.

81 On Giovanni's references to the example of Gnaeus Octavius cited by Cicero see Kent, op. cit., 39, 54–5; Preyer, op. cit., 202–4. For a slightly different perspective on this, see above, pp. 221–2.

82 C.f. his *elogio* of the churches of Florence; this is just a list noting their affiliations and resources, which as he said, he copied at the direction of Messer Mariano [Salviati], the bishop of Cortona and former prior of Santissima Annunziata, *Zibaldone* I, 65–6.

83 *Zibaldone* I, 67–78.

84 See Gilbert, "Earliest Guide."

85 Kent, op. cit., 45. As a Christian tourist Rucellai was interested in relics and martyrs, in the portrait of the Virgin by Saint Luke himself, and he repeated a story associated with a chapel in St. Peter's concerning the noblewoman who disdained to kiss the cross after the poor had done so, *Zibaldone* I, 68–9.

86 *Zibaldone* 1, 77, 61.

87 See, for example, *Zibaldone* 1, 69.

88 Ibid., 75.

89 See *Zibaldone* 1, 74, "gratioso et gentile," though he also noted the church's "colonne doppie a coppie, con begli archi." Creighton Gilbert described the Santa Costanza mosaic Giovanni so admired as "less early Christian than classical, and the nearest thing anyone could see to ancient paintings," *Italian Art*, 111. Renaissance Italians regarded mosaics as a crucial link with the ancient world; Michele Savonarola of Padua wrote in 1447 that "Giotto the Florentine . . . was the first who rendered figures modern, in a marvelous way, after the old mosaics," ibid., 208–9.

90 On Rucellai and marbles see also Preyer, op. cit., 204.

91 *Natural History*, bk. XXXVI. Speaking of the first century B.C., he observed: "When we think of these things we feel ourselves blushing prodigiously with shame even for the men of former times." He was particularly appalled by "the spectacle of 360 columns being taken to the stage of an improvised theatre that was intended to be used barely for a month, and the laws were silent"; this occurred "in the aedileship of Marcus Scaurus," 58 B.C. There are quite a number of mosaics in the Medici collections, not only of Lorenzo, but also of his father Piero, and his grandfather Cosimo.

92 On the facade see Borsi, *Alberti*.

93 *Zibaldone* 1, 72. Cosimo had created a highly original and genuinely classicizing inscription for his father's tomb shortly after inspecting the inscriptions on Roman tombs at Ostia in the company of Poggio Bracciolini.

94 Op. cit., 63.

95 On the Rucellai tomb see Kent, op. cit., 57–60; Borsi, *Alberti*; Heydenreich, "Die Cappella Rucellai." Rucellai's first reference to the chapel was in 1448, when he was undecided whether to put it in Santa Maria Novella or San Pancrazio, where it was begun in or soon after 1458; in that year the decision to give a facade to the quarter church was approved by the Bankers' Guild and Saint Antoninus.

96 "IOHANNES RUCELLARIUS PAULI.F. UTINDE SALUTEM SUAM PRECARETUR UNDE OMNIUM CUM CHRISTO FACTA EST RESURRECTIO SACELLUM HOC / AD INSTAR IHEROSOLIMITANI SEPULCHRI FACIUNDUM CURAVIT MCCCCLXVII."

97 *Zibaldone* 1, 70; Kent, op. cit., 60. On possible Roman models see Borsi, op. cit., 35, 109.

98 *Zibaldone* 1, 23–4. Giovanni also ordered a triptych from Neri di Bicci in 1455, *Ricordanze*, 28–9, which included a representation of John the Baptist, Florence's patron saint, whose appearance in Medici commissions is usually seen as evidence of their "appropriation" of civic symbols; see above, pp. 193–4.

99 See Salvini, "Frescoes in the Altana," *Zibaldone* 2, 241–52. There is no documentation concerning their date or the artist; Salvini, 250, attributed them on grounds of style to Giovanni di Francesco, c.1457–9.

100 Ibid., 242, cf. Perosa, op. cit., 136; he did not identify Cavalca as one of Giovanni's sources.

101 See Salvini, op. cit.; *Zibaldone* 2, 241–52, 247.

102 See Newbigin, *Nuovo Corpus*, xii, xxi, 225–49, especially 249.

103 See Kent, op. cit., 81–2; MAP, v, 366, 12 Aug. 1439; ibid., 368, 23 Aug. 1439.

104 Kent, op. cit., 81, compared Giovanni's figures to Pliny the

105 See the *didascalie* of the manuscript, published *Zibaldone* 1, xix, MS., ff. 30–32; cf. above, pp. 91–3.

106 *Zibaldone* 1, 21–2.

107 While we might infer more about Giovanni's character than Cosimo's from his own testimony, it is his culture and values to which the *zibaldone* provide a more secure key, and which for the purpose of understanding his oeuvre, with its strong public function, are probably more important.

108 See "Lo Zibaldone."

109 As Perosa observed in the preface to his edition of the *Zibaldone*, 1, xiii, Giovanni articulated the values common to many other Florentines. For the long list of religious texts he transcribed, see Perosa, "Lo Zibaldone," 135–7; he also noted the errors and misattributions in Rucellai's quotations. Kent's biography emphasized Rucellai the merchant and banker, engaged in elaborate financial dealings with his Strozzi father-in-law; as Goldthwaite observed in his review of the second volume, Rucellai is most unusual in being so explicit about his interest in economic affairs. A notable example of this is his recurrent reference to the institution of the Monte delle Doti; see *Zibaldone* 1, 61, unpublished MS. f. 81–2. For an overview of the contents of the unpublished sections of the *zibaldone* see *Zibaldone* 1, xix–xxv; it includes such items as "Della significhazione e cirimonie della santa messa," ff. 41–3; De' comandamenti di Dio e di più altre chose ecchlesiastiche, ff. 44–6; Pistole di Senecha, ff. 138–78.

110 *Zibaldone*, 1, 103; also 112–14, 175–6, n. 40.

111 The citations from Sallust and Cicero's *De Natura* may be direct; on the sources of the other passages see Perosa's notes, *Zibaldone*, 1, 170–76.

112 Ibid., 116.

113 See above, p. 78; below, p. 423, n. 88, and p. 424, n. 89.

114 Lanza, *Lirici toscani* 2, 277.

115 "Onde ritorno/ far possi al disiato e vero segno/ non di piacer fe alcun, ma d'ira pregno,/ con dolori infiniti e grave scorno/ . . . Chi m'era fida guida e vera stella/ di me non cura e più sempre mi nòce,/ ch'io cerco di farmi ombra al suo bel velo," ibid., 408–10. The appeal and persistence of this image is indicated by Michelangelo's use of it almost a century later: "Arrived already is my life's brief course/ Through a most stormy sea, in a frail bark,/ At mankind's common port and at the shores/ Where one accounts for one's deeds, bright or dark," *Complete Poems*, 151, no. 147.

116 Rucellai had lost his fair share of these; see Kent, op. cit., 36. His account of the important events of his lifetime, especially the Florentine wars with other states, probably gives more attention to the Florentine galleys than that of any other of his contemporaries, with the exception of the diary of Luca degli Albizzi, who was captain of the Florentine galleys during the war with Lucca. Averardo de' Medici, who was stationed in Pisa at that time, also had a good deal to say about them; see above, ch. 12. For another mercantile reflection on ships, sails, God, and fortune see the letter of Lapo Mazzei to Francesco Datini published by Origo, *Merchant of Prato*, 237.

117 On the relation of this passage to Cosimo's life, see above, ch. 2; on the use of Platonic images, see Brown, "Platonism in Fifteenth-Century Florence."

118 *Zibaldone* 1, 122; Kent, op. cit., 85. Cf. Cosimo's much more

pragmatic account in his *Ricordi* of his own escape from ill fortune; safely arrived in Venice in 1433 he observed that "ho voluto fare ricordo dell'onore che mi fu fatto per non essere ingrato in farne ricordo, e ancora perchè fu cosa da non credere, essendo cacciato di casa, trovar tanto onore, perchè si suol perdere gli amici con la fortuna."

119 *La Rinascita del paganesimo antico*, 232–8. Cf. Marco Parenti's "original" device, more a diversion than an emblem, above, pp. 109–10.

120 Preyer noted that the Medici set a fashion in Florence by using emblems on their palace toward the end of the 1440s, as they wove arms and devices into the fabric of many other buildings. This practice may have been earlier established at the court of the Este, whose cultured example Cosimo and Piero followed in other innovations, including Piero's *studiolo*. Conversely, in the extensive use of *imprese*, the Este and Sforza may, in accordance with Fraser-Jenkins's observation, "Theory of Magnificence," have followed the lead of their Medici friends. Böninger, "Diplomatie im Dienste der Kontinuität," argued on the basis of a very limited understanding of their relationship that Cosimo took over the emblem used by Sforza and his father. The evidence adduced for borrowing in either direction is too circumstantial to be conclusive. In cases which are not well documented, the frequency of such borrowings can make it difficult to reconstruct their sequence. Not all the available evidence supports Preyer's view that "Giovanni's emblems, like those of many other Florentines, were imported, not invented to express personal conceits. They were used to allude to special relationships with noble houses," op. cit., 201. The handful of cases she adduced are not entirely comparable to that of the Rucellai; for example, the Strozzi received the privilege of using Angevin symbols in their arms for their service as bankers to the Neapolitan queen, for which they became knights of the crown; Niccolò d'Este conferred the use of his diamond ring on the count of Cotignola, who was his *condottiere*, in return for military service. A similar service may have been the essential element in the privileges conferred by the Este upon the Lanfredini by letters patent; see Preyer, op. cit., loc. cit., 220. According to Ames-Lewis, "Early Medicean Devices," 130, the earliest known example of the Este use of the diamond ring on an object is in a manuscript of 1455, and Rucellai's friendship with the Este in 1446 has not been shown to have had more significance for either party than dozens of others similarly described; nor are they mentioned in his *zibaldone*, which dwells at length upon Rucellai's connections, both within Florence and beyond it. By 1464 the Medici and Sforza arms and devices were combined in the garden of the Medici palace and the decoration of the Medici bank in Milan, but in view of the nature of the relationship between the two families, described above, the Medici borrowing is most unlikely to have been viewed as a "princely concession." Piero and Lorenzo's obvious delight in obtaining the privilege of adding to their arms the emblem of the royal house of Anjou, also officially conferred with letters patent, is a very different matter, and cognate to similar royal privileges accorded Florentine citizens by the emperor, and by the Angevin and Aragonese monarchs. However, it is difficult even to speculate with much confidence when we know so little about how Florentines at this time related the conventions of foreign heraldry to themselves.

121 Op. cit., 150. A depiction of the wheel of Fortune decorated the Palazzo Vecchio by 1400; see Rubinstein, *Palazzo Vecchio*, 50.

122 The *zibaldone* indicates Rucellai's lively interest in sailing craft, even apart from their associations with Fortune. On the River Arno at the bottom of his garden, he kept "uno navicello e channai e truovomirete da peschare d'ogni ragione," and he said that he took particular pleasure in sitting at table watching the barges pass by, *Zibaldone* 1, 21–2.

123 "Die Segel-Imprese."

124 *Purgatorio* 1, 1. See also *Zibaldone* 1, 68; Alberti, *On Painting*, 78, and Andrea Bartolini's comment to Giovanni di Cosimo de' Medici on his impressions of the papal court at Rome, MAP, v, 468, 9 Nov. 1442: "credo vi ti penserai la corte è povera et malghuidata e nonè questa naviciella di Pietro in meno pericholo cche ssi fussi quando da Xpo fu socchorsa in illo tenpore . . ."

125 These devices labeled not only public buildings but also a whole range of personal possessions; in the Medici houses, paintings for private devotion, and all sorts of household objects, including silver, linen, carpets, and hangings, as well as the better known birthtrays and *cassoni*. Rucellai created with figures trimmed into his hedgerows "una festa cum molte arme della chasa, e arme de' chasati, dove à maritate le sue figliuole, e de' chasati delle nuore sue, e maximamente quelle della chasa delli Strozzi del quale è la mia honorevole compagnia, e di molte altre gentilezze." He also included several objects used by various other families as *imprese*; diamonds, dolphins, "marzochi con bandiere del comune," ships, and galleys. Cf. the use by the Del Benino of the image of the phoenix. Neri di Bicci painted this on a roundel for their palace courtyard, while Francesco del Benino celebrated in a poem the symbolism and moral exemplum of the bird consumed by flames from gazing at the sun, and then resurrected from its own ashes; see above, p. 112, and Lanza, *Lirici toscani* 1, 263–5. Marco Parenti used a circle, signifying time, as his personal device, which he had engraved on the belt-buckle he gave to Filippo Strozzi, see above, pp. 109–10. As Preyer noted, op. cit., loc. cit., men with names incorporating images used these in their *imprese*; for example, the Sacchetti emblem was a sling and stones.

126 *Zibaldone* 1, 122.

Conclusion

1 *Zibaldone* of B. Fontius, Ricc., 907, 14v: "eleganter qui tum deo jocaretur dicere solebat, patientiam domine habe in me et omnia reddam tibi."

2 *Istorie fiorentine*, 264.

3 Machiavelli, *Istorie fiorentine*, 66; cf. Najemy, "Machiavelli and the Medici," especially 566–71. Najemy interpreted this comment in terms of Machiavelli's particular view of the tension between the extraordinary individual and the historical process; the former might be admired even if the latter were to be condemned. This tension was accepted by many fifteenth-century Florentine politicians and political analysts with an interest in working the system, not overturning it.

4 See Gilbert, *Machiavelli and Guicciardini*, especially ch. 1 on Florence and Venice, and "Venetian Constitution," especially 463–77; Pesman, "Florentine Ruling Group."

5 Review of *Transformation of Virginia*, 1.

6 See Brown, *Cult of the Saints*; on the language of patronage Kent, *Rise of the Medici* and *Fathers and Friends*; Kent and Simons, introduction to *Patronage, Art and Society*.

7 While this was hardly true in practice, it was the case in terms of constitutional status and privilege.

8 Filarete, *Trattato* 2, 683–4.

9 De Roover, *Rise and Decline*, passim and table 26.

10 Landucci, *Diario*, 3. Gregorio Dati also observed in this connection, *Istoria*, 15, that "A Florentine who is not a merchant, and who has not traveled through the world, seeing foreign nations and peoples and then returned to Florence with some wealth, is a man who enjoys no esteem whatsoever."

11 This may be seen in their patronage of painting; for example, Van Eyck's wedding portrait for the Arnolfini, the Medici Van der Weyden, and the Portinari altarpiece by Van der Goes.

12 Dei, *Cronica*, especially 67–8.

13 Brown, *Language and Images of Renaissance Italy*, vii, xii. Like many recent writers on Laurentian Florence, including particularly Bullard, "Magnificent Lorenzo," she inclined to the view that the tensions between Florence's republican constitution and Medicean autocratic behavior became clear only under Lorenzo. However, she also suggested that "Cosimo's attempts to reduce the wealthy Guelf Party, and his use of his family's bank as its treasurer, anticipate his grandson Lorenzo's activities in the field of government finance, where the boundary between the public interest and Lorenzo's private interest was becoming very indistinct."

14 "Early Medici as Patrons," 35; "Golden Age," 31.

15 Ames-Lewis, *Cosimo "il vecchio,"* 1–2.

16 Bullard, *Image and Anxiety*, ix, made a similar point about Lorenzo: "Trying to remove the veil of myth from Lorenzo is like trying to remove the garments from a statue. It cannot be done. But by acknowledging the pervasive presence of myth in our perceptions of Lorenzo, we come to see his myth as a valuable signpost by which to redirect our gaze towards otherwise obfuscated aspects of the period which, upon investigation, yield new intrpretations and a bit of fresh air too."

17 "Io rido, e el rider mio non passa dentro: io ardo, el'arsion mia non par di fore," *Lettere*, 12.

18 For a subtle analysis of the social context of this ambiguity which Cosimo's case exemplifies, see Weissman, "Importance of Being Ambiguous." Calling for the recognition of a more "multi-faceted "Renaissance man,'" whose identity was shaped by "interpersonal interaction," rather than imagining a Renaissance sense of self "mechanically reflecting some automatic process of class or status socialization", 269, Weissman discerned a "purposeful, intentional use of the mechanisms of ambiguity to define and protect the self", 279, to manipulate and redefine situations in which an individual was torn by competing, often conflicting personal obligations. "Within an intensely public culture that demanded intense loyalty, devious, manipulative behavior was used to protect a coherent sense of self and to project a coherent and trustworthy image," 273, which observers equated with personal honor. This account of Renaissance attitudes is amply supported with reference to the writings of such contemporary experts on social analysis as Paolo da Certaldo, Giovanni Morelli, and Francesco Guicciardini, and further illuminated by the model of Erving Goffman's account of "impression management" in his *Presentation of Self*.

19 See, for example, Fubini, "Problemi di Politica Fiorentina," 6, on "il culto idealizzante alla memoria di Cosimo, nel cui nome vedeva compendiata l'idea di 'cosmo,' dell'ordine universale . . . l'invocazione costante a un patronato . . . se non tirannico, certo paternalisticamente controllato." See also Kent on Lorenzo, "Un paradiso habitato da diavoli."

20 On the intellectual currents of this period, see particularly Holmes, *Florentine Enlightenment*, ch. 1.

21 See De Roover, *Rise and Decline*; Rubinstein, *Government of Florence*; Clarke, *Power and Patronage*.

22 On these modifications, from among the vast quantity of literature on Lorenzo, see for example Brown, "Public and Private Interest."

23 The italics are mine.

24 Watkins, ed., *Humanism and Liberty*, 157–62, especially 158–9.

25 Cf. above, ch. 2, and Kent, *Rise of the Medici*, ch. 5.

26 See above, ch. 4, n. 6.

27 "Cosimo de' Medici come banchiere," 472.

28 Op. cit., 359–60.

29 For the literature on the Magi, and the evidence relating to the Medici family's involvement in the cult, see above, ch. 13.

30 Published Hatfield, "Compagnia de' Magi," 148.

31 On these see Strocchia, *Death and Ritual*, especially 182–8.

32 MAP, CLXIII, 41b, published Rochon, *La Jeunesse de Laurent*, 47, n. 12.

33 MAP, CLXIII, 3r–4r. Extracts of this document have been published by Fabroni, *Magni Cosmi*, and some passages are translated in Ross, *Lives of the Early Medici*, 77–81.

34 Gombrich, "Early Medici as Patrons of Art," 49–50, suggested that the associations of the medal and its inscription were imperial. Cf. McManamon, "Continuity and Change," 76–7: the Roman resonances of the title were inclusive of both republic and empire and therefore ambiguous; its primary associations were with Cicero and Camillus, but it was also awarded to Julius Caesar and Augustus.

35 "cum summa atque amplissima beneficia in rem publicam florentinam bello et pace contulerit, semperque patriam suam omni pietate conservaverit, adiuverit, auxerit eique magno usui et glorie fuierit, atque usque ad supremum vite diem ipsam in omnibus que summum virum ac civem optimum decent, non secus ac pater familias propriam domum omni cura, studio, diligentiaque gubernarit pro eius maximis virtutibus beneficia et pietas . . . ," ASF, Provv. Reg., 155m., 261v–263v, published McKillop, "Dante and *Lumen Christi*," 291–301, especially 292. See also Brown, "Humanist Portrait of Cosimo."

36 Above, pp. 190–91: "Orba parente suo patria moesta gemit . . ."

37 Paoletti, "Donatello's Bronze Doors," 47.

38 Lanza, *Lirici toscani* 2, 286.

39 Laur., Ashb. 539, 80r. Such a concept of the responsibilities of rule is not yet dead. United States President George Bush in his State of the Nation speech of 1992 observed that "we must provide for our nation in the way a family provides for its children."

40 Fabroni, *Magni Cosmi* 2, 253–4.

41 The most exhaustive study is Clearfield's "Tomb of Cosimo de' Medici"; see also Butterfield, *Verrocchio*, ch. 2, especially 36, on the uniqueness of this monument in terms of tomb typology, and on the meanings conveyed by its constituent elements; type, placement, design, materials, and epitaph.

42 Vespasiano, *Vite* 2, 190. Piero's account of the burial and funeral is from a *Libro di Ricordi* that was transcribed by Moreni before its disappearance; citations are from Clearfield, op. cit., 21–2.

43 Ibid. In a note of 1496 concerning the work for which the deceased sculptor Andrea del Verrocchio had not received proper payment, his brother Tommaso included and identified by its location "la sepultura di Chosimo appie del altare magiore in S. Lorenzo."

44 See above, p. 24, and fig. 7. The inscription on the reliquary was recorded by Vasari, Vasari-Milanesi, *Vite* 2, 234, and Richa, *Notizie istoriche* 8, 158–9: "Clarissimi Viri Cosmas et Laurentius fratres Medices neglectas diu sanctorum reliquias martyrium religioso studio ac fidelissima pietate suis sumptibus aeneis loculis condendas colendasque curarunt." The *zibaldone* of Giovanni di Andrea and Antonio di Meglio, popular poets at the center of the Medici circle, includes a memoriam to Saints Protus, Nemesius, and Iacintus, the otherwise obscure dedicatees of the Medici reliquary; see above, p. 24 and fig. 7.

45 See Ames-Lewis, "Fra Filippo Lippi's S. Lorenzo *Annunciation.*"

46 Clearfield, op. cit., 27; see also McKillop, "Dante and *Lumen Christi.*"

47 Clearfield, op. cit., 29–30; she observed that almost every crypt contained an altar dedicated to the Virgin, and the most important graves were placed nearest to it.

48 For Cosimo's extremely active role in shaping the liturgy of San Lorenzo to the commemoration of the Medici dead see Gaston, "Liturgy and Patronage," and McKillop, especially "Dante and *Lumen Christi.*"

49 Gaston, op. cit., 119.

50 McKillop, op. cit., 251, 271, 273–4. See also the list, published D'Ancona, "I begli arredi," of the church furnishings of San Lorenzo in 1393, when not one of 265 items endowed for the benefit of the donor's soul had been given by the Medici; cf. McKillop's account, "Dante and *Lumen Christi,*" especially 280–88, of the many Medici gifts of vestments and altar furniture in use by the time of Cosimo's death.

51 See, for example, Herzner, "Die Kanzeln Donatellos," discussed below, n. 63.

52 Beyer and Boucher, introduction to *Piero de' Medici*, xviii; see also Beyer, "Die Porphyry-Rotae der Medici."

53 "Dante and *Lumen Christi,*" 289–90. On the use of marbles see also Clearfield, op. cit.; Lavin, "Donatello's Bronze Pulpits," 17.

54 *Triumph of Vulcan*, especially 122–3, also 60, 75, 80. The examples she noted include the porphyry imperial tomb chests in Rome and Constantinople, the decoration of such early Christian churches as San Lorenzo in Damaso, and Abbot Suger's antique porphyry vase for the twelfth-century church of Saint Denis, near Paris. An early Renaissance instance of the use of porphyry rotae in Rome was the pavement in the nave of Saint John Lateran by Martin V, modeled after the early Christian Roman churches of San Lorenzo Fuori le Mura, Santa Maria in Cosmedin, the Aracoeli, and San Clemente; see Sperling, "Verrocchio's Medici Tombs."

55 Lavin, "Sources of Donatello's Pulpits" and "Donatello's Bronze Pulpits." For Traversari's influence on Cosimo see above, p. 87; on Traversari's thinking about the early Christian world and its possible application to the visual, see Stinger, *Humanism and the Church Fathers* and "Tempio degli Scolari." On Benedetto Accolti's translation for Cosimo of

the homilies on the Gospel of Saint John by Chrysostom, the early Christian writer in whom Traversari had kindled Cosimo's major interest, see Black, "Ancients and Moderns in the Renaissance."

56 On the central role played by this text in the development of the Florentine civic ethos see Davis, "Topographical and Historical Propaganda," and Rubinstein, "Beginnings of Political Thought." Its traditions were emphasized and preserved by their incorporation into the later histories of Florence by Villani and Dati which were staples of Florentine popular culture in Cosimo's lifetime.

57 Lavin, op. cit. The fact that the pulpits were probably not brought into the church before 1515, see Butterfield, "Documents for the Pulpits," is not immediately relevant to the patron's intention in commissioning them; cf. Vespasiano, *Vite.*

58 See Manetti, *Life of Brunelleschi*, 107, and Saalman's speculation, ibid., 147, concerning Cosimo's intentions.

59 Burns, "San Lorenzo in Florence," published a fifteenth-century plan showing Cosimo's tomb at the entrance to the *cappella maggiore*, with the altar in front of the chapel and approached by steps from behind, so that the celebrant would face the body of the church. Butterfield observed however, *Verrocchio*, 36, that it is unclear to which of several successive stages in the construction and modification of the altar this plan refers. Clearfield pointed out, op. cit., 25–6, that the same changes were made in several other churches around this time; in 1462 at Pienza; at Santa Giustina in Padua, at Santissima Annunziata in Florence and at San Salvatore just outside it, as part of an emphasis on greater lay participation in services in the early Christian tradition.

60 Lavin; Saalman, 18. Clearfield, op. cit., 28.

61 "Donatello's Bronze Pulpits," 23.

62 Ibid.; also Becherucci, *I Pergami.*

63 On these issues see Janson, *Donatello*, 209–18; Lavin, "Sources of Donatello's Pulpits"; Herzner, "Die Kanzeln"; Becherucci, *I Pergami.* See also Pope-Hennessy, *Donatello, Sculptor*, 292–313, and 349, especially n. 41. The differences in height, organization, and framing arrangements between the panels of the two pulpits have not been entirely explained. See the above citations and also Bennett and Wilkins, *Donatello*, ch. I, especially 13. Herzner's suggestion that they were intended for a grandiose free-standing tomb in front of the high altar, a commission made perhaps as early as 1457, but abandoned as a result of a religious crisis which led Cosimo to choose a more modest memorial, depends upon imagining Cosimo's sudden conversion to a position which in fact he had held all his life, and involves the arbitrary dismissal of testimony by Albertini, a canon of San Lorenzo in 1510 who had access to the church records, as well as that of Vespasiano, who had access to Cosimo. It also fails to comprehend the immense spiritual and liturgical significance of the position of Cosimo's simple tomb marker, and the philosophical and theological implications of its distinctive design. Pope-Hennessy combined Herzner's "brilliant" idea with an implausible assumption of his own, that Piero's "decorative, classicizing" taste was "the dominant force in Medici commissions after about 1455." He suggested that "work on the altar or tomb may have been suspended" because Piero did not share Cosimo's affinity for Donatello's style, op. cit., 349.

64 On this see particularly Verdon, "Donatello and the Theater." After noting the generic relationship of the spatial arrange-

ments in the pulpit panels with the relief style of column of Trajan, Verdon pointed out the very specific relationship of a number of quattrocento paintings and sculptures to the stage sets of sacred plays. Cf. above, pp. 62–5. He observed, 40, that many writers have invoked metaphors associated with the theater in describing the pulpits, particularly Seymour, who imagined their "action taking place on the precariously narrow platform of a medieval stage," customarily set up on the rood screen of a church. He also commented, 49, upon the "enigmatic fence set up in the Ascension . . . without intelligible iconographic function" and the "strange and startling" effect of "figures cascading out of the frame of a space with real rather than imaginary physical depth," by contrast with the Albertian ideal.

65 Janson, op. cit., 218; see also Pope-Hennessy, op. cit., 301, who described the scenes of Christ before Caiaphas and Pontius Pilate as among "the most moving evocations of Christ's condemnation in the whole of Western art."

66 On the Resurrection scene see Lavin, "Sources of Donatello's Pulpits," 30; also Pope-Hennessy, op. cit., 296.

67 See Saalman, "A Cosimo Portrait?" His identification of the man's features with those of the Gozzoli frescoes portrait and the posthumous medal of Cosimo is reasonably convincing; the wife's features similarly bear a broad resemblance to those of the woman in Contessina's only putative portrait. It seems to me that the argument from the function of the two figures, not identifiable with any other customary protagonists of this scene, and set apart from them, as Saalman observed, by the sharper definition of their features, is more important than that of their form. McKillop, "Dante and *Lumen Christi*," 281–2, suggested that this may be explicated by two texts from the Gospel and the Epistles which would have been read from the ambos as part of the Good Friday service.

68 *Donatello, Sculptor*, 303.

69 Lavin, "Donatello's Bronze Pulpits," 15; above, p. 119.

70 I owe these last observations, like so many others contributing to my attempt to follow Michael Baxandall's injunction to reconstruct the "intellectual and sensible world of the Renaissance," to the work of Susan McKillop; see here especially "Dante and *Lumen Christi*," 284–8. On Solomon's knot, see also Lavin, "Donatello's Bronze Pulpits"; Ames-Lewis, "Early Medicean Devices."

71 Cosimo to Ficino, *Letters* 1, 1.

72 Lavin, "Donatello's Bronze Pulpits," 17.

73 Ficino, *Opera omnia* 1, 615.

74 *Commento* on *Purgatorio* XXXIII, 15.

75 *Paradiso* XXIII, 85–93; 133–45.

WORKS CITED

Archives

Florence, Archivio di Stato
  Acquisti e Doni
  Carte Strozziane
  Catasto
  Compagnie Religiose Soppresse
  Consulte e Pratiche
  Conventi Soppressi
  Manoscritti
  Medici avanti il Principato
  Provvisioni, Registri
  Signori e Collegi, Deliberazioni
  Signori e Collegi, Missive
  Signori, Legazioni e Commissioni
  Tratte
Florence, Buonomini di San Martino
Florence, Opera del Duomo
  Arte della Lana
Florence, San Lorenzo

Manuscript Libraries

Florence, Biblioteca Nazionale
Florence, Laurenziana
Florence, Riccardiana
Milan, Ambrosiana
Paris, Bibliothèque Nationale
Rome, Vaticana

Printed Sources

Aesop, *Fables*; see Esopo.
Alberti, Leon Battista, *Opere volgari*, ed. Cecil Grayson, 3 vols., Bari, 1960–73.
——*Della famiglia*, in *Opere volgari*, ed. Grayson, vol. 1, Bari, 1960, 3–341; trans. and ed. Renée Neu Watkins, *The Family in Renaissance Florence*, Columbia, s.c., 1969.
——*Intercoenales*, trans. and ed. David Marsh, *Dinner Pieces*, Binghamton, N.Y., 1987.
——*Della pittura: On Painting*, trans. Cecil Grayson, with introduction and notes by Martin Kemp, London, 1991.
——*De Re Aedificatoria: On the Art of Building in Ten Books*, trans. Joseph Rykwert, Cambridge, Mass., 1988; Latin and Italian texts, *De Re Aedificatoria* and *Dell'architettura*, trans. and ed. G. Orlandi and P. Portoghesi, Milan, 1966.
——*Rime e versioni poetiche*, ed. G. Gorni, Milan and Naples, 1975.
——*On Painting and On Sculpture*, English and Latin texts of *De Pictura* and *De Statua*, trans. and ed. Cecil Grayson, New York, 1972.
——*Villa*, in *Opere volgari*, ed. Grayson, vol. 1, Bari, 1960, 359–63.
Albizzi, Rinaldo degli, *Commissioni*, ed. C. Guasti, 3 vols., Florence, 1867–73.
Antoninus, Saint, *Chronicon*, Lyons, 1586.
——*Summa Theologica*, Nuremberg, 1491.
——*Lettere di Sant'Antonino*, ed. Tommaso Corsetto, Florence, 1859.
——*Opera a ben vivere di Santo Antonino*, ed. Francesco Palermo, Florence, 1858.
Aquinas, Saint Thomas, *On Kingship, to the King of Cyprus*, trans. Gerald B. Phelan, Toronto, 1949.
Archivio di Stato di Firenze, *Medici avanti il Principato, Inventario* 1, Florence, 1966.
Aristotle, *Politics and Economics*, trans. E. Walford, London, 1880.
——*The Nicomachean Ethics*, Greek and English, trans. A. L. Rackham, Cambridge, Mass., and London, 1934.
——*Generation of Animals*, Greek and English, trans. A. L. Peck, Cambridge, Mass., and London, 1943.
——*The Poetics*. "Longinus": *On the Sublime*. Demetrius: *On Style*. Greek and English, trans. W. H. Fyfe, London, 1932.
Avogadro, A., *De religione et munificentia Cosmi Medicis florentini*, in *Delizie degli eruditi toscani*, ed. P. Ildefonso di San Luigi, vol. 12, Florence, 1770–89.
Barbaro, Francesco, *De Re Uxoria*, in "Francesco Barbaro: '*De Re Uxoria Liber*,'" ed. A. Gnesetto, *Atti e memorie della Reale Accademia di Scienze, Lettere ed Arte in Padova*, n.s. 32, 1915–16, 6–105.
Bardi de' Medici, Contessina, *VII lettere ai figliuoli Piero e Giovanni pubblicate per nozze Lanichelli*, ed. Mariotto da T. Casini and S. Morpurgo, Florence, 1886.
Beccadelli, Antonio, called Panormita, *Hermaphroditus*, in *Poeti Latini del Quattrocento*, ed. Francesco Arnaldi, Milan and Naples, 1964.

Belcari, Feo, *La Rappresentazione quando la Nostra Donna Vergine Maria fu annunziata dall'angelo*, ed. Nerida Newbigin, Sydney, 1983.

Bernard of Clairvaux, Saint, *Letters*, in *The Letters of Saint Bernard*, ed. and trans. B. S. James, London, 1953.

—— *The Steps of Humility*, trans. and introduced by George Bosworth Burch, Notre Dame, 1963.

Bernardino of Siena, Saint, *Le Prediche Volgari*, ed. C. Cannarozzi, vols. 1–2, Pistoia, 1934; vols. 3–5, Florence 1940; vols. 6–7, Florence, 1958; *La Fonte della Vita: Prediche volgari scelte*, Florence, 1964.

—— *Opera Omnia*, in *Sancti Bernardini Senensis Ordinis Seraphicum Minorum Opera Omnia*, ed. Iohannis De La Haye, 2nd ed., 5 vols., Venice, 1745.

Bertolini, Lucia, ed., *De vera amicitia: i testi del primo Certame coronario*, Ferrara, 1993.

Bible, King James Version; also Vulgate.

Billi, Antonio, ed. Carl Frey, *Il libro di Antonio Billi*, Berlin, 1892.

Boccaccio, *Centonovelle*, in *La Letteratura Italiana, Storia e Testi*, 8, ed. Enrico Bianchi, Carlo Salinari, and Natalino Sapegno, Milan, 1952.

—— *Decameron, Filocolo, Ameto, Fiammetta*.

—— *Genealogia Deorum, In Defence of Poetry*, ed. Jeremiah Reedy, Toronto, 1978.

Boethius, *De Consolatione, The Consolation of Philosophy*, Greek and English, trans. P. G. Walsh, Oxford and New York, 1999.

Bondanella, Peter, and Mark Musa, eds., *The Portable Machiavelli*, New York, 1979.

Bracciolini, Poggio, *Opera omnia*, ed. Riccardo Fubini, 1964.

—— *Epistolae*, in *Prosatori latini del Quattrocento*, ed. E. Garin, Milan and Naples, 1952.

—— *Facezie*, Latin and Italian, ed. and trans. Marcello Ciccuto, Milan, 1983; *The Facetiae of Poggio*, trans. Edward Storer, London, 1928.

—— *De Nobilitate*, in *Prosatori latini del Quattrocento*, ed. E. Garin, Milan and Naples, 1952.

Brucker, Gene, ed., *Two Memoirs of Renaissance Florence: The Diaries of Buonaccorso Pitti and Gregorio Dati*, New York, 1967.

—— *The Society of Renaissance Florence: A Documentary Study*, New York, 1971.

Brunelleschi, Filippo, *Il Grasso Legnaiuolo*, in Antonio di Tuccio Manetti, *Vita di Filippo Brunelleschi, preceduta dall Novella del Grasso Legnaiuolo*, ed. Domenico de Robertis and Giuliano Tanturli, Milan, 1976; English trans. with comment in Lauro Martines, *An Italian Renaissance Sextet: Six Tales in Historical Context*, New York, 1994.

—— *Sonetti*, ed. Domenico de' Robertis, with introduction by Giuliano Tanturli, Florence, 1977.

Brunelleschi, Ghigo, *Geta e Birria*, ed. C. Arlia, in *Commissioni per i testi di lingua*, Bologna, 1968.

Bruni, Leonardo, *De Militia*, trans. C. C. Bayley, in *War and Society in Renaissance Florence*, Toronto, 1961.

—— *Dialogues*, in *The Three Crowns of Florence*, ed. D. Thompson and A. Nagel, New York, 1972, 19–52; trans. from

Prosatori Latini del Quattrocento, ed. E. Garin, Milan and Naples, 1952.

—— *On the Constitution*, in *The Renaissance*, ed. E. Cochrane and J. Kirschner, Chicago, 1986, 140–44.

—— *Panegirico della città di Firenze*, ed. Giuseppe De Toffol, Florence, 1974, Latin and Italian; partial English trans. in *The Earthly Republic*, ed. Benjamin Kohl and Ronald G. Witt, Philadelphia 1978, 135–75.

Buonarotti, Michelangelo, *Complete Poems*, trans. Joseph Tusiani, New York, 1960.

Buoninsegni, Domenico, *Storie della città di Firenze dall'anno 1410 al 1460*, Florence, 1637.

Burchiello, Domenico di Giovanni, called Il Burchiello, *I Sonetti*, ed. A. Viviani, Milan, 1940.

Buser, Benjamin, *Die Beziehungen der Mediceer zu Frankreich während der Jahre 1434–1494 in ihrem Zusammenhang mit den allgemeinen Verhältnissen Italiens*, Leipzig, 1879.

Caesar, Julius, *War Commentaries and De bello civili*, ed. and trans. John Warrington, London and New York, 1958.

Cambi, Giovanni, *Istorie*, in *Delizie degli eruditi toscani*, ed. Ildefonso di San Luigi, vols. 20–30, Florence, 1785–6.

Cappelli, A., *Cronologia, cronografia e calendario perpetuo*, Milan, 1978.

Capponi, Gino, *Ricordi di Gino di Neri Capponi*, ed. G. Folena in *Miscellanea di studi offerte a A. Balduino e B. Bianchi*, Padua, 1962, 34–9.

Capponi, Neri, *Commentari di Neri di Gino Capponi di cose seguite in Italia dal 1419 al 1456*, in *Rerum Italicarum Scriptores* 18, ed. L. A. Muratori, Milan, 1731.

—— *Commentari dell'acquisto di Pisa*, Florence, 1862.

Casotti, G. B., *Prose e rime de' due Buonaccorsis da Montemagno con Annotazioni. Ed Alcune Rime di Niccolò Tinucci*, Florence, 1818.

Cassian, *Monastic Institutes*, ed. Philip Schaff, in *Nicene and Post-Nicene Fathers* 2, London, 1892.

Cavalca, Fra Domenico, *Disciplina degli spirituali col trattato delle trenta stoltizie*, ed. G. Bottari, Milan, 1838.

—— *I frutti della lingua, volgarizzamento del Dialogo di San Gregorio e dell'Epistola di S. Girolamo ad Eustochio*, ed. G. Bottari, Milan, 1837.

—— *Medicina del cuore, ovvero Trattato della pazienza*, Milan, 1838.

—— *Il Pungilingua*, ed. G. Bottari, Milan, 1837.

—— *Specchio di croce*, ed. G. Bottari, Brescia, 1822.

—— *Lo specchio de' peccati*, ed. F. del Furia, Milan, 1838.

—— *Volgarizzamento degli Atti degli Apostoli*, ed. Filippo Nesti, Florence, 1837.

Cavalcanti, Giovanni, *Istorie fiorentine*, ed. G. Di Pino; citations of vol. 2 refer to the edition of F. Polidori, 2 vols., Florence, 1838–9.

—— *The "Trattato politico-morale" of Giovanni Cavalcanti (1381–1451)*, ed. Marcella T. Grendler, Geneva, 1973.

Chambers, D. S., ed. and trans., *Patrons and Artists in the Italian Renaissance*, Columbia, s.c., 1971.

Chellini, Giovanni, *Le ricordanze*, ed. Maria Teresa Sillano, Milan, 1984.

Cianfogni, P., ed., *Memorie istoriche dell'Ambrosiano R. Basilica di S. Lorenzo di Firenze*, 3 vols., Florence, 1804–17.

Cicero, Marcus Tullius, *De senectute De amicitia, De divinatione*, Latin and English, trans. William Armistead Falconer, London and Cambridge, Mass., 1964.

——*De Officiis*, Latin and English, trans. Walter Miller, London and Cambridge, Mass., 1913.

——*Epistolae ad familiares: The Letters to His Friends*, Latin and English, trans. W. Glynn Williams, 3 vols., London and Cambridge, Mass., 1952–4.

——*De Oratore*, Latin and English, trans. E. W. S. Sutton and H. Rackham, Cambridge, Mass., and London, 1942.

——*Orator, Brutus*, Latin and English, trans. G. L. Hendrickson and H. M. Hubbell, London and Cambridge, Mass., 1939.

Cicero, Pseudo, *Rhetorica ad Herennium*, ed. and trans. H. Caplan, London and Cambridge, 1954.

Compagni, Dino, *La cronica*, ed. I. del Lungo, in *Rerum Italicarum Scriptores*, vol. 22, pt. 3, Città di Castello, 1907–16; trans. and ed. Daniel D. Bornstein, *Dino Compagni's Chronicle of Florence*, Philadelphia, 1986.

Corti, Gino, and Frederick Hartt, "New Documents Concerning Donatello, Luca and Andrea della Robbia, Desiderio, Mino, Uccello, Pollaiuolo, Filippo Lippi, Baldovinetti and others," *AB* 44, 1962, 155–7.

D'Ancona, Alessandro, ed., *Sacre rappresentazioni dei secoli XIV, XV e XVI*, 3 vols., Florence, 1872.

Da Voragine, Iacopo, *The Golden Legend,* trans. William Granger Ryan, 2 vols., Princeton, 1993.

De Angelis, Laura, et al., eds., *La civiltà fiorentina del Quattrocento*, Florence, 1993.

De Blasi, Nicola, ed., *Libro de la destructione de Troya: Volgarizzamento Napoletano trecentesco da Guido delle Colonne*, Rome, 1986.

Del Corazza, Bartolomeo, *Diario fiorentino*, ed. Roberta Gentile, Rome, 1991.

De Cossart, Michael, *Antonio Beccadelli and the Hermaphrodite*, Liverpool, 1984.

Dante Alighieri, *La divina commedia*, ed. Natalino Sapegno, Florence, 3 vols., 1956–7.

——*Convivio*, in *Le opere di Dante Alighieri*, ed. E. Moore and P. Toynbee, Oxford, 1963.

Dati, Gregorio, *Istoria di Firenze*, ed. L. Pratesi, Florence, 1904.

Dei, Benedetto, *La cronica dall'anno 1400 all'anno 1500*, ed. Roberto Barducci, Florence, 1985.

——"Una Lista di Personaggi," ed. Gino Corti, *Rinascimento* 3, 1952, 152–6.

Dictionnaire de L'Académie Française, Brussels, 1835.

The Divine Office: The Liturgy of the Hours According to the Roman Rite, 3 vols., London, 1974.

Dominici, Giovanni, *Lettere spirituali*, ed. M.-T. Casella and G. Pozzi, *Spicilegium Friburgense* 13, Freiburg, 1969.

——*Il libro d'amore di carità del fiorentino B. Giovanni Dominici, dell ordine de' predicatori*, ed. Antonio Ceruti, Bologna, 1889.

——*Regola del governo di cura familiare*, ed. D. Salvi, Florence, 1860; trans. and intro., A. B. Coté, in *On the Education of Children*, Washington, 1927.

Dufay, Guillaume, *Nuper Rosarum Flores*, in *Opera Omnia*, ed. Guglielmus de Dan, Rome, 1948, 70–6.

Encyclopaedia Universalis, Paris, 1980.

Esopo, *Favole*, from the edition of E. Chambry, Paris, 1967, with woodcuts from the edition of Manfredo Bonello, Venice, 1491, and a note by Giovanni Mardersteig, Rizzoli, 1976.

Eusebius, *The Ecclesiastical History*, Greek and English, trans. Kirsop Lake, 2 vols., London and Cambridge, Mass., 1957–9.

Fabroni, Angelo, *Magni Cosmi Medicei Vita*, 2 vols., Pisa, 1789.

——*Magni Laurentii Medicis Magnificentia Vita*, Pisa, 1784.

Ficino, Marsilio, *The Letters of Marsilio Ficino*, trans. Language Department, School of Economic Science, London, intro. by Paul Oskar Kristeller, 4 vols., London, 1975–81.

Filarete (Antonio Averlino), *Trattato di architettura*, ed. A. M. Finoli and L. Grassi, 2 vols., Milan, 1972; ed. and trans. John R. Spencer, *Filarete's Treatise on Architecture*, 2 vols., New Haven and London, 1965.

Filelfo, *Commentationes in esilio*, in *Prosatori latini del Quattrocento*, ed. E. Garin, Latin and Italian, Milan and Naples, 1952.

——*Sforziad*, in Diana Robin, *Filelfo in Milan*, Princeton, 1991.

The Florentine Fior' di virtù of 1491, trans. Nicholas Fersin with facsimiles of all the original woodcuts, intro. by L. J. Rosenwald, Washington, D.C., 1953.

Foster, Philip, "Donatello Notices in Medici Letters," *AB* 62, 1980, 148–50.

Frescobaldi, Leonardo, *Viaggi in Terrasanta*, ed. G. Angelini, Florence, 1944.

Garin, Eugenio, ed., *Prosatori latini del quattrocento*, Milan and Naples, 1952.

Gaye, G., *Carteggio inedito d'artisti dei secoli XIV, XV, XVI*, 3 vols., Turin, 1839–40.

Gherardi, Giovanni, da Prato, *Il Paradiso degli Alberti*, ed. A. Lanza, Rome, 1975.

Ghiberti, Lorenzo, *I Commentari*, ed. O Morisani, Naples, 1947.

Gilbert, Creighton, ed., *Italian Art, 1400–1500: Sources and Documents*, Englewood Cliffs, N.J. 1980. The same sources are published in their original language in Gilbert, *L'Arte del quattrocento nelle testimonianze coeve*, Florence, 1988.

Goldin, Frederick, ed., *The Song of Roland*, New York, 1978.

Giovanni dalle Celle, *Letters*, in *Lettere del Beato Don Giovanni dalle Celle, Monaco Vallombrosano, e d'altri*, ed. B. Sorio, Rome, 1845.

Giovanni dalle Celle–Luigi Marsili, *Lettere*, ed. F. Giambonini, 2 vols., Florence, 1991.

Gordan, Phyllis Walter, *Two Renaissance Book Hunters: The Letters of Poggius Bracciolinus to Nicolaus de Niccolis*, New York, 1974.

Griffiths, Gordon, James Hankins, and David Thompson, eds. *The Humanism of Leonardo Bruni: Selected Texts*, Binghamton, N.Y., 1987.

Grunzweig, A., *Correspondance de la filiale de Bruges des Médicis*, Brussels, 1931.

Guarini, Guarino, *Epistolario di Guarino Veronese*, ed. R. Sabbadini, 3 vols., Venice, 1915–19.

Guasti, Cesare, *Le feste di San Giovanni Battista in Firenze: descritte in prosa e in rima da contemporanei*, Florence, 1926.

Herzner, Volker, "*Regesti Donatelliani*," *Rivista dell'Istituto Nazionale d'Archaeologia e di Storia dell'Arte*, ser. 3, 2, 1979, 169–228.

Iacopone da Todi, *Laude*, ed. Franco Mancini, Rome and Bari, 1977.

Juvenal, *Satires*, in Juvenal and Persius, Latin and English, trans. G. G. Ramsay, London and Cambridge, Mass., 1950.

Kennedy, Clarence, "Documenti inediti su Desiderio da Settignano e la sua famiglia," *Rivista d'Arte* 12, 1930, 16–29.

Kohl, Benjamin, and Ronald Witt, eds., *The Earthly Republic: Italian Humanists on Government and Society*, Pennsylvania, 1978.

Lactantius, *The Divine Institutes*, bks. 1–7, trans. Mary Francis McDonald, Washington, 1964.

Landucci, Luca, *Diario fiorentino dal 1450 al 1516*, ed. I. del Badia, Florence 1883, repr. 1985.

Lanza, Antonio, *Lirici toscani del quattrocento*, 2 vols., Rome, 1973–5.

Lapaccini, Giuliano, *Cronaca*, in Raoul Morçay, "La Cronaca del convento fiorentino di San Marco: la parte più antica, dettata da Giuliano Lapaccini," *ASI* 1, 1913.

Latini, Brunetto, *Il tesoretto*, ed. and trans. Julia Bolton, Holloway, N.Y., 1981.

Leonardo da Vinci, *The Notebooks*, ed. J. Richter, 2 vols., New York, 1970.

Livy, *Decades (Historiae Romanae)*, Latin and English, trans. B. O. Foster et al., London and Cambridge, Mass., 1959–67.

Lopez, Robert S., and Irving W. Raymond, *Medieval Trade in the Mediterranean World*, New York, 1961.

Louis, Cameron, ed., *The Commonplace Book of Robert Reynes of Acle: An Edition of Tanner MS 407*, New York and London, 1980.

Machiavelli, Niccolò, *Lettere*, ed. F. Gaeta, Milan, 1961; trans. Alan Gilbert, *The Letters of Machiavelli*, Chicago, 1961; also trans. and ed. Peter Bondanella and Mark Musa, *The Portable Machiavelli*, New York, 1979.

——*Arte della guerra e scritti politici minori*, ed. S. Bertelli, Milan, 1960.

——*Istorie fiorentine*, ed. F. Gaeta, Milan, 1962.

Maffei, Timoteo, *In Magnificentiae Cosmi Medicei Florentini Detractores*, in *Deliciae Eruditorum*, ed. G. Lami, 12, Florence, 1742, 150–68.

Manetti, Antonio di Tuccio, *Vita di Filippo Brunelleschi, preceduta dall Novella del Grasso Legnaiuolo*, ed. Domenico de Robertis and Giuliano Tanturli, Milan, 1976; *Life of Brunelleschi*, ed. Howard Saalman, trans. C. Engass, University Park, Pa., 1970.

Martelli, Ugolino di Niccolò, *Ricordanze dal 1433 al 1483*, ed. Fulvio Pezzarossa, Rome, 1989.

Mather, Rufus, "New Documents on Michelozzo," *AB* 24, 1942, 226–31.

——"Documents, Mostly New, Relating to Florentine Painters and Sculptors of the Fifteenth Century," *AB* 30, 1948, 20–65.

Mazzei, Lapo, *Lettere di un notaro a un mercante del secolo XIV, con altre lettere e documenti*, ed., C. Guasti, 2 vols., Florence, 1880.

McSparran, F., and P. R. Robinson, eds., *Cambridge University Library MS Ff. 2. 38*, Cambridge, 1979.

Medici, Cosimo, *Ricordi*, in W. Roscoe, *The Life of Lorenzo de' Medici, Called the Magnificent*, 10th ed., London, 1898. Italian text in Angelo Fabroni, *Magni Cosmi Medicei Vita*, 2 vols., Pisa, 1789, vol. 2, 97–101.

Medici, Foligno, *Libro di memorie di Filigno de' Medici*, ed. D. Biondi de' Medici Tornaquinci, Florence, 1981.

Medici, Lorenzo, *Justification of the Commentary on his Sonnets*, extract in *The Three Crowns of Florence*, ed., D. Thompson and P. Nagel, New York, 1972, 134–47.

——*Opere scelte*, ed. Tiziano Zanato, Turin, 1992.

——*Ricordi*, in Angelo Fabroni, *Magni Laurentii Medicis Magnificentia Vita*, Pisa, 1784; trans. Renée Neu Watkins, *Humanism and Liberty: Writings on Freedom from Fifteenth-Century Florence*, Columbia, s.c., 1978, 157–64.

Merisalo, Outi, ed., *Le collezioni medicee nel 1495: Deliberazioni degli ufficiali dei ribelli, Florence*, 1999.

Milanesi, Gaetano, ed., "Lettere d'artisti dei secoli XIV e XV," in *Il Buonarroti*, 1869.

——ed., *Nuovi documenti per la storia dell'arte toscana dal XII al XV secolo*, Florence, 1901.

Morelli, Giovanni, *Ricordi*, ed. Vittore Branca, Florence, 1956.

Neri di Bicci, *Le ricordanze*, ed. B. Santi, Pisa, 1976.

Newbigin, Nerida, ed., *Nuovo corpus di sacre rappresentazioni fiorentine del quattrocento*, Bologna, 1983.

Ovid, *Epistolae, Ten Epistles of Ovid*, Latin and English, trans. W. Fitzthomas, London, 1807.

——*Metamorphoses*, Latin and English, trans. F. J. Miller, 2 vols., London and Cambridge, Mass., 1964–6.

Palmieri, Matteo, *Della vita civile*, in *Della vita civile di Matteo Palmieri: de Optimo Cive di Bartolomeo Sacchi, detto Il Platina*, ed., Felice Battaglia, Bologna, 1944.

——*Annales*, in *Rerum Italicarum Scriptores* vol. 26, pt. 1, Città di Castello, 1906–15, 131–94.

——*Libro del poema chiamato Città di vita composto da Matteo Palmieri Florentino*, ed. M. Rooke, Smith College Studies in Modern Languages, Northampton, Mass., 1927–8.

Panormita, see Beccadelli, Antonio.

Paolo da Certaldo, *Libro di buoni costumi*, ed. A. Schiaffini, Florence, 1945.

Parenti, Marco, *Lettere*, ed. Maria Marrese, Florence, 1996.

Petrarca, Francesco, *Trionfi*, in *Rime, Trionfi e Poesie Latine*, ed., Ferdinando Neri, Milan, 1951, 481–559; trans. E. H. Wilkins, *The Triumphs of Petrarch*, Chicago, 1962.

Piccolomini, Aeneas Sylvius, Pope Pius II, *I Commentarii*, ed. G. Bernetti, 5 vols., Siena, 1972–6; *Memoirs of a Renaissance Pope: The Commentaries of Pius II*, an abridgement and trans.

by Florence A. Gragg, ed. Leona C. Gabel, New York, 1959.

Piovano Arlotto, *Motti e Facezie*, ed. Gianfranco Folena, Milan and Naples, 1953.

Pitti, Buonaccorso, *Cronica*, ed. A. B. della Lega, Bologna, 1905.

Pliny the Elder, *Natural History*, Latin and English, trans. H. Rackham, 10 vols., Cambridge, Mass., 1938–52.

Poggi, Giovanni, *Il duomo di Firenze: documenti sulla decorazione della chiesa e del campanile tratti dall'archivio dell'opera*, ed. Margaret Haines, Italienische Forschungen herausgegeben vom Kunsthistorischen Institut in Florenz, 2 vols., Florence, 1988 [cit. as Poggi/Haines].

Poliziano, Angelo, *Della Congiura dei Pazzi*, ed. A. Perosa, Padua, 1958; trans. *The Pazzi Conspiracy*, in Renée Neu Watkins, *Humanism and Liberty: Writings on Freedom from Fifteenth-Century Florence*, Columbia, s.c., 1978, 171–83.

——*Detti Piacevoli*, ed. Mariano Fresta, Montepulciano, 1985.

Pontano, Giovanni, *I trattati delle virtù sociali: De Liberalitate, De Beneficentia, De Magnificentia, De Splendore, De Conviventia*, ed. Francesco Tateo, Rome 1965.

Propertius, Sextius, *Elegies*, Latin and English, trans. G. P. Godd, Cambridge, Mass., 1990.

Quintilian, *Institutio Oratoria*, Latin and English, ed. and trans. H. E. Butler, 4 vols., Cambridge, Mass., and London, 1966–9.

Renier, Rodolfo, ed., *Strambotti e sonetti dell'Altissimo*, Turin, 1886.

Rinuccini, Alamanno, *Lettere e orazioni*, ed. V. R. Giustiniani, Florence, 1953.

Rucellai, Giovanni, *Giovanni Rucellai ed il suo Zibaldone*, ed. A. Perosa, London, 1960.

Sacchetti, Franco, *Trecentonovelle*, in *Opere*, ed. V. Pernicone, Florence, 1946.

——*Il Libro delle rime*, ed. A. Chiari, Bari, 1936.

Sallust, *Catiline: Jugurthan War*, English and Latin, trans. J. C. Rolfe, Cambridge, Mass., 1931.

Salvini, Mariano, *Dialogus de Origine Ordinis Servorum ad Petrum Cosmae*, ed. P. Attavanti, in *Monumenta Ordinis Servorum Sanctae Mariae* 11, 1910, 88–112.

Seneca, Lucius Annaeus, *Letters, Epistulae Morales ad Lucilium. Selections*, Latin and English, trans. C. D. N. Costa, Warminster, Wilts., 1988.

Spallanzani, Marco, *Inventari Medicei, 1417–1465: Giovanni di Bicci, Cosimo e Lorenzo di Giovanni, Piero di Cosimo*, Florence, 1996.

Spallanzani, Marco, and Giovanna Gaeta Bertelà, eds., *Libro d'inventario dei beni di Lorenzo il Magnifico*, Florence, 1992.

Strozzi, Alessandra Macinghi negli, *Lettere di una gentildonna fiorentina del secolo XV*, ed. C. Guasti, Florence, 1877; bilingual ed. and trans. by Heather Gregory, *Selected Letters of Alessandra Strozzi*, Berkeley and Los Angeles, 1997.

Thompson, D., and A. Nagel, *The Three Crowns of Florence: Humanist Assessments of Dante, Petrarca and Boccaccio*, New York, 1972.

Tornabuoni, Lucrezia, *Poemetti Sacri*, ed. Fulvio Pezzarossa, Florence, 1978.

Toulmin Smith, L., ed., *A Common Place Book of the Fifteenth Century*, London, 1886.

Traversari, Ambrogio, *Hodoeporicon*, ed. Vittorio Tamburini, Florence, 1985.

Trexler, Richard, ed., *The Libro cerimoniale of the Florentine Republic, by Francesco Filarete and Angelo Manfidi*, Geneva, 1978.

Twain, Mark, *Innocents Abroad*, London, 1872.

Vasari, Giorgio, *Le vite de' più eccellenti pittori scultori et architettori*, ed. Gaetano Milanese, 9 vols., Florence, 1878–85, repr. Florence, 1973 [cit. as Vasari-Milanesi].

Vasoli, Cesari, ed., *Johannis Nesi adolescentis oratio de humilitate habita in fraternitate nativitatis die XI aprilis MCCCCLXVI*, in "Giovanni Nesi tra Donato Acciauoli e Girolamo Savonarola: Testi editi e inediti," in *Umanesimo e teologia tra '400 e '500, Memorie Domenicane*, n. s. 4, 1973.

Verzone, Carlo, ed., *Le rime burlesche di Anton Francesco Grazzini*, Florence, 1882.

Vespasiano da Bisticci, *Le Vite*, ed. A. Greco, 3 vols., Florence, 1970–76.

Villani, Giovanni, Matteo, and Filippo, *Croniche*, ed. I. Moutier and F. G. Dragomanni, Milan, 1848.

Virgilius, *Opera, Bucolica Georgica Aeneis: Manoscritto 492 della Biblioteca Riccardiana di Firenze*, Florence, 1969.

Volpi, G., ed., *Ricordi di Firenze dell'anno 1459*, in *Rerum Italicarum Scriptores*, vol. 27, pt. 1, Città di Castello, 1907–16.

Watkins, Reneé Neu, ed., *Humanism and Liberty: Writings on Freedom from Fifteenth-Century Florence*, Columbia, s.c., 1978.

Secondary Works

Académie Française, *Dictionnaire de L'Académie Française*, Paris, 1867.

Achenbach, "The Iconography of Tobias and the Angel in Florentine Painting of the Renaissance," *Marsyas* 3, 1943–5, 71–86.

Acidini Luchinat, Cristina, "La cappella medicea attraverso cinque secoli," in *Il Palazzo Medici Riccardi di Firenze*, ed. G. Cherubini and G. Fanelli. Florence, 1990, 82–97.

——ed., *The Chapel of the Magi: Benozzo Gozzoli's Frescoes in the Palazzo Medici-Riccardi Florence*, London and New York, 1994; trans. of *Benozzo Gozzoli: La cappella dei Magi*, Milan, 1993.

——"The Chapel of the Magi" in *idem*, 7–24.

——"The Chapel of the Magi: The Procession of the Magi," in *idem*, 39–42.

——"The Medici and Citizens in the *Procession of the Magi: A Portrait of a Society*," in *idem*, 363–70.

——"The Choirs of Angels," in *idem*, 264–7.

Ackerman, James, S., "Sources of the Renaissance Villa," in Ackerman, *The Renaissance and Mannerism*, in International Congress of the History of Art, Acts and Studies in Western Art, 4 vols., Princeton, 1963, vol. 2, 6–18.

—— *The Villa: Form and Ideology of Country Houses*, Princeton, 1990.

——*Essays in Theory and Renaissance Art and Architecture*, Cambridge, Mass., 1991.

Ady, Cecilia M., *Lorenzo de' Medici and the Balance of Power in Italy*, London, 1955.

Allegri, Ettore, and Alessandro Cecchi, eds., *Palazzo Vecchio e i Medici: guida storica*, Florence, 1980.

Allen, D. C., *Mysteriously Meant: The Rediscovery of Pagan Symbolism and Allegorical Interpretation in the Renaissance*, Baltimore, 1970.

Alpers, Svetlana, ed., "Art or Society: Must We Choose?" *Representations* 12, 1985, 1–43.

Ames-Lewis, Francis, *The Library and Manuscripts of Piero di Cosimo de' Medici*, New York and London, 1977.

——"Art History or Stilkritik? Donatello's Bronze David Reconsidered," *Art History* 2, 1979, 139–55.

——"Early Medicean Devices," *JWCI* 42, 1979, 122–43.

——"Domenico Veneziano and the Medici," *Jahrbuch der Berliner Museen* 21, 1979, 67–90.

——review of John Pope-Hennessy, *Luca della Robbia*; Hellmut Wohl, *The Paintings of Domenico Veneziano*; Marita Horster, *Andrea del Castagno*; R. W. Lightbown, *Donatello and Michelozzo*, *Art History* 4, 1981, 339–44.

——"Matteo de' Pasti and the Use of Powdered Gold," *Mitteilungen* 28, 1984, 351–62.

——"Donatello's Bronze *David* and the Palazzo Medici Courtyard," *Renaissance Studies* 3, 1989, 235–51.

——"Fra Filippo Lippi's S. Lorenzo *Annunciation*," *Storia dell'Arte* 69, 1990, 155–63.

—— ed., *Cosimo "il Vecchio" de' Medici, 1389–1464*, Oxford, 1992.

—— "Art in the Service of the Family: The Taste and Patronage of Piero di Cosimo de' Medici," in *Piero de' Medici, "il Gottoso" (1416–1469): Kunst im Dienste der Mediceer*, ed. Andreas Beyer and Bruce Boucher, Berlin, 1993, 207–20.

Ames-Lewis, Francis, and Anka Bednarek, eds., *Decorum in Renaissance Narrative Art: Papers Delivered at the Annual Conference of the Association of Art Historians*, London 1992.

——ed., *The Early Medici and their Artists*, London, 1995.

—— "Fra Angelico, Fra Filippo Lippi and the early Medici," in *The Early Medici and their Artists*, 107–24.

Arasse, D., "Annonciation/énonciation: remarques sur un énoncé pictural du Quattrocento," *Versus, Quaderni di studi semiotici* 37, 1984, 2–43.

Asselberghs, J. P., *Les Tapisseries flamandes au Etats-Unis d'Amérique*, Brussels, 1974.

Auerbach, Erich, *Mimesis: The Representation of Reality in Western Literature,* Princeton, 1968.

Avery, Charles, "The Early Medici and Donatello," in *The Early Medici and their Artists*, ed. Francis Ames-Lewis, London, 1995, 71–106.

Avesani, Rino, *Quattro miscellanee medievali e umanistiche*, Rome, 1967.

Bacci, O., and A. Della Lega, "Di Michele di Nofri del Giogante e del codice Ricc. 2734," *GSLI* 32, 1898, 328–54.

Bakhtin, Mikhail, *Rabelais and His World*, Cambridge, Mass., 1968.

Baldesi, Ludwig, *Jan van Eyck*, New York, 1956.

Baldini, Umberto, et al., *Brunelleschi e Donatello nella Sagrestia di S. Lorenzo*, Florence, 1989.

Bandini, A. M., *Catalogus Codicum Latinorum Biblioteca Medicea Laurenziana*, Florence, 1774–8.

Banker, James R., "Mourning a Son: Childhood and Paternal Love in the Consolateria of Giannozzo Manetti," *History of Childhood Quarterly* 3, 1976, 351–62.

——*Death in the Community: Memorialization and Confraternities in an Italian Commune in the Late Middle Ages*, Athens, Ga., and London, 1988.

——"The Sassetta Altarpiece," *I Tatti Studies* 6, 1993, 1–58.

Bargellini, Clara, and Pierre De La Ruffinière du Prey, "Sources for a Reconstruction of the Villa Medici, Fiesole," *BM* 111, 1969, 597–605.

Barolsky, Paul, *Infinite Jest: Wit and Humor in Italian Renaissance Art*, Columbia and London, 1978.

——"The Significant Form of Castagno's *David*," *Source* 8, 1989.

——"Naturalism and the Visionary Art of the Early Renaissance," *Gazette des beaux-arts* 139, 1997, 57–64.

Baron, Hans, "Franciscan Poverty and Civic Wealth as Factors in the Rise of Humanistic Thought," *Speculum* 13, 1938, 1–37.

——*The Crisis of the Early Italian Renaissance*, rev. ed., Princeton, 1966.

Barr, Cyrilla, "Music and Spectacle in Confraternity Drama of Fifteenth-Century Florence," in *Christianity and the Renaissance*, ed. T. Verdon and J. Henderson, Syracuse, N.Y. 1990.

——"A Renaissance Artist in the Service of a Singing Confraternity," in *Life and Death in Fifteenth-Century Florence*, ed. Marcel Tetel, Ronald G. Witt, and Rona Goffen, Durham and London, 1989, 104–119.

——*The Monophonic Lauda and the Lay Religious Confraternities of Tuscany and Umbria in the Late Middle Ages*, Kalamazoo, Mich., 1988.

Bartoli, Maria Teresa, "A Neoplatonic Pavement," in *The Chapel of the Magi: Benozzo Gozzoli's Frescoes in the Palazzo Medici-Riccardi Florence*, ed. Cristina Acidini Luchinat, London and New York, 1994, 25–8.

Battisti, Eugenio, *Brunelleschi: The Complete Work*, London, 1981.

Baxandall, Michael, "A Dialogue on Art from the Court of Leonello d'Este: Angelo Decembrio's De Politia Litteraria Pars LXVIII," *JWCI* 26, 1963, 304–26.

——"Bartholomeus Facius on Painting: A Fifteenth-Century Manuscript of the *De Viris Illustribus*," *JWCI* 27, 1964, 90–107.

——*Giotto and the Orators: Humanist Observers of Painting in Italy and the Discovery of Pictorial Composition, 1350–1450*, Oxford, 1971.

——*Painting and Experience in Fifteenth-Century Italy*, Oxford, 1972.

——*Patterns of Intention*, London, 1982.

——"Rudolph Agricola on Patrons Efficient and Patrons Final: A Renaissance Discrimination," *BM* 124, 1982, 424–5.

——"Art, Society and the Bouguer Principle," *Representations* 12, 1985, 32–43.

Bayley, C. C., *War and Society in Renaissance Florence*, Toronto, 1961.

Bec, Christian, *Les Marchands écrivains: affaires et humanisme à Florence, 1375–1434*, Paris, 1967.

—— *Les Livres des Florentins (1413–1609)*, Biblioteca di Lettere Italiane, Studi e Testi 29, Florence, 1984.

Becherini, Bianca, "Relazioni di musici fiamminghi con la corte dei Medici: nuovi documenti," *La Rinascita* 4, 1912, 94–112.

—— "Un canta in panca fiorentino, Antonio di Guido," *Rivista musicale italiana* 50, 1948, 241–7.

—— "La musica nelle 'sacre rappresentazioni' fiorentini," *Rivista musicale italiana* 53, 1951, 193–241.

—— "Poesia e musica in Italia ai primi del XV secolo," *Les Colloques de Wégimont II, 1955*, Paris, 1959, 239–59.

—— "Antonio Squarcialupi e il Cod. Mediceo-Palatino 87," in *L'ars nova italiana del trecento*, ed. Becherini, Florence, 1962.

Becherucci, L., *Donatello: i pergami di S. Lorenzo*, Florence, 1979.

Beck, James, "New Notices for Michelozzo," in *Renaissance Studies in Honor of Craig Hugh Smyth*, ed. A. Morrogh, F. S. Gioffredi, P. Morselli, and E. Borsook, 2 vols., Florence, 1985, vol. 2, 23–35.

—— "Iacopo della Quercia and Donatello: Networking in the Quattrocento," *Source* 6, 1987, 6–15.

—— "Leon Battista Alberti and the 'Night Sky' at San Lorenzo," *Artibus et historiae* 10, 1989, 9–35.

Becker, Marvin, *Florence in Transition*, 2 vols., Baltimore, 1967–8.

—— "Church and State in Florence in the Fourteenth Century," in *Florentine Studies*, ed. Nicolai Rubinstein, London, 1968.

—— "Aspects of Lay Piety in Early Renaissance Florence," in *The Pursuit of Holiness in Late Medieval and Renaissance Religion*, ed. C. Trinkaus and H. Oberman, Leiden, 1974, 177–99.

Bellosi, Luciano, and Margaret Haines, *Lo Scheggia*, Florence and Siena, 1999.

Belluzzi, A., "La Badia Fiesolana: tipologia edilizia e linguaggio architettonico," in *Richerche Brunelleschiane*, ed. P. Benigni, Florence, 1977.

Belting, Hans, *The Image and its Public in the Middle Ages: Form and Function of Early Paintings of the Passion*, trans. Mark Bartusis and Raymond Meyer, New Rochelle, N.Y., 1990.

—— *Likeness and Presence: A History of the Image before the Era of Art*, Chicago and London, 1994.

Benigni, Paola, ed., *Palazzo Neroni a Firenze: storia, architettura, restauro*, Florence, 1996.

Benigni, P., and P. Ruschi, "Il contributo di Filippo Brunelleschi all'assedio di Lucca: documenti e ipotesi," in *Convegno internazionale di studi brunelleschiani*, Florence, 1977, 55–82.

Bennett, B. A., and D. G. Wilkins, *Donatello*, Oxford, 1984.

Bentley, Jerry H., *Politics and Culture in Renaissance Naples*, Princeton, 1987.

Benvenuti Papi, Anna, "Un momento del concilio di Firenze: la traslazione delle reliquie di San Zanobi," in *Firenze e il Concilio del 1439*, ed. Paolo Viti, Florence, 1994, 191–220.

—— "I culti patronali tra memoria ecclesiastica e costruzione dell'identità civica: l'esempio di Firenze," in *La Religion civique à l'époque médiévale et moderne, Chretienté et Islam, Atti del colloquio di Nanterre, 1993*, ed. A. Vauchez, Rome, 1995, 99–118.

Berger, Peter, and Thomas Luckmann, *Social Construction of Reality: A Treatise in the Sociology of Knowledge*, Garden City, N.Y., 1966, repr. Irvington, 1980.

Bergmann, Bettina, "The Roman House as Memory Theater: The House of the Tragic Poet in Pompeii," *AB* 76, 1994, 225–55.

Bergstein, Mary, "Marian Politics in *Quattrocento* Florence: The Renewed Dedication of Santa Maria del Fiore in 1412," *RQ* 44, 1991, 673–719.

Bernacchioni, Anna Maria, "Botteghe di artisti e artigiani nel XV secolo," in *Gli antichi chiassi tra Ponte Vecchio e Santa Trinita*, ed. Giampaolo Trotta, Florence, 1992, 209–14.

Bernstein, Joanne Gitlin, "A Florentine Patron in Milan: Pigello and the Portinari Chapel," in *Renaissance Studies in Honor of Craig Hugh Smyth*, ed. A. Morrogh, F. S. Gioffredi, P. Morselli, and E. Borsook, 2 vols., Florence, 1985, vol. 2, 171–200.

Bertolini, Lucia, "Censimento dei manoscritti della *Sfera* del Dati," *Annali della Scuola Normale Superiore di Pisa*, ser. 3, 12, 1982, 665–75; 15, 1985, 889–940.

Beyer, Andreas, "Funktion und Repräsentation: Die Porphy-Rotae der Medici," in *Piero de' Medici, "il Gottoso" (1416–1469): Kunst im Dienste der Mediceer*, ed. Andreas Beyer and Bruce Boucher, Berlin, 1993, 151–67.

Beyer, Andreas, and Bruce Boucher, eds., *Piero de' Medici, "il Gottoso" (1416–1469): Kunst im Dienste der Mediceer*, Berlin, 1993.

Bizzocchi, Roberto, "Patronato politico e giuspatronati ecclesiastici: il caso fiorentino," *Richerche storiche* 15, 1985, 95–106.

—— *Chiesa e potere nella Toscana del Quattrocento*, Bologna, 1987.

—— "Concilio, Papato e Firenze," in *Firenze e il Concilio del 1439*, ed. Paolo Viti, 2 vols., Florence, 1994, 1, 109–27.

Black, Robert, "Ancients and Moderns in the Renaissance: Rhetoric and History in Accolti's Dialogue on the Preeminence of Men of his Own Time," *JHI* 13, 1982, 3–32.

—— "Piero de' Medici and Arezzo," in *Piero de' Medici, "il Gottoso" (1416–1469): Kunst im Dienste der Mediceer*, ed., Andreas Beyer and Bruce Boucher, Berlin, 1993, 43–67.

Blumenthal, A. R., "A Newly Identified Drawing of Brunelleschi's Stage Machinery," *Marsyas* 13, 1966–7, 20–23.

Blumenthal, G., "The Science of the Magi: The Old Sacristy of San Lorenzo and the Medici," *Source* 6, 1986, 1–11.

Bober, Phyllis Pray, and Ruth Rubinstein, *Renaissance Artists and Antique Sculpture: A Handbook of Sources*, Oxford, 1986.

Boccia, Lionello, "Le armature di Paolo Uccello," *L'Arte* 11–12, 1970, 55–9.

—— ed., *Armi difensive dal medioevo all'età moderna: dizionari terminologici*. Florence, 1982.

Bolgar, R. R., ed., *Classical Influences on European Culture, A.D. 500–1500*, Cambridge, 1969.

Böninger, Lorenz, "Diplomatie im Dienste der Kontinuität:

Piero de' Medici zwischen Rom und Mailand (1447–1454)," in *Piero de' Medici, "il Gottoso" (1416–1469): Kunst im Dienste der Mediceer*, ed. Andreas Beyer and Bruce Boucher, Berlin, 1993, 39–54.

Bornstein, Daniel, "Giovanni Dominici, the Bianchi, and Venice: Symbolic Action and Interpretive Grids," *JMRS* 23, 1993, 143–72.

Borsi, Franco, "The Badia Fiesolana: Culture and Architecture," in *La Badia Fiesolana*, ed. F. Borsi, G. Landucci, E. Balducci, and G. Morolli, Florence, 1976.

——— *Leon Battista Alberti*, Oxford, 1977.

Borsi, Franco, and Stefano Borsi, *Paolo Uccello*, New York, 1994.

Borsook, Eve, *The Companion Guide to Florence*, 1966; 5th ed. New York and London, 1991.

——— *The Mural Painters of Tuscany*, 2nd ed. Oxford, 1980.

——— "A Florentine *Scrittoio* for Diomede Carafa," in *Art, The Ape of Nature: Studies in Honor of H. W. Janson*, ed. M. Barasch, L. Freeman Sandler, and P. Egan, New York, 1981, 91–6.

Borsook, Eve, and Fiorella Superbi Gioffredi, eds., *The Italian Altarpiece, 1250–1550: History, Technique and Style*, Oxford, 1993.

Bossy, J., "The Mass as a Social Institution, 1200–1700," *Past and Present* 100, 1983, 29–61.

Boucher, Bruce, "Florence and Faenza at Mid-Century: The Medici and the Manfredi," in *Piero de' Medici, "il Gottoso" (1416–1469): Kunst im Dienste der Mediceer*, ed. Andreas Beyer and Bruce Boucher, Berlin, 1993, 169–80.

Bowen, Barbara, "Renaissance Collections of *facetiae*, 1344–1490: A New Listing," Pt. 1, *RQ* 39, 1986, 1–15.

Branciforte, Suzanne, "Poetry as Document: A *Popolaresco* Account of Life in Quattrocento Florence," MA Diss., University of California at Los Angeles, 1986.

——— *Ars poetica rei publicae: The Herald of the Florentine Signoria*, Ann Arbor, 1990.

Brewer, Charles, "Defrosted Architecture: The Incommensurability of Dufay's *Nuper Rosarum Flores* and the Cathedral of Santa Maria del Fiore," *JAMS* 47, 1994, 395–439.

Brock, M., "Sguardo pubblico, privato e intimo sulle immagini religiose del Quattrocento fiorentino," *Ricerche Storiche* 16, 1986, 551–64.

Brown, Alison, "The Humanist Portrait of Cosimo de' Medici, Pater Patriae," *JWCI* 24, 1961, 188–214.

——— *Bartolommeo Scala, 1430–1497: Chancellor of Florence. The Humanist as Bureaucrat*, Princeton, 1979.

——— "Pierfrancesco de' Medici, 1430–1476: A Radical Alternative to Elder Medicean Supremacy," *JWCI* 42, 1979, 81–103.

——— "The Guelf Party in Fifteenth-Century Florence: The Transition from Communal to Medicean State," *Rinascimento* 20, 1980, 41–86.

——— "Florence, Renaissance and Early Modern State: Reappraisals," review article, *JMH* 56, 1984, 285–300.

——— "Platonism in Fifteenth-Century Florence and its Contribution to Early Modern Political Thought, *JMH* 58, 1986, 383–413.

——— "Hans Baron's Renaissance," review article, *The Historical Journal* 33, 1990, 441–8.

——— "City and Citizen: Changing Perceptions in the Fifteenth and Sixteenth Centuries," in *City States in Classical Antiquity and Medieval Italy*, ed. A. Molho, Kurt Raaflaub, and Julia Emlen, Stuttgart 1991, 93–111.

——— "Cosimo de' Medici's Wit and Wisdom," in *Cosimo "il Vecchio" de' Medici, 1389–1464*, ed. Francis Ames-Lewis, Oxford, 1992, 95–114.

——— *The Medici in Florence: The Exercise and Language of Power*, Florence and Perth, 1992.

——— "Public and Private Interest: Lorenzo, the Monte and the Seventeen Reformers," in *Lorenzo de' Medici. Studi*, ed. G. C. Garfagnini, Florence, 1992, 103–65.

——— "Piero's Infirmity and Political Power," in *Piero de' Medici, "il Gottoso" (1416–1469): Kunst im Dienste der Mediceer*, ed. Andreas Beyer and Bruce Boucher, Berlin, 1993, 9–19.

——— "Lorenzo and Public Opinion in Florence: The Problem of Opposition," in *Lorenzo il Magnifico e il suo mondo*, ed. G. C. Garfagnini, Florence, 1994, 61–86.

——— ed., *Language and Images of Renaissance Italy*, Oxford, 1995.

Brown, Alison, and A. C. De La Mare, "Bartolomeo Scala's Dealings with Booksellers, Scribes and Illuminators, 1459–63," *JWCI* 39, 1976, 237–45.

Brown, Beverley, "The Patronage and Building History of the Tribuna of SS. Annunziata in Florence: A Reappraisal in Light of New Documentation," *Mitteilungen* 25, 1981, 60–146.

——— "An Enthusiastic Amateur: Lorenzo de' Medici as Architect," *RQ* 46, 1993, 1–22.

Brown, David Alan, "Leonardo and the Ladies with the Ermine and the Book," *Artibus et historiae* 22, 1990, 47–61.

——— *Leonardo da Vinci: Origins of a Genius*, New Haven and London, 1998.

Brown, Judith, *In the Shadow of Florence: Provincial Society in Renaissance Pescia*, New York, 1982.

Brown, Peter, *The Cult of the Saints*, Chicago, 1980.

——— *Society and the Holy in Late Antiquity*, Berkeley, 1982.

Brucker, Gene A., "The Medici in the Fourteenth Century," *Speculum* 32, 1957, 1–26.

——— *Politics and Society in Renaissance Florence, 1343–1382*, Princeton, 1962.

——— "The Structure of Patrician Society in Renaissance Florence," *Colloquium* 1, 1964, 2–11.

——— *Renaissance Florence*, New York, 1969.

——— "Florence and its University, 1348–1434," in *Action and Conviction in Early Modern Europe*, ed. Theodore K. Rabb and Jerrold E. Seigel, Princeton, 1969, 220–36.

——— "The Florentine *Popolo Minuto* and its Political Role, 1340–1450," in *Violence and Civil Disorder in Italian Cities, 1200–1500*, ed. Lauro Martines, Berkeley and Los Angeles, 1972, 155–83.

——— *The Civic World of Early Renaissance Florence*, Princeton, 1977.

——"A Civic Debate on Florentine Higher Education (1460)," *RQ* 34, 1981, 517–33.

——"Bureaucracy and Social Welfare in the Renaissance: A Florentine Case Study," *JMH* 55, 1983, 1–21.

——"Urban Parishes and their Clergy in Quattrocento Florence: A Preliminary *Sondage*," in *Renaissance Studies in Honor of Craig Hugh Smyth*, ed. A. Morrogh, F. S. Gioffredi, P. Morselli, and E. Borsook, Florence, 2 vols., 1985, vol. 1, 17–28.

——*Giovanni and Lusanna: Love and Marriage in Renaissance Florence*, Berkeley and Los Angeles, 1986.

——"Monasteries, Friaries, and Nunneries in Quattrocento Florence," in *Christianity in the Renaissance*, ed. Timothy Verdon and John Henderson, Syracuse, 1990, 41–62.

——"Florentine Voices from the Catasto, 1427–1480, *I Tatti Studies* 5, 1993, 11–32.

——*Renaissance Florence: Society, Culture, and Religion*, Goldbach, 1994.

"The Economic Foundations of Laurentian Florence," in *Atti del Convegno su Lorenzo de' Medici, Firenze, 1992*, ed. Gian Carlo Garfagnini, Florence, 1994, 3–15.

Brussels, Musée Communale, *Rogier van der Weyden, Rogier de le Pasture*, Brussels, 1979.

Budriesi, Roberta, *La Basilica dei SS. Cosma e Damiano a Roma*, Bologna, 1968.

Bueno de Mesquita, D. M., "The Place of Despotism in Italian Politics," in *Europe in the Later Middle Ages*, ed. J. R. Hale, J. R. L. Highfield, and Beryl Smalley, London, 1965, 301–31.

Buhler, Stephen M., "Marsilio Ficino's *De Stella Magorum* and the Renaissance View of the Magi," *RQ* 43, 1990, 348–71.

Bullard, Melissa, "The Magnificent Lorenzo de' Medici: Between Myth and History," in *Politics and Culture in Early Modern Europe: Essays in Honour of H. G. Koenigsberger*, ed. P. Mack and M. C. Jacob, Cambridge, 1987, 25–58.

——"Marsilio Ficino and the Medici: The Inner Dimensions of Patronage," in *Christianity and the Renaissance*, ed. T. Verdon and J. Henderson, Syracuse, 1990, 467–92.

——"Anxiety, Image Making, and Political Reality in the Renaissance," in *Lorenzo de' Medici Studi,* ed. Gian Carlo Garfagnini, Florence, 1992, 3–40.

——"Heroes and Their Workshops: Medici Patronage and the Problem of Shared Agency," *JMRS* 24, 1994, 179–98.

——*Lorenzo il Magnifico: Image and Anxiety, Politics and Finance*, Florence, 1994.

Bulman, Louise, "Artistic Patronage at SS. Annunziata, 1440–1520," Ph.D. Diss., University of London, 1971.

Bulst, Wolfger, "Die Ursprüngliche Innere Aufteilung des Palazzo Medici in Florenz, *Mitteilungen* 14, 1970, 369–94.

——"L'uso e trasformazione del palazzo mediceo fino ai Riccardi," in *Il Palazzo Medici Riccardi di Firenze*, ed. Giovanni Cherubini and Giovanni Fanelli, Florence, 1990, 98–129.

——"Die *sala grande* des Palazzo Medici in Florenz: Rekonstruktion und Bedeutung," in *Piero de' Medici, "il Gottoso" (1416–1469): Kunst im Dienste der Mediceer*, ed. Andreas Beyer

and Bruce Boucher, Berlin, 1993, 89–127.

Burckhardt, Jacob, *The Civilization of the Renaissance in Italy*, 1st ed. 1860, New York, 1954.

Burke, Peter, *Popular Culture in Early Modern Europe*, London, 1978.

——"The Social History of Art or the History of Images?" *Budapest Review of Books* 2, 1, 1992, 9–12.

Burns, Howard, "Quattrocento Architecture and the Antique: Some Problems," in *Classical Influences on European Culture, A.D. 500–1500*, ed. R. R. Bolgar, Cambridge, 1969, 269–87.

——"San Lorenzo in Florence before the Building of the New Sacristy: An Early Plan," *Mitteilungen* 23, 1979, 145–53.

Buser, B., *Die Beziehungen der Mediceer zu Frankreich*, Leipzig, 1879.

Butterfield, Andrew, "Verrocchio's Christ and St. Thomas: Chronology, Iconography and Political Context," *BM* 134, 1992, 225–33.

——"Documents for the Pulpits of San Lorenzo, Florence," *Mitteilungen* 38, 1994, 147–53.

——*The Sculptures of Andrea del Verrocchio*, New Haven and London, 1997.

Butters, Humphrey C., *Governors and Government in Early Sixteenth-century Florence 1502–1519*, Oxford, 1985.

Butters, Suzanne, *The Triumph of Vulcan: Sculptors' Tools, Porphyry, and the Prince in Ducal Florence*, Villa I Tatti, The Harvard University Center for Italian Renaissance Studies, Florence, 1996.

Caglioti, Francesco, "Bernardo Rossellino a Roma: i stralci del carteggio mediceo (con qualche briciola sul Filarete)," *Prospettiva* 64, 1991, 49–59.

——"Due 'restauratori' per le antichità dei primi Medici: Mino da Fiesole e Andrea del Verrocchio, e il 'Marsia,'" *Prospettiva* 73, 1994, 74–96.

——"Donatello, i Medici e Gentile de' Becchi: un po' d'ordine intorno alla 'Giuditta' (e al 'David') di Via Larga, I, II, III," *Prospettiva* 75–6, 1994, 14–49; 78, 1995, 22–55; 80, 1995, 15–58.

——*Donatello e i Medici. Saggio di storia dell'arte sul David e la Giuditta*, Florence, 2000.

Caglioti, Francesco, and Davide Gasparotto, "Lorenzo Ghiberti, il 'Sigillo di Nerone' e le origini della placchetta 'antiquaria,'" *Prospettiva* 85, 1997, 2–38.

Cagni, Giuseppe M., *Vespasiano da Bisticci e il suo epistolario*, Rome, 1969.

Callmann, Ellen, *Apollonio di Giovanni*, Oxford, 1974.

Campbell, Lorne, *Van der Weyden*, New York, 1980.

Camporeale, Salvatore, "Poggio Bracciolini contro Lorenzo Valla," *Rinascimento* 10, 137–67.

Caplow, Harriet McNeal, *Michelozzo*, 2 vols., New York, 1977.

——"Sculptors' Partnerships in Michelozzo's Florence," *Studies in the Renaissance* 21, 1974, 145–73.

Carandente, G. *I Trionfi del Primo Rinascimento*, Rome, 1963.

Cardini, Franco, and Marco Tangheroni, eds., *Guerra e guerrieri nella Toscana del rinascimento*, Florence, 1990.

Carl, Doris, "La Casa Vecchia dei Medici e il suo giardino," in *Il Palazzo Medici Riccardi di Firenze*, ed. Giovanni Cherubini and Giovanni Fanelli, Florence, 1990, 38–43.

Carmichael, Ann, *Plague and the Poor in Renaissance Florence*, New York, 1986.

—— "The Health Status of Florentines in the Fifteenth Century," in *Life and Death in Fifteenth-Century Florence*, ed. Marcel Tetel, Ronald G. Witt, and Rona Goffen, Durham and London, 1989, 28–45.

Carnesasca, Ettore, *Artisti in bottega*, Milan, 1966.

Carocci, G., "La campana di S. Marco di Firenze," *Bollettino d'arte* 2, 1908, 256–64.

Carruthers, Mary, *The Book of Memory: A Study of Memory in Medieval Culture*, Cambridge, 1990.

Casali, G., "I passaggi di proprietà nelle successioni ereditari dei possedimenti delle ville medicee," in *I Medici nel contado fiorentino*, ed. V. Franchetti Pardo and G. Casali, Florence, 1978, 47–141.

Casalini, Eugenio, "L'Angelico e la Cateratta per l'Armadio degli Argenti Alla SS, Annunziata di Firenze," *Commentari* 14, 1963, 104–24.

Cassidy, B., ed., *Iconography at the Crossroads*, Princeton, 1992.

Cattin, Giulio, "Contributi alla storia della lauda spirituale. Sulla evoluzione musicale e letteraria della lauda nei secoli XIV e XV, *Quadrivium* 2, 1958, 45–78.

Cecconi, E., *Studi storici sul concilio di firenze*, Florence, 1969.

Celenza, Christopher S., " 'Parallel Lives': Plutarch's *Lives*, Lapo da Castiglionchio the Younger (1405–1438) and the Art of Italian Renaissance Translation," *Illinois Classical Studies* 22, 1997, 121–55.

Chambers, D. S., review of Guy Lytle and Stephen Orgel, eds., *Patronage in the Renaissance*, *JMH* 56, 1984, 316–18.

Chartier, Roger, *Cultural History: Between Practices and Representations*, trans. Lydia Cochrane, Cambridge, 1988.

—— "Leisure and Sociability: Reading Aloud in Early Modern Europe," in *Urban Life in the Renaissance*, ed. Susan Zimmerman and Ronald F. E. Weissman, London and Toronto, 1989, 103–20.

—— *The Order of Books: Readers, Authors, and Libraries in Europe between the Fourteenth and Eighteenth Centuries*, trans. Lydia G. Cochrane, Stanford, 1994.

Cheles, Luciano, *The Studiolo of Urbino: An Iconographic Investigation*, University Park, Pennsylvania, 1986.

Chiarelli, C., and G. Leoncini, eds., *La Certosa del Galluzzo a Firenze*, Milan, 1982.

Chrétien, Heidi, *The Festival of San Giovanni: Imagery and Political Power in Renaissance Florence*, New York, 1994.

Ciappelli, Giovanni, "Libri e letture a Firenze nel XV secolo," *Rinascimento*, 2nd ser., 29, 1989, 267–91.

Ciappelli, Giovanni, and Patricia Rubin, eds., *Art, Memory and the Family in Renaissance Florence*, Cambridge, 2000.

—— "Family Memory: Functions, Evolution, Recurrences," in *Art, Memory and the Family in Renaissance Florence*, 26–38.

Ciseri, Ilaria, "Spiritualità e spettacolo nella Firenze del Con- cilio: cerimoniale diplomatico e sacre rappresentazioni," in *Firenze e il Concilio del 1439*, ed. Paolo Viti, 2 vols., Florence, 1994, vol. 1, 437–55.

Civai, A., *Dipinti e sculture in casa Martelli*, Florence, 1990.

Cividali, P., "Il Beato Giovanni dalle Celle," *Memorie della R. Accademia dei Lincei, Classe di scienze morali, storiche e filologiche*, ser. 5, 12, 1907, 353–477.

Clark, D. L., "Filippino Lippi's 'The Virgin inspiring St. Bernard' and Florentine Humanism," *Studies in Iconography* 7–8, 1981–2, 175–87.

Clark, Kenneth, *Civilization*, BBC-TV, Public Media Video, 1987.

—— introduction to James Hall, *Dictionary of Subjects and Symbols in Art*, New York, 1979.

Clarke, Paula, *Power and Patronage in Fifteenth-Century Florence*, Oxford, 1991.

Clearfield, J., "The Tomb of Cosimo de' Medici in San Lorenzo," *Rutgers Art Review* 2, 1981, 13–30.

Cochrane, Eric, *Florence in the Forgotten Centuries, 1527–1800*, Chicago, 1973.

Coffin, David R., *The Villa in the Life of Renaissance Rome*, Princeton, 1979.

Cohn, Samuel Kline, "The Character of Insurrection in Mid-Quattrocento Florence," in *Il Tumulto dei Ciompi: Un momento di storia fiorentina ed europea, Convegno internazionale di studi*, Florence, 1979, 1–24.

—— *The Laboring Classes in Renaissance Florence*, New York, 1980.

—— *The Cult of Remembrance and the Black Death: Six Cities in Central Italy*, Baltimore, 1992.

—— "Burckhardt Revisited from Social History," in *Language and Images of Renaissance Italy*, ed. Alison Brown, Oxford, 1995, 217–34.

Cohn, Werner, "Franco Sacchetti und das ikonographische Programm der Gewölbemalereien von Orsanmichele," *Mitteilungen* 8, 1958, 65–77.

Cole Ahl, Diane, "Renaissance Birth Salvers and the Richmond 'Judgment of Solomon,' " *Studies in Iconography* 7–8, 1981–2, 157–74.

—— *Benozzo Gozzoli*, New Haven and London, 1996.

Connell, William J., review of *I ceti dirigenti nella Toscana del quattrocento, Atti del V e VI Convegno, Firenze, 1987*, *ASI* 147, 1989, 370–71.

Conti, Elio, *L'imposta diretta a Firenze nel Quattrocento, 1427–1494*, Rome, 1984.

Cook, Elizabeth, "Figured Poetry," *JWCI* 42, 1979, 1–15.

Copenhaver, Brian, and Charles Schmitt, *Renaissance Philosophy*, New York, 1992.

Covi, Dario, "Lettering in the Inscriptions of Fifteenth Century Florentine Paintings," *Renaissance News* 7, 1954, 46–50.

—— "Four New Documents Concerning Andrea del Verrocchio," *AB* 75, 1993, 97–103.

Cropper, Elizabeth, ed., *Florentine Drawing at the Time of Lorenzo the Magnificent. Villa Spelman Colloquia 4*, Bologna, 1994.

Crum, Roger J., "Retrospection and Response: The Medici

Palace in the Service of the Medici, c.1420–1469," Ph.D. Diss., University of Pittsburgh, 1992.

—— "Donatello's *Ascension of St. John the Evangelist* and the Old Sacristy as Sepulchre," *Artibus et Historiae*, 32, 1995, 141–61.

—— "Roberto Martelli, the Council of Florence, and the Medici Palace Chapel," *Zeitschrift für Kunstgeschichte* 59, 1996, 403–18.

—— "Donatello's Bronze David and the Question of Foreign Versus Domestic Tyranny," *Renaissance Studies* 10, 1996, 440–50.

Curtius, E. R., *European Literature and the Latin Middle Ages*, trans. R. W. Trask, New York, 1953.

D'Accone, Frank, "The Singers of San Giovanni in Florence during the Fifteenth century," *JAMS* 14, 1961, 307–58.

—— "Le Compagnie dei Laudesi in Firenze durante *L'Ars Nova*," in *L'Ars nova italiana del trecento*, 3, ed. Centro di Studi Sull'Ars Nova Italiana del Trecento, Certaldo, 1970, 253–80.

—— "Music and Musicians at Santa Maria del Fiore in the early *Quattrocento*," *Scritti in onore di Luigi Ronga*, Milan and Naples, 1973, 99–126.

—— "Alcune note sulle Compagnie fiorentine dei Laudesi durante il quattrocento," *Rivista italiana di musicologia* 10, 1975, 86–114.

Dacos, N., A. Giuliano, U. Pannuti, eds., *Il tesoro di Lorenzo il Magnifico: I, Le gemme*, Florence, 1973.

Dal Poggetto, Maria Grazia Ciardi Dupré, et al., eds., *L'Oreficeria nella Firenze del quattrocento*, Florence, 1977.

Dal Prà, Laura, ed., *Bernardo di Chiaravalle nell'arte italiana dal XIV al XVIII secolo*, Milan, 1990.

Dami, B., *Giovanni di Bicci dei Medici nella vita politica, Florence*, 1899.

D'Ancona, Alessandro, *Origini del teatro italiano*, 3 vols., Turin, 1891.

D'Ancona, Paolo, "I begli arredi della Sagrestia di San Lorenzo di Firenze sullo scorcio del secolo XIV," *Miscellanea di storia dell'arte in onore di Benevenuto Supino*, Florence, 1933, 247–69.

Danilova, Irina, "La rappresentazione dell' Annunciazione nella Chiesa della SS. Annunziata in Firenze vista dall'Arcivescovo Abramo di Suzdal," in *Filippo Brunelleschi, la sua opera e il suo tempo*, Florence, 1981.

Darnton, Robert, *The Great Cat Massacre*, New York, 1984.

—— "Readers Respond to Rousseau: The Fabrication of Romantic Sensitivity, in *idem*, 215–56.

Davies, Jonathan, "Marsilio Ficino: Lecturer at the Studio Fiorentino," *RQ* 45, 1992, 785–90.

Davies, Martin, "Fra Filippo's Annunciation and Seven Saints," *Critica d'arte* 8, 1950, 356–63.

—— *The Earlier Italian Schools before 1400*, London, National Gallery Catalogue, 1961.

—— *Rogier van der Weyden*, London, 1972.

Davies, M. C., "An Emperor without Clothes? Niccolò Niccoli under Attack," *Italia medioevale e umanistica* 30, 1987, 95–148.

Davis, Charles, *Dante and the Idea of Rome*, Oxford, 1957.

—— "Brunetto Latini e Dante," *Studi medievali*, ser. 3, 8, 1967, 421–50.

—— "Topographical and Historical Propaganda in Early Florentine Chronicles and in Villani," *Medioevo e rinascimento* 2, 1988, 33–51.

Davis, Natalie Zemon, "Beyond the Market: Books as Gifts in Sixteenth-Century France," *Transactions of the Royal Historical Society* 33, 1983, 69–88.

—— "Art and Society in the Gifts of Montaigne" *Representations* 12, 1985, 24–32.

—— *Fiction in the Archives: Pardon Tales and Their Tellers in Sixteenth-Century France*, Stanford, 1987.

Davisson, Darrell, "The Iconology of the S. Trinita Sacristy, 1418–1435: A Study of the Private and Public Functions of Religious Art in the Early Quattrocento," *AB* 57, 1975, 315–34.

Dean, Trevor, "Lords, Vassals and Clients in Renaissance Ferrara," *English Historical Review* 100, 1985, 106–19.

—— "Commune and Despot: The Commune of Ferarra under Este Rule, 1300–1450," in *City and Countryside in Late Medieval and Renaissance Italy*, ed. T. Dean and C. Wickham, London, 1990, 183–97.

De Certeau, Michel, *The Practice of Everyday Life*, trans. Steven F. Rendall, Berkeley and Los Angeles, 1984.

—— *The Writing of History*, New York, 1988.

Déer, Josef, *The Dynastic Porphyry Tombs of the Norman Period in Sicily*, trans. G. A. Gillhoff, Cambridge, Mass., 1959.

Degenhart, B., and A. Schmitt, *Corpus der Italienischen Zeichnungen, 1300–1450*, Berlin, 1968.

Deimling, Barbara, " 'The Meeting of the Queen of Sheba with Solomon': Crusade Propaganda in the Fresco Cycle of Piero della Francesca in Arezzo," *Pantheon* 53, 1995, 18–28.

De La Mare, A. C., "The Shop of a Florentine 'cartolaio' in 1426," in *Studi offerti a Roberti Ridolfi*, ed. Berta Maracchi Biagiarelli and Dennis E. Rhodes, Florence, 1973, 237–48.

—— "The Library of Francesco Sassetti (1421–90)," in *Cultural Aspects of the Italian Renaissance: Essays in Honor of P. O. Kristeller*, ed. C. Clough, Manchester, 1976, 160–201.

—— "Cosimo and His Books," in *Cosimo "il Vecchio" de' Medici, 1389–1464*, ed. Francis Ames-Lewis, Oxford, 1992, 115–56.

Del Piazzo, Marcello, ed., *Protocolli del carteggio di Lorenzo il Magnifico per gli anni 1473–74, 1477–92*, Florence, 1956.

Dempsey, Charles, "Masaccio's *Trinity*: Altarpiece or Tomb?" *AB* 54, 1972, 279–81.

Denley, Peter, "Governments and Schools in Late Medieval Italy," in *City and Countryside in Late Medieval and Renaissance Italy: Essays Presented to Philip Jones*, ed. Trevor Dean and Chris Wickham, London and Ronceverte, 1990, 93–107.

D'Entrèves, A. Passerin, *Dante as a Political Thinker*, Oxford, 1952.

Denver Art Museum, *Paintings and Sculpture of the Samuel H. Kress Collection*, Denver, 1954.

Derbes, Anne, and Mark Sandona, "Barren Metal and the Fruitful Womb: The Program of Giotto's Arena Chapel in Padua," *AB* 80, 1998, 274–91.

De Roover, Raymond, "A Florentine Firm of Cloth Manufac-turers," *Speculum* 16, 1941, 1–33.

—— "Cosimo de' Medici come banchiere e mercante," *ASI*, 111, 1953.

—— *The Rise and Decline of the Medici Bank*, Cambridge, Mass., 1963.

—— "Gli antecedenti del Banco Mediceo e l'azienda bancaria di messer Vieri di Cambio de' Medici," *ASI* 123, 1965, 4–13.

—— *San Bernardino of Siena and Sant'Antonino of Florence: The Two Great Economic Thinkers of the Middle Ages*, Boston, 1967.

Desideri Costa, Leona, *La Chiesa di San Martino del Vescovo, L'Oratorio dei Buonomini e gli affreschi sulle opere di misericordia in Firenze presso le case degli Alighieri*, Florence, 1942.

D'Essling, V. M., and E. Müntz, *Pétrarque, ses études d'art, son influence sur les artistes, ses portraits et ceux de Laure, l'illustration de ses écrits*, Paris, 1902.

Diana, E., "Interventi medicei in Mugello," in *I beni culturali: dalla conoscenza storica: una prospettiva per il Mugello*, ed. V. Franchetti Pardo, Florence, 1983, 169–75.

Didi-Huberman, Georges, *Fra Angelico, dissemblance et figuration*, Paris, 1990.

Dixon, John W., "The Drama of Donatello's David: Re-examination of an 'Enigma,'" *Gazette des Beaux-Arts*, 93, 1979, 6–12.

Donato, Monica, "Hercules and David in the Decoration of the Palazzo Vecchio: Manuscript Evidence," *JWCI* 54, 1991, 83–98.

Doren, *Le arti fiorentine*, 2 vols., Florence, 1940.

Dorini, U., "Il culto delle memorie Patrie nella Repubblica di Firenze," *Rassegna nazionale* 179, 1911, 3–25.

Douglas, Mary, *Natural Symbols: Explorations in Cosmology*, New York, 1973.

Draper, James, *Bertoldo di Giovanni, Sculptor of the Medici House-hold*, Columbia, S.C., 1992.

Duffy, Eamon, *The Stripping of the Altars: Traditional Religion in England, c.1400–c.1580*, New Haven and London, 1992.

Eckstein, Nicholas, *The District of the Green Dragon: Neighbour-hood Life and Social Change in Renaissance Florence*, Florence, 1995.

Edgerton, Samuel Y., "Florentine Interest in Ptolemaic Cartog-raphy as Background for Renaissance Painting, Architecture and the Discovery of America," *JSAH* 33, 1974, 275–92.

—— *Pictures and Punishment: Art and Criminal Prosecution during the Florentine Renaissance*, Ithaca, 1985.

—— "'How Shall This Be?' Part 2," *Artibus et historiae* 16, 1987, 45–53.

Eisenbichler, Konrad, ed., *Crossing the Boundaries: Christian Piety and the Arts in Italian Medieval and Renaissance Confraternities*, Kalamazoo, 1991.

—— "Le Confraternite Laicali al tempo del Concilio," in *Firenze e il Concilio del 1439*, ed. Paolo Viti, 2 vols., Florence, 1994, vol. 1, 221–41.

Eisenbichler, Konrad, and Amilcare Iannucci, *Petrarch's Triumphs: Allegory and Spectacle*, Toronto and Ottawa, 1990.

Eisler, Colin, "The Athlete of Virtue: The Iconography of Asceticism," in *De Artibus, opuscula XL. Essays in Honor of Erwin Panofsky*, ed. Millard Meiss, New York, 1961, 82–97.

Elam, Caroline, "Lorenzo de' Medici and the Urban Develop-ment of Renaissance Florence," *Art History* 1, 1978, 43–66.

—— "The Site and Early Building History of Michelangelo's New Sacristy," *Mitteilungen* 23, 1979, 153–86.

—— "Conspicuous Construction," review of Richard Goldth-waite, *The Building of Renaissance Florence*, in *The Times Literary Supplement*, Nov. 13, 1981, 1335.

—— "Art and Diplomacy in Renaissance Florence," *Journal of the Royal Society of Arts* 136, 1988, 813–26.

—— "Cosimo de' Medici and San Lorenzo," in *Cosimo "il Vecchio" de' Medici, 1389–1464*, ed. Frances Ames-Lewis, Oxford, 1992, 157–80.

—— "Il palazzo nel contesto della città: urbanistiche dei Medici nel gonfalone del Leon d'oro, 1415–1430," in *Il palazzo Medici Riccardi di Firenze*, ed. G. Cherubini and G. Fanelli, Florence, 1990, 44–57.

Ettlinger, Helen, "The Sepulchre on the Façade: A Re-evaluation of Sigismondo Malatesta's Rebuilding of San Francesco in Rimini, *JWCI* 53, 1990, 133–43.

Ettlinger, Leopold, "Hercules Florentinus," *Mitteilungen* 16, 1972, 119–42.

Fabbri, M., E. Garbero Zorzi, and A. M. Petrioli Tofani, eds., *Il luogo teatrale a Firenze*, Florence, 1975.

Fabriczy, Cornelius von, *Brunelleschi*, 2 vols., Stuttgart, 1892.

—— "Michelozzo di Bartolomeo," *Jahrbuch der königlich preussis-chen Kunstsammlungen* 25, 1904, 34–110.

—— "Nanni di Miniato, detto Fora," *Jahrbuch der königlicher Preussischen Kunstsammlungen* 27, 1906, 74–6.

Fanelli, Vittorio, "I Libri di Messer Palla di Nofri Strozzi (1372–1462), *Convivium* 1, 1952, 57–73.

Ferrara, Miranda, and Francesco Quinterio, *Michelozzo di Bartolomeo*, Florence, 1984.

Field, Arthur, *The Origins of the Platonic Academy of Florence*, Princeton, 1988.

—— "Cristoforo Landino's First Lectures on Dante," *RQ* 39, 1986, 16–48.

—— "A Manuscript of Cristoforo Landino's First Lectures on Virgil, 1462–63 (Codex 1368, Biblioteca Casanatese, Rome)," *RQ* 31, 1978, 17–20.

Fiocco, G., "La biblioteca di Palla Strozzi," in *Studi di bibliografia e di storia in onore di Tammaro de Marinis*, Verona, 1964, 2 vols., 2, 289–310.

Flamini, Francesco, *La lirica toscana del Rinascimento anteriore ai tempi del Magnifico*, Pisa, 1891.

Fortini Brown, Patricia, "*Laetentur Caeli*: The Council of Florence and the Astronomical Fresco in the Old Sacristy," *JWCI* 44, 1981, 176–80.

—— *Venetian Narrative Painting in the Age of Carpaccio*, New Haven and London, 1988.

Foster, Philip, *A Study of Lorenzo de Medici's Villa at Poggio a Caiano*, 2 vols., Ann Arbor, 1978.

Foucault, Michel, *Madness and Civilization: A History of Insanity in the Age of Reason*, trans. Richard Howard, New York, 1965.

—— *The Order of Things: An Archaeology of the Human Sciences*, trans. of *Les Mots et les choses*, New York, 1970.

—— "Archaeology and the History of Ideas," in Foucault, *The Archaeology of Knowledge*, London, 1972, 135–40.

Franceschi, Franco, *Oltre il "Tumulto": i lavoratori fiorentini dell'Arte della Lana fra Tre e Quattrocento*, Florence 1993.

Fraser Jenkins, A. D., "Cosimo de' Medici's Patronage of Architecture and the Theory of Magnificence," *JWCI* 33, 1970, 162–70.

Frati, L., "Cantari e sonetti ricordati nella cronaca di Benedetto Dei," *GSLI* 4, 1884, 162–202.

Freedberg, David, *"The Power of Images: Studies in the History and Theory of Response,"* Chicago, 1989.

Frick, Carole, "Wedding and Conventual Trousseaux," paper presented to the Metropolitan Museum of Art, 1998.

Frosinini, C., "Il passaggio di gestione in una bottega pittorica fiorentina del primo '400: Bicci di Lorenzo e Neri di Bicci," *Antichità viva* 26, 1987, 1, 5–14.

Fubini, Riccardo, "Appunti sui rapporti diplomatici fra il Dominio Sforzesco e Firenze medicea," in *Gli Sforza a Milano e in Lombardia e i loro rapporti con gli stati italiani ed europei (1450–1535)*, Milan, 1982, 291–334.

—— "Problemi di Politica Fiorentina all'epoca del Concilio," in *Firenze e il Concilio del 1439*, ed. Paolo Viti, 2 vols., Florence, 1994, vol. 1, 27–57.

Fusco, Laurie, and Gino Corti, "Giovanni Ciampolini: A Renaissance Dealer in Rome and His Collection of Antiquities," *Xenia* 21, 1991, 7–47.

—— "The Medici as Collectors of Antiquities and the Formation of 'Princely' Taste," paper presented at the Museum of Fine Arts, Boston, 1989.

—— *Lorenzo de' Medici, Collector: The Pursuit of Antiquities and Rare Objects in the Early Renaissance*, Cambridge, forthcoming.

Gadol, Joan, *Leon Battista Alberti*, Chicago, 1969.

Gallizzi, Alessandra, "Flying Babies in Emilian Painting: Iconographies of the Immaculate Conception circa 1500," Ph.D. Diss., The Johns Hopkins University, 1991.

Gardner, J., "Altarpieces, Legislation and Usage," in *The Italian Altarpiece, 1250–1550: History, Technique and Style*, ed. Eve Borsook and Fiorella Superbi Gioffredi, Oxford, 1993.

Gardner von Teufel, Christa, "Lorenzo Monaco, Filippo Lippi und Filippo Brunelleschi: die Erfindung der Renaissancepala," *Zeitschrift fur Kunstgeschichte* 45, 1982, 1–30.

—— "From Polyptych to Pala: Some Structural Considerations," in *La pittura nel XIV e XV secolo: il contributo dell' analisi tecnica alla storia dell'arte*, ed. H. van Os and J. van Asperen de Boer, Bologna, 1983, 323–44.

Garfagnini, Gian Carlo, ed., *Giorgio Vasari: tra decorazione ambientale e storiografia artistica*, Florence, 1985.

—— ed., *Ambrogio Traversari nel VI centenario della nascita*, Florence, 1988.

—— ed., *Lorenzo de' Medici: studi*, Istituto Nazionale di Studi sul Rinascimento, Studi e Testi, 27, Florence, 1992.

—— ed., *Lorenzo il Magnifico e il suo mondo*, Florence, 1994.

Garin, Eugenio, *L'umanesimo italiano*, 8th ed., Bari, 1975.

Gaston, Robert, "Liturgy and Patronage in San Lorenzo, Florence, 1350–1650," in *Patronage, Art and Society in Renaissance Italy*, ed. F. W. Kent and Patricia Simons, Oxford, 1987, 111–33.

—— "Attention and Inattention in Religious Painting of the Renaissance: Some Preliminary Observations," in *Renaissance Studies in Honor of Craig Hugh Smyth*, ed. A. Morrogh, F. Superbi Gioffredi, P. Morselli, and E. Borsook, Florence, 1985, 253–68.

Gatti, Luca, "The *Comune Studio Libertatis* of Florence and Venice, and the Political Implications of the Pre-Medicean Restoration of the Convent of San Marco," *Quaderni di storia dell'architettura e restauro* 13–14, 1995, 37–47.

Gebhardt, Volker, "Ein Porträt Cosimo de' Medicis von Paolo Uccello," *Pantheon* 48, 1990, 28–35.

—— *Paolo Uccellos "Schlacht von San Romano,"* Frankfurt-am-Main, 1991.

—— "Some Problems in the Reconstruction of Uccello's 'Rout of San Romano,'" *BM* 133, 1991, 179–88.

Geertz, Clifford, *The Interpretation of Cultures*, London, 1975.

—— "Blurred Genres: The Refiguration of Social Thought," *The American Scholar* 49, 1980, 165–79.

Gelli, A., "L'esilio di Cosimo de' Medici," *ASI*, 4th ser., 10, 1882, 53–96; 149–69.

Gellner, E., and W. Waterbury, eds., *Patrons and Clients in Mediterranean Societies*, London, 1977.

Gilbert, Creighton, "On Subject and Not-Subject in Italian Renaissance Pictures," *AB* 34, 1952, 202–16.

—— "The Archbishop on the Painters of Florence, 1450," *AB* 41, 1959, 75–87.

—— "The Earliest Guide to Florentine Architecture, 1423," *Mitteilungen* 14, 1969, 33–46.

—— "Castagno's Nine Famous Men and Women: Sword and Book as the Basis for Public Service," in *Life and Death in Fifteenth-Century Florence*, ed. Marcel Tetel, Ronald G. Witt, and Rona Goffen, Durham and London, 1989, 174–92.

—— "Saint Antonin de Florence et l'art: theologie pastorale, administration et commande d'oeuvres," *Revue de l'art* 90, 1990, 9–20.

—— *Poets Seeing Artists' Work: Instances in the Italian Renaissance*, Florence, 1991.

—— "Ghiberti on the Destruction of Art," *I Tatti Studies* 6, 1995, 135–44.

—— "What Did the Renaissance Patron Buy?" *RQ* 51, 1998, 392–450.

Gilbert, Felix, "Bernardo Rucellai and the Orti Oricellari: A Study on the Origin of Modern Political Thought," *JWCI* 12, 1949, 101–31.

—— *Machiavelli and Guicciardini: Politics and History in Sixteenth-Century Florence*, Princeton, 1965.

——"The Venetian Constitution in Florentine Political Thought," in *Florentine Studies: Politics and Society in Renaissance Florence*, ed. N. Rubinstein, London, 1968, 463–500.

——"The Medici Megalopolis," review of Richard Goldthwaite, *The Building of Renaissance Florence*, in *The New York Review of Books*, January 21, 1982, 62–6.

——"The Other Florence," review article in *The New York Review of Books*, October 9, 1986, 43–4.

Gill, Joseph, *The Council of Florence*, Cambridge, 1959.

——*Eugenius IV: Pope of Christian Union*, Westminster, Md., 1961.

——*Personalities of the Council of Florence and Other Essays*, New York and London, 1964.

Ginori Conti, Piero, *La basilica di S. Lorenzo di Firenze e la famiglia Ginori*, Florence, 1940.

Ginori-Lisci, L., *I palazzi di Firenze nella storia e nell'arte*, Florence, 1972.

Ginzburg, Carlo, *Il formaggio e i vermi*, Rome, 1976; trans. John and Anne Tedeschi, *The Cheese and the Worms*, Baltimore, 1980.

Glasser, Hannelore, *Artists' Contracts of the Early Renaissance*, New York, 1977.

Gnocchi, Lorenzo, "Le preferenze artistiche di Piero di Cosimo de' Medici," *Artibus et historiae* 9, 1988, 41–77.

Goffen, Rona, "Masaccio's *Trinity* and the Letter to the Hebrews," *Memorie domenicane* 11, 1980, 489–504.

——*Piety and Patronage in Renaissance Venice: Bellini, Titian, and the Franciscans*, New Haven and London, 1986.

Goffman, Erving, *The Presentation of Self in Everyday Life*, Garden City, N.J., 1959.

Goldthwaite, R. A. "The Florentine Palace as Domestic Architecture," *AHR* 77, 1972, 977–1012.

——"The Building of the Strozzi Palace: The Construction Industry in Renaissance Florence," *Studies in Medieval and Renaissance History* 10, 1973, 97–194.

——*The Building of Renaissance Florence. An Economic and Social History*, Baltimore, 1980.

——review of F. W. Kent et al., *Giovanni Rucellai ed il suo Zibaldone, II. A Florentine Patrician and his Palace*, in *BM* 125, 1983.

——"The Empire of Things: Consumer Demand in Renaissance Italy," in *Patronage, Art and Society in Renaissance Italy*, ed. F. W. Kent and Patricia Simons, Oxford, 1987, 153–75.

——"The Medici Bank and the World of Florentine Capitalism," *Past and Present* 114, 1987, 3–31.

——"The Economic and Social World of Italian Renaissance Maiolica," *RQ* 42, 1989, 1–32.

——"Il contesto economico del palazzo fiorentino nel Rinascimento: investimento, cantiere, consumi," *Annali di architettura* 2, 1990, 53–8.

——*Wealth and the Demand for Art in Italy, 1300–1600*, Baltimore, 1993.

Goldthwaite, Richard A., and R. W. Rearick, "Michelozzo and the Ospedale di San Paolo in Florence," *Mitteilungen* 21, 1977, 221–306.

Gombrich, E. H., "The Renaissance Conception of Artistic Progress and its Consequence," 1955, repr. in Gombrich, *Norm and Form: Studies in the Art of the Renaissance, 1*, London and New York, 1966, 1–10.

——"A Classical Topos in the Introduction to Alberti's *Della Pittura*," *JWCI* 20, 1957, 173.

——"The Early Medici as Patrons of Art," in *Italian Renaissance Studies*, ed. E. F. Jacob, London, 1960, 35–59, repr. in *Norm and Form*.

——"Vasari's *Lives* and Cicero's *Brutus*," *JWCI* 23, 1960, 309–11.

——"Renaissance and Golden Age," *JWCI* 24, 1961, 306–9.

——"Alberto Avogadro's Descriptions of the Badia of Fiesole and of the Villa of Careggi," *Italia medioevale e umanistica* 5, 1962, 217–29.

——"The Social History of Art," in Gombrich, *Meditations on a Hobby-Horse and Other Essays on the Theory of Art*, London, 1963.

——*Norm and Form, Studies in the Art of the Renaissance, 1*, London, 1966.

——"From the Revival of Letters to the Reform of the Arts: Niccolo Niccoli and Filippo Brunelleschi, in *Essays on the History of Art Presented to Rudolf Wittkower*, London, 1967, 71–82.

——"The Leaven of Criticism in Renaissance Art: Texts and Episodes," in *Art, Science and History*, ed. C. Singleton, Baltimore, 1967, 3–42.

——*Aby Warburg: An Intellectual Biography*, London, 1970.

——*Symbolic Images: Studies in the Art of the Renaissance, 2*, London, 1972.

——*Topos and Topicality in Renaissance Art*, London, 1973.

——*The Heritage of Apelles: Studies in the Art of the Renaissance*, Ithaca, N.Y. 1976.

——introduction to *Cosimo 'il Vecchio' de' Medici, 1389–1464*, ed. Francis Ames-Lewis, Oxford, 1992, 1–4.

Gori, P., *Firenze magnifica: le feste fiorentine attraverso i secoli*, Florence, 1930.

Gorni, G., "Storia del Certame Coronario," *Rinascimento*, ser. 2, 12, 1972, 135–81.

Graf, Arturo, "Il Zibaldone attribuito ad Antonio Pucci," *GSLI* 1, 294–328.

Grafton, Anthony, and Lisa Jardine, *From Humanism to the Humanities, Education and the Liberal Arts in Fifteenth- and Sixteenth-Century Europe*, Cambridge, Mass., 1986.

Granato, Lois R., "The Location of the Armory in the Italian Renaissance Palace: A Note on Three Literary Sources," *Waffen-und Kostumkunde* 24, 1982, 152–3.

Grayson, Cecil, "The Composition of L. B. Alberti's 'Decem Libri de Re Aedificatoria,'" *Münchner Jahrbuch der Bildenden Kunst* 11, 1960, 152–61.

——"Poesie latine di Gentile Becchi in un codice bodleiano," in *Studi offerti a Roberto Ridolfi direttore de "La Bibliofilia,"* ed. Berta Maracchi Biagiarelli and Dennis E. Rhodes, Florence, 1973, 285–303.

Green, Louis, "Galvano Fiamma, Azzone Visconti and the Revival of the Classical Theory of Magnificence," *JWCI* 53, 1990, 98–113.

Greenblatt, Stephen, *Renaissance Self-Fashioning: From More to Shakespeare*, Chicago, 1980.

—— *Shakespearean Negotiations: The Circulation of Social Energy in Renaissance England*, Berkeley and Los Angeles, 1988.

Greenhalgh, Michael, *Donatello and His Sources*, London, 1982.

Greenstein, Jack, "The Vision of Peace: Meaning and Representation in Ambrogio Lorenzetti's *Sala della Pace* Cityscapes," *Art History* 11, 1988, 492–510.

—— "Alberti on *Historia*: A Renaissance View of the Structure of Significance in Narrative Painting," *Viator* 21, 1990, 273–99.

—— *Mantegna and Painting as Historical Narrative*, Chicago, 1992.

Gregory, Heather, "Palla Strozzi's Patronage and Pre-Medicean Florence," in *Patronage, Art and Society in Renaissance Italy*, ed. F. W. Kent and Patricia Simons, Oxford, 1987, 201–20.

Grendler, Paul F., *Schooling in Renaissance Italy: Literacy and Learning, 1300–1600*, Baltimore and London, 1989.

—— "Schooling in Western Europe," *RQ* 43, 1990, 775–87.

—— "Form and Function in Italian Renaissance Popular Books," *RQ* 46, 1993, 451–85.

Griffiths, Gordon, "The Political Significance of Uccello's *Battle of San Romano*," *JWCI* 41, 1978, 313–16.

Grote, Andreas, "A Hitherto Unpublished Letter on Benozzo Gozzoli's Frescoes in the Palazzo Medici-Riccardi," *JWCI* 27, 1964, 321–2.

Grubb, James, *Provincial Families of the Renaissance: Private and Public Life in the Veneto*, Baltimore and London, 1996.

Guasti, C., *Le feste di San Giovanni Battista in Firenze*, Florence, 1884.

Guenther, Ursula, "Unusual Phenomena in the Transmission of Late Fourteenth-Century Polyphonic Music," *Musica disciplina* 38, 1984, 87–118.

Guerri, D., *La corrente popolare nel Rinascimento: Berte, burle, e baie nella Firenze del Brunellesco e del Burchiello*, Florence, 1931.

Guidotti, Alessandro, "Pubblico e privato, committenza e clientela: botteghe e produzione artistica a Firenze tra XV e XVI secolo," *Ricerche storiche* 16, 1986, 535–550.

Gurevich, Aron, *Medieval Popular Culture: Problems of Belief and Perception*, New York, 1988.

Gurrieri, Francesco, ed., *La sacrestia vecchia di San Lorenzo*, Florence, 1986.

Gurrieri, Francesco, et al., *La basilica di San Miniato al Monte a Firenze*, 1988.

Gutkind, C. S., "Burchelliana," *Archivium Romanicum* 15, 1931, 9–12.

—— *Cosimo de' Medici, Pater Patriae, 1389–1464*, Oxford, 1938.

Haines, Margaret, *La Sagrestia delle Messe nel Duomo di Firenze*, Florence, 1983.

—— "La colonna della *Dovizia* di Donatello," *Rivista d'arte* 37, 1984, 347–59.

—— "Brunelleschi and Bureaucracy: The Tradition of Public Patronage of the Florentine Cathedral," *I Tatti Studies* 3, 1989, 89–125.

—— "L'Arte della Lana e L'Opera del Duomo a Firenze, con un acceno a Ghiberti tra due istituzioni," in *Opera: carattere e ruolo delle fabbriche cittadine fino all'inizio dell' età moderna*, ed. Margaret Haines and Lucio Riccetti, Florence, 1996, 267–94.

—— "Il principio di 'mirabilissime cose:' i mosaici per la volta della cappella di San Zanobi in Santa Maria del Fiore," in *La difficile eredità: architettura a Firenze dalla Repubblica all'Assedio*, ed. Narzua Dezzi Bardeschi, Florence, 1994, 38–54.

—— "Artisan Family Strategies," in *Art, Memory and the Family in Renaissance Florence*, ed. Giovanni Ciappelli and Patricia Rubin, Cambridge, 2000, 163–75.

Haitovsky, Dalia, "The Source of the Young *David* by Andrea del Castagno," *Mitteilungen* 29, 1985, 174–82.

Hale, John R., *Italian Renaissance Painting from Masaccio to Titian*, Oxford, 1977.

—— *Florence and the Medici: The Pattern of Control*, London, 1977.

—— *Artists and Warfare in the Renaissance*, New Haven and London, 1990.

Hall, James, *Dictionary of Subjects and Symbols in Art*, New York, 1979.

Hall, Marcia, "The 'Tramezzo' in S. Croce, Florence, and Domenico Veneziano's Fresco," *BM* 112, 1970, 797–9.

—— "The Ponte in Sa. Maria Novella: The Problem of the Rood Screen in Italy," *JWCI* 37, 1974, 157–73.

Hankey, Teresa, "Salutati's Epigrams for the Palazzo Vecchio at Florence," *JWCI* 22, 1959, 363–5.

Hankins, James, "The Humanist, The Banker and the Condottiere: An Unpublished Letter of Cosimo and Lorenzo de' Medici Written by Leonardo Bruni," *Renaissance Society and Culture: Essays in Honor of Eugene F. Rice, Jr.*, ed. John Monfasani and Ronald G. Musto, New York, 1991, 59–70.

—— "Cosimo de' Medici and the 'Platonic Academy,'" *JWCI* 53, 1990, 144–62.

—— *Plato in the Italian Renaissance*, 2 vols., Leiden, 1990.

—— "Cosimo de' Medici as a Patron of Humanistic Literature," in *Cosimo "il Vecchio" de' Medici, 1389–1464*, ed. Francis Ames-Lewis, Oxford, 1992, 69–94.

Hartt, Frederick, "Art and Freedom in Quattrocento Florence," in *Essays in Memory of Karl Lehmann*, ed. Lucy Freeman Sandler, New York, 1964, 114–31.

Haskell, Francis, *Patrons and Painters: A Study in the Relations Between Italian Art and Society in the Age of the Baroque*, New Haven and London, 1980.

—— *History and its Images: Art and the Interpretation of the Past*, London, 1993.

Hatfield, Rab, "The Compagnia de' Magi," *JWCI* 33, 1970, 107–61.

—— "Some Unknown Descriptions of the Medici Palace in 1459," *AB* 52, 1970.

—— review of D. S. Chambers, ed., *Patrons and Artists in the Italian Renaissance*, and Peter Burke, *Culture and Society in Renaissance Italy, 1420–1540*, *AB* 55, 1973, 630–3.

—— *Botticelli's Uffizi 'Adoration'*, Princeton 1976.

—— "Cosimo de' Medici and the Chapel of his Palace," in *Cosimo "il Vecchio" de' Medici, 1389–1464*, Oxford, 1992, 221–43.

Heers, J., *Fêtes, jeux et jouts dans les sociétés d'occident à la fin du moyen age*, Montreal, 1971.

Heikamp, D., and A. Grote, eds., *Il tesoro di Lorenzo il Magnifico*, 2 vols. Florence, 1974, vol. 2.

Henderson, John, "Le confraternite religiose nella Firenze del tardo medioevo: patroni spirituali e anche politici?" *Ricerche storiche* 15, 1985, 77–94.

—— "Confraternities and the Church in Late Medieval Florence," in *Voluntary Religion*, ed. W. J. Sheils and Diana Woord, Oxford, 1986, 69–84.

—— "Penitence and the Laity in Fifteenth-Century Florence," in *Christianity and the Renaissance*, ed. Timothy Verdon and John Henderson, Syracuse, 1990, 229–49.

—— *Piety and Charity in Late Medieval Florence*, Oxford, 1994.

Herlihy, David, "Veillir à Florence au Quattrocento," *Annales ESC* 24, 1969, 1338–52.

—— introduction to Christiane Klapisch-Züber, *Women, Family and Ritual in Renaissance Italy*, Chicago, 1985.

—— "Tuscan Names, 1200–1530," *RQ* 41, 1988, 561–82.

—— "The Rulers of Florence, 1282–1530," in *City States in Classical Antiquity and Medieval Italy*, ed. Anthony Molho, Kurt Raaflaub, and Julia Emden, Stuttgart, 1991, 197–221.

Herlihy, David, and Christiane Klapisch-Zuber, *Les Toscans et leurs familles: une étude du catasto florentin de 1427*, Paris, 1978; abridged English ed., *Tuscans and Their Families: A Study of the Florentine Catasto of 1427*, New Haven and London, 1985.

Hersey, George, *The Aragonese Arch at Naples, 1443–1475*, New Haven and London, 1973.

Herzner, V., "Die Kanzeln Donatellos in San Lorenzo," *Münchner Jahrbuch der Bildenden Kunst* 23, 1972, 101–64.

—— "Zur Baugeschichte von San Lorenzo in Florenz," *Zeitschrift für Kunstgeschichte*, 37, 1974, 89–115.

—— "Die Segel-Imprese der Familie Pazzi," *Mitteilungen* 20, 1976, 13–32.

—— "David Florentinus. II: Der Bronze-David Donatellos im Bargello," *Jahrbuch der Berliner Museen* 24, 1982, 63–142.

Heydenreich, Ludwig H., "Die Cappella Rucellai von San Pancrazio in Florenz," *Essays in Honor of Erwin Panofsky*, ed. Millard Meiss, New York, 1961, 219–29.

Heydenreich, L. H., and W. Lotz, *Architecture in Italy, 1440–1600*, Harmondsworth, 1974.

Heywood, W., *The Ensamples of Fra Filippo*, Siena, 1901.

Hill, George Francis, *A Corpus of Italian Medals of the Renaissance before Cellini*, 2 vols., London, 1930.

Hofman, G., "Kopten und Aethiopier auf dem Konzil von Florenz," *Orientalia Christiana Periodica* 8, 1942, 3–35.

Hollingsworth, Mary, "The Architect in Fifteenth-Century Florence," *Art History* 7, 1984, 385–410.

Holmes, George, "How the Medici Became the Pope's Bankers," in *Florentine Studies: Politics and Society in Renaissance Florence*, ed. N. Rubinstein, London, 1968, 357–80.

—— *The Florentine Enlightenment, 1400–1450*, London, 1969.

—— "The Emergence of an Urban Ideology at Florence, c.1250–1450," *Transactions of the Royal Historical Society* 23, 1973, 111–34.

—— *Florence, Rome and the Origins of the Renaissance*, Oxford, 1986.

Holmes, Megan, *Fra Filippo Lippi the Carmelite Painter*, New Haven and London, 1999.

—— "Giovanni Benci's Patronage of the Nunnery, Le Murate," in *Art, Memory and Family in Renaissance Florence*, ed. Giovanni Ciappelli and Patricia Rubin, Cambridge, 2000, 114–34.

Hood, William, "Saint Dominic's Manners of Praying: Gestures in Fra Angelico's Cell Frescoes at San Marco," *AB* 68, 1986, 195–205.

—— "Fra Angelico at San Marco: Art and the Liturgy of Cloistered Life," in *Christianity and the Renaissance*, ed. T. Verdon and J. Henderson, Syracuse, 1986, 108–31.

—— "The State of Research in Italian Renaissance Art," *AB* 69, 1987, 174–86.

—— *Fra Angelico at San Marco*, New Haven and London, 1993.

—— "Creating Memory: Monumental Painting and Cultural Definition," in *Language and Images of Renaissance Italy*, ed. Alison Brown, Oxford, 1995, 157–69.

Hope, Charles, "Artists, Patrons and Advisers in the Italian Renaissance," in *Patronage in the Renaissance*, ed. Guy Lytle and Stephen Orgel, Princeton, 1981, 293–343.

—— "Altarpieces and the Requirements of Patrons," in *Christianity and the Renaissance*, ed. T. Verdon and J. Henderson, Syracuse, 1986, 535–68.

—— "Religious Narrative in Renaissance Art," *Royal Society of Arts Journal* 134, 1986, 804–18.

—— "The Early History of the Tempio Malatestiana," *JWCI* 55, 1992, 51–154.

Horowitz, Maryanne Cline, "Aristotle and Woman," *Journal of the History of Biology* 9, 1976, 183–213.

Horster, Marita, *Andrea del Castagno*, London, 1980.

Hoshino, H., *L'arte della lana in Firenze nel basso medioevo*, Florence, 1980.

Hughes, Diane Owen, "Representing the Family: Portraits and Purposes in Early Modern Italy," in the symposium, *The Evidence of Art: Images and Meaning in History, JIH* 17, 1986, 7–38.

Huizinga, J., *Homo Ludens: A Study of the Play Element in Culture*, Haarlem, 1938; US ed., Boston, 1950.

Humfrey, P., and M. Kemp, eds. *The Altarpiece in the Renaissance*, Cambridge, 1990.

Hunt, Lynn, ed., *The New Cultural History*, Berkeley and Los Angeles, 1989.

Hyman, Isabelle, "New Light on Old Problems: Palazzo Medici and the Church of S. Lorenzo," *JSAH* 37, 1969.

—— *Brunelleschi in Perspective*, Englewood Cliffs, 1974.

——"Notes and Speculations on S. Lorenzo, Palazzo Medici, and an Urban Project by Brunelleschi," *JSAH* 34, 1975, 98–120.

——*Fifteenth-Century Florentine Studies: The Palazzo Medici and a Ledger for the Church of San Lorenzo*, Ann Arbor, 1977.

Ianziti, Gary, "The Production of History in Milan," in *Patronage, Art and Society in Renaissance Italy*, ed. F. W. Kent and Patricia Simons, Oxford, 1987, 299–311.

Ilardi, V., "The Banker-Statesman and the Condottiere-Prince: Cosimo de' Medici and Francesco Sforza (1450–1464)," in *Florence and Milan: Comparisons and Relations*, ed. C. H. Smyth and G. Garfagnini, 2 vols., Florence, 1989, vol. 2, 217–42.

Isaac, Rhys, *The Transformation of Virginia, 1740–1790*, Chapel Hill, N.C., 1982.

Jacks, Philip, "Michelozzo di Bartolomeo and the 'Domus Pulcra' of Tommaso Spinelli," in *Florence, Architectura, Zeitschrift für Geschichte der Baukunst*, 1996, 47–83.

Jacks, P., and V. Cafarro, *Tommaso Spinelli*, Durham, forthcoming.

Janson, H. W., *The Sculpture of Donatello*, Princeton, 1963.

——"Giovanni Chellini's *Libro* and Donatello," in *Studien zur Toskanischen Kunst: Festschrift für Ludwig Heinrich Heydenreich*, ed. Wolfgang Lotz and Lise Lotte Möller, Munich, 1964, 131–8.

——"La Signification politique du David en bronze de Donatello," *Revue de l'art* 39, 1978, 33–38.

——"The Birth of 'Artistic Licence': The Dissatisfied Patron in the Early Renaissance," in *Patronage in the Renaissance*, ed. Guy Lytle and Stephen Orgel, Princeton, 1981, 344–53.

Jarzombek, Mark, *On Leon Baptista Alberti: His Literary and Aesthetic Theories*, Cambridge, Mass., 1989.

Jayne, Emily, "A Choreography by Lorenzo in Botticelli's Primavera," in *Lorenzo de' Medici: New Perspectives*, ed. Bernard Toscani, New York, 1993, 163–78.

Joannides, P., *Masaccio and Masolino: A Complete Catalogue*, London, 1993.

——"Paolo Uccello's 'Rout of San Romano': A New Observation," *BM* 131, 1989, 214–15.

Johnson, Geraldine, "Family Values: Sculpture and the Family in Fifteenth-Century Florence," in *Art, Memory and Family in Renaissance Florence*, ed. Giovanni Ciappelli and Patricia Rubin, Cambridge, 2000, 215–33.

Jones, A. H. M., *The Later Roman Empire*, 2 vols., Oxford, 1964.

Jones, P. J., "Communes and Despots: The City-State in Late Medieval Italy," *Transactions of the Royal Historical Society*, ser. 5, 15, 1965, 71–96.

——*The Malatesta of Rimini and the Papal State*, London and New York, 1974.

Jones, Roger, "Palla Strozzi e la Sagrestia di Santa Trinita," *Rivista d'arte*, ser. 4, 1, no. 37, 1984, 9–106.

Joost-Gaugier, Christiane, "Poggio and Visual Tradition: *Uomini Famosi* in Classical Literary Description," *Artibus et historiae* 16, 1987, 91–9.

Jungmann, J. A., *The Mass of the Roman Rite: Its Origins and Development*, trans. F. A. Brunner, London, 1959.

Kallendorf, Craig, "Cristoforo Landino's *Aeneid* and the Humanist Critical Tradition," *RQ* 36, 1983, 519–46.

——*In Praise of Aeneas: Virgil and Epideictic Rhetoric in the Early Italian Renaissance*, Hanover and London, 1989.

Kaske, Carol V., "Marsilio Ficino and the Twelve Gods of the Zodiac," *JWCI* 45, 1982, 195–202.

Kemp, Martin, "From 'Mimesis' to 'Fantasia': The Quattrocento Vocabulary of Creation, Inspiration and Genius in the Visual Arts," *Viator* 8, 1977, 347–98.

——*Leonardo da Vinci: The Marvellous Works of Nature and Man*, London, 1981.

——"'Equal Excellences': Lomazzo and the Explanation of Individual Style in the Visual Arts," *Renaissance Studies* 1, 1987, 1–23.

Kemp, Wolfgang, "Visual Narratives, Memory, and the Medieval *Esprit du Système*," in *Images of Memory: On Remembering and Representation*, ed. S. Küchler and W. Melion, Washington and London, 1991, 87–108.

Kempers, Bram, *Painting, Power and Patronage: The Rise of the Professional Artist in Renaissance Italy*, English ed. London, 1992.

Kennedy, Ruth Wedgwood, *Alesso Baldovinetti*, New Haven, 1938.

Kennedy, William J., "Petrarchan Figurations of Death in Lorenzo de' Medici's Sonnets and Commento," in *Life and Death in Fifteenth-Century Florence*, ed. Marcel Tetel, Ronald G. Witt, and Rona Goffen, Durham and London, 1989, 46–67.

Kent, Dale, "I Medici in esilio: una vittoria di famiglia e una disfatta personale, *ASI* 132, 1974, 1–63.

——"The Florentine '*Reggimento*' in the Fifteenth-Century," *RQ* 4, 1975, 264–344.

——*The Rise of the Medici: Faction in Florence, 1426–1434*, Oxford, 1978.

——"The Importance of Being Eccentric: Giovanni Cavalcanti's View of Cosimo de' Medici's Florence, *JMRS* 20, 1979, 101–32.

——"The Dynamic of Power in Cosimo de' Medici's Florence," *Patronage and Society in Renaissance Italy*, ed. F. W. Kent and Patricia Simons, Oxford, 1986, 63–77.

——"The Buonomini di San Martino: Charity for 'the glory of God, the honour of the city, and the commemoration of myself,'" in *Cosimo "il Vecchio" de' Medici, 1389–1464*, ed. Francis Ames-Lewis, Oxford, 1992, 49–67.

——"Michele del Giogante's House of Memory," in *Culture and Identity in Renaissance Florence: Essays presented to Gene A. Brucker*, ed. William J. Connell, Berkeley and Los Angeles, forthcoming.

——*Fathers and Friends: Patronage and Patriarchy in Renaissance Florence*, forthcoming.

Kent, D. V. and F. W. Kent, "Two Comments of March 1445 on the Medici Palace," *BM* 121, 1979, 795–6.

——"A Self-Disciplining Pact Made by the Peruzzi Family of Florence (June 1433)," *RQ* 24, 1981, 337–55.

——*Neighbours and Neighbourhood in Renaissance Florence*, Locust Valley, N.Y., 1982.

——"Two Vignettes of Florentine Society in the Fifteenth Century," *Rinascimento* 23, 1983, 237–60.

Kent, F. W., *Household and Lineage in Renaissance Florence: The Family Life of the Capponi, Ginori and Rucellai*, Princeton, 1977.

——"'Più superba de quella de Lorenzo': Courtly and Family Interest in the Building of Filippo Strozzi's Palace," *RQ* 30, 1977, 311–23.

——"Lorenzo de' Medici's Acquisition of Poggio a Caiano in 1474 and an Early Reference to his Architectural Expertise," *JWCI* 1979, 250–57.

——"The Making of a Renaissance Patron," in F. W. Kent et al., *Giovanni Rucellai ed il suo Zibaldone*, II: *A Florentine Patrician and his Palace*, London, 1981, 9–95.

——"Lorenzo di Credi, his Patron Iacopo Bongianni and Savonarola," *BM* 125, 1983, 539–41.

——"Palaces, Politics and Society in Fifteenth-Century Florence," *I Tatti Studies* 2, 1987, 41–70.

——"Patron-Client Networks in Renaissance Florence and the Emergence of Lorenzo as 'Maestro della Bottega'," in *Lorenzo de' Medici: New Perspectives*, ed. Bernard Toscani, New York, 1994, 279–314.

——"'Un paradiso habitato da diavoli': Ties of Loyalty and Patronage in the Society of Medicean Florence," in *Le radici cristiane di Firenze*, ed. Anna Benvenuti, Franco Cardini, and Elena Giannarelli, Florence, 1994.

Kent, F. W., and Amanda Lillie, "The Piovano Arlotto: New Documents," in *Florence and Italy: Renaissance Studies in Honour of Nicolai Rubinstein*, ed. Peter Denley and Caroline Elam, London, 1988, 347–67.

Kent, F. W., and Patricia Simons, eds., *Patronage, Art and Society in Renaissance Italy*, Oxford, 1987.

Kettering, Sharon, "Patronage in Early Modern France," *French Historical Studies* 17, 1992, 839–71.

——"Gift-Giving and Patronage in Early Modern France," *French History* 2, 1988, 131–51.

King, Catherine, "Filarete's Portrait Signature on the Bronze Door of St Peter's," *JWCI* 53, 1990, 297–9.

Kirschner, Jules, "Pursuing Honor while Avoiding Sin: The *Monte delle doti* of Florence, *Studi Senesi* 89, 1977, 175–258.

Klapisch-Zuber, Christiane, "Parenti, amici, e vicini: il territorio urbano di una famiglia mercantile nel XV secolo," *Quaderni storici* 33, 1976, 953–82.

——"Zacharie, ou le père évincé: les rites nuptiaux toscans entre Giotto et le Concile de Trente," *Annales ESC* 34, 1979, 1216–43.

——"Le Nom 'refait': la transmission des prénoms a Florence (XIVe–XVIe siècles)," *L'Homme* 20, 1980, 77–104.

——*Women, Family and Ritual in Renaissance Italy*, Chicago, 1985.

——"Holy Dolls: Play and Piety in Florence in the Quattrocento," in Klapisch-Zuber, *Women, Family and Ritual in Renaissance Italy*, 310–29.

——"Compérage et clientélisme à Florence (1360–1520), *Ricerche storiche* 15, 1985, 61–76.

——ed., "Il pubblico, il privato, l'intimita; percezioni ed esperienze tra Medio Evo e Rinascimento," *Ricerche storiche* 16, 1986.

Kohl, Benjamin, "The Scrovegni in Carrara Padua and Enrico's Will," *Apollo* 142, 1995, 43–7.

Kramer, L. S., "Literature, Criticism and Historical Imagination," in *The New Cultural History*, ed. Lynn Hunt, Berkeley and Los Angeles, 1989, 97–128.

Krautheimer, Richard, with Trude Krautheimer-Hess, *Lorenzo Ghiberti*, Princeton, 2nd ed., 1970.

——*Rome: Profile of a City, 312–1308*, Princeton, 1980.

——*Early Christian and Byzantine Architecture*, New York, 1986.

Krinsky, Carol H., "A View of the Palazzo Medici and the Church of San Lorenzo," *JSAH* 28, 1969, 133–5.

Kristeller, Paul, *Early Florentine Woodcuts*, repr. London, 1968.

Kristeller, Paul Oskar, *The Philosophy of Marsilio Ficino*, New York, 1943.

——*Iter Italicum*, 6 vols., London, 1963–7.

——"Lay Religious Traditions and Florentine Platonism," in P. O. Kristeller, *Studies in Renaissance Thought and Letters*, Rome, 1956, 99–122.

——"Marsilio Ficino and his Circle," in P. O. Kristeller, *Studies in Renaissance Thought and Letters*, Rome, 1956, 99–115.

——"Marsilio Ficino as a Man of Letters and the Glosses Attributed to Him in the Caetani Codex of Dante," *RQ* 36, 1983, 1–34.

Küchler, Susanne, and Walter Melion, eds., *Images of Memory: On Remembering and Representation*, Washington and London, 1991.

Kuehn, Thomas, *Law, Family, and Women: Toward a Legal Anthropology of Renaissance Italy*, Chicago, 1991.

La Capra, Dominick, *Re-Thinking Intellectual History: Texts, Contexts, Language*, Ithaca, N.Y., 1983.

——*History and Criticism*, Ithaca, N.Y., 1985.

"Is Everyone a *Mentalité* Case? Transference and the 'Culture' Concept," in La Capra, *History and Criticism*, 71–94.

——"The Cheese and the Worms," in La Capra, *History and Criticism*, 61–9.

Lang, S., "The Programme of the SS. Annunziata in Florence," *JWCI* 17, 1954, 288–300.

Langedijk, Karla, *The Portraits of the Medici*, Florence, 1981.

Lanza, Antonio, *Polemiche e berte letterarie nelle Firenze del primo Rinascimento, (1375–1449): studi e testi*, Rome, 1972: completely rev. ed. Rome, 1987.

Lapi Ballerini, I., "The Celestial Hemisphere of the Old Sacristy and its Restoration," *BM* 129, 1987, 51–2.

——"Gli emisferi celesti della Sagrestia Vecchia e della Cappella Pazzi," *Rinascimento*, ser. 3, 16, 1988, 321–55.

——"Considerazioni a margine del restauro della 'cupolina'

dipinta nella Sagrestia Vecchia," in *Donatello-Studien* III, XVI, 1989, 102–12.

Larner, John, "The Church and the *Quattrocento* Renaissance in Geography," *Renaissance Studies* 12, 1998, 26–39.

Lavin, Irving, "The Sources of Donatello's Pulpits in San Lorenzo: Revival and Freedom of Choice in the Early Renaissance," *AB* 41, 1959, 19–38.

—— "On the Sources and Meaning of the Renaissance Portrait Bust," *Art Quarterly* 33, 1970, 207–26.

—— "Donatello's Bronze Pulpits in San Lorenzo and the Early Christian Revival," in Lavin, *Past–Present: Essays on Historicism in Art from Donatello to Picasso*, Berkeley and Los Angeles, 1993, 1–27.

Lavin, Marilyn Aronberg, "Giovannino Battista: A Study in Renaissance Religious Symbolism," *AB* 37, 1955, 85–101.

—— "Giovannino Battista: A Supplement," *AB* 43, 1961, 321–6.

—— "Piero della Francesca's Fresco of Sigismondo Pandolfo Malatesta before St. Sigismund," *AB* 56, 1974, 345–73.

—— "The Antique Source for the Tempio Malatestiano's Greek Inscriptions," *AB* 59, 1977, 421–2.

Law, John E., "Giovanni Vitelleschi: 'prelato guerriero,'" *Renaissance Studies* 12, 1998, 40–66.

Lee, Rensselaer W., "*Ut pictura poesis*: The Humanistic Theory of Painting," *AB* 22, 1940, 197–269.

Le Goff, Jacques, *The Birth of Purgatory*, Chicago, 1986.

—— *Your Money or Your Life: Economy and Religion in the Middle Ages*, New York, 1990.

Leonardi, Claudio, "San Miniato: il martire e il suo culto sul Monte di Firenze," in Francesco Gurrieri, et al., *La Basilica di San Miniato al Monte a Firenze*, Florence, 1988, 279–85.

Lerner, Gerda, *The Creation of Patriarchy*, Oxford, 1986.

Lesher, Melinda, "The Vision of St. Bernard and the Chapel of the Priors: Private and Public Images of Bernard of Clairvaux in Renaissance Florence," Ph.D. Diss. Columbia University, 1979.

Lesnick, Daniel, "Dominican Preaching and the Creation of Capitalist Ideology in Late-Medieval Florence," *Memorie Domenicane*, n. s. 8–9, 1977–8, 199–247.

—— "Civic Preaching in the Early Renaissance," in *Christianity and the Renaissance*, ed. T. Verdon and J. Henderson, Syracuse, 1990, 208–25.

Liebenwein, Wolfgang, *Studiolo: Die Entstehung eines Raumtyps und seine Entwicklung bis um 1600*, Berlin, 1977.

—— "Die 'Privatisierung' des Wunders: Piero de' Medici in SS. Annunziata und San Miniato," in *Piero de' Medici, 'il Gottoso' (1416–1469): Kunst im Dienste der Mediceer*, ed. Andreas Beyer and Bruce Boucher, Berlin, 1993, 251–90.

Lightbown, R. W., 'Giovanni Chellini, Donatello and Antonio Rossellino," *BM* 104, 1962, 102–4.

—— *Donatello and Michelozzo: An Artistic Partnership and its Patrons in the Early Renaissance*, 2 vols., London, 1980.

Lillie, Amanda, "Florentine Villas in the Fifteenth Century: A Study of the Strozzi and Sassetti Country Properties," Ph.D. Diss. Courtauld Institute of Art, University of London, 1986.

—— "Giovanni di Cosimo and the Villa Medici at Fiesole," in *Piero de' Medici, 'il Gottoso' (1416–1469): Kunst im Dienste der Mediceer*, ed. Andreas Beyer and Bruce Boucher, Berlin, 1993, 189–206.

—— "The Humanist Villa Revisited," in *Language and Images of Renaissance Italy*, ed. Alison Brown, Oxford, 1995, 193–215.

—— "The Memory of Place: *Luogo* and Lineage," in *Art, Memory and the Family in Renaissance Florence*, ed. G. Ciappelli and Patricia Rubin, Cambridge, 2000, 195–214.

Lippincott, Kristen, "The Neo-Latin Historical Epics of the North Italian Courts: An Examination of 'Courtly Culture' in the Fifteenth Century," *Renaissance Studies* 3, 1989, 415–30.

—— "The Art of Cartography in Fifteenth-Century Florence," in *Lorenzo the Magnificent: Culture and Politics*, ed. Michael Mallett and Nicholas Mann, London, 1996, 131–43.

Litta, P., *Famiglie celebri italiane: Medici di Firenze*, Milan, 1829.

Looper, M. G. "Political Messages in the Medici Palace Garden," *Journal of Garden History* 12, 1992, 255–68.

Lord, Carla, "The *Ovid Moralisé* and the Old Testament," in *A Tribute to Lotte Brand Philips: Art Historian and Detective*, ed. William W. Clark, New York, 1985.

Lydecker, Kent, "Il Patriziato Fiorentino e la Commitenza Artistica per la Casa," in *I ceti dirigenti nella Toscana del Quattrocento*, Florence, 1987, 211–21.

—— "The Domestic Setting of the Arts in Renaissance Florence," Ph.D. Diss., The Johns Hopkins University, 1988.

Lytle, Guy, and Stephen Orgel, eds., *Patronage in the Renaissance*, Princeton, 1981.

Magnani, R., *Relazioni private tra la corte Sforzesca di Milano e Casa Medici, 1450–1500*, Milan, 1910.

Maguire, Yvonne, *The Women of the Medici*, London, 1927.

Mallett, Michael, *The Florentine Galleys in the Fifteenth Century*, Oxford, 1967.

—— *Mercenaries and Their Masters: Warfare in Renaissance Italy*, London, 1974.

—— "Diplomacy and War in Later Fifteenth-Century Italy," *Proceedings of the British Academy* 67, 1981, 267–88.

—— "Some Notes on a Fifteenth-Century Condottiere and his Library: Count Antonio da Marsciano," in *Cultural Aspects of the Italian Renaissance: Essays in Honor of P. O. Kristeller*, ed. C. Clough, Manchester, 1976, 202–15.

Mallett, Michael, and Nicholas Mann, eds., *Lorenzo the Magnificent: Culture and Politics*, London, 1996.

Marsh, David, *The Quattrocento Dialogue: Classical Tradition and Humanist Innovation*, Cambridge, Mass., 1980.

Martelli, Mario, "Appunti sulla poesia volgare fiorentina negli anni del Concilio," in *Firenze e il Concilio del 1439*, ed. Paolo Viti, Florence, 1994, 2, 713–35.

Martindale, Andrew, *The Rise of the Artist in the Middle Ages and Early Renaissance*, New York, 1972.

Martines, Lauro, "La famiglia Martelli e un documento sulla vigilia del ritorno dall'esilio di Cosimo de' Medici (1434)," *ASI* 117, 1959, 19–43.

—— *The Social World of the Florentine Humanists, 1390–1460*, Princeton, 1963.

—— *Power and Imagination: City-States in Renaissance Italy*, New York, 1979.

—— *Society and History in English Renaissance Verse*, New York, 1985.

—— "The Politics of Love Poetry in Renaissance Italy," *Interpres* 11, 1991, 93–111.

—— *An Italian Renaissance Sextet: Six Tales in Historical Context*, New York, 1994.

—— "Love and Hate in Renaissance Patronage," *The Italianist* 14, 1994, 5–31.

—— "The Italian Renaissance Tale as History," in *Language and Images of Renaissance Italy*, ed. Alison Brown, Oxford, 1995, 313–30.

—— "Poetry as Politics and Memory in Renaissance Florence and Italy," in *Art, Memory and the Family in Renaissance Florence*, ed. Giovanni Ciappelli and Patricia Rubin, Cambridge, 2000, 48–63.

Massai, F., "Nicodemo da Pontremoli, ambasciatore di Francesco Sforza a Firenze al tempo di Cosimo il Vecchio," *Atti della Società Colombaria Fiorentina* 12, 1934, 133–62.

Matheson, Peter, *Cardinal Contarini at Regensburg*, Oxford, 1972.

Matthiae, G., *Mosaici medioevali delle chiese di Roma*, 2 vols., Rome, 1967.

Mauss, Marcel, *The Gift*, 1923–4; English trans. London, 1954.

Mazzoni, Guido, *I Bóti della Ss. Annunziata in Firenze*, Florence, 1923.

McClure, George W., "The Art of Mourning: Autobiographical Writings on the Loss of a Son in Italian Humanist Thought," *RQ* 39, 1986, 440–75.

McHam, Sarah Blake Wilk, "Donatello's *Dovizia* as an Image of Florentine Political Propaganda," *Artibus et historiae* 14, 1986, 9–28.

—— "Donatello's Tomb of John XXIII," in *Life and Death in Fifteenth-Century Florence*, ed. Marcel Tetel, Ronald G. Witt, and Rona Goffen, Durham and London, 1989, 146–242.

—— ed., *Looking at Italian Renaissance Sculpture*, New York, 1998.

—— "Public Sculpture in Renaissance Florence," in *Looking at Italian Renaissance Sculpture*, ed. Sarah Blake McHam, New York, 1998, 149–88.

McKillop, Susan, "He Shall Build a House for my Name: The Patronage of Cosimo de' Medici at San Marco and Some Thoughts about its Implications," unpubl. manuscript.

—— "Dante and *Lumen Christi*: A Proposal for the Meaning of the Tomb of Cosimo de' Medici," in *Cosimo 'il Vecchio' de' Medici, 1389–1464*, ed. Francis Ames Lewis, Oxford, 1992, 245–301.

—— "L'ampliamento dello stemma mediceo e il suo contesto politico," *ASI* 150, 1992, 641–713.

McManamon, John, "Continuity and Change in the Ideals of Humanism: The Evidence from Florentine Funeral Oratory," in *Life and Death in Fifteeenth-Century Florence*, ed. Marcel Tetel, Ronald G. Witt, and Rona Goffen, Durham, 1989, 68–87.

Meersseman, G. G., *Ordo fraternitatis: confraternite e pietà dei laici nel medioevo*, 3 vols., Rome, 1977.

Meiss, Millard, "An Early Altarpiece from the Cathedral of Florence," *Metropolitan Museum of Art Bulletin*, n. s. 12, 1954, 302–17.

—— "Toward a More Comprehensive Renaissance Palaeography," *AB* 42, 1960, 97–112.

—— "The Original Position of Uccello's *John Hawkwood*," *AB* 52, 1970, 231–2.

—— "Scholarship and Penitence in the Early Renaissance: The Image of Saint Jerome," in *The Painter's Choice: Problems in the Interpretation of Renaissance Art*, London and New York, 1976, 189–202.

Middeldorf, Ulrich, "Die Zwölf Caesaren von Desiderio da Settignano," *Mitteilungen* 23, 1979, 297–312.

—— review of Michael Baxandall, *Painting and Experience in Fifteenth-Century Italy*, *AB* 57, 1985, 204–5.

Miller, Julia, *Major Florentine Altarpieces from 1430 to 1450*, Ann Arbor 1983.

—— "Medici Patronage and the Iconography of Fra Angelico's San Marco Altarpiece," *Studies in Iconography* 2, 1987, 1–13.

Miles, M., *Image as Insight: Visual Understanding in Western Chritianity and Secular Culture*, Boston, 1985.

Minnich, Nelson H., "The Autobiography of Antonio degli Agli (ca. 1400–77), Humanist and Prelate," in *Renaissance Studies in Honor of Craig Hugh Smyth*, ed. A. Morrogh, F. Superbi Gioffredi, P. Morselli, and E. Borsook, Florence, 1985, 177–91.

Mitchell, Charles, "An Early Christian Model for the Tempio Malatestiano," in *Intuition und Kunstwissenschaft*, Festschrift H. Swarenski, Berlin, 1973.

Mode, Robert L., "San Bernardino in Glory," *AB* 55, 1973, 58–76.

Molho, Anthony, "A Note on the Albizzi and the Conquest of Pisa," *RQ* 20, 1967, 185–99.

—— *Florentine Public Finances in the Early Renaissance*, Cambridge, Mass., 1971.

—— "The Brancacci Chapel: Studes in Its Iconography and History," *JWCI* 40, 1977, 50–98.

—— "Cosimo de' Medici: *Pater Patriae* or *padrino*?" *Stanford Italian Review* 1, 1979, 5–33.

—— "Art and Society in *Quattrocento* Florence," paper for a conference at the Newberry Library, Chicago.

—— "Il Patronato a firenze nella storiografia Anglofona," *Ricerche storiche* 15, 1985, 5–16.

—— "American Historians and the Italian Renaissance: An Overview," *Schifanoia* 8, 1989, 9–17; reprinted *Bulletin of the Society for Renaissance Studies* 9, 1991, 10–23.

—— "Patronage and the State in Early Modern Italy," in *Klientelsysteme im Europa der Fruehen Neuzeit*, Munich, 1988, 233–42.

Molho, Anthony, Kurt Raaflaub, and Julia Emlen, eds., *City*

States in Classical Antiquity and Medieval Italy, Stuttgart, 1991.

Morandini, Francesca, "Palazzo Pitti: la sua costruzione e i successivi ingrandimenti," *Commentari* 16, 1965, 35–46.

Morçay, Raoul, "La Cronaca del convento fiorentino di San Marco: la parte più antica, dettata da Giuliano Lapaccini," *ASI* 1, 1913, 1–29.

—— *Saint Antonin, Fondateur du Convent de Saint-Marc, Archevêque de Florence, 1389–1459*, Paris, 1914.

Morpurgo, S., *I manoscritti della R. Biblioteca Riccardiana di Firenze: manoscritti italiani* 1, Rome, 1893.

Muir, E., and Weissman, Ronald F. E. "Social and Symbolic Places in Renaissance Venice and Florence," in *The Power of Place: Bringing Together Geographical and Sociological Imaginations*, ed. John A. Agnew and James S. Duncan, Boston, 1989, 81–103.

Munman, Robert, "The Evangelists from the Cathedral of Florence: A Renaissance Arrangement Recovered," *AB* 29, 1980, 207–17.

Müntz, Eugene, *Les Précurseurs de la Renaissance*, Paris, 1882.

—— *Les Collections des Médicis au quinzième siècle*, Paris, 1888.

Murray, Peter, *An Index of Attributions made in Tuscan Sources before Vasari*, Florence, 1959.

Najemy, John M., "Guild Republicanism in Trecento Florence: The Success and Ultimate Failure of Corporate Rights," *AHR* 84, 1979, 53–71.

—— *Corporatism and Consensus in Florentine Electoral Politics, 1280–1400*, Chapel Hill, 1982.

—— "Machiavelli and the Medici: The Lessons of Florentine History," *RQ* 35, 1982, 551–76.

—— "Linguaggi storiografici sulla Firenze rinascimentale," *Rivista storica italiana* 97, 1985, 102–59.

—— "The Dialogue of Power in Florentine Politics," in *City States in Classical Antiquity and Medieval Italy*, ed. Anthony Molho, Kurt Raaflaub, and Julia Emlen, Stuttgart, 1991, 269–88.

—— "The Republic's Two Bodies: Body Metaphors in Italian Renaissance Political Thought," in *Language and Images of Renaissance Italy*, ed. Alison Brown, Oxford, 1995, 237–62.

—— *Between Friends: Discourses of Power and Desire in the Machiavelli–Vettori Letters of 1513–1515*, Princeton, 1993.

Nash, J. M., "Art and Arousal," review of David Freedberg, *The Power of Images: Studies in the History and Theory of Response*, *Art History* 13, 1990, 566–70.

Natali, A., "Cosimo il Vecchio, la campagna e due tracce michelozziane," in *Antichità viva* 17, 1978, 47–62.

National Gallery of Art, Washington, D.C., *Catalogue of European Paintings and Sculpture*, Washington, D.C., 1965.

Newbigin, Nerida, "The Word Made Flesh: The *Rappresentazioni* of Mysteries and Miracles in Fifteenth-Century Florence," in *Christianity and the Renaissance: Image and Religious Imagination in the Quattrocento*, ed. Timothy Verdon and John Henderson, New York, 1990, 362–75.

—— "Il testo e il contesto dell' *Abramo e Isac* di Feo Belcari," *Studi e problemi di critica testuale* 13 1981, 13–37.

—— "Piety and Politics in the *Feste* of Lorenzo's Florence," in *Lorenzo il Magnifico e il suo mondo*, ed. G. C. Garfagnini, Florence, 1994, 17–41.

—— *Feste D'Oltrarno: Plays in Churches in Fifteenth-Century Florence*, Istituto Nazionale di Studi sul Rinascimento, studi e testi 37, Florence, 1996.

—— "The Ascension Plays of Fifteenth-Century Florence: Some Problems of Terminology and Reconstruction," in *Altro Polo: Italian Studies in Memory of Frederick May*, ed. Suzanne Kiernan, 1996, 53–82.

Nuttall, P., "Early Netherlandish Painting in Florence: Acquisition, Ownership and Influence, *c.*1435–1500," Ph.D. Diss., Courtauld Institute, University of London, 1989.

Olson, Roberta, "Brunelleschi's Machines of Paradise and Botticelli's *Mystic Nativity*," *Gazette des Beaux-Arts* 97, 1981, 183–8.

—— *The Florentine Tondo*, Oxford, 2000.

Onians, John, "Brunelleschi: Humanist or Nationalist?" *Art History* 5, 1982, 259–72.

Orgel, Stephen, *The Illusion of Power: Political Theater in the English Renaissance*, Berkeley and Los Angeles, 1975.

Origo, Iris, "The Domestic Enemy: Eastern Slaves in Tuscany in the Fourteenth and Fifteenth Centuries," *Speculum* 30, 1955, 321–66.

—— *The Merchant of Prato: Francesco di Marco Datini*, London, 1963.

—— *The World of San Bernardino*, London, 1964.

Orlandi, Stefano, "Il vii centenario della predicazione di S. Pietro Martire a Firenze (1245–1945)," *Memorie domenicane*, n. s. 21, 1946, 26–42, 59–87; n. s. 22, 1947, 31–48, 109–36, 170–211.

—— "Il Beato Angelico," *Rivista d'arte* 39, ser. 3, 4, 1954, 161–201.

—— *S. Antonino: Arcivescovo di Firenze*, 2 vols., Florence, 1959.

Ortalli, Gherardo, *"Pingatur in Palatio:" La Pittura Infamante nei secoli XIII–XVI*, Rome, 1979.

Orvieto, P. "Un esperto orientalista del '400: Benedetto Dei," *Rinascimento*, ser. 2, 9, 1969, 205–75.

Paatz, Walter, and Elizabeth Paatz, *Die Kirchen von Florenz*, 6 vols., Frankfurt, 1940–54.

Pacciani, Riccardo, "Brunelleschi e la Magnificenza," in *Ricerche Brunelleschiane*, ed. P. Benigni, Florence, 1977, 635–44.

—— "Immagini, Arti e Architettura nelle Feste di Età Laurenziana," in *'Le Tems Revient': feste e spettacoli nella Firenze di Lorenzo il Magnifico*, ed. Paolo Ventrone, Florence, 1992, 119–37.

—— "Testimonianze per l'edificazione della basilica di San Lorenzo a Firenze, 1421–1442," *Prospettiva* 75, 1994, 85–99.

Padoa Rizzo, Anna, *Benozzo Gozzoli: pittore fiorentino*, Florence, 1972.

—— "The Chapel of the Magi in Benozzo Gozzoli's Oeuvre," in *The Chapel of the Magi: Benozzo Gozzoli's Frescoes in the*

Palazzo Medici-Riccardi Florence, ed. Cristina Acidini Luchinat, London, 1994, 357–62.

Panofsky, E., *Studies in Iconology: Humanistic Themes in the Art of the Renaissance*, New York, 1939, 2nd ed. 1962.

——*Early Netherlandish Painting*, Cambridge, Mass., 1953.

——"A Letter to St. Jerome," *Studies in Art and Literature for Belle Da Costa Greene*, Princeton, 1954, 102ff.

——*Meaning in the Visual Arts*, Garden City, N.Y., 1955, repr. 1974.

Paoletti, John T., "The Bargello David and Public Sculpture in Fifteenth-Century Florence," in *Collaboration in Italian Renaissance Art*, ed. Wendy Stedman Sheard and John T. Paoletti, New Haven and London, 1978, 99–112.

——"Donatello's Bronze Doors for the Old Sacristy of San Lorenzo,"*Artibus et historiae* 11, 1990, 39–68.

——"Fraternal Piety and Family Power: The Artistic Patronage of Cosimo and Lorenzo de' Medici," in *Cosimo 'il Vecchio' de' Medici, 1389–1464*, ed. Francis Ames Lewis, Oxford, 1992, 195–219.

——"'Ha fatto Piero con voluntà del padre. . . .': Piero de' Medici and Corporate Commissions of Art," in *Piero de' Medici, 'il Gottoso' (1416–1469): Kunst im Dienste der Mediceer*, ed. Andreas Beyer and Bruce Boucher, Berlin, 1993, 221–50.

——"The Banco Mediceo in Milan: Urban Politics and Family Power," *JMRS* 24, 1994, 199–238.

——"Invisible Images of Control: Appropriation of Site and Tradition in Medici Patronage"; Renaissance Society of America, *Abstracts of the Conference*, 1995, 99.

——"Strategies and Structures of Medici Artistic Patronage in the 15th Century," in *The Early Medici and their Artists*, ed. Francis Ames-Lewis, London, 1995, 19–36.

——"Familiar Objects: Sculptural Types in the Collections of the Early Medici," in *Looking at Italian Renaissance Sculpture*, ed. Sarah Blake McHam, New York, 1998, 79–110.

Paoletti, John T., and Gary M. Radke, *Art in Renaissance Italy*, New York, 1997.

Pardo, Mary, "Memory, Imagination, Figuration: Leonardo da Vinci and the Painter's Mind," in *Images of Memory: On Remembering and Representation*, ed. Susanne Küchler and Walter Melion, Washington and London, 1991, 47–73.

Park, Katherine, "The Readers at the Florentine *Studio* According to Communal Fiscal Records (1357–1380, 1413–1446)," *Rinascimento* 20, 1980, 249–310.

——*Doctors and Medicine in Early Renaissance Florence*, Princeton, 1985.

Parronchi, Alessandro, *Paolo Uccello*, Bologna, 1974.

Passerini, L., *Storia degli stabilimenti di beneficenza e d'istruzione elementare e gratuita della città di Firenze*, Florence, 1853.

Pedretti, Carlo, "Commentary 3," in J. Richter, *The Literary Works of Leonardo da Vinci*, 2 vols., London, 1977, 318–20.

Pellecchia Najemy, Linda, "The First Observant Church of San Salvatore al Monte in Florence," *Mitteilungen* 23, 1979, 273–96.

——review of Piero Morselli and Gino Corti, *La Chiesa di Santa Maria delle Carceri in Prato*, *JSAH* 44, 1985, 184–6.

——"The Patron's Role in the Production of Architecture: Bartolomeo Scala and the Scala Palace," *RQ* 42, 1989, 258–91.

Pellegrini, F. C., *Sulla repubblica fiorentina al tempo di Cosimo il Vecchio*, Pisa, 1880.

Peristiany, J., ed., *Honour and Shame: The Values of Mediterranean Society*, Chicago, 1966.

Perosa, Alessandro, "Lo Zibaldone di Giovanni Rucellai," in F. W. Kent et al., *Giovanni Rucellai ed il suo Zibaldone II: A Florentine Patrician and His Palace*, London, 1981, 99–154.

Pesman Cooper, Roslyn, "The Florentine Ruling Group under the '*governo populare*,' 1494–1512," *Studies in Medieval and Renaissance History* 7, 1985, 69–181.

Peterson, David S., "Archbishop Antoninus: Florence and the Church in the earlier Fifteenth Century," Ph.D. Diss., Cornell University, 1985.

——"An Episcopal Election in Quattrocento Florence," in *Popes, Teachers, and Canon Law in the Middle Ages*, ed. James Ross Sweeney and Stanley Chodorow, Ithaca and London, 1989, 300–25.

Petrioli Tofani, Annamaria, ed., *Il disegno fiorentino del tempo di Lorenzo il Magnifico*, Florence, 1992.

Phillips, Mark, *Guicciardini: The Historian's Craft*, Toronto, 1977.

——"Machiavelli, Guicciardini and the Tradition of Vernacular Historiography in Florence," *AHR*, 84, 1979, 86–105.

——*The Memoir of Marco Parenti*, Princeton, 1987.

——"Benedetto Dei's Book of Lists," paper presented to a conference on Michel de Certeaux, University of San Diego, 1987.

Pieraccini, G., *La Stirpe dei Medici di Cafaggiolo*, 3 vols., Florence, repr. 1986.

Pintor, F., "Per la storia della Libreria Medicea nel Rinascimento," *Italia medioevale e umanistica* 3, 1960, 189–210.

Plesner, Johann, *L'Emigration de la campagne à la ville libre de Florence au 13e siècle*, Copenhagen, 1934.

Pochat, Goetz, "Brunelleschi and the 'Ascension' of 1422," *AB* 60, 1978, 232–4.

Poeschke, Joachim, *Donatello and His World: Sculpture of the Italian Renaissance*, New York, 1993.

Poggi, Giovanni, and I. B. Supino, "La Compagnia del Bigallo," *Rivista d'arte* 2, 1904, 8–10.

Polizzotto, Lorenzo, *The Elect Nation: The Savonarolan Movement in Florence, 1494–1545*, Oxford, 1994.

Pontani, Anna, "Firenze nelle fonti greche del Concilio," in *Firenze e il Concilio del 1439*, ed. Paolo Viti, 2 vols., Florence, 1994, 2, 753–812.

Pope-Hennessy, John, *Donatello's Relief of the Ascension with Christ Giving the Keys to St Peter*, London, 1949: repr. in *Essays on Italian Sculpture*, London, 1968, 37–48.

——"The Fifth Centenary of Donatello," in *Essays on Italian Sculpture*, 22–36.

——*Paolo Uccello*, 2nd ed., London and New York, 1969.

——"The Interaction of Painting and Sculpture in Florence in the Fifteenth Century," *Journal of the Royal Society of Arts* 70, 1969, 406–24.

——*Fra Angelico*, New York, 1974.

——"The Madonna Reliefs of Donatello," *Apollo* 103, 1976, 172–91.

——"Donatello and the Bronze Statuette," *Apollo* 105, 1977, 30–3.

——*Luca della Robbia*, Oxford, 1980.

——*The Study and Criticism of Italian Sculpture*, New York, 1980.

——"Donatello's Bronze David," *Scritti di storia dell'arte in onore di Federico Zeri*, 2 vols., Milan, 1984, vol. 1, 121–7.

——*Donatello: Sculptor*, New York, 1993.

Portioli, A., *I Gongaza ai bagni di Petriolo di Siena nel 1460 e 1461*, ed. Attilio Portioli, Mantua, 1869.

Preyer, Brenda, "The Rucellai Loggia," *Mitteilungen* 21, 1977, 183–98.

——"The Rucellai Palace," in F. W. Kent et al., *Giovanni Rucellai ed il suo Zibaldone, II: A Florentine Patrician and his Palace*, London, 1981, 155–228.

——"The 'chasa overo palagio' of Alberto di Zanobi: A Florentine Palace of about 1400 and its Later Remodeling," *AB* 45, 1983, 387–401.

——"Two Cerchi Palaces in Florence," in *Renaissance Studies in Honor of Craig Hugh Smyth*, ed. A. Morrogh, F. Superbi Gioffredi, P. Morselli, and E. Borsook, 2 vols., Florence, 1985, vol. 2, 613–30.

——"L'archittetura del palazzo mediceo," in *Il Palazzo Medici Riccardi di Firenze*, ed. Giovanni Cherubini and Giovanni Fanelli, Florence, 1990, 58–75.

——*Palazzo Corsi-Horne*, Rome, 1993.

——"Planning for Visitors at Florentine Palaces," *Renaissance Studies* 12, 1998, 357–74.

——"The Medici Palace: Lorenzo de' Medici and Questions of Style and Time," paper presented to a conference at the Metropolitan Museum of Art, New York, 1993.

——"Michelozzo e Vasari," in *Michelozzo: Scultore e architetto nel suo tempo (1396–1472)*, ed. G. Mordli, Florence, 1998, 325–31.

——"Florentine Palaces and Memories of the Past," in *Art, Memory and Family in Early Renaissance Florence*, ed. Giovanni Ciappelli and Patricia Rubin, Cambridge, 2000, 176–94.

Price, B. B., "The Effect of Patronage on the Intellectualization of Medieval Endeavours," in *The Search for a Patron in the Middle Ages and the Renaissance*, ed. David and Rebecca Wilkins, Lewiston, N.Y., 1996, 5–18.

Price Zimmerman, T. C., "Confession and Autobiography in the Early Renaissance," in *Renaissance Studies in Honor Hans Baron*, ed. Anthony Molho and John A. Tedeschi, De Kalb, Ill., 1971, 119–40.

Procacci, Ugo, "Di Iacopo di Antonio e delle compagnie di pittori del Corso degli Adimari nel XV secolo," *Rivista d'arte* 24, 1961, 3–70.

——"Cosimo de' Medici e la costruzione della Badia Fiesolana," *Commentari* 19, 1968, 80–97.

——"Come gli artisti leggevano Dante," *Rinascimento* 1969, 97–134.

Proctor, Robert E., "Quaedam Particula Perfecti," in *Renaissance Studies in Honor of Craig Hugh Smyth*, ed. A. Morrogh, F. Superbi Gioffredi, P. Morselli, and E. Borsook, 2 vols., Florence, 1985, vol. 1, 427–36.

——"The *Studia Humanitatis*: Contemporary Scholarship and Renaissance Ideals," *RQ* 43, 1990, 813–24.

Pullini, Giorgio, *Burle e facezie del '400*, Pisa, 1958.

Quint, David, "On *ingiegno*," *RQ* 38, 1985, 434.

Radcliffe, A., and C. Avery, "The Chellini Madonna by Donatello," *BM* 118, 1976, 377–87.

Raggio, Olga, and Antoine M. Wilmering, *The Liberal Arts Studiolo from the Ducal Palace at Gubbio*, New York, 1996.

Rajna, P. "Cantare dei cantari," *Zeitschrift für Romanische Philologie* 2, 1868, 220–54, 419–37.

——*Ricerche intorno ai Reali di Francia*, Bologna, 1872.

Rankin, Lois Gieschen, "Donatello's Bronze David as Paradox and Parallel: The Role of the Biblical Narrative," M.A. Diss., University of Texas at Austin, 1987.

Rao, Ida, "Ambrogio Traversari al Concilio di Firenze," in *Firenze e il Concilio del 1439*, ed. Paolo Viti, 2 vols., Florence, 1994, vol. 2, 577–98.

Réau, Louis *Iconographie de l'art chrétien*, 3 vols., Paris, 1955–9.

Ricci, P., "Una consolatoria inedita," *Rinascita* 2, 1940, 363–433.

Rice, Eugene, *Saint Jerome in the Renaissance*, Baltimore, 1985.

——"St. Jerome's 'Vision of the Trinity': An Iconographical Note," *BM* 125, 1983, 151–5.

Richa, Giuseppe, *Notizie istoriche delle chiese fiorentine, divise ne' suoi quartieri*, 10 vols., Florence, 1754–62, repr. Rome, 1972.

Ricoeur, Paul, "The Model of the Text: Meaningful Action Considered as Text," in P. Ricoeur, *From Text to Action*, Evanston, Ill., 1991.

Ridderbos, B., *Saint and Symbol: Images of St. Jerome in Early Italian Art*, Groningen, 1984.

Ridolfi, Roberto, "Le lettere dell'archivio Bartolini Salimbeni," *La Bibliofilia* 29, 1927, 193–226.

Riess, Jonathan B., "The Civic View of Sculpture in Alberti's *De Re Aedificatoria*," *RQ* 32, 1979, 1–17.

Riis, Thomas, "I poveri nell'arte italiana (secoli XV–XVIII)," in *Timore e carità: i poveri nell'Italia moderna*, Cremona, 1982, 45–58.

Ringbom, Sixten, *Icon to Narrative: The Rise of the Dramatic Close-up in Fifteenth-Century Devotional Painting*, Abö, 1965.

De Robertis, D., "L'esperienza poetica del Quattrocento," in *Storia della letteratura italiana*, 9 vols., ed. E. Cecchi and N. Sapegno, vol. 2, Milan, 1966, 439–61.

Robertson, Clare, "*Cui Bono?*: Patronage in the Italian Renaissance," review of *Patronage, Art and Society*, ed. F. W. Kent and Patricia Simons, *Art History*, 11, 1988, 570–74.

——*"Il gran cardinale:" Alessandro Farnese, Patron of the Arts*, New Haven and London, 1992.

Robin, Diana, *Filelfo in Milan*, Princeton, 1991.

Robinson, Crispin, "Cosimo de' Medici's Patronage of the

Observantist Movement," M.Phil. thesis, Courtauld Institute, University of London, 1984.

——"Cosimo de' Medici and the Franciscan Observants at Bosco ai Frati," in *Cosimo 'il Vecchio' de' Medici, 1389–1464*, ed. Francis Ames Lewis, Oxford, 1992, 181–94.

Roccasecca, Pietro, *Paolo Uccello: Le Battaglie*, Milan, 1997.

Rochon, André, *Formes et signification de la "beffa" dans la litter-ature italienne de la Renaissance*, Paris, 1975.

——*La Jeunesse de Laurent de Médici, 1449–78*, Paris, 1963.

Rocke, Michael J., *Forbidden Friendships: Homosexuality in Renais-sance Florence*, Oxford, 1997.

Roscoe, William, *The Life of Lorenzo de' Medici, Called the Magnificent*, 10th ed., London, 1898.

Rosenauer, Artur, *Donatello*, Milan, 1993.

Rosenberg, C., ed., *Art and Politics in Late Medieval and Early Renaissance Italy: 1250–1500*, Notre Dame, Ind., 1990.

Rosenthal, Earl, "A Renaissance 'Copy' of the Holy Sepulchre," *JSAH* 17, 1958, pp. 2–11.

Ross, Janet, *The Lives of the Early Medici as Told in their Corre-spondence*, Boston, 1911.

Rossi, V., "L'indole e gli studi di Giovanni di Cosimo de' Medici," *Rendiconti della Reale Accademia dei Lincei, Classe di scienze morali, storiche e filologiche* 2, 1893, 38–150.

——"Le lettere di un matto," *La Biblioteca delle scuole italiane* 2, 1905, 114–7.

Rouse, Richard H., and Mary A. Rouse, "St. Antoninus of Florence on Manuscript Production," in *Litterae medii aevi: Festschrift für Johanna Autenrieth*, ed. M. Borgolte and H. Spilling, Sigmarigen, 1988, 255–63.

Rubin, M., *Corpus Christi: The Eucharist in Late Medieval Culture*, Cambridge, 1991.

Rubin, Patricia, *Giorgio Vasari: Art and History*, New Haven and London, 1995.

——"Magnificence and the Medici," in *The Early Medici and their Artists*, ed. Francis Ames-Lewis, London, 1995, 37–50.

Rubinstein, Nicolai, "The Beginnings of Political Thought in Florence," *JWCI* 5, 1942, 198–227.

——"The *Storie fiorentine* and the *Memorie di famiglia* by Francesco Guicciardini," *Rinascimento* 4, 1953, 171–225.

——"Political Ideas in Sienese Art: The Frescoes by Ambrogio Lorenzetti and Taddeo di Bartolo in the Palazzo Pubblico," *JWCI* 21, 1958, 179–207.

——*The Government of Florence under the Medici: 1434–1494*, Oxford, 1966.

——"Florentine Constitutionalism and Medici Ascendancy in the Fifteenth-Century," in *Florentine Studies: Politics and Society in Renaissance Florence*, ed. N. Rubinstein, London, 1968, 442–62.

——"La confessione di Francesco Neroni e la congiura antimedicea del 1466," *ASI* 126, 1968, 373–87.

——"The Piazza della Signoria in Florence," in *Festschrift Herbert Siebenhühner*, ed. E. Hubala and G. Schweikhart, Würzburg, 1978, 19–30.

——review of Richard Trexler, *Public Life in Renaissance Florence, Italian Studies* 38, 1983, 87–92.

——"*Stato* and Regime in Fifteenth-Century Florence," in *Per Federico Chabod (1901–1960): I, Lo stato e il potere nel Rinascimento*, ed. S. Bertelli, Materiali di Storia, 5, Annali della Facoltà di Scienze Politiche, 17, Perugia, 1980–81, 137–46.

——"Florentina Libertas," *Rinascimento* 26, 1986, 3–26.

——"Classical Themes in the Decoration of the Palazzo Vecchio in Florence," *JWCI* 50, 1987, 29–43.

——review of F. W. Kent and Patricia Simons, eds., *Patronage, Art and Society in Renaissance Florence, BM* 1988, 706–7.

——"Lay Patronage and Observant Reform in Fifteenth-Century Florence," in *Christianity and the Renaissance*, ed. Timothy Verdon and John Henderson, Syracuse, 1992, 63–82.

——"Palazzi Pubblici e Palazzi Privati al Tempo di Brunelleschi," in *Filippo Brunelleschi, la sua opera e il suo tempo*, 2 vols., Florence, 1980, vol. 1, 27–36.

——"Cosimo *optimus civis*," in *Cosimo 'il Vecchio' de' Medici, 1389–1464*, ed. Francis Ames-Lewis, Oxford, 1992, 5–20.

——"Piero de' Medici *Gonfaloniere di Giustizia*," in *Piero de' Medici, 'il Gottoso' (1416–1469): Kunst im Dienste der Mediceer*, ed. Andreas Beyer and Bruce Boucher, Berlin, 1993, 1–8.

——*The Palazzo Vecchio, 1298–1532*, London, 1995.

Ruda, Jeffrey, "The National Gallery Tondo of the *Adoration of the Magi* and the Early Style of Filippo Lippi," *Studies in the History of Art*, National Gallery, Washington, D.C., 1975, 7–39.

——"A 1434 Building Programme for San Lorenzo in Florence," *BM* 120, 1978, 358–61.

——"Style and Patronage in the 1440s: Two Altarpieces of the Coronation of the Virgin by Filippo Lippi," *Mitteilungen* 28, 1984, 363–84.

——*Fra Filippo Lippi*, London and New York, 1993.

Ruschi, P., and P. Benigni, "Il contributo di Filippo Brunelleschi all'episodio di Lucca: documenti ed ipotesi," in *Ricerche Brunelleschiane*, Florence, 1977.

Rutherford, David, "Antonio da Rho," Ph.D. Diss., Ann Arbor, Mich., 1988.

Rykwert, Joseph, and Anne Engel, eds., *Città di Mantova Centro Internazionale d'Arte e di Cultura di Palazzo Te: Leon Battista Alberti*, Mantua, 1994.

Saalman, Howard, "Giovanni di Gherardo da Prato's Designs Concerning the Cupola of Santa Maria del Fiore in Florence," *JSAH* 18, 1959, 11–20.

——"The Palazzo Comunale in Montepulciano: An Unknown Work by Michelozzo," *Zeitschrift für Kunstgeschichte* 28, 1965, 1–46.

——*The Bigallo: The Oratory and Residence of the Compagnia del Bigallo e della Misericordia in Florence*, New York, 1969.

——"San Lorenzo: The 1434 Chapel Project," *BM* 120, 1978, 361–4.

——*Filippo Brunelleschi: The Cupola of Santa Maria del Fiore*, London, 1980.

——"The San Lorenzo Pulpits: A Cosimo Portrait?" *Mit-teilungen* 30, 1986, 587–9.

——"Strozzi Tombs in the Sacristy of Santa Trinita," *Münchner Jahrbuch der bildenden Kunst* 38, 1987, 149–60.

——review of F. W. Kent et al., *Giovanni Rucellai ed il suo Ziba done, II: A Florentine Patrician and his Palace, JSAH* 47, 1988, 82–90.

——*Filippo Brunelleschi: The Buildings*, University Park, Pa., 1993.

Saalman, Howard, and Philip Mattox, "The First Medici Palace," *JSAH* 44, 1985, 329–45.

Sabbadini, R., "Storia e critica di alcuni testi latini," *Museo italiano di antichità classica* 3, 1888–90, 401–24.

——*Le scoperte dei codici latini e greci ne' secoli XIV e XV*, 2 vols., Florence, 1905–14.

Sacchi, F. "Cosimo de' Medici e Firenze nell'acquisto di Milano allo Sforza," *Rivista di scienze storiche* 2, 1905, 340–6.

Sale, J. Russell, "An Iconographic Program by Marco Parenti," *RQ* 27, 1974, 293–9.

Salmi, Mario, *Paolo Uccello, Andrea del Castagno, Domenico Veneziano*, Paris, 1939.

——"I Trionfi e il De viris illustribus nell'arte del primo Rinascimento," *Convegno Internazionale Francesco Petrarca*, 1974, Roma, Accademia Nazionale dei Lincei, 1976.

Salvini, Roberto, "The Frescoes in the *Altana* of the Rucellai Palace," in F. W. Kent et al., *Giovanni Rucellai ed il suo Zibaldone, II: A Florentine Patrician and his Palace*, London, 1981, 241–52.

Sanesi, E., "Maestri di organo in S. Maria del Fiore (1436–1600)," *Note d'archivio per la storia musicale* 14, 1937, 171–9.

Sapegno, N., *Il Trecento*, Milan, 1960.

Saxl, F., "The Classical Inscription in Renaissance Art and Politics," *JWCI* 4, 1941, 19–31.

Scalini, Mario, "L'armatura fiorentina nel Quattrocento e la produzione d'armi in Toscana," in *Guerra e guerrieri nella Toscana del Rinascimento*, ed. Franco Cardini and Marco Tangheroni, Florence, 1990, 83–126.

Schalk, Fritz, *Das Publikum im Italienischen Humanismus*, Krefeld, 1955.

Schama, Simon, *The Embarrassment of Riches: An Interpretation of Dutch Culture in the Golden Age*, Berkeley and Los Angeles, 1988.

Schiaparelli, A., *La casa fiorentina e i suoi arredi nei secoli XIV e XV*, Florence, 1908, new ed. M. Sframeli and L. Pagnotta, 2 vols., Florence, 1983.

Schneider, Laurie, "Donatello's Bronze *David*," *AB*, 55, 1973, 213–16.

——"More on Donatello's Bronze *David*, "*Gazette des Beaux-Arts* 93, 1979, 57.

Schubring, Paul, *Cassoni: Truhen und Truhenbilder der italienischen Fruerenaissance*, 2 vols., Leipzig, 1923.

Schulz, Anne Markham, "The Tomb of Giovanni Chellini at San Miniato al Tedesco," *AB* 51, 1969, 317–32.

——*The Sculpture of Bernardo Rossellino and his Workshop*, Princeton, 1977.

Schuyler, Jane, *Florentine Busts: Sculpted Portraiture in the Fifteenth Century*, New York, 1976.

Scribner, Robert, *For the Sake of Simple Folk: Popular Propaganda for the German Reformation*, Cambridge, 1986; repr. Oxford 1994, with revised introduction.

——"Is a History of Popular Culture Possible?" *History of European Ideas* 10, 1989, 175–91.

——"Popular Piety and Modes of Visual Perception in Late Medieval and Reformation Germany," *Journal of Religious History* 15, 448–69.

Scuricini Greco, M. L., *Miniature riccardiane*, Florence, 1958.

Seay, Albert, "The Fifteenth-Century Cappella at Santa Maria del Fiore in Florence," *JAMS* 11, 1958, 45–55.

Settis, Salvatore, "Artisti e Committenti fra Quattro- e Cinquecento," *Storia d'Italia. Annali, 4. Intellettuali e potere*, Turin, 1981, 701–61.

Seymour, Charles, *Early Italian Paintings*, New Haven, 1970.

Seznec, Jean, *The Survival of the Pagan Gods: The Mythological Tradition and its Place in Renaissance Humanism*, trans. Barbara F. Sessions, New York, 1953.

Sframeli, Maria, ed., *Il centro di Firenze restituito: affreschi e frammenti lapidei nel Museo di San Marco*, Florence, 1989.

Sheard, Wendy Stedman, "Antonio Lombardo's Reliefs for Alfonso d'Este's *Studio di Marmi*: Their Significance and Impact on Titian," in *Titian 500, National Gallery Studies in the History of Art* 45, 1995, 315–57.

Shearman, John, "The Collections of the Younger Branch of the Medici," *BM* 117, 1975, 12–27.

——*Only Connect: Art and the Spectator in the Italian Renaissance*, Princeton, 1992.

Siebenhüner, H., and L. H. Heydenreich, "Die Klosterkirche S. Francesco Al Bosco im Mugello," *Mitteilungen* 5, 1937–40, 183–96, 387–401.

Silverman, Sydel, *Three Bells of Civilization: The Life of an Italian Hill Town*, New York, 1975.

Simons, Patricia, *Portraiture and Patronage in Quattrocento Florence with Special Reference to the Tornaquinci and their Chapel in S. Maria Novella*, 2 vols., Ann Arbor, 1987.

——"Renaissance Palaces, Sex and Gender: The 'Public' and 'Private' Spaces of an Urban Oligarchy," paper delivered at the Courtauld Institute, London, 1989.

——"The Art of Viewing: Quattrocento Images in Society," paper presented at the J. Paul Getty Center for the History of Art and the Humanities, Los Angeles, 1987.

——"(Check) Mating the Grand Masters: The Gendered, Sexualized Politics of Chess in Renaissance Italy," *The Oxford Art Journal* 16, 1993, 59–74.

——"Two Rucellai Altarpieces with St Jerome in the National Gallery: Patterns of Patronage," paper presented at a symposium on "Art, Memory and Family," National Gallery, London, 1996.

Sinding-Larsen, Staale, "A Tale of Two Cities: Florentine and Roman Visual Context for Fifteenth-Century Palaces," *Acta ad Archaeologiam et Artium Historiam Pertinentia* 6, 1975, 163–212.

——*Iconography and Ritual*, Oslo, 1984.

Skinner, Quentin, "Ambrogio Lorenzetti: The Artist as Political Philosopher," *Proceedings of the British Academy* 72, 1986, 1–56.

——"The Vocabulary of Renaissance Republicanism: A Cultural Longue-durée?" in *Language and Images of Renaissance Italy*, ed. Alison Brown, Oxford, 1995, 87–110.

Smith, Christine, "Originality and Cultural Progress in the Quattrocento: Brunelleschi's Dome and a Letter by Alberti," *Rinascimento*, ser. 2, 28, 1988, 291–317.

——"Cyriacus of Ancona's Seven Drawings of Hagia Sophia," *AB* 69, 1987, 16–32.

——*Architecture in the Culture of Early Humanism: Ethics, Aesthetics and Eloquence*, Oxford, 1992.

Smith, William A., "References to Dance in Fifteenth-Century Italian *Sacre Rappresentazioni*," *Dance Research Journal* 23, 1991, 17–24.

Soudek, Josef, "A Fifteenth-Century Humanistic Bestseller: The Manuscript Diffusion of Leonardo Bruni's Annotated Latin Version of the (Pseudo)-Aristotelian Economics," in *Philosophy and Humanism, Renaissance Essays in Honor of Paul Oskar Kristeller*, ed. Edward P. Mahoney, New York, 1976, 129–43.

Southern, R. W., *The Making of the Middle Ages*, London, 1953.

Spencer, John, "*Ut Rhetorica Pictura*: A Study in *Quattrocento* Theory of Painting," *JWCI* 20, 1957, 26–44.

——"The Dome of Sforzinda Cathedral," *AB* 14, 1959, 328–30.

——*Andrea del Castagno and His Patrons*, Durham, N.C., 1991.

——"A Note on Slavery," unpublished article.

Sperling, Christine, "Donatello's Bronze *David* and the Demands of Medici Politics," *BM* 134, 1992, 218–24.

——"Verrocchio's Medici Tombs," in *Andrea del Verrocchio and Late Quattrocento Sculpture*, ed. Steven Bule, Florence, 1991, 51–62.

Spicciani, A., "The 'Poveri Vergognosi' in Fifteenth-Century Florence: The First Thirty Years' Activity of the Buonomini di S. Martino," in *Aspects of Poverty in the Middle Ages*, ed. T. Riis, Stuttgart, 1981, 119–82.

Spina Barelli, Emma, "Note iconografiche in margine al David in bronzo di Donatello," *Italian Studies* 29, 1974, 28–44.

Starn, Randolph, "Francesco Guicciardini and his Brothers," in *Renaissance Studies in Honor of Hans Baron*, ed. A. Molho and J. A. Tedeschi, De Kalb, Ill., 1971, 412–16.

——*Contrary Commonwealth: The Theme of Exile in Medieval and Renaissance Italy*, Berkeley and Los Angeles, 1982.

——"A Demand for Art in Renaissance Florence: Three Recent Books," *AB* 65, 1983, 329–35.

——"Seeing Culture in a Room for a Renaissance Prince," in *The New Cultural History*, ed. Lynn Hunt, Berkeley and Los Angeles, 1989, 205–32.

Starn, Randolph, and Loren Partridge, "Representing War in the Renaissance: The Shield of Paolo Uccello," *Representations* 5, 1984, 32–65.

——*Arts of Power*, Berkeley and Los Angeles, 1992.

Steinberg, Leo, *The Sexuality of Christ in Renaissance Art and in Modern Oblivion*, New York, 1982.

Stella, Alessandro, *La Révolte des Ciompi: les hommes, les lieux, le travail*, Paris, 1993.

Stephens, J. N., *The Fall of the Florentine Republic, 1512–1530*, Oxford, 1983.

Stinger, Charles, "Ambrogio Traversari and the 'Tempio degli Scolari' at S. Maria degli Angeli in Florence," in *Essays Presented to Myron P. Gilmore*, ed. S. Bertelli and G. Ramakus, 2 vols., Florence, 1978, vol.1, 271–85.

——*Humanism and the Church Fathers: Ambrogio Traversari (1386–1439) and Christian Antiquity in the Italian Renaissance*, Albany, 1977.

Strocchia, Sharon, *Death and Ritual in Renaissance Florence*, Baltimore, 1992.

——"Death Rites and the Ritual Family in Renaissance Florence," in *Life and Death in Fifteenth-Century Florence*, ed. Marcel Tetel, Ronald G. Witt, and Rona Goffen, Durham and London, 1989, 120–45.

Strong, Roy, *Art and Power: Renaissance Festivals 1450–1650*, New Haven, 1978.

Strozzi, Beatrice Paolozzi, "Sull'Adorazione di Filippo Lippi nella cappella di Palazzo Medici," *Artistas* 5, 1993, 2–12.

——"*The Adoration of the Child* by the Workshop of Filippo Lippi," in *The Chapel of the Magi: Benozzo Gozzoli's Frescoes in the Palazzo Medici-Riccardi Florence*, ed. Cristina Acidini Luchinat, London and New York, 1994, 29–32.

Tanturli, Giuliano, "I Benci copisti," *Studi di filologia italiana* 36, 1978, 197–313.

——"Codici di Antonio Manetti e ricette del Ficino," *Rinascimento* 2, 1951, 313–29.

——"Rapporti del Brunelleschi con gli ambienti letterari fiorentini," in *Filippo Brunelleschi, la sua opera e il suo tempo*, 2 vols., Florence, 1980, vol. 1, 125–44.

Teubner, Hans, "San Marco in Florenz: Umbauten vor 1500: Ein Beitrag zum Werk des Michelozzo," *Mitteilungen* 23, 1979, 239–72.

Testaverde Matteini, Anna Maria, "La decorazione festiva e l'itinerario de 'rifondazione' della città negli ingressi trionfali a Firenze tra XV e XVI secolo," *Mitteilungen* 32, 1988, 323–52.

Thomas, Anabel, *The Painter's Practice in Renaissance Tuscany*, Cambridge, 1995.

——"Neri di Bicci's *Young St. John the Baptist Going into the Desert*," *Apollo* 143, 1996, 3–7.

——"Neri di Bicci's *Assumption of the Virgin* for S. Trìnita, Florence," *Apollo* 145, 1997, 42–51.

Thompson, E. P. "Patrician Society, Plebeian Culture," *Journal of Social History* 7, 1973–4, 382–405.

——Thomson, David, *Renaissance Architecture: Critics, Patrons, Luxury*, Manchester, 1993.

Thornton, Peter, *The Italian Renaissance Interior, 1400–1800*, London, 1991.

Tönnesmann, Andreas, "Zwischen Bürgerhaus und Residenz: Zur sozialen Typik des Palazzo Medici," in *Piero de' Medici*, *"il Gottoso" (1416–1469): Kunst im Dienste der Mediceer*, ed. Andreas Beyer and Bruce Boucher, Berlin, 1993, 71–88.

Toscan, Jean, *Le Carneval du langage: le lexique érotique des poètes de l'équivoque de Burchiello à Marino*, 4 vols., Lille, 1981.

Toschi, Paolo, *Invito al folklore italiano: le regioni e le feste*, Rome, 1963.

Trachtenberg, Marvin, "What Brunelleschi Saw: Monument and Site at the Palazzo Vecchio in Florence," *JSAH* 47, 1988, 14–44.

—— "On Brunelleschi's Old Sacristy as Model for Early Renaissance Church Architecture," *L'Eglise dans l'architecture de la Renaissance, De Architectura, Collection fondée par André Chastel et Jean Guillaume*, 1993, 9–36.

—— *Dominion of the Eye: Urbanism, Art, and Power in Early Modern Florence*, Cambridge, 1997.

Trevor-Roper, Hugh, *Princes and Artists: Patronage and Ideology at Four Habsburg Courts, 1517–1633*, London, 1976.

Trexler, Richard, "Florentine Religious Experience: The Sacred Image," *Studies in the Renaissance* 19, 1972, 7–41.

—— "Charity and the Defense of the Urban Elites in the Italian Communes," in *The Rich, the Well-Born and the Powerful*, ed. F. Jaher, Urbana, Ill., 1973, 64–109.

—— "The Episcopal Constitutions of Antoninus of Florence," *Quellen und Forschungen aus Italienischen Archiven und Bibliotheken* 54, 1979, 244–72.

—— "Honor Among Thieves: The Trust Function of the Urban Clergy in the Florentine Republic," in *Essays Presented to Myron P. Gilmore*, ed. S. Bertelli and G. Ramakus, 2 vols., Florence, 1978, vol. 1, 317–34.

—— "Florentine Theater, 1280–1500: A Checklist of Performances and Institutions," *Forum Italicum* 14, 1980, 454–75.

—— *Public Life in Renaissance Florence*, New York, 1980.

—— "Neighbours and Comrades: The Revolutionaries of Florence, 1378," *Social Analysis* 14, 1983, 53–106.

—— "The Magi Enter Florence: The Ubriachi of Florence and Venice," in *Church and Community, 1200–1600: Studies in the History of Florence and New Spain*, ed. R. Trexler, Rome, 1987, 75–167.

—— *The Journey of the Magi: Meanings in History of a Christian Story*, Princeton, 1997.

Trexler, R., and Mary Lewis, "Two Captains and Three Kings: New Light on the Medici Chapel," *Studies in Medieval and Renaissance History*, n. s. 4, 1981, 93–177.

Trinkaus, Charles, *In Our Image and Likeness: Humanity and Divinity in Italian Humanist Thought*, 2 vols., London, 1970.

Trinkaus, Charles, with Heiko Oberman, *The Pursuit of Holiness in Late Medieval and Renaissance Religion*, Leiden, 1974.

Ullmann, Berthold L., and Philip A. Stadter, *The Public Library of Renaissance Florence*, Padua, 1972.

Ullmann, W., *Principles of Government and Politics in the Middle Ages*, London, 1961.

Van Os, Henk W., et al., eds., *The Art of Devotion in the Late Middle Ages*, Princeton, 1994.

Ventrone, Paola, "Thoughts on Florentine Fifteenth-Century Religious Spectacle," in *Christianity and the Renaissance*, ed., Timothy Verdon and John Henderson, Syracuse, 1990, 405–12.

—— ed., *"Le Tems revient": feste e spettacoli nella Firenze di Lorenzo il Magnifico*, Florence, 1992.

—— "Esperienza dello spettacolo religioso nell'Europa del Quattrocento," in *Centro studi sul teatro medioevale e rinascimentale, 72 XVI Convengo, 1992*, ed. M. Chiabò and F. Doglio, Rome, 1993, 67–99.

—— "La sacra rappresentazione fiorentina: aspetti e problemi," in *Esperienze dello spettacolo religioso nell'Europa del Quattrocento, Centro Studi sul Teatro Medioevale e Rinascimentale, Atti del XVI Convegno*, Roma, 1993.

—— "L'eccezione e la regola: le rappresentazioni del 1439 nella tradizione fiorentina delle feste di quartiere," in *Firenze e il Concilio del 1439*, ed. Paolo Viti, 2 vols., Florence, 1994, vol. 1, 409–35.

—— "Lorenzo's 'Politica Festiva,'" in *Lorenzo the Magnificent: Culture and Politics*, ed. Michael Mallett and Nicholas Mann, London, 1996, 105–16.

Verde, Armando, *Lo studio fiorentino, 1473–1503: ricerche e documenti*, 3 vols., Pistoia, 1973–7.

—— "Libri tra le pareti domestiche," *Memorie domenicane* 18, 1987, 1–39.

Verdon, Timothy, "Christianity, the Renaissance, and the Study of History: Environments of Experience and Imagination," in *Renaissance*, ed. Timothy Verdon and John Henderson, Syracuse, 1990, 1–37.

—— "Donatello and the Theater: Stage Space and Projected Space in the San Lorenzo Pulpits," *Artibus et historiae* 14, 1986, 29–55.

—— "Le *spirituel vécu*: La Maddelena e l'epistemologia dell'arte cristiana," *Arte Cristiana* 74, 1986, 409–14.

Verdon, Timothy, and John Henderson, eds. *Renaissance: Image and Religious Imagination in the Quattrocento*, Syracuse, 1990.

Verellen, Till, "Cosmas and Damian in the New Sacristy," *JWCI* 42, 1979, 274–7.

Vertova, Luisa, "Cupid and Psyche in Renaissance Painting before Raphael," *JWCI* 42, 1979, 104–21.

Vickers, Brian, "Leisure and Idleness in the Renaissance: The Ambivalence of *otium*," *Renaissance Studies* 4, 1990, 1–37, 107–54.

Viti, Paolo, ed., *Firenze e il Concilio del 1439*, Biblioteca Storica Toscana, a cura della Deputazione di Storia Patria per la Toscana 29, 2 vols., Florence, 1994.

Viti, V., *La Badia Fiesolana*, Florence, 1926.

Volpi, G., *Le feste di Firenze dell'anno 1459: notizie di un poemetto del sec. XV*, Pistoia, 1902.

Wackernagel, Martin, *The World of the Florentine Renaissance Artist*, trans. Alison Luchs, Princeton, 1981.

Waddy, Patricia, *Seventeenth-Century Roman Palaces: Use and the Art of the Plan*, Cambridge, Mass., 1990.

Walsh, Martin, "Martin of Tours: Patron Saint of Medieval

Comedy," paper presented to the Annual Conference of the RSA, Harvard, 1989.

Warburg, Aby, *Gesammelte Schriften*, trans. and ed. Gertrud Bing, *La rinascita del paganesimo antico*, Florence, 1966.

Warnke, Martin, *The Court Artist: On the Ancestry of the Modern Artist*, Cambridge, 1993.

Warren, Charles W., "Brunelleschi's Dome and Dufay's Motet," *Musical Quarterly* 59, 1973, 92–105.

Watkins, Renée, "Il Burchiello (1404–48): Poverty, Politics and Poetry," *Italian Quarterly* 14, 54, 21–87.

Watson, Paul, "A *Desco da Parto* by Bartolomeo di Fruosino," *AB* 56, 1974, 4–9.

—— *The Garden of Love in Tuscan Art of the Early Renaissance*, Philadelphia, 1979.

Wàz'bínski, Zygmunt, "L'*Annunciazione* della Vergine nella chiesa della SS. Annunziata a Firenze: un contributo al modern culto dei quadri," in *Renaissance Studies in Honor of Craig Hugh Smyth*, ed. A. Morrogh, F. Superbi Gioffredi, P. Morselli, and E. Borsook, Florence, 1985, 533–49.

Wegener, Wendy, "Mortuary Chapels of Renaissance Condottieri," Ph.D. Diss., Princeton University, 1989.

—— "'That the Practice of Arms is Most Excellent Declare the Statues of Valiant Men': The Luccan War and Florentine Political Ideology in Paintings by Uccello and Castagno," *Renaissance Studies* 7, 1993, 129–67.

Weil-Garris, Kathleen, and John D'Amico, "The Renaissance Cardinal's Ideal Palace: A Chapter from Cortesi's De Cardinalatu," in *Studies in Italian Art and Architecture Fifteenth through Eighteenth Centuries*, ed. Henry A. Millon, Cambridge, Mass., 1980, 45–119.

Weinstein, Donald, "The Myth of Florence," in *Florentine Studies*, ed. Nicolai Rubinstein, London, 1968, 15–44.

—— *Savonarola and Florence: Prophecy and Patriotism in the Renaissance*, Princeton, 1970.

Weissman, Ronald F. E., *Ritual Brotherhood in Renaissance Florence*, New York, 1982.

—— "Taking Patronage Seriously: Mediterranean Values and Renaissance Society," in *Patronage, Art, and Society in Renaissance Italy*, ed. F. W. Kent and Patricia Simons, Oxford, 1986, 25–45.

—— "Brothers and Strangers: Confraternal Charity in Renaissance Florence," *Historical Reflections/Réflexions historiques* 15, 1988, 27–45.

—— "The Importance of Being Ambiguous: Social Relations, Individualism and Identity in Renaissance Florence," in *Urban Life in the Renaissance*, ed. Susan Zimmermann and Ronald F. E. Weissman, London and Toronto, 1989, 269–80.

—— "Sacred Eloquence: Humanist Preaching and Lay Piety in Renaissance Florence," in *Christianity and the Renaissance*, ed. Timothy Verdon and John Henderson, Syracuse, 1990, 250–71.

—— "Commentary, Politics and Conflict," in *City States in Classical Antiquity and Medieval Italy*, ed. Anthony Molho, Kurt Raaflaub, and Julia Emlen, Stuttgart, 1991, 345–51.

—— "Cults and Contexts: In Search of the Renaissance Confraternity," in *Crossing the Boundaries: Christian Piety and the Arts in Italian Medieval and Renaissance Confraternities*, ed. Konrad Eisenbichler, Kalamazoo, 1991, 201–20.

Welch, Evelyn Samuels, "The Process of Sforza Patronage," *Renaissance Studies* 3, 1989, 370–86.

—— *Art and Authority in Renaissance Milan*, New Haven and London, 1995.

—— *Art and Society in Italy, 1350–1500*, Oxford, 1997.

—— "The Italian Courts: An Overview," *Bulletin of the Society for Renaissance Studies* 15, 1997, 25–31.

—— "Theorising the Decorative Arts: Giovanni Pontano's *De Splendore*," paper delivered March 1997 to the conference at the Cooper-Hewitt and Metropolitan Museums of Art, *Bringing the Renaissance Home*.

Wester, Ursula, and Erika Simon, "Die Reliefmedaillons Im Hofe Des Palazzo Medici Zu Florenz," *Jahrbuch der Berliner Museen* 7, 1965, 15–91.

Westfall, C. W., "Chivalric Declaration: The Palazzo Ducale in Urbino as a Political Statement," in *Art and Architecture in the Service of Politics*, ed. L. Nochlin and H. Millon, Cambridge, Mass., 1978, 20–45.

Whitaker, Lucy, "Maso Finiguerra, Baccio Baldini and the Florentine Picture Chronicle," in *Florentine Drawing at the Time of Lorenzo the Magnificent*, ed. Elizabeth Cropper, Bologna, 1994.

White, Hayden, *Tropics of Discourse: Essays in Cultural Criticism*, Baltimore, 1978.

—— *The Content of the Form: Narrative Discourse and Historical Representation*, Baltimore, 1987.

Wilcox, Donald, *The Development of Florentine Humanist Historiography in the Fifteenth Century*, Cambridge, Mass., 1969.

Wilkins, David G., "Donatello's Lost *Dovizia* for the Mercato Vecchio: Wealth and Charity as Florentine Civic Virtues," *AB* 45, 1983, 401–23.

Wilkins, David, and Rebecca Wilkins, eds., *The Search for a Patron in the Middle Ages and the Renaissance*, Lewiston, N.Y., 1996.

Wilson, Blake, *Music and Merchants: The Laudesi Companies of Republican Florence*, Oxford, 1992.

Wilson, R. Jackson, review of Rhys Isaac, *The Transformation of Virginia, 1740–1790*, Chapel Hill, N.C., 1982, privately circulated.

Wind, Edgar, "Platonic Tyranny and the Renaissance Fortuna: On Ficino's Reading of Laws IV, 709A–712A," in *De artibus opuscula XL: Essays in Honor of Erwin Panofsky*, ed. Millard Meiss, New York, 1961, 491–6; rev. and repr. in *The Eloquence of Symbols*, ed. Jaynie Anderson, Oxford, 1983, 86–93.

—— *Pagan Mysteries in the Renaissance*, New Haven and London, 1958, rev. ed. New York, 1968.

Winter, Lois, "Paradox and Parallel," M.A. thesis, Department of Art History, University of Texas at Austin, 1991.

Witt, Ronald, *Hercules at the Crossroads: The Life, Works and Thought of Coluccio Salutati*, Durham, N.C., 1981.

Wittkower, R., "Individualism in Art and Artists: A Renaissance Problem," *JHI* 22, 1961, 291–302.

Wittkower, Rudolf, and Margo Wittkower, *Born under Saturn: The Character and Conduct of Artists: A Documented History from Antiquity to the French Revolution*, London, 1963.

Wohl, H., "Domenico Veneziano Studies: The Sant'Egidio and Parenti Documents," *BM* 1971, 635–41.

—— *The Paintings of Domenico Veneziano*, New York, 1980.

Woodhouse, C. M., *George Gemistos Plethon: The Last of the Hellenes*, Oxford, 1986.

Woods-Marsden, Joanna, "Art and Political Identity in Fifteenth-Century Naples," in *Art and Politics in Late Medieval and Early Renaissance Italy, 1250–1500*, ed. Charles Rosenberg, Notre Dame and London, 1990, 11–37.

—— *The Gonzaga of Mantua and Pisanello's Arthurian Frescoes*, Princeton, 1988.

—— "How Quattrocento Princes Used Art: Sigismondo Pandolfo Malatesta of Rimini and *cose militari*," *Renaissance Studies* 3, 1989, 387–413.

—— review of Jack Greenstein, *Mantegna and Painting as Historical Narrative, JMH* 67, 1995, 455–8.

Wright, Alison, "Piero de' Medici and the Pollaiuolo," in *Piero de' Medici, "il Gottoso" (1416–1469): Kunst im Dienste der Mediceer*, ed. Andreas Beyer and Bruce Boucher, Berlin, 1993, 129–49.

Wright, Craig, "Dufay's *Nuper Rosarum Flores*, King Solomon's Temple, and the Veneration of the Virgin," *JAMS* 1994, 395–441.

Yates, Frances, *The Art of Memory*, Chicago, 1966.

Zaccaria, Raffaella Maria, "Documenti e testimonianze inedite," in *Firenze e il Concilio del 1439*, ed. Paolo Viti, 2 vols., Florence, 1994, vol. 1, 100–08.

Zeri, Federico, *Italian Paintings: A Catalogue of the Collection of the Metropolitan Museum of Art, Florentine School*, New York, 1971.

Zervas, Diane, "Ghiberti's *St. Matthew* Ensemble at Orsanmichele: Symbolism in Proportion," *AB* 58, 1976, 36–44.

—— "Filippo Brunelleschi's Political Career," *BM* 121, 1979, 630–9.

—— *The Parte Guelfa, Brunelleschi and Donatello*, Locust Valley, N.Y., 1987.

—— "'Quos volent et eo modo quo volent': Piero de' Medici and the *Operai* of SS. Annunziata, 1445–55," in *Florence and Italy: Renaissance Studies in Honour of Nicolai Rubinstein*, ed. Peter Denley and Caroline Elam, London, 1988, 465–79.

—— *Orsanmichele a Firenze*, 2 vols., Modena, 1996.

Zippel, Giuseppe, "Il Filelfo a Firenze (1429–34)," 1899, repr. in *Storia e cultura del rinascimento italiano*, ed. Gianni Zippel, Padua, 1979, 215–53.

—— "Niccolò Niccoli: Contributo alla Storia dell'Umanesimo," in *Storia e cultura del rinascimento italiano*, ed. Gianni Zippel, Padua, 1979, 68–153.

Zorzi, L., "Figurazione pittorica e figurazione teatrale," in *Storia dell'arte italiana*, ed. G. Bollati and P. Fossati, 5 vols., 1978–82, vol. 1, *Materiali e problemi, I: Questioni e metodi*, Turin, 1978, 421–63.

—— "La scenotecnica brunelleschiana: problemi filologici e interpretativi," in *Filippo Brunelleschi: la sua opera e il suo tempo*, 2 vols., Florence, 1980, vol. 1, 136–62.

Zorzi Pugliese, O., "The Good Work of the Florentine 'Buonomini di San Martino': An Example of Renaissance Pragmatism," in *Crossing the Boundaries: Christian Piety and the Arts in Italian Medieval and Renaissance Confraternities*, ed. Konrad Eisenbichler, Kalamazoo, 1991, 108–20.

Zughaib, N. L., "The Steps to Humility, the Steps to Sovereignty: Fra Filippo Lippi's Nativity Altarpiece for the Chapel of the Palazzo Medici," in *Syracuse University Graduate Studies in Florence*, Syracuse, 1989, 92–102.

Zuraw, Shelley, "The Medici Portraits of Mino da Fiesole" in *Piero de' Medici, "il Gottoso" (1416–1469): Kunst im Dienste der Mediceer*, ed. Andreas Beyer and Bruce Boucher, Berlin, 1993, 317–39.

INDEX

Abbondanza, figure of, 113, 120; *see also* Donatello, *Dovizia*

Abyssinia, 90

Acciaiuoli, family, 89, 118, 188, 212, 351, 355; Agnolo, 138, 212, 372; Donato, 34, 109, 305; Nicola, 89, 153

account books, 70

Acidini, Cristina, 310

Ad Herennium, 92–3; *see also* Cicero

Adimari, family, 137; Bonaccorso di Filippo, 83; Giovaniello di Giovaniello, 386; Guglielmo, 176

Aesop, *Fables*, 7, 72, 73, 76–7 (fig. 29), 82, 96, 385, 427 nn.135–7

Agli, degli, family, 107, 355; Agostino di Ser Francesco di Ser Giovanni, 110; Antonio, 81, 107, 182; Barnaba, 173

Ahl, Diane Cole, 319

Alberti, family, 28, 218, 351; gardens of, 23, *see also* Gherardi, Giovanni, *Paradiso degli Alberti*; Francesco di Altobianco, 59, 73, 78, 83, 85, 90, 193, 211, 322; Francesco di Bivigliano, 342

Alberti, Leon Battista, 5, 13, 17–18, 27, 28, 43, 255, 288, 353; Certame Coronario and, 28, 359; architectural works: façade of S. Maria Novella, 354, 358 (fig. 177), 360–61 (fig. 179); *see also* Rimini, S. Francesco; Rucellai, Giovanni, façade of Palazzo Rucellai, 228, 359 (fig. 178); Rucellai, Giovanni, Holy Sepulcher (S. Pancrazio), 362 (fig. 181); Rucellai, Giovanni, San Francesco (Rimini), 353–4, 360; writings: *De Uxoria*, 28; *On the Art of Building*, 28, 192, 217, 220, 222, 225, 228, 231, 300, 309; *On the Family*, 239, 242; *On Painting*, 28, 92, 98, 102, 156, 251, 311, 342–3, 365; *On Sculpture*, 28

Albizzi, degli, family, 49, 57, 71, 218; Francesco di Albizzo di Luca di Ser Albizzo, 70; Luca, 24, 278; Maso, 191; Ormanno, 176; Rinaldo, 24, 181–2, 272–3, 276, 287, 357

Albizzo da Fortuna, 182

Aldobrandini del Nero, family, 181; Iacopo, 181

Alessandri, degli, family, 218, 356 (fig. 176); Alessandro, 24

Alexander the Great, 117

Alighieri, *see* Dante

altarpieces: form, 159; function, 144; iconography, demands of, 144

Altoviti, Nero di Bardo, 385

Amadory, Giovanni di Zanobi, shoemaker, 71, 77, 84

Ambrose, St., 114, 188, 325

Ambruoso, Fra, of the Angeli, 23

Ames-Lewis, Francis, 105, 155, 192, 254, 261, 288, 297, 338, 364; *amicizia*, perception of, *see* friendship

Andrea di Francesco, butcher, 119

Andrea delle Sargie, painter of banners and coverlets, 76–7, 104, 116; *see also* Francesco del maestro Andrea (his son)

Angelico, Fra, 12, 18, 57, 108, 150–99, 174–5, 244, 245, 251–5, 342; works in Medici collection, 251–5; *Adoration of the Magi* (Medici tondo; with Fra Filippo Lippi), 245, 252–5 (fig. 117),

311, 380; Annalena altarpiece, 11, 141, 144–5 (fig. 54), 262; Bosco ai Frati altarpiece, 11, 141, 144–6 (fig. 55); *Crucifixion* (S. Marco, chapter house), 151 (fig. 59); *Deposition*, 245, 252 (fig. 116); *Lamentation*, 157 (fig. 63); *Last Judgment*, 85, 104, 133 (fig. 45), 150; *Madonna and Child with Eight Saints* (S. Marco, east corridor) 150 (fig. 58), 175; reliquary cabinet (SS. Annunziata), 206 (fig. 86), 209, 311; S. Marco altarpiece, 11, 87, 141–53, 154 (fig. 62), 155–9, 251, 255, 311, 313, 338; *Saints Cosmas and Damian before Lysias* (S. Marco altarpiece, predella), 312 (fig. 155); *Lamentation* (S. Marco altarpiece, predella), 156 (fig. 63)

Angevin, 349, 351; *see also* Naples

Anghiari, battle of, 49, 88, 162, 185, 197, 267, 272, 277, 279–81, 341

Anjou, René of, 193; *see also* Angevin; Naples

Anne, St., 106

Annunciation, 45, 63, 64 (fig. 22), 99, 101, 104–6, 105 (fig. 35), 125, 204; *see also* Florence, SS. Annunziata

Anonimo Magliabechiano, 247

anthologies, patriotic, 89

Anthony Abbot, St., 149, 377, 468 n.111

Anthony of Padua, St., 100, 148, 468 n.111

anti-Medici party, 238; *see also* Albizzi; Pazzi

antiquity, influence of, 21, 28, 83, 225–8, 240, 281, 285–6, 320, 360

Antoninus, Archbishop of Florence (Antonio Pierozzi), 57, 60, 66, 73, 85, 87, 95–6, 151, 360; Buonomini di S. Martino and, 47; Cosimo and, 174–5, 207, 210; writings, 6–7, 117, 134, 158, 174

Antonio *calzaiuolo*, shoemaker, 44, 53, 76 (fig. 27), 78, 103

Antonio da Bacchereto, barber, 44, 78, 117

Antonio dalla Lastra, blacksmith, 112

Antonio di Guido, soapmaker, 44, 49, 53, 71, 75, 77–8, 80, 88, 90, 98, 103, 117, 157, 325, 364

Antonio di Guido di Cristofano, wool-trimmer, 74, 77

Antonio di Meglio, herald, 48, 49, 53, 62, 73, 78, 89–90, 106, 118, 202, 270, 328

Antonio di Puccio, 204; *see also* Pucci, family

Antwerp, 341

Apollo and Marsyas, 295 (fig. 143)

Apollonio di Giovanni, 81, 226 (figs. 95–6), 231 (fig. 100), 235, 299

apostles, letters of, 79; representations of, 196

Aquinas, Thomas, St., 19, 141

Aragazzi, Bartolommeo, tomb of, 166, 176

Aragonese, lords of Naples, 353; Alfonso, 214, 349; Federigo, 82, 349

archives of Florence, 15

Ardinghelli, Iacopo d'Ubaldino, 385

Aretino, Spinello, *see* Spinello Aretino

Argyropoulos, John, 24, 34, 212

Aristotle, 5, 36, 50, 220, 363; *Ethics*, 38, 214; *Poetics*, 16; *Pseudo-Economics*, 38

Armenian Christians, 90, 202, 231, 313–14; confraternity of, 66

armillary sphere, 155, 192, 264

arms and armor: description of, 61; Medici collections of, 235, 266, 271, 279, 292–3, 294 (fig. 141), 318, 342, 476 n.308

Arrighi, family: Simone d'Alessandro di Iacopo, 70; Simone di Girolamo di Giovambattista, 70

Arrigucci, Filippo d'Arrigho, 385

art and society, relation of, ix, xii, 41, 389 n.32

Arti, *see* guilds

artists: audience of, 4, 41, 254, 423 n.80; arbitration between, 30; contracts, 7, 30, 144, 333; education and reading, 113–17; letters of, 7, 332–3; patrons and, 3, 30, 111–16, chap. XIV passim; patronage networks and, 7, chap. XIV passim, 341–2; poets and, 116; scholarly advisors to, 22, 331–2; status of, 5, 6; workshop records of, 30; writings, 27; *see also* Neri di Bicci

Ascension, feast and play, 47, 63, 64 (fig. 21), 66, 115, 196, 251

astrology, 155, 156, 192–3, 297, 328, 446 n.126

Athenaeus, 29

Attendolo (da Cotignola), Micheletto, 53, 267, 275, 278; Muzio, 53, 271

Augustine, St., 47, 115; writings in Cosimo's library, 35, 36, 79, 83

Augustinian, Order, 162, 173; Observant branch, 173, 213; *see also* Fiesole, Badia

Aulus Gellius, 35

Aurispa, 29

authority, Cosimo's, 16, 19, 120, 158, 225, 305, 396 n.50

Avogadro, Alberto, *On the Religion and Magnificence of Cosimo*, 36, 213, 299

Bagno a Corsina, 319

Baldesi, Ambrogio, 56

Baldovinetti, Alesso, 209; Cafaggiolo altarpiece, 11, 87, 112, 141, 148 (fig. 57)

Baldovini, Ser Baldovino, 73

Baldus, Iohannes, *De Electione Medicis*, 36

Baptism of Christ, 254, 313, 328

Barbadori, family, 171, 355; altarpiece, 115, 333, 338; *see also* Lippi, Fra Filippo

Barbaro, Francesco, 333

Barbarossa, Frederick, 89

Barberini, Giovanni di Maffeo, 119

Bardi, family, 10, 80, 107, 166; Bartolomeo, 26, 164; Bernardo d'Andrea di Lippaccio, 74, 107; Bernardo di Giorgio, 385; chapel in S. Croce, 31, 107, 166; Contessina, *see* Medici, Contessina; Giuliano di Giovanni, *zibaldone* of, 71, 74, 80, 107; Ilarione, 164, 166; Lorenzo di Larione, 107, 219

Barducci, Ottavante, 116

Baroncelli, family: Bernardo, 108, 112; Piero di Giovanni Bandini, 385

Bartolini, family, 265–6; Andrea, 226; Andrea di Lionardo, 266–7; Damiano di Lionardo, 266; Lionardo, 48, 71, 266–7; Zanobi di Zanobi di Lionardo, 71

Bastiano, Ser, notary, 112,

battle, representations of, 264; *see also* condottiere; Uccello, Paolo

Baxandall, Michael, 5, 18, 30, 41, 98, 104, 360

Becchi, family: Gentile, 25, 283, 295, 310, 315, 320, 376, 474 n.253; Giovanni, 25

Belcari, Feo, 19, 25, 47, 59, 71, 76, 78, 102–3, 118, 119, 134, 207, 269, 320, 324, 376; letters, 87; *sacre rappresentazioni* of, 62–7;

Abraham and Isaac, 71, 101, 118, 192, 242; *King Nebuchadnezzar*, 120, 199

Bellevuoni, Mazzeo, 89

Benci, family, 10, 71, 80, 207; Bartolomeo, 80, 107; Francesco di Tommaso, 80, 107; Giovanni di Amerigo, 107, 214, 261; Giovanni di Guarnieri, 107, 111; Lorenzo di Giovanni di Taddeo, 328; Lorenzo di Tommaso, 80, 107; as patrons, 261; Tommaso di Tommaso di Giovanni di Taddeo, 80, 82, 107, 328

Bencivenni, Banco di Niccolò, 103

Benedetto da Maiano, 117, 278

Benedetto di Filippo, 385

Benedict, St., 100

Benincasa, Papi di, 385

Benino, del, family: Bernardo, 108, 112; Francesco, 108, 112; Piero, 108, 112

Bentivoglio, rulers of Bologna, 352–3

Benuccio, barber, 49

Berlinghieri, Francesco, 46

Bernard of Clairvaux, St., 6, 79, 190, 306, 315, 324–8, 384; representations of, 12, 84 (fig. 31), 284, 308, 322, 325–8 (figs. 163–4), 362, 384; writings, 55, 84, 117, 222, 325; *Steps of Humility*, 284

Bernardino, San, 59, 87, 97, 101, 105, 106, 112, 134, 169, 170, 171, 196; IHS symbol, 101–2, 115, 171–3, 309, 360, 435 n.36; Franciscan Observants, 173; Medici and, 173, 309; *see also* Medici, Cosimo, Bosco ai Frati

Berti, Antonio di Guido, soapmaker, 71

Berti, Simone di Giovanni, "lo Smunto," 421 n.54

Bertoldo di Giovanni, sculptor, 244, 482 n.10

Betti, Giovanni di Zanobi, notary, 74, 78, 81, 138

Beyer, Andreas, 262, 379

Biada, Iacopo del, 30

Biblioteca Laurenziana, 33, 69; Nazionale di Firenze, 69; Riccardiana, 69

Bicci di Lorenzo, 65

Biffoli, Bernardo, notary, 75, 78

Biliotti, Bartolo, 385

Billi, Antonio, 247

biography, problems of, 15–16

Biondo, Flavio, 225, 378

birthtrays (*deschi da parto*) of Medici family, 245, 247, 298 (fig. 146); *see also* deschi da parto

Boccaccio, Giovanni, 20, 42, 74, 79, 81–2, 89, 91, 100, 117, 285, 322; *Decameron*, 71, 300, 320; *Genealogy of the Gods*, 36

Boethius, 71, 79, 83, 363, 385

Bonaccorso di Montemagno, 72, 89

Bonaiuti, Andrea (da Firenze), 122 (fig. 41)

Bongianni, Iacopo di Borgianni, 78, 108

Boni, Leonardo, 111

Boni-Antinori, palace, 237

Boniface VIII, pope, 124

Bonvanni, Niccolò, 181, 348

books: as gifts, 73; owned by Florentines, chap. VI passim, 424 nn.97–9

Borgo S. Sepolcro, 56

Borsiad, 354

Borsook, Eve, 196

Bosco ai Frati, *see* Medici, Cosimo, commissions, architecture

Botticelli, Sandro, 244; *Mystic Nativity*, 64

Boucher, Bruce, 262

Bracciolini, Poggio, 23–6, 34–5, 43, 177, 225, 284, 322; *De Infelicitate Principum*, 27; *De Nobilitate*, 25, 27, 240; *Facetiae*, 43;

letters, 25–6, 34–5, 188, 294; translation of Lucian's *Lucius, vel de Asino*, 37

Brancacci, family: Antonio, 250; Branca, 108, 135; chapel (S. Maria del Carmine), 28, 172, 250, 355, 356; Giuliano di Tommaso, 385

Brancacci, Rinaldo, cardinal, tomb of, 176

Bridget of Sweden, St., 6, 86, 324

Brown, Alison, 234, 369

Brown, Peter, 135, 368

Brucker, Gene, 49

Brunelleschi, Filippo, 13, 21, 23, 28–30, 33–4, 172, 186, 228–9, 334, 360; author of *Il Grasso legnaiuolo*, 82, 123, 128, 426 n.129; Barbadori chapel, 171, 188, 355; cathedral cupola, 20, 28, 121 (fig. 40), 122–8, 279; designer of set machinery, 64; old sacristy, S. Lorenzo, 172, 187–97 (figs. 77–80); plan to divert Serchio river, 30, 176, 275; S. Lorenzo, 179–97 (figs. 74–80), 229, 344 (fig. 171); sculptor of competition panel for baptistery doors, 63 (fig. 20), 191–2; *see also* Manetti, Antonio, *Life of Brunelleschi*

Brunelleschi, Ghigo, 76, 81–2, 91; *see also Geta and Birria*

Brunellesco Lippi, Ser, 123

Bruni, Leonardo, 20, 23–5, 27, 44, 53, 88–9, 115, 125, 270–71, 275–6, 369; *De Militia*, 273; *History of Florence*, 36; *On the Constitution*, 27; *Panegyric to the City of Florence*, 217, 220, 224; program for the baptistery doors, 29; translation of Aristotle's *Economics*, 27, 36; translation of Plato's *Phaedrus*, 286

Bueri, de', family: Gherardo, 25; as patrons, 5; Piccarda, *see* Medici, Piccarda

Buggiano, 186, 190–91 (fig. 78), 342

buildings, patronage of, 5–6, 343

Buonarroti, Michelangelo, *see* Michelangelo

Buondelmonti, Zanobi, 331

Buoninsegni, Domenico di Leonardo, 24–5

Buonomini di S. Martino, confraternity of, 46–7 (fig. 14), 55, 134 (fig. 47), 328, 341; Cosimo and, 46–7, 120, 201, 313

Burchiello, barber: Medici relations with, 49, 82, 91, 118, 270, 314; poems by, 44, 49, 78, 80, 81–2, 109

Burckhardt, Jacob, 11, 230

burle e baie (jests and rantings), 78, 82

Burns, Howard, 194, 225

Busini, family, 231

Butters, Suzanne, 379

Byzantium, 312; *see also* Eastern influences; Greeks

Caesar, Julius, 79; *Commentaries*, 38, 83, 269, 278

Caglioti, Francesco, 266, 286

Cairoli, Giovanni, 58

Calderoni, Anselmo, 19, 49, 78, 117, 118–19, 143, 280

Calimala, Arte di (Importers and Exporters' Guild), *see* guilds, Calimala

Calixtus III, pope, 175, 178

Camaldolensian Order, 24, 87; *see also* Lippi, Fra Filippo

Camaldoli, convent of, 188, 324

Cambini, Bernardo, 119, 223, 270

Cambio, Arte di (Bankers' Guild), *see* guilds, Cambio

Cantansanti, Ser Francesco, 336, 376

Cantare dei Cantari, 48

Canticle of Canticles, 382–4

canto (street corner), 231; Canto alla Macina, 231, 314; Canto de' Carnesecchi, 337; Canto de' Medici, 231

canzoni morali, 49, 73, 116

Caplow, Harriet, 308

Caponsacchi, family, 177

cappella (choir), 211

Capponi, family, 108, 339; Gino di Neri, 217, 235, 241, 272; Neri di Gino, 15, 30, 49, 272, 277, 279–80; (?)portrait, 317 (fig. 159, no. 21); 318, 355

cardinals: Brancacci, 166; Corsini, 128; Pietro Barbo, 286; S. Marcello, 127; S. Marco, 127

Carducci, family, 248, 341, 345; *see also* Castagno, Andrea del

Carissimi, Niccolò, 239, 244, 252, 291, 300, 306, 308

Carnesecchi, family, 171; Bernardo di Cristofano, 337; Leonardo di Giovanni, *zibaldone* of, 70; Mariotto di Antonio, 266; shrine by Domenico Veneziano, 108, 337

cartography, Florentine interest in, 264, 431 n.207

Casa, della, family: Bernardo, 298; Bernardo di Ser Iacopo, 72; Lodovico d'Antonio, Ser, 83, 87

Casalini, Eugenio, 209

Cassian, 36; *Monastic Institutes*, 12, 19, 32 (fig. 8), 34, 37, 84, 149, 212

cassoni (marriage chests), 108, 112, 219, 234 (fig. 100), chap. XII passim, 279, 287, 289 (figs. 139 a, b, 140); *see also* Apollonio di Giovanni; Troy, tales of

Castagno, Andrea del, 107, 197, 205, 280–81, 341–2, 356; *David*, 52 (fig. 17), 62, 283; *Niccolò da Tolentino*, 13, 274 (fig. 129), 281; *St. John*, 245; *St. Julian and the Savior*, 207; *Uomini illustri*, 248 (fig. 113)

Castellani, family, 218, 228; Messer Matteo, 385

Castello, Cambio da, 85

catasti, 15, 42 (fig. 12), 218, 230, 405 nn.10–11

Catherine, St., of Alexandria, 98 (fig. 33), 100

Cato, 79, 113; *De Re Rustica*, 35, 299

Cavalca, Fra Giovanni, 86, 324, 362

Cavalcanti, Andrea, *see* Buggiano

Cavalcanti, family, 351; Giovanni, chronicler, 30, 71, 104, 117, 167, 223, 234, 276, 343, 363, 367; Mainardo, 355

Cavalieri, Francesco di Giovanni, 385

Celle, Giovanni dalle, 86–7, 134

Cerbaia, 320

Cerretani, Alessandro, 74

Certaldo, Ser Paolo di Ser Pace da, 127, 135

Certame Coronario, 28, 43, 80, 81, 83, 90, 138, 211, 359

Certosa, Florence (Galluzzo), 153, 212, 355

Chambers, David, 333

chancellors of Florence, 24, 27, 35, 176, 229; speeches of, 49; *see also* Bruni, Leonardo; Marsuppini, Carlo; Salutati, Francesco

chancery, papal, 24

chapbooks, 42, 43; *see also* vernacular miscellanies

charity, 19, 46–7, 127, 131–6, 189, 240, 328, 360; *see also* confraternities

Charlemagne, wars of, 117, 278; *see also Song of Roland*

Chellini, Giovanni, physician, 114, 116, 251; *see also* Donatello, *Chellini Madonna*

chess, 20, 292, 299, 386, 397 n.74

Chiaro, del, family: Giovanni, 385; Michele di Giovanni, 385

Chimento, barber, 113

Christ Child, images of, 62, 96

Christus, Petrus, *St. Jerome in his Study*, 262 (fig. 123)

Chrysoloras, Manuel, 24

Chrysostom, St. John, 102, 199–200; works by in Cosimo's library, 35, 196, 212; *Commentary on the Epistles of Paul*, 24, 196

Church Councils: Constance (1414), 27, 164; Ferrara/Florence (1438–9), 12, 63, 66, 80, 90, 103, 155, 164, 193, 196, 255, 258, 308, 312–13, 315, 350, 369, 373, 379

Church Fathers, writings of, 12, 35, 79

Ciai, family: Bartolomeo, Ser, 181–2; Bernardo, 182; Ciaio, Ser, 30, 181; Giovanni, 57, 59

Ciantellini, Giovanni di Ser Pietro, 386

Cicero, Marcus Tullius, 10, 15–6, 19–20, 29, 35–6, 93, 239–40, 359, 363, 370, 376; commentaries on five speeches of Asconius, 35; *De Amicitia*, 83, 385; *De Officiis*, 220–21; *De Oratore*, 38; *Dream of Scipio*, 286; *Letters*, 25, 34, 79; *Orator*, 38, 196, 270; *Tusculan Disputations*, 196; see also *Ad Herennium*

Cimabue, 244

Ciriaco d'Ancona, 263, 294, 309, 342

civic, Christianity, 35, 50, 87; events, 88–90, 124–6, 192, 211; good, 50, 144, 174, 201, 360, 368; participation, 50, 410 n.76; republican ideology, persistence of, x, 50–52, 221, 224, 368, 376; speeches, 51; symbols, 50, 51, 52; traditions, 88–90, 204, 207, 228; see also *entries under* Florence

Clark, David, 325

Clark, Kenneth, 331

class and class conflict, xii, 120–21, 408 n.43, 423 n.87, 440 n.106

classical culture, influence, *see* antiquity

Clearfield, Janet, 377

clientelismo and *mecenatismo*, 8, 332; see also patronage

Cocco–Donati, family: Iacopo di Niccolò, *zibaldone* of, 71, 80; Niccolò di Cocco, 80

Cohn, Samuel, 110

collecting, 4, 8, 351; see also Medici, family, collection

Colleoni, family, 353

colloquia, 34; see also symposia

Colonna, family (of Rome), 80; Gianni, 80; Guido, 89

commune, good of, 50, 144, 162, 198, 223

Compagni, Dino, 46

Concordia, St., 377

condottieri, 45, 52, 88, 207, 245, 264, 270–79, 349, 352; monuments, 470–71 n.177; see also military captains; Castagno, Andrea; Uccello, Paolo

confessions, 85

confraternities, 54–7; artisan role, 54; attendance, 54; boys' (*fanciulli*), 55; charity, 54, 134; commissions, 56 (fig. 18), 136 (figs. 48–9); *disciplinati* (flagellants; penitential), 54–6, 57, 99; *laudesi*, 54–5, 325, 413 nn.115–19; Marian devotion, 55, 157; Medici role, 57–9, 66–7; membership: of Bigallo, 55–6, 58; of the Convertite, 113; of the Holy Spirit, 177; of Jesus the Pilgrim, 56; of the Magi, 59, 177, 374, see also Magi, company; of Misericordia, 55–6, 58; of Orsanmichele, 105; of the Purification, 59, 66, 177, 340–41; of S. Bartolomeo, 314, 374; of S. Frediano, 55–6; of S. Giorgio, 113; of S. Paolo, 54; of S. Pietro Martire, 55–6, 58; of S. Zenobi, 55; of Sant' Agnese, 55, 63–5, 115, 136; of the Trinity, 137; musical performances, 55, 60, 67; paraliturgical activities, 54, 96, 284; religious education, 54; social composition, 54–7, 413 nn.108–9; suppression of, 57–8; see also Buonomini di S. Martino; *laude*

Constantinople, 90, 192, 315; see also Hagia Sophia

Consulte e Pratiche, 143, 270

contracts, artists', 7, 30, 144, 333

Copts, 313

Corazza, Bartolomeo del, 61–2, 88

Corella, Fra Domenico, 204, 208, 251, 458 nn.284–5

correttore (clerical mentor), 54

Cosmas and Damian, Saints, *see* Medici, family, saints

Councils (Constance; Ferrara/Florence), *see* Church Councils

Cresci, Pietro, da Bruggia, 262

Cristoforo, "L'Altissimo," 44–6, 116, 124, 407 n.32; *Reali*, 52

Cristoforo, Cristofano di, 116, 408 n.42

crusade, 348; see also Pius II

Crusca, Accademia della, 421 n.54

Cyprian, St., 36

Daddi, Bernardo, 94 (fig. 32)

Daedalus, 122–3, 297

Damiano, leatherworker, 113

dance, 322, 416 nn.180, 185

Danilova, Irina, 65

Dante Alighieri, 13, 19–20, 36, 42, 44, 46, 81–2, 91, 105, 162, 219, 251, 269, 356, 370, 382, 385; *Divine Comedy*, 9, 50, 79, 211, 300, 308, 325, 366, 370, 382, 384; lectures on, 81; portraits of, 76; readings of, 44

Dati, Gregorio di Stagio, 59–60, 75, 218, 349, 360; *Globe (Sfera* or *Mappamondo)*, 68 (fig. 24), 76, 79, 90, 91, 117; *History of Florence*, 218, 286, 460–61 n.7

Dati, Leonardo, 328

Davanzati, family: Giuliano, 126, 127; Mariotto, 78, 81, 108; Nicolaio di Giovanni, 108, 112

David, 82, 84, 124, 284, 300; images of, 52 (fig. 17), 62, 281 (fig. 133), 282–6; see also Castagno, Andrea; Donatello

Decembrio, Pier Candido, 271

decorum, 220–22, 273

defamation, 272, 280–81, 473 n.239; see also Castagno, Andrea

Dei, Benedetto, 70, 79, 91, 115, 218, 287, 309, 369

De La Mare, Albinia, 33, 35, 37

Delli, Dello, 108, 247–8

deschi da parto, 13, 112, 245, 247, 279, 298 (fig. 146)

Desiderio da Settignano, 30, 115, 248

devotion, *see* popular devotional literature

dialogues, 27

Diana, goddess, 109, 115

diaries, 70

Dieci di Balìa, 26, 30, 273, 276

Dietisalvi-Neroni, family, 179, 236; Francesco di Nerone, 182; Giovanni, 183; Nerone di Nigi, 25, 181, 183, (?)portrait, 317 (fig. 159, no. 27), 318; Nigi di Nigi, 236, 237 (fig. 106)

Diogenes Laertius, 24, 36

Dioskourides, *Apollo, Olympus and Marsyas*, 295 (fig. 143)

Domenico da Pietrasanta, tailor, 112, 113

Domenico da Prato, 82

Dominic, St., 150, 175

Dominican, Order, 134, 254; liturgy, 157–8; Observant branch, 151, 173; saints, 150, 156; see also Florence, S. Marco

Dominici, Fra Giovanni, 7, 57, 59, 61, 87, 95–6, 101, 131, 162

Donatello, 7, 13, 21, 23, 28–9, 33–4, 125, 244, 249, 294, 334, 339, 342–3, 344, 351; Michelozzo and, 343–5; works in Medici collection, 248–51; workshop, 114; works: *Ascension and Donation of the Keys*, 245, 250–51 (fig. 115); *Ascension of St. John to Heaven*, 194 (fig. 79); *Banquet of Herod* (Lille), 249 (fig. 114), 250; *Banquet of Herod* (Siena), 251; *Bust of a Youth*, 285 (fig. 134); *Cantoria*, 196; *Chellini Madonna*, 114 (fig. 37), 116, 251; *David* (bronze), 13, 19, 37, 52, 249, 267, 281 (fig. 133), 282–6, 299–300, 310; *David* (marble), 283, 339; decoration of old sacristy, 13, 172, 186–90, 193–7 (figs. 79–80), 344; *Dovizia* or *Abbondanza*, 113, 120 (fig. 39), 286, 344; *Judith and Holofernes*, 52, 249, 267, 281 (fig. 132), 282–6, 299–300, 310; *Madonna and Child*, 245; pulpit (Prato; with Michelozzo), 198, 344; pulpits (S. Lorenzo), 13, 105, 251, 318, 344, 379–82 (figs. 189–92); *St. George*, 61 (fig. 19); *St. John*, 245, see also Donatello, *Banquet of Herod*; tomb for John XXIII (with Michelozzo), 27, 132, 164–6 (fig. 66), 176, 344

Donato di Maestro Piero, shoe-maker, 74, 77
double entendre, 37, 370
Dovizia, figure of, *see* Donatello, *Dovizia*
Draper, James, 245, 482 n.10
Duccio, *Madonna and Child* (Uffizi), 56
Dufay, Guillaume, 126, 127

Early Christian influences, 12, 84, 142, 188, 193, 196, 208, 254,
    309, 360, 370, 377, 379
Eastern influences on Florentine culture, 90, 155, 196, 258, 293,
    308, 312–13
Ecclesiastes, 84
education: artists', 113–17; Christian, 96; humanist, 34; mercantile,
    34, 77; vernacular, 42, 77
Eight Saints, War of the, 35, 86, 167
Eisler, Colin, 196
ekphrasis, 240
Elam, Caroline, 180, 296, 353, 356
envy, 37
Ephraem, St., *Sermons*, 36
Epicureanism, 284
Epiphany, feast of, 149, 158, 162, 173, 254, 305, 313, 325, 328; *see
    also* Magi; Florence, S. Marco
equestrian monuments, 353
Este, rulers of Ferrara, 35, 237, 255, 259, 296, 349, 353–4, 364;
    Ercole, 259; Lionello, 220
Ethiopia, 90, 313, 479–80 nn.40–42
Ettlinger, Helen, 353
Eucharist, 57, 377, 378
Eugenius IV (Gabriel Condulmer), pope, 24, 47, 49, 88, 124–7,
    153, 162, 166–7, 170–71, 204, 302, 313, 325
Eusebius, 188
Eustorgius, St., 308
Evangelists: representations of, 84, 320; writings, 79, 84; *see also*
    John the Evangelist, St.
expiation, 11, 46, 132, 172, 207, 311, 358, 371, 373
Eyck, Jan van, 75, 262–4; *see also* Medici, family, Flemish artists
Ezekiel, Vision of, 206 (fig. 86), 209, 311; *see also* Jerome, St.

Faenza: Beata Umiltà of, 73; S. Giovanni, monastery, 73; *see also*
    Manfredi
Falconieri, Piero di Francesco, 205
fame, 134, 171, 218, 240, 272, 284; *see also* defamation
family and lineage, 9, 11, 230, 241
family chapels, importance of, 9, 180–83, 189, 194, 218, 355
family palaces, 108, 217–24, 226, 230–38, 347, 355
fanciulli, *see* confraternities, boys'
Farnese cup, 295
Fazio, Bartolomeo, 98, 104, 259, 263
Ferrara: Church Council of, *see* Church Council,
    Ferrara/Florence; court of, 35, 155, 259; *see also* Este
Ficino, Marsilio, 12, 33–4, 59, 90, 103, 132, 211, 212, 303, 328,
    364; translations of Plato, 36, 286
Fiesole: Badia, 36, 131, 149, 173, 178, 212–14, 213 (fig. 91), 299; S.
    Domenico, 149, 173–5, 355; S. Girolamo, 87, 161, 213, 304, 359;
    Villa Medici, 213, 303–4
Filarete (Antonio Averlino), *Treatise on Architecture*, 5, 131, 161–2,
    178, 189, 196, 207, 213, 221, 228, 239, 287, 297, 368
Filelfo, Francesco, 16, 24–5, 109, 304; *Sforziad*, 354
Finiguerra, Maso, 76, 115–16; Stefano, Lo Za, 78, 81–2, 91, 116
Fior di virtu, *see* Flowers of Virtue
flagellants, 55, 57; *see also* confraternities

Flamini, Francesco, 348
Flavius, 71
Flemish art, 262–4; *see also* Medici, family, Flemish artists
FLORENCE
City and state: archives, 15; chancellors, 24; constitution
    (republican), 351, 370; divine mission, 50, 159, 411 n.78, *see also*
    Jerusalem, Florence as; elections, 58; institutions, 410–11 n.76;
    liberty (*libertas*), 51–2, 88, 117, 276, 281–4, 291; maps, 22 (figs.
    5–6), 163 (fig. 65); schools, 42, 405 n.9, 419 n.4; symbols, *see*
    David, Hercules, John the Baptist, lily; tradition of Roman
    foundation, 50, 410 n.75; university (Studio), 33, 44, 399
    n.28
Churches, religious institutions and hospitals:
    Badia, 46, 183, 356 (fig. 175)
    baptistery, 63, 125; *Last Judgment* 133 (fig. 46), 176, 188, 191,
        193, 305–6, 379; pavement, 309 (fig. 152); tomb of John
        XXIII, 27, 164–6 (fig. 66); *see also* Ghiberti, Lorenzo
    cathedral (duomo; S. Liperata; S. Reparata; S. Maria del Fiore),
        56, 79, 81, 88–9, 106, 176, 210–12 (fig. 90); chapels, 441
        n.126; consecration, 125–7 (fig. 42), 200, 211, 353; cupola,
        121 (fig. 40), 122–8, 210; *operai*, 30, 122–4, 166, 176, 210,
        273, 400–01 n.92
    Murate, convent, 107, 261
    Orsanmichele, 44, 218; decorative program at, 105–6, 164;
        miraculous Madonna, 56, 94 (fig. 32), 106, 200; sculptural
        niches, 28, 102, 176, 247; *see also* guild
    Ospedale degli Innocenti (Foundling Hospital), 62, 111, 218
    SS. Annunziata (S. Maria de' Servi), 56, 89, 106, 108, 118, 170,
        188, 202–10 (figs. 85, 88), 280, 291, 306, 308, 311, 352–3; *see
        also* Medici, Piero di Cosimo
    S. Croce, 356; façade, 358 (fig. 177); family chapels: Bardi
        chapel, 31, 194, 355; Medici (Novitiate) chapel, 145–6, 188,
        200–02, 201 (fig. 83), 334; Pazzi chapel, 236 (fig. 10); Peruzzi
        chapel, 31, 194
    S. Egidio, 107, 337, 356–7
    S. Felice in Piazza, 63, 108, 111
    S. Felicita, 108, 111, 171, 188, 355
    S. Frediano, 56, 114
    S. Giorgio, 113
    S. Giovannino, 228, 231
    S. Iacopo sopr'Arno, 123
    S. Lorenzo, 58, 108, 179–97, 179 (fig. 74), 228, 229 (fig. 98),
        312, 377–92; family chapels, 108, 111, 180 (fig. 75), 181–3,
        184 (fig. 76), 334; liturgy, 378–9; Medici chapels, 144,
        179–86, 377; *operai*, 180–3, 334; parish and *gonfalone*, 179–80,
        see also gonfaloni, Golden Lion; pulpits, 379; tomb-marker of
        Cosimo, 309, 377–84, 378 (fig. 188); tomb of Cosimo, 383
        (fig. 193)
    old sacristy, 85, 186–97 (figs. 77–80), 247; altar, 191–2; bronze
        doors, 194–7; ceiling fresco, 192–3; stucco decorations, 85,
        193–4; tomb of Giovanni di Bicci, 190–91, 247, 309, 342,
        354, 376
    S. Lucia de' Magnoli, 339
    S. Marco, 143–59, 171–8, 179 (fig. 73), 188, 251, 305, 339;
        altarpiece, *see* Angelico, Fra; bronze bell, 173–4 (fig. 72), *see*
        Verrocchio, Andrea; cell and dormitory frescoes, 141,
        149–55, 179 (fig. 73), *see also* Angelico, Fra; chapter room
        and cloister frescoes, *see* Angelico, Fra; Cosimo's cell at, 6,
        12, 153, 155, 192, 305, 311, *see also* Gozzoli, Benozzo;
        garden, 178, 299; library, 35, 160 (fig. 64), 178; transfer from
        Silvestrines to Dominicans, 173
    S. Maria degli Angeli, convent, 23–4, 88, 133, 377

S. Maria del Carmine, 63, 172, 250, 355, 356; *see also* Brancacci, chapel

S. Maria del Fiore, *see* Florence, cathedral

S. Maria della Scala, hospital, 110

S. Maria Impruneta, 107; *see also* Madonna, of Impruneta

S. Maria Maddalena in Cestello, *sacre rappresentazioni* in, 62–3

S. Maria Novella, 5; façade, 174, 354, 355–66 (figs. 177, 179, 182); papal apartments, 125, 153, 166–7, 306, 360; Spanish chapel, 122 (fig. 41), 355; *Trinity* fresco, *see* Masaccio, *Trinity*

S. Maria Nuova, hospital, 73, 207, 356

S. Martino al Vescovo, 40 (fig. 11), 43, 46 (fig. 13), chap. VI passim; performances at, 43–6, 88; wool manufacturing district of, 43–6; *see also* Buonomini di S. Martino

S. Miniato al Monte, 73, 107, 166, 188, 202, 291; *see also* Medici, Piero di Cosimo

S. Niccolò Oltrarno, 107, 113

S. Pancrazio, 73, 358 (fig. 177)

S. Paolo, hospital, 167

S. Quaresima, 79, 91

S. Reparata, *see* Florence, cathedral

S. Salvatore al Monte, 80, 107, 346

S. Spirito, 23, 63, 111, 333

S. Tommaso, 12, 177, 197–200, 198 (fig. 82), 241, 291

S. Trinita, 172, 266, 291; Strozzi chapel, 308; Strozzi sacristy, 188; *see also* Gentile da Fabriano; Strozzi, family

S. Vincenzo d'Annalena, *see* Angelico, Fra

Palaces (family and government) 237; *see also under family palaces and individual family entries*

Palazzo Medici, *see* Medici, Cosimo, commissions, architecture, Medici palace

Palazzo Pitti, 225, 238 (fig. 108)

Palazzo del Podesta (Justice; Bargello), 231, 280

Palazzo Rucellai, 225, 236; *see also* Rucellai, Giovanni, palace

Palazzo Strozzi, 237 (fig. 107); *see also* Strozzi, family

Palazzo Vecchio (Priors; Signoria), 51 (fig. 16), 88, 106, 198, 218, 225–6, 235, 248, 280, 305–6, 325, 440 n.122; *see also* Signoria

Flowers of Virtue (Fior di virtu), 79, 86, 363, 385

Fortebracci, Niccolò, 272, 275

Fortini Brown, Patricia, 193

Fortune, 83, 90, 284, 358, 362, 363, 364–5; *see also* Petrarch; Rucellai, Giovanni

Foucault, Michel, 347

Fracassini, Francesco, factor, 170

France, king of, 228, 372

Francesco d'Agostino del Chegia, factor, 267

Francesco da Siena, marriage-broker, 114

Francesco del Maestro Andrea, son of Andrea "della Sargie," 141

Francesco di Iacopo di Gianni, apothecary, *zibaldone* of, 77

Francesco di Matteo, goldsmith, 103

Francesco di Pesello, *see* Pesellino

Francesco di Ser Andrea, 385

Francione, woodworker, 266

Francis, St., 144, 156, 200, 385

Franciscan, Order: Observant branch, 145, 167–71; saints, 144; *see also* Medici, Cosimo, commissions, architecture, Bosco ai Frati

Fraser-Jenkins, A. D., 214, 224, 333

Frediano, San, district, 114–15

Frescobaldi, family: Domenico, 90; Leonardo, 188

friendship, 7, 34, 74, 83, 117, 300, 328, 338

Friuli, 134

Frontinus, 270

Fruosino da Panzano, 341

Gaddi, Taddeo, 377

Gagliano, family: Giovanni di Francesco, 170, 205–6; Piero, 170, 205–6, 341

Gaiole, Giovanni di Domenico, 186

Galluzzo, *see* Certosa, Florence

Garden of Prayer, The, 93

Garin, Eugenio, 349

Gattamelata, 245, 271, 281

genealogies, 70

gente mezzana, 77, 112

Gentile da Fabriano, 107, 137; *Adoration of the Magi*, 172, 191, 258, 308, 310 (fig. 153), 311–12, 356; *Miracle of St. Nicholas* (Quaratesi altarpiece, predella), 137, 140 (fig. 52)

George, St., *see* Donatello

Geri, barber, 113

Gerini, Niccolò di Pietro, *Savior with Saints and Funeral Rites*, 56 (fig. 18)

Geta and Birria, 72–3, 76–7 (fig. 30), 81–2, 128, 426 nn.129–31; *see also* Brunelleschi, Ghigo

Gherardi, Giovanni, da Prato, 75, 88; *Paradiso degli Alberti*, 300, 320

Ghetti, Antonio di Ser Bartolommeo di Ser Nello, 181

Ghiberti, Lorenzo di Bartolo, 10, 21, 23–4, 28–30, 116, 248, 286, 294, 342–4, 344 (fig. 171); *Commentaries*, 20, 27, 29, 295; competition panel for first bronze doors of baptistery, 63, 342; second bronze doors of baptistery, 29, 197; reliquary for S. Maria degli Angeli, 10, 24 (fig. 7), 87, 377; *Saint Matthew*, 164, 176, 247

Ghiberti, Vittorio di Lorenzo, 115

ghiribizzi (fantasies), 78, 80

Ghirlandaio, family: David, 266; Domenico, workshop of, 47 (fig. 14)

Gianfigliazzi, Giannozzo, 276; palace, 237

Giannotti, Donato, 284

Gilbert, Creighton, 96, 110, 259, 333

Ginori, family, 179, 181–3, 452 nn.143–4; Francesco di Piero, 183; Piero, 181, 183; *see also* Florence, S. Lorenzo

Ginzburg, Carlo, 43

Giotto, 20, 31, 107, 194, 196, 244, 298; *Crucifixion*, 245; *Last Judgment* (Arena Chapel), 130 (fig. 44), 344 (fig. 170), 345 *Navicella* (Old St. Peter's), 365–6 (fig. 184)

Giovanfrancesco di Andrea, shoemaker, *zibaldone* of, 77

Giovanni, Francesco di Tommaso, priorista, 223–4

Giovanni, fringemaker, 113

Giovanni Battista, *see* John the Baptist, St.

Giovanni d'Angelo d'Antonio, painter and lute-player, 342

Giovanni da Settimo, Fra, 119

Giovanni di Cino, shoemaker, 78, 88, 91, 125, 127

Giovanni di Gherardo da Prato, 79, 82, 123

Giovanni di Giovanni, 385

Giovanni di Iacopo da Brucanese, spectaclemaker, 74

Giovanni di Maffeo da Barberino, 53

Giovanni Gualberto, St., 73, 202, 291

Girdle of the Virgin, 199, 200, 456 n.236; *see also* Thomas, St.

Girolamo da Imola, physician, 116

Giuliano da Maiano, 109, 111, 113

Giuliano di Santi, carpenter, 342

Giugni, family: Bernardo, (?)portrait, 317 (fig. 159, no. 23); Giovanni, 162; Rinieri di Niccolò, 266

Gnaeus Octavius, 221–2
Goes, van der, Hugo, 264
Golden Legend, The, see Voragine, Iacopo da
Golden Lion, district, *see gonfaloni*
Goldthwaite, Richard, 223, 230, 240
Gombrich, Ernst, 21, 197, 241, 242, 311, 331, 333, 369
gonfaloni (districts): Dragon, 197, 206; Golden Lion, 179, 183, 197, 229, *see also* Florence, S. Lorenzo; Green Dragon, 115, 197, 206
Gonfalonier of Justice, 198, 204, 209, 234, 242, 274, 291, 341, 350, 357
Gonzaga, rulers of Mantua, 21, 166, 240, 342, 349, 352; Alessandro, 244, 304; Francesco, 207; Giovanfrancesco, 28; Ludovico, 344
Gori, Zanobi di Federico, *zibaldone* of, 116
Gozzoli, Benozzo, 11, 209, 342; letters, 312, 339–41; *Adoration of the Magi* (S. Marco, Cosimo's cell), 12, 153 (fig. 61), 155, 192, 311, 339; altarpiece of the Company of the Purification, 66, 340; *Crucifixion* (S. Marco, Cosimo's cell,), 12, 99, 137, 152 (fig. 60), 153, 155, 262, 303, 339; *Journey of the Magi* (Medici palace chapel), 11–12, 308–10, 311, 316 (figs. 156–62); east wall, 317 (fig. 157); diagram of portraits, 317 (fig. 158); west wall, diagram of portraits, 317 (fig. 159); *Mystic Lamb*, 312, 327 (fig. 165); self-portraits, 312, 317 (figs. 157, 158, no. 18), 330 (fig. 166)
Greeks, 312; visit to Florence of, 80, 155, 258, 315; *see also* Byzantium; Church Council, Ferrara/Florence; Eastern influences
Green Dragon, district, *see gonfaloni*
Gregorian chant, 44, 320
Gregory, St., 74, 84, 87, 101, 117, 254
Grendler, Paul, 405 n.9, 419 n.4
Grisi, Ser Piero, 485
Guadagni, family: Bernardo, 357; Vieri, 164, 172
Gualfonda, 267
Guarino da Verona, 29, 35, 155, 259, 272, 288
Guasconi, family, 182; Biagio, 183; Filippo di Biagio, 181; Niccolò, 385; Tomasia (wife of Giovanni Rondinelli), 181; Zanobi, 181
Gubbio, ducal palace, *studiolo*, 296 (fig. 144)
Guccio, Niccolò di Meser, 385
Guelf party, 198, 200, 210; commissions of, 198, 281, 457 n.247
Guglielmo da Sommaia, 319
Guicciardini, family, 198; Iacopo, 18, 138; Piero, 270
Guidalotti, family, 355
Guidetti, Iacopo, 385
Guiducci, family: Giovanni di Guido di Michele, 385; Mario, 70
guilds (Arti), 199, 210; Medici family membership, 440–41 n.124; Calimala (Importers and Exporters), competition for baptistery doors, 28, 166, 201–2; Cambio (Bankers), 124, *St. Matthew* for Orsanmichele, 30, 164, 247; Lana (Wool), 53, 124, 210; Seta (Silk), 218
Gutkind, C. S., ix

Hagia Sophia, 188
Haines, Margaret, 122–3
Haskell, Francis, 93
Hatfield, Rab, 255, 312, 333
Hawkwood, Sir John, 91, 272–5; *see also condottieri*; Uccello, Paolo
Hector, death of, 43
Henderson, John, 58
heralds, *see* Signoria, heralds

Hercules, 82, 91, 92, 108, 283, 286–7; *see also* Pollaiuolo, Antonio
Herzner, Volker, 364
Hesperis, The, 354
historia, see istoria
Holy Roman Emperor, 89, 205, 224
Holy Sepulcher, 188; *see also* Rucellai, Giovanni
homoeroticism, 37, 284–5, 474–5 n.270
honor, 218
Hood, William, 144, 252, 311
Hope, Charles, 96–7
Horace, 104
Hospital of the Innocents, *see* Florence, Ospedale
house of memory, 240
humanism, 23–7, 34, 380; *see also* neoplatonism
Hungary, king of, 89, 224
hunting, 257, 293, 303, 308
Hyman, Isabelle, 185, 225

illiteracy, 43
images, chap. VII passim; attention in viewing, 7, 99; attitudes toward, 6, 7, 254; power of, 6, 99, 105; Nicene council on, 101; sacred, 112, chap. VII passim, 254, 433 n.10; social meaning of, 349; views of saints, 101
Immaculate Conception, doctrine, 103
imprese, 227 (fig. 97), 364, 490 n.120; *see also* Medici, family, symbols; Rucellai, Giovanni
Incarnation, 103, 308, 322
ingegno, admiration, 12–13, 22, 117, 124, 175, 186, 221, 251, 268, 343; definitions and applications, 20, 64, 124, 209, 249, 286, 308, 397 nn.66–7
Inghirami, family: Filippo, 356; Francesco di Piero, 108, 183
inheritance, laws of, 241
inscriptions, 25, 70, 207, 360, 448 n.25, 455 n.198, 489 n.96
intarsia, 30, 210, 239, 244, 250, 291, 296 (fig. 144), 309–10
intercession, 135, 338, 370, 378; images, 136–8 (fig. 50), 156
inventio, 21, 29, 62, 193, 197, 374
Isidore of Seville, St., 382
istoria, 21, 29, 102, 251, 267, 278, 297, 391 n.47
ius patronandi, 167–71, 199

Iacopo del Piccia, wool merchant, 114
Iacopo di Biagio, cloth-trimmer, 342, 459 n.304
Iacopo di Lione, saddle-maker, *zibaldone* of, 74, 77
Iacopone da Todi, 80, 85
Jerome, St., 84, 117, 362; representations of, 57, 84, 87, 247, 259 (fig. 120), 262, 322, 359; writings in Cosimo's library, 35–6, 79, 311
Jerusalem, Florence as, 50, 188, 192, 305, 411 n.78
John the Baptist, St., patron of Florence, 52, 56, 59–61, 80, 97, 100–01, 117, 142, 162, 164, 209, 247, 251, 261, 284, 304, 308, 313, 322, 324
John the Evangelist, St., 72–3, 85, 99–100, 154, 180, 190, 247, 261, 324
John XXIII (Baldassare Cossa), pope, 27, 294; tomb of by Donatello and Michelozzo, 27, 132, 164–6 (fig. 66)
jokes, Renaissance, 37; *see also* double entendre
Joseph, O. T. patriarch, 362
jousting, 61, 80, 293
Judith and Holofernes, 52; *see also* Donatello
Julian, St., 206; *see also* Baldovinetti, Alesso, Cafaggiolo altarpiece
Julius II, pope, 345
Juvenal, 34, 79, 240, 284

Kent, F. W., 230, 267, 358, 360
Krautheimer, Richard, 29, 197

Lactantius, 25, 36; *On False Religion*, 35
Laertius Diogenes, 36
"L'Altissimo," *see* Cristoforo
Lamberteschi, Ser Lamberto di Goccio, 84
Lamberti, Pietro, 355 (fig. 174)
Lana, Arte di (Wool Guild), *see* guilds, Lana
Landino, Cristoforo, 43, 104, 212, 251, 287, 328, 343, 383
Landucci, Luca, 50, 116, 119, 222, 287, 369
Lapaccini, family; Filippo, 80, 104; Giuliano, 5, 80, 175, 178, 339
Lapi, Giovanni di Tommaso, 73
Lapo di Castiglionchio, 36, 270, 364; translation of Plutarch's *Life of Themistocles*, 19
Last Judgment, 103–4, 130 (fig. 34), 132, 133 (figs. 45–6), 378
Latini, Brunetto, 50, 80, 100, 118, 269
laude, 47, 53, 83, 87, 95
laudesi, *see* confraternities
Lavin, Irving, 379
Lavin, Marilyn, 324
Lawrence, St., *see* Medici, family, saints
lay piety, 54; *see also* charity; confraternities
leisure, *see otium*
Lenzi, family, 237; Antonio, 199; Domenico, 119–20; Matteo di Jacopo, 199
letters, artists', 7, 8, 331–3; Domenico Veneziano's, 337–9; Filippo Lippi's, 333–7, 336 (fig. 169); language and form, 7, 332–3, 338; Matteo de' Pasti's, 339; personal, as evidence, 7
liberality *(liberalitas)*, 132, 135, 214, 219, 221, 223, 240, 313, 358
liberty, *see* Florence, liberty
Liebenwein, Wolfgang, 209
Lillie, Amanda, 300, 303
lily, symbol, 124–5, 209, 264, 309, 320
lineage, *see* family
Lippi, Filippino, 324, 337
Lippi, Fra Filippo, 12, 28, 107, 111, 244, 266, 353, 380; Medici and, 259–62, 333–7; letter to Giovanni di Cosimo, 336 (fig. 169); *Adoration of the Child* (Annalena), 324; *Adoration of the Child* (Camaldoli), 322, 327 (fig. 164); *Adoration of the Child* (Medici palace chapel), 12, 84, 261, 306, 308, 322–8, 326 (fig. 163), 334, 384; *Adoration of the Magi* (Medici tondo; with Fra Angelico), 245, 252–5 (fig. 117), 260 (fig. 121), 311, 334; Alessandri altarpiece, 356 (fig. 176); *Annunciation* (Martelli), 108, 261, 334, 377; *Annunciation* and *Seven Saints*, 12, 106, 260–61 (figs. 121–2), 334; Barbadori altarpiece, 115, 333, 338; Novitiate altarpiece (Medici chapel, S. Croce), 11, 145, 147 (fig. 56), 259–60, 334; *SS. Anthony Abbot and Michael*, 334, 335 (figs. 167–8); *St. Bernard's Vision of the Virgin*, 84 (fig. 31); *St. Jerome in Penitence*, 259 (fig. 120); *Tarquinia Madonna*, 333
literacy, rate and evidence of, 42
literary compilations, *see* vernacular miscellanies
literature, classical and Christian, 33–8,
liturgy, 57, 284
Livy, 79; *Decades*, 25, 36, 70
Lodi, Peace of, 53, 214, 239, 271, 284, 350
Lodovico d'Antonio, notary, 70
loggias, 171, 225, 231, 234–5
Lorenzetti, Ambrogio, 50, 118; *Allegory of Good Government*, 51 (north wall, fig. 15), 115 (east wall, fig. 38)
Lorenzo dello Stecchuto, 181
Lorenzo di Andrea, butcher, 181

Lorenzo di Bicci, 248
Lorenzo di Credi, 108, 116
Lorenzo di Tommaso, scissor-maker, 104
Lorenzo Monaco, 266, 311
Lorenzo Pisano, *De Misericordia*, 36, 383
Lotteringhi, Sandro, 75, 83, 85, 87, 89
Louis of Toulouse, St., 281; *see also* Guelf Party
Luca di Marco, 181
Lucan, 71, 385
Lucca, war with, 18, 52, 88, 265, 273–6
Lucian, *Lucius, vel de Asino*, 36
Lucretius, *De Rerum Natura*, 284
Lucullus, 223
Luke, St., 202; *see also* Evangelists
Luna, della, family: Francesco, 30; Giuliano, 363
Luther, Martin, 87

Machiavelli, Niccolò, xiii, 4, 18, 19, 23, 82, 91, 200, 224, 363, 367
Madonna and Child, images of: Annunciate, 202–4, 207, 251, 291, *see also* Florence, SS. Annunziata; del Giglio (of the lily), 125; della Misericordia (of Mercy), 56, 135, 136 (figs. 48–9); of Humility, 45; of Impruneta, 107, 162; *see also* Girdle of the Virgin
Maecenas, 190, 343
Maffei, Timoteo, abbot, 213; *Against the Detractors of Cosimo's Magnificence*, 36
Magi, company of, 57, 62, 65, 158, 173, 177, 305, 310, 313; narrative, 305, 315; representations of, 62, 252–5, 257, chap. XIII passim (figs. 156–62), 356, 374; *see also* Epiphany; Florence, S. Marco; Medici, Cosimo, Medici palace chapel frescoes
magnanimity, 240
magnificence, 189, 214, 219, 224; *see also* Maffei, Timoteo
Magnolino, chess-player, 20, 397 n.74
Malatesta, lords of Rimini, 342, 349, 352; Carlo, 141, 271; Sigismondo, 89, 108, 126, 264, 271, portrait, 317 (fig. 158, no. 6), 353, 354 (fig. 173), 360
Mallett, Michael, 271
Manelli, Count Raimondo, 222
Manetti, family, 118; Antonio, 25, 88, 186, 212; *Life of Brunelleschi*, 30, 116, 123–4, 186–8, 194, 379
Manfredi, lords of Faenza, 352
Mantegna, Andrea, 21, 240, 342
Mantua, *see* Gonzaga
marbles, 360; *see also* porphyry
Marchi, Buono di Marco del Buono di Filippo, 75
Marco del Buono, 231 (fig. 100)
Marco di Priore di Gino da Prato, notary, 89
Mark, St., 141, 150, *see also* Evangelists; Florence, S. Marco
Mark, St., of Rome, 377
Marsili, Luigi, 23, 86, 371
Marsuppini, family: Carlo, 24–5, 27–8, 288, 294; Iacopo, 266
Marsyas, representations of, 29, 294–5 (fig. 143)
Martelli, family, 10, 179, 181, 452 n.138; as patrons, 261, 339; Antonio, 33, 186, 338; Bartolomeo, 108, 334; Carlo, 108, 155; Filippo, 310; Galeotto, 266; Girolamo, 266; Roberto, 49, 108, (?)portrait, 317 (fig. 159, no. 28), 318, 339–40; Ugolino, 25, 181
Martial, 34–5
Martin V (Oddo Colonna), pope, 164, 173
Martines, Lauro, 116, 368, 406 n.14
Martini, Piero d'Agostino, 385
Martini, Simone, *Annunciation*, 101, 105 (fig. 35)
martyrs, images of, 196

Mary Magdalene, St., 205, 324

Marzocco, 91, 167

Masaccio, 21, 23, 28, 343; Brancacci chapel, 28, 65, 90, 172, 250; *desco da parto*, 245; *Sagra*, 172 (fig. 70), 247, 343; *Trinity*, 28, 86, 137, 138–9 (fig. 51), 325; *see also* Scheggia, Lo

Masi, family, 181; Ludovico, 183

Maso di Bartolomeo, 202

Masolino, 65, 172

Massaio, Piero del, 65, 161, 163 (fig. 65), 209, 218

masses, commemorative, 12, 185, 189, 191, 201, 261, 373, 376, 378–9

Matteo di Bartolo, leather-dresser, 74, 77

Matteo di Giunto, 75

Mazzi, Mariotto, pedlar, 112

mazzocchi, 279, 318

mecenatismo, 8, 332, 392 n.63

McHam, Sarah, 166

McKillop, Susan, 155, 185, 379, 442 n.12

medals, 177, 259, 352–3; *see also* Pisanello

MEDICI, COSIMO DI GIOVANNI DI BICCI, DE'
aphorisms, 38, 132, 162, 175, 475 n.270; audience, 3, 4; authority, 16, 19, 120, 158, 225, 305, 370, 396 n.50; banker, xi, 241; biography of, ix, xi; books, marginalia, 37–8; building, 5, 9, 11, 15, 36, 131; charity, 19, 47, 172; collections, 15, 292–5, 362; commune, 18, 38; death, 138–41, 242, 255, 303, 305, 375; exile, 19, 33, 34, 36, 37, 52, 89, 118, 166, 277, 284, 313; *ex libris*, 33; funeral, 10, 319, 371–2, 375–7; gardens at *casa vecchia*, palace and S. Marco, 35, 153, 178, 299–300, 303; Gonfalonier of Justice, 198, 204, 209; government, role in, manipulation of, 158, 348–51; history, interest in, 36; household, 10, 240, 306; humanism, 23–7, 34; illness (gout), 138, 234, 244, 306, 318, 444 n.64; inscriptions, 25, 177, 190, 207, 283, 377; language, 17; letters, 8, 15–20 (figs. 2, 3), 234, 241, 268, 277–8, 350, 364, 367; library, 7, 12, 33–8, 77–81, 132, 144, 158, 255; maps and cartography, 264; monasticism, 12, 212, *see also* Cassian; music, 211–12, 292; oeuvre of, x, xi, xii, 3–4, 5, 9–13, 46, 122, 200, 305, 343, 344, 357, conclusion passim; *parenti, amici, vicini*, 230–38, 318; patriarch, *paterfamilias, padrino, pater patriae*, xi, 9, 11, 15, 18, 19, 38, 117, 138, 162, 219, 230–38, 241, 271, 318, 352, 368, 375 (figs. 186–7); poem by (attr.), 20, 44, 53–4, 83, 91, 119, 133, 175, 222, 277; portraits of, 317 (fig. 158, no. 4), 318, 381–2, 383 (fig. 192); praise of, 117, 158; princely pretensions, supposed, x, xi, 158, 224, 291, 305, 348–54, 360, 370; private altar, 155, 247; protagonist of dialogues, 27; protest against, 121; public image, xi–xii, 9, 117–21, 161, 300; *ricordo*, 19, 36, 141, 277, 372; *studiolo* (study), 296; tomb, 377–84, 383 (fig. 193), *see also* S. Lorenzo; visible image, xii, 9, 372–5; visits to Ostia Antica, Padua, Venice, Verona, 25, 166, 176, 271

COMMISSIONS, ARCHITECTURE:
Badia a Fiesole, 12, 36, 212–14 (fig. 91); library, 15, 214

Bosco ai Frati, 167–71 (figs. 68–9), 176, 188, 205–6, 302, 314; altarpiece, 11, 144–5 (fig. 55)

Medici palace, 10, 12, 144, 177, 201, 214, 223, 226 (figs. 95–6), 217–38, 229 (figs. 98–9), 232 (fig. 101), 284, 353; art in, 245–99, 289, 290 (fig. 139); classical influences on, 225–8; courtyard, 231, 283; façade, 226 (figs. 95–6), 228 (figs. 98–9), 255; garden, 178, 226, 233 (fig. 102), 239, 245, 283, 299–300, 322, 362; interiors, 239, 243, 291–2; inventories, 231, 235, 239, 244–9; loggia, 231–5; plans, 243 (figs. 109–10); roundels, 285 (fig. 135), 286, 294; *see also* Medici, family, *casa vecchia*; tapestries, 295, 318, 341, 369

Chapel, 305–28 (fig. 151); altar, 309–10; altarpiece, *see* Lippi, Fra Filippo, *Adoration of the Child*; ceiling, 309, 311 (fig. 154); frescoes, 309–22 (figs. 156–62), *see also* Gozzoli, Benozzo; furniture, 306, 309–10; inscription, 310; pavement, 309

SS. Cosma e Damiano, Rome, *see* Rome, SS. Cosma e Damiano

S. Croce, Novitiate chapel, 200–02, 201 (fig. 83); altarpiece, 11, 147 (fig. 56); *see also* Lippi, Fra Filippo

S. Francesco al Bosco, *see* Bosco ai Frati

S. Lorenzo, 10, 12, 179–97 (figs. 74–6), 228, 312; Cosimo's tomb marker at, 12, 197, 255, 309, 369, 377–84, 378 (fig. 188); family chapels, 180 (fig. 75), 181–3; liturgy and Medici commemorative masses, 12, 185, 189, 378–9, *see also* commemorative masses; old sacristy, 10, 12, 85, 186–97 (figs. 77–80), 247, 376, 379; pulpits, 13, 105, 197, 380–2 (figs. 189–92); tomb of Cosimo, 383–4 (fig. 193); *see also* Florence, S. Lorenzo

S. Marco, 5, 175–8; altarpiece, 11, 141, 155–9 (fig. 62); cell frescoes, 149–55; garden, 178, 299; library, 15, 25, 27, 160 (fig. 64), 178; gifts of Cosimo's books, 35; rebuilding, 11–12, 59, 141, 171–3 (figs. 71, 73), 175–7, 178–9 (fig. 73); Cosimo's cell, 6, 12, 99 (fig. 33), 153–55, 303, 311

S. Maria degli Angeli, 10; *see also* Ghiberti, Lorenzo

S. Tommaso, 12, 197–200, 291; *see also* Florence, S. Tommaso

COMMISSIONS, PAINTING: *see also* Medici, family, Flemish artists

Angelico, Fra: *Adoration of the Magi* (Medici tondo; with Fra Filippo Lippi) 245, 252–5 (fig. 117); Annalena altarpiece, 11, 144–5 (fig. 54), 262; *Crucifixion* (S. Marco, chapter house), 59 (fig. 59); *Deposition*, 245, 252 (fig. 116); *Lamentation*, 157 (fig. 63); *Madonna and Child with Eight Saints*, 150 (fig. 58), 175; S. Marco altarpiece, 11, 87, 141, 154 (fig. 62), 155, 251, 255; *SS. Cosmas and Damian before Lysias*, 312 (fig. 155); *see also* Angelico, Fra

Gozzoli, Benozzo, 11, 339–41; *Adoration of the Magi* (S. Marco, Cosimo's cell), 12, 153 (fig. 61), 192, 339; altarpiece of the Company of the Purification, 66, 340; *Crucifixion* (S. Marco, Cosimo's cell), 12, 99, 137, 152 (fig. 60), 153, 255, 262, 339; *Journey of the Magi* (Medici palace chapel), 11, 12, 312–22 (figs. 156–62), 339–41; *see also* Gozzoli, Benozzo

Lippi, Fra Filippo, 333–7; *Adoration of the Child* (Medici palace chapel; with Fra Angelico), 12, 84, 252, 322–6 (fig. 163), 334; *Adoration of the Magi* (Medici tondo; with Fra Angelico), 252–5 (fig. 117), 260, 334; *Annunciation and Seven Saints*, 12, 260–61 (figs. 121, 122), 334; Novitiate altarpiece (S. Croce), 145–6, 147 (fig. 56), 259, 334; *SS. Anthony Abbot and Michael*, 334, 335 (figs. 167–8); *see also* Lippi, Fra Filippo

Pasti, Matteo de', 339

Pollaiuolo, Antonio, *Labours of Hercules*, 287 (fig. 136); *see also* Pollaiuolo, Antonio

Uccello, Paolo, *Battle of San Romano*, 13, 20, 264–70 (figs. 125–7); *see also* Uccello, Paolo

Veneziano, Domenico, *Adoration of the Magi* (Medici tondo), 245, 255–9 (figs. 118–19), 319; *see also* Veneziano, Domenico

COMMISSIONS, SCULPTURE:
Donatello, 248–51; *David* (bronze), 13, 19, 281 (fig. 133), 282–6; *Judith and Holofernes*, 250, 281 (fig. 132), 282–6; doors, S. Lorenzo, old sacristy, 13, 195 (fig. 80); pulpits, S. Lorenzo, 13, 105, 250, 380–82 (figs. 189–92), 492 n.63; *see also* Donatello

Ghiberti, bronze reliquary, 10, 24 (fig. 7), 88, 377; *see also* Ghiberti, Lorenzo

MEDICI, FAMILY
  amici, see Medici, family, partisans
  bank, 9–10, 143, 184–5, 197, 214, 234, 239, 261, 295, 369, 371,
    373, 376; accounts, 15; branches: Bruges, 264, 318, 341;
    Florence, 234, 356; Geneva, 318; London, 315, 341; Lübeck,
    25; Lyons, 318; Pisa, 33, 162, 292, 334; Milan, 53, 266;
    Rome, 142, 164, 271; Venice, 33, 164, 166, 170, 188; mark, 37
    (fig. 10)
  baths, curative, 319
  casa vecchia, 10, 35, 144, 224, 234, 241, 245; plans, 246 (figs.
    111–12), 252, 260, 266, 289, 292, 296, 374; garden, 299, 362
  collection of, 4, 16, 244–5, 286, 292–5
  cult of the Magi, 12, 374; *see also*, confraternity, Magi; Medici,
    Cosimo, architecture commissions, Medici palace, chapel
  dukes, 118, 238
  estates in Mugello, 35, 162, 167, 168 (fig. 67), 197, 300–04, 301
    (figs. 147–8), 319
  exile (1433–4), 19, 34, 119, 166, 198, 270, 277, 284, 309
  expulsion (1494), 118, 251, 306, 371
  factors, 168, 170, 185, 199, 267, 302, 319, 376
  family, lineage, dynasty, kin-group, 9, 11, 161, 194, 240, 312,
    318, 370
  family tree, 10 (fig. 1)
  Flemish artists, 262–4, 318, 341
  household, size and composition, 34, 132, 240, 376
  hunting, 257, 293, 303, 308, 319–20
  imprese, see Medici, family, symbols and *imprese*
  inventories, 12, 231, 235, 239; (1417/18) 34–5, 135, 144, 235,
    241, 244–9, 266, 293, 401 n.12; (1456) 241, 292, 318;
    (1464/5) 239, 241, 292; (1492) 231, 235, 241, 244–9, 265
  jousting, 258
  letters, 234, 241
  mottoes, 255, 258, 290 (figs. 139 a, b), 309, 318, 322
  palace, 10, 12, 144, 232 (figs. 92, 101–2), 201, 224; *see also*
    Medici, Cosimo, architecture commissions, Medici palace
  partisans and party (*amici, parenti, vicini*), 117, 119, 180, 183,
    209, 230–38, 305, 318, 350, 370–71; portraits of, 317 (fig.
    159), 321 (fig. 161)
  play on name, 36, 118–19, 142, 148, 158
  portraits in Medici palace chapel, 316, 317 (fig. 158), 321 (fig.
    161)
  rivalry with Strozzi, 8
  saints, onomastic, 11, 144, 149, 185, 200, 247, 260–61, 313,
    374–5, 377, 468 n.111; Cosmas and Damian, 19, 36, 46, 79,
    118–19, 141–59, 143 (fig. 53), 186, 189, 193, 201, 242, 247,
    252, 263, 303, 313, 341, 356, 373, 377, 445 n.89; Lawrence,
    149, 185, 247, 377; representations of, 11–12, 141–59 (figs.
    53–60, 62), 177, 186, 247, 284
  studioli (studies), 296; *see also under* Medici, Cosimo; Medici,
    Giovanni; Medici, Lorenzo; Medici, Lorenzo di Piero
  symbols and *imprese*, 227, 254, 287, 290 (figs. 139a, b), 364, 366,
    463 n.61; balls (*palle*), 156, 171, 178, 190, 209, 214, 227 (fig.
    97), 289, 290 (figs. 139a, b), 299, 318, 369, 372; diamond ring
    with feathers, 13, 227, 255, 260, 290 (figs. 139a, b), 292,
    309–10, 318, 354, 364, 366; falcon, 254, 257, 366; oranges
    (*mala medica; melarancie*), 119, 157, 209, 299, 303; peacock,
    254, 257, 366; Solomon's knot, 369, 380–84
  Venice, 19, 271
  villas, 162, 176, 300–04, 308, 318, 376; Cafaggiolo, 10–11, 17,
    148 (fig. 47), 167, 170, 177, 257, 300–02, 301 (fig. 147), 319,
    375, *see also* Baldovinetti, Alesso; Careggi, 10, 49, 168, 211,
    292, 302 (fig. 149), 303, 340; Fiesole, 13, 161, 303 (fig. 150);

  Poggio ai Caiano, 300, 359; Trebbio, 10, 168, 176, 257,
    300–02, 301 (fig. 148)
Medici, members of family
  Alamanno, 168–9
  Amerigo di Lapo, 178
  Andrea, *zibaldone* of, 71, 79
  Antonio, Fra, 200
  Averardo, detto Bicci, 9, 241
  Averardo di Francesco di Bicci (cousin of Cosimo), 16, 18, 20,
    30, 31, 52, 134, 140, 148, 176–7, 198, 242, 270, 275–6, 278,
    302, 334, 345, 450 n.96
  Bernardetto, 49, 88, 205, 231, 274, 277–80, 341, 357
  Bernardo d'Alammano, 328
  Bernardo d'Antonio (Bernardetto), 176, 183, 197, 207, 272
  Bernardo di Leonardo, 169
  Carlo di Cosimo, 248, 317 (fig. 158, no. 3), 342, 480 n.52
  Clarice (Orsini) (wife of Lorenzo il Magnifico), 271, 292
  Conte di Foligno, 241
  Contessina (Bardi) (wife of Cosimo), 65–6, 80, 135, 138, 170,
    194, 244, 289, 290 (figs. 139a, b), 303, 314, 317, 324, 342,
    381–2, 382 (fig. 192)
  Cosimino, 244; (?)portrait, 317 (fig. 158, no. 8)
  Damiano di Giovanni di Bicci, 11, 141, 393 n.24
  Donato, archbishop, 210, 356
  Filippo, archbishop, 210, 356
  Francesco di Averardo detto Bicci, 19, 34
  Francesco di Giuliano di Averardo, 168, 177, 198, 242, 284
  Gianfrancesco di Piero, 35–6
  Giovanni d'Antonio, 199
  Giovanni di Bicci (father of Cosimo), 10, 11, 27, 108, 142, 144,
    161, 164, 241–2, 247; tomb in old sacristy, S. Lorenzo, 12,
    26, 141, 180, 188, 191 (fig. 78), 247, 342
  Giovanni di Cosimo, 10, 12, 13, 49, 53, 118, 182, 186, 191, 221,
    242, 257, 288, 303, 320, 348, 363; bust by Mino da Fiesole,
    10, 267, 288, 289 (fig. 138); classical learning, 35, 71;
    collection of, 16, 250, 254, 288; Donatello, 254; Filippo
    Lippi, 336 (fig. 169), 337; illness of, 36; music, 211, 292;
    operaio, 124; patronage, 142, 248, 254, 264, 288, 334, 335 (figs.
    167–8), 342; portrait of, 317 (fig. 158, no. 16); *studiolo*
    (study), 296, 351; villa at Fiesole, 13, 161, 213, 242, 248, 250,
    288, 303
  Giovanni di Lorenzo di Piero, 118, 211
  Giovenco d'Antonio, 124, 273, 440–41 n.124
  Giuliano di Averardo di Francesco, 140, 149, 177, 242
  Giuliano di Piero di Cosimo, 34, 80, 107, 148–9, 183, 242;
    portrait, 317 (fig. 158, no. 13); *see also* Pazzi, conspiracy
  Itta (wife of Amerigo di Lapo), 178
  Iacopa (wife of Averardo detto Bicci), 241
  Laodomia, 229 (fig. 98)
  Leonardo di Bernardo, bishop of Forli, 169
  Lorenzo di Giovanni di Bicci (brother of Cosimo), 5, 10,
    12–13, 23–8, 36, 138, 170, 181, 240, 277, 299; death of, 49,
    156, 185–6, 190, 242; *studiolo* (study), 296; learning and
    library of, 79
  Lorenzo di Piero di Cosimo, 34, 66, 91, 231, 242, 245, 284,
    287, 292, 313, 348, 352, 368, 370–72; collection, 245, 295;
    diplomatic gifts, 296; letters (Benozzo Gozzoli), 341; letters
    (Fra Filippo Lippi), 337; portrait, 317 (fig. 158, no. 10);
    ricordo, 371; urban development by, 353
  Lucrezia (Tornabuoni) (wife of Piero di Cosimo), 47, 183, 289,
    290 (figs. 140), 292, 324; bust by Mino da Fiesole, 10, 245;
    poetry by, 47, 49, 59, 86

Maddalena (Monaldi) (wife of Averardo di Francesco), 178
Mariotto (Mari), 19, 214
Nannina, Monna, see Medici, members of family, Piccarda
Nannina, daughter of Piero di Cosimo, 81, 357
Nicola di Vieri, 25, 190, 345
Orlando di Guccio, 197, 205, 207 (fig. 87), 274, 341, 356, 368, 416 n.179
Piccarda (de' Bueri) (wife of Giovanni di Bicci), 11, 25, 140, 141, 247
Pierfrancesco di Lorenzo di Giovanni, 10, 18, 36, 188, 242, 257, 302, 319, 357, 465 n.34
Piero di Cosimo, 10–11, 13, 18, 34, 47, 101, 138, 178, 242; Benozzo Gozzoli and, 339–41; bust by Mino da Fiesole, 10, 245, 288, 289 (fig. 137), 257; Certame Coronario, 28; classical learning, 28, 35, 288; collection of, 16, 288; Domenico Veneziano and, 337–8; illness (gout), 36, 234, 244; imprese, 202, 214, 287; library, 13, 72, 73, 77–81, 211, 248, 284, 288, 297, 339; livery colours, 309; Matteo de' Pasti, 339; operaio, 30, 124, 205, 210; patronage, 161, 167, 210, 255, 262, 287–9, 290 (fig. 140); political style, 288, 290; portrait, 317 (fig. 158, no. 2); princely pretensions, supposed, x, xi, 158, 224, 291; SS. Annunziata, 11, 106, 118, 161, 197, 202–10, 208 (fig. 88), 242, 255, 291, 297; S. Miniato al Monte, 11, 73, 161, 202, 203 (fig. 84), 242, 255, 291, 297; studiolo (study), 288, 296–8
Piero di Lorenzo di Piero, 118, 244
Piero di Pierfrancesco, 35–6
Romulo, Fra, 170
Vanni, 277
Vieri di Cambio, Messer, 241, 465 n.26
meditation, 85, 95
melopee, 44
memento mori, 86, 138; see also popular devotional literature
Memling, Hans, 264
memory, 70, 95; art of, treatises, 91–3
Menocchio, Friulian miller, 43
Mercanzia (Merchants), court of, 111, 120, 176, 198, 201, 210, 313, 345
Mercato Vecchio, 81, 119, 120 (fig. 39), 197, 199, 234, 241; see also Florence, S. Tommaso
merchants, respect for, 119, 120
Merisalo, Outi, 265
meta-patronage, 356
Michael, Fra, monk at S. Maria degli Angeli, 24–5, 36
Michelangelo (Buonarroti), 4, 266, 287, 344
Michele del Giogante, 47, 53, 70, 72 (fig. 25), 73–5, 78, 91–3, 98, 133, 227, 234–5, 240, 293, 313
Michelozzi, Michelozzo di Bartolomeo, 7, 13, 29, 65, 116, 175, 314, 342; Donatello and, 164–6, 343–5; Medici and, 175–7; Badia di Fiesole, 212–14, 213 (fig. 91), see also Fiesole, Badia; Medici villas, 302–4, see also Medici, family, villas; Novitiate chapel, S. Croce, 200–02 (fig. 83), see also Florence, S. Croce; Medici palace, 228, see also Medici, Cosimo, Medici palace; pulpit (Prato; with Donatello), 198; S. Marco, 160 (fig. 64), 172 (fig. 71), see also Florence, S. Marco; SS. Annunziata, 204, tabernacle, 207–8 (fig. 88), 308; tomb for John XXIII (with Donatello), 27, 132, 164–6 (fig. 66)
Michelozzo, Niccolò, 176, 229
Milan: ambassador to, see Tranchedini, Nicodemo; dukes of, see under Sforza and Visconti
military captains, 45, 51, 88, 265, 271, 351; see also condottieri
Mino da Fiesole, 10, 245, 267, 288, 289 (figs. 137–8)
Molho, Anthony, 331

Monna Antonia, 112
Monna Lionarda, 113
Monaldi, Maddalena, 178
Montefeltro, lords of Urbino, 352, 353; Federigo, 296 (fig. 144); Guido, 49
Montemagno, Bonaccorso di, 72, 89
Monte Oliveto, Order of, 212
moral exempla, 82–3, 99
Morelli, family: Giovanni, 12, 85, 98–100, 272, 386; Girolamo, 71
Mugello, 35, 100, 140, 162, 167, 168 (fig. 67), 279, 300, 310 (figs. 147–8), 319; see also Medici, family, villas; Bosco ai Frati
Murate, convent of, 107
Muses, 93, 125
music, 67; and cathedral, 126, 211–12, 459 n.304; and Medici household, 320
Muzi, Piero di Mariano, pursemaker, 66

Nanni di Banco, 102, 125
Naples, 89, 260, 262, 333–4, 337, 351, 353
Nasi, Bartolomeo, 80
neighborhood, 54–5; Medici parish of S. Lorenzo, 179–83; Medici parish of S. Tommaso, 197–8; see also gonfalone
Nelli, family, 182; Bartolomeo di Antonio, 182
Neoplatonism, 23, 90, 120, 196, 212, 309, 370, 382
Neri di Bicci, 56, 107, 111, 248; patrons, 111–15; ricordanze, 31, 138; workshop book, 111–16, 264; Coronation of the Virgin, 65 (fig. 23); Transfiguration, 108; Virgin and Child with St. Lawrence, 114 (fig. 36)
Nero del, family: Bernardo, 74; Nero di Filippo, 74
Neroni, family, see Dietisalvi-Neroni
Nesi, Giovanni, 313, 328
Newbigin, Nerida, 416 nn.180, 187–9, 417 n.43
Niccoli, Niccolò, 23, 25–7, 29, 34–5, 190, 240; collection, 25, 294; library, 25, 35, 178
Niccolò Cieco, 44, 46, 48, 53, 75, 78, 83, 90–91, 98, 313
Niccolò Gesuato, 103
Niccolò, S., 137, 140 (fig. 52)
Nicholas V (Tommaso (da Sarzana) Parentucelli), pope, 27, 35, 178
Nicodemo, see Pontremoli, Nicodemo
Nofri, shoemaker, 113
Nori, Simone, 341

Observants, 430 n.176; see also Augustinian, Dominican, and Franciscan Orders
Office, Divine, 85
opera: importance of institution, 29, 400–01 n.92; del Duomo, 30, 122–4, 166, 176, 210, 273, 400–01 n.92, see also Florence, cathedral; Florence, S. Lorenzo, 180–81, 334; see also Medici, members of family
oral culture, 42–3
Orcagna, 94 (fig. 32)
Ordelaffi, lords of Forlì, 352
Orlandini, Bartolomeo, 279
Orosius, Paulus, 79
Orsanmichele, see Florence, Orsanmichele
Orsini, family, 271, 279, 352; Clarice, see Medici, Clarice; Paolo, 267
Orti Oricellari, 23, 320
Os, Henk van, 101
Ostia, Cosimo's archaeological expedition to, 25–6

otium (leisure) 239, 300
Ovid, 79, 385; *Epistles* (*Heroides*), 35, 36 (fig. 9), 116

Pacini, Antonio, 36
Padua, Medici stay in, 177
Pagholo di Ghuglielmo, 385
pala, see altarpieces, form
palaces, *see* family palaces; *see also* Florence, Palaces
Palagio, Guido del, 18, 86, 167, 173, 430 n.176
Paleologus, John, Byzantine emperor, 259, 312–13, 315
Palmieri, Matteo, 45, 60, 115, 118, 213, 222, 240
Panciatichi, Gabriello di Messer Bartolomeo, 386
Pandolfini, Giannozzo, 355 (fig. 175), 356
Panofsky, Erwin, 263
Panormita (Antonio Beccadelli), *Hermaphrodite*, 34, 37, 284–5
Paoletti, John, 188, 194, 198–9, 349
Paolo di Stefano, 56
Parenti, Marco, 109–10, 118, 228, 231, 234–5, 292, 364
Park, Katherine, 58
Parma, Niccolò de' Carissimi da, *see* Carissimi
parrot, 100, 320, 435 n.27
Parte Guelfa, *see* Guelf party
Partridge, Loren, 275, 277–8
Passavanti, Iacopo, 88, 134
Pasti, Matteo de', 13, 258, 339, 353
patriarchy, metaphors of, 9, 135; structures and values of, xi, 5, 18, 161, 219, 241; *see also* Medici, Cosimo, *paterfamilias, padrino, pater patriae*
patristics, *see* Early Christian influences
patron: education, 33–8; intentions, recovery of, x, xi, 3, 16, 122, 308; interaction between artist and, xii, 3, 6, chap. XIV passim; oeuvre of, 3, 8, 388 n.5, *see also* Medici, Cosimo, oeuvre; point of view of, xii, 5; self-definition, 6, 8; taste and choice, 8
patronage: buildings, 5, 343; *clientelismo* and *mecenatismo*, 8, 332, 392 n.63; corporate, 122; expiatory, 375, *see also* expiation; language of, 7, 8; letters as instruments of, 7, 234, 331, 333; models, xii, 6, 8, 41, 241; networks, 7, 234; personal relations, 7; private, 122–8, 347; public, 30, 347, *see also* guilds; reciprocity, 6, 46, 331, 333; various senses, 6, 128
patronus, 399 n.49
Paul II (Pietro Barbo), pope, 286
Paul, St., 101, 134, 196; *Epistles*, 24
Pauletti, Tomeo de', 104
Pazzi, family, 80, 88, 219; Andrea, 201, 276; chapel (S. Croce), 236 (fig. 105); conspiracy, 183, 211, 236, 291, 314; palace, 235, 236 (fig. 104); Politia de', 80, 108
peacock, 254, 320
Pelli, Ser Alesso, 14 (figs. 3, 4), 25, 35, 47, 66, 177, 207, 227, 230, 234, 302, 314, 409 n.52, 457 n.268; letters of, 16, 59, 90, 313, 319, 395 n.22
"Pennuccia," wool-carder, 42
Pentecost, feast and play, 63; performance, venues for, 34; *see also* S. Martino
Perini, Zanobi di Pagholo d'Agnolo, 91
Perosa, Alessandro, 363, 364
perspective, 279
Perugia, Baglioni palace, 259
Peruzzi, family, 108, 218, 355; Bonifazio, 248; chapel (S. Croce), 31, 108, 194; Ridolfo, 171, 248
Pesellino (Francesco di Pesello), 147, 245, 255, 259, 265; *SS. Jerome and Francis*, 245, 259
Pesello, Giuliano, 255, 273

Peter, St., 250, 261
Peter Martyr, St., 58, 153, 261
Petrarch, 13, 36, 42, 75, 80, 81–2, 192, 298, 304, 363, 370, 422 n.71; *De Viris Illustribus*, 248, 287; *Songs* and *Sonnets* (*Canzoni*), 35, 71, 76, 79; *Treatise on Fortune*, 76 (fig. 28), 298; *Triumphs* (*Trionfi*), 13, 75, 81, 86, 116, 185, 258, 297, 298 (fig. 146), 339, 341, 342, 354
phoenix, 108, 112
Piazza di S. Martino, 43–6, chap. V passim
Piccinino, Niccolò, 45, 267, 277–9; *see also* condottieri; Uccello, Paolo
Pieranimo, Piero, canon of SS. Cosma e Damiano, Rome, 142
Piero dalla Volta, blacksmith, 113
Piero della Francesca, 56, 136 (fig. 49), 354 (fig. 173)
Piero di Crescenzi, 80
Piero di Fruosino, cook, 42 (fig. 12)
Piero, Ser, di Ser Bonaccorso, 79
Piero di Sozzo, 242
Pietriboni, Pietro, 277
Pietrobuoni, Paolo di Matteo, 62
Pigli, family: Gerozzo, 315, 341; Giovanni, 104, 119, 315
Pisa: Florentine conquest of, 53, 61, 162, 217; S. Cosimo, church, 135, 143, 242; S. Francesco, church, 162
Pisanello, 258–9, 342
Pitti, family, 237; Buonaccorso, 86, 108, 119, 364; Luca, 108, 219, 225, 235, 238, (?)portrait, 317 (fig. 159, no. 33), 318, 353; palace, 237, 238 (fig. 108)
Pius II (Andreas Sylvius Piccolomini), pope, 90, 164, 223, 224, 239, 313, 348
Plato, 83, 159; *Symposium*, 285; translations, 36, 286
Platonic Academy, 212, 303; *see also* Ficino, Marsilio
Plautus, 35, 76
plebeian patrons: commissions by, 110; point of view of, xi, 41, 121, 405 n.3, 408 n.43
Pletho, Gemistus, 90, 155
Pliny, 27, 76, 221, 343, 351
Plutarch, *Lives*, 19, 27, 36, 83, 364
Poeschke, Joachim, 250, 344
political, varying conceptions of, x
Poliziano (Politian), Angelo, 15, 43, 57, 175, 190, 211, 234, 343
Pollaiuolo, Antonio and Piero, 207, 341; *Hercules*, 245; *Labours of Hercules*, 287 (fig. 136)
Pollini, Domenico, 56–7
polyphony, 55, 67, 126, 417 n.207; *see also* music
Pontano, 214, 221
Pontremoli, Nicodemo da, *see* Tranchedini
Pope-Hennessy, John, 155, 250, 382
Popoleschi, Niccolò, 348
Poppi, counts of, 279, 280
popular culture, 28, 35, 43, 55, 78, 107, 284, 406 n.20, 407 n.21, 423 n.80; characterization, 42; performances, 43
popular devotional literature, 34, 55, 57, 83–8, 117; in Cosimo's library, 79
popular piety, 95; *see also* confraternities; saints
popular poetry and texts, collections, 34, 42–3, 53, 55
popular poets, repertoire, 45, 78, 105
porphyry, 309, 351, 360, 377, 379, 479 n.24
Portinari, family, 10, 107, 207, 488 n.62; Adovardo di Giovanni, 73, 80; chapel (S. Egidio), 107, 337–8, 356–7; Folco, 107, 356–7; Pigello, 357; Tommaso, 264, 341
Prato, 198
prayers, 85

Prester John, 90, 313
Preyer, Brenda, 224, 225, 231, 237, 244, 358, 364
princes, Italian, 349–54
prioriste, 70
Priors, 30, 352, *see also* Signoria of Florence; employment of poets, 49; *familia* of, 49
prisoners, release of, 127, 376
Propertius, *Elegies*, 190, 343
prophets, O. T., 191
Prosper, 212
Protus, Hyacinthus and Nemesius, SS., 87; Medici reliquary, 24, 377; *see also* Ghiberti, Lorenzo
Psalms, 84, 211, 283–4; penitential, 79, 84, 284, 364; *see also* David
Ptolemy, 90, 192
Pucci, family, 108, 207; Antonio, *zibaldone* of, 48, 80, 81, 119; Antonio di Puccio, 204; Puccio, 357
Pulci, Bernardo, 377
Pupilli, officials, records of, 79, appendix passim, 425 n.120; *zibaldoni*, 79

quaderni, 42; *see also* vernacular miscellanies
quadernucci, 75; *see also* vernacular miscellanies
Quaracchi, 223, 362–3; *see also* Rucellai, Giovanni
Quaratesi, family, 137, 356; altarpiece, *see* Gentile da Fabriano; Giuliano, 80, 97, 101, 107, 434 n.11
Quintilian, 35, 79, 98, 220; *Institutio Oratoria*, 7, 92
Quintus Curtius, 26

reading practices, 38, 404 n.69, 406 n.18
recipes, 90
Reformation, 54, 83, 104, 368
relics, 377, 445 n.103
remedies, 90
Riccardi, Iacopo d'Anchino, 386
Ricci, family, 80; Giuliano de', *zibaldone* of, 71, 74, 80; Piero de', 76, 80
Riccialbani, Iacopo di Niccolò, 89
ricordi (diaries), 70; *see also* Medici, Cosimo; Medici, Lorenzo di Piero; Neri di Bicci
Ridolfi, Bartolo di Schiatta, 385
Ridolfi–Guidi, family palace, 237
Rimini, S. Francesco, 353, 354 (fig. 173); *see also* Malatesta, family
ringhiera, civic orations from, 51 (fig. 16), 60, 88, 115, 275
Rinieri, Filippo di Piero, 385
Rinuccini, Alamanno, 109, 284, 286
Riva, Bonvesin della, 59
Rizzo, Anna Padoa, 311
Robbia, della, Andrea, 62
Robbia, della, Luca, 28, 107, 111, 196 (fig. 81), 202, 342, 343; *cantoria*, 211 (fig. 89); *Philosophy*, 196 (fig. 81); *Twelve Labors of the Months*, 297 (fig. 145)
Robertis, De, 278
Robinson, Crispin, 170; *see also*, Medici, Cosimo, Bosco ai Frati
Roman houses and villas, 240
Rome: Coliseum, 226; Pantheon, 360, 361 (fig. 180); Sancta Sanctorum, 362; SS. Cosma e Damiano, 142–3 (fig. 53), 194; (Old) St. Peter's, 365, 379
Romuald, St., 324
Rondinelli, family, 171, 179, 181; Andrea di Rinaldo, 181; Giovanni, 181; Vieri di Andrea, 181
Roover, De, Raymond, 234, 371
rose, papal, 193, 227, 441 n.136

Roselli, Rosello, 71, 79, 107, 292, 314, 364
Rosenauer, Artur, 251
Rossellino, family: Antonio, 30; Bernardo, 83, 202, 205, 207 (fig. 87), 342, 355 (fig. 175), 356
Rossi, Bartolomeo di Giovanni, 385
Rossi, Giovanni, 303
Rossi, Roberto de', 23, 24
Rubinstein, Nicolai, 218, 348, 350
Rucellai, family, 30, 73, *see also* Orti Oricellari; Andrea, Fra, 30; Bernardo, 81, 357, 363; Cosimo, 331; Giovanni di Paolo, *see* Rucellai, Giovanni di Paolo; Luigi di Donato di Paolo di Messer Paolo, 80; Pandolfo di Giovanni, 73, 363
Rucellai, Giovanni di Paolo, x, 5, 8, 19, 20, 28, 34, 161, 162, 221–3, 239, 267, 357–66, 358 (fig. 177); collector, 362; *impresa*, 358, 364, 365 (figs. 182–3, 185), 490 n.125; patronage, 28, 30, 174, 213, 219, 228, 266, 357–66, 358 (fig. 177); works of architecture and art commissioned by: façade of S. Maria Novella, 354, 357, 358 (fig. 177), 360, 361 (fig. 179), 365 (fig. 182); fresco decoration, 362; Holy Sepulcher tomb (S. Pancrazio), 141, 188, 357, 358 (fig. 177), 360–62 (fig. 181); palace and loggia, 228, 231, 236, 358–66 (figs. 177–8, 183, 185); villa and gardens at Quaracchi, 223, 300, 362–3; *zibaldone*, 5, 8, 69, 208, 219, 221–2, 270, 275, 357–66, 490 n.122
Ruda, Jeffrey, 111, 253, 260, 324, 333
Rustici, Codex, 40 (fig. 11), 198 (fig. 82), 199

Saalman, Howard, 58, 182, 190, 194
Sabbadini, Roberto, 33
Sacchetti, Franco, 25, 81, 105–6, 116, 198, 202, 235, 273
sacre rappresentazioni (sacred plays), 55, 62–7, 96, 136, 320; *Abraham and Isaac*, 63, 101; *Annunciation*, 63–6; *Ascension*, 63–6; *Joseph*, 362; *Prodigal Son*, 66; *see also* Annunciation; Ascension; Belcari, Feo; confraternities
saints, 87, 88, 368; images of, 97; patron, *see* Medici, family, saints, Cosmas and Damian; *see also* popular devotional literature
Sallust, 79, 269, 385
Salutati, Francesco, 37, 86, 135, 248, 287, 371; library, 35
Salviati, family: Alamanno, 30, 276; Bernardo, 111; Diamante, 96, 108, 111
Salvini, Mariano, general of the Servites, 108, 111, 177, 207, 458 n.275
Salvini, Roberto, 362
Sangallo, family: Antonio da, *zibaldone* of, 108, 116; Giuliano da, 81, 310
Sanguinacci, family, 353
S. Piero al Sieve, 166–71
S. Romano, battle of, 275–9; *see also* Uccello, Paolo
Sassetti, family: Bartolomeo, 185; Francesco, (?)portrait, 317 (fig. 159, no. 24), 318, 356; Nera, 356
Savonarola, Girolamo, 23, 87, 116, 191
Scala, Bartolomeo, 34, 304, 376
Scambrilla, Matteo, 59, 304
Scarfa, dello, Martino, 348
"Scarsella in Stinche," 71
Scaurus, 221
Scheggia, Lo, 13, 109, 245, 298 (fig. 146), 319
Schiattesi, Benedetto, prior of S. Lorenzo, 183
Scolari family, 166; Filippo (Pippo Spano), 89, 470 n.162
scrapbooks, 69, 71; *see also* vernacular miscellanies
Scriptures, 84–5
Scrovegni, Enrico, 130 (fig. 34), 132, 344 (fig. 170), 345; *see also* Giotto

Sellaio, Jacopo del, *St John the Baptist*, 217 (fig. 93)

Seneca, 79, 87, 385; *Epistles*, 38, 72; *Tragedies*, 287

Serego, 353

Sernigi, Pier Francesco, 111

Serragli, Bartolomeo, 303, 336–7, 342, 477 n.321

Serristori, Antonio di Salvestro, 276

Sertini, family: Andrea, 348; Tomaso di Bartolo di Ser Tino, 385

Servites, Order, 207; Observant branch, 204; *see also* Florence, SS. Annunziata

Sforza, lords of Milan, 349, 352, 353, 354; Alessandro, 263, 346 (fig. 172); Francesco, 15, 20, 44–5, 49, 53, 72, 88, 205, 213, 221, 239, 244, 271–2, 279, 305, 348; Giangaleazzo Maria, 49, 223, 234, 239, 244, 292, 300, 303, 306, 308, 313, portrait, 317 (fig. 158, no. 5), 352; *Sforziad*, 354

Shearman, John, 190

Siena, baptistery, 251

Sigismund, St., 354 (fig. 173)

Signoria of Florence, 19, 49, 198, 201, 218, 238, 280, 306, 377; heralds, 44, 48, 60, 61, 78, 89, 409 n.63; *see also* Florence, Palazzo Vecchio; Priors

Simone di Ser Dini da Siena, 80

Simons, Patricia, 230

Sixtus IV (Giuliano della Rovere), pope, 88

Sizi, family, 198

social class/strata/orders, perceptions of, 77

Soderini, family: Niccolò, 108, 318, 372; Tommaso, 108, 219

Solomon's knot, 52, 84, 279, 382–4

Song of Roland, 278

Souzdal, Bishop Abraham of, 63–5, 314

Spano, Pippo, *see* Scolari, family, Filippo

Spencer, John, 341

Speraindio, Giovanni, 112

Spinelli, family: Antonio di Lorenzo, 211; palace, 237, 287; Tommaso, 211, 287

Spinello Aretino, *Marriage of St. Catherine*, 98 (fig. 33); copy of Giotto's *Navicella*, 365 (fig. 184)

Spini, family, 111, 355; palace, 218, 228

spiritual services, reciprocity of, 46

Squarcialupi, Antonio, 59, 211, 292, 414 n.144, 415 n.161

Starn, Randolph, 240, 275, 277–8

Statius, 385

Stoicism, 34, 371

storia, see istoria

Strabo, 90

street corner, *see canto*

Strozzi, family, 78, 308, 351; altarpiece, *see* Gentile da Fabriano; Caterina, 109; chapel (S. Trinita), 308, 356; Filippo di Matteo, 109; Matteo, 29, 270; Nofri, 172, 356 (fig. 174); palace, 222, 237 (fig. 107), 356; Palla di Nofri, 33, 166, 172, 191, 205, 257, 267, 356; Palla di Palla, 119; rivalry with Medici, 8, 236, 356; sacristy (S. Trinita), 188, 356

Strozzi, Zanobi, artist, 209

studia humanitatis, 34

Stufa, della, family, 84, 108, 182, 452–3 n.147; Agnolo, 353; Antonio di Lorenzo, 49; Lorenzo, 25; Lorenzo di Andrea di Messer Ugo, 181; Lotteringho d'Andrea, 182; Giovanni, 81, 108; Giovenco di Lorenzo, 81; Gismondo d'Agnolo di Lorenzo di Messer Andrea, 74; Sigismondo d'Andrea, 74, 81, 108, 183, 211; Ugo d'Andrea, 108, 179, 181; Ugo di Lorenzo, 182

Suetonius, 26, 192, 248

symbols, signs, 95

symposia (academies, colloquia), 34; at Alberti gardens, 23; at Orti Oricellari, 23; at S. Maria degli Angeli, 23; at S. Spirito, 23

Tacitus, 35

Taddei, family, 181

Tanaglia, Matteo di Bartolomeo, 386

Tani, Agnolo, 264, (?)portrait, 317 (fig. 159, no. 25), 318

Tazzi, Pietro, 115

Temperani, Manno, 348

Ten of War, *see* Dieci di Balia

Terence, 26, 35, 385

Teri, Francesco di Niccolo di Teri, 76, 85

Terze Rime, 85, 193, 240, 245, 297, 299–300, 306

Thebaid, 362

Three Crowns of Florence, 43, 79, 81–2, 425 nn.120–25; *see also* Boccaccio; Dante; Petrarch

Thucydides, 220

Thomas, St., 106, 177, 198–9; *see also* Florence, S. Tommaso

Tinnucci, Niccolò, 276

Tobias and the angel, 58

Tolentino, Niccolò da, 13, 49, 52–3, 265, 267, 272–4 (fig. 129), 357, 382; *see also* Castagno, Andrea; Uccello, Paolo

Tolosini, Giovanni, 71, 74

tondi, 112, 254; *see also* Lippi, Filippo; Veneziano, Domenico

Tornabuoni, family, 234; Dianora, 158, 284; Giovanni di Francesco, (?)portrait, 317 (fig. 158, no. 15); Lucrezia, *see* Medici, Lucrezia

Torelli, Filippo, 342

Torre del Castagna, 46

Toscanelli, Paolo, 25, 30, 90, 192

Tracolo da Rimini, 269

Trajan, emperor, 120; column, 105 (fig. 34), 226, 299, 360; forum, 194, 225, 299

Tranchedini, Nicodemo (da Pontremoli), Milanese ambassador, 75, 235, 272, 286, 319, 376

Trachtenberg, Marvin, 188

Traversari, Ambrogio, 10, 23–6, 29, 35–6, 133, 294, 325, 377, 379; council of Florence, 29, 196–7; *Hodoeporicon*, 24; letters, 36, 164; patristic scholarship, 24, 29

Trexler, Richard, 99, 224, 349

Trinity, the doctrine of, 103, 315, 325, 382; representations, 76, 113, 137–9 (fig. 51), 308

Triumphs, *see* Petrarch

Troy, tales of, 79, 108

Turkey, 90

Twain, Mark, 348

Ubaldini, family, 169

Uberti, family, 235, 251; Fazio degli, 71

Uccello, Paolo, 279, 342–3; *Battle of San Romano*, 13, 20, 53, 245, 264–70 (figs. 125–7, 141–2), 275–9, 374, 382; *Sir John Hawkwood*, 30, 91, 272–5 (fig. 128); *St. Thomas*, 12, 199

Ufficiali del Banco, 270, 276

Ufficiali della Notte, 474 n.270

Ulivieri di Brucolino da Ghagliano, factor, 168

Umiltà, Beata, of Faenza, 73; of Florence, 73

uomini illustri, 89, 248, 352, 466–7 n.65; *see also* Castagno, Andrea

Urbino, duke of, *see* Montefeltro

Ursina, Suor, *zibaldone* of, 119

usury, sin of, 132

Utens, Giusto, 238 (fig. 108), 301 (figs. 147–8)

ut pictura poesis, 104–6

Uzzano, family, 231; Agnolo da, 218; Niccolò da, 90, 108, 164, 171–2, 218–19, 339, 356

Valentini, Niccolaio, notary, 112
Valerius Maximus, 79
Valerius Publicola, 223
Valla, Lorenzo, *De voluptate*, 284
Vallombrosan, Order, 87, 202
Valori, family: Bartolomeo, 164, 172; Niccolò, 219 (fig. 94)
Vasari, Giorgio: *Lives of the Artists*, 27, 175, 202, 228, 247, 264–5, 279, 333, 390 n.42; *Brunelleschi and Ghiberti Presenting a Model of San Lorenzo to Cosimo*, 344 (fig. 171)
Vecchietti, Jacopo, 385
Vendetta of Christ, 75, 80, 430 n.189
Veneziano, Domenico, 12, 107, 109, 244, 324, 328, 337–9, 342, 356; Medici and, 337–9; Portinari chapel (S. Egidio), 337, 338; *Adoration of the Magi* (Medici tondo), 245, 255–9 (figs. 118–19), 319, 333, 337–9; *Carnesecchi Madonna*, 337; *Vanitas*, 259
Venice, Medici exile in, 19, 338; republican model, 367; St Mark's, 309, 449 n.72
Ventrone, Paola, 66, 349
Venuti, Comedio, notary, 223
vernacular miscellanies (anthologies, chapbooks, compilations, diaries, popular poetry, *quaderni, quadernucci, ricordi*, scrapbooks, *zibaldoni*), 55, chap. VI passim, 281, 284, appendix passim, 418 nn.1–4; belonging to the Medici, 77–81; families, 69; form and function, 42, 57, 69, 74; illustrations, 72 (figs. 25–6), 75–6 (figs. 27–8), 85; passing on of, 55, 71, 73–4, 107; patriotic anthologies, 89; plebeian compilations, 78, 82
Verrocchio, Andrea del, 111, 116, 294; *bell* (S. Marco), 173–4 (fig. 72); *Incredulity of St Thomas*, 198, 200, 457 n.247; tomb-marker (S. Lorenzo) for Cosimo, 378 (fig. 188); *Virgin and Child with Saints*, 127 (fig. 43); workshop, 76, 77 (figs. 29–30), 423 n.80
Vertova, Luisa, 289
Vespasiano da Bisticci, 9, 11, 13, 16, 20, 25, 33–6, 48, 109, 214; *Lives*, 23, 27, 223; *Life of Cosimo*, 15, 23, 132, 138, 170, 172, 188–9, 212, 230, 294, 299, 319, 343, 349, 373, 381
Vespucci, family: Anastasio, 270; Giovanni, 319
Vettori, Francesco, 91
Via de' Calzaiuoli, 46, 218

Villani, Giovanni, 42, 59; *Cronica*, 50, 179, 314
Vinci, 110
Vinci, Leonardo da, 82, 333; *Battle of Anghiari*, 280
Virgil, 35, 385; *Aeneid*, 226 (figs. 95–6), 235 (fig. 103), 299; as Dante's guide, 9; topos of bucolic pleasures, 35, 300
virtù, admiration for, 20, 22, 50, 122, 220, 224, 281, 368–9, 376, 397 n.70
Visconti, dukes of Milan, 49, 52, 89, 185, 275
Vitelleschi, Giovanni, 126, 167, 271, 333
Vitruvius, 231
Volterra, S. Girolamo, 459 n.307
Voragine, Iacopo da, *The Golden Legend*, 22, 70, 78, 88, 97–8, 102, 158, 199, 254–5, 315, 325

Warburg, Aby, 364
War magistracy: Averardo and, 30; Cosimo's service with, 26; *see also* Dieci di Balìa (Ten of War)
Wegener, Wendy, 272
Weissman, Ronald, 54
Weyden, Rogier van der, 262–4; *Crucifixion with Saints and Angels*, 346 (fig. 172), 354; *Medici Madonna*, 144, 262–3 (fig. 124); *see also* Medici, family, Flemish artists
Wilson, Blake, 67
Wind, Edgar, 349
Wohl, Helmut, 255, 338
woodcuts, 85
wool guild, *see* guilds, Lana
workers, unskilled, 42–3
Wright, Alison, 288, 341

Yates, Frances, 92

Za, Lo, *see* Finiguerra, Stefano
Zanobi di Manno, caskmaker, 114
Zecca (Florentine mint), 176
Zenobius, St., 55, 127–8
Zervas, Diane, 205
zibaldoni, *see* vernacular miscellanies
zodiac, signs, *see* astrology
Zuraw, Shelley, 28

PHOTOGRAPH CREDITS